The Wiley Blackwell Encyclopedia of Consumption and Consumer Studies

Wiley Blackwell Encyclopedias in Social Science
Consulting Editor: George Ritzer

Published

The Wiley Blackwell Encyclopedia of Globalization
Edited by George Ritzer

The Wiley Blackwell Encyclopedia of Social and Political Movements
Edited by David A. Snow, Donatella della Porta, Bert Klandermans, and Doug McAdam

The Wiley Blackwell Encyclopedia of Health, Illness, Behavior, and Society
Edited by William C. Cockerham, Robert Dingwall, and Stella Quah

The Wiley Blackwell Encyclopedia of Race, Ethnicity, and Nationalism
Edited by John Stone, Rutledge M. Dennis, Polly S. Rizova, Anthony D. Smith, and Xiaoshuo Hou

The Wiley Blackwell Encyclopedia of Consumption and Consumer Studies
Edited by Daniel Thomas Cook and J. Michael Ryan

Forthcoming

The Wiley Blackwell Encyclopedia of Social Theory
Edited by Bryan S. Turner, Chang Kyung-Sup, Cynthia Epstein, Peter Kivisto, William Outhwaite, and J. Michael Ryan

The Wiley Blackwell Encyclopedia of Gender and Sexuality Studies
Edited by Nancy A. Naples, Renée C. Hoogland, Maithree Wickramasinghe, and Angela Wong Wai Ching

The Wiley Blackwell Encyclopedia of Family Studies
Edited by Connie L. Shehan

The Wiley Blackwell Encyclopedia of Urban and Regional Studies
Edited by Anthony M. Orum

Related titles

The Blackwell Encyclopedia of Sociology
Edited by George Ritzer

The Concise Encyclopedia of Sociology
Edited by George Ritzer and J. Michael Ryan

The Wiley Blackwell Encyclopedia of Consumption and Consumer Studies

Edited by

Daniel Thomas Cook
and J. Michael Ryan

WILEY Blackwell

This edition first published 2015

Registered Office
John Wiley & Sons Ltd, The Atrium, Southern Gate, Chichester, West Sussex, PO19 8SQ, UK

Editorial Offices
350 Main Street, Malden, MA 02148-5020, USA
9600 Garsington Road, Oxford, OX4 2DQ, UK
The Atrium, Southern Gate, Chichester, West Sussex, PO19 8SQ, UK

For details of our global editorial offices, for customer services, and for information about how to apply for permission to reuse the copyright material in this book please see our website at www.wiley.com/wiley-blackwell.

Library of Congress Cataloging-in-Publication data is available for this book.

ISBN 9780470672846

Cover image: Clockwise from top left: Market stall, Cuba © Desmond Boylan/Reuters/Corbis; Women at weekly market, Romania (c) Martin Roemers/Panos; Santa Claus dolls for sale in Manila, Philippines © Romeo Ranoco/Reuters/Corbis; Shoppers in hypermarket, Poland © Piotr Malecki/Panos

Set in 10/12.5pt Minion by Laserwords, Chennai, India

1 2015

Contents

Editors vi
Contributors vii
Lexicon xv
Timeline xxi
Introduction xxv
Acknowledgments xxvii

Consumption and Consumer Studies A–Z 1

Index 579

Editors

Daniel Thomas Cook is Professor of Childhood Studies at Rutgers University–Camden, USA. He has published widely on consumer culture, childhood, and their intersections in culture and history. He is author of *The Commodification of Childhood: The Children's Clothing Industry and the Rise of the Child Consumer* (2004), and editor of several books, including *The Lived Experiences of Public Consumption* (2008). He is co-editor of the journal *Childhood.*

J. Michael Ryan is Assistant Professor of Sociology at The American University in Cairo, Egypt. He has previously taught at Facultad Latinoamericana de Ciencias Sociales (FLACSO) in Quito, Ecuador, and the University of Maryland, USA. He is co-editor (with George Ritzer) of *The Concise Encyclopedia of Sociology* (Wiley-Blackwell, 2011) and the forthcoming *Wiley-Blackwell Encyclopedia of Social Theory (*with Bryan S. Turner et al.*).* Before returning to academia, he worked as a research methodologist at the National Center for Health Statistics (which is part of the Centers for Disease Control and Prevention) in Washington, DC. His research interests include consumer culture, gender, sexualities, and globalization.

Contributors

Sharad Agarwal, *Indian Institute of Management Ranchi, India*

Melike Aktaş Yamanoğlu, *Ankara University, Turkey*

Veronika A. Andorfer, *University of Kassel, Germany*

David L. Andrews, *University of Maryland, USA*

Katsuki Aoki, *Meiji University, Japan*

Janelle Applequist, *Pennsylvania State University, USA*

Patricia Arend, *Fitchburg State University, USA*

Denis G. Arnold, *University of North Carolina, USA*

Søren Askegaard, *University of Southern Denmark, Denmark*

Lucy Atkinson, *University of Texas at Austin, USA*

Minna Autio, *University of Helsinki, Finland*

Rob Beamish, *Queen's University, Canada*

Russell Belk, *York University, Canada*

Michael M. Bell, *University of Wisconsin–Madison, USA*

Yaara Benger, *Max Planck Institute for Human Development, Germany*

Magdalena Bielenia-Grajewska, *University of Gdansk, Poland*

David B. Bills, *University of Iowa, USA*

Rebecca Bishop, *Independent scholar*

David D. Blouin, *Indiana University South Bend, USA*

Whitney Erin Boesel, *University of California, Santa Cruz, USA*

Michele Bonazzi, *University of Bologna, Italy*

Michael Ian Borer, *University of Nevada, Las Vegas, USA*

Jacqueline Botterill, *Brock University, Canada*

Gaspar Brändle, *Universidad de Murcia, Spain*

Clair Brown, *University of California, Berkeley, USA*

Nicole Brown, *University of Illinois at Urbana, Champaign, USA*

Annechen Bahr Bugge, *National Institute for Consumer Research, Norway*

Thomas C. Burr, *Illinois State University, USA*

John Edward Campbell, *Temple University, USA*

Jessica Carbino, *University of California, Los Angeles, USA*

Vince Carducci, *College for Creative Studies, USA*

Vander Casaqui, *Escola Superior de Propaganda e Marketing, Brazil*

Emma Casey, *Kingston University, UK*

Christopher Chávez, *University of Oregon, USA*

Katherine K. Chen, *City College of New York; Graduate Center, City University of New York, USA*

Chih-Chin Chen, *University of Maryland, USA*

Hélène Cherrier, *Griffith University, Australia*

Elizabeth Chin, *Art Center College of Design, USA*

Sung-Chang Chun, *Mercy College of Ohio, USA*

Hannah Clarke, *University of Arizona, USA*

Bryan C. Clift, *University of Maryland, USA*

I. Glenn Cohen, *Harvard Law School, USA*

Daniel Thomas Cook, *Rutgers University–Camden, USA*

Matteo Corciolani, *University of Pisa, Italy*

Patricia Cormack, *St. Francis Xavier University, Canada*

Natalie Coulter, *York University, Canada*

Patrick Cox, *Rutgers University, USA*

Linden Dalecki, *Kelce College of Business at Pittsburg State University, USA*

Adel Daoud, *University of Gothenburg, Sweden*

Andrea Dassopoulos, *University of Nevada, Las Vegas, USA*

Piergiorgio Degli Esposti, *University of Bologna, Italy*

Tim Delaney, *State University of New York at Oswego, USA*

Dominique Desjeux, *Paris Descartes University, Sorbonne Paris Cité, France*

Sara Di Chiazza, *Universidade Nova de Lisboa, Portugal*

Randal Doane, *Oberlin College, USA*

Paddy Dolan, *Dublin Institute of Technology, Ireland*

Paul Eisewicht, *TU Dortmund University, Germany*

Karin M. Ekström, *University of Borås, Sweden*

Susan Falls, *Savannah College of Art and Design, USA*

Mark Featherstone, *Keele University, UK*

Krisztina Fehérváry, *University of Michigan, USA*

Mary Beth Finch, *Northwestern University, USA*

Penelope Francks, *University of Leeds, UK*

Peter N. Funke, *University of South Florida, USA*

Dustin Garlitz, *University of South Florida, USA*

John Germov, *University of Newcastle, Australia*

Kevin Fox Gotham, *Tulane University, USA*

Maaike Gottfried, *DePaul University, USA*

Ove Granstrand, *Chalmers University of Technology, Sweden*

Kent Grayson, *Northwestern University, USA*

David Grazian, *University of Pennsylvania, USA*

Kjerstin Gruys, *University of California, Los Angeles, USA*

Alya Guseva, *Boston University, USA*

Clara Gustafsson, *Lund University, Sweden*

Sejung Ham, *University of Wisconsin–Madison, USA*

Markus Hadler, *Macquarie University, Australia*

Michael A. Haedicke, *Drake University, USA*

Hans Peter Hahn, *Goethe-Universität, Germany*

Benjamin Halligan, *University of Salford, UK*

Eugene Halton, *University of Notre Dame, USA*

Christoph Henning, *University of St. Gallen, Switzerland*

Aaron Hess, *Arizona State University, USA*

Clare Hinrichs, *Pennsylvania State University, USA*

Elizabeth C. Hirschman, *Rutgers University, USA*

Morris B. Holbrook, *Columbia University, USA*

Marcus Holgersson, *University of Gothenburg, Sweden*

Kim Humphery, *RMIT University, Australia*

Eva Illouz, *Hebrew University of Jerusalem, Israel*

Devon Johnson, *Montclair State University, USA*

Josée Johnston, *University of Toronto, Canada*

Ellis Jones, *Holy Cross College, USA*

Annamma Joy, *University of British Columbia, Canada*

Nathan Jurgenson, *University of Maryland, USA*

Andreas M. Kaplan, *ESCP Europe, France*

Douglas Kellner, *University of California, Los Angeles, USA*

Martha W. King, *Graduate Center, City University of New York, USA*

Andrzej Klimczuk, *Warsaw School of Economics, Poland*

Karin Knorr Cetina, *University of Chicago, USA*

Krzysztof Kubacki, *Griffith University, Australia*

Kathleen Kuehn, *Victoria University of Wellington, New Zealand*

Kalevi Kull, *University of Tartu, Estonia*

Chenjerai Kumanyika, *Clemson University, USA*

Klaus R. Kunzmann, *Emeritus, TU Dortmund University, Germany*

Craig D. Lair, *Gettysburg College, USA*

John T. Lang, *Occidental College, USA*

Beryl Langer, *La Trobe University, Australia*

Lauren Langman, *Loyola University Chicago, USA*

Jörgen Larsson, *Chalmers University of Technology, Sweden*

Stacey J. Lee, *University of Wisconsin–Madison, USA*

Ming Lim, *University of Leicester, UK*

Yu-Wei Lin, *University for the Creative Arts, UK*

Jan Logemann, *University of Göttingen, Germany*

Janet A. Lorenzen, *Williamette University, USA*

Paolo Magaudda, *Università degli Studi di Padova, Italy*

Amias S. Maldonado, *University of Texas at Austin, USA*

Lidia K. C. Manzo, *University of Trento, Italy*

Stephen T. Margulis, *Grand Valley State University, USA*

Martha A. Martinez, *DePaul University, USA*

Gary T. Marx, *Emeritus, Massachusetts Institute of Technology, USA*

Nita Mathur, *Indira Gandhi National Open University, India*

Cynthia Maurer, *Rutgers University, USA*

Christopher Mayes, *University of Sydney, Australia*

Matthew P. McAllister, *Pennsylvania State University, USA*

Matthew McDonald, *Assumption University, Thailand*

Octavio Medina, *The World Bank, USA*

Steven Miles, *Manchester Metropolitan University, UK*

Candace N. Miller, *University of Virginia, USA*

Toby Miller, *Cardiff University, UK; Murdoch University, Australia*

Murray Milner Jr., *University of Virginia, USA*

Ross Mouer, *Meiji University, Japan*

Isaac I. Muñoz, *University of Dallas, USA*

Rolland Munro, *University of Leicester, UK*

Dhiraj Murthy, *Goldsmiths, University of London, UK*

Agnes Nairn, *EM-Lyon Business School, France*

Stephanie O'Donohoe, *University of Edinburgh Business School, UK*

Cele C. Otnes, *University of Illinois, USA*

Yok-Fong Paat, *University of Texas at El Paso, USA*

Madeleine Pape, *University of Wisconsin–Madison, USA*

Aaron Passell, *Furman University, USA*

Georgios Patsiaouras, *University of Leicester, UK*

Lisa Peñaloza, *Kedge Business School, France*

Mark Allen Peterson, *Miami University, USA*

Simone Polillo, *University of Virginia, USA*

Ethan Prall, *Harvard Law School*

Harland Prechel, *Texas A&M University, USA*

Allison J. Pugh, *University of Virginia, USA*

P. S. Raju, *University of Louisville, USA*

Silver Rattasepp, *University of Tartu, Estonia*

David Redmon, *University of Kent at Canterbury, UK*

Jacqueline Reid-Walsh, *Pennsylvania State University, USA*

Lucia A. Reisch, *Copenhagen Business School, Denmark*

Raquel Barbosa Ribeiro, *University of Lisbon, Portugal*

Petra Riefler, *University of Vienna, Austria*

Viviane Riegel, *Goldsmiths, University of London, UK*

George Ritzer, *University of Maryland, USA*

Alexandra Rodney, *University of Toronto, Canada*

Chris Rojek, *City University, London, UK*

Jörg Rössel, *University of Zurich, Switzerland*

Mark Rubinfeld, *Westminster College, Salt Lake City, USA*

Joe Rumbo, *Texas State University, USA*

Julie A. Ruth, *Rutgers University–Camden, USA*

J. Michael Ryan, *The American University in Cairo, Egypt*

Michael T. Ryan, *Dodge City Community College, USA*

Robert W. Rydell, *Montana State University, USA*

Ethan D. Schoolman, *University of Michigan, USA*

Juliet B. Schor, *Boston College, USA*

Jonathan E. Schroeder, *Rochester Institute of Technology, USA*

Justin L. Schupp, *Kenyon College, USA*

Rachel Schwartz, *St. Joseph's College, USA*

Richard Sharpley, *University of Central Lancashire, UK*

Michael Siciliano, *University of California, Los Angeles, USA*

Régine Sirota, *Université Paris Descartes, France*

Leslie Sklair, *London School of Economics and Political Science, UK*

Don Slater, *London School of Economics and Political Science, UK*

Alexandra Nutter Smith, *University of Washington – Tacoma, USA*

Jennifer Smith Maguire, *University of Leicester, UK*

Isabel Soares, *University of Lisbon, Portugal*

Anna Sparrman, *Linköping University, Sweden*

Andre Spicer, *City University London, UK*

Keith Spiller, *Open University, UK*

Michael K. Stein, *University of Massachusetts, Amherst, USA*

Joel Stillerman, *Grand Valley State University, USA*

Inger L. Stole, *University of Illinois at Urbana-Champaign, USA*

Per Strömberg, *Telemark University College, Norway*

Anthony Sullivan, *University of the Arts, London, UK*

Cass R. Sunstein, *Harvard University, USA*

Yvette Taylor, *London South Bank University, UK*

Jacob Thomas, *University of California, Los Angeles, USA*

Deborah Thorne, *Ohio University, USA*

Joseph J. Tohill, *York University, Canada*

Keila Tyner, *Texas State University, USA*

Koen Van Bommel, *Vrije Universiteit, Netherlands*

Joeri Van den Bergh, *InSites Consulting, Netherlands*

Jacquelien van Stekelenburg, *VU University Amsterdam, Netherlands*

Alladi Venkatesh, *University of California, Irvine, USA*

Luca M. Visconti, *ESCP Europe, France*

Faye Linda Wachs, *California State Polytechnic University, Pomona, USA*

Randi Wærdahl, *Agder Research, Norway*

Chris Warhurst, *University of Warwick, UK*

Stephen L. Wearing, *University of Technology, Sydney, Australia*

Christine A. Wernet, *University of South Carolina, USA*

Frederick F. Wherry, *Yale University, USA*

Jennifer M. Whitmer, *University of Nevada, Las Vegas, USA*

Wendy A. Wiedenhoft-Murphy, *John Carroll University, USA*

Lauren T. Williams, *Griffith University, Australia*

Todd Wolfson, *Rutgers University, USA*

Newman Chun Wai Wong, *Midwestern State University, USA*

M .J. Xavier, *Indian Institute of Management Ranchi, India*

Jane Zavisca, *University of Arizona, USA*

Dennis Zuev, *CIES-ISCTE, Portugal*

Sharon Zukin, *City University of New York, USA*

Lexicon

Technology and New Media

Apple 19
Beauty Industry 38
Credit Cards 206
Digital-Mobile Consumption and Marketing 244
eBay 251
Edutainment 260
Facebook 277
Generation Y 321
Hollywood 353
Infomercial 363
Infotainment 364
Intellectual Property 366
Internet, The, and Consumption 368
Las Vegas 377
Marketing/Marketing Science 389
Mass Culture 407
Mass Marketing 410
Mass Media 411
Methods of Consumer Research 422
Music and Consumer Experience 435
Obsolescence: Planned, Progressive, Stylistic 451
Open Source and Consumption 455
Outsourcing 457
Peer-to-peer File Sharing 461
Popular Culture 467
Prosumption 476
Simulations 516
Social Media 519
Visual Consumption 556
YouTube 576

Globalization

Americanization 12
Capitalism 67
Coca-Colonization 89
Commodification 90
Commodity Chains 95
Consumer Cosmopolitanism 110
Consumer Society 145
Culture-Ideology of Consumerism 220
Culture Industries 222
Disneyization 246
Ecotourism 255
Fair Trade 280
Finance/Financial Markets 293
Free Trade Zones/Export Processing Zones 310
Global Justice Movement 328
Global Markets 331
Globalization and Consumption 333
Glocalization/Grobalization 338
Green Consumption 346
Homogenization and Heterogenization 356
Locavorism 387
Mass Culture 407
Mass Marketing 410
Mass Media 411
Material Culture Studies 414
McDonaldization 416
Medical Tourism 418
Modernization Theory 428
Nike 445

Occupy Movement 453
Outsourcing 457
Slow Food Movement 517
Starbuckization 524
Sweatshops 534
Tourism 549
World's Fairs and International Expositions 571

Identities

African Americans and Consumption 10
Asian Americans and Consumption 23
Beauty Industry 38
Behavioral Economics and Consumption 41
Body and Consumer Culture 49
Brand Loyalty 57
Brand Mascots 58
Brands and Branding 59
Burning Man 65
Celebrity 71
Children's Consumer Culture 75
Citizenship and Consumption 81
Class 86
Commodities 93
Commodity Racism 99
Conspicuous Consumption 101
Consumer Activism 103
Consumer Behavior 105
Consumer Socialization 144
Consumer Society 145
Consumers, Flawed 154
Consumption and Identity 162
Consumption, Postmodern 183
Consumption Rituals 187
Consumption and Sport 191
Cosmetic Surgery 202
Cultural Capital 209
Dandyism 229
Diderot Effect 243
Do-It-Yourself (DIY) 247
Downshifting 248
Education and Consumption 257
Emotions, Consumption and 263
Fashion 286
Femininities 290
Flâneur/Flânerie 295
Gay and Lesbian/Queer Markets/Marketing 313
Gender and Consumer Culture 316
Generation Y 321
Girl Culture 326
Latinos and Consumption 379
Lifestyle 383
Locavorism 387
Masculinity 403
Metrosexual 427
Mothers/Motherhood 433
Narcissism 439
Niche Marketing 443
Nostalgia 447
Pets 462
Politics and Consumer Culture 463
Popular Culture 467
Privacy 473
Prosumption 476
Quality of Life, Measurements of 481
Sexualities and Consumption 501
Teens 543
Tweens 551
Youth Culture(s) 573

Inequalities

Bankruptcy 28
Capitalism 67
Citizenship and Consumption 81
Class 86
Coca-Colonization 89
Commodity Chains 95
Commodity Racism 99
Conspicuous Consumption 101
Consumer Activism 103
Consumer Protection Agency 137
Consumer Society 145
Consumers in Emerging Economies 150

Cooperatives 200
Cultural Capital 209
Debt 235
Diderot Effect 243
Economy, Informal 252
Elias, Norbert 261
Ethical Consumption 268
Fair Trade 280
Farmers' Markets 284
Finance/Financial Markets 293
Flea Markets 296
Food Deserts 300
Frankfurt School 305
Free Trade Zones/Export Processing Zones 310
Gay and Lesbian/Queer Markets/Marketing 313
Gender and Consumer Culture 316
Gifts 324
Global Justice Movement 328
Green Consumerism 342
Green Consumption 346
Housing/Housing Markets 357
Leisure and Consumption 381
Marketplace Trust 393
Markets, Moral Aspects of 395
Marx, Karl 397
Medical Tourism 418
Modernization Theory 428
Needs, True and False 440
Needs and Wants 442
Obesity 449
Occupy Movement 453
Open Source and Consumption 455
Outsourcing 457
Politics and Consumer Culture 463
Quality of Life, Measurements of 481
Scarcity and Artificial Scarcity 489
Slow Food Movement 517
Socially Responsible Marketing (SRM) 523
Sustainable Consumption 530
Sweatshops 534
Taxes 541
Veblen, Thorstein 555
Wal-Mart 559

Key Figures

Adorno, Theodor 1
Barthes, Roland 32
Baudrillard, Jean 33
Benjamin, Walter 42
Birmingham School 47
Bourdieu, Pierre 51
Consumer Activism 103
Consumer Movements, Contemporary 128
Consumer Protection Agency 137
Consumer Resistance Movements 139
Cooperatives 200
de Certeau, Michel 230
Debord, Guy 233
Elias, Norbert 261
Frankfurt School 305
Marx, Karl 397
Veblen, Thorstein 555
Warhol, Andy 561
Williams, Raymond 569

Movements

Anti-Consumption Tactics 15
Boycotts 55
Burning Man 65
Consumer Movements, Contemporary 128
Consumer Resistance Movements 139
Cooperatives 200
Culture Jamming 226
Do-It-Yourself (DIY) 247
Downshifting 248
Ecotourism 255
Ethical Consumption 268
Fair Trade 280
Farmers' Markets 284
Gentrification 322
Global Justice Movement 328

Marx, Karl 397
Occupy Movement 453
Open Source and Consumption 455
Politics and Consumer Culture 463
Recycling 485
Slow Food Movement 517
Socially Responsible Marketing (SRM) 523
Sustainable Consumption 530

Practices

Advertising 2
Anti-Consumption Tactics 15
Arcades 21
B2B Marketing 27
Body and Consumer Culture 49
Boycotts 55
Character Licensing 74
Christmas 77
Consumer Activism 103
Consumer Behavior 105
Consumer Resistance Movements 139
Consumer Socialization 144
Consumption and Identity 162
Consumption Rituals 187
Cosmetic Surgery 202
Counterfeiting/Piracy 204
Cultural Omnivores 214
Culture Jamming 226
Dandyism 229
Death and Consumption 231
Decluttering 238
Department Stores 240
Diderot Effect 243
Do-It-Yourself (DIY) 247
Downshifting 248
Economy, Informal 252
Ethical Consumption 268
Experiential Consumption 273
Fair Trade 280
Farmers' Markets 284
Fashion 286
Flâneur/Flânerie 295
Flea Markets 296
Food 297
Fordism/Post-Fordism 301
Franchising 304
Gentrification 322
Gifts 324
Hyperconsumption 360
Leisure and Consumption 381
Lifestyle 383
Locavorism 387
Marketing/Marketing Science 389
Medical Tourism 418
Merchandising 421
Metrosexual 427
Money 430
Music and Consumer Experience 435
Open Source and Consumption 455
Outsourcing 457
Peer-to-Peer File Sharing 461
Prosumption 476
Public Relations 477
Recycling 485
Servicescapes 499
Shopping 505
Socially Responsible Marketing (SRM) 523
Stealth Marketing 526
Sustainable Consumption 530
Sweatshops 534
Waste 563
Weddings 566

Race, Gender, Body, and Sexuality

African Americans and Consumption 10
Asian Americans and Consumption 23
Barbie 30
Beauty Industry 38
Behavioral Economics and Consumption 41
Body and Consumer Culture 49
Citizenship and Consumption 81

Commodity Racism 99
Consumption and Identity 162
Consumption and Sport 191
Cosmetic Surgery 202
Cultural Capital 209
Emotions and Consumption 263
Fashion 286
Femininities 290
Gay and Lesbian/Queer Markets/Marketing 313
Gender and Consumer Culture 316
Girl Culture 326
Global Justice Movement 328
Latinos and Consumption 379
Lifestyle 383
Masculinity 403
Metrosexual 427
Mothers/Motherhood 433
Nike 445
Sexualities and Consumption 501
Warhol, Andy 561
Weddings 566

Situated Consumption

Americanization 12
Arcades 21
Authenticity 25
Big-Box Stores 45
Bricolage 63
Burning Man 65
Carnivals/Carnivalesque 69
Children's Consumer Culture 75
Cities, Visual Consumption of 79
Commodities 93
Commodity Fetishism 97
Consumers in Emerging Economies 150
Consumption in Africa 157
Consumption in China 159
Consumption in India 167
Consumption in Japan 170
Consumption, Landscapes of 173
Consumption in the Middle East/Arab World 174
Consumption in Postcommunist Countries 179
Consumption in the United States 195
Dandyism 229
Department Stores 240
Economy, Informal 252
Ecotourism 255
Farmers' Markets 284
Flea Markets 296
Food Deserts 300
Free Trade Zones/Export Processing Zones 310
Global Markets 331
Las Vegas 377
Locavorism 387
Medical Tourism 418
Occupy Movement 453
Servicescapes 499
Shopping Malls 509
Supermarkets 528
Tourism 549
Wal-Mart 559
Whole Foods Market 567
World's Fairs and International Expositions 571

Theories

Adorno, Theodor 1
Authenticity 25
Barthes, Roland 32
Baudrillard, Jean 33
Behavioral Economics and Consumption 41
Benjamin, Walter 42
Birmingham School 47
Bourdieu, Pierre 51
Commodification 90
Commodity Fetishism 97
Commodity Racism 99
Conspicuous Consumption 101
Consumer Culture, History of 118
Consumer Culture Theory (CCT) 124
Consumer Movements, History of 133

Consumer Socialization 144
Consumer Society 145
Consumers, Flawed 154
Consumption and Identity 162
Consumption, Postmodern 183
Consumption, Spectacles of 189
Coolhunting 199
Cultural Capital 209
Cultural Studies 216
Culture Jamming 226
Culture-Ideology of Consumerism 220
de Certeau, Michel 230
Debord, Guy 233
Disneyization 246
Elias, Norbert 261
Ethical Consumption 268
Experiential Consumption 273
Failing Consumption 279
Fashion 286
Fordism/Post-Fordism 301
Frankfurt School 305
Gender and Consumer Culture 316
Gifts 324
Glocalization/Grobalization 338
Governmentality and Consumer Culture 339
Homogenization and Heterogenization 356
Hyperconsumption 360
Just-in-Time Production 373
Marx, Karl 397
Material Culture Studies 414
McDonaldization 416
Methods of Consumer Research 422
Modernization Theory 428
Needs and Wants 442
Needs, True and False 440
Semiotics 492
Starbuckization 524
Symbolic Exchange 536
Symbolic Value 538

Timeline

YEAR	EVENT
4000 BC	Bartering is common method of trade
500 BC – AD 400	Greek agoras dominate Mediterranean commercial life
210 BC – AD 1450s	The Silk Road is an important trade route between Europe, Africa, the Middle East, and Asia
100 BC – AD 476	Roman Forums are leading centers of commercial activity
AD 600s	Paper money becomes common in China during the Tang Dynasty
1400s	Markets become centerplace of trading, including a number of prominent souks in the Middle East
1602	The Dutch East India Corporation was founded, progenitor of the modern corporation
1760s – 1840s	The height of the Industrial Revolution
1780s	Palais-Royal opens in Paris as first arcade
1786	First advertising agency – William Taylor – opens
1844	French Industrial Exposition of 1844 is predecessor to World's Fairs
1851	The Crystal Palace is constructed as part of the Great Exhibition of 1851
1852	Bon Marché opens in Paris as world's first department store
1859	A&P opens in the United States as first chain store
1867	First industrial assembly line is used by the meatpacking industry in Chicago
1893	World Columbian Exposition held in Chicago, making use of a "midway" and "anchor" exhibits as forerunners of shopping malls and amusement parks
1911	Hollywood produces its first film shot by Nestor Motion Picture Company
1913	First Bollywood film produced – Raja Harishchandra by Dadasaheb Phalke
1916	Market Square opens in Chicago

YEAR	EVENT
1923	Country Club opens in Kansas City, Missouri
	The Frankfurt School, associated with the Institute for Social Research, is established in Germany
1924	A&W opens first food service franchise
1936	First issue of *Consumer Reports* is published
1940s	Hotel-casinos being to appear on "strip" in Las Vegas
1945	End of WWII
1946	Levittown founded on Long Island, New York
1947	Northgate opens in Seattle, Washington
1949	Diners Club issues first universal credit card
1954	Northland opens outside Detroit, Michigan
1955	McDonald's begins franchising
	Disneyland Resort opens in Anaheim, California
1956	Southdale opens in Edina, Minnesota as world's first enclosed shopping mall
1957	First superstore opens as predecessor to Toys 'R Us
1959	First Barbie doll sold
	First free trade/export processing zone in the world established in Ireland
1962	Sam Walton opens Walmart Discount City in Rogers, Arkansas
1964	Center for Contemporary Culture Studies founded at University of Birmingham (UK) by Richard Hoggart
1964	Nike begins operations as Blue Ribbons Sports
1967	First international McDonald's open in Canada and Costa Rica
1967	*Journal of Consumer Affairs* launched
1970	First outlet mall opens outside Reading, Pennsylvania
1971	First Starbucks opens in Seattle, Washington
1974	*Journal of Consumer Research* launched
1976	Apple founded
1980	Whole Foods Market opens first store in Austin, Texas
1981	West Edmonton Mall opens in Canada
1985	Home Shopping Network is launched
1986	First Burning Man event held in Black Rock desert of Northern Nevada
1986	Slow Food Movement founded by Carlo Petrini to promote traditional and regional cuisine
1988	First Wal-Mart Supercenter opens
1989	Adbusters is founded as an anti-consumerist organization in Vancouver, Canada
1992	Mall of America opens in Bloomington, Minnesota

YEAR	EVENT
1992	First Buy Nothing Day is held in Canada as an international day of protest against consumerism
1993	Consumer Research Network of European Sociological Association begins
1995	amazon.com begins operations
1995	eBay begins operations
1996	Wal-Mart opens first cybermall
1996	Celebration, Florida opens as example of new urbanism
1997	Ericsson introduces the first device known as a "smartphone"
1997	*Consumption, Markets, and Culture* (journal) launched
1998	Google founded
1998	PayPal founded as online payment processing and money transfer service
1999	Easton Lifestyle Center opens phase I in Columbus, Ohio
1999	Battle for Seattle protests break out over WTO in Seattle, Washington
1999	Napster begins operating as a peer-to-peer file sharing service
2001	The first iPod is released by Apple, Inc.
2001	*Journal of Consumer Culture* launched
2003	iTunes store opens
2004	Child and Teen Consumption biennial international conference launched
2004	Facebook begins operations
2005	YouTube begins operations
2006	Consumer Culture Theory annual conference and consortium launched
2006	Twitter begins operations
2009	The Dubai Mall, currently the largest shopping mall in the world by total area, opens in the United Arab Emirates
2011	Occupy Movement takes off
2012	Sociology of Consumers and Consumption Section of the American Sociological Association launched
2015	*Wiley Blackwell Encyclopedia of Consumption and Consumer Studies* published

J. Michael Ryan

Introduction

The academic interest in consumption and consumer studies has its primary origins in the interwar period in Europe. The social importance of consumption to everyday life and politics, however, dates back to the beginnings of permanent settlements among humans. From the early days of bartering, to the Greek agoras, to the Roman Forums, to McDonald's, Wal-Mart, and the internet, the exchange of goods and services and their relevance as markers of individual social identity and engines of large-scale social change has, in many ways, been at the heart of human sociality.

Although consumption was once arguably more of a necessary practice to obtain needed goods and services (something it still is today), it has now also become a form of social diversion, entertainment, and lifestyle among those of us who are privileged enough to be able to take part in what some might see as its excesses. The appearance of shopping malls, the spread of local and international franchises, the appearance of the credit card, and, more recently, the internet have all pushed consumption from the margins to the center in the everyday lives of many. This push to the center has also occurred within the academy, where a growing number of institutions now offer courses, majors, and even departments devoted to the study of consumer culture.

The social-cultural study of consumers and consumption stands today as a robust area of scholarly inquiry, growing largely since the end of the last century and continuing apace as the landscapes of various consumer cultures arise and transform. Over the last two decades, scholars from around the world have produced influential theories and substantive empirical research on consumers and consumption that touch upon virtually all key aspects of social life and social thought. Recent scholarship draws upon and speaks to key questions and problems claimed within the social and cultural sciences, broadly speaking – for example, power, inequality, social differentiation and identity, ecological impact, meaning, structure and agency, and the relations between micro-interactions and large-scale patterns.

In this light, we have curated the *Wiley Blackwell Encyclopedia of Consumption and Consumer Studies* (ECCS) as an accessible and focused reference, suitable for instructors, seasoned researchers, and students alike. It is a tool and resource for those who seek thoughtful yet to-the-point discussions of key concepts, issues, and figures in this growing, expansive field. The distinctive feature of the ECCS is the diversity of voices, paradigms, and disciplines it brings to bear on the study of consumers and consumption. Renowned and emergent scholars from sociology, communication, consumer behavior, marketing, psychology, and a variety of other fields offer a breadth of perspectives and approaches to the topics they address in their respective entries. This volume has benefited not only from the fresh perspectives of advanced graduate students and early-career scholars from a variety of disciplines, but also from the expertise of well-established experts in the field of consumption. As well, we include authors from countries around the world, including Brazil, Canada, Egypt, France, Greece, Israel, Italy, the Netherlands, Norway, Peru, Sweden, the United Kingdom, and the United States, among others.

Assembling such texts from such a wide range of fields and varying national contexts into a single compact volume has proven both challenging and rewarding, with gaps and omissions of people and concepts unavoidable. We, as co-editors, have made no attempt to reconcile the perspectives and paradigms offered by the different authors, preferring to allow each to speak for her- or himself. As a reference text, the ECCS is not meant to be read cover to cover for ideological or theoretical consistency, but to offer perspectives on an open and dynamic area of inquiry. In that way, we hope to make the ECCS an open resource available for a plethora of uses and needs and another step in helping to coalesce this dynamic field of inquiry.

We hope you find the *Wiley Blackwell Encyclopedia of Consumption and Consumer Studies* to be both enjoyable as well as practical, at once handy and engaging.

Daniel Thomas Cook
Rutgers University – Camden, USA
J. Michael Ryan
The American University in Cairo, Egypt

Acknowledgments

This project is the result of the hard work of not only the editors but also the many contributors, the publishers, and the unnamed others who have been involved in its production. The primary thanks belong to the dedicated contributors who took the time and energy to write the outstanding entries that make up this work. We were truly impressed by the caliber of scholarship among them, a feature which certainly made our jobs as editors much easier. It is to them that the quality of this project is truly attributable.

We would also like to thank the outstanding team at Wiley Blackwell for their support and dedication to this project. Justin Vaughan, our publisher, has been a real source of encouragement in helping make the dream we had of producing this kind of resource into a reality. Ben Thatcher has also been an invaluable support through his attention to detail, his patience, and for being always willing to offer guidance and assistance.

A

Adorno, Theodor

VANDER CASAQUI
Escola Superior de Propaganda e Marketing, Brazil

The German researcher Theodor W. Adorno (1903–69) was one of the leading theorists of the Frankfurt School, which conceived critical media theory and has had a wide influence in communication studies across the decades. In a classical context, Adorno developed a series of sophisticated studies in his capacity as an art critic, a philosopher, a sociologist, and a musicologist.

The context of the development of his most famous thesis about media phenomena is the social scene that culminated in World War II (1939–45). Of Jewish descent, Adorno left Germany to seek refuge in the United States, where he worked with Max Horkheimer. He was influenced by the spread of Nazism and its mobilizing power, strongly supported by the use of ideological propaganda. In the United States, he observed the spread of the media industry and the culture of the "American way of life," finding similarities in how media communication influenced the political, ideological, and commercial strategies of those in positions of power. With experience of these two scenarios, he was stimulated to build a theory that criticized up front the domination of the people by the ideological apparatuses of their time.

Along with Horkheimer, Adorno wrote *Dialectic of Enlightenment* (1947), in which the concept of the culture industry is developed. With Marxist theory as a backdrop, Adorno and Horkheimer's critical theory makes an analogy of the process of manufacturing goods, of the industrial capitalism that permeated Karl Marx's analysis, with the production of cultural goods conceived as an industry, from communication via the mass media that spread throughout the twentieth century. For Marx, the capitalist mode of production created alienated workers, who were unaware of the value of their work and of the exploitation of their labor by the bourgeoisie, the owners of the means of production. For critical theory, the culture industry results in the production of mass cultural goods that lead to the alienation of the masses, who are instituted solely as consumers and manipulated according to their interests and profit goals.

The alienation of the people through the culture industry is a reading of the effects inferred from what is observed in the media's productive sphere. The result of this production would be a mass culture, somewhere between high and popular culture, which makes use of aesthetic elements from both,

The Wiley Blackwell Encyclopedia of Consumption and Consumer Studies, First Edition.
Edited by Daniel Thomas Cook and J. Michael Ryan.

emptying them of their most potent characteristics. A culture based on the commodity form, to be consumed on a large scale: this is the analysis that results from the idea of a culture industry. In short, critical theory is an Enlightenment project of rationalization of the people, in response to the non-reflexive character of the hegemonic mass culture – created to take into account leisure time for workers, and with the aim of having them conform to the status quo.

Analysis of the possible effects of cultural goods produced and promoted by the culture industry is sustained by Adorno's conception of culture, based on a hierarchy of value, in which high culture, associated with high art, has the power to form conscious and reflexive subjects, complete beings in their existence, in contrast to mass culture that alienates the subjects. The technical reproducibility would represent the loss of the artistic aura and its power of fruition; on this matter, Adorno and Walter Benjamin – the latter of whom was averse to such a deterministic reading of critical theory – sustained antagonistic beliefs.

The deterministic design of the alienated subject by the consumption of mass culture was criticized by the school of cultural studies from the 1960s and later, and by the Latin American school of communication. However, the perspective of produced culture as a commodity is a fundamental legacy of the studies of communication and consumption. Guy Debord (1995/1967) observed in the 1960s that this process of aestheticization and commodification, initially identified by Adorno, had expanded to embody culture as a whole, within the social scene that would be called the "society of the spectacle."

In the contemporary scene, the commodity form and the logic of entertainment broadly cross areas of cultural production, and can be seen in the most varied of products, from music to talk shows, from news to movies. Conceived as industries, the production spheres and/or the spheres of distribution of contemporary cultural goods, known as "creative industries," feed the perception of the importance of the contribution from Adorno, Horkheimer, and their critical theory.

SEE ALSO: Benjamin, Walter; Commodification; Debord, Guy; Frankfurt School; Marx, Karl; Mass Culture; Mass Media

REFERENCE

Debord, Guy. 1995/1967. *The Society of the Spectacle.* New York: Zone Books.

FURTHER READING

Benjamin, Walter 2002. *Selected Writings, Volume 4: 1938–1940.* Cambridge, MA: Harvard University Press.

Horkheimer, Max, and Adorno, Theodor W. 2002/1947. *Dialectic of Enlightenment: Philosophical Fragments.* Stanford, CA: Stanford University Press.

Marx, Karl. 1992/1867. *Capital. Volume 1: A Critique of Political Economy.* London: Penguin Classics.

Advertising

LAUREN LANGMAN
Loyola University Chicago, USA

Advertising is the process through which an organization or individual who provides a product or service uses a variety of announcements through signs, billboards, and mass media (that now includes the internet) to encourage people to purchase those goods or services. The average person is exposed to thousands and thousands of ads. In an election year, there will be many more ads "selling" candidates. Some claim advertising leads to social fragmentation, alienation, and the wanton destruction of the environment. But, conversely, others argue that advertising helps consumers make informed decisions and, indeed, provides people with a basis of common goals, values, and a variety of gratifications. All agree that ads are ubiquitous.

THE HISTORY OF ADVERTISING: FROM SELLING PRODUCTS TO PERSONAS

Since marketplaces first emerged, sellers have attempted to supply information to consumers to describe and promote their offerings. The beermakers of Mesopotamia may have been the first people to advertise their products. The brothels of Pompeii advertised their services with signs of stick figures representing the particular services available and the prices of each. These ads still endure. For most of the history of markets, advertising consisted of the displays of wares closely tied to the place where sales or trades took place: what you saw was what you could get, whether fruits, vegetables, clothes, jewelry, pottery, prostitutes, or metal tools. By the Middle Ages, certain trades had distinct symbols to represent their products or services – the three balls in front of the pawn shop or the striped barber pole may be the best-known examples that are still around today.

As trade began to flourish, especially after the rise of print-based literacy and newspapers, advertising and mass media soon became intertwined. In the eighteenth century, most of such advertising consisted simply of announcements of product availability and descriptions. The first newspaper ad in the United States appeared in 1702, offering an estate in Oyster Bay. About 40 years later, Benjamin Franklin printed the first magazine advertisement in the *General Magazine*, which he had founded. By the nineteenth century, advertising had become an important part of commerce. In 1841, the first ad agency opened in Philadelphia. By the Civil War, the sale of advertising space in newspapers and magazines had become a major business, pioneered in part by one William Carlton, whose agency would eventually become known as J. Walter Thompson.

For the most part, early advertisements were often flowery product descriptions telling about quality, how well items were made, functioned, and/or the "trustworthiness" of the producer. With the spread of railroads and rural mail delivery, the catalogs of Sears and Wards were delivering their goods to homes throughout the nation. Toward the end of the century, we would see the growth of the department stores that soon became major advertisers in newspapers. The displays themselves were advertisements of the "fantastic" life that could be purchased (Leach 1993). This time also witnessed the growth of "branded" household goods such as Campbell Soup, Quaker Oats, Morton Salt, and Ivory soap. Soon, outdoor signs and billboards heralding various goods, services, or events were to be found on buildings and along roads and highways. The turn of the twentieth century was marked by branded consumer products such as the Kodak Brownie or the Gillette razor. Oldsmobile was the first mass-produced car and the Wright brothers flew the world's first airplane. At the same time there was another innovation in the works: electricity was becoming widely available and it wasn't long before electrical home appliances, from vacuum cleaners to refrigerators, were being heavily advertised.

From the 1920s or so on, there were major innovations that would forever impact advertising and, in turn, society. First, the rapid growth of cities, often tied to industrialization, created vast factories with better-paid workers and markets for consumer goods and services that workers could not produce for themselves. Advertising proliferated to "help" them make "informed" choices. Second, the rapid growth of radio, and the licensing of airwaves to private companies, led to the proliferation of radio programming that sold airtime to advertisers. Soon came an explosion of regular radio programs featuring various "stars" and, in turn, larger audiences for commercials encouraging consumption. The airwaves became flooded with jingles, songs and rhymes, testimonials, endorsements, and lofty promises. Third, advertising began to change from textual descriptions to visual images and from selling the quality of the product to constructing and improving the nature of the consumer, rendering him or her a better, more attractive, desirable person. Perhaps the marker of this change came when Edward Louis Bernays, nephew of Sigmund Freud, arrived in the United States and blended psychoanalytic theory with mass media. The marker of this change came when "prominent" women marched down the Boardwalk of Atlantic City smoking "torches of liberty." After this, cigarettes began to become widely acceptable among "respectable" women – heretofore, smoking was practiced only by prostitutes. Owning and using the product came to have meanings for self-enhancement, a desirable identity, status, gaining recognition, etc. Image slowly displaced substance. Advertised products promised to make people healthier, happier, more beautiful, and more "alluring." Otherwise said, advertising began to "colonize consciousness" and transform desire such that people believed purchasing certain things would provide self-gratification that would make them happy (Ewen 1976; Ewen and Ewen 1982). Finally, as a result of what has been said, the 1920s marked an important point of transition in which the technologies of mass production joined with mass-mediated entertainment. Consumerism spread from the elites to the masses. This new complex of production, mass-mediated advertising, and consumption would constitute modern consumer society, with its elite-driven culture, extolled by advertising, in which the democratization of desire was realized.

Within 20 years, radio had joined with photography to create another form of mass media: television. While the proliferation and spread of television were delayed by World War II, by the end of the 1950s, most Americans owned a TV set. By this time, advertising had largely completed the move from selling the products to creating certain kinds of (desirable) consumer-based identities. What one wore, drove, ate, or paid money to see/hear, expressed one's group membership, identity, and "distinction." Acquisition and consumption became the means of achieving happiness (Leach 1993).

CONSUMER SOCIETY

The postwar years in the United States saw a rapid expansion of the economy and, in turn, major corporate growth, rising disposable income, and an explosion of consumerism. Between pent-up demand and the new affluence, and a proliferation of government-backed mortgages that supported vast tracts of suburban housing construction, there were demands for furnishings, appliances, cars, and a national interstate highway system. More than half the economy was now based on advertising-inspired consumer demand for goods, services, and cultural consumption, from gramophone records to foreign travel. By the 1950s, capitalism had achieved a major turning point; the consumer society had arrived.

For many social observers, consumer society and its cornucopia of goods, championed by advertising, heralded a new stage of social development and a new form of domination. The new era of unending "spectacles" and manufactured events manipulated consciousness and fostered mass compliance to the world of better living through consumption (Debord 1967/2006; Boorstin 1962). A number of cultural markers might be noted – for example, the Marlboro Man trotted across television screens and, as a result, Marlboro sales skyrocketed. Later, the Marlboro Man got lung cancer and spent the rest of his now shortened life coughing, spitting up blood, and working in anti-smoking campaigns. But to this very day, the image of his rugged individualism, accompanied by the "Western" music beat, remains etched in our consciousness. That spirit helped elect two "cowboy presidents." One of the key ways to understand consumer society has been the study of meanings and identities – namely, what academics call semiotics. Thus, for example, certain meanings, such as luxury, adventure, romance, sophistication, and even transgression, come to be associated with certain brands or items. The ads suggest that if people buy this or that, eat this or that, or travel to here or there, they can be considered classy, erudite, or sexy. The logic of advertising often borders on the "magical," in which a particular toothpaste makes you "popular" or an SUV renders you powerful. Similarly, many restaurants, theme parks, casinos, and hotels sell "themed environments" laden with meanings (Gottdiener 2002). In this realm of symbolic meanings, advertisements often challenge other advertisements and engage in what has been called "sign wars" (Goldman and Papson 1996).

THE JOYS OF SHOPPING

Why do people like to shop and how has advertising become intertwined with human desire? Is the consumer a rational hero who rationally pursues his or her desires, or a superficial fool duped and manipulated by advertising? For those influenced by Marxism, advertising's message is that buying and possessing goods satisfy desires. People have certain basic needs, they desire (1) memberships in groups, and connections with friends, family, and communities; (2) self-esteem, pride, and dignity; and (3) a sense of agency and the feeling of making an impact on the world. Furthermore (4), they hope to avoid unpleasant experiences – for example, loneliness, anxiety, or depression, etc. Advertising has insinuated itself into the individual's psyche in such a way that buying the advertised product will gratify these human longings. If one drinks the "right" cola, beer, or juice, one will have great friends or lovers. Consumption is often based on conformity to gain acceptance by others. Similarly, the "right" label (read "expensive") on one's clothes, watch, or car can enhance status and provide a sense of pride through ownership – "standing out" from other folks with lesser taste. In a world where so much of our lives is controlled by impersonal forces, one of the places where we find a range of "choices" is in consumption, choosing particular advertised brands or items that will go together in "unique combinations." Finally, for many, shopping alleviates the stresses and strains of life. "When the going gets tough, the tough go shopping." While many advertised products promise gratifications, so too do many products promise relief from various afflictions, from headaches, coughs, or nausea, to constipation or diarrhea. Indeed, a great deal of early advertising suggested many health benefits: things did go better with Coca-Cola when it actually contained coke.

Some consider the Marxists to be somewhat puritanical – any form of commodified self-indulgence is implicitly counter-revolutionary. Yet Chinese Communists gave up Mao jackets decades ago. In China today, shopping malls sprout like mushrooms. Some see consumption as a realm of fun and gratification. Whenever people have a chance to consume, they will. Twitchell (1996) claims that, despite the anti-consumerist biases of leftist curmudgeons, people do enjoy consuming advertised goods and far more people opt to "shop till they drop" than retreat to the "simple life."

> Reaching into the wallet is a much more powerful articulation of desire and belief than delivering the lecture … I think the market essentially shows this. What is being consumed is what people really do think is entertaining them, satisfying them, making them happy…, but it is the illusion that is so powerful. This illusion seems to be making American culture incredibly attractive to others and making other cultures essentially mimics of American popular culture. Whatever this stuff is in advertising, it's incredibly powerful. It's pushed all these other things like literature, art and religion aside. (Sut Jhally v. James Twitchell, n.d.)

Consumerism provides a realm of irrational release from the toils of ordered work demands. Advertising culture provides us with fun. Ritzer (1999) has similarly claimed that consumption "re-enchants" the world. Otherwise said, the world of consumption, much like religion in earlier times, becomes a way of integrating oneself into certain groups, finding esteem, dignity, and meaning.

How does advertising foster purchases, and what mediates between advertised image, purchase, and emotions? Mass-mediated images not only impact consciousness, but unconsciousness as well. Advertising's images seem to go directly from the external source to the person's emotional realms, avoiding the cortical areas of reason and reflection. Thus, if one hears the right words or songs, one feels that buying the suggested product will provide a positive feeling. Certain critics of advertising have suggested that many ads have subliminal messages and/or hidden sexual/aggressive imagery that encourage people to buy certain products – from popcorn during movie intermissions to clam dinners containing subliminal images of sex orgies. In any event, seeing or hearing ads, consciously or not, evokes certain feelings and desires. When shoppers see or seek out what was advertised, they are disposed to reproduce that feeling – and quite often the purchase does indeed make us feel better, if for only a short period.

THE BRANDED SELF

For many people, their narrative of self-identity is expressed in their style of life – their clothes, home and its décor, cars (or other forms of transportation such as bicycles, motorcycles), food preferences, cultural tastes, etc. Merchandisers today are not so much selling products made in their factories as marketing "brands" that provide the consumer with certain lifestyle-based self-identities and memberships in the "imaginary communities" of, say, North Face adventurers, Ralph Lauren sophisticates, or Abercrombie and Fitch or Fubu's subcultures of transgression (Klein 2000).

Market researchers have devoted millions of dollars to targeting particular clusters of consumers. While social class (education, income) plays a major role in what one can afford and the aesthetic tastes one appreciates, for many Americans who consider themselves "middle class," selfhood is more complex and nuanced, articulated in patterns of consumption that provide them with "distinction" (Bourdieu 1979/1984). Thus, for example, "young bohemians" (urbanites in creative occupations like advertising) might well prefer to dine in the latest storefront restaurant serving Mexican-Mongolian fusion food, while "the pool and patio" older, upper middle-class suburbanites prefer Olive Garden or Chilies. Most tastes and preferences are not simply based on income, but on how folks choose to dispose of it. Aesthetic tastes reflect lifestyles, and identities. Products for the exploding youth market promise that consumers will be "cool," acceptable, or desirable in certain subcultures, expressed in nonconformist and rebellious ways, such as the flaunting of sexual norms (for example in Abercrombie and Fitch ads/catalogues). The "marketing of cool" is a major strategy of advertising (Frank 1997).

One of the latest expressions of branded selfhood is "celebrity ware" – fashion lines "designed" and marketed by various media stars such as Jaclyn Smith, Jennifer Lopez, or Paris Hilton. Much like the magical thought known as "imitative magic" practiced among traditional peoples, the person imagines that if she – and it is mostly she – dresses like a glamorous "star," then she too will be glamorous. Moreover, she might also need to enroll in that star's exercise program and diet plan, and pick from recommended plastic surgeons.

Does advertising impact one's identity, self-image, and sexuality? A number of critics have suggested not only that the images of advertised beauty through consumption, for both men and women, might affect a person's self-esteem by defining unattainable levels of beauty with the "right" consumption of fashions, cosmetics, and accessories – that might include cars, travel, and leisure – but that, at the same time, advertising is objectifying people on the basis of race, gender, and ethnicity (see Cortese 2007). Moreover, sexualized advertising, flaunting beauty and equating it with sexuality, naturalizes "casual" sexuality as "normal," and not everyone is comfortable with that. Kilbourne (2010) has shown how much advertising has impacted the identities of young women, bombarding them with images of beauty and happiness promised through consumption, but never realized. Instead, most women do not look like the models shown – and that discrepancy often impairs their self-esteem.

THE SOCIAL CONSEQUENCES OF ADVERTISING

There is little doubt that advertising is one of the central motifs of the contemporary age; almost every product or service available to consumers is advertised somewhere. But there is little agreement as to the consequences of advertising for individuals and the society. Does consumption bring the personal happiness promised by the ads? Aristotle warned that human wants are insatiable, that wealth and possessions do not bring happiness. Tolstoy said much the same. Freud suggested that happiness came through love and work – indeed, the accumulation of goods was often compensation for what was lacking within one's self or one's relationships. Yet although advertising promises that consumption will provide idealized selfhood and the very happiness that people seek, when consumption does not gratify, people continue to buy things in the hope that the next purchase, the next "improved" version, will make them happy. Many conservatives fundamentally agree and suggest that advertising not only encourages "immoral" behavior (particularly sex), but undermines the authority of parents, teachers, and religious leaders. All too often, we moderns find out the truth from ancient religious teachings that worldly possessions are not what bring us true happiness. While it is surely the case that abject poverty and financial duress do not make people happy, after a certain point it is hard to see any relation between wealth, possessions, and happiness.

Whether or not advertising brings happiness, it does have other costs and functions. One of the most enduring critiques of advertising and consumerism comes from various leftist commentators who see advertising-dominated mass culture as an essential aspect of the status quo that sustains ruling-class interests; while the majority of people are not only exploited and alienated, but also "dumbed down," they are distracted from serious concerns and actively reproduce their own subjugation. For Marx, religion served to keep people pacified and looking forward to the next life. Today, consumerism serves much the same functions. Consumerism not only provides most of the profits for the current economic and social system, but it secures political hegemony as it entraps people within the system.

One of the most serious issues today involves political advertising – the "selling" of candidates, much like soap or toothpaste. In 1960, people who watched live on TV the debate between potential presidential candidates John F. Kennedy and Richard Nixon thought JFK had won. Radio listeners, on the other hand, gave the debate to Nixon. Henceforth, televised images have been among the most important factors in determining elections. Media consultants now play a major role in shaping political campaigns. Much like when they are selling other products, they use focus groups, surveys, and audience responses to hone political images and messages to produce the various soundbites and soundsights. Similar techniques are used to discredit the opponent. Sadly, these political advertisements, like most other ads, appeal to feelings and emotions and, as a result, serious political questions are no longer subject to genuine debates. George W. Bush was seen as a religious, "regular Joe," as a strong leader, fighting to defend American security. That his images were simulations is hardly doubted. Similarly, his "selling" of the invasion of Iraq, based clearly on what we can now see was "false advertising," has had tragic consequences. *Caveat emptor*.

As Marcuse (1964) argued, advertising has produced "artificial needs" that are "gratified" in consumption habits that foster an exaggerated concern with the self and personal pleasures; this self-centeredness leads to indifference to social costs and consequences on the larger community. Moreover, advertising fosters "one-dimensional" thought that erodes the power of critical reason and, in turn, acceptance of domination rather than human freedom. Jhally (1997) has noted that Americans constitute 6 percent of the world's population and consume 25 percent of its resources, leading to major environmental damage. We are approaching the point where our planet will no longer be able to sustain human behavior. Many experts have tied the intensity of recent hurricanes to global warming, brought on by fossil fuel emissions and industrial pollutants.

Schudson (1984) argued that the function of advertising is not simply to sell goods, but, further, advertising promotes "American realism," a notion that the "American way of life" provides more material abundance than any other society in the world; it is not only superior, but the future will be even better. Advertising, as an ideology, sells consumerism as a way of life and as displaying loyalty to consumer capitalism. Advertised consumerism has come to replace religion and/or nationalism as a basis for the rituals and beliefs that provide social cohesion and give us fundamental meaning for life.

We might note that, in the last decade or so, a new form of mass-mediated advertising has appeared – on the internet. There are at least three kinds of advertisement. When you open a web page, a number of products and services may well appear on the website. But the technology of the internet has now become so sophisticated that if, perchance, you open a certain website to check a price or gain information, various pop-up ads for that product or service will then appear wherever else you go on the web. Also, almost everyone gets loads of spam email, in which all kinds of goods are advertised and sold, from foods to clothes and books to boats. Likewise, a number of emails offer services, from vacation tours to sewer cleaning, and, indeed, a vast variety of meeting, dating, and "hook-up sites."

At the same time, advertising has been used to promote worthy causes, from anti-slavery to suffrage to anti-sweatshop movements. But so too has advertising led to alienation and social fragmentation, as well as social indifference to collective adversity as shopping malls and internet stores have replaced churches. Advertising has also led to certain ill-informed political choices and policies. Yet whatever the opinions of academics, we have seen that advertising has become a major component of the contemporary landscape.

CONCLUSION

America's move from a backwater colony to the wealthiest country in the world was dependent on the early embrace of mass production, followed by the mass distribution of advertising-laden newspapers and magazines touting the many new products available. By the early nineteenth century, the fates of the US economy and of advertising were closely intertwined. On the one hand, advertising was essential for the rapid economic development of the United States, and its current position in the world. On the other hand, some argue that advertising fosters alienation, isolation, and environmental damage. Others claim that the imaginary world offered by advertising provides a great deal of fun and enjoyment for many people. Is advertising a curse, a blessing, or perhaps in some ways both? That is the question.

SEE ALSO: Brands and Branding; Consumer Society; Department Stores; Frankfurt School; Gay and Lesbian/Queer Markets/Marketing; Hollywood; Infomercial; Mass Marketing; Mass Media; Niche Marketing; Stealth Marketing; Theming

REFERENCES

Boorstin, Daniel J. 1962. *The Image: A Guide to Pseudo-Events in America*. New York: Random House.

Bourdieu, Pierre. 1979/1984. *Distinction: A Social Critique of the Judgment of Taste*. Translated by Richard Nice. London: Routledge & Kegan Paul.

Cortese, Anthony J. 2007. *Provocateur: Images of Women and Minorities in Advertising*, 3rd ed. Lanham, MD: Rowan & Littlefield.

Debord, Guy. 1967/2006. *The Society of the Spectacle*. Translated by Ken Knabb. Detroit: Black and Red.

Ewen, Stuart. 1976. *Captains of Consciousness: Advertising and the Social Roots of Consumer Culture*. New York: McGraw-Hill.

Ewen, Stuart, and Elizabeth Ewen. 1982. *Channels of Desire: Mass Images and the Shaping of American Consciousness*. New York: McGraw-Hill.

Frank, Thomas. 1997. *The Conquest of Cool*. Chicago: University of Chicago Press.

Goldman, Robert, and Stephen Papson. 1996. *Sign Wars: The Cluttered Landscape of Advertising*. New York: Guilford.

Gottdiener, Mark. 2002. *The Theming of America*. Boulder, CO: Westview.

Jhally, Sut. 1997. *Advertising and the End of the World*. Northampton, MA: Media Education Foundation.

Kilbourne, Jean. 2010. *Killing Us Softly 4*. Northampton, MA: Media Education Foundation.

Klein, Naomi. 2000. *No Logo: Taking Aim at the Brand Bullies*. New York: Picador.

Leach, William R. 1993. *Land of Desire: Merchants, Power, and the Rise of a New American Culture*. New York: Random House.

Marcuse, Herbert. 1964. *One Dimensional Man*. Boston, MA: Beacon Press.

Ritzer, George. 1999. *Enchanting a Disenchanted World: Revolutionizing the Means of Consumption*. Thousand Oaks, CA: Pine Forge.

Schudson, Michael. 1984. *Advertising: The Uneasy Persuasion*. New York: Basic Books.

Sut Jhally v. James Twitchell. n.d. *On Advertising*. http://www.sutjhally.com/articles/jhallyvsttwitchell/:

Twitchell, James B. 1996. *Adcult: The Triumph of Advertising in American Culture*. New York: Colombia University Press.

African Americans and Consumption

NICOLE BROWN
University of Illinois at Urbana-Champaign, USA

African American consumerism deals with the meanings, beliefs, and values that African Americans associate with individual or group consumption. African Americans have a deep, complicated, and at times tumultuous relationship with consumerism that engages topics which include culture, citizenship, and identity. This relationship fuses together the desire of African Americans for access to material goods/services and a desire for acknowledgment and treatment as first-class citizens within the United States. Within the historical context of slavery, consumerism has functioned in various ways: (1) as an oppressive mechanism, with African Americans serving as commodities; (2) as a tool of resistance that would, in some cases, lead to systemic change; and/or (3) as a vehicle with which to mask systems of oppression by minimizing indicators of material deprivation.

Lizabeth Cohen (2003) argues that during the Cold War era through the 1970s, the public and private sector were interconnected through the creation of the "citizen consumer" (as a result of a booming economy, suburbanization, etc.) and that this connection helped perpetuate democratic ideals and had the unintentional effect of providing a consumer space of resistance for marginalized groups, specifically African Americans. The Welfare Rights Movement of the 1960s and 1970s, which was spearheaded by African American women, had among its primary goals the securing of what it felt were citizenry rights to participate in the economic system, and believed that government benefits should be made available to allow the poor to more equally engage as consumers.

Historically used as a tool for those marginalized by the traditional political system, consumerism as a tactic of political activism can be seen among those who are disenfranchised from the vote and who go otherwise unacknowledged as citizens, and among those distrustful of government and political institutions. African Americans have a long history of resisting such marginalization by engaging consumerism for political purposes, including access to the marketplace, via employment and consumer spaces.

In 1900, Booker T. Washington founded the National Negro Business League, an organization which sought to support black entrepreneurship and black capitalism. Shortly thereafter, African Americans near Tulsa, Oklahoma were building what would later be known as "Black Wall Street." The Greenwood district of Tulsa was the wealthiest black city in America and was home to a broad and successful array of black-owned businesses and a thriving black middle class before being burned down in a race riot in 1921. White mobs infiltrated the district and destroyed more than 35 city blocks, leaving more than 10,000 people homeless. Also during this time, the Garvey Movement would encourage African Americans to patronize black-owned businesses created specifically to serve the black consumer. Between 1929 and 1941, African Americans sustained pickets and boycotts which began in Chicago and led to a national movement referred to as "Don't Buy Where You Can't Work" campaigns. The early 1930s boycotts were heavily concentrated in the north of the country and served as the model of black activism precipitated by the Great Depression. The necessary conditions for this movement were severe unemployment, discrimination against African Americans, and a high concentration of African Americans in a central location. In many cases, these job campaigns were the result of grassroots neighborhood efforts.

During the 1950s and 1960s, the United States witnessed increased collective action of African Americans in consumer spaces through boycotts and selective patronage campaigns. Boycotts, such as those conducted in the 1960s in Montgomery (Alabama), Philadelphia (Pennsylvania), and Greensboro (North Carolina), for instance, addressed a variety of consumer issues, including inequities in products and services, inequitable facilities, and hiring practices, all of which had political and civil rights implications and applications. There was also a shift in boycott initiation from local efforts to national Civil Rights organizations, organizations which previously, during the 1930s, were somewhat hostile toward boycotts as a tactic in political action. African Americans were beginning to be acknowledged by white businesses as a viable and profitable consumer bloc.

Robert Weems (1998) provides ample examples of the exploitation of African Americans as consumers. During the 1970s, African Americans were exploited by the white movie industry, as the influx of "blaxploitation" films saved Hollywood producers like MGM from financial ruin. In advertising, white businesses looked for African American dollars to compensate for their losses, as was the case with African American cosmetics in the wake of falling Avon profits. Also, white businesses exploited black media to reach African American consumers and, once sufficiently entrenched in the market, deemed black media inefficient, as was the case with *Ebony* magazine and other publications intended for a minority audience. These black-owned and directed businesses were used until they were financially dependent and then subsequently dismissed. During this period, white-owned and operated businesses showed interest in servicing the black community only after these companies were hemorrhaging, and, in essence, had nothing to lose.

After the 1970s, with decreased momentum and support for national collective buying power campaigns and boycotts, African American consumerism began to lose its efficacy as a collective political strategy. According to the Selig Center for Economic Growth, in 2012 African Americans' collective purchasing power exceeded US$1 trillion. Though much of those African American dollars make their way to non-black businesses, there continues to be an expansion of black-owned businesses.

Often with discussions of African American consumerism comes the critique of conspicuous consumption, particularly when discussing consumers from lower socioeconomic status. While it is true that African Americans spend disproportionately on goods and services, what should also be considered within this discussion are the increased costs of obtaining these goods and services, particularly in lower-income African American neighborhoods, where these consumers may pay higher rates and entry/access fees. What also must be considered are the reasons for this type of consumption and how African Americans, particularly those of lower socioeconomic status, are making meaning of their consumer practices within the context of a society that is still hostile toward these consumers. Elizabeth Chin (2001) discusses the consumption practices of low-income African American children, and concludes that, as consumers, the children are able to construct their own meaning toward objects, even in the face of social, political, and economic constraints. For example, in the case of white Barbie dolls, the girls in Chin's ethnography recognize their marginalized position within society, juxtaposed against the lavish, privileged life of white Barbie. However, even as they articulate these disconnects, they still demonstrate agency in their play by adapting the dolls' hair and clothes to be more reflective of their lived experiences as black girls living in an impoverished east coast urban neighborhood.

Today, with the expansion of media, we also see the cooptation of black culture through the music, fashion, and jargon within popular culture. In many ways, African American culture has been commodified and transformed into a sanitized, depoliticized version of itself for consumption by the masses of consumers, who are predominantly white. What is removed in this commodification process of black culture and bodies is the historical roots of African American culture. For example, hip hop has now become synonymous with popularized gangsta rap/pop and much of the music that is produced for the national and global "masses" that claims to invoke black culture is created by white multinational production companies, which control the narratives as well as the profits. Also related to black culture and music, it was during the early 2000s that there was much debate within the National Basketball Association (NBA) regarding the "infiltration" of hip hop culture via its players. On the one hand, hip hop culture was used to explain what was perceived as an increase in violence among its players and, on the other hand, it was used by advertising agents to sell sports-related products. Despite these efforts of cooptation and commodification, African Americans continue to use consumption as a way of expressing identities and resisting distorted narratives.

SEE ALSO: Citizenship and Consumption; Consumption and Identity

REFERENCES

Chin, Elizabeth. 2001. *Purchasing Power: Black Kids and American Consumer Culture*, Minneapolis: University of Minnesota Press.

Cohen, Lizabeth. 2003. *A Consumers' Republic: The Politics of Mass Consumption*. New York: Alfred A. Knopf.

Weems, Robert, Jr. 1998. *Desegregating the Dollar: African American Consumerism in the Twentieth Century*. New York: New York University Press.

FURTHER READING

Collins, Patricia Hill. 2006. "New Commodities, New Consumers." *Ethnicities* 6(3): 297–317.

Davis, James. 2007. *Color in Commerce: Race, Consumer Culture, and American Literature, 1893–1933*. Ann Arbor, MI: University of Michigan Press.

Newman, Benjamin, and Brandon Bartels. 2011. "Politics at the Checkout Line: Explaining Political Consumerism in the United States." *Political Research Quarterly* 64(4): 803–817.

Patillo-McCoy, M. 1999. *Black Picket Fences*. Chicago: University of Chicago Press.

Americanization

VIVIANE RIEGEL
Goldsmiths, University of London, UK

Americanization can be defined as the propagation of US ideas, customs, social patterns, industry, and capital around the world. It is a powerful unidirectional process stemming from the United States that tends to overwhelm competing processes (e.g., Japanization) as well as the strength of local (and glocal) forces that might resist, modify, or transform American models into hybrid forms. Moreover, the notion of Americanization is tied to a particular nation – the United States – but it has a differential impact on many specific nations. Americanization is a process that is central to globalization, but is not its equal (Ritzer 2010).

Americanization is inclusive of forms of US cultural, institutional, political, and economic imperialism. For example, we can include under this heading the worldwide diffusion of the American industrial model and the later global proliferation of the American consumption model; the marketing of American media, including Hollywood film and popular music; the selling of American sports such as NFL football and NBA basketball abroad; the transnational marketing of American commodities, including blue jeans and computer operating systems; the extensive diplomatic and military engagement with Europe, Asia, the Middle East, and South America; the training of many of the world's military, political, and scientific elites in American universities; the expansion of the American model of democratic politics; and the development and use of the international labor market and natural resources by American corporations.

On the surface, Americanization involves some characteristics and values related to the American way of life. The shopping mall, for example, is closely linked to the importance of the automobile in the functioning of US society, as well as to the value Americans place on their automobiles. In some cases, success throughout the world depends on playing up the American roots and characteristics as an important part of the product, while in other cases it involves playing them down or even striving to obliterate them – to the extent that things like a pair of Levi jeans, a can of Coca-Cola, a set of Mickey Mouse ears, or a Malibu Barbie Beach House come to be disconnected from their American roots and become forms that fit anywhere and everywhere. It means they can move effortlessly from one culture to another and be sold widely in all cultures.

Many critics of globalization focus on the perspective of the Americanization of world culture and the perils of the dominance of American culture throughout the world. Much of the discussion about cultural effects of globalization has centered on the extent to which increased cultural communication tends to produce a homogeneous global culture.

GLOBALIZATION AND AMERICANIZATION

Globalization can be analyzed culturally, economically, politically, or institutionally. At the extremes, in the realm of culture, globalization can be seen as a form of transnational expansion of common codes and practices (homogeneity), or it can involve the interaction of many global and local cultural inputs to create a kind of pastiche, or a blend, leading to a variety of cultural hybrids (heterogeneity). The trend toward homogeneity is often associated with cultural imperialism or the growing international influence of a particular culture. There are many varieties of cultural imperialism, including those that emphasize the role played by American culture, the West, or core countries. In opposition to this perspective, Robertson (1995) supports the concept of "glocalization," by describing a series of cultural hybrids resulting from the interpenetration of the universal and the particular.

In the homogenization view, barriers that prevent flows that would contribute to making cultures look alike are weak, and global flows are strong. In its extreme form, homogenization, which is also known as convergence, advances the possibility that local cultures can be shaped by other more powerful cultures or even a global culture. This perspective is reflected in several concepts and models, such as the global culture, Americanization, and, more importantly, the McDonaldization theory (Ritzer 2010).

George Ritzer's theory regards globalization from the perspective of consumer-side phenomena. What happens, from this view, is the further homogenization of consumption through globalization. The growth dynamic of globalization, according to the sociologist, takes place through three other processes: capitalism, Americanization, and McDonaldization. Capitalism frames Americanization and McDonaldization; the three can be read politically as symbolically identical, especially by opponents – for example, those who seek to blow up McDonald's sites in protest against America and/or capitalism.

HISTORY OF THE RELATION BETWEEN AMERICANIZATION AND CONSUMPTION

As regards the seventeenth and eighteenth centuries, a fresh interest in the global history of consumption has reintegrated the Indian Ocean and China into a history of material culture previously monopolized by Britain and Holland. The career of Indian cottons epitomizes this more interactive understanding of the entanglement between East and West. Whereas recent accounts of the eighteenth century emphasize mutual entanglements – with Britain as much in the role of follower as of leader – the multidirectional flow of consumer cultures, and dispersed centers of technologies and creativity, the Americanization story remains a one-way street. By the 1930s, dreams of a better material life were circulating throughout society. These would be reaped in the affluent 1950s and 1960s, and reinforced by American consumer culture, but they were not solely a foreign import. Thus, the Nazi regime and business together created anticipatory desires for a world of material comfort that outlived war and destruction and that families took with them into the postwar years. During the twentieth century, it was as if the world had shrunk. The central axis for transnational flows was then focused between the United States and Europe, the "irresistible Empire: America's advance through twentieth-century Europe" (de Grazia 2005), symbolized by Hollywood and the supermarket.

Consumerism as a new lifestyle in contemporary society, imported from the American way of life, means that consumption is crucial for self-fashioning and lifestyle, the actualization of the self, and the rise of a consumer-citizen. Americanization and global consumerism are not necessarily the same; local cultures play an active role in shaping the global. Consumerism rose to prominence during the Cold War and expressed the anxieties of observers about the pathologies of consumer society rather than the realities of how people lived their lives in affluent societies. Victoria de Grazia has placed consumption at the center of her account of the United States as a hegemonic "market empire" after World War II (de Grazia 2005). The interest in Americanization and its twin "global consumerism" continues to treat the United States as origin and center. It is a self-critical inversion of the "Rise of the West," which replaces the positive *telos* of liberty, law, and commerce with a negative one of unbounded materialism. If many regions and traditions have shaped the world of goods, it may be too simple to view "consumerism" as an alien import, or to focus on the ethical responsibility of affluent consumers in the North.

Such perspectives from the margins of globalization point to the limitations of a simple binary between the local (authentic, diverse, free) and the global (artificial, standardized, imposed). US consumer culture, with its limitless territorial and social ambition, is contrasted with "old bourgeois" Europe, bounded by class and nation. Inevitably, this approach highlights a clash between material civilizations rather than affinities or continuities. Cultural transfer was never a one-way street. Americanization, too, occurred at the margins and took hybrid forms, as Europeans picked certain aspects and fused them with their inherited traditions. The American idea of creating peace by going out and selling goods went one step further than the British imperial mission of spreading civilization through commerce. Advertisers and businessmen continued where missionaries and free traders had been before. Best practice and material comfort replaced the gospel and the promise of atonement, but the global mission of leading people up the ladder of consumption to a higher plane continued. Class cultures were, perhaps, more entrenched in Europe, but it was not the case that divisions across race, income, and region were simply erased in the United States by the idealized American way of life (Cohen 2003).

SEE ALSO: Coca-Colonization; Disneyization; Globalization and Consumption; Glocalization/Grobalization; McDonaldization; Starbuckization

REFERENCES

Cohen, Lizabeth. 2003. *A Consumer's Republic: The Politics of Mass Consumption in Postwar America*. New York: Alfred A. Knopf.

de Grazia, Victoria. 2005. *Irresistible Empire: America's Advance through 20th-Century Europe*. Cambridge, MA: Belknap Press.

Ritzer, George. 2010. *Globalization: A Basic Text*. Chichester, UK: Wiley-Blackwell.

Ritzer, George, and Michael Ryan. 2004. "Americanisation, McDonaldisation, and Globalisation." In *Issues in Americanisation and Culture*, edited by Neil Campbell, Jude Davies, and George McKay, 41–60. Edinburgh: Edinburgh University Press.

Robertson, Roland. 1995. "Glocalization: Time–Space and Homogeneity–Heterogeneity." In *Global Modernities*, edited by Mike Featherstone, Scott Lash, and Roland Robertson, 25–44. London: Sage.

Anti-Consumption Tactics

ANDREA DASSOPOULOS
University of Nevada, Las Vegas, USA

The rise of mass consumerism through the twentieth century triggered numerous critiques and challenges that have positioned consumption practices as key areas of struggle. Anti-consumption movements and subcultures have emerged to resist the declining quality of life created by consumer culture and to issue a moral critique of unsustainable consumption. They oppose the ideology of consumerism, which supports an inherently oppressive, global capitalist system by persuading people to consume more than they need. Advanced industrial societies have the potential to satisfy real human needs, but consumerism is oppressive because it manipulates needs and wants. Advertising leads consumers to believe that happiness lies within consumer choices, and, in pursuit of happiness, they act irrationally in order to be able to consume more. These irrational behaviors include working more hours than necessary for survival, disposing of still useful products, and creating environmental destruction. Anti-consumption groups engage in a variety of tactics, such as dumpstering, squatting, stealing, performance acts, culture jamming, consuming ethically, and brand boycotting.

The types of tactics individuals engage in depend on their motivations for anti-consumption. Motivations for anti-consumption vary, but generally fit within five types. Personal motivations include the desire to liberate oneself from the system. Moral motivations stem from feeling a personal responsibility not to cause harm through excessive consumption; those with activist motivations use their anti-consumption practices to subvert or challenge the entire capitalist system. Identifactory motivations describe an individual's desire for authenticity by aligning practices with ideals, and social motivations describe the desire for community and solidarity with other anarchists.

Reducing consumption or abandoning material possessions has a long history in ancient philosophies and religions. Voluntary simplicity is a movement that promotes voluntary asceticism as the means of attaining a sustainable and more fulfilling life. Although there are inherent political implications for voluntary simplicity, it tends to be inwardly directed. Voluntary simplifiers are motivated to improve their own lives by shedding the burden and stress of consumer culture and minimizing their own impact on the environment. Voluntary simplifiers develop their individual ethical consumer identities through interaction with the broader movement. Others take on an explicitly activist identity and view their anti-consumption as a tool to resist and ultimately challenge consumer culture. Anti-consumption as resistance involves adopting an oppositional lifestyle as a tactical resistance. Lifestyle tactics are the individual choices that demonstrate resistance to the dominant culture.

The most visible critics of consumer culture are contemporary anarchists. Coherent consumption practices of activists and subcultures reflect ideological values, create cohesion, and mark membership to groups. The anti-consumption of anarchists is a lifestyle orientation. Anarchists abstain from excessive consumption that they deem has derived from capitalist interests, such as the purchase of hygiene products. They view the hygiene industry as creating a false expectation of how the human body should smell and look in order to sell unnecessary products.

Do-it-yourselfers (DIY) and freegans are among the anarchist groups that are part of a larger global anti-capitalist movement. They challenge the cultural value system that creates social and ecological crisis by creating alternative consumption cultures that are ecologically minded and organized around a lifestyle of mutual aid and reuse. Dumpster diving, or dumpstering, is scavenging for food and useable items in dumpsters and waste bins. It is an important act of solidarity and identity formation. Freegans, whose name is a portmanteau of "free" and "vegan," survive by finding food and useable items in dumpsters and by freely sharing their findings with local communities. Freegans expose the vast amounts of non-perished food that is discarded daily; in the United States, an estimated 40 percent of all food is discarded uneaten. Loosely organized freegan coalitions, such as Food Not Bombs, create meals out of dumpstered food and host public feedings that are free and open to anyone who is hungry. By freely sharing meals, freegans create alternative social relations that are not dependent on markets and status.

Dumpster diving both is a practical means for surviving outside traditional consumer culture and draws attention to the excess and waste found within capitalist societies. In advanced capitalist societies, consumer goods create a surplus value that can only be maintained if unsold, yet perfectly useable, products are discarded rather than distributed to those in need. Freegans redistribute those items in order to create a culture that realizes human needs. Scavenging in one form or another has always been a part of human life, but freegans explicitly frame dumpster diving as a political statement and lifestyle.

Freegans base their lifestyle on the moral assumption that all humans have a right to basic necessities of food and shelter and that they also have a responsibility to minimize their impact on the planet. Beyond dumpster diving, they promote other alternative consumption practices. For instance, they avoid fossil fuel dependence whenever possible by using bicycles for transportation or converting diesel cars to run on used vegetable oil. They also advocate squatting in abandoned buildings because surplus housing should not exist when people are homeless. Since freegans minimize their participation in consumer culture, they do not have to work as much. Working minimal hours is part of their anti-capitalist ideology. Work, especially in retail, contributes to the system that they find inherently exploitative.

Anti-consumption politicizes mundane acts, such as eating. Veganism, a lifestyle of not consuming animals or animal products, becomes an oppositional stance against a consumer culture that endorses meat and dairy consumption as part of a healthy diet yet supports an exploitative and unsustainable agriculture industry. Lifestyle practices become idealized in anarchist communities and can be contradictory and controversial. Lifestyle tactics are imperfect; the complexity of immersion within the capitalist system makes it difficult to live in a completely ethical way. Thus individuals negotiate their lifestyle choices through public discourse and trial and error. As a lifestyle, anti-consumption brings consumer critiques into everyday experiences instead of only at isolated, high-profile demonstrations. Freegans build collective identity around their shared consumptive practices.

Sharing and gifting are the basis of the alternative culture they are trying to create. Anarchists oftentimes will open infoshops, or storefronts, where they will offer free goods, classes, and literature with a DIY organizing principle. A DIY principle motivates individuals to produce their own goods and services whenever possible rather than purchase the products and expertise of alienated labor. DIY principles lead to self-organized networks of individuals that trade skills and services for mutual good. DIY networks allow everyone to take advantage of the collective knowledge and skills of the group, largely helping to sustain oppositional lifestyles. They are able to produce and consume the things that they need in an ethical way, such as bike repair, medical care, farming, hunting, making clothes, and home brewing.

Culture jamming is another tactic employed by anti-consumption activists. Culture jamming is a rhetorical protest that uses advertising against itself. It has been promoted by the activist magazine *Adbusters*, which creates "subvertisements" that look and feel like recognizable advertisements but that offer scathing critiques of consumer culture. Culture jamming can also include acts of corporate billboard vandalism, brandalism, trademark infringement, and parodies. The flood of brand marketing that consumers are exposed to daily makes culture jamming an important tactic that resonates with people from diverse backgrounds. Culture jammers resist the imposition of advertising into all aspects of human life. Corporations have the resources to impose themselves without consent and increasingly become more insidious. Street artists participate in brand vandalism, or brandalism. Acts of brandalism include painting over existing billboards or modifying a corporate message to alter the meaning in such a way that it tarnishes the brand's public image.

Culture jammers also utilize performance art as a tactic for public protest. Street theater that satirizes the ills of consumption, such as that of Reverend Billy and the Church of Stop Shopping, raises awareness. Reverend Billy takes on the persona of a charismatic minister and causes a spectacle inside corporate shopping spaces. He prays for consumers to abandon their ways. He predicts that the end of humanity will come from manic consumption. He uses a humorous and disruptive technique for delivering his anti-consumption message. Other public performers, such as the Yes Men, use parody to expose the irrational logic behind consumer culture. The Yes Men impersonate real corporate executives and present themselves in a way that they feel reveals their true and sometimes hideous intentions. Parodic performance art has potentially alienating effects on its audience; thus there is not a consensus on its effectiveness as an anti-consumption tactic.

Boycotting is another tactic, one that works from a reformist assumption. Collective actions that boycott products can pressure corporations to modify unethical practices. Successful boycotts require a critical mass that can publicly shame the company as well as create significant impacts on profits.

Collaborative consumption is another anti-consumption tactic. Broadly defined, collaborative consumption is the development of sharing economies, among friends or strangers. Some examples include free and fee-based hospitality exchanges, book swaps, microlending, car sharing, ride sharing, bike sharing, child care exchange, and food exchange. These exchanges are made easy and more convenient through resource sharing websites; earlier forms of sharing economies, such as communes and collectives, required co-presence, and deeper commitment or immersion into a community or lifestyle. Websites exist to facilitate peer-to-peer exchange for practically any imaginable service or good; sometimes participants in these networks use the website to earn a little extra money from their idle possessions, while others exist simply to connect people with mutual interests. Collaborative consumption relies on social networks and peer communities to function; it is a lifestyle that is compatible with networked individuals and not explicitly oppositional, although it does promote alternative social relationships.

Collaborative consumption is meant to be a more sustainable way of consuming because it is based on usage rather than ownership. Collaborative consumption depends on four basic conditions: critical mass, idling capacity, belief in the commons, and trust. The network has to be large enough to be self-sustaining and to offer enough options to people. The second condition is that there must be enough idling capacity, meaning there have to be enough resources to share. The third condition necessary, the belief in the commons, is the shared belief that resources belong to all people, a notion at odds with private property. This belief comes into conflict with "tragedy of the commons" theory, which, when unregulated, means that humans will maximize resources to their own benefit and deplete the commons. This notion is based on scarcity of goods, but the common resources found within social networks are not scarce and are only strengthened by more use. The final necessary condition for collaborative consumption to be successful is trust between strangers. Trusting strangers is not new to the internet. Humans rely on strangers every day to accomplish basic survival; however, that trust is mediated through bureaucratic systems and individuals are held accountable for violations of trust. Collaborative consumption creates decentralized, peer-to-peer trust that challenges individuals' comfort levels by demanding they evaluate trustworthiness themselves, based on pieces of information made available through websites. Collaborative consumption websites proliferate, indicating an overall trend toward a sharing economy.

SEE ALSO: Boycotts; Consumer Culture; Consumer Resistance Movements; Culture Jamming; Do-It-Yourself (DIY); Globalization and Consumption

FURTHER READING

Botsman, Rachel and Roo Rogers. 2011. *What's Mine Is Yours: How Collaborative Consumption Is Changing the Way We Live*. London: Collins.

Cherrier, Helene. 2008. "Anti-Consumption Discourses and Consumer-Resistant Identities." *Journal of Business Research* 62: 181–190.

Cronin, James M., Mary B. McCarthy, and Alan M. Collins. 2012. "Covert Distinction: How Hipsters Practice Food-Based Resistance Strategies in the Production of Identity." *Consumption Markets and Culture* 1–27. doi:10.1080/10253866.2012.678785.

Littler, Jo. "Beyond the Boycott: Anti-Consumerism, Cultural Change and the Limits of Reflexivity." *Cultural Studies* 19(2): 227–252.

McClish, Carmen L. 2009. "Activism Based in Embarrassment: The Anti-Consumption Spirituality of the Reverend Billy." *Liminalities: A Journal of Performance Studies* 5(2): 1–20.

Pentina, Iryna, and Clinton Amos. 2011. "The Freegan Phenomenon: Anti-Consumption or Consumer Resistance?" *European Journal of Marketing* 45(11/12): 1768–1778.

Portwood-Stacer, Laura. 2012. "Anti-Consumption as Tactical Resistance: Anarchists, Subculture, and Activist Strategy." *Journal of Consumer Culture* 12(1): 87–105.

Apple

VIVIANE RIEGEL
Goldsmiths, University of London, UK

Apple Inc. is an American multinational company that designs and markets consumer electronics, software, and personal computers. The company's best-known hardware products include the Macintosh computers, the iPod, iPhone, and iPad. Apple software includes the iOS operating system, the iTunes media browser, and the iCloud online storage. Its brand logo is an apple fruit with a bite taken out of it.

According to the Forbes Global Leading Companies (2013), by 2013 Apple had a worldwide annual revenue of US$171 billion, with more than half of it coming from the iPhone category. Its overall market value in May 2013 was US$416 billion, making it the most valuable company in the US market (it had been public since 1980 on NASDAQ). The 2013 BrandZ Report ranked Apple as the most valuable brand in the world, with a brand value of US$185,071 billion.

Apple was established on April 1, 1976 by Steve Jobs, Steve Wozniak, and Ronald Wayne, in Cupertino, California. By the end of the 1970s, Apple had a staff of computer designers and a production line. On January 24, 1984, Apple launched the Macintosh, and its debut was announced by the now famous US$1.5 million television commercial "1984," considered a watershed event for Apple's success. Steve Jobs resigned from the company one year later and only returned in 1997, when he began restructuring the company's product line. In 2001, Apple opened the first of its official Apple Retail Stores and introduced the iPod, opening a new way to do business in the technology market and starting its revolution in other spheres. The company shifted its emphasis to mobile electronic devices with other products, such as the iPhone (2007), the App Store (2008), and the iPad (2010).

The history of the company shows that innovation and quality were the basis for its development and growth. There are elements in the history of Apple that formulate classic hero myths, with both its founders and its various products as the heroes. For reasons as various as its philosophy of comprehensive aesthetic design to its distinctive advertising campaigns, Apple has established a unique reputation in the consumer electronics industry. This includes a customer base that is devoted to the company and its brand, translating the company's and the brand's value into engagement and loyalty. This loyalty from Apple users has been characterized as an instance of brand community (Muñiz and O'Guinn 2001).

Along with this emotional community that supports the brand, Apple has also reached a position of market dominance in the music and smartphone businesses. The iPod and iTunes have changed the reality of the music industry and its competition. In addition, the advancement of the iPhone and the iPad have made competitors, such as Nokia, Motorola, Samsung, Microsoft, and Google, change their tactics, creating new horizons in the technology market, as they not only focus on smartphones, tablets, and its devices, but also target the consumer experience and its diverse social relations. The importance of Apple in the tech world can be understood by the impact of products such as the iPod, iPhone, and iPad in the market, combining both innovation and passion. Apple became a dream factory, transforming the experience of buying a product into something magical; an idea into something concrete. These products revolutionized the market, spreading Apple's influence beyond computer technology, reaching into the music industry with the iPod, and into the mobility process with the iPhone and iPad, both advances also representing an important change in the way people began to interact daily through the internet.

The Apple brand became stronger, not only concerning its technical attributes, but mainly because consumers were relating more emotionally to the brand, with all its products and devices. Apple's rise in brand value can be attributed to the way it has created a seamless omnichannel experience for customers. By keeping consumers at the center of everything it does, Apple tries to anticipate what they want next and break new ground in terms of both design and performance.

We can look at how this interaction with the Apple brand offers consumers the opportunity to increase their cultural capital, by giving them devices that help them to accumulate knowledge and skills – which are the essence of cultural capital, according to Bourdieu (1987). Apple has labored to cultivate a strong brand personality based on the ideas of nonconformity, innovation, and creativity. A theme of the company's emotional branding strategy is the hope it cultivates in people of the sort of person they could be by virtue of using the company's products. The idea of Apple users as standouts from the masses was introduced in the company's first commercial, which aired only once, during the 1984 Super Bowl broadcast. With ads like these, Apple suggests that daring to be different (by purchasing an Apple product) opens up the possibility for one to do great things. Advertising and marketing strategies have highlighted these associated characteristics, like the "Think Different" campaign. This trend continues today in commercials that appeal to people's desire to be valued and admired as artistically creative, culturally relevant, and intellectually engaging. In today's digitally mediated world, where social networking is the norm, the promise of such narcissistic pursuits and outcomes is a key part of Apple's brand strategy. "Be your best 21st century you!" recent ads seem to shout.

Apple is a good example of brand strategy that supports the unique position of the company and its products in the global market. Even if the personal computer market is dominated by PC computers using operating systems and software from Microsoft, and although Apple currently has less than 4 percent of the personal computer market, its customers are distinguished by their fierce loyalty to the brand and their personal identification with Apple.

SEE ALSO: Brand Loyalty; Cultural Capital; Digital-Mobile Consumption and Marketing

REFERENCES

Apple official website: www.apple.com

Bourdieu, Pierre. 1987. "The Forms of Capital." In *Handbook of Theory and Research for the Sociology of Education,* edited by John G. Richardson, 241–258. New York: Greenwood Press.

Brand Z. 2013. Top 100 Most Valuable Global Brands 2013. Available at: http://www.wpp.com/wpp/marketing/brandz/brandz-2013/.

Forbes Global Leading Companies. May 2013. Available at: http://www.forbes.com/companies/apple/.

Muñiz, Albert M., Jr., and Thomas C. O'Guinn. 2001. "Brand Community." *Journal of Consumer Research* 27(4): 412–433.

Arcades

KLAUS R. KUNZMANN
Emeritus, TU Dortmund University, Germany

Arcades are covered passageways with shops, stalls, cafés, or restaurants, usually in the front of private and public buildings in high-density inner-city quarters of European and some Asian cities. They protect shop owners and their goods, customers, residents, and *flâneurs* from sun and rain. The name stems from the architectural term "arcade," which describes a series of columns or pillars forming a gallery or a colonnade. In Roman times the architectural form of the arcade was also used in more functional buildings, such as aqueducts or city gates.

The idea of the arcade and the passageway goes back to the covered oriental market (*souk*). Early arcades were built in Mesopotamia and Egypt. Such oriental markets can still be found in cities like Sana'a in Yemen, Bursa in Turkey, Marrakech in Morocco, and Aleppo in Syria. From there, the architectural feature spread around the world. They were particularly popular in Italy and in other Mediterranean regions of Europe. They can also be found in other regions of the world – for example, in North Africa, Latin America, and even in China and Taiwan.

Arcades represent the transition space between public and private spaces. They are buffer zones between private spheres and public representation. The pathway under the arcade is public, while the spaces behind the pathway are private. Arcades reflect city building regulations, established and enforced by powerful civic leadership or feudal emperors. For aesthetic or functional reasons, and on the basis of professional guidance by influential city builders, be it architects, engineers, or surveyors, arcade design regulations controlled the street fronts of privately developed buildings.

Arcades are still an attractive feature of many cities in Europe. Traditional forms of arcades and passageways were deliberately designed and built in city building processes during the Renaissance and Baroque eras. In Victorian times, such arcades were built in the United Kingdom (e.g., London, Newcastle-upon-Tyne). Well preserved and maintained and economically still functioning, inner-city arcades can be found in many cities in Italy (e.g., Lucca, Bologna, Turin), Spain (Pamplona), and Germany (e.g., Münster, Freudenstadt). A special form of arcade can be seen in renowned shopping galleries such as the Galleria Vittorio Emanuele II in Milan, or the Galleria Umberto I in Naples, or the Galleries St. Hubert in Brussels, and the passages in Paris.

Arcades have architectural, functional, as well as economic and social dimensions. Architecturally, arcades give order to the urban fabric by controlling the dimension and the use of ground floors along inner-city streets. They hold back individual building styles to a common harmonious and equalizing urban concept. In a way, arcades reflect a democratic civic spirit of architecture. They force individual landowners and property developers to follow a common rule when developing buildings along an inner-city shopping street. Arcades contribute much to the local and cultural identity of a city.

Functionally, arcades operate as showrooms and meeting spots alike. They are covered locations for grocery shops, boutiques, and fashion outlets, for workshops and service activities, for antiquity shops and galleries; they accommodate cafés and restaurants using sections of the semi-public covered pathway for tables and chairs. Often, they are also used as shelters for inner-city bus stops and taxi lines. No carriages and equestrians in former times and no cars, tramways, or bicycles today disturb the promenading and shopping along the walkways.

Economic activities in arcades represent the local economy. Arcades are locations for buying and selling, for showing products and offering services. They are much appreciated pathways through the inner city from which to enjoy the consumption of daily demand or specialized clothes and goods. Arcades also serve as places for communication and social interaction, for information exchange, for chatting and for gossip. They are meeting spots and public urban catwalks to show and to be seen. They hide and they make visible. Arcades are also urban spaces of slowness. At least for a while, they slow down city life.

In modern times, the virtues of shopping arcades have been rediscovered. Arcades attracted renewed interest among investors developing inner-city shopping centers. Newly built and set in scene with voluptuous light arrangements, and with a big choice of shops and food courts, contemporary shopping precincts encourage and seduce visitors to consume in fancy air-conditioned environments, protected from rain and sun, and undisturbed by traffic noise. Often, to benefit from the spirit of traditional colonnades, such new shopping areas are even labeled arcades. They have been developed in many European cities, both large and small, by specialized developers (such as ECE) – for example, in Berlin (Potsdamer Platz Arkaden, Steglitz Arkaden), Klagenfurt (Austria), Copenhagen, Stockholm, Beijing, Shanghai, Seoul, and Taipei, as well as in "winter cities" or on city-like cruise ships. However, such modern arcades are not public, or even semi-public, spaces; they are private spaces fully controlled by modern security devices.

Jonas Geist (1985), an architectural historian in Berlin, has written the most comprehensive compendium on arcades as an architectural building type in the 1970s. Arcades in the Parisian version of passages – covered lanes in Haussmannian housing blocks with a mixture of shops, galleries, and restaurants – inspired Walter Benjamin (1981) to embark on his *Arcades Project*, a collection of intellectual reflections on time and on the metropolis, on the architecture of consumption, and on the *flâneur*, the citizen strolling in the glass-ceilinged passages, observing the market and exploring the conditions of life in the metropolis. *The Arcades Project* has become one of the most influential texts of the twentieth century in cultural criticism. Many authors in subsequent writings about the role of consumption in the city, such as Marc Jayne (2006), Steven Miles (2010), Roberta Sassatelli (2007), and Sharon Zukin (2004), refer to Benjamin and his seminal explorations into the soul of the metropolis and its citizens. They all explore the forces that have made shopping so important in modern city life, the rise of consumer culture, and the key role consumption plays for social status, and they describe the urban spaces where consumption happens.

By the beginning of the twenty-first century, the excesses of suburbanization and urban sprawl, as well as changing family values and the technology-driven forces of a new urban economy, had favored a renaissance of the desire to live in densely built-up inner cities. Market research forecasts that more than 25 percent of future consumers will turn to online shopping. Assuming that this form of virtual shopping will gradually increase its share in consumption habits, a further revival of arcades in modern cities can be expected. Online shopping will require the existence of showrooms in attractive locations, where shoppers can see and touch the goods, and, above all, try on the items of clothing they have selected in electronic catalogues. Arcades offer the perfect environment for such practice. They provide the right ambience for the window-shopper, where he or she can perfectly combine a visit to a real, nonvirtual online shop, sheltered from rain and heat, with a cappuccino and with meeting friends and face-to-face business contacts in an attractive neutral urban environment.

SEE ALSO: Benjamin, Walter; *Flâneur/Flânerie*; Shopping; Shopping Malls

REFERENCES

Benjamin, Walter. 1981. *The Arcades Project*. Cambridge, MA: Belknap Press.

Geist, Johann Friedrich. 1985. *Arcades: The History of a Building Type*. Cambridge, MA: MIT Press.

Jayne, Mark. 2006. *Cities and Consumption*. London: Routledge.

Miles, Steven. 2010. *Spaces for Consumption*. London: Sage.

Sassatelli, Roberta. 2007. *Consumer Culture: History, Theory and Politics*. London: Sage.

Zukin, Sharon. 2004. *Point of Purchase: How Shopping Changed American Culture*. London: Routledge.

FURTHER READING

Kunzmann, Klaus R. 2011. "Spaces of Consumption." In *The Routledge Companion to Urban Design: Roots, Influences, and Trends*, edited by Tridib Banerjee and Anastasia Loukaitou-Sideris, 391–404. London: Routledge.

Asian Americans and Consumption

STACEY J. LEE and SEJUNG HAM
University of Wisconsin–Madison, USA

Asian Americans make up 5.8 percent of the total population in the United States and are the fastest-growing racial group there; there was an increase of 46 percent from the 2000 census to the 2010 census. The growth in the Asian American population has led to an increasing interest in the subject of Asian American consumption among scholars from a range of academic disciplines. Popular discussions of Asian Americans often characterize them as a monolithic group, but the reality is that Asian Americans are highly diverse in terms of ethnicity, language, religion, social class, generation, educational attainment, political affiliation, and other identities. Such diversity makes it difficult to speak about a single Asian American pattern of consumption or consumer identity. As with other groups, patterns of consumption are influenced by a host of factors, including social class, age, and cultural identity. Furthermore, Asian American consumption represents a form of cultural expression and reflects Asian American aspirations and longings.

Marketing scholars have identified Asian Americans as an important consumer market in the twenty-first century. Consumer research groups view Asian Americans as a powerful consumer base because of the high levels of education and high incomes among certain segments of the Asian American population. In efforts to tap into this consumer base, marketing scholars focus on identifying patterns of consumption and common needs among Asian Americans. Entrepreneurship in this group has been on the rise and Asian American-owned businesses are both buyers and sellers of a range of products related to everything from technology to beauty supplies. The fact that a large number of Asian Americans are foreign-born has been found to shape consumption in significant ways. Many Asian American households, for example, watch both Asian television and US television. Korean soap operas are popular among Korean Americans across age groups and are growing in popularity among other Asian American groups as well. Because many Asian Americans still have family in their homelands, they are frequent consumers of international phone services and air travel. According to a report by a major consumer group, Asian Americans are major users of new technologies, with larger percentages of the Asian American population than any other ethnic grouping having laptops, tablets, cellphones, broadband at home, and wireless connectivity (Nielson Company 2012).

While marketing scholars are interested in patterns of Asian American consumption in order to better target the relevant markets, scholars in anthropology, cultural studies, sociology, and education are interested in what Asian American consumption says about identity, aspirations, and belonging. National boundaries are now becoming increasingly blurred and the number of transnational migrants who belong to more than one society is on the rise. Asian American consumption reflects the global flows of information, goods, and money across borders. Because of the ongoing connections that Asian Americans have with their native countries, there has been a growth in the number of businesses that center on the transnational flow of goods between the United States and various Asian countries. The Filipino Balikbayan box, a giftbox that Filipinos send to friends and relatives in the Philippines, is one example of a formalized and regulated form of transnational remittance and there are shipping companies that specialize in shipping Balikbayan boxes.

Asian American youth are heavy consumers of technology, media, music, fashion, and other products from Asia. The well-known "Hello Kitty" boom among Asian Americans is one example of transnational consumption. Buying "Hello Kitty" products at stores in Chinatowns and Japan towns is related to creating and affirming an Asian American identity for girls and young women across Asian ethnic groups. Another recent example is consumption of Korean popular culture (K-pop) that arose through transnational flows throughout Pacific Asian countries and in Asian American communities. Research on South Asian American youth suggests that they are active consumers of transnational music and fashion, which they transform by blending with urban American popular cultural forms (Maira and Soep 2005; Shankar 2008). The consumption of transnational popular culture may reflect the lack of Asian American figures and/or presence of stereotypical Asian American figures in the US media (Park 2004).

Asian American consumption is a complicated phenomenon that reflects both the desires and the needs of this growing and diverse group. The large number of Asian Americans from immigrant backgrounds means that their tastes are influenced by their homelands. Given the overall growth in the Asian American population and the affluence of certain segments of this group, the subject of Asian American consumption is likely to grow in interest among scholars across disciplines.

SEE ALSO: Youth Culture(s)

REFERENCES

Maira, Sunaina, and Elisabeth Soep, eds. 2005. *Youthscapes: The Popular, the National, the Global.* Philadelphia: University of Pennsylvania Press.

Nielson Company. 2012. "State of the Asian American Consumer: Growing Market, Growing Impact." Accessed June 16, 2014. http://www.nielsen.com/content/dam/corporate/us/en/microsites/publicaffairs/StateoftheAsianAmericanConsumerReport.pdf.

Park, Jung Sun. 2004. "Korean American Youths' Consumption of Korean and Japanese TV Dramas and Its Implications." In *Feeling Asian Modernities: Transnational Consumption of Japanese TV Dramas*, edited by Koichi Iwabuchi, 275–298. Hong Kong: Hong Kong University Press.

Shankar, Shalini. 2008. *Desi Land: Teen Culture, Class, and Success in Silicon Valley*. Durham, NC: Duke University Press.

FURTHER READING

Jung, Eun Young. 2009. "Transnational Korea: A Critical Assessment of the Korean Wave in Asia and the United States." *Southeast Review of Asian Studies* 31: 69–80.

Authenticity

KENT GRAYSON
Northwestern University, USA
MATTEO CORCIOLANI
University of Pisa, Italy

An authentic market offering is something that is sold in the marketplace, and whose market value is based wholly or partly on a belief that the offering has a particular kind of real, truthful, or genuine connection with something that is important or special to the consumer. The market for authenticity has existed for centuries (Jones 1992; Mukerji 1983). Today's consumers can view a range of marketplace offerings as being authentic, including tourist attractions, products, brands, and characters on television shows. Consumers can also be influenced by the perceived authenticity of entities that develop and sell market offerings, including corporate executives, celebrity endorsers, salespeople, and characters in advertisements.

Judgments of authenticity are inherently subjective. Depending on a variety of factors (including a person's expertise and personal goals), different observers can apply different criteria and can come to different conclusions about a market offering's authenticity. Even in the case of market offerings that many think are objectively authentic (such as art objects in museums), expert judgments about authenticity can differ, depending on subjective criteria (Phillips 1997). Some have therefore argued that there is no single kind of authenticity (Wherry 2006), and that the term "authentic" can refer to different types of judgments in different contexts. In this entry, we discuss two well-known types.

One kind of authenticity relates to whether the market offering is believed to have a factual and physical link with something important to the consumer. Those who market tourist attractions and memorabilia often prominently promote physical links – for example, by emphasizing that a museum is authentic because a historical figure actually lived at the museum site, or that an article of clothing is authentic because a famous celebrity actually wore it. Physical links can also be important for judging the authenticity of more commonplace products. For instance, a Japanese car manufactured in Japan is likely to be viewed as being more authentically Japanese than a Japanese car manufactured in the United States.

Another perceived factual connection that influences perceptions of authenticity is a perceived connection between personality and behavior. For example, consumers can view a market offering as being authentic to the extent they believe it reflects the true personality of a company, brand, or spokesperson. Similarly, consumers view company representatives (such as CEOs or salespeople) as being authentic if they believe these representatives are behaving in a way that is true to their personality. Perceptions of authenticity can therefore be undermined if consumers suspect that the marketer has engaged in activities merely to get consumers to buy, and not as a reflection of the company's true personality. This is one reason why an increase in sales for a product or brand can lead to perceptions of inauthenticity.

Related to being true to one's self is the question of whether a market offering is unique or original. Originality is linked to authenticity because of a common assumption that being true to one's personality often means expressing one's uniqueness, as in the performance of blues music for instance (Grazian 2003). Also related to being true to one's self is the question of whether a company, its products, and its representatives have been consistent over time. Consistency is linked to authenticity because of a general belief that a person's true character is unlikely to change over time. If a company has changed over the years (and especially if it changes dramatically), it is harder to believe that its behavior continues to reflect its personality.

A second kind of authenticity relates to whether the market offering is believed to physically resemble something important or otherwise valuable to the consumer. Here, the connection is not physical but is perceptual. This meaning of authenticity is frequently used when describing replica art objects, restored historical artifacts, facsimiles of brands and products, and places that were created to look like other places. In this sense, market offerings are authentic to the extent that they truly resemble what they are meant to represent and therefore create a sensory experience for consumers that is the same as looking at the real thing.

Consumer judgments of authenticity can sometimes be enhanced by the assessment of legitimate authorities who can verify whether a market offering actually has the claimed physical connection or truly resembles what it claims to resemble. Yet, even when consumers believe that something is authentic, this belief may not be sufficient to encourage a purchase. For example, consumers do not value all companies that are true to the founder's personality; they also have to believe that the personality is attractive for other reasons. Similarly, a physical connection is not valuable unless the connection is with a person, place, or time period in which consumers have an interest. And, a perfect copy of something does not have value to a consumer unless the thing being copied is valued by the consumer.

SEE ALSO: Celebrity; Counterfeiting/Piracy

REFERENCES

Grazian, David. 2003. *Blue Chicago: The Search for Authenticity in Urban Blues Clubs*. Chicago: University of Chicago Press.

Jones, Mark. 1992. *Why Fakes Matter*. London: British Museum Press.

Mukerji, Chandra. 1983. *From Graven Images: Patterns of Modern Materialism*. New York: Columbia University Press.

Phillips, David. 1997. *Exhibiting Authenticity*. Manchester: Manchester University Press.

Wherry, Frederick. 2006. "The Social Sources of Authenticity in Global Handicraft Markets: Evidence from Northern Thailand." *Journal of Consumer Culture* 6(1): 5–32.

B

B2B Marketing

RAQUEL BARBOSA RIBEIRO and
ISABEL SOARES
University of Lisbon, Portugal

Business-to-business (B2B) marketing concerns marketing activities between organizations: companies, governments, institutions, or NGOs. B2B marketing particularities, when compared to the most common typology of marketing relations, known as business-to-consumers or B2C, mean fewer customers but more stakeholders, more complex decisions, larger quantities, and higher sums of money involved, product customization, and the prevalence of rational motivations, oriented either for profit or for the public interest.

B2B marketing was formerly known as industrial marketing, referring to the transactions of products, raw materials, and supplies for other businesses. Having gained serious scholarly interest from the 1960 onward, B2B marketing accounts for relatively few scientific contributions when compared to B2C marketing, as Grewal and Lilien (2012) note. Besides the generalist marketing journals, research on B2B marketing is found in specialized journals, including *Industrial Marketing Management*, the *Journal of Business and Industrial Marketing*, and the *Journal of Business-to-Business Marketing*.

In B2B, consumers are titled customers or clients. B2B markets are characterized by relatively few, yet powerful, customers whose acquisitions are considerable in terms of units, volume, and value. Frequently, a small number of customers represent a high share of the total demand. In contrast to individual consumers and households, these customers have distinct objectives: increasing profits, reducing costs, satisfying multiple stakeholders simultaneously (final consumers, employees, actionists), and complying with legal obligations and the public good. Rationality and efficiency prevail in decision making, which is chiefly oriented to best price choices. Impulsive buying is less frequent. The demand in B2B marketing is strongly affected by factors such as final consumers' demand, public expenditure, and macroeconomic indicators. Organizational demand is, however, more inelastic than that of individuals given its more complex processes and contracts, which slow down reaction to changes.

The most important customers exert various forms of power over their providers,

The Wiley Blackwell Encyclopedia of Consumption and Consumer Studies, First Edition.
Edited by Daniel Thomas Cook and J. Michael Ryan.

often determining prices, sales conditions, deadlines, and product customization details. Purchase procedures are usually formalized, routinized, multistage, and requiring advanced technical expertise from the parties involved. Actors implicated in a B2B negotiation can be initiators (those who detect the need and start the process: users), influencers and consultants (technical staff advising the upper hierarchies: engineers, lawyers), deciders (management and administration), approvers (financial analysts and accountants), buyers (procurement), and auditors.

Traditional B2B marketing presumes a close customer/supplier relationship and the use of a sales force for both research and communication. Whereas in the past transactions used to be personal and private, future directions include high technology, online marketing, and social networks. B2B marketing already accounts for more than 80 percent of e-commerce, with CRM and data analysis being important and increasingly developing research matters. Globalization and cultural differences pose pressing challenges to this area. Collaborative marketing is forecasted as another relevant trend.

SEE ALSO: Marketing/Marketing Science

REFERENCE

Grewal, Rajdeep, and Gary L. Lilien. 2012. *Handbook on Business to Business Marketing*. Cheltenham, UK: Edward Elgar Publishing.

FURTHER READING

Kotler, Philip, and L. Kevin Keller. 2012. *Marketing Management: Analysis, Planning, and Control*. 14th ed. Upper Saddle River, NJ: Prentice Hall.

Zimmerman, Alan, and Jim Blythe. 2012. *Business to Business Marketing Management*. New York: Routledge.

Bankruptcy

DEBORAH THORNE
Ohio University, USA

In 1800, the United States Congress penned the country's first bankruptcy laws, which, not surprisingly, paralleled those of the United Kingdom. Bankruptcy was limited to businesses, and the principal objective was to ensure that any assets recaptured from debtors were equally distributed among creditors. The financial well-being of the creditor, rather than the debtor, was the focus.

Fast-forward a little over 200 years. In the United States today, there are six different types (or chapters) of bankruptcy; each type is described within the corresponding chapter of the US Bankruptcy Code. Approximately 99 percent of US bankruptcies are either Chapter 7 or Chapter 13, the overwhelming majority of which are considered "personal" bankruptcies, filed by individuals and families rather than by corporations or municipalities. Debtors who file Chapter 7 relinquish all their eligible assets in exchange for discharge of their debts. Chapter 13 requires debtors to repay a portion of their debts, usually over a five-year period, after which time the remaining debt is discharged. Unlike two centuries ago, the primary purpose of bankruptcy today is to protect debtors from the collection attempts of their creditors.

The number of Americans filing bankruptcy continued a relatively unabated climb throughout the 1980s and 1990s. In 1996, a notable milestone was reached: more than one million petitions were filed that year. In 2005, in an effort to curtail bankruptcies, President George W. Bush signed into law extensive bankruptcy reforms; proponents argued that by increasing the cost and complexity of filing bankruptcy, numbers would decline. Prior to the reforms taking effect in October of that year, indebted Americans flooded bankruptcy courts and more than two million petitions were filed. In 2006, however, numbers did in fact drop by more than two-thirds to approximately 617,000. But the declining number of bankruptcies was short-lived: by 2008, filings once again surpassed one million.

Using occupational status, educational levels, and home ownership to determine socioeconomic status, the majority of American debtors who file personal bankruptcy are from middle-class households. Warren and Thorne (2012) argue that, within the bankrupt population, income is an unreliable measure of socioeconomic status because the vast majority (well over two-thirds) of filers report job problems and declines in income in the two years before filing. The median unsecured debt owed by petitioners is nearly $34,000, or about 1.2 times their median household income. Because extreme debt severely undercuts a household's wealth, creates familial hardships, and generally reduces life chances, it is critical that debt is included when determining the socioeconomic status of a bankrupt household.

Theoretically, bankruptcy, by its very nature, should be a powerful mechanism for upward social mobility because in a very short period of time (especially in the case of Chapter 7), large amounts of debt are discharged, thereby increasing household wealth almost overnight. Research by Porter and Thorne (2006) suggests that only about two-thirds of personal bankruptcies successfully increase a household's socioeconomic status – one year after bankruptcy, more than one-third of petitioners report that their financial circumstances are the same as, or worse than, the day they filed. This is most often the case for filers who face chronic employment, chronic medical problems, or who are over 65. Another factor that may impede upward mobility post-bankruptcy is the fact that bankruptcy remains on the credit report for 10 years, which often makes it very difficult to secure housing, transportation, employment, and loans, further undermining the likelihood that a filer can financially rebound.

The greatest percentage of bankruptcy filers are in their middle years: between the ages of 25 and 55. However, since the early 1990s, there has been a significant increase in the percentage of filers aged 65 and over. Among these older debtors, high interest and fees on credit cards, as well as illness and injury, are the two leading reasons cited for filing bankruptcy (Thorne 2010).

In the United States, there is a persistent assumption that people who file bankruptcy experience no shame and are seeking protection from their creditors because they are fiscally unskilled and profligate. Research, however, suggests something altogether different. Indeed, the stigma of bankruptcy continues to thrive. According to Thorne and Anderson (2006), to minimize the shame of bankruptcy, debtors often rely on common stigma management techniques, such as hiding their circumstances from others, differentiating themselves from filers whom they believe fit the stereotype of the "deadbeat debtor," and providing justifications and explanations for their financial failure. Research also suggests that families are quite reluctant to file bankruptcy and postpone doing so for as long as possible: more than four in ten households report that they seriously struggled with their debts for *more* than two years before they conceded and filed (Lawless et al. 2008). Further, reckless spending does not top the list of reasons for filing bankruptcy; instead, debtors report filing because of job loss, illness or injury, and separation or divorce (Warren and Tyagi 2003). These factors, which correlate with consumer bankruptcy, reflect structural changes within America's social safety net, resulting primarily from laws that explicitly shift economic risk onto individuals. For example, since the mid-1970s, there has been extreme volatility and instability in household income; households frequently require two wage earners to make ends meet; pensions have been replaced by unpredictable and often inadequate 401(k)s; the mortgage lending industry was, for many years, virtually unregulated, allowing for the proliferation of subprime and other precarious mortgage loans; and the cost of health care and health insurance has surpassed what most Americans can afford (Hacker 2008).

Behind every bankruptcy petition are living, breathing people – single moms, working couples, children, retired debtors. The massive debt that typically precedes bankruptcy and the process of filing often take a considerable toll. Thorne (2012) studied bankrupt couples and described how management of household debt prior to filing is overwhelmingly the responsibility of the wife. This chore often creates high levels of emotional distress and anxiety, leading some women to consider suicide as a way to escape the extreme pressure. Couples also report that the strain of the debt prior to bankruptcy causes extraordinary levels of stress, insomnia, depression, and marital dissatisfaction. Interestingly, after bankruptcy, the same couples report lower levels of stress, insomnia, and depression, while levels of marital satisfaction increase.

Clearly, bankruptcy is a complex experience. Most debtors describe extreme emotional distress, and filing bankruptcy does not necessarily guarantee a return to financial stability. That said, many debtors do emerge from the process with better emotional health, stronger marriages, and a clean financial slate which enables them once again to participate in and contribute to the US economy.

SEE ALSO: Class; Consumer Behavior; Debt; Finance/Financial Markets

REFERENCES

Hacker, Jacob S. 2008. *The Great Risk Shift: The New Economic Insecurity and the Decline of the American Dream*. New York: Oxford University Press.

Lawless, Robert M., Angela K. Littwin, Katherine M. Porter, John A. E. Pottow, Deborah K. Thorne, and Elizabeth Warren. 2008. "Did Bankruptcy Reform Fail? An Empirical Study of Consumer Debtors." *The American Bankruptcy Law Journal* 82: 349–405.

Porter, Katherine, and Deborah Thorne. 2006. "The Failure of Bankruptcy's Fresh Start." *Cornell Law Review* 92: 67–127.

Thorne, Deborah. 2010. "The (Interconnected) Reasons Elder Americans File Consumer Bankruptcy." *Journal of Aging & Social Policy* 22: 188–206.

Thorne, Deborah, 2012. "Women's Work, Women's Worry? Debt Management in Financially Distressed Families." In *Broke: How Debt Bankrupts the Middle Class*, edited by Katherine Porter, 136–153. Stanford, CA: Stanford University Press.

Thorne, Deborah, and Leon Anderson. 2006. "Managing the Stigma of Personal Bankruptcy." *Sociological Focus* 39: 77–97.

Warren, Elizabeth, and Deborah Thorne. 2012. "A Vulnerable Middle Class: Bankruptcy and Class Status." In *Broke: How Debt Bankrupts the Middle Class*, edited by Katherine Porter, 25–39. Stanford, CA: Stanford University Press.

Warren, Elizabeth, and Amelia Warren Tyagi. 2003. *The Two-Income Trap: Why Middle-Class Mothers and Father Are Going Broke*. New York: Basic Books.

Barbie

AGNES NAIRN
EM-Lyon Business School, France

Barbie is a consumer and a cultural icon that continues to attract contradiction and controversy nearly six decades after her launch in 1959. At first sight, the 11.5-inch plastic doll, owned by the Mattel Corporation, is a ubiquitous and timeless consumer success story. Two Barbie dolls are sold every second across 150 countries, with more than one billion incarnations in existence; 90 percent of girls in the United States under the age of 10 own at least one, and the average number of Barbies per child is ten in the United States, seven in the United Kingdom and Italy, and five in France and Germany. As a collector's item, Barbie also seems to be an appealing and enduring investment: the original 1959 Barbie that sold for US$3 in 1959 fetched €27,000 in 2006.

However, 2005 saw a drop in sales of 18 percent worldwide and 30 percent in the United States, when a new range of sassier Bratz dolls from MGA muscled its way into Barbie's market space. Meanwhile, Mattel's 2009 US$30 million investment in a six-story flagship Barbie store in Shanghai failed to provide sufficient returns and was closed down just two years after its opening. The Barbie brand, it transpired, could not be stretched to encompass premium-priced designer fashion, a theme bar, or bridal accoutrements – at least not in China. Moreover, despite the creation of a Chinese Barbie called "Ling," it seems that her "I Can Be" mentality and opulent spending habits do not represent a good cultural fit for contemporary Chinese femininity. In Saudi Arabia, the doll has been banned since 2003 because, according to the Committee for the Propagation of Virtue and Prevention of Vice, she does not fit with the ideals of Islam.

Yet for many Western cultures, Barbie offers some highly positive attributes as a youth role model. Unlike her baby doll predecessors, which encouraged girls to see themselves primarily as mothers, Barbie invited children to project their own adulthood aspirations. Barbie has offered girls 108 different careers over the years, ranging from "pet vet" or software engineer to tennis star or president, thus arguably representing a strong, feminist vision of unlimited career opportunities for women. Yet, despite this, Mattel maintains that girls themselves persist in displaying more interest in her looks than in her skills, attitudes, or ambitions; to accommodate their customers' alleged penchant for Barbie's signature long, blond hair they have created a disembodied "Barbie Head" that can simply be coiffed and made up. Her personality and drive are consigned to irrelevance, and even her body is cast into oblivion.

This body, however, has been the site of the most heated debate. If her 11.5-inch plastic self were to be built life-size and to scale, she would have a 39-inch bust, an 18-inch waist, and 33-inch hips. Standing at 5 foot 9 inches and weighing 110 pounds, she would have a BMI of 16.24 and be classified as anorexic. Slumber Party Barbie, introduced in 1965, attracted particular opprobrium for encouraging eating disorders, as she came with a bathroom scale permanently set at 110 pounds and a book entitled *How to Lose Weight*, with directions inside stating simply, "Don't eat." The limited range of Barbie's ethnic origins has also been criticized, with commentators noting that diversity comes into play only when it does not entail significantly displacing white, blond Barbie. Indeed, the current "Dolls of the World" range represents rather crass national stereotypes, such as a Spanish Barbie dressed in flamenco costume, rather than real aspirational role models, while every "I Can Be" Barbie career girl on the current brand website is both blond and white.

Perhaps the most interesting part of Barbie's cultural status is that little girls themselves often reject her violently, cutting off her hair, mutilating her body, and even putting her in the microwave. The reasons for rejection are complex and multifaceted. Ironically for an adult doll, she is shunned as "babyish," as girls receive their first Barbie aged 2 or 3 so that, by age 7, disavowing Barbie becomes a symbolic rite of passage. Equally ironically for a doll that has allegedly penetrated male-dominated workplaces, her infantilization is bound up with her hyperfemininity: many children see her as strictly for "girly girls." She is also spurned for "inauthenticity" both because she is "plastic" and because she is multiple and ubiquitous – just too much.

In an attempt to keep Barbie alive for another generation, Mattel is currently leveraging movie hits such as *Twilight* and *The Hunger Games* to create new personalities and possibilities for her. Will Barbie live to celebrate her 100th birthday? As a nostalgic collector's item certainly; as a girl's playmate – perhaps.

SEE ALSO: Children's Consumer Culture; Gender and Consumer Culture; Girl Culture

FURTHER READING

Nairn, Agnes, Christine Griffin, and Patricia Gaya Wicks, 2008. "Children's Use of Brand Symbolism: A Consumer Culture Theory Approach." *European Journal of Marketing* 42(5/6): 627–640.

Rand, Erica. 1995. *Barbie's Queer Accessories*. Durham, NC: Duke University Press.

Rogers, Mary F. 1999. *Barbie Culture*. New York: Sage.

Barthes, Roland

MING LIM
University of Leicester, UK

Roland Barthes (1915–80) is a familiar name to readers of cultural and literary theory, but he remains, for many, a somewhat enigmatic figure. As a cultural critic and a semiologist, his method of analysis can appear, as the translator of the 1957 edition of *Mythologies*, Annette Lavers, puts it, "highly poetic and idiosyncratic." This entry aims to clarify his early work, specifically his arguments relating to myth and the uses of semiology in cultural analysis.

Barthes was born in Cherbourg, France and enjoyed a distinguished career in French academia: in his mid-30s and 40s, he held positions at the Centre National de la Recherche Scientifique and eventually, at 61, took up the Chair in Literary Semiology at the Collège de France. Barthes was trained in linguistics, philosophy and psychoanalysis, and his work exercised formidable influence across the Anglophone world throughout much of the 1980s and 1990s and has earned an enduring place in the history of thought, particularly in departments of literary theory, comparative literature, media, and culture.

Barthes argued that the books and films we read and watch, the foods we eat, the entertainment we indulge in, and the advertising we consume were often uncritically accepted as natural and unmysterious. He wanted to debunk what he called the "essential enemy" (1972/1957, 9) or the "bourgeois norm" of this kind of attitude toward cultural ideas and products. A fundamental issue in all of Barthes' work centers on the meaning and the mechanics of myth. The notion of myth has a language in its own right, with its own rules, codes, and shades of meaning, and is not one that comes automatically or intuitively to mind to contemporary readers and audiences of literary theory. Because myth is a language, according to Barthes, it can be learned and mastered in order to interrogate and clarify the myriad activities one associates with everyday life. Barthes claims for "myth" a universal status: he is unapologetic about the notion that everything and anything can be classified as myth as long as it is "conveyed by a discourse" (1972/1957, 109). All objects in our world, as long as they can be talked about, become social. In this way, all matter always has the potential to be discoursed about and, hence, to be mythic. In this sense, myth is "social usage" of matter (p. 109).

Myth, for Barthes, is material that is *worked over*, loaded (like a gun, say), ready for firing off rockets of meaning. In other words, it plays with the well-known distinction between "signifier" and "signified" in a new way. Those familiar with Saussure will remember that the "signified" is the concept (the category or group of animals, e.g., "cats"), the "signifier" is the mental image we have of it, and the third term that links both is the "sign" (the word "cat"). Explained in this way, it would not be, strictly speaking, inaccurate to say that the signifier *expresses* the signified; instead, it is the *sign* that expresses the correlation between the two terms. The signifier, in fact, is empty, in Barthes' view; it is the sign that gives meaning to the signifieds.

Myth operates on two levels: it leverages on this semiological system I have just explained and also plays with another layer, what Barthes calls the "metalanguage." That is to say, myth (as a language in its own right, as mentioned earlier) has the power to speak about the first language or semiological system. Furthermore, myth encompasses both systems of meaning – both languages, as it were – in itself to form a *global sign* that does away with the first system. In this way, myth becomes greater than either the signifier (the grammatical utterance) or the signified (the concept). The signifier is, in myth, already a sum of signs: "In myth, the signifier is already formed by the signs of the language" (1972/1957, 117). Barthes proposes a new word for this phenomenon: "signification." This nomenclature is useful to the extent that it combines meaning (the signified) and form (the signifier).

Myths, in other words, are complex structures. On the one hand, they require historical, cultural, and political understanding. On the other, myth is simply a way of saying something that transcends specific values: it has a global resonance that is not easily summarized or even articulated. What we call "globalization" today is surely a vindication of Barthes' explanation of how images of all kinds are saturated with a global significance that deserves more detailed semiological scrutiny.

SEE ALSO: Adorno, Theodor; Advertising; Capitalism; Consumer Culture; Glocalization/Grobalization; Semiotics

REFERENCE

Barthes, Roland. 1972/1957. "Myth Today." In *Mythologies*. Translated by Annette Lavers. London: Vintage.

FURTHER READING

Bennett, Pete and Julian McDougall. 2013. *Barthes' Mythologies Today: Readings of Contemporary Culture*. New York: Routledge.
Harland, Richard. 1999. *Literary Theory from Plato to Barthes: An Introductory History*. Basingstoke, UK: Macmillan.

Baudrillard, Jean

DOUGLAS KELLNER
University of California, Los Angeles, USA

Jean Baudrillard (1929–2007) first emerged as an important theorist of consumption and the consumer society. His early work in these areas focuses on what he called the system of objects, the consumer society, and a critique of the political economy of the sign. These texts combined neo-Marxian social theory with the sort of cultural semiotics associated with Roland Barthes, the critique of everyday life associated with Henri Lefebvre, and the radical critique of existing consumer society by Guy Debord and the Situationists (see Kellner 1989).

During the late 1960s, Baudrillard began publishing a series of books that would eventually make him world famous. Influenced by Henri Lefebvre, Roland Barthes, Georges

Bataille, and Guy Debord and the French Situationists, Baudrillard undertook serious work in the field of social theory, semiology, and psychoanalysis and published his first book *The System of Objects* in 1968, followed by *The Consumer Society* in 1970, and *For a Critique of the Political Economy of the Sign* in 1972. These early publications are attempts, within the framework of critical sociology, to combine the studies of everyday life initiated by Lefebvre and Debord and the Situationists with a social semiology that studies the life of signs in social life (see Genosko 1994). Along with Lefebvre, Debord, and the Situationists, Baudrillard was suggesting that the contemporary stage of capitalism is distinguished from earlier socioeconomic formations precisely by the increased importance of commodity culture within both production and social reproduction (i.e., the ways in which society reproduces itself in individual thought and behavior). On this view, one cannot properly understand history, politics, economics, or any social phenomena without grasping the role of culture and commodification within the social logic of contemporary capitalist societies. From this perspective, Baudrillard provides provocative rethinking of the role of commodity culture and the consumer society within contemporary capitalism.

His first published book, *The System of Objects* (1996/1968), investigates the new system of mass consumption bound up with the explosive proliferation of a brave new world of consumer goods and services. The project operates within the framework of a subject–object dialectic where the subject faces a world of objects which attract, fascinate, and sometimes control the individual's perception, thought, and behavior. The analyses presuppose the theory of the commodification of everyday life under capitalism advanced by Marxists like Lukács and semiological theories in which objects are interpreted as signs that are organized into systems of signification, developed by Barthes and others (see Kellner 1989).

Baudrillard took on the ambitious task of describing the contours and dominant structures of the new system of objects, while indicating how they condition and structure needs, fantasies, and behavior. *The System of Objects* itself is highly systematic, exploring first the system of *functional objects* (consumer goods), followed by studies of systems of seemingly *non-functional objects* (antiques, collections) and *metafunctional objects* (gadgets and robots), concluding with an important inquiry into "the socio-ideological system of objects and consumption." The book is animated by a sense that Baudrillard is describing a *new* social order which he describes variously as a "new technical order," a "new environment," a "new field of everyday life," a "new morality," and a new form of "hypercivilization." He frequently uses the terms "modernity" and "modern" to describe the new environment; thus he interprets the rise of the system of objects and consumer society under the sign of modernity (whereas later he will describe the genesis and contours of what will eventually be called a "postmodern" world). The text is full of interesting insights and anticipations of his later work. Indeed, the framework of a perceiving and desiring subject facing a world of objects and signs will define the trajectory of Baudrillard's thought through the present.

The starting point of Baudrillard's *oeuvre* is thus our familiar system of objects in which we are surrounded by objects of everyday life. Individuals in all societies have always organized their everyday life through the production, arrangement, and use of objects, and Baudrillard attempts to describe the distinguishing features of our contemporary system of objects and what differentiates it from previous societies. In his view, the new environment is more abstract, more homogeneous, and less embedded with personal and traditional significance than the previous world of objects. The new world of objects and signs is at once more functional, differentiated, and complex, and more subject to manipulation and control than the traditional world of objects. The new technical world imposes new demands and challenges and elicits contradictory responses.

Life in the system of objects for the early Baudrillard is divided into a private sphere and a public sphere; if the home is the center and locus of the private sphere, the car is the key object in which I emerge into and traverse through the public sphere. For Baudrillard, the home is the unmoving locus of my own spatial existence; the car takes me through time and space in the public sphere. Speed is the car's privileged modality and the source of both pleasure and power as I careen through the city and countryside (one has to have observed driving in France during the period when Baudrillard wrote this to get the full resonance of his position). The car represents a masculine world of danger and adventure compared to the feminine world of the home and domesticity, thus reproducing a bipolar gender system.

Although Baudrillard describes the system of objects as a system of commodities which constitute a consumer society – and focuses his description on types of commodities, advertising, credit, modes of consumption, and so on – there is little historical discussion of the emergence of the system of objects from the development of capitalism. Baudrillard's study is distinguished by a critical scrutiny of the structure of the system of objects and the ways that it differs from the traditional object worlds. He also carries through cultural analyses à la Barthes of the mythologies surrounding such objects as furniture, mirrors, clocks, colors, glass, collections, the automobile, gadgets, robots, and so on. Also of interest is his discussion of the ways that consumption, credit, and advertising produce a new morality that shifts from a productivist (work) ethic to a consumerist (leisure) ethic of fun and gratification. These analyses permit discussion of the subjective projections and responses involved in the system of objects and provide a framework for his analysis of the consumer society that would occupy him in his next book.

Baudrillard's second book *The Consumer Society* (1996/1970) continues his systematic theoretical and empirical investigations of objects and activities in the new world of consumption and technique. While *The System of Objects* contains a rather theoretical analysis of the structure and ambience of the world of objects, *The Consumer Society* presents more concrete sociological analysis of the new worlds of leisure and consumption for a more popular audience. This book contains analyses of the structure and nature of commodities and objects, a theory of consumption, and studies of the mass media, sex, and leisure; it concludes with some observations concerning the nature of contemporary alienation. The project is animated by the conviction that deeper understanding of consumption is needed to understand the fundamental dynamics of neocapitalist societies. While capitalism focused its energies on developing a system of mass production during the nineteenth and early twentieth centuries, beginning in the 1920s the issue of mass consumption and the management of consumer demand became of paramount importance (see Ewen and Ewen 1982).

Everyday life, Baudrillard suggests, is defined more by the manipulation of commodities and messages and the organization and display of domestic goods – and thus by interaction with objects – than by social interaction with other people. Baudrillard focuses on the "logic of social differentiation," whereby individuals distinguish themselves and attain social prestige and standing through the purchase and use of consumer goods. He argues that the entire system of production produces a system of needs that are rationalized, homogenized, systematized, and hierarchized. Rather than an individual commodity (or advertisement) seducing a consumer into purchase (which he equates with the primitive notion of *mana*), one is actually induced to buy into an entire system of objects and needs through which one differentiates oneself socially and yet integrates oneself into the consumer society. He suggests that this activity can best be conceptualized by seeing the objects of consumption as *signs* and the consumer society as a system of signs: "In this way a washing machine *serves* as equipment and *plays* as an element of comfort, or of prestige and so on. It is the latter that is specifically the field of consumption … A need is not a need for a particular object as much as it is a 'need' for difference (the *desire for social meaning*" (Baudrillard 1996/1970, 106–107).

Baudrillard stresses in *The Consumer Society* how consumption is based upon an unending desire for objects and unlimited renewal of needs, suggesting that the imperatives of an entire system of needs and objects require a vast *labor* to learn about the products, to master their use, and to earn the money and leisure to purchase and use them. Consumption is thus *productive activity* which requires education and effort. Consequently, Baudrillard proposes that consumption is not primarily to be interpreted in relation to pleasure or to the satisfaction of needs, but as a mode of social activity whereby one inserts oneself into the consumer society, conforming to socially normative behavior and signifying that one is a player in the society of consumption.

In the language of Lévi-Strauss, Baudrillard is suggesting that consumption is not largely derived from the realm of nature but from culture, and should be interpreted as a system of signs organized by codes and rules rather than a "natural" satisfaction of needs through goods. Thus, for Baudrillard, commodities and consumption constitute a "global, arbitrary and coherent system of signs, a *cultural* system which substitutes a social order of values and classifications for a contingent world of needs and pleasures, the natural and biological order" (1996/1970, 111). He continues: "Marketing, purchasing, sales, the acquisition of differentiated commodities and object/signs – all of these presently constitute our language, a code with which our entire society *communicates* and speaks of and to itself" (p. 112). The consumer can therefore not avoid the obligation to consume because it is consumption that is the primary mode of social integration and is the primary ethic and activity within the consumer society. The consumer ethic and "fun morality" thus involve active labor, incessant curiosity and search for novelty, and conformity to the latest fads, products, and demands to consume.

Thus, on this view, consumption is not the free activity of an autonomous subject, but is constrained by the order of production that produces and manages a system of needs and by the order of signification that determines the relative social prestige and value of the system of goods. Yet the effects of politically organized consumers, Baudrillard suggests, could be tremendous, since consumer revolt could bring to a halt the dynamics of contemporary capitalism. Such revolts, however, have been manifested only "in a few strikes among American housewives and in the sporadic destruction of commodities (May 1968, the *No Bra Day* where American women publically burned their bras)," Baudrillard stating that "in general the consumers, as such, are unconscious and unorganized, just as workers may have been at the beginning of the nineteenth century. As such, consumers have been glorified, flattered and eulogized as 'public opinion,' that mystical, providential and '*sovereign*' reality" (1996/1970, 121–123).

Baudrillard concludes by valorizing "multiple forms of refusal" which can be fused in a "practice of radical change" (1996/1970, 295) and he alludes to the expectation of "brutal eruptions and sudden disaggregations" which "in a fashion as unforeseeable but certain, as in May 68, will come to shatter this white mass [of consumption]" (p. 316). On the other hand, in his conclusion Baudrillard also describes a situation where alienation is so total that it cannot be surpassed because "it is the very structure of the consumer society" (p. 307). His argument is that in a society where everything is a commodity that can be bought and sold, alienation is total. Indeed, the term "alienation" originally signified "to sale," and in a totally commodified society where everything is a commodity, alienation is ubiquitous, because everything has its price and is for sale. Moreover, the conclusion describes "the end of transcendence" (a phrase borrowed from Marcuse) where individuals can neither perceive their own true needs or another way of life (pp. 307ff).

Baudrillard's problematic here is particularly close to the work of the Frankfurt School, especially that of Herbert Marcuse, who had already developed some of the most far-reaching critiques of the consumer society. Like Lukács and the Frankfurt School, Baudrillard employs a mode of thought whereby the commodity and commodification become a totalizing social process that permeates social life. Following the general line of critical Marxism, Baudrillard argues that the process of homogenization, alienation, and exploitation constitutes a process of *reification* in which objects come to dominate subjects, thereby robbing people of their human qualities and capacities. For Lukács, the Frankfurt School, and Baudrillard, reification – the process whereby human beings become dominated by things and become more thing-like themselves – comes to dominate social life.

In a sense, Baudrillard's early work can be read as an account of a higher stage of reification and social domination than that described by the Frankfurt School. Baudrillard goes beyond the Frankfurt School by applying the semiological theory of the sign to describe the world of commodities, media, and the consumer society and, in a sense, he takes its theory of "one-dimensional society" to a higher level. Eventually, Baudrillard will take his analysis of domination by signs and the system of objects to even more pessimistic conclusions, where he concludes that the problematic of the "end of the individual" sketched by the Frankfurt School has reached its fruition in the total defeat of the subject by the object world. Yet in his early writings, Baudrillard has a somewhat more active theory of consumption than that of the Frankfurt School, which generally portrays consumption as a passive mode of social integration. By contrast, consumption in Baudrillard's early writings is itself a kind of labor, "an active manipulation of signs," a way of inserting oneself within the consumer society and working to differentiate oneself from others. Yet this active manipulation of signs is not equivalent to postulating an active subject which could resist, redefine, or produce its own signs, thus Baudrillard fails to develop a genuine theory of agency, resistance to consumer capitalism, or alternative values and ideals to the existing society, projects he will take up in later works.

In the consumer society, consumption thus replaces production as the central mode of social behavior and social organization from which standpoint society can be interpreted and critically analyzed. Baudrillard thus conceives consumption as a mode of being, a way of gaining identity, meaning, and prestige in contemporary society. In later works, he further elaborates semiotic theories of signs and signification which he uses to analyze and critique the consumer society, thus adding a semiological dimension to previous neo-Marxian critiques of the consumer society. In *For a Critique of the Political Economy of the Sign* (1972), Baudrillard discusses problems with both standard bourgeois and Marxian analyses of commodities, consumption, and needs, while arguing that a sociologically oriented semiology could help to develop more adequate perspectives. Though critical of classical Marxism, these studies are not as dismissive as his later works, starting with *The Mirror of Production* (1975), and can be read as an attempt to strengthen and reconstruct the Marxian critique of political economy.

Later, Baudrillard will become infamous for his theories of simulation and simulacra and argument that contemporary societies are being propelled into new hyperreal and virtual worlds (see Kellner 1989), which indeed have come to pass in our new digitized media and social networking societies. In Baudrillard's later writings, however, he does not discuss consumption, commodities, and the consumer society in the same language as in his earlier more sociological work; instead he veers to a cultural metaphysics, sometimes associated with postmodern theory. There are reasons, however, why those interested in consumption and the consumer society could find important analyses and ideas in Baudrillard's work, as I have attempted to show in this entry.

SEE ALSO: Barthes, Roland; Commodification; Debord, Guy; Frankfurt School; Marx, Karl; Semiotics

REFERENCES

Baudrillard, Jean. 1996/1968. *The System of Objects*. London: Verso.

Baudrillard, Jean. 1996/1970. *The Consumer Society*. London: Verso.

Baudrillard, Jean. 1981/1972. *For a Critique of the Political Economy of the Sign*. St. Louis, MO: Telos Press.

Baudrillard, Jean. 1975. *The Mirror of Production*. St. Louis, MO: Telos Press.

Ewen, Stuart, and Elizabeth Ewen. 1982. *Channels of Desire*. New York: McGraw-Hill.

Genosko, Gary. 1994 *Baudrillard and Signs*. London: Routledge.

Kellner, Douglas. 1989. *Jean Baudrillard: From Marxism to Post-Modernism and Beyond*. Cambridge, UK: Polity.

FURTHER READING

Barthes, Roland. 1962/1957. *Mythologies*. New York: Hill and Wang.

Beauty Industry

JENNIFER M. WHITMER
University of Nevada, Las Vegas, USA

The beauty industry, which includes the sale of cosmetics, fragrances, and toiletries, today is a multibillion dollar global industry. The pursuit of beauty has a long historical tradition. Cultures throughout history have established beauty norms and methods for achieving them. However, the mass beauty industry which developed with the advent of modern consumer culture did not come to prominence until the years leading up to and following World War I, particularly as US business firms began to capitalize on the extant beauty culture and a modernist cultural understanding of the malleability of the body, transforming what had been a craft into a capitalist industry.

Because the mass beauty industry encompasses a heterogeneous array of products, the commercial beauty industry can claim many roots, including perfumeries, salons, pharmacies, and drugstores, as well as theatrical makeup. However, although there was a small trade in beauty products and services throughout the nineteenth century, prior to the rise of the beauty industry, beauty practices took place largely within the household. Due to the influence of Puritanical morality, the excessive use of cosmetics, particularly color cosmetics, was frowned upon in the early history of the United States as evidence of loose moral character. However, women continued to use cosmetics which were meant to improve or preserve the condition of the skin. The traditional Christian morality which characterized the beauty culture of the nineteenth century did not fit with the modern consumerist ethos of the twentieth century. Nineteenth-century America connected beauty and morality, whereas, by the early twentieth century, beauty marketing was beginning to link the consumption of beauty products to modernist ideals of scientific progress, individual expression, and the liberation from traditional social norms. The concept of the body as malleable, to be changed through the use of consumer goods, was central to this transformation. Modern shifts in fashion and technology made the use of cosmetics and beauty services more widespread and acceptable. Higher incomes and more leisure time allowed individuals to invest in beautifying themselves, while transportation technologies allowed companies to sell to more people and communications technologies allowed for beauty norms to be diffused to the masses.

The beauty industry has always attracted debate and criticism. In the earliest years of mass marketization, the use of color cosmetics was seen as a falsehood and a vanity, as well as evidence of women's frivolity and irrationality. As the twentieth century developed and the use of cosmetics became normalized, criticism of the industry turned to its colonial impact, as well as to its contribution to racially homogenized and oppressive beauty norms.

Early advertising portrayed the beauty industry as having a democratizing impact: beauty, glamour, and luxury were accessible to any woman with the right products, rather than by virtue of class background. However, the ideals popularized by the industry for much of the twentieth century emphasized whiteness above all else, and the beauty industry was highly segregated by race. In the United States before World War I, this opened opportunities for African American entrepreneurs, such as Annie Malone and C. J. Walker, to develop successful businesses which emerged to serve African American communities and which stressed beauty as an expression of racial pride and uplift. However, in the face of the Depression and competition from large white-owned firms, which began capitalizing on the African American market, many of these companies were unable to survive. Companies serving the African American population instead stressed beauty ideals that aligned with white ideals, including lighter skin, straight hair, and European features. The beauty industry is no longer so clearly segregated, but whiteness continues to dominate as a beauty ideal. Similarly, as US and European firms began to make serious attempts to move into non-Western markets following World War II, they contributed to a similar homogenization of beauty norms worldwide, flattening cultural distinctions. Western firms today are perhaps more attuned to local tastes and culture – for instance, hiring local actors and models for advertising in different markets. However, they continue to promote Western cultural messages regarding beauty and consumption.

Some of the most vocal critics of the beauty industry have come from feminist circles. In general, there have been two schools of feminist thought: one is rooted in second-wave feminist thought and a second is rooted in feminist cultural studies. Historically, second-wave feminist critiques of the beauty industry frame it as a patriarchal force that sustains women's subordination by defining their personhood according to how closely they are able to align themselves to homogeneous, unattainable, unnatural ideals of beauty. From this perspective, the beauty industry sustains itself by manufacturing false needs and creating insecurities in women. Women are made to spend large quantities of time and money on treatments and products which are often useless and potentially dangerous. Thus, the pursuit of beauty represents a form of physical as well as symbolic violence enacted on women's bodies; the pleasure many women feel in beautifying is to be read as a form of false consciousness, and the current proliferation of the beauty industry represents a backlash against women's success in the public sphere.

Academics working in the tradition of feminist cultural studies, such as Rosalind Gill, Michelle Lazar, Angela McRobbie, and Kathy Peiss, have focused on the contradictions inherent in the beauty industry, including women's capacity for agency and pleasure within an oppressive system. These authors pointed to the history of feminine culture behind the beauty industry, the career success women have had in the beauty industry in contrast with other businesses, and the personal pleasures and social benefits women find in self-aestheticization. Rather than framing the proliferation of the beauty industry as pure feminist backlash, these analyses examine how the industry has historically traded on an image of woman as a liberated, modern, self-actualizing consumer, acknowledging feminist ideals while reducing women's freedom to the freedom to consume. Within this context, women's self-aestheticization cannot be understood purely as evidence of false consciousness, but as a means of engaging with cultural meanings of gender and femininity in ways that may be self-fulfilling even as, at the same time, they reproduce patterns of women's subordination.

The growth of the men's segment of the beauty market further complicates the relationship between gender and beauty. Although the use of cosmetics has historically been associated with women in Western societies, pre-industrial beauty products were largely unisex. However, the mass beauty industry exaggerated a tendency toward gender differentiation through branding practices which aligned women's use of cosmetics with feminized ideals of glamour, beauty, and luxury. The beauty industry still relies on aspirational messages in marketing its products, but in contemporary brand culture, the emphasis in beauty marketing is on developing relationships between brands and consumers and on how products can be made relevant to individuals' lives and self-projects. With the expansion of consumer culture and the tendency toward the aestheticization of the body, there has been a push toward increasing men's use of beauty products. Although initially stigmatized as unmasculine, men's beauty consumption is increasingly normalized.

SEE ALSO: Body and Consumer Culture; Cosmetic Surgery; Gender and Consumer Culture

FURTHER READING

Gimlin, Debra. 2002. *Body Work: Beauty and Self-Image in American Culture*. Berkeley: University of California Press.

Jones, Geoffrey. 2010. *Beauty Imagined: A History of the Global Beauty Industry*. Oxford: Oxford University Press.

Lazar, Michelle. 2006. "'Discover the Power of Femininity!' Analyzing Global 'Power Femininity' in Advertising." *Feminist Media Studies* 6(4). doi:10.1080/14680770600990002

Peiss, Kathy. 1998. *Hope in a Jar: The Making of America's Beauty Culture*. New York: Henry Holt.

Behavioral Economics and Consumption

LUCIA A. REISCH
Copenhagen Business School, Denmark
CASS R. SUNSTEIN
Harvard University, USA

The standard economic model of consumer behavior is simple: rational "econs" (Thaler and Sunstein 2008) choose the best things they can afford within their budget constraints. The mathematical model is essentially a constrained optimization situation for a set of considered consumption bundles, the evoked set. This model accounts for factors that influence choices, primarily time (current availability), other goods (opportunity costs), and consumption circumstances (perhaps including diminishing marginal utility). The model assumes that attitudes, values, social norms, and other mental representations are included in a consumer's preferences. While the model recognizes distinctive features or potential anomalies of consumption – such as bandwagon or cascade effects, Veblen effects, habits, addiction, limited information processing – it assumes that the biases and heuristic strategies that have been identified in empirical consumer research are generally unimportant in real-world markets. This assumption is supported by a further set of assumptions about economic agents: that they are motivated (solely) by expected utility maximization, are generally governed by purely selfish concerns, and have consistent time preferences and fungible income and assets. Later versions of the standard model have relaxed some of these assumptions in order to incorporate the notion of cognitive limitations in economic actors (in 1956, the psychologist Herbert Simon introduced the concept of bounded rationality), the fact that information is not free (economics of information), the existence of unselfish motivations (emphasized by Gary Becker), and the influence of formal and informal institutions on choice (institutional economics). Nonetheless, the model of the consumer as *econ* persists in this work.

While the aforementioned precepts can be valuable for mathematical economic analysis, they do limit the explanatory power and practical relevance of standard economic models. This is the strength and utility of behavioral economics (BE): it is based on an empirically and theoretically well-grounded set of psychological principles and derives its results from empirical methods such as field and lab experiments, as well as survey research. BE explicitly revises rational choice models by identifying specific departures from them. While rational choice models continue to have explanatory power, psychological plausibility is producing more realistic models of consumer behavior. At the same time, these models can be more complex, which makes applying them a challenge.

The rise of BE in studying, explaining, and modeling consumer behavior can be traced to the 1970s. In 1974, Daniel Kahneman and Amos Tversky showed that people use mental short cuts (heuristics) in evaluating risks, including, for example, the availability heuristic, which means that people assess probabilities by asking about which events come readily to mind. Kahneman and Tversky made another seminal contribution with their 1979 work on prospect theory, which proposed an alternative to expected utility theory. From prospect theory, it emerged that people dislike losses more than they like equivalent gains (loss aversion), which greatly affects their choices; what counts as a gain or loss is determined by the reference point, which can be manipulated (for example, by sellers). Another key publication was Richard Thaler's "Toward a Positive Theory of Consumer Choice" (1980) which helped develop

BE's theoretical groundwork, with particular emphasis on mental accounting (consumers put money in different mental accounts, such as savings, school, and vacation, and spend accordingly) and the endowment effect (by which consumers value goods that they have more than they value the same goods in the hands of others).

The 1980s, 1990s, and 2000s witnessed a stream of groundbreaking research on human biases (e.g., optimism bias, status quo bias, and availability bias, as well as myopia, understood as a focus on the short term) and also on the power of contexts, defaults, priming, and framing. The research showed that producers can manipulate consumers in multiple ways. BE experienced broad public recognition in the mid-2000s, when public officials became interested in new policy instruments. Behaviorally informed regulation, such as "nudging" (Thaler and Sunstein 2008), was introduced into academic discourse and was soon applied to policy in fields ranging from healthy eating and weight loss to saving for retirement, standard terms in consumer contracts, acceptance of offshore wind farms, energy conservation, and many more. Some countries, such as the United Kingdom and the United States, have appointed "behavioral insight teams" within their governments, whose task it is to put policy programs and tools to the test prior to their actual implementation. Nudging as a policy tool has given rise to debate over both the effectiveness and legitimacy of "libertarian paternalism" in light of behavioral findings.

BE is sometimes criticized as being empirically rich, but theory poor – a claim that is hard to accept, or is at least overstated, considering both the rich psychological and economic body of theoretical work on which it is built and the fact that it remains a nascent field. In consumer research, consumer policy, and environmental policy, BE has refreshed and expanded the debate on behavioral assumptions, consumption models, and effective and efficient policy instruments. Moreover, BE is closely related to other recently developing areas of economics, primarily neuroeconomics and experimental economics, both of which contribute innovative methodological approaches to the development of BE research and policy application.

SEE ALSO: Consumer Behavior; Methods of Consumer Research

REFERENCES

Kahneman, Daniel, and Amos Tversky. 1974. "Judgment under Uncertainty: Heuristics and Biases." *Science* 185(4157): 1124–1131.

Kahneman, Daniel, and Amos Tversky. 1979. "Prospect Theory: An Analysis of Decision under Risk." *Econometrica* 47(2): 263–291.

Simon, Herbert. 1956. "Rational Choice and the Structure of the Environment." *Psychological Review* 63: 129–138.

Thaler, Richard H. 1980. "Toward a Positive Theory of Consumer Choice." *Journal of Economic Behavior and Organization* 1: 39–60.

Thaler, Richard H., and Cass R. Sunstein. 2008. *Nudge: Improving Decisions about Health, Wealth, and Happiness*. New Haven, CT: Yale University Press.

Benjamin, Walter

ANDREA DASSOPOULOS
University of Nevada – Las Vegas, US

Walter Benjamin's (1892–1940) diverse intellectual influence extends throughout the humanities and social sciences. Most often, he is recognized as a literary critic or a philosopher associated with the Frankfurt School. His work covers a wide range of subjects, such as history, modernity, religiosity, art, literature, and technology, though most of it was published and translated posthumously.

He earned a doctorate in Switzerland in 1919, but was unable to secure an academic position, eventually working odd freelance jobs as a translator and literary critic. He befriended poet and playwright Bertolt Brecht, with whom he collaborated and shared leftist and Marxist ideals. He was born to a wealthy Jewish family in Berlin and fled to Paris when the Nazis took power in 1933. While in Paris he continued to do freelance work for the Frankfurt School and corresponded frequently with his friends and colleagues Theodor Adorno and Gershom Scholem. He was interned briefly in a French prison camp in 1939 and, following his release, spent the next few months trying to flee France across the Pyrenees mountains into Spain. His attempts to escape were thwarted by customs officials, who sent him back to France. In despair, he took his own life in 1940. After the war, Adorno and Scholem generated a revived interest in his work. Benjamin left behind fragmented works and a legacy that continues to be debated as more of his voluminous work becomes published, translated, and scrutinized. His earliest works remain unpublished, but were significant for establishing his critical philosophy and to the development of the critical theory of the Frankfurt School. He was among the first to critique mass culture and to identify its relationship to consumer culture.

Benjamin was influenced by the philosopher Georg Simmel, who wrote about the contradictions of metropolitan life and people's meaningful interactions with objects in the city. For Simmel, the introduction of money forever changed social interactions and was the source of alienation and the breakdown of community bonds and atomization in the city, but money was also the source of great cosmopolitan freedom and cultural cultivation. Benjamin wanted to build on Simmel's ideas and tackle the contradictions of the city. His time in Paris inspired his unfinished yet prodigious *Arcades Project*; for 13 years, he methodically collected information about the city's nineteenth-century arcades (*passages couverts*). Adorno had become critical of the *Arcades Project* because it lacked mediation; Benjamin had collected a large volume of artifacts, which he presented without interpretation or theoretical mediation, thus imbuing them with mystic quality. The project aimed to map the psychosocial spaces of nineteenth-century Paris in the context of the changes brought about by capitalism. Benjamin conceived the project as a "dialectical fairytale," wherein one generation imagines the next within itself. The arcades were lines of shops with glass roofs. Technological advances in construction and lighting created a dramatic environment where people could stroll, be seen, and gaze upon others. The arcades as a novelty and as a public space became a prominent pastime of nineteenth-century Parisians and the beginning of consumerism. Within the arcades are new experiences and commodities to consume. Extending Marx's explanation of commodity fetishism, Benjamin critiques the experience of the arcades for its ephemeral quality meant to distract and occupy the masses, thus hiding the exploitative nature of consumerism.

Benjamin also was deeply influenced by Charles Baudelaire's presentation of the *flâneur* as the painter of modern life. The arcades promoted *flânerie*, or aimless strolling. The gentlemen *flâneurs* and lady *flâneuses* of the arcades played a pivotal role in the urban culture. They became intoxicated by the possibilities of the city, drawn further and further into aimless exploration, ultimately leading to unsatisfied desires. Fleeting fashion and the experience of boredom were novel in the arcades and distinct from any time period before them. Aimless wandering through the well-lit shops aroused the senses and provided stimulation and excitement. However, beneath the experience of novelty was a transformation of life by the commodity form. The *flâneur*, a result of the transformation of society through modernism, was self-aware and thus played a dual role as both a participant in consumerism and a detached observer who could proffer a cultural critique.

Benjamin's most influential essay "The Work of Art in the Age of Mechanical Reproduction" (1935) explores changes in the consumption of art. Benjamin argued that in capitalist societies, art is elevated to a sacred status because of its unique "aura" that is the product of its manual production and the historical context in which it was produced. However, the technical process of reproducing art creates images that bear resemblance to the original work, but lack the sacred aural qualities. As these modes of artistic production grow more prominent, specifically photography and film, they become the preferred choice of the masses, and the industries that create them have a captive audience. For fellow Frankfurt School members, especially Theodor Adorno, the creation of mass culture represented a form of oppression. Adorno argued that culture industries turned authentic artistic expressions into commodities, stripping them of their revolutionary and utopian potential, denigrating popular culture and creating an audience of passive dupes susceptible to ideological domination.

While Benjamin recognized the rise of culture industries and the loss of traditionally produced art, he held a more ambivalent position on the mass production of art, which he viewed as irreversible. The highly individualistic experience of viewing art objects and appreciating their transcendent qualities would be replaced by the collective appreciation of mass-produced films and photographs. Thus, he found some potentially progressive features in the shift from manual to mechanical production. Rather than elevate the art to cultic status, to be revered and to be the exclusive domain of the bourgeoisie, it becomes demystified and available for all. The masses could now consume images of the contemporary world and participate in public discourses. Benjamin thought that film had a democratizing potential and the ability to produce social critique. Through mechanical reproduction, art appreciation departs from the ritualistic elements that had always defined it and becomes political. However, within the politics of art is the history of domination and exploitation. Benjamin feared that, rather than produce political critique, art also had the potential to ignite reactionary tendencies. Mass culture dissociates from history and context, and so the viewer is also detached. The evaluation of art is merely the evaluation of its aesthetic presentation, and the manipulation of aesthetics to serve fascism was a consequence of mass culture.

Benjamin's final text, the fragmented essay "On the Concept of History" (1940), has had competing interpretations, largely depending on the interpreter. It has been seen as both historical materialist and theological in character and as some combination of both. Benjamin sought to redefine both terms and establish a new relationship to the past. He created historical intelligibility through the use of new methods of presenting images of the past as a montage. This method presented history as dialectical rather than as a progression of time. Any understanding of the now is contrasted to an understanding of a then, which is different from a simple temporal understanding, which Benjamin believed impeded social action by giving an illusion of undirected progress. The essay aims to explore our responsibility to the past through the examination of Paul Klee's painting *Angelus Novus*. Benjamin describes the painting as an angel looking toward the past as a singular event that has left a pile of wreckage, rather than as a chain of events. His interpretation of the painting exposes his understanding of human history as constructing human consciousness; the remnants of our past catastrophes are the foundation upon which we stand. He argues for a historical materialism that enlists theology. His introduction of religiosity was taboo among traditional Marxists and has contributed to criticism that his critical theory is ambiguous and contradictory. Benjamin reconciles historical materialism and theology, however, with the search for the aural, authentic experience. The Marxist critique and call to action center around the experience of debased culture, alienation, and universal class struggle. Benjamin thought that rational society created a spiritual alienation that needed to be reconciled. He did not see mysticism and materialism as irreconcilable positions, though he was aware of the controversy that this rhetoric could stimulate. Had he had the opportunity to complete this work, he may have clarified the philosophical underpinnings of his position, though the context of his writing, in isolation and facing the devastation of the war, compelled him to confront the philosophy of history.

SEE ALSO: Adorno, Theodor; Arcades; Commodity Fetishism; *Flâneur/Flânerie*; Frankfurt School

REFERENCES

Benjamin, Walter. 2002. *The Arcades Project*, edited by Rolf Tiedemann. Cambridge, MA: Belknap Press.

Benjamin, Walter. 2007. *Illuminations: Essays and Reflections*, edited by Hannah Arendt. New York: Schocken Books.

FURTHER READING

Eagleton, Terry. 1981. *Walter Benjamin or Towards a Revolutionary Criticism*. New York: Verso.

Kellner, Douglas. 1989. *Critical Theory, Marxism, and Modernity*. Baltimore, MD: Johns Hopkins University Press.

Kohlenbach, Margarete. 2002. *Walter Benjamin: Self-Reference and Religiosity*. New York: Palgrave Macmillan.

Big-Box Stores

ETHAN D. SCHOOLMAN
University of Michigan, USA

A big-box store is a physically large retail establishment, often part of a chain, whose size allows for enormous quantities of goods to be sold under one roof. Big-box stores are associated with a range of contemporary consumption phenomena: strong emphasis on low prices, outsourcing of manufacturing to countries with inexpensive, non-unionized labor, consistent retail environments regardless of geographical location, suburban sprawl and automobile-centered transportation, and the advent of "one-stop shopping." As their dominance has grown, big-box stores have attracted both praise for making groceries and household goods cheaper and easier to buy, and criticism for their alleged role in the decline of small, independent businesses and traditional downtowns.

Since the early 1960s, when the first Wal-Mart, Kmart, and Target stores were opened, the big-box store has become a ubiquitous form of retail architecture. A largely US phenomenon, the first Wal-Mart store appeared in 1962 in Arkansas, followed by four Target stores near Minneapolis, Minnesota, and a Kmart outside Detroit, Michigan. These companies were soon joined by others, such as Fred Meyer in the Northwest, Meijer in Michigan, and FedMart in California. As the suburbs boomed and Americans became increasingly reliant on the automobile, companies associated with big-box stores experienced explosive growth. Led by Kmart, with 2000 stores, and Wal-Mart, with nearly 1000, more than 10,000 big-box stores, averaging between 45,000 and 60,000 square feet, had opened by the mid-1980s. While Kmart, Wal-Mart, and Target stores contained a huge range of goods, from groceries to clothing to furniture and electronics, the big-box model was also adopted by companies that focused on one kind of good. Often called "category killers," these companies included Home Depot and Lowe's (construction and home improvement), Barnes & Noble and Borders (books and music), Staples, OfficeMax, and Office Depot (office supplies), and Best Buy and Circuit City (electronics). By the end of the twentieth century, many major companies behind the big-box model owned multiple stores in every major metropolitan area in the United States, and the size of the average big-box store had also grown significantly. In 2008, the typical Home Depot was approximately 125,000 square feet, and a Wal-Mart "supercenter" could be as large as 250,000 square feet, or over 5 acres. Increasingly, big-box stores are found in countries other than the United States, such as Mexico and China, where companies such as Wal-Mart expect most of their growth to take place over the next 50 years.

The economic, social, and environmental benefits and costs of big-box stores have been the subject of significant debate. According to proponents of big-box stores, the model has made an extraordinary variety of foodstuffs and goods available to consumers who otherwise would not be able to afford them. Shopping at big-box stores, supporters say, is not only more affordable, but also more convenient, and thus time-saving: everything you need is in one place. Large companies also often argue that big-box stores are an important source of jobs in distressed communities, employing hundreds of people who otherwise might have to move elsewhere in order to find work.

Against these claims, critics make a number of points. First, the low prices at big-box stores do not take into account environmental and social externalities that may result from the production process. To the extent that dry goods, in particular, at big-box stores are largely manufactured in developing countries, these products may represent the export of pollution and other externalities from wealthy countries to poor. Second, big-box stores may not create new jobs so much as represent a transfer of retail jobs from independent businesses to larger companies. By competing with small businesses, companies like Wal-Mart and Target – which can absorb large losses in order to attract customers – have thus arguably been integral to the decline of traditional downtowns, and the loss of the social and economic benefits that such downtowns have been thought to provide. Finally, critics have argued that the environmental impacts of big-box stores are significant, not just because of their role in suburban sprawl, but also because shopping at big-box stores is part and parcel of a lifestyle that facilitates overconsumption, waste, and disposability.

SEE ALSO: Department Stores; Hyperconsumption; Needs and Wants; Shopping Malls; Wal-Mart

FURTHER READING

Mitchell, Stacy. 2006. *Big-Box Swindle: The True Cost of Mega-Retailers and the Fight for America's Independent Businesses.* Boston, MA: Beacon Press.

Vedder, Richard, and Wendell Cox. 2006. *The Wal-Mart Revolution: How Big-Box Stores Benefit Consumers, Workers, and the Economy.* Washington, DC: AEI Press.

Birmingham School

TODD WOLFSON
Rutgers University, USA

The Birmingham School, formally known as the Centre for Contemporary Cultural Studies (CCCS) at the University of Birmingham, was an innovative academic enterprise, which led the emergence and development of the field of cultural studies across the latter half of the twentieth century. The CCCS and the intellectual tradition it inspired reimagined how we understand culture and domination, cultivating groundbreaking work focused on the areas of media and communication, youth culture, class, gender, race, and the politics of representation. The Birmingham School includes the work of noteworthy British scholars such as Raymond Williams, Stuart Hall, Paul Willis, Dick Hebdige, and Angela McRobbie.

Established as a postgraduate research institute by Richard Hoggart in 1964, the initial goal of the Birmingham School was to challenge the cultural elitism of literary theory as well as the positivism of British Sociology, creating an approach that had three components. As Hoggart explained of the different elements of this new field of inquiry, "one is roughly historical and philosophical; another is, yet again roughly, sociological, the third, which will be the most important – is the literary critical" (1970, 255). With a broad agenda and diverse methodologies, the Birmingham School developed a variety of critical approaches for the analysis of cultural artifacts. Perhaps the most enduring legacy of the School is the reconceptualization of popular culture as a site of resistance and negotiation for marginalized and disempowered groups. Building on the work of Antonio Gramsci, this perspective imbued popular cultural forms with a new importance, as scholars no longer designated mass culture solely as a mass distraction, but instead re-read pop culture in relationship to power, domination, and resistance.

From the beginning of the project, the Birmingham School was decidedly political, particularly because it emerged in the shadows of the rising New Left in Britain in the postwar 1950s (Shulman 1993). The British New Left was broadly socialist in orientation, with a strong anti-imperialist and anti-racist bent, and one of the central struggles was the Campaign for Nuclear Disarmament (CND). Many of the founders and leaders of the New Left became founding members of the CCCS, including Hoggart, literary theorist Raymond Williams, historian E. P. Thompson, and the second director of CCCS, Stuart Hall. In fact, the *New Left Review*, the principal journal of the New Left, was first edited by Hall, and routinely published the works of Thompson and Williams, among others (Shulman 1993).

In the initial period of the CCCS, Hoggart and Williams played critical roles in the intellectual life of the Centre. Both men were involved in projects focused on working-class education and socialist politics, and the work of the CCCS was an intellectual extension of this vision. The fundamental texts in this formative period were Hoggart's *The Uses of Literacy* (1957), Williams's *Culture and Society* (1958) and *The Long Revolution* (1961), and Thompson's *The Making of the English Working Class* (1964). These canonic texts influenced the early agenda of the Centre, which focused on historical and critical inquiries into working-class institutions and struggles; and opposition to elitist notions of education and culture that emerged from T. S. Eliot and F. R. Leavis, two towering conservative intellectual figures in English society.

In 1968, Stuart Hall took over from Hoggart as the director of the CCCS. In the ensuing years, Hall's intellectual trajectory had a strong influence on the direction of the Birmingham School. This period of the CCCS was punctuated by the scholarship of French theorist Louis Althusser's structural Marxism, and, following this, by the writing of Italian Marxist Antonio Gramsci. Gramsci, a leader in the Communist Party of Italy, was imprisoned by Benito Mussolini's fascist regime. In jail he wrote *The Prison Notebooks*, in which he aimed to understand how the elite fight to retain control of society through cultural institutions. Building on the work of Marx and Lenin, he argued that the ruling elite work to forge a form of hegemony or domination through ideas and culture that induce a form of consent of the governed. Importantly, this hegemonic rule is always open and contested by counter-hegemonic forces; thus there is a constant struggle over ideas and cultural institutions. This complex of ideas became a critical building block for the CCCS and cultural studies more broadly, and turned CCCS scholars toward mass media and popular culture as critical sites to study both domination and resistance.

In this period, many cultural studies scholars also moved away from a singular approach to class, focusing more squarely on other forms of oppression, including gender and race. For instance, Angela McRobbie, Dorothy Hobson, and other women associated with the CCCS developed the Women's Studies Group within the Centre, and together they published *Women Take Issue* (1978; also see Shulman 1993). In general, the 1970s was a rich period of scholarship for the Birmingham School, which included works like Dick Hebdige's *Subculture: The Meaning of Style* (1979), Paul Willis's *Learning to Labour: How Working Class Kids Get Working Class Jobs* (1977), and the co-authored work by Stuart Hall, Chas Critcher, Tony Jefferson, John Clarke, and Brian Roberts, *Policing the Crisis: Mugging the State and Law and Order* (1978).

Across the next two decades, cultural studies continued to develop as a critical new field of inquiry, particularly in Britain and the United States. As the field grew, it became less tied to the CCCS, as new sites of study developed, building on the Birmingham approach. In 2002, senior management at the University of Birmingham proposed to shut down the CCCS. Students and faculty at the school and across the globe protested against the closure, but despite the controversy, the Centre was shut down. Although the physical Centre that Hoggart envisioned and Stuart Hall carefully nurtured no longer exists, the intellectual approach that was associated with the Birmingham School has had far-reaching effects. The scholars and scholarship of the Birmingham School forged British cultural studies, while impacting a host of other disciplines and fields of study from anthropology and sociology to political theory, media studies, education, and literary theory.

SEE ALSO: Class; Marx, Karl; Mass Culture; Mass Media; Popular Culture; Williams, Raymond; Youth Culture(s)

REFERENCES

Hall, Stuart, Chas Critcher, Tony Jefferson, John Clarke, and Brian Roberts. 1978. *Policing the Crisis: Mugging the State and Law and Order*. New York: Holmes and Meier.

Hebdige, Dick. 1979. *Subculture: The Meaning of Style*. London: Routledge.

Hoggart, Richard. 1957. *The Uses of Literacy*. London: Chatto & Windus.

Hoggart, Richard. 1970. *Speaking to Each Other. Vol. 2: About Literature*. London: Chatto & Windus.

Shulman, Norma. 1993. "Conditions of their Own Making: An Intellectual History of the Centre of Contemporary Cultural Studies at the University of Birmingham." *Canadian Journal of Communication* 18(1). Available at: http://www.cjc-online.ca/index.php/journal/article/view/717/623.

Thompson, Edward P. 1964. *The Making of the English Working Class*. New York: Pantheon.

Williams, Raymond. 1958. *Culture and Society*. London: Chatto & Windus.
Williams, Raymond. 1961. *The Long Revolution*. London: Chatto & Windus.
Willis, Paul. 1977. *Learning to Labour: How Working Class Kids Get Working Class Jobs*. New York: Columbia University Press.
Women's Study Group, eds. 1978. *Women Take Issue: Aspects of Women's Subordination*. London: Hutchinson.

Body and Consumer Culture

KEILA TYNER
Texas State University, USA

In recent decades, social scientists have placed much importance on understanding the body, particularly as a site whereby the individual connects to and interacts with the social world around them. Much of this theorizing on the body takes into account one of two distinct approaches, the first of which is the notion that "we have a body" (Featherstone 2006), implying that the body is a separate entity from the true inner self. The second approach involves a more complex understanding of how the body is lived in or the experience of embodiment whereby the body is an integrated aspect of the true inner self – that is, "we are a body" (Featherstone 2006). Contemporary reflections on these seemingly divergent understandings of the body suggest that an integrated approach is possible (Turner 2006) and called for in further theorizing on the body within the context of consumer culture.

Traditional Cartesian thought considers the body a subordinate object to the superior subject of the mind (i.e., subject–object relationship). Here, the mind is a distinct and separate entity from the body, exerting control over the body – "we have a body." Cartesian understanding of the body is situated on this binary construction of mind/body, whereby personhood, self, and identity are viewed as independent of the human body. "In Cartesian view of the world, though vision is privileged as the sense that connects the self to the physical and material environment in which the self is located, bodily sensation is not seen to influence or contaminate perception" (Howson 2004, 3). This philosophical dualism underpins traditional Western epistemology and has been the basis for much further theorization of the role the body plays in relation to notions of the self.

Foucault's (1977) notion of the docile body and Giddens's (1991) conception of the reflexive project of the body are key theories that focus on the mind exerting control over the body. For Foucault, the docile body is one that adheres to cultural mandates of appropriateness and is a body that is necessarily controlled by the mind by way of the internalized general other (i.e., the panoptic gaze). The docile body is one that follows socially normalized gender roles and subsequent bodily appearances associated with those gender roles. As such, feminist scholars have often used Foucault in theorizing the ways in which women have internalized patriarchal social structures that subjugate the female self and the female body. Within this context, the body is under the constant surveillance and control of the mind and therefore bodily related projects are concentrated.

Giddens (1991) refers to the reflexive project within late modernity, whereby social actors consider and invest in body projects to enhance self-identity. Here, the body becomes a malleable and flexible site for manipulating the contours of the body in addition to identity. Consumption plays a critical role in this self-affirming and self-defining endeavor for positioning the individual within society.

According to Shilling (2005), "the body is not only a source of and location for society, but is a vital *means* through which individuals are *positioned* within and *oriented towards* society" (p. 11). This view of the body serves as a "multidimensional medium" for understanding and exploring societal interactions and meanings, particularly in understanding how "we are a body." Shilling's approach also underscores the importance of the embodied individual's agency in intervening and shaping the meaning of the social environment.

From a phenomenological perspective, sociologist Merleau-Ponty (1962) argues that the body is the vehicle through which the world is understood and interpreted, and, thus, mind and body function together to inform experience. Perception of the environment through the bodily senses plays the important role of mediating the interconnectedness of the mind and body. Within this context, the embodied individual is an active agent in the creation of meaning and understanding of society.

Additionally, Bourdieu (1984) posits that the embodied individual is an active agent in producing meaning within and about society, much like Merleau-Ponty, but further argues that society also shapes this meaning and understanding of the world. Particularly, Bourdieu's notion of *habitus* places much importance on the dynamic and interlocking roles of agent and society in shaping meaning. According to Bourdieu, habitus is informed by an individual's social location and consists of "the collective culture into which people are ingrained" (Howson 2004, 100). This collective culture shapes individual taste and preferences, which are then reified within that particular social field. Bourdieu understands social fields as "constituted by organized spaces which each possess their own regulative principles" as opposed to social life at large being governed by a single culture (Shilling 2005, 61). In this way, "the amount of body work done on the body by different classes in order to enhance self-presentation is 'proportionate to the chances of material or symbolic profit they can reasonably expect from it'" (Shilling 2005, 63). Therefore, an understanding of the world through the body is based on an individual's social location, which is in part informed by social class, family, occupation, and other social groups.

Regardless of the theoretical approaches of "we have a body" or "we are a body," the fact remains that we are dressed bodies; we present our bodies and therefore ourselves to the world as dressed, which, according to anthropologists, is true of all known human cultures (Entwistle 2001). Here, dress refers to intentional body modifications and/or supplements to the body that may be perceived (i.e., communicated and understood) by others (Roach-Higgins and Eicher 1992). As such, the "dressed person is a *gestalt* that includes body, all direct modification of the body itself, and all three-dimensional supplements added to it" (p. 13). Meanings of dress are socially and culturally bound and therefore shift over time and across cultures. As a situated bodily practice, dressing the body is an endeavor that allows for the creative presentation of the self and identity to the social world (Entwistle 2001), an endeavor that is particularly consumer-oriented within present Western culture.

The consumption of various products plays a symbolic role in defining social reality and guiding appropriate behavior within that social context (Belk 1988). Consumption choices are often made on the basis of what a product means and how those meanings expand and strengthen one's sense of self. According to Belk, the term "self" refers to how a person subjectively perceives who he or she is. Research suggests that the body and personal identifying characteristics and attributes (e.g., feelings about the body and appearance) represent defining aspects of the core self (Ahuvia 2005). Exploring and understanding the body are important to consider in relation to consumer culture because bodily related consumption is a form of symbolic consumption, where such consumption plays a role in shaping meanings of the self and identity in symbolic interactionist terms. Specifically, Goffman (1959) positions the body as the central vehicle within the micro social order (Entwistle 2001) and, as such, the dressed body then becomes the medium through which social actors enact agency in presenting the self and identity to others.

The marketplace is rife with choices for managing the dressed body, such as diet aids (e.g., diet pills, appetite suppressants, etc.), exercise videos and equipment to shape the body, cosmetics and beauty-related products including cosmetic procedures (both surgical and nonsurgical), fashion and apparel, tattooing and piercing services, and tanning services – to name a few. Consumption choices made for the purpose of dressing the body then become part and parcel of the individual identity project, connecting the body with the social world and other social actors. Here, such consumption choices for managing the dressed body become symbolic props used to signify identity and specific social roles of the actor.

The body itself also can become a commodity, a corporeal form of exchange value. Obvious examples include sex workers (Bernstein 2007) and fashion models (Entwistle and Wissinger 2006), but can include, as well, athletics, film and theater performance, and almost any use of imagery in the service of promotional culture.

SEE ALSO: Beauty Industry; Consumption and Identity; Cosmetic Surgery; Metrosexual; Obesity

REFERENCES

Ahuvia, Aaron C. 2005. "Beyond the Extended Self: Loved Objects and Consumers' Identity Narratives." *Journal of Consumer Research* 32: 171–184.

Belk, Russell W. 1988. "Possessions and the Extended Self." *Journal of Consumer Research* 15: 139–168.

Bernstein, Elizabeth. 2007 "Sex Work for the Middle Class." *Sexualities* 10(4): 473–488.

Bourdieu, Pierre. 1984. *Distinction: A Social Critique of the Judgment of Taste*. Cambridge, MA: Harvard University Press.

Entwistle, Joanne. 2001. "The Dressed Body." In *Body Dressing*, edited by Joanne Entwistle and Elizabeth Wilson, 33–58. New York: Berg.

Entwistle, Joanne, and Elizabeth Wissinger. 2006. "Keeping Up Appearances: Aesthetic Labour in the Fashion Modelling Industries of London and New York." *The Sociological Review* 54(4): 774–794.

Featherstone, Mike. 2006. "Body Image/Body without Image." *Theory, Culture & Society* 23(2–3): 233–236.

Foucault, Michel. 1977. *Discipline and Punish*. New York: Vintage.

Giddens, Anthony. 1991. *Modernity and Self-Identity: Self and Society in the Late Modern Age*. Oxford: Polity.

Goffman, Erving. 1959. *The Presentation of the Self in Everyday Life*. Garden City, NY: Doubleday Anchor Books.

Howson, Alexandra. 2004. *The Body in Society: An Introduction*. Malden, MA: Blackwell Publishing.

Merleau-Ponty, Maurice. 1962. *Phenomenology of Perception*. London: Routledge & Kegan Paul.

Roach-Higgins, Mary Ellen, and Joanne Eicher. 1992. "Dress and Identity." *Clothing and Textiles Research Journal* 10(4): 1–8.

Shilling, Chris. 2005. *The Body in Culture, Technology and Society*. Thousand Oaks, CA: Sage.

Turner, Bryan. 2006. "Body." *Theory, Culture & Society* 23(2–3): 223–229.

Bourdieu, Pierre

VIVIANE RIEGEL
Goldsmiths, University of London, UK

Pierre Bourdieu (1930–2002) was a French sociologist who had considerable influence in the humanities in general, and the social sciences in particular. His sociological work focused on the analysis of the mechanisms of reproduction of social hierarchies. Bourdieu emphasized the importance of cultural and symbolic factors in this reproduction and criticized the primacy given to economic factors in Marxist conceptions. His theory of practice sought to show that social agents develop strategies based on a small number of provisions acquired through socialization. The two components of his constructivist structuralist perspective are the agent and the structure, between which there is interplay. The social world is made up of the objective structures of culture and language (structuralism), is built (constructed) by agents, and conditions the actions of the agents. The main elements in Bourdieu's theory of practice to explain how this interplay takes place are *habitus*, capital, and field.

Bourdieu's major works on the theory of practice are *Esquisse d'une théorie de la pratique* (Outline of a Theory of Practice, 1972) and *Le Sens pratique* (The Logic of Practice, 1980). His works on cultural practices are an essential part of his sociological perspective, and led to the publication in 1979 of *La Distinction: critique sociale du jugement* (Distinction: A Social Critique of the Judgment of Taste). This is his best-known and most important work in the sociological field and, according to the International Sociological Association, is one of the 10 most important sociological publications of the twentieth century.

Bourdieu's contribution to studies of consumption opens up an approach that tries to reconcile the more pessimistic classical heritage with recognition of the fact that consumption is indispensable in modernity. For him, the importance of consumption studies lies in the identification of signs of distinction through an analysis of what we consume and how we consume (Bourdieu 1984). His work influenced contemporary authors on studies of consumption: Campbell (1987), Miller (1987), Featherstone (1991), and Slater (1997).

In his major work, *Distinction* (1984), Bourdieu analyzes the mechanisms of social reproduction by which societies maintain, through time, structures of order between social groups and power relations between one group and another. For him, the structural difference of class that exists in Western capitalist society is an objective reflection of the subjective intent of social distinction. Individuals strive to improve their social positions through the logic of practice and the manipulation of goods and cultural representations of their position within the social field. The possibilities of the choices an individual has arise from a sociocultural heritage internalized by individuals, from their class habitus, and from what they learn from social practices.

Bourdieu's concept of habitus refers to the unconscious dispositions and the classificatory schemes by which we acquire cognitive structures, preferences which are manifest in the individual's sense of the appropriateness and validity of their taste for cultural goods and practices – art, food, hobbies, and so on. Habitus is also inscribed onto the body, in the form of esteem for the body, pitch, tone of voice, and so on; hence class taste is embodied. This system of enduring embodied structures is created in response to objective conditions and acquired through socialization. One important feature of habitus is that the actor can be transcended through reflexivity, since habitus exerts its strongest influence through unconscious structures, and reflexivity is able to escape its determinations. We can never be completely free of our habitus (it is a structured and structuring structure, which is classifiable through a class of conditionings), but we can be free enough to interrupt the reproduction of class structures.

The concept of habitus is an important tool for thinking about the relationship between consumption, distinction, and social identity. Through it, the subject progresses from a disposition to the practice of developing in her everyday life signs, for example of etiquette, that differentiate her from other individuals; this enables us to understand the effect of conditioning on consumption practices. Thus, the position that an individual occupies in the social structure will be expressed – not only, but also – through his consumption practices. The habitus affects choices about what and how to consume, practices that relate to lifestyle and personal tastes, which are bound to the issue of cultural capital and forms of social presentation.

The habitus structure creates both a system of schemes generating classifiable social practices and a system of schemes of perception and appreciation, a set of dispositions of tastes. Taste, which is part of the essence and the fickleness of a person, is found in the object. Objects, used in the interaction between subjects, are the elements that construct the habitus of the group.

The historical and social dimension given by Bourdieu (1984) to the question of taste reveals that, through scientific observation, it is possible to analyze cultural needs as the product of upbringing and education. This process of acquisition of taste ends up functioning as one of the distinctive elements and as a criterion for the identification of individuals, though it is often naturalized and emptied of meaning as a social and historical process. In contrast to the idea of "natural taste," which means that no part of taste is learned or studied, Bourdieu shows how people can be socially evaluated for their display of taste and the aesthetic norms that fit certain parameters of the social hierarchy for social rather than for natural reasons.

For Bourdieu, there is homology between the fields of production of goods and of taste, through the dynamics of the fields of distinction between social classes. It creates a hierarchy in the "universe of stylistic possibilities," according to the recognition earned by a particular authority within her own field. Given the accessibility that any individual has in relation to the elements considered "human," which highlight sensory pleasure and sensual desire, the process of distinction occurs within a system of judgments based on these elements. Mainly, there is a subordination in the system to the representation of objects that are considered more beautiful or superior. Bourdieu (1984) states that there is no such thing as universal beauty, because beauty is plural and is conditioned by an actual judgment in relation to the class to which it refers. There is a clear distinction between the use of illegitimate objects, fruits of repetition which, from an aesthetic point of view, are common and vulgar, and the original, superior objects, of which the former are a copy.

Through classifiable practices, Bourdieu (1984) explains the system of classified and classifying practices of distinctive signs, or what he calls lifestyle. According to his theory, the practices engendered by the different habitus appear as systematic configurations and, once perceived by agents, are endowed with the schemes of perception and appreciation (taste), which are necessary in order to identify, interpret, and evaluate their pertinent features and their function as lifestyle.

Consumption and lifestyle preferences involve discriminatory judgments which, at the same time, identify and render classifiable our own particular judgment of taste to others. Particular constellations of taste, consumption preferences, and lifestyle practices are associated with specific occupation and class categories. This makes it possible to map out the universe of taste and lifestyle, with its structured oppositions and finely graded distinctions, which operates within a particular society at a particular point in history.

Bourdieu presents the connection between these principles of action and classification (habitus + taste + lifestyle) with mainly cultural and symbolic capitals, in order to explain the power they exert for individuals who possess them. Those who have a high volume of economic capital (industrialists, commercial employers) have a taste for expensive goods. Those who possess a high volume of cultural capital (higher education teachers, artistic producers) have a taste for differentiated cultural goods. Those low in both economic and cultural capital (semi-skilled, skilled, unskilled workers) have a taste for popular goods. The concept points to the way in which, in parallel to economic capital which is immediately calculable, exchangeable, and realizable, there are also modes of power and processes of accumulation based on culture and symbols. Cultural capital works as a classifier and hierarchical element in the social context, and Bourdieu (1987) points to three forms in which it can be analyzed: the embodied state (style of presentation, mode of speech, beauty, etc.), the objectified state (cultural goods), and the institutionalized state (such as educational qualifications).

In his analysis of the various manifestations of distinction within society, Bourdieu (1984) states that consumption depends not only on the financial resources of the consumer, their economic capital, but also on their social capital within the web of personal and institutional relationships in which they are inserted, and on their cultural capital, their set of knowledge and tastes which reflects both personal and collective characteristics. The different styles and labels of fashionable clothing and goods that an individual consumes, while they are subject to change, imitation, and copying, are a set of clues that are used in the act of classifying consumers. Moreover, individuals also possess symbolic capital as signs of the dispositions and classificatory schemes that reflect their origins and trajectory through life. The signs are present not only in the objects they consume but are also manifest in the body, so it is not just a question of what clothes are worn but how they are worn.

Bourdieu's principles of classification and cultural capital contribute to the position takings – the fields – that are formed within the society. In *The Field of Cultural Production* (1983), he shows how the social world can be divided into fields through the differentiation of social activities and the formation of social subareas specializing in the performance of a given social activity, such as the artistic field or the political field. A field is a grouping in which each element in the group is subjectively defined in terms of its relations and oppositions to other elements. Any given field is, to varying degrees, autonomous from other social structures, and this autonomy is developed on two levels: the subjective level of sociological reflexivity and the objective level of institutions that establish their own separate hierarchies of success. A field is analyzed as an arena of conflict, struggle, and competition for scarce resources and symbolic recognition related to the specific type of capital that governs success in the field.

The analysis of consumption practices through Bourdieu's approach is based on the autonomy of particular practices, which need to be understood in terms of the internal dynamic, structuring principles, and processes that operate within a particular field. Bourdieu, however, did not recognize an autonomous field in the sphere of consumption, and in his scheme there was no place for consumer creativity. His tendency was to view consumption as a reflection of the economic hierarchy, so any subjective experience that contradicts this perspective is seen as a type of false consciousness.

On the basis of Bourdieu's theory, Featherstone (1991) developed a richer and more complex conception of the consumer. First, he recognizes the autonomy of the field of consumption, and, second, he carves out a place for individual creativity by relying on Bourdieu's analysis of the role of *cultural intermediaries* ("taste makers" in Bourdieu's original) who provide symbolic goods and services. Motivated by an embodied discomfort and lacking economic and cultural capital, this new cultural intermediary adopts a new way of life and consciously educates his own taste and lifestyle (Featherstone 1991). Thus the consumer is able to appropriate consumer objects creatively rather than being controlled through them. Featherstone also suggests going beyond Bourdieu's theory of practice, and postulates that lifestyle can be a choice rather than something that is imposed structurally.

SEE ALSO: Consumer Culture; Cultural Capital; Lifestyle; Marx, Karl

REFERENCES

Bourdieu, Pierre. 1972. *Esquisse d'une théorie de la pratique: précédé de trois études d'ethnologie Kabyle [Outline of a Theory of Practice: Preceded by Three Studies of Kabylian Ethnology]*. Geneva: Droz.

Bourdieu, Pierre. 1979. *La Distinction: critique sociale du jugement [Distinction: A Social Critique of the Judgment of Taste]*. Paris: Minuit.

Bourdieu, Pierre. 1980. *Le Sens pratique [The Logic of Practice]*. Paris: Minuit.

Bourdieu, Pierre. 1983. "The Field of Cultural Production; or, The Economic World Reversed." *Poetics* 12(4–5): 311–356.

Bourdieu, Pierre. 1984. *Distinction: A Social Critique of the Judgment of Taste*. Translated by R. Nice. London: Routledge & Kegan Paul.

Bourdieu, Pierre. 1987. "The Forms of Capital." In J. G. Richardson (ed.), *Handbook of Theory and Research for the Sociology of Education*. New York: Greenwood.

Campbell, Colin. 1987. *The Romantic Ethic and the Spirit of Modern Consumerism*. Oxford: Blackwell.

Featherstone, Mike. 1991. *Consumer Culture and Postmodernism*. London: Sage.

Miller, Daniel. 1987. *Material Culture and Mass Consumption*. Oxford: Blackwell.

Slater, Don. 1997. *Consumer Culture and Modernity*. Cambridge, UK: Polity.

Boycotts

KATHLEEN KUEHN
Victoria University of Wellington, New Zealand

Boycotts are the strategic avoidance of a person, country, organization, product, or service, usually to express dissatisfaction with a particular set of practices. They are a form of protest, the goal typically being to effect some change nonviolently through the application of economic pressure. Designed to punish offending or unfavorable behavior, boycotts are a popular form of consumer and political activism. The converse, "buycotting," is the purposeful consumption of certain companies, products, or services. As a positive form of endorsement, buycotts direct spending at a particular firm or service not only to incentivize favorable behaviors by rewarding them, but to punish competing firms that do not meet the same values or standards.

The term's etymology derives from Captain Charles Boycott, an Irish land agent who evicted tenant farmers unable to pay high rents after a poor harvest year in 1878. As news of the evictions spread, Boycott's own workers formed the Irish Land League and, as a union, collectively refused to harvest his fields. Local service providers – including traders and the postal service – supported the strike by refusing to do business with Boycott, as well. The term "boycott" earned widespread use for organized isolation, appearing in several newspapers by 1880 – the same year the socially ostracized Boycott resettled in England.

As one of the earliest forms of consumer protest, the application of economic pressure through organized refusal predates the term's coinage. Organized boycotts of British tea and textile imports in the eighteenth century precipitated the American Revolution, while English abolitionists in the 1790s and the National Negro Convention in 1830 boycotted commodities produced by enslaved labor. The civil rights movement effectively used economic pressure as a political tool, most notably in the 1955 Montgomery bus boycott. Women in particular have historically used boycotts to achieve rights, recognition, and other social changes in contexts where they otherwise had little power. Local Housewives' Leagues throughout the Progressive era organized boycotts to demand fair wages and cost of living increases; they also used their domestic responsibilities to lobby for safer food practices and price controls, motivating events like the 1902 mass kosher meat boycotts in New York City.

Political boycotts include the German and Italian boycott of Hollywood films during World War II, the Arab League's boycott of Israeli products and services since 1948, and Olympic Games boycotts in the 1930s, 1970s, and 1980s against fascism, South African apartheid, and the Soviet invasion of Afghanistan, respectively. More recent consumer boycotts have been waged against Nestlé (for promoting baby formula over breast milk in developing countries), Nike (for its use of sweatshop labor), BP (for the 2010 Gulf oil spill), the fur and timber industries (for inhumane treatment of animals and deforestation practices), and Chick-fil-A, the Salvation Army, and Target Corporation (for discrimination against lesbian, gay, bisexual, and transgender people). The anti-consumerist International Buy Nothing Day, founded by *Adbusters* magazine, aims its protest at consumer capitalism generally by boycotting consumption of any form on the busiest shopping days of the year.

The actual effects of boycotts vary across context. Greenpeace's 1995 Shell Oil boycott reduced sales in Germany by nearly 40 percent, while the United Students against Sweatshops' boycott of clothing manufacturers has successfully renegotiated fair trade contracts with factory workers. While firms can sustain financial damage, the most effective boycotts are not necessarily those that cripple sales but those that negatively affect the firm's image – particularly when a firm's reputation is already in decline. Research also suggests that relatively few organizations ever concede to a boycott's demands. This raises questions about who actually benefits most from the organized refusal to consume certain products. Abstaining from goods made by low-waged or child labor often means the loss of what little income such workers do earn, particularly since the offending manufacturers will often respond by closing down and relocating elsewhere. The low stakes involved continue to make boycotts a popular avenue for consumer activism, however, particularly in an era where social media networks make it easier than ever to spread messages at an increasingly rapid pace and with minimal effort.

SEE ALSO: Consumer Activism; Ethical Consumption; Politics and Consumer Culture

FURTHER READING

Friedman, Monroe. 1999. *Consumer Boycotts: Effecting Change through the Marketplace and Media*. New York: Routledge.

Harrison, Rob, Terry Newholm, and Deirdre Shaw, eds. 2005. *The Ethical Consumer*. London: Sage.

Brand Loyalty

CLARA GUSTAFSSON
Lund University, Sweden

Brand loyalty became a key concept in consumer research in the 1990s, having been a central aspect of consumer-level branding in marketing management research since the late 1960s. The traditional definition of brand loyalty is concerned with a consumer's repeat purchase of a certain branded product or service. As a rule, research on the concept also argues that the repeat purchase needs to be combined with a favorable attitude toward the brand. This definition is usually followed by further labeling of the research presented – whereby it is described as *behavioral*, or *attitudinal*. In other words, research on brand loyalty tends to focus either on the repeated repurchasing of the brand or on the consumer's attitude to the brand. The choice of methods in a consumer research setting varies, and is often of a qualitative orientation. Marketing management research on brand loyalty uses mainly quantitative methods. Noticeably, stores and brands make extensive use of so-called *loyalty programs* or *loyalty cards* to retain consumers.

Brand loyalty has gained international reputation as a meaningful branding concept largely because of its prominent role in the highly influential *brand equity* construct. Brand equity is often used to describe how the brand, in itself, adds value to a company. Consumer-based brand equity, in Aaker's (1991) seminal theory, consists of four components: brand loyalty, perceived quality, brand awareness, and brand associations. Brand loyalty is considered the most important of the four. While largely agreeing with the above definition of brand loyalty, qualitatively oriented consumer research has moved away from perceiving brand loyalty as originating in the management of the brand's communication toward consumers. Generally, the role of the consumer's relationship with the brand is focused on the analysis of qualitative consumer data.

Interestingly, their relatively new presence in the online environment has provided challenges for brands in the quest for brand loyalty, because consumers can easily compare prices and switch brands online. Recent research on brand loyalty online has therefore often added the dimension of *brand trust* to the brand equity construct to better address loyalty *online*. In the brand trust literature, brand loyalty is generally considered an antecedent of brand trust. Further, the two concepts of loyalty and trust share common qualities in relation to consumer vulnerability through their brand relationships, opening up questions on the brand's ethics communication toward the loyal or trustful consumer.

In her groundbreaking article "Consumers and Their Brands," Fournier (1998) argues that there is a need for a different view of brand loyalty, which would allow, for instance, loyalty to be connected with love, passion, and the brand's connection to the self as part of attitudinal loyalty. In other words, she questions the marketing discipline's previous conceptions of brand loyalty as centered on strongly affective, positive, voluntary, and strenuous relationships on the part of consumers toward their brands. Instead, she argues that consumers' brand loyalty will take on more forms, and relate to a greater number of brands in consumers' lives, than previously conceived. Present research on brand loyalty, which is not centered on the brand equity construct, is influenced by this argument. It is about seeing the consumer's role as an active co-producer of brand value as well as a receiver of information from brand management.

However, the brand loyalty concept is always strongly linked to brand equity. In consumer research, the components of brand loyalty (i.e., continuous repurchase of, and a favorable attitude to, the brand) are generally recontextualized so that they apply to a specific, readily observable, context in which consumers interact socially and culturally with their brand. A useful way of doing this has been through the study of *brand communities* – existing among enormously devoted owners of, for example, a car or a computer of a certain brand. An immediate goal of the research on brand communities is to reconceptualize brand loyalty to include brand relationships. However, an important reason why these community contexts are seen as rich examples of brand loyalty practices is that Aaker's four consumer-based brand equity components are all affected by the presence of strong brand communities.

SEE ALSO: Brands and Branding; Consumer Behavior; Consumer Culture Theory (CCT)

REFERENCES

Aaker, David. 1991. *Managing Brand Equity*. New York: Free Press.

Fournier, Susan. 1998. "Consumers and Their Brands: Developing Relationship Theory in Consumer Research." *Journal of Consumer Research* 24: 343–373. doi:10.1086/209515.

FURTHER READING

Arnould, Eric J., and Craig J. Thompson. 2005. "Consumer Culture Theory (CCT): Twenty Years of Research." *Journal of Consumer Research* 31: 868–882. doi:10.1086/426626.

Chaudhuri, Arjun, and Morris B. Holbrook. 2001. "The Chain of Effects from Brand Trust and Brand Affect to Brand Performance: The Role of Brand Loyalty." *Journal of Marketing* 65: 81–93. doi:10.1509/jmkg.65.2.81255.

Gustafsson, Clara. 2005. "Trust as an Instance of Asymmetrical Reciprocity: An Ethics Perspective on Corporate Brand Management." *Business Ethics: A European Review* 14(2): 142–150. doi:10.1111/j.1467-8608.2005.00398.x.

Holt, Douglas, B. 2002. "Why Do Brands Cause Trouble? A Dialectical Theory of Consumer Culture and Branding." *Journal of Consumer Research* 29: 70–90. doi:10.1086/339922.

Jacoby, Jacob, and Robert W. Chestnut. 1978. *Brand Loyalty: Measurement and Management*. Chichester, UK: Wiley.

McAlexander, James H., John W. Schouten, and Harold F. Koenig. 2002. "Building Brand Community." *Journal of Marketing* 66: 38–54. doi:10.1509/jmkg.66.1.38.18451.

Muñiz, Albert, and Thomas C. O'Guinn. 2000. "Brand Communities." *Journal of Consumer Research* 27: 412–432. doi:10.1086/319618.

Brand Mascots

REBECCA BISHOP
Independent scholar

A brand mascot is an embodied personification of the values and qualities of a particular brand identity. Presented as emblematic of the personality of a brand or product, brand mascots have long been used as a means of engaging consumers and of differentiating products in the marketplace. Featured in advertisements since the late nineteenth century, brand mascots have become an integral feature of consumer culture and are now beginning to develop an online presence in the world of social media.

The first instance of creating a mascot to represent a brand is attributed to André and Edouard Michelin, who worked with artist Marius Rossillon to produce the Michelin Man, or Bibendum, in 1898. In 1916 US brand Planter's released its mascot, Mr. Peanut, an anthropomorphic nut dressed in top hat and spats; and, also in the United States, the cartoon figure referred to as the Jolly Green Giant was created to represent Green Giant Peas in 1925. Shortly afterward, a further range of enduring brand mascots entered consumer culture. Kellogg's produced elfin icons Snap, Crackle, and Pop in 1936; Tony the Tiger was created for Kraft in 1951; and the Pillsbury Doughboy was produced for Pillsbury in 1965. Each of these early mascots has maintained a presence in the consumer marketplace of the twenty-first century and has become a recurring image in the world of brand marketing.

A number of brand mascots feature in global consumer culture, pointing to the significant geographical reach of these iconic figures. Mickey Mouse, created by Walt Disney and Ub Iwerks in 1928; Ronald McDonald, made a mascot of the McDonald's company in 1963; and the M&M's Spokescandies, produced for Mars Incorporated in 1995, are all examples of mascots with a strong international presence and a universally recognized image. This global reach in itself has produced a series of debates about the spread of the products, values, and meanings of Western consumer culture in the non-Western world, and of the appropriation of iconic brand mascots and images by local consumer markets.

No longer confined to the print, television, and billboard sites of traditional advertising, mascots Mickey Mouse, Ronald McDonald, the Jolly Green Giant, and Tony the Tiger now have their own Facebook pages and Twitter accounts. This move toward creating a social media presence for brand mascots highlights an enduring belief of product advertisers in the power of mascots in engaging consumers; in addition, it highlights the way in which traditional marketing practices are being absorbed and reworked in the context of contemporary digital culture.

SEE ALSO: Brand Loyalty; Brands and Branding; Consumer Behavior; Consumer Culture; Glocalization/Grobalization; McDonaldization

FURTHER READING

Arvidsson, Adam. 2006. *Brands: Meaning and Value in Media Culture*. New York: Routledge.

Holt, Douglas B. 2004. *How Brands Become Icons: The Principles of Cultural Branding*. Boston, MA: Harvard Business School Press.

Sivulka, Juliann. 2012. *Soap, Sex, and Cigarettes: A Cultural History of American Advertising*. Boston, MA: Wadsworth, Cengage Learning.

Brandalism: *SEE* ANTI-CONSUMPTION TACTICS

Brands and Branding

JONATHAN E. SCHROEDER
Rochester Institute of Technology, USA

Brands and branding have emerged as key concepts in marketing, management, and strategy. Branding refers to the process of bringing attention to a product, company, concept, person, or cause. The American Marketing Association defines brands as a "name, term, sign, symbol, or design, or a combination of them, intended to identify the goods and services of one seller or group of sellers and to differentiate them from those of competition." Brands and branding have transcended the traditional implications of trademark to occupy a central place in corporate strategy and cultural life. They are not just managerial tools or marketing concepts; they represent a contested ideological, managerial, and scholarly arena. Understanding brands and branding involves an awareness of basic cultural processes which include historical context, ethical concerns, consumer response, and regulation.

Recent research on brands and branding has expanded to include cultural, sociological, and theoretical analysis which both complements and complicates corporate, economic, and managerial approaches. Brands have representational and rhetorical power both as valuable cultural artifacts and as engaging and deceptive bearers of meaning and value, reflecting broad societal, cultural, and ideological codes. Brands are not only mediators of cultural meaning; they themselves have become ideological referents that shape cultural rituals, economic activities, and social norms. For example, strong brands constantly develop prescriptive models for the way people talk, think, and behave – their goals, thoughts, and desires. Brands may supplant the cultural spheres of religion, politics, and myth, as they generally promote an ideology linked to economic, political, and theological models that equate consumption with happiness.

Research and thinking about brands and branding can be divided into four perspectives: corporate perspectives, consumer perspectives, cultural perspectives, and critical perspectives. These four perspectives demonstrate the growing interdisciplinary interest in brands, and how brand research sheds light on basic issues of consumer agency, consumer behavior, and consumer culture. They also signal a move away from a focus on the consumer–brand dyad, toward broader sociocultural and theoretical concerns. Studies that extend brand research into cultural and historical realms may provide an essential bridge between our understanding of value residing within the product or producer intention and the value wholly created by individual consumers or brand communities.

Key issues in contemporary research in brands and branding include: (1) conceptual and ideological tensions between corporate brand management and research into brand culture; (2) theoretical issues of brands from interdisciplinary perspectives; (3) brands in transition economies such as China, India, and post-Soviet Russia; and (4) debates over consumer agency, co-creation, and consumer exploitation within the global brand culture. Greater awareness of the associations between the traditions and conventions of culture and the production and consumption of brands helps us to position and understand branding as a global representational system.

The *corporate perspective* represents the majority of branding research and thinking. Many of the world's biggest companies and most highly valued brands, such as Apple, BMW, Coca-Cola, and Sony, are seen as corporate brands rather than corporate entities, each valued more for its intangible brand attributes than for any other assets. These corporate brands are an increasingly important, powerful, and visible part of culture. Within the corporate perspective, models of brand identity, brand image, and brand equity are central to understanding issues such as brand DNA, brand essence, and brand value. Also, one can speak of a brand culture within a corporation, with reference to how closely the organization aligns with brand values – so-called "living the brand."

Basic branding strategy generally implies that branding decisions work together with a number of other branding elements, including the brand's core essence, the brand's personality and positioning, and the brand's execution, which may include advertising, promotion, and social media. From a corporate perspective, branding is largely about communicating a message interpreted in line with the brand owner's intention. Within the corporate perspective, global branding marks an increasingly important topic. Although branding experts often agree on which features make a brand global – the use of the same name worldwide, and similar positioning strategies and marketing mixes in target markets – there exist some disagreements about the limits to which a brand must go before it can be christened "global." Some maintain that absolute, undiluted standardization of brand strategy and marketing mix is essential.

Brand identity refers to the strategic intention of the brand – what the brand manager imagines the brand to be. Brand identity contributes to models of brand equity, strategic brand management, brand leadership, and living the brand programs. *Brand image* concerns the image of the brand in the mind of the customer and in the marketplace. Brand image forms the basis for understanding advertising, brand community, and market segmentation models. *Brand equity* refers to the value of the brand, generally considered a function of the awareness of the brand and the positive attitudes, beliefs, and feelings about the brand. Counterfeiting remains a significant problem within the corporate perspective.

Consumer research has shown that brands are interpreted in multiple ways, prompting an important and illuminating reconsideration of how branding works. The *consumer perspective* has shifted attention from corporate perspectives toward a consumer perspective in order to understand the roles of brands and branding in the everyday lives of consumers, and the roles brands play in consumer culture. Consumers are seen to construct and perform identities and self-concepts, trying out new roles and creating their identity within and in collaboration with brand culture. From a consumer perspective, brands can be understood as communicative objects. Cultural codes, ideological discourse, consumers' background knowledge, and rhetorical processes have been cited as influences in branding and in consumers' relationships to brands.

Key concepts within the consumer perspective include brand relationships, brand community, and brand tribes. *Brand relationships* encompass how consumers form relationships and attachments to brands, fostered by strategic brand communication, and negotiated by consumers. *Brand communities* and *brand tribes* refer to groups of followers of a brand, who often get together, online or in person, to celebrate their favored brand. Brand communities are marked by shared ideals about the brand, brand routines and rituals, and a sense of obligation to the brand (Muñiz and O'Guinn 2001).

Global branding and the consumer perspective often overlap. From the consumer perspective, a global brand is one interpreted by brand actors worldwide, including employees, consumers, and the media. In other words, the global status of brands is constituted by worldwide recognition, sales, or brand awareness. Accordingly, global branding refers to brand discourses on a global scale. These discourses include advertisements, brand communities, fan blogs, investment analyses, media commentaries, official brand websites, and trade fairs (Zhiyan, Borgerson, and Schroeder, 2013).

The *cultural perspective* considers brands as part of culture rather than primarily a management tool. A cultural perspective reveals how branding has opened up to include cultural, sociological, and theoretical inquiry that both complements and complicates the economic and managerial analysis of branding. An emphasis on culture forms part of a larger movement within the brand research canon, reinforcing a basic premise that culture and history can provide the necessary context for corporate perspectives of the interaction of branding with consumers and society.

Brand research from a cultural perspective occupies the theoretical space between strategic concepts of brand identity and consumer interpretations of brand image, shedding light on the gap often seen between the corporate and consumer perspectives. The cultural perspective emphasizes brand heritage, history, and legacy and how these create associations, meaning, and value. Brand culture focuses on how brands share stories, build community, and solve problems. As cultural forms, brands evolve in accordance with changes in the historical, geographical, and social context. From this perspective, cultural, ideological, and political environments influence the process of building brands, brand meaning, and brand value (Schroeder and Salzer-Mörling 2006). Along these lines, brand culture has been defined as "the cultural codes of brands – history, images, myths, art, and theatre – that influence brand meaning and value in the marketplace" (Schroeder 2009, 124). Brands, understood as cultural forms, reflect people's ideologies, their lifestyles, and their cultural values.

Critical perspectives on brands provide an important reflective point of view, revealing how, beyond their strategic roles, brands function as ethical, ideological, and political objects. This perspective is not merely critical for critique's sake – a critical perspective on brands remains essential for understanding the powerful roles brands play in consumers' lives and in cultural discourse. Key critical concepts include aesthetic labor, double exploitation and working consumers, and globalization's negative aspects. Aesthetic labor involves how consumers co-create brand meaning and value through owning, displaying, discussing, and promoting brands, often via online platforms such as Facebook. This labor has led to concerns over the double exploitation of workers in that, first, their labor is exploited for pay, and then their aesthetic labor is exploited for free, turning them into working consumers. From this perspective, if brands are co-created by consumers and companies, then consumers ought to benefit economically from the value they help create for brands.

A common criticism of brands and branding focuses on globalization and its homogenizing effects on local and indigenous economies and markets. From a critical perspective, global brands often represent imperial desires, colonizing weaker local brands without global budgets or brand strategists and leading to a global brand landscape in which Western brands dominate. In addition, the rise of superbrands may lead to less consumer choice. The conspicuous consumption of brands, including luxury brands, may lead to consumer discontent through making social inequality more visible in daily life, particularly for young consumers. Another line of criticism concerns the expansion of brands and a branding logic into a wide range of institutions, including hospitals, nations, politics, and personal lives. Social media tends to encourage branding in one's own online life via Facebook, Twitter, and other platforms. Brand relationships and brand communities have been criticized as fostering relationships with corporate for-profit entities, as well as celebrity brands, rather than with friends and family, promoting online brand communities over local communities.

These four brand perspectives encompass how brands articulate, embody, and embrace cultural contradictions and existential tensions (Holt and Cameron 2010). Furthermore, as can be seen in the impact of Western brands on global culture, global branding practices influence local culture. A thorough analysis of brands derives not only from networks of users, producers, and other brand builders, but also from local and global events, such as definitive events in a nation's history, consumer boycotts, and anti-globalization movements.

Brands, brand meanings, and brand values can be understood as cultural, political, and ideological forms, and brand researchers and others are encouraged to develop multiple perspectives to understand brands as a fundamental aspect of contemporary consumer culture. Crucial concerns for future work on brands and branding include the growth of social media and digital culture, co-creation of brands, brand measurement and value, brands in emerging economies, and the psychological, interpersonal, and cultural effects of consumers' relationships to brands.

SEE ALSO: Advertising; Brand Loyalty; Commodities; Conspicuous Consumption; Consumer Resistance Movements; Cultural Studies; Global Markets; Mass Marketing; Visual Consumption; Warhol, Andy

REFERENCES

Holt, Douglas, and Douglas Cameron. 2010. *Cultural Strategy: Using Innovative Ideologies to Build Breakthrough Brands*. Oxford: Oxford University Press.

Muñiz, Albert M., Jr., and Thomas C. O'Guinn. 2001. "Brand Community." *Journal of Consumer Research* 27(4): 412–432.

Schroeder, Jonathan E. 2009. "The Cultural Codes of Branding." *Marketing Theory* 9(1): 123–126.

Schroeder, Jonathan E., and Miriam Salzer-Mörling, eds. 2006. *Brand Culture*. London: Routledge.

Zhiyan, Wu, Janet Borgerson, and Jonathan Schroeder. 2013. *From Chinese Brand Culture to Global Brands: Insights from Aesthetics, Fashion and History*. Basingstoke, UK: Palgrave Macmillan.

FURTHER READING

Hatch, Mary Jo, and Majken Schultz. 2008. *Taking Brand Initiative: How Companies Can Align Strategy, Culture, and Identity through Corporate Branding*. San Francisco: Jossey-Bass.

Kornberger, Martin. 2010. *Brand Society: How Brands Transform Management and Lifestyle*. Cambridge, UK: Cambridge University Press.

Lury, Celia. 2004. *Brands: The Logos of the Global Economy*. London: Routledge.

Manning, Paul. 2010. "The Semiotics of Brand." *Annual Review of Anthropology* 39: 33–49.

Bricolage

DUSTIN GARLITZ
University of South Florida, US

Bricolage is a type of construction achieved by using whatever materials are at hand, or the act of creating something from a diverse range of available materials. More generally, bricolage essentially stands for do-it-yourself, and in the field of contemporary consumer studies it can be thought of as a theoretical foundation of do-it-yourself (DIY) culture. The individual who practices bricolage is known as a bricoleur, and is regarded as a sort of Jack-of-all-trades.

In his 1962 book *La Pensée sauvage*, translated into English and published in 1966 as *The Savage Mind*, structural anthropologist Claude Lévi-Strauss introduced the cultural concept of bricolage, which was originally intended to intellectually characterize mythical thought. In a translator's note in *The Savage Mind*, the individual who practices bricolage, the bricoleur, is described as someone "who undertakes odd jobs and is a Jack-of-all-trades, or a kind of professional do-it-yourself man" (Lévi-Strauss 1966/1962, 17). In his 1966 essay "Structure, Sign, and Play in the Discourse of the Human Sciences," philosopher Jacques Derrida (1978/1966) critiqued Lévi-Strauss's concept of bricolage and its bricoleur, developing his own semiotic theory of deconstruction in the process, as he also did in his 1967 work *Of Grammatology* (Derrida 1998/1967). Philosophers Gilles Deleuze and Félix Guattari incorporated the notion of bricolage in their 1972 work *Anti-Oedipus: Capitalism and Schizophrenia*, which finds that in postmodernism the schizophrenic is the universal producer, and that there is not a need to distinguish between the act of producing and the actual product itself. Deleuze and Guattari found that, when Lévi-Strauss defined bricolage, he did so "in terms of a set of closely related characteristics" such as "the possession of a stock of materials or of rules of thumb that are fairly extensive, though more or less a hodge-podge," were "multiple and at the same time limited." Moreover, it applied to the "ability to rearrange fragments continually in new and different patterns or configurations," which as a consequence were indifferent "toward the act of producing and toward the product," and "toward the set of instruments to be used and toward the over-all result to be achieved" (Deleuze and Guattari 1983/1972, 7).

At the level of bricolage and identity, Lévi-Strauss found in *The Savage Mind* that, while the bricoleur may never complete his or her task, he or she always put part of the self in the process. Cultural and media theorist Dick Hebdige, an exponent of the Birmingham School of cultural studies in Britain, has written on style as bricolage in his 1979 book *Subculture: The Meaning of Style*, and on the consumer identity of the bricoleur. Hebdige finds that the concept of bricolage, as originally introduced in anthropology by Lévi-Strauss, helps to explain how distinct rituals of consumption, through style, and by a subculture, can simultaneously disclose their secret identity and communicate their forbidden meanings, or how commodities employed in subcultures demarcate a subculture from more orthodox cultural formations. Hebdige finds that bricolage can be used to explain how subcultural styles are constructed from the bottom up. He highlights how, in contemporary cultural studies, British scholar John Clarke has stressed the way in which prominent forms of discourse, most notably fashion, are radically adapted, subverted, and extended by the subcultural bricoleur.

In the context of style, subcultures, and rituals, Clarke (2006) adapted the term bricolage to refer to the construction of unofficial styles in opposition to more widely held values and practices of society. In the generating of style, Clarke finds that fashion is a basic form of discourse to which the subcultural bricoleur must continually refer. Clarke finds the practitioner of subcultural bricolage, like Lévi-Strauss's bricoleur in the context of mythical thought, constrained by the existing meanings and communication of signs within such discourse grounded in semiotics. He theorizes of a level where "the objects, the 'gear' used to assemble a new subcultural style must not only already exist, but must also carry meaning organised into a system coherent enough for their relocation and transformation to be understood *as a transformation*" (Clarke 2006, 149). It is found that there is no point to this "if the new assemblage looks exactly like" and "carries the same message as" what had previously existed. Also, where the aspects of Lévi-Strauss's intellectual bricolage of mythical thought were "mainly natural objects, naturally available for contemplation," Clarke finds that those objects adapted by the subcultural bricoleur are "physically appropriated – worn and used – and they are commodities, produced originally for specific markets" (2006, 149). In other words, he finds that their pretransformational existence was predicated on the presence of other groups, thought of as intersecting with a dominant class who would have originally purchased, employed, and expressed their own lifestyle through such objects functioning as signs in the greater semiotic system of mass society.

SEE ALSO: Birmingham School; Do-It-Yourself (DIY); Fashion; Semiotics

REFERENCES

Clarke, John. 2006. "Style." In *Resistance through Rituals: Youth Subcultures in Post-War Britain*, edited by Stuart Hall and Tony Jefferson, 147–161. London: Routledge.

Deleuze, Gilles, and Félix Guattari. 1983/1972. *Anti-Oedipus: Capitalism and Schizophrenia*. Translated by Robert Hurley, Mark Seem, and

Helen R. Lane. Minneapolis: University of Minnesota Press.
Derrida, Jacques. 1978/1966. "Structure, Sign, and Play in the Discourse of the Human Sciences." In *Writing and Difference*, translated by Alan Bass, 278–293. Chicago: University of Chicago Press.
Derrida, Jacques. 1998/1967. *Of Grammatology*, corrected ed. Translated by Gayatri Chakravorty Spivak. Baltimore, MD: Johns Hopkins University Press.
Hebdige, Dick. 1988/1979. *Subculture: The Meaning of Style*. London: Routledge.
Lévi-Strauss, Claude. 1966/1962. *The Savage Mind*. Chicago: University of Chicago Press.

Burning Man

KATHERINE K. CHEN
City College of New York; Graduate Center, City University of New York, USA

In 1986 Burning Man started as an intimate San Francisco beach bonfire. This annual event now attracts more than 69,000 people to the Nevada Black Rock Desert, where they form the week-long Black Rock City. Named after the celebratory bonfire of a neon-lit wooden statue located at the city's center, Burning Man espouses 10 principles of radical inclusion, gifting, decommodification, radical self-reliance, radical self-expression, communal effort, civic responsibility, Leave No Trace, participation, and immediacy. These countercultural guidelines emphasize forming relations with others; event goers, dubbed "participants," collaboratively produce the event's activities. Eschewing corporate sponsorship, the event and its organization's US$26 million budget are fueled by ticket sales and donations. The Black Rock City LLC, a for-profit organization led by one of the event's original cofounders, coordinates the year-round activities, such as working with volunteers, law enforcement, government officials, and suppliers. With its large volunteer ranks, the organization operates more like a voluntary association than a for-profit organization.

Studies of various Burning Man phenomena all highlight participants' agency in meaning-making activities. Burning Man's emphasis on expression encourages participants to expand their identities through prosuming the event, exploring spirituality, breaking norms, and altering emotions. To re-enchant consumption, participants reject commercialism and monetary exchange. Instead, they practice prosumption by simultaneously producing and consuming the event. To acculturate newcomers to this unfamiliar activity, the Burning Man organization has articulated a logic, or belief and practices, directing efforts toward creating an inclusive community. Inspired by examples recounted in stories or experienced in person, participants prosume Burning Man by volunteering for the organization, coordinating theme camps that collaborate around a motif (e.g., Black Rock Roller Disco, Thunderdome, etc.), and constructing art that invites audience involvement. In doing so, they gain prestige in the gift economy which advocates giving without expectation of reciprocation.

Some participants explore their individuality via alternative forms of expression. Although not overtly religious, Burning Man also facilitates individualized spirituality via sacred spaces created through rituals and art projects, including the adorning and burning of a temple devoted to deceased loved ones. For example, some men sport handmade costumes that incorporate "feminine" elements, subverting gender norms; some women participate in an annual topless bike ride celebrating the female form. Under these conditions, surveyed participants reported that they were less likely to suppress emotions and more likely to readjust their thinking to control emotions at the event than elsewhere.

Recent research has documented the dissemination of Burning Man practices, including prosumption, into everyday life via Burning Man regionals or local organizations that coordinate gatherings based on Burning Man principles, and Burning Man-inspired projects that promote civic engagement or artistic prosumption. In addition, the Black Rock Arts Foundation, a nonprofit organization founded by Burning Man organizers, funds art in local communities. As these groups proliferate, they promote the acceptance of Burning Man's style of prosumption and organizing practices across mainstream society.

SEE ALSO: Anti-Consumption Tactics; Authenticity; Carnivals/Carnivalesque; Culture Jamming; Do-It-Yourself (DIY); Gifts; Prosumption

FURTHER READING

Chen, Katherine K. 2009. *Enabling Creative Chaos: The Organization behind the Burning Man Event*. Chicago: University of Chicago Press.

Chen, Katherine K. 2011. "Lessons for Creative Cities from Burning Man: How Organizations Can Sustain and Disseminate a Creative Context." *City, Culture and Society* 2(2): 93–100. doi:10.1016/j.ccs.2011.05.003.

Chen, Katherine K. 2012. "Artistic Prosumption: Cocreative Destruction at Burning Man." *American Behavioral Scientist* 56(4): 570–595. doi:10.1177/0002764211429362.

Chen, Katherine K. 2012. "Charismatizing the Routine: Storytelling for Meaning and Agency in the Burning Man Organization." *Qualitative Sociology* 35(3): 311–334. doi:10.1007/s11133-012-9229-1.

Clupper, Wendy. 2009. "The Erotic Politics of Critical Tits: Exhibitionism or Feminist Statement?" In *Political Performances: Theory and Practice*, edited by Susan C. Haedicke, Deirdre Heddon, Avraham Oz, and E. J. Westlake, 251–267. New York: Rodopi.

Gilmore, Lee. 2010. *Theater in a Crowded Fire: Ritual and Spirituality at Burning Man*. Berkeley: University of California Press.

Green, Denise N., and Susan B. Kaiser. 2011. "From Ephemeral to Everyday Costuming: Negotiations in Masculine Identities at the Burning Man Project." *Dress: Journal of the Costume Society of America* 37(1): 1–22. doi:10.1179/036121112X13099651318548.

Kozinets, Robert V. 2002. "Can Consumers Escape the Market? Emancipatory Illuminations from Burning Man." *Journal of Consumer Research* 29(1): 20–38. doi:10.1086/339919.

McRae, Kateri, S. Meghan Heller, Oliver P. John, and James J. Gross. 2011. "Context-Dependent Emotion Regulation: Suppression and Reappraisal at the Burning Man Festival." *Basic and Applied Social Psychology* 33(4): 346–350. doi:10.1080/01973533.2011.614170.

Sherry, John F., Jr., and Robert V. Kozinets. 2007. "Comedy of the Commons: Nomadic Spirituality and the Burning Man Festival." *Consumer Culture Theory* 11: 119–147.

Turner, Fred. 2009. "Burning Man at Google: A Cultural Infrastructure for New Media Production." *New Media & Society* 11(1–2): 73–94.

Buy Nothing Day: *SEE* Consumer Resistance Movements

C

Capitalism

ROB BEAMISH
Queen's University, Canada

The term "capital," as a noun referring to the funds individuals or corporations use as the basis for financial operations, was first employed in 1709 within "An Act for Enlarging the Capital Stock of the Bank of England." "Capitalism," representing a system where capital is advanced to increase wealth, did not come into use until William Thackeray's 1854 novel *The Newcomes*.

Capitalism may refer to an economic, political, and/or social system (e.g., feudalism, capitalism, communism), a broad historical period, or specific forms within that period (e.g., mercantile, industrial, finance, monopoly, or late capitalism). It is often politically encumbered through association with Marx's and other socialist or communist critiques of capitalism (although Marx never used "capitalism" in *The Communist Manifesto* or *Capital*, and first employed it in his late 1870s correspondence). Werner Sombart (1991) tried to depoliticize the term, maintaining that it was an analytical concept applicable to a specific socioeconomic system.

As such, capitalism is a system that provides for needs and wants, animated by a particular ethos; coordinated and organized by established practices, regulations, and laws; and privileging particular types of knowledge (e.g., scientific, technical, and instrumentally rational). Capitalism's ethos involves a historically unique approach to acquisition, positive attitudes toward unfettered competition, and the predominance of goal-rational action (Weber 1927/1923, 352–368). Capitalist production is not directly aimed at human need; it centers on abstract value and potentially unlimited accumulation. Each economic unit competes to extend its economic power as far and as advantageously as possible within the existing legal system.

While forms of capitalism existed in the ancient world, in thirteenth-century Italy, and in the Low Countries, Weber (1927/1923, 275–278) identified five criteria characterizing capitalism as a "pure type" in the modern era.

First, capitalism exists when "the provision of everyday wants" is met through capitalist enterprise. The whole economic system would collapse if those enterprises ceased their productive activities.

Second, capitalism depends on rational calculation and precise accounting. It is the first economic or social system aimed at the pursuit of unlimited wealth, where everything

The Wiley Blackwell Encyclopedia of Consumption and Consumer Studies, First Edition.
Edited by Daniel Thomas Cook and J. Michael Ryan.

is viewed in terms of accumulation: people are producers or consumers; nature is a repository of resources; the enhancing of managerial techniques, technical capacities, and performance outcomes is constantly required; progress involves the creation of new wants, better technology, reduced costs, and increased speeds of capital circulation. Firms calculate the components and costs of production – for example, raw material, machinery, wages, transport, advertising – and the potential consumer demand to ensure, as far as possible, profit maximization. Enterprises determine when and how far they can extend their economic reach while complying with existing law. Goal-rational action pervades capitalism as people, objects, and events are evaluated in terms of means or ends.

Third, capitalism presupposes an enduring, predictable legal system. Entrepreneurs, enterprises, and managers must be certain of property and ownership rights, their easy purchase and sale, and enforceable contracts. Agents of capital must have the legal freedom to undertake the production of any product or service where profit appears attainable and be able to pursue that objective through a variety of organizational forms.

Fourth, capitalism presupposes the presence of individuals "who are not only legally in the position, but are also economically compelled, to sell their labor on the market without restriction" (Weber 1927/1923, 277). Capitalism could not exist and develop without "such a propertyless stratum … a class compelled to sell its labor services to live." Living "under the compulsion of the whip of hunger," Weber maintained, enabled employers to "unambiguously [determine workers' wages] by agreement in advance."

Finally, capitalism requires the complete commercialization of economic life, whereby the primary goal is the gaining and expanding of economic advantage while building commercial wealth. Of critical importance are the sale and purchase of shares in an enterprise or particular property. Through share ownership, individuals or corporations gain access to capital resources well beyond a single individual's wealth, enabling firms to dominate increasingly larger markets and ultimately globalize their activities. The stock market provides the opportunity for wealth through shrewd investment and moves capital to areas of anticipated need and growth; the fluctuation of share values also measures the efficiency and profitability of enterprises over the short and long term.

Capitalism entails a number of dynamic tensions involving power, control, and freedom. Although capitalism has flourished in periods of war, it requires sufficiently long periods of social and political stability for investors, speculators, and producers to make long-term plans with some confidence. Capitalism requires the personal, internal control of individuals' actions, along with institutional regulation – Michel Foucault's notion of disciplining docile bodies – with ultimate power residing in the legal system. Thus, despite certain rhetoric to the contrary, capitalism requires a strong, stable state, although state powers must be limited. There is a constant tension and shifting of the balance of power between private and public sectors.

State power must be restricted so that individuals or firms may engage in saving, risk taking, and profit making activities without the fear of arbitrary state intervention or the confiscation of property. At the same time, particularly after the 1929 depression, private enterprise has depended on the state and public sector for key infrastructural resources, policies, laws, and security. The state, even the neoliberal one, plays a major role in managing the financial environment within which corporations act: for example, governments establish the money supply;

determine interest rates; influence access to credit; implement budgets (including deficits and deficit financing); set rates for progressive income and corporate taxes; influence currency value; regulate securities exchanges; establish tariff rates and trade policies; legislate collective bargaining rights, minimum wage, unemployment insurance; fund and oversee education; and are increasingly involved in health care. The state is a major economic actor.

The emergence and early development of sociology within industrial capitalism are not mere coincidence. Capitalism's social impact and its analytical ethos provided the substance and form for sociology to develop as an empirically based and theoretically informed critical discipline.

SEE ALSO: Class; Commodity Fetishism; Glocalization/Grobalization; Marx, Karl; Mass Culture

REFERENCES

Sombart, W. 1991. *The Economics and Sociology of Capitalism*. Edited by R. Swedberg. Princeton, NJ: Princeton University Press.

Weber, M. 1927/1923. *General Economic History*. Translated by F. H. Knight. Glencoe, IL: Free Press.

Carnivals/Carnivalesque

LAUREN LANGMAN
Loyola University Chicago, USA

Émile Durkheim (1858–1917) noted how laws and norms require transgression to be affirmed, how a society of saints requires sinners to affirm moral boundaries, and how this is often done through public spectacles of punishment or an encapsulated realm of transgression. For Victor Turner (1920–83), a social structure necessarily creates an "anti-structure," with alternative values and practices which are generally kept apart from mainstream society. But, on occasion, often celebratory festivals, there is toleration for, if not acceptance of, what is generally considered deviant, transgressive, and indeed prohibited. Public celebrations of the transgressive have been part of Western society since the highly expressive, orgiastic Dionysian festivals of ancient Greece provided frenzied homage to the god who gave humanity wine and whose rituals included hearty drinking, singing, dancing, and a lot of cavorting.

Life in the Middle Ages was generally nasty, brutish, and short, especially for poor peasants and townspeople who lived under oppressive political and economic conditions. Yet there were collective festivals, fairs, and carnivals that were times of widespread merriment, joy, and laughter. These were often connected with various kinds of transgressions of moral norms and values like modesty and deference to authority, and with celebration of the body in the form of indulgence in food, drink, and sexual acts. These kinds of rituals acted as pressure valves to preserve the social order. For Mikhail Bakhtin (1968) the carnival became a popular festival, one that emerged from the ordinary people and not from the religious festivals and holidays of the church or the jousts, tournaments, and feasts of the feudal elites. Carnival was a liberating time and place where the otherwise forbidden was tolerated and accepted, often with the aid of large quantities of drink. There was mass transgression in word and deed, which might include overeating, cursing, the scatological, and quite often sexual license. Carnival provided a utopian moment of respite from the ordinary, a moment of utopian equality and community between the classes when the peasants might parody, lampoon, or berate the clerical elites who were thereby "brought down to earth."

Modern Western society, like any other, relegated transgressions to the margins. Following World War II, suburbanization and consumerism brought with them new forms of alienation which were often expressed in artistic/literary protests of transgression against the vapid materialism, repression, and emptiness of consumer society. In the 1950s and early 1960s the Beat Generation, through their writing and transgressive lifestyles celebrating drugs and sex, protested against the sterility, conformity, and repression of society. The 1960s saw widespread anti-war protests and the growth of a massive counterculture celebrating drugs, sex, and rock and roll through transgressive celebrations that extolled heretofore forbidden pleasures, including nudity and sexuality, against the repressive norms and alienation of the social order.

These moments provided an alternative to the otherwise typical forms of domination, alienation, dehumanization, and fragmentation of community that had been lamented by Marx, Weber, and Durkheim (see Langman 2012). Festivals provided gratifying identities and meanings in contrast to the sterile conformity of mass culture and empty consumerism. But, as these various countercultures began to flourish, it was not long before capitalism transformed the cultural protests at the alienation and dehumanization of consumer society into profitable commodities. In other words, carnivalization came to profit from the mass marketing of cultural protests against itself. For example, the anger and perhaps nihilism of punk music as protest were successfully co-opted, as many artists were highly successful and punk fashions and accessories became profitable.

Part of the magic and secret of consumerism has been its ability to turn everything into a marketable commodity, including collective transgressions that had been critiques of consumerism. Carnivalization now represents the mass marketing of what Marcuse (1964) called "repressive desublimation" whereby erotic toleration sustained consumer society and reproduced the very social condition of a class society and its various kinds of domination. Consider, for example, the rise of "porn chic." While pornography may not necessarily be a festive celebration of groups, the potential for monetizing transgressive eroticism has created a market for such practices. We have seen a carnivalization of everyday life where what may have been transgressive is now quite acceptable. The mass marketing of erotic toys and accessories now includes home parties (typically involving suburban housewives) where vibrators, flavored lubricants, and edible panties have displaced the sale of Tupperware. The proliferation of video cameras, mobile phones, and the internet has seen a flourishing of "sexting" and do-it-yourself amateur porn where people upload their own videos to various sites. Finally, a number of erotically oriented social media have emerged to dispense with lunch meetings, pub crawls, and singles parties in order to find sexual partners. Such sites are strictly for immediate erotic encounters, sexual gratification with "NSA" (no strings attached).

In a similar vein, spring break vacations to places like Cancún for almost endless drinking and partying, with dancing that includes erotic grinding, belly shots, and the like, in a sense routinize the carnivalesque and make it part of a rite of passage for many people of college age. In addition, the New Orleans Mardi Gras has become synonymous with breast baring in exchange for cheap necklaces. Various Caribbean resorts cater to adult only, clothing optional, hook up retreats.

In recent years, however, some expressions of carnivalization have been embraced by various political activists to protest what they see as injustice and to foster social change, from critiques of global inequality to more local patterns of protests against patriarchy, racism, and homophobia. In the "Battle of Seattle" in 1999 and other similar anti-globalization movements, the use of puppetry, performance, and masking was a key element of the public face of the movement. For a number of years, the animal rights group PETA (People for the Ethical Treatment of Animals) has used nude pictures of famous stars to say that they would rather go naked than wear fur. Many anti-war movements have used nudity as a form of protest; for example, during the anti-Iraq war demonstrations a group of topless women pleaded for "Boobs Not Bombs" (Feminist Activism 101 2013). The Ukrainian group Femen goes topless to protest sex trafficking, patriarchy, global inequality, and injustice, while the Russian rock group Pussy Riot protested against Putin in a Russian Orthodox church. Gay pride parades, replete with leather daddies, dykes on bikes, S&M outfits, or sometimes no outfits, have helped to normalize gay lifestyles and to foster the acceptance of LGBTs into the mainstream of society. The annual Burning Man festival combines elements of spectacle, transgression, do-it-yourself, and commercialism. Hence, the carnivalesque can be co-opted but it continues on its path of disruption and critique in ever-changing forms of expression. It is now an integral part of consumer society.

SEE ALSO: Body and Consumer Culture; Burning Man; Consumption, Spectacles of

REFERENCES

Bakhtin, Mikhail. 1968. *Rabelais and His World*. Bloomington: Indiana University Press.

Feminist Activism 101. 2013. "The Naked Body – A Tool of Protest." Accessed July 15, 2014. http://www.feministactivism101.com/2013/11/the-naked-body-a-tool-of-protest.html.

Langman, Lauren. 2012. "Alienation, Entrapment, and Inauthenticity: Carnival to the Rescue." In *Alienation and Carnivalization*, edited by J. Braun and L. Langman, 53–75. New York: Routledge.

Marcuse, Herbert. 1964. *One Dimensional Man*. Boston, MA: Beacon.

Celebrity

CHRIS ROJEK

City University, London, UK

Celebrity may be defined as the accumulation of attention capital. Most commonly, it is understood to be a quality of individuals. However, it may also refer to social groups (sports teams, pop groups, business management partnerships) and social events (the Olympics, the World Series, the FIFA World Cup). With respect to individuals, there are three types of celebrity. *Ascribed celebrity* refers to social impact that reflects bloodline, whereby hereditary titled individuals, such as kings, queens, emperors, ladies, duchesses, and so forth, are positioned in the social hierarchy to automatically command enlarged respect and deference. *Achieved celebrity* refers to social impact that derives from recognized talents and accomplishments; successful sports stars, musicians, actors, comedians, and authors are pre-eminent in this social category. *Celetoids* are individuals who attain intense bursts of fame. The term is an amalgamation of "celebrity" and "tabloid" (newspaper); this gives a clue to the meaning of the phenomenon by highlighting the pivotal role of media communication in the process.

The attention capital of celetoids is not principally a matter of innate talent or learned accomplishment. More properly, it is the dividend of external investment. Celetoids are creations of the public relations–media hub

(PR – media hub), especially mass circulation print and electronic news outlets and reality TV production companies. For the sake of clarity, a further distinction should be made between *short life* and *long life* celetoids. The former refers to individuals who command the media horizon for a finite period and then disappear into complete obscurity. The latter refers to individuals constructed by the PR – media hub who extend media visibility for the duration.

Historians of celebrity generally agree that the profile of celebrity culture has been trending upward for more than a century (Gundle 2008; Inglis 2010). Rationales for the expansion of celebrity fall into supply-side and demand-side accounts. Supply-side accounts fasten on the commercial value of attention capital. According to this way of thinking, the multiplication of celebrity in social consciousness is chiefly the result of the proliferation of media outlets. Hence, attention capital is indissolubly coupled with commercial imperatives. Commercial interests construct the celetoid as a means of capital accumulation. Thus, the celetoid is the latest iteration of the requirement of capital to conquer new physical and cultural space, just like the mass spectacle that preceded it. For the vested interests, celetoid culture is an attractive low-cost option for capital accumulation, since reality TV does not pay performers and is usually based in static production sets, rather than involving expensive location schedules.

Supply-side accounts question the common-sense assumption that social encounters between achieved celebrities, celetoids, and audiences are natural. They do so by insisting that cultural intermediaries are now decisive in the communication and refinement of attention capital. Cultural intermediaries refer to business managers, speech coaches, body stylists, public relations experts, dieticians, and security staff who manage encounters between celebrities and the public. In the days of the Hollywood studio system, executives took great pains to construct the "picture personality"; it was a form of exposure management that ensured that the film personality presented to the public in magazines and interviews was consistent with the screen personality. The Hollywood new wave of the late 1960s undermined studio power and altered the balance between film executives and movie personalities. This was part of a wider movement of artistic liberalization in the entertainment sector that extended to popular musicians, who renegotiated recording contracts on more favorable terms and created their own record labels; team sports players, who gained more contractual independence from their clubs; and novelists, who ceased to be bound to renewable book contracts with publishers.

The undoubted merits of the supply-side perspective are outweighed by the tendency to see the demand for celebrity as the product of the strategy of cultural intermediaries and media manipulation. This is unsatisfactory because the audience is finally represented as impressionable and passive. Demand-side accounts seek to correct this. They operate on three fronts. First, the rise of celebrity culture is portrayed as filling the emotional gap for social positioning and direction caused by the decline of organized religion. Many of the rituals of celebrity culture seem to echo the rituals of religion, for example the sacred importance attributed to relics (locks of hair, nail clippings, autographs, clothing, and other possessions), sites of nativity and death, and pilgrimages. In addition, some celebrities are regarded as possessing superhuman powers which parallel the supernatural powers attributed to some religious figures. Like religious figures, celebrities provide followers with a sense of transcendence and escapism from the mundane aspects of life.

Second, demand for celebrities is explored as a matter of narcissistic identification and hero worship. The attention capital of stars is regarded as entertaining and attractive. The magnification of celebrity culture by the media produces a strong propensity for the audience to emulate this behavior. Pinsky and Young (2009) refer to this as "the mirror effect." Since some forms of well-publicized celebrity behavior often test boundaries and work on the edge of legality, emulation of this type is regarded as contributing to personal disorientation and social malaise. Psychologists have developed this line of thought by introducing the concept of *celebrity worship syndrome* (CWS) (Maltby and Day 2011). This behavioral syndrome refers to an excessive or morbid interest in celebrities. Celebrity harassment, stalking, hate crime, and murder are regularly explored as examples of the fan's overidentification with a celebrity.

Third, the role of celebrities in transferring informal life coaching tips to personal and work relations is posited as a reason for the multiplication of celebrity. The logic here is that, in many developed economies, service work employs a significantly larger portion of the labor force than agriculture or the manufacturing and extractive industries. Of course, the ratio of service workers to other sectors varies in different countries. For the purposes of analysis, a proportion of 6–8 out of 10 is not an unreasonable benchmark in the economically advanced bloc. Service sector workers depend on communication, information, persuasion, and cognate "people skills" to be effective. Who are the people that are given the greatest financial rewards and status rankings for the possession and adroit practice of these skills? Superstars. According to this line of reasoning, then, celebrities equip the crowd with tips on grooming, speech, lifestyle, and impression management that transfer to the world of work and personal relationships.

The humanizing effect of celebrities has been amply recognized by commercial interests in consumer culture. Celebrity endorsement of commodities switches attention capital from the entertainment sector to high street or shopping mall retailing. Screen glamour is redefined as a commercial asset so that the commodity that is the subject of endorsement is presented as a symbolic extension of the celebrity. The practice raises additional questions of exposure management. *Celebrity vamping* refers to the deflation of celebrity endorsement. It follows from the overextension of a celebrity in endorsing too many products, so that the law of diminishing returns applies. It also connects up with supply-side arguments which maintain that celebrities are now prize assets in governance and control. The widespread deployment of celebrity figures to endorse political candidates and parties is an example of this. So too is the application of Hollywood staging and glamour-enhancing techniques in presidential, senatorial, and congressional election campaigns.

In general, the attitude of the media to celebrities is condescending. It presents celebrity culture as the new opiate of the people. Dedicated celebrity magazines, TV channels, and blog sites are often taken as evidence of trivialization and malaise. What this fails to recognize is the important role that celebrity culture plays in providing escapism and transcendence in societies dominated by bureaucratic, rational, and secular standards. It is also the case that celebrities can operate as successful role models. For example, Nelson Mandela's role in heading peace and reconciliation in South Africa, George Clooney's campaign against human rights abuse in Sudan, and Angelina Jolie's humanitarian work as UNHCR (United Nations High Commissioner for Refugees) goodwill ambassador are widely regarded as providing positive benchmarks of citizenship and leadership.

SEE ALSO: Cool; Cosmetic Surgery; Narcissism

REFERENCES

Gundle, Stephen. 2008. *Glamour*. Oxford: Oxford University Press.
Inglis, Fred. 2010. *A Short History of Celebrity*. Princeton, NJ: Princeton University Press.
Maltby, John, and Liza Day. 2011. "Celebrity Worship and the Incidence of Elective Cosmetic Surgery." *Journal of Adolescent Health* 49: 483–489.
Pinsky, Drew, and Mark Young. 2009. *The Mirror Effect: How Celebrity Narcissism Is Endangering Our Families – and How to Save Them*. New York: HarperCollins.
Rojek, Chris. 2001. *Celebrity*. London: Reaktion.

Character Licensing

CYNTHIA MAURER
Rutgers University, USA

Character licensing is the use of fictional characters to sell merchandise through one or more manufacturers, whereby the manufacturing company purchases the license for the character to produce various products. Most often linked to children's goods and media, licensed characters often come from popular culture and appeal to both children and adults, thus reaching a wide consumer audience.

In traditional character licensing, companies sought a license to use a property – that is, an image, story, or likeness – which had enjoyed prior success as character in a comic, movie, or television show (Engelhardt 1986). Character holders thought it smart to receive free advertising in exchange for the rights to their character and often did not charge for the use of their characters (Schneider 1987). The most successful traditional character licensing took place in 1977 when Kenner Toys bought the exclusive worldwide toys and games rights for the *Star Wars* movies. Initially, movies were profitably inconsistent in regard to character licensing, and manufacturers became hesitant to invest in movies (Schneider 1987). Kenner Toys' investment to license various characters from the first *Star Wars* movie, as well as the sequels, proved one of the more profitable character licensing endeavors.

Strategies for licensing changed in the 1980s. A company called Those Characters from Cleveland created a new character, Strawberry Shortcake, based not on the prior success of an entertainment show, but on survey data for girls. The image of Shortcake was printed on greeting cards and made into toys well before it appeared on television. In the years that followed, many companies attempted the same "Shortcake Strategy" (Engelhardt 1986) of creating and disseminating a character *before* the success of the television show or movie. The case of Strawberry Shortcake demonstrated that a character could be created and loved separately from any particular medium or product by virtue of the creation of a backstory that the intended audience can relate to. This is something that requires considerable coordination between the creator of the character and the producer of goods, fusing image and material production.

Traditional character licensing continues alongside newer strategies, as exemplified by Nickelodeon Network's Spongebob Squarepants cartoon character which appeals to audiences of all ages. After the show was a confirmed success, Nickelodeon began licensing the characters for video games, food, clothing, toys, school supplies, and bed decorations (Hendershot 2004). Either way, characters tend to add value to products and thereby capture higher prices in the marketplace than nonlicensed goods.

SEE ALSO: Advertising; Brand Mascots; Children's Consumer Culture

REFERENCES

Engelhardt, Tom. 1986. "The Strawberry Shortcake Strategy." In *Watching Television: A Pantheon Guide to Popular Culture*, edited by Todd Gitlin, 68–110. New York: Pantheon.

Hendershot, Heather. 2004. "Nickelodeon's Nautical Nonsense: The Intergenerational Appeal of Spongebob Squarepants." In *Nickelodeon Nation: The History, Politics and Economics of America's Only TV Channel for Kids*, edited by Heather Hendershot, 182–208. New York: New York University Press.

Schneider, Cy. 1987. *Children's Television: The Art, the Business, and How It Works*. Chicago, IL: NTC Business.

Children's Consumer Culture

ANNA SPARRMAN
Linköping University, Sweden

Over the past half century, research on children and consumption has expanded and changed both theoretically and methodologically. As a research area, children's consumer culture was established and developed from the 1990s onward. It has progressed in parallel with the development of the social construction of children and childhood, as presented by the "new" sociology of and history of childhood (today called child studies or childhood studies). The new sociology of childhood provided a severe critique of the lack of focus on children in disciplines such as anthropology, history, sociology, and feminism. Moreover, it challenged the supremacy of psychological theories when researching children. The most important contribution of the new sociology of childhood, however, was the changing view of children as situated social members of and actors in society.

Critique similar to that expressed in the sociology of childhood has also been aimed at consumer research. As pointed out by consumer and childhood researcher Daniel Thomas Cook (2008), children have consistently been neglected in consumer theories. Likewise, between the 1950s and 1990s, developmental psychology and social behaviorism were the predominant theoretical approaches for investigating and understanding children's consumer behaviors.

Theoretically, children's consumer culture aligns with the change in approach to seeing children as situated social actors and meaning makers in society. The research focuses mainly on cultural consumption, social and cultural contexts, lived cultures, symbolism, and children's meaning making. Qualitative methods such as ethnography, qualitative interviews, and focus groups, as well as analytical methods such as narrative analysis, discourse analysis, and interpretive analysis, are favored. In this way, children's consumer culture is aligned with consumer culture theory (CCT), which sets out to study consumer identities, marketplace cultures, sociohistoric patterns of consumption, and consumers' interpretive strategies.

However, the topic of children and consumption often leads to so-called moral panics. Central to these panics are children's potential vulnerability and presumed need for protection against the consumer society. Advertising, sexy clothing, and pop stars have all been subject to larger panics initiated by consumer organizations, churches, the political left as well as right, child psychologists, or parents and teachers. Political liberals, marketing practitioners, market research, and academics studying children's consumer culture tend to view children as well informed and agentive consumers, a position that has created some confusion, with differences in approaches noted by scholars such as David Buckingham (2007). Market practitioners and researchers present children as savvy and knowing consumers, whereas academic research tends to focus on the complexities and contradictions of children's consumption (for example, parental involvement in consumer decisions, children's access to or lack of money, ethnicity, gender, relations between the local and the global), on children as both competent and innocent actors/consumers, and on legislation. Academic research is not against "protection," but suggests solutions such as consumer education and consumer literacy instead of prohibition and legislation, even though the latter solutions are sometimes accepted.

The policies and legislation regulating children's consumption and consumer cultures constitute an important topic for children's consumer culture, as does child labor. Questions such as when, where, and at what age children are allowed to earn and spend money or to open savings accounts depends on the social as well as national context. In many countries, tourism is a resource for children's wage earnings, as is babysitting to earn pocket money and selling cookies to finance school class trips. In *Pricing the Priceless Child* (1985), sociologist Viviana Zelizer points out how children have been economically valued during different historical periods. Today children are used as commodity objects in advertising that targets both adults and children. Furthermore, research on children's use of money has shown that children differentiate between types of money: their own money, money given as gifts, and earned money.

Children's relation to money and their economic value as objects in consumer markets constitute a somewhat neglected research area, even though the market segments for children are expanding. Research shows that children's consumer culture is growing across the globe through the so-called Disneyfication of everyday life, and McDonaldization of food consumption. Children worldwide are celebrating the same commercial holidays, such as Halloween and Valentine's Day, and visiting similar amusement and theme parks. Having a birthday party more or less constitutes the Western world's view on what constitutes a good childhood. Nonetheless, when research is focused on children's practices and meaning making, the findings reveal national as well as local diversity. The cultural meanings of consumption thereby signal plurality, fluidity, and hybridity rather than continuity. Still, children's consumer markets are highly gendered and sexualized, which limits children's consumer choices. How children and parents deal with this has been, and is being, investigated by researchers in the area of children's consumer culture.

Restricted access to money means that children use negotiation strategies in order to act on consumer markets. Weekly or monthly allowances are negotiated. What jeans to buy or which food to buy in the supermarket is negotiated. There is a thin line between what is looked on as children's negotiations and children's "nag factor" or "pester power." These factors show that most shopping is done on behalf of children by adults rather than by children themselves. The purchasing power belongs to adults, while the power of negotiation belongs to children. As pointed out by historian of child consumer researcher Gary Cross (2004), a great deal of consumption for children stems from parents' or grandparents' childhood nostalgia. Parents' consumption for children is enveloped in parents' own childhood memories, and in love and the desire to help their children fit into various social and cultural contexts.

The main benefactor of the field of children's consumer culture is without doubt consumer and history of childhood researcher Daniel Thomas Cook. He has framed the research area historically by investigating how market practitioners established the notion of childhood as a market and of children as individual consumers, pointing out how consumer theories have consequently ignored children; and the importance of studying the cultural and symbolic values of children's material cultures. Theoretically merging child studies and consumer studies, Cook has also argued in favor of qualitative methods focusing on children's meaning making.

Cook's call to emphasize children's meaning making and cultural consumption has generated new knowledge, suggesting multidirectional influences between child and adult consumption and introducing new theoretical concepts. The notion of "situated child consumption," introduced by Anna Sparrman and Bengt Sandin (2012), emphasizes situating *or placing* child consumption within different practices, be they found in everyday life, politics, markets, local or global settings, or tied to specific historical periods. Concepts such as "prosumption," which highlights children's double roles as producers and consumers, are emerging, as is "childity." The concept of childity elaborates on age, which has been a main focus in behavioral studies of child consumption. Childity, however, questions how it is possible to see that a child is a child when information about age is lacking. Market-created categories like the "tween" – which defines the period between childhood and teenagehood – are both integrated and contested as a theoretical concept by academic scholars. The theoretical and methodological explorations of children's consumer culture have the potential to influence and change the direction of research in the area of child studies.

SEE ALSO: Consumer Culture Theory (CCT); Consumption and Identity; Money; Nostalgia; Prosumption; Teens; Tweens

REFERENCES

Buckingham, David. 2007. "Selling Childhood? Children and Consumer Culture." *Journal of Children and Media* 1(1): 15–24.

Cook, Daniel Thomas. 2008. "The Missing Child in Consumption Theory." *Journal of Consumer Culture* 8(2): 210–243.

Cross, Gary. 2004. *The Cute and the Cool: Wondrous Innocence and Modern American Children's Culture*. Oxford: Oxford University Press.

Sparrman, Anna, and Bengt Sandin. 2012. "Situated Child Consumption: An Introduction." In Situating Child *Consumption: Rethinking Values and Notions of Children, Childhood and Consumption*, edited by Anna Sparrman, Bengt Sandin, and Johanna Sjoberg, 9–31. Lund, Sweden: Nordic Academic Press.

Zelizer, Viviana. 1985. *Pricing the Priceless Child: A Changing Social Value of Children*. New York: Basic Books.

FURTHER READING

Arnould, Eric J., and Craig J. Thompson. 2005. "Consumer Culture Theory (CCT): Twenty Years of Research." *Journal of Consumer Research* 31(4): 868–882.

Buckingham, David. 2011. *The Material Child*. Cambridge, UK: Polity.

Cook, Daniel Thomas. 2010. "Commercial Enculturation: Moving beyond Consumer Socialization." In *Childhood and Consumer Culture*, edited by David Buckingham and Vebjørg Tingstad, 63–79. Basingstoke, UK: Palgrave Macmillan.

Christmas

PATRICK COX
Rutgers University, USA

Christmas as it is practiced today in the United States is as much a festival of consumerism as of religious rites. Much ado is made annually in the media over the "real" meaning of Christmas, though historically the holiday has had less to do with religion than is often thought today. This consumerism has had more to do with the popularity of the celebration in England and the United States than with religion, though religious and consumerist celebrations of the holiday developed in tandem into the modern Western Christmas festival, particularly since the seventeenth century.

Modern Christmas celebrations have roots in mid-winter festivals throughout Europe, most notably Saturnalia in Rome and Yul in Scandinavia. These festivals were raucous affairs that lasted from a few days to several weeks and typically involved rites and symbols meant to afford relief from the darkest and coldest days of the year during which they were held. These included evergreens, fire, and lavish feasting and drinking. In England and the United States in the nineteenth century, Christmas festivities turned from public festivals to domestic celebrations centered around family and consumption. The holiday quickly caught on as a family affair emphasizing children, food, and gift-giving following the publication of Charles Dickens's *A Christmas Carol* in 1843 and the circulation of images of the royal family in England celebrating a secular Christmas with a Christmas tree and presents.

Twentieth-century commodification of Christmas has been well noted. Russell W. Belk (1987) has written of the secularization of Christmas and of consumption itself as a religion over which Santa Claus presides as deity. Brian Sutton-Smith (1986) has specified Christmas consumerism as "the festival of toys," noting, "Every Christmas there is the annual parental demonstration of conspicuous consumption" (1986, 20) calling attention to the centrality not only of consumerism but also of children to Christmas celebrations. The links between childhood and consumerism at Christmastime are clear and cannot be overlooked. Modern Christmas celebrations arose in the mid to the late nineteenth century concomitant with a modern conception of childhood as a special stage of life and the center of the domestic sphere. Today, many of the rituals, media, and gift-giving at Christmas are centered around children.

The most recognizable symbol of the holiday, Santa Claus, has been theorized to act as a buffer between children and consumerism as part of an illusion of presents made by elves and arriving on a sleigh, shielding children from knowledge of toys as products in the marketplace purchased on credit, thereby preserving the protected space of childhood distinct from the adult world. This use of Santa can be said to cleanse Christmas of the taint of consumerism, at least for children, making the rampant consumerism of Christmas more acceptable as a festival to share with children. Yet Santa himself is a market product: the widespread popularity of his image has largely been the result of its use in commercial advertising and the ritual linkage of Santa with children explicitly asking for presents.

SEE ALSO: Children's Consumer Culture; Consumption Rituals; Gifts

REFERENCES

Belk, Russell W. 1987. "A Child's Christmas in America: Santa Claus as Deity, Consumption as Religion." *Journal of American Culture* 10: 87–100.

Sutton-Smith, Brian. 1986. *Toys as Culture*. New York: Gardner Press.

FURTHER READING

Bartunek, Jean M., and Boram Do. 2011. "The Sacralization of Christmas Commerce." *Organization* 18(6): 795–806.

Nissenbaum, Stephen. 1996. *The Battle for Christmas*. New York: Alfred A. Knopf.

Cities, Visual Consumption of

DENNIS ZUEV
CIES-ISCTE, Portugal

The idea of visual consumption focuses on the graphic or optical aspects of the commercial world, including the acts of looking and seeing and the production of images and messages. Visual consumption can be exemplified by walking in the red light district in Amsterdam, watching a Euroleague football game, browsing the internet, gazing at advertising posters at the bus stop, gaping at skyscrapers in Shanghai, looking at museum exhibitions in Dubai, or watching a gay pride parade in São Paulo.

Visual consumption is a key attribute of an experience economy where images and visual texts have become important parts of making sense of various human experiences. In visual consumption the underlying sociological issues of status display, emerging taste publics, and social differentiation play an important role in understanding how visual consumption can be managed and governed. Visual consumption is driven by the laws of decoding of visual texts by taste publics which possess knowledge of optical, graphic, aesthetic, ideological, and linguistic codes. Advertising plays a prominent role in the visual consumption landscape as it represents an important institution in routinizing, or establishing, the primacy of image consumption over physical or tactile consumption.

The starting point for understanding visual consumption, as Schroeder (2002) suggests, is the image. Simultaneously, one can also consider starting from simple interrogation of the influence of the exterior visual design of objects and texts ranging from the promotion webpage of Google Glass to the iconic silhouette of a Kalashnikov AK-47 assault rifle, which has affected the design of over 100 other models worldwide and became a pop-culture icon (Chivers 2010). Distinguishing between the visual consumption of web imagery, of real-life objects and imagery, and of staged and natural displays offers some inroad into understanding the dynamics of visual consumption. At the same time, one has to be aware that hybrid forms of visual consumption are possible and often present – that is, the image of the product (such as a destination in tourism) can be consumed online via web-based imagery of landscapes or a virtual tour during e-booking of a hotel – before actual, "direct" experience.

Internet-related lifestyles such as blogging and social networking involve galaxies of images – images that are shared, discussed, and collectively or individually consumed. YouTube videos, for instance, are produced and consumed by anonymous masses of users. Film-sharing online services provide opportunity for video and film viewing in the format of home video and laptop screen, when the stream of film can be controlled and interrupted, unlike in a real cinema setting.

Scholars observe a shift to amateur production and aesthetic codes related to new media visual consumption, often attributed to increasingly wide accessibility of digital video and photo recording devices. The consumption of images follows the logic of digital production, as when images are stored in digital memory archives and can be retrieved instantaneously. One has to be mindful that the peculiarities of local visual consumption culture and popular sentiments can be mobilized in the marketing of visually based consumer products which expand the official propaganda domain, such as in the promotion of the online game *Resistance War Online* which was based on the anti-Japanese sentiments of the Chinese public (Nie 2013).

Cities emerge as significant centers of the modern visual sphere (Nathansohn and Zuev 2013), as they provide diverse venues for the spectacles and imagery to be produced and consumed – from shopping centers and trendy art venues to street guerrilla art and performances (Hannigan 1998; Miles 2010). Spectacles are large-scale events which privilege visual interaction and which can range from commercially produced sport or music shows to street parades and protests. However, these spectacles are not limited to displays or performances staged for commercial purposes. Consumption of staged and natural displays is closely connected with traveling and tourism, and therefore nations seek to promote their national iconic landscapes for consumption, for example Torres Del Paine national park in Chile, the Grand Canyon in the United States, or wild beaches in Portugal, and organize events representing the place, such as Rio Carnival in Brazil or the Victory Day military parade in Moscow, Russia. The tourist search for unspoiled nature and authentic cultural displays leads them to the most inaccessible places for visual consumption because "holidays last longer in snapshots" (Kodak slogan, quoted in Schroeder 2002, 74). This is particularly relevant for hard-to-access places or places consumed in a group of family or friends. For instance, Antarctic landscapes are subject to rather homogeneous consumption principles dictated by the logic of Antarctic tourism operators (IAATO), which allows for only a limited number of places to be visited and thus visually consumed.

Visual consumption is accompanied by leisure consumption – that is, fun, pleasure, and entertainment. Tourism is one of the most widespread visually supported lifestyles in the sense that tourists travel in order to see or experience the places visually and structure their experience anchored sensorially to photographs and videos. In the analysis of tourism the concept of gaze has been particularly influential in conceptualizing the tourist's experiences (Urry 2002) where the tourist is seen as a visual consumer of places.

The changing aesthetics of visual production pattern new modes of visual consumption. Visually based lifestyles such as traveling, shopping, blogging, and social networking limit the intimate connection with the produced image: the paper photo cannot be deleted while the digital ones can be. With new technologies and devices such as the smartphone, visual consumption has become even more ubiquitous as well as more mobile and portable.

SEE ALSO: Advertising; Consumption, Spectacles of; Experiential Consumption; Tourism; Visual Consumption

REFERENCES

Chivers, C. J. 2010. "How the AK-47 Rewrote the Rules of Modern Warfare." *Wired* 1 November. http://www.wired.com/magazine/2010/11/ff_ak47/all/1?pid=3451.

Hannigan, John. 1998. *Fantasy City: Pleasure and Profit in the Postmodern Metropolis*. New York: Routledge.

Miles, Steven. 2010. *Spaces for Consumption: Pleasure and Placelessness in the Post-Industrial City*. London: Sage.

Nathansohn, Regev, and Dennis Zuev. eds. 2013. *Sociology of the Visual Sphere*. New York: Routledge.

Nie, Hongping Annie. 2013. "Gaming, Nationalism and Ideological Work in Contemporary China: Online Games Based on the War of Resistance against Japan." *Journal of Contemporary China* 22(81): 499–517.

Schroeder, Jonathan E. 2002. *Visual Consumption*. London: Routledge.

Urry, John. 2002. *Tourist Gaze*. London: Sage.

Citizenship and Consumption

KATHLEEN KUEHN
Victoria University of Wellington, New Zealand

Traditionally, citizenship and consumption have been relegated to oppositional spheres of human activity. At the one end, citizenship denotes association to a nation or state in which recognized members are granted a specific set of rights and responsibilities to participate in political life. As it describes activities performed in the "public sphere," citizenship constitutes some allegiance to a governing body that, in turn, entitles its denizens to varying levels of sovereignty, rights, and protections. Consumption, at the other end, refers to activities of exchange performed in the "private sphere" of the marketplace. To practice consumption is to satisfy one's personal needs and desires through the use, purchase, or accumulation of goods, services, and other resources. Beyond occupying activities within the public and private realms, citizenship and consumption are ostensibly motivated by qualitatively different value systems. As a social ideal, citizenship – particularly in Western democracies – is rooted in classical liberal values of collective responsibility and a commitment to the larger social good or "commons." To prioritize communal values as a fundamental task of citizenship, however, requires some restraint of individual rights. As the eighteenth-century philosopher Jean-Jacques Rousseau (1947/1762) argued, civil society functions best when sovereign citizens bind themselves to the social contract, that is, members willingly relinquish certain impulses, rights, and desires for the greater good. In this sense, good citizenship implies a degree of sacrifice to elevate the larger public interest. Conversely, consumption has long been viewed as an embodiment of rampant individualism and unrestrained freedom of choice, whereby purchasing decisions are treated as an expression and reflection of one's own self-interest. In short, the outwardly focused citizen is diametrically opposed to the inwardly focused consumer, whose primary commitments are centered on the self.

More recently, economic and cultural historians have challenged the long-held mythical distinction between citizenship and consumption, arguing that it constructs an evolutionary history that assumes human beings have, over the course of modern time, transformed (or devolved) from once morally virtuous citizens to amoral selfish consumers. Histories of consumer culture acknowledge that citizenship and consumption, as well as the public and private, have never been wholly separate. They note that the recognition of rights (political, economic, civil, and social), identification, and equality – foundational components of democratic citizenship – have long been located in the private sphere of consumption. Wartime rationing, boycotts, and the fair trade movement indicate just some of the more common ways in which consumption practices have been infused with civic values. Contemporarily, political consumerism ranges from pragmatic alternative shopping behaviors (e.g., ethical consumption, the localvore movement) to direct forms of public advocacy (e.g., letter writing, sit-ins) to anti-consumerist critiques (e.g., culture jamming, Occupy movement). While the relationship between citizenship and consumption may predate modern times, the consumer-citizen hybrid can be located historically as early as the eighteenth century, when prewar colonial boycotts of British imports functioned as a stepping stone to political independence. As Lizabeth Cohen describes in *A Consumer's Republic* (2003), the late nineteenth to mid-twentieth century especially marked a time where the collective mobilization of consumers, acting as citizens, effected vast social and political changes. During these years, consumers approached the market as both an alternative sphere for action and a site responsible to civic demands. As the intensification of industrial manufacturing both created and facilitated the struggles of early organized labor, Progressive era reforms constructed a direct relationship between public and private rights as a response to laissez-faire capitalism's exploitative effects. Demands for shorter work weeks, minimum wages, and fair prices were at least partly lobbied for on the grounds that better work conditions would produce better consumers; in other words, less time at work for fair pay and safer environments guaranteed more leisure time and resources to share in the promises of consumption.

By the 1930s, US President Franklin D. Roosevelt's appropriation of Keynesian economics was informing post-Depression New Deal policies in the United States, which legitimized government intervention in facilitating mass consumption as a means of economic growth. As federal revitalization programs promoted consumption as a civic obligation, emergent consumer rights organizations simultaneously demanded federally regulated protections from unscrupulous big business. As part of the 1933 National Industrial Recovery Act, Congress officially recognized consumers, for the first time in modern history, as legitimate subjects warranting their own set of guaranteed federal protections and rights by instituting the Consumer Advisory Board, and later the Consumers' Counsel. Designed to safeguard consumers from the profit driven motives of private industry, these consumer advocacy organizations successfully lobbied for protections against credit lenders, dangerous products, deception, and other health and safety risks.

The practices of constructing consumer issues as matters of the public interest continued through World War II, as mandated rationing and price controls – particularly in the United States – equated consumption practices with one's civic or patriotic duty. Women in particular took up the role of consumption managers to serve the war from the home front by actively reorganizing their shopping routines around government restrictions placed on commodities such as sugar, tires, and gasoline. Mobilizing around responsible consumption in times of war, famine, or other disasters paralleled the social contract of democratic citizenship, whereby the "good citizen" willingly relinquished certain rights, impulses, or desires for the benefit of the greater good. In the 1960s–1970s, Ralph Nader spearheaded similar reforms to the mid-twentieth-century consumer advocacy efforts; his exposé of the US automobile industry's poor safety record famously ignited widespread movements around corporate and state accountability to consumers. The grassroots investigative work of "Nader's Raiders" lobbied Washington on behalf of consumers to successfully overhaul the Federal Trade Commission, helping to create new consumer protection agencies and driving the passage of new environmental, food, and public safety laws.

Beyond issues of rights, protections, or even good citizenship, consumption has also been historically leveraged as a political tool by marginalized segments of the population as a gateway to accessing full political, economic, and social rights. Women in nineteenth-century Europe and the United States, for example, engaged the rituals of shopping and consumption as a means of liberation from both the doldrums of domesticity and the confines of patriarchal gender relations. As twentieth-century industrialization democratized access to the marketplace through the availability of cheaper goods, the shift to mass consumption also enabled the working and the emerging middle classes to symbolically participate in the lifestyles once reserved for social elites and aristocrats. Immigrant populations, similarly, saw mass consumption as a pathway to cultural assimilation; the strategic purchase of domestic goods became a sign of national loyalty, patriotism, and a means of accessing the full rights of citizenship.

Political and economic behaviors converged again in the growing postwar struggle for racial equality during the twentieth-century Civil Rights movement. African American soldiers returning from war, who had just risked their lives for freedoms to which they were not entitled, helped catalyze the movement's widespread protests against racial segregation. Civil rights activists used the market strategically to demand recognition, rights, and access to the public sphere via boycotts and lunch counter sit-ins at whites-only establishments, and through their investments in cooperative models and minority owned businesses. Importantly, these tactics were not anti-capitalist or even anti-consumption, but rather treated the market as a site where obtaining the rights of democratic citizenship could be achieved.

A period of post-World War II affluence further leveraged the market in socially productive ways as citizens approached mass consumption as a means of expanding and distributing economic prosperity to all members of society. This approach integrated consumption with the promises of democratic freedom, the idea being that increased consumption created more jobs and thus elevated the financial security of all citizen-consumers equally. In the decades that followed, however, the need to keep consumption rates commensurate with new production efficiencies drove a consumer culture that altered the ways in which consumer citizenship has been previously articulated. Commodities came to provide new meaning and connection as traditional sites of community and identification dissolved alongside an increasingly mobile and global society. Whereas labor politics, class affiliation, or geography once served as a primary site of social identification, the mass segmentation of consumers into marketable demographics helped fill this new void by reframing consumption away from the goals of economic egalitarianism toward a practice centered on fulfilling individual desires as a central task of meaning making and identity.

By the 1970s, sweeping deregulation, privatization, free trade, and other market reforms further altered the relationship between citizenship and consumption. These changes were largely informed by the shift from a Keynesian model of deficit spending toward the neoliberal framework of market liberalization. Influenced by the economic theories of Friedrich Hayek and Milton Friedman, this paradigm extolls the virtues of an unfettered marketplace free from government regulation. Positing that public needs are met most effectively and efficiently through private enterprise, the government's primary responsibility to a free society is to foster the appropriate conditions necessary for competition. In accordance with the logic of classical liberalism, the application of free market principles to social life presents the responsibilities of citizenship in consumerist terms.

An emphasis on rationality, free choice, and personal responsibility has thus rearticulated economic choice as the primary expression of political will and desire; where one dollar equals one vote, a universal or common consumer interest now undergirds popular conceptualizations of citizenship. Accountable for the decisions freely made in a marketplace of unlimited choice, the ideal consumer becomes synonymous with the good citizen as one who empowers both herself and her community through the purchasing decisions she makes. This version of the good citizen – the citizen-consumer – is someone who maximizes the self not through society or collective action, but through private and individual choices made in the spheres of lifestyle and consumption. Unlike post-New Deal citizens who engaged government as an ally for the purpose of harnessing consumption to elevate the greater social good, contemporary citizen-consumers engage government with the same economic rationality as is brought to the market. To summarize: whereas the citizen-consumer was at one time constructed by a set of collective or shared goals, contemporary notions of good citizenship are defined by the individual choices one makes in the marketplace.

The turn toward responsible consumption as self-empowerment which emerges in the context of market liberalization and privatization simultaneously explains (as it also enables) the rise of corporate social responsibility (CSR) in recent years. As state investment in social services and welfare programs declined through the 1980s and 1990s, the corporate citizen stepped in to fulfill some of the roles previously performed by the state. Corporate social responsibility is typically deployed as an umbrella term for private initiatives or investments that go above and beyond the goals of profit making to foster ethical business practices, a positive environmental impact, or some larger social benefit. Ethical and ecological initiatives are one of the most common forms of corporate social responsibility to emerge since the turn of the twenty-first century, illustrated by companies as wide-ranging as Starbucks, Twenty-First Century Fox, Dawn, and BP. Mass recycling programs, green products, hybrid automobiles, and other innovations designed to reduce individual and industrial carbon footprints have, somewhat paradoxically, helped create a new mass market for sustainable goods. As many critics argue, corporate environmentalism merely "greenwashes" issues like climate change and is not enough to reverse the long-term ecological damage to the planet. From this perspective, ethical consumption may not be so much a sustainable way of facilitating real social or environmental benefits as it is a way for companies to build brand loyalty and more consumption. After all, the proliferation of green products is not about limiting consumption but rather about overconsuming new *kinds* of products, reinforcing the belief that such issues can in fact be better resolved through shopping than through government regulations or structural reforms.

One of the most common CSR initiatives that bridges civic virtues and consumption is cause related marketing (CRM); here, a mutually beneficial association is established between private firms and charitable or nonprofit organizations with the shared goals of generating revenue and awareness for both parties. As an avenue for political consumerism, CRM campaigns are often a private means of addressing social needs long deemed matters of public concern. One of the most financially successful and ubiquitous CRM campaigns, Susan B. Komen for the Cure, raises US$55 million annually for breast cancer research and awareness through global partnerships with firms as diverse as Yoplait, American Airlines, Dell, and *SELF Magazine*. Another popular CRM initiative, Product Red, has raised over US$210 million to help fight AIDS in Africa since 2006 by licensing its logo to popular brands like Gap, Motorola, and Apple. Office Depot's anti-bullying program and Starbucks' "Ethos Water" and "Shared Planet" environmental campaigns are other examples of how responsible, virtuous consumers direct their everyday purchases toward funding important social causes.

While these campaigns have certainly generated awareness and publicity for issues that might otherwise have gone unaddressed, cause marketing has also confronted its own share of backlash. On the one hand, critics have objected to the asymmetrical benefits between the sponsoring corporation and its funding recipients. For example, the Komen Foundation has been publicly criticized for the small percentage of funds it dedicates to "finding a cure" in comparison to the take-home salaries of its executive officers; Product Red's lack of funding transparency and exorbitant marketing costs have generated similar critiques. Others argue that CRM merely puts a "brand aid" on important social issues and is incapable of adequately addressing the structural inequities of wealth and power that undergird many of the global issues these campaigns aim to redress. Moreover, the industrial manufacturing processes or products behind many CRM campaigns are often responsible for the very problems that the sales are intended to ameliorate. Many of Komen's "pink ribbon" partners – including fast food chains and processed foods and cosmetics companies – sell products that contain the very harmful chemicals, carcinogens, and toxins thought to increase the risk of cancer. Further to these critiques are the negative implications that marketized philanthropy has for social issues deemed unmarketable, for example domestic violence, incest, and sexual abuse. This point raises questions about what types of causes or individuals in need are excluded when social and civic concerns cannot be monetized. Importantly, cause marketing thus highlights a primary tension that arises when consumption and citizenship are conflated: if every dollar spent is equal to a vote, then social groups privileged with more purchasing power inevitably have more political power to effect the types of changes they deem worthy. As decreased public funding continues alongside the increase in privatized welfare, social organizations must orient their image so as to attract private investment rather than the citizens they are designed to serve.

To be sure, contemporary forms of political consumerism exist that direct their aims a bit more explicitly at the redistribution of power and equality; the fair trade movement, for one, has been particularly successful in protecting workers' rights by persuading manufacturers and distributors of imported commodities to guarantee fair prices, safe working conditions, and living wages. Particularly in the developing world, some fair trade agreements have had positive material effects on low-waged workers. United Students against Sweatshops (United States), a national student labor organization with representation on over 150 US college campuses, has also successfully lobbied universities to cut their contracts with manufacturers that employed sweatshop labor in the production of university apparel. However, it is not just consumption that is equated with civic values; conversely, political processes too have come to be guided by the logic of consumer choice. Image management has become of central importance to voters over the past several decades and, for some voters, the carefully packaged personality of a candidate transcends his stance on important issues. In this sense, electoral politics has become increasingly difficult to distinguish from other forms of branding.

As political scientists have noted with some concern, the rising importance of political branding requires that electoral candidates conform to the logic of the marketplace in terms of how their message is sold to the citizen as a consumer of politics. Whether or not the reduction of politics into market spectacle negatively affects a deeper understanding of political issues is debatable. On the one hand, the careful packaging of political personalities may be able to generate interest in a way traditional politics has not succeeded in doing. One need look no further than US President Barack Obama's 2008 aspirational campaign platform of "Hope and Change" to see how making politics marketable helped capture the youth vote. On the other hand, this logic also encourages the passive consumption of social movements, for example armchair activism and "clicktivism." Moreover, political values have been opened up to commodification, as evidenced by the appropriation of anti-war songs in automobile TV advertisements, and the commercial use of iconic images of radical figures like Malcolm X and Che Guevara to adorn tee shirts, hats, and other merchandise. As the stuff of citizenship continues to be packaged in commercial form, and as citizens vote on image over information or issues, the long-term consequences of these practices for democracy become a question of pressing importance.

Whether or not political rights and identities can stand in opposition to the market continues to drive the debate over the political efficacy of consumer-citizenship today. Some research contends that citizens find consumption a more empowering way to promote social change than traditional democratic processes (e.g., voting). At the same time, critics blame the focus in consumer culture on the acquisition of material goods, self-interest, and individualism for civil society's decline. These latter criticisms, of course, are oftentimes based on false nostalgia for some ideal civic culture of the past that has likely never existed.

SEE ALSO: Ethical Consumption; Green Consumption; Politics and Consumer Culture; Socially Responsible Marketing (SRM)

REFERENCES

Cohen, Lizabeth. 2003. *A Consumer's Republic.* New York: First Vintage.

Rousseau, Jean-Jacques. 1947/1762. *The Social Contract.* Translated by Charles Frankel. New York: Hafner.

FURTHER READING

Mukherjee, Roopali, and Sarah Banet-Weiser. 2012. *Commodity Activism.* New York: New York University Press.

Soper, Kate, and Frank Trentmann. 2008. *Citizenship and Consumption.* Basingstoke, UK: Palgrave Macmillan.

Class

JACOB THOMAS and KJERSTIN GRUYS
University of California, Los Angeles, USA

Social class is an essential focus of analysis for scholars in multiple academic fields, including sociology, anthropology, cultural studies, and history. The term "class" refers to a mode of social stratification by which people are grouped into a set of hierarchical social categories. The word stems from the sixteenth-century Latin word *classis*, used by census takers to categorize Roman citizens by wealth. Groups of people have been categorized along many different lines throughout history and across cultures, such as by culture, caste, politics, nobility, or land ownership. However, by the late eighteenth century, the term "class" had largely replaced other classifications as the primary means of organizing society into hierarchical divisions.

Today, the term "social class" is commonly understood in vertical, relative terms of socioeconomic status, such as through the common three-stratum model, which includes (1) a very wealthy and powerful upper class of elites; (2) a middle class of professional workers, small business owners, and low-level managers; and (3) a lower class, who rely on frequently unstable and/or dangerous low-paying wage jobs for their livelihood, and who often experience poverty.

THEORIES OF CLASS

Theoretical and analytical conceptions of class generally align with one of two classic sociological perspectives: that of Marxism, which is associated with the nineteenth-century writings of Karl Marx, or that of structural functionalism, which is associated with the twentieth-century writings of Max Weber.

Marxist perspectives focus on class hierarchies as having emerged through conflict over power and resources, in which class status is based on a group's relationship to "the means of production." In *The German Ideology* (1972/1932) Karl Marx argued that class differences, whether they existed between serfs and feudal lords, or between industrial workers and factory owners, necessarily lead to material conflict between these groups. Marx's vision of class conflict predicts that revolution through class conflict will fundamentally restructure the organization of society. Marx applied this theory retrospectively to explain why capitalism emerged from feudalism, and also used it to predict that the working class would some day overthrow the capitalist order, replacing capitalism with a classless socialist society in which human needs rather than profit would motivate production.

Contemporary scholars influenced by Marx emphasized how class emerges through conflict between people as to what is valuable, and often focus on tensions within the class system that might destabilize it and lead to class conflict. For example, Melvin Tumin (1953) argued that only those in privileged classes are able to reproduce and protect their status by defining what skills are most valued in society, such that the disadvantaged are unable to demonstrate that they possess these skills. Critics of Marxist approaches to class conflict often argue that Marx's singular focus on economic relationships overlooks other ways that social groups may experience social inequality and conflict, such as by gender or race/ethnicity.

In contrast to the Marxist focus on conflict, inequality, and revolution, Weberian perspectives tend to emphasize how social class has the functional role of creating order and legitimacy within society. Max Weber challenges Marx's assertion that class position is determined by the means of production, arguing instead that class position is determined by a person's skills and education. He claimed that noneconomic forms of identity – such as those tied to culture, religion, and/or politics – *combined* with economic factors to shape class identities. In his essay "Class, Party, and Status" (1953) Weber conceptualized a three-component theory for understanding social hierarchies as the interplay between *class* (a person's economic position in society), *status* (a person's prestige, honor, or popularity in society), and *power* (a person's ability to influence change, despite the resistance of others).

Contemporary scholars influenced by Weber tend to view class as a consistent and stable category across space and time, and emphasize how class functions to create stability and authority in society. For example, Kingsley Davis and Wilbert E. Moore (1945) argue in "Some Principles of Stratification" that classes emerged such that people could consistently occupy needed positions and segments in society where they could contribute the most. By this logic, hierarchical classes ensure that society will maintain efficient and functional stability. Critiques of the Weberian perspective often argue that focusing on the function of hierarchical social classes ignores the important issue of increasing social inequality and decreasing social mobility.

Both Marx and Weber describe class inequality as undesirable. However, where Marx argued that class inequality would disappear only with the revolutionary dissolution of capitalism and private property, Weber believed that the solution to inequality lay in providing equal opportunity within a competitive capitalist system.

CLASS AND CONSUMPTION

Class status is closely tied to consumption practices, not only because spending power increases with wealth and resources, but also because consumption practices are tied to class identity and are linked to the reproduction of class inequality. Thorstein Veblen's (1994/1899) theory of conspicuous consumption speaks to consumption as an expression of class identity and status, such that economic wealth is translated into social status through the display of expensive leisure activities and ostentatious spending. Importantly, Veblen notes that individuals emulate the consumption practices of those above them in class status, causing a trickle down of high-status goods from rich elites through the middle class and finally into the lower class. This pattern of consumption becomes an ongoing fashion cycle as elites chase after the next new and expensive goods, after abandoning those that are no longer exclusively high status.

Pierre Bourdieu's (1984) theory of social distinction further links consumer preferences to the reproduction and legitimization of class hierarchies. Bourdieu defines social class along the lines of economic, cultural, and social resources, called capital. Economic capital includes income and assets; cultural capital includes one's cultural interests, purchases, and activities; while social capital includes one's social network. Adding nuance to Veblen's theory of trickle-down consumption practices, Bourdieu notes that class differences in consumer preferences (which he refers to as "tastes") are used by the dominant upper class to both distance themselves from the "tasteless" lower classes and to justify their own cultural dominance. Noting that one's aesthetic tastes are not inherent but are socially conditioned by class membership, Bourdieu contends that class inequalities appear to be the natural result of the lower classes' poor taste, when, in fact, dominant classes define legitimate tastes around their own consumption practices.

In the US context, inequality between class groups has steadily increased in the past several decades, as a small number of upper-class elite – increasingly referred to as "the one percent" – have acquired greater and greater control over economic resources. Future research on social class demands that scholars pay attention to the social processes and structures that either increase or decrease social mobility. There is also a demand for future research examining how class status intersects with other social statuses, such as gender and race/ethnicity, among others.

SEE ALSO: Conspicuous Consumption; Cultural Capital; Marx, Karl; Veblen, Thorstein

REFERENCES

Bourdieu, Pierre. 1984. *Distinction: A Social Critique of the Judgement of Taste*. Cambridge, MA: Harvard University Press.

Davis, Kingsley, and Wilbert E. Moore. 1945. "Some Principles of Stratification." *American Sociological Review* 10(2): 242–249.

Marx, Karl. 1972/1932. *The German Ideology*. In *The Marx–Engels Reader*, edited by Robert C. Tucker. New York: Norton.

Tumin, Melvin M. 1953. "Some Principles of Stratification: A Critical Analysis." *American Sociological Review* 18(4): 387–394.

Veblen, Thorstein. 1994/1899. *The Theory of the Leisure Class*. New York: Penguin.

Weber, Max. 1953. "Class, Status, and Party." In *Class, Status and Power*, edited by Reinhard Bendix and Seymour Martin Lipset. Glencoe, IL: Free Press.

FURTHER READING

Marx, Karl. 1972. *Capital: A Critique of Political Economy*. In *The Marx–Engels Reader*, edited by Robert C. Tucker. New York: Norton.

Parsons, Talcott. 2010. *Essays in Sociological Theory*. New York: Simon & Schuster.

Weber, Max. 2002. *The Protestant Ethic and the "Spirit of Capitalism": And Other Writings*. Harmondsworth, UK: Penguin.

Coca-Colonization

VANDER CASAQUI
Escola Superior de Propaganda e Marketing, Brazil

The term "coca-colonization" has no well-defined origin; it became visible with the publication of Reinhold Wagnleitner's book *Coca-Colonization and the Cold War: The Cultural Mission of the United States in Austria after the Second World War* (1994). Without a precise definition, the term refers to the process of the Americanization of culture, carried out mainly through the process of reconstruction of Europe after the destruction of World War II. As a major funder of this reconstruction, the United States expanded its influence in Europe, through the presence of military force, large corporations, consumer goods, and a diversity of cultural products, thus building hegemony adjusted to the new postwar times. In his book Wagnleitner elaborates a view of these phenomena through the evidence of the American presence in Austria, his home country.

The period post-World War II was the time of polarization of global power into two major blocs, under the leadership of the United States and the Union of Soviet Socialist Republics (USSR). The dispute between these two great powers, which remained until the fall of the Berlin Wall at the end of the 1980s, was marked by threats of nuclear attack from both sides, the space race, rivalry in sports competitions like the Olympic Games, and – especially in relation to consumer studies – by the cultural influence of these great powers on the countries that constituted their power blocs. Consumption was one of the most visible elements of the US presence, distributed on a large scale through the products of its culture industry (cinema and television series) and the goods and services produced by the food, clothing, technology, and other industries. Among the most readily identified products of American culture was perhaps its main symbol of consumption, the soft drink brand Coca-Cola.

The meaning of coca-colonization, in a wider reading, is related to the vision of a ubiquitous American presence, through the dissemination of goods, commodities, and the American way of life, as a new form of colonization, supported by a spectacular society, where the symbolism of consumption is seen as a form of power. In the world of global communication, the symbolic power associated with consumption is the target of clashes, not only in European societies, but also in Latin American and Eastern societies. In this context, youth movements and organizations of cultural resistance correspond, therefore, to the perspective of consumption as a symbolic territory of confrontation and political articulations.

Hardt and Negri (2000) developed the concept of *empire* to address the political, economic, and cultural transformations in postmodernity, and to show how notions of imperialism, biopower, and resistance correspond to this context. The authors address the globalization process which intensified after the collapse of the Soviet bloc, with the fall of the Berlin Wall, and discuss the influence of globalized empires, especially that of the United States, as a threat to the sovereignty of nation-states. The power of US hegemony, which transcends geographic boundaries, could overlap local sovereignties.

In this context, the recurring targets of local reactions in the face of this perception of threat – together with the economic crisis, political instability, lack of jobs, and the risk of cultural homogenization – are the symbols of global consumption. Because of its close identification with the American nation and its global expansion, the Coca-Cola brand is one of the most frequent targets of revolt groups and anti-globalization movements, in the micro-conflicts between hegemonies and counter-hegemonies that characterize the scene described by the authors.

The practice of culture jamming (according to Klein 2002), or the appropriation and subversion of the icons of global consumption to express criticism of the political and economic system they represent, is identified with the term "coca-colonization." In the contemporary context, a quick search in digital media allows you to access images from the iconic soft drink brand in a resignified form, shifted from the symbolic universe fueled by its advertising. For decades, the Coca-Cola brand has been associated with the image and the youth imaginary, in an intrinsic relationship with the imaginary of happiness; in the resignified images, the contesting spirit of youth demarcates its otherness. Slogans like "Enjoy Capitalism," "Enjoy Coca-Colonization," "Coca-Colonization Breeds Resistance," accompanied by images that reveal the hidden side of the imaginary of the brand, subvert the incitement to its consumption, once they turn into calls to resistance and opposition to the capitalist system, globalized culture, and consumer society. Other terms that relate to critical readings of global consumption, economic order, and imperialist logic that they represent are "McDonaldization" and "Starbuckization."

The backdrop to this process of assimilation and subversion of the signs of consumption is the social dynamics predicted by Mikhail Bakhtin's (1986) theory of language, where the sign is ideological, and its meanings are objects of symbolic disputes. Through the discourses produced in these disputes, it is possible to observe worldviews and rhetorical strategies of agents and powers represented in a society. The Coca-Cola brand is one of the privileged places for this observation; the term "coca-colonization" is a statement of the consumer's interest in political and social debate.

SEE ALSO: Consumer Resistance Movements; Culture Industries; Culture Jamming; Globalization and Consumption; McDonaldization; Starbuckization

REFERENCES

Bakhtin, Mikhail M. (Voloshinov). 1986. *Marxism and the Philosophy of Language*. Cambridge, MA: Harvard University Press.

Hardt, Michael, and Antonio Negri. 2000. *Empire*. Cambridge, MA: Harvard University Press.

Klein, Naomi. 2002. *No Logo*. New York: Picador.

Wagnleitner, Reinhold. 1994. *Coca-Colonization and the Cold War: The Cultural Mission of the United States in Austria after the Second World War*. Chapel Hill: University of North Carolina Press.

FURTHER READING

Debord, Guy. 1995/1967. *The Society of the Spectacle*. New York: Zone.

Flusty, Steven. 2004. *De-Coca-Colonization: Making the Globe from the Inside Out*. New York: Routledge.

Commodification

ALEXANDRA NUTTER SMITH
University of Washington – Tacoma, USA

Commodification refers to the process by which goods or services that were previously valued for their use are assigned an economic value and become exchangeable items (commodities). In capitalist societies, things like human labor, natural resources, and even cultural expression become tradable entities; frequently, relationships also take on commercial meaning. This exchange value is not something that is intrinsic to these goods and services, but is rather the result of the neoliberal drive to expand the circulation of capital. With origins in Marxist political economy, commodification has become an important concept in various scholarly applications of critical theory (including areas of inquiry such as sociology, feminist theory, environmental studies, and media studies). In social science and cultural studies, "commodification" is generally used interchangeably with "commoditization," although other areas may separate the two by defining "commoditization" as the process by which formerly distinct goods become homogenized in the eyes of consumers.

One effect of commodification has been an increasing focus on consumer activity rather than on production-side concerns, a phenomenon that Marx called commodity fetishism. In consumer culture, the conditions of producers and their labor are obscured in the exchange of goods and services, so that the meaning of goods and services is instead founded on the economic (or objective) value of a commodity in comparison to other commodities. This understanding of meaning, in turn, further encourages and legitimates commodification since the process generally goes unquestioned by consumers (a desirable situation for those who control the means of production and who thus benefit financially from maximizing the circulation of capital). The resulting logic of commodification – a characteristic of neoliberalism – has given rise to a society where commodities seem to be more important than workers.

In order to maintain this logic of commodification, radical ideas and images are stripped of their revolutionary meaning and instead imbued with monetary value. Expressions and artifacts that once held meaning as challenges to the dominant consumer culture or status quo are frequently co-opted and remade into commodities that reinforce the primacy of markets. For example, the music and fashion of Britain's subcultural punk scene originated in rebellion against an increasingly conservative British society in the mid-twentieth century. Over time the countercultural meaning of these artifacts was diminished as major record labels sought to sign punk bands and the punk aesthetic became integrated into mainstream fashion. The end result was not just a commodification of the artifacts in question but also the neutralization of a potential threat to the hegemonic commodity economy. Maintenance of social dominance through commodification is a characteristic of what Guy Debord called the "society of the spectacle," in which hegemonic culture sterilizes revolutionary sentiment and incorporates it back into the mainstream.

Less explicitly revolutionary elements of a culture can also be commodified. Generally, cultural expressions of marginalized or "othered" groups are appropriated by a dominant culture, where their context is obscured and they are assigned financial value. Examples of commodification of otherness abound, including the conversion of yoga from a spiritual practice to one that focuses primarily on physical exercise and values a particular fashion aesthetic, or the adoption of the images and sound of black soul, blues, and hip hop artists by white musicians. Feminist scholar bell hooks has described this process as "eating the other," and it legitimates the appropriator's dominance by offering this recognition of marginalized cultures as a sign of inclusiveness or progressive political change. In reality, however, commodification of the other rarely goes beyond the mere ascription of commercial worth.

In media studies, the function of mass communication as an instrument of commodification has been a topic of much theorizing and research. Not only are media texts themselves commodities, but the presence of advertising and consumerist ideology therein serves to support the process of commodification throughout society. Because media are a primary source of cultural pedagogy, consumers of media products "learn" the logic of commodification from a young age. Political economist Dallas Smythe suggested that audiences do "work" when they consume media texts, because they are exposed to various promotional messages and, more broadly, to pro-consumerist ideology. The audience becomes a commodity that media corporations can sell to advertisers, thus realizing a profit that in some cases exceeds the revenue generated from selling the media products themselves.

Critical environmentalists identify a trend toward the commodification of nature. Formerly, natural resources such as minerals, water, and clean air were not considered commodities, but the expansion of capitalism has led to these resources being reimagined as carriers of monetary value. Nonhuman animals are used for food, clothing, and product testing. Even genetic material becomes a commodity when corporations attempt to patent genetically modified organisms. When access to such resources is limited to those who have the financial means to acquire them, commodification reinforces or exacerbates social inequality.

As with any hegemonic force, commodification is constantly being contested and negotiated by those who resist – either in whole or in part – the social status quo. Igor Kopytoff suggests that one such site of negotiation is any society's collective decision to identify some artifacts as singularly unique, either because they are powerful symbols of power or are in some way sacralized; such items cannot be traded for anything else and are thus noncommodifiable. (Kopytoff, it should be noted, uses the term "commoditization" rather than "commodification.") The gift economy, wherein the circulation of goods is fluidly based on altruism rather than transaction, is also a resistant force. An example of an experimental and radical gift economy in the United States is the annual Burning Man event, during which a city of 69,000 people is collectively built and disassembled in the Nevada desert. The community is guided by an ethos summarized in 10 principles, including gifting and decommodification. While at Burning Man, participants freely share things that are heavily commodified in mainstream society, including food, music, other services, and trinkets. Future scholarly work on commodification will be likely to focus on digital media and online communities. The dynamic and interactive characteristics of Web 2.0 have expanded the opportunities for the exploitative commodification of labor. In particular, those who participate in social media (such as Facebook, Pinterest, or Tumblr), upload content to video sharing sites like YouTube, or provide consumer reviews (on commercial sites like Amazon or Zappos) are doing unpaid work that ultimately benefits those who control these outlets. Additionally, information and personal data have also been subjects of commodification as those with the means to do so have monetized them. Another potential application of this concept is in the continued study of so-called conscious or compassionate consumerism, where consumers seek to uncover at least some of the conditions of production with the intent of rewarding those that are less environmentally damaging or socially inequitable (for example, the movement to end sweatshop working conditions or the desire to purchase organic food items). In these cases, it is precisely the concern over buying more just or eco-friendly products that is commodified, often resulting in the ascription of a higher market value.

SEE ALSO: Burning Man; Commodities; Commodity Fetishism; Consumer Culture; Consumption, Spectacles of; Debord, Guy; Gifts; Marx, Karl

FURTHER READING

hooks, bell. 1992. *Black Looks: Race and Representation*. Boston, MA: South End.

Kopytoff, Igor. 1986. "The Cultural Biography of Things: Commoditization as Process." In *The Social Life of Things: Commodities in Cultural Perspective*, edited by A. Appadurai, 64–91. Cambridge, UK: Cambridge University Press.

Marx, Karl. 1990/1906. *Capital*. Vol. 1: *A Critique of Political Economy*. New York: Penguin.

McAllister, Matthew P. 1996. *The Commercialization of American Culture: New Advertising, Control, and Democracy*. Thousand Oaks, CA: Sage.

Smythe, Dallas W. 1981. "On the Audience Commodity and Its Work." In *Dependency Road: Communications, Capitalism, Consciousness, and Canada*, 22–51. Norwood, NJ: Ablex.

Commodities

LUCA M. VISCONTI
ESCP Europe, France

In its wider and current sense, a commodity is any material (product) or immaterial (service, experience, and brand) artifact with a value (functional, symbolic, and/or hedonic) that is produced and eventually traded on the market and made consumable for either companies or end consumers. Marx (1967/1867) proposed a threefold articulation of such value: the value of the incorporated labor, the value in use, and the subsequent value in exchange generally reflected by the market price of the commodity.

In line with its Latin root *commoditas* – meaning advantage, convenience – a commodity is an object that is expected to benefit whoever consumes it, individually or collectively. However, assuming that notions of commodity and benefit implicate each other is the basis of an enduring theoretical confrontation.

On the one hand, the established approach to commodities reflects the perspective of liberal economics and the cognitive sciences. By adopting an engineering driven, analytical, and rational perspective, they corroborate the idea that commodities are marketable objects aimed at satisfying human wants and needs. Within this frame, commodities are usually defined narrowly to indicate those goods that customers perceive as banal, undifferentiated, and standardized (Kotler and Keller 2012). Examples can be raw materials, components, low differentiable products/services, and goods in an advanced life cycle stage. Stemming from this perspective, scholars observe that commodities have implications for both customers and producers. Customers tend to have a simplified decision-making process (price driven, low involvement, routine bound), demonstrate low loyalty, and live a diminished consumption experience since commodities are centered on features and benefits (Schmitt 1999) more than on singularized personal meanings (Appadurai 1986). Because of presumed high product substitutability, producers of commodities see their competitive advantage eroded, have to align prices, and therefore enjoy limited profit margins. Strategies to cope with the "commodity trap" (Kotler and Keller 2012, 311) include, at an industry level, collective actions and, at a company level, attempts at differentiation via branding, co-construction, relationship management, and innovation to avoid commodification.

On the other hand, a critical perspective on commodities, which is rooted in sociocultural and postcolonial studies, contends that consumer culture does not aim to liberate human beings from their wants and needs. Instead, its purpose is to subjugate them to an endless chain of insatiable desires (Belk, Ger, and Askegaard 2003), the reason being that in Western consumer culture subjectivity is tightly constructed through the goods we consume (Belk 1988). Within this framework, commodities are defined extensively to incorporate each and every consumable object traded on the market. Thus, they are a synonym for material goods and constitute the outcome of commodification. The sociocultural notion of commodities is therefore broader, at a consumer level (thus excluding industrial markets), and embedded in ideological meanings. The critique advanced by these theorists is twofold. First, in line with Marx (1967/1867), they attack commodity fetishism, that is, the psychological and emotional dependence that consumers may show for commodities (Ellis et al. 2011), and envision a liberatory revolution that has already surfaced in forms of consumer resistance, voluntary simplicity, and social movements around the globe (e.g., Adbusters, the Freecycle Network, the Burning Man, and many more). Second, and more radically, they contest the fact that commodification has progressively incorporated all the domains of social life. Among others, gender, ethnic, family, religious, sexual, professional, and generational cultures are all reified (i.e., commoditized) and become exchangeable on the market (Slater 1997).

Future research has the responsibility to advance current understanding about: (1) the possible effects – individual as well as societal – of any successful attempt to defetishize commodities (Coles 2011); (2) how emergent systems of ownership (sharing, in particular) intersect commodities; (3) how commodities may sustain transformative practices, improving personal and collective well-being – a concern that stands at the heart of the *transformative consumer research* stream (Mick et al. 2012); (4) the role of commodities at the bottom of the pyramid; and (5) the contextualization of commodities in different market cultures, including the transnational aspects tied to the global commodity chain (GCC).

Over six centuries, the term "commodity" has become a battlefield for multiple disciplines and rival ideologies. By interrogating its definition, it is possible to examine the progressive stratification of Taylorism and its concern for the efficiency of production; the amelioration of the material life of societies entering, and leaving, the industrial revolution; the Marxist critique; and the postcolonial contestation unveiling the domination of the most developed countries over the developing world. As such, while progressively fragmenting into a plethora of meanings, the notion of commodity has acquired a pejorative valence that addresses either low involvement, standardized consumer goods or the excesses of materialism.

SEE ALSO: Anti-Consumption Tactics; Capitalism; Commodification; Commodity Fetishism; Consumer Culture; Consumption and Identity; Cultural Studies; Marx, Karl

REFERENCES

Appadurai, Arjun, ed. 1986. *The Social Life of Things*. Cambridge, UK: Cambridge University Press.

Belk, Russell W. 1988. "Possessions and the Extended Self." *Journal of Consumer Research* 15: 139–168.

Belk, Russell W., Güliz Ger, and Søren Askegaard. 2003. "The Fire of Desire: A Multisited Inquiry into Consumer Passion." *Journal of Consumer Research* 30: 326–351.

Coles, Benjamin. 2011. "Commodities." In *Encyclopedia of Consumer Culture*, vol. 1, edited by

Dale Southerton, 214–218. Thousand Oaks, CA: Sage.
Ellis, Nick, James Fitchett, Matthew Higgins, Gavin Jack, Ming Lim, Michael Saren, and Mark Tadajewski. 2011. *Marketing: A Critical Textbook*. London: Sage.
Kotler, Philip, and Kevin Lane Keller. 2012. *Marketing Management*, 14th ed. Harlow, UK: Pearson.
Marx, Karl. 1967/1867. *Capital: A Critique of Political Economy*. Vol. 1: *The Process of Capitalist Production*. New York: International Publishers.
Mick, Glen D., Simone Pettigrew, Cornelia Pechmann, and Julie L. Ozanne, eds. 2012. *Transformative Consumer Research for Personal and Collective Well-Being*. New York: Routledge.
Schmitt, Bernd H. 1999. *Experiential Marketing: How to Get Customers to Your Company and Brands*. New York: Free Press.
Slater, Don. 1997. *Consumer Culture and Modernity*. Cambridge, UK: Polity.

Commodity Chains

THOMAS C. BURR
Illinois State University, USA

Commodity chains constitute the underlying socioeconomic structures of economic globalization. Scholars use the metaphor of a chain to describe the complex series of steps in the production and distribution of a given product. Terms for these phenomena abound: sociologists examine "commodity chains"; marketers study "supply chains"; geographers analyze "production networks"; and French agricultural economists research *filières* (Gereffi 2005; Bair 2009). Increasingly scholars use the term "value chains" to emphasize the added value at each stage: usefulness for consumers and profit for producers. Despite this terminological proliferation, the term "commodity chain" is best known.

World system theorists originally argued that commodity chains constitute the individual strands of the capitalist world economy (Bair 2009). Gereffi and Korzeniewicz (1994) developed this concept further, originally defining three levels of analysis, then adding a fourth. For any particular chain, the first issue is analyzing the input–output structure – the series of steps taken to make that commodity. Minimally there are four stages: raw materials production, manufacturing, distribution, and consumption. In practice, each stage has many substages; for instance, manufacturing can involve parts production and assembly. The second issue is territoriality, the locations through which the chain moves. Transformations in communications and transportation technologies since World War II, including satellite technology, the internet, containerization, and port upgrading, have dramatically reduced shipping costs, making possible the global dispersion of production, distribution, and consumption for many products (Gereffi 2005; Dicken 2011). While commodity chains can operate on local, regional, or national scales, most published research is on global commodity chains (GCCs), focusing on assembled products such as automobiles and electronics or on tropical products consumed mostly in temperate zones such as chocolate, coffee, and tea. The third issue is governance; scholars focus on the *lead firm* which coordinates and has the most power over the entire chain, and which usually profits the most from it. Finally, Gereffi later acknowledged that institutional environments structure GCCs.

Most research focuses on the third issue, lead firm governance. Originally, Gereffi and Korzeniewicz (1994) suggested a twofold typology. *Producer driven* chains or networks are traditional structures of early capitalism. Manufacturers control production and distribution; such a system could consist of raw materials companies, large manufacturers, wholesalers, and small retailers. These scholars argue that large retailers (not end consumers) as buyers have increasingly superseded producer driven chains since the late nineteenth century. In the 1860s department stores were the first large retailers; chain stores continued the trend in the 1890s; and "super" markets continued retail innovation in the 1930s (Hamilton, Senauer, and Petrovic 2011). Thus, the post-World War II globalization of commodity chains by *big-box* retailers such as Walmart, Target, and Home Depot represents an intensification of long trends in the development of buyer driven chains. In either type, the driving firm tends to be a transnational corporation (TNC).

Much research attempts to analyze the wide variation in GCCs. Recently Gereffi, Humphrey, and Sturgeon (2005) have suggested that three variables – transaction complexity, codifiability of information, and capability of suppliers – lead to a continuum of five types of increasingly enmeshed relations between firms along the chain. Arm's length or market-based transactions involve firms trading mostly through simple, easily changeable transactions. In modular networks, suppliers produce complex products through generic machinery. Relational networks consist of mutual dependence between suppliers and buyers, while in captive networks suppliers are very dependent on buyers. Finally, in vertical integration one company simply owns and controls enterprises along the entire chain.

While research on commodity chains' institutional environments could be developed (Bair 2009), some research already exists. Much focuses on how global political-economic institutions, especially the World Trade Organization, and regional intergovernmental associations such as NAFTA, MERCOSUR, and others, govern all firms (Schmitz 2004; Gereffi 2005). Other research analyzes the importance of national institutional environments for transnational corporations (Lane and Probert 2009; Dicken 2011); since GCCs regularly cross international borders, lead firm coordination is extremely complex. Most firms rely heavily on their home state (Dicken 2011) for international support, but these states' laws and traditions also constrain large firms. Finally, Neilson and Pritchard (2009) analyze regional producers' institutions in coffee and tea.

Commodity chain analysis has increasingly moved away from its neo-Marxist roots to the issue of economic development, about which world system theorists have always been extremely skeptical. Some note that globalization accomplished through GCCs can lead to the economic development of entire countries (Hamilton, Senauer, and Petrovic 2011), especially by *upgrading* or moving *down* the chain – for instance, instead of producing raw materials, companies will start processing, which allows them to capture more value (Gereffi 2005). East Asian countries have become a global *supply base* from which large retailers can order an increasing array of products, driven by demand in developed countries (Hamilton, Senauer, and Petrovic 2011).

Meeting demand, or what consumers want, is the entire purpose of commodity chains, yet attention to consumers has long been minimal. However, historians, sociologists, and geographers have begun to examine consumption. Dicken (2011) emphasizes the role of consumers. He argues that the flow of products and information from producers, and the flow of money and information from consumers, mean that chains are better termed *commodity circuits*. Recently sociologists have shown how consumer activism can influence the nature of the products that consumers purchase and use by influencing the behavior and structure of firms in commodity chains (Schurman and Munro 2009). Finally, historians of Latin America have recently applied the chain concept to different commodities over the last five centuries, analyzing how social influences on demand affect suppliers in chains devoted to such diverse products as tobacco, bananas, chocolate, and rubber (Topik, Carichal, and Frank 2006).

Many topics that relate to globalization and consumers also relate to commodity chains. The distribution of production overseas makes possible outsourcing, which has had devastating consequences on employment and income equality in rich, developed countries, but also resulted in extremely low prices to consumers for a wide range of products. The fair trade movement effectively creates alternative, socially just structures to mitigate the exploitation of labor in global commodity chains. However, while GCC scholars note the links between chains and these issues (Gereffi 2005), they rarely develop these links.

SEE ALSO: Capitalism; Commodities; Fair Trade; Globalization and Consumption; Outsourcing

REFERENCES

Bair, Jennifer. 2009. "Global Commodity Chains: Genealogy and Review." In *Frontiers of Commodity Chain Research*, edited by Jennifer Bair, 1–34. Stanford, CA: Stanford University Press.

Dicken, Peter. 2011. *Global Shift: Mapping the Changing Contours of the World Economy*, 6th ed. New York: Guilford.

Gereffi, Gary. 2005. "The Global Economy: Organization, Governance, and Development." In *Handbook of Economic Sociology*, 2nd ed., edited by Neil J. Smelser and Richard Swedberg, 160–182. Princeton, NJ: Princeton University Press.

Gereffi, Gary, and Miguel Korzeniewicz, eds. 1994. *Commodity Chains and Global Capitalism*. Westport, CT: Greenwood.

Gereffi, Gary, John Humphrey, and Timothy Sturgeon. 2005. "The Governance of Global Value Chains." *Review of International Political Economy* 12(1): 78–104.

Hamilton, Gary, Benjamin Senauer, and Misha Petrovic. 2011. *The Market Makers: How Retailers Are Changing the Global Economy*. Oxford: Oxford University Press.

Lane, Christel, and Jocelyn Probert. 2009. *National Capitalisms, Global Production Networks: Fashioning the Value Chain in the UK, US, and Germany*. Oxford: Oxford University Press.

Neilson, Jeff, and Bill Pritchard. 2009. *Value Chain Struggles: Institutions and Governance in the Plantation Districts of South India*. Oxford: Wiley-Blackwell.

Schmitz, Hubert. 2004. *Local Enterprises in the Global Economy: Issues of Governance and Upgrading*. Cheltenham, UK: Edward Elgar.

Schurman, Rachel, and William Munro. 2009. "Targeting Capital: A Cultural Economy Approach to Understanding the Efficacy of Two Anti-Genetic Engineering Movements." *American Journal of Sociology* 115(1): 155–202.

Topik, Steven, Carlos Carichal, and Zephyr Frank, eds. 2006. *From Silver to Cocaine: Latin American Commodity Chains and the Building of the World Economy, 1500–2000*. Durham, NC: Duke University Press.

Commodity Fetishism

MATTHEW P. MCALLISTER
Pennsylvania State University, USA

"Commodity fetishism," a term coined by Karl Marx in *Capital*, has been expanded beyond the commodity itself in consumer culture studies to apply to issues of branding, advertising, and media economics. The concept has arguably become more relevant in an era of integrated marketing, licensing, and digital media.

For Marx, commodity fetishism referred to how the social relations and production processes of a thing, including the dynamics of labor, were masked by commodification, thus decontextualizing the commodity and making it seem autonomous from its means of production. In commodification, relations between people are hidden, while relations between things become naturalized.

Describing this process as "transcendent," "metaphysical," "mysterious," "fantastic," "magic," and "necromancy," Marx borrowed the fetishism metaphor from religion. He saw a fetish as analogous to a totem, which becomes infused with supposed magical qualities, a construction that denies its human origins (Marx 1967/1867, 76–81). The masking of production contexts and the resulting perception of the commodity's autonomy and agency may be viewed as a "double mystification" (Mosco 2009, 131). In this sense, the concept has an intrinsic ideological component.

As Jhally (1987) notes, Marx wrote of this process before the development of image-based advertising and advanced consumerism. However, with the gap in meaning inherent in industrialized commodities, characteristics of consumer culture both accentuated the deflection from the production context and filled this contextual gap through the added symbolic meaning provided by branding and advertising, thus emphasizing the agentic power of the commodity even more.

Traditional advertising very rarely discusses production elements of brands and products, but instead focuses on consumption orientations. Thus the *externalities* of production – or the social costs of production including labor and animal policies, the support of oppressive corporate and governmental regimes, and the environmental impact – are for the most part downplayed and ignored in advertising. Trends in green marketing may be more likely to highlight production elements (e.g., using recycled materials) than traditional advertising, although even then the emphasis in green advertising is often on appeals to environmentally friendly consumption practices (energy-efficient use) rather than on production practices. A fetishistic quality may also be said to be inherent in the political economy of traditional advertising-supported media, especially commercial broadcast television, given that audiences serve as a form of labor power through exposure to advertising (and are subsequently sold to advertisers via television ratings). This is an audience commodification process that is naturalized as pure entertainment.

Commodity fetishism as discussed by critical advertising scholars also highlights what Raymond Williams called advertising's qualities as a "magic system," a metaphor that fits nicely with the idea of a fetish. Here the production context gap of commodities is filled with claims about symbolically constructed attributes when commodities are sold and marketed as brands, even beyond their material function. As Williams (1980) famously wrote, advertising plays up the nonmaterial promises of brands since "society is quite evidently not materialistic enough" (p. 185). Stated in a Marxian way, then, advertising symbolically constructs the social and cultural attributes of material products to enhance their *use value* through increased *brand value* (and, ultimately, also increasing exchange value). By connecting brands to social values and desires, it is hoped that consumers will believe that the acquisition of brands will offer these social benefits. An advertisement for a brand of paper towels may not just tout its ability to clean a spill, but also demonstrate how its use may lead to, or at least is consistent with, good motherhood.

Commodity fetishism influences or is concordant with a variety of work in consumer culture. The concept is central to Debordian "spectacle" (Debord 1995/1967) given the decontextualizing and totalizing nature of both phenomena. Naomi Klein's 1999 book *No Logo* arguably pointed to a crisis of commodity fetishism in the 1990s, although the term itself is never mentioned in the work.

The book highlights the disconnect of image-based brands that emphasize empowering messages in their advertising (i.e., the Nike brand slogan "Just Do It") while simultaneously engaging in especially exploitative globalizing labor practices. The subsequent anti-corporate protests and pranks, while not necessarily enduring, signaled a boiling point in the disconnects and injustices of fetishization.

Commodity fetishism has also been applied to such diverse modern phenomena as mobile phones (McGuigan 2009), media licensing (Meehan 1991), and integrated marketing/digital media (McAllister 2011; Fuchs 2012). The latter focuses on the increased branding tools that the internet and social media introduce, enabling marketers to create sophisticated digital worlds of branding symbols and to expand the reach and narrative power of advertising icons and campaigns. The increased emphasis on database and personalized marketing may increase the symbolic power of brands as appeals are refined and molded for individual consumer proclivities. At the same time, the production and distribution power of digital media empower critics to highlight exploitative labor practices and the hypocrisy of advertising.

SEE ALSO: Advertising; Commodification; Consumer Resistance Movements; Debord, Guy; Marx, Karl; Williams, Raymond

REFERENCES

Debord, Guy. 1995/1967. *The Society of the Spectacle*. Translated by D. Nicholson-Smith. New York: Zone.

Fuchs, Christian. 2012. "Towards Marxian Internet Studies." *tripleC: Communication, Capitalism & Critique* 10(2): 392–412.

Jhally, Sut. 1987. *The Codes of Advertising: Fetishism and the Political Economy of Meaning in the Consumer Society*. New York: Routledge & Kegan Paul.

Klein, Naomi. 1999. *No Logo: Taking Aim at the Brand Bullies*. New York: Picador.

Marx, Karl. 1967/1867. *Capital: A Critique of Political Economy*. Vol. 1: *The Process of Capitalist Production*. New York: International Publishers.

McAllister, Matthew P. 2011. "Consumer Culture and New Media: Commodity Fetishism in the Digital Era." In *Media Perspectives for the 21st Century*, edited by Stylianos Papathanassopoulos, 149–165. London: Routledge.

McGuigan, Jim. 2009. *Cool Capitalism*. New York: Pluto.

Meehan, Eileen R. 1991. "'Holy Commodity Fetish, Batman!' The Political Economy of Commercial Intertext." In *The Many Lives of the Batman: Critical Approaches to a Superhero and His Media*, edited by Roberta E. Pearson and William Uricchio, 47–65. New York: Routledge.

Mosco, Vincent. 2009. *The Political Economy of Communication*, 2nd ed. Thousand Oaks, CA: Sage.

Williams, Raymond. 1980. *Problems in Materialism and Culture: Selected Essays*. London: Verso.

Commodity Racism

ELIZABETH CHIN
Art Center College of Design, US

The term "commodity racism" is most closely associated with McClintock's *Imperial Leather* (1995), in which she argues that, in the late 1800s, evolutionary and teleological formulations of racism were packaged into commodities. Mass production and distribution allowed these products and their embedded ideas to reach the masses in a way that scientific racism could not. Taking soap as her primary object of analysis, McClintock shows how seemingly innocuous products were imbued with deeply fetishized qualities, including the ability to confer racial uplift while simultaneously identifying the darker races as backward and in need of the care and attention of colonialist regimes.

Commodity racism, as defined by McClintock, is certainly one key manifestation of the intersection of race and commodification, but commodities and race intersect in other ways that are important and can be considered as commodity racism, particularly in the United States. Slavery itself must be understood as commodity racism since it was racism itself that justified turning people into commodities. The end of slavery provoked massive changes with regard to race, commodities, and consumption in the United States (Wilson 2005). As African Americans moved into the consumer sphere as agents and actors, ambivalence about these social and economic changes resulted in commodified cultural forms including the minstrel show and mammy memorabilia.

In the late nineteenth century, the practice of exhibiting native and indigenous people created a spectacle of race while commodifying the people on display and physicalizing the idea of racial hierarchy. Invariably those on display were labeled as both primitive and nonwhite. One of the most famous and contentious cases of such display involves the "Venus Hottentot," South African !Kung woman Sarah Baartman. More recently a number of scholars working in adoption studies have argued that Asian children, in particular, are racialized and commodified in specific ways by Western adoptive parents (Briggs 2012). Racialized stereotypes about Asian tractability and intelligence frame the construction of Asian children as attractive adoptees, and the adoption industry itself is increasingly commoditized. Furthermore, many adoptive parents make use of commodified and racially problematic markers of Asianness when teaching their adoptees about their natal cultures. New industries such as culture camps and heritage tours have emerged to fulfill the desire generated by the growing practice of transnational adoption. Mail order brides and sex tourism constitute additional ways in which social relationships are shaped by racist notions constructed through the commodification of people.

Commodity racism leverages commodities in service of racist agendas. Manring (1998) shows, in an analysis of Aunt Jemima, the degree to which white nostalgia for slavery was packaged and mass marketed through a pancake mix. Introduced shortly after the Civil War, Aunt Jemima drew on images of the prewar South as a place of gracious hospitality and loyal slaves. Although whites could no longer have slaves, Manring argues, they could have a slave in a box in the form of Aunt Jemima, whose backstory included choosing to remain with her master through thick and thin, and taking joy and pride in serving her pancakes to all visitors to the plantation. The familiar figures of Uncle Ben and Rastus (the smiling chef on the Cream of Wheat container) are examples of similar images that persist into the present. Globally any number of skin lightening creams and toothpaste brands use racial commodification as brand identities and selling strategies. These include Colgate-Palmolive's "Darkie Toothpaste," which until the early 1990s depicted a googly-eyed black caricature as its emblem. After much pressure, the brand name was changed to "Darlie" and the image was revised, though it remains troubling for many.

Commodity racism is deeply gendered. For girls, dolls have been powerful vectors for commodity racism. Bernstein (2011) views dolls as a means through which notions of race were commodified and performed. Whiteness for Bernstein is fundamentally constructed as one of "racial innocence," while the negative elements of guilt and badness are projected onto blackness. Using black and white dolls, children from the 1800s onward have been enmeshed in social dynamics that encourage them to perform and enact these dichotomies using dolls as actors in the larger social drama. Barbie, of course, is a key symbol of whiteness and commodifies race as well. This is something that black children understand quite deeply and they also understand that the ideologies built into their toys are part of the larger world around them (Chin 2001). In the realm of masculinity, commodity racism is increasingly an issue in the world of sports. Here black men are the commodities consumed by largely white audiences, producing huge sums of wealth, in addition to mass quantities of media imagery (Leonard and King 2012). It is worth noting that the cover of Leonard and King's volume features an image by the visual artist Hank Willis Thomas, whose work explores race and commodification.

Until recently, most work on commodity racism focused primarily on instantiations of whiteness or blackness. A group of papers brought together by King directly address commodity racism, covering a wide range of new ground, including Hawaii and Australia, expanding understandings of both race and commodification (Denzin 2009).

SEE ALSO: African Americans and Consumption; Asian Americans and Consumption; Brand Mascots; Commodity Fetishism; Latinos and Consumption

REFERENCES

Bernstein, Robin. 2011. *Racial Innocence: Performing American Childhood from Slavery to Civil Rights*. New York: New York University Press.

Briggs, Laura. 2012. *Somebody's Children: The Politics of Transracial and Transnational Adoption*. Durham, NC: Duke University Press.

Chin, Elizabeth. 2001. *Purchasing Power: Black Kids and American Consumer Culture*. Minneapolis: University of Minnesota Press.

Denzin, Norman K., ed. 2009. *Studies in Symbolic Interaction*, Vol. 33. Bingley, UK: Emerald.

Leonard, David J., and C. Richard King. 2012. *Commodified and Criminalized: New Racism and African Americans in Contemporary Sports*. Lanham, MD: Rowman & Littlefield.

Manring, M. M. 1998. *Slave in a Box: The Strange Career of Aunt Jemima*. Charlottesville: University Press of Virginia.

McClintock, Anne. 1995. *Imperial Leather: Race, Gender, and Sexuality in the Colonial Contest*. New York: Routledge.

Wilson, Bobby M. 2005. "Race in Commodity Exchange and Consumption: Separate but Equal." *Annals of the Association of American Geographers* 95(3): 587–606. doi:10.2307/3693958.

Conspicuous Consumption

JULIET B. SCHOR
Boston College, US

The term "conspicuous consumption" entered the sociological lexicon via Thorstein Veblen's biting analysis of the spending patterns of the rich and nouveau riche in the late nineteenth century. *The Theory of the Leisure Class* (1899) is an account of how these groups spent enormous energy and money constructing an ostentatious style of life. They built and decorated ornate homes, adorned their persons with clothing and jewelry, designed elaborate carriages, and employed large numbers of servants dressed in expensive uniforms. Throughout, the principles of waste, luxury, and ornamentation ruled the choices they made. The motive that animated their efforts was the desire for social esteem, which itself was dependent on the possession of wealth. But having money was not enough: it must be put "in evidence," or become conspicuous. Without a public display of superfluity, there is no socially sanctioned method of convincingly proving the size of one's bank account. That need for public display is caused by the combination of what contemporary theorists call moral hazard (a strong incentive to lie about how much money one has) with complex, unwritten rules of gaining social status (e.g., boasting is counterproductive, nonchalant display being the preferred method). Because these are ongoing features of wealth-based status systems, the concept of conspicuousness continued to be important long after the Veblenian era had passed.

The theory of conspicuous consumption is the centerpiece of Veblen's larger analysis of class society and its relation to styles of life and work. Relying on a stylized history of "savage," "barbarian," and "civilized" societies, Veblen argued that the emergence of classes in the barbarian era (roughly synonymous with feudal Europe and Asia) led to the use of wealth as the primary basis of males' social esteem, in contrast to military prowess. Wealth originally reflected booty gained in war but, over time, came to be valued for its own sake, even to the extent that inherited wealth was more valued than wealth gained through personal accomplishments. Veblen believed that the desire to attain status, or social esteem, eventually became the dominant motive in individuals' decisions about work and consumption, eclipsing even biological or physical pressures to consume.

In a status system based on wealth, the credibility and verifiability of individuals' claims to status become significant issues. Particularly before the era of paper money, wealth was not easily transportable, and ensuring its safety also militated against the public display of money itself. Therefore proxy measures of wealth holding developed, chief among them the abilities to forgo productive labor and to consume luxuriously, or what Veblen termed *conspicuous leisure* and *conspicuous consumption*. While status accrues in the first instance to the male head of household, wives and servants engaged in vicarious leisure and consumption. Their idleness and adornment with expensive jewels, furs, and livery are powerful testaments to the pecuniary position of their husbands and masters.

For both leisure and consumption, public visibility is central. In Veblen's day, when the rich gave elaborate dinner parties, they had their menus published in the newspapers. Today, expensive homes are pictured in popular magazines or television shows. This argument explains why furnaces are far less important as status goods than are watches, and why some people pay as much for a handbag as a mattress. There is a need to put spending "in evidence" because public display solves the informational problems associated with wealth-based status competitions.

In contrast to standard accounts of consumption as a functional and satisfying cultural expression, in Veblen's account there is a frustrating aspect to spending, because all status is positional and the goal of the game is to *waste*. The dynamic part of his theory involves the trickle down of status goods through the layers of the social hierarchy. The rich are the first adopters of new and expensive products. As incomes rise, groups farther down the social hierarchy mimic the spending patterns of those above them. Luxuries turn into necessities with lower status, because everyone owns them, and the rich move on to the next new or more expensive thing. Absolute increases in spending yield social value only when they improve relative position. When increases in the standard of living are general, they are like a treadmill, merely keeping people from falling behind.

SEE ALSO: Bourdieu, Pierre; Brands and Branding; Class; Cultural Capital; Veblen, Thorstein

REFERENCES

Bourdieu, Pierre. 1984. *Distinction: A Social Critique of the Judgement of Taste*. Cambridge, MA: Harvard University Press.

Campbell, Colin. 1994. "Conspicuous Confusion? A Critique of Veblen's Theory of Conspicuous Consumption." *Sociological Theory* 12(2): 34–47.
Schor, Juliet B. 1998. *The Overspent American: Upscaling, Downshifting, and the New Consumer*. New York: Basic Books.
Veblen, Thorstein. 1994/1899. *The Theory of the Leisure Class*. New York: Penguin.

Consumer Activism

JOSEPH J. TOHILL
York University, Canada

Consumer activism is the collective use of consumer purchasing power for political ends. It encompasses a wide range of actions by people who make consumption choices (about products and producers) with the goal of changing market or institutional practices and/or influencing corporate and public policymakers. The ultimate goal of consumer activists is usually to create what they see as a socially just marketplace or to redress some form of inequality within capitalist societies. They are motivated by either a concern for the larger public welfare (e.g., a desire to stop the harmful effects of agricultural pesticides on public health), or narrower private or personal interests (such as the effects of such pesticides on their immediate family), or both.

Philosophically, consumer activism is premised on a belief that consumption is an inherently political act embedded in a complex web of economic and social relations. This belief establishes a framework and prescription for collective action that make use of the market power of consumers. At times, consumer activists have called on consumers to take action to assist a group to which they belong (e.g., early twentieth-century housewives' cost-of-living protests), but more often they call for action from consumers on behalf of others (as in fair trade and anti-sweatshop campaigns). Recognizing the connections between their choices as consumers and labor rights, corporate behavior, the environment, and human rights, consumer activists practice a form of long-distance solidarity that links them not only to like-minded consumers but also to distant workers, employers, environments, and nations.

Consumer activism can serve a variety of political ends or causes, although it is mostly associated with liberal, social democratic, or progressive politics. Historically, it has been an important tactic in diverse social movements, including abolitionism, civil rights, gay rights, and environmentalism. However, consumer activism has also served nonprogressive causes, such as the Nazi boycott of Jewish businesses in the 1930s.

As a form of political participation outside of the realm of formal politics, consumer activism has opened up new arenas for citizen participation in public life. In fact, it calls into question the public/private divide that ordinarily defines what constitutes political participation because it recognizes seemingly nonpolitical or private arenas (such as the market or the home) as venues for political action. The traditional gender division of labor in capitalist societies has made consumer activism an important form of political participation for women, in particular. As low-risk political activity, it has also appealed to oppressed groups and those marginalized by traditional political systems and voting, such as African Americans denied the vote in the Southern United States under Jim Crow.

The most common form of consumer activism, the boycott, involves collectively shunning goods and services produced or sold by particular firms, industries, nation-states, or (on occasion) ethnic groups. Another common activity is the buycott, through which activists encourage the consumption of particular goods or brands for moral, ethical, or political reasons. Such actions have a relatively low threshold for participation; they usually require little personal sacrifice or risk.

Although consumer activism is commonly associated with the emergence of modern consumer capitalism in the twentieth century, it has a longer history dating back to the birth of consumer society in the eighteenth-century North Atlantic world. A notable early example was the boycott of British goods during the American Revolution. During the nineteenth century, disparate groups mobilized consumers' collective purchasing power for causes such as the abolition of slavery and the promotion of labor rights. Such groups, however, did not identify themselves as consumer activists.

Several factors in the early to mid-twentieth century – especially the increasing importance of consumption in everyday life, the shift toward the consumption-oriented economic theories most associated with the Keynesian revolution, and the maturation of consumer capitalism – fostered the growth of more self-conscious consumer activism and consumer groups and a focus on consumers themselves as the beneficiaries of collective action. Organized consumer movements emerged in many Western countries by mid-century and globally thereafter to protect and promote the rights of consumers.

Historically, consumer activism has been mostly associated with the affluent countries of North America and Western Europe, though it has also played an important role elsewhere (as in India's Swadeshi movement). The last three decades of the twentieth century witnessed a rise in consumer activism in the developing countries of Southeast Asia, Latin America, Africa, and the former Soviet bloc.

Successful consumer activism has often engendered fierce resistance. Notably, the growth and success of consumer activism globally in the 1960s and 1970s led to a backlash, particularly in the United States, from conservatives and corporate interests pushing an anti-regulatory agenda. This backlash blunted the social democratic agenda of the global consumer movement and narrowed its vision to a focus on freedom of choice in the marketplace rather than expanding market access to raise living standards. In recent years, corporate retail giants like Walmart have portrayed consumer activism as irrelevant and have promoted themselves as representing the consumer interest (narrowly conceived as price consciousness) through their enormous buying power.

In spite of this, scholars and commentators have noted a marked rise in consumer activism (increasingly referred to by social scientists as political consumerism) in the 1990s and early twenty-first century. Green and ethical consumerism, fair trade, socially responsible investing, culture jamming, and anti-sweatshop campaigns are among the dominant forms of consumer activism today.

The efficacy of consumer activism is often difficult to measure and therefore open to debate. Although many, if not most, consumerist campaigns such as boycotts fail or only partially achieve their stated goals, their success can also be measured by the degree to which they mobilize consumer citizens for collective action and publicize, popularize, and politicize causes.

SEE ALSO: Boycotts; Consumer Movements, Contemporary; Consumer Movements, History of; Consumer Resistance Movements; Culture Jamming; Ethical Consumption; Fair Trade; Green Consumption; Politics and Consumer Culture

FURTHER READING

Cohen, Lizabeth. 2003. *A Consumer's Republic: The Politics of Mass Consumption in Postwar America*. New York: Vintage.

Glickman, Lawrence. 2009. *Buying Power: A History of Consumer Activism in America*. Chicago, IL: University of Chicago Press.

Hilton, Matthew. 2009. *Prosperity for All: Consumer Activism in an Era of Globalization*. Ithaca, NY: Cornell University Press.

Micheletti, Michele. 2010. *Political Virtue and Shopping: Individuals, Consumerism, and Collective Action*, rev. ed. New York: Palgrave Macmillan.

Stolle, Dietlind, and Michele Micheletti. 2013. *Political Consumerism: Global Responsibility in Action*. Cambridge, UK: Cambridge University Press.

Tohill, Joseph, and Louis Hyman, eds. 2015. *Shopping for Change: Consumer Activism in North American History*. Toronto: Between the Lines.

Consumer Behavior

RUSSELL BELK
York University, Canada

It is only within the affluent consumer societies that have developed over the past century or so that consumer behavior could emerge as a research topic. Today our behavior as consumers is a key focus throughout the social sciences and humanities. It is of interest in disciplines and institutions ranging from governmental economic policy units to consumer goods corporations to academic departments of history, geography, anthropology, psychology, sociology, business, cultural studies, and others. But the term is most commonly associated with marketing departments in business schools, where consumer behavior courses are required and where consumer research dominates PhD dissertations and faculty research. It is the subject of many textbooks used in marketing, communications, and advertising departments of universities and, with a focus on journal articles and conference presentations, consumer behavior is most strongly represented in the *Journal of Consumer Research*, the *Journal of Consumer Psychology*, the conferences and publications of the Association for Consumer Research, the Society for Consumer Psychology, and the Consumer Culture Theory (CCT) Consortium. Attempts to understand consumer behavior differ in approach depending on whether the researcher favors the psychological side of the discipline or the more sociological and anthropological side, which has become attached to the CCT banner ever since a review article by Arnould and Thompson (2005) created this label. Both the presumed nature of the consumer and the methods used to investigate consumer behavior differ between these two groups of researchers, with the former being more experimental and the latter more ethnographic. They are therefore treated separately in this entry, with the greater emphasis on the CCT understanding of consumer behavior.

CONSUMER PSYCHOLOGY

In a review of consumer psychology by Loken (2006), the major research topics identified were categorization, inferences, affect, and persuasion. Categorization includes brand classification, goals and motivational bases for consumer judgments, and information processing. Inferences are said to be cognitive and experience-based judgments (e.g., judging product quality based on advertising, brand names, and product appearance). Consumer affect, or feelings and mental attitudes toward a brand or company, is generally regarded to be the key focal variable within consumer psychology and is studied as a surrogate for brand choice. Finally, persuasion is measured as brand attitude change resulting from various types of promotion. Taken together, these topics suggest that consumer psychology views the consumer as an information processor and decision maker deciding about brand purchases.

In a more recent summary of consumer psychology, Ariely and Norton (2009) focused on what they call "conceptual consumption." By this they mean that consumer behavior has shifted from consuming products like food to consuming concepts like the images of various brands of bottled water or automobiles. They consider four categories of conceptual consumption that affect choices: expectancies, goals, fluency, and regulatory fit. Expectancies involve the influences of what the consumer expects to experience; for example, a familiar brand name on a beer enhances our perception of its taste. Goals are held to influence consumer behavior in forming intentions (e.g., to exercise daily and eat a moderate number of calories in order to lose weight). Fluency involves the ease with which brand stimuli can be processed. Familiar and easily pronounceable symbols and brands, for example, are found to be regarded more favorably. Lastly, regulatory fit has to do with the degree to which goals and preferences are aligned with behavior. With high degrees of regulatory fit, consumers are found to devote more effort to information processing tasks and to better control their consumption behavior and avoid excess. Compared to the information processing orientation of Loken's (2006) review, the conceptual consumption research reviewed by Ariely and Norton (2009) tends to focus on behaviors more than attitudes. It is part of what is sometimes called judgment and decision-making research – an area of decision theory that is intent on showing the biases that lead consumers to make suboptimal choices.

Both variants of consumer psychology focus primarily on consumer brand choice as a function of information available. Both hold laboratory experimentation to be the epitome of good consumer research methods. Such research specifies and tests hypotheses by randomly assigning subjects (most often college students) to treatment conditions. Statistical analysis leads to supporting or rejecting these hypotheses. It has become common to report multiple 2×2 variable experiments demonstrating the hypothesized results in various ways and establishing factors that mediate or moderate the results, as well as showing boundary conditions where the effect no longer holds.

CONSUMER CULTURE THEORY

Consumer culture theory implies both an interest in the influence of culture on consumption and an interest in studying the consumption-centered life that has come to be called consumer culture. It is not, however, a theory. After publishing their position paper summarizing 20 years of consumer culture research in the *Journal of Consumer Research*, Arnould and Thompson (2005) clarified that they should have said "theoretics" rather than "theory" because they didn't mean to imply that a singular theory had emerged from the body of research they reviewed. In their initial article they detailed four areas into which existing CCT research may be categorized: consumer identity projects, marketplace cultures, the sociohistoric patterning of consumption, and mass-mediated marketplace ideologies (together with consumers' interpretive strategies). In contrast to the great majority of consumer psychology research, in all of these areas of research the specific in situ contexts in which the field research is carried out are important. CCT research methods typically include some combination of depth interviews, observations, and participant observation. Rather than the numerically scaled and measured variables of surveys and experimental research, the data of CCT research is normally words and images. As the title of the paper by Arnould and Thompson (2005) indicates, the field was already 20 years old when they wrote their survey. The event that marked the beginning of this period in 1985 and 1986 was a group of researchers who engaged in an extended field project called the Consumer Behavior Odyssey. While this project launched ethnographic methods within marketing departments in business schools, Sydney Levy and others had conducted research based on depth interviews and qualitative methods since the 1950s, and Ernest Dichter and others had begun qualitative "motivation research" about the same time. However, the academic legitimacy of CCT research was given a big boost by the Odyssey project and subsequently by the CCT article.

The first of the four areas of CCT research identified by Arnould and Thompson (2005), *consumer identity projects*, highlights the fact that, rather than averaging consumers together, CCT research pays attention to the meanings and understandings of each individual studied and aggregates findings over individuals only after this individual level of understanding has been achieved. Identity projects are forged from the marketplace of brands as consumers intentionally or unintentionally, knowingly or unknowingly, pursue aims of achieving a particular, if changing, ideal self or selves. Consumption objects and experiences are seen as expressive of individual and collective selves and may be vehicles that act as an archive of past personal and shared consumption histories. Illustrative here is work developing the concept of the "extended self," largely consisting of possessions and certain other people with whom we identify (Belk 1988). Jean Anthelme Brillat-Savarin said "Tell me what you eat and I will tell you what you are," and Ludwig Andreas Feuerbach simplified this to "Man is what he eats." The extended self goes farther and proposes that you are what you eat, wear, drive, watch, and otherwise consume, as well as the company you keep. This might also be taken as indicative of being a member of a consumer society or marketplace culture that values such consumption-based self-expression.

The marketplace cultures aspect of CCT research emphasizes the cultural influences on consumer behavior as well as the emplaced contextual locus of CCT research. This line of research also emphasizes the groups and communities that are variously termed consumption communities, brand communities, brand cults, brand tribes, idiocultures, microcultures, or subcultures of consumption. Examples include such diverse groups as Harley-Davidson owners' groups, *Star Trek* fans ("Trekkies"), and Apple enthusiasts. As these examples suggest, besides ethnically or geographically defined cultures, brand affinities, lifestyles, and leisure interests also define the cultural and subcultural groups of interest. Status, cultural capital, mythologies, rituals, age, and group identity are among the theoretical lenses used in such studies. Thus rituals like Christmas celebrations have become largely secular celebrations of consumption, and even anti-consumption festivals like Burning Man have failed to allow consumers to "escape the market." The rise, commercialization, and global spread of St. Patrick's Day, Mother's Day, Halloween, Cinco de Mayo, and Valentine's Day are also illustrative of the increasing interpenetration of consumption and cultural rites. Marketers have become the chief promoters of such expansion as a vehicle for selling ever more goods tied to these celebrations. And, because gift purchases and festival foods and drinks are typically more lavish and luxurious than everyday consumption, high-end consumer purchases are stimulated by such activity.

CCT work on the sociohistoric patterning of consumption most explicitly addresses the nature and effects of consumer culture. Specific attention to social class, gender, ethnicity, and family structure characterizes such studies. Postassimilationist studies of ethnic identities as mediated by consumption choices are a focus of studies of globalization. Resistance, hybridity, and "glocalization" are among the alternative strategies that immigrants and local cultures have been found to employ. Historical research on the emergence and spread of consumer culture is also a part of this category of CCT research. Critical theoretic and neo-Marxist views of consumption often take a sociohistorical view of consumption and emphasize that self-definition has shifted from production to consumption. At the same time, such research is likely to examine commodity chains of distribution that implicate consumers in the labor and resource bases of their consumption. Thus, for example, if running sneakers are made by child labor working under sweatshop labor conditions or diamonds are extracted by brutality and human exploitation, creating a consumer consciousness of these linkages is one of the objectives of such research. Such studies also consider the environmental and health effects of consumption activities.

The study of mass-mediated marketplace ideologies encompasses not only consumer interpretations of advertising and other mass communications, but also investigations of a variety of other ways in which marketplace ideologies are conveyed and fostered. These ideologies range from micro messages to buy this product or adopt that look to more macro messages to adopt a lifestyle or a general orientation to consume, participate in fashion, or subscribe to global consumption trends. Nonadvertising means of communicating such ideologies include retail "servicescapes," entertainment, music, fashion industry promotions, consumption spectacles and events, video games, and other aspects of popular culture. Consumers are increasingly seen as active agents or co-producers of such ideological activity rather than being seen as passive dupes. This agency includes ideological resistance, boycotts, "culture jamming," and word-of-mouth activity that often reworks and repurposes commercial messages. Thus, research in this area frequently employs not only semiotic and literary criticism perspectives but also audience response and critical theoretic perspectives. Examples here include work showing that consumer activists often disparage and alienate the consumers on whose behalf they are ostensibly working, and studies showing how Turkish women have turned stigmatized veiling practices, transforming these ostensibly modest garments into high fashion.

CONSUMER BEHAVIOR AS STUDIED IN OTHER DISCIPLINES

Consumer behavior and consumer culture have inescapably come to dominate the lives, hopes, and ambitions of the majority of the world's population. Consumption is to contemporary life what the Catholic Church was to life in the Middle Ages in Europe. As such, it is not surprising that consumption has become a significant topic for research and theorizing in a variety of disciplines. Historical studies of consumer culture in Europe were first inspired by Fernand Braudel (1982/1979) and have examined its development in an increasing variety of global locales (e.g., Brewer and Porter 1993). Both historical and contemporary consumption have attracted not only historians, but sociologists, anthropologists, and marketing scholars as well. For example, the precommunist history of consumer culture in China has been studied alongside contemporary Chinese consumption in the wake of the country's recent dramatic economic rise. Ottoman coffeehouses have been studied as crucibles of consumer culture. And nineteenth-century Mormon pioneer diaries have been studied to examine the role of possessions as memory markers in the covered wagon and handcart exodus of Mormons from the Midwest to the West.

Sociology has been interested in consumer behavior at least since Veblen's *The Theory of the Leisure Class* was published in 1899 and Simmel's (2004/1907) *The Philosophy of Money* was first published in 1907. A variety of consumption topics have been investigated within sociology, including the commodification of childhood in the clothing industry, urban consumption spaces, theme parks, food cultures, and globalization. The *Journal of Consumer Culture* is a sociology journal devoted to such consumption studies. Pierre Bourdieu's work on cultural capital as a basis for social stratification has been especially influential in recent consumer research.

The area of anthropology most devoted to contemporary consumer behavior is material culture studies, including the prolific work of Daniel Miller (e.g., 2010). There has also been anthropological interest in tourist behaviors as they impact both hosts and guests as well as virtual consumption in online worlds and games. The edited volume *The Social Life of Things* has been influential as well. Grant McCracken's (e.g., 1988) work also stands out in consumer anthropology. Alan Fiske (1991) is another influential anthropologist of consumption, although his work has had more impact in psychology than in material culture studies. The *Journal of Material Culture* specializes in such work. There is a related field of economic anthropology.

A variety of other disciplines also have some interest in consumption. They include economics, economic psychology (and its *Journal of Economic Psychology*), positive psychology, evolutionary psychology, clinical psychology, human and cultural geography, gender studies, cultural studies, and English literature. Other areas emerging with an interest in consumer behavior include neuroscience and human–computer interaction studies (e.g., Wood and Solomon 2009; Molesworth and Denegri-Knott 2012; Belk and Llamas 2013). The internet has not only provided new media for promotion and new avenues for selling and playing, it has also created more instantaneous, global, and interactive ways of being a consumer. In terms of the presentation of self, social media, blogging, photo and video sharing sites, and various consumer forums and rating sites have made the project of self-promotion much more intense and enveloping. These have also spawned seemingly addictive tendencies to participate for fear of missing out or appearing uninteresting. These addictive tendencies are also evident in massively multiplayer online role playing games (MMORPGs) and online gambling.

Among the topics of current interest across these disciplines are social media, online consumer behavior, globalization, materialism, and consumer well-being. As societies have opened up to consumption with the fall of the Iron Curtain, growing affluence, and increasingly global flows of goods, people, and ideas, it has been possible to examine both the positive and negative effects of growing consumer culture as well as cultural differences impacting these effects. Recent economic downturns, wars, and natural disasters have precipitated studies of downward consumption trends as well. And global warming and global pollution have highlighted our fragile environment and the significance of consumer culture in causing and addressing these critical human issues.

As a pervasive and defining phenomenon of contemporary life, consumer behavior has clearly attracted equally pervasive and widespread research attention. Whether it is intended to help marketers, consumers, the environment, or society understand its obsession with consumption, the study of consumer behavior is one of the most active areas of academic, business, and governmental research.

SEE ALSO: Consumer Culture; Consumer Culture Theory (CCT); Marketing/Marketing Science

REFERENCES

Ariely, Dan, and Michael Norton. 2009. "Conceptual Consumption." *Annual Review of Psychology* 60: 475–499.

Arnould, Eric, and Craig Thompson. 2005. "Consumer Culture Theory: Twenty Years of Research." *Journal of Consumer Research* 31: 868–882.

Belk, Russell. 1988. "Possessions and the Extended Self." *Journal of Consumer Research* 15: 139–168.

Belk, Russell, and Rosa Llamas, eds. 2013. *Routledge Companion to Digital Consumption.* London: Routledge.

Braudel, Fernand. 1982/1979. *The Wheels of Commerce.* London: Collins.

Brewer, John, and Roy Porter, eds. 1993. *Consumption and the World of Goods.* London: Routledge.

Fiske, Alan. 1991. *Structures of Social Life: The Four Elementary Forms of Human Relations.* New York: Free Press.

Loken, Barbara. 2006. "Consumer Psychology: Categorization, Inferences, Affect, and Persuasion." *Annual Review of Psychology* 57: 453–485.

McCracken, Grant. 1988. *Culture and Consumption.* Bloomington: Indiana University Press.

Miller, Daniel. 2010. *Stuff.* Cambridge, UK: Polity.

Molesworth, Mike, and Janice Denegri-Knott, eds. 2012. *Digital Virtual Consumption.* London: Routledge.

Simmel, Georg. 2004/1907. *The Philosophy of Money*, 3rd ed. Edited by David Frisby. Translated by Tom Bottomore and David Frisby. London: Routledge.

Wood, Natalie T., and Michael Solomon, eds. 2009. *Virtual Social Identity and Consumer Behavior.* Armonk, NY: M. E. Sharpe.

FURTHER READING

Slater, Don. 1997. *Consumer Culture and Modernity.* Cambridge, UK: Polity.

Stearns, Peter. 2001. *Consumerism in World History: The Global Transformation of Desire.* London: Routledge.

Consumer Cosmopolitanism

PETRA RIEFLER
University of Vienna, Austria

Consumer cosmopolitanism describes the extent to which a consumer: "(a) exhibits an open-mindedness towards foreign countries and cultures, (b) appreciates the diversity brought about by the availability of products from different national and cultural origins, and (c) is positively disposed towards consuming products from foreign countries" (Riefler, Diamantopoulos, and Siguaw 2012, 287).

The origins of the term cosmopolitanism, which consists of the words *cosmos* (world) and *politis* (citizen), date back to the early classical periods of Greek thought. Over centuries, the term has been used to describe individuals who break free from the boundaries of locality and who wish to distinguish themselves by a willingness to engage with and borrow from other cultures (Hill 1998). In a contemporary perspective, cosmopolitans are seen as people who identify themselves as members of a global community rather than a specific nation-state. These are people who tend to travel, to be unprejudiced, to be interested in the unknown, and to use broader reference frames of values than those of their local community. Importantly, this broader reference frame represents a reflective distance to the locality rather than an alienation. Cosmopolitan consumers are not disengaged from the city or village they live in: they can be involved in local activities and groups despite their global background.

Inspired by sociologists (e.g., Hannerz 1990; Holt 1997) who characterize cosmopolitans as consumers of the exotic, the other, the original, and the authentic, the concept of consumer cosmopolitanism has recently been introduced to literature which specifically focuses on the market-related activities of cosmopolitan individuals (Cannon and Yaprak 2002). Market-related activities, such as particular tastes and consumption choices, are used as a vehicle to express a cosmopolitan lifestyle. In particular, their open-mindedness renders cosmopolitan consumers receptive to ideas and habits from other cultures and nations which translate into their consumption choices. They distinguish themselves as consumers through their appreciation for diversity of market offerings as opposed to the sameness of contemporary global markets. Cosmopolitan consumers value the availability of culture-bound, small-scale, and regional products. While recognizing that ease of daily life delivered by global well-known brands thanks to consistent quality and service around the world, these consumers also opt for regional and unfamiliar products as these enable them to consume and experience the authentic. To achieve this consumption goal, cosmopolitan consumers purposefully go to off-touristic places, eat ethnic food, drink local beer, and try things they have never seen before. At home, they read foreign newspapers, watch foreign-language TV channels, or listen to cultural music (Riefler et al. 2012). These consumers are willing to accept some purchase risk as a trade-off for experiencing new or unfamiliar things and are therefore a target group for unknown, new, or innovative brands.

For marketers, consumer cosmopolitanism represents a psychographic segmentation base that can be used to target consumers in international markets. Such cross-national segmentation criteria are particularly relevant in the contemporary globalized marketplace, where companies try to match product attributes to customer attitudes, values, and lifestyles in multiple countries. Cosmopolitan consumers can be found around the world and constitute a growing segment, as more and more people are enabled to travel or connect virtually to the world outside their locality. Their demographic profile is young, well-educated, and residing in cities.

Regarding the question of what makes people and consumers cosmopolitan, literature agrees that the exposure to foreign cultures is central for cultivating open-mindedness. According to this view, a cosmopolitan orientation can be socialized and fostered by travel, life, or work abroad, and contact with people with diverse cultural backgrounds. However, the presence of a multicultural environment does not guarantee the development of a cosmopolitan orientation. Some authors suggest that a personal disposition to an open-minded orientation is contingent for becoming cosmopolitan. More research on drivers of cosmopolitanism will be needed to shed more light on antecedents as well as consequences of consumer cosmopolitanism.

SEE ALSO: Authenticity; Citizenship and Consumption; Global Markets; McDonaldization

REFERENCES

Cannon, Hugh M., and Attila Yaprak. 2002. "Will the Real-World Citizens Please Stand Up! The Many Faces of Cosmopolitan Consumer Behavior." *Journal of International Marketing* 10(4): 30–52.

Hannerz, Ulf. 1990. "Cosmopolitans and Locals in World Culture." *Theory, Culture & Society* 7(2): 237–251.

Hill, Jason D. 1998. "Creating the Self: Toward a Cosmopolitan Identity." PhD diss., Purdue University.

Holt, Douglas B. 1997. "Poststructuralist Lifestyle Analysis: Conceptualizing the Social Patterning of Consumption in Postmodernity." *Journal of Consumer Research* 23(4): 326–350.

Riefler, Petra, Adamantios Diamantopoulos, and Judy A. Siguaw. 2012. "Cosmopolitan Consumers as a Target Group for Segmentation." *Journal of International Business Studies* 43(3): 285–305.

FURTHER READING

Prince, Melvin, ed. 2012. *Globalization and the Cosmopolitan Consumer*. New York: Business Expert Press.

Consumer Culture

DON SLATER
London School of Economics and Political Science, UK

Consumer culture sits alongside several influential descriptions of modern Western society (such as media society, market society, mass culture) that attempt to sum up and evaluate the specificity of the modern West. The phrase therefore can be used in three different ways.

First, it can be used as a description of how consumption is organized in modern societies, and the importance of consumption to those societies. Consumer culture is usually invoked to argue that consumption has become centrally important to identities, values, social reproduction, political order, and much more, and that modern people live out their social lives more through their identities as consumers than as, say, workers or citizens.

Second, it can be viewed as discourses or debates through which people have articulated key concepts and issues in modern experience such as choice, freedom, individualism, needs and wants, value, and so on. In this sense, describing the modern West as a consumer culture might be a way of asserting a liberal vision of individual choice on the basis of uncontested private preferences (consumer sovereignty) or a way of arguing that collective political interests are being masked by individualistic fetishization of material things. In either case, consumer culture has provided an idiom through which to debate the central values and visions of modern life.

Third, the term can be considered as performative, in that consumer culture is neither the real social organization of consumption nor merely ideas about it; rather, the term has been central to the actual production of what it means to be modern, and to critical thought and practice. For example, political battles over public utilities such as electricity and water in nineteenth-century cities were fundamentally altered by recasting residents as consumers.

Underlying all three uses of the term is a distinction between consumption and consumer culture: consumption applies in general to the use of material and symbolic resources in the reproduction of social relations and practices, and can be treated as a necessary aspect of any social organization. However, consumption is organized differently in every social order, with different ways of relating production, distribution, and consumption, and different roles and meanings attached to often very distinct categorizations of consumption (e.g., ritual uses of things as opposed to mundane ones). Consumer culture, then, refers to a specific organization of consumption that is generally associated with the rise of modern Western commercial culture, or more recently with the rise of an affluent society that is strongly focused on purchased goods. By the same token, consumer culture is often associated with the globalization of the values and identities associated with Western (or specifically American) consumer culture to other regions, regarded either as a sign of progressive modernization or as a new form of (cultural) imperialism. This relates to a further confusion about the term: it is often treated as synonymous with consumerism, which has two entirely opposite meanings: consumerism means either an oppressive obsession with consumption and materialism (equating to a negative evaluation of consumer culture) or a desire to protect the consumer through regulation of products (hence to replace the values governing consumer culture with truth and rationality).

FEATURES OF CONSUMER CULTURE

Although the phrase itself is fairly recent (like consumer society, certainly not in use before the 1920s, and not common until the postwar period), we can trace its core components at least to the seventeenth century as battlegrounds for the forging of modern institutions and practices. Hence consumer culture is fundamentally defined by the presumed centrality of consumption to social life, and through this to the centrality of the role and identity of being a consumer. The claim implied in the phrase is that people derive their value, their social place and meaning, and their status through their capacity to act as consumers, and that they understand and organize their own capacities and projects in terms of being a consumer – such as their ability to exercise choice on the basis of knowledge of their own needs, of available goods and tastes, and of market prices and access to goods. The consumer identity may exist alongside other identities, but dominates and inflects them: I might also see myself as a father or an intellectual, but in a consumer culture those identities would also partly depend on my relationship to consumption values and consumer identities (e.g., in providing for my family or in relating to my students as choosing consumers). By the same token, deprivation, exclusion, and inequality are largely experienced, it is claimed, through lack of access to the material culture that will sustain a desired lifestyle and social participation. Only very extreme views have argued that people are reduced to the consumer identity in their entirety; more usually, consumer mentalities and values are seen as symptomatic of modern tendencies to, inter alia, materialism, calculative rationality, hedonism, or freedom and autonomy, and therefore as indications of what is good or bad in modern life.

Any characterization of the consumer and consumer culture is therefore bound to be evaluative, as we will see in the next section. In this section we can at least try to be more neutral and ask what kinds of values and practices are usually glimpsed in the idea of consumer culture, however it is evaluated. First, as stated, consumer culture has at its core individual consumers, or consumers as part of intimate, private relations (mainly families) who choose things on the basis of their own sense of needs and desires, and their knowledge of available goods and their properties, as well as their knowledge of wider material cultural trends such as brands, tastes, fashions, and lifestyles that knit groups of goods together. This presumes both knowledge and formal freedom: the consumer in a consumer culture does not enact already ascribed identities (as, for example, in premodern sumptuary regulation or in religious prescription of consumption practices such as kosher or halal regulation); consumers have rather to stabilize identities and practices under conditions of little regulation or certainty.

Second, the consumer has to meet most needs through the market. Consumer culture is generally associated not only with an increased range and quantity of goods but with increased commerce and market mediation. Very little is produced by consumers for direct consumption; rather consumer skills concern the ability to shop intelligently and to make choices on the basis of knowledge of commercial representations (advertisements, shop displays) and experiences of goods. Where consumers produce their own goods, this is regarded as either residual tradition or as niche marketing (having a bread-making hobby is an opportunity to buy lots of specialist goods on the market) or as new forms of prosumption (a move *within* the logic of consumer culture). The centrality of market mediation also connects consumer culture to new forms of representation and expertise, and to a generalized aestheticization of everyday life and commercial practice. That is to say, advertising, design, marketing, and branding are complex practices, largely occasioned by the importance of market exchange, that fashion the material and sensuous properties of things in particular ways, and these developments are also often described as consumer culture.

Third, consumer culture is – largely by virtue of market mediation – deemed to be impersonal. The model for consumer culture is mass consumption, in which goods are not produced for known users but rather mass produced for homogenized aggregates. Targeted or niche marketing still corresponds to depersonalized demographics; on the other hand, if goods can be directly customized for each individual shopper it is arguable that the term consumer culture would no longer apply. Consumer culture is impersonal in another – generally positive – sense: access to goods is on the basis of ability to pay, not on the basis of who you are. For example, civil rights movements could argue that excluding people from consumer goods such as restaurants and buses on the basis of skin color was abhorrent.

Finally, consumer culture assumes that needs and wants are unlimited and insatiable. Whereas most other social organizations of consumption assume that insatiable or excessive desire is pathological (except under specific ritual circumstances), the premise of consumer culture is a dynamism in which consumers are stimulated by an expanding world of goods to imagine ever more complex lifestyles and identities, in response to which producers generate ever more inventive goods and properties. This view is largely shared by both liberal proponents of market society and capitalism and by quite a range of critics such as Marx and Simmel, both of whom saw that modern progress involved an open-ended dialectic of needs and use values, or of subjective and objective culture. The critique of insatiability has usually rounded on the way this dialectic has been subverted by capitalist relations, or has been based on ecological critiques of the unsustainability of this dialectic.

CONSUMER CULTURE AS MORAL/POLITICAL JUDGMENT

Critics and advocates of consumer culture would generally agree on these defining features, but the complexity of their assessments and the range of positions that can be adopted on this basis go beyond brief summary. Most importantly, consumer culture has served to deliver judgments on the entire direction of Western modernization; therefore it is clear that most uses of the idea have pointed in different directions and to diverse issues.

There are many grounds on which the idea of consumer culture has served to characterize Western progress and development. It is important to recover these views, particularly as consumer culture has so often been commonsensically assumed to sum up all that is wrong in the modern world – its materialism, debased tastes, false consciousness, and so forth. The contrary view generally starts from one or more of three positions: (1) that consumer culture indexes an increase in material comforts delivered to individuals in relation to their own desires which can only be denied to others on dubious grounds, as in, how can we deny consumer culture to newly industrialized countries (NICs) on ecological grounds after the West has enjoyed these gains for a century or more? (2) that consumer culture produces a virtuous dynamic between supply and demand that fuels political stability and economic development on the basis of maximum freedom; and (3) that the increasing complexity of material culture produces increasing moral, aesthetic, and cultural sophistication in consumers (more "refinement" as Simmel would have it). The costs of these arrangements are counted in inequality, and in the externalities of production, but the values internal to the idea of consumer culture have appeared for centuries to be integral to modern progress: they are corrosive of premodern privilege and inherited status; they are developmental; and they promote self-determined choices by knowledgeable individuals. Much of this view is incorporated in the ideal of consumer sovereignty which was long employed to distinguish Western arrangements from both competing totalitarian systems and from traditional or theocratic ones.

These connections between choice, freedom, and progress, and between commerce and consumption, have underpinned liberal traditions (and many critical traditions) from Bernard Mandeville onward, and are clearly articulated in Hume and Adam Smith: the ideas still recognizable in the notion of consumer culture (if not the term itself) were central to characterizing the modern West as dynamic and rational in comparison to the *ancien régime*. By contrast, the use of the idea of consumer culture to critique capitalist modernity started equally early, and came in numerous brands; in all cases, consumer culture was castigated not (only) as problematic in itself but as symptomatic of modern decline or pathology. We can analytically isolate two kinds of critique: reactionary and progressive.

On the one hand, notions of an emergent consumer culture early came to label all that was wrong with modernity and modern values: whereas premodern society was associated with values and identities organically rooted in a natural order, consumer culture indicated a world turned upside down, in which people could exercise choice on the basis of mere purchasing power, without breeding, cultural values, or collective responsibility (Tocqueville very early connected consumption to increasing privatization and the loss of the political). Hence, the figure of the modern consumer was closely associated with satires of the nouveau riche, whose consumption was governed by meaningless wealth and slavish emulation of their "betters." This divorce between material culture and cultural value extends to figures like Thorstein Veblen and F. R. Leavis, and is generally connected to critiques of mass production: consumer culture involves standardized goods that are as inauthentic as their buyers. Indeed, consumer culture is really a contradiction in terms, and is not properly a culture at all: it can only be a shallow materialism based on money rather than value.

On the other hand – though often with considerable overlap – radical critiques deployed consumer culture concepts to castigate not the unleashing of the masses but their subjectification to capitalist obfuscation. From this perspective, the consumer is not a figure of freedom and choice but the site of manipulation and functional co-optation into the capitalist system. This position is most strongly associated with the Marxist tradition, and latterly the Frankfurt School, but also with a wider radicalism (from situationism through to more recent anti-globalization movements) and with non-Marxist critics of the postwar affluent society. From these perspectives, consumer culture cannot be a system of free choice by knowledgeable and developing individuals; to the contrary, it is a system for producing and manipulating needs so as to render individual subjectivity functional to capitalist economic growth and political stability. The figure of the consumer represents a reorganization of the self so as to fit into the needs of social reproduction.

This is generally tied to some account of alienation, reification, or fetishization in that the production of desire and representations of desire are an intrinsic result of the market system. Finally, consumer culture is related to increasing political passivity, loss of agency, and foreclosing of critical consciousness as people become consumers focused on private and insatiable desires rather than collective interests and projects.

It is important to recognize that during one of the most important and explicit periods of research into consumer culture it was almost entirely synonymous with ideology; consumer culture had absolutely nothing to do with choice or needs in the semiotic tradition or in Baudrillardian styles of postmodernism, and the "culture" part of consumer culture had no analytical role in critical thought. Consumer culture was actually an ideological structure which replaced or orchestrated social processes, such that consumption could never be about social practice; it could only be about the play of coded signs. There have of course been more optimistic versions of postmodernism and poststructuralism, including much of the work of cultural studies in the 1970s and 1980s, in which consumer culture may well be a semiotic playground of loosened and inconsequential meanings and identities, but that reconstitutes consumption as a space of freedom and creativity, and provides resources for the production of new identities and practices (as in subcultural politics). On the other hand, the past two decades or so of consumption studies have dropped the notion of consumer culture almost entirely, opting rather for detailed empirical studies of specific consumption practices that do not aim to subsume all consumption under overarching narratives of consumer culture: even if there are shared values and identities that could meaningfully be labeled consumer culture, we get more understanding by looking in detail at how they are constituted than by treating them simply as local instances of a macro structure.

POSTCONSUMER CULTURE?

The idea that we live in a society dominated by consumption and the figure of the consumer has a long history but arguably reached a peak first in the long northern postwar boom, during which mass production not only fueled increasing material affluence, but in which the centrality of consumer-driven demand was institutionalized in Keynesian governance policies; and second in the rise of both neoliberalism and postmodernism in the 1980s, each in its own way a story about the domination of individual desire over the allocation of social resources, and about the unreality of "the social" compared to the desires of the individual.

If we look at consumption theory and commercial practices since the 1980s, it seems initially as if we are faced with the triumph of commercialism but ironically at the cost of a kind of implosion of the very idea of consumers and consumer culture. At the very least, we might ask whether the idea of consumer culture still has much value either as a description of contemporary consumption or as a discursive figure through which to debate social values. We might look at the fate of the idea of consumer culture through four interrelated developments: branding, prosumption, globalization, and ecological critiques. All four in different ways dissolve the specificity of the consumer identity on which the very idea of consumer culture has depended.

First, product branding originally referred to semiotic and marketing tools that would give the product a distinguishable identity based on its mode of distribution (from design through advertising through sales representation), addressing consumers specifically and distinctly as consumers. Contemporary branding is rather different, addressing the entire social life of goods, and therefore the entire social life of buyers, not just their moment of shopping and commodity purchase and use. The brand, as much contemporary theory argues, is a total social phenomenon, an interface between markets and users. Indeed, a product that merely addresses the consumer is deemed to be doomed to failure: brand consultancies for some time have employed ethnographers, coolhunters, trend spotters, and increasingly social media spaces and associated analytics which bring together commodities and social worlds, and therefore rely less on the identity of the consumer, and much less on moments of shopping and buying.

Second, prosumption is just one concept that points to the extent to which companies operate on the buyer not as passive consumer but as someone who invests various forms of labor in the use of goods, so that they do work which can be harnessed for value creation; in some accounts this is value creation which is not only useful (and of course free) but also increasingly necessary to capitalism. While this still assumes the centrality of consumption and demand to capitalist reproduction, the function is not secured through the figure of the consumer, or not the consumer as a distinguishable identity. If we add to this the extent to which digital media have progressively blurred distinctions between producers, curators, consumers, and fans, and between production and consumption more generally (if I curate a music fansite, and even produce music in relation to that particular music scene, and find that the economic value of my goods is close to zero, am I meaningfully either a consumer or a producer?), then it is hard to see how the idea of consumer culture can continue to outline dominant motifs and issues of contemporary consumption. Consumption, again, might still be central, even more central; but the idea of consumer culture made other claims about choice, market mediation, needs, and impersonality that no longer seem to tease out the important issues.

Third, the story of globalization and consumption has conventionally been told as a narrative of cultural imperialism in which the culture-ideology of consumerism (Sklair 1991) or McDonaldized rationalization (Ritzer 2013) is universalized. This picture has usually been qualified through dialectics of local and global (such as glocalization) but the focus has remained on consumer culture as a northern export that localities more or less successfully resist, or that firms more or less skillfully adapt to local circumstances. Particularly in the case of Sklair and Ritzer, the argument is distinctly about consumer culture rather than simply marketing strategies: both are stories about the apparently irresistible spread of the underlying values (or ideology) of consumer culture. Ethnographies of specific consumption (indeed transnational studies of McDonald's) show clearly how different and localized understandings and uses fog the same commodity, but also show people encountering the same commodity through extremely diverse roles and values which are not easily reducible to that of a consumer. When they do invoke the tropes of consumer culture, they are often radically re-interpreted or ironic or expressive of complex responses to Western modernity in the name of alternative modernities. More fundamental and more recent, however, are increasing studies of the formation of middle classes in NICs across the world, in which massive class formation under conditions of increased affluence does not produce the same or even similar focus on the consumer, or certainly not in a form easily assimilable to the story of consumer culture within Western modernization.

Finally, the past two decades have shown increasing concern with a range of issues that are directly related to consumption in many people's minds – above all, climate change and energy use, and food risks (including the turn to organics). The point for this discussion is not that people are turning away from consumption as a result of moral and political choices; there is very little evidence for that. Rather, there is evidence that a different set of values other than free choice have had to enter into the calculations of both producers and consumers: values such as care and responsibility, future orientation, moral obligations, collective interdependencies, none of which sits within any meaningful understanding of consumer culture, and all of which invoke identifications other than, or at least additional to, the standard figure of the consumer.

SEE ALSO: Baudrillard, Jean; Brands and Branding; Capitalism; Children's Consumer Culture; Consumer Culture, History of; Consumer Culture Theory (CCT); Consumer Society; Consumption and Identity; Culture-Ideology of Consumerism; Frankfurt School; Globalization and Consumption

REFERENCES

Ritzer, George. 2013. *The McDonaldization of Society*, 7th ed. Thousand Oaks, CA: Sage.

Sklair, Leslie. 1991. *Sociology of the Global System*. Baltimore, MD: Johns Hopkins University Press.

FURTHER READING

Lury, Celia. 2011. *Consumer Culture*, 2nd ed. Cambridge, UK: Polity.

Sassatelli, Roberta. 2007. *History, Theory and Politics*, 2nd ed. London: Sage.

Slater, Don. 1997. *Consumer Culture and Modernity*. Cambridge, UK: Polity.

Consumer Culture and Body: *SEE* BODY AND CONSUMER CULTURE

Consumer Culture, Children's: *SEE* CHILDREN'S CONSUMER CULTURE

Consumer Culture and Gender: *SEE* GENDER AND CONSUMER CULTURE

Consumer Culture and Governmentality: *SEE* GOVERNMENTALITY AND CONSUMER CULTURE

Consumer Culture, History of

PAOLO MAGAUDDA
Università degli Studi di Padova, Italy

Although the notion of consumer culture did not emerge in Western culture until after World War II, the historical rise of a recognizable set of cultural values and norms associated with consumption certainly goes back to earlier stages of the modern era. Since the 1990s, the historiography of consumption has emphasized that a specific culture of consumption was the driving force in the process of industrialization in the late eighteenth and early nineteenth centuries. It has also been argued that earlier forms of consumer culture can be traced further back to the second half of the sixteenth century or even to the Renaissance.

While the acts of buying and using goods in a meaningful social way have no doubt existed since the beginning of civilization, historians of consumption commonly assume that a proper culture of consumption developed only in modern societies as a long-term and progressive process. Consumer culture represented a crucial cultural feature in the development of the modern Western world. Its historical emergence could also be interpreted as the result of a specific social configuration, in which the relationship between the symbolic world and material resources started to be mediated through the market and to assume a central role in socio-cultural reproduction, in the fulfillment of personal needs and the use of material objects (see Slater 1997, 8). Over the centuries, the main features of this consumer culture have been the growth of a materialistic attitude, a tendency to develop forms of social competition through goods, and also an increase in the meaningfulness of these goods to express identity and social belonging.

After the seventeenth century in particular, this culture of consumption, based on the processes of social stratification, emerged as an influential force, sustaining the formation of modernity, the development of trade and mercantilism, and the adoption of the monetary economy: in sum, it has accompanied the entire rise of modern capitalism. In the nineteenth century, the spread of consumer culture was a prerequisite for the industrial revolution and, consequently, for the diffusion of the industrial mass production of standardized goods, as well as the transformation of cities and the process of urbanization. It thus became an important symbolic dimension in the emergence of the bourgeois and middle classes. In the twentieth century consumer culture evolved into a crucial facet of society, acquiring a pre-eminent role in the evolution of contemporary global culture. As the historian William Leach (1993) has pointed out with reference to the United States, in the first part of the twentieth century we assisted in a wide social effort to promote an orchestrated and coherent culture of consumption as a system of values, practices, and imageries based on the desire of material objects and the acquisition of goods to fulfill needs and to achieve prosperity and self-realization in society.

THE BIRTH OF CONSUMER CULTURE: RENAISSANCE, ROYAL COURTS, AND BOURGEOIS CLASSES

While early historical accounts concerning the consumer society simplistically assumed that the importance of consumption had just been a consequence of changes in production that occurred with the nineteenth-century industrial revolution, contemporary historiography (e.g., Sassatelli 2007; Trentmann 2012) has pointed out that explicit forms of consumer culture have accompanied the evolution of the modern world, at least since the early modern era. The formation of modern societies was accompanied by the emergence of both new cultural models, through which people interacted with commodities, and new ways of generating collective identities and social distinction thanks to the consumption of goods. The local markets held in European cities in the late Middle Ages were one of the first phenomena in which modern consumption attitudes can be recognized. The French historian Fernand Braudel (1982/1979) located the earliest forms of modern consumer culture within Italian Renaissance cities, and in particular in Lorenzo de' Medici's Florence, where people started to develop materialistic attitudes and to adopt material goods as tools of social competition.

However, it was only in the late seventeenth century that the historiography of consumer culture identified some of the key moments in the evolution of modern consumption habits, by looking at the social changes occurring in England and in other European countries, which were the main players in the nascent international trade with "exotic" colonies. One of the more convincing descriptions of the emergence of consumer culture in the period focuses on the court of Elizabeth I in late sixteenth-century England. The anthropologist Grant McCracken (1988) points out that Elizabeth consolidated power over her kingdom by using the magnificence of courtly ceremony and stimulating social competition between nobles through the material acquisition of luxury goods and fashion. It is in this period that we can recognize a more systematic emergence of what Thorstein Veblen (1899) noted as a crucial feature of consumer modernity: conspicuous consumption, namely, the strategic use of material goods to achieve or display social status. From the time of Elizabeth I onward, the focus on competition through consumption and the role of consumption in the processes of social differentiation became determinants in consumer culture, initially among the nobles and eventually in wider sectors of society in a trickle-down pattern.

Luxury goods are the point of departure in the German historian and sociologist Werner Sombart's (1967/1913) historical interpretation of the development of consumer culture. According to the reconstruction in his seminal study *Luxury and Capitalism*, luxurious products have played a decisive role in the creation of markets and modern merchant capitalism since the late Middle Ages and, consequently, they have been decisive in the birth of the modern consumer culture. On the one hand, luxurious consumption had been made possible by the transformation of the feudal economy into a capitalist economy, which allowed the accumulation of those resources needed for investments in international trade and in the exploitation of colonies. On the other hand, the trade with colonies was directly stimulated by a new consumer demand for luxury goods such as spices, textiles, perfumes, and precious stones. As early as in the sixteenth and seventeenth centuries, these new material resources circulated through an early capitalistic economy led to a profound rearrangement of the cultural classification of goods and also stimulated the recognition of material objects as a means of self-expression and social distinction.

COLONIAL COMMERCE, SOCIAL COMPETITION, AND HEDONISM

The role of luxury and colonial products was not solely a matter of economic value. These new and rare goods were also important for the cultural changes they gave rise to in consumers' mentality and in their attitudes toward material objects. Historians of consumption have highlighted this aspect by focusing on the role of new colonial goods that arrived for the first time in Europe as early as the fifteenth century, such as sugar, tea, and coffee. Cultural sociologist Chandra Mukerji (1983) argued that, when they were commercialized in Europe, these new colonial goods needed to be completely contextualized by the attribution of a new set of values and ethical projections, depending on local consumers' knowledge and social norms. The diffusion of these commodities forced growing sections of the population to deal with new objects and new meanings of consumption, and introduced the pressure to develop cultural competence in regard to the classification and evaluation of these goods.

A major historical reconstruction of the emergence of consumer culture coincides with the unfolding of a revolution in consumption among the eighteenth-century English middle class. As the historical economist Neil McKendrick (1982) has shown in detail, it is possible to recognize a major revolution of consumption within English society in this period, involving not only primary commodities but also and especially luxury goods, apparel, and furniture. A real difference from previous periods was that this revolution involved the middle class and was characterized by explicit imitative forms of consumption related to forms of class competition and the desire for social mobility. McKendrick exemplifies this change in relation to the commercialization of the Wedgwood potteries, which were a great commercial success with the middle class, thanks to Josiah Wedgwood's marketing strategies and the forms of sponsorship he put in place. These potteries were used officially by British and European royal families, and for this reason their possession started to be considered a sign of social advancement by the emerging bourgeois class. The consumption of these objects, usually held in the homes of nobles, was explicitly and consciously assumed to be a means of upward social mobility of the growing middle class.

The rise of the relevance of consumer culture in social processes was not only dependent on forms of emulation relating to social aspiration, but it was also related to other cultural developments. In this regard, the historical sociologist Colin Campbell (1987) argued that in nineteenth-century England, a new cultural attitude marked by materialism and hedonism permeated society, opening the way for a different approach to commodities. In Campbell's view, the cultural influences of Romanticism were the basis for the development of a new consideration of commodities, clothes, and other personal belongings, which started to be identified as tools to foster the imagination, desire, and individual fulfillment. Overturning the perspective of Max Weber – according to which the rise of capitalism was linked to an ascetic style shared by the emerging bourgeois classes – Campbell argued that it was rather a focus on desire, material hedonism, and expressiveness through goods to stimulate a new way to consume, and therefore to generate a new demand for goods, that was essential for the development of capitalism. Consumer culture incorporated wider cultural transformations as romantic ideas grew in popularity (thanks especially to the popular success of the literary character of Dorian Gray, created by Oscar Wilde), and consumption legitimated not only hedonism, but also aesthetic enjoyment and the idea that consumption represented a sphere of self-expression and identity formation in the modern experience of society.

The rise of an autonomous and self-aware consumer culture was a long journey during which major changes relating to the transition from the feudal world to modern societies were accompanied by profound transformations in the cultural values associated with commodities and consumption. With the advancement of modernity, consumption became more and more influential in both stimulating the development of the capitalist system and defining boundaries, distinctions, and homologies between the new social classes of the emerging capitalistic society.

CITIES, DEPARTMENT STORES, AND ADVERTISING

If the period from the late Middle Ages to the start of the mid-nineteenth century was a period during which material goods acquired a role in social distinction and self-expression, and which saw the emergence of a materialistic attitude in society, then the era between the mid-nineteenth and the early twentieth centuries was a time of rapid and intense change. During these few decades, at least three profound transformations in production and everyday life accompanied the rise of consumption: the process of industrialization and the spread of the mass production of goods; urbanization and the new lifestyles emerging within huge modern cities; and, lastly, the evolution of advertising. It was in this period that advertising acquired its modern configuration and laid the foundations for the further symbolic role ads would acquire in modern culture after the world wars.

There is no doubt that, in the second half of the nineteenth century, the rapid shift of population from the countryside to large cities was instrumental in the transformation of the infrastructures, spaces, and culture of consumption. German sociologist George Simmel offers vivid accounts of the changes occurring in urban life in late nineteenth-century Berlin, which was characterized by a multiplication of aesthetic and sensory stimulation. Dress styles and fashion reflected and encouraged individualism as well as a new sense of affinity between different people, highlighting how consumer culture has been a crucial dimension in the shaping and expression of identity within the changing context of individualized modern societies (Simmel 1904/1895). As for Paris, the social theorist Walter Benjamin (2002/1927–40) offered powerful pictures of the typical Parisian *passages*, road corridors with numerous shops and windows exhibiting luxury goods. These *passages* were described by Benjamin as "landscapes of consumption," reflecting the significant role of commodities and shopping in Parisian society and heralding the autonomous spectacle of commodities in the culture and social practices of the time.

This age was full of innovations in consumption and marketing, including the introduction of department stores. They were characterized by large, well-kept, enclosed public buildings in which commodities were displayed in a very attractive way. One of the earliest and most famous department stores was the Bon Marché, which opened in Paris in 1852 and was renovated sumptuously at the end of the century with the help of the engineer Gustave Eiffel (Williams 1982). The department stores introduced the idea that consumers were not forced to buy anything and that they were not required even to interact with saleswomen; all this contributed to affirm the idea that goods could constitute an autonomous spectacle, independent from the act of buying, in a similar way to exhibits in museums.

The latter half of the nineteenth century was also, and above all, characterized by the advent of modern advertising, which started to assume the role of the engine of trade in the economy of mass-produced goods, together with the earliest marketing techniques and strategies. Advertisements had appeared since the seventeenth century, accompanying the publication of newspapers and magazines, but they had remained for a long time informative in tone and factual in content. From the late nineteenth century, ads started to become more and more attractive, adopting metaphors and allusions, and beginning to use the technique of symbolic association that would be recognized by Roland Barthes (1972/1957) in the postwar period as typical of popular modern mythologies. It was, therefore, during this period that advertising stopped just selling products and began to offer lifestyles and dreams, taking on the role of a really powerful player in contemporary cultural flows.

FROM THE "CONSUMER SOCIETY" TO THE AGE OF THE INTERNET

The historian of consumption Frank Trentmann (2012) argued that the historiography on consumer culture can be divided into two broad streams. On the one hand are the studies that deal with ancient history, focusing mainly on Europe from the Renaissance to the beginning of the twentieth century. On the other hand are the researchers who place a dominant emphasis on World War II onward, and especially on North America and US society. In effect, there is no doubt that the gravitational center of consumer culture in this latter historical phase shifted from

Europe to the United States, where many innovations in consumption have appeared, including shopping malls. But, even more relevant, consumption in itself came to be recognized as one of the main dimensions to measure the growth of individual and social wellness.

The first shopping mall was opened in Minnesota in 1956, paving the way for the creation of larger and larger cathedrals of consumption and of an entire way of life based on suburbs and the use of private cars. In the postwar decades the centrality of consumption in American cultural life was also reflected in the pop art movement, particularly in the work of Andy Warhol, who transformed objects of everyday consumption and advertising (i.e., a soup can or a soap box) into pieces of art. In the 1950s and 1960s, the consumer society became a common way to account for the fact that desiring, buying, and using commodities was at the core of everyday social experience, predominantly in the United States but also in the rest of the capitalist Western world. Since then, thanks especially to TV broadcasting, consumer culture has started to be more and more inextricably intertwined with the global media industry and the world of entertainment. Television advertising was increasingly important both commercially and for its ability to permeate popular culture and people's imaginations. Since the 1980s companies' logos and brands have acquired a pervasive presence in everyday life, and have attained the status of a sort of global iconic language in the West and in many underdeveloped countries as well.

At the same time, the pervasiveness of consumption generated distinctive critical voices, particularly with reference to the way in which consumer culture was corrupting the supposed traditional values of society. In the United States, public figures such as John K. Galbraith and Vance Packard condemned the culture of consumption as a carrier of excessive individualism and vacuous interpersonal relationships; in Europe, intellectuals such as Theodor Adorno and Marx Horkheimer identified a sort of spiritual impoverishment in consumer society compared to the achievements of European cultural traditions.

Since the 1990s, many of these concerns have become common arguments of political movements that are critical of the processes of globalization. With a different, but sometimes overlapping, critical perspective on the world of consumption, groups active in the protection of consumer rights have gained visibility, especially after the 1960s. In addition, thanks to their actions in the postwar decades, new regulations defending the rights of consumers were enforced in many Western countries. However, the advancement of ethics and democracy within consumer culture can also be interpreted as the unfolding of the effects produced by a "new spirit of capitalism" (Boltanski and Chiapello 2005/1999) – that is, the tendency of late twentieth-century capitalism to reinforce itself by incorporating criticisms in order to further expand its power, such as the introduction of ethical principles into business and commerce.

In recent years, several new perspectives and specific concerns have enriched the understanding of the evolution of consumer culture. Among them, it is worth mentioning the role of gender in the construction of consumer culture, particularly in the shaping of the everyday domestic consumer practices. Another crucial topic has been the politicization of consumption, such as in the case of boycott actions, which have been increasingly important in political activism, especially in the form of an anti-capitalistic attitude shared by the anti-globalization movements. Moreover, growing attention has been devoted to the way in which social differences such as class, age, ethnicity, or group membership influence the development of consumer culture, for example the way children's consumption has become a rising area of commodification. Finally, the evolution of consumer culture today intersects with the internet and digital personal communication. While the ongoing process of the digitalization of consumption has already produced huge effects on markets, practices, and cultures – such as in the exemplary case of digital music – the mutual shaping of consumer culture and digital media has yet to completely unfold all its potential consequences on culture and society.

SEE ALSO: Advertising; Americanization; Benjamin, Walter; Capitalism; Consumer Culture; Consumer Movements, Contemporary; Consumer Movements, History of; Consumer Society; Department Stores; Fashion; Frankfurt School; Globalization and Consumption; Mass Culture; Mass Media; Shopping Malls

REFERENCES

Barthes, Roland. 1972/1957. *Mythologies*. London: Paladin.

Benjamin, Walter. 2002/1927–40. *The Arcades Project*. Cambridge, MA: Belknap.

Boltanski, Luc, and Ève Chiapello. 2005/1999. *The New Spirit of Capitalism*. London: Verso.

Braudel, Fernand. 1982/1979. *The Wheels of Commerce: Civilization and Capitalism, 15th–18th Century*. New York: Harper & Row.

Campbell, Colin. 1987. *The Romantic Ethic and the Spirit of Modern Consumerism*. Oxford: Blackwell.

Leach, W. 1993. *Land of Desire: Merchants, Power, and the Rise of a New American Culture*. New York: Pantheon.

McCracken, Grant. 1988. *Culture and Consumption: New Approaches to the Symbolic Character of Consumer Goods and Activities*. Bloomington: Indiana University Press.

McKendrick, Neil. 1982. "Josiah Wedgwood and the Commercialization of the Potteries." In *The Birth of a Consumer Society: The Commercialization of Eighteenth-Century England*, edited by N. McKendrick, J. Brewer, and J. H. Plumb, 100–145. Bloomington: Indiana University Press.

Mukerji, Chandra. 1983. *From Graven Images: Patterns of Modern Materialism*. New York: Columbia University Press.

Sassatelli, Roberta. 2007. *Consumer Culture: History, Theory and Politics*. London: Sage.

Simmel, George. 1904/1895. "Fashion." *International Quarterly* 10: 130–155.

Slater, Don. 1997. *Consumer Culture and Modernity*. Cambridge, UK: Polity.

Sombart, Werner. 1967/1913. *Luxury and Capitalism*. Ann Arbor: University of Michigan Press.

Trentmann, Frank, ed. 2012. *The Oxford Handbook of the History of Consumption*. Oxford: Oxford University Press.

Veblen, T. 1899. *The Theory of the Leisure Class*. London: Macmillan.

Williams, Rosalind. 1982. *Dream Worlds: Mass Consumption in Late-Nineteenth-Century France*. Berkeley: University of California Press.

Consumer Culture and Politics: *SEE* POLITICS AND CONSUMER CULTURE

Consumer Culture Theory (CCT)

SØREN ASKEGAARD
University of Southern Denmark, Denmark

Consumer culture theory (CCT) is a stream of research focusing on consumption patterns as a social and cultural practice. Scholars who espouse CCT are predominantly, albeit not exclusively, employed in marketing or management departments in universities and business schools in Europe and North America, though there is a growing interest in this type of research in Latin America, for example. Based on the legacy of earlier social psychological approaches to the symbolic nature of consumer behavior as expressed in, for example, the work of Sidney Levy from the 1950s, CCT slowly grew from the early 1980s onward as an increasingly significant addition to the traditional econometric and cognitive psychological approaches to the study of consumer decision making and consumer behavior in business schools.

CCT is also an emergent formalized scholarly association which has organized its own annual conference since 2006. Its most significant and prestigious publication outlet is the *Journal of Consumer Research*, although this is shared with consumer researchers working from the more dominant perspectives of cognitive psychology/behavioral decision theory and econometric modeling of consumer behavior. Other outlets with significant contributions from CCT scholars are the journals *Consumption, Market and Culture*, *Journal of Consumer Culture*, *Journal of Macromarketing*, *Journal of Marketing*, *Journal of Marketing Management*, *Journal of Retailing*, and *Marketing Theory*. Edited volumes such as the book series "Research in Consumer Behavior" and "Interpretive Marketing Research" from Routledge should also be mentioned.

AXIOLOGY

Consumer culture, according to the definitional article by Arnould and Thompson (2005), "denotes a social arrangement in which the relations between lived culture and social resources, and between meaningful ways of life and the symbolic and material resources on which they depend, are mediated through markets" (p. 869). Consequently, consumption phenomena can be understood only though their inscription in the sociocultural context in which they exist and, furthermore, they must be seen in relation to the full consumption cycle including acquisition, possession, consumption, and disposition. The aim is to theorize the dynamics driving such consumption cycles as well as the social logics at stake on a micro, meso, or macro level. Contexts are thus not ends in themselves but are regarded as important as the field in which consumption phenomena unfold as real and lived experiences. While the significance of the sociocultural context makes CCT scholars predominantly oriented toward methods that allow for a profound conceptualization (most often ethnographic and/or phenomenological approaches), there is an openness toward a multiplicity of methods and representations, including those based on survey or experimental data (Arnould and Thompson 2005). Most recently, the CCT field has added research in market systems, still from a cultural perspective, to its axiological point of departure, since it has become increasingly clear that an understanding of consumption practices in a modern capitalist economy is deeply intertwined with market systems of production, distribution, and exchange.

HISTORY

The earliest roots of consumer culture theory are difficult to locate. It might be fair to say, however, that authors such as Thorstein Veblen on conspicuous consumption and Georg Simmel on fashion were among the earliest social theorists to take up consumption as a central social phenomenon. However, in terms of its institutional linkage with business schools and marketing departments, the initial foundation of what was to become consumer culture theory arose as a follow-up to the marketing research interest in motivational theory in the 1950s. Most significantly, from this period, Sidney Levy argued for the symbolic nature of consumption, contributing a more social-psychological framework of the relationship between consumption and lifestyle to Veblen's and Simmel's predominantly class-based sociological theories. Levy's insights were all but forgotten during the following couple of decades until revived by the prominent paradigmatic debates in the marketing discipline during the 1970s and 1980s. An early and, in many accounts, decisive event was the 1981 conference on symbolic consumer behavior organized in New York. A reading of the proceedings from this event demonstrates that culturally oriented consumer research was initially just as much a study of the consumption *of* culture as a study of consumer culture, since it was predominantly a reaction against classical approaches within consumer research, which emphasized a utilitarian perspective that was ill equipped to account for more aesthetically oriented consumption. This initial interest in the symbolism and experiential pleasures of consumption of performances and products of the culture industries gave the early years of this type of consumer research a distinctly humanistic ethos. Many of the initial research projects dealt with cinematographic, musical, or similar types of aesthetic consumption.

Sherry (1991) provided the first general overview of what he terms "the interpretive turn in consumer research," and discusses the relationship of this emergence of a new consumer research tradition with the quest for an alternative paradigm for market and consumer research. He evokes three major domains of "postmodern consumer research" that are characterizing the alternative movement. First, he makes reference to a critical stream of research which predominantly focuses on historical and macrosocial dimensions of consumption and consumer research. This historically and critically interested stream of research later played a relatively weak role in the CCT movement (Askegaard and Scott 2013), although change may now be coming (see below). Second is a "culturological" strand of research, which refers to an emerging interest in naturalistic inquiry and phenomenologies of consumer experiences, as expressed through the mythological "consumer odyssey," where leading proponents of a cultural approach to consumer research undertook a transcontinental journey into marketplaces and consumer lifeworlds across America – a truly "manifestary" moment in the history of CCT (Bode and Østergaard 2013). And, third, a number of scholars are working with communicative perspectives, which refers to work rooted in structuralist or semiotic perspectives in the analysis of consumer meanings in relation to commercial imagery, notably advertising.

THE BIRTH OF THE CCT CONCEPT AND ITS RESEARCH DOMAINS

As the CCT stream of research gained a foothold within consumer research in general, there was a growing curiosity about what the domain exactly stood for in terms of theory building. In 2005 a seminal article by Arnould and Thompson (2005) not only coined the term, but established CCT as a brand that has since designated the research community. They suggested that four distinct but related areas could be the basis for theory building. *Consumer identity projects* allegedly constitute the largest area of research, looking into how contemporary reflexive consumers make use of market-related resources to forge a coherent, if also complex and diversified, self-identity. If this stream of research has a distinctly individual focus, the theory building relating to *marketplace cultures*, conversely, looks at how consumers, through activities tied to the marketplace, build particular cultural communities, analyzed in terms of subcultures, brand communities, or neo-tribalistic consumer networks. The *sociohistoric patterning of consumption* is the third of the four domains in which CCT is argued to contribute to theory building. This reflects the interest of CCT scholars in the structural and institutional forces shaping consumption patterns, whether it is different types of social stratification, gender, ethnicity, or other such institutional factors. The fourth and final domain is called *mass-mediated marketplace ideologies and consumers' interpretive strategies*. Here, the influence from media theory and critical theory is obvious, since the focus is on the ideological shaping of consumer culture meanings through commercial imagery, servicescapes, and so on. However, a particular focus on consumer agency is retained, through investigations of the strategies used by consumers to turn a variety of popular culture texts, including commercial messages, into resources for their own life situation though active reinterpretation.

The consequence of the publication of this synthesizing article was that CCT rapidly gained status as the common denominator for a large number of researchers in the community. However, a number of scholars, especially those representing the critical tradition and/or the European scene, expressed their discontent with what they saw as the article's hegemonizing definition of the research field and an unfortunate focus on the work published in the *Journal of Consumer Research*, which thereby excluded the rich scholarly output in other journals. As a consequence, the two authors of the original CCT-defining article returned with a qualifying article after the first CCT conference (Arnould and Thompson 2007). Here, they tried to elaborate on their understanding of the CCT field, underlining their own distance from any attempt to provide a totalizing narrative of what CCT is and is not, as well as referring to philosopher Richard Rorty in the argument that the "theory" in CCT should be understood as a "conversational vernacular rather than a cumulative body of knowledge" (Arnould and Thompson 2007, 6). They also tried to alter the impression of CCT research being defined exclusively by the four above-mentioned domains by adding another four domains of research as "interstitial linkages" between the existing four. Most significantly, they underlined the dynamic character of CCT as a research field.

CRITIQUE

CCT has been the subject of both internal and external critique. First, a number of researchers who were part of the interpretive consumer research community prior to the establishment of the CCT brand have refused to adopt the label, arguing that it lacks a critical stance on neoliberal market institutions and the consumerist ideology. A similar critique has been raised by scholars completely outside the consumer research domain, for example from economic anthropology (see Askegaard and Scott 2013).

Similar critiques have been raised from within the field, albeit framed more in terms of lack of focus on the institutional and macrosocial framings of consumer culture. Thus, it has been argued that the existential-phenomenological legacy of the CCT field, the establishment of the phenomenological depth interview as the primary research instrument and the consequent overestimation of consumer agency, has led to a certain neglect of the effects of social forces that are not directly felt or expressed by the consumer subjects. From this response, it is also clear that the CCT field is moving toward an increasing focus not just on the consumer as a market actor but on more complex institutional systems of market interaction as constitutive of consumer culture. Thus, there is a growing willingness among CCT scholars to consider consumer culture not just from the perspective of consumers' individual and collective agency, but as inscribed in a market system. Consequently, influences from institutional theory, actor network theory, and assemblage theory are becoming increasingly significant.

SEE ALSO: Consumer Culture; Consumer Culture, History of; Consumer Society

REFERENCES

Arnould, Eric J., and Craig J. Thompson. 2005. "Consumer Culture Theory (CCT): Twenty Years of Research." *Journal of Consumer Research* 33: 868–882.

Arnould, Eric, and Craig Thompson. 2007. "Consumer Culture Theory (and We Really Mean Theoretics): Dilemmas and Opportunities Posed by an Academic Brand Strategy." *Research in Consumer Behavior* 11: 3–22.

Askegaard, Søren, and Linda Scott. 2013. "Consumer Culture Theory: The Ironies of History." *Marketing Theory* 13(2) (special issue on "Consumer Culture Theory: History, Perspectives and Prospectives"): 139–147.

Bode, Matthias, and Per Østergaard. 2013. "'The Wild and Wacky Worlds of Consumer Oddballs': Analyzing the Manifestary Context of Consumer Culture Theory." *Marketing Theory* 13(2) (special issue): 175–192.

Sherry, John F., Jr. 1991. "Postmodern Alternatives: The Interpretive Turn in Consumer Research." In *Handbook of Consumer Behavior*, edited by T. Robertson and H. Kassarjian, 548–591. Englewoods Cliffs, NJ: Prentice Hall.

Consumer Experience and Music: *SEE* Music and Consumer Experience

Consumer Movements, Contemporary

WENDY A. WIEDENHOFT-MURPHY
John Carroll University, USA

Although consumer activism has a long and significant history in the United States from the boycotts of British goods leading up to the American Revolution to the union label and white label buycotts of the American Federation of Labor and the National Consumers' League during the Progressive era, the Great Depression marks the birth of the contemporary consumer movement (Glickman 2009; Hilton 2007; Sorenson 1941). It was during the late 1920s that scientific experts began using the tactic of testing products to ensure their safety for consumers and established two consumer organizations in the United States, Consumers' Research and Consumers Union, the latter of which remains central to the consumer movement today. Unlike the focus of earlier forms of consumer activism, which tended to stress how the purchasing decisions of consumers affected the wages or working conditions of laborers, the contemporary consumer movement positions the interests of the consumer as its predominant concern. These consumer interests include objective product information regarding quality, standards, and price. A diverse constituency, independence from business and political parties, a decentralized organizational structure, and single-issue campaigns are some of the reasons why the consumer movement has survived for almost a century. While product testing may be the foundation of the contemporary consumer movement, currently one can argue that the consumer movement is rediscovering the tactics of earlier forms of consumer activism, particularly boycotts and buycotts, and legitimizing these tactics with scientific research.

There are also signs that participants in the current US consumer movement are not just a handful of scientific experts and formal organizations operating "inside the Beltway" (Mayer 1989, 53–54), but include consumers themselves, creating initiatives at the local or grassroots level. This entry describes the contemporary consumer movement in linear fashion, addressing the key periods when it has been most vocal and active. In general the contemporary US consumer movement has been most successful when its goals and interests receive wide support from the public and from the federal government (Pertschuk 1982, 13), such as in the 1920s and 1930s, the 1960s and 1970s, and since the 1990s.

1920S–1930S: CR, CU, PRODUCT TESTING, AND CONSUMER INFORMATION

In 1927 Stuart Chase, an accountant, and Frederick Schlink, a mechanical engineer, published *Your Money's Worth*, a book that argued that American consumers were victims, manipulated by corporations and advertisers and coerced into purchasing inferior products due to lack of information and standardization. The success of the book encouraged the authors to create Consumers' Research (CR) in 1928, a professional organization dedicated to product testing and consumer education. CR published *Consumers' Research Bulletin*, a magazine that provided subscribers with objective information on products the organization tested in its laboratories. The *Bulletin* proved so popular that its subscriptions soared from 565 in 1927 to 42,000 in 1932 (Mayer 1989, 20–21). Riding this wave of consumer interest in product testing, Schlink and CR board member Arthur Kallet published the book *100,000,000 Guinea Pigs: Dangers in Everyday Foods, Drugs and Cosmetics* in 1933. Kallet and Schlink argued that consumers were unwitting guinea pigs that corporations used to test the health and safety of their often poisonous products because of the lack of government oversight. Their book inspired the passage of the Wheeler–Lea Act in 1938, which gave the Federal Trade Commission power to regulate false advertising and food, drugs, cosmetics, and therapeutic devices advertisements.

While CR might have represented the interests of consumers, it did not embrace them as active participants in the consumer movement, but as due-paying members who needed its expertise in order to make rational decisions in the marketplace. The focus of CR on product price and quality was deemed too narrow by some, particularly those who wanted consumers to form an alliance with labor similar to earlier forms of consumer activism. Interestingly, CR's own workers went on strike in 1935 after CR fired three of its employees who organized a chapter of the American Federation of Labor's Technical, Editorial and Office Assistants Union. Several of these workers formed their own organization, Consumers Union (CU), which became larger than CR in just one year. As a union shop CU was more radical than CR and it supplied consumers with information on both products and workplace conditions. CR became increasingly conservative over the years, "searching for subversives in the consumer movement" (Glickman 2009, 213). One of its executives became the director of research for the House Committee on Un-American Activities (HCUA). However, CU also became less radical by the 1940s, eliminating information on workplace conditions as a result of anti-communist sentiment (Glickman 2009, 198–215; Mayer 1989, 21–22). Today CU is best known for its popular publication *Consumer Reports*, a product-testing guide on a variety of middle-class household items and automobiles, and has an operating budget of over US$150 million in revenues. In general CU endorses rather than challenges consumerism (Hilton 2007, 126, 132).

The Great Depression provided the context for the popularity of CR and subsequently CU – consumers needed unbiased advice and information on how to manage their household budgets when their paychecks were being stretched. According to Helen Sorenson, the Great Depression brought people "rather suddenly to a realization that they have problems in consumption as well as in production" (1941, 4). Consumers were able to secure representation in two key New Deal programs: a Consumer Advisory Board (CAB) in the National Recovery Administration (NRA) and a Consumers' Counsel (CC) in the Department of Agriculture. In 1934 the National Emergency Council (NED) established a Consumers' Division to manage CAB and CC and established local consumer councils across the country. The inclusion of consumers alongside labor and business in these New Deal advisory groups was significant, if not practical, as these programs sought to implement Keynesian economic policies, such as government restrictions on production, which would result in higher prices for consumers. However, it was difficult for the voice of consumers to be as strong as those of business and labor because of a lack of organization and a coherent message. It was also difficult to simply identify who a consumer was exactly. For example, the local councils created by the Consumers' Division of the NED were composed of a diverse range of individuals, including a member of a women's group that addressed consumer issues, a county agent, a dietitian, a home economist or educator, a farmer, a middle- or lower-class housewife, a manual worker, and a member of a consumer cooperative. While these individuals were all consumers it is questionable if they all had the same interests or could speak with one voice for "the consumer." In the end, the most significant accomplishment of New Deal consumer representation was that standards and grades for consumer goods developed by CAB were integrated into many NRA codes (Cohen 2003; Mayer 1989; Sorenson 1941).

In addition to product-testing agencies other consumer groups were active during the 1920s and 1930s including the Consumers' National Federation, the League of Women Shoppers, and, most notably, the National Consumers' League (NCL). The NCL was established in 1899, utilizing the tactic of the *buycott* or the "positive boycott" in its efforts to educate consumers, help workers, and eradicate sweatshop production. The NCL created a white label, which was attached to goods that were produced in safe and healthy work environments, and a white list that included the names of stores that treated their employees fairly. Composed mainly of educated middle- and upper-class women, the NCL did its own investigative work to ensure that manufacturers and retailers were abiding by its labor and health standards. NCL members used their expertise to help win a Supreme Court case, *Muller v. Oregon*, which limited the number of hours a woman could work to 10 per day. During the New Deal era the NCL remained active in politics, working on behalf of the NRA to establish maximum work hours and minimum wage codes and lobbying in support of the 1938 Fair Labor Standards Act. Though not as popular as product-testing organizations, the NCL demonstrated that consumers were not simply concerned with their own self-interests, but those of workers, and that women were important actors in the consumer movement (Cohen 2003; Storrs 2000).

1960S–1970S: NADER, CORPORATE ACCOUNTABILITY, AND CONSUMER PROTECTION

While the consumer movement did not disappear in the 1940s and 1950s, it was certainly less active and vocal than it was during the 1920s and 1930s due to a hostile political environment. Consumers were mobilized to participate on the home front during World War II, but their activities were centered on rationing, recycling, and planting victory gardens as the federal government established price controls on thousands of commodities (Cohen 2003). The Cold War and HCUA accusations affected consumer groups that supported organized labor, though CU's membership increased rapidly after World War II from less than 100,000 in 1945 to over 700,000 in 1953 as it abandoned its radical roots (Glickman 2009, 269). Perhaps the most significant moment of consumer activism during the 1940s and 1950s was the Montgomery bus boycott in 1955, which marked the culmination of years of Jim Crow streetcar protests by African Americans and the beginning of the Civil Rights movement.

The consumer movement gained remarkable momentum in the mid-1960s and early 1970s in regard to federal legislation and regulation, with the successful passage of the Federal Cigarette Labeling and Advertising Act (1965), the National Traffic and Motor Vehicle Safely Act (1966), the Consumer Product Safety Act (1972), and the Magnuson–Moss Warranty and FTC Improvement Act (1975). According to Michael Pertschuk, former chairman of the Federal Trade Commission (FTC), these successes were a result of strong support from the public and the state as well as a coalition of consumer advocates in Congress, an entrepreneurial congressional staff, aggressive investigative and advocacy journalists, organized labor, and nonprofit entrepreneurs like Ralph Nader (Pertschuk 1982, 23). Indeed, Ralph Nader emerged as the contentious leader of the consumer movement during the 1960s with the publication of his book *Unsafe at Any Speed* in 1965, which documented the human and social costs of dangerously designed automobiles, like General Motors' Corvair. Nader stressed the unfair economic playing field that corporations created and was critical of how the federal government refused to challenge the concentration of corporate power. Nader assembled law students and undergraduates – known as "Nader's Raiders" – in the late 1960s to investigate the failure of government agencies, such as the FTC and the FDA, to protect consumers from dangerous products, and founded the public interest group Public Citizen in 1972. Nader's public interest crusades have focused on a variety of issues, including nuclear power safety, food safety, product liability, air and water pollution, and government accountability.

The success of the consumer movement was short-lived as its power weakened in the late 1970s. Corporations united and gained strength as they instituted their "revolt against regulation" and categorically defeated the efforts of the consumer movement to create a federal Consumer Protection Agency (Pertschuk 1982, 59). According to Glickman, this defeat signaled the rise of the New Right and the triumph of free market ideology (Glickman 2009, 279). Predictably, the consumer movement began to wane in such a political environment, losing support in the 1980s as government regulation was viewed as unnecessary interference in the economy that restricted consumer choice.

1990S–TODAY: SHOPPING FOR SOCIAL JUSTICE AND ENVIRONMENTAL SUSTAINABILITY

During the 1990s the consumer movement shifted its attention away from government regulation and toward trying to achieve social change using the marketplace itself. Consumers became political and shopping was politicized as people became concerned about how their decisions in the marketplace affected the environment, culture, and labor on a global scale. Political consumerism emerged as "actions by people who make choices among producers and products with the goal of changing objectionable institutional or market practices" (Micheletti 2003, 2). Instead of trying to fight capitalism the consumer movement decided to use free market ideology to its advantage through the tactic of the buycott, which recommends purchasing particular consumer products instead of avoiding them. The 1990s witnessed what has been called the *certification revolution*, as a variety of products began to display labels to inform consumers about their origins at the point of purchase. Labeling schemes target five areas: ecology, fair trade, organic food, forestry, and marine life. Manufacturers are responsible for the cost of certifying their products through independent nonprofit organizations or government agencies, though some engage in less accountable self-certification schemes to market their own products. Perhaps the most recognizable and successful label today is the fair trade one that can be found on a variety of products from coffee to bananas to chocolate. The mission of fair trade is to eradicate global poverty, which it attempts to do by mobilizing the purchasing power of consumers in developed countries to help improve the wages and working conditions of producers in developing countries by purchasing fair trade labeled goods. The cost of fair trade products is typically 10 percent higher than the cost price of the products, the difference in which is considered a "social premium" that provides developmental assistance to disadvantaged producers (Nicholls and Opal 2004, 6). Fair trade organizations, including the Fairtrade Labeling Organizations International, the European Fair Trade Association, and the Fair Trade Federation, guarantee label certification and compliance, develop markets for fair trade products, and assist in the importing and retailing processes. According to Fair Trade USA, the number of fair trade products for sale in the United States is currently over 10,000 and the sale of fair trade goods was up 63 percent in 2011.

The rise of political consumerism is not without challenges. Those on the left consider it the triumph of neoliberal values and a sign of the decline of the state, while those on the right view it as a form of socialism that interferes with free trade (Micheletti 2003, 3). Some question whether the individual actions of consumers even constitute collective action or if changing individual shopping habits can save the world if existing institutions are not altered. Purchasing eco-friendly laundry detergent does not challenge consumerism – we are still buying, albeit with ethical considerations. Yet others wonder if the consumer should be at the center of political consumerism as they argue it is not the consumer, but organizations, that are the main agents responsible for this phenomenon. These organizations "make the ethical consumer visible" and "seek to connect the forms of care and concern already embedded in everyday consumption practices into wider networks of collective solidarity" (Barnett et al. 2011, 97, 93). Finally, some think that the ethical consumer is a myth because it is not so much consumer demand as corporate supply that makes political consumerism successful. In other words, corporations are making the decision to sell fair trade coffee, not individual consumers (Devinney, Auger, and Eckhardt 2010, 3). Whether consumers are aware of purchasing ethical products or not, it is evident that most businesses are not threatened by this current wave of the consumer movement and seem happy to support political consumerism as long as it improves their reputations and profit margins.

Although political consumerism can be considered mainstream, as ethical products can be found on the shelves of big-box stores like Walmart and Target, there are more radical elements of the consumer movement today that target the ideology of consumerism and capitalism. Culture jammers, like Adbusters, use discursive action to undermine the meaning of corporate logos and advertisements. Adbusters promotes Buy Nothing Day on the Friday following Thanksgiving and was instrumental in organizing the Occupy Wall Street protests. Individuals active in the voluntary simplicity movement also confront consumerism by downshifting their lifestyles, reducing their spending and the amount of time they work, and potentially increasing their happiness and wellbeing. Downshifters engage in a variety of activities to avoid participating in the formal economy, such as freecycling, dumpster diving, wildcrafting, and hunting and gathering their own food. Others practice collaborative consumption, sharing what they already own with family, friends, and neighbors in order to reduce consumption and build community.

SEE ALSO: Anti-Consumption Tactics; Consumer Activism; Ethical Consumption; Fair Trade

REFERENCES

Barnett, Clive, Paul Cloke, Nick Clarke, and Alice Malpass. 2011. *Globalizing Responsibility: The Political Rationalities of Ethical Consumption*. Oxford: Wiley-Blackwell.

Cohen, Lizabeth. 2003. *A Consumers' Republic: The Politics of Mass Consumption in Postwar America*. New York: Knopf.

Devinney, Timothy, Pat Auger, and Giana Eckhardt. 2010. *The Myth of the Ethical Consumer*. Cambridge, UK: Cambridge University Press.

Glickman, Lawrence. 2009. *Buyer Power: A History of Consumer Activism in America*. Chicago, IL: University of Chicago Press.

Hilton, Michael. 2007. "Social Activism in an Age of Consumption: The Organized Consumer Movement." *Social History* 32: 121–143.

Mayer, Robert. 1989. *The Consumer Movement: Guardians of the Marketplace*. Boston, MA: Twayne Publishers.

Micheletti, Michele. 2003. *Political Virtue and Shopping: Individuals, Consumerism, and Collective Action*. New York: Palgrave.

Nicholls, Alex, and Charlotte Opal. 2004. *Fair Trade: Market-Driven Ethical Consumption*. London: Sage.

Pertschuk, Michael. 1982. *Revolt against Regulation: The Rise and Pause of the Consumer Movement*. Berkeley: University of California Press.

Sorenson, Helen. 1941. *The Consumer Movement: What It Is and What It Means*. New York: Harper & Brothers.

Storrs, Landon. 2000. *Civilizing Capitalism: The National Consumers' League, Women's Activism, and Labor Standards in the New Deal Era*. Chapel Hill: University of North Carolina Press.

Consumer Movements, History of

INGER L. STOLE

University of Illinois at Urbana-Champaign, USA

A modern consumer culture first emerged in the United States after the Civil War, in connection with massive changes in the production, distribution, and marketing of goods. By the turn of the twentieth century, intersecting concerns about labor conditions and production processes in the nation's factories had already given rise to the first American consumer movement. Formed in 1899, the National Consumers League worked relentlessly on behalf of workers and consumers. Operating in many states, the organization conducted regular factory inspections and lobbied for local and federal laws that would improve conditions in the workplace. In order to carry the league's white label, garments had to be produced in factories that refused to employ children and that paid their employees fair wages and treated them well. In acknowledging the economic significance of consumers and actively working in their interest, Kathryn Kish Sklar (1998, 25) argues, the National Consumers League helped translate consumption into political action and elevated consumers into political participants.

In addition to concerns about working conditions, the absence of laws to protect the public from dangerous, and largely unregulated, additives and chemicals also drew activists' attention. Work on what would eventually become the 1906 federal Pure Food and Drugs Act began in 1892, when a group led by Dr. Harvey W. Wiley launched a crusade against adulterated food and drugs. By 1904, *Collier's* had assigned the successful muckraker Samuel Hopkins Adams to conduct a thorough investigation of the nostrum industry. Adams exposed a proprietary industry that lined its pockets by selling worthless, even dangerous, medicines to the public. Assisted by an agricultural chemist and pharmaceutical experts, he concluded that people were consuming huge amounts of alcohol, opiates, and narcotics that often made them even sicker. Not surprisingly, groups such as the National Wholesale Liquor Dealers Association and the Proprietary Medicine Association opposed any attempt at regulation, and their deep coffers and skill at enlisting powerful representatives in Congress prevented legislation from being passed.

The situation appeared to be at a standstill when Upton Sinclair's book *The Jungle* was published in 1906. The bestseller unveiled unethical and unsanitary conditions in the meatpacking industry that were resulting in sales of contaminated meat to consumers. Although Sinclair's call for labor reform fell largely on deaf ears, his plea for stricter regulation of meat gained massive support. As meat sales kept dropping, President Theodore Roosevelt came out in support of a meat inspection bill, which was written into law in 1906. That success lent renewed support to demands for regulation of food and drugs, a crusade now supported by the American Medical Association and several women's organizations. In 1906 the Food and Drugs Act finally made all forms of misbranding, including falsification of drug labels, illegal. It was a substantial victory for the Progressive era's consumer movement. More than anything, and in combination with other consumer-related victories, its passage demonstrated that consumer interests finally had a voice in politics. In the words of Ralph M. Gaedeke (1972, 58), it "did a great deal to dissolve the old nineteenth-century American habit of viewing political issues solely from the standpoint of the producer."

By the end of World War I, organized consumer activity had tapered off. No longer pushing for major federal regulation, consumer organizations were now focused primarily on retail prices and sanitary issues. Although the National Consumers League remained active, it moved beyond its white label campaign, leveraging its political power to secure minimum wage and fair labor standards. Surviving strands of progressive thought continued to influence social and political thinking, however, and by the 1930s, a new consumer movement had appeared on the scene.

Advertising had been a relatively new phenomenon in the early twentieth century, and few could have predicted its immense growth. Consequently, it was not regulated by the 1906 Food and Drugs Act. By the late 1920s, however, advertising had become the main form of communication between manufacturers and consumers, and a problematic one at that. Advertisers, presenting themselves as both coach and confidant, "guided" consumers through the task of choosing the "right" products and preyed on their fears and insecurities. People were told that bad breath, old-fashioned furnishings, and the "wrong" cigarette brands could hinder their professional and social success, and that if they failed to use or wear certain products they would not be able to keep up with modern society, much less get ahead (Marchand 1986, chap. 1).

In 1927 Stuart Chase and F. J. Schlink published a book that would ignite a new wave of consumer activism. *Your Money's Worth: A Study in the Waste of the Consumer's Dollars* exposed fraud and manipulation by American manufacturers and argued that, because advertising failed to provide sufficient product information, people were wasting their hard-earned money. Inefficiency in buying, the authors contended, was a direct result of consumers' lack of knowledge. Consumers in the marketplace were forced to rely on advertising propaganda that provided them with almost no factual information. Urging the public to educate themselves about the perils of such marketing devices, Chase and Schlink called for structural reform. By 1929, widespread interest in the book and in the *Consumers' Club Commodity List*, a newsletter that rated various branded products based on laboratory testings, spurred the formation of Consumers' Research. The new organization employed technical experts and had its own laboratory for testing consumer products. It generated a proliferation of articles and bestselling books on consumer-related issues, and received solid support from a range of professional organizations, including the General Federation of Women's Clubs, the American Home Economics Association, and the National League of Women Voters. It also cultivated friendly relations with members of the Consumer Advisory Board in Franklin D. Roosevelt's short-lived National Recovery Administration. In the mid-1930s, however, labor disagreements led some of the members to split off from Consumers' Research, resulting in the creation in 1936 of Consumers Union, with Colston E. Warne as its president.

The Federal Trade Commission Act of 1914 had given the Federal Trade Commission (FTC) jurisdiction over advertising, but only in cases where one business used advertising to gain an unfair advantage over another. This meant that the FTC lacked the authority to intervene on consumers' behalf when they were wronged, even harmed, by false and misleading advertising. Thus there was considerable momentum for stricter advertising regulation by the time of Roosevelt's inauguration in 1933. In June of that year, a bill to amend the 1906 Food and Drugs Act was introduced in Congress. The measure, which received input from Consumers' Research during its preparatory stages, proposed new labeling laws and mandatory grading of goods to help guide consumers in the marketplace. It also sought to empower the Food and Drug Administration to prohibit the false advertising of any food, drug, or cosmetic. Advertisers were immediately drawn to a stipulation that defined an advertisement as deceptive if it used "ambiguity or inference" to create a misleading impression. Major manufacturers generally had no objection to a ban on false advertising, but their reaction to the proposed ban on "ambiguity and inference" was strong and adverse. It was exactly the use of clever advertising to create enough ambiguity for consumers to infer the desirability of one product over another, even if none existed, that drove most of the consumer industry, and thus much of capitalism in general. They recognized, however, that this rationale for advertising might sound hollow to consumers, especially in the midst of a severe economic downturn, so they did their best to avoid discussing the issue directly. If anything, they argued, consumers should be grateful because advertising had brought them conveniences and cheaply mass-produced products. Consumer activists were equally unhappy with the bill, complaining that it did not go far enough in terms of providing consumer protection.

One section of the bill addressed the consumer movement's demand for product quality standards, to provide the public with purchasing guidance that was more informative than brand advertising. Not surprisingly, because standardization and mandatory grading of consumer goods posed a direct threat to brand advertising, the proposal was met with the same level of opposition as the proposal for advertising regulation. This set the stage for a five-year legislative battle, with congressional hearings on several revised versions of the bill. Helping the advertising industry's cause were a set of well-developed public relations and lobbying strategies and considerable influence over the commercial mass media. Few among the general public were fully informed about the issues at stake. With each new version of the bill, industry concerns took the front seat, and the issue of consumer protection, which had been the original impetus for the measure, gradually faded from the agenda. Despite demands from consumer groups, New Dealers, and government regulatory agencies, advertisers survived the battle with surprising ease. The Wheeler–Lea Amendment to the Federal Trade Commission Act was passed in 1938, but it only minimally affected existing advertising practices. The grading proposal never made it into law.

It was several decades before the United States experienced a new surge of intense consumer activism. In the 1960s and early 1970s, consumer organizations enjoyed steady support for their demands, and a variety of national consumer groups emerged, each with specialized interests, and some with charismatic leaders. The most influential person in what would come to be known as the third wave of consumer activism was undoubtedly Ralph Nader. In 1963 the young lawyer published *Unsafe at Any Speed*, a highly acclaimed and widely discussed exposé of the auto industry and its utter disregard for consumer safety.

Nader later transformed his interest in consumer issues into a movement that could effectively counter the power held by business in the marketplace. With help from associates, he uncovered abuses against individual consumers, and in 1968 he recruited a taskforce of students to investigate the FTC, which was being manipulated by business to such an extent that it was unable to fulfill its mandate. Hoping to invigorate the citizenry to fight corporate power and make businesses accountable to the people, Nader experimented with new strategies for action. His efforts had a strong impact: between 1967 and 1973, Congress enacted more than 25 laws to regulate corporate conduct in the consumer and environmental fields. The 1978 defeat of legislation to create a consumer advocacy agency was a watershed moment. The idea of a Department of the Consumer, to parallel the Departments of Commerce and Labor, had first been introduced back in the early 1930s. Under Nader's leadership, however, attention shifted from the creation of an agency without regulatory powers to one entrusted with monitoring the activities of other government agencies and with the authority, if necessary, to intervene in their regulatory decision making on consumers' behalf. In spite of massive support from consumer organizations, including the Consumer Federation of America and a newly invigorated Consumers Union, the plans were thwarted by commercial interests. Arguing that the proposed agency would create a new bureaucracy, increase the complexity of regulatory hearings, and force the disclosure of trade secrets, business interests once again used their powerful lobbying arm to defeat the plan. Organized consumer efforts to expand the FTC's regulatory powers and regulate the commercial targeting of children, led by the group Action on Children's Television, met a similar fate. By the late 1970s, most of the gains that had been made in the early part of the decade were lost.

Some of the activist momentum survived into the 1980s, but it quickly lost ground under the neoliberal policies that were put in place during the Reagan presidency. Deregulation of the telecommunications industry provided advertisers with new and expanded venues. In the business-friendly regulatory climate that followed, mass media became increasingly reluctant to discuss issues that might cast their commercial benefactors in a negative light.

In the 1990s consumers rose in unison once again, this time with a global vision. While this wave of activism is commonly referred to as "the anti-globalization movement," that does not mean that its proponents were xenophobic or nationalistic; they simply found common ground in opposing global policies that served investors and corporate interests. The interconnectedness of factory conditions, child labor, excessive commercialization, and environmental concerns demanded corporate accountability on a global level. Concerns over labor conditions and public health harked back to the Progressive era; the issue of overcommercialization and labeling of genetically altered foods echoed concerns that had been voiced in the 1930s; and the movement's outcry over environmental exploitation around the world reflected consumer demands that had been voiced some 30 years earlier. And, while it might appear that a century of consumer activism had come full circle, it was also evident that a new battle had just begun.

SEE ALSO: Consumer Activism; Consumer Culture, History of; Consumer Society

REFERENCES

Chase, Stuart, and F. J. Schlink. 1913. *Your Money's Worth: A Study in the Waste of the Consumer's Dollars*. New York: Macmillan.

Gaedeke, Ralph M. 1972. "The Muckraking Era." In *Consumerism: Viewpoints from Business, Government, and the Public Interest*, by Ralph M. Gaedeke and Warren W. Etcheson, 57–59. San Francisco, CA: Canfield.

Marchand, Ronald. 1986. *Advertising the American Dream: Making Way for Modernity, 1920–1940*. Berkeley: University of California Press.

Nader, Ralph. 1965. *Unsafe at Any Speed: The Designed-In Dangers of the American Automobile*. New York: Grossman.

Sklar, Kathryn Kish. 1998. "The Consumers' White Label Campaign and the National Consumers' League, 1898–1918." In *Getting and Spending: European and American Consumer Societies in the Twentieth Century*, edited by Susan Strasser, Charles McGovern, and Matthias Judt, 17–35. New York: Cambridge University Press.

FURTHER READING

Cohen, Lizabeth. 2003. *A Consumers' Republic: The Politics of Mass Consumption in Postwar America*. New York: Vintage.

Glickman, Lawrence B. 2009. *Buying Power: A History of Consumer Activism in America*. Chicago, IL: University of Chicago Press.

Stole, Inger L. 2012. *Advertising at War: Business, Consumers and Government in the 1940s*. Urbana: University of Illinois Press.

Consumer Protection Agency

MARTHA W. KING
Graduate Center, City University of New York, USA

Consumer protection agencies exist around the world to protect the interests of consumers. They are commonly established as the result of advocacy by consumer organizations and movements and are most generally designed to ensure the rights of consumers are acknowledged and protected. From the perspective of free market capitalists, the market should automatically protect consumer interests through competition and the balancing forces of supply and demand. But both consumer advocates and economists have argued that market imperfections or failures, such as monopolies or inadequate information, justify a range of government interventions to protect consumers. Consumer protection advocates and agencies recognize that profit seeking companies will avoid sharing information that might detract from profits but might be important for consumers to know, especially in relation to safety and health. Prime concerns of the consumer protection movement, which were subsequently taken up by protection agencies, include prices, fair trade competition, transparency, fraud, and regulation of advertisers.

US President John F. Kennedy's speech on consumer rights and his declaration of a "Consumers' Bill of Rights" in 1962 is seen as a high point in the history of consumer protection because it was the first time an elected leader had so emphatically embraced consumer rights. The anniversary of his speech, March 15, is now celebrated internationally as World Consumer Rights Day by the consumer movement to raise awareness. Subsequently, President Johnson appointed a White House adviser on consumer affairs in 1964. The US government first considered a Consumer Protection Agency in 1969.

Through to the late 1970s, it seemed that Americans were poised to benefit from a mass consumer movement and its advocacy for a federal agency. But the congressional margin of support for a federal agency was not large enough to overcome a veto by President Gerald Ford. At that time, the vision for the Consumer Protection Agency was as a clearinghouse for consumer complaints and as an advocate of consumer interests, to be led by a presidentially appointed leader. The demise of this legislation has been attributed to lobbying efforts of business and the work of the US Chamber of Commerce, the Business Roundtable, the Grocery Manufacturers Association, the National Association of Manufacturers, and the American Enterprise Institute. The agency, with a proposed budget of $15 million, was criticized as big government, overly burdensome and regulatory, and too bureaucratic. Through the Carter and Reagan administrations (1977–89), consumer protection efforts were significantly reduced in the United States. The Federal Trade Commission considers itself a consumer protection agency.

When President Barack Obama revived interest in this issue after the 2008 financial crisis, attention to consumer protection rose significantly and increasingly focused on consumer protection in the realm of financial services. The Consumer Financial Protection Bureau (CFPB), established in July 2011, consolidates most federal consumer financial protection authority in one place and is intended to protect people from unfair, deceptive, and abusive financial practices. The CFPB's authority begins with the ability to issue regulations under a host of consumer protection laws, exercising supervisory and enforcement authority over banks, savings associations, and large asset credit unions, as well as all consumer mortgage companies, payday lenders, and private education lenders. Elizabeth Warren, then a Harvard law professor and now a US senator representing Massachusetts, crafted the plans for the CPFB, building on the decades-old plan for a US CPA and adding the protection of consumers in financial markets.

The 2008 financial crisis increased the international community's interest in consumer protections for financial services as an element of global economic security. The World Bank created a Global Program on Consumer Protection and Financial Literacy in 2010. The program has conducted diagnostic reviews of consumer protection in 12 countries and action plans for improving consumer protection in two countries, Azerbaijan and Latvia. In 2012 the World Bank issued a set of "Good Practices for Financial Consumer Protection" which included recommendations relating to financial literacy and consumer empowerment, dispute resolution, competition, and disclosure and sales practices.

In 1985 the United Nations adopted the UN Guidelines for Consumer Protection. The UN's guidelines reflect the advocacy of Consumers International, a federation of 240 nongovernmental organizations in 120 countries, values such as the right to safety, redress, and to be informed, and a set of consumer responsibilities such as critical awareness and social responsibility. In 2011 the G20 issued "High Level Principles for Financial Consumer Protection," and the OECD launched a Task Force on Consumer Financial Protection.

There are also a series of regional networks devoted to consumer protection, such as the European Union's Consumer Protection Cooperation Network and the European Consumer Centres Network, the African Consumer Protection Dialogue, the Central American Council on Consumer Protection, the Caribbean Consumer Council, the Consumer Forum of East Asian Nations, the Iberoamerican Forum of Consumer Protection Agencies, and the ASEAN Coordinating Committee on Consumer Protection of Southeast Asian countries.

The International Consumer Protection and Enforcement Network (ICPEN) is a coalition of consumer protection agencies from more than 50 countries. Plans for the ICPEN, created to enforce fair trade and monitor cross-border transactions of goods and services, emerged in 1991 at the initiative of the Danish consumer ombudsman. It operates with a rotating presidency held by member countries' consumer agencies. The network does not address product safety or the regulation of financial services. Its strategies include generating and sharing information on consumer protection issues; sharing best practices in legislative and enforcement approaches to consumer protection; combating cross-border breaches of consumer protection laws; and facilitating effective cross-border remedies. ICPEN also launched the website at www.econsumer.gov for consumers to lodge complaints regarding cross-border transactions and foreign governments.

SEE ALSO: Consumer Activism; Consumer Movements, Contemporary; Consumer Movements, History of; Fair Trade

FURTHER READING

Cohen, Lizabeth. 2003. *A Consumer's Republic: The Politics of Mass Consumption in Post-War America*. New York: Vintage.

Glickman, Lawrence. 2009. *Buying Power: A History of Consumer Activism in America*. Chicago, IL: University of Chicago Press.

Harris, Richard. 1989. *The Politics of Regulatory Change: A Tale of Two Agencies*. New York: Oxford University Press.

Consumer Research, Methods of:

SEE Methods of Consumer Research

Consumer Resistance Movements

VINCE CARDUCCI
College for Creative Studies, USA

Consumer resistance movements are collective efforts, both formal and informal, that use the power of the marketplace either as a means of expression or to bring about some kind of change. Consumer resistance movements, often in wealthy nations of the global North, can be anti-consumerist as a general orientation, such as *Adbusters* magazine's annual Buy Nothing Day and the broader trend of "do-it-yourself," or activist, targeted to achieve economic or political goals, as in the United Students Against Sweatshops (USAS) efforts to pressure American colleges and universities to adopt fair labor and environmentally friendly practices in their purchasing and service operations. Consumer resistance movements and consumer resistance in general have a long history, and have garnered popular attention in recent years with the publication of Naomi Klein's book *No Logo: Taking Aim at the Brand Bullies* (1999).

An element of consumer resistance is built into the process of market exchange. Classical economics sees exchange as the balancing of supply on the producer's part and demand on the consumer's part in the assignment of value mediated through the mechanism of price. The consumer, in effect, resists completing the exchange transaction until equilibrium has been achieved in the form of a mutually agreed-upon price. Neoclassical economics introduces the concept of marginal utility into the decision-making process, focusing on the rational calculation of choices to be made in allocating scarce resources between a myriad of needs, desires, and purchase options and the opportunity costs of selecting one versus another. For example, one may forgo the value of current news information in favor of the satisfaction of caffeine in opting for a cup of coffee in the morning instead of the daily paper. The calculation of marginal utility can be realized in a number of ways: resisting one product and opting for another in the same category, resisting a product in one category and opting for one in another category, or not completing any transaction at all. Negotiating the margins of utility in order to overcome consumer resistance is central to modern sales tactics and marketing theory from the producer's perspective (Olivier 2009).

Albert O. Hirschman's (1970) concepts of exit and voice are useful for parsing the varieties of consumer resistance and their organization into movements. Hirschman associates *exit*, the refusal to buy a firm's product or service, with economics; he associates *voice*, the expression of disapproval either directly to a firm or indirectly through more oblique channels, with politics. Exit may be expressed either by leaving the market entirely or by simply choosing another product, essentially the operation of the invisible hand of the self-regulating market. Voice is more complex and visible, as it seeks to consciously register dissatisfaction in the hope of effecting change either in the product or the producer. Exit and voice can commingle as when a consumer boycott is coupled with a letter writing campaign, public demonstration, or other tactic meant to garner media attention or instigate regulatory action. Anti-consumerist movements such as Buy Nothing Day are exit, whereas activist movements such as USAS are voice.

Another example of consumer resistance in the form of exit is the voluntary simplicity movement. As a contemporary form of asceticism, voluntary simplicity encompasses a number of practices to reduce one's level of consumption as a way to disengage from market transactions, from lowering the number and types of possessions, particularly those considered extraneous or luxurious, to increasing self-sufficiency, in the form of home production and other do-it-yourself methods. The power of voice as a form of consumer resistance can be further seen in the rise of conscientious consumption as a social movement – that is, consumers who, as markets have matured, possess information and affluence and who factor such considerations as environmental sustainability, workplace equity, point of origin, and so on into virtually every purchasing decision across a broad range of product and service categories, with the full expectation that producers will supply their demands (Stehr 2008).

Perspectives on consumer resistance differ depending on which side of the transaction the interested party sits. For producers, consumer resistance is a barrier to completing a transaction that needs to be overcome. For consumers, resistance is a form of agency, the assertion of sovereignty in the marketplace. The nature of the resistance also varies. It can be purely economic – producer and consumer are simply unable to come to terms with respect to the determination of price and value. It can be based on anxiety, for example fear on the consumer's part that a product or service poses a physical threat or other serious disadvantage. It can even be moral, a refusal to engage in certain kinds of consumption transactions based on principled concerns for such questions as ecological sustainability, social responsibility, and national ideology, among other things.

If a modern understanding of consumer resistance from the producer side is grounded in classical economics, then its opposite can be seen through the theoretical lens of the Marxist tradition and its romantic antecedents. For Marx, commodity consumption is the site of mystification, alienation, and exploitation within the capitalist system, a mechanism whereby workers unwittingly reproduce their inequality through the purchase on the market of the surplus value (that is, the fruits of their labor in commodity form) that has been appropriated from them by the bourgeoisie. Nineteenth-century utopian socialists sought to create exchange networks that would ameliorate the abuses of the modern division of labor, constituting a resistance to the burgeoning commodity system in the form of what is now known as *solidarity economics*. Marxism directly inspired some of the models, such as the Arts and Crafts movement founded by William Morris, while others are more accurately described as fellow travelers, such as the British cooperative movement of Robert Owen.

Consumer resistance in this vein is often characterized as politics carried on by other means. This can take the form of mass protests against material scarcity and rising prices, going back at least to the plebeian bread riots of ancient Rome. Or it could assume more of a moral dimension, as in the later resistance to and social unrest in the face of the increasingly monopolized distribution of corn and other grains in the nascent capitalist market economy in eighteenth-century England; E. P. Thompson (1971) has characterized these events as a breach of trust on the part of the patron classes in neglecting to provide for those in the community who are less fortunate. Consumer resistance as alternative political action is also evident in the sugar boycott of the late eighteenth and early nineteenth centuries in protest at the Caribbean slave trade under the British empire: middle- and upper-class women who otherwise lacked voting privileges expressed their political will by refusing to purchase the sweetener imported from colonial plantations under production conditions that were perceived to be tainted with what the abolitionists termed "Brother's blood."

Indeed, boycotts are one of the main forms of collective consumer resistance, and their exercise is sometimes referred to as "negative political consumerism," a term that recognizes their reactive nature in the exchange process (Micheletti 2003). Monroe Friedman (1999) notes that boycotts are a frequently used tactic for those outside the conventional power structure. Their use as an alternative means of political action has historically been to achieve either economic or social justice. The former is typically the concern of consumers, while the latter is often the concern of minorities. Examples of economic justice boycotts include the protests against high meat prices during the Great Depression and coffee in the 1970s. Examples of social justice boycotts include the "Don't Buy from Where You Can't Work" boycotts for equal employment opportunity, which also occurred during the Great Depression, and the celebrated Civil Rights movement bus boycotts of the 1950s. Most consumer boycotts have historically been directed against commodities, such as meat, grapes, and coffee. They have also tended to be more market-oriented, that is, directed to effecting change by impacting a target's sales revenues, giving economic leverage to those mounting the action. Contemporary consumer boycotts, on the other hand, tend to be more media-oriented, seeking to have an effect by damaging the target's reputation or brand image.

Recent examples of market-oriented consumer boycotts include those mounted against Nestlé for its alleged exploitative sale of baby formula in less developed countries, and Nike for unfair labor practices, outsourcing, and environmentally unfriendly production practices. Faith-based groups have also organized boycotts of television programs, products, and brands to protest what they perceive to be anti-family values. The 2012 campaign against J. C. Penney for its endorsement deal with lesbian celebrity Ellen DeGeneres is an example.

Parodies of brand names and marketing slogans are among the primary and more effective tools used in organizing contemporary media-oriented methods of consumer resistance. These actions are known by the term "culture jamming," after the technique of electronically interfering with broadcast and radio signals for military or political purposes. Common culture jams include subverting commercial advertising and other promotional messages by altering copy and images and appropriating brand identities.

The opposite of boycotts, "buycotts," have additionally appeared, seeking to offer support for products deemed admirable from such perspectives as ecological sustainability or fair trade, known as green and blue consumerism respectively. These actions are forms of "positive political consumerism" (Micheletti 2003) in recognition of their proactive aspect. Other examples include "Buy American" and similar campaigns, which employ nationalist ideology to promote the purchase of certain products. Implicit in these types of actions is resistance to the consumption of products offered by perceived foreign competitors.

In light of these trends, many companies have adopted corporate social responsibility (CSR) programs as a tactic for overcoming certain kinds of consumer resistance. CSR takes many forms and seeks to mediate between the mandates of pure profitability and broader social concerns (Werther and Chandler 2010). The simplest and arguably most traditional practice is corporate philanthropy in which a firm offers financial or in-kind support to target communities or other stakeholders. A common practice in this regard is to devote a certain portion of revenues to specific causes such as the arts, the environment, or at-risk communities as a way to demonstrate concern on the part of the corporation, the intent being to garner support for the firm's overall mission and thereby minimize consumer resistance. A more recent development is social accounting, in which organizations open their operations to external review to certify compliance with various standards that are typically monitored by third parties, including ISO 14000 and 9000, the Fair Labor Association, and the Forest Stewardship Council. Another recent trend is to integrate CSR into the business plan as a form of socially responsible marketing. Firms that have done this include Fair Trade-certified purveyors of coffee, tea, and cocoa, for example Pete's Coffee and Divine Chocolates, and anti-sweatshop apparel manufacturers, for example Fair Indigo and Maggie's Organic Fibers.

These practices have engendered further consumer resistance based on skepticism with respect to the firms' true commitment to CSR. The terms "greenwashing" and "bluewashing" describe what are perceived as disingenuous efforts on the part of corporations to act in environmentally and socially responsible ways respectively. The label has been used to describe Starbucks, for example, in that even though it is, as its promotional communications claim, the world's largest purchaser of Fair Trade-certified coffee, the company's financial commitment to the category constitutes only a tiny fraction of its total supply. Another criticism of Starbucks pertains to its use of internally determined criteria for CSR rather than third-party certification, a charge which is leveled against many corporations and their perceived green- and bluewashing practices.

Recently, a new form of business organization has emerged termed the B (for benefit) corporation, whose purpose is to create value for society at large as well as for shareholders. B corporations typically report performance to their socially responsible objectives using third-party certified criteria rather than those they might develop internally. Maryland was the first US state to permit such corporate organization in 2010, with several other states having since allowed similar types of corporate charters. Examples include Namaste Solar, an employee-owned cooperative based in Boulder, Colorado, which designs, installs, and maintains solar electric systems for homes, businesses, nonprofits, and government, and Green Building Services, based in Portland, Oregon, a provider of sustainable building services and tools to benefit business, the community, and the environment. These operations are typically small and locally based, often capitalizing on consumer resistance to large multinational corporations as part of their value proposition.

Some researchers see the ostensible antagonism between producer and consumer, on which the concept of consumer resistance is based, as an outmoded dialectic, particularly with the blurring of these roles within the information economy, a process known in the social sciences as de-differentiation. Increasingly, the cycles of production and consumption are coming together, with users producing the goods and services they consume. This can be seen most clearly in social media such as Facebook, Pinterest, Tumblr, and Twitter, and in massively multiplayer online games (MMPOGs), such as *World of Warcraft* and *Happy Farm*, in which time spent online is taken up with providing content that constitutes one's form of entertainment and self-expression while simultaneously creating value for the for-profit enterprises that provide the software services. Even so, some semblance of consumer resistance persists in the do-it-yourself practices of hacker spaces, Maker Faires, urban farming, and the like. This activity is sometimes referred to as prosumption, a portmanteau of the words "production" and "consumption" (Ritzer and Jurgenson 2010).

SEE ALSO: Boycotts; Consumer Activism; Culture Jamming; Do-It-Yourself (DIY); Downshifting; Ethical Consumption; Fair Trade; Markets, Moral Aspects of; Politics and Consumer Culture; Prosumption; Socially Responsible Marketing (SRM)

REFERENCES

Friedman, Monroe. 1999. *Consumer Boycotts: Effecting Change through the Marketplace and the Media*. London: Routledge.

Hirschman, Albert O. 1970. *Exit, Voice, and Loyalty: Responses to Decline in Firms, Organizations, and States*. Cambridge, MA: Harvard University Press.

Klein, Naomi. 1999. *No Logo: Taking Aim at the Brand Bullies*. New York: Picador.

Micheletti, Michelle. 2003. *Political Virtue and Shopping: Individuals, Consumerism, and Collective Action*. New York: Palgrave Macmillan.

Olivier, Richard L. 2009. *Satisfaction: A Behavioral Perspective on the Consumer*, 2nd ed. Armonk, NY: M. E. Sharpe.

Ritzer, George, and Nathan Jurgenson. 2010. "Production, Consumption, Prosumption: The Nature of Capitalism in the Age of the Digital 'Prosumer.'" *Journal of Consumer Culture* 10:13–36. doi:10.1177/1469540509354673.

Stehr, Nico. 2008. *Moral Markets: How Knowledge and Affluence Change Consumers and Products*. Boulder, CO: Paradigm.

Thompson, E. P. 1971. "The Moral Economy of the English Crowd in the Eighteenth Century." *Past & Present* 50: 76–136.

Werther, William B., Jr., and David Chandler. 2010. *Strategic Corporate Responsibility: Stakeholders in a Broader Environment*, 2nd ed. Thousand Oaks, CA: Sage.

Consumer Socialization

KARIN M. EKSTRÖM
University of Borås, Sweden

Consumer socialization has attracted researchers' attention over the years, and in particular during the 1970s when public policy issues regarding the effect of television advertising on children was discussed. Most research has focused on how children are socialized during childhood and adolescence. John (1999) provides a comprehensive overview of 25 years of research on the consumer socialization of children. A common definition of consumer socialization in marketing is Ward's (1974): "the process by which young people acquire skills, knowledge, and attitudes relevant to their functioning as consumers in the marketplace" (p. 2). Socialization is believed to be particularly strong during childhood, as children become consumers. However, consumer socialization is a lifelong process (e.g., Ward 1974; Ekström 2006). This is particularly important to recognize as society changes and consumers continuously have to learn new skills to function as consumers, for example internet banking skills. Berger and Luckmann (1967) distinguish between primary socialization, which takes place during childhood, and secondary socialization, which occurs subsequently. There are a few studies on socialization of the elderly, but a lack of studies regarding adult consumer socialization. Adult consumer socialization is about learning new roles, for example being a spouse or a parent. Riesman and Roseborough (1955) introduced the concept "resocialization" to describe when an individual has to relearn patterns of behavior. Rather than recognizing continuous lifelong learning, it implies more drastic changes and the learning of new roles. Resocialization has been used in relation to institutionalization to describe correction of behavior derived from earlier socialization.

Definitions and meanings of socialization in general, and consumer socialization specifically, are discussed by Ekström (2006). One crucial component is to conform to societal requirements or norms. Moschis (1987) writes: "from a social perspective, an individual can be said to be socialized when he or she has learned to think and feel according to society's expectations" (p. 23). However, membership in society is something that is acquired, not something an individual is born into. Berger and Luckman (1967) state: "he is born with a predisposition towards sociality, and he becomes a member of society" (p. 149). In marketing, consumer socialization is about functioning in the marketplace (e.g., Ward 1974). Research on consumer socialization has focused in particular on how to become effective consumers.

Another important component of socialization is social interaction. Secord and Backman (1964) argue that only changes that have their origin in interaction with other people are products of socialization. A majority of research has focused on the family as the socialization agent or involved a few socialization agents such as family, friends, or mass media. Research on families would benefit from a reciprocal view in that family members and generations socialize each other.

Most studies on consumer socialization have focused on learning. The consumer socialization process has been described with cognitive developmental theories (e.g., John and Whitney 1986) and social learning theories (e.g., Moschis 1987). Researchers have also advocated a combination of modeling, reinforcement, and social interaction (often focusing on family communication). Overall, there is too little research on the processes through which consumer socialization occurs. Instead of studying how learning is acquired, the focus in research has been on the content of learning. The socialization processes may be difficult to capture since the socialization agent or the person socialized may not be aware of the processes. Often "socialization takes place indirectly as an unintended, or at least, as an implicit consequence of an ongoing relationship" (Tallman, Marotz-Baden, and Pindas 1983, 25). It is hard to know when consumer socialization begins and when it is completed. In fact, since it is lifelong, it is a continuous process that will never be concluded.

SEE ALSO: Brands and Branding; Children's Consumer Culture; Mass Marketing

REFERENCES

Berger, Peter L., and Thomas Luckmann. 1967. *The Social Construction of Reality*. Harmondsworth, UK: Penguin.

Ekström, Karin M. 2006. "Consumer Socialization Revisited." *Research in Consumer Behavior* 10: 71–98.

John, Deborah Roedder. 1999. "Consumer Socialization of Children: A Retrospective Look at Twenty-Five Years of Research." *Journal of Consumer Research* 26: 183–213.

John, Deborah Roedder, and John C. Whitney Jr. 1986. "The Development of Consumer Knowledge in Children: A Cognitive Structure Approach." *Journal of Consumer Research* 12: 406–417.

Moschis, George P. 1987. *Consumer Socialization: A Life Cycle Perspective*. Lexington, MA: Lexington.

Riesman, David, and Howard Roseborough. 1955. "Careers and Consumer Behavior." In *Consumer Behavior*, Vol. 2: *The Life Cycle and Consumer Behavior*, edited by Lincoln Clark, 1–18. New York: New York University Press.

Secord, Paul F., and Carl W. Backman. 1964. *Social Psychology*. New York: McGraw-Hill.

Tallman, Irving, Ramona Marotz-Baden, and Pablo Pindas. 1983. *Adolescent Socialization in Cross-Cultural Perspective: Planning for Social Change*. New York: Academic Press.

Ward, Scott. 1974. "Consumer Socialization." *Journal of Consumer Research* 1: 1–16.

Consumer Society

STEVEN MILES
Manchester Metropolitan University, UK

A consumer society is a society in which the buying and selling of goods and services is its defining characteristic. The emergence of a consumer society has had a fundamental effect on how people live in the developed world; it has created a logic of its own to the extent that it would appear difficult to imagine a society that is not driven by consumption. The existence of a consumer society has fascinated scholars in a wide range of disciplines including sociology, anthropology, history, economics, cultural studies, and human geography. These disciplines have sought to comprehend the evolution of a society that was defined in the past by the satisfaction of needs and that has come to be defined by the satisfaction of wants. It is this distinction that underpins the consumer society as an ideological entity in which our sense of individuals as citizens is fundamentally tied to the kind of society in which we live.

The consumer society is in part the product of global economic processes that are founded on an almost universal commitment to the free market. Global capitalism is perpetuated through the maintenance of artificial consumption levels built on the promotion of artificially created desires. These desires are played out at a private level, but collectively they allow for a degree of spending for the maximization of private profit. In the twentieth century, the market became the underpinning socioeconomic characteristic of developed societies and the consumer society is the social consequence of this process.

As much as politicians might portray the market as a neutral entity in which freedom and choice predominate, this process is highly ideological in nature. The market defines reality and the dominant reality it defines is that of a consumer society. The hegemony of the consumer society is facilitated by the degree of choice that the consumer society appears to provide. In a consumer society, the degree of choice made available to the consumer to, say, buy a pair of jeans or a computer tablet is artificial and immense. The market depends on the constant reproduction of such choice (through, for example, the compulsory obsolescence of electronic goods). It also depends on the implicit assumption that happiness can be achieved through the freedoms that that choice provides. In effect, as members of the Frankfurt School such as Herbert Marcuse recognized, people come to recognize themselves in and through their commodities – they find "their soul" in what it is they consume and as such they are tied to the ideology that underpins the society in which they live.

The recognition that the consumer society exists may logically lead us to the conclusion that consumption has a more fundamental role in tying us to the social structures than might previously have been imagined. Social theorists have traditionally prioritized production as opposed to consumption as the driving force of social change. Karl Marx's theory of social change is one of historical materialism. For Marx transitions in technology and production determine the nature of socioeconomic development and it is through these developments that the everyday realities of social life are determined. Marx saw the commodity not as a product to be consumed at the level of the individual but as one that was sold on the market in exchange for money. From this point of view, the whole capitalist system was objectified through the commodity, which in turn reproduced a certain set of social relations. What is interesting about this for a discussion of a consumer society is that Marx also argued that the dominance of the commodity and of a market driven by exchange resulted in a sort of "false consciousness." The working classes are alienated from each other by a false sense that the natural way to behave is to happily compete with each other for commodities. In this context, the commodity externalizes the products of human labor from the laborer. Commodities become external to the self, and more and more objects are bought and sold for exchange on the marketplace. Through what Marx called commodity fetishism, objects become treated with a particular reverence to the extent that, to the consumer, it appears that anything is possible in a consumer society.

In the above context the actual experience of the consumer society is one that is underpinned by the nature of the relationship between structure and agency: how the individual negotiates through the structures laid out for him or her by the broader society. In other words, everyday life is a product of a society underpinned by the consumer system. That system is ideologically powerful inasmuch as it appears to define the parameters within which we can conduct our everyday lives and yet we are able, or at least we feel able, to construct a sense of ourselves through the opportunities that the consumer society provides. In this respect, the consumer society can only be understood in reference to questions of identity. The longevity of the consumer society is dependent on a set of circumstances in which consumers feel, consciously or subconsciously, that they can achieve a state of belonging through the social structures provided by the consumer society. It is on this basis that the consumer society is reproduced. Life in a consumer society is therefore very much about a set of compromises in which the individual seeks to protect their individuality while ensuring that individuality is suitably corroborated through group membership. Georg Simmel (1957) thus argued that the individual balances a psychological tendency toward imitation with the personal desire for differentiation so that fashion, for example, effectively provides the individual with a sense of stability in an essentially unstable world.

Perhaps the most concerted discussion of the consumer society is that of Jean Baudrillard in *The Consumer Society* (1998/1970). Baudrillard is interested in how individuals become wedded to a way of thinking about the world that is determined by "formal rationality." In other words, people's relationship to the consumer society is calculated in nature: consumption offers them a means to an end, the end (however partial and temporary) being the sense of happiness that consumer goods can offer. But such thinking is ultimately illusory, for Baudrillard, in that all goods basically signify the same thing. The problem here is that "needs" are not inherent or natural. A consumer does not *need* a new pair of expensive training shoes, although it might suit his or her frame of mind to think that he or she does. It can thus be argued that real and artificial needs cannot be distinguished from each other. In other words, there are no actual "needs" at all. The consumer society constructs a sense of what these needs should be: as consumers, as citizens of the consumer society, we are subject to a system of needs that has been constructed for us. The consumer society ties us into a system in which we are in turn implicated.

In effect, the consumer society creates its own kind of sociability in which we as consumers conform to the consumerist logic that it creates. The question of choice plays a key role in this process, as choice effectively becomes a proxy for freedom. But the freedom the consumer society offers us is at best partial. It is an inherently limited freedom as it can only exist within the parameters defined by the consumer society. The consumer society appears to be democratic, but the democracy it is founded on is accessible only to those people who are economically able to fully engage with the consumer society. It is in this sense that, for many, the consumer society is no more than symbolic. It obliges us to be involved in the democracy it constructs, and it obliges us to aspire to the sets of identities with which it associates itself. In this sense it is as oppressive as it is democratic, as it can never possibly deliver on all the promises it makes.

The reality is that a consumer society is by its very nature an unequal society. Those who are apparently unable to make choices in a consumer society on economic grounds are ironically the very same individuals, given the way in which the mass media constantly reinforces the values that a consumer society propagates, who are most obliged to engage in that society. The price to pay for consumer freedom is therefore excessive. A consumer society gives the consumer a sense of liberation and security while exacerbating the oppression of others. In some senses, then, the consumer society is a spectacular illusion. It convinces us all that we can belong, but it rarely delivers on this promise. In considering the socially divisive nature of the consumer society Zygmunt Bauman (1998) deploys the notion of the "flawed consumer" and argues that, in a consumer society, what it means to be poor is no longer defined by a person's work status but by their limited ability to consume in a society that obliges them to do so.

The consumer society is a society in which consumption, and not work, becomes a primary focus for everyday life. This process is reinforced not just in the way we think about the world, but also through the physical manifestation of the consumer society. The consumer society has come to be ingrained in the very physicality of the society in which we live so that we are left with very little choice but to partake in what it has to offer. The point here is that a consumer society becomes more than the sum of its parts. Its physical manifestation is not dependent on how far retail opportunities come to define the urban landscape, but rather on the broader ideological expression of that landscape so that it becomes very difficult for consumers to imagine a society in which they would do anything else but consume.

The consumer society is perhaps most visibly manifested through the city, which from this point of view has arguably become little more than a unit for the efficient maximization of consumption. Thus, we find a cityscape increasingly defined by opportunities to consume – by shopping malls, multiplex cinemas incorporating bookshops and cafés, and sports stadia that have become an experience in their own right above and beyond the sports they house. Such spaces provide a mirror of the society in which we live. However, this tells only half the story, as the power of the consumer society is in fact largely symbolic. In a postindustrial world in which economic possibilities are increasingly constrained, the service driven economy appears to be particularly attractive. It is therefore incumbent on policymakers to ensure that their city is competitive in this context. It is essential that the city is represented as being an energetic (usually cultural) place to be, and free market capitalism deems that consumption must provide the means of achieving this. As such, there is a danger that cities, or at least the decision makers responsible for the future of those cities, are putting too many eggs in the consumption basket. In committing to the world of choice that apparently characterizes the consumer society, there is a danger that the consumer society is manifested as an increasingly homogenized society. A city or society defined by consumption arguably undermines the sense of discovery and excitement that makes such places special in the first place.

We are surrounded by a society in which consumption is the orthodoxy and yet it remains highly questionable whether consumption can fulfill what we expect of it. And the irony of all this is that, as individuals, we are arguably complicit with this process. Rather than being the victims of a consumer society duped into consuming in particular ways, as members of the Frankfurt School may have argued in the past, it might be suggested that contemporary consumers are actually content to give up some freedoms in order to access another set of freedoms which the consumer society provides. So, for example, many cities are highly policed by CCTV. On the one hand, this might be considered to represent an assault on human rights. On the other, such measures may be deemed by the individual, subconsciously at least, to be acceptable so that they are free to maximize their opportunities to consume.

We could come to the conclusion that the consumer society manipulates us into consuming in particular ways. This reflects a fear that the political right has hijacked the notion of the consumer as being at the forefront of a society (to the extent that in the 1980s the British prime minister Margaret Thatcher went so far as to proclaim that there was no longer any such thing as society, only individuals – men, women, and families) built around the individual's engagement with the "free" market. However, there is a contrary view. One suggestion is that the consumer society may actually provide the basis for a new form of consumer driven citizenship. Garcia Canclini (2001) has therefore suggested that the arena of consumption contributes to the integrative and communicative rationality of society. In an increasingly atomized world consumption comes more to the fore in determining what constitutes a shared identity. Public life is filtered through the market more so than it is through the state. From this point of view there is potential for a more positive reimagining of the consumer society as a site of cognitive value in which the individual's relationship to the consumer society becomes much more proactive and less motivated by personal gain.

It is important to understand that the consumer experience cannot be understood in isolation as a purely personal experience. Consumption isn't merely a matter of choice (as some marketers tend to imply); the degree of that choice is predetermined by the ideological dimensions of the consumer society. As such, in critically considering the impact of the consumer society on people's everyday lives, it is essential to remember that consumption potentially plays a key social role in enhancing a sense of disenfranchisement, for example among young people, who are under incredible pressure to consume in particular ways, but who simply do not have the resources to do so.

Economically at least, the consumer society is built on the assumed benefits of a persistent growth in material living standards. This may have brought with it an upward spiral of aspirational affluence, but what it has not apparently brought is a parallel change in values. Despite ongoing debates about healthy eating, recycling, and the environment, for example, there is no sense that a postconsumer society in which the individual rises above the pressures of the consumer society to become less self-centered and more altruistic is around the corner. Even in times of global economic downturn consumers apparently continue to aspire to the trappings of the consumer society, believing that they can find some sense of fulfillment around the next corner. The consumer society is reproduced by the fact that the point of satisfaction is never reached. As such, in a consumer society consumers are arguably left in a state of constant limbo, perpetually unfulfilled by a world of short-term fixes and "solutions" that simply reaffirm their loyalty to the very social system that strips them, or indeed us, of our individuality.

SEE ALSO: Adorno, Theodor; Baudrillard, Jean; Capitalism; Citizenship and Consumption; Commodities; Commodity Fetishism; Consumption and Identity; Homogenization and Heterogenization; Marx, Karl

REFERENCES

Baudrillard, Jean. 1998/1970. *The Consumer Society: Myths and Structures*. London: Sage.

Bauman, Zygmunt. 1998. *Work, Consumerism and the New Poor.* Buckingham, UK: Open University Press.

Canclini, Nestor Garcia. 2001. *Consumers and Citizens: Globalization and Multicultural Conflicts.* Minneapolis: University of Minnesota Press.

Simmel, Georg. 1957. "Fashion." *American Journal of Sociology* 62: 541–548.

FURTHER READING

Campbell, Colin. 1987. *The Romantic Ethic and the Spirit of Modern Consumerism.* Oxford: Blackwell.

Douglas, Mary, and Baron Isherwood. 1982. *The World of Goods.* New York: Norton.

Marcuse, Herbert. 1964. *One-Dimensional Man.* Boston, MA: Beacon.

Marx, Karl. 1990. *Capital: A Critique of Political Economy,* Vol. 1, 2nd ed. Harmondsworth, UK: Penguin.

Miller, Daniel. 1987. *Material Culture and Mass Consumption.* Oxford: Blackwell.

Ritzer, George. 2010. *The McDonaldization of Society 6.* Thousand Oaks, CA: Pine Forge.

Slater, Don. 1997. *Consumer Culture and Modernity.* Cambridge, UK: Polity.

Consumers in Emerging Economies

SHARAD AGARWAL and M. J. XAVIER
Indian Institute of Management Ranchi, India

Emerging economies are nations with social or business activities in the process of rapid growth and industrialization. This rapid growth and development have led to the increase in income of the residents of these countries, which in turn has led to a splurge in consumption among the populations of these nations.

Emerging economies commonly refer to the BRIC countries (Brazil, Russia, Indian, and China) and has more recently included MIKT countries (Mexico, Indonesia, South Korea, and Turkey). According a report by the World Bank (Global Development Horizons 2011), BRIC countries plus South Korea and Indonesia will lead the world's economy by 2025 with more than half of all global growth, which makes it imperative to study them from the consumption perspective in order to understand and analyze the consumer habits and patterns in these economies. In this entry, we will focus on consumer patterns from an Indian perspective.

Since the early 2000s, the Chinese economy has experienced phenomenal growth, which has helped it to become the second largest economy in the world next only to the mighty United States. As projected by Goldman Sachs (quoted in Chen et al. 2012) and depicted in Table 1, the average GDP growth expected by India and China between 2020 and 2025 is around 7.7 and 6.6 percent respectively; the advanced economies of the United Kingdom and United States will experience a GDP growth rate of 1.4 and 2.1 percent respectively during the same period; and some European economies (Italy and Germany) are even expected to experience a GDP growth of less than 1 percent. These figures denote the growth in demand expected from the consumers in emerging economies, which will be much higher than those in the advanced economies.

INDIAN CONSUMER CATEGORIES

In 2050, India's population is projected to be around 1.69 billion, while that of China will be around 1.31 billion. The household consumption in any economy depends upon the income levels of the households. As suggested by Beinhocker, Farrell, and Zainulbhai (2007), Indian households can be classified into four broad categories, on the basis of household income. The first category, "deprived," comprises households with annual incomes of less than INR90,000 (US$1 = INR65, approx.). This category consisted of

Table 1 Projected GDP growth (%)

	2006–15	*2015–20*	*2020–25*
Advanced economies			
France	1.8	1.8	1.7
Germany	1.7	1.1	0.6
Italy	1.5	1.4	0.9
Japan	1.1	1.3	1.5
UK	2.3	1.8	1.4
US	3.8	2.3	2.1
Emerging economies			
Brazil	3.9	3.8	3.7
China	5.5	8.4	7.7
India	4.5	7.1	6.6
Russia	4.3	3.2	3.1

Source: Chen et al. 2012

around 54 percent of all Indian households in 2005 and is expected to fall to around 22 percent by 2025. This fall in the "deprived" population indicates the expected increase in consumption from this segment, as many move up the economic ladder. The second category is termed "aspirer," with annual incomes in the range of INR90,000 to INR200,000. This class is also expected to decrease from its share of around 41 percent (in 2005) to 36 percent by 2025. The third category is termed "middle class," which includes households earning in the range of INR200,000 to INR1,000,000. This class is expected to grow from its share of around 5 percent (in 2005) to around 41 percent by 2025. This great Indian middle class, as it is called, is expected to be the major consumer of all modern products and services, as it broadly comprises an educated generation working in diversified industrial sectors. The fourth category is termed the "rich" class, with average annual household incomes greater than INR1,000,000. The share of this category of households is expected to be around 2–3 percent by 2025. This class consists of industrialists, entrepreneurs, and professionals who are niche segment consumers and aspire to maintain a world-class lifestyle, choosing premium products and brands across their consumption patterns.

To elucidate the pattern of consumer spending, we explain spending by the Indian consumer across different product categories in the year 2011, along with projections for spending in the year 2016. As depicted in Table 2, food and groceries constitute the lion's share in total spending by the Indian consumer – namely, 69.1 percent in 2011 and projected to decrease slightly to 63 percent by 2015. This decrease in the share of the food and grocery segment, alongside an increase in areas such as consumer electronics and IT, jewelry and watches, restaurants, etc., denotes a shift in lifestyle consumption patterns among consumers in emerging economies.

BOTTOM-OF-PYRAMID CONSUMERS

Following the seminal work of Prahalad and Hart (2002), there has been a rising interest in so-called "Bottom-of-Pyramid" (BoP)

Table 2 Consumer spending (2011 vs. 2016), in US$ billion

Category	*2011*	*Percent (2011)*	*2016*	*Percent (2016)*
Food and groceries	325.0	69.1	425.0	63.0
Apparel	35.0	7.4	50.2	7.4
Jewelry and watches	25.6	5.4	44.2	6.5
Consumer electronics and IT	22.7	4.8	42.8	6.3
Pharmacy	14.0	3.0	23.6	3.5
Furnishings and furniture	9.1	1.9	17.1	2.5
Restaurants	8.8	1.9	15.8	2.3
Footwear	4.5	1.0	8.3	1.2
Beauty services	1.3	0.3	3	0.4
Health/fitness services	1.0	0.2	2.5	0.4
Others	23.0	4.9	42.5	6.3
Total (US$bn)	470.0	100.0	675.0	100.0

Source: Adapted from *The Marketing White Book* 2012–13, 75

consumers across the world. This term refers to the approximately four billion people in the world, including more than 732 million in India itself, with a per capita income of less than US$2 per day or less than US$1500 per year. The needs and demands of BoP consumers were traditionally neglected and were severely underserved by the consumer product companies. This segment of the population has unique needs, constraints, challenges, and resources, and the majority of them live outside the confines of the formal economy (London 2008). This consumer segment together accounts for US$5 trillion of the total consumer market, and their aggregate purchasing power suggests significant opportunities for market-based approaches to better meet their needs, increase their productivity and incomes, and empower their entry into the formal economy (WRI 2007). The majority of these four billion people live in villages across the world. With the spread of mass media such as radio and television, these consumers are now well aware of the products and services available to their counterparts in cities, and hence they themselves aspire to have access to similar services.

The traditional business models of companies have failed to serve these consumers, which would involve adopting innovative models of production, sales, distribution, and logistics to make it possible for the global corporations to serve the BoP consumers profitably. To successfully serve the BoP consumers in the emerging economies, companies are required to develop the markets rather than just exploit them. One initiative along this line was undertaken by Hindustan Unilever (project Shakti), a door-to-door selling operation, which attempted to provide work for large numbers of people in poor rural communities (Xavier et al. 2008).

SEE ALSO: Consumer Behavior; Consumption in China; Consumption in India

REFERENCES

Beinhocker, Eric D., Diana Farrell, and Adil S. Zainulbhai. 2007. "Tracking the Growth of India's Middle Class." *McKinsey Quarterly* 3: 51–61.

Chen, Vivian, Ben Cheng, Gad Levanon, Ataman Ozyildirim, and Bart van Ark. 2012. "Projecting Global Growth." *Economics Program Working Papers 12–02*. New York: The Conference Board, Economics Program.

Global Development Horizons. 2011. "Multipolarity: The New Global Economy." Available at http://siteresources.worldbank.org/INTGDH/Resources/GDH_CompleteReport2011.pdf.

London, Ted. 2008. "The Base-of-the-Pyramid Perspective: A New Approach to Poverty Alleviation." *Academy of Management Proceedings* 1: 1–6.

Prahalad, C. K. and Stuart Hart. 2002. "The Fortune at the Bottom of the Pyramid". *Strategy+Business* 26: 54–67.

The Marketing White Book 2012–13: One Stop Guide for Marketers. 2012. New Delhi: Business World.

WRI. 2007. "The Next 4 Billion Market Size and Business Strategy at the Base of the Pyramid." Available at http://web.mit.edu/idi/idi/n4b_executive_summary_graphics.pdf.

Xavier, M. J., Raja, J. and S. Usha Nandhini. 2008. "Impact Assessment of a Rural Women's Micro Entrepreneurship Project using Path Analysis Models." *IIMB Management Review* 20(2): 215–227.

Consumers, Failed

ISAAC I. MUÑOZ
University of Dallas, USA

A consumer society is one in which participants adhere to the idea of consuming products and services rather than producing them. This type of contemporary society, with its unspoken but understood moral rules, expects its members to give in to the temptations of the marketplace. In fact, its members (consumers) are expected to participate regularly, as consumption offers a means of re-establishing normalcy, especially during economic downturns. This consumer-driven economic re-investment is what sociologist Zygmunt Bauman calls "consumer-led recovery."

At the center of the consumer psyche lies one of the core tenets of Maslow's Hierarchy of Needs, self-improvement. Out of this ideology of self-improvement the paradox of choice emerges: in other words, fashion, which subsequently begets obsolescence. Understanding the difference between fashion and obsolescence in such a society necessitates an understanding of its passive participants, those flawed consumers, collateral casualties of consumerism, and underclass or failed consumers. Although these terms are often used interchangeably, measuring their distinctions yields more meaningful insights by which to evaluate these nonconsumers.

Mainstream consumers and corporations at large perpetuate a certain view of collateral damage that neglects an entire class of consumers, who are labeled the underclass; this group's place on societal maps of social divisions is essentially nonexistent. According to Carl Schmitt, this population is off-limits in relation to all other classes and class hierarchy. In other words, their weight is so miniscule that there is no chance of their being re-admitted to a "normal" consumer society. People in this group tend to be grouped based on a behavioral definition that would indicate that they include school dropouts, the unemployed, and those on welfare, as well as beggars, homeless people, alcohol and drug addicts, and street criminals. Herbert J. Gans (1972) suggests that the above definition should be flexible and somewhat fluid. But what is important to understand about the underclass is that these are people seen as completely useless or, in a consumer society, as failed consumers. They are failed consumers because they are disturbing a consumption society that should be otherwise harmonious (at least theoretically), as they neither produce nor consume, instead being parasitic on the "normal" consumer, so in essence they should not count as consumers at all. For the consumer society, this is a sentence tantamount to nonexistence.

Failed consumers and the underclass share a lack of participation in a consumer society. What separates the typical failed consumers from the underclass is that the former are simply nonconsumers, not unemployed. They are called failed because they are unable to participate in one (if not the most crucial) of their responsibilities, being an active and successful participant of a consumer society. Furthermore, these consumers are failed because they are not (and most likely will not be) able to experience the full happiness that comes from living actively in a consumer society. Thanks to the media (marketers and advertisers in particular), lavish consumption is seen as a sign of success. The innovation of upcoming fashion styles renders current products obsolete; the possession of specific products reflects the lifestyle a given consumer aims to project and, theoretically, their associated happiness. Since happiness goes hand-in-hand with self-improvement, the pursuit of this feeling is constant, and therefore active consumers will never become bored.

The issue with the paradigm of constantly pursuing happiness via consumption is the discrepancy and gap it creates between flawed consumers, the underclass, and normal or active consumers. While active consumers will continue to gain more because of their access to opportunities based on their societal status, flawed consumers and the underclass will continue to be at a disadvantage and therefore will not be able to be an active part of society. The concern with not having access to the same opportunities may lead flawed consumers to take short cuts, following what Bauman calls their "inner demons" based on the stress of needing to consume.

The underclass of society, failed consumers, have a long way to go in order to be thought of as active participants. The struggle a consumption society has with these consumers is that they believe being a flawed consumer is a choice – especially in a free economy. They believe these people are being grouped together because of their wrong individual choices, and their life catastrophes and defeats serve as proof of this. Lastly, they are termed failed because they lack the three things needed to be a part of a consumer society: wit, will, and effort.

SEE ALSO: Consumers, Flawed; Culture-Ideology of Consumerism; Politics and Consumer Culture

FURTHER READING

Bauman, Zygmunt. 2007. *Consuming Life*. Cambridge, UK: Polity.

Belk, Russell. 1985. "Materialism: Trait Aspects of Living in a Material World." *Journal of Consumer Research* 12(December): 265–280.

Gans, Herbert. 1972. "The Positive Functions of Poverty." *The American Journal of Sociology* 78(2): 275–289.

McCracken, Grant. 1986. "Culture and Consumption: A Theoretical Account of the Structure and Movement of the Cultural Meaning of Consumer Goods." *Journal of Consumer Research* 13(June): 71–84.

Consumers, Flawed

ALLISON J. PUGH and CANDACE N. MILLER
University of Virginia, USA

"Flawed consumers" is a term coined by the theorist Zygmunt Bauman to signify prevailing social discourse about poor consumers, or those who, by virtue of their limited means, cannot participate fully in the consumer culture of the contemporary West. While not in extensive usage, the term captures what other scholars have also set out to do: portray and explain how low-income people are pathologized and marginalized as consumer society expands.

Bauman developed this concept in his monograph *Work, Consumerism, and the New Poor* (1998). In earlier production economies, social acceptance and status rested upon participation and success in the labor force, and the poor were marginalized by claims that they lacked a work ethic. Under this rubric, however, the poor were still nominally useful as a reserve labor resource. But in the elaborated consumer economies of the late twentieth century, the level of production became less dependent on a large labor force in the developed world. Unable to participate fully in contests of consumption with standards set by others far away from poor communities, the poor were now castigated as flawed consumers, with neither social position nor, given the fixity of their predicament, even redeeming potential as some sort of reserve army of consumers-to-be. Bauman argued that social prestige came to be conferred upon the rich, not merely the industrious. The concept of flawed consumer depended on the definition of consumer, emphasizing the relational quality of such notions as poverty.

The implications of the concept extend to arenas of family and politics. While the work of quantitative scholars suggests that low-income caregivers spend proportionately more on their children than do the more affluent, this is not necessarily evidence that the notion of "flawed consumers" does not hold sway, but rather implies that the concept influences the buying practices of low-income caregivers. Researchers have found that low-income consumers engage in a sort of "shielding consumption" to ensure that their children can participate in peer culture, and to mute the effect of their own poverty on their children's experiences; through consumption, they seek to deflect characterizations of being "flawed consumers" (Pugh 2009). Low-income caregivers have long been condemned for being unable to provide for their families appropriately. In a context in which consumption forms the bedrock of economic, social, and political activity, low-income people become not just flawed consumers but flawed mothers. Elaine Power's welfare-reliant informants asserted that one of their highest priorities was to help their children fit in with their peers, even if they had to sacrifice buying household items, food, or personal items for themselves in order to do so (Power 2003). The low-income women in Edin and Lein's landmark study *Making Ends Meet* (1997) also said they felt compelled to spend what it took to make their kids feel normal. At the same time, this priority conflicts with the reality of available resources in many low-income households in the West, not least in the United States, where, according to the US Census, more than 22 percent of children lived in "food insecure homes" in 2011.

In the political sphere, the flawed consumer concept also reverberates. Bauman explored the consequences of this new framing of the poor for social support for the welfare state. Formerly justified as a way to maintain this reserve army of laborers upon whom the economy sometimes depended, welfare benefits which provide (however nominally) for flawed consumers can no longer depend on economic arguments for their rationale. In addition, other scholars have noted the contradictory implications of consumer culture for social patterning. In the American case, the paradox of consumer culture's promise of a newly egalitarian society is juxtaposed with its divisive practices of segregating consumers by purchasing power and accentuating what distinguishes them. Those who are economic outcasts by virtue of their inability to consume risk being "flawed citizens" as well, constraining their claim to social personhood (Cross 2000; Cohen 2003).

Aspects of the concept of flawed consumer remain unsettled. Bauman's definition relied on a fairly narrow definition of consumption as strictly buying, or acquisition; indeed, he also referred to the poor as nonconsumers who were unable to buy the goods and services the market offers. Yet, as we have seen above, caregivers do stretch budgets to ensure their child has at least some of the commodities of childhood that peer culture deems worthy. In addition, participation in consumer society can also include such practices as fantasy, playing, shoplifting, talking about products, even scavenging dumpsters, as Chin put it in *Purchasing Power* (2001). This wider net catches the poorest members of society within its reach, suggesting that it is not that the poor do not consume that makes them subject to the discourse of flawed consumers, it is that they cannot consume enough, or that they do not consume regularly (Pugh 2004). Additionally, those who do not consume the right things may be perceived as flawed consumers (Nightingale 1993; Bourgois 1995; Schor 1998). Australian homeowners viewed nearby renters as flawed consumers, for example, for failing to adopt the ethical and moral values implied by home ownership (Cheshire, Walters, and Rosenblatt 2010).

Bauman relies on broad-brush characterizations of the producer and consumer eras to make his point, but the discourse of flawed consumers taps into a scholarly project that transcends his work. Further research might profitably delve into the implications of pathologizing low-income consumers in other arenas of social life, such as work, education, and art; the disciplinary effect of this sort of discourse on consumers of greater means; and how the flawed consumer image is deployed and experienced in daily life.

SEE ALSO:
Consumer Culture; Hyperconsumption

REFERENCES

Bauman, Zygmunt. 1998. *Work, Consumerism and the New Poor*. Buckingham, UK: Open University Press.

Bourgois, Philippe. 1995. *In Search of Respect*. New York: Cambridge University Press.

Cheshire, Lynda, Peter Walters, and Ted Rosenblatt. 2010. "The Politics of Housing Consumption: Renters as Flawed Consumers on a Master Planned Estate." *Urban Studies* 47(12): 2597–2614.

Chin, Elizabeth. 2001. *Purchasing Power: Black Kids and American Consumer Culture*. Minneapolis: University of Minnesota Press.

Cohen, Lizabeth. 2003. *A Consumer's Republic: The Politics of Mass Consumption in Postwar America*. New York: Knopf.

Cross, Gary, 2000. *An All-Consuming Century: Why Commercialism Won in Modern America*. New York: Columbia University Press.

Edin, Kathryn, and Laura Lein. 1997. *Making Ends Meet: How Single Mothers Survive Welfare and Low-Wage Work*. New York: Russell Sage Foundation.

Nightingale, Carl. 1993. *On the Edge: A History of Poor Black Children and Their American Dreams*. New York: Basic Books.

Power, Elaine. 2003. "Freedom and Belonging through Consumption: The Disciplining of Desire in Single Mothers on Welfare." Paper presented to the British Sociological Association annual conference, University of York.

Pugh, Allison J. 2004. "Windfall Child Rearing: Low-Income Care and Consumption." *Journal of Consumer Culture* 4(2): 229–249.

Pugh, Allison J. 2009. *Longing and Belonging: Parents, Children and Consumer Culture*. Berkeley: University of California Press.

Schor, Juliet. 1998. *The Overspent American: Upscaling, Downshifting and the New Consumer*. New York: Basic Books.

Consumption in Africa

HANS PETER HAHN
Goethe-Universität, Germany

In the past African societies have been studied by anthropologists, who were merely interested in local communities, where production, distribution, and consumption form an entity. As a consequence of the bias toward subsistence economy, the global entanglements of African markets have long been understudied. Even within the mainstream of the so-called transatlantic studies, Africa was mostly considered as a provider of slaves. However, since Roman times, Africa has also participated in global markets as a consumer. In early modern times, European traders reported difficulties in selling the goods they had brought with them on their vessels, because they did not meet the tastes of consumers in Africa. From the sixteenth to the nineteenth centuries, the varieties of cloth, jewelry, and ironware offered by European traders on West and East African shores changed frequently, following rapid changes in African ideas about fashion and style (Miller 1986). As these practices indicate, the consumption of global goods has been part and parcel of African economies for a long time. It is therefore legitimate to speak about an almost forgotten "genealogy of consumerism" (Prestholdt 2008), which redefines the place of African societies in the context of emergent global markets.

Furthermore, consumption in Africa still is considered by many Western experts as an obstacle to development or, even worse, as a threat to global environment, in particular with regard to energy consumption. Development on the continent was closely associated with production and the export of raw materials, but not with consumption. Consumption, and notably consumption of imported goods, was considered a burden for the national economies.

As a result of this double bias, in anthropology and in development discourse, current practices of consumption on the African continent have remained almost unnoticed. Africans consume and they do so in spite of the low levels of income on the continent. The majority of Africa's consumers apply pragmatic strategies to deal with limited resources. In the period between 1980 and 2000, the standard of life and consumption declined for most African countries. Studies of households in Africa have shown that, at least in many rural areas, each individual has no more than 100 items (Hahn 2008), in sharp contrast to consumer societies, where the number of items possessed by each individual is at least 10 times as high. The low number of possessions in Africa reflects the standard of life and the difficulties in accessing consumer goods. It also indicates a limited interest in spending available resources on material goods (Hart 1987).

A good share of the consumer goods offered on African markets and in shops comes from overseas. In many domains, for example electronic devices or automobiles, Africa depends entirely on imports from other continents. Given its low income levels and weak purchasing power, hardly any of the foreign products are specifically designed for Africa. African consumers experience the limitations of global markets because they have to deal with products that are hardly ever designed to fit the standards and priorities of their lives. The current rise in the importation of Chinese goods, like enamelware and plastics, is a good example: these objects have been designed for Chinese households and are now offered without any modification almost everywhere in Africa.

Against this background of economic marginalization and nonexistent design for African needs, the conceptual framework of cultural appropriation is able to explain how people in Africa deal with the objects of mass consumption available to them. In many African societies there are clear definitions about the adequate contexts and the appropriate usages of these things. The assignment of meaning relates imported objects to gender and age, but also to functions of previously known everyday objects. Cultural appropriation refers to the consumers' social actions in defining usages, contexts, and meanings of foreign objects. The result is the embedding of these things in local communities, sometimes by promoting totally new definitions of these objects' roles (Hahn 2012).

The longstanding experience with imported goods and the deeply rooted self-consciousness of market participants can be explained by the history of acquiring and consuming such goods. The earliest reports about the unintended side effects of European commodities, including complaints about worthless knick-knacks and alcoholic beverages sold by Portuguese traders, were written in the sixteenth century by the Angolan ruler king Alfonso. But the consumption of Western goods was also a highly controversial topic during colonial times. The acquisition of the "modern" clothing and paraphernalia of the colonizers, like the pith helmet, was considered as a provocation and led to a certain disdain of Europeans for those Africans who managed to imitate the colonizers' habits. Obviously, there was a subversive aspect in these consumption patterns. Today the subversion of Western norms is still celebrated in the context of the Congolese fashion known as "La Sape" (Gandoulou 1984).

From the consumers' perspective, there are more issues than economic weakness and absence of design. Consumers in Africa are well aware that foreign products have a lure, but they also constitute a link between Africa and the producers' nations. Africans manage to articulate their cultures and their values through the consumption of foreign goods and through giving new meaning to these objects (Comaroff and Comaroff 2009). Consumption thereby becomes a means of negotiating cultural and power relations and of self-consciously redefining them.

SEE ALSO: Consumption in the Middle East/Arab World; Culture-Ideology of Consumerism; Globalization and Consumption; Glocalization/Grobalization

REFERENCES

Comaroff, John L., and Jean Comaroff. 2009. *Ethnicity, Inc.* Chicago, IL: University of Chicago Press.

Gandoulou, Justin-Daniel. 1984. *Entre Paris et Bacongo*. Paris: Centre Georges Pompidou.

Hahn, Hans P. 2008. "Consumption, Identities and Agency in Africa – Introduction." In *Consumption in Africa: Anthropological Approaches*, edited by H. P. Hahn, 9–41. Berlin: LIT.

Hahn, Hans P. 2012. "Cultural Appropriation: Power, Transformation, and Tradition." In *Travelling Goods, Travelling Moods: Varieties of Cultural Appropriation*, edited by C. Huck and S. Bauernschmidt, 15–35. Frankfurt: Campus.

Hart, Keith. 1987. "Commoditisation and the Standard of Living." In *The Standard of Living*, edited by A. Sen and G. Hawthorn, 70–93. Cambridge, UK: Cambridge University Press.

Miller, Joseph C. 1986. "Imports at Luanda, Angola 1785–1823." In *Figuring African Trade: Long Distance Trade in Africa in the Nineteenth Century (c. 1800–1913)*, edited by G. Liesegang, H. Pasch, and A. Jones, 164–246. Berlin: Reimer.

Prestholdt, Jeremy. 2008. *Domesticating the World: African Consumerism and the Genealogies of Globalization*. Berkeley: University of California Press.

Consumption and African Americans: *SEE* AFRICAN AMERICANS AND CONSUMPTION

Consumption and Asian Americans: *SEE* Asian Americans and Consumption

Consumption and Behavioral Economics: *SEE* Behavioral Economics and Consumption

Consumption in China

DOMINIQUE DESJEUX
Paris Descartes University, Sorbonne Paris Cité, France

Consumption in China has basically followed the same trend as the United States in the 1920s and Europe during the *Trente Glorieuses*, the years of reconstruction and consumer development that followed World War II, just before the 1973 oil crisis. This has led to strategic government intervention to ensure the best conditions for consumer development in China, the growth of a middle class that drives this consumption, and the establishment of seven major consumer markets between 1980 and 2013: mobility, energy, luxury goods, body care, home furnishings, and products for children and for senior citizens. The market for senior citizens is expanding rapidly because of the aging of the Chinese population: those aged over 65 will increase from 27 percent of the population in 2015 to 37 percent in 2040, and this growth will be accompanied by a services market to cater for their needs.

All this has not been without strain. The Chinese demand for consumer goods has led to a strong demand for raw materials, energy, and proteins in the world market. This has been a source of economic, political, ecological, and military tension; for example, in 2010 and 2011 there was military tension with Japan over the supply of rare earth minerals that were necessary in the manufacture of new communications technologies.

FAST-GROWING CHINESE MIDDLE CLASS WITH LIMITED BUYING POWER

Between 1980 and 2012 Chinese economic growth and the accompanying lifestyle transformations have, from a macrosocial point of view, followed a process very similar to that of postwar Western economies, even though its political system is completely different from Western-style democracies. The infrastructure put in place by the state has fostered the development of the mobility of individuals, goods, and information, which is required for the development of mass consumption. As a result of this greater mobility, cities are growing, and along with this the need for more housing, cars, and retail sales. Western companies that have set up in China include Carrefour from France, Tesco from Great Britain, and Walmart from the United States.

Consumption has developed as the Chinese middle class has expanded. In 2012 it comprised approximately 400 million people, including 130 million in the upper middle class, with incomes ranging from US$5000 to US$30,000 per year. The lower middle class was composed of 270 million new consumers, with incomes of between US$3000 and US$5000. It is the urban middle class that sustains the huge growth in Chinese domestic consumption.

However, the development of consumption in China has run into two problems: the limited effectiveness of the social protection system and consumer credit. Since 2008, the government has begun implementing a system of social protection. However this system is still very inequitable, providing more benefits for employees of large companies, officials, and certain urban trades. Peasants, migrant workers, and many small business employees do not really benefit from the welfare state. In fact, the lack of a universal social protection system means that Chinese families have a very high savings rate, representing about 25 percent of their income; most prefer to save for their retirement and against the risk of illness rather than spending all their income. A large proportion of Chinese people still prefer to seek credit for consumption from their networks of family and friends, which is cheaper and safer than borrowing from banks, but not always as readily available.

SOCIAL INEQUALITIES AND LUXURY CONSUMER GOODS

Today China has 152 billionaires and more than a million millionaires. The most numerous are in Beijing, Guangzhou, and Shanghai, the three major cities of the east coast, but there are also fortunes being made in Henan and Sichuan, areas located further west. Their consumption of luxury goods is focused to a large extent on products related to the body, such as perfumes, clothing, and alcoholic beverages, as well as products related to the presentation of self, such as bags, shoes, jewelry, and watches. French brands like Chanel, Louis Vuitton, and Dior are popular with Chinese millionaires and the upper middle class.

CONSUMPTION IN THE PROCESS OF DIVERSIFICATION

Even though as a percentage of GDP it is in relative decline, domestic consumption is growing. There were 20 million vehicles manufactured in China in 2013, compared to 600,000 in 2000. It is shifting from a luxury car market to a greater proportion of popular vehicles, thanks to the production of Chinese brands.

In housing, products that require electric power are increasing; the use of appliances in the kitchen is booming, with refrigerators, washing machines, rice cookers, microwaves, and dish sterilizers. Certain appliances, however, such as ovens and vacuum cleaners, are not showing rapid expansion. The living room is where most televisions, computers, video game consoles, phones, other internet devices, and battery chargers can be found, with a certain number used in the bedroom. The bathroom is less connected to the boom in electronics, but it has been significantly modernized by the upper middle class. Bathtubs are still rare, remaining luxury items.

The body care and makeup markets exploded in the mid-1990s. Today both Western and Chinese brands offer a complete range of beauty products, with particular importance given to skin whitening products. Makeup is also a good reflector of social distinctions, as Chinese women invest differing amounts of time and money in caring for different parts of the body, including the face, hair, hands, and feet. How the body is presented is a very ambivalent subject in China. It is an object of transgression, of pleasure, of constraint, of power, of concern, and of social distinction. It can be used to track the invisible mutations that run through Chinese society.

The food market is also changing, with the development of large-scale distribution. In terms of fresh produce, some vegetables and fruits are still sold loose, but much is now sold in cellophane packaging. In some supermarkets it is possible to find prepared dishes, which are very convenient for young working couples, whether they have a child or not, who have little time to spend in the kitchen, unlike their parents. The demand for milk and yogurt has exploded since 2005.

Supermarket shelves also offer imported wines from France, Australia, Italy, and Chile, alongside traditional Chinese alcohols and wines such as the Great Wall label. Consumption in the supermarket is a good monitor of the effects of globalization.

Another large new market is education for the only child, which is reflected particularly in the growing number of private schools. Competition in schools has become more and more intense, as middle-class families seek to give their children as many advantages as possible to help them enter the best Chinese and American universities. Children's rooms and living rooms are full of toys destined for a one-child market, and social practices, such as food provisioning, have also undergone a cultural change (Jing 2000).

Products relating to the use of sustainable and alternative energy sources, including solar panels and electric cars, also constitute an emerging market.

CONCLUSION

Overall, absolute poverty in China has decreased dramatically over the past 30 years. A Chinese middle class has emerged, and a rich ruling class has developed. This all adds up to a transformation of patterns of life and consumption at the cost of an increase in social inequalities. The Gini coefficient rose from 0.41 to nearly 0.5 in urban areas from 2006 to 2009 (Aglietta and Bai 2012, 287).

This means that the study of consumption should not be limited to psychological analysis of the consumer; it is also a means of analyzing the complexities of family interplay, political systems, markets, lifestyles, and geopolitics. It is important to understand how the growth of Chinese consumption has an impact, for example in terms of rising prices, on all our daily lives, especially in the West.

SEE ALSO: Conspicuous Consumption; Consumption in Japan; Consumption in Postcommunist Countries; Consumption in the United States

REFERENCES

Aglietta, Michel, and Guo Bai. 2012. *China's Development: Capitalism and Empire*. London: Routledge.

Jing, Jun, ed. 2000. *Feeding China's Little Emperors: Food, Children and Social Change*. Stanford, CA: Stanford University Press.

FURTHER READING

Davis, Deborah S., ed. 2000. *The Consumer Revolution in Urban China*. Berkeley: University of California Press.

Desjeux, Dominique. 2006. *La Consommation*. Paris: Presses Universitaires de France.

Li, Cheng, ed. 2010. *China's Emerging Middle Class: Beyond Economic Transformation*. Washington, DC: Brookings Institution.

Zheng Lihua and Dominique Desjeux, eds. 2002. *Entreprises et vie quotidienne en Chine: Approches interculturelles* [Businesses and Daily Life in China: Intercultural Approaches]. Paris: L'Harmattan.

Consumption and Citizenship:

SEE CITIZENSHIP AND CONSUMPTION

Consumption and Death:

SEE DEATH AND CONSUMPTION

Consumption and Education:

SEE EDUCATION AND CONSUMPTION

Consumption and Emotions:

SEE EMOTIONS AND CONSUMPTION

Consumption, Ethical: *SEE* Ethical Consumption

Consumption, Experiential: *SEE* Experiential Consumption

Consumption, Failing: *SEE* Failing Consumption

Consumption and Globalization: *SEE* Globalization and Consumption

Consumption, Green: *SEE* Green Consumption

Consumption and Identity

ROLLAND MUNRO
University of Leicester, UK

The subject of identity concerns the interpretation of our *relations* with each other and with the world. While each of us might focus first on what it is we want to be or do, or on how we experience things or what we have in terms of personal possessions, the topic of identity revolves around ways in which significant others settle questions about who we are. Where we hang out, with whom we affiliate, what we do, and what we buy are all grist to the mill of "placing" one another as *this* or as *that*.

Historically the topic was oriented toward notions of unity and belonging. In seeking to tie collectivities (or groups) to *place*, identity covers the widest possible range of membership possibilities, from warring nationalities to rival neighborhood gangs and from union member to a regular of a local club or bar. However, more modern meanings treat patterns of consumption as displays of belonging and so extend identity toward how we are "figured" by others in our day-to-day conduct. Hence we can be seen by others as the *same* as them, or as *different*. Or, in terms of typifications at work, we are read as someone who get things done, or as someone out for themselves.

Much of this kind of figuring or placing of people is no longer just a matter of place, but more what the sociologist Erving Goffman calls *face*. Hence identity not only reflects how we arrive marked by ability, gender, age, ethnicity, and class, but is affected from moment to moment in how our conduct is read by others. Here Goffman (1959) draws attention to *facework*, for example by widening our smile on greeting someone, or by timing a wave when passing in the street. His studies of "infractions" and "front," and his distinction between "front stage" and "backstage," are seminal here.

In all, this identity has gravitated into becoming a question of *performance* as much as it was earlier perceived to be a matter of intrinsic qualities or essence. For instance, Cappellini and Parsons (2012) found mothers enacting their motherhood through self-sacrifice and abnegation in the kitchen. Instead of being secured at birth or molded by upbringing and culture, identity is seen today by many as liquid, malleable, and indeterminate. As such it is open to displays that advertise belonging, difference, and other forms of relationality.

This is where the ties to consumption become critical. Following an argument that goods are the "building blocks" of lifeworlds, Friedman (1990, 327) went on to show how they act as constituents of selfhood, of social identity. Earlier, coming out of anthropology, the work of Mary Douglas proved to be highly influential in contemporary understandings of consumer culture. Arguing that people advertise their *belonging* through goods, in both senses of the word, Douglas and Isherwood (1979) reversed the way economics had displaced culture as determining consumption by drawing attention to the "expressive" nature of materiality. As Douglas argued, consumption "uses goods to make firm and *visible* a particular set of judgments in the fluid processes of classifying persons and events" (1979, 67).

Key to contemporary understandings is the recognition that identity is *motile* (Munro 2004) to what we consume. A first way to grasp this is to contrast when facework is treated as happening in accordance with norms against when it is read as "strategic conduct." Emphasizing the "neglected situation," Goffman's (1959) subtle writings illustrate how people draw on *institutions* (like that of shaking hands, playing host, or "civil inattention") to make their displays. The nub of *The Presentation of Self in Everyday Life* is to show how minutely custom and ritual are open to calculation and manipulation.

As such, identity differs from self inasmuch as it is *reflexive* to institutions – ways of doing that are conceived broadly in terms of precedent and custom. Odd or unusual ways can be treated as infractions under whatever forms of social surveillance are in place. For these reasons, what is at stake over identity is often vital, even when the acts themselves seem tangential and transient. So, too, the work of "situating" persons (and deeming their conduct to be "in place" or "out of place") is also more intricate wherever interactions are swift and numerous. Hence, as is often the case either in the workplace or in city life, questions of identity do in fact intensify even when the encounter is "thin."

It is precisely this emphasis on how we *consume* institutions that distinguishes Goffman's work from neoliberal ideologies that make identity out to be a matter of personal choice. For all that strategic conduct affects readings of identity, it should be remembered that identity is never in the say of an individual. The temptation to reduce identity to notions of self should be avoided. While each of us can be reflective about how we conduct ourselves, it is the audience that judges performances. Identity is granted by others.

The upshot has been to bring about a profound shift in theory away from the dominant trope of *production* toward registering who is consuming what. Of the many topics covered elsewhere in this Encyclopedia, identity is perhaps most affected by the rising interest in consumption. Indeed, it is fair to suggest that much of the impetus behind the turn to consumption stems from the insights noted above. Previous generations had regarded consumption as the "mirror of production" (Baudrillard 1975). The assumption was that, aside from the wealthy whose choice was less constrained, people for the most part put up with what they could get. The idea that production could actually be led by consumption was a novel idea indeed.

This turn to consumption has oriented theory away from its earlier grip by functionalism, as well as broadening empirical methodology, bringing ethnography and opinion surveys on board with earlier forms of observation and experiment. Earlier views of personhood tended to revolve around the premise that identity is *produced* – and produced mainly through what sociologists called "structures," such as class, ethnicity, or the division of labor. Identity, in this view, was formed by where you came from, your background, or what you did. All this settled your role in life. True, parents and teachers had an educating influence, but since their identities had already been produced, the effects were marginal in the wider scheme of things.

Treated merely as the obverse side of production, consumption thus played second fiddle. The purchase of goods in particular was largely understood to reflect identities that were already well established. This led to stereotypical views of Italians eating pasta because they were Italian and the French eating baguettes because they were French. Similarly, girls played with dolls because they were girls and boys played with bricks because they were boys. So, too, the upper echelons of the class system patronized high culture, such as opera and painting, while the working classes were presumed to indulge in gin palaces and music halls.

The central problem of such views is not only their triviality. Or even their falsity – nowadays most Euro-Americans happily eat pasta and baguettes. What is particularly problematic for production theories is to explain change. If people were only "bearers of culture," then it would follow that consumption patterns would be stable, if not fixed, over time. Veblen was the first to challenge this picture of the status quo, showing how the new rich in the United States used leisure as a means to display their wealth. Rose's (1990) depiction of how the wealthy elite in Pennsylvania "cathected" to horses is a landmark study of displays of leisure, from the library to foxhunting.

Earlier lines of explanation for changes in consumption had relied on the notion of emulation. Models of social mobility held that those seeking to rise in terms of class would do so by copying the consumption patterns of those in the class above them. This model overlooked a reverse direction in which soap operas and football now cut across all classes as major forms of entertainment. Indeed, a salutary insight into the limitations of the emulation view is the much quoted example of the rising middle classes growing fat while the upper classes slimmed down. As a means of preserving difference, those with "old money" abandoned overeating and body bulk was left instead to display new wealth.

A major explanation for changes in consumption focused on modernity, particularly on advances in technology. Just as mass production techniques made products like cars more widely available by reducing their cost of production, it was also expected that innovation would bring novel goods to the market, such washing machines or televisions. As people became "modern," the expectation was that mass production would produce mass consumption; and, indeed, many homes built from the 1930s to the 1970s replicated the more or less identical suburban box with the same set of white goods.

Zygmunt Bauman's (1972/1966) critique of these ideas of mass consumption is key here. Functionalist views tend to assume consumption works upwards in layers, from what is physiologically necessary for safety and survival toward esteem and self-actualization. This, as Heidegger points out, overlooks the way in which consumption can become an end in itself: "The circularity of consumption for the sake of consumption is the sole procedure which distinctively characterizes the history of a world which has become an unworld" (1973, 107). Taking to task the reliance placed on Abraham Maslow's hierarchy of needs (later interpreted into its pyramid form), Bauman pointed out that "Being needs" were of a different nature. To the contrary of any actualization of goals satisfying people, their accomplishment seems rather to incite further aspirations. Far from representing an apex at the top of a needs triangle, Being needs appear to expand exponentially.

What is most radical about the contemporary turn to consumption is not then the focus on what we buy – critical for identity making as such displays are – rather it is the change in *explanation* for why we are consuming what we do. For instance, David Hume, the Scottish philosopher of the Enlightenment, was early in arguing that social cohesion was driven by habit, a consumption view refined later into the notion of habitus by Marcel Mauss, Émile Durkheim's nephew, and deployed even more influentially today by followers of Pierre Bourdieu.

Bourdieu's (1986) most famous work today is *Distinction*, in which he demonstrates how *class* is consumed in France as much as it is simultaneously reproduced. Just as Veblen had shown leisure was deployed as a means of making one class distinct from other, Bourdieu drew together compelling evidence to show that the taste for high culture goods like opera not only depends on upbringing, but is used to emphasize difference and so place others in terms of class.

Bauman's voluminous work on identity takes this matter of explanation one stage further. What he comes close to arguing is that it is identity that we consume. And, if we go on to include self-identity, perhaps it is all that we consume. Contrary to ideas that marginalize it as a mere byproduct of production, identity has turned out to be pivotal to consumption. Friedman's (1990) study of immigrants to the United States, for instance, showed how they spend a greater than expected proportion of their incomes on food and drink branded as American. For all their relative poverty, it is also important to immigrants to enjoy a sense of belonging.

Issues over identity arise here in the related topics of division, discrimination, and exclusion. *Division* is endemic to identity, with one category, such as that of white-collar workers, traditionally set above another, in this case blue-collar workers. Identities are also divided, in attempts to change organizational cultures, between those who "deliver" and "time-wasters" who do not (Munro 2004). While many ethnographers of the workplace report how employees divide themselves up between "them" and "us" and scorn "them over there," division is also a ubiquitous feature of the politics of everyday life.

Discrimination follows division. Immigration debates, in particular, often revolve around the issue of keeping migrants out of an area in order to preserve jobs for the population who are already living there. If being born on the wrong side of the tracks or with the "wrong" hair color no longer carries the stigma it once did, I have to report that I know of few academics who make the "A-list" parties for celebrities and the super-rich. More pointedly, discrimination over identity involves such figures as the "progressives" (those who display their willingness to go along with the changing times) standing against those denigrated as "Luddites" or "dinosaurs" (those seeming to stand in the way of progress by nostalgically looking back to notions of community and tradition).

If consumption is now the engine of identity, *exclusion* remains at its heart. Inclusion for some invariably entails exclusion for others, as every schoolchild knows. While it should never be seen as inevitable, exclusion concerns those who are prevented from doing what they wish to do by virtue of their omission or expulsion from a favored group. With many disadvantaged by disability, and even more excluded through prejudice, identity more generally can affect the distribution of resources – who marries whom and who gets given what – as well as the allocation of work – who gets to go to the better parties or do the better jobs. Preference, promotion, and patronage all run through lines of identity.

The Civil Rights movements in the United States focused attention on what has come to be known as *identity politics*. This came to the fore where marginalized groups (minorities) banded together with a program that petitioned for their rights to be treated equally with those of others (the majority). Where identity politics departs radically from earlier forms of collective identity is in pressing for recognition on the very grounds on which recognition has been denied. This is to say that it is *as* women, *as* blacks, and *as* pensioners that marginalized groups demand recognition. Respect and dignity are called for on the basis of difference, not on the premise of being the same.

Division, discrimination, and exclusion can also be traced to power effects. Power is typically identified with those influential enough to get others to do things for them, a view that has some credence in the nature of hierarchy as well as in the fees celebrities receive nowadays to promote products. In the tradition of conflict sociology, however, persons are granted *agency*, a form of power that comes into being only when they are representing a class, status group, or party in a struggle for domination and legitimation between classes, genders, generations, and ethnicities. Someone without identity has no power, nothing to struggle for, and in consequence seemingly has no place in the world.

In contrast, the influential French writer Michel Foucault argued that power is not held but rather is *exercised* through knowledge. Drawing on examples like that of doctors becoming disciplined through imposing on patients their "medical gaze," Foucault (1973) explains how power circulates through persons by virtue of their consumption of the kind of discourse that grants sovereignty to experts in their field. Consequently experts see themselves as arbiters of taste and judgment, rather than recognize that they act as relays of authority. Subjugation affects all of us, even those who are at the pinnacle of their profession.

Notions like sovereignty (even weak versions such as the consumer is king) contribute to the fashionable idea of multiple identities, such as Alfred Schutz's proposal that the ruthless businessman by day becomes the loving father by night. In opposition to advocating multiple identities, Munro (2004) has argued that identity is better understood as "punctualized." This view follows up Heidegger's thesis of humans acting as a "standing reserve" to technology, but goes on to suggest how much of our consumption is "on call." As Munro asserts, people make identities "visible and available" to those they wish to impress or to whom they feel subordinate. Men can display themselves, for instance as the "new male," by doing the cooking and the washing up, or employees may make a "cultural performance" of supporting a quality initiative if that is the agenda of the month.

Some reserve has to be put on the thesis that identity is all we consume. For instance, the fact that many major corporations now brand themselves as "ethical" evidences how far consumption has taken on a moral force. A burgeoning range of studies explore how social movements such as fair trade, the Soil Association, and Friends of the Earth form around such matters as the nonexploitation of developing countries, organic food, and buying locally. So, too, exponents of healthy living may advocate the gym or campaign against the ubiquity of sugar in ready meals. Sugar is, of course, notorious for its addictive qualities but, even here, one has to be careful about what exactly is being consumed. Vitellone's (2011) study of heroin addicts, for instance, suggests how compassion for sufferers enters the picture as much as what users call the "rush."

SEE ALSO: Citizenship and Consumption; Consumer Behavior; Consumer Socialization; Emotions and Consumption; Metrosexual

REFERENCES

Baudrillard, Jean. 1975. *The Mirror of Production*. Translated by Mark Poster. St. Louis, MO: Telos.

Bauman, Zygmunt. 1972/1966. "A Note on Mass Culture: On Infrastructure." In *Sociology of Mass*

Communications, edited by Denis McQuail, 61–74. Harmondsworth, UK: Penguin.
Bourdieu, Pierre. 1986. *Distinction: A Social Critique of the Judgement of Taste*. Translated by Richard Nice. London: Routledge.
Cappellini, Benedetta, and Elizabeth Parsons. 2012. "(Re)Enacting Motherhood: Self-Sacrifice and Abnegation in the Kitchen." In *Routledge Companion to Identity and Consumption*, edited by A. A. Ruvio and R. W. Belk. New York: Routledge.
Douglas, Mary, and Baron Isherwood. 1979. *The World of Goods: Towards an Anthropology of Consumption*. New York: Basic Books.
Foucault, Michel. 1973. *The Birth of the Clinic: An Archaeology of Medical Perception*. London: Tavistock.
Friedman, Jonathan. 1990. "Being in the World: Globalization and Localization." *Theory, Culture & Society* 8(4): 311–328.
Goffman, Erving. 1959. *The Presentation of Self in Everyday Life*. New York: Doubleday.
Heidegger, Martin. 1973. *The End of Philosophy*. New York: Harper & Row.
Munro, Rolland. 2004. "Punctualising Identity: Time and the Demanding Relation." *Sociology* 38(2): 293–311.
Rose, Dan. 1990. "Quixote's Library and Pragmatic Discourse: Toward Understanding the Culture of Capitalism." *Anthropological Quarterly* 63(4): 155–168.
Vitellone, Nicole. 2011. "Contesting Compassion." *Sociological Review* 59(3): 579–596.

Consumption in India

NITA MATHUR
Indira Gandhi National Open University, India

Consumption studies in India are of particular salience because of the peculiar juxtapositioning of traditional values emphasizing frugality, voluntary poverty, and sense of community with the practice of consumption emphasizing, among others, lavishness, ostentation, and individuation. A niche is carved out in which traditional values and the practices of consumption get mutually constituted. Many of the moralistic concerns of consumption are based on scriptural injunctions that lie deep in people's psyche, and to a large extent influence their decisions and/or choices. Nearly all the main religions in the country press for altruism, sharing, benevolence, and abstemiousness – which are antithetical to the very grain of consumption. Gandhi (1910) reiterated that it is necessary to control one's indulgences. He came down heavily on the ideology promoting sovereignty of money over human spirit, and maintained that the compulsive need to expand the vast captive market lay at the root of colonial domination in India. It is often argued that the fancy products that dominate the market space project an illusion of prosperity which camouflages the reality that large sections of the population are living under conditions of poverty and deprivation.

The economic reforms of the 1990s, which lifted restraints on foreign trade in a phased manner, marked a watershed and pronounced change in the lifestyles of many people. While in the period of the command and control economy, consumption was essentially necessity-based, economic liberalization brought with it a rise in conspicuous consumption and the concomitant emergence of consumer society. The report of the National Sample Survey on Household Consumer Expenditure in India carried out by the National Sample Survey Organization (NSSO) for the period January–June 2004 confirmed an overall rise in consumption including that of luxury goods. The 68th round of NSSO for the period July 2011–June 2012 recorded monthly per capita expenditure (MPCE) of 1281.45 rupees for rural India and 2041.68 rupees for urban India (i.e., average urban MPCE exceeds average rural MPCE by 87.4%). Five quinquennial surveys concluded by the NSSO in the period 1987–1988 to 2009–2010 indicate a decline in the share of food over the years by 10 percentage points to 53.6 percent in the rural sector, and by about 16 percentage points to 40.7 percent in the urban sector. In a major policy change in 2012, the Indian government allowed up to 51 percent direct foreign investment in multibrand retail which is expected to pave the way for the entry of global brands to India; these will usher in major changes in the nature and scale of consumption in the country. McKinsey Global Institute's 2007 report foretells that real consumption per capita in India will be US$1064 by 2025, making it the fifth largest consumer market in the world. Indian retail chains are consolidating their realty, brands, market shares, and locations as they seek to expand their share of organized retail, particularly in the supply chain for food and groceries (see Kalhan 2007). The prominent growth in consumption originated in and is expected to be sustained by the dynamic and risk taking middle and upper classes.

A fairly large section of people in Indian cities are, increasingly, adopting lifestyles incorporating, for example, the replacement of train travel with air travel, the preference for purchasing commodities online and/or from malls and retail stores over local shops, the prioritization of consumer products and guilt-free shopping, and so on that have hitherto characterized ways of life in affluent nations. The robustness of domestic and international tourism, the telecommunications sector, the food and hotel industries, and aggressive and competitive marketing reflect a transformation in the consumption profile of people in India. The younger generation tends to avail themselves of livelihoods in large towns and cities which in turn accentuate the demand for consumer goods. Some of them migrate to work abroad, lured by the prospect of a better life, interpreted by those who have had modest beginnings as one free from a sense of deprivation, and by those who have had relatively comfortable beginnings as given to a hedonistic lifestyle. Migration from India to affluent nations has a backlash effect in that it contributes to the spread of consumer culture in India through the bringing of luxury commodities into the domestic market and through engaging in joint ventures with foreign companies via capital transfer to the domestic economy.

The new consumers are largely cosmopolitan in their outlook and lifestyle, global in their aspirations, and demanding of leisure time services (such as tourism, hospitality in hotels, etc.). Distraught with the former protectionist policies, they celebrate material prosperity and their newly acquired ability to choose commodities and realize long-held aspirations of consumption. The consuming class serves as the major market for Western commodities and services – clothes and accessories, cosmetics, upmarket cuisine, electronic gadgets, films, music, and so on – for two reasons: their marked expansion in purchasing power and their penchant for Western commodities and services. Not only metropolitan cities but also smaller cities and towns house restaurants, leisure enclaves, and multiple malls that display visual signs of wealth and affluence by presentation of more than necessity and luxury goods.

Many companies cater to these fashion demands and regularly change the merchandise in their stores to keep pace with the latest trends and choices of people, and diversify the products they already have in the market to meet the demands of people from different economic and social groups. Product diversification is an important means of meeting the demand of a large section of people belonging to distinct or different social and economic groups. In anticipation of the saturation of urban markets, most of the major companies target the rural market with the awareness of people's low per capita spending and tough competition from local indigenous products.

The challenge to gain the confidence of the rural masses is compounded by their beliefs, longstanding familiarity with and tradition of using local indigenous products, and by their price sensitivity (Mathur 2007). The consumption decisions of people are largely informed by the media – films, television, magazines, and advertising – which promotes lifestyles and accords central position to images and ideas drawn from the global culture economy. The media promotes the purchase of goods that define one's newly acquired wealth or else reinforce one's superior middle-class status (Ganguly-Scrase and Scrase 2009).

The predominant public culture of consumption, which is driven by the market and the media and which informs the consumption decisions of people, significantly assigns critical value to images and ideas drawn from the global cultural economy. Indian consumers are differentiated in terms of purchasing capacity, local cultures, and the ideals and ideologies that influence their consumption decisions. The cultural politics of consumption, whereby goods get transacted as a kind of social currency, is framed by demographic profile, local cultural differences, and consumers' propensity to consume. The diversity and heterogeneity in the country create not one but multiple social and cultural niches. Unlike consumers elsewhere, Indians prefer products that align with their own local culture in terms of logic, emotions, lifestyle, values, beliefs, and social practices, yet make them feel connected to the global world. Retailers have to work ingeniously to cater to differentiated demands for unique versions of a product or to develop distinct marketing strategies that convince diverse categories of people that the product answers the needs of their social and economic niche. This calls for the reconciling of global brand narratives with particular understandings of "Indianness" (Mazzarella 2003) and the balancing of a sense of Indianness with that of an international connection. Local cultures negotiate with consumer culture in such a way that both undergo change as they assimilate to each other. As much as Indian consumers have accepted foreign brands, several international brands have demonstrated sensitivity to local tastes. Many of those who cannot afford to buy a branded product will purchase a cheaper one that closely resembles the original, believing that others will not be able to make out the difference. Integrating the credit needs of customers with every product category will enhance consumption across different classes in society.

Market forces, however, have tended to subordinate personal emotions, a sense of community, contentment with what is available, self-reliance, and nurturance, to isolationism, competition, and strife. Individuals lose their community-based identity to anonymity and individualism in a market driven society as they engage in a competitive display of consumption. They seek to compensate for a sense of loss resulting from being separated from their communities by surrounding themselves with consumer goods and leading a life of luxury in which reflection finds no place. The challenge is to identify ways to strengthen the emotional connection of consumers so that they do not end up living in self-obsessed cocoons.

SEE ALSO: Brands and Branding; Commodity Fetishism; Conspicuous Consumption; Glocalization/Grobalization; Shopping Malls

REFERENCES

Gandhi, Mohandas Karamchand. 1910. *Hind Swaraj or Indian Home Rule*. Translated by M. K. Gandhi. Accessed June 25, 2014. http://www.soilandhealth.org/03sov/0303critic/hind%20swaraj.pdf. (Originally published in the Gujarat columns of *Indian Opinion*, December 11 and 18, 1909.)

Ganguly-Scrase, Ruchira, and Timothy Scrase. 2009. *Globalisation and the Middle Classes in*

India: The Social and Cultural Impact of Neoliberal Reforms. London: Routledge.
Kalhan, Anuradha. 2007. "Impact of Malls on Small Shops and Hawkers." *Economic and Political Weekly* 40(22): 2063–2066.
Mathur, Nita. 2007. "Consumerism." In *Alternative Economic Survey: India*. New Delhi: Daanish.
Mazzarella, William. 2003. *Shoveling Smoke: Advertising and Globalization in Contemporary India*. Durham, NC: Duke University Press.
McKinsey Global Institute. 2007. "The 'Bird of Gold': The Rise of India's Consumer Market." Accessed June 25, 2014. http://www.mckinsey.com/insights/asia-pacific/the_bird_of_gold.

FURTHER READING

Mathur, Nita. 2010. "Shopping Malls, Credit Cards and Global Brands: Consumer Culture and Lifestyle of India's New Middle Class." *South Asia Research* 30: 211–231.

Consumption and the Internet:

SEE Internet, the, and Consumption

Consumption in Japan

PENELOPE FRANCKS
University of Leeds, UK

Japanese people are famed as hard workers and heroic savers, and until relatively recently little attention was paid to their lives as consumers of the products of their labor and frugality. A long Marxist tradition in Japanese historical studies viewed ordinary people as too poor to engage in anything beyond subsistence consumption, while modern economists concentrated on trying to understand a savings rate that appeared to contrast so sharply with that of the spendthrift West. However, by the 1980s, Japanese consumers, wielding the financial resources afforded them by the "miracle" economic growth of the postwar decades, were too visible in the global centers of luxury shopping to be ignored any longer. Anthropologists and sociologists led the way in exploring their use and enjoyment of goods – in forms sometimes similar to those of their Western counterparts and sometimes distinctive – and eventually even economists began to recognize that domestic markets for consumer goods must have played a role in Japan's remarkable rise to economic superpower status. Analysis of the role of consumption in mediating Japan's response to Western modernity has opened up new research fields in areas such as gender, material culture, and fashion, and it is clear that many of the challenges now posed by the growth of consumption in, for example, China and India had already been confronted by the modernizing Japan of the nineteenth and twentieth centuries.

Scholars of the early modern Tokugawa period (1600–1868) had never doubted the role of marketed consumer goods in facilitating the vibrant urban culture of the time. Some of the largest cities in the seventeenth-century world were to be found in Japan. The growing mercantile wealth that urbanization generated fueled growth in both production and consumption. Extensive sumptuary regulation largely failed to curb the expenditure of the urban merchant classes on the elaborate silk clothing, multicourse dining, and beautifully crafted household goods deemed inappropriate to their status. The familiar woodblock prints of the period abound in references to fashionable consumer goods, and the techniques of product placement and advertisement were by no means unknown to the great artists of the era.

The growth in urban demand for goods stimulated production in rural areas (as opposed to towns), where producer households combined agriculture with manufacturing activity for the market. Production was coordinated by an expanding network of traders and entrepreneurs based in the villages, through which goods reached the markets and, increasingly, the shops of the towns and cities. However, rising incomes in the countryside, together with the expansion of travel and tourism brought about by the regular passage of regional lords and their retinues to and from the Tokugawa shogun's capital at Edo (Tokyo), diffused urban consumer tastes among the better-off throughout the country. Growing numbers of guidebooks detailed what to see, what to buy, and which shops and restaurants to visit in the cities, while the returning officials and servants of local lords brought back souvenirs embodying the urban tastes they had acquired. Village shops and traveling peddlers brought "populuxe" versions to country dwellers even in quite remote parts of the country.

Though by no means entirely uninfluenced by goods and ideas from outside Japan, this growth in consumer demand took place largely in isolation from developments elsewhere, which included the industrial revolution and the first steps toward mass production and consumption in Europe and North America. With the opening of the country to increased contact with the West from the 1850s, Japanese people were faced with a whole new range of consumption possibilities. After initial fads for all things Western, a more selective response emerged, incorporating Western-style items into existing patterns and lifestyles. Men began to don hats and overcoats, eventually adopting the Western-style suit as the uniform of white-collar work. Many women continued to wear kimono, though now accessorized with new hairstyles and makeup, and increasingly made from fabrics embodying new techniques, materials, and designs. Japanese-style meals, based on rice, continued to be preferred both at home and in the best restaurants, but Western treats, such as sugar-based snacks or German-style beer, were soon being enjoyed alongside them.

As urbanization and industrialization proceeded through the late nineteenth and early twentieth centuries, the production of processed foodstuffs and manufactured consumer goods steadily expanded to meet growing urban and, to a lesser extent, rural demand. This process was dominated by Japanese-style products (soy sauce, sake, kimono fabrics) but also involved Western-style treats, accessories, and gadgets (confectionery, shoes and hats, watches, and bicycles) that could be accommodated alongside them. Although the small local shop remained the source of most everyday goods, retail facilities expanded and modernized. The great dry goods emporia that had emerged in the cities during the Tokugawa period transformed into department stores which served to "educate" their customers about Western-style goods while also acting as purveyors of fashion in all manner of Japanese-style items – as did the expansion of print media and the accompanying advertising in newspapers and women's magazines. Shopping as a serious leisure activity became much more widespread, as provincial cities established their own versions of Tokyo's Ginza and mail order brought the department store into rural homes.

By the interwar period (1918–41), the development of the urban infrastructure was requiring new solutions to the frictions between Japanese ways of life and the conveniences and pleasures offered by Western-style products. The suburban "dream house" of the emerging white-collar couple provided the environment in which to combine electrical gadgets in kitchen and living room with the comfort and familiarity of Japanese-style dining and sleeping arrangements. Intellectuals engaged in agonized debate over the perceived clash between Japanese values and identity and the consumption of Western-style goods, but ordinary consumers do not seem to have experienced the same dilemmas, as they absorbed cinema and baseball, beer and ice cream into their everyday lives. At the macrolevel, domestic consumption remained the most significant contributor to output growth until the onset of depression and war-related austerity in the 1930s.

After World War II, anxiety over consumption issues faded. The steady increase in household incomes made it possible both to save for the future and to enjoy an ever-widening variety, quantity, and quality of goods. However, the uses to which this new abundance was put continued to be conditioned by past approaches to consumption and by a social and institutional life in some ways particular to Japan. The housewife emerged as the key figure in household spending decisions, managing the acquisition of the electrical appliances that came to fill Japanese homes and ensuring the safety and healthiness of her family's consumption. The purchase of gifts and travel souvenirs, often used to cement hierarchical relationships, continued to take up a significant share of consumer expenditure. After-work socializing in company-based groups sustained entertainment districts that dated back to the Tokugawa period. While a huge advertising sector flourished, and department stores and fashion chains created a vivid urban shopping scene, the small shop continued as the basis of a multilayered wholesale and retail structure, resisting the spread of the supermarket. At the aggregate level, the persistently high cost of food and housing in a land-scarce environment biased overall consumption patterns, although the high savings rate of the postwar decades does not appear particularly "unique" in comparison to much of the rest of the developed world. Nonetheless, the Japanese domestic market of the second half of the twentieth century remained distinctive and difficult to penetrate, not just because of trade restrictions but also because of a consumer attachment to quality, differentiation, and niche consumption conditioned by a long history of approaches to goods.

As a result, Japanese consumers came to be recognized as some of the most serious and demanding in the world. The frenetic consumerism that characterized the period of the "bubble economy" in the 1980s became legendary and makers of luxury goods everywhere relied on the spending power of the yen. However, with the collapse of the bubble, consumption and saving again became problematic issues for households and government. Efforts to encourage consumers to spend their way out of recession largely failed, although the savings rate fell back to a more "normal" level and consumer debt (once unmentionable) became a concern as employment prospects worsened. Nonetheless, Japanese consumers continued to console themselves with goods, so that, for example, "nostalgic" products which embodied conceptions of a lost world of social and family life became fashionable must-haves in the late twentieth century. Hence, while population aging suggests that it is the "gray" consumer market to which producers should now be looking, the temples to consumerism in the hearts of Japanese cities are still, as in the Tokugawa period, the places to go for street fashion and the display of an array of goods and services the equal, in quality and variety, of any in the world.

SEE ALSO: Cities, Visual Consumption of; Consumption in China; Department Stores; Lifestyle

FURTHER READING

Clammer, John. 1997. *Contemporary Urban Japan: A Sociology of Consumption*. Oxford: Blackwell.

Francks, Penelope. 2009. *The Japanese Consumer: An Alternative Economic History of Modern Japan*. Cambridge, UK: Cambridge University Press.

Francks, Penelope, and Janet Hunter, eds. 2012. *The Historical Consumer: Consumption and*

Everyday Life in Japan, 1850–2000. Basingstoke, UK: Palgrave Macmillan.
Garon, Sheldon, and Patricia MacLachlan, eds. 2006. *The Ambivalent Consumer: Questioning Consumption in East Asia and the West*. Ithaca, NY: Cornell University Press.
Sand, Jordan. 2003. *House and Home in Modern Japan: Architecture, Domestic Space, and Bourgeois Culture, 1880–1930*. Cambridge, MA: Harvard University Press.
Tobin, Joseph, ed. 1992. *Re-Made in Japan: Everyday Life and Consumer Taste in a Changing Society*. New Haven, CT: Yale University Press.

Consumption, Landscapes of

J. MICHAEL RYAN
The American University in Cairo, Egypt

George Ritzer (2005) has built upon his notion of cathedrals of consumption to describe what he terms "landscapes of consumption," or "geographic areas that encompass two, or more, cathedrals of consumption" (p. 149). This definition can be extended to define landscapes of consumption as *locales that encompass two or more cathedrals of consumption that allow, encourage, and even compel people to consume*. The prototypical example of this would be the Las Vegas strip – an area where multiple cathedrals of consumption exist side by side in the same geographic setting and entice consumers not only through their individual appeal, but also through the techniques made possible by their synergistic proximity.

Elsewhere, Ritzer, Ryan, and Stepnisky (2005) have extended the idea of landscapes of consumption with their case study of Easton Town Center in Columbus, Ohio. They argue that Easton serves as a prototype of a consumer setting that is becoming increasingly prevalent – one that seeks to simulate the look and feel of a nostalgic small-town America. By encompassing two or more landscapes of consumption within one setting, Easton is able to expand the spectacle of landscape to a community level (Ryan 2005).

Sharon Zukin (1991) has also contributed much to the idea of landscape. She uses the term "landscape" to describe a configuration of material geographic surroundings and their related social and symbolic practices. She argues that landscape is the major cultural product of our time and that landscape and power are deeply and intricately connected. Through this, large-scale, bureaucratic, economic structures attempt to impose a new order upon an existing geographic location. Although there is sometimes resistance to these attempts, ultimately capital wins out and landscapes are imposed. Zukin also argues that landscapes, contrary to the assertions of many postmodern social theorists, tend toward "repetition and singularity" and not toward ephemeral aestheticism.

Consumer researchers have developed their own, broader sense of landscape. For example, some have noted a shift in how shopping malls are designed. While they were at one time constructed to maximize efficiency and functionality, now they are designed largely to create spectacle and attract, and reattract, consumers. Other consumer researchers have developed terms to help describe these settings such as "servicescape," "brandscape," and "retroscape." John Sherry, in his analysis of the brand outlet "Nike Town Chicago" (1998), argues that what he calls the brandscape (an example of the broader concept of servicescape) is not merely the result of designer intention and spatial layout, but that its form and significance also depend upon the activity of consumers who imaginatively and physically experience the brand as it is laid out in geographic space.

SEE ALSO: Consumption, Spectacles of; Shopping; Shopping Malls

REFERENCES

Ritzer, George. 2005. *Enchanting a Disenchanted World: Revolutionizing the Means of Consumption*, 2nd ed. Thousand Oaks, CA: Pine Forge Press.

Ritzer, George, J. Michael Ryan, and Jeff Stepnisky. 2005. "Innovation in Consumer Settings: Landscapes and Beyond." In S. Ratneshwar and David G. Mick (eds.), *Inside Consumption: Frontiers of Research on Consumer Motives, Goals, and Desires*, 292–308. London: Routledge.

Ryan, J. Michael. 2005. "Easton: A 21st Century (R)evolution in Consumption, Community, Urbanism, and Space." MA thesis, University of Maryland, College Park, MD.

Sherry, John F., Jnr. 1998. "Nike Town Chicago and the Emplaced Brandscape." In *Servicescapes: The Concept of Place in Contemporary Markets*, edited by John F. Sherry. Chicago, IL: NTC Business Books.

Zukin, Sharon. 1991. *Landscapes of Power: From Detroit to Disney World*. Berkeley: University of California Press.

Consumption and Latinos: *SEE* Latinos and Consumption

Consumption and Leisure: *SEE* Leisure and Consumption

Consumption in the Middle East/Arab World

MARK ALLEN PETERSON
Miami University, USA

The Middle East refers to a broad geographic region whose borders shift according to North American and European geopolitical interests. Currently, the term is used to describe a belt of Muslim-majority countries stretching from Morocco in the west to Afghanistan or even Pakistan in the east. The bulk of consumption studies has focused on those countries with strong historical ties to the colonial and postcolonial West (Turkey, Egypt, Morocco, Lebanon), and to those states that rose to positions of extreme wealth in the twentieth century through extraction of oil (Dubai, Saudi Arabia).

Throughout most of its history, the Middle East has been primarily rural, producing grain, cotton, sesame, olive oil, oranges, soap, and other goods for consumption in urban centers and trade with Europe and Asia. In antiquity, great trade routes carried goods across the Arabian peninsula from Spain in the far west to China and Japan. The most significant of these was the Incense Route, which brought frankincense and myrrh from Hadhramaut, the easternmost kingdom of South Arabia, to Gaza, a port north of the Sinai Peninsula on the Mediterranean Sea. The Incense Route also carried gems, gold, ivory, pearls, spices, and textiles which originated in Africa, India, and East Asia. Both the Nabatean kingdom (encompassing much of modern-day Jordan and Syria) and the South Arabian kingdom grew tremendously wealthy through the transport of goods destined for lands beyond the Arabian Peninsula. Evidence suggests that both in Nabatean and South Arabian cities, class distinctions emerged marked by cosmopolitan habits of consumption – that is, the adoption of the tastes and styles (and thus goods) of the societies with which the merchants traded.

Mecca, where Islam originated, was itself a city that depended on trade. Located in an area not suitable for agriculture, Mecca produced little except leather; it survived by extensive trade, which brought in cereals, oil, silk, wine, and luxury goods for local consumption. Commerce and the development of credit institutions, including the use of money for paying wages, converted Meccans from the traditional Bedouin system, which organized society by kinship, to one in which kinship was cross-cut by economic class. A hierarchical system emerged consisting of clusters of rich merchants, their families, and various dependents, ranging from client families to wage laborers to slaves, many of whom were related by blood. Class distinctions were marked by styles of dress and consumption practices. Some of the Prophet Muhammad's injunctions seem to have been intended to undermine these practices, particularly the forbidding of usury, ban on consumption of intoxicants, and requirement that people redistribute 10 percent of their wealth to the poor.

There are few studies as yet of consumption during the Abbasid, Safavid, and Mughal empires, although all engaged in extensive trade. Islamic sharia placed restrictions on certain modes of exchange and forms of consumption (for example, pork and intoxicants), and as new goods entered the market their position under sharia had to be scrutinized. Coffee, for example, was alternately forbidden and permitted by various Islamic jurists even as it became a staple of Middle Eastern consumption.

By the Ottoman period, many of the cities of North Africa, West Asia, and the Gulf were connected by complex trade routes that brought luxury goods to feed increasingly cosmopolitan tastes, including tulips, tobacco, clocks, and firearms. As the industrial revolution transformed production in Europe, the consumption of inexpensive calicoes and Manchester cloths arose among peasants. In this multicultural, multilinguistic cosmopolitan society, European and Asian goods were not necessarily distinguished as "foreign" and the meanings Ottomans applied to various kinds of consumer goods are still a matter of considerable scholarly debate.

In countries like Egypt, however, which were under the rule of a series of foreign conquerors from Alexander the Great until the mid-twentieth century, the adoption of the language and tastes of the ruling class was clearly an important means of social mobility. For the ruling class, consumption became a significant mode of maintaining connection with the societies from which they or their forebears came, whether it was Greece, Rome, or Turkey. At the same time, the consumption of imported goods, and local imitations of these, became part of a system through which upper-class Egyptians displayed their participation in the culture of the ruling classes, thus converting economic capital into social status.

COLONIAL CONSUMPTION

The rise of European colonialism, beginning with the conquest of Egypt by the French empire of Napoleon Bonaparte in 1798, led to dramatic economic changes in the region. The British seized Egypt from France, while the French remained in control of Morocco, Algeria, and Tunisia. European economic influences were also strong in West Asia and, after the fall of the Ottoman empire at the end of World War I, France ruled outright in Syria and Lebanon, while Britain gained direct control of Palestine, Jordan, and the kingdom of Iraq, which it formed out of previously distinct Ottoman provinces.

European colonialism was initially less a political project than an economic one. European states sought to control the extraction of raw materials as well as to monopolize consumer markets. In Egypt, for example, they would buy raw cotton, ship it home to be machine woven into textiles, then sell the woven cloth at prices that undermined local producers. Some Egyptians grew quite wealthy through collaborating with British merchants and banks, and later with the colonial administrations. For this class, the consumption of imported European goods became an important marker of their status.

As the colonial system penetrated more and more of Middle Eastern life, introducing police forces, bureaucracies, and regulations, it also created schools and other institutions which sought to turn Egyptians into industrious, productive, and obedient members of colonial society in part through the inculcation of European norms, including tastes. Anglophone and Francophone Arabs and Turks visited European-style coffee houses and restaurants and shopped at specialty stores filled with imported European goods. These changes were not without their critics, who noted the economic pressures European fashions placed on families. For example, given continually changing fashions, mothers could no longer pass their clothing on to their daughters, and clothing ceased to be a good investment for dowries.

"Modern" department stores emerged in the Middle East not long after their appearance in Europe. Known as *grands magasins* in North Africa and *bonmarşeler* in Turkey and the Levant, these originally catered for the hundreds of thousands of Europeans settled in the great Middle Eastern capitals between the 1850s and the 1940s. The greatest of these, Orosdi-Back, opened its first store in Istanbul in 1857, and in Cairo in 1858, followed by branches in Aleppo, Beirut, Tunis, Bizerta, Sfax, Baghdad, and Basra, as well as industrial cities in western and central Europe, and in Japan. Others followed suit, including Cicurel and Omar Effendi in Egypt, Surbaji in Syria, and Wertheim in Istanbul.

The emergence of these department stores dramatically changed consumption habits in the urban Middle East. First, in cities like Alexandria, Cairo, Damascus, and Istanbul, where there would often be five or seven such stores operating, they offered a visible indicator of the highly stratified class society of the cities, with high-end trendsetting stores at the top, reaching down to the upper middle classes and even the aspiring middle class. Second, their size and rococo splendor often served as models of the modernization of these cities. The sultans of Istanbul pointed to them as evidence that the city was European, not Asian, and they were central to the khedive of Egypt's plan to create a "Paris on the Nile." Third, they introduced new tastes and types of goods. Beginning primarily as ready-to-wear clothing stores, they gradually introduced European-style shoes, hosiery, cosmetics, costume jewelry, watches, leatherware, household goods, glassware, travel goods, ironware, and furniture. In some cases, such as the introduction of gramophone records, attention to local tastes was required, and stores would partner (or in some cases own) local recording studios and record production factories.

Perhaps the most important change was the introduction of "shopping" as a leisure pursuit through which people viewed goods and engaged in social interaction with others of their class. Initially, shopping was an activity performed by men. Gradually, department stores staffed by multilingual saleswomen – usually from local Jewish populations – came to be seen as safe places for women to go, first European women, then gradually upper-class women from the local community.

POSTCOLONIAL AND NATIONALIST CONSUMPTION

Many historians date the end of colonialism in the Middle East with the Egyptian seizure of the Suez Canal in 1956, then the most important trade resource in the region. With the collapse of colonial control, a tension developed between locally made goods and foreign imports. Efforts to create new states increasingly involved efforts to build up local productivity and export trade, and to rely less and less on foreign goods.

Cheap, accessible, locally made goods were available through emerging manufacturing sectors. These competed with even less expensive goods from manufacturing centers in Asia, and high-end Western goods which usually remained the standard against which others were measured. Sweeping nationalizations of foreign property occurred, and waves of nationalism overtook industry and commerce. Yet, while the new states often urged people to buy local to support national development, many working-class families could afford only cheap imports, while upper-class families often continued to prefer Western products when available. It was the middle classes that created and sustained consumptive national self-assertion, including shopping at new national department stores like 'Awf and Misr lil-Muntajat al-Misriyya. In strongly nationalist states, like Turkey, these new sites of consumption forced the old European department stores out of business by the 1940s, while in other states they lingered on into the 1960s.

Nationalism was particularly connected to industries involving local foods and languages. Advertisements in Arabic, Turkish, Persian, and other local languages began to appear in the 1930s, and by the 1960s Arabic ads aimed at local middle-class audiences dominated the scene. While upper-class families might buy European magazines in French or English, most were limited to magazines in the local languages of Arabic, Persian, or Turkish. This led to the emergence of regional hubs, such as Egypt, as the center for the production of Arabic films. Even here, though, the growth of dubbing and subtitling industries allows local films to compete with Hollywood movies in high-end theaters, and Bollywood musicals and Hong Kong action films at the low end.

The twentieth century saw the rise of oil wealth in several Middle Eastern countries, with Iraq, Libya, Saudi Arabia, United Arab Emirates, Kuwait, and Qatar emerging as among the world's most productive oil economies. In some of these countries, such as Libya prior to its 2012 revolution, and Iraq before the Second Gulf War, political and tribal elites controlled the oil wealth, imported consumer goods were controlled, and as much as 25 percent of the population lived in poverty. In others, such as Qatar, Kuwait, and the UAE, a small hereditary aristocracy controls the wealth, which is distributed to citizens in the form of free health care, education, and sometimes income. Qatar and the UAE have established themselves as specialized geographic zones for global elite consumption, constructing vast and opulent complexes of hotels, leisure spaces, convention centers, and shopping malls carrying consumer goods from all over the world. But citizens in these countries make up less than half the population; a large population of foreign labor, predominantly South Asian, also exists. These populations do not enjoy the benefits of citizens, live separately, and import large amounts of consumer goods, especially foodstuffs, from their homelands.

Another key issue in postcolonial consumption was remittances. The late twentieth century saw a significant rise in labor migration. Much of this was regional, in which workers traveled from less wealthy economies to work in the oil-rich countries of the Gulf, such as Moroccans and Egyptians traveling to the United Arab Emirates. In other cases, this involved populations moving from Middle Eastern countries to labor in North America or Europe. Often migrant workers are drawn from economically marginalized groups, such as Kurdish Turks or Moroccan Haratines traveling to Europe. The flow of remittances offers opportunities for advancement from paying bribes for better jobs or to ease license regulations to start a business, to purchasing property, paying private school fees, or purchasing the consumer goods needed for weddings.

GLOBAL AND MULTILOCAL

The globalization of the world economy has created a situation in which more and more international goods flow into the region at every possible price level, from cheap plastic toys and textiles to top-line fashions and high-end electronics. Facilitated by the very states that used to oppose them, these goods compete with local manufacturing, but create an unprecedented range of consumer choices. Contemporary consumption in Middle Eastern countries is shaped by the flood of international goods into the region, but has also been marked by three key trends: multilocalism, Islamic chic, and resistant consumption.

Multilocalism involves efforts by multinational or global companies to see their brands, goods, and services recognized by consumers as local brands, goods, and services. This strategy serves multiple purposes: reliance on local infrastructure and management personnel is cheaper than importation and management by transnational professionals; customers are believed to build stronger brand loyalty if the brand is understood as being local; and companies will more successfully weather anti-Western boycotts. In Morocco and Egypt, McDonald's spent years establishing local infrastructures so that everything it sold could be locally produced: local staff were trained in all aspects of restaurant management; advertising was in local languages; and local popular actors and singers endorsed the products. Other companies, like Coca-Cola, compromised, running its flagship drink Coke as a global brand but the Fanta fruit drink line as a local brand in each market.

Multilocal strategies are strengthened by the fact that many stores featuring global brands are locally or regionally franchised. For example, the Kuwaiti Alshaya Group operates Middle Eastern franchises of almost 50 global brands, including Body Shop, Foot Locker, Peugeot, and Starbucks. New shopping malls, as opulent as anything offered in Europe or North America, appeared in Dubai, Kuwait, Cairo, Istanbul, and other major regional cities to showcase these upscale brands, while other shopping centers cater to regional and Asian markets.

The globalization of production, communication, and design technologies, and the relatively cheap and rapid systems of transportation in the late twentieth century, also meant that local alternatives to global chains are of increasingly high quality. One consumer niche not initially fed by the global market was the reassertion of Islamic identity. As upper-class women who grew up on fashion magazines such as *Redbook* and *Cosmopolitan* chose to veil themselves, they sought ways to accessorize attractively. The "Islamic chic" movement seeks to reimagine clothing that meets various interpretations of modest dress in terms of international styles. Demand for stylish clothing that asserts an Islamic identity led to the establishment of a new global consumption trend, with centers in Dubai, New York, and Paris. Many of these companies have been founded and are operated by women.

Alongside the reassertion of Islamic identity as a personal fashion statement is the notion of deliberate consumption of non-Western goods as an anti-Western political statement. Upscale versions of traditional coffee houses vie with Starbucks at shopping malls and hotels. Frequent boycotts of North American and European brands are called in support of the Palestinian cause. And specifically anti-Western alternative products like Mecca-Cola allow consumers to embrace the notion of global modern networks of consumption while rejecting specifically American global dominance of these networks.

SEE ALSO: Americanization; Consumption in Africa; Globalization and Consumption; Glocalization/Grobalization

FURTHER READING

Abaza, Mona. 2006. *Changing Consumer Cultures of Modern Egypt: Cairo's Urban Reshaping*. Leiden, Netherlands: Brill.

Hattox, Ralph. 1985. *Coffee and Coffeehouses: The Origins of a Social Beverage in the Medieval Near East*. Seattle: University of Washington Press.

Kupferschmidt, Uri M. 2007. "Who Needed Department Stores in Egypt? From Orosdi-Back to Omar Effendi." *Middle Eastern Studies* 43(2): 175–192.

Peterson, Mark Allen. 2011. *Connected in Cairo: Growing Up Cosmopolitan in the Modern Middle East*. Bloomington: Indiana University Press.

Quataert, Donald. 2000. *Consumption Studies and the History of the Ottoman Empire*. Albany: State University of New York Press.

Ram, Uri. 2001. "Liquid Identities: Mecca Cola versus Coca-Cola." *European Journal of Cultural Studies* 10: 465–484.

Rice, Gillian, and Mohammed Al-Mossawi. 2002. "The Implications of Islam for Advertising Messages: The Middle Eastern Context." *Journal of Euromarketing* 11(3): 79–91.

Wolf, Eric. R. 1951. "The Social Organization of Mecca and the Origins of Islam." *Southwestern Journal of Anthropology* 7(4): 329–356.

Consumption, Open Source and:

SEE Open Source and Consumption

Consumption in Postcommunist Countries

KRISZTINA FEHÉRVÁRY
University of Michigan, USA

Postcommunist countries are those countries that were once characterized by centrally planned economic systems whose twin goals were modernization and an equitable distribution of national wealth across the population. Thus, "postcommunist" refers to places where communist rule collapsed (as in the former Soviet Union and Eastern Europe in 1989–91). It also refers to places where the communist party continues to hold political power but has embraced market reforms and opened up the nation's economy to global forms of commerce (as in China, Cuba, and Vietnam). The bulk of scholarship on post-communist consumption has focused on the former Soviet Union and Eastern Europe, although there is a rapidly growing scholarship on consumer culture in China, as well as some on smaller non-European countries.

COMMUNIST CONSUMPTION

During the Cold War, it was commonly assumed that communist societies were plagued by constant shortages of consumer goods and that the goods that were produced were of shoddy quality. Both shortages and shoddy goods were, ostensibly, caused by the inefficiencies of central planning and communist ideologies of austerity and anti-individualism. Since the 1990s, a voluminous scholarship has emerged that documents the robust material culture produced during the communist era by state factories and collective workshops, and also by private entrepreneurs operating in a variety of conditions – from an illegal black market to state condoned forms of private production. This production took many forms and produced a variety of consumer goods, including badly made goods but also goods of relatively high quality (many of which were exported to capitalist countries). Despite Euro-American stereotypes of gray and colorless consumer landscapes, communist production included colorful advertising in print, posters, and television spots, and featured substantial use of branding. Many communist countries permitted some apolitical media to flourish, from talent shows on television to magazines for automobile aficionados and fashion. Finally, a much overlooked aspect of communist consumption was one that was ideologically central: the principle that the population had a right to adequate food, shelter, education, medical care, and other basics, from access to books, theater, and museums to the provision of public transportation, athletic facilities, and even vacation resorts – all heavily subsidized by the state to make them affordable. This promise was never fully realized in any country, especially in the case of housing; moreover, forced dependence on the state for basic provisions in some places had tragic consequences (malnutrition, crowding, and other markers of poverty). Nonetheless, in many communist countries these modernization policies provided ever greater numbers of the population with a modern life in the form of ready-to-wear clothing, indoor plumbing, universal education, inexpensive foodstuffs, as well as new consumer technologies like radios, televisions, and, for some, private cars. Over time, people's experiences with communist forms of consumption (as well as the success of illicit production) generated expectations of "normal" middle-class lifestyles that capitalist economic systems were supposed to deliver. These expectations for consumption were defined by standards of living in prosperous capitalist countries.

NOSTALGIC AND NATIONALIST CONSUMPTION

After the fall of communism in Eastern Europe and the Soviet Union, consumers in these countries clamored for commodities they had long known about and had occasionally experienced firsthand. They favored commodities produced for populations in developed nations over familiar local brands or those from countries allied under communist economic trade agreements. "Socialist" brands rapidly disappeared from store shelves as producers were either bought up by Western competitors or driven under by the collapse of trade networks and the loss of consumer interest. Fairly quickly (especially in the former East Germany), this disappearance of familiar brands, especially of foodstuffs, became a cause for consternation. The dismay over the loss of familiar commodities from one's childhood (from favorite candies and laundry detergent to pop songs and board games) echoed wider concerns that all things that had been of value under the old regime (including legal, medical, economic, and other professional knowledge and experience) were being undermined. Scholars of the resulting phenomenon, known by the misnomer of "nostalgia" throughout the former Soviet bloc, argued that people searched out lost goods in part to reassert the value of the things they had once produced and consumed, things that represented their own personal histories. As a market emerged, familiar "socialist" branded products were reintroduced as "originals" along with their familiar jingles and advertising slogans. Ironically, many of these brands were now owned by Western companies.

A different but parallel trend was the nationalist-tinged rejection of Western or foreign brands that had flooded store shelves after the fall of communism, and the assertion that local or national products (especially foodstuffs) were superior in taste and quality because they were "ours." For many East European countries in the mid to late 2000s, entry to the European Union precipitated new anxieties about foreign versus nationally produced consumer goods, in part because EU regulations interfered with local modes of production. In response, people turned again to the valorization of home brands and also began to brand the local as "artisanal" or promoted the value of *terroir*.

DIVERGING CONSUMPTION AFTER COMMUNISM

In most of these countries, the introduction or intensification of "free" market mechanisms had the effect of increasing the availability of consumer goods, in terms of sheer quantity as well as of quality and variety. However, these market mechanisms combined with the withdrawal of state subsidies meant that the purchasing power of different sectors of the population within each country began to diverge widely, creating new and often extreme economic inequalities. In China, where the Maoist regime had kept most of the population at very low levels of consumption (although there were wide differences between rural and urban areas), the population as a whole has seen standards of living rise despite dramatic increases in social and economic inequalities. In other parts of the postcommunist world, especially the post-Soviet states where development during communism had been fairly advanced, many people have seen their purchasing power and standard of living go down, not up. Some postcommunist countries have become among the poorest places on earth; Moldova, for example, is one of the world's principal (illegal) exporters of kidneys to consumers from wealthier countries. At the same time, despite several economic crises crippling the living standards of the rank and file, post-Soviet Russia has become home to many of the world's billionaires. And China's communist party continues to promote policies allowing for the emergence of incredibly wealthy individuals. In most of these countries, an emergent middle class struggles to maintain its position. Thus, the shift from relatively homogeneous forms of consumption to widely differentiated forms of consumption after communism both reflects and helps to constitute new social stratifications.

The extensive privatization of once state-owned industries and services has had an enormous effect on consumption practices. With the loss of state subsidies, costs for basic goods like food, shelter, and utilities (especially heat) have skyrocketed, eating up a huge proportion of pensioners' fixed incomes or the incomes of working-class families. Populations have become further divided and subdivided into those who can pay for privatized and specialty services and those who cannot. As state facilities fall into disrepair, private gyms and fitness salons, upscale medical and dental clinics, and private degree granting institutions have proliferated. Meanwhile, the average citizen continues to think that the state should be responsible for providing for all of its citizens. While religious and other charity organizations work to help the poor and disenfranchised, many people blame those who are unable to consume at a respectable level for their own predicament.

SHIFTS IN GLOBAL CONSUMPTION

Many of the changes in consumption practices of the last two decades in postcommunist countries have little to do with their "communist" past, but are part of general developments across the globe. Some have to do with globalizing economic policies such as free trade agreements, the rise of corporate power and of corporate branding practices. Many global brands have a significant presence in these countries, although the prohibitive expense of some of these brands means many consumers appreciate counterfeits that are within their means. The rise of new technologies that have come to dominate consumer experience generally, such as the cellphone, the laptop computer, and the internet, are also central here. Indeed, postcommunist countries were early adopters of cellphones, in part because infrastructure for land-line telephones was underdeveloped and authorities (fearful of anti-state mobilization) limited access to private telephones. Internet use is high, although internet shopping is curtailed by concerns about financial transactions over the internet and also by high shipping costs.

The rapid increase in economic inequalities in postcommunist countries *appears* dramatic relative to the limits placed on such inequalities during state socialism, but is driven by processes that have been global in scope for decades. The rise in social and economic stratification is both produced by and reflected in consumption. While people in concrete, high-rise housing developments from the communist era are often from diverse income groups, cities increasingly exhibit forms of spatial segregation similar to cities elsewhere. More affluent citizens have bought into new, luxurious high rises and gated developments, or have created new suburbs of single-family houses. The poor live in ghettoizing sections of cities or move to rural, economically depressed areas where housing is cheap but services nonexistent. Similarly, shopping venues tend to cater to different sections of the population. Mega malls opened in major cities throughout the communist world, frequented by the new middle classes and elites. They are a sharp contrast to open-air markets where vendors sell a wide variety of inexpensive goods. Big-box stores have increasingly forced out small shops, such as local butchers. In more prosperous areas, corporate brand name chains such as McDonald's and more recently Starbucks are replacing local haunts. At the same time, bakeries, beauty salons, restaurants, and shops have proliferated for consumers across much of the income spectrum, with corresponding differences in what they offer. Another dramatic site of consumer difference is in transportation, as public transportation has become aligned with poorer classes (except in metropolitan cities). Private cars (or motorbikes in postcommunist Asia) are critical for middle-class distinction, but also as necessary forms of mobility for shopping, leisure travel, not to mention for employment. Petrol alone constitutes a major element of middle-class consumption.

Income divides are also notable in differing valuations of time. While scholars of the communist period noted the enormous amounts of time most of the population spent in waiting (for goods, in administrative offices, and so forth), the postcommunist economy tends to differentiate people according to the value of their time. For example, while the quality of much public transportation has declined, new toll highways have been built for those who can pay the often prohibitive fares to speed through the countryside – avoiding the traffic on the old, two-lane roads. Services too, such as prepared foods, cleaning and gardening, cater to those consumers with money but who do not wish to engage in time-consuming domestic tasks. The increasing commodification of goods and services after state socialism, however, has been accompanied by the revival of older forms of do-it-yourself practices. Some people grow their own vegetables, can fruit obtained through exchanges, and make their own shampoos, clothing, and furniture as a mode of survival. These subsistence practices contrast with newer middle-class versions framed as hobbies or forms of connoisseurship, as groups of men for example gather to produce home-made sausage or specialty alcohols, often outsourcing the labor-intensive parts but labeling the final result to offer as gifts or to enjoy themselves.

SEE ALSO: Consumption in China; Global Markets; Globalization and Consumption

REFERENCES

Berdahl, Daphne. 1999. *Where the World Ended: Re-Unification and Identity in the German Borderland.* Berkeley: University of California Press.

Caldwell, Melissa L., ed. 2009. *Food and Everyday Life in the Postsocialist World.* Bloomington: Indiana University Press.

Farquhar, Judith. 2002. *Appetites: Food and Sex in Postsocialist China.* Durham, NC: Duke University Press.

Fehérváry, Krisztina. 2013. *Politics in Color and Concrete: Socialist Materialities and the Middle Class in Hungary.* Bloomington: Indiana University Press.

Verdery, Katherine. 1996. *What Was Socialism, and What Comes Next?* Princeton, NJ: Princeton University Press.

Consumption, Postmodern

ALLADI VENKATESH
University of California, Irvine, USA

The origins of postmodernism cannot be traced to a single source or set of circumstances. At first glance, the different trails may appear diffused, disparate, and disconnected. A closer look might reveal a common pattern woven by those different threads. Postmodernism is generally viewed as a reaction against, or rejection of, modernist tendencies in philosophy, social and cultural theory, literature, and politics. Postmodernism is closely related to poststructuralism, whose origins are slightly different but whose arguments are very similar – so much so that in the eyes of many, postmodernism subsumes poststructuralism and therefore they are treated interchangeably. The last quarter of the twentieth century witnessed the most intense excursions into postmodern ideas.

In architecture, where postmodernist tendencies were first noticed, there was a reaction against modernist definitions of form and style, questioning the emphases on universalism, functionalism, and rationalism. Postmodern architecture considered the modernist approach to be too rigid, and argued for greater fluidity of design, the mixing of styles, and local variability. In literature, postmodernism was a reaction against the entrenched notions of the Western canon. It has given rise to the poststructuralist movement away from the signifier to the signified, and toward displacement, difference, and dispersal instead of rigid origins and representations of human nature. In politics, postmodernism rejected neoclassical liberalism and triggered intense debates on gender and ethnic issues. At the global level, it has induced the postcolonial discourse.

Postmodernism can be considered a rejection of what Lyotard (1984) terms metanarratives of modernism and (equally importantly) products of the Enlightenment. These grand themes of modernism include rationalism in philosophy; the pursuit of science as the only path to ultimate truth and human advancement; and the individual subject as the most powerful and universal self, whose destiny is to conquer and establish decisive superiority over nature. Postmodernism argues that for all its claims of enlightened humanism and progress, the results of modernism are hardly salutary. The realm of science has become a hegemonic regime of dogma and is dismissive of alternative sources of knowledge; human progress has been equated with oppressive industrialism; individualism has become basically a phallocentric ideology; and Western/European narratives have become the master discourse. Once postmodernism gained the necessary momentum and provided the umbrella under which marginal(ized) discourses could take refuge, other submovements followed in its footsteps. These groups consisted mainly of feminists, (multi)cultural anti-essentialists, and postcolonial critics. Postmodernism pointed out that there is a world beyond science and instrumental rationality and that human experiences are embedded in culture, language, aesthetics, art, symbols, and visual forms.

During the 1990s postmodernism came under attack from various quarters. The criticism can be summarized as follows: (1) it promotes a spurious relativism and an "anything goes" philosophy; (2) it is anarchic and self-indulgent; (3) it incites anti-science thinking and throws the baby out with the bath water; (4) it is intentionally blind to scientific contributions to human health and happiness; (5) its claims are false and unsustainable within any reasonable discourse; (6) it is very elitist and does not serve the disadvantaged and the marginal sections of society; (7) it is essentially an integral part of the hegemonic Western discourse and may not apply to many non-Western cultures where a majority of the global population lives.

There is no question that there has been a slowing down of postmodernist writings in the last decade or so. Does it mean that postmodernism has become less relevant or is it the case that postmodern ideas have met with success and are being slowly absorbed into the mainstream? It is probably a bit of both. Certainly, in cultural studies and derivatively in the study of consumer culture, postmodernist ideas may have had the greatest impact.

Modernist thought tended to privilege production as the handmaiden of the capitalist industrial machine, for production meant the creation of value within the social order. Correspondingly, consumption was viewed as a value-destructive function serving no useful purpose in the industrial economy. Postmodernism exposed the absurdity of this position by simply pointing out that production and consumption are two sides of the same economic coin and by posing the question of what the value of production is, if what is produced is not consumed. Postmodernism has elevated the discourse on consumption critically and analytically as an inevitable and highly significant condition of contemporary social order. Postmodernism views consumption as a complex social phenomenon and the postmodern vocabulary includes such wide-ranging topics as aesthetics, sign value, cultures of consumption, fragmentation, hyperreality, everyday life experiences, consumer identities, liberatory consumption, and the like – terms that were either nonexistent before or remained at the margins of social science discourse. In the face of these developments, traditional theories of consumption based on positivist psychology and economic utility theories have been found to be quaint and inadequate. Somewhat surprisingly, the Frankfurt School – with its scathing attack on culture industries – seems to have missed a critical opportunity, for it failed to recognize the central and essential role of consumption in modern societies. Postmodernism was the first to recognize that consumption is a positive social activity despite the fact that marketers exploit consumers to gain economic advantage, while Marxist economists and feel-good patronizing sociological critics consider consumption as wasteful. For postmodernists, consumption could be a liberatory force if consumers were allowed to pursue their consumptive goals as part of their everyday life experiences.

Postmodernism affects consumerism in two ways: first, by creating a sense of pastiche which involves an "ironic mixing of existing categories and styles," and second by rendering the "consumer lifestyle itself as a kind of work of art" (Solomon, Bamossy, and Askegaard 2002, 561, 563). Recent works on postmodernism suggest that modernistic and mechanistic notions of aesthetics have given way to paradoxical sensibilities in aesthetic experiences, including the juxtaposition of opposites, a lack of quest for unity, and a search for hybridity, theatricality, and a mixing of aesthetic objects. While modernity does allow for mixing and blending, the aim of such activities is unification or convergence to a central idea. The postmodernistic ideal would look for mingling without unification. The ultimate goal of art (and therefore aesthetic experience) in modernism is to attain some sort of (Kantian) sublime, while under postmodernism it is closer to what Bourdieu (1984) calls "both transgression and an element of personal/social distinction" (p. 34). Thus "high art" and "low culture" can mingle in popular consumer imagination and reach their substance in consumption objects. One of the driving ideas of postmodernism is that instead of (or in addition to) looking for universal and objective standards of aesthetic taste, consumers look for personal perspectives that may run counter to such standards.

Our notions of everyday life rely on the seminal ideas of Lefebvre (1971) and de Certeau (1984). These authors, in their own way, distinguish "the space of experience and its everyday life with its embodied interactions" (Miles 2005, 29) from more abstract and impersonal notions of economy and culture. They are mainly concerned that life in modern industrial cultures can become very structured and devoid of human content. In such a culture, the rational order is represented by the industrial structure and the nonrational order is oriented toward the private nonwork life. The structures of work environments are such that they are stripped of humanistic appeals, while individual workers or consumers need to escape from such an oppressive environment. Perhaps the individual can find relief by directly participating in such endeavors and by seeking experiences in everyday consumption practices. To meet consumers' needs, the marketing enterprise provides opportunities for sensory consumption through everyday products. Sometimes, as the critics of market culture argue, this is done with excessive zeal rather than appropriate sensitivity. The question is: do consumers buy into the marketing system to meet their aesthetic and emotional needs?

Kozinets (2002) suggests that consumers resort to some sort of Bakhtinian carnivalesque-type escapism, as depicted in his work on "burning man." On the other hand, Mackay (1997) takes a more inclusive view, arguing, for instance, that consumption activities can be studied as part of everyday life, as being integral to consumers' identity construction and creative pursuits. "Rather than a passive, secondary, determined activity, consumption is increasingly seen as an activity with its own practices, tempo, significance, and determination" (p. 4). While everyday life refers to "routine activities and control of ordinary people as they go about their day-to-day lives," Mackay also sees consumers as being "endlessly creative in the appropriation and manipulation of consumer goods" (p. 5).

Numerous writers on the postmodern have advanced the idea that everyday life in Western consumer culture has become aestheticized, as boundaries between high art and popular culture and between different styles (of art, architecture, etc.) have been effaced. Research on aestheticization processes occurring in consumer culture has focused largely upon aesthetic principles integral to the design of products and corporate images and has not paid sufficient attention to the aesthetic nature of the consumption experience itself. Nevertheless, some exceptions can be found: (1) Holt's (1995) classification of consumption practices into experience (i.e., an aesthetic or emotional reaction to a consumption object), integration, classification, and play, using the game of baseball as exemplar; (2) Peñaloza's (1999) work on the experiential and spatial dimensions of consumption in a particular retail setting (Nike Town); (3) Schroeder's (2002) perspective on visual consumption as a means of sensory communication and experiential system; and (4) Brown, Hirschman, and Maclaran's (2001) exposition of contemporary aesthetics as a postmodern condition.

Although the marketing and consumer literature on aesthetics is somewhat limited, it is not insignificant. On the marketing side, Schmitt and Simonson (1997, chap. 1) focus on brand images and identity issues through the management of product and/or corporate aesthetics. Their main arguments are related to how strategic branding can be employed to interact with product attributes and what impacts they have on customer sensory experiences, and how this system of interaction creates brand appeals and ultimately brand differentiation in the marketplace. Thus the emphasis is on the aesthetic appeal of ad presentation, that is, its creative execution.

From the consumer side, as everyday objects become commodified through mass production and lose their aura, a natural tendency appears to be to elevate them from ordinary to extraordinary status, or to (re)aestheticize objects. In the 1980s consumer research began to move away from a cognitive paradigm to an interpretive one. People started to introduce such terms as consumer experiences, meanings, symbols, images, and cultural categories, and a host of other similarly evocative terms which stood in stark contrast to product attributes, brand loyalty, lifestyle marketing, and other analytical categories that are measurable and quantifiable. A major move in this direction came in the mid-1980s when authors began to examine how postmodern culture influences consumption patterns. In fact, consumption systems were themselves viewed as culturally coded systems. Research has begun to address how consumers' understanding of products and brands derives from the meanings that consumers attach to them. A question that arises is: where do the meanings come from and how are they attached to consumable objects and consumer environments? The fact that any given culture forms the basis of relevant symbolic systems and aesthetic representations means that these symbolic systems transcend into sensory experiences – which is the basis of postmodern consumption.

SEE ALSO: Commodification; Commodities; Commodity Fetishism; Disneyization; Hyperconsumption

REFERENCES

Bourdieu, Pierre. 1984. *Distinction: A Social Critique of the Judgment of Taste*. Cambridge, MA: Harvard University Press.

Brown, Stephen, Elizabeth C. Hirschman, and Pauline Maclaran. 2001. "Presenting the Past: On Marketing's Re-production Orientation." In *Imagining Marketing: Art, Aesthetics and the Avant-Garde*, edited by Stephen Brown and Anthony Patterson, 145–191. New York: Routledge.

de Certeau, Michel. 1984. *The Practice of Everyday Life*, translated by Steven Rendall. Berkeley: University of California Press.

Holt, Douglas B. 1995. "How Consumers Consume: A Typology of Consumption Practices." *Journal of Consumer Research* 22(June): 1–16.

Kozinets, Robert V. 2002. "Can Consumers Escape the Market? Emancipatory Illusions from Burning Man." *Journal of Consumer Research* 29(June): 20–38.

Lefebvre, Henri. 1971. *Everyday Life in the Modern World*. Translated by Sacha Rabinovitch. London: Allen Lane.

Lyotard, Jean-François. 1984. *The Postmodern Condition: A Report on Knowledge*. Minneapolis: University of Minnesota Press.
Mackay, Hugh. 1997. "Introduction." In *Consumption and Everyday Life*, edited by Hugh Mackay, 1–12. London: Sage.
Miles, Malcolm. 2005/1997. *Art, Space and the City*. London: Routledge.
Peñaloza, Lisa. 1999. "Just Doing It: A Visual Ethnographic Study of Spectacular Consumption Behavior at Nike Town." *Consumption, Markets and Culture* 2(4): 337–400.
Schmitt, Bernd, and Alex Simonson. 1997. *Marketing Aesthetics: The Strategic Management of Brands, Identity, and Image*. New York: Free Press.
Schroeder, Jonathan E. 2002. *Visual Consumption*. New York: Routledge.
Solomon, Michael R., Gary Bamossy, and Soren Askegaard. 2002. *Consumer Behavior: A European Perspective*. Harlow, UK: Financial Times/Prentice-Hall.

FURTHER READING

Baudrillard, Jean. 1995. "Transaesthetics." In *The Transparency of Evil: Essays on Extreme Phenomena*, translated by James Benedict, 14–19. New York: Verso.
Featherstone, Mike. 1991. *Consumer Culture and Postmodernism*. Newbury Park, CA: Sage.

Consumption Rituals

JULIE A. RUTH
Rutgers University–Camden, US
CELE C. OTNES
University of Illinois, USA

Consumption rituals are performative events that are often planned, repeated over time within a social group or culture, and characterized by intensive use of goods and services. Drawing on research in sociology and anthropology, Rook (1985) explicates the concept of ritualistic consumption and its structural elements: ritual scripts, performance roles, audience, and artifacts. Ritual scripts provide normative guidelines pertaining to an occasion's storyline and expected performances of the main protagonist(s) and observers. Ritual artifacts are objects imbued with symbolic and even sacred meaning, and are often excluded from everyday consumption.

For example, a holiday celebration such as Christmas or Diwali is a consumption ritual because it commemorates an important cultural time; includes people who are typically not present at everyday gatherings; features foods, objects, and activities reserved for the occasion; and involves performance roles distinct from everyday actions. Social and cultural meaning making occurs through the performance of consumption rituals and can transform people's identities as they portray key roles, particularly those associated with rites of passage (e.g., Latin American Quinceañera celebrations which symbolize the transition from child to young woman; Ghanaian funeral practices which offer the living and the dead opportunities for new social identities). Through their symbolism, consumption rituals add to the cultural biographies of ritual artifacts (e.g., a family heirloom used in weddings across generations).

Also important to rituals are their social and individual functions, such as order, transformation, and communitas (Driver 1991). Order refers to the ability of a ritual to structure people's actions within a consumption ritual (e.g., scripts and sequenced actions associated with a wedding celebration) and over time by marking significant life events such as birth, coming of age, marriage, parenthood, becoming an elder, and death. Transformation refers to the ability of a consumption ritual to enact change in participants, ranging from momentary and often inconsequential ways (feeling lethargic from feasting) to more extraordinary and permanent changes (initiation to manhood rituals including circumcision of Xhosa teenage boys in South Africa). Communitas refers to the potential for ritual to strengthen social bonds between participants, their social networks, and cultural communities.

The most visible types of consumption rituals are associated with rites of passage, holidays, and gift giving. For example, in most cultures weddings are elaborate rites associated with extraordinary consumption, such as special clothing for main participants and audience members, food, transport, decorations, and the transfer of wealth and materiality between participants. Wedding artifacts oftentimes reflect the religious and/or secular origins of these events. For example, Christian weddings may feature bibles and communion artifacts; likewise, Jewish weddings often take place under a chuppah, or flower bedecked arch. Nevertheless, given the increasing ease with which people move and sociocultural information spreads, weddings are likewise becoming more diverse with respect to cultures and participants. For example, interest in the "white wedding" has risen across the globe, in some instances overshadowing local traditions. At the same time, there is a rise in the combining of cultural traditions in ways that might have been taboo in the past. These include adopting ritual elements associated with the ethnic or religious heritages of both partners – as in an American wedding ceremony combined with Buddhist rituals such as symbolic food offerings for ancestors, or a Catholic ceremony occurring under a chuppah. Likewise, some ritual scripts for marriage are being appropriated for other occasions (e.g., the "prom-posal," during which male and female US high schoolers stage elaborate surprise invitations to attend a prom event).

Gift giving is a consumption ritual that is often embedded within ritual occasions. Sherry (1983) introduced a three-stage model of gift giving consisting of *gestation* (all activities prior to the actual gift exchange), *prestation* (ceremonial presentation and emotional reaction of the recipient), and *reformulation* (the relational impact of the exchange). Ruth, Otnes, and Brunel (1999) find that giver–recipient relationships can be strengthened, affirmed, negatively confirmed, weakened, or even severed through gift exchange. Recent research examines gifts between communities (rather than individuals) that are guided by moral rather than interpersonal considerations.

While many consumption rituals take place inside the home and other prescribed ritual sites (e.g., houses of worship), recent research has shifted its focus to other venues. For example, festive performances such as New Year's Eve celebrations in capital cities accentuate the event's fantasy, whereas thrill performance activities such as rafting, mountain climbing, and safaris emphasize the uncertainties and realism of nature. In addition, recent research has focused on consumption rituals in marketspace settings, exploring the ways in which consumer experience is shaped by ritual language; choreographed servicescapes such as American Girl stores; and conventions and merchandise that support identity play among members of fan communities such as *Star Trek* enthusiasts. At the same time, scholars are exploring how rejection of the marketplace plays a role in consumption rituals, for example Burning Man (Kozinets 2002) and the nature of rituals used by consumers who are shedding possessions associated with significant private or public meaning.

Consumer cultures are replete with changes in meaning making as existing consumption rituals are appropriated, revised, and transformed. Future research will continue to examine the ways artifacts, scripts, roles, participants, and occasions shape consumption rituals and their sociocultural meaning.

SEE ALSO: Burning Man; Consumer Culture; Consumption and Identity; Experiential Consumption; Gifts; Weddings

REFERENCES

Driver, Tom. 1991. *The Magic of Ritual.* New York: HarperCollins.

Kozinets, Robert V. 2002. "Can Consumers Escape the Market? Emancipatory Illuminations from Burning Man." *Journal of Consumer Research* 29: 20–38.

Rook, Dennis W. 1985. "The Ritual Dimension of Consumer Behavior." *Journal of Consumer Research* 12: 251–264. Accessed June 17, 2014. https://www2.bc.edu/~woodsiar/CB%20Chap%201%20Rook%20Ritual%20Dimensions%20.pdf.

Ruth, Julie A., Cele C. Otnes, and Frederic F. Brunel. 1999. "Gift Receipt and the Reformulation of Relationships." *Journal of Consumer Research* 25(4): 385–402.

Sherry, John F., Jr. 1983. "Gift Giving in Anthropological Perspective." *Journal of Consumer Research* 10(2): 157–168.

Consumption and Sexualities: *SEE* SEXUALITIES AND CONSUMPTION

Consumption, Spectacles of

EUGENE HALTON
University of Notre Dame, USA

The word "spectacle" means something that is viewed or seen, with the connotation of something impressive being displayed, a "show" to be viewed by numbers of people. The early spectacles of ancient Greece and Rome ranged from theatrical and athletic events, gladiatorial combats and wild beast shows, to civic commemorations. The Roman practice of "bread and circuses," described by the satirist and poet Juvenal, where free wheat and entertainments were provided to curry political favor, may be an early example of spectacles of consumption in one sense in which it is used today – a medium of consumption-linked entertainment as a way of life. The rise of modern sports in the nineteenth century gave birth to the growth of professionalized spectator sport in the twentieth century as a form of consumption.

Both the terms "spectator" and "consumer" connote taking something in, involving a passive relation rather than productive activity or participation. Theater, developing out of ritual in ancient Greece, is another word related to looking at, and represents the transformation from what Lucien Levy-Bruhl described as participation consciousness characterizing tribal peoples, to more marked separation of the production of an event from its visual consumption by spectators in civilizations.

The term "spectacles of consumption" may refer to specific events linked with consumption or to a more general sense of consumption as a pervasive visualizing ideology which presents life as a spectacle. This latter sense of consumption as a larger-than-life visual enactment expressive of the dynamics of capitalism is an outlook associated with a group of French Marxist intellectuals known as the "situationist international," whose notable members included Guy Debord and Raoul Vaneigem.

Debord's book *The Society of the Spectacle*, first published in 1967, draws attention to the ubiquity of spectacle in modern life, not only as an event, but as a primary medium of capitalism, culture, and consumption. In his view the culture of the spectacle enables social life as *being*, which became commodified to *having* in an earlier stage of capitalism, and then being further degraded to *appearing*: "all 'having' must now derive its immediate prestige and its ultimate purpose from appearances" (2002/1967, chap. 1, par. 17). The appearances take on a fetishized life of their own as representations of the ruling economic order, as "a vast inaccessible reality that can never be questioned. Its sole message is: 'What appears is good, and what is good appears'" (chap. 1, par. 12).

Hence spectacle, in its mediated appearances such as commercial television, systematically destroys the capacity for genuine encounter:

> Imprisoned in a flattened universe bounded by the *screen* of the spectacle that has enthralled him, the spectator knows no one but the *fictitious speakers* who subject him to a one-way monologue about their commodities and the politics of their commodities. The spectacle as a whole serves as his looking glass. (2002/1967, Chap. 9, par. 218)

Critic Jerry Mander similarly saw the spread of commercial television as a form of confinement of experience through passive spectatorship, and argued that "The autocracy can exist in the technology itself" (1978, 97).

French situationist Vaneigem notes that, if a life is priceless, its value is reversed in consumer society because:

> by the lights of the spectacle such riches can only be described as intolerable poverty. For consumer society poverty is whatever cannot be consumed. The reduction of people to consumers is thus an enrichment: the more things we have, the more roles we play, the more we *are*. So decrees the organization of appearances. (2012/1967, 121)

Hence spectacle can act as illusory appearance designed to mask the underlying transformation of life and social relations into commodities to be consumed.

Spectacles of consumption also can mean specific places, such as theme parks, malls, Las Vegas, and spectator arenas, as well as events, such as Black Friday shopping after Thanksgiving or the Super Bowl. Mark Gottdeiner has written on the rise of a range of spectacular built environments in his 2001 book *The Theming of America*, and in other works. George Ritzer's book *Enchanting a Disenchanted World* (2004) also deals with the theme of spectacle and "cathedrals of consumption."

The role of the spectator has also enlarged far beyond the confines of being present at the spectacle. The sheer proliferation of screens, from television to hand-held devices, also enables consumption, through advertising, celebrity, and "spectacleness" itself, to permeate everyday conduct all of the time. More information is available to people, but more commercializing of information, both in form and content, is also delivered. Constantly updated Facebook profiles provide information, but also illustrate how the self can become a spectacle, an appearance to be looked at within commercialized electronic space.

The summer Olympics has a global television audience in the billions, and the cost and complexity of its opening ceremonies have been growing ever more spectacular. Yet the 2012 Super Bowl perhaps best exemplifies spectacles of consumption as events as well as a dominant cultural ideology. It was viewed by an average of 111.3 million Americans, more than 33 percent of the population, and was the most watched program in US history. An additional 100 million viewers from other countries watched the game. Some 114 million American viewers tuned into the halftime show by Madonna, three million more than for the game and the largest halftime audience thus far. Madonna entered the stadium on a dais pulled by what looked like ancient Roman slaves, a spectacle reminiscent of a scene from the movie *Cleopatra*, starring Elizabeth Taylor. It was perhaps the perfection of a spectacle within a spectacle referencing spectacle to the society of the spectacle. Antidemocratic hierarchy and domination appeared, not to reveal the alienating dynamics of spectacle that Debord had criticized, but to sell them as commodified entertainment. It was the culmination of the process whereby people would learn, as Aldous Huxley put it in 1958, to "love their servitude." The National Anthem was sung by the *American Idol* winner, further cementing celebrity, spectacle, and patriotism.

The new commercials introduced specifically for the Super Bowl are closely watched and enjoyed, and are just as essential to the spectacle as the football game and halftime entertainment. In the decade from 2001 to 2010, total commercial time jumped from 40 minutes to almost 48 minutes (Steinberg 2011). Advertising for the 2012 game was sold out over a year in advance, with commercials averaging US$3.5 million per 30-second ad, a new record. But the next year the rate went up again to an average of US$4 million, and had a record 164 million Americans watching at least six minutes of the event. By all appearances spectacles of consumption continue to grow unabated.

SEE ALSO: Debord, Guy; Experiential Consumption; McDonaldization; Theming; Visual Consumption

REFERENCES

Debord, Guy. 2002/1967. *The Society of the Spectacle.* Translated by Ken Knabb. http://www.bopsecrets.org/SI/debord/index.htm.

Gottdiener, Mark. 2001. *The Theming of America*, 2nd ed. Boulder, CO: Westview Press.

Mander, J. 1978. *Four Arguments for the Elimination of Television.* New York: HarperCollins.

Ritzer, George. 2004. *Enchanting a Disenchanted World.* New York: Sage.

Steinberg, Brian. 2011. "Super Bowl Ad Creep Gave Viewers Nearly 48 Minutes of Commercials Last Year." *Ad Age* Jan. 18. http://adage.com/article/special-report-super-bowl/super-bowl-ad-creep-gave-viewers-48-minutes-ads-year/148261/.

Vaneigem, Raoul. 2012/1967. *The Revolution of Everyday Life.* Oakland, CA: PM Press.

Consumption and Sport

DAVID L. ANDREWS and BRYAN C. CLIFT
University of Maryland, USA

In the twenty-first century, sport represents a popular and prominent aspect of what is a pervasive consumer culture (Horne 2006). The concerted commercialization of sport has been a process that can be traced back, at the very least, to the rapidly urbanizing mass culture of the early to mid phases of the industrial revolution. However, it has only been since the end of World War II that broader enmeshed economic, social, cultural, and technological transformations have drastically reshaped the sporting landscape according to the dictates of a seemingly unrelenting, corporate-led culture of consumption. Within this moment, the combined processes of corporatization, commodification, spectacularization, and celebritization have rendered sport a vivid expression of a late capitalist economy, within which cultural products and processes have played an ever more pivotal role (Jameson 1998). From its basic internal logic as competitive athletic practices, the pervasive commodification of sport as a culture industry has led to its re-engineering as primarily a mode of commercial entertainment. Hence, contemporary sporting events (specifically those high-profile, meticulously structured, and heavily financed physically based contests between teams and/or individuals) are illustrative of an economic formation characterized by an inextricably conjoined *commercialized culture* (the manufacturing of cultural practices and services for profit) and *culturalized economy* (an increased reliance on the cultural realm as a source of capital accumulation).

Sport is unequivocally a significant sector within late capitalism's flexible regime of accumulation (Andrews 2006). Nonetheless, it cannot be considered an economic or cultural monolith. Its incorporation into the consumerist order, which is defined and dominated by corporate and media interests, has transformed it into a multifaceted and intertextual amalgam that can be experienced, and thereby consumed, in myriad forms. These include event attendance, media viewership, or the purchase of the ancillary commodities and services through which sport leagues, teams, and celebrities become materialized and/or embellished in the minds and lives of the consuming populace. Crucial to understanding the consumption of sport, as Crawford (2004) observed, are fans, audiences, and spectators, for it is consumers who contribute to the generation of the atmosphere at venues, create alternative ways to view sport in homes or other establishments, publish fanzines, participate in radio discussions, contribute to internet sites, and generate expressions through social media (Dart 2012). Sporting content is also communicated through a variety of commercially oriented delivery platforms (either through the selling of the sporting content to consumers, the auctioning and delivery of sport audiences to corporate advertisers, or oftentimes both), ranging from print and televisual media, to new social media conduits. Furthermore, the intertextual and multiplatform constitution of the sport sphere is complicated and compounded by its mutually constitutive relations with other culture industry domains (each of which incorporates its own intertextual and multiplatform relations). As Crawford (2004) observed, the incorporation of sport into the emergent cultural economy has increased opportunities for people to engage in and to consume sport, both via the growing market of sport-related consumer goods and services, and expanding mass media technologies. Invoking Debord (1994/1967), it is thus possible to argue that spectacularized sport commodities have colonized all aspects of social life: from team branded baby apparel worn in an individual's formative years; through the directly experienced and/or mass-mediated sporting successes and failures, trials and tribulations that provide untold emotive value and symbolic meaning to many people's very existences; to even the team logo-adorned coffin into which the perpetually loyal deceased is laid to rest.

The changing nature of sport, through the mid and late twentieth century and into the early twenty-first century, has brought about significant changes within the realm of sport involvement and spectatorship. Indeed, as Bourdieu (1978) argued, the professionalization of sport delivered back to ordinary people, as paying customers or spectators, the commodified iterations of practices that were once sources of their enjoyment and that they had directly controlled. Nonetheless, and despite the corporate organization and ownership of major sporting entities, many sport fans express a proprietary relationship with the sports and teams they follow. This is because – and perhaps more so than comparable cultural forms incorporated into the machinations of the late capitalist order (i.e., popular music, literature, and film) – for many people sport retains an aura that allows it to transcend the very real commercial forces and relations with which it is now constitutively framed. Furthermore, despite engaging in very real consumptive practices as part and parcel of their everyday sporting involvements, many supporters demonstrate open hostility toward what is perceived to be the commercial colonization and corruption of *their* game. For instance, some English football fans balk at the very reference to their teams as brands, others eschew the refashioned club logos on their replica shirts, and some even show an indifference toward the new wave of moneyed owners (many of whom are American magnates) who have oftentimes rescued their beloved clubs from being economically unsustainable. Much of the disdain exhibited by such fans derives from a sense that the new model of sport ownership, organization, and delivery fails to account for the traditions, values, and ethos of the game. Theirs is a sense of resigned disillusionment that sport is under threat from the relentless march of unashamed packaging, promotion, and presentation that positions it as nothing more than a consumer choice within the expanding commercial leisure economy (Andrews 2009).

Within this context, the very notion of the sport spectator has become complicated by residual and emergent experiences and expectations. Giulianotti (2002) captured this bifurcation within his taxonomy of professional football spectators, wherein (and among other insights) he positioned the traditional football "supporter" in contradistinction to the more contemporaneous football *flâneur*. Whereas the former displayed an ingrained personal and emotional investment in the team, its spatial location, and the community of supporters of which they were a part, the latter displays a relatively indifferent, and most likely ephemeral and highly mediated relationship with football, the sport being used as a marker of the *flâneur*'s urbane and cosmopolitan lifestyle until it loses its cultural cachet and is replaced by the next sign of cultural sophistication. Recognizing the competing consumer subjectivities operating within the contemporary sport context, Roger Goodell, the National Football League's Commissioner, recently characterized the Washington Redskins' audience as "millions of fans and consumers": the loyal supporters or fans being a constituency that can be almost guaranteed because of their traditional or "hot" relationship with the team and sport, whereas the "cool" *flâneurs* or consumers required enticing away from competing commercialized leisure options (Giulianotti 2002).

One aspect of contemporary sport culture that has opened on new consumption opportunities and experiences over the past decade or so has been that of social media. New social media technologies (such as Twitter, Facebook, YouTube, Vine, Instagram) are now invaluable and unavoidable aspects of the corporate sport landscape. They are vital mechanisms through which marketing and promotional initiatives reach the consuming public (Dart 2012). Moreover, for consumers, new social media represent a cultural space which affords them the potential to influence the creation of meanings associated with sport and to develop new democratized patterns of interaction that can (at times) circumvent established hierarchies of media communication (Dixon 2011). Such "sport chatter" (Whannel 2009) is distinct from statistical information, formal reporting, and material consumption, and provides occasion for fans to exchange analyses of events, tactics, players, and performances blended with anecdotes, banter, and reminiscences. Moreover, such engagements can evolve into the creation of new practices and traditions associated with being part of a sporting community (Dixon 2011). Furthermore, fans using social media become *prosumers* (Ritzer, Dean, and Jurgenson 2012) in that they are no longer purely consumers of media content, but actively produce media content that shapes, however minutely, the meanings circulating within the sporting culture industry. The rise of the prosumer – what Ritzer refers to as the "coming age of the prosumer" – signals an increased importance (sport) producers place on the end user or prosumer within the realization of commodities and services. More readily and recently associated with advocates of social media than other realms, the sport prosumer represents the largely autonomous, uncontrollable, and unpaid manner in which fans produce and consume the user-generated online content that powers social media technologies. Going beyond the passive consumption of sport, prosumers contribute to the social media universe in myriad ways that accelerate and intensify the feedback loops that add to the constitution and production of sport media, marketing, and promotional discourse. Consequently, the fan endeavoring to exist and operate productively within the social media universe necessarily participates in the *trending* dimensions of prosumers' commentaries, which may lead to reconsiderations, or even reworkings, of commercial marketing and promotional strategies and practices (Ritzer, Dean, and Jurgenson 2012). This new patterning in the production of sporting consumption effectively ties together more closely the individual elements of the production–text–audience triad of cultural production.

While the commodification of sport and spectator identities as vehicles for the promotion of the cultural industry ushered forward highly mediated productions of sport and the expansion of sport into other forms of consumption, contemporary (sporting) promotional culture cannot completely control the production of meaning and structuring of relationships of objects, people, events, and experiences (Wernick 1991). With the creative utilization of sporting objects, events, and experiences in the, at times, oppositional practices of the everyday (Willis 1990), the positioning of the sport fan or consumer as the irrelevant end point in the triad of cultural production must be reconsidered (Crawford 2004). For, as new social media technologies attest, the symbolic production of sport's symbolic economy and experiential spaces is indebted not solely to promotional devices, but also to the various ways in which people productively engage in practices of symbolic manufacture and exchange, such as the nurturing and circulation of expressions of individual and communal identity, and associated feelings of belonging (Dixon 2011). Evidently, analyses of contemporary sport fandom cannot simply reduce the sporting consumer to being a compliant or passive dupe of consumer culture.

SEE ALSO: Commodities; *Flâneur/Flânerie*; Leisure and Consumption; Popular Culture; Prosumption

REFERENCES

Andrews, David L. 2006. *Sport–Commerce–Culture: Essays on Sport in Late Capitalist America*. New York: Lang.

Andrews, David L. 2009. "Sport, Culture, and Late Capitalism." In *Marxism, Cultural Studies and Sport*, edited by B. Carrington and I. McDonald, 213–231. London: Routledge.

Bourdieu, Pierre. 1978. "Sport and Social Class." *Social Science Information* 17(6): 819–840.

Crawford, Garry. 2004. *Consuming Sport: Fans, Sport and Culture*. London: Routledge.

Dart, Jon. 2012. "New Media, Professional Sport and Political Economy." *Journal of Sport & Social Issues*. doi:10.1177/0193723512467356.

Debord, Guy. 1994/1967. *The Society of the Spectacle*. Translated by D. Nicholson-Smith. New York: Zone.

Dixon, Kevin. 2011. "A 'Third Way' for Football Fandom Research: Anthony Giddens and Structuration Theory." *Soccer & Society* 12(2): 279–298.

Giulianotti, Richard. 2002. "Supporters, Followers, Fans, and Flâneurs: A Taxonomy of Spectator Identities in Football." *Journal of Sport & Social Issues* 26(1): 25–46.

Horne, John. 2006. *Sport in Consumer Culture*. New York: Palgrave Macmillan.

Jameson, Frederic. 1998. *The Cultural Turn: Selected Writings on the Postmodern 1983–1998*. London: Verso.

Ritzer, George, Paul Dean, and Nathan Jurgenson. 2012. "The Coming of Age of the Prosumer." *American Behavioral Scientist* 56(4): 379–398.

Wernick, Andrew. 1991. *Promotional Culture: Advertising, Ideology and Symbolic Expression*. London: Sage.

Whannel, Garry. 2009. "Between Culture and Economy: Understanding the Politics of Media Sport." In *Marxism, Cultural Studies and Sport*, edited by B. Carrington & I. MacDonald, 68–87. London: Routledge.
Willis, Paul E. 1990. *Common Culture: Symbolic Work at Play in the Everyday Cultures of the Young*. Milton Keynes, UK: Open University Press.

Consumption in the United States

MICHAEL K. STEIN
University of Massachusetts Amherst, USA

Consumption in the United States refers to the material and symbolic importance of consuming goods and services for the economy and the identity of the United States. This contemporary meaning has two important features. The first is the central role that the consuming of goods, increasingly purchased with credit, plays in the American economy. The second feature is the ideology of consumerism and the cultivation of the consumer as a political, social, and economic category or subject. These two features have, significantly, developed in the postwar period and remain central to understandings of the American way of life today. The American dream reflects these features and projects a vision of the good life that is attainable by those who are willing to work hard in a land of opportunity. In addition, consumer choice is seen as an important dimension of personal freedom and political claims on the right and left of the political spectrum evoke consumer choice as an important value. Practices of consumption are therefore important sites for the production of social meaning and serve as markers of status and as venues for self-creation.

Prior to the emergence of the American consumer society that is recognizable today, consumption had a number of important meanings and associations that help to inform our current understanding of consumption in the United States. To consume has long meant to use up, waste, or destroy. This is reflected in our understanding of eating whereby the food or drink that is consumed is transformed from energy into sustenance. It is also used to express the condition of being emotionally overwhelmed, such as being consumed with jealousy or anger. When we are consumed by an emotion, our capacity for thinking clearly has been destroyed. In addition to eating, material objects can also be consumed by flames or other material processes. For similar reasons consumption was used to describe aspects of disease, and tuberculosis became known as consumption for its pulmonary symptoms. In the late nineteenth and early twentieth centuries sanatoriums were built in many regions of the United States to treat and segregate patients with consumption.

As these examples indicate, consumption has both positive and negative historical connotations. Consuming food provides us with valuable nutrients while tuberculosis threatens our lives. Unsurprisingly, contemporary consumption in the United States has positive and negative dimensions as well. A growing standard of living is very appealing, and access to the good life is considered positive. Consumer movements secured increased protections, accountability, and equal access for many Americans and these achievements certainly improve the lives of everyday people. At the same time, however, these movements and the legal apparatuses they generated institutionalized the logic of consumption, reinforcing its centrality to the American vision of the good life. Although this vision is appealing to many people and encouraging of desire, the economic reality of ever-increasing consumption entails a logic of infinite expansion in a world of finite resources. This limitation, perhaps even paradox, is at the heart of environmental critiques of consumption in the United States and raises serious questions about the sustainability of consumption as a way of life. Despite this paradox, political leaders from both parties continue to advocate for domestic and international policies that reaffirm the centrality of consumption in the American way of life. The political and economic development of the United States has discursively unfolded on the terrain of consumption.

Throughout the history of the United States the buying and selling of goods played an important political role in the development of the country. Strong resentment by colonists against British taxes on goods resulted in the Boston Tea Party and helped to politicize the purchase and sale of goods. Colonists found themselves associated with each other as customers in spite of their geographic separation. Both domestic and imported goods began to give rise to colonial grievances explicitly and contributed to the spirit of revolution. Boycotts also served as an important act of resistance in the push for independence.

The politicization of goods is an undeniable constant throughout American history. Politicized buying evolved alongside the economic development of the United States, often connecting the consumption of goods with the conditions of their production. This played an important role in the development and tactics of the labor movement and identity politics. Demographic targeting and market segmentation provided a diversity of products that allowed individuals to express themselves through the purchase of goods, to find meaning in the consumer choices they made, and to give voice to their political and social grievances. In this way consumption is a site not only where goods and services are used up but also where social meaning is produced. Consumption remains an important site for political, ethical, and social claims and contestation in the United States.

While we can identify the politicization of goods in the United States from the colonial era to the present, there are important differences between the economies of the colonial customer and the contemporary consumer that we must consider. The universality and measurability of wealth and labor endemic to capitalism brought about the industrial revolution, mass society, and the production of an ever-increasing number of goods to satisfy human needs and desires. In many ways the current era of globalization is an extension of the logic and processes of capitalism throughout the world. As productive economic power increased, the consumer-based economy became increasingly important in the early twentieth century. Corporations looked for new methods of persuasion, giving birth to the public relations and advertising industries. Despite the economic setbacks of the Great Depression and the shift to wartime production during World War II, the consumer republic flourished in the postwar period. Between the late 1940s and early 1970s good paying jobs and consumer purchasing power were within the reach of large segments of the population, creating the impression of a dream fulfilled. Today nostalgia for this era casts a long shadow over contemporary American society, reflecting the enduring promise and appeal of consumption in the United States.

During the latter half of the twentieth century the consumer economy played a pivotal role in the transformation of the physical landscape of the country. The desire for single-family home ownership in the postwar period gave rise to a sprawling landscape of suburbs extending from the periphery of cities into surrounding rural areas. The automobile industry was at the forefront of this transformation, producing cars that allowed workers to commute to work from their suburban homes each day. The collapse of distance and time that automobiles unleashed would not have been possible without the dynamic development of the Interstate Highway System and of numerous state and local roads. Linking suburban, urban, and rural areas reduced the time it took to transport goods, services, and workers, reconfigured the geography, and opened up new possibilities for capital and American culture.

Consumption in the United States continues to play a central role in the collective mythos and economic structure of the country. However, challenges to the longevity and promise of this way of life abound. The decline of wages, rising inequality, and growing personal debt have reduced the ability of many Americans to achieve the level of economic success and material comfort that had been available to previous generations. The environmental and social costs of consumption are mounting, and sustainability of this way of life is in doubt. Despite these challenges, however, consumption in the United States will remain a defining feature of the American way of life for the foreseeable future.

SEE ALSO: Citizenship and Consumption; Commodity Fetishism; Consumer Society; Culture-Ideology of Consumerism; Symbolic Value

FURTHER READING

Breen, Timothy Hall. 2004. *The Marketplace of Revolution: How Consumer Politics Shaped American Independence*. New York: Oxford University Press.

Cohen, Lizabeth. 2003. *A Consumer's Republic: The Politics of Mass Consumption in Postwar America*. New York: Knopf.

Graeber, David. 2011. "Consumption." *Current Anthropology* 52(4): 489–511. doi:10.1086/660166.

Leach, William. 1993. *Land of Desire: Merchants, Power, and the Rise of a New American Culture*. New York: Vintage.

Consumption, Visual: *SEE* VISUAL CONSUMPTION

Cool

LIDIA K. C. MANZO
University of Trento, Italy

In recent years the term "cool" has increasingly become a universal phenomenon, the ideal language of popular (and youth) culture, and a source of constant innovation. Arguably, it has had an important influence on many institutions, from media and education to the real estate market and the economy itself.

The word "cool" was apparently first used by the jazz saxophonist Lester Young (1909–59). This predominantly black jazz scene in the United States, and among expatriate musicians in Paris, helped popularize notions of cool in America in the 1940s, giving birth to Bohemian, or Beatnik, culture. Through the 1950s, "cool" was reified in American literature for example, in one of the most penetrating studies of the hipster, *The White Negro* (1957). In this essay, Norman Mailer asserted that the only way to resist conformity was by being a hipster, whose tastes for jazz, sex, drugs, and black slang and mores were distinctly cool. Interestingly, the 1960s and 1970s anti-establishment, hedonistic movements of the United States were symbolized by the adoption of hippy fashion, which also heralded the adoption of cool by the masses. Throughout the 1970s, in fact, the moral world of hippies and counterculturalists evolved into a form of revolution that was more personal, practical, and immediate, a revolution played out in the practice of everyday life, most notably Binkley's *Getting Loose* (2007). Here, the trajectory of the counterculture was not something to be fought for, but something to be relaxed "in the moment," a philosophy of life, and the practicing of a looser and more "authentic" way of living. Thus, cool became a global phenomenon which morphed into the broader popular culture. Indeed, as this process penetrated into larger social practices, it commanded the attention of more conventional social and economic power, converting liberationist desire into more established modes, most insidiously consumption.

Cool, as a cultural category in its own right, apparently has no single meaning, and the idea of "coolness" falls into different categories (e.g., language, self-presentation, artistic expression, values, attitudes). Indeed, cool is not something that is inherent in artifacts themselves, but rather in people's attitude toward them. The clothing designer Levi Strauss found out the hard way that cool is not an intrinsic property woven into the blue denim of its jeans: it was the way that their wearers perceived Levi's that made them cool, and within a few years that perception would be imperceptibly stolen away by Calvin Klein and Tommy Hilfiger. What originally made Levi's cool in the 1950s was that they were garments associated with the working classes, and for a middle-class kid to wear them symbolized an act of rebellion. Once an expression of rebellion, as offered by glamorous terrorists, gangsters, and wasted rock musicians, as Pountain and Robins (2000) state, cool came to depict, in fact, a "murky and contradictory" image: "on the one hand, it is egalitarian and hedonistic in temperament. On the other hand, it is fascinated by violence, drugs and criminality and mesmerized by the sight of naked power" (p. 178).

Cool is now very much linked to commodities and the aesthetics of designer labels and niche brands. As faith in the revolutionary potential of "authentic" counterculture combined with the development of a new ideology of consumption, cool became the language of advertising and thus entered the mainstream as a marketing strategy. The determination of what is cool oscillates between peer judgments and conceptions and corporate promotion. In a March 1997 *New York Times* article, Malcolm Gladwell unveiled the triumphant circularity of "cool hunting" – that is, the search for authenticity among the urban poor by marketers, cultural reporters, or style runners – in which the act of discovering what is cool is itself what causes cool to take flight. Such a phenomenon represents a closed loop, whereby not only can the uncool not see cool but cool cannot even be adequately described by them. A special mix of six characteristics, compiled by Superbrands (UK) Ltd., included style, innovation, originality, desirability, uniqueness, and "authenticity" as components of cool that were recognized and adjudicated by people from the "street," who supposedly can spot trends well ahead of marketers.

While authenticity has been understood as the truest hallmark of cool behavior, Thornton's analysis of the dance music scene (1995), for instance, focuses more on the exclusivity of cool, whereby authenticity is used to express superior taste and disdain for the mainstream. Urgently seeking cool for their products, businesses, services, and advertising, they are themselves prime exponents of the cool lifestyle. They are what French sociologist Pierre Bourdieu (1984) referred to as cultural intermediaries.

SEE ALSO: Authenticity; Consumption and Identity; Coolhunting; Cultural Intermediaries; Fashion; Popular Culture; Youth Culture(s)

REFERENCES

Binkley, Sam. 2007. *Getting Loose: Lifestyle Consumption in the 1970s*. Durham, NC: Duke University Press.

Bourdieu, Pierre. 1984. *Distinction: A Social Critique of the Judgment of Taste*. London: Routledge.

Pountain, Dick, and David Robins. 2000. *Cool Rules: Anatomy of an Attitude*. London: Reaktion Books.

Thornton, Sarah. 1995. *Club Cultures: Music, Media, and Subcultural Capital*. Cambridge, UK: Polity.

Coolhunting

NATALIE COULTER
York University, Canada

"Coolhunting" is a term coined within marketing circles. It came to the attention of the public when social commentator Malcolm Gladwell wrote an essay for the *New Yorker* on March 17, 1997, entitled "The Coolhunt." Coolhunters are marketing professionals who "hunt" the streets to determine what is "cool." In his article Gladwell describes how marketers seek knowledge from the street (often urban, minority youth), and then define, interpret, and repackage "cool" to sell to corporations, who in turn try to leverage this knowledge in the marketplace. Gladwell characterizes the coolhunt as a "collection of spontaneous observation and predictions that differ from one moment to the next, and from one coolhunter to the next."

Gladwell acknowledges that the difficulty with hunting cool is that cool is in a perpetual cycle of obsolescence. Coolhunting itself is paradoxical, because, once something is discovered by the marketing professionals to be cool, it is appropriated and sold as cool and hence loses its coolness. Gladwell refers to this dynamic as "chase and flight," a term often used to describe the fashion theory of sociologist Thorstein Veblen. In looking for the origin of trends in the street rather than in the corporate boardroom, coolhunting expects fashion and coolness to trickle up the social scale, rather than the top-down, upper- to lower-class, movement traditionally theorized by sociologists. An American Public Broadcasting System documentary film, *The Merchants of Cool* (2001), written by Rachel Dretzin and directed by Barak Goodman, follows coolhunters in their pursuit as they enter the spaces of young people to ask them specific questions about their tastes, styles, and values.

Coolhunting differs from traditional forms of market research in that it takes the information from those deemed "cool," or what trend researcher Irma Zandt calls the "alpha consumers" (Grossman 2003), as authoritative marketing knowledge. As not all individuals are cool, the job of the coolhunter is to determine who is cool within a particular social grouping. Coolhunting represents a deepening of market research into young people's cultures, as well as the fetishization of young people as the driver of society's tastes and styles. In essence, coolhunting is the elusive attempt to commodify what Sarah Thornton (1996) calls subcultural capital, "being in the know" in a particular scene.

Since its initial entrée into public consciousness, coolhunting has faced criticism, mainly for its failure to identify profitable trends and its lack of robustness as a research approach. This has led some to argue that the marketers themselves were lured, like those to whom they sought to sell, by the promise of coolness (Grossman 2003).

SEE ALSO: Bourdieu, Pierre; Brands and Branding; Cool; Fashion; Teens

REFERENCES

Gladwell, Malcolm. 1997. "The Coolhunt." *New Yorker*, March 17: 78. Accessed June 26, 2014. http://www.newyorker.com/archive/1997/03/

17/1997_03_17_078_TNY_CARDS_000378002.
Grossman, Lev. 2003. "The Quest for Cool." *Time* 162(10): 48.
Thornton, Sarah. 1996. *Club Cultures: Music, Media and Subcultural Capital.* Hanover, NH: University Press of New England.

Cooperatives

PIERGIORGIO DEGLI ESPOSTI
University of Bologna, Italy

A cooperative, commonly referred to as a "co-op," is a voluntary association that is organized for the mutual benefit of a particular social, economic, and/or cultural agenda(s). The venerable idea of cooperative enterprise originated in Europe during the Middle Ages. In fact, the merchant guilds and trade associations of the Hanseatic League were built on the idea of cooperation. As the legitimacy of aristocratic regimes based on monarchic or theocratic rule declined and European territories gained political independence, the idea of the cooperative took root and spread. The cooperative principle is a historical and core ideal of the Swiss nation. The relics of medieval commons which can be seen in present-day European forest cooperatives offer proof of the cooperative's deep history.

While various cooperative efforts have their roots in ancient civilization, the modern cooperative movement began primarily as a response to industrial capitalism. Those concerned about the problems created by industry looked to a variety of private and public efforts to provide greater security and equity for those whose lives were being turned upside down by powerful economic changes. Economic theorists such as Mills, Pareto, and Walras were prominent in regard to the notion of cooperation. Mills (1852) emphasized the equality of workers as shareholders with the capability of electing or dismissing the management. Walras (1865) defined cooperatives according to their two main goals: the creation of capital and the redistribution of wealth to the members.

While cooperatives are economic enterprises, they are at the same time socially oriented. However, in some countries, cooperatives and nonprofit organizations are defined together under the social or civic economy. A cooperative is a legal entity that is democratically owned and controlled by its members; therefore, an interconnected relationship exists between consumers, producers, and employees. Cooperatives are founded on the seven cooperative principles: voluntary and open membership; democratic member control; economic participation by members; autonomy and independence; education, training, and information; cooperation between cooperatives; and a concern for community. Unlike traditional businesses where the emphasis is on profit margins, cooperatives embrace principles of openness, integrity, and social responsibility. Such a focus promotes harmony rather than hostility. The nature of traditional business pits consumers, producers, and employees against each other as a result of the competing and independent goals (profit) of each entity. The democratic operation of cooperatives allows for a longer lifespan than other, more traditional, types of enterprises.

While various forms of cooperation have always existed in civil societies, the modern cooperative movement has its roots in the early industrial revolution as a response to industrial capitalism. The byproduct of this response is the dualistic nature of cooperatives: their economic goal of making profits and their social goal of redistributing wealth. Cooperatives differ from nonprofit organizations in their handling of surpluses. In cooperative enterprises, surpluses may be paid to members in the form of patronage returns proportional to the business done by each member of the cooperative. Nonprofit organizations, by nature and law, are precluded from distributing any surplus to members. Several types of cooperatives exist, including nonprofit community organizations, consumer cooperatives, worker cooperatives, and housing cooperatives (Fay 1908).

There are altogether eight different types of cooperatives. Housing cooperatives are "a legal mechanism for ownership of housing where residents either own shares ... or have membership and occupancy rights" (IACETE & KWF Trust n.d.). Utility cooperatives were created to deliver public utilities to their members and to reinvest any residual profit in infrastructure or to distribute it to members in the form of capital credits. In agricultural cooperatives farmers pool their resources for mutual economic benefit. Credit unions provide financial services, much like a bank, but are not for profit and adhere to the seven cooperative principles. Federal cooperatives consist of members that are themselves cooperatives. Cooperative wholesale societies organize bulk purchases, while a cooperative union develops solidarity between societies. The latter type of cooperative exists primarily for moral and ethical purposes. Finally, cooperative political movements are cooperatives that form political networks from within to better represent member interests.

Cooperatives differ from country to country; for example, the Italian and the Japanese systems are very different. The Italian cooperative movement is more complex than that of Britain or Germany. It involves several political parties, idealistic ambitions, many product sectors, and strong, efficient networks of cooperatives. Unlike in many other countries, as early as 1900 the Italian cooperative movement was developing along three major political and religious lines: communist/socialist; Catholic social; and liberal democratic (or red, white, and green, respectively). In contrast, Japan has a long history of informal rural mutual assistance groups which arose during the Edo period (1603–1867) among less economically powerful individuals. Like the Canadians and the Americans, the Japanese quickly realized the potential of the European cooperative model and first applied it in German Raiffeisen-inspired agricultural credit unions. By 1900, many industrial cooperatives had been voluntarily established by landowners and wealthy farmers but they failed to develop as expected (Klinedinst and Sato 1994). In 1947, after a major attempt by the Japanese government to force farmers to join agricultural associations during World War II, a law was passed that supported the creation of autonomous, voluntary, and democratic cooperatives called *nokyos* (Yamashita 2008).

The cooperative sector is considerable. The world's 300 largest cooperatives have a turnover of US$1.1 trillion annually, which is roughly equal to Spain's gross national product. In Sweden and Switzerland, cooperatives account for about 20 percent of the country's GNP. A recent statistical report comparing cooperative and conventional business ownership worldwide shows that, compared to 328 million people who own shares, there are one billion member-owners of cooperative enterprises. Throughout the world, individuals and communities have created a cooperative self-help organization named the International Co-operative Alliance (ICA).

SEE ALSO: Consumer Activism

REFERENCES

Battilani, Patrizia, and Harm G. Schröter, eds. 2012. *The Cooperative Business Movement, 1950 to Present*. Cambridge, UK: Cambridge University Press.

Fay, Charles Rye. 1908. *Co-operation at Home and Abroad: A Description and Analysis*. London: P. S. King.
IACETE & KWF Trust. n.d. "About IACETE Housing Co-operative Societies." Bangalore: Indian Agriculture College, Education, Non-Education, Teachers, Employees and Karmikas Welfare Foundation Trust. Accessed June 30, 2014. http://iacete-trust.org/faqs.html.
Klinedinst, Mark, and Hitomi Sato. 1994. "The Japanese Cooperative Sector." *Journal of Economic Issues* 38(2): 509–517.
Mills, John Stuart. 1852. *Principles of Political Economy*, 3rd ed., Vol. 2. London: Longman.
Walras, Léon. 1865. *Les Associations populaires de consommation, de production et de crédit* [Popular Associations of Consumption, Production and Credit]. Paris: Dautur.
Yamashita, Kazuhito. 2008. "The Agricultural Cooperatives and Farming Reform in Japan (1)." Tokyo Foundation. Accessed June 30, 2014. http://www.tokyofoundation.org/en/articles/2008/the-agricultural-cooperatives-and-farming-reform-in-japan-1.

FURTHER READING

Black, Lawrence, and Nicole Robertson. 2009. *Consumerism and the Co-operative Movement in Modern British History: Taking Stock*. Manchester: Manchester University Press.
Gurney, Peter. 1996. *Co-operative Culture and the Politics of Consumption in England, 1870–1930*. Manchester: Manchester University Press.

Cosmetic Surgery

JANELLE APPLEQUIST
Pennsylvania State University, USA

Often confused with plastic surgery, cosmetic surgery has become a popular sphere of consumption in the United States and beyond. Plastic surgery is performed to reconstruct physical defects resulting from disorders, accidents, and disease. Cosmetic surgery is performed on areas of the head or body that work properly, but are felt to be lacking in comparison to an aesthetic "norm"; this makes it an elective procedure. Academically, the consumption practices of cosmetic surgery have been researched most often in the context of feminism, including critical debate as to whether procedures such as breast augmentation are meant to benefit one's own understanding of the self, or to fulfill the desire to perform for society in terms of physical appearance.

Women (who make up 90 percent of all procedures) are the main focus of the consumer culture that is cosmetic surgery, as voluntary procedures such as implants, tummy tucks, face lifts, and liposuction have become more normalized. Cosmetic surgery itself, and the consumer's desire for physical perfection, existed well before the 1900s, but the marketing and advertising of the surgery became apparent after World War I. As the physical injuries of soldiers led surgeons to develop new procedures for physical reconstruction of the body, another group of surgeons emerged that catered to the desire for beauty. This created the distinction between plastic and cosmetic surgery.

Studies on the consumer appeals of cosmetic surgery emphasize that the "choice" to undergo risky surgeries may not be a choice at all. Researchers have analyzed cosmetic surgery advertisements since the 1990s, and have consistently found that the advertising discourse emphasizes an unattainable Western beauty ideal, where thin bone structure, large breasts, and striking facial features lead to the attainment of greater social capital and acceptance. In the advertisements, women are consistently positioned in a way that normalizes a multimodality of body parts being emphasized alongside the consumer's happiness; this allows the idealized body to become a form of commodity in terms of the economic exchange required to achieve the desire for perfection. In terms of consumption, the industry of cosmetic surgery is unique in that it exists across two separate forms of social activity: medicine and beauty/fashion. Yet, the choice presented to consumers is not one that emphasizes the medical risks associated with invasive procedures, but rather highlights the potential to gain more self-confidence in regard to socialized ideals of beauty.

Cosmetic surgery is a significant purchase decision on the part of the consumer, as the annual US$10 billion industry sells full body lifts for US$20,000 or, for those with less spare cash, cheek implants for $3000. The most employed marketing tactic is that of the commodification of the body, whereby "before" and "after" photos of satisfied customers are used to sell consumers not only the procedure, but also the notion of how a "good" or "bad" body part looks. Previously available only to the extremely wealthy and to Hollywood celebrities, cosmetic surgery has become an option that is accessible by anyone – clinics now offer payment plans and in-house medical loans. For example, General Electric's CareCredit offers financing for more than 150,000 clinics worldwide with a loan interest rate of almost 27 percent.

The media has amplified the normalization of cosmetic surgery, as reality television shows have focused on the concept of the makeover since the early 1990s. US shows such as *Extreme Makeover*, *The Swan*, and *Dr. 90210* have enabled "everyday" individuals to receive numerous surgeries within a two-month period in exchange for their participation. These participants are often removed from their everyday lives, including their loved ones, in an effort to "hide" their natural appearance until a special reveal at the end of each program presents the new and improved individual to their family and friends. In other cases, the media unintentionally supports the cosmetic surgery industry. The overwhelming cosmetic surgery trend of 2012 was the upper arm lift, with the procedure being performed on 15,000 individuals, up an impressive 4000 percent since 1999. First Lady Michelle Obama has been credited with the popularity of the procedure, as women on social media outlets began discussing their desire to achieve her arm structure which they had observed on her appearance at her husband's first address to Congress in 2008.

In the current research on the consumption of cosmetic surgery the decision to have a procedure is understood as an aspect of the individual, reflexive construction of self-identity. Often theorized according to Michel Foucault's "body politics," cosmetic surgery is regarded by academics as an experience that the consumer uses to perform particular social discourses, via bodily reflexivity and self-imagery. Cosmetic surgery consumption is an area that merits prompt deliberation and investigation, as the industry continues to expand toward the tourism industry. Cosmetic surgery tourism is becoming more commonplace in the United States, offering individuals the opportunity to have surgery followed by recuperation in an exotic location or specialized retreat, including options to embark on African safaris and tropical getaways while receiving Brazilian butt lifts, facial implants, and thigh reconstructions. Whatever one's opinion on the procedures and their purposes, this booming industry is not going away anytime soon – which reflects its importance in our current cultural sphere.

SEE ALSO: Beauty Industry; Fashion; Mass Marketing; Medical Tourism

FURTHER READING

Foucault, Michel. 1978. *Discipline and Punish: The Birth of the Prison*. New York: Pantheon.

Haiken, Elizabeth. 1997. *Venus Envy: A History of Cosmetic Surgery*. Baltimore, MD: Johns Hopkins University Press.

Martinez Lirola, Maria, and Jan Chovanec. 2012. "The Dream of a Perfect Body True:

Multimodality in Cosmetic Surgery Advertising." *Discourse & Society* 23(5): 487–507.
Sanchez Taylor, Jacqueline. 2012. "Buying and Selling Breasts: Cosmetic Surgery, Beauty Treatments and Risk." *Sociological Review* 60: 635–653.

Counterfeiting/Piracy

JACQUELINE BOTTERILL
Brock University, Canada

Counterfeiting and piracy are consumer culture quagmires. By definition they refer to legal boundaries drawn around copying in market societies. To counterfeit is to copy or imitate in an unfavorable way. Piracy contravenes copyright, or the legal control extended to authors and producers over the reproduction of their creations. The assertion of these legal boundaries involves the separation of private rights from public interests, which is rarely clear-cut because each is profoundly intertwined in the other.

Counterfeiting is old and prevalent in all human cultures, yet becomes both apparent and politicized in societies that construct and inscribe authorship, publishing, and private property rights in law. Premodern oral cultures copied stories, songs, and plays with few concerns. According to popular culture historian Peter Burke (2009), these works had no ascribed authors. When sixteenth-century artists replicated master paintings, they were understood to be apprentices, not forgers. Literary critic Northrop Frye (2007) argues that Milton's poetry is a likely suspect of contravention, remarkable less for the author's rhetorical distinctiveness than for his reliance on the Bible, itself protected under contemporary copyright law. Poststructuralist literary critics such as Jacques Derrida challenge the very idea of an original, authentic, or genuine text. They reason that meaning occurs only in the context of other meaning and interpretation. Texts are a circuit of infinite regression in which declaring an original entry point is impossible.

Others disagree. Two distinctive arguments are advanced to justify the construction of an original source and to protect the item from indiscriminate copying. One view sees authentication and reproduction control as a means of creating a greater social good. For example, modern economies emerged from control over the copying of money. European elites secured control over expanding paper money economies in the eighteenth century by putting forgers to death. The first forms of domestic American bills circulated in the 1700s in the colony of Massachusetts carried the statement "To counterfeit is death." Control over the replication of money created centralized economies that were open to the potential for abuse by the few, yet also enabled widespread tax systems for more equal distribution of resources, funded public projects, and limited inflation (Mihm 2007).

The second view regards copyright legislation as the champion of individual rights. Copyright acknowledges the singularity of creative expression and supports artists' claim to profit from their creative labor. These popular values are difficult to untangle from the printing press, which enabled the production, distribution, and sale of information on an unprecedented scale. France established publishing monopolies. Britain extended copyrights to publishers and individual authors. The 1710 Statute of Anne described copying "without the consent of the authors or proprietors" as a "great detriment" and ruin to "them and their families," and therefore awarded copyright to authors for 14 years, after which the author's works became public.

Today, copyright is expansive. Its extension to corporations brought many changes. Copyright typically spans a lifetime plus

70 years. Corporations, which can exist in perpetuity, claim that, to maintain a competitive position, provide jobs, and pay out to shareholders, long-term control of profitable innovations is required. Pharmaceutical industries, for example, seek to prevent drugs being classified as generic. Artists frequently sell their copyright to corporations for cash advances and marketing support. Intellectual property rights have become more assertive in late modern economies where much productive force stems from creative, information, knowledge, and symbolic commodities. Conflict occurs because ideas, titles, categories, and fashion are viewed as integral public resources exempt from copyright. So too in contemporary economies have the commodities' symbolic or sign values – trademarks, logos, brands – become valuable. Infringement of these signs is considered as seriously as the counterfeiting of goods (Dinwoodie and Janis 2008).

These expansions prompt debate over whether copyright creates an excessive surplus on public interest. Critics point to examples deemed disproportionate, such as Tiffany's control over a shade of blue, the copyrighting of the sounds for sonic logos, and private control of genetic material, like the strain of cancer-prone mice produced and owned by Harvard University. During the Olympic Games large sections of public space come under the control of the International Olympic Committee and sponsors who can exercise authority over behavior and speech. Some contemporary artists feel that copyright limits their creative appropriation of music styles (Gaylor 2008). Court cases in which corporations assert copyright over parody and satire raise concerns about limits to free speech, political criticism, and the ability to have a laugh (e.g., *Campbell v. Accuff-Rose Music*, 92–1292, 510 U.S. 569 (1994)).

Business associations, trade committees, nations, and pan-national associations argue that counterfeit controls are not powerful enough to stem the rising tide of fake goods. Advertising campaigns, special reports, and news documentaries circulate to inform the public of the scope, escalation, and associated risks of the global counterfeit economy. Counterfeiting is linked to loss of profit, jobs, taxes, national competitiveness, and sovereignty. Counterfeiting is said to leach trust from markets by deceiving consumers and calling into question the quality of goods. Counterfeit pharmaceuticals, foods, toys, electronic components, car, airplane, and military vehicle parts bring with them potential dangers, health risks, and threats to national security.

In the late twentieth century a global division of labor was struck in which US companies assumed responsibility for product research, design, and marketing, while manufacturing was undertaken offshore, most commonly in China. Contracts ensured that offshore producers met standards of production, but could not control workers' knowledge of the goods or their desire to create replicas for sale in China or distributed globally at prices below those of the originals. Counterfeiting can provide jobs and goods that are difficult to acquire under other means, and therefore counterfeiters are sometimes cast as modern-day Robin Hoods (Hennessey 2012). A fuller understanding of counterfeiting is also supported by recent studies that focus on US and EU demand for counterfeit goods. Large numbers of consumers do not feel deceived but report that they are active shoppers who seek out contraband goods, to stretch their dollars and enjoy entry into the high-end fashion scene without making extortionate investments (Swami, Chamorro-Premuzic, and Furnham 2009).

Piracy emerges as a special category of counterfeiting in the context of digital technologies that have forged new global linkages and support reproduction on a scale well beyond that of the printing press. The employment of digital technologies to copy and share copyrighted software, music, film, TV programs, published material, live performances, and photographs is common. The Motion Picture Association of America condemns popular file sharing platforms like Pirate Bay and applauds the persecution of its operators, but eliminating Pirate Bay has been difficult. Its founders find popular support in their claim that communities have the right to share personal libraries. The closure of Pirate Bay provokes sympathetic hacktivists to continually renew the site when it is shut down.

Controlling counterfeiting and piracy is a challenge. The penalties vary from case to case and nation to nation. Judges exercise discretion over fines that typically focus on compensation. Generally, copying that generates no or low income, or few losses, such as for personal use and the sharing of privately held material like record collections, results in lower fines. Copying or copyright infringement for commercial gain or to avoid licensing fees on a wide scale, such as internet file sharing platforms or distributing copyright materials (software, publications) through an expansive organization, can be subject to large fines, amounting to hundreds of thousands, sometimes millions, of dollars. Counterfeiting and piracy remain highly politicized murky zones of consumer culture because private and public interests are difficult to balance, and the question of the ownership of culture continues unabated.

SEE ALSO: Brands and Branding; Consumer Activism; Intellectual Property

REFERENCES

Burke, Peter. 2009. *Popular Culture in Early Modern Europe*. Aldershot, UK: Ashgate.

Dinwoodie, Graeme D., and Mark D. Janis. 2008. *Trademark Law and Theory: A Handbook of Contemporary Research*. Cheltenham, UK: Elgar.

Frye, Northrop. 2007. *The Great Code: The Bible and Literature*. Toronto: Penguin Canada.

Gaylor, Brett. 2008. *RiP! A Remix Manifesto*. Video, 84 min. National Film Board of Canada.

Hennessey, William. 2012. "Deconstructing Shanzhai – China's Copycat Counterculture: Catch Me If You Can." *Campbell Law Review* 34(3): 609–627.

Mihm, Stephen. 2007. *A Nation of Counterfeiters: Capitalists, Con Men, and the Making of the United States*. Cambridge, MA: Harvard University Press.

Swami, Viren, Tomas Chamorro-Premuzic, and Adrian Furnham. 2009. "Faking It: Personality and Individual Difference Predictors of Willingness to Buy Counterfeit Goods." *Journal of Socio-Economics* 38(5): 820–825.

Credit Cards

ALYA GUSEVA
Boston University, USA

Credit cards were invented and mass issued for the first time in the United States after World War II, although their emergence can be traced back to the early 1900s and the rise in consumer lending. This was when the first mass-produced consumer goods were made available to Americans, including automobiles, pianos, sewing machines, and, with the availability of electricity, electrical appliances. Sears was one of the pioneers of installment credit to buy household goods through its catalogue, but smaller stores were not far behind: they frequently kept an open book account for their most frequent and loyal customers. Early credit cards were issued by merchants such as department stores, gas stations, and hotel chains to their own customers, so the cards tied the consumer to a particular retailer or, at least, to a particular brand (Shell Oil cards could be used in Shell stations across the country, for example). Retailer-procured consumer credit was not the sole source of credit cards, however. In 1914 Western Union introduced a paper charge card to assist in money transfers. The card identified the customer and the account from which the charge was later deducted.

The term "credit card" was initially coined by Edward Bellamy, a writer and a socialist, in his 1881 futuristic novel *Looking Backward: 2000–1887*. In his vision of a utopian society, credit cards would entirely replace cash; they would not be a means of borrowing, however, but just a way workers were compensated based on the work credit they had earned. Diners Club cards, first offered in 1949, copied the name and became known as the first credit cards, though, technically, this was a misnomer. Diners were not credit but charge cards: the balance always had to be settled in full each month. The innovation of Diners Club was to move beyond the limitations of a one-card one-merchant model: the cards were accepted by many different restaurants, first in New York, and later in other major cities. They were marketed to business travelers, who appreciated the cards as a means not only of paying for meals, but also of conveniently keeping track of expenses through card purchase slips.

Credit cards inherited their present look – a rectangular piece of plastic with raised letters and numbers – from Charga-Plates, which appeared in 1928. Charga-Plates were made out of metal, like dog tags, with account information embossed in raised letters and numbers so that it could be transferred onto a paper slip with the use of carbon paper. But it was only in 1958 that American Express issued a plastic version of a Charga-Plate, similar to the cards we have today. Several American banks tried setting up their own card systems in the late 1940s and 1950s (most unsuccessfully, though). One of them was Bank of America. The first credit cards with the BankAmericard logo were issued in 1958, and in 1976 the brand was renamed Visa.

The credit card has been viewed as a protagonist of the global spread of American consumerism in the rest of the world. Ritzer (1995) called the global dissemination of credit cards an instance of "McDonaldization," a process, like that of the diffusion of American fast food, characterized by efficiency, calculability, predictability, control, and displacement of personal relationships by nonhuman technology. More recent comparative research on the global spread of credit cards underscores the limits of globalization and the power of local contexts in shaping such a seemingly standard product as a credit card (Rona-Tas and Guseva 2014). New markets for credit cards are often faced with a significant degree of resistance from both prospective cardholders and merchants. Credit card markets are called "two-sided markets," where each side, prospective cardholders or merchants, is waiting for the other side to join first. It makes little sense for an individual to carry a card if no or very few merchants accept payment by card. Similarly, with very few cards in circulation, merchants would not be interested in accepting them. When the numbers of cardholders and card accepting merchants reach a certain – tipping – point, the market starts growing effortlessly, the sheer number of cardholders attracting new merchants and vice versa. At the dawn of the American market, card issuing banks mailed unsolicited cards to unscreened individuals (who had not applied for them or even knew what the cards were) in order to saturate the market enough to attract merchants. While these practices were successful in jump-starting the US market, they were also very costly to the banks, which incurred losses as a result of rampant defaults and fraud. In an attempt to disseminate cards in postcommunist countries like Russia, Ukraine, and Hungary, local banks relied instead on outright coercion: they distributed cards in connection with transferring previously cash-based salaries and social benefits to direct deposit schemes, and targeted employees of large enterprises, government workers, doctors, teachers, students, those in the military, and retirees. In some countries banks also successfully lobbied states to make card acceptance mandatory in most or all merchant locations.

The recent emergence of Chinese UnionPay cards, first as the basis for the domestic payment system, and later as a global competitor to Visa and MasterCard, is an example of successful resistance to globalization. In just over 10 years (starting in 2002) China developed a brand that has already overtaken Visa and MasterCard in terms of the number of cards issued globally. Recently it has even surpassed MasterCard in terms of global transaction volume. The Chinese example is instructive because China initially viewed credit cards in quite different terms, not just as another consumer service best delivered by market actors, but as a key element of the national financial and economic system and as a tool of economic modernization. India is also on its way to developing the RuPay national payment system. Russia, too, has announced that it is creating a national payment system based on a domestic card brand. Such efforts by the BRIC countries (Brazil, Russia, India, and China) signify the end of the era of global dominance by US-based multinational credit card networks.

As in all consumer credit markets, credit card issuers are faced with the problem of information asymmetry in selecting borrowers. Modern screening practices – credit reporting and the use of numerical credit scores – help lenders estimate risk, reject bad applicants, and price credit cards for the rest of the application pool. But stratifying people according to the risk they pose for lenders, and making the cost of credit cards dependent on their perceived risk, amplifies inequality: when the poor can access only more expensive, higher-interest credit cards, they are more vulnerable to default. Manning (2000) observes the sharp rise in the use of credit cards as a means for the heavily indebted middle class and the working poor to pay for family emergencies and medical bills, and to compensate for unemployment. When credit cards offer to help the poor pay for necessities or emergencies which the shrinking welfare state no longer pays, deceptively low minimum payments coupled with high interest rates lock them into a vicious cycle of overspending, crushing indebtedness, and hopeless destitution. An average American has three or four credit cards (plus about four more retail and one charge card, such as American Express or Diners) with a total outstanding debt of US$4000. However, since around 45 percent of American households are "convenience users" of credit cards who pay their balance in full each month to avoid interest charges, the average outstanding debt among "revolver" households is much higher, at US$11,575 (Manning 2000).

Compared to the installment credit prevalent in the United States in the early 1900s and in the postwar period, which was tied to the purchase, and required borrowers to be employed and to pay regular monthly payments – a form of forced savings or "budgetism" (Calder 1999) – general purpose revolving credit cards encourage consumption that is free from the internalized discipline of continuous labor in order to meet the rigid schedule of repayments, and for that reason alone can easily lead to overspending. Empirical studies confirm that consumers spend more when they pay with a credit card compared to when they pay in cash. This tendency to encourage overspending places credit cards in an imagined moral hierarchy of American consumer credit above fringe lending like payday loans and pawn shops, but below installment credit and, particularly, below mortgages, the backbone of American home ownership, which, in turn, is at the core of the American dream.

SEE ALSO: Consumption in the United States; Debt; Finance/Financial Markets; Globalization and Consumption; McDonaldization; Money

REFERENCES

Calder, Lendol. 1999. *Financing the American Dream: A Cultural History of Consumer Credit*. Princeton, NJ: Princeton University Press.
Manning, Robert. 2000. *Credit Card Nation*. New York: Basic Books.
Ritzer, George. 1995. *Expressing America: A Critique of the Global Credit Card Society*. Thousand Oaks, CA: Sage.
Rona-Tas, Akos, and Alya Guseva. 2014. *Plastic Money: Constructing Markets for Credit Cards in Eight Postcommunist Countries*. Stanford, CA: Stanford University Press.

FURTHER READING

Evans, David, and Richard Schmalensee. 1999. *Paying with Plastic: The Digital Revolution in Buying and Borrowing*. Cambridge, MA: MIT Press.
Guseva, Alya. 2008. *Into the Red: The Birth of the Credit Card Market in Postcommunist Russia*. Stanford, CA: Stanford University Press.
Nocera, Joseph. 1994. *A Piece of the Action: How the Middle Class Joined the Money Class*. New York: Simon & Schuster.

Cultural Capital

ANDRZEJ KLIMCZUK
Warsaw School of Economics, Poland

The concept of cultural capital was first introduced by French sociologists Pierre Bourdieu and Jean-Claude Passeron in 1970 in their study on school education and differences in children's outcomes. Bourdieu and Passeron (1990/1970) found that middle-class parents equip their children with cultural capital, which consists of a variety of language, social, and cultural skills. Schools require the possession of these skills to achieve educational success, and are not able, through teaching, to pass these competencies on to working-class children. As a result, school grades, even though they seem to be objective, in fact reflect and contribute to economic inequality. Finally, working-class children can see that the educational success of their middle-class peers is legitimated by symbolic or economic inheritance rather than being the result of hard work.

Bourdieu further developed the concept of cultural capital as part of his theory of structure and agency in his later works. He shows that individuals can use many forms of capital, with which they are unequally equipped. The crucial forms are economic capital (money and tangible objects suitable to produce goods and services, infrastructure), social capital (social position and networks of more or less institutionalized relationships), cultural capital (lifestyle, acquired or consumed cultural objects, skills, customs, language, education, taste, social origin), and symbolic capital (prestige, honor, attention, fame, recognition; Bourdieu and Wacquant 1992). The most important of these is symbolic capital, where symbols are used to legitimize ownership of other forms of capital and symbolic violence against the lower social classes. Forms of capital can be partly converted so they can be better used in different fields and social contexts. A field can be any structure of social relations that includes individuals or groups competing for positions within that field (for example, education, work, art, consumption, law, science, family). Capitals are collected and transmitted as an inheritance by members of different social classes to the next generation and can be used to produce or reproduce inequality and consumption patterns.

Bourdieu (1986) describes three subtypes of cultural capital: embodied, objectified, and institutionalized. Embodied capital consists of resources that are consciously acquired by the personal investment of time and effort and is passively inherited by family socialization. This capital expresses itself through habitus, that is, individual character and way of thinking. The habitus is also determined by the internalization of norms and values inherited from one's family in accordance with patterns that have been established in a given social class. Objectified cultural capital includes physical objects owned by an individual. Cultural goods such as art and literature are instruments that may be converted into economic capital by buying and selling or to cultural capital by using and consuming them if their users have proper embodied skills. Institutionalized cultural capital consists of acquired and socially recognizable educational competencies, for example academic credentials or qualifications. Institutional recognition is important in the labor market as it allows for the comparison of job applicants.

In *Distinction* (1984) Bourdieu develops his social stratification theory on the basis of taste, which he regards as a part of cultural capital. He claims that aesthetic preferences are transmitted by generations so young people are directed toward behaviors and positions that are appropriate to their social class, and taught an aversion toward other behaviors. Tastes in food, culture, and presentation reflect trends in individual consumption and how they fit into classes of a given society. Each class has its own consumer interests and positions that meet these needs through newspapers, artists, and hairdressers, for example. Taste differentiation implies claims to authority and authenticity. For example, cultural elites, the dominant class (owners of capital, high-level managers, professors, artists), show their learned characteristics and properties as natural and innate. Their tastes are presented through symbolic violence in order to dominate the other social classes. These processes are manifested, for example, in luxury or the freedom of practicing and admiring art for art's sake. For all those outside this class, they are at best incomprehensible and at worst exclusive, for example as reflected in abstract painting, music without rhythm or melody, or novels with no traditional form and structure. Below this "high" culture is the "average" individual's taste for musicals, light opera, and amateur photography. At the bottom of the hierarchy is popular taste, or taste of necessity, which reflects the impossibility of sharing or imitating the supposed selfless taste of the dominant classes. Popular taste is oriented toward pleasure, usability, and functionality; it gravitates toward pleasant images of attractive people, rock and country music, undemanding stories, photographs of pleasurable moments of everyday life. For example, a choice of olive oil over vegetable oil indicates an orientation to a more "knowing" position, a healthy consumer as opposed to one who seeks instant gratification. This is the difference between a luxury and a necessity (Paterson 2006). It also shows consumer awareness of brands and of their role in the construction of lifestyle and cultural identity.

Cultural capital can be confused with concepts of human and creative capitals, of pecuniary emulation, and of a variant definition of cultural capital employed in economics and urban studies. The idea of human capital was developed by James Coleman (1988) in his studies on educational institutions. Human capital is composed of knowledge, skills, and competencies that are an effect of the use of social capital. For example, parents can use their social contacts to choose a school for their children that will increase their chance of educational success. Human capital is different from cultural capital in that it represents the cultural characteristics of individuals and the possibility of the conscious acquisition of identity. Meanwhile cultural capital primarily describes the possession of class culture and identity from primary groups such as family, friends, and neighbors.

Richard Florida (2002) introduced creative capital theory to highlight that it is not only people, education, and social contacts that are important to the development of geographic regions. He argues that economic growth occurs in places that are preferred by creative people, places that are innovative, diverse, and tolerant. Creative capital theory thus differs from human capital theory by identifying a type of human capital, creative people, as being key to economic growth; and by identifying factors that shape their location decisions. Creative capital is characterized by thin social capital that is not blocking the creative activity of individuals and is open to immigrants and diversity, whereas cultural capital can be understood as relating to thick social capital, exclusion, and limitation by traditions. Moreover creative capital can be interpreted as an effect of art education on those who produce and distribute cultural goods, while cultural capital is the effect of cultural education that encourages aspirational lifestyles and the tendency to consume. Bourdieu's concept of cultural capital should be distinguished from Thorstein Veblen's (2009/1899) idea of "pecuniary emulation" which describes the competition for prestigious and expensive signs of distinction. For Bourdieu it is status groups, not individuals, that aim to monopolize cultural capital. He also highlighted that cultural capital must be legitimate and not only fashionable. Moreover, for Bourdieu, prestigious cultural goods not only lose their value with time and trickle down the class hierarchy but are reproduced with cultural hierarchies over long periods of time. Bourdieu's concept should be also distinguished from the cultural capital interpretations of economists and urbanists, who sometimes use it to describe collections of aesthetic or moral knowledge, cultural heritage, diversity, and sustainability, or as the economic benefits of arts spending in the cultural and creative industries (Throsby 2001).

The concept of cultural capital was further developed by other scholars. In her studies on fandom Sarah Thornton (1995) coined the term "subcultural capital" to describe a subtype of capital that is not common across an entire culture but is specific to a subculture or fan culture. Matt Hills (2002) describes media and sports "fan cultural capital" as dominated by male and middle-class groups. Roberta Sassatelli (2007) describes "consumer capital" as a relatively autonomous form of capital. This capital is based on practices of consumption that create a structure for the standardization of taste. Sassatelli argues that consumer capital can be the result of consumer experiences from the past that are related to the consumer's class and formal education, including influences from market (global brands and mass media) and nonmarket (social movements) institutions. Consumer capital also includes consumer practices as indicators of the tastes and opinions of different experts (for example, fashion journalists, architects, environmentalists) who try to influence consumer choices.

SEE ALSO: Bourdieu, Pierre; Class; Consumer Socialization; Education and Consumption

REFERENCES

Bourdieu, Pierre. 1984. *Distinction: A Social Critique of the Judgement of Taste*. London: Routledge.

Bourdieu, Pierre. 1986. "The Forms of Capital." In *Handbook of Theory and Research for the Sociology of Education*, edited by John G. Richardson, 241–258. New York: Greenwood.

Bourdieu, Pierre, and Jean-Claude Passeron. 1990/1970. *Reproduction in Education, Society and Culture.* London: Sage.
Bourdieu, Pierre, and Loïc Wacquant. 1992. *An Invitation to Reflexive Sociology.* Chicago, IL: University of Chicago Press.
Coleman, James S. 1988. "Social Capital in the Creation of Human Capital." *American Journal of Sociology* 94: S95–S120.
Florida, Richard L. 2002. *The Rise of the Creative Class: And How It's Transforming Work, Leisure, Community and Everyday Life.* New York: Basic Books.
Hills, Matt. 2002. *Fan Cultures.* London: Routledge.
Paterson, Mark. 2006. *Consumption and Everyday Life.* London: Routledge.
Sassatelli, Roberta. 2007. *Consumer Culture: History, Theory and Politics.* Los Angeles, CA: Sage.
Thornton, Sarah. 1995. *Club Cultures: Music, Media and Subcultural Capital.* Oxford: Polity.
Throsby, David. 2001. *Economics and Culture.* Cambridge, UK: Cambridge University Press.
Veblen, Thorstein. 2009/1899. *The Theory of the Leisure Class: An Economic Study of Institutions.* Oxford: Oxford University Press.

Cultural Intermediaries

JENNIFER SMITH MAGUIRE
University of Leicester, UK

Cultural intermediaries perform the work of mediating how goods are perceived by others (end consumers, and other market actors including other cultural intermediaries). Their work – which is often symbolic and immaterial – involves framing particular material products, services, and behaviors as "good" or socially esteemed; thus, cultural intermediaries rely on claims of professional expertise in matters of taste and value relative to specific cultural fields. Research on cultural intermediaries has highlighted such issues as the blurring of work and leisure, the conservatism of "creative" work, the significance of cultural capital and personal disposition for professional credibility, and the material practices involved in the promotion of consumption. The concept is especially useful for foregrounding the agency and everyday practices of market actors, which are often overshadowed by the agency of consumers, and the power of macrostructures and institutions in the study of the production of consumer culture.

The starting point for this area is usually Pierre Bourdieu's *Distinction: A Social Critique of the Judgment of Taste* (1984), in which cultural intermediaries are identified as exemplars of the new petite bourgeoisie in 1970s France. Cultural intermediaries act as needs merchants and taste makers, mediating between the fields of production and consumption by orchestrating a match between goods produced and consumer needs and desires. They do so by drawing on established ideas of good taste and the forms of media at their disposal, thereby popularizing "high" culture and expanding middle-brow culture. More broadly, cultural intermediaries and other members of the petite bourgeoisie embody and promote a lifestyle that valorizes fun and pleasure: a role that Bourdieu likens to a "transmission belt" (1984, 365) which converts others to a new ethos that is fit for the contemporary consumer economy. Class position is significant in this account: with high cultural capital but a more precarious social position than the established middle class, cultural intermediaries have both knowledge of legitimate culture and the motivation to legitimate – and master – new forms of culture as a basis for claiming social distinction. Beyond class position, Bourdieu also locates cultural intermediaries in what he regards as new forms of work: typically, media-related occupations.

A Bourdieusian approach has been critiqued for viewing cultural intermediaries as altogether new and homogeneous, and for speculative claims about their role in reshaping consumer subjectivities. In contrast, more recent research has been concerned with the long-term development and contemporary variations of cultural intermediary work. Informed by actor network theory, new economic sociology, cultural economy, and Michel Foucault's theorization of governmentality, this second wave of research focuses on the material practices involved in processes of value formation and the "qualification" of goods (Callon, Méadel, and Rabeharisoa 2002). Here, the impact of cultural intermediaries is conceived in terms not of a transmission belt, but of the governmental work of mobilizing the attachments of consumers and other market actors to particular goods.

Methodologically, the orientation of such research is ethnographic and/or historical, with interviews, field observations, and archival work used to explore the "devices and dispositions" (du Gay 2004) that cultural intermediaries employ. Empirical foci include cultural intermediaries' particular day-to-day practices, types of knowledge and attitudes, and the occupational conventions and tools they use to identify and contextualize goods as worthy and desirable for an intended market or audience. An occupational focus remains a common mode of research design: case studies include such groups as advertising and branding practitioners, social marketers, fashion and television programming buyers, personal trainers, and retailers of clothing, books, and furniture. However, a small but growing body of work explicitly investigates the multiplicity of "regimes of mediation" (Cronin 2004), with attention given to the interconnections and variations between and within different cultural intermediaries in various commodity chains, urban spaces, and cultural fields.

As this field of research continues to develop, there is a need for greater conceptual clarity and empirical investigation on at least three fronts with regard to the shared features and points of differentiation that characterize cultural intermediaries. First, cultural intermediaries are defined by their work in framing goods for others, but differ in the devices they employ and the constraints they must negotiate in shaping tastes and adding symbolic value. Of particular note is the increasing attention to the role of nonhuman actors in these processes, with regard to how cultural intermediaries are enabled and constrained by the goods and devices with which they work. Second, cultural intermediaries are distinguished by their claims to expertise, but differ in their degrees of professionalization, autonomy, and influence. More research is needed on the significance of affect, disposition, and habitus in a cultural intermediary's performance of expertise and ability to serve as a surrogate for and reader of an intended market. Third, cultural intermediaries are implicated in the construction of legitimacy as a way to stratify culture and mobilize the actions of others, but differ with regard to the relative success and durability of their impact. Further consideration of the category of the legitimate is required.

As research on cultural omnivores makes clear, the category of good taste is not synonymous with a traditional bourgeois canon; despite evidence of changing patterns of taste, there has been scant investigation of the mechanisms by which those changes have taken place. Along these lines, future research could unpack and detail the impact of cultural intermediaries' devices and consuming passions and preferences on the codification, circulation, and potential transformation of the criteria by which legitimacy is articulated in today's marketplace.

SEE ALSO: Bourdieu, Pierre; Cultural Omnivores; Governmentality and Consumer Culture; Symbolic Value

REFERENCES

Bourdieu, Pierre. 1984. *Distinction: A Social Critique of the Judgment of Taste*. Cambridge, MA: Harvard University Press.

Callon, Michel, Cécile Méadel, and Vololona Rabeharisoa. 2002. "The Economy of Qualities." *Economy and Society* 31(2): 194–217.

Cronin, Anne. 2004. "Regimes of Mediation: Advertising Practitioners as Cultural Intermediaries?" *Consumption, Markets and Culture* 7(4): 349–369.

du Gay, Paul. 2004. "Devices and Dispositions: Promoting Consumption." *Consumption, Markets and Culture* 7(2): 99–105.

FURTHER READING

Nixon, Sean, and Paul du Gay. 2002. "Who Needs Cultural Intermediaries?" *Cultural Studies* 16(4): 495–500.

Smith Maguire, Jennifer, and Julian Matthews. 2012. "Are We All Cultural Intermediaries Now?" *European Journal of Cultural Studies* 15(5): 551–562.

Smith Maguire, Jennifer, and Julian Matthews, eds. 2014. *The Cultural Intermediaries Reader*. London: Sage.

Cultural Omnivores

JENNIFER SMITH MAGUIRE
University of Leicester, UK

Cultural omnivores are people whose consumption tastes range widely across both elite and popular genres; they differ from people with "univorous" tastes, which are narrowly restricted to either highbrow, middlebrow, or lowbrow activities and preferences. While omnivorousness is not limited to elite groups, high-status individuals are more likely to be omnivores, and have therefore been of especial interest to researchers. Historically, popular or "low" cultural forms were shunned by elite groups; today, however, research finds that individuals with exclusively highbrow tastes ("snobs") are a rarity. In contrasting the figure of the omnivore with the snob, research on cultural omnivores suggests how patterns of elite taste have changed in contemporary consumer cultures, and offers insights into the relationship between class, taste, and cultural capital.

The study of cultural omnivores builds on the theoretical and empirical work of Pierre Bourdieu and others; the specific term comes from Richard Peterson (Peterson and Simkus 1992; Peterson 2005). Examining survey data on arts participation in the United States, Peterson and colleagues found that high-status respondents were more likely than others to include highbrow genres (such as opera) in their musical tastes, and also more likely to include non-highbrow genres, such as country music. On the basis of the prevalence of omnivorous tastes within the high-status respondents, Peterson's work suggested that elite taste had been redefined as an ability to appreciate the aesthetic dimensions of a wide range of cultural forms, and not only those of highbrow culture.

Subsequent studies in North America, Europe, and Australia have explored how omnivorous tastes (for example, in music, literature, and art) are patterned by various factors. The methodological reliance on survey data for much of this research tends to measure omnivorousness in terms of volume (liking a greater number of genres than other individuals) and composition (liking forms that cross cultural boundaries). The research broadly confirms that individuals with higher levels of education and income, and in higher-status social positions, are more likely to have a greater diversity and volume of tastes than others. Omnivorous tastes are also more common in urban and younger consumers.

Survey research, however, is poorly equipped to capture the manner in which people practice their preferences, which is central to Bourdieu's conceptualization of taste (1984) as expressed through *how* one consumes, not simply *what* one consumes. Here, much has been gained from the studies of omnivorousness that employ interpretive methods (typically, interviews or textual analysis), which broadly agree that what distinguishes omnivores is a "particular discriminating orientation towards taste" (Warde, Wright, and Gayo-Cal 2008, 149). Interpretive research, furthermore, contributes insight into the fluidity of boundaries around legitimate culture, and the criteria on which legitimacy is constructed, including notions of the new and the authentic; the normative value (and potential prestige) of displaying diverse tastes; and the social significance of individuals' dislikes – not just likes – for constructing class identities via omnivorous tastes. Through such research, a more nuanced description of omnivorousness continues to develop. A simplistic dichotomy of high-status omnivores versus low-status univores has been replaced by a better understanding of how and in what ways omnivorous tastes are exhibited across different groups.

While research has largely focused on omnivores themselves, further attention to the sociohistorical factors underlying the rise (and future decline) of omnivorousness as a dominant mode of "good taste" in Western consumer cultures is still required. These factors include the expansion of higher education, the commercialization of highbrow cultural forms, and the aestheticization of everyday life, which have increased the accessibility of elite culture; and globalization, liberalism, and identity politics, which have increased the accessibility and legitimacy of diverse cultural forms and practices. In this context, a discerning disposition coupled with cultural tolerance, which regards any genre as potentially worthy of aesthetic assessment, becomes an especially valuable form of cultural capital.

As yet underexamined is the question of how these factors – and others – shape changing patterns of taste in emerging and maturing consumer cultures in non-Western nations such as India and China. Also underexamined are the mechanisms involved in constructing, legitimating, and circulating new definitions and repertoires of good taste, and new, socially esteemed mentalities about taste and consumption. These mechanisms include various forms of lifestyle media, especially those explicitly aimed at high-status consumers, and cultural intermediaries, whose professional work as taste makers relies on their own discerning mentalities.

Cultural omnivorousness has been linked to the democratization of culture, in that it is associated with a greater openness and acceptance of diversity, echoing discussions of cosmopolitanism. Nevertheless, culture and taste remain potent sites and tools of social stratification, as this area of research makes clear. If knowledge of and participation in highbrow culture are no longer exclusive markers of distinction, then omnivorousness – the connoisseurship of seemingly anything – offers a means of demonstrating distinction without appearing to be antidemocratic, of being elite but not (appearing to be) elitist.

SEE ALSO: Authenticity; Bourdieu, Pierre; Cultural Capital; Cultural Intermediaries; Leisure and Consumption

REFERENCES

Bourdieu, Pierre. 1984. *Distinction: A Social Critique of the Judgment of Taste*. Cambridge, MA: Harvard University Press.

Peterson, Richard A. 2005. "Problems in Comparative Research: The Example of Omnivorousness." *Poetics* 33: 257–282. doi:10.1016/j.poetic.2005.10.002.

Peterson, Richard A., and Albert Simkus. 1992. "How Musical Tastes Mark Occupational Status Groups." In *Cultivating Differences: Symbolic Boundaries and the Making of Inequality*, edited by Michèl Lamont and Marcel Fournier, 152–186. Chicago, IL: University of Chicago Press.

Warde, Alan, David Wright, and Modesto Gayo-Cal. 2008. "The Omnivorous Orientation in the UK." *Poetics* 36(2–3): 148–165. doi:10.1016/j.poetic.2008.02.004.

Cultural Studies

TOBY MILLER
Cardiff University, UK; Murdoch University, Australia

Since the 1970s, cultural studies has been both an irritant and a master trope in the humanities and qualitative social sciences, blending and blurring textual analysis with social and cultural theory and empirical ethnography, and focusing on the margins of power rather than reproducing established lines of force and authority. For example, rather than researching canonical works of art, governmental leadership, or quantitative social data, cultural studies devotes time to subcultures, popular media, music, clothing, environmental representations, and sport. It does so with strong commitments to class, gender, racial, sexual, and cosmopolitan equality and justice, bringing together and incarnating various tendencies that productively splinter the human sciences: Marxism, feminism, queer theory, and postcolonialism.

In addition to this conceptual and political trajectory, cultural studies has an interesting spatial one as well. Anglophone readers may associate it with Britain and the United States, but cultural studies has equally vibrant and generative traditions that emanate from Latin America, Asia, and Africa. Some of these histories are interlocking, but others are quite autonomous, in keeping with the history of political, economic, linguistic, and educational colonialism. It is no surprise that several leading practitioners have moved between different parts of the world (for instance, Néstor García Canclini, Argentina–Mexico; George Yúdice, US–Costa Rica; Meaghan Morris, Australia–Hong Kong; Tony Bennett, UK–Australia; Stuart Hall, Jamaica–UK; John Nguyet Erni, Hong Kong–US; Andrew Ross, UK–US; Paula Chakravartty, Canada–US; Paul Smith, UK–US; and Yuezhi Zhao, China–Canada).

Cultural studies places value on how culture is used and transformed by ordinary and marginal social groups. It regards such people not simply as consumers or as victims of corporate and governmental power, but as potential and actual producers of new social values and cultural languages that have the potential to challenge elites. How did this development come to pass?

Cultural studies emerged from changes in the etymology of culture and its governmental and commercial significance. The principal shift actually predates cultural studies by centuries, but definitively established the conditions for its possibility. The concept of culture emerged from the Latin word *colare*, which implied tending and developing agriculture as part of subsistence. With the appearance of capitalism's division of labor, culture came both to *embody* instrumentalism and to *abjure* it, via the industrialization of farming on the one hand, and the cultivation of taste on the other. In keeping with this distinction, culture has usually been understood in two registers, via the social sciences and via the humanities – truth versus beauty. What was a heuristic division in the sixteenth century became substantive over time. Eighteenth-century German, French, and Spanish dictionaries bear witness to a metaphorical shift into spiritual cultivation. As the spread of literacy and printing saw customs and laws passed on, governed, and adjudicated through the written word, cultural texts supplemented and supplanted physical force as guarantors of authority. With the industrial revolution, populations became urban dwellers; food was imported, cultures developed textual forms that could be exchanged, and consumer society emerged through horse racing, opera, art exhibits, masquerades, and balls.

The impact of this shift was indexed in cultural labor: *poligrafi* in fifteenth-century Venice and hacks in eighteenth-century London wrote popular and influential conduct books. These works of instruction on everyday life marked the textualization of custom and the emergence of new occupational identities. Anxieties about cultural invasion also date from this period, via Islamic debates over Western domination.

Culture became a marker of differences and similarities in taste and status, explored interpretively and methodically. In the humanities, culture is judged by criteria of quality and meaning, as practiced critically and historically. In the social sciences, the focus is on culture's sociopolitical norms, as explored psychologically or statistically. But culture is also a crucial economic category. In the past, it provided an index of life in agricultural and manufacturing societies. Now it is at the very center of profit and loss, through television, the internet, sex, fashion, music, and sport.

We can contrast the view of hegemonic powerbrokers, who see culture as a route to economic efficiency, with that of cultural studies, which questions power and subjectivity rather than using them to extract surplus value from ordinary people or to educate them into obedience. Cultural studies seeks to audit the denial, assimilation, and invention that occur each time words such as "nation," "community," or "society" are brought into discourse, moving away from essentialist definitions of national identity and toward plural accounts of person and polity.

Historically, the humanities have articulated population differences through *symbolic* means (for example, which class has the cultural capital to appreciate high culture, and which does not). Conversely, the social sciences have articulated population differences through *social* means (for example, which people are affected by TV messages, and which are not). Cultural studies problematizes both projects. It questions the idea of knowledge that is purportedly produced for its own sake but frequently serves dominant socioeconomic elite interests, whether through policy advice or professional training.

Cultural studies thus mounts a comprehensive challenge to academic business as usual. In addition, its investment in the popular makes waves in the extramural world, because weighing in on the social and intellectual significance of telenovelas or football games sidesteps universities' historical task of criticizing entertainment in the name of elevating audiences and readers.

Cultural studies is a tendency across disciplines, rather than a discipline itself. This is evident in practitioners' expressed desires to simultaneously refuse definition, insist on differentiation, and sustain conventional departmental credentials (as well as pyrotechnic, polymath-like capacities for reasoning and research). Cultural studies' continuities come from shared concerns and methods: the concern is the reproduction of culture through structural determinations on subjects versus their own agency, and the method is historical materialism.

Cultural studies is programmatically animated by subjectivity and power – how human subjects are formed and how they experience cultural and social space. It takes its agenda and mode of analysis from economics, politics, media and communication studies, sociology, literature, education, the law, science and technology studies, anthropology, and history, with a particular focus on gender, race, class, and sexuality in everyday life, commingling textual and social theory under the sign of a commitment to progressive social change.

While categorical devices from the social sciences are deployed in cultural studies as grids of investigation, their status as machines that can obliterate or obscure difference and similarity is brought into question. At its best, cultural studies produces an intellectual polyphony that draws out contradictions and dissonances through grounded analysis, gender theory, ethnography, history, postcolonial theory, material objects, and policy, animated by a desire to reveal and transform those who control the means of communication and culture, and undertaken with a constant vigilance over one's own *raison d'être* and modus operandi.

Attempts to list what counts as cultural studies are fraught, especially when they engage in an absolute binarization (cultural studies frequently disavows binary oppositions for failing to acknowledge the logocentric interdependence of supposed opposites, such as that whiteness depends for its sense of self on blackness, for example). But binaries are useful things to draw on, criticize, and revise, like other forms of scholarly inclusion and exclusion.

On one side of academia lies cultural studies, boasting a commitment to articulate knowledge with social change. This tendency represents the will to link the professoriat with social movements as primary loci of power, authorization, and responsibility. On the other side more conventional disciplines reside, boasting a commitment to articulate knowledge with social reproduction. This second tendency represents a will to link the professoriat with universities and professions as a primary locus of power, authorization, and responsibility. Where cultural studies is about a transformation of the social order, conventional research and teaching are dedicated to its replication. One is to do with academic activism, the other with academic parthenogenesis. One likes to be naughty and to engage in outbursts, the other prefers to be staid and to make pronouncements.

The political significance of popular cultural practices is exemplified in subcultures. Subcultures are spaces under culture, simultaneously opposed to, derivative of, and informing official, dominant, governmental, commercial, bureaucratically organized forms of life – a shift away from culture as a tool of domination and toward culture as a tool of empowerment. This move wants to find out how the socially disadvantaged use culture to contest their subservient position. Historical and contemporary studies conducted through the 1960s and 1970s on slaves, crowds, pirates, bandits, and the working class emphasized day-to-day noncompliance with authority.

For example, UK research into teddy boys, mods, bikers, skinheads, punks, school students, teen girls, and Rastas identified truants, dropouts, and magazine readers – people who deviated from the norms of school and the transition to work by entering subcultures – as its magical agents of history. Such studies examined the structural underpinnings to collective style, investigating how their bricolage subverted the achievement-oriented, materialistic, educationally driven values and appearance of the middle class. The working assumption was that subordinate groups adopt and adapt signs and objects of the dominant culture, reorganizing them to manufacture new meanings. Consumption was the epicenter of such subcultures; paradoxically, it also reversed members' status as consumers. They become producers of new fashions, inscribing alienation, difference, and powerlessness on their bodies. For instance, the decline of the British economy and state across the 1970s was supposedly exemplified and contested in punk's use of rubbish as an adornment: bag liners, lavatory appliances, and ripped and torn clothing.

There is a paradox and possibly a contradiction in cultural studies' engagement with such anticorporate tropes, because commodified fashion and convention learned to respond almost gratefully to subcultures: capitalism appropriated the appropriator. Even as the media and politicians announced that punks were folk devils and set in train various moral panics about their effect on society, the fashion and music industries were sending out spies to watch and listen to them as part of a restless search for new trends to market. Whenever the politics of spectacle is used effectively by social movements, advertising agencies watch on and parrot what they see using much more effective methods.

The need for awareness of this double-edged investment in commodities, as objects of resistance whose very appropriation can then be recommodified, makes socioeconomic analysis via critical political economy theoretically a good ally of representational analysis via cultural studies. But a certain tendency on both sides has maintained that the two approaches are mutually exclusive: one is concerned with structures of the economy, the other with structures of meaning. This need not be the case. Historically, the best critical political economy and the best cultural studies have worked through the imbrication of power and subjectivity at all points on the cultural continuum.

Ideally, blending the two approaches might heal the division between fact and interpretation and between the social sciences and the humanities, under the sign of a principled approach to cultural democracy. There are signs of such a merger. At a moment when the global North uses culture as a selling point for deindustrialized societies, and the global South does so for never industrialized ones, cultural studies is coming to focus on a nimble hybrid approach governed not by the humanities or the social sciences, but by an agenda of *cui bono*? Who benefits and loses from governmental and corporate maneuvers, who complains about the fact, and how can we learn from them?

This commitment to social and cultural justice, as well as academic theorization and research, has proven magnetic to many subordinate groups entering academia for the first time since the mid-1960s. Hence cultural studies' popularity not only at the conventional scholarly metropoles in the United States and the United Kingdom, but in Colombia, Brazil, Turkey, India, and other important sites that are all too accustomed to being theorized and analyzed and all too *un*familiar with being regarded as the *sources* of ideas, not merely places for their application. At the same time, it has also thrived in the context of a more reformist, even reactionary formation, which rejects the field's past as a form of insurrectionary semiotic reading and instead favors hitching itself to the new surge in cultural industries represented by public policies and investment patterns. For people operating within cultural studies' less radical wing, this has involved consultancies on behalf of the media, museums, copyright, pornography, schooling, and cultural precincts. Their methods – archival research, questionnaires, and Foucauldian theory – emphasize the foundational nature of government in the creation of the liberal individual (understood as per not US politics but US education, i.e., a person open to new ideas delivered in a rational form and reasoned manner). There has been a considerable amount of traffic between this new perspective and instrumental policy people and scholars, who argue for an efflorescence of creativity, cultural difference, import substitution, and national and regional pride and influence, thanks to new technologies and innovative firms – with capitalism an ally, not a foe.

This has also produced a new model of consumer freedom that derives from subcultural politics, even though they share little in terms of commitments to social justice. The working assumption is that the culture industries are being overrun by individual creativity. It is a Marxist/Godardian fantasy. People fish, film, fornicate, and finance from morning to midnight. Media technologies obliterate geography, sovereignty, and hierarchy in an alchemy of truth and beauty. A deregulated, individuated world makes consumers into producers, frees the disabled from confinement, encourages new subjectivities, rewards intellect and competitiveness, links people across cultures, and allows billions of flowers to bloom in a postpolitical cornucopia. Consumption is privileged, production is discounted, and labor is forgotten.

For some, this turn appears like a reactionary form of incorporation. New commercial trends are sometimes embraced by cultural studies in a way that no longer appears critical, so embedded is this fulsome reception within corporate logics or popular rhetoric. Perhaps cultural studies has been tamed, co-opted, and commodified. For other critics, however, this represents the maturation of the field and its increased relevance to the everyday hopes and needs of an instrumental student body and a democratically responsive polity.

SEE ALSO: Cultural Capital; Culture Industries

FURTHER READING

Abbas, Abbas, and John Nguyet Erni, eds. 2005. *International Cultural Studies: An Anthology*. Oxford: Blackwell.

Aguilar, Miguel Ángel, Eduardo Nivón, María Ana Portal, and Rosalía Winocur, eds. 2009. *Pensar lo contemporáneo: de la cultura situada a la convergencia tecnológica* [Thinking the Contemporary: From Local Culture to Technological Convergence]. Barcelona: Anthropos; Mexico City: Universidad Autónoma Metropolitana.

Banks, Mark, Rosalind Gill, and Stephanie Taylor, eds. 2013. *Theorising Cultural Work: Labour, Continuity and Change in the Cultural and Creative Industries*. London: Routledge.

Hammer, Rhonda, and Douglas Kellner, eds. 2009. *Media/Cultural Studies: Critical Approaches*. New York: Lang.

Lewis, Tania, and Emily Potter, eds. 2011. *Ethical Consumption: A Critical Introduction*. London: Routledge.

Miller, Toby, ed. 2006. *A Companion to Cultural Studies*. Oxford: Blackwell.

Culture-Ideology of Consumerism

LESLIE SKLAIR
London School of Economics and Political Science, UK

While the idea of consumerism as an ideology has been familiar in the social sciences for several decades, the concept of the culture-ideology of consumerism as a key component in a theory of capitalist globalization is of relatively recent origin. It was initially proposed by Sklair in 1991 (see Sklair 2002) and refers to the transformation of excessively above-subsistence consumption from a sectional practice of the rich throughout human history to a globalizing phenomenon directed at the mass of the population in the era of capitalist globalization. Its emergence can be explained in terms of two historically unprecedented factors. First, capitalism entered a qualitatively new globalizing phase in the 1950s, facilitated by the electronic revolution. Substantial increases were made possible in the productivity of factories and systems of extraction and processing of raw materials, accompanied by vastly greater efficiencies in product design, marketing, financing, and the distribution of goods and services. These processes, driven by new types of globally integrated transnational corporations and organized politically by an embryonic transnational capitalist class, first took root in the United States but soon spread around the world. Second, new mass media and communications technologies made it very easy for new consumerist lifestyles to become the dominant motif for these media, which became in time extraordinarily efficient vehicles for disseminating the culture-ideology of consumerism globally.

By the second half of the twentieth century, for the first time in human history, an increasingly globalizing capitalism was sufficiently productive to provide an above-subsistence package of material possessions and services to almost everyone in the First World and to privileged groups elsewhere. Capitalism, particularly in its neoliberal phase from the 1980s, promised that eventually everyone in the world would get rich as long as they followed the precepts of the so-called free market. People were persuaded that the culture-ideology of consumerism was what a happy and satisfying life was all about. In a powerful empirical study of the increasing hours and more intensive nature of work in the United States since the 1950s, Schor (1991) demonstrated how capitalist consumerism led North Americans and other groups elsewhere into a Faustian bargain whereby those who can find relatively well-paying employment work longer and longer hours so that they can afford to buy more and more consumer goods and services, or at least qualify for credit to do so. Without two key inventions of the twentieth century – the shopping mall and the credit card – the culture-ideology of consumerism would not have been possible and, as the many lists of shopping malls available on the internet demonstrate, these are now truly global phenomena.

Ideas of Americanization and cultural and/or media imperialism are important elements in any discussion of the culture-ideology of consumerism. Through Hollywood, and the globalization of the movies, via Madison Avenue, from where "captains of consciousness" created the modern advertising and marketing industry (see Ewen 1976), to the more geographically diffuse but ideologically monolithic television networks and the mainstream of the World Wide Web, the consumerist elites of the corporate world have assumed leadership of the culture-ideology of consumerism in the interests of the private profits that capitalist globalization brings. The universal availability of the mass media has been rapidly achieved through relatively cheap hardware, first radios, then TVs, and now computers and mobile phones with online facilities that totally penetrate the developed world, almost totally penetrate cities elsewhere, and are beginning to penetrate deeply into the countryside even in the poorest places. Thus, the potential of global exposure to global communication, the dream of every merchant in history, has arrived. The process by which people learn what to want, which used to occur mainly in the home and the school, is increasingly taking place through what the theorists of the Frankfurt School had so acutely termed the "culture industry."

The net effect of the culture-ideology of consumerism appears to be the creation of twin crises of capitalist globalization – namely class polarization and ecological unsustainability – that threaten to destabilize the global capitalist system as a whole. These crises feed off each other and they are both unintended and extremely unwelcome consequences of the culture-ideology of consumerism as it has colonized the world under conditions of capitalist globalization. The implications of an unrestrained culture-ideology of consumerism for the future of the planet are plain for all to see, and it appears increasingly unlikely that this dilemma can be resolved while the conditions of capitalist globalization prevail.

SEE ALSO: Advertising; Culture Industries; Globalization and Consumption; Glocalization/Grobalization; Mass Marketing

REFERENCES

Ewen, Stuart. 1976. *Captains of Consciousness: Advertising and the Social Roots of Consumer Culture*. New York: McGraw-Hill.

Schor, Juliet. 1991. *The Overworked American: The Unexpected Decline of Leisure*. New York: Basic Books.

Sklair, Leslie. 2002. *Globalization: Capitalism and Its Alternatives*. Oxford: Oxford University Press.

Culture Industries

BERYL LANGER
La Trobe University, Australia

When it was coined by Max Horkheimer and Theodor Adorno in the 1940s, the term "culture industry" was inherently critical. "Culture" evoked a sphere of artistic "creation" viewed as an end in itself, "industry" a sphere of factory production subject to the means–ends logic of economic rationality. The industrial production of "culture" was thus viewed as a travesty. That this is no longer the case is evidenced by routine use of the term "culture industries" in the social sciences, in cultural studies, and in cultural policy and labor market documents, although the term still generates debate at the margins.

The meaning of "culture" that gave the idea of a culture industry its critical edge came into English usage between the last decades of the eighteenth century and the middle of the nineteenth. As Raymond Williams argues in *Culture and Society* (1976/1957), the word "culture" took on new meaning in response to the increasingly rationalized, commodified, and environmentally polluted life world brought into being by the industrial revolution, and the social and political changes consequent to democracy. Culture (fine art, poetry, music) was conceptualized as a transcendent sphere of inspired creation which offered both a refuge from industrial society and a critical space from which it could be judged. The separation of culture and commerce drew on religious tradition (money as the root of all evil) and on the romantic idea of the creative artist as a free spirit, which gave rise to the opposition between bohemia and business.

The mass production of culture for consumption by the burgeoning proletariat saw the emergence of an opposition between "mass culture" and "popular" or "folk" culture, premised on notions of authenticity and moral value. Culture produced for the purposes of generating profit – a legitimate activity in the economic sphere – was positioned as inferior to culture embedded in lived experience and produced by ordinary people themselves. Pierre Bourdieu's (1993/1983) designation of the field of cultural production as "the economic world reversed" captures the way in which value was accorded to culture produced by "inspired genius" or embedded in popular tradition rather than produced for commercial gain.

These historically constituted distinctions between the categories of "culture," "popular culture," and "mass culture" gave rise to hierarchical understandings of cultural value, which framed taken-for-granted assumptions about which kinds of activities were worthwhile and which institutions were worthy of public or philanthropic funding. These assumptions also formed the background of later Anglo-American interpretations of the Frankfurt School critique as an "elitist" defense of "high culture" mounted through an attack on the cultural preferences of "ordinary people" – interpretations that still have currency, even while it is clear from remarks on gallery visiting and classical music in "The Culture Industry" essay that Horkheimer and Adorno (2002/1947) were no less critical of high culture and its audiences. In contrast to mass culture's *conservative* critics, the Horkheimer–Adorno argument was not that democratization lowered cultural standards, but that the industrially standardized, controlled, and commodified production of culture for "the masses" was profoundly undemocratic. Their fundamental objection to the "culture industry" was that it extended capitalist domination and exploitation beyond work to leisure time and individual consciousness.

Where Horkheimer and Adorno considered the distinction between high and mass culture irrelevant, given the subjection of all culture to the commodity form, longstanding assumptions about which kinds of cultural activities were worthwhile and which institutions were worthy of public or philanthropic funding had been framed in terms of this hierarchical distinction. The building of publicly funded art museums, concert halls, and public libraries in the nineteenth century was premised on the belief that culture – "great" art, music, and literature – enriched people's lives and put them in touch with "higher" values. The idea that these cultural institutions were a public good that should be subsidized by the state, whereas the popular entertainments consumed by "ordinary" people were merely private pleasures for which they as consumers should pay, persisted unchallenged until the 1980s, when a combination of technical, structural, and ideological factors destabilized the hierarchy.

Just as the definition of culture as a sphere of higher value was produced by the historical intersection of technological, economic, and social changes, so too was the shift in meaning that made *culture industries* a neutral rather than a critical term. In the final decades of the twentieth century, the opposition between culture and society lost its relevance for all but a critical minority, as the transition to consumer capitalism and new information technologies made the production and consumption of culture central to the economy. The concurrent shift from Keynesian to neoliberal economics elevated the moral status of money, making all areas of life, including culture, equally "accountable." At the same time, the relation between the academy and popular culture had changed; whereas earlier generations had viewed popular culture from the outside, and by implication from above, the post-sixties generation was more likely to share its codes and values. Social science and humanities academics who had grown up watching television and listening to rock music found the Frankfurt School critique elitist and out of touch with contemporary culture's complex interplay of resistance and affirmation. Moreover, the idea of a single culture industry churning out standardized mass culture was being rendered obsolete by technological advances that allowed small-scale production for niche markets – a process that would intensify with the revolution in information communications technology.

The term "culture industries" first entered policy debate in 1982, when UNESCO published *Cultural Industries: A Challenge for the Future of Culture*, a report on research contracted in the 1970s in response to "the new industrial revolution in culture" resulting from the massive expansion of the production and distribution of messages and symbols. While crediting Horkheimer and Adorno with identifying the implications of industrialization and the ascendance of capitalist logic within the sphere of culture, the report argued that the scale and complexity of technological innovation and economic incorporation since the 1940s meant that it was no longer possible to speak in terms of a unified culture industry or to confine analysis to criticism. Given the place of cultural industries in the system of production of the most widely distributed cultural goods, understanding how this system worked was essential to the UNESCO project of cultural development. A series of questions was posed: how are cultural products conceived, selected, given form, manufactured, distributed, and consumed? What is their relation to other forms of cultural communication? What is the relation between their economic and symbolic value?

Another key moment in the emergence of a discourse on culture industries took place in London in 1983, when the Greater London Council organized a conference to reconsider cultural policy in terms that focused on the media and popular culture rather than on Art. The impetus was both economic and ideological. The concentration in London of such industries as publishing, newspapers, music, television, film, advertising, and information technology made culture in the broad sense an important part of the urban economy and a major area of employment. The conference also challenged the established order of arts funding as elitist, and argued for a more inclusive definition of culture that encompassed popular forms delivered by the market rather than the state – a policy agenda with theoretical support from the emerging field of cultural studies.

Popular culture was at the core of the cultural studies project, which mobilized the concept of cultural industries against the idea of culture as a transcendent realm. In a paper delivered at the GLC conference and later published in the first issue of the *Journal of Cultural Studies*, Nicholas Garnham argued for a paradigm shift in cultural analysis from definitions of culture as a site of individual excellence and "Art" to a redefinition focused on popular culture and the media. Cultural policy premised on an idealized concept of culture as inspired creation was criticized as marginal, elitist, and inadequate to understanding a society in which most people accessed culture as goods and services delivered by the market. Culture – defined as "the production and circulation of symbolic meaning" – was positioned as a material process of production and exchange that was not separate from society but part of it; cultural industries were those institutions using industrial modes of production and organization to produce and disseminate symbols in the form of cultural goods and services, usually as commodities (Garnham 1987, 25).

In the 1980s the term was used in relation to the production of cultural content such as newspapers, books, television, film, and music. Policy discussion on cultural industries was largely concerned with their economic importance to cities and nations in the developed world which were losing their manufacturing base in a globalizing labor market, and with social equity questions in relation to funding cultural practices that were of interest only to elites. These issues continue to shape discussion of cultural policy, even as what has been called the "culturalization" of the economy has expanded the category of culture industry beyond the boundaries of cultural production as defined in earlier phases of capitalism.

Underpinning the nuances of social theoretical debate on what is variously described as "postmodernity," "reflexive modernity," and "consumer capitalism" is a general agreement that economic and cultural processes have become inextricably entwined and mutually inflected. While consumer goods have always carried symbolic as well as use value, competition for market share is increasingly conducted in terms of meaning rather than function. Given the importance of brands as signifiers of identity and lifestyle, industrial production and distribution are now as much the circulation of signs as of objects. Conversely, the logic of branding and promotion is intrinsic to the operation of cultural institutions like universities and art museums, once they can no longer rely on their presumed contribution to the public good to guarantee economic support. Exhibitions, festivals, and annual events generate income for cultural institutions and cities. There is no culture without commerce and no commerce without promotional branding.

Since the early 2000s there has been a further discursive shift. The fact that reliance on information technology, design, and digital imaging is shared across the culture/commerce divide has given rise to the term "creative industries." Broader and more diffuse than "culture industries," "creative industries" is used in relation to discussion of a "new economy" based on ideas and intellectual property. Like "culture industries," it first appeared in policy documents, for example of the Creative Industries Task Force established in the Department for Culture, Media and Sport (DCMS) by the British Labour government in 1997, to map the creative industries and measure their contribution to the British economy. Creative industries were defined as "those activities which have their origin in individual creativity, skill and talent and which have the potential for wealth and job creation through the generation and exploitation of intellectual property" (DCMS, quoted in British Council 2010, 16), including advertising, design, designer fashion, software, computer games, and electronic publishing.

Whereas the culture industry discourse shifted the focus of cultural policy from creative artist to audiences, creative industries are defined in terms of their dependence on individual creativity and talent. This is not a return to the romantic idea of the artist as outsider, but rather a blurring of the distinction between commercial and fine art and the emergence of a new concept of the creative worker as central to postindustrial economies. As Richard Florida (2002, 6) has argued, "the creative individual is no longer viewed as an iconoclast," but as "the new mainstream." This elision of culture and economy can be viewed critically, as in Judith Kapferer's (2010) thesis of a shift from a culture debating society to a culture consuming one, or positively, as in Steven D. Tepper's (2012) argument that the "explosion of choice" supported by digital technology contributes to the emergence of citizen engagement in curating their own cultural experience. There is also continuing debate on whether the project-based organization of creative industries and the valorization of creative workers as continuously seeking new challenges serve to legitimize precarious conditions of employment.

SEE ALSO: Adorno, Theodor; Commodification; Frankfurt School; Mass Culture; Popular Culture

REFERENCES

Bourdieu, Pierre. 1993/1983. "The Field of Cultural Production; or, The Economic World Reversed." In *The Field of Cultural Production*. New York: Columbia University Press.

British Council. 2010. *Mapping the Creative Industries: A Toolkit*. London: British Council. Accessed July 14, 2014. http://www.britishcouncil.org/mapping_the_creative_industries_a_toolkit_2-2.pdf.

Florida, Richard. 2002. *The Rise of the Creative Class*. New York: Basic Books.

Garnham, Nicholas. 1987. "Concepts of Culture: Public Policy and the Cultural Industries." *Cultural Studies* 1(1): 23–37.
Horkheimer, Max, and Theodor Adorno. 2002/1947. "The Culture Industry: Enlightenment as Mass Deception." In *The Dialectic of Enlightenment*. Stanford, CA: Stanford University Press.
Kapferer, Judith. 2010. "Twilight of the Enlightenment: The Art Fair, the Culture Industry, and the 'Creative Class.'" *Social Analysis* 54(2): 9–27.
Tepper, Steven J. 2012. *Engaging Art: The Next Great Transformation of America's Cultural Life*. Hoboken, NJ: Taylor & Francis.
UNESCO. 1982. *Cultural Industries: A Challenge for the Future of Culture*. Paris: United Nations. Accessed July 10, 2014. http://unesdoc.unesco.org/images/0004/000499/049972eo.pdf.
Williams, Raymond. 1976/1957. *Culture and Society 1780–1950*. Harmondsworth, UK: Penguin.

FURTHER READING

Hesmondhalgh, David. 2007. *The Cultural Industries*, 2nd ed. London: Sage.

Culture Jamming

KATHLEEN KUEHN
Victoria University of Wellington, New Zealand

Culture jamming is a form of rhetorical protest through pranking, hoaxes, hacking, and other types of sabotage. The concept derives from the radio jamming techniques of pirate citizens band (CB) radio operators who intentionally disrupted transmissions between sender and receiver by introducing noise into the signal. The guerrilla communications tactics of culture jamming, however, are rooted in the tenets of social activism and aim to reclaim independent thought and public spaces from the control and influence of ubiquitous media culture. Although the modes of disruption vary, culture jamming reconstructs new messages from existing ones; it aspires not only to generate critical awareness of social issues but to challenge the status quo by eliciting alternative frames for thinking. Importantly, culture jammers distinguish their acts from pointless vandalism; as social activists, the perpetrators of these creative crimes are motivated by a larger sense of purpose beyond destruction for its own sake. Shepard Fairey's "Obey" campaign, Banksy's urban graffiti, "Billionaires for Bush," and the anti-consumerist magazine *Adbusters* mark some of the more popular culture jams in recent years.

Generally, culture jamming reacts to the loss of control over information and representation in an era of profit driven corporate media ownership and a standardized system of cultural production. As a political tool, it responds to what Adorno and Horkheimer identified as the culture industry's depoliticizing effects on the masses, an idea later expanded upon in Guy Debord's highly influential *Society of the Spectacle*. In an "empire of signs" where images, aesthetics, and consumption take primacy over debate, deliberation, and natural environments, subversive techniques become the necessary means for breaking through the clutter of a 24/7 visual media spectacle. Engaging consumer capitalism on its own terms, pranks and other high jinks intend to liberate audiences from the pervasive corporate and political influence that increasingly governs what to believe, who to be, and what to buy.

In his seminal introduction to culture jamming, Mark Dery (1993) outlines four main modes: subvertising, billboard banditry, media hoaxing, and audio agit-prop. The first, *subvertising*, is the practice of satirically altering a recognizable advert, political message, logo, or image through spoof or parody. By closely mimicking the original, subvertisements undermine the power of advertising by "uncooling" it; they construct "demotions" (or "antipromotions") that invite viewers to rethink the originally intended message. Popular subvertisements include *Adbusters'* "Joe Chemo" spoof (an anti-smoking campaign featuring the "Joe Cool" Camel receiving cancer treatment) and "Reality for Men" (a mockery of Calvin Klein's "Obsession" campaign which poses "normal" bodies).

A second but related mode, *billboard banditry*, hijacks outdoor ad spaces on a larger scale. The "Brandalism" project's team of underground street artists, for example, has refaced over 30 billboards across five UK cities to reclaim the visual landscape from advertisers. Subvertising and billboard banditry both aim to provoke the transformation of passive consumers into active receivers by asking viewers to recognize the corporate strategies behind mediated messages, while calling attention to the commodification of public space.

Media hoaxing is another mode of culture jamming that involves pranking or tricking journalists into covering elaborately staged deceptions as actual news stories and revealing mainstream media's attention to spectacle over issues that actually matter. New York City performance artist Joey Skaggs notoriously staged a number of such hoaxes, such as his elaborate 1976 "Cathouse for Dogs" performance which successfully convinced local media outlets to cover the launch of his (fake) animal brothel (earning WABC-TV an Emmy nomination for the story it never retracted). More recently, the activist saboteurs The Yes Men have penetrated the realms of big business and political organizations through highly styled antics. Like other modes of culture jamming, they appropriate media's own orientation toward spectacle as a mechanism for raising awareness around important stories or events that would otherwise go unreported. By creating fake websites, posing as corporate executives, or engaging in other coordinated pranks, The Yes Men have been able to provide citizens with a backstage glimpse into how powerful people make important everyday decisions affecting society. They have successfully infiltrated the World Trade Organization, the Republican National Convention, and BBC World. In the latter case, member Andy Bichlbaum appeared on British national television in 2004 as a Dow Chemical representative to claim full responsibility for the 1984 Bhopal gas leak, promising reparations for disaster victims. The prank ultimately forced the real Dow Chemical company to release a public statement addressing the issue.

Dery's fourth mode of culture jamming, *audio agit-prop*, is best exemplified by the experimental music of Negativeland, which coined the term "culture jamming" in its 1984 *JAMCON '84* album. The band deconstructs media culture (and copyrights) by appropriating its content to produce politically themed sound collages from news clips, speech samples, and other recordings. Formally, these mash-ups mimic what now passes as "objective journalism," for example overused soundbites, biased reporting, and an emphasis on entertainment value.

Playful subversion as social critique can be located as far back as the alternative folk culture of medieval carnival. Its more commonly recognized predecessor, however, is the 1950s Situationist International (SI). Situationists were an organized group of European revolutionaries, artists, and public intellectuals who responded to postwar Europe's growing conservatism and exploding consumer culture via *détournement*: the "detouring" of intended messages through their reclamation and subversion. They encouraged the creation of "authentic" situations through spontaneous actions that the machinations of mass culture could not easily replicate or appropriate. Designed to awaken the masses from their spectacle-induced passivity, such activities included improvisational public performances, billboard banditry, and the nonsensical juxtapositions of popular imagery (e.g., Guy Debord's collage of a bare breasted Stalin). In the United States, radical Yippie pranktivists engaged similar tactics to disrupt the status quo, as in their 1968 attempt to nominate a pig for the presidential candidacy.

Critics challenge culture jamming as an ineffective and paternalistic form of resistance. Christine Harold (2007) argues that subversive parodies do little more than reduce the power of advertising to an overly simplified cause–effect relationship; this logic assumes that all consumers (except jammers themselves!) are passive dupes of popular media culture who interpret dominant messages the same way. Merely advocating a message of "Just say no to consumer culture" fails to provide an alternative outlet for action, and thus has little efficacy in a historical moment where consumer capitalism dominates the new global order. Therefore, whereas parodies and pranks might uncover some hidden truths about capitalism, Harold's point is that they fail to produce any new truths on which alternative ways of being might replace the existing order of things. Her critique of *Adbusters* points out that the magazine's brand as an "antibrand" actually operates along the same marketing logics as the very corporations the publication mocks, raising the question of whether culture jamming can ever escape the systems of commodification it critiques. This point can be seen in the way pranksterism has been reappropriated by guerrilla marketers themselves as a way of ambushing consumers with corporate messages through seemingly noncorporate strategies. Moreover, the mainstreaming of satire and parody on popular cable programs like *The Daily Show* and *Colbert Report* also presents new challenges to the efficacy of subversion as a political tool.

SEE ALSO: Consumer Activism; Consumer Resistance Movements

REFERENCES

Dery, Mark. 1993. *Culture Jamming: Hacking, Slashing, and Sniping in the Empire of Signs*. Open Magazine pamphlet. Accessed June 30, 2014. http://markdery.com/?page_id=154.

Harold, Christine. 2007. *OurSpace: Resisting the Corporate Control of Culture*. Minneapolis: University of Minnesota Press.

FURTHER READING

Klein, Naomi. 2009. *No Logo*, 3rd ed. New York: Picador.

Lasn, Kalle. 2000. *Culture Jam: The Uncooling of America*. New York: Quill.

D

Dandyism

MICHELE BONAZZI
University of Bologna, Italy

The term "dandyism" refers to a British cultural movement of the late nineteenth century, within the Victorian era. It was a doctrine of elegance, finesse, and originality which was primarily concerned with language, sophisticated manners, and dress. An aphorism coined by the writer Gabriele D'Annunzio, one of the leading representatives of the Italian movement, perfectly sums up its essence: "living life as a work of art." For that reason, "being dandy" became an expression not only of sophisticated dress, but of a proper lifestyle that expressed itself in every aspect of existence, such as attitude and personal tastes, and was superior from the point of view of social and cultural capital. This way of life was driven by a determination to stand out from the stereotype of the ordinary bourgeois man, and its aim was to rise above social conventions and the common way of thinking. In this sense, the dandy played a leading role in the society of his time, as an actor on a theater stage, shocking the audience with his eccentric and provocative style.

This type of mentality had been conceived by the cultural and artistic movement of the Pre-Raphaelites, for example with the painter Dante Gabriel Rossetti. In England, Beau Brummell and Oscar Wilde are often regarded as the embodiment of the figure of the dandy in the collective imagination. Dandyism became a cultural movement in Europe, mainly because of its attraction for the art world. Hungary was the native land of the famous dandy, the composer and citizen of the world Franz Liszt, while in Spain there was the multitalented surrealist painter Salvador Dalí.

Driven by the constant need to distinguish himself from the masses (Simmel 1911), the dandy felt the need to express his singularity and to affirm his narcissistic personality. He took delight in defying the moral norms of society; his targets were the conservative and orthodox ideas of the middle class. As Wilde wrote in *The Picture of Dorian Gray*, "there is only one thing in the world worse than being talked about, and that is not being talked about" (Wilde 1981, 141). In this sense, it was irrelevant whether the public response to him was positive or negative: the dandy was focused on the importance of being noticed.

SEE ALSO: Consumption and Identity; Cultural Capital; *Flâneur/Flânerie*; Narcissism

The Wiley Blackwell Encyclopedia of Consumption and Consumer Studies, First Edition.
Edited by Daniel Thomas Cook and J. Michael Ryan.

REFERENCES

Simmel, Georg. 1911. *Philosophische Kultur* [Cultural Philosophy]. Leipzig: Kröner.

Wilde, Oscar. 1981. *The Picture of Dorian Gray*. In *The Portable Oscar Wilde*, edited by R. Aldington and S. Weintraub, 138–391. Harmondsworth, UK: Penguin.

FURTHER READING

Barbey d'Aurevilly, Jules. 1988. *Of Dandyism and of George Brummell*. New York: PAJ.

de Certeau, Michel

DOMINIQUE DESJEUX

Paris Descartes University, Sorbonne Paris Cité, France

One of Michel de Certeau's great virtues was the attention he paid to other people, as Luce Giard reminds us in the book she edited in 1987, a year after his death. This is reflected in his work through a never ending search for otherness, his quest for an invisible presence. De Certeau was one of the great experts on mysticism, and his quest was close to that of earlier mystics in their constant search for the hidden presence of God. Himself a Jesuit, he followed the spiritual exercises of St. Ignatius of Loyola, by which adherents apply prudence with respect to illusions, discernment of the meaning of life, and liberation of the self as a means of being more available to others. These characteristics are often also demanded of a social science researcher. They are that much more effective in de Certeau's work in that they are associated with physical and intellectual mobility.

Michel de Certeau was born in 1925. He traveled constantly between the provinces and Paris, between France and the Americas, between institutions – from the Jesuits to EHESS (École des Hautes Études en Sciences Sociales) in Paris, with stops at Berkeley and Université Paris VII – and, especially, between intellectual fields, from mystics like Jean Joseph Surin, a seventeenth-century Jesuit, to the exploration of daily routine and the ordinary life. These activities plunged him into the heart of the consumer society, which he approached from the perspective of the "dominated."

De Certeau's principal work, which was carried out in collaboration with Luce Giard, Marie Ferrier, and Pierre Mayol, bears on *L'Invention du quotidian* (The Invention of the Daily Routine) (1994). This research was conducted between 1974 and 1977 at the request of La Délégation Générale à la Recherche Scientifique et Technique (DGRST), a public research funding organization in France. De Certeau was one of the pioneers of ROD (research on demand), which shows how investigations financed by bodies outside of the university can give rise to original theories. In particular, he was one of the first sociologists from the 1970s onward to show that the consumer is not passive but active, that there is a culture associated with the daily routine, and that this ordinary culture comes back to a practice which consists of turning away from the order imposed on the dominated actors through mass distribution or other commercial means.

It is on this precise point, of domination relations, that de Certeau distinguishes himself from Michel Foucault, who highlights the effect of imposition to the detriment of the "ruse" (cunning), of a "bricolage" (patchwork arrangement), and de Certeau's reinterpretation that the dominated actors, those from the grassroots, can produce and create, even faced with domination. This is why he does not limit the figure of the consumer to that of someone resisting, since resistance supposes a passive rather than an active actor. Resisting is opposing without creating.

Thus, the consumer observed by de Certeau in the process of bricolage and *perruque* (personal use of the employer's equipment) in his workshop is already paving the way for the new consumer of the twenty-first century who, affected by the economic crisis from 2008 onward, must engage in new behavior (for example, retrieving discarded appliances by the roadside); engage in nonmonetary exchange systems and, increasingly, in transactions over the internet, with actors from the same region, to compensate for limited purchasing power; or collect unsold vegetables at the end of the day at street markets in the big cities.

The key to de Certeau's method is to start with daily practices, those that we may observe at home and in the kitchen, that is, those that develop within the small spaces of the daily routine. As Luce Giard wrote in her introduction to volume 1 of *L'Invention du quotidien*, Michel de Certeau's objective is to create theory out of routine daily practices.

At the heart of this theory of consumption as an analyzer of the daily routine are two central concepts: strategy and tactics. Strategy is the practice of the strong. The strong may be a firm, a political institution, a research body, or an army which creates a power struggle in seeking to manipulate the dominated actors. Such strategies are related to a space, to a place that the strong seeks to besiege. As in military theory, the tactic is the response of the weak to the strong: it is based on movement; it tries to take advantage of opportunities. It resembles the Chinese military strategist Sun Zi's 2500-year-old theory which stressed the need to take the situation into account in order to develop a tactic with which to confront the enemy.

In contrast, de Certeau's theory can be differentiated from the strategic sociology developed by Michel Crozier in *Le Phénomène bureaucratique* (*The Bureaucratic Phenomenon*) in 1963, in which power is a relationship which makes all actors play, with some actors having more or fewer advantages in the game. For de Certeau, on the contrary, power is an asset and, therefore, the dominated actor has no power, but he or she has sufficient cunning, creativity, and mobility to confound and play with the rules that seek to impose the dominant institutions on him or her.

Michel de Certeau viewed consumption as the site of a power struggle, and in this sense, his perspective is close to that of Pierre Bourdieu, but it is in opposition to marketing which apparently magically turns reality into a world with no power struggles or domination.

SEE ALSO: Bourdieu, Pierre; Bricolage; Consumption, Postmodern

REFERENCES

Crozier, Michel. 1963. *Le Phénomène bureaucratique* [*The Bureaucratic Phenomenon*]. Paris: Seuil.

de Certeau, Michel. 1980. *L'Invention du quotidien* [The Invention of the Daily Routine]. Vol. 1: *Arts de faire* [Arts of Doing]. Paris: UGE.

de Certeau, Michel, Luce Giard, and Pierre Mayol. 1994. *L'Invention du quotidien* [The Invention of the Daily Routine]. Vol. 2: *Habiter, cuisiner* [Living, Cooking]. Paris: Gallimard.

Giard, Luce, ed. 1987. *Michel de Certeau*. Paris: Centre Georges Pompidou, Cahiers pour un temps.

Death and Consumption

MAAIKE GOTTFRIED
DePaul University, USA

Death and consumption intersect at the practical need to dispose of a human corpse and the oft-accompanying ritual. In the modern capitalist West this universal and basic human responsibility has become a multibillion-dollar industry whose main actors and transactions are sanctioned and regulated by state governments and federal agencies.

Before the Second Industrial Revolution (1860s–1920s), those charged with handling this responsibility were largely unpaid female relatives of the deceased and the craftsmen they employed to supply elements deemed essential for the ritual that took place in the homes of the bereaved. Scientific and technological advances of the late nineteenth and early twentieth centuries hastened and legitimated the move of corpse disposal from the domestic sphere to that of the professional and the commercial. The rise of modern hospitals saw increasing numbers of people dying outside the home for the first time in history. Embalming became popular and increasingly more scientific after the bodies of fallen soldiers were chemically preserved during the American Civil War (1861–65) in order to withstand transport to their families. Soon embalmers offered their services with the promise of both increased public safety by preventing corpse decay and thus the spread of disease, and the emotional relief of seeing a loved one in a state of seeming somnolence before burial. Their specialized knowledge of anatomy and chemicals required to correctly embalm a body, along with an awareness of their unique position to offer new services to the bereaved, led embalmers to pursue professional status through occupational licensing, specialized schools, and state laws regarding corpse disposal.

In modern times, the Western death ritual is located within the purview of the funeral home, a commercial establishment offering a nondomestic centralized space in which to sell the bereaved services and merchandise related to the legal, practical, religious, and cultural requirements of corpse disposal and bereavement. In the United States, many cultures and religions have accepted the funeral home and the commodification of death rituals. Despite widespread acceptance, however, this sentiment is far from universal. The religious laws, customs, and traditions of Orthodox Judaism, for instance, do not allow for any incorporation of consumption into the death ritual; a society of local Jewish volunteers is responsible for cleaning and ritually purifying the body for burial without preservative techniques. Where it is legal, there is also a growing nonreligious do-it-yourself death care movement, in which adherents assume responsibility over the preservation and disposal of the body of the deceased and the funeral ritual.

The modern funeral home is the locus of death and consumption, where many aspects of a death ritual are commodified. Such commodities include the professional services of funeral directors, embalming, the use of space within the funeral home for the ritual, the receptacles used to contain the corpse such as a casket or urn, floral arrangements, the services of a cemetery or crematorium for final disposal, sentimental keepsake items, clothing and grooming of the deceased, obituaries, the presence and services of religious leaders, and the ground in which one will ultimately rest. These elements can be purchased and uniquely combined to design a funeral of one's traditions and/or desires. Guided by religious and cultural standards, many survivors use the presentation of the death ritual as a way to honor the dead, retain social status for the deceased and surviving family, assuage unpleasant emotions about the death, reconcile changing relationships and social roles, and provide comfort and solace to mourners.

Consumption in the context of death is unique in that many consumers are in a heightened emotional state during the process, and the services and products purchased will neither be directly used, nor directly enjoyed, by the purchaser. For this reason, the Federal Trade Commission has paid special attention to the death care industry, enacting legislation in the last decades of the twentieth century to regulate interactions between service providers and potential customers in the name of consumer protection from potentially predatory business practices. Governmental legislation has also served to expand the industry to allow multinational corporations as well as internet-based retailers of funeral merchandise and cremation services to enter the market.

Research has focused on the increasing personalization, standardization, and secularization of death rituals; cultural methods of controlling death anxieties; the social and psychological reasons for consumption after a death; and the effects of state and federal legislation on service providers and consumers.

SEE ALSO: Consumer Culture; Consumption Rituals; Emotions and Consumption

FURTHER READING

Laderman, Gary. 2003. *Rest in Peace: A Cultural History of Death and the Funeral Home in Twentieth Century America*. New York: Oxford University Press.

Debord, Guy

DAVID REDMON
University of Kent at Canterbury, UK

Guy Debord (1931–94), the founding member of the social revolutionary organization Situationist International, is most famous for his polemic *The Society of the Spectacle* – a montage of theoretical writings which analyzed the transformation of a society organized around production and manufacturing into one organized around the consumption of "an immense accumulation of spectacles." According to Best and Kellner (1997, 81), Debord sought to update the Marxian emphasis on class struggle, capital, and factory work by directing attention to the accumulation of capital through a series of integrated images that manufacture reality. Capitalism recreates space in its own image in a wide range of venues, from the total institutions of packaged tourist resorts, to the malls across America, to the fabricated fantasies of Las Vegas, Disneyland, and New Orleans' Mardi Gras. Media institutions, such as CNN, MTV, Fox News, CBC, ARTE, and the BBC, have become fully integrated forms of "infotainment": commodified installations of reality television and celebrity ethos that merge subjectivity with consumer culture. This global merger of ubiquitous image and subjectivity creates a "spectacular" society. Spectacular society, according to Debord, is an apparatus of fabricated social relations in which institutions socialize people by manipulating their relationship to images; it is a reified world where consumers and producers are alienated from each other and can experience their social world only through the accumulation of spectacles. Debord (1994/1967) writes: "The spectacle is the moment when the commodity has attained the total occupation of social life. The relation to the commodity is not only visible, but one no longer sees anything but it: the world one sees is its world." All that remains from the spectacle are representations of life.

In spectacular society, life becomes a fully integrated network of consumer gadgets and apps (iPhones, Facebook, Amazon, Google, Verizon); leisure is reduced to shopping, and the logo or brand becomes the dominating category of status and prestige for people. The apparatus of surface appearances produces a coherent glossy image that hides, or even erases, the rational techniques of manufacture and the content behind the façade; all that remains is the desire to possess the signifier of the sign. In other words, the spectacle does not socially control its subjects by force, but through the pacification of creativity and the consensus of collective desire. The spectacle extends its subtle forms of normalization and domination by inspiring in its subjects the desire to conform to images in magazines, advertisements, commercials, and movies. "The spectacle," Debord notes, "is the moment when the commodity has attained the total occupation of social life" (Debord 1994/1967, ch. 2, thesis 42). The spectacle is a chain of images that flattens and reduces landscapes to a vacuum of TGI Friday's, Applebees, GAP, Abercrombie & Fitch, glistening billboards, and Starbucks located next to fast-food restaurants and chain hotels.

Debord is adamant in pointing out that spectacular society is socially constructed by an apparatus of modern specialists: advertisers, city council planners, international financial institutions, corporations, special economic zones, architects, fashion designers, and so on. Therefore, he claims, it is imperative to understand that the spectacle is vulnerable to disruption and eventual eradication. The concept he applies to this possible transformation is *détournement*. *Détournement* is a conceptual and physical tactic employed by opponents of the spectacle who desire to alter, destroy, and replace it with a more humane alternative that advocates creativity and full participation in one's life. Jeff Ferrell, a US sociologist, utilizes *détournement* in his books *Empire of Scrounge* (2006) and *Tearing Down the Streets* (2002) as a way to introduce the pillars of contemporary *cultural criminology* in sociology. Ferrell uses microscale examples of *détournement*, such as resignifying or inverting the intended meaning of advertisements through graffiti or street art; reclaiming streets, parks, or abandoned gardens so that the public can participate in them; and mapping and reinventing the city on one's own terms by scrounging disposable commodities as acts of subversion. "A world now awash in mass-produced images made possible an aesthetic confrontation with mass production and mass society itself" (Ferrell 2006, 149). *Détournement* and *dérive* make pleasure, passion, and surprise possible through chance encounters. *Dérive* wanderings resist the spectacle by creating relationships based on actual lived experiences, drifting, and self-creativity.

Examples of macrolevel *détournement* against the spectacle also exist, however. The actions of May 1968, especially in Paris, provided the defining moment for Situationism; the historical rupture that transpired could not be attributed directly to a crisis in the economy. Students, communists, Maoists, Situationists, anarchists, and workers revolted with disparate goals. Universities temporarily shut down, nationwide strikes occurred, and riots broke out in the streets of Paris. There among the rioters was Guy Debord, and several quotes from his *Society of the Spectacle* manifesto appeared as written graffiti on city walls (Merrifield 2005). Contemporary examples of macrolevel *détournement* include international social movements against global capitalism and neoliberalism, such as Critical Mass and Reclaim the Streets. The twentieth-century birth date of these contemporary movements can be pinpointed to January 1, 1994, when the Zapatistas rose up "against neoliberalism and for humanity." Similar movements subsequently erupted in Seattle, Washington, against the World Trade Organization on November 30, 1999 – exactly five years after Debord's suicide. Appropriately, masked anarchists joined local activists and citizens to damage the spectacle. Targets included the spectacular images that Debord sought to eradicate, the pillars of the global spectacle themselves: McDonald's, Starbucks, Nike Town, and banks were all vandalized, windows were smashed, and graffiti was painted: "Fuck the WTO," "Stop sweatshops," and, perhaps most famously, "We are winning?"

The tension between spectacular resistance and the reproduction of the spectacle persists with the international Occupy movement and the US government's bailout of corporate banks, the NSA's international network of spectacular spying through everyday telecommunication systems, and the Electronic Frontier Foundation's attempt to counter the NSA. Likewise, influential contemporary social theorists such as Thomas Mathiesen and Zygmunt Bauman invoke Debord's theories in their discussions of "synoptical society" and "liquid society." Debord's continuing presence in the world of espionage, everyday activism, and academia suggests that his terms "spectacle" and *détournement* are perhaps more appropriately intertwined than originally imagined.

SEE ALSO: Capitalism; Consumption, Spectacles of; Mass Media

REFERENCES

Best, Steven, and Douglas Kellner. 1997. *The Postmodern Turn*. New York: Guilford.

Debord, Guy. 1994/1967. *The Society of the Spectacle*. New York: Zone.

Ferrell, Jeff. 2002. *Tearing Down the Streets*. New York: Palgrave Macmillan.

Ferrell, Jeff. 2006. *Empire of Scrounge*. New York: New York University Press.

Merrifield, Andy. 2005. *Guy Debord*. London: Reaktion.

Debt

JAN LOGEMANN
University of Göttingen, Germany

Debt and credit are central to nearly all economic processes, but they have become particularly vital to the functioning of modern consumer economies. While there are many forms of debt, this entry will focus on the development of household debt and consumer credit in the modern era, neglecting public debt and commercial loans. Consumer debt expanded dramatically during the twentieth century, when a variety of new financial products and technologies, from installment loans to credit cards, became important marketing tools that facilitated the spread of mass consumption. Traditional social, moral, and legal restrictions on debt increasingly gave way to a widespread acceptance, starting in the late nineteenth century, of debt as an integral part of middle-class consumption. Proponents of credit expansion have pointed to its role in smoothing life cycle consumption, in fostering aggregate demand, and in "democratizing" access to a growing world of consumer goods. Critics, by contrast, point to the growing phenomenon of overindebtedness and personal bankruptcies, the precarious nature of a debt financed lifestyle, the degree of surveillance and disciplining involved with new modes of credit scoring and reporting, as well as to the overall lack of sustainability of a consumer economy built on debt, as evidenced by the financial crisis of 2007–8.

Personal debt for consumption purposes, however, has a long history which predates modern consumer societies (Gelpi and Julien-Labruyère 2000), and historians caution against notions of a supposed bygone era of thriftiness and solid cash sales. Class biases often informed nineteenth-century discussions of debt, and, while working-class debt was frequently stigmatized, the Victorian era gentleman (the creditworthiness of women remained widely restricted in most countries until the 1970s) naturally enjoyed credit with many businesses (Horowitz 1985). While numerous usury laws kept banks in the United States out of the business of consumer lending, legitimate pawnshops and illegitimate loan sharks, as well as (by the end of the century) semi-legitimate payday lenders, would meet the demand (Woloson 2009). Many smaller stores offered informal credit accounts in ledger books to regular customers to be settled periodically. In Britain and Germany, specialized hire purchase stores and check trading companies began to offer household goods on credit, while US companies such as Singer secured the international success of their sewing machines through direct marketed sales on a payment plan (Logemann and Spiekermann 2010). By the turn of the century, legal and economic debates about the need to (de)regulate consumer credit could be found across the Atlantic world.

Between the two world wars, the United States saw a shift from traditional forms of lending to new forms of organized consumer credit that would set the standard for much of the twentieth century. Legal reforms allowed for the creation of small-loans banks specializing in consumer debt, while department stores and other retailers increasingly began to offer and advertise installment loans with low down payments and regular monthly rates. The spread of many new consumer goods, but particularly of the automobile, depended heavily on new sales financing models through specialized banks set up by car companies. While European countries and Japan also saw changes, such as the introduction of credit checks issued by retailer consortiums, debt financed consumption remained on a comparatively limited scale there. More importantly, consumer debt was becoming part of a respectable and modern middle-class consumer lifestyle in the United States. The onset of the Great Depression, with its surprisingly low default rates on many consumer loans, did little to change this.

Some historians see the 1930s and the Roosevelt administration's New Deal response to the depression as a watershed that made the United States an increasingly debt centered consumer society. New Deal policies helped expand the mortgage market, one of the most important aspects of household debt, and promoted home modernization loans. Under the emerging Keynesian paradigm, credit became an increasingly important tool in regulating aggregate demand. Economists argued that consumer debt would increasingly become a means not of alleviating household deficits, but rather of shoring up household capital in the form of an increasing stock of durable goods. While World War II restrictions such as Regulation W dampened credit growth somewhat until the late 1940s, expanding consumer debt became widely seen as a means to ensure postwar growth and to expand the reach of the mass consumer economy.

Indeed, postwar America saw a tremendous growth in (partially government subsidized) consumer debt with the expansion of mortgage and installment credit, the increasing involvement of commercial banks in the business of small personal loans, and the introduction of new technologies such as the credit card by the 1950s and 1960s (Hyman 2011). This expansion in credit was unmatched in other consumer economies in Europe and Japan, where an emphasis on saving and capital accumulation tended to dominate economic reconstruction policies, and social strictures on debt financing remained more prominent. Many American commentators, by contrast, celebrated credit as a great "democratizer" that offered nearly everybody, regardless of class, access to the abundance of the American way of life – instant gratification without delay.

Rather than being a source of hedonist indulgence, consumer debt was increasingly recognized as a disciplining force in the lives of consumers. Regular installments forced households to budget conscientiously, but contemporary critics such as William Whyte and Kenneth Galbraith questioned whether the bill collector should really play such a central role in conceptions of the good life. Debt furthermore allows for specialized data collection that retailers began to exploit for marketing purposes during the 1920s. The growth of credit reporting agencies after World War II further made consumers ever more "legible" to marketers and financial institutions. Whereas reputation and standing within the community increasingly mattered less, the all-important – if more impersonal – credit score came to loom large in the lives of consumers by the 1970s.

US consumer legislation during the 1960s and 1970s, however, was less concerned with the ways in which growing debt impacted the lives of consumers and more with safety and equality of access. The federal Truth in Lending Act of 1968, thus, forced retailers to clearly state interest rates and loan conditions. The Equal Credit Opportunity Act of 1974 sought to remedy widespread discriminatory practices on the basis of race and gender. Women and African Americans, for example, had long been excluded from access to many forms of consumer debt, most notoriously mortgages (Cohen 2003). While European countries had also expanded credit access during the postwar economic boom era, by contrast government policy, many retailers, as well as consumers in France, West Germany, and other countries long retained a more conservative and restrictive stance toward debt financed consumption (Effosse and Gaillard 2010).

The precarious nature of debt financed consumption in the United States became ever more evident during the 1980s as wage inequality grew and many households struggled with unsustainable financial situations, leading to a marked increase in personal bankruptcies, which had been made easier by previous legal reforms. At the same time, new financial tools such as home equity loans and the aggressive marketing of consumer debt to lower-income families and college students made indebtedness increasingly pervasive (Manning 2000). Additionally, a "fringe banking" industry of pawnshops and payday and auto title lenders expanded that catered – at often exorbitant interest rates – to recent immigrants, inner-city residents, and other populations underserved by commercial banks and other established lenders.

Overindebtedness, often discussed during the 1990s as a problem of middle-class, status-oriented, "overspent" Americans, was more often the consequence of "passive indebtedness" following sudden unemployment or illness than the result of consumerist splurges or conspicuous consumption. Medical debt and student loans were among the most pressing debt burdens on many households, reflecting the growing importance of medical and educational expenses in consumer budgets overall. At the beginning of the twenty-first century, many Americans felt the need to compensate for a comparatively underdeveloped welfare state by incurring debt – a pattern that some scholars argue is characteristic of the American political economy in general (Prasad 2012).

Today, consumer indebtedness is a phenomenon present in all developed consumer economies; there has been a global transfer of credit instruments, and even traditionally frugal Japanese consumers often carry a heavy debt burden (Horioka 2012). Still, comparative and transnational scholarship has recently highlighted the exceptional role of America's propensity to consume on debt and disinclination to save (Garon 2012). While the United States has been a widely discussed reference point for modern mass consumption, its policy approach toward credit expansion and its social and cultural acceptance of consumer debt have not been universally shared across European and Asian societies (Logemann 2012). The economic crisis of 2007–8, by contrast, has again underscored the fragility and potential unsustainability of consumer societies that are too heavily debt centered.

SEE ALSO: Bankruptcy; Conspicuous Consumption; Credit Cards; Finance/Financial Markets; Markets, Moral Aspects of; Money

REFERENCES

Cohen, Lizabeth. 2003. *A Consumers' Republic: The Politics of Mass Consumption in Postwar America*. New York: Knopf.

Effosse, Sabine, and Isabelle Gaillard. 2010. *Consommer à crédit en Europe au XXe siècle* [Consuming on Credit in Twentieth-Century Europe]. Paris: ESKA.

Garon, Sheldon M. 2012. *Beyond Our Means: Why America Spends while the World Saves*. Princeton: Princeton University Press.

Gelpi, Rosa-Maria, and François Julien-Labruyère. 2000. *The History of Consumer Credit: Doctrines and Practice*. New York: St. Martin's.

Horioka, Charles. 2012. "Japan and the Western Model: An Economist's View of Cultures of Household Finance." In *The Development of Consumer Credit in Global Perspective*, edited by Jan Logemann, 243–256. New York: Palgrave Macmillan.

Horowitz, Daniel. 1985. *The Morality of Spending: Attitudes toward the Consumer Society in America, 1875–1940*. Baltimore: Johns Hopkins University Press.

Hyman, Louis. 2011. *Debtor Nation: The History of America in Red Ink*. Princeton: Princeton University Press.

Logemann, Jan. 2012. *The Development of Consumer Credit in Global Perspective: Business, Regulation, and Culture*. New York: Palgrave Macmillan.

Logemann, Jan, and Uwe Spiekermann. 2010. "The Myth of a Bygone Cash Economy: Consumer Lending in Germany from the Nineteenth Century to the Mid-Twentieth Century." *Entreprises et Histoire* 59(2): 12–27.

Manning, Robert D. 2000. *Credit Card Nation: The Consequences of America's Addiction to Credit*. New York: Basic Books.

Prasad, Monica. 2012. *The Land of Too Much: American Abundance and the Paradox of Poverty*. Cambridge, MA: Harvard University Press.

Woloson, Wendy A. 2009. *In Hock: Pawning in America from Independence through the Great Depression*. Chicago: University of Chicago Press.

Decluttering

HÉLÈNE CHERRIER
Griffith University, Australia
RUSSELL BELK
York University, Canada

It is not clear precisely when clutter became a problem in the homes of middle-class consumers, but during the 1990s and 2000s a variety of professional organizers, self-help books, and online sites began to address the problem. The international bestseller *Organizing from the Inside Out* by Julie Morgenstern (2000) and *Clear Your Clutter* by Karen Kingston (1998), *Clean Sweep* by Alison Haynes (2004), and *Teach Yourself Decluttering* by Bernice Walmsley (2006) illustrate society's preoccupation with clutter and organizing. Television shows in the United Kingdom and United States also emerged focusing on the problems of hoarding and the necessity for professional decluttering (Belk 2014). As clutter was progressively problematized (Frost and Steketee 2010), hoarding became a formally recognized psychiatric disorder in DSM-5 (*The Diagnostic and Statistical Manual of Mental Disorders*). Nevertheless, both clutter and hoarding are social judgments, and were not seen as problems in the object-crowded rooms of the Victorian era. While the American television show *Hoarders* started out as an entertaining look inside cluttered homes, the producers quickly concluded that their subjects had serious problems that required counseling more than cleansing (Paxton 2011).

In consumer culture, decluttering aims at clearing out the mess, disorder, and complications that often accompany material accumulation and also nonmaterial accumulation on computer hard drives and corporate records. With the proliferation of material offerings and affordability, consumers are increasingly trapped in a disorganized and chaotic material presence. Belk, Seo, and Li (2007) discuss how "clutteraholics" find it impossible to personally dispose of cluttering objects due to lack of time and organization skills and deep symbolic meanings attached to possessions.

Decluttering is an episodic practice with a beginning but no definitive end. Prior to decluttering, individuals may not realize that others judge their environment as cluttered or overcrowded. After initial decluttering, the space – physical and/or mental – has been transformed from disordered and messy to ordered and tidy and a plan is set in place to keep it so. However, clutter often returns, necessitating episodic decluttering, sometimes ritualized, such as spring cleaning, transitional cleaning (when children leave home), or letting go of emotionally charged possessions, as when older individuals move to smaller residences.

Decluttering is also a social practice. As a social practice, decluttering is entrenched in shared understandings and the development of common modes of appropriate conduct. For example, hoarders often question the idea of disposal, perceiving it as counterproductive to the process of acquiring and preserving symbolic representations of their past (Cherrier 2010; Cherrier and Ponnor 2003; Lepselter 2011). Although meaningful to hoarders, their cluttered space is socially and culturally seen as disorder, impurity, or dirt that needs to be organized to fit societal norms of comfort and cleanliness (Shove 2003). Polluting aspects of material clutter partly derive from major world religions. In Judeo-Christian scriptures, Abraham warned against the evils of material excess and Jesus repeatedly urged his followers to seek their treasures outside of material things, considering earthly excess to lead to deadness of the heart (Shi 1985). Decluttering is thus deeply rooted in the social, cultural, and symbolic presentation of how one's life and home should be. In popular culture, television shows such as *Hoarders* and The Learning Channel's website "Hoarding: Buried Alive," combined with numerous decluttering makeover shows, reiterate the social imperative to declutter.

Decluttering has some therapeutic characteristics. For example, Belk and colleagues found that people feel better about themselves and their environment after having partially decluttered their home (Belk, Seo, and Li 2007). Studies of simple living and downsizing support the view that reorganizing to achieve material simplicity promotes well-being and happiness (Cherrier and Murray 2007) and helps focus on "what is important" (Alexander and Ussher 2012). However, simply decluttering the number of possessions does not seem to improve one's life if it is not paired with a modified attitude toward material possessions (Alexander and Ussher 2012).

Based on beliefs that mainstream marketing contributes to clutter, Cristol and Sealy (2000) discuss marketing simplicity strategies to declutter the number of products, brands, and decisions in customers' lives. The strategies involve replacing, repackaging, repositioning, and replenishing. However, competing strategies strive to rent or sell consumers more storage space (Arnold and Lang 2007; Cwerner and Metcalfe 2003).

SEE ALSO: Consumer Culture; Downshifting; Needs and Wants; Waste

REFERENCES AND FURTHER READING

Alexander, Samuel, and Simon Ussher. 2012. "The Voluntary Simplicity Movement: A Multi-National Survey Analysis in Theoretical Context." *Journal of Consumer Culture* 12(1): 66–86.

Arnold, Jeanne, and Ursula Lang. 2007. "Changing American Home Life: Trends in Domestic Leisure and Storage among Middle-Class Families." *Journal of Family Economic Issues* 28: 23–48.

Belk, Russell W. 2014. "Ownership and Collecting." In *Oxford Handbook of Hoarding and Acquiring*, edited by Randy O. Frost and Gail Steketee. Oxford: Oxford University Press.

Belk, Russell W., Joon Yong Seo, and Eric Li. 2007. "Dirty Little Secret: Home Chaos and Professional Organizers." *Consumption Markets & Culture* 10(2): 133–140.

Cherrier, Hélène. 2010. "Custodian Behavior: A Material Expression of Anti-Consumerism." *Consumption Markets & Culture* 13(3): 259–272.

Cherrier, Hélène, and Jeff B. Murray. 2007. "Reflexive Dispossession and the Self: Constructing a Processual Theory of Identity." *Consumption Markets & Culture* 10(1): 1–30.

Cherrier, Hélène, and Tresa Ponnor. 2003. "A Study of Hoarding Behavior and Attachment to Material Possessions." *Qualitative Market Research* 13(1): 8–23.

Cristol, Stephen, and Peter Sealy. 2000. *Simplicity Marketing: End Brand Complexity, Clutter, and Confusion.* New York: Free Press.

Cwerner, Saulo, and Alan Metcalfe. 2003. "Storage and Clutter: Discourses and Practices of Order in the Domestic World." *Journal of Design History* 16(3): 229–239.

Frost, Randy O., and Gail Steketee. 2010. *Stuff: Compulsive Hoarding and the Meaning of Things.* Boston, MA: Houghton Mifflin Harcourt.

Lepselter, Susan. 2011. "The Disorder of Things: Hoarding Narratives in the Popular Media." *Anthropological Quarterly* 84(4): 919–947.

Paxton, Matt. 2011. *The Secret Life of Hoarders.* New York: Perigee.

Shi, David E. 1985. *The Simple Life: Plain Living and High Thinking in American Culture.* Athens, GA: University of Georgia Press.

Shove, Elizabeth. 2003. *Comfort, Cleanliness, and Convenience: The Social Organization of Normality.* Oxford: Berg.

Department Stores

KEITH SPILLER
Open University, UK

Department stores were the first all-purpose shops housing extensive ranges of products. Late nineteenth-century department stores were significant in the transition from an economy centered on production to one based on consumption (Lancaster 1995). Prior to the emergence of the department store, the urban milieu was very different – there were numerous small and specialist stores and shopping involved traversing from store to store. Department stores sold mass-produced commodities in bulk and, while they did sell high-end expensive goods, most stores were intent on making a quick and profitable turnover. Alongside their commercial imperative, the stores were also influential in introducing a number of new social protocols, as well as having a lasting effect on the urban landscape. Department stores helped to introduce new sensibilities and ways of shopping to the middle classes, who in turn became the new cultural intermediaries for the emerging cultures of consumption. The stores also helped to cultivate international appeal and notoriety, for example Parisian "chic," New York "sophistication," and Western "modernity."

The first department stores took their inspiration from the nineteenth-century Great Exhibition and World Fairs hosted by cities such as London, New York, and Paris (Laermans 1993). Adopting the presentation techniques promoted at the exhibitions, department stores utilized display cabinets, walkways, decor, and architecture to convey alluring sensations of awe and wonder to their customers. Indeed, coupled with the "everything under one roof" approach (Lewis 1983), stores displayed objects with the added advantage that they were also available for purchase. Paris, recognized as a leading city in the development of the stores, was home to one of the most significant stores of this time, the Bon Marché. Like many of the big nineteenth-century department stores, the Bon Marché began life as a *magasin de nouveautés* – a general store selling dry goods, textiles, and fabrics, which quickly expanded as a result of economic demand. Textile manufacturing had moved to large-scale production and retail outlets were needed to sell the high volume of goods produced. The Bon Marché, under the proprietorship of Aristide Boucicaut, was to the forefront of exhibition-style display and helped to fundamentally change the nature of retailing. In 1867 Boucicaut bought the buildings adjacent to his store and employed architect Louis-Auguste Boileau to design Paris's first purpose-built department store. The store opened in 1872.

Along with other Parisian department stores such as Galeries Lafayette, the Bon Marché's impressive classical stone façade and ability to match its imposing exterior with spectacle, popular appeal, and ultimately sales made it one of the most copied and reproduced department store designs throughout the late nineteenth and early twentieth centuries. The façades of stores – large imposing buildings with ornate crevices and trestles, and gigantic windows – were designed to suggest prominence and status. Indeed, department store windows introduced and fortified the concept of window shopping. Internally, the architecture continued the grandiose theme; modern technologies such as mechanical escalators and lifts carried thousands of consumers between different floors. During the 1890s between 15,000 and 18,000 customers visited the Bon Marché daily. Few, if any, buildings in nineteenth-century Paris could have facilitated the movement of such vast numbers of customers. Other innovations established by the department store include resting areas, libraries, restaurants, and some of the first public toilets – again all modern advances for nineteenth-century consumers. Parisian department stores also promoted consumption as a leisure activity. Much like Walter Benjamin's *flâneur*, consumers walked and admired and, in turn, were happy to be admired – all without an overriding pressure to purchase (Benjamin 1999).

Department stores also had an influence on their immediate social, cultural, and geographical settings. The cosmopolitanism, the reputation, and the standing of cities were often dependent on the presence of a store. If a city had a department store, it was seen to be modern and as a place of fashion or technological innovation. Consumers traveled to department stores from other cities, as well as from surrounding rural areas. In some cases they even traveled internationally, drawn by the attractions and commodities of particular stores (Spiller and Linehan 2006). Indeed, in many cities streets and districts became synonymous with consumption, retail, and fashion, for example Oxford Street in London and Fifth Avenue in New York City. Department stores were magnets in drawing people and businesses to these developing districts of commerce and consumption. A modern sense of self was being offered by the stores through the imagery and desires that were paraded in their windows and their displays.

One identity that received unprecedented attention was the fashionable bourgeois woman. Department stores were deliberate in focusing their attentions on her (Bowlby 1985). As Zola (2006/1883) explicitly illustrates in his descriptions of the Parisian department store, the ambience, architecture, and display all served to tantalize women's senses. During the nineteenth century no self-respecting bourgeois woman would venture into the city without a male chaperon – although the sizable number of bourgeois women working and volunteering in the city at this time is often neglected (Nava 1996). Despite women's relative exclusion from the city, department stores were socially accepted spaces in which they could socialize, congregate, and move freely (Domosh 1996). The cultural significance of the stores was to give rise to new feminized spaces within the city (Barth 1980). Yet, these spaces also posed some new social problems. Suffering from "feminine weakness," women were on occasion found to be incapacitated by kleptomania, a "modern" illness perpetuated by the extensively, if not exclusively, male domain of shop owners, the police, and the judiciary. The argument was that the heightened sense of desire felt by bourgeois women left them unable to withstand temptation. It was a rather convenient diagnosis that helped to disguise the capitalistic bent of a growing consumer culture (Nava 1996). Other novel changes initiated by the department store included the "civilizing" effect whereby all goods were marked with a price, thus eliminating opportunities to haggle or removing any misunderstanding of price (Fredriksson 1997). The ordered sense of the stores was also accentuated by staffed counters, where goods were stored behind counters and viewed only on request. Such forms of display took inspiration from the Great Exhibitions; however, during the twentieth century most counters disappeared in the move to self-selection and with the reduction of staff employed in the stores.

The progression to modernity that was offered by the department store brought about a remarkable shift in society's approach to consumption and the city. Department stores brought much to the urban experience through their notions of spectacle and value and irrevocably changed cityscapes and reputations. The stores also taught consumers new ways to shop and the appreciation of new social etiquettes. However, by the 1960s the stores' influence began to wane as a result of the rise of supermarkets, chain stores, specialist shops, television, and more recently the internet. Nonetheless, department stores do survive in many cities today and, despite their falling cultural significance, their continued presence indicates the popularity and success of this business model, as well as their sustained influence on consumer culture.

SEE ALSO: Benjamin, Walter; Consumer Culture; Consumer Culture, History of; Symbolic Value

REFERENCES

Barth, Gunther. 1980. *City People: The Rise of Modern City Culture in Nineteenth Century America.* Oxford: Oxford University Press.

Benjamin, Walter. 1999. *The Arcades Project.* Translated by Howard Eiland and Kevin McLaughlin. Cambridge, MA: Belknap.

Bowlby, Rachel. 1985. *Just Looking: Consumer Culture in Dreiser, Gissing and Zola.* New York: Methuen.

Domosh, Mona. 1996. "The Feminized Retail Landscape: Gender Ideology and Consumer Culture in Nineteenth Century New York City." In *Retailing, Consumption and Capital: Towards the New Retail Geography*, edited by Neil Wrigley and Michelle Lowe, 257–270. London: Longman.

Fredriksson, Cecilia. 1997. "The Making of a Swedish Department Store Culture." In *The Shopping Experience*, edited by Pasi Falk and Colin Campbell, 111–135. London: Sage.

Laermans, Rudi. 1993. "Learning to Consume: Early Department Stores and the Shaping of the Modern Consumer Culture (1860–1914)." *Theory, Culture & Society* 10: 79–102.

Lancaster, Bill. 1995. *The Department Store.* Leicester, UK: Leicester University Press.

Lewis, Russell. 1983. "'Everything under One Roof': World Fairs and Department Stores in Paris and Chicago." *Chicago History* 12(3): 28–47.

Nava, M. 1996. "Modernity's Disavowal: Women, the City and the Department Store." In *Modern Times: Reflections on a Century of English Modernity*, edited by M. Nava and A. O'Shea, 38–76. London: Routledge.

Spiller, Keith, and Denis Linehan. 2006. "Beacons of Modernity: Department Stores, Modernity and the Urban Experience in Mid-Twentieth Century Ireland." *Irish Geography* 39(2): 143–158.

Zola, Émile. 2006/1883. *Au Bonheur des dames (The Ladies' Delight)*. London: Penguin.

FURTHER READING

Crossick, Geoffrey, and Serge Jaumain. 1999. *Cathedrals of Consumption: The European Department Store, 1850–1939*. Aldershot, UK: Ashgate.

Leach, William. 1984. "Transformations in a Culture of Consumption: Women and Department Stores, 1890–1925." *Journal of American History* 71(2): 319–342.

Proctor, Robert. 2002. "The Department Store in Paris 1855–1914: An Architectural History." PhD thesis, University of Cambridge.

Diderot Effect

JANET A. LORENZEN
Williamette University, USA

Grant McCracken (1986, 1988) argues that when a familiar consumption pattern is disrupted, by a fine gift for example, individuals will seek to establish a new pattern of consumption which conforms to the level of quality and status represented by the gift. McCracken calls this the Diderot effect, named after French philosopher Denis Diderot (1713–84) who wrote an essay entitled "Regrets on Parting with my Old Dressing Gown; or, A Warning to Those who Have More Taste Than Money" (1964/1772). On receiving a new dressing gown as a gift from a friend, Diderot found that it compelled him to redecorate his entire study because the new dressing gown made everything else in the room look old and shabby by comparison. The Diderot effect is thus a mechanism for overconsumption; the attempt to purchase goods which fit together in some subjectively coherent way results in expansive consumer spending and continual trading up. Caught up in this process of the Diderot effect, individuals are also attempting to fulfill their ideal of a good life through the purchase of particular consumer goods.

Establishing a new consumer pattern is an ongoing process enabled by "bridging goods" – or unique objects that connect individuals to their hopes and ideals (McCracken 1986, 1988, 2006). McCracken (1988) describes many different kinds of bridging goods including both commodified and noncommodified objects (e.g., flags) and how they may be used as bridges to past, present, or future ideals. However, his work is primarily employed to explain the ways in which unique or exceptional consumer goods link people to their ideal future. Because individuals cannot achieve their ideals today, they project them into the future, often in the form of consumer goods that they hope to attain. McCracken (1988) refers to this as "displaced meaning." Thus the consumer goods that individuals covet represent and shelter their ideals. If the goods are purchased, they serve as a demonstration of the purchaser's commitment to those ideals; however, ideals are never completely fulfilled and go on to be displaced onto other goods. The Diderot effect can be seen as an attempt to match one's consumption pattern to a particular bridging good which represents the good life. Unfortunately this process never ends, as new bridging goods are identified over time.

SEE ALSO: Conspicuous Consumption; Consumption and Identity

REFERENCES

Diderot, Denis. 1964/1772. *Rameau's Nephew and Other Works*. Indianapolis: Bobbs-Merrill.

McCracken, Grant, 1986. "Culture and Consumption: A Theoretical Account of the Structure and Movement of the Cultural Meaning of

Consumer Goods." *Journal of Consumer Research* 13(1): 71–84.
McCracken, Grant. 1988. *Culture and Consumption: New Approaches to the Symbolic Character of Consumer Goods and Activities*. Bloomington: Indiana University Press.
McCracken, Grant. 2006. "The Evocative Power of Things: Consumer Goods and the Preservation of Hopes and Ideals." In *The Earthscan Reader on Sustainable Consumption*, edited by Tim Jackson, 263–277. New York: Earthscan.

Digital-Mobile Consumption and Marketing

JESSICA CARBINO
University of California–Los Angeles, USA

Technological change spans beyond the introduction of new inventions. With the emergence of new technologies, new industries arise, markets change, and individuals adopt new social norms. The birth of the information age occurred in the late 1970s with the development of computers. The rise of the internet in the late 1990s and ultimate adoption of computer technology by individuals brought the information age into full bloom. The information age, now more commonly referred to as the digital age, represents a shift from a more traditional economy to an economy based upon information transmitted via computer.

The primary adopters of the internet were initially white, male, and highly educated. Today 85 percent of Americans have access to the internet. As with all areas of social life, however, social stratification influences digital consumption. Social stratification scholars have long been concerned about a new form of social inequality emerging: a digital divide. The digital divide represents the gap between those individuals who have limited or no access to the internet and internet users. As a result of unequal access, the digital divide may be particularly problematic because certain groups may not be able to consume information or be exposed to certain opportunities.

Scholars also are concerned about the global nature and implications of the digital divide, including a North–South divide. The North–South divide characterizes unequal technological development in Western nations, such as European countries and the United States (North), relative to developing countries in Africa, Latin America, and some parts of Asia (South). For example, only 15 percent of individuals in Africa have internet access whereas 61 percent of individuals in the Americas have internet access. The causes of the digital divide are complex and can be attributed to physical, infrastructural, financial, and cultural differences across countries. Growth differences in internet access exist as well. For example, Asian countries are experiencing the most rapid growth in mobile phone usage.

Individuals who historically have not had access to the internet or digital media, such as minorities and socioeconomically disadvantaged individuals, are using their smartphones to gain information and access the internet. While race differences in internet access are now largely diminished due to the emergence of the smartphone, many groups still lack internet access. Today the primary negative predictors of internet use are age (being 65 years of age or older), having lower levels of education (less than a high school degree), and low household income (less than US$20,000 per year).

Although smartphones theoretically help to close the digital consumption gap for groups that have historically had limited access to the internet, they are not an ideal solution. Unlike wired internet access, activities that are now primarily performed via the internet that are critical to daily life, such as filing a job application or taking a course online, are far more difficult, if not impossible, to perform on a smartphone.

Researchers suggest that the effects of digital consumption are also far-reaching in terms of economic consequences. In fact, some suggest that a new form of capitalism may be emerging due to digital consumption. In the late 1970s, the term "prosumer" entered the lexicon to describe the behavior between consumers and companies. In a prosumption-based market, consumers create value for companies but do not receive any salary for their labor. At the same time individuals stand to potentially gain through engaging in both production and consumption behavior in an online setting. For example, individuals who sell goods on eBay may be listing their items on the site, monitoring their auctions, and paying a fee, but the individual also has a forum to sell goods that otherwise may never have been sold.

Social relationships are a major part of the consumption and marketing process. While the digital era presents many marketing challenges, companies have a vast wealth of information at their disposal to understand the activities and desires of consumers. The tacit knowledge that companies have access to includes consumer interests, shopping patterns, transactional and payment information, and feedback via reviews and chat rooms. Businesses therefore are better able to target their demographic base of interest. Digital marketing may be preferable for many companies because they are able to analyze in real time whether customers like their products. Companies may also manipulate various campaigns and experiment with different strategies to determine what is most desirable to consumers.

Since the advent of the digital era, power in multiple areas of business has shifted. Marketing is one area of business that has been particularly impacted by changes in digital consumption. Businesses are interested in knowing how they can better reach customers, both through matching with those who are searching for their products and searching for customers who may find their products appealing. Unlike traditional marketing that is focused on the business and its products, digital marketing is based largely on the needs and desires of the customer. "Customerization" is a newer term coined in the area of marketing. With customerization, customers design the product and the business acts as the space or resources by which customers create what they want. Examples of customerization could include individuals designing their own computer on an Apple site or creating a blog on a host like Wordpress.

The two primary forms of digital marketing are pull and push. Pull marketing involves companies providing information to consumers. For instance, when consumers look for a certain item, marketers will have paid for advertisements to present items that match the search request as well as potentially related items. In push marketing, consumers do not seek the information directly and businesses send them information via advertisements. As a result of increased information provided to businesses through consumers' data, online pull strategies may be more effective in the digital era.

Pricing has also largely been affected by digital consumption. Traditionally, companies creating and distributing the products were responsible for setting prices. Customers, however, now control price setting. Customers have the ability to compare prices across a variety of platforms and make more informed choices. Nevertheless, increased knowledge is not the only form of power customers wield. Due to the ability of individuals to share information online with other consumers in chat rooms or reviews, customers are able to exert a great deal of control over prices. The disruptive influence of digital consumption extends to the influence of intermediaries in the marketplace. The influence of intermediaries, such as real estate brokers and car salespeople, is now more limited because of customers' direct access to information.

The digital age is described as a disruptive environment for traditional businesses. According to pundits, the growth of online marketplaces has negatively impacted many traditional retail establishments. While consumers arguably benefit from increased competition and options, traditional retailers may not be able to compete with significantly lower-priced goods available on online sites such as Amazon. For example, major video stores such as Blockbuster have gone out of business due to the rise of Netflix and online video streaming.

With the introduction of the mobile phone, media such as newspapers are also now consumed primarily through digital sources. The effects of digital media consumption are particularly disruptive for media, such as print media, that were already experiencing decreases in their traditional customer base. While many associate the decline in print media consumption primarily with newspapers, other print media, such as magazines, have also experienced a major decline in consumption. Although many have speculated that the decline in print media consumption may largely be associated with a decline in interest in reading generally, the data related to reading suggests that individuals still enjoy reading. Print media may therefore be experiencing a major decline due to the overwhelming use of digital media to access news sources and magazines rather than due to changes in time use preferences.

SEE ALSO: Consumption in Africa; Prosumption

FURTHER READING

Caumont, Andrea. 2013. "Twelve Trends Shaping Digital News." *Pew Research Internet Project.* http://www.pewresearch.org/fact-tank/2013/10/16/12-trends-shaping-digital-news/.

Dijk Van, Jan, and Kenneth Hacker. 2003. "The Digital Divide as Complex and Dynamic Phenomenon." *The Information Society* 19(4): 315–326.

Rainee, Lee. 2013. "The State of Digital Divides." Pew Research Internet Project. http://www.pewinternet.org/2013/11/05/the-state-of-digital-divides-video-slides/.

Ritzer, George, and Nathan Jurgenson. 2010. "Production, Consumption, Prosumption: The Nature of Capitalism in the Age of the Digital 'Prosumer'." *Journal of Consumer Culture* 10(1): 13–36.

Wind, Jerry, and Vijay Mahajan. 2002. *Digital Marketing: Global Strategies from the World's Leading Experts.* New York: Wiley.

Zickuhr, Kathryn. 2013. "Who's Not Online and Why." *Pew Research Internet Project.* http://www.pewinternet.org/2013/09/25/main-report-2/.

Disneyization

J. MICHAEL RYAN
The American University in Cairo, Egypt

Disneyization, a phrase popularized by Alan Bryman (2004), is "the process by which the principles of the Disney theme parks are coming to dominate more and more sectors of American society as well as the rest of the world" (p. 1). Disneyization is composed of four central elements – theming, hybrid consumption, merchandising, and performative labor.

Theming is the coherence lent to a location or institution by the overarching application of a focal narrative. Museums, amusement parks, hotels, towns, and malls are all examples of social locations that have been themed. Although theming has its roots in themed attractions and grand exhibitions such as the world's fairs, it was Disneyland that popularized theming, especially by transforming themed attractions into themed environments and by providing a more permanent site. Theming also works through the principles of adjacent attraction and differentiation to allow those who employ it to compete in the entertainment economy.

Hybrid consumption is "the general trend whereby the forms of consumption associated with different institutional spheres become interlocked with each other and increasingly difficult to distinguish" (Bryman 2004, 57). It serves two general purposes – to create a destination, to entice people to stay longer in a given setting, and consequently to increase their spending. The ideas of hybrid, or de-differentiated, consumption were used long before Disney, most notably with the advent of the supermarket and department store, but once again it was Disney that helped to demonstrate the synergistic consumer opportunities available through hybrid consumption. Numerous examples – casinos, cruise ships, sports stadia, zoos – highlight the growing ubiquity of this practice.

Merchandising is "the promotion of goods in the form of or bearing copyright images and logos, including such products made under license" (Bryman 2004, 79). It is a form of franchising whereby businesses are able to garner further revenue from images and associations that have already attracted the attention, and likely the money, of the consumer. Synergy is key to merchandising such that promoting one entity is usually helpful in promoting others. For example, the inclusion of toys related to the latest blockbuster movie in a child's fast-food meal is likely to increase sales at both the fast-food restaurant and the box office. The movie industry, television networks, and sports teams are all particularly successful at taking advantage of this process.

Performative labor refers to the type of emotional management and theatrical performances that are required of employees, particularly those in the service industry. Such labor can be seen as a form either of surface acting or of deep acting, but both are meant to help differentiate what are likely otherwise largely indistinguishable goods in an increasingly service-oriented society. Performative labor also appeals to the principle of consumer sovereignty whereby businesses must guarantee customer satisfaction in order to ensure their repeat business.

SEE ALSO: Emotions and Consumption; McDonaldization; Theming

REFERENCE

Bryman, Alan. 2004. *The Disneyization of Society*. Thousand Oaks, CA: Sage.

Do-It-Yourself (DIY)

RANDAL DOANE
Oberlin College, USA
JOE RUMBO
Texas State University, USA

The do-it-yourself (DIY) spirit associated with anti-corporatism and alternative music scenes was first articulated in sociological circles in Vance Packard's (1961) celebration of the "do-it-yourself" handyman (p. 76). DIY in general refers to a range of consumer practices in which individuals or groups demonstrate self-reliance in the production (and consumption) of material objects, representations, and cultural events.

The articulation of the DIY and anti-establishment spirit emerged in the late 1960s, and coincided with a shift from DIY material practices to the production, distribution, and consumption of culture. Advocates of lifestyle movements extolled the virtues of naturalness and authenticity, in newsletters and small-batch consumer goods, for an ethically reflexive clientele (Binkley 2007). The DIY spirit was also manifest in the intentional communities of Haight-Ashbury in San Francisco and elsewhere, as well as the Vortex Festival (1970 and 1971), the Rainbow Gathering (established 1972), and more recently the Burning Man Festival (established 1986). On remote sites, festival revelers constructed temporary autonomous spaces to celebrate free love, egalitarianism, cooperation, and altered states of consciousness.

Coincidentally, rock music in the mid-1970s adopted new scales for concerts and heightened artifice and, in turn, produced a DIY backlash in the form of punk rock. In punk, the DIY ethos celebrated the amateur, the interpreter, and the auteur. Punks started their own fanzines, established independent record labels, formed bands, and created a network of venues to pursue the joys of (semi-)popular music. The effects were aesthetic, corporeal, and political: punk revolted against the virtuosity of progressive rock and, counter to the "smile on your brother" demeanor of stoned-out hippies, punks "costumed themselves as post-apocalyptic street urchins with a dystopian outlook fueled by amphetamines" (Roberts and Moore 2009, 22–23). DIY punks celebrated their autonomy, industriousness, and a life relatively free of corporate influence.

The DIY ethos held sway in other musical genres too. In its commercial ascent from the 1970s through the 1990s, rap music and hip-hop culture engaged similar questions about authenticity, self-representation, and entrepreneurship (Negus 2004) – see, for example, the FUBU (For Us By Us) clothing line. In addition, the rave scene adopted the DIY ethos of rap "composition" (that is, putting together) of found materials in novel aesthetic forms for collective celebration.

With respect to material consumption, the DIY ethos has contemporary resonance in buy-local and eat-local movements, urban garden associations, and "time dollar" economic systems. Through these DIY arrangements, consumers pursue healthier diets, self-discovery, and a heightened sense of community (Schor 2011). Whether such consumer reflexivity can morph into a larger social movement remains to be seen.

SEE ALSO: Authenticity; Burning Man; Consumer Movements, Contemporary; Ethical Consumption; Lifestyle; Mass Culture; Music and Consumer Experience

REFERENCES

Binkley, Sam. 2007. *Getting Loose: Lifestyle Consumption in the 1970s*. Durham, NC: Duke University Press.

Negus, Keith. 2004. "The Business of Rap." In *That's the Joint! The Hip-Hop Studies Reader*, edited by Murray Forman and Mark Anthony Neal, 607–625. New York: Routledge.

Packard, Vance. 1961. *Status Seekers*. New York: Vintage.

Roberts, Michael, and Ryan Moore. 2009. "Peace Punks and Punks against Racism: Resource Mobilization and Frame Construction in the Punk Movement." *Music and Arts in Action* 2(1): 21–36.

Schor, Juliet. 2011. *True Wealth: How and Why Millions of Americans Are Creating a Time-Rich, Ecologically Light, Small-Scale, High-Satisfaction Economy*. New York: Penguin.

Downshifting

JÖRGEN LARSSON
Chalmers University of Technology, Sweden

The concept of downshifting spread in the United States during the 1990s, starting with

Amy Saltzman's book *Down-Shifting: Reinventing Success on a Slower Track* (1991). The main idea is to focus less on paid work and to cut out unnecessary expenditures, in order to have time to do more of the things one wants to do. Ideas about an ascetic or simple life are well known in most major religions, as well as in literature. One example is Henry David Thoreau's *Walden* (1855), which describes a simple life in the forest far removed from urban stress, and which is still popular today. Downshifting is a form of voluntary simplicity – a term which was introduced in the 1930s by one of Mahatma Gandhi's followers and which became widespread after Duane Elgin used it in the title of his 1981 book, *Voluntary Simplicity: Toward a Way of Life That Is Outwardly Simple, Inwardly Rich*.

Shaw and Newholm (2002) make a distinction between two types of voluntary simplifiers: downshifters and ethical simplifiers. Downshifters are motivated mainly by self-centered reasons, usually the aim to improve their quality of life. Ethical simplifiers are motivated mainly by environmental and/or social concerns. A quite different group are the involuntary simplifiers, a category which has also become more common in many OECD countries as a result of financial crises.

Downshifting can be defined as a long-term strategy to improve the quality of one's life, involving significantly less income or consumption in relation to one's potential level. The lifestyle of the downshifter can be very frugal and yet remain mainstream. The key point is that income and consumption levels are significantly lower in comparison to an individual's potential level, typically the level he or she had before downshifting. Common practical changes that lead to lower incomes include working part-time in order to gain more leisure time; departing from a managerial position; leaving a city for a lower-paid job in the countryside; changing to a lower-paid but more meaningful job; or becoming self-employed in order to gain greater autonomy.

The concept of downshifting has gained importance in a context of long working hours and frequent overtime work. Reports of stress, time pressure, consumerism, the rat race, and problems of maintaining a balance between work and personal life are commonly aired in the popular media. Downshifting can be viewed as a reaction to our work-oriented consumer culture; it is a term that captures the dream of a lifestyle with more leisure time and a better work–life balance (Schor 1998). Surveys on work hour preferences reveal a widespread wish for shorter hours even when this means a cut in pay. Those who have taken this step appear to have improved their lives; in one study 87 percent of simplifiers report being happier compared to before they downshifted (Alexander and Ussher 2012).

However, implementing downshifting on one's own, without the backing of family and friends or of supporting societal structures, is fraught with major difficulties. One difficulty is that many workplaces are organized around full-time work schedules which do not allow cuts in working hours. Another difficulty is that work and consumption are central to shaping our identities, both through being a professional in a certain field of work and through the consumption possibilities that one's salary allows.

Because of the many different difficulties or obstacles, downshifting is not a possibility for everyone. Rather, it is a private adaptation in the absence of a general solution. However, if a sufficient number of pioneers can overcome these obstacles, it might change the norms that currently determine work and consumption which would make it easier for others aspiring to downshift. Some countries have introduced a right to reduce work hours along with a cut in pay. This is usually mainly for parents with preschool children, but in the Netherlands all employees have the right to request to work part-time (Moss 2012).

SEE ALSO: Anti-Consumption Tactics; Burning Man; Conspicuous Consumption; Consumer Society; Do-It-Yourself (DIY)

REFERENCES

Alexander, Samuel, and Simon Ussher. 2012. "The Voluntary Simplicity Movement: A Multi-National Survey Analysis in Theoretical Context." *Journal of Consumer Culture* 12(1): 66–86.

Elgin, Duane. 1981. *Voluntary Simplicity: Toward a Way of Life That Is Outwardly Simple, Inwardly Rich*. New York: Quill.

Moss, Peter, ed. 2012. *International Review of Leave Policies and Related Research 2012*. Accessed June 25, 2014. http://www.leavenetwork.org/fileadmin/Leavenetwork/Annual_reviews/2012_annual_review.pdf.

Saltzman, Amy. 1991. *Downshifting: Reinventing Success on a Slower Track*. New York: HarperCollins.

Schor, Juliet B. 1998. *The Overspent American: Why We Want What We Don't Need*. New York: Basic Books.

Shaw, Dierdre, and Terry Newholm. 2002. "Voluntary Simplicity and the Ethics of Consumption." *Psychology & Marketing* 19(2): 167–185.

Dumpster Diving: *SEE*

ANTI-CONSUMPTION TACTICS

E

eBay

NEWMAN CHUN WAI WONG
Midwestern State University, USA

eBay (ebay.com) is an international online auction platform with a headquarters in San José, California. In 1995 the founder of eBay, Pierre Omidyar, listed a broken laser pointer as a test on his personal auction website, but got an actual offer, and as the traffic to his website increased, Omidyar saw the potential of developing eBay into an enterprise. The original name of eBay was AuctionWeb, and was later changed to eBay representing Omidyar's consulting firm, Echo Bay. eBay has expanded globally since 2008. In addition to the United States and Canada, eBay offers localized sites in Europe and Asia Pacific, including the United Kingdom, France, Germany, Italy, Australia, Hong Kong, India, and New Zealand. Over the years, eBay has developed from a start-up company in the dot-com bubble to become the world's largest virtual marketplace.

eBay does not have a physical store or sell any tangible products, but provides a virtual platform on which individuals and businesses buy and sell a wide range of products and services. It is free to register as an eBay member and purchase goods on eBay. eBay charges sellers a small amount to list items, and a percentage of sales when an item is sold. In addition to the traditional auction listing, sellers may list items at a fixed price (Buy It Now) or for bargaining (Buy It Now or Best Offer). eBay's feedback system allows buyers and sellers to rate their experience with each other as "positive," "neutral," or "negative," and leave a brief comment. Some popular listing categories on eBay include collectables, jewelry, motors, music, sports, technology, and toys. Nearly anything can be listed on eBay, as long as it is not on the list of prohibited or restricted items, such as tobacco, alcohol, drugs, firearms, and gambling items. Examples of services listed on eBay are custom logo design, remote computer repair, and home improvement services.

eBay is a socially responsible company. It promotes sustainable consumption by facilitating the exchange of previously owned goods, and much of this used merchandise would otherwise go into landfill or recycling. eBay has also introduced various environmental initiatives. For instance, eBay's campus in San José installed enough solar panels to supply 18 percent of its power needs, and it provides shuttles between San Francisco and the San José campus to get more vehicles off the road. eBay also acquired

The Wiley Blackwell Encyclopedia of Consumption and Consumer Studies, First Edition.
Edited by Daniel Thomas Cook and J. Michael Ryan.

and partnered with WorldofGood.com to develop a fair trade platform for handcrafted products from cooperatives and nonprofit organizations in developing countries. Other social enterprises of eBay include MicroPlace, a global microfinance platform, and eBay Foundation. The eBay empire also includes PayPal, StubHub, and Half.com.

SEE ALSO: Globalization and Consumption; Green Consumption; Internet, The, and Consumption; Shopping

FURTHER READING

Denegri-Knott, Janice, and Mike Molesworth. 2010. "Love It. Buy It. Sell It.': Consumer Desire and the Social Drama of eBay." *Journal of Consumer Culture* 10: 56–79. doi: 10.1177/1469540509355025.

Hasker, Kevin, and Robin Sickles. 2010. "eBay in the Economic Literature: Analysis of an Auction Marketplace." *Review of Industrial Organization* 37: 3–42. doi: 10.1007/s11151-010-9257-5.

Economy, Informal

OCTAVIO MEDINA
The World Bank, USA

Whether a firm enters informality is often a result of the benefits and costs it derives from doing so. Both becoming and remaining formal entail a series of costs, which could also be seen as the benefits of informality. Registering a firm, paying the license fees, and generally going through the procedures required to open a business might deter individuals from doing so, and constitute entry costs. Labor regulations and taxes, on the other hand, are the costs of remaining formal. Naturally, informality also has its costs, namely the possibility of being caught by the relevant authorities, and the lack of access to the goods provided by the state. Penalties for firms and workers operating informally can be stiff, ranging from monetary fines to closure. In addition, an informal firm cannot use government services and institutions such as the police or the judicial system to protect its activities. This has a significant effect on property rights, since informal firms will lack the ability to enforce contracts judicially, therefore increasing the risk for the firm. Both as a result of this increased risk and of their inability to enter legal agreements, informal firms usually have more limited access to capital markets and financing.

Although informal economies by definition do not follow the laws and regulations established by the relevant political authority, they are far from being lawless. Informal rules, often based on custom or tacit agreement, set the framework for the exchange of goods and services. Arbitration and enforcement of these rules need not be absent, either. As Sudhir Alladi Venkatesh says in *Off the Books* (2008), neutral third-party arbitrators often play the role of judges, and para-institutions created and controlled by local actors (for instance, gang leaders or bosses) serve as de facto justice systems. Whereas the former require the mutual trust of all parties in the transaction, the latter can be imposed by force.

Whereas every activity in an informal economy involves breaking laws, it is relevant to separate those activities into two groups: illicit and licit. The latter involves any activity that is legal, such as fixing a car or providing cleaning services, but is carried out absent of compliance with the law (for example, by not paying sales taxes). The former, on the other hand, involves activities that are illegal and thus *must* be carried out informally; prostitution or the selling of drugs belong in this group. The borders between licit and illicit informality, and between these and formality, can be rather fluid. Individuals with a formal job may engage in informal activities that would otherwise not be profitable in order to supplement their wages, for example.

The traditional view of the informal labor market rests on the idea of duality, present along several levels. On the one hand, it is the dichotomy between large, capital-intensive firms and small firms that utilize relatively more labor. On the other, it is the contraposition between workers with high levels of human capital and low-skilled laborers, which naturally leads to the competing worlds of salaried workers in well-paid jobs and underemployed individuals working for subsistence.

Firms must face the decision of either complying with all laws and regulations, facing higher wages and lower capital costs, or choosing to enter the informal sector and face the inverse. Workers who choose to stay in the formal labor market compete for a supply of jobs that is below optimal, and the rest face unemployment or informal employment, very often at salaries below the minimum wage. The empirical evidence we have suggests that for similarly skilled workers working in the formal or the informal sector, the differences in wages can be quite high (Fields 1990, in Loayza 1994).

Fields divides the constraints to formality into two separate types: institutional and market. The former are created by the political system, whereas the latter are a result of the behavior of workers and firms. Minimum wage laws, high firing costs, and social security contributions are all institutional reasons. On the other hand, wage differentials could also appear due to market reasons. For instance, firms might choose to increase workers' salaries by a certain percentage if they expect the workers' productivity to increase by more than that.

For most of history, and especially since the end of the industrial revolution, economic growth has been accompanied by a growing rate of urbanization. This phenomenon accelerated in the twentieth century, during which most of the world's societies made the transition from predominantly rural to urban. The migration patterns and massive shifts in labor from countryside to cities were the inspiration for the first explanations of the informal sector. The tone of these, mostly written during the 1950s and 1960s, was intrinsically related to the idea of an excess supply of labor in urban environments, or an industrial reserve army. Given the lack of salaried job opportunities in cities, migrants from the countryside had to resort to self-employment and other poorly paying jobs that left them effectively marginalized. Whereas the concept of marginalization was mainly applied to the developing world, and especially Latin America (Peattie 1987), similar ideas existed in the advanced economies.

Often, however, predictions turned out to be worse than reality. The idea of a static supply of city jobs that would never be able to match the mass of migrants gave way to a reality where these marginalized workers adapted to and became part of the urban economy. Instead of the anticipated revolutions and riots, there were shantytowns and subsistence.

This gradual evolution toward a large and permanent informal sector in many cities of the developing world allowed for a change in paradigms and the appearance of new conceptualizations. British anthropologist Keith Hart was the first to use the term "informality" as way to describe the situation he observed in many African urban economies. As quoted by Peattie (1987), Hart asked in 1973 whether "the 'reserve arm of urban unemployed and underemployed' really constitute a passive, exploited majority in cities like Accra, or do their informal economic activities possess some autonomous capacity for generating growth in the incomes of the urban (and rural) poor?" Hart's siding with the latter option paved the way for a new conception of the informal economy as something more akin to "popular entrepreneurship in which lack of capital resources (is) compensated by the ingenuity and motivation of the people involved," as explained by Portes and Schauffler (1993). Thus, it was through the creation of small informal firms that the large masses of the urban poor were able to subsist. The popularity of the informal sector concept in academic and policy circles was boosted by the ILO (International Labour Organization) missions to Kenya, and later on Colombia, which adapted Hart's terminology to define informality as a "way of doing things," involving features such as "ease of access," "small scale operation," or "labor intensive" nature. The ILO effectively left the door open for the debate on whether informality was a "stopgap for welfare or a seedbed for capitalism."

The regional employment research program of the ILO in Latin America (PREALC in its Spanish acronym) further adapted these ideas and proposed a definition of informality based on the *object* of economic activity. Whereas for regular, formal firms the target was to make a profit and accumulate money, the goal of the informal firm is to provide enough income for the subsistence of the owner and his or her immediate family or social circle. Hart's "popular entrepreneurship" gives way to the idea that informality is a simple, rational decision in order to guarantee survival.

ALTERNATIVE VIEWS

Structural articulation: Informality as an integral part of the system

Structural articulation is a theory born as an answer to the excessive focus on marginality of the traditional view and optimistic descriptions of the informal entrepreneur. It sees the informal and formal labor markets less as opposites and more as complementary sides of the same coin, although not necessarily in a positive fashion. Structuralists link the formal–informal dichotomy to traditional themes of Marxist political and economic thought, such as whether some modes of production are the dominant ones or how different classes compete. The school focuses on the dense relationships and interdependencies between the informal and formal economies, often reaching the conclusion that they are effectively one, for they need one another in order to exist.

Under this approach, formal sector firms benefit from the existence of informality, because the informal sector supplies a whole array of cheap goods and services that are key to the survival and functioning of formal firms and workers, thus providing a large implicit subsidy to the formal sector. This allows formal firms to pay wages that fall below the cost of basic needs and increase profit margins. The relationship between informality and formality is thus exploitative. As Peattie (1987) puts it, informal firms that seem to carry out activities that differ on many levels from those of the formal sector "may be in actual function simply the disreputable and less-visible production end of the established firms." Far from playing a marginal role, in this view informal labor is embedded into the system itself. Formal firms play into it too, by hiding the practice of subcontracting unregulated services and hiring informal workers from the books.

Mercantilism: Informality as a result of state coercion

Whereas traditional theories generally speak of informality as being a result of structural trends, the following points to the main culprit: the state. Popularized by Peruvian economist Hernando de Soto in his book *The Other Path* (1989), this strand of theory – mainly based on the Latin American experience – contends that informality is a result of the mercantilistic behavior of the state. As Portes and Schauffler (1993) put it, "the state survives by granting the privilege of legal participation in the economy to a narrow elite. Informality is the popular response that successfully breaks down this legal barrier." In this sense, informality becomes the real economy, the rational response of individuals who refuse to cooperate with excessive government regulation. Informal workers are no longer a marginalized underclass, but rather a group of small entrepreneurs who defy the restrictive policies of the state. While de Soto acknowledges the role of mass migration from rural to urban areas, he blames regulation as the main constraint for integrating the urban informal sector.

In a sense, de Soto brings back Hart's visualization of the informal sector as a dynamic world of entrepreneurs, but adding the clear contraposition to the oppressive power of governments and regulation. The main difference lies in that, whereas Hart, and later PREALC, described informal sector activity as labor intensive, and low in capital, productivity, and value added, de Soto sees the informal worker as an "economic hero who manages to survive and even prosper despite state oppression."

SEE ALSO: Counterfeiting/Piracy; Global Markets

REFERENCES

Fields, Gary S. 1990. "Labour Market Modelling and the Urban Informal Sector: Theory and Evidence." works.bepress.com.

Loayza, Norman V. 1994. *Labor Regulations and the Informal Economy*. Washington, DC: World Bank.

Peattie, Lisa. 1987. "An Idea in Good Currency and How It Grew: The Informal Sector." *World Development* 15(7): 851–860.

Portes, Alejandro, and Richard Schauffler. 1993. "Competing Perspectives on the Latin American Informal Sector." *Population and Development Review* 19(1): 33.

Soto, Hernando de, and Peru Instituto Libertad y Democracia Lima. 1989. *The Other Path: The Invisible Revolution in the Third World*. New York: Harper & Row.

Venkatesh, Sudhir Alladi. 2008. *Off the Books: The Underground Economy of the Urban Poor*. Cambridge, MA: Harvard University Press.

Ecotourism

RICHARD SHARPLEY
University of Central Lancashire, UK

The term "ecotourism" defies precise definition. Indeed, since it was popularized by Hector Cellabos-Lascuráin in the early 1980s (Sharpley 2006), such has been the variety of tourism activities, experiences, and products to which it has been applied that it has become almost meaningless. Nevertheless, definitions of ecotourism abound. Fennell (2013), for example, describes it simply as "a type of tourism based on an interest in the natural history attractions of a destination" (p. 323). In so doing, he not only acknowledges the breadth of the concept, but also confirms, as Cellabos-Lascuráin first proposed, that it is primarily a nature-based form of tourism consumption. However, this definition is problematic. Not only does it fail to distinguish between ecotourism and other forms of tourism, such as nature, wildlife, adventure, or rural tourism, which are to a greater or lesser extent dependent on the consumption of the natural environment, but it also fails to acknowledge two distinctive perspectives on ecotourism.

On the one hand, many definitions emphasize the role of the tourist in ecotourism consumption. Thus, ecotourism is considered to be "*responsible travel* to natural areas which conserves the environment and improves the welfare of local people" (International Ecotourism Society 2012; emphasis added), although it is recognized that ecotourists vary in their motivations, values, and sense of responsibility. Weaver (2005), for example, distinguishes between "hard" and "soft" ecotourists, or those who are highly committed to sustainability and seek challenging, prolonged interactions with nature compared to those who seek briefer, service-intensive experiences. On the other hand, a supply perspective reveals the roots of ecotourism in the alternative tourism school, regarding it as a solution to the environmental, economic, and social problems commonly associated with more traditional mass forms of tourism development. Consequently, ecotourism is defined by a number of development-related objectives, including minimizing local environmental and sociocultural impacts; promoting and supporting environmental and cultural conservation; enhancing environmental awareness among both visitors and local communities; generating income for local people; and engaging and empowering local people in tourism development and management (see Honey 2008).

Taking these two perspectives together, ecotourism can be broadly considered as a form of low-impact (responsible or "non-consumptive") tourism based on the natural environment which seeks to promote environmental awareness and local sustainable development. Whether these characteristics are reflected in practice, however, remains debatable. Not only is the prefix "eco" attached to innumerable tourism products, places, and experiences that vary significantly in their environmental credentials, from projects based on sound social and environmental objectives to holidays that simply occur in natural areas, to the extent that it has become a relatively meaningless, overused label. A number of specific criticisms may also be leveled at the concept of ecotourism that challenge its fundamental principles.

First and foremost, as with all services, tourism experiences are created at the point of consumption; the nature of the experience is therefore determined by the manner of its consumption. Thus, the production of "true" ecotourism experiences is largely dependent on the existence of the "ecotourist." However, despite rapid growth in the demand for experiences marketed as ecotourism and surveys that point to increasing environmental consciousness on the part of tourists, there is little evidence to suggest that those participating are motivated by strong environmental values or a sense of environmental responsibility. Typically, ecotourism is consumed for more egocentric reasons, such as enjoyment of nature or the wilderness or escape from modern life, while stated preferences for eco-friendly holidays are rarely manifested in practice (Sharpley 2006). In other words, many of those who consume so-called ecotourism experiences may not legitimately be described as ecotourists.

Second, and reflecting a criticism of tourism development more generally, many commentators point to the consumptive nature of ecotourism. Inevitably, the development and consumption of tourism utilize often fragile or scarce resources while ecotourism in particular, promoted as a sustainable approach to tourism, is susceptible to the inherent ambiguity and contradictions of the concept of sustainable development, to which it is explicitly linked. More specifically, it is suggested that ecotourism is a Western construct: "because the origins of ecotourism lie in Western ideology and values, and its practice is frequently dominated by Western interests, the advocacy of ecotourism as a universal template arise from Western hegemony" (Cater 2006, 24). Consequently, ecotourism is seen as a form of ecocolonialism in which nature and local culture are commodified, packaged, and sold to tourists seeking alternative or authentic experiences. Not only may natural areas be transformed from either wilderness or life sustaining resources into a marketable commodity with exchange value, but local communities, far from being empowered, may also become a commodity that is viewed and consumed by tourists.

Third, and related, ecotourism is often accused of being an explicit form of "greenwashing," that is, resorts, accommodation providers, or tourism companies may adopt the "eco" label in order to attract more visitors, yet not engage in sound environmental practices. This is not uncommon. Surveys consistently show that, in general, the great majority of products marketed as "green" do not reflect this description, hence the criticism by many that ecotourism is just a marketing label. Nevertheless, a number of accreditation schemes exist that, acknowledging sound environmental credentials, go some way to addressing the "greenwashing" phenomenon. Moreover, despite these criticisms, not only is ecotourism one of the fastest growing sectors of tourism but there is also no doubt that "true" ecotourism experiences, at least at the destination level, may be found.

SEE ALSO: Commodification; Consumer Culture; Ethical Consumption; Markets, Moral Aspects of; Tourism

REFERENCES

Cater, Erlet. 2006. "Ecotourism as a Western Construct." *Journal of Ecotourism* 5(1–2): 23–39.

Fennell, David A. 2013. "Ecotourism." In *The Routledge Handbook of Tourism and the Environment*, edited by Andrew Holden and David A. Fennell. Abingdon, UK: Routledge.

Honey, Martha. 2008. *Ecotourism and Sustainable Development: Who Owns Paradise?* 2nd ed. Washington, DC: Island.

International Ecotourism Society. 2012. "What Is Ecotourism?" Accessed June 25, 2014. http://www.ecotourism.org/what-is-ecotourism.

Sharpley, Richard. 2006. "Ecotourism: A Consumption Perspective." *Journal of Ecotourism* 5(1–2): 7–22.

Weaver, David B. 2005. "Comprehensive and Minimalist Dimensions of Ecotourism." *Annals of Tourism Research* 32(2): 439–455.

Education and Consumption

JÖRG RÖSSEL
University of Zurich, Switzerland

Education can be defined as the learning of general basic skills (reading, writing), specific instrumental skills (accounting, techniques of a certain craft), factual knowledge, and finally socialization into values, norms, and social behavior based on teaching. Furthermore, in contemporary societies education also includes the certificates issued by educational organizations.

With regard to consumption, education is important in mainly two respects. First, consumer education means the teaching of the different skills, knowledge, and norms which are important for achieving a consumer's goals. These goals range from being able to utilize a certain appliance like a washing machine, to attaining particular health standards, to sustainable consumption. Different actors, like state agencies, companies, schools, consumerist organizations, and other social movements, are involved in consumer education.

The second aspect is the empirical and theoretical relationship between certain measures of education (e.g., years of schooling) and different forms of consumption. On the one hand, there is research on education and its impact on general orientations, for example the assumption that those with a higher education have a stronger future orientation and a greater ability to defer gratification. This thesis is often cited in the literature; nevertheless, the empirical evidence overall does not support it (Wood 1998). On the other hand, this discussion is especially prominent in specific fields of consumption, like food and healthy lifestyles, culture and the arts, as well as ethical and political consumption, where most empirical research on the relationship between education and consumption is undertaken and theoretical explanations of this relationship are put forward. The discussion in these three fields will therefore be presented in the remainder of this entry.

FOOD AND HEALTHY LIFESTYLES

In the field of food and healthy lifestyles, there is an enormous amount of literature dealing with the relationship between education and consumption. Education is often taken as an exchangeable indicator of socioeconomic position. However, in some studies the effects of class, occupation, income, and education are separated. It turns out that education, which is rather stable over a lifetime, is usually the best socioeconomic predictor of nutritional behavior. In the majority of studies the focus is on the determinants of healthy food consumption, which has a clear impact on obesity, morbidity, and mortality. In this field there are several well-established empirical generalizations on the impact of education: persons with higher education and their children tend to consume less fat and sugar; to drink alcohol moderately; to eat more fruits, vegetables, and dietary fiber; and to have a broader knowledge about food. There is also some evidence that higher-educated persons have a higher probability of being vegetarian or at least of eating less meat. This research is usually very empirical in its orientation. There are two main explanations for the relationship between education and healthy food consumption: first, education enhances food knowledge, which tends to lead to healthier lifestyles (Wardle, Parmenter, and Waller 2000); and, second, education shapes motivations toward food consumption, for example decreasing the importance of sensory appeal (Steptoe and Wardle 1999).

In contrast to this focus on health, many areas of food consumption and the importance of education therein remain relatively unexplored, so only one exemplary study is mentioned here. In a fascinating study on eating out, Warde and Martens (2000) show that persons with higher education tend to eat out much more frequently than others (with friends and kin and at commercial places). Furthermore, they tend to frequent a greater variety of restaurants and are especially open to diverse ethnic cuisines. This study shows that food consumption is not only about health, but also about aesthetics and taste.

CULTURE AND THE ARTS

Consumption of artistic goods and services, which are defined by their primarily aesthetic orientation, is often subsumed under the label of cultural consumption. An established result in this field of research is the fact that higher-educated persons are strongly overrepresented among the audiences of artistic fields which are deemed highbrow, like art museums, classical music, and opera. Recent research has accumulated evidence for different countries which shows that they are not only overrepresented among audiences in highbrow fields, but also tend to be active in nearly all other areas of cultural consumption, apart from TV and radio. This is also true for taste patterns. In particular,

Richard Peterson has put forward the idea that those with a high class position and high education tend not to be highbrow snobs, who despise everything but highbrow culture, but cultural omnivores, exhibiting a broad taste range beyond highbrow genres (Peterson and Kern 1996). This pattern was empirically demonstrated for several countries, but there tend to be counter-examples like Germany or Finland. Finally, empirical research has even shown educational differences with regard to the mode of consumption: higher-educated persons tend to consume highbrow culture with a stronger analytical orientation and derive more emotional satisfaction from consuming it (Rössel 2011); they also have a more formal and reflexive orientation toward cultural consumption.

The explanations for the specific tastes and consumption practices of persons with higher education focus on two mechanisms. First, it is assumed that education is one source of skills and knowledge (cultural capital), which enable consumers to enjoy complex works that are rich in references (Bourdieu 1984). Second, education may be a predictor of cultural tastes and participation because they are a signal of social status.

ETHICAL AND POLITICAL CONSUMPTION

Ethical consumption is defined by its adherence to certain principles like sustainability, social justice, or religious orientations. Political consumption attempts to influence powerful actors by buycotting or boycotting certain goods and services. There is clear evidence that persons with higher education participate more strongly than other groups in such forms of consumption (Koos 2012). Therefore, some authors argue that this is a behavior which empowers higher-class persons and endows them with an ethically legitimated form of distinction. The main explanations of the educational gap refer, on the one hand, to the knowledge and skills linked to education that are necessary for grasping social and political issues and, on the other hand, to the institutions in which civic skills are practiced and which are often linked to education, like educational institutions and workplaces.

Despite the voluminous literature discussing the relationship between education and consumption, there are still important desiderata for future research: first, the extension of this discussion to further fields, like food consumption apart from healthy food; second, the analysis of the changing impact of education and other indicators of socioeconomic status on consumption; and, finally, the precise clarification and empirical testing of the causal mechanisms linking education and other indicators of socioeconomic status with different forms of consumption.

SEE ALSO: Bourdieu, Pierre; Boycotts; Class; Conspicuous Consumption; Cultural Capital; Cultural Omnivores; Ethical Consumption; Food; Lifestyle

REFERENCES

Bourdieu, Pierre. 1984. *Distinction: A Social Critique of the Judgement of Taste*. Cambridge, MA: Harvard University Press.

Koos, Sebastian. 2012. "What Drives Political Consumption in Europe? A Multi-Level Analysis of Individual Characteristics, Opportunity Structures and Globalization." *Acta Sociologica* 55: 37–57.

Peterson, Richard A., and Roger M. Kern. 1996. "Changing Highbrow Taste: From Snob to Omnivore." *American Sociological Review* 61: 900–907.

Rössel, Jörg. 2011. "Cultural Capital and the Variety of Modes of Consumption in the Opera Audience." *Sociological Quarterly* 52: 83–103.

Steptoe, Andrew, and Jane Wardle. 1999. "Motivational Factors as Mediators of Socioeconomic Variations in Dietary Intake Patterns." *Psychology and Health* 14: 391–402.

Warde, Alan, and Lydia Martens. 2000. *Eating Out: Social Differentiation, Consumption and Pleasure*. Cambridge, UK: Cambridge University Press.

Wardle, Jane, Kate Parmenter, and Jo Waller. 2000. "Nutrition Knowledge and Food Intake." *Appetite* 34: 269–275.

Wood, Michael. 1998. "Socio-Economic Status, Delay of Gratification, and Impulse Buying." *Journal of Economic Psychology* 19: 295–320.

Edutainment

PATRICK COX
Rutgers University, USA

The term "edutainment" encompasses a category of consumer products designed for children and intended to be educational and entertaining at the same time. Though educational materials can also be entertaining in formal school settings, the category of edutainment is primarily applied to products sold to parents for use in the home. There are a range of consumer products that fall into the broad category, including computer games, magazines, books, toys, as well as media products such as television shows and audio recordings. As the category appeals to parents' desires to advance their children's intellect at an earlier age, edutainment is as much a marketing conceit as a classification of actual products.

It is useful to consider edutainment not simply as specific products designed for children for educational purposes but as an approach to childrearing and childhood itself. This entails, on the one hand, an extension of education as something that takes place beyond the walls of formal schooling into homes, daycare centers, parks, and television sets: any place where children engage with consumer products. This suggests an increase in the importance given to learning in Western society as well as a diminishment of the value of play without something to redeem it: places and products intended for "just play" are decreasing or are being filled with products designed to instruct and be played with simultaneously. On the other hand, edutainment entails a conception of childhood as a time when play permeates times and spaces formerly preserved for formal education. In this regard, edutainment marks a significant divergence from older models of education and childrearing toward a view of children needing to be entertained and happy. Just as edutainment implies a need for children to advance intellectually at an earlier age, it also preserves the idea that playfulness is a necessary part of development in the childhood years. Edutainment products, then, reflect both parents' competitive drive for children to succeed through earlier and more frequent education, as well as a contradictory wish to preserve play as part of a carefree childhood not driven by adult ideals of advancement.

Learning through play is not an entirely new concept. Many late nineteenth- and early twentieth-century developmental psychologists, most notably Lev Vygotsky and Jean Piaget, believed that learning took place through play, and Friedrich Fröbel operationalized the idea in his creation of the first kindergarten. The twentieth and twenty-first centuries saw the rise of the child consumer and of digital culture which have both contributed to the increased prominence of the edutainment category of products. Many toys are now marketed at children as strictly "fun" while the same advertisements contain messages to parents that the toys are in some way "good" for children. Digital culture has allowed for the creation of educational websites and online games. These digital forms of edutainment have contributed significantly to gamification which, by inserting gaming elements into previously nongaming realms, is strongly linked to edutainment.

SEE ALSO: Children's Consumer Culture; Education and Consumption

FURTHER READING

Buckingham, David. 2007. *Beyond Technology: Children's Learning in the Age of Digital Culture*. Cambridge, UK: Polity.

Buckingham, David. 2007. "That's Edutainment! New Media, Marketing and Education in the Home." In *Children, Media, and Consumption: On the Front Edge*, edited by K. M. Eckström and B. Tufte, 33–45. Gothenburg: Nordicom, Göteborgs Universitet.

Piaget, Jean. 1976. "Mastery Play." In *Play: Its Role in Development and Evolution*, edited by Jerome Bruner. New York: Basic Books.

Vygotsky, Lev S. 1976. "Play and Its Role in the Mental Development of the Child." In *Play: Its Role in Development and Evolution*, edited by Jerome Bruner. New York: Basic Books.

Elias, Norbert

PADDY DOLAN
Dublin Institute of Technology, Ireland

Norbert Elias (1897–1990) was born into a Jewish middle-class family in Germany, where he initially trained in philosophy before making a deliberate move toward sociology. Elias fled Germany in the 1930s and wrote *The Civilizing Process* (recently published as *On the Process of Civilisation*) in London; it was eventually published in 1939 (Mennell 1998). His other significant work in the context of consumer culture includes *The Court Society* (2006), and *Quest for Excitement* (2008) written with Eric Dunning. His work synthesized concepts developed by earlier social thinkers such as Freud, Veblen, Simmel, Durkheim, Weber, and Mannheim, among others (Kilminster 2007).

Elias's theories stress connections between people across space and time. He examines civilizing processes (Elias 2012) in a technical, rather than normative, sense from the Middle Ages up to the nineteenth century, using successive editions of etiquette texts as his main source of data. He argues that over this long time period new standards of civilized conduct developed in an unplanned but structured way. Competition between aristocratic houses in France led to an eventual monopoly of the means of violence and taxation by a single royal house. Kings remained anxious about their control of territory and the degree of loyalty from other nobles. This led to the "courtization" and pacification of knights, who were increasingly obliged to attend the king's court and compete for his favors in displays of status competition. This cultural change included an emphasis on more refined conduct at table. Consumption practices, especially but not only in relation to eating, demanded greater self-control of emotions, and advancing thresholds of shame regarding any transgressions of the developing codes. Through mutual observation at court, a social constraint toward self-restraint occurred. These changes were propelled partly by a "pressure from below" as the various social classes became more interdependent with urbanization and the growth in trade.

The refinement and elaboration of consumption rituals were in response to both rising middle classes from below and status competition between members of the nobility. The court model of conduct eventually became a style to be emulated by other groups, though the degree of emulation or resistance depended on the integration of the social classes as power chances changed at particular historical moments. In many ways, Elias prefigures Bourdieu in that he uses concepts of distinction and habitus relationally. As more and more people became more interdependent for the fulfillment of needs and functions (themselves socially generated), the figuration (fluid network of mutually dependent people) became denser and longer, so that people had to observe and steer their own conduct to a greater extent, and new cultural codes emerged as guides.

As the social classes became less unequal, people found it more difficult to recognize their emotional experiences as an outcome of social relations. Emotionally stable and controlled conduct was increasingly expected in all interpersonal relations, not just those toward social superiors. Emotions became identified with the interior of the person, as the need to control emotions fell on the self to a greater extent. This feeling of separateness from others produced what Elias called the *homo clausus* (closed person) condition. This individualization of society is also largely unplanned from a long-term perspective, though parents then did try to socialize children to meet more emotionally controlled standards. In the field of consumption, the consumer has also become associated with a more individualized subjectivity, occurring within unplanned figurational dynamics (Dolan 2009).

Elias's other contribution to understanding consumption, or more broadly leisure, concerned the growth in the "pleasure of the eye" or the spectacle as source of pleasure (2012, 196–197). Because children learn that they cannot touch everything they desire, they gradually develop an appreciation of imagined pleasure through spectating and other forms of more detached enjoyment. Elias relates this moderation of emotions and impulses to the growth of imaginary pleasures served by music, cinema, art, and sport. In *Quest for Excitement*, Elias and Dunning examine this special enclave of emotional generation and release as "controlled decontrolling of emotions." Watching sport and films, reading novels, or listening to music are forms of mimetic pleasure in that they allow access to pleasurable emotional experiences that have become more difficult to recreate in modern society. Wouters (2007) has also extended Elias's ideas to argue that an informalization process has occurred in the West since the late nineteenth century. As social classes become even more interdependent and less unequal, a pronounced blending of aesthetic and emotional styles advances. A relative emancipation of formerly repressed feelings requires a heightened and more flexible form of self-control in order to face fears and embrace risk in consumption practices.

The figurational approach developed by Elias sees consumption as a fluid set of practices related to particular forms of habitus and cultural codes produced through long-term webs of social bonds.

SEE ALSO: Bourdieu, Pierre; Class; Conspicuous Consumption; Consumption and Sport; Emotions and Consumption; Veblen, Thorstein

REFERENCES

Dolan, Paddy. 2009. "Developing Consumer Subjectivity in Ireland: 1900–80." *Journal of Consumer Culture* 9 (1): 117–141.

Elias, Norbert. 2006 (1969). *The Court Society*. Dublin: University College Dublin Press.

Elias, Norbert. 2012 (1939). *On the Process of Civilisation*. Dublin: University College Dublin Press.

Elias, Norbert, and Eric Dunning. 2008 (1986). *Quest for Excitement: Sport and Leisure in the Civilising Process*. Dublin: University College Dublin Press.

Kilminster, Richard. 2007. *Norbert Elias: Post-Philosophical Sociology*. London: Routledge.

Mennell, Stephen. 1998. *Norbert Elias: An Introduction*. Dublin: University College Dublin Press.

Wouters, Cas. 2007. *Informalization: Manners and Emotions since 1890*. London: Sage.

Emotions and Consumption

EVA ILLOUZ
Hebrew University of Jerusalem, Israel
YAARA BENGER
Max Planck Institute for Human Development, Germany

Until the 1960s, the same assumptions that had governed the sphere of production were those that were used to understand the black box of the consumer and of consumption conceived as an economic practice. Consumption was the act of "buying" and it was viewed as a rational utilitarian practice conducted under capitalism's tendency to produce, standardize, and rationalize. In many ways, the field of consumer studies which subsequently developed was nothing but a vast attempt to revise and reject the assumption of a rational actor. Various paradigms – semiotic, postmodern, symbolic, and post-Marxist – all conceived of consumption as a complex cultural practice, imbued with meaning, symbols, and rituals. One of the most effective critiques of the utilitarian paradigm of consumption has been the Bourdieuian notion of "habitus," which locates consumer choices in "tastes" and systems of preferences that are shaped by class position, which translates in the body and in a matrix of cognitive and preconscious judgments. This theoretical move has contributed much to integrate class and culture in consumer choices, and made these choices expressions of wasteful strategies as conspicuous consumption, distinction, and competitive envy. Yet, if we examine the developments of consumer culture of the last 20 years, the Bourdieuian notion of habitus was also imbued with strong rationalist overtones and has obscured a fundamental dimension of consumption, namely the fact that it has been increasingly oriented toward the production of emotions, moods, and sensorial experiences. Such emotional experiences, albeit connected to class habitus, transcend them, cut across and rework class hierarchy and distinctions. In other words, while some emotions are more likely to motivate class-based consumption than rational goals – envy or status anxiety for the socially insecure groups – the claim here is that emotion has also been a dimension cutting transversally across class groups.

Emotion is a psychological entity, but only inasmuch as it is the condensed experience of cultural definitions of personhood as they are expressed in relationships that are concrete and immediate, but always culturally and socially defined. Given that emotion, as a concept, encompasses the individual and the social, the cognitive-cultural, the bodily, and the motivational, it is a powerful category for the analysis of the culture of consumption. This is true not only because it accounts for the phenomenology of consumption but more crucially because it clarifies the actual historical development of the phenomenology of consumption. It accounts for the ways in which the many cultural and economic entrepreneurs who brought about consumer culture conceived of consumers and of the role of emotions in making commodities an increasingly important aspect of the performance and experience of identity and subjectivity.

EMOTION AS AN INDEPENDENT CATEGORY OF CONSUMPTION

At first blush, postmodern sociology of consumption would seem to enable us to move away from the rational-instrumental overtones of Marxian sociology, with Baudrillard (1998), for example, discussing the concept of "desire," stressing the passionate and unconscious components of consumption in order to explain "both the engine and the chief cultural characteristic of consumption" (Illouz 2009, 381). However, this theory relies on a vague philosophical notion of "desire" as the need "for something that is lacking" and is not able to specify the social dynamic of such desire. Nor is it able to link together the logic of production of commodities with the logic of consumption. A more satisfactory account of the emotional dimension of consumption is one that simultaneously connects the emotional dimension of the consumer experience and the process of producing commodities (Illouz 2009), thus making emotion at once a cultural category and a knowledge practice for those in charge of the processes of transforming commodities into cultural goods, as well as an actual commodity consumed for different reasons and possibly in different ways from other commodities.

THE CREATION OF THE CONSUMER AS AN EMOTIONAL AGENT

One crucial point which the sociology of consumption has disregarded is the historical process through which the consumer was conceptualized in emotional terms. Actually, the consumer is not simply an actor waiting to buy commodities, but a product of the knowledge systems, marketing sciences, and advertising strategies which shaped the beliefs of the people who sold and bought products (see Lash and Lury 2007). Following the creation, from the late nineteenth century, of a private psychological self and identity intensely preoccupied with its emotions, the formation of the consumer sphere was also accompanied by a new – emotional – conceptualization of the consumer.

Starting from the first decades of the twentieth century, with Freudian views as a strong tailwind, marketing science started developing, based on the belief that commodities have greater appeal when they carry symbolic and emotional meanings. The practice which became known as "branding" is the deliberate association of products and trademarked names with ideas, concepts, cultural icons, collective symbols, and myths which activate emotional meanings. As early as the 1920s, American advertisers applied a direct "personal" tone, moving from descriptive data to subjective motivations and emotional arguments. Increasingly, advertisements emphasized consumers – their lifestyles, enjoyment, and satisfaction – rather than the actual material product. Following the growing focus on the individual and the shared perception of emotions as "the lowest common human denominator," a close cooperation emerged between economists and psychologists from the 1930s onwards. This consolidated the view of the consumer as driven by emotions and of emotional states as a basic incentive for consumption: people buy if they envy the possessions of others or if they are bored with their own, if they wish to please someone they love, if they are anxious about their health and well-being, and so forth (Marchand 1985).

Simultaneously, while consumerism was converting into a mass culture practice, this "mass" was exposed to the therapeutic discourse, becoming aware of and preoccupied with emotions, and increasingly convinced that one's emotional interiority defines one's self-identity. Freudianism and consumer culture worked hand in hand to build up an ideal individual, who perceives his or her self-identity and lifestyle as a property and resource, which should be managed and cultivated through self-reflection and self-fashioning (Illouz 2008).

Post-World War II economic expansion required new methods for mass marketing and led to an acceleration in the cooperation between psychology and economics. During the 1940s and 1950s, Ernest Dichter, an Austro-American psychologist, started applying psychoanalytic theory not for relieving personal anxieties or solving psychological difficulties, but for unraveling consumers' behavior, and is therefore considered to be the foundering father of motivation research (Berger 2010). In accordance with changes in the psychology discipline, motivation research evolved to become market research, which combined behavioral theories and relied more and more on the rising field of cognitive psychology, wishing to better understand and influence consumers' behavior. Thus emotions were conceptualized as a motivational force and from the late 1970s their role in decision-making processes was receiving increasing importance in light of new insights brought from behavioral economy. In the following decades, theories of consumer behavior further emphasized the influence of emotions on consumers' satisfaction, their cognitive responses and choices, guiding advertising and product design.

Advertising culture did not merely manipulate emotions to increase consumption, by doing so it constructed the consumer as an emotional entity transforming material acquisition into a cultural and emotional experience. Drawing from theories and experiments from psychology, economy, and neuroscience, the practice of "emotional branding" reinforced the conceptualization of the consumer as an emotional actor and helped achieve the perception of the market as a source supplying consumer strategies for achieving emotional authenticity, emotional meaning, and self-realization. The connection between "authenticity" and consumption would be one of the most fruitful points to activate consumer culture. It would affect not only the aura around objects but also the practice itself of buying, making it less the attempt to fulfill a clear emotional need than a diffuse and ongoing practice to shape the self and its interiority.

EMOTION AND THE SEMIOTICS OF CONSUMPTION

Semiotics has long claimed that commodities are offered as signs for something else. In Barthes' famous analysis of Panzani pasta, "connotation" – the excess meaning added to a commodity – is what bestows on a commodity its meaning. Subsequent analyses of advertisements confirmed that we purchase commodities not only for their function but also for what they mean in an economy of social relationships (Appadurai 1988; Baudrillard 1998). After World War II, the commodity underwent a dematerialization process – which followed the shift from a goods economy to a service and informational economy – and a new generation of scholars emphasized the significance of the nonmaterial (aesthetic/symbolic) components of commodities, claiming that the sign became an autonomous aspect of the very process of production of the commodity. This approach pointed to the fact that in addition to the increasing intangibility of commodities, material commodities gained value from their aesthetic and symbolic components, such as their design and branding (Lash and Urry 1994; Amin and Thrift 2004).

In these approaches, emotions explain the allegedly irrational aspects of consumption and are viewed as the paramount motivation to buy, regardless of the cost–benefit value. However, if consumption is less about utilitarian satisfaction than it is about the symbolic meaning of commodities, it does not make the act of consumption into an emotional experience proper. A commodity could be consumed for its emotional meaning (e.g., this pasta signals Italian warmth), without making the experience of eating an ipso facto emotional experience.

It was not until the 1990s that properly emotional experiences were identified and labeled as such by sociologists of consumption. In order to distinguish this category from the semiotic one, we would call this a *performative emotional consumer experience*. This emotionally performative aspect of commodities came to the fore when scholars began to ask how the commodity itself translates directly into an emotional experience: the way the cigar generates masculine self-confidence or lingerie the experience of femininity and sensuality. Two basic responses ensue. First, once the commodity is embedded in emotional meaning for the goal of attracting consumers, emotion becomes a main motivational engine for consumption, implicating cognitions, affect, evaluation, and the body ("He believes a cigar is a sign of power, masculinity, and control; he enjoys smoking cigars because he wishes to express his masculinity; he feels self-confident when smoking a cigar"). Once commodities are not evaluated in terms of their mere functionality but in terms of their meaning, consumption is not only the act of owning or having a material property, but a way of *doing, expressing, reproducing* identity ("He buys cigars in order to intensify his masculinity and strengthen his self-confidence"). Thus consumption becomes a performative dimension of emotional subjectivity.

Second, commodities acquire different values and personal meanings according to the specific relationship in which they are exchanged (Appadurai 1988; Zelizer 2005). In this sense, experiences of consumption are always connected to the social relationships they signal and constitute, which in their turn produce intense emotional work ("She is looking for a new bra for her date – one that will make her feel sexy and confident, but that won't be too tacky and make a wrong impression on her date"). Therefore, consumption becomes part of wider social chains and emotional practices (Illouz 2009). In these two cases emotion is not merely the motivational force for consumption, based on the semiotic value of the commodity – rather it is constituted through the act of consumption. The commodity (with its symbolic meaning) is no longer external and uniform – rather it depends on the interaction with the consumer, in order to co-produce subjective emotional effects.

Once the emotionally performative dimension of goods was recognized, meaning that consumption was seen as an emotional performance, which generates real emotional experiences, and not merely as a semiotic act, the concept of consumer experience helped identify a category *sui generis* of consumer acts whose purpose was explicitly emotional. In her *Window Shopping: Cinema and the Postmodern* (1993) Anne Friedberg defined the concept of commodity-experience as intangible commodities delivered through an aesthetic activity which creates a subjective effect on the consumer-spectator. As such, commodity-experience is detached from the act of production or from a concrete service and rather objectifies the consumer and operates on her or him. Window shopping, for example, is distinguished from the act of buying, but it is an activity which provides diversion and a sense of freedom and individual choice, while (potentially, at least) transforming the spectator into a desirous consumer. Thus the mobilized gaze is in fact commodified (Friedberg 1993).

Indeed, in late capitalism many commodities are being sold as forms of experiences and experiences have increasingly become commodities. Especially in mass culture, leisure and tourist industries offer intangible goods that are manufactured in a standardized way but generate singular experiences for different consumers. Package tours are a good example of this as they produce a standardized mobility through defined sites, converting the "sightseeing" experience into a commodity (Friedberg 1993). The notion of commodity-experience resonated in the economics and marketing literature during the 1990s and 2000s, when a new emphasis was placed on intangible goods and particularly services and experiences (Pine and Gilmore 1999; Vargo and Lusch 2004). Marketing sciences increasingly perceived the consumer as seeking memorable experiences and emotional intensity, thus boosting goods with an experiential dimension.

EMOTIONS AS COMMODITIES

The argument so far has been that emotions motivate consumption and that consumption in turn shapes our emotional world and identity. It follows from these two propositions that a third essential connection between emotion and consumption should be recognized: emotions are the very commodity produced and purchased. Thus we can define emotional commodities as products that are designed to create emotions, moods, and affects and are consumed for this purpose (Illouz forthcoming). This capacity of late capitalism – to produce and supply emotions as commodities – was missed by the sociological analysis of consumption as a social and semiotic act. This process was stimulated by the pervasiveness of the psychological discourse which considerably objectified emotional categories, and made them worthy as objects in themselves, thus facilitating their commodification, and, by turning emotions into objects of preoccupation and management for achieving self-realization and emotional authenticity, enhancing consumers' demand for emotions (Illouz 2008).

The concept of emotional commodities extends Friedberg's commodity-experience in two main ways: first, it emphasizes the fact that specific and defined emotions are the actual economic end, in the eyes both of the producer and of the consumer, while commodity-experience merely aims to stimulate and seduce the consumers' desire on their way to a concrete act of consumption or to make profit out of a vague experience. For example, when buying a music mood compilation ("nostalgic" or "romantic" music), in purchasing a workshop on anger control, or in acquiring a pill to reduce social anxiety, one is purchasing a defined emotional state, quite different from the amusement park whose purpose is to supply a general mood.

Second, as a result of the concrete emotional aim the concept encompasses much more than the "mobilized gaze," since emotional commodities operate through diverse sensual and cognitive channels. This is evident for example in the vacation resort industry. The Club Med industry emerged within the context of new psychological thought on the modern conception of stress and relaxation (Benger forthcoming). Starting from the 1950s Club Med sold to a new middle class avid to use and consume leisure time, a new experience of relaxation. The production of relaxation demanded new and more sophisticated strategies than the mere sightseeing experience and thus it entailed new conceptions of architecture, ambience design, and management (Benger forthcoming; Illouz forthcoming).

In contrast to the case of emotional branding, where emotions which presumably exist prior to the act of consumption are manipulated by the industry strategically, the emotional promises of emotional commodities are actually delivered: consumers demand specific emotional experiences or moods and these are delivered to them in a way which is interpreted as subjective and authentic. In this sense, emotional commodities enhance a major characteristic that was attributed in the last decade to intangible goods, services, skills, and knowledge (Vargo and Lusch 2004), namely the intersecting of the roles of producer and consumer or co-production. In the co-production logic (1) the value of the commodity depends on the experience itself and is thus "defined by and cocreated with the consumer" (Vargo and Lusch 2004, 6), and (2) products are no longer an arbitrary choice forced on consumers, but an outcome of broader cultural processes that design objects and desires, emotions and economics.

Emotion has played a crucial role in the historical development of consumer culture, not only as the connotation of the commodity in advertising culture, but also as the form which the production, marketing, and consumption of goods have taken. In many ways we can say that a late capitalist commodity contains congealed emotions, not congealed time. It is the crucial role of emotion in the nexus of capitalist market–media culture–technology which explains why consumer culture is a way of objectifying subjectivity, and vice versa, a way of making objects into pure subjectivity.

SEE ALSO: Consumer Culture, History of; Consumption and Identity; Experiential Consumption; Leisure and Consumption; Semiotics

REFERENCES

Amin, Ash, and Nigel Thrift. 2004. *The Cultural Economy Reader*. Oxford: Blackwell.

Appadurai, Arjun, ed. 1988. *The Social Life of Things: Commodities in Cultural Perspective*. Cambridge, UK: Cambridge University Press.

Baudrillard, Jean. 1998. *The Consumer Society: Myths and Structures*. London: Sage.

Benger, Yaara. Forthcoming. "Exploring the Production of Relaxation in Club Med Resorts." In Rethinking the History of Capitalism: How Emotions Became Commodities, edited by Eva Illouz.

Berger, Arthur Asa. 2010. *The Objects of Affection: Semiotics and Consumer Culture*. New York: Palgrave Macmillan.

Friedberg, Anne. 1993. *Window Shopping: Cinema and the Postmodern*. Berkeley: University of California Press.

Illouz, Eva. 2008. *Saving the Modern Soul: Therapy, Emotions and the Culture of Self-Help*. Berkeley: University of California Press.

Illouz, Eva. 2009. "Emotions, Imagination and Consumption: A New Research Agenda." *Journal of Consumer Culture* 9: 377–413.

Illouz, Eva. Forthcoming. Rethinking the History of Capitalism: How Emotions Became Commodities.

Lash, Scott, and Celia Lury. 2007. *Global Culture Industry: The Mediation of Things*. Cambridge, UK: Polity.

Lash, Scott, and John Urry. 1994. *Economies of Signs and Space*. London: Sage.

Marchand, Roland. 1985. *Advertising the American Dream: Making Way for Modernity, 1920–1940*. Berkeley: University of California Press.

Pine, Joseph, and James Gilmore. 1999. *The Experience Economy: Work Is Theatre and Every Business a Stage*. Cambridge, MA: Harvard Business School Press.

Vargo, Stephen L., and Robert F. Lusch. 2004. "Evolving to a New Dominant Logic for Marketing." *Journal of Marketing*, 68: 1–17.

Zelizer, Viviana A. 2005. *The Purchase of Intimacy*. Princeton, NJ: Princeton University Press.

Ethical Consumption

VERONIKA A. ANDORFER
University of Kassel, Germany

Scholars and practitioners alike use the term "ethical consumption" in reference to consumers who satisfy their own needs and desires but are at the same time mindful of the consequences their consumption practices have on the environment, on animals, and on other human beings. Having evolved at the beginning of the 1980s, initially mainly focusing on the environmental consequences of consumption, the concept is now applied more broadly to denote a growing field of consumer practices and interdisciplinary research.

A variety of other terms is often used synonymously, albeit with slightly different connotations. To name but the most common ones: green consumption and green consumerism, sustainable consumption, responsible consumption, socially conscious consumption, political consumption/political consumerism. The main difference between the terms "consumption" and "consumerism" is that the former focuses on private consumer choice and individual consumer concerns, while the latter focuses on consumer social movements and consumer activism, consumer manipulation, and ideologies in systems of consumer capitalism (Gabriel and Lang 2006, 8–9). It is often hard to draw clear boundaries between these two terms as they overlap in the day-to-day discourses on ethical consumption.

Widening the narrow scope of green consumption to include a broader array of ethical concerns has triggered contributions from scholars in agronomy, anthropology, business and marketing, consumer studies, economics, ethics and philosophy, geography, political science, psychology and social psychology, sociology, and sustainability studies. The manifestations of ethical consumption in everyday life are as diverse as the disciplines in which they are studied. Common examples include buying organic, local, or fair trade products; boycotting clothes manufactured in sweatshops; investing in green companies; recycling waste; or committing to community-supported agriculture. At times, consumer practices of voluntary simplicity, anti-consumption, and slow living are also linked to ethical consumption. Highlighting the main issues on the topic, different types of ethical consumption, historical developments, key research areas, and critical remarks to the field are considered in this entry.

TYPES OF ETHICAL CONSUMPTION

Ethical consumption is often seen as a "convenient catch-all phrase" (Lewis and Potter 2011, 4) for a plethora of consumer concerns and actions that go beyond considerations of product price and quality to include the political, social, and environmental consequences when acquiring, using, or disposing of goods and services. Most commonly, scholars distinguish between positive buying (also called "buycotting," Friedman 1996), that is, consumers buying goods and services to reward companies for their (ethical) strategies, and negative buying (also called boycotting), that is, consumers deliberately refraining from buying goods and services to achieve certain (ethical) objectives. Ethical practices that go beyond the purchase or boycott of ethical products (e.g., lobbying) are summarized as *consumer action*. In addition, examples of ethical lifestyles of voluntarily cutting down on overall consumption are classified as anti-consumerism, or voluntary simplicity.

Other types of ethical consumption include sustainable consumer habits, relationship purchasing, and comparative ethical ratings. Recycling, waste management, energy and water conservation are summarized as sustainable consumer habits (Papaoikonomou, Ryan, and Valverde 2011, 213). The category of relationship purchasing includes examples of community-supported agriculture and other consumer cooperatives where members take part in the development and implementation of ethical strategies (Harrison, Newholm, and Shaw 2007). Finally, examples of green/ethical consumer guides, ethical consumer magazines, and ratings of companies, products, and services in terms of their ethical characteristics run under the heading of comparative ethical ratings (Harrison et al. 2007).

HISTORICAL DEVELOPMENTS

The historical roots of the two classical types of ethical consumption – boycotts and buycotts – can be traced back to the eighteenth and nineteenth centuries. Some of the more prominent examples include the boycott of English goods by the Boston Tea Party in 1773 or the buycott of the White Label Campaign in 1899, when US women's consumer leagues rewarded department stores for their good labor conditions with a label (Lewis and Potter, 2011, 6).

Gabriel and Lang (2006) identify four waves of consumer activism, starting with the cooperative movement of English working-class people to meet their needs for high-quality and affordable food in 1844. This was followed by the value-for-money movement in the United States at the beginning of the twentieth century with the aim of informing and educating consumers to get their money's worth. The third wave is named "Naderism" after Ralph Nader, a US lawyer active in the empowerment of consumers against the alleged manipulation and systematic disinformation of consumers by businesses. Finally, with the rise of alternative consumers in the 1970s and 1980s, concerns for the detrimental impacts of affluent lifestyles on the environment appeared on the agenda. So-called "green" consumption became mainstream in the 1990s. Since then a broader ethical turn has linked ethical consumption to popular critiques of globalization and global social justice, overconsumption, materialism, and unsustainable lifestyles (see also Lewis and Potter 2011, 7).

Scholars discuss several reasons for the rise in ethical consumption at the turn of the twenty-first century (e.g., Harrison et al. 2007; Lewis and Potter 2011; Newholm and Shaw 2007): increasing media coverage on the impact and risks of affluent lifestyles; state withdrawal from traditional areas of civic responsibilities, with a subsequent upsurge of nongovernmental organizations (NGOs) and other forms of collective action that open up new ways for citizens to engage in issues of personal concern; growing affluence and higher levels of education; the long-term shift from materialist values of basic needs to postmaterialist values of self-fulfillment and care for others; expressing personal concerns and issues of self-image through consumption in today's consumer culture.

KEY RESEARCH AREAS

The rise of everyday ethical consumption practices is matched by an increasing interest in this topic by scholars in the humanities and the social sciences. Especially since the beginning of the 2000s researchers have published more and more academic work on the topic (Papaoikonomou et al. 2011). Key research questions cover a spectrum ranging from aspects of individualized ethical consumption decisions at one end to structural and collective aspects of ethical consumption at the other end.

The philosophical basis of ethical consumption is a key research area within consumer ethics. Focusing on ethical consumption in terms of personal moral conduct, scholars apply different philosophical theories to evaluate ethical consumption, discuss the meaning of "ethical" in ethical consumption, and explore its dimensions of morality. Much empirical research has focused on identifying and categorizing the ethical consumer. Early on, scholars in business and marketing began to profile ethical consumers and to establish related market segments based on sociodemographics (gender, income, education, etc.) and personality characteristics. Empirical evidence tentatively suggests that ethical consumers are likely to be female, have higher incomes and higher levels of education, and score high on values of universalism, solidarity, or religiousness.

As these findings proved to be rather unstable, scholars moved on to the question of which factors determine individual ethical consumption. Drawing on the concepts of *attitudes*, modified versions of the attitude–intention–behavior framework (mostly Ajzen's theory of planned behavior) are often applied to model ethical consumption practices. Empirical studies suggest that controlling for a subjective norm and perceived behavioral control, positive attitudes toward ethical consumption positively influence ethical consumption behavior or related behavioral intentions. Especially in research on green consumption, much scholarly work and discussion have concentrated on the effect of environmental concern as a general attitude toward pro-environmental consumption practices and whether its effect decreases as behavioral costs increase (the so-called low-cost hypothesis, Diekmann and Preisendörfer 2003). Empirical evidence of the low-cost hypothesis is mixed, and the link between environmental concern and behavior is often found to be weak, pointing to complementary determinants in ethical consumption.

Concomitant are discussions about the gap between what consumers say (in surveys) and what they do (in the marketplace), known as the attitude–behavior gap. Some scholars argue for a refinement of theories to better account for the link between attitudes and behavior (e.g., Newholm and Shaw 2007, 257–258), while others argue for the application of methods other than surveys (e.g., field experiments, discrete choice experiments) to take the problem of socially desirable answers into account (e.g., Devinney, Auger, and Eckhardt 2010, 56–60).

Influenced by Schwartz's norm-activation model and the theory of planned behavior, *norms* are also identified as key determinants of ethical consumption. Empirical evidence shows that the personal norm of feeling morally obliged to consume in an ethical manner exerts a positive effect on ethical consumption. Closely linked are questions of labeling ethical products and consumers' trust in these certification schemes. Here, empirical studies show that knowledge and high-quality information reduce consumers' skepticism about ethical consumption; results also suggest a positive effect of consumers' trust in labels.

Studies of consumers' willingness to pay (WTP) a premium for the ethical features of products are prevalent among standard economic approaches to consumer behavior. Concentrating primarily on product price and budget restriction, consumers are assumed to choose the product alternative that gives them the highest expected utility per cost unit. Consumers reveal their preference in choosing the more expensive ethical product, and consequently it is assumed that these consumers gain additional utility from the ethical attributes. Estimating consumers' WTP, researchers apply various forms of stated-preference methods (e.g., contingent valuation, discrete choice experiments) and field experiments. Empirical evidence shows that consumers are indeed willing to pay an ethical premium, for example for organic and fair trade products.

Scholars mainly in consumption studies have turned to the concept of identity in analyzing ethical consumption. Drawing on the work of Bauman (1988) and Giddens (1991), who see consumption as an identity project central to the individual expression of self-meaning and the personal selection of self-image in late modernity, empirical studies find that ethical consumption is understood as a means to express moral concerns and to construct a (consumer) identity as a moral person.

Other areas of key interest are conspicuous consumption, class, and distinction (Lewis and Potter 2011, 13). Connected to the arguments of Veblen (1899) and Bourdieu (1984) that consumption practices can serve as a means to prove, retain, and reinforce social distinction and power structures in society, ethical consumption is discussed as an elite project of social distinction. Empirical evidence suggests that consumers with higher social status or higher class positions are more prone to ethical consumption.

Issues of space and place have been taken up by scholars of human and cultural geography (Lewis and Potter 2011, 13–16). Studies focus on questions of commodity chains starting at the producer side of ethical consumption, caring at a distance, food miles, and, more recently, on the networks and organizations shaping ethical consumption (Clarke 2008). Criticizing the individualistic bias and the predominant model of ethical consumers as rational actors in research on ethical consumption, scholars in geography and other disciplines argue that ethical consumption is primarily determined by macro factors of networks, organizations, political regulations, and market structures that provide the infrastructure of ethical consumption, and less by factors on the level of individual consumer choice.

Moving toward the other end of the spectrum, it is questions of civic engagement and collective action that point to the collective and contextual aspects of ethical consumption. Key issues in studies on political consumption and political consumerism evolve around consumption as voting and consumer sovereignty, consumer citizenship, and empowerment (Gabriel and Lang 2006 chap. 10); and individualized collective action (Micheletti 2010). From this perspective ethical consumption practices are linked to individuals' political concerns and serve as a means for political change beyond traditional approaches of political participation – potentially at the expense of (national) government responsibility or crowding out other means of political change that might be more effective. However, empirical evidence for these assertions is inconclusive. Normative concerns have also been raised that only the wealthy can afford to vote on ethical issues in the marketplace (Littler 2011, 34). From a social movement perspective, (boycotting) campaigns of consumers or NGOs highlight the social dilemma of engaging individuals in the (costly) provision of public goods such as human rights, biodiversity, and animal welfare.

CRITICAL REMARKS

Ethical consumption has not gone uncriticized. Objections are frequently made as to the field's unclear boundaries: it is considered too loose, too fragmented, and too opaque to be meaningful (e.g., Devinney et al. 2010; Littler 2011). A commonly accepted definition and an integrated theoretical framework are missing in research; in everyday life, different ethical practices might contradict each other, for example saving on food miles and buying fair trade products from faraway places (Littler 2011, 28).

A second common objection raises the question of effectiveness: does ethical consumption make a difference? Can consumers change (unethical) markets? While proponents of ethical consumption answer in the affirmative, critics consider ethical goods to be niche products unfit for the mass market: a means for consumers to assuage guilt about their consumption, and a means for companies to make more profit and to practice "greenwashing." Devinney et al. (2010, 36), for example, find the image of the ethical consumer greatly exaggerated by activists, and emphasize that consumers do not change the moral conduct of markets – it is the producers who make the rules.

A third objection points to the notion of ordinary consumption habits being "unethical" when contrasted with ethical consumption practices. Critics stress that many consumers frame their ordinary consumption in moral terms; focusing solely on ethical consumption turns a blind eye to the less spectacular forms of day-to-day consumption.

ACKNOWLEDGMENT

Many thanks go to Jörg Rössel and Patrick Schenk for helpful comments on earlier versions of this entry.

SEE ALSO: Boycotts; Citizenship and Consumption; Consumer Activism; Consumer Movements, History of; Fair Trade; Green Consumption; Sustainable Consumption

REFERENCES

Bauman, Zygmunt. 1988. *Freedom*. Milton Keynes, UK: Open University Press.

Bourdieu, Pierre. 1984. *Distinction: A Social Critique of the Judgement of Taste*. London: Routledge and Kegan Paul.

Clarke, Nick. 2008. "From Ethical Consumerism to Political Consumption." *Geography Compass* 2(6): 1870–1884.

Devinney, Timothy M., Pat Auger, and Giana M. Eckhardt. 2010. *The Myth of the Ethical Consumer*. Cambridge, UK: Cambridge University Press.

Diekmann, Andreas, and Peter Preisendörfer. 2003. "Green and Greenback: The Behavioral Effects of Environmental Attitudes in Low-Cost and High-Cost Situations." *Rationality and Society* 15(4): 441–472.

Friedman, Monroe. 1996. "A Positive Approach to Organized Consumer Action: The 'Buycott' as an Alternative to the Boycott." *Journal of Consumer Policy* 19: 439–451.

Gabriel, Yiannis, and Tim Lang. 2006. *The Unmanageable Consumer*. London: Sage.

Giddens, Anthony (1991) *Modernity and Self-identity*. Cambridge, UK: Polity.

Harrison, Rob, Terry Newholm, and Deirdre Shaw. 2007. "Introduction." In *The Ethical Consumer*, edited by Rob Harrison, Terry Newholm, and Deirdre Shaw, 1–8. London: Sage.

Lewis, Tania, and Emily Potter. 2011. "Introducing Ethical Consumption." In *Ethical Consumption. A Critical Introduction*, edited by Tania Lewis and Emily Potter, 3–23. New York: Routledge.

Littler, Jo. 2011. "What's Wrong with Ethical Consumption?" In *Ethical Consumption. A Critical Introduction*, edited by Tania Lewis and Emily Potter, 27–40. New York: Routledge.

Micheletti, Michele. 2010. *Political Virtue and Shopping. Individuals, Consumerism, and Collective Action*. New York: Palgrave Macmillan.

Newholm, Terry, and Deirdre Shaw. 2007. "Studying the Ethical Consumer: A Review of Research." *Journal of Consumer Behaviour* 6: 253–270.

Papaoikonomou, Eleni, Gerard Ryan, and Mireia Valverde. 2011. "Mapping Ethical Consumer Behavior: Integrating the Empirical Research and Identifying Future Directions." *Ethics & Behavior* 21(3): 197–221.

Veblen, Thorstein. 1899. *The Theory of the Leisure Class*. New York: Macmillan.

Experiential Consumption

MORRIS B. HOLBROOK
Columbia University, USA

ELIZABETH C. HIRSCHMAN
Rutgers University, USA

In the 1960s and 1970s, most consumer researchers – following the formulations of such influential thinkers as Howard and Sheth or Bettman – embraced an essentially rational model of the buyer as a decision maker who processed various informational inputs (cognitions or C) to produce brand preferences (affect or A) that resulted in purchase commitments (behavior or B). These C-A-B formulations drew heavily on the work of attitude researchers (e.g., Ajzen and Fishbein) and emphasized the role of tangible brand attributes (features or F) in shaping beliefs (perceptions or P) that led to likes and dislikes (affect or A). Such F-P-A approaches were kissing cousins of the ubiquitous C-A-B models insofar as they hinged on the rational economic aspects of buying choices.

During the early 1980s – reflecting the work of such earlier pioneers as Abbott, Alderson, Dichter, Levy, Kotler, Jacoby, and Woods – Holbrook and Hirschman (1982) proposed an expansion of the C-A-B scheme to include aspects of what they called an "experiential view" that focused on fantasies (not just cognitive beliefs or perceptions but also various dreams, daydreams, unconscious material, symbolic meanings); feelings (not just affect in the form of likes and dislikes but also various emotions such as love, hate, joy, sorrow, anger, fear, acceptance, disgust); and fun (not just purchases but also various activities involved in using a product as part of one's daily life). Further, as inputs into such consumption experiences, these authors recognized the hitherto neglected roles of hedonic aspects (rather than merely utilitarian benefits) (Hirschman and Holbrook 1982); symbolic meanings (rather than just tangible features) (Hirschman and Holbrook 1981); aesthetics, play, spirituality, or ethics as types of intrinsic value (in addition to the more extrinsic types of economic or social value) (Holbrook 1999); and neglected offerings in the arts and entertainment (beyond the conventional preoccupation with such functional products as detergents, toothpaste, yoghurt, or home appliances) (Hirschman and Holbrook 1981).

This expanded substantive focus required the adoption of new methods. In that spirit, Hirschman and Holbrook proposed the incorporation of various interpretive approaches drawn from the humanities, semiology, hermeneutics, comparative literature, and so forth (Hirschman 1986, 1989; Holbrook and Hirschman 1993). They took pains to justify these more pluralistic or "postmodern" methods within the context of more traditional neopositivistic approaches (Hirschman and Holbrook 1992). But they departed rather freely from the conventional toolkit of restrictively scientistic procedures to engage in some of the more free-spirited aspects of approaches such as subjective personal introspection or SPI (Holbrook 1995). Hence this focus on consumption experiences included such applications as the interpretation of films, analysis of television shows, personal encounters with the arts and entertainment, and psychoanalytic insights drawn from long-term psychotherapy or from the "dark side" of consumer behavior.

All this followed from a basic commitment to an expansion of the old decision-oriented focus to include aspects of the experiential perspective. This view sees the consumer as something more than a rational information-processing choice-generating calculating machine (i.e., a computer) and someone more like a hedonic feelings-centered fun-oriented flesh-and-blood living creature (i.e., a human animal). Holbrook and Hirschman encouraged an expanded F-F-F view that built on the old C-A-B framework to incorporate various hitherto neglected aspects of fantasies (e.g., unconscious meanings), feelings (e.g., emotional responses), and fun (e.g., leisure pursuits) – as well as the broadened sphere of relevant experiences that these entailed, such as the aforementioned experiences with high culture (art) and popular culture (entertainment), but also those pertaining to fashion and shopping. This perspective advocates an integration or synthesis of the otherwise divergent C-A-B and F-F-F perspectives into a suitably holistic view of the consumer.

In time, the experiential view has caught on among scholars and among those who write managerial self-help books under the rubric of "experiential marketing." With rare exceptions, the latter have paid little attention to the origins of the ideas that they have borrowed in the service of creating, proposing, or explaining various successful marketing campaigns for such offerings as Starbucks, JetBlue, Nike, the Hard Rock Café, Disney World, Apple, or Krispy Kremes. But certainly one can track the success of the experience-oriented advice offered by these managerial gurus in the frequency with which television commercials, print advertisements, storefronts, corporate logos, billboards, websites, blogs, tweets, and other media have begun to insist on the importance of consumption experiences as the root of consumer satisfaction, the basis for customer loyalty, and the foundation for commercial success in such product categories as air travel ("Experience Italy with Alitalia!"); cruise ships ("Come experience everything that makes a Celebrity cruise a true departure"); hotels ("MGM Grand Offers Maximum Food & Beverage Experience"); electronics ("Experience the Undeniable Power of Panasonic Plasma"); cultural events ("Carnegie Hall Proudly Invites You To An Exciting One Night Only Musical Experience"); and even financial services ("Experience the value of fixed-income investing at Fidelity"). (For further details and examples, please see Holbrook 2009.)

SEE ALSO: Consumer Behavior; Consumer Culture; Consumption, Spectacles of; Cultural Studies; Emotions and Consumption; Fashion; Leisure and Consumption; Semiotics; Symbolic Value

REFERENCES

Hirschman, Elizabeth C. 1986. "Humanistic Inquiry in Marketing Research: Philosophy, Method, and Criteria." *Journal of Marketing Research* 23(3): 237–249.

Hirschman, Elizabeth C., ed. 1989. *Interpretive Consumer Research.* Provo, UT: Association for Consumer Research.

Hirschman, Elizabeth C., and Morris B. Holbrook, eds. 1981. *Symbolic Consumer Behavior*, Ann Arbor, MI: Association for Consumer Research.

Hirschman, Elizabeth C., and Morris B. Holbrook. 1982. "Hedonic Consumption: Emerging Concepts, Methods, and Propositions." *Journal of Marketing* 46 (3): 92–101.

Hirschman, Elizabeth C., and Morris B. Holbrook. 1992. *Postmodern Consumer Research: The Study of Consumption as Text.* Newbury Park, CA: Sage.

Holbrook, Morris B. 1995. *Consumer Research: Introspective Essays on the Study of Consumption.* Thousand Oaks, CA: Sage.

Holbrook, Morris B., ed. 1999. *Consumer Value: A Framework for Analysis and Research.* London: Routledge.

Holbrook, Morris B. 2009. "Manufacturing Memorable Consumption Experiences from Ivy and Ivory: The Business Model, Customer Orientation, and Distortion of Academic Values in the Post-Millennial University." In *Memorable Customer Experiences: A Research Anthology*, edited by Adam Lindgreen, Joëlle Vanhamme, and Michael B. Beverland, 267–290. Burlington, VT: Gower.

Holbrook, Morris B., and Elizabeth C. Hirschman. 1982. "The Experiential Aspects of Consumption: Consumer Fantasies, Feelings, and Fun." *Journal of Consumer Research* 9 (2): 132–140.

Holbrook, Morris B., and Elizabeth C. Hirschman. 1993. *The Semiotics of Consumption: Interpreting Symbolic Consumer Behavior in Popular Culture and Works of Art.* Berlin: Mouton De Gruyter.

FURTHER READING

Debord, Guy. 1967. *The Society of the Spectacle.* Translation by Donald Nicholson-Smith. New York: Zone Books.

Falk, Pasi, and Colin Campbell, eds. 1997. *The Shopping Experience.* London: Sage.

F

Facebook

DHIRAJ MURTHY
Goldsmiths, University of London, UK

Facebook is an online social networking site, which as of spring 2014 had more than 1.2 billion users and had recently celebrated its 10th birthday. The site seeks to foster interactions between "friends" through updates, sharing photographs, and playing games together. Facebook has become a household name, not only because of its large user base, but also its prominent use in social movements (including the Arab Spring in 2012), elections (e.g., the 2012 American presidential election), and the 2011 UK riots (Baker 2012). Though Facebook initially began as a social network for college students, it has become ubiquitous among diverse demographic groups in both developed and developing countries.

Facebook, like other online social networking sites, is built upon "profiles" which contain photographs, basic to detailed demographic data, employment and educational history, relationship information, and information about a user's hobbies, musical preferences, favorite movies, and other social preferences. The medium has made commonplace the term "friending," which involves inviting someone to connect with you on the medium. Friends on Facebook are able to see each other's profiles as well as any "status updates," usually one- to two-line social updates. Facebook relies on the production and consumption of large amounts of "user-generated content" which can include low-effort content such as clicking a button to "like" a photograph.

Advertising and marketing are central to Facebook's revenue and one's experience of Facebook involves the consumption of "dynamic ad insertion" (Okazaki and Taylor 2013). Additionally, there is "buzz" marketing, where companies generate buzz through an "outrageous" or eye-catching campaign (Freeman and Chapman 2008), attempts to generate viral sharing, liking, and commenting on Facebook. Because of the medium's historical skew toward younger users, these forms of product marketing have been particularly successful.

Some critics of Facebook view the medium as placing primacy on a multitude of information being disseminated "second-hand" at the expense of singularly directed communication. Others argue that it creates a social pressure toward self-disclosure and that Facebook may be a site of shifts in social communication from the private to the public (Lange 2007). Specifically, one's existence on Facebook usually ranges in a spectrum from semi-public to public because

The Wiley Blackwell Encyclopedia of Consumption and Consumer Studies, First Edition.
Edited by Daniel Thomas Cook and J. Michael Ryan.

of the fact that friends or friends of friends often have privacy settings which allow some level of public access to their profiles. One implication of this existence is the decrease in exclusivity of "personal" information (e.g., one's love life). Additionally, Facebook applications and linked websites can post automatically on one's wall, sharing with friends location information, current activity, or a purchase. These have fostered electronic word-of-mouth (eWOM) consumption, where friends are encouraged to endorse products and activities to their friends.

Because of this push toward disclosure, one's Facebook profile can be quite contemporaneous. These very regular interactions can foster what Licoppe (2004) describes as a "connected presence." The perception that others are always there as a listening audience helps Facebook build a perceived community. For critics, this could be viewed as troublesome in that it places primacy on the seemingly banal. For proponents, this can be viewed as a means for one's extended friend network to gain access to what Goffman referred to as a person's "backstage," a part of their life which is normally not on public display.

Ultimately, Facebook has tremendous influence on what content is being consumed on the Internet. For example, the virality of the controversial Kony 2012 video (http://www.youtube.com/watch?v=Y4MnpzG5Sqc), which sought to bring to justice the internationally wanted Ugandan war criminal Joseph Kony, was influenced strongly by viral sharing of the video among Facebook friends. Many Facebook users then posted the video as a status update and changed their photo to a Kony 2012 banner. Facebook's social spaces have become particularly important across many demographic lines, and one-third of US adults get their news from Facebook. However, there are also segments of backlash, "Facebook fatigue," against the pervasiveness of Facebook, as illustrated by movements such as the 2010 "Quit Facebook Day." Survey research found that 23% of American teens polled in 2013 found Facebook to be the most important social site to them, a figure down from 42% in 2012. Some fear that "Facebooking" may be affecting the interaction of co-present individuals, in that they may place priority on Facebooking the moment rather than "living" in it. Facebook has also been criticized for the ease of its use in cyberbullying and its circulation of controversial videos (including beheading videos). Regardless of the potential downsides surrounding Facebook, the medium has become ubiquitous for many and has profoundly shaped economic, political, and cultural consumption.

SEE ALSO: eBay; Social Media; YouTube

REFERENCES

Baker, Stephanie Alice. 2012. "From the Criminal Crowd to the 'Mediated Crowd': The Impact of Social Media on the 2011 English Riots." *Safer Communities* 11(1): 40–49.

Freeman, Becky, and Simon Chapman. 2008. "Gone Viral? Heard the Buzz? A Guide for Public Health Practitioners and Researchers on How Web 2.0 Can Subvert Advertising Restrictions and Spread Health Information." *Journal of Epidemiology and Community Health* 62(9): 778–782.

Lange, Patricia G. 2007. "Publicly Private and Privately Public: Social Networking on YouTube." *Journal of Computer-Mediated Communication* 13(1): 361–380.

Licoppe, Christian. 2004. "'Connected' Presence: The Emergence of a New Repertoire for Managing Social Relationships in a Changing Communication Technoscape." *Environment and Planning D: Society and Space* 22: 135–156.

Okazaki, Shintaro, and Charles R. Taylor. 2013. "Social Media and International Advertising: Theoretical Challenges and Future Directions." *International Marketing Review* 30(1): 56–71.

FURTHER READING

Hong, Sounman, and Daniel Nadler. 2012. "Which Candidates Do the Public Discuss Online in an Election Campaign? The Use of Social Media by 2012 Presidential Candidates and Its Impact on Candidate Salience." *Government Information Quarterly* 29(4): 455–461.

Khamis, Sahar, and Katherine Vaughn. 2012. "We Are All Khaled Said: The Potentials and Limitations of Cyberactivism in Triggering Public Mobilization and Promoting Political Change." *Journal of Arab & Muslim Media Research* 4(2–3): 145–163.

Noueihed, Lin, and Alex Warren. 2012. *The Battle for the Arab Spring: Revolution, Counter-Revolution and the Making of a New Era*. New Haven, CT: Yale University Press.

van Dijck, José. 2009. "Users Like You? Theorizing Agency in User-Generated Content." *Media, Culture & Society* 31(1): 41–58.

Failing Consumption

PAUL EISEWICHT
TU Dortmund University, Germany

Failing consumption sums up the manifold problems that consumers encounter in the process of everyday consumption and the ways they resolve them. Purchasing and using a good, the social actor (qualified for being a consumer) projects and executes an action for satisfying a need or want. Consumption implies two modern myths of success: first, the good can be used in the projected manner, and second, the purchased good answers the consumer's need. As modern life is characterized as one of extensive consumption, people's capacity to act successfully depends strongly on the typified expectation of successful consumption.

However, the course of everyday consumption masks its risk of failing, which is inherent to every action due to the general uncertainty under which social actors act (see Bagozzi and Warshaw 1990). The risk which is masked by routine (via the typified expectation that typified problems of consumption are solved by corresponding typified actions) can become a problem. If the problem cannot be resolved, consumption fails. In consequence of a relevant but unresolved problem, this can lead on to a cross-situational crisis as failed solutions point to dysfunctional routines (including those of problem solving).

Failing consumption can arise in the stages of consumer decision making (see Blackwell, Miniard, and Engel 2006), each of which produces specific risks to successful consumption. First, the recognition of needs and wants can be disturbed due to overlapping and opposing needs and wants. Therefore it can be a problem for the social actor to construct an adequate and clear projection of the targeted consumption. Also, gathering and evaluating information can fail if consumers do not have access to information and sources necessary for their purchase decision. In another case, if the consumer has contradicting information, this can lead to problems of reliability, validity, and compatibility of information. This can result in consumer confusion, which more generally addresses the problem of information overload. So the consumer can be trapped in a process of gathering, organizing, contesting, and evaluating ever new and opposing information.

The decision to make a purchase represents another risk factor as an imagined projected action needs to be realized (and this necessarily means making a decision for a specific offer and against others). Problems during the purchase raise questions of qualification and authorization to buy. To purchase a good means that buyer and seller negotiate the terms of the transaction: this includes the transfer of money to the seller as well as the transfer of a good to the buyer. This addresses problems of offered, preferred, or hindered ways of transaction, ways of packing/unpacking, sending/receiving, and so forth, as well as problems with involved intermediate organizations (e.g., credit institutions, delivery services, or customs).

With the transaction the buyer becomes a consumer, in a narrow sense, as the user of a good. The comparison of expectations and usage of the good can be a source of dissatisfaction. This can be due to defective functions or a discrepancy between perceived usage and promised satisfaction. Further problems regard the frequency and effort for the maintenance of the good. Finally, problems regarding the storage or disposal of a good can arise if there are legal requirements or if the good cannot be stored, disassembled, packed, or transported as expected.

If the risks turn into problems, there are several types of routines to solve these problems, including the attribution of causes for the perceived dissatisfaction, and subsequent patterns of action (e.g., complaints). Failing consumption refers to two conceptions of problems: first, the problem of the action (as the action should solve a problem but can fail to do so), and second, action as a problem (as there are manifold possibilities for acting and people need to choose between actions but can choose for the better or the worse).

From this perspective, consumption in affluent societies can be seen as a problem of managing different wants rather than a problem of satisfying needs. The general problem for consumers, being confronted with the various shopping channels, the range of goods, and the plurality of sense making, is to bring together the increasingly complex structure of their needs with the symbolic and material contingency that is inherent in consumption (see Leiss 1988). In other words: consumption is a constant struggle between wanting to have and having to choose, which is a characteristic consequence for the disembedded individual in contemporary society.

SEE ALSO: Boycotts; Consumer Behavior; Consumers, Flawed; Needs and Wants

REFERENCES

Bagozzi, Richard P., and Paul R. Warshaw. 1990. "Trying to Consume." *Journal of Consumer Research* 17(2): 127–140.

Blackwell, Roger D., Paul W. Miniard, and James F. Engel. 2006. *Consumer Behavior*, 10th ed. Mason, OH: Thomson/South Western.

Leiss, William. 1988. *The Limits to Satisfaction: An Essay on the Problem of Needs and Commodities.* Montreal: McGill-Queens University.

Fair Trade

MARY BETH FINCH
Northwestern University, US

The fair trade movement is a values-based consumer movement that strives to empower disadvantaged workers and promote more equitable international trade relations. It is based upon two central premises: on the one hand, unfettered capitalism leads to the exploitation of the most vulnerable participants in the global market; on the other hand, the market is the best avenue for improving the lives of disadvantaged workers. Fair trade is, thus, in the precarious and somewhat paradoxical position of being both "in and against the market." Two primary goals of the movement are to create consumer demand for products made under nonexploitative conditions and to facilitate the process by which the workers who supply these products reach these consumers. Drawing upon Polanyi's analysis of market embeddedness (1944), fair trade can be understood as attempting to "re-embed" relationships between producers and consumers.

Though all proponents of fair trade aim to transform business practices and harness consumer power for the benefit of workers, there is no single definition of fair trade.

The fair trade movement is a loosely organized system of advocacy groups, certifying organizations, producer groups, wholesalers, retailers, and religious organizations. The various groups have different concerns and interests and this shapes how each defines fair trade. Granted, there is widespread agreement that basic fair trade principles include ensuring living wages and safe working conditions for producers, promoting environmental sustainability, supporting community development, respecting cultural diversity, shortening the supply chain, and building long-term relationships among producer groups and wholesalers. However, there is debate – and indeed contention – within the movement over precisely which practices are required to meet the threshold necessary to qualify as "fair trade."

To appreciate the complexities of defining fair trade, it is helpful to consider the history of the movement. Although food commodities such as coffee, tea, and chocolate currently dominate the fair trade market, the initial emphasis was on handicrafts produced by inhabitants of financially depressed nations. The fair trade movement is typically traced to the 1940s when efforts to import products from artisans in struggling countries emerged simultaneously in Europe and the United States (Nicholls and Opal 2005). In Western Europe, the Oxford Committee for Famine Relief (later Oxfam) began bringing in goods made by artisans from countries in Eastern Europe that had been devastated by World War II. Edna Ruth Byler is credited with starting the movement in the United States when she began selling crafts made by poor women in Puerto Rico. In conjunction with the Mennonite Central Committee, Byler's project developed from her selling these products out of the trunk of her car into an organized retail operation (which is now Ten Thousand Villages). Also around this time in the United States, the Church of the Brethren formed the organization SERRV which, like Oxfam, focused on products from Eastern Europe. Until the 1980s these efforts to trade directly with producers in poorer countries were carried out by alternative trade organizations. During this time products were typically sold through catalogues and through world shops.

The movement changed drastically in 1988 when the first fair trade labeling system was created by the Dutch development agency Solidaridad, using the label Max Havelaar, which led to similar labels being created throughout Europe and North America. Because these labels enabled consumers to identify the fair trade items among conventional products, it allowed fair trade products to move more easily into mainstream markets. At this point agricultural commodities, such as coffee, were a growing sector in fair trade. The move into more mainstream retail outlets precipitated the growth of agricultural commodities over handicrafts within the movement. Another consequence of the labeling system was the need to build consensus about the meaning of fair trade and codify the practices and standards. The uniqueness of handicrafts versus the fungibility of agricultural commodities necessitates distinct systems of regulation. Indeed, throughout the 1990s separate sets of certifying organizations emerged.

In the case of agricultural commodities, it is the product itself that is certified. Products are primarily regulated by setting a minimum price that must be paid for a crop as well as including an additional "social premium" cost, which is paid directly to the cooperative. The social premium is earmarked for community development and capacity building. Fairtrade International (formerly Fairtrade Labeling Organizations, FLO) and Fair Trade USA (formerly Transfair USA) are the main organizations that oversee this process. Because there is no standardization with respect to handicrafts, a different certification process is needed. In this case, it is the producer group or retailer that is identified as complying with fair trade practices. These groups are regulated through membership in oversight organizations. The most important of these are the World Fair Trade Organization and the Fair Trade Federation in the United States. While the goal behind both types of labeling is to promote fair trade principles, the systems for handicrafts and agricultural commodities generally operate parallel to each other.

In recent years fair trade has been growing at a remarkable rate. For instance, Fair Trade International reported approximately US$6.3 billion in annual sales in 2011, up from US$4 billion in 2008. Moreover, as of 2011 there were approximately 1000 producer groups that include over 1.2 million farmers and workers engaged in fair trade production. While coffee and cacao remain the largest segment of the fair trade market, an increasingly wide array of crops are eligible for fair trade certification; these include quinoa, spices, sugar, cotton, and flowers. Another growing segment of the fair trade market is composite products, multiple ingredient items which are eligible for the fair trade label because they meet a certain threshold for containing fair trade-certified ingredients. For instance, fair trade cosmetics, shampoo, ice cream, and root beer are all available. Similarly, the range of styles and products available in the handicrafts market is rapidly expanding. In earlier stages the handicrafts tended to be culturally specific to the producer group (e.g., weavings from Guatemala or baskets from Ghana). The design of handicraft items is increasingly moving toward more "Westernized" and "contemporary" designs.

Given the drastic changes in the movement since its beginning, it ought not to be surprising that internecine debates have broken out about the fundamental principles of fair trade. Indeed, contention about the definition of fair trade has led to a proliferation of fair trade labels and certifying organizations. The disagreements largely revolve around maintaining ideological purity versus growing the movement.

A particularly fraught issue is the extent to which fair trade must remain committed to supporting small farmers and cooperatives. This is evident in the debate over whether or not crops produced on plantations should be eligible for fair trade certification. Certifying products from large-scale plantations is a significant shift in fair trade practices. The prevailing argument of proponents of including plantations in the fair trade system is that doing so will extend the economic benefits of fair trade to a substantially larger number of workers and communities. The main focus is on rapidly growing fair trade. Those who oppose certifying crops produced on plantations argue that it completely undermines the spirit of the movement. They argue that fair trade is about creating a particular model of trade and that the vision should not be compromised. If plantation-produced crops are eligible for fair trade, they maintain it will drive the small farmers, those whom fair trade was created to protect, out of business. Purity of vision is valued over expansion. The debate about whether to allow coffee grown on plantations to be certified led to Fair Trade USA (which supports including plantations) making the very controversial decision to split from Fair Trade International in 2012.

The mainstreaming of fair trade is a further source of concern and contention. While placing fair trade products in mainstream retail outlets obviously increases sales significantly, it not clear that it is in the greater interest of the movement to be working with companies that are not committed to fair trade principles. Again, it is a question of growth versus a commitment to alternative markets: are the increased sales enough to justify working with companies that support the very business model that fair trade fights against? Critics argue that the mainstreaming of the fair trade movement has led it to be depoliticized and diluted (Low and Davenport 2007). Many also see the shift toward more mainstream designs in the handicraft markets as undermining the movement. The source of concern is that it makes producers' livelihood dependent on the whims of consumers. Moreover, maintaining a long-term commitment to producer groups is challenging when they are making items that are only trendy for a short amount of time. A further dimension of the debate around mainstreaming fair trade is the extent to which it matters whether or not fair trade principles are a motivating factor for consumers. On the one hand, there are those who argue that fair trade is a political project and that it is important for consumers to support the underlying mission. The goal is not just to sell more products but also to help consumers understand the problems with conventional markets. On the other hand, there are those who contend that the focus should be on quality and the inherent desirability of the products instead of principles. They argue that the goal is to help the producers become self-sufficient and that the only way to do this is to make a product that people want to buy, regardless of the politics involved.

Evaluating the extent to which producers benefit from fair trade is the focus of a great deal of research. The assessments are generally mixed. When looking at agricultural commodities, it is clear that fair trade results in significant economic gains for producers, both in terms of higher earnings and the value of social premiums. This is evident in both analyses of the aggregate data and multiple case studies (Jaffe 2007; Linton 2012; Lyon and Moberg 2010). It is not the case, however, that all producers benefit; nor does the fact that producers are making more money always mean they are making enough to sustain a decent lifestyle. Increased income is, however, only one piece of the fair trade mission. Research indicates that the fair trade movement is lacking with respect to the larger ideological issues. Beyond the higher prices, many of the farmers involved in fair trade production have little understanding of fair trade or its purpose. Likewise, many do not feel a sense of belonging to or ownership over fair trade as a movement despite the benefits they receive from it.

Measuring the impact of fair trade on handicraft groups is somewhat more challenging because prices for the products are not standardized and the alternative is frequently unemployment, as opposed to selling the items at a "conventional price." The majority of the artisans are women, many of whom have no other opportunity for employment. Further, the handicraft producers are particularly apt to gain the "intangible benefits" that come from working in a cooperative such as social support, a sense of empowerment, and personal development. Ethnographic research has shown that indeed artisans can reap significant financial and social gains from their participation in fair trade (Littrell and Dickson 2010). Again, not all assessments are positive.

The consequence of fair trade marketing practices has also received substantial scholarly attention. Fair trade sales strategies rely heavily upon biographies and images of the producers. Indeed, it is considered common wisdom among fair trade retailers that it is the "story" that sells the product. While the focus on telling consumers about producers may be rooted in an effort to bridge the gap between producers and consumers and decommodify the products, the effect may be quite different. Critics suggest that much of fair trade marketing is highly exploitative and perpetuates the producers' status as "Other."

Some argue that dominant fair trade marketing practices shift the commodification from the products to the producers, which is even more deeply problematic. Moreover, they may reinforce consumers' position of power since consumers are privy to more knowledge of the producers than the producers have of them (Wright 2004). So far this discussion around fair trade marketing has been predominantly theoretical. One opportunity for future research is to consider consumers' reception of the marketing. Indeed, there is an overall need for more research on fair trade consumers.

The fair trade movement is clearly beset with a multitude of challenges. The split between FLO and Fair Trade USA highlights the deep ideological divisions within the movement. Whether or not the movement will continue to exist as a single movement is not yet clear. Fair trade, it seems, is at a crossroads.

SEE ALSO: Citizenship and Consumption; Consumer Movements, History of; Ethical Consumption; Globalization and Consumption; Sustainable Consumption

REFERENCES

Jaffe, Daniel. 2007. *Brewing Justice: Fair Trade Coffee, Sustainability, and Survival*. Berkeley: University of California Press.

Linton, April. 2012. *Fair Trade from the Ground Up: New Markets for Social Justice*. Seattle: University of Washington Press.

Littrell, Mary A., and Marsha A. Dickson. 2010. *Artisans and Fair Trade: Crafting Development*. Sterling, VA: Kumarian Press.

Low, William, and Eileen Davenport. 2007. "To Boldly Go … Exploring Ethical Spaces to Re-politicise Ethical Consumption and Fair Trade." *Journal of Consumer Behavior* 6: 336–348.

Lyon, Sarah and Mark Moberg, eds. 2010. *Fair Trade and Social Justice: Global Ethnographies*. New York: NYU Press.

Nicholls, Alex, and Charlotte Opal 2005. *Fair Trade: Market-Driven Ethical Consumption*. London: Sage.

Polanyi, Karl. 1944. *The Great Transformation*. New York: Rinehart.

Wright, Caroline. 2004. "Consuming Lives, Consuming Landscapes: Interpreting Advertisements for Cafedirect Coffees." *Journal of International Development* 16: 665–680.

Farmers' Markets

CLARE HINRICHS
Pennsylvania State University, US

Farmers' markets take place periodically in fixed locations, with farmers and sometimes other artisans convening to sell their goods directly to customers. Street and open air markets are certainly not new. They have flourished worldwide and continue to be important sites for selling and buying food throughout the global South. What is new in the late twentieth and early twenty-first centuries are the resurgence and reconstitution of farmers' markets in the global North as alternative spaces for food consumers who may feel disenchanted or disenfranchised by the increasingly globalized, industrialized food and agricultural system. Promoted by national policies, extension services, local governments, food writers, bloggers, planners, and activists, farmers' markets have burgeoned as favored venues where eaters can find fresh, local, and sustainably produced fruits and vegetables, meats, cheeses, and specialty foods. According to the US Department of Agriculture, the number of farmers' markets in the United States increased more than 300 percent between 1994 and 2012, from 1755 to 7864. They are located unevenly across the landscape, with urban and suburban areas having more customer traffic and higher densities of farmers' markets than rural areas.

Research on the re-emergence of US farmers' markets around the 1980s focused on their role in supporting livelihoods and diversifying markets for producers struggling to succeed in conventional commodity markets. Farmers' markets have subsequently been studied as sites of consumption politics and practice within the growing local, sustainable food movement. The social embeddedness of exchange at farmers' markets, as distinct from the marketness and instrumentalism of more conventional market settings, helps to explain the presumed virtue and appeal of farmers' markets (Hinrichs 2000). The possibility of direct engagement between food producers and consumers at farmers' markets, especially face-to-face interaction, represents the crucial contrast to the more convenient, but standardized, customer experience at commercial chain supermarkets. In shopping at farmers' markets, consumers pursue ideals of localness, quality, authenticity, and legitimacy, both in their actual encounters with farmers and their purchase of food, although such ideals may remain contingent and only partially fulfilled (Smithers, Lamarche, and Joseph, 2008).

Considerations of class and morality influence understandings of farmers' markets as consumption sites. Even as farmers' markets now serve as the anti-supermarket shopping experience, they are often dominated by the interests and tastes of elite "alternative" consumers, for whom the performative purchase and luxury consumption of artisanal cheese, wildcrafted mushrooms, and heritage tomatoes construct a "foodie" identity and lifestyle. In this sense, farmers' markets are sites where higher-income consumers can deploy and augment their cultural capital through knowledgeable engagement with the total farmers' market experience. For some consumers, farmers' market shopping itself becomes a form of serious leisure that is all the more compelling given the multiple sensory experiences of a "good" farmers' market – tasty samples of products, the aroma of novel prepared foods, seeing interesting people and meeting friends, possibly enjoying live music or other performances. National survey research in the United States found that shoppers who enjoyed cooking and cooked frequently and also had another adult in the household were more likely to patronize farmers' markets, while those for whom cost was the most important characteristic of food were less likely to shop at farmers' markets (Zepeda 2009).

Concern about the democratic dimensions of farmers' markets centers on their accessibility, geographically, economically, culturally, and politically, to lower-income consumers. Retail supermarkets may epitomize the ersatz abundance of the industrialized, globalized food and agricultural system, but their comparative absence in many low-income communities – both urban and rural – limits food consumption options for consumers in those places. In this context, the material presence and cultural and economic viability of farmers' markets serving low-income consumers align with a political ecology of consumption, health, and bodies that addresses more fundamental human concerns than cultivating a foodie identity or culture. For lower-income consumers, farmers' markets can have transformative and emancipatory potential simply by making healthy, fresh, local, and affordable food available where it is otherwise scarce. However, the politics of determining what "good" foods should be sold at a given farmers' market underscores the continuing resonance and challenge of class and culture. Prioritizing, for instance, collards or cave-aged cheeses can reveal social class and other tensions as food consumers and producers at particular farmers' markets navigate potentially different interests around food prices, preferences, and choices. In this sense, issues of food justice and sustainable consumption can intersect forcefully and not always comfortably at farmers' markets (Alkon 2008).

Farmers' markets have a long history and diverse geographic manifestations as sites of consumption. Building on knowledge about identities, culture, and class dynamics at farmers' markets, future research should consider how consumption practices and consumer experiences at farmers' markets either promote or impede the adaptive learning and collective capacity building for challenges, such as climate change.

SEE ALSO: Authenticity; Class; Downshifting; Food; Markets, Moral Aspects of

REFERENCES

Alkon, Alison Hope. 2008. "From Value to Values: Sustainable Consumption at Farmers Markets." *Agriculture and Human Values* 25: 487–498.

Hinrichs, C. Clare. 2000. "Embeddedness and Local Food Systems: Notes on Two Types of Direct Agricultural Market." *Journal of Rural Studies* 16: 295–303.

Smithers, John, Jeremy Lamarche, and Alun E. Joseph. 2008. "Unpacking the Terms of Engagement with Local Food at the Farmers' Market: Insights from Ontario." *Journal of Rural Studies* 24: 337–350.

Zepeda, Lydia. 2009. "Which Little Piggy Goes to Market? Characteristics of U.S. Farmers Market Shoppers." *International Journal of Consumer Studies* 33: 250–257.

Fashion

ANTHONY SULLIVAN
University of the Arts, London, UK

Although fashion is often conflated with dress and style, most accounts agree that it is distinct from both because of its temporal logic of change, where particular forms or styles of dress are replaced for social and aesthetic rather than for practical reasons.

In general usage, *fashion* refers to almost anything (from philosophy to architecture) which is subject to changing cycles of popularity and the establishment of collective norms or styles which make them démodé or à la mode, of their time or not, "in fashion" or "out." Sapir (1931) argues that styles which achieve a permanence "crystallize" into the customs which make new fashion possible. This takes us on to the definition of style: understanding not just what to wear but how to wear it. "Stylishness" is therefore attributed to someone who has the "cultural capital" know-how or "taste" (Bourdieu 1984) to make the right judgment calls. Sapir's work also explains the notion of classic style as something enduring and resistant to fashion's restless pursuit of change and its short-term fads.

Dress, the broadest term, serves three purposes. First, practical functionality: given the climate and the seasons, dress protects us from the elements, for example cold, wind, and rain. Second, modesty or display: concealing or revealing the genitalia and breasts or a mix of these contrary impulses, as in the accentuation achieved by the Tudor codpiece and modern push-up bra or low-slung jeans. Finally, dress acts as a means of symbolic or cultural adornment expressing custom, social status, and identity. Thus, since the Victorian era, black has signified mourning in Britain; the suit conventionally expresses bourgeois status for men, and the hijab symbolizes Muslim women's identity. These functions of dress are widely seen as universal to all societies. But while fashion, like dress, can take many forms including clothing, makeup, jewelry, scarification, tattoos, or other bodily modifications, what distinguishes fashion is its constant rhythm of stylistically driven change. Based on the seasonal requirements of dress – autumn/winter and spring/summer – for each period fashion engenders changing styles of dress which move through birth, innovation, or introduction to "early adoption" through a cycle of widespread mass diffusion, acceptance, or saturation followed by decline and eventual obsolescence (Davis 1992). So while one of last year's summer dress trends might be short and lacy, the following year long printed sleeveless maxis may be "in" while the former is "out" of fashion.

Historically speaking, a range of authors concur that fashion emerged as a distinct practice in the West from around the fourteenth century. The decline of the rural isolation and social stability of feudalism was central to fashion's emergence, as the static nature of dress reflected unchanging status and occupation. Thus the more fluid social hierarchy and social mobility of urban capitalist modernity produced a new dynamic mode of adornment. Wilson (2003) argues that "the European city in the early stages of mercantile capitalism ... saw the birth of ... something qualitatively new and different ... Fashion is dress in which the key feature is rapid and constant changing of styles" (pp. 4–5). Fashion, as "the child of capitalism" (p. 7), emerged out of everyday encounters in Western city streets as a means of identifying the self. Accordingly, the modern concept of individual identity is tied to fashion, since it is one of the ways we can mark out and position ourselves socially. So fashion can be used to reveal, conceal, feign, or manipulate many aspects of identity from gender and sexuality to ethnicity, class, age, and subcultural affiliation.

Significantly, the term "dress" is also applied to the customary styles of groups of people ethnically, regionally, or nationally. National dress, for example, though socially constructed and increasingly subject to fashionable change through globalization, changes relatively slowly and often imperceptibly. By contrast, fashion exists where the pace of stylistic change and its perception are clear, creating a sense of newness, self-renewal, and subjective freedom. However, not all accounts share this view of the origins of fashion. Some argue that this perspective is ethnocentric, privileging Western cultural experience. But this argument can itself be leveled at definitions of fashion whose vagueness, or historical and spatial nonspecificity, universalizes it.

In classic sociological accounts, fashion's logic of change or mutability (Simmel 1971; Veblen 1994) is driven by emulation in class terms. Here higher social classes initiate new fashions which are copied and gradually "trickle down" through the social hierarchy. When "inferior" classes catch up with the fashion of their "superiors," a competitive desire for differentiation or "distinction" (Bourdieu 1984) drives the latter's take-up of new styles. This ongoing competitive game of similarity and difference in fashion, exemplified in the Paris of the Second Empire (1852–70), propels its dynamic of change and a cycle of aesthetic obsolescence in which the rate of replacement of clothing exceeds dilapidation (Barthes 1990).

The dominance of Parisian haute couture, from Rose Bertin and Worth to Dior, lasted from the mid-eighteenth until the mid-twentieth century when three interrelated changes reshaped fashion: the decline of couture "trickle-down" diffusion and the dictatorship of the designer, the rise of youth and teenage consumption in the 1950s and 1960s, and the growth of men's fashion in the 1980s. The convergence of the postwar baby boom and an economic upturn produced a new dynamic in fashion – "bubble-up" youth styles from the street. These challenged "trickle-down" fashion from couture, as teenagers' active or productive consumption of music and fashion produced new group identities or youth subcultures. From bikers and teddy boys to mods, skinheads, and punks, subcultural style gave fashion more complex stylistic rhythms and cycles. Fashion in the singular, dictated by the designers, became fashions in the plural. Decentralization or polycentrism was encouraged still further by globalization and digitalization. Jet travel and the internet turned Tokyo, Moscow, Rio, Mumbai, and Hong Kong into new fashion centers. By the 1990s subcultures blended into mainstream sartorial culture, creating a dissonant, fluid, and hybrid era of postmodern style and identity play.

These developments dramatically impacted on men. After the "Great Masculine Renunciation" (Flugel 1930), men's withdrawal from fashion in the nineteenth century, their centrality to subcultures reintroduced a minority of men to fashion. Within the context of the shift to a postmodern consumer culture, men's re-engagement with fashion in the late twentieth century was reinforced by new representations of masculinity in men's magazines. These legitimized male display, promoting menswear and grooming sales. The broader significance of this on masculinity remains the subject of some debate.

The word "fashion" is used both as a noun, applied to fashionable clothing and accessories, and as a verb, "to fashion," and this syntactical duality is a useful starting point for the deeper analysis of fashion as a complex and hybrid cultural, artistic, and a commercial phenomenon. The verb "to fashion" raises the question as to who makes fashion and the importance of practices of fashioning the body as embodied material acts. For Simmel (1971) fashion negotiates the modern tension between the individual and society, and contrary impulses to conformity and difference. As a social and cultural force fashion has to be made, and making it is both an individual and a collective act, a balance of agency and structure on many levels, for example between the commercial imperative, the needs of the industry as producers to sell garments and looks, and the desire of consumers to express themselves in the context of existing ideologies and discourses, ways of thinking and acting, whether in terms of gender, age, class, or sexuality.

Here it is important to stress that what is being fashioned is an embodied look. Visual culture, images, and representations of fashion in magazines, film, advertising, and on the internet, especially blogs, remain its central mode of diffusion. Thus both contemporary music and celebrity culture form key sites for the performance of fashion as an embodied spectacle. But here considerable tensions arise as fashion is both an immaterial and a material phenomenon. As "a situated bodily practice" beyond representation, image, or discourse, fashion is a lived, embodied reality (Entwistle 2000). Crucially, this dynamic has led to three waves of feminist critique of the gender and representational politics of fashion (Negrin 2008). The industry is accused of enforcing damaging, sexually objectifying male standards and ideals of femininity via images and garments, including the corset and stiletto heels, and cosmetic surgery and other bodily regimes. Fashion is said to fix women as the object of the male gaze or look. Though rejected as too simplistic by many third-wave feminists, controversy over eating disorders, crash dieting, and an imputed link to images of super-thin models, "the size zero debate," a rehabilitated sexist or "raunch culture," and persistent disturbingly high levels of rape and sexual assault of women globally have rekindled feminist critiques.

Two other intractable issues face fashion: the questionable ethics of an industry largely based (outside the bespoke tailoring and couture sectors) on globally outsourced sweated labor, and, finally, the ecological challenge presented by "fast fashion" and the need to "green" an industry which designs and promotes fashionable obsolescence.

SEE ALSO: Bourdieu, Pierre; Capitalism; Cultural Capital; Ethical Consumption; Obsolescence: Planned, Progressive, Stylistic; Veblen, Thorstein

REFERENCES

Barthes, Roland. 1990 (1967). *The Fashion System*. Berkeley: University of California Press.

Bourdieu, Pierre. 1984. *Distinction: A Social Critique of the Judgment of Taste*. Cambridge, MA: Harvard University Press.

Davis, Fred. 1992. *Fashion, Culture, and Identity*. Chicago, IL: Chicago University Press.

Entwistle, Joanne. 2000. *The Fashioned Body: Fashion, Dress and Modern Social Theory*. Cambridge, UK: Polity.

Flugel, John C. 1930. *The Psychology of Clothes*. London: Hogarth Press.

Negrin, Llewellyn. 2008. *Appearance and Identity: Fashioning the Body in Postmodernity*. Basingstoke, UK: Macmillan.

Sapir, Edward. 1931. "Fashion." In *Encyclopaedia of the Social Sciences*, Vol. 6, 139–144. New York: Macmillan.

Simmel, Georg. 1971 (1904). "Fashion." In *Georg Simmel on Individuality and Social Forms*, edited by Donald N. Levine, 294–323. Chicago, IL: University of Chicago Press.

Veblen, Thorstein. 1994 (1899). *The Theory of the Leisure Class*. New York: Penguin.

Wilson, Elizabeth. 2003 (1985). *Adorned in Dreams: Fashion and Modernity*. London: I.B. Tauris.

Fast Food

ANNECHEN BAHR BUGGE
National Institute for Consumer Research, Norway

Fast food is often described as simple snacks served from restaurants, snack bars, kiosks, bars, or shops. A characteristic of these types of dishes is that they are quick to prepare, serve, and eat. Also often known as "street food," due to portability and informality, fast food can be traced back to the ancient Roman cities and so is not exclusively tied to the hamburger, pizza, and hot dog meals arising in the nineteenth and twentieth centuries.

The American fast food concept has been a particularly successful innovation in the post-World War II era, although the first commercial hot dog stand opened in New York in 1871. The idea of quick, ready-made, and portable food reached Europe when the first snack bars were established in American and European cities. These were alcohol-free restaurants with young people as their main patrons. The snack bar concept arose along with the rise of teenage culture, in which young people sought out their own places that catered to their cultural and culinary tastes. Food and food establishments became symbols of social and cultural identity for young people, marking them off from adults and "adult culture," and making the fast food restaurant emblematic of this youth culture. When the American hot dog reached Europe in the 1950s, it became a very fashionable food to eat among many young people, as did the hamburgers from McDonald's and Burger King in the 1970s.

McDonald's originated from a small drive-in restaurant which was run by the McDonald brothers until taken over in 1955 by Ray Kroc, who developed it into the concept familiar today. According to Ritzer (1993), McDonald's not only revolutionized the restaurant industry and started new food trends, it also changed American society and gradually the rest of the Western world through a process he calls "McDonaldization," which emphasizes efficiency, calculability, predictability, and control. McDonaldization refers to the ways in which these principles, originating in the realm of fast food, have spread through various areas of social life.

In recent years, there has been increased social resistance toward this type of food and associated eating habits, which contribute to food-related illnesses such as obesity and diabetes. Grassroots groups have sought to question both the nutritional and the social value of fast food. The international slow food movement (http://slowfood.com/) was established in Italy in 1989 and is now represented in over 150 countries. The health and social impact of fast food has become the subject of a number of books and films, notably Morgan Spurlock's (2004) film *Super Size Me* and Eric Schlosser's (2001) book *Fast Food Nation*. Both of these contributions to the public debate provide a fairly pessimistic picture of modern human beings and their food and eating habits, as well as the effects of McDonaldization on society as a whole. With animated, child-targeted films such as *Over the Hedge* (2006), *Ratatouille* (2007), and *Wall-E* (2008), criticism of dining and living patterns, of the treatment of nature and the environment, as well as of the consumer society's logic itself, continues to proliferate.

In view of the wide-ranging criticism of fast food, it is not surprising that consumer studies show an increasing negativity toward conventional fast food with its high content of fat, sugar, and salt. A consequence of this is that an increasing number of slow food-themed fast food outlets are being established in many Western countries. The food being sold is characterized as fresh, healthy, organic, and ethically produced.

SEE ALSO: McDonaldization; Slow Food Movement; Teens

REFERENCES

Ritzer, George. 1993. *The McDonaldization of Society*. Thousand Oaks, CA: Pine Forge Press.
Schlosser, Eric. 2001. *Fast Food Nation: What the All-American Meal Is Doing to the World*. London: Penguin.

FURTHER READING

Lupton, Deborah. 1996. *Food, the Body and the Self.* London: Sage.
Monatanai, Massimo. 1996. *The Culture of Food.* Oxford: Blackwell.
Pollan, Michael. 2009. *In Defense of Food: An Eater's Manifesto*. New York: Penguin.

Femininities

ALEXANDRA NUTTER SMITH
University of Washington – Tacoma, USA

The various manifestations of gender identity presented by people who identify as women are collectively called *femininities*. Such manifestations may include particular mannerisms, modes of dress, and a range of behaviors relating to interpersonal relationships and social roles. While essentialized views of gender identity along a masculine–feminine dichotomy are still common, awareness and acceptance of nontraditional and transgressive modes of femininity are growing. Thus the word is pluralized to indicate the existence of more than one femininity rather than a one-size-fits-all mode. (This is similar to the way that the word feminism is often transformed into "feminisms" in order to recognize the impossibility of having one feminism that addresses the concerns of all women.) Femininities calls to mind the potential differences between life experiences for women of different intersectional identities; women's lived realities may differ based on identity traits like ethnicity, age, ability, and sexuality, necessitating recognition of different types of femininity.

Thus there are many forms of femininity (many femininities), but the traits that have historically been deemed most acceptable in patriarchal society include beauty, softness, compassion, and nurturing; traits associated with masculinity, on the other hand, include strength, aggressiveness, competitiveness, and intelligence. Within heavily mediated consumer societies, images of "correct" femininity are often problematically utilized as drivers of commercial activity, an issue which will be explored further below.

In her foundational feminist text, *The Second Sex*, first published in 1949, Simone de Beauvoir argued that rather than being biologically determined, gender identities are socially constructed. Biological sex, on the other hand, refers to anatomy and chromosomes and is a wholly distinct trait from gender; there is no predetermined correlation between the two. Instead, historical associations of feminine traits with genetic females and masculine traits with genetic males have reified the sex–gender association. We currently recognize that individuals of all sexes (female, male, and intersex) may identify as women, but typically when someone's gender identity diverges from the accepted correlation (i.e., male/masculine or female/feminine) they may be referred to as transgender (or said to be suffering from gender dysphoria).

The persistent association of "feminine" behavior with female sex has been so prevalent over time that gender roles have been naturalized. Many have come to believe that there is an essential and biological link between being female and exhibiting feminine traits. The strength of this link is visible at the site of motherhood, where a person's physical ability to birth a child is assumed to be evidence of the existence of traditionally feminine behaviors such as soothing, nurturing, and care-taking. However, biological motherhood and socially constructed mothering roles do not necessarily correspond and women whose behavior diverges from the maternal femininity, or who choose to forgo reproduction, are often viewed as being outside the norm, or deviant.

By conforming to the socially accepted range of gender-related behavior (in one's appearance, attitude, or social roles), women are performing gender. Over time such performances normalize the idea of a static gender binary, and simultaneously obscure the instability and socially constructed nature of gender behavior. Feminist philosopher Judith Butler writes about this "gender performativity" in *Gender Trouble* (1990), arguing that when we act out gender, we sustain and give power to the dominant (patriarchal) narrative about gender, the effect of which is to minimize acceptance of gender fluidity or nonconforming femininities.

Many feminists, especially those of the so-called "second wave" of feminism, have identified the sex–gender association as a patriarchal construct, advanced by males/men to preserve their longstanding dominance in society. A new generation of feminists (sometimes called the "third wave") have sought to reclaim even traditional femininities and find empowerment in the autonomous adoption of activities (such as domestic crafts, mothering, or girly modes of dress) that have at various times been denounced as externally (patriarchally) imposed limitations. This movement toward finding liberation in femininity has unfortunately been co-opted by the dominant forces in capitalist society and rebranded as postfeminism. The problematic message of postfeminism – or what Susan J. Douglas (2010) calls "enlightened feminism" – is that women's struggles to achieve equality have been successful, and that women and girls now live in a world where they are able to make a legitimately autonomous choice to conform to traditional modes of femininity (especially with regard to the norms of self-presentation, which dictate that one should make oneself attractive to straight men) without necessarily being victims of patriarchy. Postfeminism's "girl power" refrain has become a powerful tool of manipulation for corporations, who use women's desire to embody a particular kind of femininity as leverage to lead them into consumer activity. As particularly adept commodifiers of femininity, the beauty and fashion industries (playing on women's physical insecurities), along with producers of food and home goods (playing on women's domestic insecurities), have been the worst perpetrators of this manipulation. The power of corporate interests coupled with the ready accessibility of narratives about femininity have led to advertisements that are saturated with messages about and images of "correct" feminine traits.

As they are a set of culturally defined characteristics, femininities are not homogeneous across cultural lines. Different cultures have divergent views regarding the acceptable range of femininities, often based on history, economic development, religion, and the relative strength of patriarchy. Women in certain societies may thus feel compelled by social norms to conform to a certain set of behaviors that would seem unacceptable to women outside those. Femininities that diverge too sharply from dominant cultural ideals are still subject to judgment and "othering." Such gender behaviors are considered transgressive, as they pass over the boundaries of social acceptance. Those who identify as queer and as women, but choose not to self-present in a sexy or "femme" manner, those who eschew marriage or motherhood, or those who exhibit a high degree of outspokenness, strength, or competitiveness, may still find themselves labeled as deviant.

Gender behavior and femininity, then, is a sociocultural process, learned over time through exposure to various institutions, including the family, schools, religion, and mass media. These lessons may not be harmonious. For example, messages about "feminine" and "masculine" practices are frequently embedded in media texts like advertisements, news coverage, and entertainment media. A near-constant exposure to media messages might counteract the lessons of parents or religious leaders.

Media culture in consumer societies often defines femininity as a bodily property. A characteristic assertion of postfeminism is that a woman can attain power by presenting herself in an appropriately "sexy" manner. The surveillance of women's bodies thus becomes a central concern of media outlets, advertisers, and lifestyle experts who feel free to comment on their cleanliness, smoothness, thinness, and attire. The capitalist drive to maximize commercial transaction has given rise to a new limitation for women: the commodification of femininities. Advertisers are adept at hailing women who associate with many different feminine personas (the businesswoman, the tomboy, the athlete, the bombshell, etc.). The surveillance of women's bodies also occurs during pregnancy, when media outlets feel free to monitor and comment on celebrities' weight gain (and subsequent weight loss after childbirth), fashion, and self-care. The message for regular women is the same as above: there is a physical ideal for pregnant women's bodies, and they must be regulated to achieve that ideal. Again, the regulation is usually attached to consumer activity and the acquisition of a range of products designed to keep one's body in line. Diverse femininities are reduced to one-dimensional caricatures: the "butch" lesbian, the hot Latina, the blissfully domestic stay-at-home mom, the subservient Asian woman, and so forth. These stereotypes leave little room for the exploration of alternatives. Of particular concern is the underrepresentation of nonconforming femininities, especially those that include disability, advanced age, or a refusal to conform to beauty ideals; because these are difficult to commodify they are often excluded from media altogether.

While much research and theorizing on the topic of femininities have addressed the problematic nature of the unfounded and socially constructed but persistent linkages between sex and gender and the function of femininity as a limiting structure for women in patriarchal society, there may have been some recent movement toward a more expansive definition. Femininities are frequently understood today as potentially encompassing traits that previously have been coded as masculine. Women are allowed to enact behaviors and pursue roles that were once reserved for men, although still within a (new but possibly more spacious) set of socially acceptable parameters. For example, girls and women may be athletes as long as they still take care to be attractive to men. Women may have careers as long as they are still attentive mothers. It is permissible for a woman to be a desiring sexual agent as long as her sexuality is nonthreatening to the gratification of straight males.

SEE ALSO: Body and Consumer Culture; Commodification; Consumption and Identity; Girl Culture; Masculinity; Mothers/Motherhood

REFERENCES

Butler, Judith. 1990. *Gender Trouble*. New York: Routledge.

de Beauvoir, Simone. 1989/1949. *The Second Sex*. New York: Vantage Books.

Douglas, Susan J. 2010. *Enlightened Sexism: The Seductive Message That Feminism's Work Is Done*. New York: Times Books.

Finance/Financial Markets

KARIN KNORR CETINA
University of Chicago, USA

Finance has evolved historically as a distinctive system of activities. If production, consumption, and distribution or exchange – the market interface between production and consumption – are three different spheres of economic activity, then finance is a fourth sphere. It fulfills a specialized function: that of supplying and controlling *credit*. In a capitalist economy, credit needs to be obtained before a production cycle can start; credit, Keynes argued, is prior to production (e.g., Shapiro 1985, 77). Only after production has been financed can it result in employment income, part of which can then be used to generate savings. Credit can be obtained through two channels: *bank lending* and *financial markets*. Manufacturing-oriented economies – such as that of continental Europe, or more specifically Germany – historically developed a financial organization in which bank lending dominated. In Anglo-Saxon countries such as the United States a different pattern emerged, one placing less emphasis on bank lending, while important credit channels were provided by money and securities markets.

The core activities in financial markets are *investment* and *speculation*. This follows directly from the credit core of finance. What are bought and sold in financial markets are not consumer goods but *financial instruments* (e.g., stocks, bonds, currencies) that directly or indirectly provide credit to a borrower (e.g., firms, states) from which the lender hopes to get dividends, interest payments, or value changes of a credit instrument that will become more profitable over time. Thus, the buying or selling of a financial instrument initiates an engagement or contract that lasts as long as one holds the instrument, and it invariably involves risk (since the future is uncertain, outcomes cannot be guaranteed). Once a financial instrument is purchased, the buyer's fate is tied to the credit receivers and their economic policy and success. Financial market actions are thus relationship-initiating (or -ending) time transactions that connect the fates of lenders, borrowers, and the market, binding them to future outcomes. A financial market does not exist when two or more individuals are prepared to enter into an exchange transaction, but rather when these actors are prepared to enter into promissory engagements: claims and commitments exercised over time based on the *promise* of future outcomes.

The forward-oriented thinking of investors and speculators points to a feature of financial thinking that works quite differently from economic thinking. The latter combines a household form of reasoning (Swedberg 2011) and the idea of individual interest optimization enshrined in the notion of economic man. Financial thinking, in contrast, requires "*financial imagination*" (Knorr Cetina forthcoming, chap. 1); it turns around the future potential value of an object whose present value may be negative. *Risk is a positive value* in that kind of thinking – risk is the daring venture one needs to undertake for profits to be made – though one also attempts to contain it by offsetting transactions (e.g., through swaps and options). Marx offered an interesting formulation of this future-oriented thinking, which he denounced (1981, 596; cited in Henwood 1997, 22). He maintained that in a credit-based economy, "*a negative quantity*," for example government debt, "*appears as capital*" – the creditor advancing the money to the government sees it as a future earnings stream. And once the connection between a "nothing" and the "something" of promised future income is made, negative or zero values may come to be seen as positively valued commodities that can be bought and sold in financial markets – others may want to own Marx's negative values as a source of future earnings. In the past, the association between debt and future benefits has opened the door for the intensification of credit and for widespread securitization. Securitization is the packaging of a variety of debts into saleable financial market instruments that promise investors a future income stream, resulting, for example, from the interest that debtors pay for the credit they received. Before the financial crisis of 2008–09, new mortgage-based instruments of this sort, together with low interest rates and government guarantees of loans, made more credit available to homeowners in the United States and helped create a housing bubble. When the bubble burst and homeowners defaulted on their loans, these instruments became "toxic," leading to the credit and banking crisis in the United States and elsewhere.

Investors and speculators reflecting on potential rather than actual value must envisage how, and in what direction, a potential can be realized. With this they anticipate and unleash molecular episodes of capitalist transformation (positive or negative). Financial capitalism does not let the future happen; it nudges it into a particular direction by creating windows of opportunity in the *present* for the creation of *futures* that will yield profit and capitalize on unrealized possibilities. The promises that underlie such transformations do not just serve motivational purposes; they also become stories that circulate in discourse and talk. *Financial analysts* make stories out of the promises of future development, while also analytically and quantitatively investigating the conditions, circumstances, and parties involved in the realization of those futures. "*Information is everything*" in this area, but what counts as information knowledge is not what has been consensually established to be true, as in the natural sciences, but what is new. Information is continually consumed and loses value once it has been absorbed in prices and replaced by new information. This *consumption epistemics*, and the role played by the imagination, brings finance closer to other areas of consumption than production. Thus financial markets are leading the shift toward a postmodern knowledge society in which specialized logics of consumption are emerging that appear, penetrate, and reconfigure knowledge.

SEE ALSO: Capitalism; Consumer Society; Debt; Global Markets; Marx, Karl; Modernization Theory

REFERENCES

Henwood, Doug. 1997. *Wall Street: How It Works and for Whom*. London: Verso.

Knorr Cetina, Karin. Forthcoming. Maverick Markets: The Virtual Societies of Financial Markets.

Marx, Karl. 1981. *Capital: A Critique of Political Economy*, vol. 3. Translated by David Fernbach. New York: Vintage.

Shapiro, Milton M. 1985. *Foundations of the Market-Price System*. Lanham, MD: University Press of America.

Swedberg, Richard. 2011. "The Household Economy: A Complement or Alternative to the Market Economy?" CSES Working Paper Series, Paper #58. http://www.economyandsociety.org/wp-content/uploads/2013/08/wp58_Swedberg_HouseholdEconomics.pdf.

Flâneur/Flânerie

STEPHEN L. WEARING
University of Technology, Sydney, Australia

The original *flâneur* was regarded as a new kind of urban dweller who had the time to wander, watch, and browse in the public spaces of the emerging modern city (Benjamin 1973) – a poet, an artist, and a "stroller." The *flâneur* wandered the city watching the urban milieu, observing people, and window-shopping. However, in the act of strolling the *flâneur* did not just observe life but was seemingly engaged in an "archaeological" process of unearthing the myths and "collective dreams" of modernity (Frisby 1986, 224). The *flâneur* was a gentleman who stood wholly outside the production process (Wilson 1995) and was away from home and in search of difference.

The *flâneur* was unquestionably male, and *flânerie* was a way of experiencing and occupying space that was available only – or predominantly – to men. As Wolff (1985) points out, "There is no question of inventing the *flâneuse*: the essential point is that such a character was rendered impossible by the sexual divisions of the nineteenth century" (p. 45). According to this view, the *flâneur*'s freedom to wander at will through the city is essentially a masculine freedom. Thus the very idea of the *flâneur* reveals it to be a gendered concept (Wilson 1995, 65). But while the signs and symbols he searched for through his use and observations of space may have been those of the collective, the *flâneur* remained detached from what he observed. He chose not to engage with either the people or the places he visited; therefore his way of seeing and being in space was highly idiosyncratic and individualistic – it was not interactive. The *flâneur*, then, is "a figure of solitude" and anonymity; in the "labyrinth" he becomes passive and placatory – "[t]he *flâneur* represented not the triumph of masculine power but its attenuation," says Wilson (1995, 74). Moreover, the *flâneur*'s way of seeing is singular in its interpretation; his lens, and thus understanding, is unchanging.

With the rise of consumer culture in more recent times, all of these characteristics, it has been argued, seem to fit the contemporary tourist – or rather established conceptualizations of the tourist (Urry 2002). We see the nineteenth-century literary construction of the *flâneur* as a forerunner of the twentieth-century tourist. When applied to tourism, the tourist-*flâneur* is conceptualized as being at the center of the phenomenon, observing on his terms. It is necessary to move away from considering tourism solely in terms of the figure of the *flâneur* to recognize the lived complexity of modern consumer culture and to develop a framework for investigating the ways in which the *flâneur* can be constituted and inscribed both in space and on the self. In particular, it is argued, it becomes necessary to conceptualize the *flâneur* not as one-dimensional and monolithic, but as one who is many-faceted and constructed through use, visual consumption, imagination, and experience. The challenge, then, is to envision a more nuanced version of the *flâneur* for tourism and the tourism experience – one that is capable of providing the basis for an understanding of lived tourist cultures. To this end, Wearing and Wearing (1996) argue that the idea of the *choraster* is potentially more fruitful than that of the *flâneur*.

SEE ALSO: Lifestyle; Tourism; Visual Consumption

REFERENCES

Benjamin, Walter. 1973. *Charles Baudelaire: A Lyric Poet in the Era of High Capitalism*. Translated by Harry Zohn. London: New Left Books.

Frisby, David. 1986. *Fragments of Modernity: Theories of Modernity in the Work of Simmel, Kracauer and Benjamin*. Cambridge, MA: MIT Press.

Urry, John. (2002) *The Tourist Gaze*, 2nd ed. London: Sage.

Wearing, Betsy, and Wearing, Stephen. (1996) "Refocussing the Tourist Experience: The Flâneur and the Choraster." *Leisure Studies* 15(4): 229–243.

Wilson, Elizabeth. 1995. "The Invisible Flâneur." In *Postmodern Cities and Spaces*, edited by Sophie Watson, and Katherine Gibson, 59–79. Oxford: Blackwell.

Wolff, Janet. 1985. "The Invisible Flâneuse: Women and the Literature of Modernity." *Theory, Culture and Society* 2: 37–45.

Flea Markets

JOEL STILLERMAN
Grand Valley State University, USA

Flea markets are open air or semi-enclosed markets featuring used, antique, or new goods and including stalls housing individual merchants. They diverge from standard retail formats because they feature independent vendors, include new and used goods, rely on cash transactions, have a nonstandardized visual presentation, and governments weakly monitor sales and tax compliance. The Paris Flea Market of the 1870s was the first flea market (Miller 1988). Researchers agree that flea markets fill a gap in retailing, though they diverge in their foci on entrepreneurial opportunities for vendors, vendors' sale strategies and motivations, and shoppers' experiences.

Flea markets offer income earning or investment opportunities to low-income individuals, members of immigrant ethnic communities with little access to formal employment, or employed individuals seeking supplementary income. Low-income vendors include downwardly mobile professionals, immigrants whose legal status or language skills limit their access to formal employment, or members of ethnic minorities facing labor market discrimination. Employed vendors view sales as either a hobby or a profession; those in the latter group search for items via newspapers, catalogues, estate sales, yard sales, and wholesalers (Barros Nock 2009; Maisel 1974).

Novice and veteran vendors differ in sales strategies. Novices liquidate assets due to economic misfortune; veterans source goods through various channels and store merchandise in garages or warehouses. Veterans may "trick" novices by buying their merchandise "for a song" and reselling it for a profit. Experienced dealers develop detailed knowledge of prices, features of goods, and effective sales strategies (Sherry 1990; Maisel 1974).

Shoppers and vendors haggle over prices, feigning ignorance or knowledge of a good's "true" value to gain economic advantage or simply to enjoy this ritualized encounter. Vendors engage in "lateral cycling" of used goods or hard-to-sell new products, thereby shifting their status from "trash" to "treasure" if purchasers appreciate their "uniqueness." Vendors seek sociability, freedom, and autonomy through entrepreneurship. Shoppers appreciate markets' carnivalesque atmosphere, the "thrill of the hunt," and socializing at markets (Maisel 1974; Sherry 1990; Gregson and Crewe 2003).

Flea markets are in-between or "liminal" spaces because they feature new and used goods, are formal businesses relying on cash sales, and include "role fluidity": vendors and shoppers each make purchases for resale. Because of their liminal status, recreational features, appealing rituals, and economic advantages, these markets "humanize" the retail experience, in contrast to sterile, standardized retail formats (Sherry 1990; Barros Nock 2009).

SEE ALSO: Consumption Rituals; Economy, Informal; Homogenization and Heterogenization; Recycling; Waste

REFERENCES

Barros Nock, Magdalena. 2009. "Swap Meets and Socioeconomic Alternatives for Mexican Immigrants: The Case of the San Joaquin Valley." *Human Organization* 68: 307–317.

Gregson, Nicky, and Louise Crewe. 2003. *Second-Hand Cultures*. Oxford and New York: Berg.

Maisel, Robert. 1974. "The Flea Market as an Action Scene." *Journal of Contemporary Ethnography* 2: 488–505. doi: 10.1177/089124167400200405.

Miller, H. Max. 1988. "Patterns of Exchange in the Rural Sector: Flea Markets along the Highway." *Journal of American Culture* 11: 55–59.

Sherry, John F., Jr. 1990. "Dealers and Dealing in a Periodic Market: Informal Retailing in Ethnographic Perspective." *Journal of Retailing* 66: 174–200.

Food

LAUREN T. WILLIAMS
Griffith University, Australia
JOHN GERMOV
University of Newcastle, Australia

Food has existed from the beginning of life on Earth: those first organisms arising from the primordial soup needed a food source in order to grow and replicate. Food can be defined from a biological perspective as substances sourced from animals or plants that can be eaten by humans and other animals to obtain the nourishment used for body maintenance, growth, and reproduction. In the physiological sense, "consumption" is the act of ingesting food and beverages. These definitions, which stem from medical and nutritional sciences, only tell part of the story of food and eating, and tend to overlook the social factors that influence why we eat the way we do. In any given society, all that is potentially edible is not eaten – illustrating the important role culture plays in the social construction of food and food consumption.

Social anthropologist Claude Lévi-Strauss (1964/1969) maintained that a key feature of what makes us human is our ability to transform the "raw" (nature) into the "cooked" (human culture); that is, the preparation and consumption of food occur through human culture, which involves rules, values, and meanings that shape what is considered edible and how it should be eaten. In a similar vein, Claude Fischler (1988) describes food as a bridge between nature and culture, transforming things of nature into "food" considered fit for human consumption. It comes as little surprise then that food habits, preferences, and cuisines vary considerably between cultures and can change over time.

INTRODUCING THE SOCIAL APPETITE

The paradox of eating is that it is both a highly individual as well as a social act. At the individual level, beyond hunger and the physiological need for sustenance, we each possess an appetite; that is, personal preferences to consume particular foods. Yet this seemingly everyday, taken-for-granted individual appetite does not occur within a social vacuum; it arises within a social context of cultural, political, religious, geographic, and economic factors that affect what and how we eat (Mennell 1996). In this sense, our food choices reflect our "social appetite" – that is, the social patterning of food production, distribution, preparation, and consumption (Germov and Williams 2008).

The act of eating is an inherently social activity, both in the sense that multiple social interactions have been involved in the production, distribution, and preparation of food by the time it is fit for consumption, and also given that eating often takes place in the company of others, whether it is the family meal, a fine dining experience, or a casual meal among friends. Commensality – that is, eating at a shared table – along with the provision of food for others carries strong emotional and social meanings (Fischler 2011). The existence of cultural preferences for particular foods, food rituals (birthdays, weddings, wakes), the etiquette of dining, and food taboos (such as the sacred cow in India and kosher food among Orthodox Jews) are all indicators of the social origins of food and eating.

In the early years of the twentieth century, Georg Simmel (1910/1997) noted that the individual act of eating was enveloped by "social forms" or patterns that shaped the way food was consumed, whereby people ate at designated times, were governed by social codes of behavior about how to eat (use of cutlery and manners), or followed particular rituals during religious and communal feasts. Sociologist Norbert Elias (1939/2000) explored the development of manners and etiquette in relation to eating, showing that over time Western societies exhibited a long-term trend of what he termed "civilizing processes" – a patterned shift from the external social control of people's behavior toward internal self-restraint.

FOOD AND IDENTITY

Food and social identity are closely entwined, and are most strongly evidenced in ethnicity, gender, and class. Indeed, the first introduction many people have to foreign cultures is through national cuisines (Italian, Thai, Chinese, Indian, and so on), and such cuisines can form strong associations with national identity, as evidenced by the spread of these cuisines with migration.

The gendered construction of food preparation and consumption has been widely studied, exploring the relationship between women and the provision of food for spouses, children, and the aged; with others noting gender preferences for particular types of food and diets (Charles and Kerr 1988; DeVault 1991), and the implications of food habits for women's body image in the context of Western preferences for a "thin ideal" of slender female bodies (Germov and Williams 2008).

Food can also be used as a means of distinguishing between social classes and as a marker of class identity (Bourdieu 1979/1984). The extent to which the social appetite operates today is possible due to the luxury afforded by the economic success of modernity, which has resulted in a broadening of food choice. Popular phrases such as "latte-drinking society" or "cappuccino culture" illustrate that the way in which a beverage is prepared, presented, and consumed acts as a marker of social class. While citizens of Western societies in particular have access to more food variety than they could ever hope to consume, it should be noted that populations in some developing countries, and subpopulations within affluent countries, are characterized by food insecurity. Food insecurity was defined at the World Food Summit in 1996 as the lack of available, affordable, and accessible food that meets both nutritional and cultural needs. The inclusion of cultural preferences in the definition acknowledges the important social role played by food.

ETHICAL CONSUMPTION AND ALTERNATIVE FOOD MOVEMENTS

Examining the social appetite brings into focus the degree to which people's food choices are an outcome of their environment (social structure) or of personal choice (agency). In the context of food, social structure refers to the way in which food is produced and distributed, and includes public policies, government regulation, and the farming, manufacturing, and marketing methods of food companies. While social structure plays a definite role in access to food, it is also subject to modification.

A potent example of how people can exercise their agency and shape the social appetite can be seen in alternative food movements, such as organics, fair trade, animal welfare, vegetarianism, sustainable agriculture, and Slow Food. Often subsumed under the broad banner of "ethical consumption," such movements attempt to promote collective action and individual behavior change through the exercise of (ethical) consumption choices (Micheletti 2010). For example, the Slow Food Movement is a global alternative food network that aims to raise awareness of the impacts of industrialized, mass-produced food, with a focus on cultural diversity, sustainability, fair trade, and the pleasures of eating as a social experience with family and friends. Slow Food arose to counteract fast food and fast life, by attempting to revalue "food time" – the time we spend on preparing, sharing, and consuming food.

THE RISE OF FOOD STUDIES

Food is as fundamental to our social and personal life as it is to our physical survival. While much has been written about food, scholarly interest in the social aspects of food, particularly food habits, identity, and the social impact of consumption, is relatively recent. While food was occasionally studied by social scientists, such as Georg Simmel's "Sociology of the Meal" (1910), Lévi-Strauss's *The Raw and the Cooked* (1964), and Mary Douglas's "Deciphering a Meal" (1972), it was from the 1980s onward that a significant shift toward food studies can be traced, with groundbreaking sociological works such as Pierre Bourdieu's *Distinction: A Social Critique of the Judgement of Taste* (1979/1984) and a series of books by Murcott (1983), Mennell, Murcott, and van Otterloo (1992), and Mennell (1996). It is speculated that the lack of significant attention to food studies up to that time reflected the taken-for-granted, everyday, and gendered nature of food preparation, which led to it being considered a somewhat mundane topic, unworthy of intellectual pursuit. By the late twentieth and early twenty-first century, though, the study of the symbolic, societal, material, and political aspects of food had become the commonplace province of many disciplines, from sociology and anthropology to cultural studies, psychology, human geography, social history, and public health nutrition, in addition to the burgeoning interdisciplinary field of food studies.

SEE ALSO: Bourdieu, Pierre; Conspicuous Consumption; Cultural Capital; Elias, Norbert; Ethical Consumption; Fair Trade; Fast Food; Slow Food Movement

REFERENCES

Bourdieu, Pierre. 1979/1984. *Distinction: A Social Critique of the Judgement of Taste*. London: Routledge & Kegan Paul.
Charles, Nickie, and Marion Kerr. 1988. *Women, Food and Families*. Manchester, UK: Manchester University Press.
DeVault, Marjorie L. 1991. *Feeding the Family: The Social Organization of Caring as Gendered Work*. Chicago, IL: Chicago University Press.
Douglas, Mary. 1972. "Deciphering a Meal." *Daedalus: Journal of the American Academy of Arts and Sciences* (Winter): 61–82.
Elias, N. 1939/2000. *The Civilizing Process*, rev. ed. Oxford: Blackwell Publishing.
Fischler, Claude. 1988. "Food, Self and Identity." *Social Science Information* 27: 275–292.
Fischler, Claude. 2011. "Commensality, Society and Culture." *Social Science Information* 50: 528–548.
Germov, John, and Lauren Williams, eds. 2008. *A Sociology of Food and Nutrition: The Social Appetite*, 3rd ed. Melbourne: Oxford University Press.
Lévi-Strauss, Claude. 1964/1969. *The Raw and the Cooked*. New York: Harper & Row.
Mennell, Stephen. 1996. *All Manners of Food: Eating and Taste in England and France from the Middle Ages to the Present*, 2nd ed. Chicago: University of Illinois Press.
Mennell, Stephen, Anne Murcott, and Anneke H. van Otterloo. 1992. *The Sociology of Food: Eating, Diet, and Culture*. London: Sage.
Micheletti, Michelle. 2010. *Political Virtue and Shopping: Individuals, Consumerism, and Collective Action*, rev. ed. New York: Palgrave Macmillan.
Murcott, Anne, ed. 1983. *The Sociology of Food and Eating*. Aldershot, UK: Gower.
Simmel, Georg. 1997/1910. "Sociology of the Meal." In *Simmel on Culture: Selected Writings*, edited by David Frisby and Mike Featherstone, 130–136. London: Sage.

Food Deserts

ALEXANDRA RODNEY
University of Toronto, Canada

A "food desert" is a disadvantaged urban or rural geographic area in which residents have restricted access to healthy, affordable, fresh food from a supermarket. Food deserts may be served only by fringe retailers (e.g., convenience stores) with higher prices and a scarcity of nutritious food. Research into the existence and health implications of food deserts began in the 1990s following a report produced by the Department of Health in London (Beaulac, Kristjansson, and Cummins 2009). Food deserts are an important public health issue because they contribute to social disparities in health outcomes. People generally shop at outlets closest to them and the foods most readily available in food deserts are increasingly fast-food options. These are high in sugar, fat, and calories, putting residents living in food deserts at greater risk for obesity and chronic diseases. In contrast, larger stores such as supermarkets generally offer healthier choices and lower overall prices. Residents in areas with supermarkets are more likely to purchase fruit and vegetables.

Compelling evidence shows that food deserts exist in the United States, while the existence of food deserts in the United Kingdom and Canada is highly debated (Beaulac, Kristjansson, and Cummins 2009). More than 23 million Americans live in food deserts, with 75 percent of these in urban areas (ERS 2009). In order to qualify as a food desert in the United States, a census tract must have a poverty rate of at least 20 percent and at least 33 percent of the population must have restricted access to a healthy, affordable food outlet (defined as living more than 1 mile away from a supermarket or large grocery store in urban areas and more than

10 miles away in rural areas) (USDA 2014). Food deserts are found in communities with greater racial segregation and economic deprivation. They are prevalent in areas with a high proportion of low-income African American and Latino residents. These groups are also more likely to suffer from diet-related diseases such as type 2 diabetes.

Public awareness of food deserts has been growing, along with policy interventions designed to remediate food deserts. For example, the Obama administration's White House Task Force on Childhood Obesity has identified the challenge of bringing healthy and affordable foods to food deserts as one aspect of solving the obesity problem in the United States. Its Healthy Food Financing Initiative provides tax breaks and financing for stores and markets selling healthy food in underserved areas. However, critics have noted that merely increasing availability ignores sociodemographic factors and other aspects of the food environment that lead to unhealthy food choices and the prevalence of obesity.

Future research directions involve addressing gaps in knowledge about how residence in a food desert affects shopping patterns, food intake, and nutritional health outcomes. Specifically, longitudinal qualitative research is warranted in order to track populations over time. Further research is also necessary in countries other than the United States, within and across geographic areas, in terms of food item and supermarket availability. Finally, few studies have examined the influence of other healthy food retailers on life in a food desert.

SEE ALSO: Fast Food; Food; Shopping; Supermarkets

REFERENCES

Beaulac, Julie, Elizabeth Kristjansson, and Steven Cummins. 2009. "A Systematic Review of Food Deserts." *Preventing Chronic Disease: Public Health Research, Practice and Policy* 6(3): 1–10.

ERS. 2009. "Access to Affordable and Nutritious Food." *ERS Report Summary*. Washington, DC: Economic Research Service, US Department of Agriculture.

USDA. 2014. *Food Access Research Atlas*. Washington, DC: United States Department of Agriculture. http://www.ers.usda.gov/data-products/food-access-research-atlas/about-the-atlas.aspx#.U5nQ_HJdWSo.

Fordism/Post-Fordism

HARLAND PRECHEL
Texas A&M University, USA

Fordism and post-Fordism emerged from Taylorism and other forms of scientific management that formalized control over the labor process. Formal control over the labor process was accelerated when Henry Ford and his engineers applied the principles of scientific management to the entire labor process. *Fordism* represents two critical changes in the historical process of fragmenting tasks and increasing the division of labor in order to increase efficiency and control of the labor process. First, whereas Taylorism developed work rules to standardize the production of parts, Fordism brought these standardized parts to the worker, which further separated conception from execution by specifying how to assemble the parts. Second, using the assembly line to bring work to the worker made it possible to increase the pace of work. While Ford implemented these production principles elsewhere, they were manifested in the most extreme form at the Ford River Rouge Complex, which became the largest integrated factory in the world when it was completed in 1928.

Fordist production enabled Ford to pay higher wages while maintaining high profits. His capacity to pay higher wages than other capitalists permitted Ford to be more selective when hiring workers and to impose stricter work standards on them. Ford also created internal labor markets by establishing job classifications and hierarchies that allowed workers to be upwardly mobile within the company. These internal labor markets created competition among workers, which divided workers against one another and reduced solidarity. Fordism also entailed a mode of state regulation that attempted to institutionalize economic growth and stability by limiting workers' rights, creating a welfare state, and implementing Keynesian economic policies. However, Fordism also exacerbated one of the fundamental contractions of capitalism: overproduction and underconsumption.

By the 1920s, business leaders identified three interrelated problems that undermined stable capitalist growth and development. First, the current level of consumption would not sustain mass production. Second, fragmentation of the labor process and low wages created social unrest, which encouraged unionization and strikes. Third, the middle and working classes were increasingly resistant to corporate power. Business leaders were aware of a fourth problem, which was largely ignored until it was temporarily solved in the 1950s: wages for most workers did not permit them to consume beyond the level required for subsistence (Bernstein 1960). As a result of the disparity between earning and spending power, much of the consumption of automobiles in the 1920s was done at the expense of necessities such as clothing and food or by mortgaging family properties (Lynd and Lynd 1929).

To overcome these impediments to capital accumulation, capitalists expanded their focus from industrial production to social engineering. A core component of this strategy created and disseminated an ideology that shifted personal satisfaction from work to satisfaction from consumption. However, the social values and emerging working-class solidarity presented obstacles to this transformation in consciousness. To create a culture of mass consumption, advertisers were employed to replace the idea that people are members of families, communities, and classes with the idea of a mass where individuals "could locate their needs and frustrations in terms of consumption of goods rather than the quality and content of life (work)" (Ewen 1976, 43). The self-appointed "captains of consciousness" also developed advertising strategies to eradicate the social values of ethnic immigrants, who tended to be conservative in their consumptive habits, by making them "ashamed of their origins and, consequently, the habits and practices that betrayed them as alien" (Ewen 1976, 43). Advertisers identified individual character flaws and presented the consumption of mass-produced goods as the solution to their individual shortcomings. To illustrate, by the mid-1920s, advertisers claimed that modern living robbed women of their natural beauty and that mass-produced beauty products would restore it.

Although the Great Depression of the 1930s presented new obstacles to capitalists' efforts to create a culture of mass consumption, the New Deal policies of the Roosevelt administration promoted consumerism, especially in the housing industry. A central component of this policy initiative was the 1938 amendment to the National Housing Act, which created the Federal National Mortgage Association, also known as Fannie Mae. This quasi-government organization was established to create a secondary mortgage market by purchasing insured loans from the Federal Housing Administration. These organizational and political–legal arrangements increased the amount of capital available to banks, which allowed them to sell more mortgages. Increasing capital for home ownership was further advanced by the post-World War II veteran benefits program. By the 1950s, home ownership had become a core component of US consumer capitalism and the "American Dream." Subsequent modifications to housing policy further increased the flow of capital into financial markets, thereby increasing the capacity of the working classes to participate in the American Dream.

However, the limitations of Fordism became apparent in 1973 when the oil crisis and the economic downturn resulted in an abrupt halt to US capitalist growth and development. This capital accumulation crisis represents a historical turning point and the transition to *post-Fordism*. The emergent organizational and political–legal arrangements restructured the production process, increased the role of the state in balancing production with consumption, accelerated globalization, and facilitated the emergence of giant multinational corporations and financial institutions that exercise control over trade, domestic companies, and some nation-states.

Despite agreement that a transition occurred, there is considerable debate among social scientists over how to characterize this form of social organization. In contrast to those who characterize post-Fordism as global corporate dominance, other scholars view this transition as creating a more flexible form of economic organization and increasing individualism and pluralistic lifestyles. There is also considerable debate over whether post-Fordism represents a historical transition or modifies previous trends. Still other scholars challenge the broad generalizations in post-Fordist theory for denying the complex and heterogeneous causal processes that operate in different places in the global economy (Hall et al. 1995).

However, there are two issues that separate Fordism from post-Fordism. During the Fordist era, inequality declined and workers' wages provided the primary means to consume industrial commodities. In contrast, during the post-Fordist era, inequality increased to historic record levels and consumption was increasingly based on credit. Although the increase in consumer credit occurred in many economic sectors (Manning 2010) during the post-Fordist era, it reached record levels in the housing industry after the political–legal arrangements were redefined in ways that permitted finance capital to enter the secondary mortgage market.

Although scores of articles and books have been written on the 2008 meltdown of the mortgage-backed securities market, little attention has been given to why this particular form of consumerism became widespread in the late twentieth century. The answer to this question lies, in part, in the state's response to the crisis that emerged in the manufacturing sector in the mid-1970s and early 1980s (Prechel 2000). After the Reagan administration provided massive subsidies in the form of tax breaks to manufacturing corporations, the financial, insurance, and real estate (FIRE) segment of the economy maintained that these policies were biased and lobbied government officials to pass policies that advanced their capital accumulation agendas. The resolution of this conflict between capitalist class factions included policies that facilitated capitalism growth and development in the energy, housing, and financial sectors of the economy. Although these policies succeeded in restoring capitalist growth and development in the short term (i.e., 1990s and early 2000s), they had adverse consequences for individuals and societies throughout the global economy in the long term. By the first decade of the twenty-first century, it was clear that the creation of financial instruments in the energy and housing sectors created opportunities and incentives for corporate managers to engage in financial malfeasance (Prechel and Morris 2010).

The meltdown of financial markets in 2008 and the subsequent Great Recession raise important questions about the capacity of post-Fordist consumer capitalism to sustain capitalist growth and development in the long term. The challenge of post-Fordism is how to create a balance among contradictory – or, at least, the seemingly incompatible – agendas of realizing corporate capital accumulation goals, reducing dependence on credit while sustaining a middle-class lifestyle, sustaining the natural environment, generating sufficient state revenues to subsidize aspects of the economy that are not in the commodity form but are necessary to sustain capitalism (e.g., education, transportation, utilities), and limiting risk-taking behavior by managers in large and complex corporations.

SEE ALSO: Class; Consumption in the United States; Marx, Karl; Taxes

REFERENCES

Bernstein, Irving. 1960. *The Lean Years*. Baltimore, MD: Penguin.

Ewen, Stuart. 1976. *Captains of Consciousness: Advertising and the Social Roots of the Consumer Culture*. New York: McGraw-Hill.

Hall, Stuart, David Held, Don Hubert, and Kenneth Thompson. 1995. *Modernity*. Cambridge, UK: Polity.

Lynd, Robert, and Helen Lynd. 1929. *Middletown: A Study in Contemporary American Culture*. New York: Harcourt Brace.

Manning, Robert. 2010. *Credit Card Nation*. New York: Basic Books.

Prechel, Harland. 2000. *Big Business and the State: Historical Transitions and Corporate Transformations, 1880–1990s*. Albany, NY: State University of New York Press.

Prechel, Harland, and Theresa Morris. 2010. "The Effects of Organizational and Political Embeddedness on Financial Malfeasance in the Largest US Corporations: Dependence, Incentives and Opportunities." *American Sociological Review* 75: 331–354.

Franchising

DAVID B. BILLS
University of Iowa, USA

Franchising is a business arrangement in which a parent company contracts with one or more smaller firms to grant or sell to them the right to distribute its products, implement its processes, or use its trade name. The recent development of franchising in the United States and elsewhere is characterized by steady to rapid growth in the number of franchised establishments, their increased levels of employment and sales, and their proliferation beyond the restaurant and retailing sectors in which they have been historically most prevalent into virtually all areas of contemporary economies.

The relationship between franchisors and franchisees is based on a contract that specifies the legal responsibilities and mutual expectations of each party to the contract. Still, the fact that the franchise relationship is so nearly an exclusive one means that the franchisors and franchisees share many common interests. Franchisors acquire a generally reliable means to expand their businesses, while franchisees acquire a measure of independence, sense of ownership, and reduced risk. Franchising permits the exploitation of efficiencies from scale economies. It allows the establishment of a parent company to share the overhead costs of such factors as marketing, advertising, and monitoring. These costs are often prohibitively expensive for a freestanding establishment. About 80 percent of the time, the franchisee buys the business or a share of the business, but often the parent company retains ownership. This pattern varies a great deal across industries.

There are two principal types of franchising, product franchising and business format franchising. The United States Department of Commerce defines product and trade name franchising as "an independent sales relationship between supplier and dealer in which the dealer acquires some of the identity of the supplier." It defines business format franchising as "an ongoing business relationship between franchisor and franchisee that includes not only the product, service, and trademark, but the entire business concept itself – a marketing strategy and plan, operating manuals and standards, quality control, and a continuing process of assistance and guidance." Product franchising (such as beverage bottling) is older and larger in sales value in the United States than business format franchising, although the share of franchise sales in the product franchising sector is declining. Business format franchising, the most common kinds of which are quick service restaurants, lodging, retail food, and table/full service restaurants, is, however, more widespread than product distribution franchising, producing about four times as many establishments and jobs.

The franchising sector in the United States has grown large, and in the early 2010s was continuing to outpace most of the private sector economy in both job growth and sales growth. While discrepancies in the definition of franchising often lead to inconsistent estimates, there are in the order of 900,000 franchises in the United States, representing some 3000 franchise systems. Franchised businesses in the United States generated about US$2.1 trillion in output in 2011. Franchising's share of total sales is much higher in some industries, but the format has spread to all corners of the economy. About 8 million Americans are directly employed in franchises. Over half of these individuals are employed in restaurants. Other sectors of high franchise employment include automobile and parts dealers, accommodation, business services, and gas stations and auto repair. Using several financial and economic indicators, *Entrepreneur* magazine in 2013 ranked America's top franchises as Hampton Hotels, Subway, JiffyLube, 7-Eleven, Supercuts, Anytime Fitness, Servpro, Denny's, McDonald's, and Pizza Hut.

While developed primarily in the United States, the reach of franchising is increasingly global. In Australia, for example, a greater share of retailing employment consists of employees in franchises than is the case in the United States (53 percent versus 41 percent). The inroads of franchising to such nations as China, India, and Brazil, while small as a share of overall economic activity, are in absolute terms already quite significant.

SEE ALSO: B2B Marketing; Commodity Chains; McDonaldization

FURTHER READING

Birkeland, Peter M. 2002. *Franchising Dreams: The Lure of Entrepreneurship in America*. Chicago, IL: University of Chicago Press.

Dant, Rajiv P., Marko Grünhagen, and Josef Windsperger. 2011. "Franchising Research Frontiers for the Twenty-First Century." *Journal of Retailing* 87: 253–268.

Dicke, Thomas S. 1992. *Franchising in America*. Chapel Hill: University of North Carolina Press.

Frankfurt School

LAUREN LANGMAN
Loyola University Chicago, USA

For Marx, the defining moment of the nineteenth century was the rise of industrial capitalism, which had transformed the nature of work, governance, values, and indeed the routines of everyday life. Capitalism spread throughout the world; it overthrew dynastic rule, battered down traditions, ended the "idiocy of rural life," and, above all, created vast wealth – at least for capitalists. However, this wealth was based on the sale of commodities that were produced by workers who sold their labor to capitalists for wages; thus labor became a commodity that greatly increased the value of raw materials turned into commodities for markets. But workers received very little of that increased value as wages; indeed, workers lived in poverty and destitution. Marx's fundamental concern was not simply the exploitation or poverty of the workers, but the alienation, objectification, and estrangement that left workers powerless, without recognition or dignity as human beings, bereft of community, and incapable of realizing their nature as members of the human species.

Marx believed that given the contradictions of capitalism, and its vast inequality, workers would eventually organize, mobilize, and overthrow the system. But that never happened. By the early twentieth century, capitalism itself had undergone a number of fundamental transformations, not least of which was the mass production of consumer goods and the increased wages that enabled workers to afford such goods. As Henry Ford said, he wanted to build a car that his well-paid workers could afford. Moreover, at the same time, a mass culture in movies, magazines, and radio had emerged. Consumerism and mass media thwarted revolutionary movements.

The Communist Party's orthodox Marxism focused almost exclusively on economics. (Marx himself had noted the importance of culture and ideology.) But elsewhere, Marxist thought was itself undergoing transformation in order to understand the new realities of the twentieth century. Karl Korsch, in *Marxism and Philosophy* (1923), argued for the enduring importance of philosophy within Marxist theory. At about the same time, Georg Lukács's seminal work, *History and Class Consciousness*, had a major impact in Marxist circles. Finally, in the 1930s, Marx's 1844 manuscripts appeared, which showed his concerns with alienation.

Given the exhaustion of classical Marxist theory rooted in early nineteenth-century factory production, in the 1920s a group of German scholars formed the Institute for Social Research and laid the foundations of what would become known as the Frankfurt School of Critical Theory – an attempt to update Marxian critique to explain the then present age by drawing upon Weber's theories of rationality and Freudian psychology. Following World War I, Germany had to pay France massive reparations; and later, as a result of the economic crises of world capital, unemployment grew, as did inflation. There were violent conflicts between left and right. The Weimar government was weak, and by 1933 the Nazis had come to power. How could one of the most culturally advanced countries in the world, a nation whose art, literature, and music were universally applauded, witness massive mobilizations for the irrational, nihilistic Nazi party led by Adolf Hitler? This question informed the research and thinking of the Frankfurt School and provided valuable insights. They underlined the important role of an authoritarian character for those with a psychological predisposition to follow a charismatic, controlling father figure who promised much in exchange for obedience, and national greatness over humiliation. Moreover, whatever else might be said of the Nazis, they understood how to use the new mass media of film and radio to disseminate their propaganda to brilliant effect, particularly blaming communists, socialists, and Jews for the adversities that had befallen Germany. Given this atmosphere, and the fact that many of the members of the Frankfurt School were in fact Jewish socialists, the members left Germany and eventually settled in the United States. As the war ended, the scholars of the Frankfurt School began to shift their attention to the changing nature of twentieth-century capitalism, especially the rapid rise of mass media and consumerism.

THE CULTURE INDUSTRIES

Their earlier studies of the appeal of fascism and the role of mass-mediated film and radio propaganda informed the work of the Frankfurt scholars. They established a number of traditions that still inform our view of contemporary consumer society, especially the nature of consumer-based identities, the nature of mass media, and how advertising as psychologically informed propaganda fostered "artificial desires" to be gratified though consuming various goods, services, or experiences. Moreover, just as the production of commodities meant alienation for the worker, so the consumption of commodities led to alienation for the consumer who had become an object to be manipulated, their consciousness and desires being colonized so that they might consume more goods.

Horkheimer and Adorno argued that the "culture industry" – the agglomeration of radio, film, Broadway musicals, magazines (and eventually television) – needed to be understood in much the same way as any other form of standardized mass production, like cars, appliances, or apparel. And thus, in the culture industry, standard themes were endlessly recycled and, regardless of the variations, the good guy always got the gal (at least if she was the "decent" kind of gal); and the good guys, cowboys, soldiers, and private detectives always got the bad guys, often via violent spectacles, ranging from the sheriff taking out the bad guys, to James Bond's forces overtaking those of the arch-villain or the soldiers beating the enemy.

The primary goals of the culture industry were to produce profits for its producers and for the advertisers who utilized mass media to disseminate "information" about their products, and to promulgate an implicit worldview that extolled the United States and its capitalist system while demonizing communist or socialist alternatives. For the most part, the culture industries mass produced and distributed deception, eroded the capacity for critical thought and independent judgment, and reinforced tendencies for conformity. Much of that deception was based on the promise of psychological gratification that might be found in consumption – to which we now turn.

CONSUMERISM

In a number of his writings, Erich Fromm noted the historical changes in the nature of character structure and commented that, by the twentieth century, the increasingly typical character type was what he called the "marketing character," the person who molds themselves into the desirable image of the society in order to sell themselves as a commodity to either sell other goods, advance within organizations, or perhaps seduce a lover. They are always seeking to buy what is new, what is good and desirable, what promises to enhance the self. Such people are highly conformist and often use displays of monetary wealth and status to display that conformity; however, at heart, such characters tend to be quite empty and devoid of a rich inner life or any independence of thought, or able to criticize the social or political world around them. Thus, Fromm pioneered the psychosocial aspects of consumerism and conformity.

Herbert Marcuse's *One-Dimensional Man* (1964), one of the most important critical books of the twentieth century, remains a foundation for critical theories of consumption. Marcuse carefully illustrated how the mass media, especially the news media, promoted one-dimensional, conformist thought incapable of either self-reflection or critique of social practices. One of the most important aspects of contemporary society, for Marcuse, was its capacity to socially construct and engender "artificial needs": for example, the need to consume goods in order to create and articulate an identity in which one's very selfhood is located in one's clothes, dwellings, furnishings, tastes in travel, and leisure activities (including, ironically enough, cultural consumption). Consumption was a new form of social control.

While humans may require shelter, do they need huge mansions? No, the need for "conspicuous consumption" (Veblen 1899) was an attempt to display the worthiness of oneself as embodied in a material form rather than more immaterial aspects of self such as kindness, empathy and caring for others, decency in relationships, and perhaps charitable contributions of time or money for the less fortunate. While the production of artificial needs well serves a society whose advanced technologies can produce a plethora of goods and services, such "needs" may actually impair the capacity to gratify more basic needs, especially the need for relationships to other people, creative self-expression, and the freedom to make "genuine" choices of self and lifestyle independently of social standards – especially standards for mass-marketed consumer-based selfhood.

One of the most important of Marcuse's insights was the charting of the transformation and colonization of sexual desire. For Freud, civilization itself depended on the repression of sexuality so that people might work together, sublimating desire, to minimize social conflict and channel creative energies toward social ends. But for Freud, that sublimation required a repressive superego, and the price of our civilization was guilt and personal suffering. Wilhelm Reich, however, argued that Freud had conflated civilization with its specific capitalist forms; rather, it was capitalist civilization, not civilization in general, that required repression in order to instill conformity and compliance into the working classes lest they become revolutionaries.

For Marcuse, however, advanced capitalism based on consumerism required a relaxation of restraints such that people might forsake ascetic values such as thrift and prudence and wantonly indulge in consumerism; thus a great deal of the consumer economy is based on "impulse buying," although, to a large extent, these impulses have already been insinuated within the character. Consumerism required relaxation of restraints, especially sexual constraints, and there was greater toleration of sexual gratification in order to serve what Marcuse called "repressive de-sublimation." Sexual desire was no longer repressed but became the goal of compulsive work that would enable the consumption of various goods that promised more and better sexuality. Of course, these would include cars, clothes, accessories, sophisticated culinary tastes, and even the fashioning of one's body using diet, trainers, and ultimately plastic surgeons. But for Marcuse, this meant that sexuality has moved from repressed to repressing, and, notwithstanding the appearance of "freedom" in a more "relaxed" and "tolerant society," consumer-based sexual freedom largely served to entrap the person within a consumer society that provides ersatz gratifications in lieu of genuine freedom and happiness. The mass production of commodities embodying cultural meanings claims the entire person, especially the inner qualities of mind that might enable opposition to the status quo which in fact thwarts and limits genuine freedom, individualism, and creative self-realization – yet this one-dimensional society seems so "reasonable."

CONCLUSION

While the Frankfurt School represented an initial attempt to come to grips with the new intertwining of mass media, culture, and consumerism, it generated a number of critiques. Perhaps the most serious of these criticisms was the view that the mass media turn people into mindless robots, "cultural dupes" devoid of agency. The tradition of critical cultural studies that began in Birmingham, UK, argued that people actively code and decode media and negotiate the meanings and understandings of cultural products. And thus mass culture may not simply produce conformity, but may actually provide the materials by which particular subcultures based on "style" can reject and reverse intended meanings.

By the latter part of the twentieth century, consumerism had become the dominant way of life in most of the advanced societies of the world. It is in this context that postmodernism arose, especially the work of the sociologist Jean Baudrillard, whose many works extolled the semiotics of consumer society and symbolic values that have displaced the society of production-based exchange value, since all goods signify the same things. For Baudrillard, consumer society with its endless spectacles and simulations challenged many of the Frankfurt School's ideas: for example, the extent to which people were duped by advertising – people are actors within a system in which freedom of choice is ubiquitous, and the pleasures of consumption are experienced as "real" rather than alienated (the situation as interpreted by scholars). People pursue happiness; the "fun morality" based on the possession and exploitation of things becomes dominant.

Given the valuable insights that the Frankfurt School has provided, yet given its limitations, where do we go from here? At this point, we might note the work of Douglas Kellner who has attempted to revise, update, and make relevant the legacies of the Frankfurt School. He has argued that mass media, the culture industries, and consumerism be understood dialectically – that is, they may act to secure domination through deception and diversion, and suggest "artificial needs" gratified through consumption that serve to secure conformity and reproduce domination. But at the same time, various media may indeed include critical subtexts that do critique domination. Consider, for example, the extent to which major progressive shifts in attitudes and values regarding women, ethnic minorities, homosexuals, and so on have been impacted by the media and its celebrities – many of whom have been both role models for and outspoken critics of traditional stereotypes.

The Frankfurt School was the earliest comprehensive theory of mass media, the culture industries, and consumerism. But as a theory driven by the rise of fascism and then the postwar explosion of mass culture and mass consumption, that theory has required considerable revisions for our current society that is now shaped by the fiscal crises of capitalism, economic stagnation, and the potential environmental catastrophes facing us. Given the many critiques that have been made, and the revisions that are currently underway, the Frankfurt School will continue to stimulate students of media and consumerism.

SEE ALSO: Adorno, Theodor; Consumption, Postmodern; Marx, Karl; Mass Culture; Mass Media

REFERENCES

Korsch, Karl. 1923/1972. *Marxism and Philosophy*. London: New Left Books.

Veblen, Thorstein. 1899. *The Theory of the Leisure Class: An Economic Study of Institutions*. New York: Macmillan.

FURTHER READING

Fromm, Erich. 1947. *Escape from Freedom*. New York: Holt Rinehart.

Horkheimer, Max, and Theodor Adorno. 1944/2002. *The Dialect of Enlightenment*. Stanford, CA: Stanford University Press.

Jay, Martin. 1973. *The Dialectical Imagination*. Boston, MA: Little, Brown.

Kellner, Douglas. 1992. *Critical Theory, Marxism, and Modernity*. Baltimore, MD: Johns Hopkins University Press.

Marcuse, Herbert. 1964. *One-Dimensional Man*. London: Routledge.

Free Trade Zones/Export Processing Zones

CHRISTOPH HENNING
University of St. Gallen, Switzerland

Export processing zones (EPZs), also called free trade zones, are industrial islands of exception within global capitalism. They aim to attract foreign direct investment (FDI) offshore, into designated areas in developing countries with special legislation (or rather deregulation). Here, goods and services are produced directly for the global market, circumventing the usual embeddedness into local legal codes and cultural norms. The International Labor Organization (ILO) in Geneva, which has monitored EPZs for decades now, due to their often problematic working conditions, defines EPZs as "industrial zones with special incentives set up to attract foreign investors, in which imported materials undergo some degree of processing before being (re)exported again" (ILO 2003, 9).

The main local factor is "cheap but disciplined labor" (McCallum 2011, 15), whereas raw materials, production technology, and knowledge are imported into these zones by foreign investors – in most cases by the international companies themselves, who take care not to spread their technological knowledge to the host countries too openly (Milberg and Amengual 2008, 21). The products are seldom sold on the local market, but are directly taken back to the global market. Hence, the links to the local country are minimal, both forward (selling to) and backward (buying from the local market). In many cases the legal codes and labor regulations are less strict in these zones, compared to the situation in the company's home country, but also compared to the developing country itself. Unions are often not allowed and members are even persecuted in some countries. This has given rise to serious criticism from NGOs (nongovernmental organizations) and unions (e.g., ICFTU 2004; Rosselson 2007). In the meantime, some companies have introduced corporate social responsibility (CSR) programs (Milberg and Amengual 2008, 48ff.). However, EPZs remain a contested topic in the global economic and political debate. As one NGO, the Fair Labor Association, noted in 2007, "monitoring alone is an inadequate tool to create sustainable change in working conditions" (cited from Milberg and Amengual 2008, 48). Milberg and Amengual imply that as long as regulations and codes of conduct remain private (that is, not politically enforced), it depends on consumers and consumer pressure groups how far fairer practices will or will not be realized. Awareness of the politics of EPZs is therefore of prime importance for an ethics of consumption.

Most EPZs are located in Asia, South America, or Africa, and the vast majority of the workforce is female (estimates range up to 90 percent; see ILO 2003, 6). Some believe the reason for this is that women cost less and tend to be more "compliant" (ICFTU 2004, 11f.). The main industries involved are textiles and clothing (Milberg and Amengual 2008, 10), but increasingly also higher-value goods (electronics, for example) or services (such as finance or tourism; ILO 2003, 2). It is estimated that at the moment there are roughly "3000 zones in 135 countries, accounting for over 68 million direct jobs and over $500 billion of direct trade-related value added within zones" (McCallum 2011, 2). According to Milberg and Amengual (2008), however, this only amounts to 0.2 percent of global employment.

What are the reasons for introducing EPZs? Two parties seem to profit from them: multinational companies and governments in developing countries (which are not identical to their "nations" or populace). The main advantages for multinational companies are the low labor costs, the low level of unionization, and low taxes and tariffs (if any at all). Together with good infrastructure (zones are often located at ports etc.) provided by the local government, but also with high mobility due to the low level of engagement in the host country, this allows for higher profit margins. But what is in it for the governments? Several factors may count here. First, these zones provide jobs which may occupy an otherwise underemployed labor force. Second, they "catalyze" a region economically (ILO 2003, 12) by linking the zones to the rest of the country, attracting more foreign capital and leading local producers too to develop an export orientation. Finally, attracting foreign direct investment is often assumed to have an impact on economic growth, and growth in turn is said to have an influence on overall development – at least, this is the story orthodox economic theory and the Washington Consensus have told in the last decades. These parties therefore have to be seen as the third actor involved. Free trade, or export-oriented growth, is a position "that for decades has been promoted by the IMF, the World Bank and powerful economists" (McCallum 2011, 3). In a way, then, EPZs are the direct manifestation of the general belief in the "myth of free trade" (Shaikh 2007). The belief is that free trade will automatically benefit everyone – if not immediately, then maybe later.

On a closer view, however, the three hopes that Southern governments associated with the idea of EPZs (more and better jobs, increased growth due to more exports and links to the local market, and a push toward overall development) are only partly fulfilled. An ethical assessment therefore has to remain ambiguous. In fact, the EPZs did provide jobs in those areas, sometimes even with better wages compared to the local wage rate (but still at a very low rate), with working conditions remaining a matter of concern as employers exert a "downward pressure on wages and labour standards, the so-called race to the bottom" (McCallum 2011, 2). Second, EPZs have in many cases increased the exports of developing countries, but the bulk of profits continue to flow to the multinational company and benefits to the host country are limited. Third, EPZs do enhance trade, but with questionable impacts on the host as EPZs prove to be a "sledgehammer method" of introducing "free trade."

In the end, the global effects of the EPZs show what the "classical" theory of competitive advantage (Shaikh 1980, 2007) would predict, namely that in international trade absolute differences matter and only the stronger party is able to appropriate the gains from an economic transaction. It is no wonder that Western countries, which today enforce free trade on others, themselves protected their own markets while they industrialized (and continue to do so even today, see Raffer 1987, 1f., 134ff.). So, introducing EPZs is a dubious way to contribute to global justice.

SEE ALSO: Capitalism; Fair Trade; Global Markets; Sweatshops

REFERENCES

ICFTU. 2004. "Behind the Brand Names. Working Conditions and Labour Rights in Export Processing Zones." Geneva: International Confederation of Free Trade Unions. www.newunionism.net/library/internationalism.

ILO. 2003. "Employment and Social Policy in Respect of Export Processing Zones (EPZs)." GB.286/ESP/3. Geneva: International Labour Organization.

McCallum, Jamie K. 2011. "Export Processing Zones: Comparative Data from China, Honduras, Nicaragua and South Africa." ILO Working Paper 21. Geneva: International Labour Organization.

Milberg, William, and Matthew Amengual. 2008. "Economic Development and Working Conditions in Export Processing Zones: A Survey of Trends." ILO Working Paper 3. Geneva: International Labour Organization.

Raffer, Kuniber. 1987. *Unequal Exchange and the Evolution of the World System.* London: Macmillan.

Rosselson, Ruth. 2007. "Export Processing Zones or Exploiting People Zones?" *Ethical Consumer,* 106 (May/June 2007). Accessed July 26, 2014. www.ethicalconsumer.org/commentanalysis/fairtrade/exportprocessingzones.aspx.

Shaikh, Anwar. 1980. "On the Laws of International Exchange." In *Growth, Profits, and Property: Essays in the Revival of Political Economy,* edited by Edward J. Nell, 204–235. Cambridge, UK: Cambridge University Press.

Shaikh, Anwar. 2007. "Globalization and the Myth of Free Trade." In *Globalization and the Myth of Free Trade: History, Theory, and Empirical Evidence,* edited by Anwar Shaikh, 50–68. Abingdon, UK: Routledge.

FURTHER READING

Muench, Richard, and Christian Dressel. 2011. *Das Regime des Freihandels: Entwicklung und Ungleichheit in der Weltgesellschaft.* Frankurt am Main: Campus.

G

Gay and Lesbian/Queer Markets/Marketing

JOHN EDWARD CAMPBELL
Temple University, USA

"Gay marketing" or "gay and lesbian marketing" refers to advertising campaigns designed to appeal to gay male and/or lesbian consumers, whether these advertisements are explicit or coded. Because advertising appeals targeted at gay male and/or lesbian consumers are seldom inclusive of bisexual or transgender people, the term "LGBT marketing" is not generally used by either marketing professionals or scholars (Chasin 2000; Sender 2004; Campbell 2005). The term "gay marketing" can be used to indicate advertising campaigns aimed specifically at gay male consumers, lesbian consumers, or gay male and lesbian consumers more broadly. Gay marketing is part of a larger shift in the advertising industry during the latter half of the twentieth century away from so-called "general market" appeals to advertising campaigns aimed at specific "niche markets" or "target markets" (Turow 2006). Gay marketing appeals take the form of advertisements or sponsored content in gay-oriented publications (e.g., *The Advocate*, *Out*, *Instinct Magazine*, *Curve*, *MetroSource*) and on gay-oriented websites (e.g., PlanetOut.com and Gay.com), direct mail solicitations, coded advertisements appearing in the commercial media, and, more recently, open appeals to gay consumers in the mainstream media (Gross 2001; Sender 2004; Campbell 2005; Ostrow 2012).

The historical development of gay marketing is fundamentally intertwined with the emergence of national gay publications (Chasin 2000; Gross 2001; Sender 2004). In the 1970s, when marketers started conceptualizing gay men as a potentially lucrative market, advertisers wishing to reach these consumers had to position their appeals in gay publications because many mainstream publications refused ads containing the words "gay" or "homosexual" (Sender 2004). A national venue for gay advertisements did not emerge until the mid-1970s when David Goodstein purchased the *Los Angeles Advocate* and transformed it into the national gay publication *The Advocate*, promoting a new image of gay men as affluent, cultured, and conspicuous consumers (Gross 2001; Sender 2004). According to Sender, two developments in 1979 increased marketer interest in reaching out to gay consumers. The first development was the founding of Rivendell Marketing, a media sales company for gay publications with a national scope.

The Wiley Blackwell Encyclopedia of Consumption and Consumer Studies, First Edition.
Edited by Daniel Thomas Cook and J. Michael Ryan.

The second development was the National March on Washington for Lesbian and Gay Rights on October 14, 1979. Attended by an estimated 79,000 demonstrators, the rally "alerted marketers to a sizable cluster of potential consumers" (Sender 2004, 32). Notably, the Second National March on Washington for Lesbian and Gay Rights on October 11, 1987 and the March on Washington for Lesbian, Gay, and Bi Equal Rights and Liberation on April 25, 1993 were both used by marketers as opportunities to survey gay consumers (Badgett 2001).

Although major corporations shied away from marketing to gay consumers in the 1980s due largely to the AIDS crisis, corporate interest in courting the gay market increased in the early 1990s after several marketing surveys constructed an image of gay men and lesbians as economically prosperous and highly loyal consumers (Sender 2004). The most influential of these marketing surveys were the 1988 Simmons Market Research Bureau survey of the readership of eight papers produced by the National Gay Newspaper Guild and the 1990 Overlooked Opinions survey of the readership of major gay publications as well as attendees of major Gay Pride events (Baker 1997). Both surveys "disproportionately represented the politically active and the affluent," thereby generating an estimate of gay wealth that was greatly exaggerated (Baker 1997, 13). The survey by Overlooked Opinions estimated the total annual income of the gay community at US$514 billion, an estimate scholars consider to be grossly inflated (Baker 1997; Sender 2004). In 1993, Yankelovich Partners conducted a more comprehensive survey, finding that the incomes of gays and lesbians were comparable to the general population, and, in fact, gay men had an average annual income slightly lower than that of heterosexual men (Baker 1997). Notably, a 2013 study from the Williams Institute found that lesbian, gay, and bisexual Americans are more likely to live in poverty than heterosexual Americans (Badgett, Durso, and Schneebaum 2013). However, the Simmons Market Research and Overlooked Opinions surveys had already received significant publicity, fostering a fallacious image of gays and lesbians as affluent, hedonistic, and DINKs (Double Income, No Kids) with no familial responsibilities to "hamper their job advancement or accumulation of wealth" (Badgett 2001, 1). Although scholars would later deconstruct this image of gay wealth (Badgett 2001; Gross 2001; Sender 2004), its currency in the popular press proved politically damaging to LGBT civil rights efforts. This was demonstrated in Colorado in 1992 when champions of an anti-gay ballot initiative used the figures from the Overlooked Opinions survey to support their claims that gays and lesbians do not need "special rights" (Hardisty and Gluckman 1997).

This image of affluence among gay and lesbian consumers led to a proliferation of advertising agencies targeting gay consumers in the 1990s. By the end of the decade, major advertising agencies, such as Countrywide Porter Novelli in Britain, had established special divisions to target the gay market. This image of gay affluence also prompted major corporations to sponsor gay social events, as long as those events were not overtly "political." For instance, in 1994 Miller Brewing Company along with Continental Airlines signed on to be among the first corporate sponsors of Gay Games IV and Cultural Festival in New York City (Baker 1997). Most significant was the explosion of corporate advertising in gay magazines by major corporations such as Seagram and PepsiCo, fostering the production of several upscale, "glossy" national gay and lesbian publications, including *Out* and *Genre* (both launched in 1992), which were quickly followed over the next few years by *Ten Percent*,

POZ, *Urban Fitness*, *Men's Style*, *Wilde*, and *50/50*. Even the first national gay publication, *The Advocate*, experienced a complete revamping in the 1990s, transforming into a glossy, high-profile publication, cleansed of all its sexually explicit and politically radical content (Gross 2001; Sender 2004).

This new economic desirability of the gay market also resulted in direct-mail campaigns by large corporations. The first such campaign was conducted by MCI in 1993, shortly followed by AT&T in 1994 (Baker 1997). Unlike the MCI campaign, the AT&T mailing campaign made explicit references to gay and lesbian identity and utilized gay iconography, including the rainbow flag. By the mid-1990s, major marketing firms were not just advertising to the gay community, they were classifying gay men and lesbians in their consumer databases under the rubric of the "gay market" (Chasin 2000). Banks even began offering gay men and lesbians credit cards based on their sexual identity. The most well known of these is the Rainbow Card originally offered by Travelers Bank in 1995, which donated a portion of the profits to national LGBT organizations (Sender 2004). By the end of the 1990s, online affinity sites such as Gay.com and PlanetOut.com became important platforms for advertising to gay consumers as well as for conducting market research on the LGBT community (Campbell 2005).

Initially, executives at major corporations worried that reaching out to gay and lesbian consumers would alienate straight consumers, especially religious fundamentalists who objected on moral grounds to anything associated with homosexuality (Sender 2004). Thus marketers developed an advertising technique employing coded appeals only recognized by gay and lesbian consumers. Michael Bronski referred to these coded advertisements as "gay window ads," and Michael Wilke termed this marketing technique "gay vague" (Sender 2004). A frequently cited example of "gay vague" advertising is Volkswagen's 1997 television commercial for the Golf titled "Sunday Afternoon." Featuring Trio's 1982 hit song "Da Da Da," the commercial shows two young men driving around town aimlessly in a VW Golf. Sender's research shows gay viewers read the two male characters as a gay couple, while straight viewers read these characters as roommates (2004). More recently, some major corporations have placed openly "gay ads" in the mainstream media. A noteworthy example is JCPenney's 2012 Father's Day print advertisement featuring two actual gay dads (Todd Koch and Cooper Smith) playing with their kids. Although the ad sparked a protest from the conservative parenting group One Million Moms, it did not appear to generate concern among heterosexual consumers in general. This led some marketers to proclaim the mainstream market as "gay friendly" (Ostrow 2012).

LGBT scholars have been careful to point out the problematic assumptions underlying gay marketing appeals: consumption is based principally on identity and identity cannot be reduced to a single dimension. As critics have noted, reducing gays and lesbians to their sexual identity alone fails to recognize the complex ways sexuality intersects with race, ethnicity, class, gender, and physical ability. Equally problematic is the fact that this marketing practice partially calls into existence the very thing it claims to have only recognized. As Sender (2004) explains, "the gay community, on a national scale at least, is not a preexisting entity that marketers simply need to appeal to, but is a construction, an imagined community formed not only through political activism but through an increasingly sophisticated, commercially supported, national media" (p. 5). Chasin (2000) argues that gay men and lesbians only started to conceptualize themselves as part of a national gay community in 1977 as a result of a nationwide boycott of oranges and juice from the Florida Citrus Commission, whose spokeswoman, Anita Bryant, led an anti-gay rights campaign in Dade County, Florida. LGBT scholars suggest that the formation of a national LGBT community was only possible after a national gay media was in place, and such media was only possible once there was sufficient advertising interest to support national gay publications (Chasin 2000; Gross 2001; Sender 2004).

Although marketers have thus far avoided acknowledging the role they play in constructing the gay market, they have recognized that not all gays and lesbians earn more than their heterosexual counterparts. Thus, for marketers it is increasingly important to identify and segment affluent gays (notably white professional gay men and lesbians) from less economically attractive segments of the LGBT community, including working-class gay men and lesbians, gay people of color, gay people with disabilities, and transgender people (Chasin 2000; Sender 2004; Campbell 2005). This has led some scholars to express concern over the impact of marketing segmentation on LGBT civic engagement (Chasin 2000; Campbell 2005).

SEE ALSO: Advertising; Lifestyle; Niche Marketing; Sexualities and Consumption

REFERENCES

Badgett, M. V. L. 2001. *Money, Myths, and Change: The Economic Lives of Lesbians and Gay Men*. Chicago, IL: University of Chicago Press.

Badgett, M. V. L., Laura E. Durso, and Alyssa Schneebaum. 2013. "New Patterns of Poverty in the Lesbian, Gay, and Bisexual Community." Los Angeles, CA: Williams Institute. Accessed October 2, 2014. http://williamsinstitute.law.ucla.edu/wp-content/uploads/LGB-Poverty-Update-Jun-2013.pdf.

Baker, Dan. 1997. "A History in Ads: The Growth of the Gay and Lesbian Market." In *Homo Economics: Capitalism, Community, and Lesbian and Gay Life*, edited by Amy Gluckman and Betsy Reed, 11–20. New York: Routledge.

Campbell, John. 2005. "Outing PlanetOut: Surveillance, Gay Marketing, and Internet Affinity Portals." *New Media and Society* 7(5): 663–683.

Chasin, Alexandra. 2000. *Selling Out: The Gay and Lesbian Movement Goes to Market*. New York: St. Martin's.

Gross, Larry. 2001. *Up from Invisibility: Lesbian, Gay Men, and the Media in America*. New York: Columbia University Press.

Hardisty, Jean, and Amy Gluckman. 1997. "The Hoax of 'Special Rights': The Right Wing's Attack on Gay Men and Lesbians." In *Homo Economics: Capitalism, Community, and Lesbian and Gay Life*, edited by Amy Gluckman and Betsy Reed, 209–222. New York: Routledge.

Ostrow, Joanne. 2012. "Ads Aim Marketing at Gay Audience: Moving Past 'Gay Vague.'" *Denver Post*, June 17. Accessed 26 July, 2014. http://www.denverpost.com/ci_20859201/moving-past-gay-vague-ads-aim-marketing-at.

Sender, Katherine. 2004. *Business, Not Politics: The Making of the Gay Market*. New York: Columbia University Press.

Turow, Joseph. 2006. *Niche Envy: Marketing Discrimination in the Digital Age*. Cambridge, MA: MIT Press.

Gender and Consumer Culture

EMMA CASEY
Kingston University, UK

Consumption has not traditionally been a central concern for feminist academics. Until the 1990s it was rare to find articles in feminist journals written specifically about consumption and textbooks on consumption frequently rendered gendered accounts of consumption to a few pages on "the body" or household expenditure. Indeed, it is only relatively recently that social scientists have begun to produce dedicated studies of gendered consumption practices. The wider experiences of women's lives as consumers both at home and in public life have often been overlooked in favor of accounts that have mapped the rise of consumerism alongside the unfolding of capitalist societies. While these accounts have undoubtedly been hugely influential, not least in reversing the trend for prioritizing accounts of production over those of consumption, they have also helped to bolster an academic study of consumption which has largely produced "ungendered" accounts of the consumer. In response to this dearth, feminist consumption scholars have often looked to a broad range of academic disciplines and studies – such as anthropology, history, and cultural studies – in order to make sense of the particular relevance of consumption to women's lives. Gendered accounts of consumption have also sought to advance many of the possibilities offered by classic texts and theories of consumption and in particular have echoed early critical readings of the ultimately disappointing and dissatisfying outcomes of consumer societies.

In many ways, the relative absence of dedicated accounts of gendered consumption is surprising, given the prevalence of consumption in women's lives throughout the twentieth century and especially following the consolidation of "mass consumption" in the United Kingdom and the United States. Many descriptions of the new middle-class suburbs which emerged in the United Kingdom in the 1930s and in the United States in the 1950s and 1960s, for example, were packed with references to the lure and appeal of new mass-produced consumer goods, many of which were advertised and marketed as easing the labor of housework. Feminist scholars have argued that, during the twentieth century, the rapid advancement of mass consumerism and the increase in demand for consumer goods were triggered not only by postwar affluence, but also by a new demand for goods that help to enhance gender and class identities. Homes during this time thus became significant markers of class and status and the responsibility for "getting it right" fell predominantly to women. The intense visibility of consumption and its growing association with demonstrating good taste, status, and high standards of housekeeping and motherhood, combined with intense scrutiny and increasingly high standards, competition, and a never-ending expansion of "choice," have been famously depicted in contemporary dramas such as *Desperate Housewives* and *Mad Men*. Here the "allure" of consumption, and particularly its association with suburban living, is presented as deeply unsatisfying and alienating.

In her famous feminist study of middle-class women living in 1960s suburbia, Betty Friedan remarked on the paradox between the insatiable lure of mass consumer society and the notable increase in cases of depression. Following the work of neo-Marxist thinkers who had previously demonized the stupefying, vacuous, and soulless characteristics of mass consumption, Friedan shifted the emphasis by arguing that the false promise of pleasure and freedom supposedly on offer in capitalist consumer economies has a particularly devastating effect on great swathes of women for whom the promise of consumption conflicts with the reality of a "life half lived." She writes: "Each suburban wife struggled with it alone. As she made the beds, shopped for groceries, matched slip-cover material, ate peanut butter sandwiches with her children, chauffeured Cub Scouts and Brownies, lay beside her husband at night – she was afraid to ask even of herself the silent question – 'Is this all?'" (1965, 13).

Writing before the advent of the second-wave feminist movement, Friedan argued that women's dissatisfaction and disappointment in the consumption-fueled lifestyle that had failed in its promise to offer fulfillment and happiness were intensified by the fact that women were left without a vocabulary to adequately describe their unhappiness; the "problem" for Friedan is thus one which "has no name." Friedan notes the dramatic increase in the use of antidepressants during this time, particularly by middle-class women.

Friedan's work not only paved the way for a wide variety of work into feminist accounts of contemporary culture, but also offered one of the first and most potent critiques of consumer society at a time when the lure of consumerism was just beginning to take hold. In many ways, the text echoes earlier neo-Marxist critiques of mass consumerism that sought to expose the myth of the American Dream. However, it also offers one of the first serious studies of consumption in intimate life and, moreover, from the perspective of women.

Despite the influence of Friedan's work, other more recent research examining the relationship between gender and twentieth-century consumption has examined in more detail some of the ways in which suburban women reclaimed consumer culture as a means of addressing some of the structural details underpinning their everyday lives. For example, production is prevalent in Alison Clarke's pioneering study of Tupperware parties in 1960s suburban America (2001). Clarke considers how middle-class women used the Tupperware industry as a means of taking control of their own finances by becoming Tupperware "entrepreneurs." Thus Tupperware parties became important spaces where suburban housewives, confined to the domestic sphere because of constraining gender roles, were offered an opportunity for the pursuit of economic independence and a pleasurable leisure space separate from the family.

Clarke considered that Tupperware embodied values of domesticity, mass consumption, and feminine identity and represented a new form of consumption which bridged traditional modernist boundaries of, for example, domesticity/commerce; work/leisure; friend/colleague; consumer/employee; thrift/excess, and so on. From this perspective, consumption becomes something which is more than simply a facet of public life and instead is recognized as an omnipresent activity, deeply entrenched in intimate, everyday routines and rituals; in the material culture of domestic life. For Clarke, efforts to reveal the detail of the intimate experiences of particular types of mainstream consumption help to enhance understandings of the broader experiences of modernity. The recent rise of the "mumtrepreneur" – mothers who have set up their own "at home" companies – and the success in the 1990s and 2000s of Ann Summers parties echo the early days of Tupperware as a route to financial independence which integrates with the demands of home.

Other authors have drawn attention to the important role of consumerism in facilitating spaces where women could be relatively free to participate in public life and to utilize consumption, becoming active in the production and construction of their own identity practices. Thus, in her essay "Alice in the Consumer Wonderland" (1984), Erica Carter marks out department stores as one of the first public spaces where women could roam independently – without a male chaperone. Furthermore, department stores such as Selfridges in London, which opened in 1909, were some of the first places to employ women in any great number.

For middle-class women, consumption has sometimes been used as a tool to carve out a pleasurable space and time for a self that exist separately from traditional demands of the home and family. However, for working-class women, consumption, and especially mass consumption, can intensify everyday stresses and anxieties since participation in the consumer society becomes fraught with difficulties for low-income women.

It is interesting that during the second-wave British feminist movement of the 1970s and 1980s, some feminist scholars began to emphasize the home and domestic life as a site for academic scholarship. In keeping with the mantra that "the personal is political," many feminists sought to uncover the personal experiences of women's lives which had hitherto been overlooked. For many, this meant demonstrating the home to be a key site of women's oppression. Ann Oakley's pioneering study of housework is important here (1974). Focusing on an almost entirely overlooked but entrenched aspect of women's everyday personal lives, Oakley's study cements housework as a key aspect of industrial society – as an activity which is frequently described as even more monotonous and alienating than assembly line work. Oakley argues that consumption is best understood as an extension of housework, as a key part of the everyday routines of homemaking in capitalist society. Delphy and Leonard's influential work is another good example of this. In their seminal text *Close to Home* (1984), they argue that as "managers of the home," women have found themselves responsible for a whole raft of complex household management tasks the outcomes of which reinforce exploitation and oppression and the privileging of the position of men within the family.

The idea that consumption is an extension of women's unpaid labor is one which has also been picked up by contemporary academics. For example, Celia Lury (1996) argues that a key part of women's consumption practices lies in the physical, *bodily* changes that consumption provokes. Describing consumption as a type of unpaid labor, Lury argues that shopping for makeup, clothes, and beauty products is an extension of women's work or the "work of femininity." Other authors have also discussed the ways in which consumption becomes part of the everyday work of household budgeting, particularly for women. In *Feeding the Family* (1991), her study of the practices and routines of feeding the family, Marjorie DeVault argues that the women in her study were determined to make up money resources that they lacked – via increasingly effective and complex budgeting – in order that they might be able to demonstrate the sort of care for others that they felt was expected of them.

Often the pressure to achieve this on a limited budget was a cause of deep anxiety and stress and other authors have made connections between poverty and the exclusionary effects of consumption. This emphasis on women's work of consumption has often overlapped into more contemporary research into the use of material objects as a way of further displaying love and care for others, particularly children, via consumer goods. Certainly, in late modern capitalist societies, the burden of responsibility for managing a frequently tight household budget still falls predominantly on women. Furthermore, as a number of authors have pointed out, consumption is often seen as a means of creating and developing a respectable feminine identity for self and family. Beverley Skeggs (1997), for example, argues that homes and bodies are spaces where respectable "caring" selves are (re)presented, where "class is lived out in the most omnipresent form" (p. 90), and where women are constantly under the gaze and surveillance of others. The interlinking of class and gender identities has proven to be a central argument in much contemporary literature on gender and consumption.

The idea that the consumption choices of working-class women are constantly assessed for their merit and "value" by middle-class others and that class and gender are reproduced and reformed via consumption has been the topic of a number of recent key studies. Allison Pugh (2004), for example, in her study of "windfall" child rearing in low-income families, argues that the challenge of child rearing on a tight budget is intensified by a constant fear of children missing out on material goods or being marked as "out of place." For example, the sort of financial rewards or treats, including regular pocket money, that might be taken for granted in a middle-class family are far less likely to be an option for low-income families. Pugh describes the anxiety and stresses experienced by low-income women as they attempt to "make ends meet." Other authors have similarly described the plethora of strategies that low-income women adopt in order to be able to care for their children via consumption in a way that they feel is appropriate and expected of them, for example by gambling (Casey 2008).

Women in particular have increasingly utilized consumption as a means of displaying status, value, and "betterment" (Casey and Martens 2007). These particular uses of consumption have been intensified by ever increasing ubiquitous images of the ideal home. One of the consequences of the dramatic proliferation of "labor-saving" devices for the home has been a parallel increase in expectations and standards of cleanliness and tidiness and ever more unattainable ideals of "perfection." Homes thus become important spaces for displaying and providing evidence of care, love, and sophistication. In her study of women and their kitchens, Elizabeth Silva (2007) describes the ways in which women utilize their kitchens in order to display a specific gendered identity of style and care. Adapting Bourdieu's model of cultural capital, Silva argues that in addition to kitchens demonstrating both economic and cultural capital via the display of goods, women hold – and express – an emotional attachment to the display of kitchens. She writes of kitchens as part of the construction of women's narratives of self, citing the example of Janet: "I stayed in this kitchen for about six hours. Janet made sure the door leading to the lounge remained shut. I was not meant to see the rest of the house. Making me come into the house through the back door had been part of Janet's narrative of herself. This was part of how she wanted to show herself to me. Everything looked sparkling clean" (p. 147). Consumption thus offers a means of dealing with many of the contradictions inherent in late capitalist societies. This is especially the case for women, for whom status – and specifically feminine identity practices of care, cleanliness, display, and budgeting – can be enhanced (see Casey and Martens 2007).

SEE ALSO: Body and Consumer Culture; Children's Consumer Culture; Femininities; Mothers/Motherhood

REFERENCES

Carter, Erica. 1984. "Alice in the Consumer Wonderland." In *Gender and Generation*, edited by Angela McRobbie and Mica Nava, 185–214. London: Macmillan.

Casey, Emma. 2008. *Women, Pleasure and the Gambling Experience*. Aldershot, UK: Ashgate.

Casey, Emma, and Lydia Martens, eds. 2007. *Gender and Consumption: Domestic Cultures and the Commercialisation of Everyday Life*. Aldershot, UK: Ashgate.

Clarke, Alison. 2001. *Tupperware: The Promise of Plastic in 1950s America*. Washington, DC: Smithsonian.

Delphy, Christine, and Diana Leonard. 1984. *Close to Home: A Materialist Analysis of Women's Oppression*. London: Hutchinson.

DeVault, Marjorie L. 1991. *Feeding the Family: The Social Organization of Caring as Gendered Work*. Chicago, IL: University of Chicago Press.

Friedan, Betty. 1965. *The Feminine Mystique*. Harmondsworth, UK: Penguin.

Lury, Celia. 1996. *Consumer Culture*. Cambridge, UK: Polity.

Oakley, Ann. 1974. *The Sociology of Housework*. London: Martin Robertson.

Pugh, Allison J. 2004. "Windfall Child Rearing: Low-Income Care and Consumption." *Journal of Consumer Culture* 4: 229–249.

Silva, Elizabeth. 2007. "Gender, Class, Emotional Capital and Consumption in Family Life." In *Gender and Consumption: Domestic Cultures and the Commercialisation of Everyday Life*, edited by Emma Casey and Lydia Martens, 141–162. Aldershot, UK: Ashgate.

Skeggs, Beverley. 1997. *Formations of Class and Gender*. London: Sage.

Generation Y

JOERI VAN DEN BERGH
InSites Consulting, The Netherlands

Generation Y, or Gen Y, refers roughly to those born between 1980 and 1996, so named due to their following Generation X. Also known as "the Millennials," as the first generation to come of age in the new millennium, they have many other nicknames, such as Generation Why, Generation Search, Generation Next, the Net generation, the digital natives, the dot-com generation, Echo Boomers, etc. Regardless of label, they share the experience of being the children born of the children of the Baby Boom generation.

Marketers and other observers attribute many characteristics to this generation, many of whom now are becoming parents themselves. They are thought to have been inculcated with a sense of individual empowerment, and perhaps entitlement; a generation who are impatient with standard work practices and pathways of promotion and reward. In part this attitude toward work and life is said to have been cultivated by Baby Boom parents who tended to treat them more as equals, valuing their opinions in decision making, from family life to consumer purchases, compared to earlier generations. As "stimulus junkies," they have a shorter attention span and an irrepressible need for instant gratification. Gen Y get along well with their parents. They report fewer fights with mum or dad than older adults say they had with their own parents when they were growing up. A consequence of Gen Y's closeness with their parents and the "boomerang" trend (living longer at their parents' home) is the increasing and enduring influence of youngsters on the family purchases (Van den Bergh and Behrer 2013).

Marketing-wise, Gen Y consumers tend to seek to personalize brands by combining competitors' brands with personality traits that reflect their own identity. Since these consumers are known to be selectively loyal to those elements of brands that touch their hearts and that keep their promise, brand managers and companies strive to fit their product offerings into the complex identity of "Gen Yers," rather than the other way around. A good deal of the revolution in brands, in prosumption (co-created products/content), and in retailing can be attributed to the influence of Generation Y.

SEE ALSO: Authenticity; Brands and Branding; Cool; Nike; Teens

REFERENCE

Van den Bergh, Joeri, and Mattias Behrer. 2013. *How Cool Brands Stay Hot: Branding to Generation Y*, 2nd ed. London: Kogan Page.

FURTHER READING

Reisenwitz, Timothy H., and Rajesh Iyer. 2009. "Differences in Generation X and Generation Y: Implications for the Organization and Marketers." *Marketing Management Journal* 19(2): 91–103.

Twenge, Jean M. 2006. *Generation Me: Why Today's Young Americans Are More Confident, Assertive, Entitled – and More Miserable Than Ever Before*. New York: Free Press.

Yarrow, Kit, and Jayne O'Donnell. 2009. *Gen BuY. How Tweens, Teens and Twenty-Somethings Are Revolutionizing Retail*. San Francisco, CA: Jossey-Bass.

Gentrification

AARON PASSELL
Furman University, USA

Ruth Glass is normally credited with coining the term "gentrification" in 1964 to describe an apparently novel kind of neighborhood change taking place in London at the time. To Glass, gentrification meant "working class quarters … invaded by the middle classes," housing upgraded – both structurally and in terms of social status – only ending when "all or most of the original working class occupiers are displaced and the social character of the district is changed" (Glass 1964, in Lees, Slater, and Wyly 2008, 4). The displacement of lower-income households, particularly those of color and immigrants, remains a key concern of progressive scholars of urban processes, but gentrification has come to mean many more things, too, in the half century since Glass's original formulation.

NECESSARY CONDITIONS AND PROCESS

Gentrification is primarily an urban process and generally involves a number of necessary conditions. First, it presumes that there is some population who wants to move into the neighborhood in question from elsewhere. By the 1980s, urban scholars had clearly identified a "back to the city" trend among some educated, middle-class professionals, mostly progressive, young, and white. Rejecting the suburban values of their parents' generations, these new city dwellers are seeking a distinctly urban lifestyle.

Second, the target neighborhood must have cheap housing, "good bones," and a good location. Relatively cheap housing is the primary pull factor for the first phase of new residents; they get affordable access to urban amenities. The housing is usually poorly maintained and often systemically disinvested – failing to meet building codes and in tax arrears. Good bones means that the existing structures and neighborhood pattern must correspond with the aesthetics of the relatively high cultural capital group for whom a move to the city holds some appeal. Even if they are going to be substantially renovated, the buildings must show the potential to become desirable. This can mean anything from forgotten gems (reclaiming Victorian houses that have faced neglect or been split up into apartments) to the raw authenticity of industrial spaces (converting warehouses into lofts). In terms of location, the neighborhood must be accessible to the workplaces and other urban amenities that gentrifiers frequent.

Third, a gentrifying neighborhood, to be described as such, must be inhabited by people who are low income by comparison to those who will ultimately move in. These neighborhoods are usually working class to poor, dominated by people of color, and have a high crime rate, at least by reputation. In Glass's terms, the "gentry" are moving in and replacing these lower-status populations. Critics of gentrification point out that these demographic and structural conditions are often portrayed in the pro-gentrification media as defining a "frontier," wild territory to be tamed by mainstream newcomers (Smith 1996). Current residents are disproportionately renters who are easily displaced by rising rents. Homeowners in these neighborhoods are often elderly and living on fixed incomes, thus at risk from property tax increases that come with the improvements to the housing around them.

The causes of gentrification, on the other hand, are less clear and are contingent on a range of historical and local factors. Neil Smith (1996) made a powerful argument for a structural account of gentrification, claiming that where a "rent gap" existed – a difference between the profits actually being realized from the investment in a neighborhood and those potentially realized – gentrification would occur. This claim has proved difficult to measure and, furthermore, conceives of individuals simply as rational actors, not accounting adequately for choice or culture (see Lees, Slater, and Wyly 2008). Structural factors associated with global, national, regional, and local political economies certainly play a role in initiating gentrification, but individual actors and the dispositions and commitments they carry with them do too.

The typical stages of gentrification are widely recognized, even clichés. The first gentrifiers – the "pioneers" – tend to possess significant cultural capital but less economic capital; artists and musicians, for example. They may appropriate local "third spaces," like bars, and transform unused spaces into art and performance venues, but they are unlikely to invest significant financial capital themselves simply because they do not have it. They are followed by people with a little more money, such as recent college graduates employed in culture industries, who are drawn by an urban lifestyle but still face challenges in finding a place in the city, either because of moderate salaries in the early stages of their careers or other characteristics. Gay communities, for example, are sometimes involved at this stage.

The arrival of this second group begins to significantly change the character of the neighborhood because the new residents put upward pressure on the delivery of city services, such as sanitation and policing, which the previous residents lacked the political power to do. Improved services, in turn, push up rents. The presence of these new residents, moreover, encourages small-scale retail – coffee shops, restaurants, boutiques – that increases the appeal to the middle class.

The presence of these intermediates, the services that follow them, and those that they demand make the neighborhood a potential destination for more established professionals, sometimes with families. This final stage is the one at which financial capital really gets invested in the neighborhood, transforming it through the purchase of real estate and its remodeling. Rents increase steeply, sales prices increase steeply, and property taxes shift upward, threatening the tenure of those on fixed incomes. Larger-scale retail – grocery stores catering to upper-middle-class tastes and budgets – shows up as smaller-scale retail proliferates, consecrating the new neighborhood's changed status through consumption practices.

GENTRIFICATION DEBATES

There are important ongoing debates about the causes of gentrification, the variety of its manifestations, and whether it necessarily causes harm to the lower-income households living in the neighborhood before the process begins. Lees, Slater, and Wyly (2008) usefully distinguish between "production explanations" for gentrification and "consumption explanations." The production side, exemplified by Neil Smith mentioned above, argues that the individual and institutional decisions that, in the aggregate, constitute gentrification are fundamentally constrained and enabled by structural conditions in local economies, real estate law, and politics. The consumption side focuses instead on the motivations behind the choices of gentrifiers, locating them in broader cultural shifts. Gentrification-like processes have been identified in many places, inspiring research on rural gentrification, new-build gentrification, and super gentrification, among others (Lees, Slater, and Wyly 2008, 139).

Research on the harm caused by displacement associated with gentrification has proved inconclusive, in part because the displaced are, by their very definition, no longer there to be studied. In fact, whether displacement occurs or not has proved difficult to demonstrate. Scholars like Lance Freeman (2005; Freeman and Braconi 2004) and Jacob Vigdor (2002) suggest that the poorest residents of gentrifying neighborhoods may actually be less likely to leave than others, arguing that we should be concerned about poverty *in place*, as much as displacement. As local retail changes and rents rise, low-income residents may find themselves "shelter poor" – dedicating so much of their income to housing that they cannot afford other necessities.

GENTRIFICATION AS CONSUMPTION

Gentrification is an important issue for consumption studies both in the sense of using city space and of using it up. If neighborhood "upgrading" is possible without causing displacement and deprivation, then gentrification in its damaging form is only one use of city space; a further return to the city could occur without displacement under the right circumstances. Japonica Brown-Saracino (2009) calls "social preservationists" people who move into neighborhoods explicitly valuing their distinct characteristics and trying to preserve them, despite their own disrupting presence. Similarly, Aaron Passell (2013) has asked whether underpopulated historic neighborhoods in older American cities can accommodate new residents without interfering with the lives of those already there or nearby. But if the adaptive reuse of existing neighborhoods is necessarily exclusionary, it needs to be understood as *using up* neighborhood resources upon which the population in place depends. Either way, consumption practices are central to the process, both in the sense of the appropriation of urban space and in regard to retail's reinforcement of neighborhood demographic shifts.

SEE ALSO: Cities, Visual Consumption of; Housing/Housing Markets; Starbuckization

REFERENCES

Brown-Saracino, Japonica. 2009. *A Neighborhood That Never Changes: Gentrification, Social Preservation, and the Search for Authenticity.* Chicago, IL: University of Chicago Press.

Freeman, Lance. 2005. "Displacement or Succession? Residential Mobility in Gentrifying Neighborhoods." *Urban Affairs Review* 40(4): 463–491. doi:10.1177/1078087404273341.

Freeman, Lance, and Frank Braconi. 2004. "Gentrification and Displacement: New York City in the 1990s." *Journal of the American Planning Association* 70(1): 39–52. doi:10.1080/01944360408976337.

Lees, Loretta, Tom Slater, and Elvin Wyly. 2008. *Gentrification*. New York: Routledge.

Passell, Aaron. 2013. "Historic Districts and Neighborhood Change: Does Designation Lead to Gentrification?" Eastern Sociological Society Annual Meeting, Boston, MA.

Smith, Neil. 1996. *The New Urban Frontier: Gentrification and the Revanchist City*. London: Routledge.

Vigdor, Jacob. 2002. "Does Gentrification Harm the Poor?" *Brookings-Wharton Papers on Urban Affairs* 133–173.

FURTHER READING

Shaw, Kate. 2008. "Gentrification: What It Is, Why It Is, and What Can Be Done about It." *Geography Compass* 2(5): 1697–1728. doi:10.1111/j.1749-8198.2008.00156.x.

Gifts

RÉGINE SIROTA
Université Paris Descartes, France

In order to address work on gifts, one must engage with Marcel Mauss's famous essay "The Gift," published in 1924. Mauss demonstrates the construction and maintenance of social ties through the cycles of exchange – giving, receiving, and reciprocating – which put at stake mechanisms of obligation and reciprocity. A gift can be considered as a total social fact, in the Durkheimian sense, in that it involves economic and social dimensions (i.e., emotional, religious, magical, utilitarian, legal, and moral) which place obligations on all involved. In German, "gift" can mean poison, pointing to the implicit social threat the gift relationship can pose to the making and breaking of social relationships. A gift thus can be considered as an analyzer of social relationships, on the one hand, and as an analyzer of consumer practices and circulation of things on the other hand. A circulating thing retains the "spirit" of the people among which it has circulated, thus preserving its history and relational origins.

While Mauss's demonstration was initially made by highlighting the competitive "potlatch" practices of indigenous societies from the West Coast of North America, numerous studies have since shown that the fundamental mechanism for building (and threatening) social links also applies to contemporary social practices and arrangements. The power and importance of gifts are particularly evident in rituals linked to the life cycle or to calendar cycles such as weddings, religious holidays, and birthdays. Anthropologists, philosophers, sociologists, economists, psychologists, and consumer science specialists have addressed this question. Indeed the relationship between giver and receiver, on the one hand, and between gift and commodity, on the other, is both expressed and symbolized through the exchange of presents. Gifts are subject to constant social invention as a market society evolves and combines material artifact and symbolism making. Gifts allow for the expression and marking of social rank, collective identity, and individuality, as well as the expression of affection, while simultaneously affirming and denying market values and commercial relationships.

During its social trajectory, an object undergoes a symbolic transformation, from the time it is made or purchased to its election to the rank of gift, up to the moment when it is presented and received. When analyzing Christmas gifts in the town of Middletown, Theodore Caplow (1982) shows how the subtlety and hierarchy of kin networks manifest themselves through the language of gifts, which express the degree of proximity and intimacy linking individuals to each other, whether it be within the kinship network or a wider social network. Paradoxically, such exchanges obey rules that are generally implicit. And this implicit character of the rule contributes to the efficacy of the mechanism of linkage regulation, thus euphemizing the obligation.

Such exchanges are part of the process of socialization. It is through the exchange of gifts that the codes of civility organizing social life and the building of identity are learned. The shaping of this identity begins at birth with gifts celebrating the arrival of a new individual that, for example, mark gender identity or signify the transmission of cultural capital. This is validated with successive birthday presents, which contribute throughout the life cycle, from childhood into adulthood, to the construction, reinforcement, and celebration of identity, whether it be within the family circle or a peer group, marking the evolution of social networks. Women play a particular role in the process, through the provision, selection, and appropriate allocation of a present.

Thus, gift exchange helps us understand how economic, social, and emotional mechanisms are combined to build social links through the transmission and maintenance of belonging and economic and cultural transformation.

SEE ALSO: Consumer Socialization; Emotions and Consumption

REFERENCES

Caplow Theodore. 1982. "Christmas Gifts and Kin Networks." *American Sociological Review* 47 (June): 383–392.

Mauss, Marcel. 1924/2012. *L'Essai sur le don: Forme et raison de l'échange dans les sociétés archaïques*, vol. 6. Paris: PUF.

Mauss, Marcel. 1954. *The Gift: Forms and Function of Exchange in Archaic Society*. Translated by Ian Cunninson. Glencoe, IL: Free Press.

FURTHER READING

Cheal, David. 1987. "Showing Them You Love Them: Gift Giving and the Dialectic of Intimacy." *The Sociological Review* 35(1): 150–169.

Godbout, Jacques T., and Alain Caillé. 1992. *L'Esprit du don*. Paris: La Découverte.

Godbout, Jacques T., and Alain Caillé. 1998. *The World of the Gift*. Translated by Donald Winkler. Montreal: McGill-Queen's University Press.

Girl Culture

JACQUELINE REID-WALSH
Pennsylvania State University, USA

Despite much contemporary interest, the term "girl culture" is not (yet) included in the *Oxford English Dictionary* (*OED*). Defining "girl culture" is not a simple task, as the individual components are themselves complex concepts with shifting meanings. The word "girl" can be traced back to the Middle Ages in both English and German, where the idea of a set chronological age or even sex or gender being associated with the term is undermined by the definitions. In the 1300s the term (usually in the plural) referred to a child or young person of either sex. Beginning in the late 1300s "girl" began to be associated with the female sex: some matter-of-fact and some derogatory, referring to a young or relatively young woman, a woman of any age, a female child, a sweetheart, a prostitute, a female servant, a female slave, and an effeminate man. The question of who is a "girl" continues to be asked today with variability of chronological age being a constant feature. Who is included and excluded? Does it matter if a girl is of preschool age, between the ages of 10 and 14, or a young adolescent as defined by the UN Population Council, or 18 and at the age of consent in many countries and at the far edge of American adolescence? If the UN definition of child is applied, the age limit rises to 29, so young and not so young women are then included.

Similarly, culture cannot be simply defined. As cultural theorist Raymond Williams notes in *Keywords* (1976), the eighteenth-century German philosopher von Herder brought in the idea of culture in the plural to circumvent European assumptions of a direct progress of society culminating in their own. This is the basis of the common twentieth-century anthropological and sociological uses. During this time period, some established compounds began to be associated with popular culture and subcultures, including café culture, drug culture, and youth culture. Yet, the first reference to girls' culture in the *OED* is 2002, referring to Goth girls.

Based on these components, some feminist cultural studies scholars, notably Angela McRobbie, sought to identify and describe examples of girl cultures. Her initial groundbreaking work, cowritten with Jenny Garber in "Girls and Subcultures" in the mid-1970s (see McRobbie 1991), investigates the apparent absence of girls in mid-twentieth-century British subcultures. McRobbie and Garber observe that girl culture tended to operate in the home. There was space for a great deal of the new teenage consumer culture within the confines of the their bedrooms, two main areas of consumption being magazines and popular music. They conclude that girls' participation in youth cultures could best be understood as moving away from the classic subcultural terrain marked out as oppositional and creative. Girls negotiate different leisure and personal spaces from boys. These in turn offer them different possibilities for resistance, negotiations of perceived status, and accommodating young sexualities.

In the twenty-first century, our understanding of girl cultures is broader. Girl culture is not monolithic, but often divided by age groups – such as baby girls, little girls, tween girls, teenage girls, young women, and so on. Neither is the concept "cultural" specific, although by default it is still mainly Anglo-American or European. One way to approach girl culture is by understanding social practices and social relations in relation to commodity objects such as "girl talk," ranging from chatting on the princess phone, to talking or texting words and images on cellphones. Another is to focus on rites of passage, such as prom, Bat Mitzvahs, or Quinceañeras as a means to engage in cross-cultural study. Yet another way is to study material culture directed at girls, such as clothes or toys. Examining specific media directed at girls, ranging from print media such as books, comics, and magazines, to television and film, to music and to digital media, also provides insight into how girls interact with each other, with adults, and with cultural products, in an effort to make meaning in their lives. Whatever the approach, there are several overarching and contradictory themes in terms of popular understanding of girl culture, which include moral and media panics about (early) sexuality, dismissing or devaluing girls' culture, perceived ephemerality, as well as loss and nostalgia.

Research on girl culture, however, emphasizes the importance of girls' agency in terms of practices, locations, and objects. This may support conventional and unconventional femininities in material and virtual spaces like ballet class, skateboard parks, (computer) gaming on different platforms, and so on. Also some DIY (do-it-yourself) girl culture practices encompass the past and present, such as writing diaries or blogs, creating artifacts such as scrapbooks or zines, or writing stories or online fan fiction. Girl cultures are not limited to the young, either. If participating in popular culture is a dominant requisite, then the term can include middle-aged women, such as those who shop at stores directed toward young women or engage in *Twilight* fandom.

Recently girl culture has emerged as an interdisciplinary field of academic study not only in Canada, England, the United States, and Australia, but internationally. As marks of the maturity of the area in universities, there are graduate courses and programs in girl culture, and numerous academic studies, including dissertations being written. Moreover, research sources are being produced that range from reference books to a journal called *Girlhood Studies* (begun in 2008). There are also supporting structures emerging, such as a listserv and an association, as well as specific conferences being held on different aspects of girl culture.

SEE ALSO: Barbie; Body and Consumer Culture; Gender and Consumer Culture; Tweens

REFERENCES

McRobbie, Angela, ed. 1991. *Feminism and Youth Culture: From "Jackie" to "Just Seventeen."* Boston, MA: Unwin Hyman.

Williams, Raymond. 1976. *Keywords: A Vocabulary of Culture and Society*. New York: Oxford University Press.

FURTHER READING

Driscoll, Catherine. 2002. *Girls: Feminine Adolescence in Popular Culture and Cultural Theory.* New York: Columbia University Press.

Mitchell, Claudia, and Jacqueline Reid-Walsh, eds. 2008. *Girl Culture: An Encyclopedia*, vols. 1 & 2. Westport, CT: Greenwood Press.

Reid-Walsh, Jacqueline. 2011. "Girlhood." In *Keywords for Children's Literature*, edited by Philip Nell and Lissa Paul, 92–95. New York: New York University Press.

Global Justice Movement

PETER N. FUNKE
University of South Florida, USA

The Global Justice Movement (GJM) is an umbrella term for the diverse and amorphous set of associated and loosely networked organizations, groups, and movements – mostly from the political left – including anti-war, labor, environmental, feminist, peasant, indigenous, and student groups, that oppose corporate globalization and neoliberal capitalism, imperialism and war. The GJM arguably peaked around the turn of the twenty-first century, with massive international mobilizations and protests as well as the launching of the dynamic, yet chaotic, World Social Forum (in 2001), spurring local, national, and regional social forums across the globe. The more recent 2011 "Arab Spring," however, along with the Occupy Wall Street protests and ongoing anti-austerity protests, can be regarded as outgrowths of the GJM's cycle of protest.

The GJM is distinguishable from a rightwing critique of globalization that emphasizes the importance of parochial national identities, interests, and nation-centered alternatives. The plethora of social movement organizations, networks, and groups that make up the GJM, on the other hand, oppose the particular neoliberal, market-driven type of globalization and the subsequent expansion of corporate and financial power. Extremely diverse in terms of issues, strategies, and goals, the GJM advocates and fights for "greater equality, dignity, democracy, devolution of power, autonomy, peace, sustainable living, environmental protection, and social justice at the local, national, and transnational levels and across economic, political, social, cultural and environmental spheres" (Reitan 2013, 324).

HISTORICAL LINEAGE

For many, the GJM signifies a new cycle of contention, distinct yet related to past movements and protest cycles. It is often contrasted to the "Old Left" of industrial trade unions and political parties, which converged around the central class struggle of bourgeoisie and proletariat, and which differed from the "New Left" concerns with identity politics, civil rights, gender, and environmental concerns. In contradistinction, the GJM represents an attempt to bring together the various historical parts of the political left, forging linkages and synergies across the fractured landscape of the "old" and "new" left.

The GJM emerged in the wake of the implementation and consolidation of global neoliberal restructuring policies that began in the 1970s in the global South. These policies usually demand the implementation of orthodox capitalist economic policies, including the commodification of publicly owned industries, services, and resources, as well as the deregulation and liberalization of trade in goods and services. Moreover, these go beyond the strictly economic realm and encroach on cultural, ecological, political, and social issues. Often enforced and administered through international or regional institutions on behalf of its member states, the structural adjustment programs of the International Monetary Fund (IMF), as well as trade liberalization policies overseen by the World Trade Organization (WTO), galvanized protests and uprisings that gave birth to the GJM.

Since the earlier so-called "bread riots" of the 1970s and 1980s against the IMF in the global South, the GJM has been most visible when demonstrating at the meetings of international institutions such as the WTO, the IMF, or the Group of Eight meetings. For example, it organized massive protests against the WTO summit in Seattle in 1999, shutting down the ministerial conference; against the Iraq War on February 15 and 16, 2003, which saw 10–20 million people demonstrating against the looming invasion worldwide; and against Group of Eight meetings such as those in Genoa (2001), Gleneagles (2005), and Heiligendamm (2007). While the 1999 "Battle for Seattle" has become iconic in the birth of the GJM in the global North, consolidating the global resistance to neoliberal policies, it was the Mexican Zapatista uprising against the North American Free Trade Agreement in 1994 that initiated the GJM's cycle of contention. The Zapatista, with its radically democratic and pluralist approach, prefigures much of what would become the GJM writ large. The Zapatista outlook is epitomized in its slogan, "One no and many yeses," capturing the unified "no" to neoliberalism, while acknowledging the diversity and plurality of alternatives, needs, aspirations, tactics, or ways of living and doing. This perspective arguably undergirds the GJM's own self-understanding of collectively rejecting neoliberalism while embracing a plurality of alternative worlds, thus allowing for linkages and convergences while guaranteeing the participating groups' autonomy.

Beyond protest mobilizations, groups and movements of the GJM have also attempted to create less reactive, "merely" protesting forms of organizing and mobilizing. The establishment of a network of independent media centers in 1999, as well as the emergence of the social forum process since 2001, are characteristic examples of attempts by the GJM to create communication and convergence space and processes that seek to function as switchboard and relay venues to withstand the ebb and flow of protest cycles, to thicken linkages and networks across space and time, and to further coalesce the GJM. Moreover, the World Social Forum has served as a vital nurturing ground of the GJM and has also galvanized global networks such as Via Campesina, the World March of Women, and Jubilee 2000/Jubilee South, which in turn have become central pillars of the broader GJM.

CORE CHARACTERISTICS OF THE GJM

The combination of seven interlinked factors epitomizes the novelty and distinctiveness of the GJM. First, the affiliated groups are opposed to a neoliberal form of globalization and broadly agree that neoliberal globalization has benefited multinational corporations and finance capital at the expense of human rights and democracy, basic labor laws, environmental codes, fair trade, and sustainable development. Second, the GJM recognizes the immanent influence of the dynamics and imperatives of neoliberal globalization in local, national, and regional environments and thus understands the subsequent necessity of interlinking local to global spheres of struggle. Third, the GJM is defined by the networking of diverse movement traditions (including the labor movement, new social movements, indigenous and peasant movements) and operating levels (ranging from neighborhood groups, city and regional projects, to global networks) from the global North and South. Fourth, a remarkable and broadly accepted diversity of individuals, groups, and networks describes the GJM. This distinctive multifariousness ranges from the affiliated groups' particular substantive foci (e.g., anti-racist, environment, indigenous, labor, media, women), tactics and strategies (e.g., holding counter-summits; organizing demonstrations; nonviolent direct action; [symbolic] property destruction), to their medium-term objectives (e.g., documenting and reporting; conducting specific welfare enhancing activities and programs; establishing autonomous zones, social and workers' centers; building networks and movements) and long-term horizons (e.g., systemic reform or revolution). Fifth, the dominant organizational model is based on networked or rhizomatic structures, grassroots democracy, and prefigurative politics that eschew representative and hierarchical structures. Sixth, the struggles for alternatives to neoliberalism are based less on concrete blueprints than on "search processes and experiences" based in everyday practices. Seventh, the GJM relies on and has reappropriated new information communication technologies, in particular the internet, while at the same time converging for face-to-face interactions most prominently in social forums such as the now biannual World Social Forum.

CHANGES AND FUTURE OF THE GJM

Today, the characteristic GJM of the 1990s/2000s seems to be weakening, possibly entering a phase of introspection as numbers of demonstrators and participants in forums and collectives, as well as at protests against international institutions, are declining. Some have claimed that the lack of coherent goals and strategies, as well as the organizational limitations of openness and horizontality, diversity, and consensus decision making that define the GJM, are leading to transient networks that present challenges to movement building and long-term growth. Others argue that the GJM is experiencing so-called spill-out or spill-over effects, "emptying" into the anti-war movement or more locally or nationally based protests. A third line of research regards the Arab Spring, the Occupy Wall Street movement, as well as the anti-austerity protests in Europe as part of the broader GJM's cycle of contention, understanding these as projects of and for global democratization and emphasizing the changing nature of the GJM since its inception. From its birth in the 1990s to the recent "homecoming" to the global North of military overstretch and deep economic crisis, the GJM has morphed from a more protest-oriented anti-neoliberalism movement (at the time also referred to as an anti- or alter-globalization movement), to a movement incorporating the global peace and justice movement, to, most recently – and in the wake of the Arab Spring and Occupy Wall Street – a movement that might be "congealing into a counter-hegemonic project of and for *global democratization*" (Reitan 2013, 324; italics in original).

SEE ALSO: Anti-Consumption Tactics; Capitalism; Class; Fair Trade

REFERENCE

Reitan, Ruth, ed. 2013. *Global Movement*. London: Routledge.

FURTHER READING

Conway, Janet. 2013. *Edges of Global Justice: The World Social Forum and Its "Others."* London: Routledge.

Della Porta, Donatella, ed. 2007. *The GJM: Cross-national and Transnational Perspectives*. Boulder, CO: Paradigm Publishers.

Funke, Peter N. 2012. "The Rhizomatic Left, Neoliberal Capitalism and Class: Theoretical Interventions on Contemporary Social Movements in the Global North." *International Critical Thought* 2(1): 30–41.

Gitlin, Todd. 2012. *Occupy Nation: The Roots, the Spirit, and the Promise of Occupy Wall Street*. New York: HarperCollins.

Hardt, Michael, and Antonio Negri. 2004. *Multitude: War and Democracy in the Age of Empire*. New York: Penguin Press.

Juris, Jeffrey, and Alex Khasnabish, eds. 2013. *Insurgent Encounters: Transnational Activism, Ethnography, and the Political*. Durham, NC: Duke University Press.

Pleyers, Geoffrey, and Alain Touraine. 2001. *Alter-Globalization: Becoming Actors in a Global Age*. Malden, MA: Polity.

Shihade, Magid, Cristina Flesher Fominaya, and Laurence Cox. 2012. "The Season of Revolution: The Arab Spring and European Mobilization." *Interface* 4(1) (special issue): 1 – 16.

Tarrow, Sidney. 2005. *The New Transnational Activism*. Cambridge, UK: Cambridge University Press.

Global Markets

P. S. RAJU
University of Louisville, USA

The term "global markets" refers to the notion that companies have to increasingly look to international markets, beyond their traditional comfort zone, for growth and profitability. Theodore Levitt argued that standardization of many aspects of marketing was the cornerstone of globalization (Levitt, 1983). However, researchers mostly agree that globalization in marketing today requires a judicious combination of both standardization and adaptation to local conditions to market effectively. A broad term, "global markets" is the subject of numerous books in global marketing management. Generally, these include discussions of various aspects of global marketing such as the global environment (economic, financial, cultural, political, and legal), marketing research and segmentation in global markets, global market entry strategies (exporting, licensing, contract manufacturing, joint ventures, etc.), marketing strategies for each element of the marketing mix (namely product, price, communication, and distribution/logistics), and other aspects of general management in global markets.

Future growth for many companies that traditionally have worked in developed economies can often be found in the "emerging economies," such as China, India, and Brazil, which represent opportunities in many sectors – from fast food, to automobiles, to technology. In these areas, the political climate has shifted in recent decades, becoming increasingly supportive of the capitalistic philosophy with respect to consumption, at least on the surface. China is a prime example, but this is also true of several countries in Eastern Europe. Another factor in the emergence of global markets stems from communications technology, especially with respect to smartphones and the internet, which have impacted the dynamics of markets in terms of reach and interactivity. Consumers today tend to be aware of developments around the world and many desire to own things that formerly were restricted to the more affluent Western markets. Relatedly, new middle classes are becoming prominent in emerging economies and less developed countries, and they anchor consumer culture both economically and symbolically. Another key factor in the rise of global markets has been the collusion between governments and business and the efforts to build supranational trade arenas, such as the European Union and the North American Free Trade Agreement, as well as other "zones" like the Pacific Rim and the arrangements between North and South America.

Companies often engage in cross-cultural analysis to understand global markets before they enter them, which involves an extensive examination of many factors, such as differences in spoken language, consumption patterns, market segments, usage patterns for products and services, decision-making patterns and evaluative criteria, group influence and word of mouth, economic, social, and marketing environment, marketing research opportunities, and the regulatory environment (Schiffman, Kanuk, and Weisenblit 2010). Over a half century ago, Ernest Dichter (1962) wrote a pioneering article in which he encouraged companies to understand the "world consumer" and capitalize on international opportunities.

Raju (1995) expanded upon and extended Dichter's framework by positing four major aspects of consumer behavior within the global market: the A–B–C–D paradigm, involving Access, Buying behavior, Consumption characteristics, and Disposal. Access includes understanding factors governing consumers' access to a product or service. These factors might include economic aspects such as income distribution, or affordability within a culture and physical access barriers posed by the distribution system and the infrastructure within the country. Buying behavior involves understanding perceptions, brand loyalty and store loyalty, marketing-related attitudes, and social norms. Consumption characteristics involve understanding product and service consumption, traditional versus modern orientation within the culture, social class influences, and urban versus rural differences in consumption. Disposal involves understanding options consumers have for reusing or disposing of products and the cultural attitudes toward the environmental and social responsibility aspects of product disposal. Essentially, this framework involves a step-by-step analysis of how the consumer deals with a product or service from initial contact to the consumption and disposal of the product and can be a useful approach to understanding differences in global markets.

The two main approaches that companies use to market their products and services in global markets are standardization and adaptation (Schiffman, Kanuk, and Weisenblit 2010). Depending on the particular product or service, companies use varying degrees of standardization and adaptation in global markets. A judicious mix of the two strategies, called a "mixed strategy," is often the best. In general, standardization is often less expensive and more efficient and is used by companies desiring a uniform global image, while adaptation is a more creative approach which allows the company to use a decentralized organizational structure while being sensitive to local values and customs. While companies might be able to standardize the product and promotion (especially advertising) aspects of their business more easily, it is generally more difficult to standardize the price and place (distribution) aspects of the business in global markets.

Even with the product and promotion decisions, companies might decide to use a standardization strategy for one and an adaptation strategy for the other. Each company strives to choose the best overall strategy for its product or service and situation. Companies like McDonald's, General Electric, Nestlé, Coca-Cola, KFC, and Colgate use various combinations of standardization and adaptation as part of their global strategy. Reasons for companies to adapt a product to local conditions might include simplification of the product for use in less affluent and less educated countries, modifications for climate and infrastructure reasons, modifications to suit local customs, tastes, preferences, and shopping habits, and any legal restrictions on product design. Reasons to adapt promotion (advertising) might include local values and superstitions, language barriers, legal restrictions, and literacy levels. Changes in pricing in global markets are often governed by the purchasing power of consumers and purchasing habits, labor and material costs, and competition within a country. Lastly, changes in distribution (place) strategies are often based on the infrastructure of the country and technology which might influence the efficiency of distributing products within the country; buying habits and availability of different types of stores; types of middleman customarily used in the culture; and the functions and roles of these middlemen.

SEE ALSO: Consumer Culture; Consumption Rituals; Globalization and Consumption; Symbolic Value

REFERENCES

Dichter, Ernest. 1962. "The World Customer." *Harvard Business Review* (July/August): 113–122.

Levitt, Theodore. 1983. "The Globalization of Markets." *Harvard Business Review* (May/June): 92–102.

Raju, P. S. 1995. "Consumer Behavior in Global Markets: The A-B-C-D Paradigm and Its Application to Eastern Europe and the Third World." *Journal of Consumer Marketing* 12(5): 37–56.

Schiffman, Leon G., Leslie Lazar Kanuk, and Joseph Weisenblit. 2010. *Consumer Behavior*, 10th ed. Upper Saddle River, NJ: Prentice-Hall.

Globalization and Consumption

CHIH-CHIN CHEN and GEORGE RITZER
University of Maryland, USA

Globalization has become an increasingly important academic concern. There are many academic definitions of globalization, but the one employed here defines it mainly as a process that involves "increasing liquidity and multi-directional flows of objects, ideas, and people around the globe" (Ritzer 2010a, 2). Beyond definitions, a wide range of images has been created to get a sense of this process, including a "global village" (McLuhan 1964) and the "global age" (Albrow 1996). These concepts, as well as many others, offer unique perspectives on the nature, mechanisms, and effects of globalization, but they all share the view, clear in the definition above, that the world is becoming more interconnected and global flows are increasingly less likely to be hindered (Friedman 2007). However, Friedman and others take this view too far when they think in terms of a "flat world." While there has been an increase in global flows, barriers remain that impede the flows and make the world far from flat. Furthermore, nation-states, businesses, and other entities continually create new barriers designed to benefit them and to adversely affect others, and which, in the process, slow down, or completely block, global flows of many sorts. In terms of Friedman's image, they create numerous hills, if not mountains, on the global landscape. Nonetheless, it is the flows and not the barriers that define globalization today and those flows, in turn, play a major role in shaping the world's political, cultural, economic, and social landscape.

The masters of social theory, especially Karl Marx and his followers, as well as contemporary theorists and empiricists, have, at least until very recently, operated with a "productivist bias." This is true, as well, of analyses of globalization as reflected in the enormous body of work on such topics as the world system (Wallerstein 1974/2011) and neoliberalism. Also reflective of this productivist bias is a large body of work that focuses on such topics as outsourcing, economic sanctions, subsidies, and trade tariffs. However, most of this work has downplayed or ignored the ways in which globalization has involved and profoundly affected not only production but also consumption. For example, the growing importance of the BRIC countries (Brazil, Russia, India, and China) is seen in both the flow of large industrial companies into these countries because of the comparative advantages in production offered to such companies, and in the fact that the BRICs are increasingly important markets for those companies' consumer goods and services of all types.

Global sites of production have become increasingly important to corporations such as General Motors, Toyota, BMW, and Apple. In addition, such corporations are increasingly attracted to the consumer markets in many parts of the world. As a result, many of them are generating an increasing proportion of their revenues outside of their home markets. For example, more than 70 percent of General Motors' sales occur outside of the United States and 64 percent of Apple's revenue is generated outside of America. It is very clear that consumer products are flowing throughout the world to the very remotest areas of the globe. However, it is not just the corporations oriented to production that are globalizing; so, too, are those that focus on consumption, including giants in this domain such as Wal-Mart, IKEA, and McDonald's. IKEA opens 15 new stores a year globally and is making inroads into the Middle East, South America, and Asia. McDonald's has been opening one new restaurant in China every day for the past three years. Walmart has more than 10,000 units from its own company as well as acquisitions from other companies worldwide. Its most recent expansion has been in South Africa, India, and China. In the process, all of these consumption-oriented corporations are bringing with them increasing consumption, as well as, more broadly, the kind of "consumer society" we usually associate with the United States.

While a productivist bias continues to this day, an increasing number of social theorists and researchers have been taking greater notice, especially since the end of World War II, of the increasing importance of consumption. However, the notion that we are increasingly living in a consumer society did not acquire its long overdue recognition until several decades later. Most notable was Jean Baudrillard's *The Consumer Society: Myths and Structures* (1998), which, although it was published in France in 1970, was not translated into English until 1998. This book not only provided the label "consumer society," which we increasingly apply to contemporary societies in the developed world, but it also offered an important critical analysis of that society. An essential feature of consumer society is that people's "identity and status are acquired and social inclusion or integration is considered to be achieved through participation in consumer activity" (Smart 2010, 39). As pointed out above, the idea of a consumer society is most closely associated with the United States where consumption and consumption-related economic activities are high and have been rising dramatically. In 2012, total spending on advertisements in America, an economic activity obviously intrinsically associated with consumption, had already exceeded US$154 billion. In addition to the United States and other Western societies, other parts of the world such as Brazil and China are also experiencing a similar expansion in consumption. There is a comparable prospective scenario for India's emerging markets, the emerging middle class, and the reshaping of consumer behavior there. It is safe to say that in the developed world consumption has come to occupy the center of many people's economic, cultural, and social lives, and this focus on consumption is rapidly flowing to many other parts of the world. However, there are many countries in the less developed world, especially those inhabited by the "bottom billion," that are relatively unaffected by global flows related to consumption (Collier 2007).

Not only has consumer society spread around much of the world in the global age, but so too have the major objects of consumption – goods and services of all types. One particularly good example is Apple's products, including iPhones and iPads, although Apple is being supplanted in the global market for such products by companies such as Samsung. Beyond the global spread of goods and services of all types is the global dissemination of sites of consumption, especially the newer ones that Ritzer (2010b, 6) has called the new "means of consumption" (or the "cathedrals of consumption"), defined as the new "settings or structures that enable us to consume all sorts of things." Among the globalized new means of consumption (most of which were invented in the United States and then exported to other parts of the world) are shopping malls and mega malls, chain (sometimes themed) restaurants (e.g., McDonald's, Hard Rock Café), Las Vegas-style casinos and casino strips such as those found on Macau, cruise ships, superstores (e.g., Wal-Mart), and Disney amusement parks as well as those modeled on them. These are all recently developed settings and business models that are aimed at better enabling, if not coercing, consumers into consuming products and services in larger quantities, greater diversity, and in a far more efficient manner. These settings have been successfully exported, replicated, and are now firmly ensconced in many parts of the world. Thus, not only have consumer society and consumer goods and services globalized, but so too have the settings in which much consumption takes place, as well as the mechanisms they use to induce people not only to be consumers, but to be "consumed" by consumption (Barber 1995).

These settings have contributed to the global spread of a variety of consumption processes. For example, the spread of supermarkets has brought with it what DeGrazia (2005) calls "supermarketing," including the increasingly ubiquitous process of filling carts with food as one traverses the market and then paying at a checkout counter (often now a self-service process). "Walmartization" has caused the shuttering of many small shops and forced consumers to buy many different products in one setting. McDonald's has brought high speed and efficiency to the process of eating, most notably through the use of drive-through windows. The latter has, in turn, led to more meals being consumed in automobiles en route to some other locale. There are many other examples of such relatively new consumption processes and they are increasingly found in more parts of the world. However, the most important changes in the consumption process – and they are inherently global – are those occurring online in a wide range of digital marketplaces. Amazon.com, one of the most prominent online sites, provides a global online marketplace with 182 million active user accounts for retailing worldwide. It employs 109,800 employees and reported a revenue of US$61.09 billion in 2012.

Such global connectedness and the possibility of anonymity provided by information technology have also led to the creation of several global black markets online: Silk Road, The Farmer's Market, etc. These websites are operated through TOR (The Onion Router) to keep the server anonymous and use alternative payment methods such as Bitcoin to evade back-tracing from law enforcement. These sites provide a marketplace for illegal drugs and contraband goods, among other things.

Consumers themselves have been globalized in various ways and senses. For example, they are increasingly accustomed to buying goods and services that emanate from many other parts of the world. In doing so, they often make their purchases on sites that were created elsewhere and use mechanisms (e.g., credit cards) that are similarly global. Consumers are especially globalized on global consumption sites on the internet, where they can purchase goods and services from virtually anywhere in the world. It is also important to mention global tourism as a way in which consumption has been globalized. Tourists, basically consumers of tourism, increasingly traverse the world in search of experiences and souvenirs.

The flows associated with consumption that are an increasingly integral part of globalization can be both positive (e.g., medical advances in the form of new technologies and pharmaceuticals) and negative (e.g., fast food that has adverse health effects). The unprecedented global flow of a wide array of goods and services is seen as a positive development by large numbers of consumers, as well as the corporations that manufacture and sell these. Many newcomers to the world of global consumption welcome the influx of goods and services. However, there are many criticisms of this as well, such as the unequal ability of the lower classes in some parts of the world, as well as great swathes of the world as a whole, to participate in consumer society. Another set of criticisms is aimed at the environmental problems caused by the boom in global consumption. The global division of labor and the "race to the bottom" have worked hand in hand to satisfy the consumer demand of high-income countries (HICs), at the expense of the health of citizens and the environment of low-income countries (LICs). Such environmental risks and concerns are not present in HICs or LICs alone, but also in international communities and transnational civil societies.

There are also concerns about the detrimental effects of global consumer society on consumers themselves. For example, the corporate-imposed homogeneity of many global products, services, processes, and consumption sites has led Ritzer (2007) to label them as "nothing," that is, as social forms that are centrally conceived, controlled, and devoid of distinctive substantive content. The nothingness that tends to be produced and exported globally by the leaders of consumer society stands in contrast to, and threatens, the "somethingness" associated with local culture. "Something" is defined as social forms that are locally conceived and controlled, and that are rich in distinctive and substantive content. Included here are local products, services, and sites of consumption (such as open-air markets). Although these survive, they are progressively being marginalized and their very existence is threatened by their globalized alternatives. As they decline and disappear, there is increasing homogeneity in global consumer culture.

The proliferation of goods, services, and consumption sites associated with globalization leads to a "monumental abundance" of all of them. That is, many parts of the world are experiencing a great increase in nothingness in the realm of consumption (and elsewhere). In addition to the threat this poses to the somethingness associated with local culture, this abundance envelops many of those in less developed societies who produce the goods that meet the definition of nothing and who offer "nothing" services in settings that have those same characteristics. The problem here is that the poor in the less developed parts of the world produce many of these things, but they cannot afford to buy them. Similarly, they work in and around settings (tourist locales) that they cannot afford to utilize. While many of these goods, services, and settings may meet the definition of nothing, they are nevertheless considered highly desirable by most in the developed and less developed world. Thus, the global poor cannot afford these things even though they are led to desire them, are surrounded by them, and are deeply involved in their production and provision.

One of the key characteristics of the development of a global consumer society is the global spread of credit and credit cards. Those who are affluent enough can use credit almost anywhere in the world, usually by using the same credit card everywhere they go. All the major credit card companies (Visa, MasterCard, American Express, Discover) have partner countries and territories (there are over 200 of them). The credit card has become a global medium of exchange. However, this convenience has contributed to hyperconsumption and hyperdebt. Hyperconsumption involves consuming more than one wants, needs, and can afford, while hyperdebt involves incurring more debt than one wants, needs, and is able to repay (Ritzer 2012). Average American household credit card debt for indebted households (excluding ones without debt) in 2012 was $15,956, and the average household debt (including credit card) was $54,000. The use of credit cards, and the tendency to go into credit card debt, is especially great in the United States. In fact, Garon (2012) contrasts the US love affair with debt to the resistance to it in other parts of the world. Nevertheless, other nations, especially the United Kingdom, are as deeply enmeshed in the world of credit cards and debt as is the United States. Credit made possible by government support is making consumers in the US and UK more prone to go into consumer credit card debt than those in Japan, even though Japan is at a similar stage of development.

Hyperconsumption and hyperdebt not only immiserate individuals and households, but they also have national and global consequences. The crash of the US economy in 2007–08 and the ensuing global economic crisis were evidence of the economic mayhem debt can bring to the world. They are also proof that the global financial system is ever more intertwined and that both good and bad financial flows move around the world quickly and easily. Because of globalization, the entire global market is tightly interconnected; each change in a single market is likely to cause ripples in every other market. Economic disasters such as the one mentioned above can cause a massive economic tsunami around the world, crippling, if not completely destroying, many markets. Ulrich Beck has analyzed world risk to society; he sees credit and finance as being among the major risks humans are facing now and are likely to face in the future (Beck 2008).

Like most Marxists, Leslie Sklair is highly critical of the global expansion of capitalism. While most Marxists continue to operate with a productivist bias, Sklair is unique in also according great significance to consumption. Specifically, he gives great importance in the global spread and success of capitalism to the existence and spread of what he terms the "culture-ideology of consumerism." He argues that capitalism, specifically TNCs (transnational corporations) and TCCs (transnational capitalist classes), is not only exporting production systems and their products, but also a "culture ideology of consumerism" involving the "overdeveloped hedonism" prevalent in Western societies through, especially, cultural and media imperialism (Sklair 2002, 164). By exporting such hedonistic consumerism, capitalism has been able to create an increasing global demand for its products. Capitalism is not satisfied by simply subsuming these markets under its production regime; it also seeks to transform more and more of those who exist in these markets into consumers and, if possible, hyperconsumers of the regime's products. It has long ceased to be sufficient to focus on production; it is now at least as important to create ever more global consumers and an ever-increasing need and desire to consume.

SEE ALSO: Culture-Ideology of Consumerism; Glocalization/Grobalization; Homogenization and Heterogenization; McDonaldization; Obesity

REFERENCES

Albrow, Martin. 1996. *The Global Age: State and Society beyond Modernity*. Cambridge, UK: Polity.

Barber, Benjamin R. 1995. *Jihad vs. McWorld: How Globalism and Tribalism Are Shaping the World.* New York: Ballantine.
Baudrillard, Jean. 1998. *The Consumer Society: Myths and Structures.* London: Sage.
Beck, Ulrich. 2008. *World at Risk.* Cambridge, UK: Polity.
Collier, Paul. 2007. *The Bottom Billion.* New York: Oxford University Press.
DeGrazia, Victoria. 2005. *Irresistible Empire.* Cambridge, MA: Belknap.
Friedman, Thomas L. 2007. *The World Is Flat: A Brief History of the Twenty-first Century.* New York: Macmillan.
Garon, Sheldon. 2012. *Beyond Our Means: Why America Spends while the World Saves.* Princeton, NJ: Princeton University Press.
McLuhan, Marshall. 1964. *Understanding Media: The Extensions of Man.* New York: McGraw-Hill.
Ritzer, George. 2007. *The Globalization of Nothing 2.* Thousand Oaks, CA: Pine Forge Press.
Ritzer, George. 2010a. *Globalization: A Basic Text.* Malden, MA: Wiley-Blackwell.
Ritzer, George. 2010b. *Enchanting a Disenchanted World.* Thousand Oaks, CA: Sage.
Ritzer, George. 2012. "Are We Consuming beyond Our Means? The Debate Over, and Resistance to, Excessive Consumption and Debt." *Contemporary Sociology: A Journal of Reviews* 42(1): 59–62.
Sklair, Leslie. 2002. *Globalization: Capitalism and Its Alternative.* Oxford: Oxford University Press.
Smart, Barry. 2010. *Consumer Society: Critical Issues and Environmental Consequences.* London: Sage.
Wallerstein, Immanuel. 1974/2011. *The Modern World-System I.* Berkeley: University of California Press.

Glocalization/ Grobalization

J. MICHAEL RYAN
The American University in Cairo, Egypt

Glocalization can be defined as the interpenetration of the global and the local, resulting in unique, hybrid outcomes (Robertson 1992). It is not the imposition of the global on the local nor is it the resistance of the local to the global, but rather a blending of the two to create a distinctly new phenomenon. And while the degree of dominance/survival of one over the other can vary greatly, glocalization still reflects the creation of a new hybrid form. Thus, proponents of glocalization argue that globalization is not leading to greater global sameness but rather creating opportunities for greater global difference.

Glocalization is rooted in the postmodern notions of hybridity, diversity, plurality, and pastiche. According to Robertson (1992, 1994), glocalization means that the world is becoming increasingly diverse and that it is sensitive to those differences. Cosmopolitanism is embraced. It sees individuals and local cultures as creative agents easily able to adapt and innovate. Social processes are thus viewed as relational and contingent, not unidirectional and imperialistic. On the level of consumption, commodities and the media are not seen as imposing uniformity but rather as providing means by which local realities can self-selectively create and refashion identities and communities. It is a generally positive view of globalization, particularly as it relates to consumption.

Grobalization is a term coined by sociologist George Ritzer (2007). It is meant to serve as a companion to the widely employed concept of glocalization. While glocalization represents the unique combinations resulting from the interpenetration of the global and the local, grobalization represents "the imperialistic ambitions of nations, corporations, organizations, and the like and their desire, indeed need, to impose themselves on various geographic areas" (p. 73). Thus, glocalization would be most closely associated with postmodern, pluralistic ideas of heterogeneity and hybridity, whereas grobalization represents a modern, imperialistic, and homogenizing perspective more closely associated with cultural convergence.

Grobalization theorists would generally argue that the world is becoming increasingly less diverse as transnational economic, cultural, political, and social entities seek to impose their influence throughout the world. The agent in this perspective has relatively little power to maneuver within, between, or around structures. Their ability to construct their own identity and world are seriously impinged on by the growing forces of grobal powers, particularly commodities and the media. Social processes are deterministic and overwhelm the local, limiting its ability to interact with, much less act back against, the global. This stands in stark contrast to theories of glocalization which give great power to the agent who they see as having increased opportunities to construct their identity in new and diverse ways by using commodities and the media to produce new and different phenomena. They view social processes as two-directional, with the local interpenetrating with the global rather than simply being overwhelmed by it.

Grobalization theorists critique defenders of glocalization on many grounds but one of their strongest arguments is that there really is little, if any, of the purely local left in the world today. That is, there is little in the world these days that is not, in some way, already affected by grobalization and hence no longer purely local. Whether it is using materials from another part of the world or even simply emphasizing the local more as a reaction against grobalization, Ritzer (2007) argues that we are "witnessing the *death of the local*, at least as we have known it" (p. 159, italics in original).

It is important to note that no value judgments are intended for either glocalization or grobalization. They are meant as social tools to help us understand social processes, not to judge them. Many things which are glocal (as well as local) can be "bad" (e.g., discrimination), while many things which are grobal can be "good" (e.g., the spread of medical technology).

SEE ALSO: Globalization and Consumption; Homogenization and Heterogenization

REFERENCES

Ritzer, George. 2007. *The Globalization of Nothing 2*. Thousand Oaks, CA: Pine Forge Press.

Robertson, Roland. 1992. *Globalization: Social Theory and Global Culture*. London: Sage.

Robertson, Roland. 1994. "Globalization or Glocalization?" *Journal of International Communication* 1: 33–52.

Governmentality and Consumer Culture

CHRISTOPHER MAYES
University of Sydney, Australia

Governmentality describes the practice of government that uses tactics, knowledges, and procedures to "conduct the conduct" of individuals and populations (Foucault 2007, 29ff.). Operating continually, yet at a distance, governmentality mobilizes an ensemble of power relations and mundane objects. Food labels, smartphones, carbon offsetting, online genomics, and countless other consumer objects and practices serve as avenues through which conduct is conducted.

Michel Foucault first introduced the term in his 1977–78 Collège de France lectures, published in English as *Security, Territory, Population* (2007). In these lectures Foucault articulates the practice of governing a people as distinct from governing the nation-state. Unlike state rule, which extends laws over juridical subjects within a territory, governmentality operates within intricate relations among individuals, objects, and populations. This mentality of governance is diffuse rather than hierarchical and requires specific knowledge of human behavior and populations to make them governable realities. Foucault traces the historical interaction of the knowledge of population and the practices of governance from the Christian pastor through to the behavioral economics of the Chicago School's neoliberal theory.

Foucault's analysis of neoliberal governmentality in his 1978–79 lectures, published as *The Birth of Biopolitics* (2008), is especially relevant for examining consumer culture in relation to political economy. While Jean Baudrillard provides important insights into connections between an economy based on consumption and the aestheticization of social relations (1998), and Marxist critiques uncover the alienating effect of commodity fetishism, Foucault's analysis of neoliberal and human capital theory exposes the politicization of life through consumption practices that enlist individuals and populations as allies in procedures and strategies of security, responsibility, and subject production.

The central point of reference in neoliberal governmentality is *Homo œconomicus* (Lemke 2001, 200). Foucault describes *Homo œconomicus* as a highly governable and responsive subject (2008, 270). This governability is enabled by a specific knowledge of humans as free and choosing, based on economist Gary Becker's human capital theory and entrepreneurial choice (Becker 1993, 115). Entrepreneurial choice transforms human labor from being purchased or embedded in the production of a commodity into a choice made by the laborer (Dilts 2011, 135). The subject does not exchange labor for a wage, but invests their human capital in order to receive an income. As such, *Homo œconomicus* has an entrepreneurial relation to the self and activity. The self becomes capital that can be invested to generate a return, producing and increasing the value of the self (Foucault 2008, 226). All choices and activities of life, not just labor, are transformed into investments and incomes that "may or may not improve human capital" (Foucault 2008, 230). Thus consumption becomes investment.

In rethinking the subject in consumer society as an entrepreneur who is obliged to be free and invest in their self, the subject becomes governable through modifications in the choices available in the surrounding environment (Gordon 1991, 43; Foucault 2008, 270). Consumer choice and the environment in which it is made become a primary domain through which individuals and populations are governed toward ends such as health, security, environmental sustainability, or social justice.

CONSUMPTION AS PRODUCTION

Neoliberal governmentality characterizes *Homo œconomicus* as an empty subject without attributes other than the capacity for freedom and choice. In consuming, the subject produces itself. Foucault writes that "we should think of consumption as an enterprise activity" (2008, 226), through which the individual is produced. The integration of consumption into productive activity rejects Marxist notions of alienation that distinguish "worker" from "consumer" (Dilts 2011, 137). In contrast, *Homo œconomicus* is a vacant subject that is produced through enterprising choice. There is no division or alienation of a self that is a consumer on the one hand and a producer on the other (Foucault 2008, 226). The subject may feel dissatisfaction with an investment that does not meet their expectations but there is not alienation, only more choosing and further consumption practices to redress investment expectations.

CONSUMPTION AS RESPONSIBILITY

With the blurring of boundaries between production and consumption, the subject is left responsible to guard them (Binkley 2006). The emphasis on self-investment in neoliberal governmentality requires the consumer to be responsible for that choice. Enterprise in neoliberal governance multiplies individual freedoms within the parameters of "a notion of responsible self-management" (McNay 2009, 61). Through the remapping of individual freedoms as responsible self-management in neoliberal governmentality, free choice and consumption become mechanisms of governance (Rose 1999). Thus, the incentive to use freedom (in a rational and responsible way) rather than a ban or law is mobilized to encourage individuals to transform the self into an enterprise directed toward ends of individual and population health, security, and economic prosperity.

CONSUMPTION AS SECURITY

Security concerns over terrorism, global climate change, gun control, obesity, and fossil fuel depletion are governed through a variety of mechanisms. However, a primary strategy of neoliberal governmentality to manage threats to population security is to facilitate incentives to choose in the direction of security. Foucault's emphasis on governing through choice and freedom is conditioned by responsibility and security. The responsible investor is not only the good citizen that secures their own future but also one who becomes "an active agent in the provision of security" for the wider population (Rose 1999, 166). There are certainly violent and oppressive strategies employed that extend beyond consumer choice. However, within neoliberal and consumer societies, manipulation of individual choice through incentives and disincentives continues to be a key governmental tactic.

It is important to note that governmentality is not a totalizing explanation for all consumer, population, or governmental activities, nor does governmentality seamlessly conduct the conduct of individuals and populations through practices such as consumption. It is an agonistic strategy that flexibly responds to points of resistance and emergent needs.

SEE ALSO: Consumer Behavior; Lifestyle; Politics and Consumer Culture

REFERENCES

Baudrillard, Jean. 1998. *The Consumer Society: Myths and Structures*. London: Sage.

Becker, Gary. 1993. *Human Capital: A Theoretical and Empirical Analysis, with Special Reference to Education*, 3rd ed. Chicago, IL: University of Chicago Press.

Binkley, Sam. 2006. "The Perilous Freedoms of Consumption: Toward a Theory of the Conduct of Consumer Conduct." *Journal for Cultural Research* 10(4): 343–362.

Dilts, Andrew. 2011. "From 'Entrepreneur of the Self' to 'Care of the Self': Neo-liberal Governmentality and Foucault's Ethics." *Foucault Studies* 12: 130–146.

Foucault, Michel. 2007. *Security, Territory, Population: Lectures at the Collège de France 1977–78*. Translated by Graham Burchell. Edited by Arnold I. Davidson. New York: Palgrave Macmillan.

Foucault, Michel. 2008. *The Birth of Biopolitics: Lectures at the Collège de France, 1978–79*. Translated by Graham Burchell. Edited by Michel Senellart, François Ewald, and Alessandro Fontana. New York: Palgrave Macmillan.

Gordon, Colin. 1991. "Governmental Rationality: An Introduction." In *The Foucault Effect: Studies in Governmentality*, edited by Graham Burchell, Colin Gordon, and Peter Miller. Chicago, IL: University of Chicago Press.

Lemke, Thomas. 2001. "'The Birth of Bio-politics': Michel Foucault's Lecture at the Collège de France on Neo-liberal Governmentality." *Economy and Society* 30(2): 190–207.

McNay, Lois. 2009. "Self as Enterprise: Dilemmas of Control and Resistance in Foucault's The Birth of Biopolitics." *Theory, Culture and Society* 26(6): 55–77.

Rose, Nikolas. 1999. *Powers of Freedom: Reframing Political Thought*. Cambridge, UK: Cambridge University Press.

Green Consumerism

MADELEINE PAPE
University of Wisconsin–Madison, USA

Consumer behavior is increasingly being highlighted as one of the central causes of environmental degradation. Whereas in the past the agendas of environmental organizations focused primarily on changing the practices of destructive industries, in recent decades there has been a shift toward asking individual consumers to take responsibility for the consequences of their consumption practices (Spaargaren and Mol 2008). Long-term environmental challenges with global reach, such as climate change, resource depletion, and pollution, are now frequently linked to the daily lifestyles and choices of individuals and households, particularly those of high-income nations.

This change in focus has coincided with the emergence of long-term "sustainable development" goals within national and global responses to environmental degradation. Sustainable development is often defined as economic and social development that meets human needs now without compromising the ability of future generations to meet their needs (WCED 1987). Broadly speaking, sustainable development recognizes the social consequences at the local and global levels associated with the production and consumption patterns of modern capitalist societies. It became institutionalized at the United Nations World Summit on Environment and Development in 1992, which produced a nonbinding agreement on sustainable development for developed and developing countries entitled *Agenda 21* (United Nations 1992). Green consumerism forms a key part of the sustainable development paradigm, focusing primarily on the environmental and social consequences associated with individual consumer behavior (Hobson 2002).

In the phrase "green consumerism," the word "consumerism" refers to the powerful ideology driving the consumption habits of individuals and households, under which consumption becomes an end in itself, leading to the reproduction and maintenance of a whole array of social relations (Bauman 2007). The word "green" refers to the ways in which the purchase and use of consumer goods and services transform the surrounding environment, either directly or indirectly. However, this simplified definition entails a number of assumptions. Most importantly, it assumes that the responsibility for the environmental impacts of consumerism falls primarily on the individuals and households directly engaged with it (Stern 1997). Similarly, it implies that action taken at the individual or household level can be instrumental in meeting long-term environmental challenges. These are assumptions that have been debated at length by social scientists engaged in research around consumerism and environmental sustainability.

KEY DEBATES

The concept of green consumerism is to some scholars and environmentalists a contradiction in terms, and to others a fitting solution given the firmly entrenched practices and economic structure of modern consumer societies. Social scientists are in a position to analyze and critique the ways in which governments, businesses, and other organizations employ discourses around green consumerism. In both practice and theory, the idea of green consumerism swings between, on the one hand, the idealism and radicalism of the environmental movement and, on the other, the rational and market-focused nature of neoliberal economic thought (Jackson 2005). However, the mainstream compatibility and appeal of green consumerism, particularly in the realm of national, international, and corporate sustainability agendas, make it quite different from earlier environmental movements.

The tension inherent in the concept of green consumerism is revealed in conflicting understandings over its implications for social and environmental practice. One basic contestation is over whether the concept should refer to consuming differently or whether, instead, it should be about consuming less. These two positions can be summarized as "efficiency" versus "sufficiency." The "efficiency" argument is primarily an economic interpretation of green consumption, emphasizing the use of market forces to achieve better environmental outcomes. Sustainable consumer goods embody this interpretation. The "sufficiency" position supports radical overhaul of the values of individual consumers away from materialist and consumption-heavy lifestyles, and is associated with movements such as "voluntary simplicity" and "simple living."

A related tension can be seen in the work of social scientists around green consumerism. The central question for social scientists is whether or not consumer practices have a role to play within solutions to environmental crises. The response to this question typically falls along a continuum between two broad positions. The first is that of "ecological modernization," which, similar to the efficiency position, argues for the positive contribution that the right kind of production and consumer practices could make toward sustainability solutions. At the opposite end of the spectrum is "demodernization," which has a view similar to that of the sufficiency position. Demodernists see consumerism as a fundamental cause of environmental crises. According to this stance, any proposed solution that includes consumerism can only serve to perpetuate modern society's trajectory toward ecological destruction. In between are those who accept that consumer behavior will at least be a part of an initial solution, but who remain skeptical of its capacity to form the basis of fundamental and enduring change. This group typically views the abandonment of the present modern consumer lifestyle and associated institutional structures as a gradual and uncertain process.

ECOLOGICAL MODERNIZATION THEORY

The central premise of ecological modernization theory is that if the structural design faults that have led to environmental destruction can be restored, then the institutions of modern society can be made compatible with environmental sustainability (Mol and Spaargaren 2000). Through a process of institutional evolution, the modern organization of production and consumerism can move toward recognizing and reflecting ecological concerns. This area of environmental sociology developed from the earlier risk society work of Ulrich Beck, and key social scientists include Arthur Mol and Gert Spaargaren from the Netherlands, and Americans Maurie Cohen and David Sonnenfield.

According to Mol (1996), the ecological modernization process hinges upon the "emancipation" of "ecological rationality" (p. 303). The problem with the environmental movement in the 1970s was that the key institutions of modernity – particularly those relating to industrial structure, economic relations, and scientific-technological developments – continued to be defined narrowly in rationalized economic terms. By contrast, Mol argues that over the 1980s and 1990s "environment-induced institutional transformations" (p. 303) occurred that reflected enlightened self-interest and the recognition of humankind's dependence upon the natural world. Maintaining environmental health became equated with preservation of a sustenance base, enabling ecological concerns to shape decisions within economic, technological, political, and social realms.

An important implication of ecological modernization theory is that it foresees capitalism as compatible with environmental sustainability. The idea of a "green capitalism" was first put on the ecological modernization agenda by Joseph Huber in the early 1980s. Since that time there has been some evidence that a "green capitalism" is not beyond the realm of possibility. Many industries have restructured their operations in line with what has come to be known as "industrial ecology," whereby environmental issues are embraced as opportunities to access new markets and to improve efficiency. Green consumer goods are another such case of green capitalism in practice.

Ecological modernization theorists in more recent years have adopted a more nuanced stance toward the green potential of capitalism, placing greater emphasis on the need for different relations of production and an alternative economic order (Mol and Spaargaren 2000). But the characterizing feature of ecological modernization theory remains the rationalization of environmental relations, whereby ecological concerns are incorporated into existing institutional structures, inspired by a logic of self-preservation.

Deep ecologists and some social scientists contest ecological modernization on two main grounds. First, they argue that it fails to recognize the inherent value of environmental preservation for its own sake. Second, they argue that there is little evidence that modern institutional structures and lifestyles shaped by capitalism and driven by a cycle of production and consumerism can be reconciled with long-term environmental sustainability.

CONSUMPTION AND DEMODERNIZATION

Scholars and environmentalists who fall under the category of demodernization argue that there can be no such thing as a "green" consumerism. According to this view, consumerism is inextricably linked to capitalism and, by association, to ecological destruction. Environmentalists such as Murray Bookchin argue against the ecological modernization perspective and suggest that true environmental sustainability demands fundamental change in the values and institutions that shape modern society, rather than an improvement of them. Since green consumerism initiatives fail to challenge the existing consumer-oriented way of life and associated production systems, such commentators argue that green consumerism can only lead to superficial change in the impact of humankind upon the environment (Hobson 2002).

Other demodernization perspectives attack the notion of economic growth, and thus the idea that we can achieve a greener future through "better" consumerism. The sociologist Allan Schnaiberg (1980) offered an organizational critique of growth known as the "treadmill of production." According to this framework, capitalist societies are driven by a self-reinforcing logic of overproduction, economic uncertainty, and a sidelining of environmental and social concerns. Ecological economists Nicholas Georgescu-Roegen and Serge Latouche offer a related and increasingly prominent critique of growth known as "de-growth," arguing that growth is not socially or economically necessary and ultimately bumps up against the second law of thermodynamics.

Political science scholars have also contributed to the argument that consumerism is not compatible with environmental sustainability, and that there must be a transition toward alternative institutions and values. Michael Maniates (2002) equates green consumerism with the "individualization of responsibility" (p. 33), whereby consumers are asked to take individual action on environmental issues rather than work toward the necessary collective solutions to the problems. Central to these political science debates on sustainability is the notion of citizenship, its diminished relevance within postmodern societies, and its potential to revive collective action on environmental issues. Andrew Dobson (2003) proposes the framework of "ecological citizenship," within which individuals are encouraged to put their responsibilities toward the environment and other people ahead of their own materialistic concerns. Green consumerism may be attractive for its compatibility with individual freedom, but it is those individualistic values that must be challenged for environmental sustainability to be achieved.

A MIDDLE POSITION ON CONSUMPTION

Given the deeply embedded place of consumerism within modern societies, both in economic and in social terms, other social scientists call for green consumerism to be viewed critically, but still optimistically. While not seeing green consumerism as the centerpiece of a shift toward an environmentally sustainable future, they nonetheless argue that consumer practices do have an important political role to play. From this perspective, political consumerism can be one of a number of strategies or actions that contribute to social change, countering the argument that green consumerism can only be individualized and anti-collective (Willis and Schor 2012). Instead, a politicized green consumerism can be linked with wider social and environmental activism and is a means through which consumers can transform the practices of corporations and business entities.

There is also the view that green consumerism is a legitimate practice even when not inspired by green values. Some green consumers are inspired solely by self-interest, such as vegetarians or organic shoppers concerned with health or food quality (Micheletti and Stolle 2012). This is what leads Michael Bell (2012) to advocate "virtual environmentalism": individuals choosing to adopt environmentally sustainable practices, but perhaps not with noble motivations in mind. From this perspective, the key focus for environmentalists and policymakers becomes establishing the institutional conditions that make environmentally sustainable choices cheap, convenient, and enjoyable.

As green consumerism evolves and becomes more normalized as a consumer practice, social scientists have the opportunity to perform the role of analyzing whether or not this is indeed translating into more widespread social change. Empirically, this is taking the form of studies of consumer behavior and attitudes as well as research on institutional and organizational practices (see Micheletti and Stolle 2012; Willis and Schor 2012). Much of this work is interdisciplinary, drawing on sociological and political theory as well as social psychology, economics, and human ecology. It continues to be characterized by the divided views on green consumerism reviewed here. Nonetheless, it is all research motivated by the desire to advance the cause of environmental sustainability, highlighting the important role that social scientists have to play in this transition.

SEE ALSO: Citizenship and Consumption; Ethical Consumption; Green Consumption; Politics and Consumer Culture; Sustainable Consumption

REFERENCES

Bauman, Zygmunt. 2007. *Consuming Life*. Cambridge, UK: Polity.

Bell, Michael M. 2012. *An Invitation to Environmental Sociology*, 4th ed. Thousand Oaks, CA: Pine Forge Press.

Dobson, Andrew. 2003. *Citizenship and the Environment*. Oxford: Oxford University Press.

Hobson, Kersty. 2002. "Competing Discourses of Sustainable Consumption: Does the 'Rationalization of Lifestyles' Make Sense?" *Environmental Politics* 11(2): 95–120.

Jackson, Tim. 2005. "Live Better by Consuming Less? Is There a 'Double Dividend' in Sustainable Consumption?" *Journal of Industrial Ecology* 9(1–2): 19–33.

Maniates, Michael. 2002. "Individualization: Plant a Tree, Buy a Bike, Save the World?" In *Confronting Consumption*, edited by Thomas Princen, Michael Maniates, and Ken Conca, 43–66. Cambridge, MA: MIT Press.

Micheletti, Michele, and Dietlind Stolle. 2012. "Sustainable Citizenship and the New Politics of Consumption." *The ANNALS of the American Academy of Political and Social Science* 644: 88–119.

Mol, Arthur P. J. 1996. "Ecological Modernization and Institutional Reflexivity: Environmental Reform in the Late Modern Age." *Environmental Politics* 5: 302–323.

Mol, Arthur P. J., and Gert Spaargaren. 2000. "Ecological Modernization Theory in Debate: A Review." *Environmental Politics* 9(1): 17–49.

Schnaiberg, Allan. 1980. *The Environment: From Surplus to Scarcity*. Oxford: Oxford University Press.

Spaargaren, Gert, and Arthur P. J. Mol. 2008. "Greening Global Consumption: Redefining Politics and Authority." *Global Environmental Change* 18: 350–359.

Stern, Paul C. 1997. "Toward a Working Definition of Consumption for Environmental Research and Policy." In *Environmentally Significant Consumption: Research Directions*, edited by Paul C. Stern, Thomas Dietz, Vernon R. Ruttan, Robert H. Socolow, & James L. Sweeney, 12–35. Washington, DC: National Academy Press.

United Nations. 1992. *Results of the World Conference on Environment and Development: Agenda 21*. UN Conference on Environment and Development, Rio de Janeiro. New York: United Nations.

WCED. 1987. *Our Common Future (The Brundtland Report)*. World Commission on Environment and Development. Oxford: Oxford University Press.

Willis, Margaret M., and Juliet B. Schor. 2012. "Does Changing a Light Bulb Lead to Changing the World? Political Action and the Conscious Consumer." *The ANNALS of the American Academy of Political and Social Science* 644: 160–190.

Green Consumption

LUCY ATKINSON
University of Texas at Austin, US

Green falls under a larger category of consumer orientations that are often referred to as "sustainable consumption." This can be defined as "the use of services and related products which respond to basic needs and bring a better quality of life while minimizing the use of natural resources and toxic materials, as well as emissions of waste and pollutants over the life cycle of the service or product so as not to jeopardize the needs of future generations" (Norwegian Ministry of the Environment 1994). In green consumption scholarship, the term remains inexactly defined and is often criticized for a lack of clarity, precision, and consistency. For example, fair trade products are generally thought of in terms of their social responsibility factors, but the standards governing fair trade also incorporate issues of environmental stewardship and protection.

Green consumption assumes multiple forms and encompasses a variety of consumer practices, including fair trade purchasing, community-supported agriculture, and consumer localism. It can be informed by a number of motivations, simultaneously individual and private as well as community oriented and public. Green consumption is often used interchangeably with other terms, including responsible consumption, ecologically concerned consumption, socially responsible consumption, ethical consumption, and political consumption.

It has its roots in the early days of the environmental movement in the 1960s and 1970s and gained strength in the 1980s and 1990s, in part because of high-profile events like the *Exxon Valdez* oil spill in 1989 off the coast of Alaska and the success of consumer boycotts of aerosol products with environmentally damaging CFCs (chlorofluorocarbons). Marketers responded to the growing green sentiment with environmentally friendly products, like biodegradable trash bags, but soon faced considerable backlash from consumers in connection with "under-performing green products and over-zealous promotional claims" (Crane 2000, 278). Green consumption gained mainstream prominence in the 2000s, and, unlike earlier incarnations that were viewed as countercultural, fringe endeavors, today's green consumer lifestyle is much more accessible and conventional (Ottman 2011). Contemporary green offerings run the gamut of product categories from organic food and personal care to appliances, cars, home furnishings, and renewable energy, and can be found in most retail stores. As of 2010, the majority of organic food in the United States is sold by conventional retailers like Wal-Mart, Costco, and Target, rather than through natural food stores.

WHO ARE THE GREEN CONSUMERS?

Research into green consumption has paid considerable attention to understanding who are the green consumers and to segmenting them into groups for the purposes of marketing. Major marketing firms like Roper Starch Worldwide, Ogilvy & Mather, and the Natural Marketing Institute have identified several subgroups of green consumers, depending on their commitment to green buying and environmental values, with descriptive names varying from firm to firm. Each segment indicates a breakdown of green commitments among US consumers. At one end are individuals who are least likely to buy green products. These "basic browns," or "green rejectors," are likely to view green products as ineffective and overpriced. At the other end are "true blue greens," or "super greens," who are optimistic about the positive impact green products can have on the environment and are committed to issues of sustainability. In between, representing about two-thirds of consumers, are moderately green consumers who range in their commitment to green products, but are more amenable to issues of sustainability than the lowest segment.

Of these segments, only the greenest of greens, accounting for between 10 and 15 percent of consumers, can be relied on regularly to engage in green consumption. The remaining consumers are inconsistent in their green purchasing patterns: although they claim some degree of environmental concern, they don't always follow through on these green interests. This attitude–behavior gap between what consumers say they value and how they actually spend their money is often referred to as the "green gap." In an effort to understand the nature of this discrepancy, scholars have looked to various psychological, cognitive, and situational factors for explanation.

In the early stages of market segmentation, demographic factors were the primary focus as a means of predicting and explaining green consumption choices. Variables including gender, age, income, education, family makeup, and marital status, for example, were explored as a way to segment consumers and develop predictive models of green consumer behavior. Although demographics remain useful antecedents, the majority of research indicates that these variables are inconsistent and weak as predictors of green consumer orientations. For example, market research consistently indicates that men are more knowledgeable about environmental issues, but women are more concerned about the environment.

Environmental concern has been an antecedent of interest since the early investigations into green consumption in the 1970s, and has been shown to have a positive association with environmentally responsible consumer patterns. For example, greater concern for the environment is positively related to purchasing organic food, green cosmetics, and products in recycled packaging; however, these patterns of association are weak and explain only a moderate amount of variance in green consumer behaviors.

A more consistent predictor of green consumer behavior is environmental knowledge. Environmental knowledge refers to what people know about the environment and has been conceptualized as having two components: (1) abstract, or having to do with environmental issues, problems, causes, and solutions; and (2) concrete, or having to do with knowledge that can be used and acted upon. Both kinds of knowledge have demonstrated positive relationships with green consumer behavior, with abstract knowledge being stronger and more consistent. Conversely, a lack of environmental knowledge has been shown to be negatively correlated with green consumption behaviors. Despite these positive relationships, there are some studies indicating environmental knowledge is only weakly or inconsistently related to environmentally motivated consumption. These inconsistencies remain an underexplored area of green consumption research.

In an effort to look beyond cognitive influences on green consumption, many scholars have turned to attitudes and beliefs as more effective predictors. Altruism, in particular, is seen as a meaningful antecedent to green consumption. Altruism has been conceptualized as having prosocial, communitarian values and is often decomposed into social altruism (concern for the well-being of others) and biospheric altruism (concern for the well-being of nonhuman elements of the environment). A more precise conceptualization of pro-environmental values has been offered by the New Ecological Paradigm, or NEP (Dunlap et al. 2000). The NEP reflects a constellation of values that views humans as having an equal relationship with nature, rather than a dominant one. Both altruism and the NEP have been shown to positively predict environmentally friendly behaviors, but with variability in the kinds of behaviors. For example, more pronounced pro-environmental values were more associated with conserving behaviors, like recycling and curbing water consumption, and less likely to be associated with acquisition-focused behaviors, like buying low-energy light bulbs.

Another strain of inquiry into green consumption focuses on consumer responsibility and efficacy. Past studies have shown that individuals vary in the degree to which they feel personally responsible for any environmental problems as well as the degree to which they feel they can personally effect change. Evidence regarding the impact of perceived responsibility is mixed, whereas evidence supporting the role of efficacy is more consistent. In terms of the former, it was assumed that as individuals become more aware of environmental issues they would increasingly feel more responsible for resolving them. Studies have shown that this positive correlation remains elusive, and that individuals continue to ascribe substantial responsibility to institutional actors, like the government, or to abstract entities, like a prototypical consumer. With regard to the latter, personal efficacy connotes the degree to which individuals believe their actions will have meaningful impact on resolving environmental issues. Perceived consumer efficacy has been shown to be positively related to environmentally responsible consumer choices, such as opting for environmentally safe products, recycling newspapers, and contributing to environmental groups.

Like most forms of consumption, green consumption is susceptible to social forces. Green consumers are influenced by family, friends, and other influential agents in their decision to engage in environmentally responsible consumer choices. Drawing on social identity theory, studies have shown that stronger identification with environmental consumers – for example, organic food purchasers – leads to more positive evaluations and knowledge of organic brands. Social influences are also felt on green consumption behaviors as a result of social norms, or those practices and behaviors that are thought to be accepted and expected within a particular social group. Considerable research has shown that social norms can exert considerable influence over green consumption choices. When individuals believe that the majority of others in their social group are engaging in particular green consumer behaviors, such as reducing energy consumption, then they are more likely to adopt the behaviors as well. However, social norms have been shown to backfire and result in unintended consequences. For example, messages that indicate how widespread are certain environmentally unfriendly behaviors, such as littering, can have the unintended effect of suggesting the behavior is commonplace, thereby normalizing it and making it appear less socially unacceptable.

Like many consumption choices, social status and prestige are integral components of green consumption. From the perspective of evolutionary psychology, research on competitive altruism and costly signaling reinforce the status-related motives of green consumption. Compared to conventional, non-green products, green products often cost more and are less effective. As a kind of competitive altruism, green consumers can publicly signal their environmental concern by opting for these less efficient green products, thereby broadcasting to others their concern for the environmental and collective good in exchange for increased status and prestige. This costly signaling also allows green consumers to signal their wealth and their ability to incur costs, since many green products entail a sacrifice in terms of higher price or reduced quality and efficacy.

Social influences are also felt in the domain of green consumption via opinion leadership and market mavenism. Opinion leaders, defined as individuals who hold sway over others, seek to influence purchase behaviors of other consumers in specific product categories. Related though distinct, market mavens are also influential consumer forces, but their knowledge is broader and more general. Whereas opinion leaders exert influence within a particular product category, mavens are influential across categories and display greater generalized consumer knowledge, interest, and innovation across multiple categories. Although limited, existing studies indicate that green opinion leaders are more likely to engage in environmentally friendly consumer behaviors, such as recycling, reducing energy consumption, and using biodegradable products, and are also willing to pay more for green products. Similarly, market mavens are also more likely than non-mavens to seek out information about green products, particularly advertising and other persuasive messages about available green items.

In addition to attitudes and values, ethical orientation has been found to offer additional insight into green consumption choices. Specifically, three ethical orientations have been examined: deontological ethics, consequentialist ethics, and virtue ethics. Within deontological ethics, individuals act ethically because it is the right thing to do, regardless of the outcome. According to consequentialist ethics, ethical conduct is defined by the outcome of consequences or actions. In the case of green consumption, it means two green consumers with different ethical orientations might be motivated to make very different green consumption choices. For example, a green consumer motivated by a deontological orientation might choose to build a new, environmentally friendly house and outfit it with the latest green products. Conversely, a green consumer motivated by the consequentialist perspective might choose to buy from existing housing stock on the premise that it is better to reuse and recycle existing materials, even if they are environmentally inferior, than to harvest natural resources to build new structures. In both scenarios, ethically minded green consumers consider self-interest to be an obstacle to altruism and ethical behavior.

A third perspective, virtue ethics, offers a different point of view and acknowledges that enlightened self-interest holds a place in caring for others (Barnett, Cafaro, and Newholm 2005). Whereas consequentialist and deontological approaches focus on duties and responsibilities, virtue ethics is concerned with the good life and how to achieve it. The good life is one that leads to well-being, maximizes moral self-realization, and fosters harmonious social relations and intellectual development (Cafaro 2001). Virtue ethics offers an explanation for why green consumers might consume in prosocial ways, but might also be motivated by self-interest.

Compared to non-green consumers, individuals who opt for environmentally friendly products and services tend to be information seekers. Green consumers enjoy being informed about products and services and use this information to make informed buying choices. This information seeking, however, is qualified by a heightened sense of distrust, particularly of advertising and other persuasive communication (Shrum, McCarty, and Lowrey 1995). Past research indicates that green consumers are highly skeptical of advertising and will not buy products from companies whose advertising they dislike.

GREEN CONSUMPTION AND GREEN MARKETING

As the number of green product and service offerings increases, so too does the number of green marketing messages. Green marketing seeks to inform and persuade consumers about environmentally friendly options via a number of means, including product labeling and advertising. Eco-labels or certification labels help consumers differentiate between green and non-green choices by emphasizing various green attributes, such as being made from recycled materials. Eco-labels serve as signals of environmental quality, backing up credence claims that cannot be verified directly by the consumer (Atkinson and Rosenthal 2014). Eco-labels vary widely in terms of their rigor and credibility; some are carefully regulated by government entities (e.g., USDA organic) or nonprofit groups (e.g., Fair Trade), while others are largely meaningless and unsubstantiated (e.g., "100% natural"). Labels vary in the degree to which consumers trust them and find them useful.

Green advertising – the inclusion of environmentally friendly features and attributes as a persuasive selling point – has also seen a resurgence. Content analyses of magazine, television, and trade publications indicate that the overall volume of green advertising has risen since the 1980s. However, a recurring criticism of green advertising is that it relies on superficial and unsubstantiated claims at best, misleading and deceptive claims at worst (Baum 2012; Kilbourne 1995). To protect consumers from false green advertising, in the United States the Federal Trade Commission has spent the last several years revisiting its Green Guides, which advise marketers on making claims about green product attributes that are truthful and nondeceptive.

MODELS OF GREEN CONSUMPTION

In an effort to predict green consumer behaviors and identify relevant antecedents, several different explanatory models have been developed. Each model seeks to account for a variety of influences, from attitudes and values to perceived efficacy and social norms. The Theory of Planned Behavior (TPB), one of the more commonly used models to explain green consumption, focuses on intentions to behave in environmentally friendly ways, and the attitudes, beliefs, and norms that influence these intentions (Sparks and Shepherd 1992). The TPB links individuals' attitudes toward green consumer behavior to their perceived ability to carry out the behavior along with the perceived social pressure to engage in green behavior.

The Value–Belief–Norm model (Stern 2000) builds on the TPB by accounting for the role played by individual values. The model depicts a causal chain and proposes that environmental behaviors are the result of values, such as altruism, which influence beliefs, like the New Ecological Paradigm, which in turn activate pro-environmental norms and behaviors, including activism and private-sphere behaviors.

The Reasonable Person Model (Kaplan 2000) was developed to deal with those behavioral changes that are considered harder to achieve or mitigate, such as reducing automobile use. Rather than focusing on altruism and sacrifice as motivating factors, it makes space for self-interest and personal gain. This model assumes individuals want to know about the world around them, to be involved in it, and to feel capable of operating effectively in it. When applied to the environment, the model suggests that if consumers are presented with information that outlines opportunities for learning, discovery, and participation, then self-interest will lead them to more environmentally friendly choices.

SEE ALSO: Ecotourism; Ethical Consumption; Fair Trade; Green Consumerism; Sustainable Consumption

REFERENCES

Atkinson, Lucy, and Sonny Rosenthal. 2014. "Signaling the Green Sell: The Influence of Eco-Label Source and Argument Specificity on Consumer Trust." *Journal of Advertising* 43(1): 33–45.

Barnett, Clive, Philip Cafaro, and Terry Newholm. 2005. "Philosophy and Ethical Consumption." In *The Ethical Consumer*, edited by Rob Harrison, Terry Newholm, and Deirdre Shaw, 11–24. London: Sage.

Baum, Lauren M. 2012. "It's Not Easy Being Green … Or Is It? A Content Analysis of Environmental Claims in Magazine Advertisements from the United States and United Kingdom." *Environmental Communication* 6(4): 423–440.

Cafaro, Philip. 2001. "Economic Consumption, Pleasure, and the Good Life." *Journal of Social Philosophy* 32(4): 471–486.

Crane, Andrew. 2000. "Facing the Backlash: Green Marketing and Strategic Reorientation in the 1990s." *Journal of Strategic Marketing* 8: 277–296.

Dunlap, Riley E., Kent D. Van Liere, Angela G. Mertig, and Robert Emmet Jones. 2000. "New Trends in Measuring Environmental Attitudes: Measuring Endorsement of the New Ecological Paradigm: A Revised Nep Scale." *Journal of Social Issues* 56(3): 425–442.

Kaplan, Stephen. 2000. "New Ways to Promote Proenvironmental Behavior: Human Nature and Environmentally Responsible Behavior." *Journal of Social Issues* 56(3): 491–508.

Kilbourne, William E. 1995. "Green Advertising: Salvation or Oxymoron?" *Journal of Advertising* 24(2): 7–19.

Norwegian Ministry of the Environment. 1994. Oslo Roundtable on Sustainable Production and Consumption. http://www.iisd.ca/consume/oslo000.html.

Ottman, Jacquelyn A. 2011. *The New Rules of Green Marketing: Strategies, Tools, and Inspiration for Sustainable Branding*. San Francisco, CA: Berrett-Koehler.

Shrum, L. J., John A. McCarty, and Tina M. Lowrey. 1995. "Buyer Characteristics of the Green Consumer and Their Implication for Advertising Strategy." *Journal of Advertising* 24(2): 71–82.

Sparks, Paul, and Richard Shepherd. 1992. "Self-Identity and the Theory of Planned Behavior: Assessing the Role of Identification with 'Green Consumerism'." *Social Psychology Quarterly* 55(4): 388–399.

Stern, Paul C. 2000. "New Environmental Theories: Toward a Coherent Theory of Environmentally Significant Behavior." *Journal of Social Issues* 56(3): 407–424.

H

Hollywood

LINDEN DALECKI
Kelce College of Business at Pittsburg State University, USA

Hollywood – a name coined by real estate developer H. J. Whitley in 1886 – refers both to the Los Angeles, California district developed by Whitley and to a set of evolving motion picture industry firms, players, practices, technologies, and modes of finance, production, and distribution that emerged in and around the district. The heavy concentration of activities in Hollywood (Los Angeles) related to the motion picture industry – and eventually to the mediated entertainment sector more generally – resulted in an economic cluster effect that continues to drive industrial efficiencies and offer access to specialized talent, technology, and other resources. Despite increasingly online workflows, contemporary Hollywood-based entertainment media firms continue to maintain a global competitive advantage over entertainment media firms based elsewhere.

In 1916 the Harvard-based applied psychologist Hugo Münsterberg – a pre-World War I Prussian-Jewish American émigré – published *The Photoplay: A Psychological Study*, widely recognized as the first serious work in the field of film theory. Münsterberg's text is remarkable for touching on aspects of film aesthetics; film mechanics; the narrative and psychological import of editing transitions; physiological and psychological aspects of human perception; the notion of screenplays as relatively less crucial than stage plays to the final rendering of the experience consumed by the audience and the relatively higher import of the director to the rendering of the entertainment; the layout of an analogical cognition/film framework; and his discussion of popular film as amalgamating "highbrow" and "lowbrow" audiences. Thus, though not widely disseminated until a reissue of the book in 1970, Münsterberg's theoretical writings on film presage many themes and concerns explored in much greater depth – and in a wider range of directions – by later film theorists.

Major post-Münsterberg developments in the realm of film theory, analysis, and research include Soviet montage theory, which emphasized the psychological effects of jarring editorial juxtapositions – as articulated by filmmaker/theorists such as Sergei Eisenstein, Lev Kuleshov, Dziga Vertov, and Vsevolod Pudovkin in the 1920s. Subsequent landmarks in theory include Rudolf Arnheim's 1932 exploration of aesthetic properties unique to film, Walter Benjamin's

The Wiley Blackwell Encyclopedia of Consumption and Consumer Studies, First Edition.
Edited by Daniel Thomas Cook and J. Michael Ryan.

argument in 1936 that all mechanically reproduced art lacks aura and authenticity, and Max Horkheimer's 1937 notion that critical theory should be engaged with challenging the social order, all of which set the stage for Theodor Adorno and Max Horkheimer's 1944 articulation of "the culture industry," wherein Hollywood films are generally viewed as ideologically fascistic lowbrow product designed to dupe an unsuspecting mass viewership into accepting the hegemonic political status quo. Despite "hegemonic-ideology-unpacking," in some form or another, as the dominant approach to Hollywood cinema studies – and screen studies more generally – within the Western academy from the 1970s until recent years, increasingly prominent work by a new constellation of scholars has offered and continues to explore a countervailing set of approaches. These methods range from narrative construction analysis, star-genre marketing formulations, management process analysis, diffusion studies of screen technologies, regulatory and policy analysis, studies on the impact of conglomeration on Hollywood, distribution and marketing studies (domestic and international, theatrical and other distribution "windows"), stylistic analysis, media cross-promotion studies, studies of the impact of digital production and distribution formats on the industry, perception studies, fan studies, to transmedia and media-convergence studies. In their introduction to *Media Industries: History, Theory, and Method* (2009), Jennifer Holt and Alisa Perren articulate a "media industries studies" approach which simultaneously recognizes the historical and continuing importance of early approaches to the study of "mass media" while synthesizing many of the more recent approaches outlined above.

American motion picture operations were initially attracted to Los Angeles in the early 1900s because of the generally sunny weather there and to avoid motion picture patent claims that were being heavily enforced in the New York area by Edison Manufacturing Company. Subsequent milestones include the evolution from short-form cinema of attractions toward long-form silent narrative feature films by the late 1910s, the emergence of "The Big 5" (the major Los Angeles-based film studios) in the 1920s, and the success of the feature narrative "talkie" (film with spoken dialogue) *The Jazz Singer* in 1927, which signaled the birth of "classical Hollywood cinema" and the arrival of the sound era. The extremely rapid adoption of sound across the entire industry was significant not only in terms of domestic casting, production, distribution, and consumption but also in terms of how "talkies" impacted Hollywood's ability to market product to non-English-language markets, versus the silent cinema, which simply required the substitution of title cards in the language of the foreign market. In addition to a number of 1920s off-screen sex scandals that tarnished Hollywood's image, outside interest groups became concerned about the potential effect of mature sound-film content on young filmgoers. Thus, from 1930 to 1968 – largely to avoid being subjected to government censorship – the Motion Picture Producers and Distributors of America (the MPPDA was a trade association representing the interests of the major studios) adopted a production code that detailed what was acceptable and what was not acceptable content for motion pictures produced for domestic audiences. The MPPDA was rebranded as the Motion Picture Association of America (MPAA) in 1945. Though still responsible for the domestic film rating system, more recent MPAA activities have largely focused on lobbying against trade barriers in key foreign markets such as France and China.

By the early 1930s, each of the major studios tended to be associated with commercial and artistic dominance in a specific genre, having a set of production values and a specific "house style," and stars who were under contract at the particular studio – typically for seven-year terms. Though not exclusively, Warner's was principally associated with the low-budget gangster film, MGM with the high-budget musical, Paramount with the sex comedy, Columbia with the screwball comedy, and Universal with the low-budget horror film. The year 1935 saw the merger of Fox Film and Twentieth Century Pictures into Twentieth Century-Fox and the box office dominance of its major child star, Shirley Temple. Temple starred in a string of hits for Twentieth Century-Fox – where she was under contract – and in several hits for other major studios to whom she was "loaned out" (assigned to the competing studio for a fee). The enormous success of Disney's animated color feature *Snow White* in 1937 illustrated the commercial viability of the animated color feature and the emerging importance of media synergy – given the cross-promotion between the blockbuster film and the hit soundtrack – and the ever-increasing importance of the "family film" whose appeal is mainly to children, but which also contains more complex coded elements that appeal to older filmgoers.

The Paramount Decree of 1948 – resulting in the divestment of studio-owned exhibition venues – along with the growth of broadcast television as a home-viewing format in the 1950s, combined to cause the demise of the classical Hollywood studio system. The arrival of "teenpics" and drive-in theaters in the 1950s engendered teens as an expanding theatrical target market. The industry placed greater importance on big-budget franchise filmmaking in the mid-1960s through the mid-1970s – especially following the success of the James Bond series (UK-produced by Saltzman/Broccoli) and *The Godfather* and *The Godfather II* – and also shifted to nationwide saturation theatrical distribution and nationwide TV teaser campaigns following the approaches of – and the success of – *Billy Jack* in 1974 and *Jaws* in 1975.

Though the four film franchises mentioned in the above paragraph are too adult-themed to be considered "family films," from a marketing standpoint these franchises set the stage for increasingly "family-friendly" mega-franchises with acute media cross-promotion, intense merchandising, and high production value sequels – as in the case of *Star Wars* (1977) and *Raiders of the Lost Ark* (1981). New delivery formats in the era include the diffusion of multiplex and megaplex theaters, which coincide with the growth of home-viewing formats such as cable TV and VHS in the 1980s. From a corporate structure standpoint, ever-increasing media conglomeration was instigated in the mid-1980s with News Corp's acquisition of 20th Century Fox and launch of Fox-TV. From a digital post-production standpoint, the widespread adoption of computer-generated imagery (CGI), special-effects-driven films followed on the success of *Jurassic Park* in 1993. In an increasingly global market, *Jurassic Park* and subsequent successful family-friendly, action-intensive motion picture mega-franchises rely on foreign territories for the bulk of their revenues. In terms of digital delivery and production, the adoption of DVD by consumers and the rapid growth of digital motion picture production coincide in the mid-1990s/early 2000s. More recently, the growth of direct-download and mobile technology in the mid-2000s and the theatrical success of *Avatar* (3D) in 2009 – and the subsequent growth of 3D mega-franchises and adoption of digital projection by exhibitors – have many industry players and observers debating what the future dominant screen format(s) will be.

SEE ALSO: Advertising; Children's Consumer Culture; Consumer Culture Theory (CCT);

Disneyization; Merchandising; Popular Culture; Teens

REFERENCES

Holt, Jennifer, and Alisa Perren, eds. 2009. *Media Industries: History, Theory, and Method*. Chichester, UK: Wiley-Blackwell.
Münsterberg, Hugo. 1916. *The Photoplay: A Psychological Study*. New York: D. Appleton & Co.

FURTHER READING

Doherty, Thomas. 2002. *Teenagers and Teenpics: The Juvenilization of American Movies in the 1950s*. Philadelphia, PA: Temple University Press.
Elberse, Anita. 2013. *Blockbusters: Hit-making, Risk-taking, and the Big Business of Entertainment*. New York: Henry Holt & Co.
Münsterberg, Hugo. 1970/1916. *The Film: A Psychological Study. The Silent Photoplay in 1916*. New York: Dover Publications.
Münsterberg, Hugo (author), and Allan Langdale (editor). 2002/1916. *Münsterberg on Film: The Photoplay: A Psychological Study and Other Writings*. New York: Routledge.
Perren, Alisa. 2013. *Indie, Inc.: Miramax and the Transformation of Hollywood in the 1990s*. Austin: University of Texas Press.
Schatz, Thomas. 2010. *The Genius of the System: Hollywood Filmmaking in the Studio Era*. Minneapolis: University of Minnesota Press.

Homogenization and Heterogenization

J. MICHAEL RYAN
The American University in Cairo, Egypt

Those who see the world as ever more homogenized argue that more of the world is growing increasingly similar. They see the global spread of things like McDonald's, Starbucks, Wal-Mart, Puma, Lady Gaga, and Hollywood as evidence that local differences are being washed away by universal sameness. As global organizations, corporations, and political and economic domination – particularly that of the United States – increase their reach, the ability of local governments, cultures, and individuals to resist becoming the same is weakened.

One of the paradigmatic theories of global homogeneity is the McDonaldization thesis. George Ritzer (2010) coined the term "McDonaldization" to describe a process by which the principles of the fast-food industry are coming to dominate more and more sectors of US society as well as the rest of the world. Building on Weber's model of rationalization and the iron cage, Ritzer argues that the principles of the fast-food industry – namely efficiency, calculability, predictability, and control by nonhuman technology – are the modern-day paradigm for global homogeneity.

As opposed to those who see greater homogenization on a global level as a result of the increasing presence of global sameness, the heterogenization argument is supported by those who see this sameness as a vehicle for greater diversity. They argue that although the same restaurants, brands, and so on are indeed more ubiquitous on a global level, they are being adapted in different ways to meet local needs and traditions. Thus, global sameness is, in fact, simply a vehicle for global difference. Whereas homogenization tends to carry a negative connotation of globalization, heterogenization tends to see it in a more positive light.

One of the paradigmatic theories of this way of thinking is that of glocalization. Roland Robertson (1992) popularized this idea with the meaning that the interpenetration of the global and the local results in unique hybrid outcomes. Thus, it is not a question of the global dominating the local or the local resisting the global but rather the ways in which the two interact that is at the heart of globalization. This idea is rooted in postmodern notions of hybridity, plurality, diversity, and pastiche. Individuals are seen as creative agents able to self-select and refashion their identities and communities using the infusion of globally dispersed phenomena.

The growing consensus among globalization scholars is that while there is merit in components of both the homogenization and the heterogenization arguments, the reality is probably a complex interaction of the two. Douglas Goodman (2007), for example, has noted that "the question as to whether globalization increases cultural homogeneity by establishing common codes and practices or whether it increases a heterogeneity of newly emerging differences seems now, to many analysts, to have been answered. Globalization does both. What appears to be a dichotomy is, in fact, complementary" (p. 24).

Uri Ram (2004) has persuasively argued for a shift away from the homogenization–heterogenization dichotomy to a "structural-symbolic construct" (p. 11). Ram's argument is that both homogenization and heterogenization are occurring at a global level but that they are doing so at different levels of influence. Homogenization is more representative of the structural level – there are more physical McDonald's buildings, credit cards, shopping malls, etc. – while heterogenization is more representative of the symbolic level – the ways in which hamburgers are eaten, TV shows are understood, and so forth.

Ram uses the example of national flags to illustrate his point. On a structural level most flags of the world are the same. Most have the same general shape, are flown from poles, and are used as a symbol of national identity. On a symbolic level, however, there is great variety. The colors, symbols, and designs are specific to each country. Thus, flags represent a global sameness on the structural level but a sameness that in turn allows for the expression of symbolic difference.

SEE ALSO: Glocalization/Grobalization; McDonaldization

REFERENCES

Goodman, Douglas J. 2007. "Globalization and Consumer Culture." In *The Blackwell Companion to Globalization,* edited by George Ritzer, 330–351. Oxford: Blackwell.

Ram, Uri. 2004. "Glocommodification: How the Global Consumes the Local – the Case of McDonald's in Israel." *Current Sociology* 52(1): 11–31.

Ritzer, George. 2010. *The McDonaldization of Society 6*. Thousand Oaks, CA: Pine Forge Press.

Robertson, Roland. 1992. *Globalization: Social Theory and Global Culture*. London: Sage.

Housing/Housing Markets

HANNAH CLARKE and JANE ZAVISCA
University of Arizona, USA

Housing is among the most costly and significant of consumer possessions, as well as a staging ground for various consumption practices. Yet housing has been largely overlooked in consumption studies, perhaps because it occupies a liminal status between consumption and production. In market societies, housing is an investment with exchange value as well as a commodity with use value. The sense of housing as investment in turn fuels housing consumption, by providing a powerful rationale for spending and indebtedness in pursuit of the owner-occupied home.

Housing shares with other consumer commodities the potential to embody an extension of self, as well as to signal attachment to – or distinction from – a particular social group. The home and the practices of domesticity it engenders demarcate the boundaries between private and public, feminine and masculine, consumption and production.

By providing a sense of privacy and control, the home satisfies the craving for ontological security that arose as modernity eroded the systems of kinship and transition that previously provided people with their sense of place in society (Dupuis and Thorns 1998).

Intensive consumption practices – and consumer spending – are required to transform the physical properties of a house into the cultural embodiment of a home, what McCracken (1989) refers to as "symbolic property," reflecting the cultural logic of what makes a home "homey." This transformation involves maintenance, renovation, and decoration of the physical structure of the home; accumulation and display of consumer objects like furniture and appliances within the home; and consumption practices that take place in the home, such as eating and entertaining. The use and upkeep of the home thus provide a constant stimulus to further consumer spending.

Like other consumer objects, housing reflects and reinforces social class and status distinctions. Class position can be inferred from housing to the extent that financial resources enable or constrain housing consumption. Housing can also be constitutive of class, as housing-based wealth is itself a financial resource that can be leveraged to support other types of consumption. However, the relationship between housing and social class is not purely economic. The home provides a rich canvas upon which to inscribe status aspirations and distinctions. For example, gentrifiers who purchase an old home in an "up-and-coming neighborhood" signify cultural capital as well as class position when they choose to either embrace its history and character, or tear it down to build something new. Just as with other consumer goods, such choices send out socially mediated signals from which one's tastes and lifestyle may be read beyond the implied economic status.

These cultural meanings of home are not isomorphic with home ownership. However, ownership does change people's relationships to their homes in ways that favor certain consumption practices. Home ownership makes a difference in how much of themselves and their resources people choose to invest in their living space. Ownership fosters an overall sense of pride and responsibility in one's home, but it also allows for practical and cosmetic transformations to the existing structure – renovating a kitchen, changing an interior color scheme, or adding a deck – to be experienced as inalienable personal accomplishments, as well as long-term investments. In some societies, ownership is also a key signifier of middle-class status, and requisite for a sense of full social and civic inclusion.

Home ownership has developed historically in a progressive relationship with consumer culture. Nineteenth-century moralists, alarmed by the expansion of the world of goods and easy consumer credit, framed homes and durable furnishings as a virtuous redirection of spending away from more frivolous consumer items. Home mortgages fit Victorian sensibilities about productive versus consumptive debt. Interest-bearing loans were seen as justified only when invested in production, and homes were viewed as productive because the acquired commodity is real estate that tends to increase in market value over time. The investment of familial capital in home ownership is supposed to provide returns that are not only economic, but civic and moral. Home ownership ideology maintains that, by giving people an economic stake in their homes as valuable property, homeowners also become invested in their communities, and in the social and political relations that underlie the housing market. Home ownership thus became enshrined in policy and public discourse as the most prudent of all consumer expenditures.

Cultural studies of the housing market highlight the social construction of both demand and supply in an economic field coordinated in large part by the state (Bourdieu 2005). The terms "housing consumer" and "housing market" entered popular discourse less than a century ago. According to historian Richard Harris (2009), the housing consumer was born in the shift from custom homes, built by contractors for clients, to readymade homes, built by speculative builders for anonymous potential buyers. The fact that more people bought homes than built them enabled housing to become a standardized commodity. While homes themselves did not become uniform, the way they were consumed did. The commodity is not just the home itself, but a standard package that includes amenities such as built-in appliances, and mortgage financing to facilitate the purchase. This emerging market required a shift in consumer demand. Harris is one of few scholars to address "the willingness of consumers to buy into the new housing regime." He attributes this in part to a growing sense of home ownership as a means of self-expression. This had long been true for women, but a growing market in "do-it-yourself" supplies now cast men in the role of "handy" home improvers, who would co-create the owner-occupied home through productive leisure.

The most powerful rationale for home ownership, however, remained investment and wealth accumulation. Ronald (2008) describes this orientation as "the consumption of housing as property." A revolution in housing finance has reinforced this investment interpretation of housing consumption. The main turning points were the introduction of federally insured, amorticized loans in the United States in the 1930s, and the emergence of mortgage-backed securities in the 1970s. From the 1930s, mortgage loans were framed as a savings vehicle, forcing homeowners to pay toward a rent-free future. More recently, home transitioned from a savings vehicle to provide security in old age in a home owned free and clear, to an investment vehicle from which equity could be extracted on demand. And if home had once been primarily a place to live, which also happened to be an asset, for some it became a financial instrument first, and a personal dwelling second. Flexible mortgages and home equity loans, which allow housing wealth to be spent without selling or vacating the home, further blurred the boundaries between investment and consumption.

Thus, the home became integral to the "financialization of daily life" (Cook, Smith, and Searle 2009). This perspective highlights the cultural meanings embedded in financial decision making and the performative nature of housing markets. Consumer decision making in housing and mortgage markets, like other consumption choices, is influenced as much by social and emotional factors as by rational, utility-maximizing ones. The connection between home and identity now extends to the financial dimension of home ownership and sense of oneself as a savvy investor (or duped debtor). This change in meaning contributed to radical shifts in home purchase decision making and the attendant escalation of mortgage indebtedness. The ongoing mortgage market crisis challenges a fundamental assumption of the investment rationale for housing consumption – that real estate continuously increases in value. With investment, many consumers have painfully learned, comes risk, undermining the basis for ontological security that remains core to the meaning of home. This crisis of meaning as well as economy is the focus of much emerging scholarship on housing consumption.

SEE ALSO: Commodification; Debt; Do-It-Yourself (DIY); Finance/Financial Markets

REFERENCES

Bourdieu, Pierre. 2005. *The Social Structures of the Economy*. Cambridge: Polity.

Cook, Nicole, Susan J. Smith, and Beverley A. Searle. 2009. "Mortgage Markets and Cultures of Consumption." *Consumption Markets & Culture* 12(2): 133–154. doi:10.1080/10253860902840958.

Dupuis, Ann, and David C. Thorns. 1998. "Home, Home Ownership and the Search for Ontological Security." *The Sociological Review* 46(1): 24–47. doi:10.1111/1467-954X.00088.

Harris, Richard. 2009. "The Birth of the Housing Consumer in the United States, 1918–1960." *International Journal of Consumer Studies* 33: 525–532. doi:10.1111/j.1470-6431.2009.00797.x.

McCracken, Grant. 1989. "'Homeyness': A Cultural Account of One Constellation of Consumer Goods and Meanings." In *Interpretive Consumer Research*, edited by Elizabeth C. Hirschman, 168–183. Provo, UT: Association for Consumer Research.

Ronald, Richard. 2008. "Between Investment, Asset and Use Consumption: The Meanings of Homeownership in Japan." *Housing Studies* 23(2): 233–251. doi:10.1080/02673030801893099.

Hyperconsumption

PIERGIORGIO DEGLI ESPOSTI
University of Bologna, Italy

The term "hyperconsumption" is linked with the concept of a "new modernity," which can be defined as a "civilization of desire" (Lipovetsky 2005). Its birth can be dated to the second half of the twentieth century. The features of this concept are clearly identifiable in a capitalist matrix, that is, the incessant creation of new needs, aggressive forms of marketing, and an empowerment of demand. This leads to a new age characterized by the emergence of consumer capitalism as replacement for an economy based on production. On the one hand, this process of change has brought significant benefits, such as increased possibilities for consumption, new concepts of space and time, and in general more opportunities for individuals to increase their social well-being. On the other hand, this new era is characterized by new pathologies, such as a bulimic approach to consumption, uncontrollable forms of entropy, and a constant search for satisfaction that seems elusive and out of reach.

An important reference for understanding the evolution of hyperconsumption is found in Thorstein Veblen's idea of conspicuous consumption (1899). He pointed out how the wealthy showed their superiority compared to other classes through a consumption based on ostentation and waste. At the same time, those who belonged to the lower classes were trying to emulate the same lifestyle and behavior as the upper classes. In the society of hyperconsumption, the scenario is changed and the ways in which individuals relate to consumption are becoming more complex. For that reason, the "trickle-down" pattern (Davis 1992) or the system of preferences described by Pierre Bourdieu (1979) are no longer applicable because they do not account for the multiple and nonlinear forms of hyperconsumption.

The roots of this hyperconsumption society are identifiable in Max Weber's theory about Western society (1922). The bureaucratization system, based on the idea of extreme rationality, led individuals to feel they were trapped in an "iron cage." There are no means of escape from this process of regulation; the only possibility is to be shifted from one rational system to another with the same characteristics. This theory will be central to introducing George Ritzer's criticism of the hyperconsumption society. Starting from the concepts of rationality and irrationality, Ritzer analyzes the globalization process, comparing it to his own ideas of "McDonaldization" (Ritzer 1993) because they are both based on the four principles of efficiency, calculability, predictability, and control exercised by mechanical technology on human beings. This process can lead to dangerous side effects. According to Ritzer, the component of irrationality may have as a result not only the dehumanization of social processes but also the disenchantment that Max Weber, drawing inspiration from Schiller's ideas, had indicated as a peculiarity of the bureaucratization of Western society. Ritzer, continuing on the path outlined by Weber, points out that this process of disenchantment is linked to the loss of the quality of goods due to the prevailing homogenization and standardization that are intrinsic characteristics of globalization.

The new era in which we are living is characterized by a progressive spectacularization of the consumption universe that leads to a romantic form of capitalism, as highlighted by Campbell (1987), and to a new form of aesthetic based on "difference, ephemerality, spectacle, fashion, and the commodification of cultural forms" (Harvey 1989). Linked to this semantic and cultural transformation, spectacularization is well represented by the "cathedrals of consumption" (Ritzer 2005) that are the embodiment of a "society of simulation" (Baudrillard 1981), where the barriers between the real and the imaginary merge to become indistinguishable. This "spectacularization of consumption" approach is characterized by a loss of authenticity and irreversible standardization. The challenge, then, is to understand if it is possible to recover a sense of enchantment and uniqueness that seems to be dematerialized in a contemporary society of consumption.

SEE ALSO: Bourdieu, Pierre; Consumption, Spectacles of; Globalization and Consumption; Veblen, Thorstein

REFERENCES

Baudrillard, Jean. 1981. *Simulacres et simulation*. Paris: Galilée.

Bourdieu, Pierre. 1979. *La Distinction: Critique sociale du jugement*. Paris: Minuit.

Campbell, Colin. 1987. *The Romantic Ethic and the Spirit of Modern Consumerism*. Oxford: Basil Blackwell.

Davis, Fred. 1992. *Fashion, Culture and Identity*. Chicago: University of Chicago Press.

Harvey, David. 1989. *The Condition of Postmodernity: An Inquiry into the Origins of Cultural Change*. Oxford: Blackwell.

Lipovetsky, Gilles. 2005. *Hypermodern Times*. Cambridge: Polity.

Ritzer, George. 1993. *The McDonaldization of Society: An Investigation into the Changing Character of Contemporary Social Life*. Thousand Oaks, CA: Pine Forge Press.

Ritzer, George. 2005. *Enchanting a Disenchanted World: Revolutionizing the Means of Consumption*. Thousand Oaks, CA: Pine Forge Press.

Veblen, Thorstein. 1979/1899. *The Theory of the Leisure Class: An Economic Study of Institutions*. London: Unwin.

Weber, Max. 1922. *Wirtschaft und Gesellschaft. Grundriss der verstehenden Soziologie*. Tübingen, Germany: J. C. B. Mohr.

I

Identity and Consumption: *SEE* CONSUMPTION AND IDENTITY

Infomercial

TIM DELANEY
State University of New York at Oswego, USA

An infomercial is a program-length commercial, designed to resemble regular television programming, that informs or instructs and may often include a discussion or demonstration of specific products, or a product line, to an audience. It is the combining of the two words "information" and "commercial" that leads to the term "infomercial." An infomercial is an extended advertisement designed to encourage people to consume commercial products or services via a demonstrative and controlled environment. Infomercials often involve testimonials from celebrities, or ordinary folks, who claim to have used the product and enjoyed highly positive results. Infomercials are characteristically accompanied by marketing sales pitches, such as: "But wait … There's more!" and "Call right now and we'll double your order at no extra cost!"

In the earliest days of television, commercial companies created their own shows so that they would have a medium through which to promote their goods and services. The US Federal Communications Commission (FCC) eventually got involved and placed limits on how much advertising can take place on any given show. Among the earliest versions of an infomercial in the United States was the advertising of Ginsu steak knives, which were promoted as being capable of cutting through anything. The first full-length infomercial in the United States aired in the 1970s on XETV, based in the San Diego area, with a one-hour program advertisement on Sundays on homes for sale in the local area (see SmallBusiness.com 2010). While the FCC limited commercial time to 18 minutes per hour in the 1970s, XETV was located in Mexico and broadcast its programs in English to an American audience to avoid US communications laws.

Teleshopping, a variation of infomercials, became popular in the United Kingdom during the 1980s; it remains popular throughout many parts of the world today. In the United States, infomercials arose following the passage of the Cable Communications Policy Act of 1984, which, among other things, deregulated television commercial airing policies (FCC 1984). Initially, infomercials were aired late at night or in the very

The Wiley Blackwell Encyclopedia of Consumption and Consumer Studies, First Edition.
Edited by Daniel Thomas Cook and J. Michael Ryan.

early hours of the morning. Over time, their popularity and the saturation of cable television outlets led to a proliferation of infomercials. Some stations show only infomercials, while others rely on infomercials for the majority of their programming hours.

The popularity of infomercials seems most improbable, considering that many people regard commercials as unwanted intrusions into their viewing pleasure. The popularity of recording devices (i.e., DVRs and TiVo) is partially explained by viewers' desire to bypass commercials completely. Despite this, millions of viewers tune into infomercial programming and, as a result, infomercials represent a money-making machine for many companies. *Consumer Reports* (2010) indicates that infomercials reduce marketing costs to as little as one-tenth the size of a traditional advertising campaign. Infomercials generate billions of dollars worldwide in annual sales and cover a diversity of products ranging from fitness workouts and juicers, to psychic hotlines, blankets that serve as bathrobes, and spray-on hair.

SEE ALSO: Advertising; Commodities; Consumer Behavior; Stealth Marketing; Visual Consumption

REFERENCES

Consumer Reports. 2010. "Should You 'Buy This Now!'?" Accessed 26 July, 2014. http://www.consumerreports.org/cro/magazine-archive/2010/february/shopping/infomercial-products/overview/infomercial-products-ov.htm.

FCC. 1984. "Public Law 98–549 – Oct. 30, 1984." Federal Communications Commission. Accessed 26 July, 2014. http://transition.fcc.gov/Bureaus/OSEC/library/legislative_histories/1286.pdf.

SmallBusiness.com. 2010. "Infomercial." http://smallbusiness.com/wiki/Infomercial.

Infotainment

LAUREN LANGMAN
Loyola University Chicago, USA

One crucial aspect of modern life has been concern with broader events and people who live in social worlds beyond our local community or nation. Thus news has become a commodity that is provided by organizations and consumed by audiences. The definition of "hard news" remains vague. Media scholarship has raised questions about the "objectivity" of hard news that is often slanted for political purposes and/or skewed for entertainment value and that shades into "infotainment," that is, "information-based media content or programming that also includes entertainment content in an effort to enhance popularity with audiences and consumers" (Demers 2005). In a consumer society, providers of hard news must compete with each other for viewers/readers against a vast number of other, softer, more entertaining kinds of sources of information (lifestyle, history, health, etc.).

Driven by competition for audience share, and thus revenue, news is packaged in ways that generate appeal, presented by "attractive" newsreaders with good looks and "pleasing personalities." Some of these newsreaders may become celebrities and in turn garner publicity and themselves become subjects of infotainment. A society that values a "fun morality" and privatized hedonism means that many people are more concerned with the personal pleasure and gratification that come from media entertainment than with "serious" information concerning death, destruction, disasters, poverty, and misery that is depressing and beyond one's ability to change. The growth of infotainment, concerns with lifestyle, and obsession with celebrity gossip need to be understood as part and parcel of contemporary consumer society and its tendency to commodify everything, including "gratifying" news and information.

A major segment of infotainment thus consists of "soft news" that is concerned with popular culture, lifestyle, entertainment and leisure, and, of course, celebrity gossip; it focuses on revelations and "secrets" about celebrities' private lives and relationships, troubles, and especially lurid accounts of their sex lives, often enough accompanied by revealing and suggestive images. A great deal of the information part of infotainment is based on prurience, if not voyeurism. Thus, pictures of the breasts of Janet Jackson or Kate Middleton can became major (pseudo)events that arouse popular interest and debate. These "displays" displace far more serious events (Anderson 2004).

The ultimate goal of information or news in an infotainment frame is to produce pleasure or the promise of pleasure. Industries provide cultural products whose goal is primarily to make the consumer happier rather than better. For the individual, it provides a relatively pleasant form of escapism. Having "inside" knowledge can give consumers/viewers a feeling of specialness and empowerment by knowing about celebrity "private" affairs. Moreover, many idealize and glorify celebrities insofar as they embody fame, riches, magnificent lifestyles, and seemingly boundless sexual gratification (Rojek 2001). At the same time, knowledge of their transgressions, foibles, weaknesses, and tragedies has somewhat of an equalizing effect to the extent that falling from grace demonstrates that wealth, beauty, and fame are no guarantee of success.

Infotainment, as an integral part of the corporate-owned "culture industries," serves to distract attention from the more serious events, public affairs, and issues. A Gresham's law of information seems to be operating here whereby soft news and infotainment displace hard news and information. Large segments of the population are quite unaware, or little interested in, how the political economy operates today, and how it largely serves the interests of large corporations and the elites who run and own them – even while most incomes are stagnant or declining. The malfeasance of elites garners little attention and thereby has little entertainment and economic value for the news market.

In the contemporary age of smartphones, video cameras, and YouTube, people have become more proactive and may themselves be used to foster mass action and then provide important news – as happened in the Arab Spring/Occupy movements when images of political protests were transmitted throughout the world, or when pictures of disasters are uploaded as they take place. Such "bottom up" hard news is ever more available. But at the same time, most of what people post to internet sites consists of what they find amusing, from dancing cats to vacation adventures or homemade pornography. Hence, the consumption of news is negotiated and people actively decide what they want to see and interpret, and indeed what they may want to provide as information, infotainment, or whatever comes in between.

SEE ALSO: Celebrity; Consumption, Spectacles of; Frankfurt School; Infomercial; Mass Media

REFERENCES

Anderson, Bonnie. 2004. *Newsflash*. San Francisco: Jossey-Bass.

Demers, David. 2005. *Dictionary of Mass Communication and Media Research: A Guide for Students, Scholars and Professionals*. Spokane, WA: Marquette Books.

Rojek, Chris. 2001. *Celebrity*. London: Reaktion Books.

FURTHER READING

Postman, Neil. 1985. *Amusing Ourselves to Death*. New York: Viking Penguin.

Reinemann, Carsten, James Stanyer, Sebastian Scherr, and Guido Legnante. 2012. "Hard and Soft News: A Review of Concepts, Operationalizations and Key Findings." *Journalism* 13(2): 221–239.

Intellectual Property

OVE GRANSTRAND
Chalmers University of Technology, Sweden
MARCUS HOLGERSSON
University of Gothenburg, Sweden

A property can be defined as a resource with some form of assigned ownership, and an intellectual property is then a property of intellectual or intangible character. An intellectual property right (IPR) is a legally codified right created and used to assign ownership to intellectual resources such as knowledge, technologies, brand names, and other types of intellectual creations.

IPRs constitute a family of temporary, restricted, and transferable or licensable rights to exclude others from commercializing someone's intellectual or intangible creations or inventions under certain conditions. The main types of IPR are *patent rights* to technical inventions, *copyrights* to creations in various arts (including software as a kind of border case), *design rights* to physical artistic and handicraft forms or designs, *trademark rights* to signs, designs, identity marks, or expressions that identify a certain entity, product, or service, and *trade secret rights* to trade secrets. Other types are, for example, *database rights* and *breeding rights*.

An intellectual creation typically has at least to be new and distinctive to qualify for IPR protection. Different legal frameworks apply to different IPRs, and these to some extent vary over time and across countries, for example in terms of legal strength and enforceability against infringers and counterfeiters. As an example, the legal framework for patents typically stipulates that in order for an invention to be patentable, it has to be new to the world, nonobvious to a person skilled in the technological area in question, and applicable or useful at least to some people.

Most IPRs are temporary by statute. For example, the maximum lifetime is 20 years for patents (with some exceptions), 50 to 100 years after the creator's death for copyrights, and 14 (US) to 25 (Europe) years for design rights. Trade secret rights differ in that they are unregistered and could be kept indefinitely (although they could also leak quickly), and trademark rights differ in that they could be prolonged indefinitely by renewing them. Thus, trademark rights and their associated brand values could become very valuable over time, such as the Apple brand, which has been valued at US$98 billion (Interbrand 2013).

IPRs are granted mainly to incentivize investments in creation and commercialization of new intellectual resources, and to incentivize the disclosure of informational resources (trade secret rights being an exception). In other words, various IPRs are granted in order to improve the provision of innovations of various kinds to the benefit of consumers and society in general, a society that is thereby being served by self-interested innovators in the spirit of a capitalist economic institution. IPRs are justified mainly on this type of utilitarian grounds, although they may in addition be justified on moral grounds (e.g., that creators should have entitlement to the fruits of their creative labor). Trademarks, as a special case, are also justified for their ability to communicate information and images to the public at large and thereby also to help protect consumers from being misled about the origin or quality of a product or service.

The desired economic benefits of IPRs do not come without costs, however. The classic criticism of IPRs – patent rights in particular but also copyrights – is that they give too strong competitive advantages, leading to monopolistic behavior (e.g., high prices) and inefficient static competition with ensuing losses for consumers as well as for the society at large. The counterargument is that, given properly balanced IPRs, the temporary loss of static competitive efficiency is outweighed by gains in dynamic efficiency in the form of an increased flow or supply of innovations to the benefit of consumers. This counterargument is in turn increasingly challenged – see below.

Traces of the use of and rights to trademarks and secrecy arrangements go back thousands of years. Plagiarism and distortion of literary works were reacted against in ancient Greece. However, patent-like arrangements did not really appear until the fourteenth and fifteenth centuries, with the first codified patent laws in Venice in 1474. The following centuries saw the introduction and adoption of laws, statutes, and ordinances for different IPRs in various countries (e.g., patent laws were adopted in 1623 in England, 1790 in the United States, 1871 in Japan, and 1984 in China). More recently, a so-called pro-patent era started in the United States in the early 1980s, and then spread to other industrialized countries, making IPR issues a key concern for business strategy and government policy. The US-sponsored Agreement on Trade-Related Aspects of IPRs (TRIPS) in the mid-1990s further spread, strengthened, and harmonized the IPR regimes around most of the world, contributing to vast increases in numbers of IPRs applied for and granted. In 2013 more than two million patent applications and more than four million trademark applications were filed worldwide.

The strengthening of IPR systems has also strengthened old as well as new types of legal, economic, and political critiques targeted at various IPR types, patents and copyrights in particular, for being counterproductive, inferior to alternatives, and prone to political capture by corporate interests and industrialized countries. IPRs restrict the *freedom to operate* for others than the owners and legitimate users. The restrictions have traditionally applied to the operations of making, selling, and using goods and services protected by IPRs, but increasingly apply also to the operations of creation and invention, thereby counteracting their intended functions. A number of reforms and other remedies have been proposed and practiced, including the use of so-called *fair, reasonable, and non-discriminatory* (FRAND) commitments in the patent area, *creative commons* in the copyright area, and *open design* in the design area. Many if not most of these remedies are essentially schemes for licensing IPR usage rights. In general, well-functioning license markets are essential to the efficient performance of IPR systems for provision of innovations. Trade and transfer of dispersed complementary intellectual resources are needed since contemporary innovation is increasingly cumulative, open, distributed, multitechnological, systemic, and IPR intensive.

SEE ALSO: Apple; Brand Loyalty; Brands and Branding; Capitalism; Counterfeiting/Piracy; Markets, Moral Aspects of; Open Source and Consumption; Peer-to-Peer File Sharing

REFERENCE

Interbrand. 2013. *Best Global Brands 2013*. New York: Interbrand.

FURTHER READING

Granstrand, Ove. 1999. *The Economics and Management of Intellectual Property: Towards Intellectual Capitalism*. Cheltenham, UK: Edward Elgar.

Jaffe, Adam B., and Josh Lerner. 2004. *Innovation and Its Discontents: How Our Broken Patent System Is Endangering Innovation and Progress, and*

What to Do about It. Princeton: Princeton University Press.
Lessig, Lawrence. 2001. *The Future of Ideas: The Fate of the Commons in a Connected World*. New York: Random House.
Merges, Robert P. 2011. *Justifying Intellectual Property*. Cambridge, MA: Harvard University Press.

Internet, The, and Consumption

DENNIS ZUEV
CIES-ISCTE, Portugal

Internet-mediated consumption has become one of the essential features of modern life. The penetration of the internet has caused unprecedented growth in computer-mediated consumption practices and an increase in electronic tribes structured around consumer interests, and has led to the emergence of a new e-consumption ethos.

When discussing the relationship between consumption and the internet, two processes have to be distinguished: consumption of the internet as a service and commodity and consumption via the internet. Consumption of the internet and its related services by different publics has also been studied as internet use. At the same time, consumption via the internet may be encountered in academic literature as digital consumption, online consumption (e-consumption), or e-shopping. The latter type of consumption is related to the habits, tastes, and tendencies of computer-mediated consumption of various goods and services. In computer-mediated consumption one can be engaged in purchasing material goods via online payments and getting the goods later by post, or receiving commodities and services in digital form or mediated/consumed by means of computer technology.

The internet has stimulated the growth of consumer-to-consumer sales all over the world. In countries with a growing internet penetration rate the population is increasingly shopping online, buying a whole range of goods and services: consumer goods, food products, books, tickets, or making hotel reservations. For instance, China alone had 245 million online shoppers in 2013. The attractiveness of online shopping is explained by its convenience: the opportunity to do everyday grocery shopping without disrupting one's working rhythm or spending time in queues. Some companies offer online-only discounts, and tickets can be considerably cheaper when bought online and in advance, although such online discounts may eventually lead to purchasing services or goods not originally intended. Many offline retailers offer discounts on their goods ordered online and shipped with no additional cost to the consumer. However, the tendency to shop online has varied globally depending on existing internet penetration rates, levels of societal trust, general economic welfare, and culture of trade.

Consumption via the internet leads to the emergence of virtual communities, or e-tribes, bringing to the fore issues of trust, reputation, and culture-specific trade communication. Such giants of online sales as Amazon and eBay have given rise to the emergence of similar websites in many countries, such as Alibaba and Taobao in China. The latter became successful local e-trading platforms, pushing global brands out of the market due to a better understanding of local consumer behavior or specificity of trade. For instance, while eBay had many restrictions, Taobao allowed for greater ease and personal communication via instant messaging between two consumers. This specific trait of Taobao made it popular in China, where trade and personal relationships are inextricably linked together. Websites that deal with sales of secondhand goods or online auctions allow people to meet prior to purchase or rely on a carefully designed system of references and other reputation signals that facilitate interaction and subsequent transaction. The internet has affected not only retail trade practices but also the tourism industry.

As Dorsey, Steeves, and Porras (2004) noted, travel has become the internet's second largest area of commerce after computer technology. At the same time, the internet has considerably eased the process of ticket purchases, which has led to the success of low-cost airlines like Ryanair, easyJet, and AirAsia, with travelers making their bookings over the internet; and which allowed some airlines to make low-fare offers, increasing the overall sales of tickets and attracting new customers.

Another development has marked the impact of the internet on tourism – namely the emergence of computer-mediated hospitality networks and apartment rental sites, which represent the alternative tourism sector. Such websites as Couchsurfing or Airbnb allow people to find free accommodation in other cities or rent out their residences as tourist accommodation; they present a challenge to the conventional hospitality and hotel industry. Despite Airbnb's popularity, it is actually illegal due to short-term rent regulations and the commercial transactions involved. Couchsurfing, on the other hand, has lost a share of its dedicated users after becoming a commercial (but free membership) venture. Both companies maintain websites that rely largely on references made by other users/customers to establish mutual trust. The hosting experience of the couchsurfer starts online, by browsing through dozens of online profiles of potential hosts to find the ideal one. Then personal communication with the chosen host is enabled by secure email service, at which point hosts can choose to show the place where the guests are to spend their time. Thus users can pre-visualize their future destination and literally "shop" online, selecting hosts that they would like to stay with or spend time with. This kind of "shopping" online is, however, subject to a number of factors related to successful impression management, personal compatibility, profile design, and physical availability. The Airbnb website, which functions on a commercial basis, displays the apartment for rent online; incongruences can later be reported by the customers/guests and may have negative social and commercial repercussions for the owner. The service of providing one's place overnight can be considered as a component in alternative tourism, catering to a certain group of tourists who prefer the comfort of an apartment and the authenticity of a real lived-in space in contrast to the commercial space of a hotel.

High-speed internet connection has facilitated changes in many aspects of human behavior, as the high speed allows streaming of videos that no longer need to be bought. This has changed the habit of buying videos to viewing them online via free online services or online cinemas. However, legal measures have prevented many websites from offering free online viewing. At the same time, there are websites that are not tightly regulated and have not been shut down. YouTube, one of the largest video repositories of fiction films, music videos, amateur videos, documentaries, family videos, and educational videos, has become a hub for online visual entertainment and promotion of political ideologies. YouTube's potential audience is taken advantage of by advertising companies that run obligatory commercials before the start of each video. Advertising on the internet occupies a considerable share of the advertising business and many free internet-related start-ups and social networking sites have been able to support themselves by means of advertising. Although TV advertising remains the dominant mode, the web video ad share has grown rapidly. The internet has not only facilitated the growth of new business avenues but has given a new dimension to activities that have long been socially stigmatized or illegal.

Pornographic imagery and virtual sex consumption have become another lucrative aspect powered by the internet. Not only does it provide free visual materials, but it also creates exclusive membership clubs and aids the prostitution industry. For instance, one of the brothels in Prague, called "Big Sister," from 2005 to 2010 advertised itself as the world's unique reality sex show. Sex was free if visitors agreed to perform for the web, but sex performed in the club was not exclusively with prostitutes and couples could visit as well and perform in front of the webcams, receiving monetary compensation. The videos produced were archived and sold at a subscription rate of US$23 per month. This example demonstrates how the internet has blurred the borders between private and public, while bringing opportunities for new commercial ventures.

The internet has stimulated the commodification of sex and made illegal prostitution in many countries an easy-to-manage online-based business, where intermediaries (pimps) can be avoided. The internet has also provided a platform for a much darker side of the flourishing global sex industry – child pornography and child prostitution. It is not just images related to sex experience that are circulated but also words and narratives; these lead to online forums where information exchange is conducted and online orgies can be performed. Commercial sex has found the internet to be a new medium where social networks between sex suppliers and sex buyers can be organized; the internet's anonymity enables sellers of sex to reach different types of customers, allowing them to establish a personal connection before actual offline interaction.

Intimate encounters for romantic purposes have also been commodified by means of numerous dating websites that allow men and women to seek partners across geographical and cultural borders. For some, such websites are an opportunity to communicate and avoid loneliness rather than seek a real long-term partner.

With the growth in popularity of death-match games like Doom or Quake, strategy games, and multiplayer online role-playing games, internet cafés (bars, clubs) have turned into important settings, providing online gaming facilities to youth. Although the internet itself is not considered to be addictive, some of its applications are; and online gaming is one of the most addictive activities on the internet, with no clear gender differences. A study by Wan and Chiou in Taiwan (2006) showed that gamers demonstrate strong interest in role playing of online games, in which they often do things that they dare not do in real life. The researchers conclude that "at the conscious level addicted players might seek self-presentation in an anonymous, relaxing, and secure space, but unconsciously, they might actually have an unsatisfied need for self-presentation due to their poor self-image in real life" (p. 765). For online consumers of games and digital sex, the internet becomes an alternative arena for personal self-expression and the expression of suppressed emotions and desires.

The internet has provided countless opportunities for diverse forms of entertainment or sports. Gambling has found its reincarnation with the growth of the internet. Online gambling and its different forms, including betting, online casinos, and online poker tables, have become among the internet's most lucrative businesses. One of the most popular forms of online gambling is poker, since it allows players to play against each other and not against the "house," with the card room making its money through "rake" and through tournament fees. An individual can play at several tables against different players at the same time. Another source of income for an experienced player is online coaching – teaching others how to play poker online. In many countries online gambling is illegal; the only measure that can regulate online gambling is the closure of websites by national authorities, but gamblers cannot be blocked from playing and can play on any site they have access to. The internet has changed habits in illegal activities such as gambling, prostitution, and sales of illegal products. It is more difficult to control these activities when they move into the internet domain.

Consumption in the internet age has to deal with the process of dematerialization, when cultural goods, artifacts, entertainment, and products can be consumed and practiced online. However, as some current research shows, consumers do not switch entirely to digital consumption, abandoning old habits. Although the internet has made obsolete some of the traditional intermediate settings or places related to trade and consumption, such as ticket booths, shops, cashiers, and so on, it does not completely exclude personal relations, which are crucial for consumer-to-consumer purchases, nor does it provide the full sensorial experience of places, things, and people. The internet comes to supplement certain forms of media consumption, such as cinema watching or events that can be now watched online. But it can gradually substitute for certain mass media such as hard-copy newspapers. However, it will not be able to substitute for the additional value of such forms of collective consumption as spectacle or event watching, which are to be experienced directly and which engage not only the visual and auditory senses but the haptic, olfactory, and taste senses too. As some scholars point out, material goods still occupy a relevant position in digital products (like music) and materiality becomes crucial in shaping consumers' practices.

Looking on the positive side, the internet has made sharing and collaborative consumption possible. People can reach each other online for the purposes, for example, of organizing collective purchases in order to get a group discount or engaging in new communities and networks. Apart from discounts, it has allowed people to share or exchange goods that they do not need any more – such as child-related products, clothes, and furniture – thus contributing to "green" consumption. One of the most important aspects of internet sharing concerns digital commodities – videos, music, information, photos. No longer is it necessary to buy films, books, or photos; they can be downloaded at no cost through pirate websites, torrent sites, or online libraries. As discussed by Ritzer and Jurgenson (2010), there is a trend toward unpaid rather than paid labor and toward offering products at no cost, when the system is marked by a new abundance where scarcity once predominated. With the rise of the web-based sharing economy new values come to replace those of capitalist consumption: access becomes more important than ownership, abundance replaces scarcity, and effectiveness comes to substitute for efficiency.

SEE ALSO: Digital-Mobile Consumption and Marketing; eBay; Prosumption; YouTube

REFERENCES

Dorsey, Elizabeth R., Leslie H. Steeves, and Luz Estella Porras. 2004. "Advertising Ecotourism on the Internet: Commodifying Environment and Culture." *New Media & Society* 6(6): 753–779.

Ritzer, George, and Nathan Jurgenson. 2010. "Production, Consumption, Prosumption." *Journal of Consumer Culture* 10(1): 13–36.

Wan, Chin-Sheng, and Wen-Bin Chiou. 2006. "Why Are Adolescents Addicted to Online Gaming? An Interview Study in Taiwan." *CyberPsychology & Behavior* 9(6): 762–766.

FURTHER READING

Burns, Neal M., Terry Daugherty, and Matthew S. Eastin. 2010. *Handbook of Research on Digital Media and Advertising: User Generated Content Consumption.* Hershey, PA: Information Science Reference.

Hughes, Donna. 1999. "The Internet and the Global Prostitution Industry." In *Cyberfeminism: Connectivity, Critique and Creativity,* edited by Susan Hawthorne and Renate Klein. North Melbourne, Australia: Spinifex Press.

Sharp, Keith, and Earle, Sarah. 2003. "Cyberpunters and Cyberwhores: Prostitution on the Internet." In *Dot.cons: Crime, Deviance and Identity on the Internet*, edited by Yvonne Jewkes, 36–52. Cullompton, UK: Willan.

J

Just-in-Time Production

KATSUKI AOKI and ROSS MOUER
Meiji University, Japan

Just-in-time production (JITP) was conceived at the Toyota Motor Company in 1938 by Ki-ichiro Toyoda. That vision evolved into what is now known as the "Toyota Production System" (TPS), owing mainly to the efforts of Tai-ichi Ono during the 1950s. JIT is one of two pillars of TPS; the other is "autonomation" (automation with a human touch), which was developed by Sakichi Toyoda. JITP is a system used by manufacturers to order and obtain processed parts through a highly developed network of subcontracting firms. JITP represents a further development of the Ford production system that facilitated the transition from mass production to small lot sizes, and reduced the cost of holding large inventories of the parts required on conveyor-based assembly lines. JITP calls for the right parts to be supplied to the production line by suppliers only at the time they are needed and only in the amount needed. JITP relies on the use of *kanban*. The *kanban* is a material flow control mechanism to communicate effectively with internal and external operations on issues such as adjusting inventory levels, production schedules, and lead times for the delivery of parts. *Heijunka* (production leveling) also plays a key role in JITP, with the aim of leveling out the quantity of parts that are sent up the supply chain, thereby smoothing flow on the production line.

Variants of Toyota's *kanban* system are widely used in Japan. The Nissan Production Way provides information regarding the quantity and delivery time for parts electronically rather than through the display of the paper-based *kanban*. Although Toyota started to use electronic *kanban* in the 1990s, it continues to use paper *kanban*. Nissan also uses a more synchronized system for the supply of large module components, a process that is sometimes called a "just-in-sequence" (JIS) system. JIS systems are more popular among Western automotive makers such as Volkswagen and Daimler. In the 1990s such manufacturers began to use this system in conjunction with supplier parks – an approach whereby several suppliers for module components establish their own assembly plant near the maker's final assembly plant. The supplier park system is considered to be a solution for many Western firms who work with parts suppliers that are more geographically dispersed than is the situation in Japan.

"JITP" refers more broadly to a variety of comprehensive manufacturing systems

The Wiley Blackwell Encyclopedia of Consumption and Consumer Studies, First Edition.
Edited by Daniel Thomas Cook and J. Michael Ryan.

in which the *kanban* system is only one component. Two features central to JITP are a many-tiered array of subcontractors (*keiretsu*) and the notion of ongoing improvement (*kaizen*) designed to raise quality and lower waste. The first evolved as Japan's economy grew after World War II, and is marked by the establishment of longstanding collaborative relations between makers and subcontractors. The second is widely found in Japanese manufacturing and is best known in Japan through the quality control circles that emerged in the 1960s and 1970s. The two are linked by the high degree to which parts are standardized in order to allow for "continuous production" to be maintained as new products are developed and marketed. Related to this are systems that allow an entire production line to be stopped in order to "get it right." If parts supplied on time do not fit the strict specifications, down time (i.e., a major waste item) increases. Therefore, a high level of coordination between final assemblers and suppliers is required. When fine-tuned, the TPS allows for reducing costs by eliminating waste across the whole supply chain process as much as possible.

In a certain sense, the TPS is a fairly straightforward, albeit complex, system that has been transferred abroad and is no longer unique to Toyota. However, it seems to have worked in Japan's large manufacturing firms in good measure owing to the training of the workforce. Those who have visited such assembly plants will notice the great intensity and energy demanded of employees on the shop floor. Long-term employment for core employees allows for the necessary acquisition of company-specific skills (knowledge) and the inculcation of company rules and ideology to occur. There is a constant need to keep employees motivated, and part of that occurs through a regimentation that is sometimes difficult to implant among workers in other cultures. The other facet provided by having a shared corporate vocabulary is the ability to communicate with great efficiency. This is particularly important in a tiered production system in which *kaizen* plays a significant role. The production of small batches requires the slight but frequent modification of parts, and that can efficiently be done only through the smooth coordination of operations up and down the supply chain. The importance of in-house knowledge has been widely noted in discussions of the width and depth of skills, the uses of internal labor markets, and the role of multiskilling in lean production.

When considering corporate culture, the history of subcontracting in Japan should be noted. A very elaborate system of subcontracting has existed in Japan since the Tokugawa period in what are now referred to as localized industries (*jiba sangyo*), which included the production of ceramic goods, pottery, lacquer ware, baskets, gloves, silk textiles, and many other products. Once into the twentieth century and modern manufacturing, some firms, most notably Toyota, began to conceive of ways to raise productivity and quality by innovating with production systems for textiles, machinery, and other goods while also relying on traditional outsourcing networks.

SEE ALSO: Commodity Chains; Fordism/Post-Fordism; Outsourcing

REFERENCES

Imai, Masaaki. 1986. *KAIZEN: The Key to Japan's Competitive Success*. New York: McGraw-Hill.

Monden, Yasuhiro. 1998. *Toyota Production System: An Integrated Approach to Just-in-Time*, 3rd ed. Norcross, GA: Engineering & Management Press.

Ohno, Taiichi. 1988. *Toyota Production System: Beyond Large-Scale Production*. New York: Productivity Press.

Shingo, Shigeo. 2005. *A Study of the Toyota Production System from an Industrial Engineering Viewpoint*. Boca Raton, FL: Taylor & Francis.

Womack, James P., Daniel T. Jones, and Daniel Roos. 1990. *The Machine That Changed the World: Based on the Massachusetts Institute of Technology 5-Million Dollar 5-Year Study on the Future of the Automobile*. New York: Rawson Associates.

L

Las Vegas

MICHAEL IAN BORER
University of Nevada, Las Vegas, USA

The image of Las Vegas, Nevada, USA is often more important than its reality, at least for those who do not live beyond the neon glow of the Strip's mega casino-resorts. The neon-infused Strip of Las Vegas – a four-mile stretch of concrete littered and glittered with hybrid amusement parks/resorts/casinos – dominates public perceptions of the once sleepy Wild West mining town. Images of the Strip abound in popular narratives from movies (e.g., *Oceans 11*, *Casino*, *The Hangover I*), television shows (e.g., *Vega$*, *Las Vegas*, *CSI*), and other pop culture media. These imagined narratives often support the images of Las Vegas as a place defined by and designed for adult consumption and entertainment. The dominant venues for consumption in Las Vegas are replicas of other places that span both national boundaries and historical time periods. An unsettling "kaleidoscopic" (Baudrillard 1988) narrative emerges from the odd juxtaposition of Pharaoh's Egypt, the Roman Empire, Caribbean Pirates and their displaced Sirens, South Pacific Volcanoes, the Emerald City, New York City, Paris, Venice, Monte Carlo, medieval castles, and grand temples to the patriarchs of consumer capitalism (e.g., Donald Trump and Steve Wynn). And that's just the Strip. The sprawling suburbs that stretch outward toward the mountains from the Strip are populated with Mediterranean-style houses on streets and in developments with names that are indicative of other regions and non-desert climates (e.g., Tuscany Village, Spanish Trails, and Providence).

In the 1990s into the 2000s, Las Vegas was the fastest growing city in the United States, with more hotel rooms than any city in the world. The population in Clark County (which is comprised of Las Vegas proper and the surrounding areas in the Valley including the Strip as well as the City of Henderson) grew from a little less than 500,000 in 1980 to about 2 million in 2010. This intense and rapid growth has put stresses on the city's physical and social infrastructure. The water levels of Lake Mead and the increased usage of water by residents are key concerns for the city's sustainability. The ubiquity of water in pools and fountains at Strip resorts (as well as the Wynn's faux waterfall and rainforest spectacle) divert attention from the sustainability issues in a city built in one of the driest deserts in the United States (Futrell 2001). Consumption and

The Wiley Blackwell Encyclopedia of Consumption and Consumer Studies, First Edition.
Edited by Daniel Thomas Cook and J. Michael Ryan.

hedonism tend to outweigh environmental issues.

Despite the massive increase in population, the city's and county's entertainment options are still strongly focused on the approximately 40 million visitors that Las Vegas hosts each year, the vast majority of whom stay on or near the Strip. Perhaps due to the mainstreaming of gambling across the United States in many cities and via online venues, the motivation of visitors to Las Vegas has changed. Any consideration of Las Vegas as a postmodern "fantasy city" (Hannigan 1998) or "cathedral of consumption" (Ritzer and Stillman 2001) needs to take into account that most tourists come to Las Vegas not to gamble but to be entertained and amused and to escape their everyday routines and roles, according to the Las Vegas Convention and Visitors Authority (2012).

Entertainment options have expanded in kind, with various Cirque de Soleil shows on offer. Restaurants run by or associated with celebrity chefs are common at many of the resorts, with some (e.g., Mandalay Bay, Cosmopolitan, MGM Grand) providing a collection of fine dining restaurants with multicultural and multiethnic culinary offerings. Perhaps the biggest change in consumption patterns is connected to the rise of the nightclub (as well as the dayclub). Upscale clubs that feature celebrity DJs can be found along the Strip resorts. Club goers not only pay for admission (from nothing to upwards of US$200, depending on night, DJ, and gender) but can also purchase table service starting at US$10,000 at many venues. Though locals can and sometimes do participate in the entertainment amenities of the Strip, they tend to be geared toward and patronized by visitors. Local weekly papers tend to be filled with pictures of and advertisements for clubs and restaurants, presented in easy-to-read large fonts and sexually oriented visuals (e.g., young women mouthing bottles of champagne, muscular men in tight T-shirts).

North of the Strip, the Downtown Project – founded by Ton Hsieh, the CEO of Zappos (an internet-based footwear retail company), and funded by US$350 million of venture capital investment – has created even more consumption opportunities for locals and visitors alike. The recently labeled Freemont East Entertainment District resides across Las Vegas Boulevard from the Freemont Street Experience (which sports the world's largest television screen as a canopy). The new district is home to bars and restaurants intended to serve non-gambling cultural omnivores, "creative class" Strip-phobes, and West Coast hipsters.

SEE ALSO: Cities, Visual Consumption of; Consumption, Landscapes of; Consumption, Spectacles of; Cultural Omnivores; Tourism

REFERENCES

Baudrillard, Jean. 1988. *America*. London: Verso.

Futrell, Robert. 2001. "The Expendable City: Las Vegas and the Limits of Sustainability." *Humboldt Journal of Social Relations* 26: 81–112.

Hannigan, John. 1998. *Fantasy City: Pleasure and Profit in the Postmodern Metropolis*. New York: Routledge.

Ritzer, George, and Todd Stillman. 2001. "The Modern Las Vegas Casino-Hotel: The Paradigmatic New Means of Consumption." *M@n@gement* 3: 83–99.

FURTHER READING

Borer, Michael Ian. 2011. "The Las Vegas Paradox: From Exceptional to Emblematic." *ASA Community and Urban Sociology Newsletter* 23(3): 1, 14–17.

Douglass, William A., and Paulina Raento. 2004. "The Tradition of Invention: Conceiving Las Vegas." *Annals of Tourism Research* 31: 7–23.

Fox, William L. 2005. *In the Desert of Desire: Las Vegas and the Culture of Spectacle*. Reno: University of Nevada Press.

Gottdiener, M., Claudia Collins, and David Dickens. 1999. *Las Vegas: The Social Production of an All-American City*. Oxford: Blackwell.

Latinos and Consumption

LISA PEÑALOZA
Kedge Business School, France
CHRISTOPHER CHÁVEZ
University of Oregon, USA

Latinas (feminine) and Latinos (masculine) make up a diverse diaspora configured at the nexus of Native American peoples, Europeans, Blacks, and Asians. Its geographic coordinates span Latin America, the United States, the Caribbean and Mediterranean regions, and a few Southeast Asian nations, such as the Philippines, as a result of the historical legacy of Spanish and Portuguese colonization, emigration, shared linguistic traditions, values, national policies, and most recently, marketing programs. Like other diasporas, its communities are marked by internal and external social relations, with strong political and economic inflections. A major distinction lies between the nations where Latinas/os constitute a majority and others where Latinas/os are a minority, although identities in both social domains reflect unique configurations of national residence, subcultural affiliation, and community and market aggregation. For example, in the United States, where Latinas/os are the largest minority, strong national roots remain among immigrants and descendants who consider themselves Mexican American, Cuban American, etc.

At the same time, the umbrella terms "Hispanic" and "Latina/o" convene a pan-national, pan-cultural, socio-market formation. In the United States, the "discovery" of a cohesive and identifiable consumer segment called the Latina/o market has been closely tied to the emergence of a nationally connected Spanish-language broadcast industry, which required that the audience be reconstituted in ways that promote the ideal of linguistic and cultural unity while suppressing differences between people with diverse nationalities, histories, geographic locations, ages, generations, social classes, languages, religions, and levels of acculturation. This construction of a unified Latina/o market has drawn heavily on institutional discourses including official census data as well as third-party research conducted by or on behalf of media industries.

Today, the Latina/o market has taken on a global dimension as consumers, corporations, and media institutions have become more transnational in nature. However, the effects of Latina/o identity on consumption are ambivalent. As consumer-citizens, Latinas/os are said to be in a better position to convert buying power into political power. However, by positioning Latinas/os as equal participants in the marketplace, consumer discourses obscure growing inequalities occurring at a global level. Despite some gains, Latinas/os continue to lag behind whites in income and education in the United States. In contrast, nations where Latinas/os are the majority are characterized by a mix of uneven economic development, political difference, and postcolonial social relations marked by the continued struggles of indigenous peoples.

Latinas/os are actively targeted in marketing discourses, and their enactments of identity and community constitute a consumer culture characterized by a dynamic bricolage of activism and cultural production. Consumer activism has changed with technology from the boycotts against the Frito Bandito promoting Frito Lay chips in the 1960s to the mix of online furor and amusement in response to Tecate's 2004 playful advertisement countering the stereotype of Latinas as hot and sexy with the caption, "Finally, a cold Latina." Latina/o cultural production has critiqued, negotiated, and appropriated consumer culture with examples ranging from José Marti's and Pablo Neruda's poems indicting multinational corporations for pilfering resources, to literary accounts peppered with product references by Ana Castillo, Isabel Allende, and Emma Perez, to the pedagogical insights of Ariel Dorfman and Chela Sandoval, and the political analyses of Enrique Trueba and Néstor García Canclini.

Latina/o consumer culture studies reflect multiple disciplinary perspectives and methods. Research flourishes on a host of topics including globalization, postcolonial development, immigration and acculturation, language ideologies, political incorporation, remittances, transnational family dynamics, marketing representations, and social media participation by a growing list of must-read authors such as Ernesto Galarza, Américo Paredes, Gloria Anzaldúa and Cherríe Moraga, Rodolfo Acuña, David Montejano, Henry Triandis, José Limón, Vicki Ruiz, Rina Benmayor, Carla Trujillo, Richard Delgado and Jean Stefanic, Amado Padilla, Norma Alarcón, Ramón Saldívar, Anghy Valdivia, Marta Tienda, Silvia Pedraza-Baily, Arlene Dávila, and Bárbara Robles.

Among the many paradoxes of consumer culture are mainstream–margin relations, the mixed legacy of market legitimation and distortion, and bittersweet immigration and remittance flows. While Latina/o consumer culture can be empowering, the homogenizing forces of the marketplace threaten to erase local identities. It is vital to track who is producing and consuming Latina/o culture, as signs and values drawn from ritual holidays and everyday life are packed into consumer objects and activities by and for Latinas/os and non-Latinos. Being targeted as a market brings social legitimacy, yet it comes with a price, as markets do not value all aspects of this diverse identity and culture. Latina/o activists and organizations continue to work for issues not connected with markets, such as neighborhood safety, political representation, and economic enfranchisement.

Future directions in research and scholarship include documenting the forces and effects of globalization, examining persistent traditions and change in families, and comparing the characteristics and experiences of Latinas/os within and across nations in the diaspora. As South and Central American nations continue to grow, they may become the center of the diaspora. Ultimately, much work needs to be done to better understand the complex development of Latina/o identity and community as played out in consumption.

SEE ALSO: Advertising; Anti-Consumption Tactics; Consumer Activism; Consumption, Landscapes of

FURTHER READING

Canclini, Néstor García. 2001. *Consumers and Citizens: Globalization and Multicultural Conflicts*. Minneapolis: University of Minnesota Press.

Chávez, Christopher. 2012. "Hispanic Agencies and Profits of Distinction: An Examination of the Advertising Industry as a Field of Cultural Production." *Consumption, Markets, Culture* 15(3): 307–325.

Del Valle, José. 2009. "US Latinos, la Hispanofonia, and the Language Ideologies of High Modernity." In *Globalization and Language in the Spanish-Speaking World*, edited by Clare Mar-Molinero and Miranda Stewart, 27–46. London: Palgrave MacMillan.

Dorfman, Ariel. 1983. *The Empire's Old Clothes: What the Lone Ranger, Babar, and other Innocent Heroes Do to Our Minds*. New York: Pantheon Books.

Peñaloza, Lisa. 2007. "Mainstreet USA Revisited: Market Targeting, Latino/a Consumer Culture, and Community." *International Journal of Sociology and Social Policy* 27(5/6): 234–249.

San Juan, Jr., E. 2002. *Racism and Cultural Studies: Critiques of Multiculturalist Ideology and the Politics of Difference*. Durham, NC: Duke University Press.

Sandoval, Chela. 2000. *Methodology of the Oppressed*. Berkeley: University of California Press.

Leisure and Consumption

STEPHEN L. WEARING
University of Technology, Sydney, Australia
MATTHEW MCDONALD
Assumption University, Thailand

Leisure and consumption have always been intimately linked, in the same way as work and production are. During the industrial Protestant era, consumption and leisure were seen as indulgent, decadent, feminine pursuits not worthy of serious intellectual analysis. One reason for this was that production, commerce, and industry were embodied in the concept of work, emphasized by the dominant culture of the time as central to the development of good character. Consumption, however, was seen as an inconsequential activity engaged in during one's leisure time.

These circumstances have since been reversed so that the dominant culture in Western societies now revolves around consumption as opposed to production. The shift from a "producer society" to a "consumer society" has meant that work and the work ethic have now been subsumed by leisure and the construction of lifestyle, both of which have become key to the formation of self-identity (Bauman 2005, 23–42). Evidence for this can be seen in the falling away of the "heroes of production" – the "self-made men," corporate founders, pioneers, explorers, and colonizers – to the "heroes of consumption" – film, music, and sporting stars – whose excessive expenditure, luxurious lifestyles, and narcissism are exalted in the mass media (Baudrillard 1970/1998, 45–46). As a consequence, there has been a growing interest in topics such as the mass media, sport, tourism, cultural studies, and consumerism because of the increasingly influential role these aspects of modern life play in understanding Western society and social behavior (Marshall 1998, 364).

Historically, work and leisure were seen as two separate realms. Marxist theorists argued that leisure was a capitalist ploy to ensure class control; as such, leisure was held to create the illusion of freedom and self-determination which is the necessary counterbalance to the real subordination of workers in the labor process (Rojek 1985). The relationship between the market and the idea of free time has trivialized leisure in capitalist society – when not working, people fill their free time with consumerism in the form of passive amusements and entertainments that disengage them from themselves and shift responsibility for their free time into the realm of the marketplace. Corporations have responded by manipulating people's leisure into a consumption process for the enlargement of capital. This has undermined the very meaning of leisure – from a concept having use value for the individual and society, to a phenomenon that exists primarily to create exchange value for corporations.

McDonald, Wearing, and Ponting (2008) maintain that the dominance of consumer culture saw it reinvent leisure as consumption. Leisure, they argue, has become the key to consumer cultures and its significance can be seen in the amount of time and money spent each year on products and services related to leisure. The average person in the United Kingdom now spends more time watching television (and its concomitant advertising) and shopping than any other leisure activity (Gershuny 2011). In 2005 the United States Census Bureau found that American households spent US$425 billion at restaurants, $400 billion on vehicle purchases, $250 billion on clothing, $200 billion on furniture and appliances, $150 billion on entertainment, $100 billion on electronics, $100 billion on gambling at casinos, and $60 billion on alcohol (Quinn 2008). When taken together, household leisure/consumer spending adds up to a staggering sum of money. In order to entice consumers to continually spend, businesses invest billions of pounds each year in the marketing and advertising of their leisure products and services.

The pursuit of the leisured society saw the enabling of a consumer culture that made consumption central to the construction of lifestyle. Within this context, consumption is the process by which consumer goods and services are created, bought, and used. For consumer culture to flourish, leisure (not by its nature a commercial activity) is required to be commodified to become an activity that is purchased and governed by the market economy with a focus on profit. The leisure experience then becomes a commodity to be bought, sold, and manipulated with this market fundamental in mind. With the emphasis on personality as a symbolic force, peer targeting, and the creation of images and narratives, an orthodoxy of play is established that is governed by marketers. As advertising molds leisure preferences, the experience derived from leisure becomes irrelevant in the face of consumption for consumption's sake; it is best encompassed in the term "conspicuous consumption."

The impact of commodified leisure on individual identity can be far ranging. Sociological theory, such as poststructuralist and critical perspectives, assume the role of the individual to be predetermined by the power relations of wider society. "Thus, these theoretical perspectives present leisure in modern industrial society as a deterrent to, rather than a facilitation of, a creative sense of individual identity." The romantic ideal of self-expression and fulfillment through leisure becomes a false consciousness or ideology, a justification for increased consumerism and compensation for inequality of opportunity in the market sector (Wearing and Wearing 1992, 8).

The arguments of modernity suggest that in the capitalist society of the new millennium, commodification of time and leisure facilities, equipment, and activities present us with an endless array of choice but an inability to satisfy that choice since the freedom to choose is dictated by the economy. Linder (1970) further explored this issue of freedom by proposing the possibility that economic growth causes an increasing scarcity of time. This creates a consumption maximum, owing to increasing time poverty, which is the result primarily of all the servicing and maintenance work required by consumption goods. People in capitalist societies devote large amounts of time to the consumption of goods and services. To service this desire people are required to work longer hours and so the cycle of work and spend continues unabated – the work and spend treadmill – and this process begins to greatly reduce the duration and quality of free time (Schor 1991). This has occurred despite the prophecy of many post-World War II economists that technological sophistication and material wealth, aided by expanding global markets, would enable society to enjoy more free time as opposed to work.

The work and spend arguments pose a direct challenge to the classical notions of leisure, so much so that Godbey (1989) argues that in capitalist society what has actually increased is anti-leisure. This has occurred as people's desire to work and spend on consumption has increased, evidenced by the high incidence of overtime, more dual job holding (moonlighting), increased time spent commuting, and increases in unpaid work such as house cleaning and child care. This desire to work and spend has meant that very little time and energy is then available for serious leisure and this has created a decrease in activities that require significant spans of concentration and time commitment to produce pleasure (Stebbins 2009). In many respects, our inability to satiate our material desires has led to the dominance of work in many people's lives.

In the tourism literature the concept of otherness is an accepted model of the phenomenon. This model has its underpinning in a power relationship in which Western developed countries use economic resources to construct tourist destinations as places for exotic voyeurism of a different and inferior culture. Through the commodification of these places and the use of their indigenous inhabitants as servants in the commercialized process, the tourist endeavor then eventually becomes a cannibalistic one. The tourist culture assumes the form of a powerful hegemony that submerges, ingests, and eventually eclipses the other culture of the host nation. What began as an attraction due to its difference and otherness becomes merely more of the same dominant culture with its identities and values intact.

SEE ALSO: Commodification; Conspicuous Consumption; Experiential Consumption; Tourism

REFERENCES

Baudrillard, Jean. 1970/1998. *The Consumer Society: Myths and Structures*. Translated by Chris Turner. Thousand Oaks, CA: Sage.

Bauman, Zygmunt. 2005. *Work, Consumerism and the New Poor*. Maidenhead, UK: Open University Press.

Gershuny, Jonathan. 2011. "Time-Use Surveys and the Measurement of National Well-Being." University of Oxford/Office of National Statistics. Accessed July 26, 2014. http://www.ons.gov.uk/ons/rel/environmental/time-use-surveys-and-the-measurement-of-national-well-being/article-by-jonathan-gershuny/index.html.

Godbey, Geoffrey. 1989. "Anti-leisure and Public Recreation Policy: A View from the USA." In *Freedom and Constraint*, edited by Fred Coalter, 74–86. London: Comedia/Routledge.

Linder, Staffan. 1970. *The Harried Leisure Class*. New York: Columbia University Press.

Marshall, Gordon. 1998. *Oxford Dictionary of Sociology*, 2nd ed. Oxford: Oxford University Press.

McDonald, Matthew, Stephen Wearing, and Jess Ponting. 2008. "Narcissism and Neoliberalism: Work, Leisure and Alienation in an Era of Consumption." *Loisir et Société/Society and Leisure* 30(1): 489–510.

Quinn, James. 2008. "The Shallowest Generation." Accessed July 6, 2014. http://www.financialsensearchive.com/editorials/quinn/2008/1103.html.

Rojek, Chris. 1985. *Capitalism and Leisure Theory*. London: Tavistock.

Schor, Juliet. 1991. *The Overworked American: The Unexpected Decline of Leisure*. New York: Basic Books.

Stebbins, Robert A. 2009. *Leisure and Consumption: Common Ground/Separate Worlds*. Basingstoke, UK: Palgrave Macmillan.

Wearing, Betsy M., and Stephen L. Wearing. 1992. "Identity and the Commodification of Leisure." *Leisure Studies* 11: 3–18.

FURTHER READING

Cook, Daniel Thomas. 2006. "Leisure and Consumption." In *A Handbook of Leisure Studies*, edited by Chris Rojek, Susan M. Shaw, and Anthony J. Veal, 304–316. Basingstoke, UK: Palgrave Macmillan.

MacCannell, Dean. 1976, *The Tourist: A New Theory of the Leisure Class*. London: Macmillan.

Lifestyle

MARK FEATHERSTONE
Keele University, UK

The idea of *lifestyle* originates in the work of the Austrian psychoanalyst Alfred Adler who discussed the idea in his 1929 work, *Problems of Neurosis* (1999a), and then later in texts such as *Individual Psychology* (1999b). Following its appearance in Adler's work, the term gradually found its way into American and British popular vernacular, and is now understood to mean a person's general approach to life, especially through their consumption choices. Adler's understanding of lifestyle – or *Lebensstil*, the style of life – builds upon the classical Freudian view of the formation of the ego. For Adler, lifestyle accompanies the growth of the ego and represents an orientation toward the world which colors the individual's experience of life and shapes their thoughts, feelings, and behaviors. Extending Freud's general theory of the influence of family upon individual psychology, Adler explains that lifestyle is inherited from the child's environment and earliest encounters with the world. In this respect it is shaped by past events and experiences and influences how the individual comes to understand the present. However, the individual's inherited lifestyle also influences their trajectory into the future because the way in which we approach life impacts upon the outcome of our social encounters.

In this way it is possible to see Adler's concept of lifestyle as an adaptation of the Freudian idea of the ego-ideal, or later, Lacan's notion of the imaginary, in that it represents the individual's self-identity and image of themselves which they then try to live up to in their social encounters. In the process of living up to their sense of identity, Adler (1999b) explains, the individual must pursue a *fictional final goal*, which represents the imaginary end of their lifestyle, in order to maintain a sense of direction in their life. Thus, Adler's idea of lifestyle is not simply concerned with the ways in which family history plays itself out across generations in such a way that the individual's behavior is determined by the past, but also focuses on the kinds of transformations that are made possible through the self's interaction with its own fictional final goal. However, Adler (1999b) is clear that the success of lifestyle transformations relies on social cooperation and he identifies the good or adjusted lifestyle as being based in a positive attitude to others, cooperation, and wider society. By contrast, the individual with a maladjusted lifestyle holds a negative attitude to others and finds it impossible to cooperate with them. The result of this, for Adler, is that the maladjusted individual will struggle to realize their fictional final goal, or may abandon this idea entirely as being entirely unrealistic. In this way the maladjusted individual possesses a poor sense of self, because they have failed to develop a functional lifestyle and instead operate through a deep sense of inferiority. On the basis of this sense of inferiority, which Adler links back to past experiences of others, the maladjusted individual feels cheated by an unfair society and expects to be cheated in future encounters. The result of this is the emergence of one of Adler's maladjusted types – a ruling or tyrannical person, who seeks to dominate everybody around them, a "getting" person who takes but never gives, or a recluse who abandons society and social activity.

Centrally, what these negative individual types emphasize, and what we should take from Adler's concept of lifestyle more generally, is the importance of a constructive relationship between self and society in enabling positive individual development. This is important because it contrasts sharply with contemporary common-sense understandings of lifestyle which tend to emphasize the individual and their self-creative activity outside of any social relation and especially through consumer choices. In this understanding of lifestyle, which we might argue has been inherited from American social and political thought concerned with what Herbert Hoover called rugged individualism, the individual is very much a self-made person. However, this is a particular version of the idea of lifestyle which opposes the classical understanding of the term. For example, long before Adler coined the term "lifestyle," Plato, in *Protagoras* (1996), wrote about self-development through reference to the Socratic maxim to know thyself (p. 43). Here, the only life worth living is the examined life. Yet there is no sense in which this lifestyle that is committed to self-knowledge is solipsistic, because the Socratic self-project is rooted in the need for discussion, debate, and dialogue, which allows the individual to evolve, develop, and find their own truth. In this way we can again see that lifestyle, which here represents the development of the individual from ignorance toward enlightenment, entails a good relationship with other people and society. By contrast, Plato's understanding in *The Republic* (1991) of the worst kind of lifestyle, the life of the tyrant, is similar to Adler's later vision of the dominant person, who is absolutely focused on the self and regards other people as objects to be used and abused. The cost of this lifestyle is, of course, loneliness, fear, paranoia, and an unsustainable life.

However, where the ancient conception of lifestyle emphasized the need for the individual to find their place within the whole, whether this was understood in terms of the *polis* or the *cosmos*, the modern understanding of the term recognizes the struggle between the individual and the collective, and projects this sense of struggle into a vision of self-making opposed to community. In relating this struggle back to the modern revolution, which saw people emancipated from medieval social conditions, Anthony Giddens (1991) explains that individuals were forced to make their own way in the world. Under conditions of what Giddens calls a post-traditional universe, the modern individual is plunged into a state of uncertainty, where self-making is no longer a choice, but rather a necessity. Here, when identity is a problem instead of a given, lifestyle becomes a response to the homelessness of the self, which must develop its own passage through life, and situate itself in the world. In essence, this is Adler's understanding of the idea of lifestyle – the way in which the individual both creates itself and finds its place in the world. However, where Adler's view is that in order to create itself the individual must place itself in the social context, other modern thinkers of lifestyle, perhaps most notably Friedrich Nietzsche, presented the individual, and individual becoming, as absolutely opposed to the collective, which was understood in terms of a mass, or herd, that would destroy the possibility of individual development. In order to illustrate Nietzsche's particular view of lifestyle, and lifestyle in opposition to community, we need only consider his adaptation of Plato's cave myth in his *Thus Spoke Zarathustra* (1974). When Nietzsche's hero, the hermit Zarathustra, emerges from the cave to explain to people that God is dead, and they have entered the future – what Giddens calls the post-traditional universe – they mock him, and tell him he is mad. Nietzsche's response is to present Zarathustra as a man of the future who must continue to become and develop *in spite* of the masses who want to hold him back and subject him to the tyranny of the majority. Where Plato's original cave myth was about enlightenment, and the problem of the other within the cave was incidental, in Nietzsche's version of the story the tyrannical mediocrity of the mass is blown up, and perhaps for the first time captures what would become the modern version of lifestyle where becoming and self-actualization rely on opposition to the suffocating collective.

From this point in history onward perhaps the key element of the idea of lifestyle concerns self-making in rebellion against the rationality of wider society. For example, we find this tendency in twentieth-century theories of subculture, where consumption, style, and the manipulation of symbols are employed in the name of lifestyle and a form of self-realization that is opposed to parent culture. Before the theorists of subculture, such as Dick Hebdige (1979), started to write about youth lifestyles, we find a similar idea of lifestyle as the pursuit of self-actualization through difference in the works of Max Weber (1992) who was, of course, a follower of Nietzsche, and later Pierre Bourdieu (2010), who explored the idea of the middle-class lifestyle. In the case of the former, Weber sought to complicate the Marxist idea of class by showing how this category of identity was also informed by differences in status that were defined by the pursuit of different lifestyles. Indeed, Weber's use of the term "styles of life" in *Economy and Society* (1992) has led the American sociologist Dennis Wrong to suggest that it was Weber, rather than Adler, who was responsible for the introduction of the term "lifestyle" into vernacular English (Giddens 1991, 81). Indeed, Weber remains an important figure in the genesis of the term, and his influence is clearly present in Bourdieu's work, and specifically *Distinction* (2010), where lifestyle is once again presented as a form of self-making defined by the ability to distinguish oneself from others. Here, Bourdieu follows Weber in showing how the middle classes manipulate signs, symbols, and culture more generally in order to distinguish themselves from others, who may possess less valuable cultural resources.

In Bourdieu's work this use of cultural politics for the purpose of self-actualization through distinction constitutes lifestyle proper because high-value culture cannot be simply purchased, but rather must be lived through immersion in education which endows the individual with the necessary habitus to distinguish him/herself from others. Here, the self is an aesthetic exercise, a work of art, created through lifestyle choice which the individual lives through their habitus or form of life. In emphasizing the culture work of lifestyle in this way, Bourdieu presents an alternative version of the concept which we find in, for example, the Frankfurt School writers, such as Adorno and Horkheimer (1997), who explored the ways in which modern life was played out through culture in the mid-twentieth century. Here, lifestyle is no longer an escape from what they saw as an overly rationalized society, but rather the form the overly rationalized society itself takes when it is transformed into a consumer society. Although the lifestyle of the capitalist individual remains tied to distinction and the need for self-realization in their work, what they suggest is that the focus on lifestyle is only necessary because the capitalist individual is mutilated by the production processes of capitalism. Destroyed and alienated by capitalist work, the capitalist individual tries to save some sense of self through lifestyle choice which transforms them into a pseudo-individual. In more recent work, the British sociologist Mike Featherstone (2007) has argued that the late-capitalist expansion of the consumer society has resulted in the emergence of a kind of carnival of choice and proliferation of lifestyles. On the one hand, capitalist individuals are free to make themselves through aesthetic practice, but on the other hand, their choice is limited by the options made available by markets. In this respect it is possible to see that the consumer model of lifestyle represents a market-oriented version of the concept based upon older understandings of the term defined by Adler and before him the ancient Greeks.

SEE ALSO: Adorno, Theodor; Birmingham School; Bourdieu, Pierre; Consumer Society; Frankfurt School

REFERENCES

Adler, Alfred. 1999a. *Problems of Neurosis: A Book of Case Histories*. London: Routledge.

Adler, Alfred. 1999b. *Individual Psychology*. New York: Harper.

Adorno, Theodor W., and Max Horkheimer. 1997. *Dialectic of Enlightenment*. London: Verso.

Bourdieu, Pierre. 2010. *Distinction: A Social Critique of the Judgement of Taste*. London: Routledge.

Featherstone, M. 2007. *Consumer Culture and Postmodernism*. London: Sage.

Giddens, Anthony. 1991. *Modernity and Self-Identity: Self and Society in the Late Modern Age*. Cambridge: Polity.

Hebdige, Dick. 1979. *Subculture: The Meaning of Style*. London: Routledge.

Nietzsche, Friedrich. 1974. *Thus Spoke Zarathustra*. London: Penguin.

Plato. 1991. *The Republic*. New York: Basic Books.

Plato. 1996. *Protagoras*. Oxford: Oxford University Press.

Weber, Max. 1992. *Economy and Society*. Berkeley: University of California Press.

Locavorism

MICHAEL A. HAEDICKE
Drake University, USA

The term *locavore* refers to a person who mainly or exclusively eats locally produced foods. This term and the related concept of *locavorism* gained traction in popular culture and in food activist communities in the early twenty-first century. Culturally, locavorism is often framed as a form of ethical consumer resistance to the control of food by transnational corporations, as well as a personally rewarding activity. However, locavorism in practice highlights some of the limitations and contradictions of consumer-based social change efforts.

While locavorism is a recently minted word, the idea of local eating as a virtuous consumer choice has a longer history. In his classic *The Unsettling of America* (1977), the agrarian writer Wendell Berry inveighed against the "estrangement of consumer and producer," which he blamed on the specialized and production-oriented character of modern industrial agriculture and food policy (p. 37). More recently, critics of globalization, such as Slow Food Movement founder Carlo Petrini, have promoted local eating as a way to preserve regional food cultures in a global economy. Locavorism has also figured prominently in the work of popular food writers. In *The Omnivore's Dilemma*, Michael Pollan described his efforts to create a family meal by hunting and foraging for food in the San Francisco Bay area. The novelist Barbara Kingsolver and the Canadian writers Alisa Smith and J. B. MacKinnon have also written book-length memoirs about their decisions to eat a locavore diet. These popular works discuss the time and effort that is involved in securing locally produced foods, but they also attribute numerous satisfactions to local eating, including increased freshness and flavor of food, enhanced knowledge of food production and seasonality, and richer relationships with neighbors in the surrounding community.

Locavorist advocacy is also supported by ethical arguments that have to do with environmental sustainability and community welfare. Supporters have argued that eating a local diet conserves energy and eliminates pollution by reducing the distance that food travels from farm to fork. The "food miles" argument, however, is challenged by others who claim that decentralized, small-scale food distribution systems may be less efficient than ones that achieve economies of scale in fuel use, and that locavore consumers typically buy food from a variety of locations, which consumes more fuel. Locavores have also asserted that buying food from local producers keeps food dollars circulating within communities, contributes to the welfare of local businesses, and nurtures civic identity and community economic independence. On the other hand, critics note that eating locally may deprive producers in food-exporting countries of market opportunities upon which they depend and contribute to widening global inequality.

Despite the contested nature of these ethical arguments, locavorism has contributed to changes in food retailing and marketing arrangements. Farmer's markets were rare in the 1970s and 1980s, but now exist in significant numbers across the United States. In 2012, the US Department of Agriculture's *National Directory of Farmer's Markets* listed over 7,800 markets in operation. The nonprofit organization Local Harvest has also identified nearly 1,500 community-supported agriculture (CSA) operations in the country. Research indicates that consumers are attracted to these operations not only because of ethical beliefs, but also because they enjoy interacting with farmers and other shoppers in settings that differ from the predictable and highly rationalized environments of many grocery stores. On the other hand, the relatively high prices charged at many markets and CSAs may exclude less affluent consumers and contribute to economic polarization in food consumption. An increasing number of supermarkets and mainstream restaurants have also begun to advertise "locally produced" items as part of a marketing strategy that emphasizes fresh, wholesome foods. In the supermarket industry, for example, Whole Foods Market has built its identity in part on its support for local farmers. These developments have made local eating possible for a wider range of consumers, but they have also raised concerns about the co-optation of locavorism by corporate interests. Particular concerns include the flexibility of the term *local*, which businesses are free to define as they see fit, and the possibility that local producers may adopt environmentally and socially damaging methods in order to meet the demands of the mainstream food industry, as has occurred in the organic foods sector.

SEE ALSO: Farmers' Markets; Ethical Consumption; Slow Food Movement; Whole Foods Market

REFERENCE

Berry, Wendell. 1977. *The Unsettling of America*. San Francisco: Sierra Club Books.

FURTHER READING

Alkon, Alison Hope. 2012. *Black, White, and Green: Farmers Markets, Race, and the Green Economy*. Athens, GA: University of Georgia Press.

Hess, David J. 2009. *Localist Movements in a Global Economy*. Cambridge, MA: MIT Press.

McWilliams, James E. 2009. *Just Food: Where Locavores Get It Wrong and How We Can Truly Eat Responsibly*. New York: Little, Brown.

Singer, Peter, and Jim Mason. 2006. *The Way We Eat: Why Our Food Choices Matter*. Emmaus, PA: Rodale.

M

Marketing/Marketing Science

RAQUEL BARBOSA RIBEIRO and ISABEL SOARES
University of Lisbon, Portugal

Marketing is the scientific knowledge and procedures used to persuade consumers to behave according to the objectives set by organizations and individuals. To attain these goals, organizations and individuals offer value to consumers, that is, ways of satisfying their needs and desires, in a relational process of intended reciprocal benefit. Such objectives can encompass selling products, changing attitudes and behaviors, ensuring satisfaction, and motivating adherence to causes.

Consumers are pivotal to the notion of marketing, a derivative of "market," narrowly defined as demand. Amply, market is the network of players (providers, suppliers, partners, stakeholders, competitors etc.) intervening in the value exchange process between organizations or individuals and their consumers. Related terminology for consumers includes *buyers*, *purchasers*, *users*, *clients*, and *customers*. From the standpoint of marketing, voters, donors, members, fans, and supporters can also be consumers. Influencers and prescribers are relevant agents as far as the market is concerned.

The first notions regarding marketing can be traced to the industrial revolution, and were further developed in the United States in the first decades of the twentieth century. After World War II, a period of mass market expansion, marketing became a consistent managerial practice and a recognized academic subject. Wilkie and Moore (2003) locate the foundation of the field between 1900 and 1920 and its formalization between 1920 and 1950. The National Association of Teachers of Marketing and Advertising was formed in 1924 in the United States, followed by the American Marketing Society in 1930. Both merged into the American Marketing Association in 1937. The *American Marketing Journal* was first published in 1934 and the *Journal of Marketing* appeared in 1936. From 1945 interest grew in theorizing the field, expressed in the proliferation of books and journals dedicated to marketing.

Schools of marketing thought, as identified by Shaw and Jones (2005), are divided into two main periods. Before 1955, they were represented by the marketing functions school (the activities of marketing), the marketing commodities school (the classification of goods related to marketing functions), and the marketing institutions school (the

The Wiley Blackwell Encyclopedia of Consumption and Consumer Studies, First Edition.
Edited by Daniel Thomas Cook and J. Michael Ryan.

actors of marketing functions). Between 1955 and 1975, academics such as Wroe Alderson helped instigate a paradigm shift from traditional to modern schools of marketing: marketing management, marketing systems, consumer behavior, macro-marketing, and exchange.

The marketing management school introduced seminal concepts in marketing. Coined in 1960, E. Jerome McCarthy's terms *marketing mix* and the *4Ps* (Product, Price, Placement, Promotion) identified the principal decisions marketing managers take to develop long-term strategies and short-term tactical programs. Marketing-mix variables were for a long time considered the key elements of the marketing plan, a managerial document set for three to five years and revised annually, which summarizes the resources and decisions an organization needs in order to accomplish its marketing objectives.

The product, either a good or a service, received most of the attention in the study of the marketing mix. Product life cycle, Chester R. Wasson's conceptual instrument, assumed that products go through different stages (introduction, growth, maturity, and decline), ranging from acceptance to costs and profits, each of which entails differentiated marketing strategies.

Every product is associated with a certain utility package for the consumer, that is, benefits that are the reason for its acquisition and that may go beyond its material value. "Marketing myopia," Theodore Levitt's expression of 1960, claimed that it would be more important for businesses to meet their customers' needs rather than to focus on selling products, thus revealing the concept of customer orientation which became a cornerstone of marketing. As Charles Revson, Revlon's founder, stated, "in the factory we make cosmetics, and in the drugstore we sell hope" (Kotler 1988).

Still within the marketing management school, marketers worked on new ways to distinguish their products from others on consumers' minds, upon realizing that competition was fierce. Strategies such as positioning, intended to simplify consumption choices, were therefore developed. Positioning is the set of main and distinctive traits that define the image of an organization, product, or brand. It is determined by consumers' expectations, the organization's offer, and competitors' attributes. The result should be a positioning statement with key messages and customer value propositions to be used for communication with the target audience.

Moving beyond the improvement of the marketing offer, the school of marketing management explored the potentials of unattended demand. Consumers' differences were considered in order to develop cost-effective strategies and attain better results as far as the organization–consumer relationship is concerned. Generated by this perspective, market segmentation is the process through which organizations identify and separately deal with distinct types of consumers (segments) and their different needs and profiles. Usual criteria for segmenting markets are demographics, socioeconomic and psychological variables, and shopping behavior patterns. Differentiated offers, positioning, and strategies are developed in line with the particulars of each segment, in what is known as targeting. Within market segmentation, niches are smaller, albeit substantial, segments with a restricted number of consumers with very specific needs, who tend to be considered highly profitable or influential.

A later development of the school of marketing management, Philip Kotler's "analysis, planning and control," entered marketing in 1967. Overall, based on their knowledge of the market (gained from organizational diagnosis, market analysis, competitor evaluation, and consumer research), marketing managers define the offer to the market (in the form of products, services, or others), make decisions about such offers (including product specifications, packaging, branding, pricing, distribution and logistics, communication, and customer service), negotiate the best terms with the business partners (suppliers, distributors, financial institutions, etc.), elaborate a budget, schedule and implement decisions (sales, promotion, logistics), assess results, and correct mistakes.

After marketing management, Alderson's subsequent contribution was the school of marketing systems, which dealt with the interaction between micro- and macromarketing. It recognized the importance of articulating marketing activities with the organization's broad environment. This environment entails demographic, economic, natural, technological, political-legal, and social-cultural variables that may affect the marketing network. A marketing network consists of the organization and its supporting stakeholders (customers, employees, suppliers, distributors, and partners) with whom it builds mutually beneficial relationships.

While marketing management matured and systems declined, the school of consumer behavior concerned itself with the economic, psychological, and sociological scientific knowledge required for understanding needs, desires, and satisfaction. Behavioral contributions grew in the marketing field in the 1960s, coexisting alongside developments in mathematics and statistically based models applied to marketing research. Together, qualitative and quantitative techniques provided marketers with instruments that enabled them to perform complex and comprehensive analysis and thus forecast consumers' beliefs, preferences, and actions.

The school of macromarketing rekindled the contributions of the school of marketing systems by highlighting the reciprocal impact of marketing in society and vice versa. Movements, policies, and macroeconomic development were taken into account. The school of exchange, on the other hand, encompassed both commercial transactions and generic human interactions, such as motivations and values between parties in a complex social context. These schools paved the way for the expansion of the marketing field proposed by Kotler after 1975.

From 1975 to 2000, marketing scholars, namely Kotler and his coauthors, further expanded the limits of marketing from business to all forms of human activity, not only economic but also social, political, religious, and personal. Marketing's widened scope began to include experiences, events, personalities, places, properties, information, and ideas as well. Concurrently, variables such as political power, public opinion, participants, physical evidence, process, and personalization were added to the marketing-mix concept. This progressive "marketization of everything" has, however, been, both academically and ethically controversial.

Major topics stemming from this paradigm change include nonprofit organizations, societal impact, and stakeholders. Social marketing, a branch of marketing that gained relevance in this period, considers the use of marketing strategies to influence a public to voluntarily accept, change, or abandon behaviors for the sake of individuals and society. Marketing is presently considered relevant to companies in all business areas, nonprofit organizations, governments and public services, nongovernmental organizations, political parties, and individuals.

Kotler and Keller (2012) describe three stages in the evolution of marketing, from product centered (Marketing 1.0), to consumer based (Marketing 2.0), to value oriented (Marketing 3.0). In the contemporary stage, Marketing 3.0, organizations propose functional, emotional, and spiritual value to consumers through the use of collaborative strategies and technological innovations destined to meet the goal of making the world a better place.

Originally designed as an instrument for developing offers to consumers and persuading them to buy, marketing evolved to the value creation paradigm, a management attitude that assumes a consumer-centric and relational perspective based on value, used either for profit or for nonprofit purposes. Marketing is now conceptually more devoted to the interests of consumers and to the interests of stakeholders, which are increasingly ruling organizations' decisions, than to profit making only. In this line of action, corporate social responsibility (CSR) refers to the organizational commitment to improve the well-being of the community. For instance, increasing environmental concerns and consumers' growing awareness of these issues leads organizations to develop and communicate environmentally friendly practices.

In more recent decades, services have gained importance in the economy of most countries, posing new challenges to marketers as the world becomes increasingly globalized and consumers acquire more power. Contemporary sub-areas of marketing thought include services marketing, CRM (customer relationship management), and customized or personalized marketing.

Services suppose different types of relations between clients and organizations. In services like transportation or tourism, consumer and provider are present and relate in the same physical place. In other cases, the service is provided remotely (online sales, home banking), or through machinery and equipment (ATM). Conceived for dealing effectively with various forms of interaction, relationship marketing, developed during the 1990s, aims at building long-term, valuable relations with consumers, partners, and stakeholders, for reciprocal preference and benefit.

A derivation of relationship marketing, CRM is a strategy for gathering, processing, and managing relevant information about consumers (or customers) and their relation with the organization in the light of maximizing their loyalty. CRM, technologically supported by database analysis and data mining tools, can help organizations identify and address their best customers, develop targeted marketing activities and campaigns, improve customer management, optimize information, and reduce costs. CRM also provides the basis for effective customization and personalization. In contrast to mass-marketing strategies, which address consumers in an undifferentiated way, customization and personalization seek to please consumers with offers adapted to their particular needs and desires. Expensive, "pure" customization is practiced by relatively few organizations (e.g., in the area of luxury goods and services or in business-to-business [B2B] marketing), but mass customization, a process allowing consumers to partly choose or co-create the attributes of their products from a set of predefined options, is expanding. The participation of consumers, not only in production but along all stages of the marketing strategy (known as collaborative marketing), has rocketed over the last years, especially due to online marketing possibilities.

More than a marketing tool, online marketing is an expanding sub-area of marketing itself. A mere distribution channel for electronic commerce, in the early days of the internet, it now encloses any marketing activity, from research to advertising and CRM. Therefore, virtual communities, social media, viral marketing, and search engine optimization (SEO) are forecast to be prominent topics in the future of marketing.

SEE ALSO: B2B Marketing; Brands and Branding; Consumer Behavior; Digital-Mobile Consumption and Marketing; Mass Marketing; Niche Marketing; Socially Responsible Marketing (SRM)

REFERENCES

Kotler, Philip. 1988. *Marketing Management: Analysis, Planning, and Control*, 6th ed. Upper Saddle River, NJ: Prentice Hall.

Kotler, Philip, and L. Kevin Keller. 2012. *Marketing Management: Analysis, Planning, and Control*, 14th ed. Upper Saddle River, NJ: Prentice Hall.

Shaw, Eric H., and D. G. Brian Jones. 2005. "A History of Schools of Marketing Thought." *Marketing Theory* 5: 239–281. doi:10.1177/1470593105054898.

Wilkie, William L., and Elizabeth S. Moore. 2003. "Scholarly Research in Marketing: Exploring the '4 Eras' of Thought Development." *Journal of Public Policy & Marketing* 22(2): 116–146. doi:10.1509/jppm.22.2.116.17639.

FURTHER READING

Kotler, Philip. 2011. "Philip Kotler's Contributions to Marketing Theory and Practice." *Review of Marketing Research* 8: 87–120. doi:10.1108/S1548-6435(2011)0000008007.

Kotler, Philip, Hermawan Kartajaya, and Iwan Setiawan. 2010. *Marketing 3.0: from Products to Customers to the Human Spirit*. Hoboken, NJ: Wiley.

Marketplace Trust

KENT GRAYSON
Northwestern University, USA
DEVON JOHNSON
Montclair State University, USA

Marketplace trust involves at least two exchange partners: one who is doing the trusting (the truster) and another who is being trusted (the trustee). For marketplace trust to exist, the truster must believe that the trustee has implicitly or explicitly agreed to do something – usually, to perform some activity on behalf of the truster, or to provide a product and/or service to the truster. Trust is defined as the truster's belief that the trustee will meet the expectations of the exchange agreement. For example, if a customer expects that a repair professional will arrive at a particular time on a particular day and will perform a specific repair in the customer's home, it can be said that the customer trusts the repair professional.

Trust focuses only on trustee actions that the truster believes are volitional and relevant to the exchange agreement. An exchange partner is therefore unlikely to "trust" that a repair professional's own refrigerator will work or that the professional's heart will beat. Neither of these activities is likely to be viewed as volitional on the part of the trustee, or relevant to the exchange agreement. In the marketplace, trust plays a role not only in exchange relationships between customers and company representatives, but also in relationships between representatives (for example, when they are cooperating on a joint venture) and in relationships between customers (for instance, when they are sharing product use information on an online community). Customers may also trust a brand or an entire organization rather than (or in addition to) an individual company representative. In such cases, customers often trust an anthropomorphized (and therefore imagined) entity.

When striving to meet the expectations of an agreement, trustees may face unexpected or unintended contingencies that limit their willingness or ability to live up to the agreement's expectations. Many definitions of marketplace trust therefore also include the truster's expectation that, if such contingencies arise, the trustee will respond only after weighing the truster's needs equally to (or more heavily than) the trustee's own needs. For instance, a repair professional who gets into an automobile accident before arriving at a customer's home might prefer to set aside customer obligations until he or she deals with the police and calls the insurance company. Yet a customer may trust that a repair professional in that situation will balance these new priorities with the customer's needs – for example, by informing the customer of the delay before calling the insurance company, or by immediately arranging for an alternative repair professional to visit the customer's home at the designated time.

Those who study marketplace trust have proposed that trust is comprised of three subdimensions. The first is honesty (or credibility), which is the belief that an exchange partner keeps promises and tells the truth. The second is benevolence, which is the belief that an exchange partner truly cares about the other partner and is not focused solely on personal gain. The third is competence trust, which is the belief that an exchange partner has the knowledge and ability to perform the agreed-upon tasks. Separate from these three subdimensions, researchers have also conceptualized trust in terms of two different psychological processes. One process is more cognitive. It is the truster's calculation of the probability that the trustee will meet expectations, based on a systematic assessment of the trustee. The second psychological process is more affective. It is based on a heuristic or impressionistic assessment of the trustee's character, which allows the truster to develop a more emotionally based decision or intuition about whether an exchange partner will meet expectations.

Trust is necessary only to the extent that the truster believes there is some chance that the trustee will decide not to meet the agreement's expectations. Because this belief is often grounded in truth, trustees sometimes do not live up to the expectations and therefore demonstrate that the truster's trust was misguided or misplaced. Some theorists (e.g., Williamson 1993) note that a good exchange agreement should obviate the need for trust by offering potential benefits (or imposing potential costs) that make it irrational for a trustee to fall short of expectations, and which therefore reduce to zero the chance that the trustee will decide not to meet the obligations of the agreement. This is an influential theoretical perspective, and it is true that the incentives contained within an exchange agreement can influence the likelihood that an exchange partner will comply. However, there is some evidence that mere compliance without trust can limit the likelihood of constructive partner behaviors that are not specified in the exchange contract, such as the extent to which exchange partners are willing to work creatively with one another (Bidault and Castello 2010). Furthermore, it is often impossible to design an agreement that perfectly balances incentives for truster and trustee (Holmström 1979) and exchange partners in the real world are never perfectly rational. Therefore, there is always a chance that a trustee will decide not to behave as agreed. The more a truster believes this chance exists, the more trust is needed before the truster will be willing to accept the agreement.

Because exchange agreements usually specify or suggest expected behaviors for all exchange partners, partners often simultaneously play the role of truster and trustee. Just as customers must often trust company representatives, company representatives must trust customers to pay for products and services, behave appropriately in retail environments, and use products as instructed. Company representatives often expect even more from customers who engage in co-production or co-creation activities such as helping a company to improve existing products or to develop new ones. When an exchange agreement requires all exchange partners to trust as part of the agreement, this does not necessarily mean that all partners will need to trust (or will be willing to trust) in the same ways and at the same levels.

Trust can be fostered by a variety of causes, such as the level of perceived similarity between truster and trustee. It can also influence a range of truster beliefs and behaviors, such as a greater willingness to purchase from the trustee. Whether these drivers lead to trust (and whether trust leads to certain outcomes) may be affected by a number of characteristics. These include whether or not the truster has a longstanding relationship with the trustee and the extent to which the truster has a trusting personality. Trustees also use different technologies to interact with trusters, each of which encourages or hinders the development of trust in different ways. For example, if a repair professional interacts with a customer primarily by email and text messages, trust will develop in a different way than if the interactions are primarily in person or by telephone. Trust is also influenced by the level of trust that trusters have in the technologies used by trustees. For example, trust in a surgeon will be influenced by how much the patient trusts the surgical equipment used, and trust in an online brokerage firm will be influenced by how much the investor trusts the firm's web interface and the timeliness and precision of its trading engine.

The norms and institutions of the broader social context can also foster or undermine trust in an exchange relationship. For example, a customer's trust in a repair professional can be influenced by the customer's trust in the politicians who regulate the industry in which the professional works, the executives who operate the firm at which the professional is employed, and the lawyers and judges responsible for punishing those who violate agreements in the marketplace. There is some debate about the influence of the broader social context on trust between exchange partners. Some have suggested that more trust in the social context strengthens the foundation for trust in exchange relationships while others have argued that it relaxes the need for it.

SEE ALSO: B2B Marketing; Prosumption

REFERENCES

Bidault, Francis and Alessio Castello. 2010. "Why Too Much Trust Is Death to Innovation." *MIT Sloan Management Review* 51(4): 33–38.

Holmström, Bengt. 1979. "Moral Hazard and Observability." *The Bell Journal of Economics* 10(1): 74–91.

Williamson, Oliver. 1993. "Calculativeness, Trust, and Economic Organization." *Journal of Law and Economics* 36(1): 453–486.

Markets, Moral Aspects of

FREDERICK F. WHERRY
Yale University, USA

Markets offer arenas for affirming and contesting right and wrong behavior, but they also do more than that by providing the stages where people enact and put on display the principles of their shared morality. Social scientists James Scott (1976) and Viviana Zelizer (2011) offer useful examples of how moral concerns infuse and steer market transactions. In *The Moral Economy of the Peasant* (1976), Scott noted that the villagers he studied have their own "notion of economic justice and their working definition of exploitation – their view of which claims on their product were tolerable and which intolerable" (p. 3). Scott moves us away from a mechanical analysis of capital–labor relations to the realm of how people are categorized and what rights and obligations are attached to what categories of persons. Scott and Zelizer recognize that work, compensation, and inviolable property rights depend on compelling moral content that emerged from sacred rituals.

Viviana Zelizer (2011) has challenged our understandings of morality and markets in her studies of the insurance industry. Pricing life in the insurance market was not merely a mathematical calculation for the actuarial tables. Marketers and sales agents relied on large-scale societal shifts in how people categorized and valued their children. Parents struggled over what it would mean to insure a priceless life at a monetary price, and spouses contemplated whether receiving monetary compensation after the death of a spouse – a reward for the loss of a sacred life – was immoral. The answer to the industry's growth was not to rid social life of its transcendental concerns but to respect and extol those concerns as deeply connected with what the market had to offer.

The intertwining of markets, morality, and social life result in fundamentally transformed contractual exchanges. It is not only that markets transform norms but also that norms and narrative tropes transform transactions. Kieran Healy and Kimberly D. Krawiec (2012) have studied how organ exchange works. Their inquiry delves into a marketized transaction with life-and-death consequences. New ways of organizing organ donations mobilize people's moral concerns while binding them in businesslike contracts. The organ transaction is neither a pure form of gift exchange (an altruistic donation to save lives) nor a pure form of market exchange (a contractual exchange between strangers to make money and satisfy wants). They describe the arrangement where a patient and a donor happen to have incompatible kidneys. What is the most efficient morally satisfying way to allow the donor to give her kidney to someone else with whom she is compatible? The patient and donor can be matched with another pair and have a simultaneous swap of their kidneys using a morally infused market mechanism.

The trope of "the gift of life" facilitates recruitment, moral commitment, and practical compliance (Healy and Krawiec 2012, 105). The mixing of the altruistic with the contractual is deliberate, and it is the symbolic work of the mixing that enables the exchange to proceed. Indeed, contracts themselves may enable these kinds of exchanges to expand the number of participants; however, these contracts work not because they are legally enforceable (they are not) but, rather, because they serve as a symbol of credible commitment in a "life-giving" ritual.

Morally noxious exchanges do occur, however. Philosopher Debra Satz (2008) has pointed to the challenge of morally good exchanges taking place where there are conditions of inequality. Can people freely choose the limits of an exchange if they suffer under extreme inequality? Is choice an individual decision if there are collective spillover effects? In other words, if a person lives in a community where people have decided to sell their kidneys for money, it may be harder for individuals to obtain a loan if they themselves are not willing to make similar sales. The idea of what assets an individual holds depends on the changed understanding about what assets people in such a situation carry (in their person). Such sociological treatments join Michael J. Sandel's *What Money Can't Buy* (2012) in indicting the market for corruptions to childhood, families, and community life. Sandel argues that markets violate the principle of fairness: people paying, rather than waiting, for national citizenship, for a higher priority in a doctor's schedule of appointments, and for public theater tickets that everyone else has to stand in a queue to obtain. He then attends to the corruption that occurs when adopted children are bid on, their value demeaned, or when the altruistic incentive to help those in need becomes polluted by market logics, rendering charity and mutual aid as suboptimal practices. Even when market logics start off as benign, he argues, they tend toward the malignant as the more powerful market values crowd out the nearly defenseless moral ones. These critical understandings of morality in markets exemplify the variety of perspectives on the moral dimensions of economic life.

SEE ALSO: Children's Consumer Culture; Commodification; Medical Tourism

REFERENCES

Healy, Kieran, and Kimberly D. Krawiec. 2012. "Custom, Contract, and Kidney Exchange." *Duke University Law Journal* 62. Accessed June 25, 2014. http://papers.ssrn.com/sol3/papers.cfm?abstract_id=2176410.

Sandel, Michael J. 2012. *What Money Can't Buy: The Moral Limits of Markets*. New York: Farrar, Straus & Giroux.

Satz, Debra. 2008. "The Moral Limits of Markets: The Case of Human Kidneys." *Proceedings of the Aristotelian Society* 108(3): 269–288.

Scott, James C. 1976. *The Moral Economy of the Peasant: Rebellion and Resistance in Southeast Asia*. New Haven: Yale University Press.

Zelizer, Viviana A. 2011. *Economic Lives: How Culture Shapes the Economy*. Princeton: Princeton University Press.

FURTHER READING

Durkheim, Émile. 2005/1900. *Professional Ethics and Civic Morals*. New York: Routledge.

Marx, Karl

ROB BEAMISH
Queen's University, Canada

Born in Trier, Germany's oldest city, located closer to Paris than Berlin, Karl Marx (1818–83), the eldest surviving son in a family of nine children (five reached adulthood), grew up in an environment saturated with the spirit of the Enlightenment, the French Revolution, and a republican worldview. Encouraged to become a lawyer like his father, Marx entered the University of Bonn in 1835, spending time writing romantic poetry to Jenny von Westphalen, his future wife, engaging in student hijinks, and studying law and philosophy.

Transferring to the University of Berlin in 1836, Marx joined the *Doktorklub* – a group of left-Hegelian students, writers, and academics – and intensively studied Georg Wilhelm Friedrich Hegel's philosophy. Considering an academic career, Marx completed a dissertation at the University of Jena in 1841 comparing Democritean and Epicurean philosophies of nature. Marx's professorial ambitions diminished when Bruno Bauer, a potential advocate, lost his position over a satire the two wrote that portrayed Hegel as the Antichrist.

With few academic prospects, Marx joined the liberal-oriented *Rheinische Zeitung* in 1842, quickly becoming its editor. Embroiled in the real, practical issues of Prussian life, Marx tired of left-Hegelian speculative philosophy and turned to French socialists for new perspectives. Following the newspaper's government closure in 1843, Marx relocated to Paris and experienced workers' lives firsthand. Familiar with Friedrich Engels' journalism, Marx met Engels in August 1844, the two men beginning their lifelong collaboration.

"RICARDO TURNED SOCIALIST, HEGEL BECOME ECONOMIST"

Building on Ludwig Feuerbach's critique of religion and German idealism, Marx began his own materialist-inspired critique of philosophy in 1843. In "Towards the Critique of Hegel's *Philosophy of Right*: Introduction,"

Marx first identified the proletariat as the "class with *radical chains*," possessing "a universal character," which would emancipate all spheres of society (Marx and Engels 1927, 619–620). Marx also began a comprehensive study of political economy, developing his insights into class, the economy's impact on social existence, and the internal, dialectical contradictions that generate revolutionary change.

Amid rumors in 1851 that Marx's "Economics" was published, Ferdinand Lassalle eagerly anticipated "the three volume monster of Ricardo turned socialist, of Hegel become economist – since this must unify both and you will unify both" (cited in Beamish 1992, 166). The fragmentary, early drafts for a proposed two-volume critique of political economy, penned in 1844 and published posthumously in 1932 as "The Economic and Philosophic Manuscripts," present Marx's first integration of Hegel and political economy.

In those manuscripts, Marx emphasized "[t]he greatness in Hegel's *Phenomenology of Mind* … the dialectic of negativity as its moving and creating principle." Based on his reading of Adam Smith, Jean-Baptiste Say, Frédéric Skarbek, Heinrich Osiander, Pierre Boisguillebert, James Mill, and David Ricardo, Marx materialized Hegel's conception of alienated existence as "the self-creation [*Selbsterzeugung*] of humankind as a process, objectification [*Vergegenständlichung*] as opposition [*Entgegenständlichung*], as alienation [*Entäußerung*] and the overcoming of this alienation," applauding Hegel's insights into "the essence of labor" and humankind's creation "as the result of its *own labor*" (Marx and Engels 1932a, 156).

Marx and Engels formalized this "negative ontology" (Schmidt 1971) – humankind's mediate relation to nature, rooted in labor – in the 1845, unpublished draft manuscript, *The German Ideology*:

> [Our premises] are not arbitrary ones, not dogmas, but real premises … [R]eal individuals, their activity and the material conditions under which they live. … One can distinguish humankind from animals by consciousness, by religion, by whatever one wants, but humans distinguish themselves from animals as soon as they begin to *produce* their means of subsistence. … Insofar as humans produce their means of subsistence, they indirectly produce their material life itself. (Marx and Engels 1932b, 10)

In the 1844 manuscripts, "proceeding from political economy's assumptions," presupposing "private property; the separation of labour, capital, and land, and likewise of wages, profit, and capital; the division of labour; competition; the conception of exchange value, etc.," Marx noted that political economy shows:

> the worker sink[ing] to the level of a commodity, the most miserable commodity; that the worker's misery stands in inverse proportion to the power and volume of his or her production, that the necessary consequence of competition is the accumulation of capital in a few hands, thus the restoration of monopoly in a more terrible form; and that, finally, the distinction between capitalist and landlord, between agricultural worker and industrial worker, disappears and the whole of society must split into the two classes of *owners of property* and propertyless *workers*.

Intertwining political economy and Hegel, Marx developed his own conception of alienated labor:

> The worker becomes poorer the more wealth he or she creates, the more his or her production increases in power and magnitude. The worker becomes an increasingly cheaper commodity the more commodities he or she produces. The *devaluation* [*Entwertung*] of the human world grows in direct proportion to the *valorization* [*Verwertung*] of the world of things. Labour produces not only commodities, it also produces itself and the worker as a *commodity* and it does

> so in the same proportion in which it produces commodities in general. (Marx and Engels 1932a, 81–82)

In capitalist production, workers are alienated from the products of their labor, the production process, other workers, and the true being of humanity (i.e., humankind's full creative capacities).

For almost 30 years, Marx struggled with how to present capitalism's underlying, dialectical tensions and internal contradictions. Between 1857 and 1859, Marx drafted 10 different plans. In a three-volume plan, the first would contain six books: capital, landed property, wage labor, the state, international trade, and world market. The "critique and history of political economy [and] the socialist object" constituted the second volume, and a "short historical sketch of the development of economic categories and relations a third." The book on capital, projected at 100 pages, would address "1. value, 2. money, 3. capital in general (production process of capital, circulation process of capital, unity of the two or capital and profit, rent)" (cited in Beamish 1992, 55). That one book became *Capital*'s three volumes, totaling more than 2400 pages.

By 1867, Marx decided to begin with the most basic relation critical to his analysis – the commodity. *Capital*'s opening chapter is its most challenging; along with the chapter on the labor and valorization processes explaining Marx's theory of surplus value, it is fundamentally important to the entire critique. Marx unfolds each dialectical opposition integrated within the commodity: form and substance, natural and social, abstract and concrete. The material commodity, "the elementary form" of capitalist production, encapsulates capitalism's social relations of production (Marx 1867, 1).

The commodity's substance is concrete, living labor-power congealed into a material form (a use value). Made to exchange, a commodity's use value is also socially determined – it must be useful to someone else to be exchanged (commodities are simultaneously material and social relations). The equivalence of one commodity for another (its exchange value) is not directly part of its material form but the substance common to each – the abstract, simple, socially necessary labor time congealed in each (their value).

As the form of exchange developed from simple, through extended and general to the money form, the real foundation of the social relations of production appear in an inverted form in capitalist production. To find an appropriate analogy, Marx (1867, 42) turned to the world of religion, Christianity in particular, and its "cult of abstract man" to explain "the fetishism of the commodity world or the objective appearance [*gegenständlichen Schein*] of the social determinations of labour." Under capitalism, the social relations of production appear to be a *sui generis* reality in which the social interaction among the producers is mediated by their products – by things. In *Das Kapital*'s first edition, Marx's terminology is more Hegelian and the alienation theme more overt than in the French or subsequent German editions: "The personal relationship [*Beziehung*] is concealed in the thingly [*sachliche*] form. … The producers' own social movement possesses, for them, the form of a movement of things under the control of which they stand, instead of controlling it" (Marx 1867, 38–39).

> The social relationships of their labors *are* and *appear* not as the immediate, social relationships [*Beziehungen*] of persons through their labor, rather as *thingly relations* [*sachliche Verhältnisse*] of persons or *social relations of things*. … The relations of the private workers to the totality of social labor objectifies itself opposite them and therefore exists for them in the *form of objects*. (Marx 1867, 39–40)

But, Marx (1867) continues, this misleading "form [*Gestalt*] of the social processes of life, i.e. the material processes of production, will strip off its mystical veil [*Nebelschleier*] once it stands as the product of free socialized [*vergesellschafteter*] persons under their conscious, planned control" (p. 40), ending the alienated existence of capitalist production.

THE MANIFESTO AND MODERNITY

The anonymous 23-page *Manifest der Kommunistischen Partei*, rolling off the League of the Just's London presses in February 1848, captured the essential dynamics of industrial capitalism as its prodigious potential was becoming obvious. Throughout the debates among socialists hosted by the League in 1847, Marx's views had prevailed. Writing the League's new manifesto moved Marx from relative obscurity in Brussels to becoming a leading European socialist.

With powerful rhetoric and imagery, Marx demonstrated the importance he placed on class consciousness among workers. "A specter moves throughout Europe – the specter of communism. All the powers of old Europe have formed a holy alliance to exorcise the specter" (Marx and Engels 1934, 9). But, Marx continued, it is time to set the record straight and "meet this nursery tale of the specter of Communism with a manifesto of the party itself." Through a carefully crafted history, Marx presented the two great titans confronting one another – bourgeoisie and proletariat.

The *Manifesto* recognizes the bourgeoisie's breathtaking accomplishments as "far surpassing Egyptian pyramids, Roman aqueducts, and Gothic cathedrals," creating "more massive and more colossal productive forces than have all preceding generations together." Marx underscored the structural imperatives impelling the bourgeoisie's constant revolutionizing of the mode of production, "pitilessly" tearing asunder Europe's "motely feudal ties" leaving "naked self-interest" and "callous 'cash payment'" as the only connection between individuals, turning "personal worth into exchange value" (1934, 12).

The *Manifesto* also captures the essence of modernity:

> All fixed, fast-frozen relations, with their train of ancient and venerable prejudices and opinions, are swept away, all new-formed ones become antiquated before they can ossify. All that is solid melts into air, all that is holy is profaned, and man is at last compelled to face with sober senses his real condition of life and his relations with his kind. (Marx and Engels 1934, 13)

In "conjuring up such gigantic means of production," the bourgeoisie "is like the sorcerer who no longer controls the powers of the nether world he has called up by his spells." Crises of overproduction and "[m]asses of laborers" crowded into factories, "grow[ing] in strength," create the conditions for revolutionary change (1934, 13). Modern industry "cuts from under its feet the very foundation on which the bourgeoisie produces and appropriates products. What the bourgeoisie therefore produces, above all, are its own grave-diggers. Its fall and the victory of the proletariat are equally inevitable" (p. 20).

FROM "MARXISM" TO THE MEGA AND DIFFERENT "MARXES"

When the first International Workingmen's Association (1864–76) broke up, a "Marxist movement" was already emerging. But as an ideology, "Marxism" faced two obstacles.

First, Marx had never published a systematic statement of his ideas. Aside from his journalism, some early essays, *The Holy Family* (1845), *The Poverty of Philosophy* (1847), the *Manifesto* (1848), *Wage-Labour and Capital* (1849), *Class Struggles in France* (1850), *The Eighteenth Brumaire of Louis*

Napoleon (1852), *Herr Vogt* (1860), and portions of his "Economics," – *Towards the Critique of Political Economy* (1859), and two German editions and a French, serialized translation of *Capital's* first volume (1867, 1873, 1872–75) – Marx had published little of his lifetime's work (for example, just a portion of his posthumously published manuscripts – early study notebooks, *The German Ideology*, the 23 notebooks of 1861–63, and *Grundrisse* – totals almost 4000 pages).

Second, because Marx integrated German idealism, political economy, and French revolutionary thought – somewhat incompatible intellectual traditions – his ideas are complex. Moreover, they were in a continuous state of flux, making it impossible to definitively state *What Marx Really Meant*, to use G. D. H. Cole's 1934 book title.

"Marxism" was a conscious creation (although it ultimately led to several "Marxisms" espoused by different political groups). Engels, Karl Kautsky, Eduard Bernstein, August Bebel, Franz Mehring, Marx's daughters, Jenny, Laura, and Eleanor (two Marx children died in infancy and son Edgar at 8), and others created "Marxism" to guide and motivate socialist revolutionaries.

The core was the *Communist Manifesto* and Marx's 1859 preface to *Towards the Critique of Political Economy*. Engels' 1886 pamphlet *Socialism: Utopian and Scientific* was equally important. Those texts, along with Engels' eulogy to Marx comparing Darwin's discovery of the laws of organic nature to the laws Marx discovered in the development of the social world, framed within the period's intellectual context, led to a highly positivistic Marxism. Viewed alongside Engels' proposed ontology in *Dialectics of Nature*, "Orthodox Marxism" suggested that capitalist breakdown was a scientifically established inevitability. The base–superstructure relationship Marx sketched in his 1859 Preface was interpreted in a highly mechanistic manner, leading to an overt economic determinism.

But Engels et al. also provided the means for challenging Orthodox Marxism. Committed to bringing Marx's full legacy to the socialist movement, Engels, Kautsky, Bernstein, and Bebel transcribed, edited, and published significant parts of Marx's literary estate including several early essays, the 1858 "Introduction" to Marx's projected, entire critique of political economy, volumes two and three of *Capital*, the three-volume *Theories of Surplus Value*, and most of the Marx–Engels correspondence. More would follow.

With Lenin's support, David Ryazanov – founder of the Institute for Marxism-Leninism and a victim of Stalinism in 1938 – began editing a comprehensive, scholarly edition of Marx's manuscripts. Twelve volumes of the *Marx–Engels Gesamtausgabe* (MEGA) appeared before Joseph Stalin terminated the project.

The first MEGA included texts that challenged not only Orthodox Marxism as the representation of Marx's ideas but, more importantly, undermined dialectical materialism – Marxism-Leninism's official ideology. The key texts were the 1844 manuscripts and Marx's accompanying *Exzerpthefte* (notebooks).

Originally prepared for MEGA but published in limited quantity in 1939 as *Grundrisse der Kritik der politischen Ökonomie (Rohentwurf)* (Foundations for the Critique of Political Economy [Rough Draft]) and a second, "appendix" volume in 1941, the Institute published Marx's (1857–58) seven-notebook draft and outlines of his entire, extremely ambitious, project. The *Grundrisse* reinforced Hegel's relevance throughout Marx's struggle to conceptualize and present his critique, the ongoing development of Marx's negative ontology, and his conception of alienation.

In order to give access to Marx's work to people other than scholars, from 1923 to 1948 Ryazanov, followed by Vladimir Adoratsky, published a 30-volume Russian-language collected works – *Marx–Engels Sochineniya*. A 42-volume second edition (1955–66) became the basis for the German Democratic Republic's (GDR) 43-volume (in 45 books) *Marx–Engels Werke* (1956–90). Fifty volumes constitute the English-language collected works (1975–2005).

In 1972, the Socialist Unity Party in the former GDR, along with the Soviet Communist Party and the Institute for Social History in Amsterdam, launched a second MEGA. Following the end of Soviet-style communism in 1990, an International Marx–Engels Foundation and the Institute in Amsterdam took over the leadership of the proposed 122-volume project.

Although the full literary estate is not yet published, enough is available to demonstrate that Marx was a gifted, synthetic thinker but that he did not author a single, clear system. Viewed positively, Marx's works remain extremely suggestive, stimulating considerable thought and debate. Seen negatively, it is difficult to definitively determine what is most important. Numerous authors have presented the "real Marx," though each is quite different (e.g., "Young Marx," "Scientific Marx," "Orthodox Marx," "Revisionist Marx," "Hegelian Marx," "Structuralist Marx," "Postmodernist Marx"). Although some distortions are politically motivated, most authors are simply trying to present Marx's work as a clear, consistent whole, but to reach that goal they focus on specific aspects and bring the other parts, which are not fully consistent with the chosen focal point, into line. The result is a consistent whole but it masks the tensions, revisions, and reconceptualization within Marx's unfinished project. In the end, Marx's oeuvre is misrepresented.

Part of Marx's difficulties was the complex, dynamic nature of industrial capitalism itself, but conceptualizing and presenting that system was equally problematic. At different times Marx thought he had discovered the key (or keys) to understanding and explaining capitalism, but even as he gave Engels *Capital*'s first proofs, he was writing an appendix to clarify the commodity chapter. Despite his struggles, Marx was clear on what not to do, making several scathing critiques of others' approaches (e.g., Bruno and Edgar Bauer, Max Stirner, Ludwig Feuerbach, J. P. Proudhon, Karl Vogt, and Adolph Wagner). Three points result.

First, reading Marx's criticisms of others shows the approaches he fully rejected while simultaneously giving insight into his own.

Second, when reading Marx or citing his work, identifying the work, when it was written, and where it stands within the whole corpus of his project is crucial. Marx's ideas evolved and although one can cite statements that appear contradictory, once the context of each is known, the contradiction disappears. When Marx wrote something and the statement's context are as important as what he wrote.

Finally, rather than treating Marx's work as Holy Scripture, it is best viewed as it really is: an unfinished, dynamic, unstable, dialectical whole that contains many strengths and insights but also some lacunae. The most glaring is the absence of a theory of consciousness formation. Ironically, although Marx began with Hegel's *Phenomenology* and recognized idealism's potential contribution to the active side of Feuerbach's materialism, Marx never pursued the question of how workers' class consciousness would actually develop and what obstacles it would face. Thus, although there are hints of how a phenomenological, existential, or social-constructionist dimension to his work could be developed and integrated into his critique of political economy, the "subjective" side of Marx's theory was never developed and remains its greatest omission.

Although much has changed since 1883, even now Marx's negative ontology, his conception of the commodity and the insights it yields, his position on alienated labor, and the structural dimensions of his theory all remain highly relevant. Marx's critique of political economy is not the final word on contemporary capitalism but it remains an excellent place to start.

SEE ALSO: Capitalism; Class; Commodities

REFERENCES

Beamish, Rob. 1992. *Marx, Method and the Division of Labor*. Chicago: University of Illinois Press.

Marx, Karl. 1867. *Das Kapital* (Capital), vol. 1. Hamburg: Otto Meissner.

Marx, Karl, and Friedrich Engels. 1927. *Marx-Engels Gesamtausgabe* (Marx-Engels Complete Works), pt. 1, vol. 1. Berlin: Marx-Engels-Verlag.

Marx, Karl, and Friedrich Engels. 1932a. *Marx-Engels Gesamtausgabe* (Marx-Engels Complete Works), pt. 1, vol. 3. Berlin: Marx-Engels-Verlag.

Marx, Karl, and Friedrich Engels. 1932b. *Marx-Engels Gesamtausgabe* (Marx-Engels Complete Works), pt. 1, vol. 5. Berlin: Marx-Engels-Verlag.

Marx, Karl, and Friedrich Engels. 1934. *Manifesto of the Communist Party*. London: Martin Lawrence.

Schmidt, Alfred. 1971. *The Concept of Nature in Marx*. London: New Left Books.

Masculinity

AMIAS S. MALDONADO
University of Texas at Austin, USA

Masculinity refers to the social roles, behaviors, and meanings traditionally associated with male bodies in a given society at any point in time. Because masculinity refers to a set of socially defined traits, it emphasizes gender over biological sex and allows us to understand cultural variations in "what it means to be a man." Masculinity is not an internal facet of identity but produced within societal institutions and daily interactions (Kimmel 2000). Briefly, masculine practices differ across four dimensions.

First, masculinity varies by culture. Some cultures encourage a masculinity that is stoic and must be proved through sexual conquest or physical skill and domination. Some cultures may have political participation, emotional availability, or economic provision as key components of masculinity. Historically, Western men were seen as producers or laborers and frivolous or domestic consumption was feminized.

Second, masculinity varies within a society. Several different meanings of masculinity comprised of different masculine practices may all coexist in the same society. Sociology has explored how class, ethnic, and sexual identity shape an individual's gender identity. For example, what it means to be a man may be very different for a young poor gay Latino man and an older, upper middle-class black man with a family. However, both practices of masculinity are deeply affected by the white heterosexual masculine ideal.

Third, masculinity varies over time. Historians have often pointed to industrialization, urbanization, new technology, or the positionality of a country in geopolitics as macro social processes which have shifted definitions of masculinity.

Finally, practices associated with masculinity may change over the individual's life course. As men shift from teenagers to husbands to fathers and grandfathers, socially accepted definitions of normative manhood change as well. For example, athletic prowess and sexual promiscuity are a central part of adolescent masculinity, but are less central to adult masculinity practices, which privilege economic provision, fatherhood, and personal responsibility.

One cannot view masculinity as an unchanging constant essence universal to all men. Gender must be seen as a fluid, dynamic assemblage of meaning and behaviors that is performed and embodied in a variety of ways. By pluralizing the term *masculinities*, we acknowledge that the term means different things to different people at different times.

HEGEMONIC MASCULINITY

The formation of personalized masculine identities does not happen in a social vacuum. Gender identities are always constructed in a field of power: all masculinities are not created equal. In every culture there exists an ideal version of masculinity that all men are expected to measure themselves against. The sociologist Raewyn Connell (1987) termed this "hegemonic masculinity." Hegemonic masculinity is defined as an ideal set of masculine practices that collectively justify male domination in any given society. While no man completely embodies hegemonic masculinity, their own versions of masculinity must always contend with the attributes of it. For example, if a society sees athleticism as an essential part of the ideal man, then men lacking physical prowess are aware of this failure to "measure up" and may decide to compensate for this with another facet of hegemonic masculinity such as sexual promiscuity.

This brings up an important point. According to Connell, hegemonic masculinity is always "constructed in relation to various subordinated masculinities as well as in relation to women" (1987, 183). Definitions of masculinity are constructed not only in relation to the hegemonic ideal, but in reference to each other: masculinity is always relational. At the most basic level, men often construct their ideas of what it means to be a man as whatever is not feminine. According to men, what men are is whatever women are not. This "anti-femininity" aspect of masculinity is one of the most influential and universal characteristics of masculinity across cultures and time.

"DOING" MASCULINITY

While early child gender socialization is influential in the construction of an individual's gendered identity, gender is not completely embodied nor completely static. Many sociologists see gender as less a fixed component of identity that individuals bring with them into interactions and more a *product* of those interactions. In Candace West and Don Zimmerman's seminal article "Doing Gender" (1987), they argue that "a person's gender is not simply an aspect of what one is, but … it is something that one does, and does recurrently, in interactions with others" (p. 140). We constantly "do" gender, performing activities and exhibiting traits that coincide with prescribed masculine/feminine gender identities. This is a performance that men continue throughout their lives, and is less a response to internalized norms or personality preference and more a navigation of the consistent demands of others to act in a recognizably masculine way. In sum, gender is not an expression of a concrete identity buried within us at birth; rather, it emerges out of interactions from the social demands put upon us by others.

MASCULINITY AND CONSUMPTION

Historically, masculinity and consumer consumption have not been strongly associated. Men were expected to grow up, marry, and support their wives financially. As part of this gendered arrangement, women did most of the household purchasing. After World War II, however, masculinity in the West began to be more intimately linked with consumerism. For one thing, the postwar economic boom meant many men felt that providing for their families was no longer enough. Due to the relational aspect of masculinity, men began to feel pressure to keep up with escalating standards of family consumption. Whereas before, material goods or luxuries were seen as frivolous at best and unmanly at worst, now, men were judging their own manhood by whether their families could afford new technologies such as dishwashers, microwaves, and color televisions.

Furthermore, the birth of these modern domestic conveniences created conditions where men questioned their roles as economic providers to their "unproductive" spouses. Barbara Ehrenreich (1983) says that during this period the "playboy philosophy" emerged. This philosophy encourages men to display their financial success not through a house or a wife, but through luxury commodities such as fine cars and cologne or imported liquor and cigars. In effect, Ehrenreich argues, this new philosophy allows single men to gain social status by refashioning consumerism and luxury consumption as masculine.

MASCULINITY AS CONSUMABLE PRODUCT

A society undergoing change may experience a state of anomie, or normlessness. In these periods gender roles are fluid. Given masculinity's relational character, disturbing the fixed hegemonic ideal produces a "crisis" in masculinity. Over the past hundred years, scholars have documented how consumption can be a key part of men's attempts to solidify their own masculine identity specifically and male domination in general. For example, Michael Messner (2007) has documented how the growth of sports culture – centered upon the consumption of mass spectacle and the purchase of team memorabilia – originally rose from a concern about the emasculating effects of industrialization and corporate capitalism.

In more recent years, societal changes – most notably feminism and globalization – have further eroded the economic and social dominance men previously took for granted. The results are new crises in masculinity. The marketplace has offered a plethora of consumer options for men looking to "buy masculinity." Take the proliferation of erectile enhancement advertisements and products. Ads for Viagra or Cialis create a narrative of a masculinity in crisis which can only be shored up through the purchase of their products. This is again linked to the increasing consumerism associated with masculinity and reinforces connections between masculinity, sexual performance, and phallocentric sexuality.

Men have also begun to consume aesthetic surgery and beautification products. Since women are now recognized as desiring sexual subjects, men have increasingly grown more concerned with their physical appearance due to the connection between masculinity and sexual desirability. This manifests itself in the growing number of men who undergo aesthetic surgery and who purchase cosmetic goods. At first, men who undertook this consumptive aesthetic of bodily care had to carve out a new identity – "metrosexuals." But recent research suggests that concern for one's aesthetic body (as opposed to one's functional body) may not necessarily be emasculating, as some men see no contradiction between their masculinity and their beautification practices.

The consumption of masculinity can also intersect with racial stereotypes. Today's mass marketing of hip-hop culture can be seen as the commercial production and packaging of hypermasculine tropes of black rage for white consumption, who constitute the larger consumers of the genre. By positioning "dangerous" black masculinity as a consumable object through the purchase of music, media, or dress, this both reifies the connection between masculinity and violence/misogyny and allows non-white men to position their own masculine practices as preferable over this performance of criminal, violent masculinity.

SEX AS COMMODITY

One final aspect of consumption and masculinity is the pervasive consumption of sexuality as a commodity among men. Normative masculinity is deeply connected to heterosexuality, male control of women's bodies, and the belief that normal men have a virtually infinite appetite for sexuality. As such, buying sex and sexual materials displays heterosexuality, objectifies women as a purchasable commodity, and mediates the disjuncture between the unquenchable sexual thirst associated with masculinity and the reality of the sexual economy where men rely on women to actually have sex.

The most pervasive example of this is prostitution. While prostitution is not new, scholars have only recently begun to uncover the complex motivations men have when purchasing sex. For example, in Gloria Gonzalez-Lopez's (2005) work on transnational Mexican sexualities, older male members in some Mexican families purchase sexual services for younger members as a rite of passage to manhood. Purchasing sex is seen as allowing these young men sexual "experience." Additionally, the ritual of the transaction allows these men to engage in promiscuous sex with women while still maintaining the gender system that stigmatizes women who have premarital sex. In China, sex consumption is also a ritual associated with masculinity. But instead of functioning as a rite of passage, sex consumption becomes a way for business partners to bond and develop trust as well as being a political statement against what they perceive as a dominating social morality. Finally, there has been a transnational turn in prostitution where men from First World countries engage in "sex tourism," traveling to the global South in search of cheap, racially eroticized sex workers.

While pornography is an equally ancient product, it has become increasingly mainstream and pervasive. Feminists and other critics have raised concerns about its effect on romantic relationships and culture in general, highlighting the ways in which pornography's commodification of sexuality and intimacy can create isolation, mistrust, and lack of interest in real sexual partners. Some psychologists contend that, for some men, a compulsive interest in the consumption of pornography can eventually become an addiction. As video technologies have become ubiquitous and inexpensive, there has also been a rise in amateur-produced pornography. Here men produce, share, and even sell their videotaped sexual experiences to other men as a performance of their masculinity.

SEE ALSO: Conspicuous Consumption; Femininities; Gender and Consumer Culture; Sexualities and Consumption

REFERENCES

Connell, R. W. 1987. *Gender and Power*. Stanford, CA: Stanford University Press.

Ehrenreich, Barbara. 1983. *The Hearts of Men*. New York: Doubleday.

Gonzalez-Lopez, Gloria. 2005. *Erotic Journeys*. Berkeley: University of California Press.

Kimmel, Michael. 2000. *The Gendered Society*. New York: Oxford University Press.

Messner, Michael. 2007. *Out of Play*. Albany, NY: SUNY Press.

West, Candace, and Don H. Zimmerman. 1987. "Doing Gender." *Gender and Society* 1(2): 125–151.

FURTHER READING

Brubaker, Sarah J., and Jennifer A. Johnson. 2008. "'Pack a More Powerful Punch' and 'Lay the Pipe': Erectile Enhancement Discourse as a Body Project for Masculinity." *Journal of Gender Studies* 17(2): 131–146.

Collins, Patricia Hill. 2005. *Black Sexual Politics*. New York: Routledge.

Feasey, Rebecca. 2009. "Spray More, Get More: Masculinity, Television Advertising and the Lynx Effect." *Journal of Gender Studies* 18(4): 357–368.

Holliday, Ruth, and Allie Cairnie. 2007. "Man made Plastic." *Journal of Consumer Culture* 7(1): 57–78.

Zheng, Tiantian. 2006. "Cool Masculinity: Male Clients' Sex Consumption and Business Alliance in Urban China's Sex Industry." *Journal of Contemporary China* 15(46): 161–182.

Mass Culture

PATRICIA CORMACK
St. Francis Xavier University, Canada

Mass culture is a foundational concept in the study of consumerism and consumer society. It is also one of the most widely defined and debated, rooted in the issues of who generates culture and who is the audience or consumer of cultural goods.

In his lexicon of the new vocabulary of modernity, Williams (1983) discusses the notion of the "masses" as both a negative and a positive cultural force. On the one hand, the masses of ordinary people represent expanding democracy, literacy, and social action, while, on other hand, they represent the lowering of taste standards and potentially a politically manipulated multitude. As he points out, the generally negative connotation of the word "mass" derives from its etymology – undifferentiated, amorphous, and easily shaped.

Historically, mass culture refers to changes that accompanied industrial production and consumption. In England, France, and the US, industrial production and trade were developed enough by the middle of the nineteenth century to allow the establishment of large department stores and mail-order catalogues. Household durables and processed foods became more affordable. Henry Ford is often credited with demonstrating the inherent connection between production and the creation of a broad consumer market, through his combination of mass auto production (leading to lower costs per unit) and higher wages for his workers. Up to this point, consumption of a wide variety of goods was limited to the relatively small leisure class. Now, as consumers, the "masses" too were to influence what constituted culture and cultural goods in the marketplace – film, literature, architecture, art, food, fashion, entertainment – or, more generally, "taste."

From the 1930s through the 1950s, mass society and culture were central themes of European and American intellectual debate. Cultural critics of a conservative bent, as well as those of a Marxist persuasion, argued that the mass production of goods implied, respectively, either the production of goods toward a degraded mass taste, or the production of degraded masses toward consumption. For the elitist or conservative critics, mass production and the participation of the working classes in cultural life meant a necessary lowering of tastes, as ordinary people were unable to appreciate complex cultural objects, practices, and texts. A new hyper-democracy threatened to replace the traditional social and political leadership of the elite over the masses. For these critics, mass culture undermined all the vital aspects of the good society – quality, reflection, liberty, beauty, and temperance.

Marxist critics of mass culture were concerned with what was lost from the "bottom" end of the cultural spectrum – folk culture and workers' knowledge of their material world – as well as threats to high culture. For example, Frankfurt School members viewed capitalist culture as the production of needs that follow on and mirror production itself. This position is rooted in Marx's argument that needs must be explained by way of the productive conditions in which they arise. The capitalist productive process (homogenized, deskilled, routinized, predictable) has a leveling effect not only on products (cheap, easy to produce), but also on the worker/consumer. Workers are enslaved mentally and spiritually by the products they make and come to desire products from the "culture industry" – predictable, simple and formulaic movies, novels, music, and the like – that further depoliticize and pacify the masses. Some other Frankfurt School thinkers, like Walter Benjamin (1968/1936), argued that the techniques of modern mechanical reproduction (especially photography) could help the working classes see through elite cultural objects and practices by bringing art closer to them, ultimately radicalizing the masses. His use of Marx emphasized the dynamic place of new technologies in the progress of history, rather than the static role of ideology used to justify a particular period of production.

Concomitant with mass culture is the advent of mass marketing – both in the sense of marketing directed at a general or typical type of consumer and in the sense of the use of mass media technologies to reach a broad audience. As far back as the nineteenth century, grand openings of the new huge and ornate department stores were media events. Many critics of mass marketing suggest that it does more than merely communicate to and persuade audiences; it helps constitute social types. The social status of housewife, child, teenager – even the good citizen – has similarly been explained as a product of mass commercial culture. For much of the twentieth century, Western governments championed mass consumption as a civic duty in that economic expansion was considered the key to a stable society.

Ironically, from the 1950s through the 1970s, critiques of mass culture became themselves objects of mass consumption. John Kenneth Galbraith and Vance Packard became widely read, arguing that productive processes and marketing generated wasteful and irrational mass consumers. The back cover of Packard's book, *The Hidden Persuaders* (1957), gives us a clue as to the intended reader: "Why your wife buys 35% more in the supermarket than she intends." Wilson Brian Key's best-selling *Subliminal Seduction* (1973) claimed that hidden messages in advertisements appealed to unconscious sexual and aggressive drives in the consumer. Christopher Lasch's *The Culture of Narcissism* (1979) blamed mass culture for the decline of American civilization in general.

More recent discussions of mass culture have shifted emphasis from a manipulated mass to the agency and creativity of consumers. For Jean Baudrillard (1985), mass audiences make nonsense of the "truths" they consume, deflecting political manipulation by treating it as entertainment. Empirical case studies of consumers have found that mass audiences of cultural objects generate diverse, even conflicting and resistant interpretations and uses of these objects. Janice Radway (1987) found that women readers of mass romance novels used these novels to cope with and also resist family demands on their time and space. Women readers of "trashy" romance novels, African American viewers of popular situation comedies, and working-class fashionable youth were found to take up mass cultural objects toward their own ends.

Historians have pointed to consumption as a rallying point for social organization and political change – through the twentieth century American housewives used their consumer power to control prices and African Americans fought for civil rights with organized boycotts. Critics like Lynne Joyrich (1996) have revisited the 1950s and 1960s academic writing on mass culture, finding it filled with themes that betray an underlying misogynist formulation of the "masses" as a feminine and weak cultural force threatening to undermine patriarchal rationality – that is, the privileged social position of these writers themselves.

Perhaps the most serious threat to the idea of "mass culture" comes from general changes in production, marketing, and advertising. On the one hand, massive levels of consumption persist and consumption remains pervasive in everyday life. But marketing now works to fragment and differentiate audiences/consumers. Moreover, ordinary people are more and more the producers of cultural goods (by way of the internet, for example). That there is a "mass audience" or "massified" consumer seems less plausible, while the masses as agents of social change are evidenced in the capacity of social movements to make use of media from a grassroots level. Clearly, the idea of mass culture is a dynamic one, and should be carefully considered within the context of a changing consumer culture.

SEE ALSO: Adorno, Theodor; Benjamin, Walter; Consumer Culture; de Certeau, Michel; Popular Culture; Veblen, Thorstein

REFERENCES

Baudrillard, Jean. 1985. "The Masses: The Implosion of the Social in the Media." *New Literary History* 16(3): 577–589.

Benjamin, Walter. 1968/1936. "The Work of Art in the Age of Mechanical Reproduction." In *Illuminations*. Translated by Harry Zohn. Edited by Hannah Arendt. New York: Schocken Books.

Joyrich, Lynne. 1996. *Re-viewing Reception: Television, Gender, and Postmodern Culture*. Bloomington: Indiana University Press.

Key, Wilson Brian. 1973. *Subliminal Seduction*. Englewood Cliffs, NJ: Prentice Hall.

Lasch, Christopher. 1979. *Culture of Narcissism: American Life in the Age of Diminishing Expectations*. New York: Norton.

Packard, Vance. 1957. *The Hidden Persuaders*. New Yorker: Simon & Schuster.

Radway, Janice. 1987. *Reading the Romance: Women, Patriarchy, and Popular Literature*. London: Verso.

Williams, Raymond. 1983. *Keywords: A Vocabulary of Culture and Society*, rev. ed. Oxford: Oxford University Press.

FURTHER READING

Ewen, Stewart. 1976. *Captains of Consciousness: Advertising and the Social Roots of Consumer Culture*. New York: McGraw-Hill.

Galbraith, John Kenneth. 1958. *The Affluent Society*. New York: Houghton Mifflin.

Horkheimer, Max, and Theodor W. Adorno. 2002. *Dialectic of Enlightenment*. Stanford, CA: Stanford University Press.

Mass Marketing

KRZYSZTOF KUBACKI
Griffith University, Australia

The Industrial Revolution of the late eighteenth and early nineteenth centuries transformed manufacturing processes, enabling the emergence of mechanized production of a larger quantity of consumption goods in a cheaper and faster way. Thanks to mass production, by the late nineteenth century Western societies witnessed the growth of many companies to the size where they could no longer directly serve increasing numbers of their customers, who were spread over large geographical areas. At the beginning of the twentieth century, some of the early commercial efforts concentrated on what was then called "the marketing problem" (Jones and Monieson 2008), that is, how to move goods from the place where they were manufactured to the final consumer in the most efficient way. In the first half of the twentieth century, a growing number of competitors in many consumer markets shifted the emphasis away from mass production lines and the technological abilities to manufacture consumer goods (supply), toward activities that were designed to stimulate consumer demand. The so-called *marketing mix*, including not only products but also places (distribution channels), pricing, and promotion, became the heart of the emergence of mass marketing.

Mass marketing is a strategy based on the assumption that consumers have similar needs and wants (Elliot, Rundle-Thiele, and Waller 2014). It is the opposite of niche marketing. Mass marketing considers that all potential consumers are alike. An undifferentiated marketing mix is provided to cater the needs and wants of one market – the same product, price, place, and promotion. This approach is often referred to as a shotgun approach. Mass marketing helped bring high volumes of products at low prices to a wide swath of consumers and reached its heights in the three decades after World War II. Production capabilities developed to support the war effort in the United States provided many American companies with large-scale production and communication technologies, well-developed transport networks, and significant financial resources to supply products to the recovering markets of Europe and Japan. Newly emerging global markets created an opportunity and ideal conditions for mass marketing of standardized products which could appeal to large groups of people, of whom many had the same or very similar unmet basic needs. Moreover, the benefits of mass marketing, such as wide coverage and economy of scale (manufacturing of large volume of products at a low cost per unit), proved to be irresistible in particular to many companies manufacturing fast-moving consumer goods (FMCG) such as processed food, toiletries and cosmetics, and consumer electronics.

Mass marketing requires mass production, promotion, and distribution, in addition to reasonably low pricing. While the Industrial Revolution led to the emergence of mass production, mass consumption, and mass market economy, the second half of the twentieth century witnessed the emergence of mass media which fuelled further growth in the utility of mass marketing. Promotion of similar products to large groups of customers required communication tools thought to deliver promotional messages. Mass marketing promotion hence tends to concentrate on the use of advertising and public relations through mass media such as television, radio, some outdoor media (e.g., billboards), and more recently the internet, the effectiveness of which requires measurement as part of a large feedback loop. Impact often is measured through the metrics of reach (the number of people exposed to the message) and frequency (the number of times they were exposed to it).

Mass promotion remains relevant in a broader sense – it is an effective tool to create brand awareness, build goodwill, and facilitate interaction between the company and its markets. The delivery of a large quantity of products to large markets also requires relatively efficient distribution systems, with many distributors, wholesalers, and large retailers (e.g., supermarkets and department stores) specializing in assorting and delivering FMCG to geographically dispersed customers. Mass-marketed FMCG need to be available to as large a group of potential consumers as possible at a maximum convenience. The effectiveness of mass distribution can be measured through the level of market coverage in relation to a saturation level. Finally, mass marketing companies make profits by selling large volume of goods at low prices, so profit per unit sold is kept to a minimum to maximize the market appeal of the product.

Mass marketing has changed quite significantly since the latter decades of the twentieth century. One of its main drawbacks is that it focuses on generalities of products rather than the specificity of customers, rarely matching the two. While mass marketing remains widely and often successfully used by many large, multinational FMCGs manufacturers such as Coca-Cola, Procter & Gamble, Unilever, or Nestlé, newer marketing approaches and tools – such as market segmentation, services marketing, and service-dominant logic, online marketing, relationship marketing, direct marketing or niche marketing – offer alternative ways of marketing products. Some marketing experts predict that the growing number of smaller market segments (fragmentation of markets and media) and more and more precise target marketing will eventually lead to the collapse of mass marketing (Brown 1995). Yet many of the benefits of one-to-one marketing (e.g., database marketing) and mass marketing have been combined to develop mass customization – the use of new technologies (e.g., the internet and computerized manufacturing systems) to deliver the low cost per unit of standardized products from mass marketing with the convenience of individually customized elements of the marketing mix, including the rise of prosumption – the productive consumption of individual consumers. Despite the predicted collapse of mass marketing it is successfully coexisting along with other marketing approaches and evolving from a dominant marketing approach in the mid twentieth century to one of several strategies in the contemporary marketing toolkit.

SEE ALSO: Marketing/Marketing Science; Mass Media; Niche Marketing

REFERENCES

Brown, Stephen. 1995. *Postmodern Marketing*. London: Routledge.

Elliot, Greg, Sharyn Rundle-Thiele, and David Waller. 2014. *Marketing*, 3rd ed. Brisbane: Wiley.

Jones, D. G. Brian, and Monieson, David D. 2008. "Origins of the Institutional Approach in Marketing." In *The History of Marketing Thought*, vol. III, edited by Mark Tadajewski and D. G. Brian Jones, 125–144. London: Sage.

Mass Media

MICHAEL SICILIANO and KJERSTIN GRUYS
University of California, Los Angeles, USA

Mass media have been a core social institution throughout modern history and in contemporary life. The term "mass media" refers to an array of technological systems, industries, cultural forms, and practices of production and consumption characterized by the transmission of information from a few producers to large groups of consumers. Technologically, mass media include the printing press, telegraphy, telephony, music recording, film projection, radio and television transmission systems, and the World Wide Web or internet. Cultural forms associated with mass media include cinema, recorded popular music, newspapers, broadcast journalism, popular literature, television programming, video games, computer software, and advertisements.

HISTORICAL IMPORTANCE AND EARLY RESEARCH

Mass media enable information and cultural forms to be experienced by many social groups across diverse geographic and sociocultural contexts. Scholars in cultural/media studies, communications, sociology, and anthropology have long explored how common experiences of mass media lead to shared meanings, attitudes, and beliefs, and also how these shared meanings lead to the formation of social groups. Many early studies of mass media emphasized the effects of mass media upon mass audiences. For example, the advent of the printing press in the sixteenth century – among the earliest forms of mass media – enabled the formation of the imagined communities of nation-states through the circulation of information. Many other varieties of mass media began their development in the mid- to late nineteenth century, a timeframe that coincides with the late nineteenth-century consolidation of Europe into nation-states, the rise of mass manufacturing, and, later, mass consumption. This period of dramatic social transformation and upheaval – coupled with the later use of film, radio broadcasts, and newspapers as propaganda tools during both world wars – shaped much of the early scholarly inquiry on mass media.

From the interwar period onward, early research began along these lines, often presenting mass media as either an enslaving propaganda tool or a potentially emancipatory technology. Famous works arising from this period include the neo-Marxist work of the Frankfurt School (e.g., Benjamin 1968; Horkheimer and Adorno 1947) and Paul Lazarsfeld's empirical research on media influence (Lazarsfeld and Katz 1955). The Frankfurt School theorized a grand role for mass media within contemporary capitalism wherein the industrialization of cultural production – exemplified by mass media – facilitated capitalist domination by creating passive consumers whose cognition appeared "forcibly retarded." Lazarsfeld's work, in contrast, suggested a comparably diminished role for mass media, in which consumers actively shape the diffusion of the intended messages of media.

MAJOR TRENDS IN MASS MEDIA RESEARCH

Following these early studies, contemporary scholarly research on mass media often emphasizes either the *reception* or the *production* of mass media. Reception studies emphasize the consumption of media products and tend to stress the agency of audiences in their use and interpretation of mass media. Rather than passively absorbing media content without thought, mass media audiences are in fact quite active and often "resistant" to meanings encoded in media, interpreting mass media content proficiently, sometimes in unexpected ways. Contemporary audiences may, for instance, refashion available media through the production of fan magazines and websites, fan-written fiction (fan-fic) that employs pre-existing characters, "remixes" that recombine existing music or video, and other audience- or user-produced texts. The agency of the "active" audience, however, is not without limits, as mass media simultaneously structure society by framing and providing the languages through which people discuss and understand historic events, politics, gender relations, and myriad other aspects of social life. For example, Paul Willis's *Common Culture* (1990) and William Gamson's *Talking Politics* (2002) illustrate how mass media provide the raw materials from which people produce their own, distinctive opinions and cultural practices.

Studies of media production often focus on industry-level, social-structural, or technological forces that shape the content or aesthetic form of mass media. For instance, sociologists and economists frequently study the relation between media ownership and diversity in media content. Legal scholars and social scientists note the effects of intellectual property and labor law upon both content and career opportunities for those working within mass media industries. Recently, scholars in the social sciences have also turned toward the study of evaluation and measurement systems that mass media producers use in order to make sense of their target audiences. For example, scholars in a variety of fields have begun to study the social construction of sales charts, measures of audience attention, and what Lucien Karpik terms "judgment devices" (2010: 44–45) such as awards and certifications of quality. Though many of these studies arise from apolitical points of view, other scholars – such as those rooted in feminist and/or Frankfurt-inspired Marxist critical theories – view media production as one means by which powerful groups maintain their power.

In some fields, such as anthropology, sociology, cultural studies, and media studies, scholars unite studies of production and reception. Notably, sociologists such as Wendy Griswold and Joshua Gamson advocate holistic approaches to the production and reception of media. Respectively, these scholars argue that researchers must consider all aspects of the "cultural diamond" of producers, consumers, cultural objects, and cultural frames (Griswold 1987) or the production, content, and reception of media objects (Gamson 1994). Holistic approaches to mass media attend, at once, to the aforementioned structuring and structured aspects of media production and the practices by which consumers demonstrate agency as they integrate media objects into their daily lives.

FUTURE DIRECTIONS IN RESEARCH AND THEORY

Future research and theorization must grapple with the rise in digital media technologies over the past 15 years. New media technologies such as the internet, Web 2.0, social media, and widespread mobile computing problematize the adjective "mass." Though these forms of media transmit information on a massive scale, they simultaneously promote fragmentation of media consumption and increase differentiation among consumers. This results in what might be termed micro-audiences or micro-publics, as opposed to the twentieth century's mass publics or mass audiences. The theoretical inheritance left by the twentieth century leaves scholars with little in the way of describing, explaining, or interpreting the activities of massively fragmented masses of media consumers despite the fact that researchers now have access to overwhelming amounts of information, often called "big data," generated by users of digital media technologies.

Additionally, digital media depend upon advertisers for revenues and much of contemporary advertising and marketing rely upon the social media activities of audiences such as sharing information and user-generated media content. In this light, audiences take on new relevance. Rather than being merely consumers, they are also producers of media content. Scholars have recently begun to approach the study of media audiences as an extension of the study of unpaid labor. This new development suggests an increased blurring between studies of media reception and studies of media production.

Looking forward, the study of mass media continues to cut across disciplinary lines, encompassing a variety of theoretical and methodological approaches. This stems, no doubt, from mass media's multifarious character, increasingly global reach, and the globalized industrial structures of media industries. For example, scholars in the humanities continue to focus on the qualitative interpretation of particular media objects while quantitative social scientists often focus on the circulation of information through the use of large sets of data culled from the internet. Future work may do well to draw links between interpretivist, phenomenological, or critical approaches to media with more positivist approaches that make use of increasingly "big" datasets.

SEE ALSO: Frankfurt School; Mass Marketing; Social Media

REFERENCES

Benjamin, Walter. 1968. "The Work of Art in the Age of Mechanical Reproduction." In *Illuminations*. Boston, MA: Houghton Mifflin Harcourt.

Gamson, Joshua. 1994. *Claims to Fame: Celebrity in Contemporary America*. Berkeley: University of California Press.

Gamson, William. 2002. *Talking Politics*. Cambridge: Cambridge University Press.

Griswold, Wendy. 1987. "A Methodological Framework for the Sociology of Culture." *Sociological Methodology* 17: 1–35.

Horkheimer, Max, and Theodor Adorno. 1947. *Dialectic of Enlightenment*. New York: Herder and Herder.

Karpik, Lucien. 2010. *Valuing the Unique: The Economics of Singularities*. Princeton, NJ: Princeton University Press.

Lazarsfeld, Paul, and Elihu Katz. 1955. *Personal Influence*. New Jersey: Transaction Publishers.

Willis, Paul E. 1990. *Common Culture: Symbolic Work at Play in the Everyday Cultures of the Young*. Boulder, CO: Westview.

FURTHER READING

Adorno, Theodor W. 1991. "On the Fetish Character in Music and the Regression of Listening." In *The Culture Industry*, edited by J. M. Bernstein. London: Routledge.

Material Culture Studies

SUSAN FALLS
Savannah College of Art and Design, USA

A broad interdisciplinary endeavor addressing empirical and theoretical questions, material culture studies examine the dynamic role things play within social organization and in subjective experience. It is partly through our interactions with material culture (at times referred to as "goods," "commodities," "objects," "artifacts," or even "stuff") that we both interpret and insert ourselves into the world, and thus it is an extremely significant, but oddly under-examined area of research, perhaps because, as many scholars have pointed out, the ubiquity of material culture makes it easy to overlook. If you are reading this book, you are likely surrounded by material culture designed, produced, advertised, exchanged, and consumed in the context of late capitalism; since most commodities contain an aspect of materiality, studies of material culture intersect with work on consumption and political economy.

The history of material culture scholarship is grounded in nineteenth-century museum work, anthropology, archaeology, collecting and exhibition practices, colonialism, and consumerism (Buchli 2002). As the methods of studying human society were revised, the notion of "culture" underwent critique from fields such as anthropology, literary criticism, and geography, and as the use of linguistic and structuralist theory to explicate nonlinguistic "texts" became increasingly fatigued, new questions have appeared about the nature, function, and study of materiality (see Hicks and Beaudry 2010).

The term itself suggests a paradox: "material culture" simultaneously presents material and ideological (cultural) potentialities that can be observed and understood using the tools of the hard sciences, historical, political, and economic analysis, and/or anthropological, sociological, psychological, philosophical, and even literary lenses. Scholars have attempted to reconcile these approaches by exploring (or exploding) the many dichotomies associated with material culture such as production versus consumption, sign versus meaning, gift versus commodity, and object versus subject. Of especial utility to consumer studies have been inroads in research related to identity, global exchange and circulation, inequality, value, agency, capitalism, branding, commodification, and the nature of materiality itself. Much of this work pushes Bourdieu's practice theory (1977) to examine how we not only produce but are produced by the commodities with which we interact.

Contemporary studies draw upon a variety of methods, theories, and concerns to explicate material culture and materiality in general, sometimes through close study of particular objects (Ingold 2012; Miller 2005; Myers 2002). And, with theoretical room for degrees of materiality, even immaterial things like money, math, and social media are included in texts on material culture. Since there are increasingly more immaterial commodities, such as data or service, developments toward immateriality take on special salience for consumption studies. Work that takes on spatial, symbolic, ethnographic, and phenomenological dimensions of material culture also informs consumption studies. The commodity chain approach, for example, tracks the movement of goods through various nodes of activity – production, distribution, consumption, and divestment – and its concomitant regimes of value, be they economic, semiotic, political, or otherwise. Studies on the symbolic nature of goods may use large-scale statistical analysis or linguistic metaphors, usually based in the semiotic analysis derived from Saussure to reveal how material culture can be used to produce, claim, reflect, or read identity along the lines of race, class, gender, nationality, religion, generation, ethnicity, and so on. Ethnographic studies, poised to reveal a subjective relationship with material culture, examine how people interpret material culture in surprising ways. From more philosophical quarters, actor–network theory (ANT) considers objects as they perform on social networks; thing theory uses a creative, interdisciplinary approach to examine how things become objectified and how they assert their presence; and phenomenological approaches connect the sensual to political, economic, and cultural shifts. The *Journal of Material Culture* is a chief resource for following trends and debates in this area.

Future directions in research, theory, and methodology will benefit from a continued critical review of the notion of materiality itself as well as the cognitive action – objectification – required to recognize it in the first place. New investigations include: To what extent and how can material culture be said to embody human characteristics, such as agency, desire, or emotion? Is material culture a universal category? What is the relationship of the virtual to the material? How are images, intellectual property, capital, theory, technology (digital or otherwise), and the body and/or self best understood as special instantiations of material culture? Theorizing an object as an event, process, or field will energize an ontological discussion, but will also advance an approach that takes material culture as a spectacularization of national, political, economic, or historical dynamics but that does not require us to keep things artificially steady. And lastly, shifting away from Saussurean semiosis in favor of an Austinian linguistic paradigm or Peircian semiotic will reveal more about what material culture does in addition to what it means. Answers to these questions impact consumption studies in refiguring our understanding of subject–object relations, processes of acquisition and divestment, as well as interpretation, resistance, and alienation.

SEE ALSO: Brands and Branding; Capitalism; Commodities; Commodity Chains; Consumer Culture; Marketing/Marketing Science; Semiotics; Symbolic Value

REFERENCES

Bourdieu, Pierre. 1977. *Outline of a Theory of Practice*. Cambridge, MA: Harvard University Press.

Buchli, Victor. 2002. "Introduction." In *The Material Culture Reader*, edited by Victor Buchli, 1–22. Oxford: Berg Publishers.

Hicks, Dan, and Mary Beaudry, eds. 2010. *The Oxford Handbook of Material Culture Studies*. Oxford: Oxford University Press.

Ingold, Tim. 2012. "Toward an Ecology of Materials." *Annual Reviews of Anthropology* 4: 427–442.

Miller, Daniel, ed. 2005. *Materiality*. Durham, NC: Duke University Press.

Myers, Fred, ed. 2002. *The Empire of Things: Regimes of Value and Material Culture*, edited by Joan K. O'Donnell and Jane Kepp. School of American Research Advanced Seminar Series. Santa Fe: SAR Press.

McDonaldization

CHIH-CHIN CHEN and GEORGE RITZER
University of Maryland, USA

McDonaldization is George Ritzer's (2013) modern theoretical adaptation of Max Weber's theory on rationalization. Where Weber uses bureaucracy as the model for the process of rationalization, Ritzer uses the fast-food restaurant, especially McDonald's, as the contemporary paradigm of the process. He defines McDonaldization as "the process by which the principles of the fast-food restaurant are coming to dominate more and more sectors of American society as well as of the rest of the world" (Ritzer 2013, 1).

The principles are *efficiency*, defined as the optimum method of getting from one point to another; *calculability*, which designates an emphasis on the quantitative aspects of products and services such as size, price, and speed; *predictability*, or the assurance that products, services, and settings will be very similar, if not entirely identical, over time and in all locales; and *control*, the power exerted over both customers and employees of McDonaldized settings.

These four principles have in various ways and forms found their way into most organizations and institutions in American society, as well as into many other parts of the world. This makes McDonaldization a major aspect of, and force in, the process of globalization. It is a key example of what Ritzer (2007) calls "the globalization of nothing."

Ritzer's critique of McDonaldization is to be found not in the four principles per se, but rather mainly in the idea of *the irrationality of rationality*. McDonaldization has provided many benefits for management, but many disadvantages for consumers (as well as for workers in McDonaldized systems). For example, the efficiency of the restaurant often results in inefficiency for customers.

McDonald's customers must often wait in line or find themselves stuck in a traffic jam in the drive-through lane. Walmart and Costco customers must often buy things in bulk and some of it proves unnecessary and inefficient to transport and store. Automated phone services often keep callers waiting and being transferred from one extension to another, when they could have received much more efficient service from trained customer service representatives. Seemingly efficient methods and processes often prove inefficient for customers, and sometimes even for organizations and their employees.

In a McDonaldized society, more and more work is being performed by the consumers themselves. For example, they take on the work of bank tellers when using ATMs, the work of waiters and buspersons when ordering, eating, and cleaning up in the fast-food restaurants, and the work of customer service representatives when working their way through automated phone directories. Customers are forced to perform more and more work, but they are not paid for their labor. In other words, the focus should be on "prosumers."

McDonaldized settings can also be seen as disenchanted, from the perspective of consumers (Ritzer 2010). That is, they have lost (if they ever had) their magic. Every process, object, and interaction is spelled out, structured, and routinized to the minutest detail and followed closely by both employees and customers. The excitement of the unknown, the mystery of the unpredictable, and people's idiosyncratic interactions are controlled or eliminated by McDonaldized systems. Those who manage McDonaldized settings care less about how good and enjoyable their services and goods are; rather, they focus more on such things as the number of customers served and products sold. McDonaldization's pursuit of quantity has reduced or eliminated its ability to create magical experiences through, for example, the pursuit of authenticity and quality.

McDonaldization has produced "islands of the living dead" (Ritzer 2003), as opposed to Weber's "iron cage." McDonaldization has transformed many settings into individual islands of McDonaldized processes and rules, but there is no overarching bureaucratized society with an iron cage (at least not yet) that compels all settings to operate in the same way. The efficiency produced in one setting may not be replicated in another setting. Thus, people move from island to island (e.g., fast-food restaurant to Wal-Mart) and are led to act like the "living dead" in each setting. Governed by the principles of McDonaldization, each island deadens people by restricting their freedom to think and act independently. The only true freedom available to people is in the non- or less-McDonaldized spaces between islands of the living dead.

In spite of its numerous problems, McDonaldization has its advantages. It has helped to produce monumental abundance for society. A wide variety of goods and services have become accessible to portions of society that found it difficult or impossible to obtain them in the past, at least at affordable prices. For example, medicines and other essentials for survival are now provided to more people than ever, and this is made possible by McDonaldizing the processes and organizations involved in the production of pharmaceuticals. The speed by which goods and services are delivered has increased significantly (e.g., Fedex). The convenience of efficiency also appeals to people who are working longer and have less time to spare. McDonaldized settings' uniform treatment of employees and customers also decreases discrimination based on race, sex, and class.

There are many examples of resistance to the expansion of both McDonald's restaurants and McDonaldization. Some (such as McLibel) directly target McDonald's by pointing out its environmental, cultural, and health threats to society. Others choose to tackle the process itself and the ideology behind it. The Slow Food movement is the most famous organization seeking to protect and promote traditional ways of food production, preparation, and consumption from the threat of the McDonaldized system. Less noticeable struggles in local communities are reported by the media from time to time.

Some approaches, such as "Starbuckization," "IKEAization," and "eBayization," offer alternative explanations and paradigms to deal with the changing landscape of society, especially consumption. Starbuckization offers a softened image of McDonaldization with dramaturgical performances making the customers feel welcome, rather than being harried and rushed as in the case of McDonald's. IKEAization emphasizes the transfer of work from employees to customers. In that, it exemplifies prosumption as well as the process in McDonald's of putting customers to work. eBayization offers an alternative picture of market-directed activity (rather than McDonaldization's centrally controlled system), a variety of products (as opposed to McDonald's limited and predetermined menu), and unpredictable offerings (in contrast to McDonald's predictable products). Even though all of these processes offer interesting and useful perspectives, their structure and leading principles continue to rely heavily on the principles of McDonaldization. Starbucks' success is built on the premise of selling coffee in a McDonaldized grab-'n-go fashion; it would never be able to sustain itself on the revenue from the relatively few sit-in customers. IKEA's products are highly McDonaldized and can even be thought of as pushing the control over customers (really prosumers) into new geospatial settings (e.g., customers are likely to assemble furniture at home in accord with instructions provided by IKEA). eBay's variety and unpredictability are made possible by utilizing a highly McDonaldized infrastructure and interface for all listings and sales.

SEE ALSO: eBay; Globalization and Consumption; Glocalization/Grobalization; Homogenization and Heterogenization; Starbuckization; Wal-Mart

REFERENCES

Ritzer, George. 2003. "Islands of the Living Dead: The Social Geography of McDonaldization." *American Behavioral Scientist* 47(2): 119–136.

Ritzer, George. 2007. *The Globalization of Nothing 2*. Thousand Oaks, CA: Pine Forge Press.

Ritzer, George. 2010. *Enchanting a Disenchanted World*, 3rd ed. Thousand Oaks, CA: Pine Forge Press.

Ritzer, George. 2013. *The McDonaldization of Society 7*. Thousand Oaks, CA: Pine Forge Press/Sage.

Medical Tourism

I. GLENN COHEN and ETHAN PRALL
Harvard Law School, USA

Medical tourism is the travel of patients from a "home country" to a "destination country" in order to seek medical treatment, often for financial reasons. It has become a booming business over the last two decades, with hundreds of thousands of patients moving internationally and millions of dollars in annual revenue accruing to hospitals in a number of developing nations (Cohen 2013a). Medical tourism takes many specific forms, and it can be analyzed according to different categories: for instance, type of service versus type of legal or ethical issue involved. The type of service generally involves either services illegal in both the home and destination countries, services illegal only in the home country ("circumvention tourism"), or services legal in both countries but cheaper or easier to access in the destination country (Cohen 2010a). Legal and ethical issues arise with respect to each of these different types of service.

When services are legal in both the home and destination countries, medical tourism may be motivated by patients' desire to save costs (especially for uninsured patients), to avoid extensive waiting lists, to take advantage of coverage options by a private medical insurer in the home country, or to access a service unavailable in the home country but covered by government-sponsored health insurance (as in the EU). Among the ethical and legal issues this kind of tourism raises is whether the tourist patient receives proper care abroad and follow-up care upon returning home. Furthermore, what baseline governs the assessment of proper care? Is it the care to which the patient is morally entitled, or the care that they are capable of purchasing at home? What are the effects on medical malpractice recovery (Cortez 2008; 2010; Cohen 2010b)?

There are also questions about the ramifications of medical tourism for health care (and consequently patient care) in the home country. Arguments here generally involve whether domestic regulations that drive patients abroad will nevertheless provide a net benefit to them by providing access to health care they would not otherwise receive. Further questions surround the effects of medical tourism on the cost and quality of health care in the home country, and whether increased competition will lead to a race to the top or to the bottom in these categories (Cohen 2010b).

Finally, this kind of medical tourism raises questions about the moral obligations of citizens of the home country to citizens of the destination country. Given that most medical tourists travel from wealthier countries to poorer ones, does medical tourism crowd out indigenous people's access to medical care, and if so, is that unethical? Empirical evidence about the actual affects of medical tourism on health care systems in developing nations is contested and underdeveloped, and there are serious normative questions regarding the obligations of home countries if effects are negative, which in turn may depend on more macro theories of global justice.

Resolving these issues depends, among other things, on coming to grips with the proper place of markets in society, the relationship between enfranchisement and a nation's medical policies, and the propriety of paternalism, as well as practical judgments about the impact of medical tourism on health care systems, the extent of market externalities, and the appropriate means of enforcement.

Regulatory proposals to address these issues vary from information-providing proposals to proposals that restrict patient choice. Procedural barriers often stand in the way of legal remedies for patients, especially in non-plaintiff-friendly legal systems. Regulatory solutions include prohibiting tourism or including mechanisms for insurance or compensation of patients. These issues relate directly to the regulation of health insurance, which presents issues of its own, including questions about the propriety of regulations that prohibit coverage for procedures undergone abroad, the incentives provided by some private insurers to seek treatment abroad, and the coverage that some countries (e.g., in the European Union) provide for cross-border health care (Cohen 2010b).

Circumvention tourism adds new concerns to those just discussed because it involves seeking services that are illegal in the home country. These medical tourists sometimes seek out abortion and assisted suicide services abroad when those procedures are illegal in the home country. Additionally, access to assistive reproductive technologies and commercial surrogacy is severely limited in many countries, resulting in "fertility tourism." Others seek out experimental therapies not approved in the home country, such as stem cell therapies (Cohen 2012a).

Among the issues raised by this kind of medical tourism are the exploitation of poor venders in destination countries, the neonatal and other costs for medical systems in the home country when patients return, the commodification of reproduction and sexuality, and paternalistic arguments for protecting patients. Furthermore, there are questions about the corrupting effects of circumvention tourism upon attitudes in the home country regarding the practice in question. Among the possible interventions home countries can implement to discourage these activities are the extraterritorial criminalization of obtaining these services abroad, and, in the case of fertility tourism, the refusal by the home country to recognize certain legal statuses for children born via these practices (Cohen 2012a).

The final category of medical tourism involves tourism for services illegal in both the home and destination countries. Organ transplantation is the best example of this type of tourism. The venders are often poor residents of developing countries that may have formal prohibitions on selling organs but where extensive black markets persist. There is good evidence from medical and anthropological studies that poor venders who sell an organ experience negative health and financial outcomes. Potential means for curbing "transplant tourism" include professional self-regulation, extraterritorial criminalization, insurance regulation limiting follow-up care in the home country (including payment for medication to avoid tissue rejection), as well as proposals to increase the supply of organs in patients' home countries (Cohen 2013b).

Taking a step back and looking at regulatory practice at a more macro level, we see a dramatic divergence across nations and even across states within a nation. For example, in the United States, Texas has restricted insurers from promoting medical tourism, while California has allowed insurers to cover medical tourism so long as the programs meet specific guidelines (Cohen 2010a). Proposed home country regulatory solutions to medical tourism problems often emphasize the importance of channeling proposals, in particular an independent accreditation or reporting process for venders. Destination countries also can regulate medical tourism, but conflicts of interest between the poor, who would generally benefit from regulation, and those who control the regulatory apparatus often inhibit regulation (Cohen 2012b). Cooperation between home and destination countries via international agreements is also possible, but the interests arrayed against the regulation of medical tourism and the relative laxity of international law on the subject remain significant obstacles to cooperation (Cohen 2010a; 2012b).

SEE ALSO: Economy, Moral Aspects of; Ecotourism; Ethical Consumption

REFERENCES

Cohen, I. Glenn. 2010a. "Medical Tourism: The View from Ten Thousand Feet." *Hastings Center Report* 40: 11–12.

Cohen, I. Glenn. 2010b. "Protecting Patients with Passports: Medical Tourism and the Patient-Protective Argument." *Iowa Law Review* 95: 1467–1566.

Cohen, I. Glenn. 2012a. "Circumvention Tourism." *Cornell Law Review* 97: 1309–1398.

Cohen, I. Glenn. 2012b. "How To Regulate Medical Tourism (And Why It Matters For Bioethics)." *Developing World Bioethics* 12: 9–20.

Cohen, I. Glenn. 2013a. "Introduction." In *The Globalization of Health Care: Legal and Ethical Issues*, edited by I. Glenn Cohen. New York: Oxford University Press.

Cohen, I. Glenn. 2013b. "Transplant Tourism: The Ethics and Regulation of International Markets for Organs." *Journal of Law, Medicine, and Ethics* 41(1): 269–285.

Cortez, Nathan. 2008. "Patients Without Borders: The Emerging Global Market for Patients and the Evolution of Modern Health Care." *Indiana Law Journal* 83: 71–132.

Cortez, Nathan. 2010. "Recalibrating the Legal Risks of Cross-Border Health Care." *Yale Journal of Health Policy, Law, & Ethics* 10: 1–89.

Merchandising

DANIEL THOMAS COOK
Rutgers University–Camden, USA

Merchandising refers mainly to retail practices that seek to sell and promote products. Perhaps the most common form of merchandising is the display and physical grouping of goods in terrestrial selling space. More broadly, merchandising can include the promotion of related goods through physical or visual juxtaposition and association, such as when a film and a food product or food chain are merchandised together. Modern merchandising took shape largely in response to the rise of the large-scale department store and dry goods store in the United States from the late 1800s into the early twentieth century (Leach 1993). In these emporia of products, the arrangement of goods served both practical and tactical ends whereby customers could locate similar goods, such as lingerie, outerwear, or kitchen utensils, in a defined area. The contemporary supermarket stands as exemplar and key site of merchandising encountered on an everyday basis.

Common merchandising tactics include: purposeful placement of products on certain shelves (i.e., eye level for adults, near the floor for children); "end caps," which are displays of particular products at the end of an aisle so as to draw attention to them; "strategic adjacencies" whereby different kinds of goods likely sought after by the same kind of customer are placed near each other (e.g., baby foods and things for mothers might be placed across the shopping aisle from diapers and other baby products); and anchor merchandising whereby highly sought-after goods are located toward the back of stores so as to lead customers past displays of less popular goods to entice purchases.

A convenience for the customer, merchandising also functions as technology of identity and desire to the extent that the characteristics and presumed preferences of particular consumers or categories of consumers are encoded in the placement and display of goods – sometimes defining cultural-consumer categories like "teens" or "homemaker." In the 1930s, for instance, the "toddler" child arose as a merchandising category at a time when it was being recognized as a phase in the early life course of childhood (Cook 2000). Similar affinities between merchandising categories and social identity can be found for consumers based on age, gender, race/ethnicity, sexuality/sexual orientation, and for just about any other self-identified affiliation.

Merchandising has its counterpart in digital spaces with pop-up advertisements, filter bubbles, and complex algorithms like those employed by Netflix and Amazon to target consumers based on past purchases and search activities.

SEE ALSO: Department Stores; Marketing/Marketing Science; Shopping Malls; Supermarkets

REFERENCES

Cook, Daniel Thomas. 2000. "The Rise of 'the Toddler' as Subject and as Merchandising Category in the 1930s." In *The New Means of Consumption*, edited by Mark Gottdiener, 111–130. Lanham, MD: Rowman & Littlefield.

Leach, William. 1993. *Land of Desire: Merchants, Power and the Rise of a New American Culture.* New York: Pantheon.

FURTHER READING

Cook, Daniel Thomas. 2003. "Spatial Biographies of Children's Consumption." *Journal of Consumer Culture* 3(2): 147–169.
Underhill, Paco. 2000. *Why We Buy: The Science of Shopping.* New York: Simon & Schuster.

Methods of Consumer Research

MAGDALENA BIELENIA-GRAJEWSKA
University of Gdansk, Poland

Observing the multidimensionality of consumer research, purchasers' preferences can be analyzed by taking different issues into account. Since one's decisions are guided by, among other things, psychological, social, biological, linguistic, and cultural determinants, consumer research may encompass various areas of study that offer extensive investigation possibilities. Applying diversified methodologies, it is possible to view consumer behavior in different ways, by concentrating on selected determinants or their outcomes in studying how people behave in purchase-related situations.

6S MODEL OF METHODS IN CONSUMER STUDIES

The diverse methods used in investigating the market can be categorized by taking into account the key determinants underlying the processes of investigation. Thus, the 6S model – encompassing stage, setting, sense, stimulus, stakeholders, and scope – can be treated as a complex approach for considering how consumer studies can be investigated. First of all, it should be mentioned that consumer research encompasses studies on different actions related to consumer behavior, in all stages of purchasing activities (pre-purchase, purchase, and post-purchase processes). Thus, consumer research investigates different phases of clients' exposure to the offered merchandise or service, studying how customers learn about products, how they recognize them among competitive merchandise, and how they shape their behavior toward selected items in the post-purchase period. Moreover, consumer research takes into account various stages of researching consumers' behavior. Thus, different methods are required for preparing investigations, selecting research samples, preparing research tools, conducting research activities themselves, collecting data, interpreting data, and presenting them to the public. In addition, research tools may be divided by taking into account the stage of research they are used for or the type of contact intended with respondents.

As far as the research stage is concerned, the tools used in introductory research may include projective techniques that concentrate on eliciting various responses from customers. For example, by presenting a drawing or a word/text, customers are asked to create associations, make some selections, or express their emotions. These techniques are often used by researchers as primary methods that offer the possibility to create more advanced research tools to study some aspects of consumer behaviors in greater detail.

Second, with regard to setting, consumer research may involve similarities and differences of consumer behavior in different purchasing situations and loci; thus, the focus of investigation can be devoted to online and offline behaviors of customers as well as to different places where products are offered, taking into account their outstanding characteristics, such as size, color, and arrangement of the sales area.

As far as stakeholders are concerned, consumer research may be focused on the type of offered merchandise or service and how the given product, because of its features, requires selected methods and tools for attracting customers' attention. In addition, research may concentrate on the product itself or the brand, determining how the relation between these notions and customers is established. Experimental tools may also be selected by analyzing the target consumers in investigations. For example, observing the role of social online networking tools among young customers, and the application of Facebook, Twitter, and other online communication options may prove useful in reaching young customers and eliciting responses from them.

Moreover, customer research may focus on studying a selected sense for determining customer behavior, or how various senses are engaged in the way people recognize and select products. Thus, such studies involve tactile, auditory, or visual aspects of perceiving different products or services. It should be remembered that senses are related to stimuli, especially as far as channels and methods of communication are concerned.

Regarding stimulus, the tools used in consumer research can be categorized by taking into account the inducement used in research (e.g., verbal, auditory, olfactory, or pictorial). For example, consumer research may involve the application of verbal representation (e.g., words, sentences, texts) as well as pictorial notions (e.g., pictures, drawings) in inquiring into the way someone behaves.

In addition, consumer studies can vary by taking into account the scope of investigation (e.g., local, regional, national, and international). For example, cross-cultural studies, directed at showing similarities and differences among consumers located in different countries, have to rely on methodologies that facilitate the collection of data in diversified environments.

QUALITATIVE AND QUANTITATIVE APPROACHES

Methods of consumer research can be classified by taking into account different typologies. One of the possible classifications is applying the notions of quality and quantity in investigating the way individuals perform in purchasing situations. In the case of consumer research, *qualitative studies* are used to research how and why certain decisions are made by analyzing consumer behavior and its determinants. This type of research is flexible in nature, offering the possibility of adjusting the methods and tools to the changing conditions of the environment. Scientists relying in their investigations on qualitative studies can select different methods to collect data, such as observation, interview, or desktop research. On the other hand, *quantitative research* focuses on collecting data (using mathematical and statistical tools) to investigate, for example, how many customers have purchased the merchandise or want to buy the product in the future, or to observe the tendencies in purchasing behaviors (whether it is rising or falling). They include such methods as mathematical models, factor analysis, regression analysis, and break-even analysis. For example, factor analysis is employed to research a relatively high number of variables, facilitating the selection of a small number of variables that can be further researched to study some aspects of consumer behavior (e.g., purchasing preferences). Regression analysis can be used to estimate and forecast consumer behaviors, basing the calculation of predicted behaviors on current ones. Consumer research can also benefit from the methods used in econometrics and operational research. In addition, quantitative studies often rely on testing hypotheses; in the case of consumer research, they can be used to check how estimated consumer behavior matches actual behavior when the data analysis has been done. Another option for extensive research is to use both qualitative and quantitative studies, such as the approach of mixed methods or exploratory sequential design.

DOMAINS OF STUDY AND CONSUMER RESEARCH

Methods used in consumer studies can also be classified by taking into account different domains of research such as marketing studies. The application of marketing investigations to studies on consumers may involve implementing marketing strategies. These tools comprise, among others, gathering secondary and primary research data, undertaking qualitative and quantitative research, and such techniques as interviews, focus groups, and observations.

Other domains that offer methodologies for consumer research include communication and linguistics. One such methodology is the different types of discourse analysis, used for studying the main characteristics of discourse and its relation to the social world. One approach is critical discourse analysis (CDA), which is an interdisciplinary research tool used primarily to study various features and functions of text and talk; it takes into account the economic, cultural, social, and political conditions that shape reality and the way stakeholders perceive different issues presented in different forms of communication. Observing the demands of consumer research, CDA can be performed at different levels to observe the way certain issues are created and presented to consumers in verbal and nonverbal channels of communication. Such analyses may include the study of verbal and pictorial methods of interacting with customers, in online and offline settings, analyzed from the micro, macro, and meso approach. The micro perspective of CDA in consumer research focuses on studying the usage of single words and phrases in shaping customers' attitude to products or services. The word/phrase analysis may encompass studies on the role of metaphors in cognition, perception, and selection of offered merchandise. The meso dimension may focus on larger pieces of information, such as texts, and the way they are perceived by purchasers. The macro dimension encompasses the analysis of relatively large informational content, such as corporate websites, promotional campaigns, and the whole organizational communication policy. Other types of research or scientific subdomains used in language or communication studies can be useful to investigate consumer behavior – such as corpus studies, ethnolinguistics, sociolinguistics, and psycholinguistics. There are also interdisciplinary methods, used, for example, in communication as well as organizational research, such as narrative analysis and storytelling. In storytelling, researchers rely on stories or other forms of narrative produced by consumers to observe their attitudes toward products or services. In addition, methods relying on ethnography (e.g., ethnography of communication) concentrate on cultural issues and cultural phenomena, showing the role of societies and cultures in shaping customer behaviors.

Methods in consumer research can also be divided by considering the sphere of interest (e.g., identity or relations). For example, relations can be studied through the prism of network theories. The application of network perspectives to research on organizations and their stakeholders results from various reasons determining the modern life of companies. One of them is the interest in postmodern organizational studies, focusing on the dynamic nature of companies, the semiotic character of communication, and the changeability of the surrounding environment. Another reason is the popularity of networks in shaping the performance of organizations; modern companies do not exist in a vacuum but have to actively respond to the dynamic situations taking place at both internal and external levels. The third determinant is the increasing role of technology, visible in the importance accorded to technological advancement and online sources of communication. All the above-mentioned factors have led to the popularity of actor–network theory (ANT) in researching organizations. ANT is an approach that stresses the importance of both the human being and objects, broadly understood, in creating and determining the performance of individuals and organizations. This approach highlights the fact that both human and nonhuman actors can be researched in studies on organizations. Thus, both animate and inanimate participants in networks are studied, together with the way they shape the characteristics of the groups and communities they are part of. For example, in the case of organizations, it is possible to study the role of human actors (e.g., managers, employees, and customers) and nonhuman network participants (computers, telephones, and furniture) in shaping corporate dialogue (Bielenia-Grajewska 2011). Narrowing the focus of investigation to consumer research, ANT offers the opportunity to study how both animate and inanimate actors determine the behaviors and preferences of customers. The application of ANT in consumer research may encompass, for example, studies on the role of space or furniture in shops and their implication for purchasing. Another possible field of investigation using the ANT approach is to concentrate on the semiotic aspect of consumer–company organization or the role of social networking tools in shaping customer behaviors in a selected context.

INTERDISCIPLINARY METHODS IN CUSTOMER RESEARCH

Observation is a very popular technique for checking the way individuals behave in market-related situations. One can distinguish between disguised and nondisguised observation. In disguised observations, individuals are not aware that they are being observed by the researcher. Conversely, nondisguised observation focuses on collecting data when an individual is aware that he or she is under scrutiny. Observation may also be performed in different roles by the researchers. For example, a scientist may be an active participant in observation or a passive observer of activities. Observation can also be categorized by taking into account the type of setting under study. Observation in a natural setting involves research taking place where individuals live, work, or stay on an everyday basis. On the other hand, observation in created settings involves the invention of a specific research environment.

Observation may also be planned or unplanned. Planned observation has a fixed structure, with the flow of observation being carefully planned by a researcher before the actual observation takes place. Unplanned observation focuses on how subjects perform in a given setting, without any scenario or stages that have to be taken into account.

As far as other techniques of consumer research are concerned, some scientists use the techniques of questioning, either face to face or at a distance. These include questionnaires (open and closed answers), surveys, and interviews. Other methods of consumer research involve, for example, sending questionnaires to respondents by regular or electronic mail. In addition, methods of consumer research can also be classified by taking into account the channel used for engaging respondents – whether offline and online, for example. To the first group belong such methods of communication as face-to-face interviews, phone interviews, and sending questionnaires by regular post. As far as the online dimension of research is concerned, there are different forms of e-consumer research, such as online interviews and surveys, conducted at websites, forums, or using different forms of social networking tools.

In addition, consumer studies can also be researched from the perspective of professionals, being specialists in a given consumer domain. For example, expert panels are devoted to gathering a given number of individuals to elicit their knowledge. Methods in consumer studies may be categorized by the number of variables studied as well as the relation between them. As Mazzocchi (2008) describes, such methods as structural equation models offer the possibility of studying dependent and explanatory variables as well as latent ones. The incorporation of factor analysis into a regression model offers a more complex way of studying different variables. When researchers want to observe how consumption changes in the face of changing factors, consumer panels turn out to be an effective information source (Mazzocchi 2008). In this technique, individuals are interviewed over time by taking part in surveys to check how their preferences evolve.

PERSPECTIVES FOR THE FUTURE: NEUROSCIENCE AND CONSUMER RESEARCH

The growing role of neuroscience in various modern disciplines has also concerned modern management and has led to the development of international neuromanagement, with such subdomains as international neurobusiness, international neurostrategy, neuromarketing, neuroentrepreneurship, and neuroethics (Bielenia-Grajewska 2013). There are two main areas of study that contribute, in terms of findings and research methods, to the neuroscientific approach to consumer studies – neuromarketing and consumer neuroscience.

Neuromarketing includes looking at the way the brain reacts to marketing stimuli. Neuromarketing studies include, among other things, investigations of how certain brain areas react to marketing-related stimuli and, consequently, shape customers' preferences and subsequent purchasing decisions. In neuromarketing the focus is often placed on reward-related brain areas (e.g., the nucleus accumbens and orbitofrontal cortex), since they are said to reflect the choices made by consumers. For example, if merchandise causes a higher response in the nucleus accumbens, it shows a preference for the product (Haynes 2011).

Another important neuromanagement study is neuroethics. Its application in the field of consumer research is popular for many reasons. One of them is the way the research is conducted and whether ethics is respected when subjects are tested with the use of neuroscientific equipment. Another layer of investigation can be the attitude of stakeholders to such aspects as organizational performance as corporate social responsibility (CSR). Thus, researchers can study how corporate policies related to moral issues are perceived by individuals, and how this perception shapes their purchasing decisions. As far as the neuroscientific tools used in consumer research are concerned, scientists rely on noninvasive techniques since these do not involve risks for participants. For example, functional magnetic resonance imaging (fMRI), a neuroimaging technique relying on magnetic resonance, is employed to observe brain activities. In fMRI testing, a participant is placed in a special machine and asked to lie still for 60–90 minutes. The first stage

(6–15 minutes) of an experiment is devoted to doing anatomical/structural scans of the brain. Later stages concentrate on the active participation of a subject in an experiment. The subject may be asked to do some activities such as answering questions or selecting pictures. For example, a stimulus appears on a screen and the participant is asked to select the button with the correct response. While the tasks are executed by the participant, the BOLD signal (blood oxygen level depending) is recorded, which allows the observer to see which brain areas are active and which are inactive when certain activities are performed. The data obtained are later compared with the control scans from the first stage of the experiment (Kenning, Plassmann, and Ahlert 2007).

SEE ALSO: Consumer Behavior

REFERENCES

Bielenia-Grajewska, Magdalena. 2011. "A Potential Application of Actor Network Theory in Organizational Studies: The Company as an Ecosystem and Its Power Relations from the ANT Perspective." In *Actor–Network Theory and Technology Innovation: Advancement and New Concepts*, edited by Arthur Tatnall, 247–258. Hershey, PA: Information Science Reference.

Bielenia-Grajewska, Magdalena. 2013. "International Neuromanagement." In *The Routledge Companion to International Management Education*, edited by Denise Tsang, Hamid H. Kazeroony, and Guy Ellis, 358–373. Abingdon, UK: Routledge.

Haynes, John-Dylan. 2011. "Brain Reading: Decoding Mental States from Brain Activity in Humans." In *Oxford Handbook of Neuroethics*, edited by Judy Illes and Barbara J. Sahakian, 3–14. Oxford: Oxford University Press.

Kenning, Peter, Hilke Plassmann, and Dieter Ahlert. 2007. "Applications of Functional Magnetic Resonance Imaging for Market Research." *Qualitative Market Research: An International Journal* 10(2): 135–152.

Mazzocchi, Mario. 2008. *Statistics for Marketing and Consumer Research*. London: Sage.

FURTHER READING

Fitchett, James, and Andrea Davies. 2013. *Consumer Research Methods*. Thousand Oaks, CA: Sage.

Helander, Martin G., and Khalid Halimahtun. 2012. "Affective Engineering and Design." In *Handbook of Human Factors and Ergonomics*, edited by Gavriel Salvendy, 569–595. Hoboken, NJ: John Wiley & Sons.

Levy, Sidney J. 1999. *Brand, Consumers, Symbols and Research*. Thousand Oaks, CA: Sage.

Ryan, Michael J. 1982. "Behavioral Intention Formation: The Interdependency of Attitudinal and Social Influence Variables." *Journal of Consumer Research* 9: 263–278.

Stone, Merlin, Alison Bond, and Bryan Foss. 2004. *Consumer Insight: How to Use Data and Market Research to Get Closer to Your Customer*. London: Kogan Page.

Metrosexual

BENJAMIN HALLIGAN
University of Salford, UK

A metrosexual is commonly understood, in the United States and British use of the term, to be a young man who engages in self-grooming to the betterment of his appearance without concern about meeting expectations of masculine patterns of behavior. That is, the metrosexual male will attend to his clothes and hair, will employ hair conditioners, skin creams and moisturizers, fake tans and hair dyes, with the understanding that this will render him more attractive to the opposite sex. Such traditionally female concerns with appearance are not perceived to be a self-imposed feminization, and so a challenge to his heterosexuality, but rather an enhancement of his sexual potential, his "pulling power." Hence, the term "metro"-sexual is a play on "heterosexual" so as to make clear that attentiveness to personal appearance in this way does not signal homosexual attraction.

It is conjectured that females, encountering the metrosexual male, find evidenced a concern with outward appearance, and thus the potential of the male to be "arm candy" (i.e., an attractive public partner), and preferable to the rough and ready males otherwise available (unmoisturized, clothed in a utilitarian manner, haircuts standardized and manageable, and carrying the sweat and wear of the day). This concern for appearance, furthermore, has been surmised as indicative of intelligence, character, and a general concern for others (i.e., the "sensitive man"; not homophobic or racist or given to violence; a reader; familiar with domestic chores), and a creative temperament (the so-called "Renaissance man" and then "new man" of the late 1980s and onwards).

Metrosexuality also denotes upward mobility: freed from the blue-collar environs of the building site, the factory floor, the lorry cab, and so on, the metrosexual male comes to understand the importance of affective labor in the white-collar environs of the office and boardroom, and the upscale café. The metrosexual represents an economic progression from the male role models adopted by the earlier generations of an industrial period. With embourgeoisement comes the migration from rural to urban areas, and the consolidation of city-center lifestyles, and so the phenomenon of metrosexuality is understood to germinate and occur in the centers of society – the metropolitan areas and their forms of lifestyles. Indeed, the earliest uses of the term "metrosexual" in the popular press, in the mid-1990s, coincide with urban regeneration and the repopulation of formerly desolate city centers. However, the metrosexual clearly claims a cultural antecedent in the "dandy," famously personified by George Bryan "Beau" Brummell of early eighteenth-century Britain.

Such themes of current modes of male presentation and upward mobility underlie the advertising campaigns for male skin moisturizers (which are often provided with the caveat that they are related to shaving), hair conditioners, and the sexualization of the male body in advertisements for male underwear. In this way, the social dividend of upward mobility – sexual activity – is understood to be available via a new beauty regime and form of public display, and new concerns of self-presentation, now appropriate to the social spaces of the urban conurbation.

SEE ALSO: Conspicuous Consumption; Consumption and Identity; Dandyism; Fashion; *Flâneur/Flânerie*

FURTHER READING

Coad, David. 2008. *The Metrosexual.* New York: SUNY Press.

Edwards, Tim. 2005. *Cultures of Masculinity.* London: Routledge.

Modernization Theory

MARTHA A. MARTINEZ
DePaul University, USA

Modernization theory is a social science paradigm created after World War II by researchers in the United States to explain the increased importance of "Third World" or "developing" countries, comprised mostly of former colonial territories in Asia, Latin America, and Africa. The theory, heavily based on the nineteenth-century sociological perspective known as functionalism, considers societies to be similar to complex biological organisms. It assumes that all societies are involved in a linear, evolutionary process that transforms traditional societies into modern ones, often labeled as "progress" or "development." "Modern" societies are defined as fitting the characteristics of the United States and Western Europe during the mid-twentieth century – all other types of societies are characterized as traditional.

The basic characteristics of a modern society are as follows: high levels of industrialization and urbanization, nuclear family structure, high rates of spatial and economic mobility, self-sustained economic growth through local demand, and high levels of mass consumption. Democratization was also seen as integral to the modernization process, as only societies with liberal democracies had achieved high levels of modernization. The theory did not consider economic, social, and political equality between men and women to be a part of modernization.

Modernization theory asserts that transitions from traditional to modern societies are systemic and organic, and the modernization of one area positively affects that of others – industrialization increases modern consumption, which in turn transforms social values, leading to an increase in entrepreneurship and economic activity. All societies are theorized to converge to a similar modern structure, eradicating local differences. The transition from the traditional to the modern is thought to be a natural internal process for all societies. Contact with and help from Western societies are seen as instrumental in this process, a view in which "underdeveloped" countries can learn from Western history to find shorter, less painful paths toward the ideal of modernization. Elites of all kinds are seen as the key actors of the modernizing process as they are positioned as the class that adapts technologies, assimilates values and patterns of actions, and imports financial, industrial, and educational models to the needy and needful nations.

An alternative to Marxist ideas, the US government used modernization theory as a framework for international policy that justified various interventions in developing countries. In 1960 Walt Rostow identified a lack of investment capital as one of the main obstacles for the development of traditional societies and proposed foreign aid as a tool to solve this problem. Not surprisingly, foreign aid has become a cornerstone of US foreign policy and a key tool for influencing those societies without military intervention. The US government has also used modernization theory to justify close relationships with nonsocialist authoritarian regimes under the assumption that capitalism, industrialization, and an alignment with US interests will lead to democratic development.

Many intellectuals and politicians in "developing" countries found modernization theory both condescending and ethnocentric. As a challenge to the theory, social scientists developed dependency theory, which holds that contact between Western and so-called underdeveloped countries creates financial, technological, and industrial dependencies that are the real obstacles to modernization. Power imbalances between former colonies and imperial rulers create a captive, extractive, and exploitative relationship that perpetuates stagnation and underdevelopment. Saddled with this dependency, underdeveloped countries can never become engines of their own growth and will always lag behind the developed world. Modernization theory then becomes a justification for new forms of cultural and economic imperialism.

At the end of the 1980s modernization theory lost influence as a social science paradigm. The fall of the Soviet Union and the implosion of most communist regimes made it less important for the United States to directly fight socialism with government programs. Instead, neoliberalism became the dominant paradigm for international political relations, placing emphasis on free trade and economic liberalization as the sources of development. Simultaneously, globalization has proved many of the assumptions of modernization theory invalid, particularly those related to the superiority of the West and the predicted conversion to a single type of modern society.

One area in which modernization theory continues to have some influence is environmental sociology. In a limited application of the original theory, ecological modernization theory is focused on finding an answer to the crisis created by excessive industrial development. It holds that further modernization is the solution to environmental problems created by rapid industrialization – the continuous process of the rationalization of production will lead to the development of increasingly environmentally friendly technologies, which in turn will solve our current resource and pollution problems. The theory is criticized for ignoring that new technologies cannot counteract the expansion of conspicuous consumption around the world.

SEE ALSO: Americanization; Behavioral Economics and Consumption; Capitalism; Globalization and Consumption

FURTHER READING

Carolan, Michael S. 2004. "Ecological Modernization Theory: What About Consumption." *Society and Natural Resources* 17: 247–260.

Przeworski, Adam, and Fernando Limongi. 1997. "Modernization: Theories and Facts." *World Politics* 49 (January): 155–183.

Spaargaren, Gert. 2000. "Ecological Modernization Theory and Domestic Consumption." *Journal of Environmental Policy and Planning* 2(4): 323–335.

Money

SIMONE POLILLO
University of Virginia, USA

While money sits at the intersection of culture, politics, and economics, it is sociology that has generated some of the most novel insights over the past few decades. Like the broader field of economic sociology within which it is located, the sociology of money has grown by leaps and bounds, benefiting from the theoretically eclectic and multi-method nature of the field. Remarkably though, and in this respect unlike economic sociology, this growth was not achieved by defining the sociological study of money in opposition to mainstream economics. Rather, it resulted from theoretical concerns generated within sociology itself. This is partly because economists (at least economists working within the neoclassical mainstream) have long stopped treating money as a topic worthy of exploration in its own terms. Since the demise of the German Historical School at the turn of the twentieth century, economists have embraced marginal analysis, utility functions, and general equilibrium. Money subsequently ceased capturing the attention of the mainstream: when it was analyzed, it was in the context of critiques of monetary policy. Concerned with "real" as opposed to the "financial," economists gave money little analytical attention.

But the internal impetus driving the development of the sociology of money depended in greater part on the important theoretical status of its object of analysis in sociology at large. To be sure, Talcott Parsons's cozy intellectual agreement with economics never stopped sociologists from going beyond the social consequences of economic institutions and probing the social conditions that made those economic institutions possible to begin with. But initially, this was not the case with money. Drawing from the critical tradition dating back to Marx and Simmel that considered money as the "great leveler" of social distinctions, sociologists were taken more by the metaphorical potential of money than by the sociological challenges it represented. Later, anthropologists inspired by the work of Karl Polanyi and the substantivist school of economic anthropology delineated a great divide between societies where economic exchange was subsumed under societal regulation, and modern, "market" societies where money acquired a life of its own. Money became a symbol of some of the defining concepts of the discipline, such as the division of labor (where money was understood to facilitate exchange across distant social networks), modernity (where money was understood as breaking down community and favoring anonymous exchange instead), and the impersonality of markets as opposed to the depth of community bonds (where the narrative similarly depicted money as infusing a logic of cold calculation into exchanges that were originally governed by reciprocity and mutual obligation).

In spite of the impeccable intellectual pedigree of this lineage, scholars investigating different realms of monetary production and exchange became increasingly unhappy with what they saw as its constraining limitations. The new sociology of money was thus born out of dissatisfaction with the inability of existing sociological assumptions to explain important aspects of money.

Early shots against the idea that money worked as a great equalizer were fired by empirical analyses of the power elite, especially in the United States, and then in the context of productive controversies about the effects that radical changes in the broader economy were allegedly having on finance. Both within specific financial markets and within the financial sector as a whole, scholars began documenting the gradual displacement of traditional banks by new financial actors, some of which were created by nonfinancial institutions (e.g., General Motors), others evolving out of pre-existing financial arrangements (e.g., institutional investors), yet others emerging from competing financial centers outside the United States (especially London and the "petrodollar" market). The complex picture drawn by these analyses, and later somewhat imprecisely crystallized under the rubric of "financialization," revealed the multilayered nature of financial instruments, and perhaps less explicitly, but with deeper empirical implications, sketched the contradictory nature of the relationship between money and political authority. As the international foundations for monetary stability inscribed in the Bretton Woods regime were quickly eroding, money seemed to multiply, with new pools of capital becoming the basis for speculative maneuvers aimed at weakening the power elite (the junk bond revolution initiated by Michael Milken can be understood in this vein), and yet failing to change the rules of the game without some accommodating moves by political authorities and regulatory agencies (as investigations of the case of Milken similarly revealed).

With this expansion of the financial sector as a backdrop, the sociology of money took off in two directions. Historical sociologists of capitalism like Geoffrey Ingham, in the wake of studies of the traditionally *commercial* nature of British capitalism, returned to the original controversy over money that had displaced it from economics as a subject of study, and rebuilt a "state-centered" or neo-chartalist theory of money (Ingham 2004). In this view, money is an institution, backed by an authority that establishes a system of accounting for value that all those who are subject to the authority then have to accept. And in modern capitalism, whatever currency the state will ask its citizens to pay taxes in, that currency will become money. The nature of modern money is "chartalist": it is a token claim to value whose unit of account and acceptability is enforced by the state through fiscal policy. What matters to money is that it is denominated in the monetary units prescribed by the state. This state-centered perspective as a consequence puts much emphasis on the fiscal origins of money, and the coercive aspects of revenue extraction. Moreover, it turns a critical eye on perspectives emphasizing the multiplication of monetary and financial media associated with financialization.

The second direction in which the sociology of money developed drew not so much from the political economy tradition of understanding the relationship between states and markets, but from the cultural sociology of the economy. Rather than investigating what it takes for a stable money to become the basis for the measurement of value, this cultural sociology of money directed attention to how individuals negotiate the potentially contradictory logics implied by self-interested and collective goals, and between morality and market-based exchange. While important ethnographic and structural studies of financial markets revealed the different cultural and moral orientations that emerge in different institutional contexts, it was with the work of Viviana Zelizer that the study of the moral aspects of money began attracting the attention of scholars from other subdisciplines within sociology.

The premise of Zelizer's approach is that we can understand money only if we focus on actual social practices, and that these social practices reveal that people constantly transform or "earmark" money (Zelizer 1994). Thus, in turn-of-the-century United States, just as the federal government attempted to tighten control over the dollar, money "multiplied both within households and in public settings. Even prisons debated the right kind of money for inmates, while some orphan asylums and foster care supervisors proposed a separate currency for dependent children," to give a few examples (1994, 17).

The systematic analysis of the ways social relations affect money yields a startling conclusion: modern money is special-purpose, its uses restricted by normative and cultural constraints; the fact that it takes multiple forms and shapes *is* its core aspect. Money always comes to be invested with local significance in and of itself. Where its previous, specialized purposes are questioned, individuals engage in frantic efforts to create new distinctions congruent with the social relations at hand.

Zelizer's later work systematizes her perspective with the concept of "circuits of commerce." The focus is on three aspects: a set of bounded social relations that are demarcated from relations with outsiders; a set of meanings and practices attached to those relations; and a distinctive kind of media that circulates within the circuit. A variety of examples share such features: migrant remittance networks and rotating credit and savings unions; local currencies and microcredit schemes. This perspective, in turn, has motivated a variety of new and original work, focusing, for instance, on how money and commercial exchange rely on dramaturgical performances that, depending on the nature of the transaction, communicate important aspects about the underlying relationship between the parties (such as mutual commitment or the authenticity of the product) (Wherry 2008); on how global flows of capital follow actual social networks between investors and hosts, mediated by political institutions and cultural understandings (Bandelj 2011); and on how the value of difficult-to-price objects, like works of art, results more from the kinds of narratives that critics and artists build around themselves and the art they produce/sell than from market forces narrowly driven by cost–benefit considerations (Velthuis 2007).

Important challenges remain nonetheless. One is to systematically theorize the relationship between, on the one hand, the macro-determinants of money, and the push toward stability and uniformity that attention to the political origins of money quickly reveals; and on the other hand, the micro-sociology of money, especially its finding that, upon scrutiny, money's homogeneity quickly disappears in social interactions, whether those interactions are mundane or take place in official financial arenas. In this vein, work by Lainer-Vos (2013) examines the sociotechnical mechanisms that turn government bonds into instruments of national attachment; Delaney (2012) investigates how organizational and occupational culture affects how people think about money, and thus how they use it. As money continues being at the center of intellectual attention as well as public debate, there is no doubt that even more exciting developments lie ahead for the sociology of money.

SEE ALSO: Capitalism; Economy, Moral Aspects of; Finance/Financial Markets; Governmentality and Consumer Culture

REFERENCES

Bandelj, Nina. 2011. *From Communists to Foreign Capitalists: The Social Foundations of Foreign Direct Investment in Postsocialist Europe*. Princeton, NJ: Princeton University Press.

Delaney, Kevin J. 2012. *Money at Work: On the Job with Priests, Poker Players and Hedge Fund Traders*. New York: New York University Press.

Ingham, Geoffrey. 2004. *The Nature of Money*. Cambridge, UK: Polity.

Lainer-Vos, Dan. 2013. *Sinews of the Nation: Constructing Irish and Zionist Bonds in the United States*. Hoboken, NJ: John Wiley & Sons.

Velthuis, Olav. 2007. *Talking Prices: Symbolic Meanings of Prices on the Market for Contemporary Art*. Princeton, NJ: Princeton University Press.

Wherry, Frederick F. 2008. *Global Markets and Local Crafts: Thailand and Costa Rica Compared*. Baltimore, MD: Johns Hopkins University Press.

Zelizer, Viviana. 1994. *The Social Meaning of Money*. New York: Basic Books.

Mothers/Motherhood

STEPHANIE O'DONOHOE
University of Edinburgh Business School, UK

"Mother" is a fundamentally relational identity: it comes into being with the creation or arrival of a child, who is produced in turn by some form of interaction between a man and a woman and is often raised by parents living together. From the moment a pregnancy is made public, a mother-to-be typically finds herself renegotiating relationships with others – including family, friends, colleagues, health professionals, and even strangers – and is subject to broader societal norms and cultural discourses of motherhood. Indeed, the term "expectant mother" may be misleading, privileging as it does the expectations that mothers have, rather than the expectations to which they are subjected. Thus mothering as an experience is intertwined with motherhood as an institution or an ideal. As Thomson et al. (2011) observe in the context of the United Kingdom, despite the veneer of equality provided by contemporary discourses of "parenting," raising children is still seen primarily as a mother's work. Thus, mothering involves agency in both senses of the word – choices have to be made, and made in the interests of a child who is vulnerable and dependent, at least in the early years. This duty of care, combined with concerns about raising children in a risk society, leads to mothers being held morally and socially responsible for virtually every aspect of children's lives (Cook 2013). It is hardly surprising, then, that the archetypes of the good and bad mother loom large in societal and cultural discourse, and that the struggles to be (and be seen as) a good mother feature prominently in many studies of mothering experiences.

Motherhood is not just socially constructed; it has to be materialized, and good mothering in consumer culture involves "getting THINGS right" (Miller 2011). The extent to which goods and consumption pervade experiences of mothering, particularly in contemporary Western markets, is highlighted in edited collections drawing on a range of disciplines (Taylor, Layne, and Wozniak 2004; Cook 2013; O'Donohoe et al. 2014). Even before conception, women are encouraged to take food supplements such as folic acid in anticipation of pregnancy, and expectant mothers are surrounded by often conflicting prescriptions about what food and drink to consume and what to avoid in order to protect their baby. Recent decades have challenged the sequestration of the pregnant body, and while that may be liberating in some respects, it has also led to new aesthetic norms, heightened by popular and celebrity culture creations such as the "yummy mummy," so that pregnant women find their dress, grooming, and body shape subject to greater surveillance than in previous generations. Early motherhood is not just a period of intensive acquisition as baby goods are bought, borrowed, or gifted; it ushers in another phase of consumer socialization, as women learn what to provide for their baby from many sources including friends, family, retailers, books, magazines, advertising, and other mothers encountered in person or via online networks such as Mumsnet. Limited product knowledge, combined with an overwhelming array of alternatives and moral discourses surrounding the good mother can leave new mothers feeling confused and vulnerable, even if they have the economic wherewithal to buy what they think is best. How can they tell which is the safest car seat or mattress, for example, and what should they feed their baby? If mothers work outside the home, what child-care solution is best? As their children grow, new preoccupations emerge: how educational are their children's toys, how much screen time is too much, or should they move home to gain access to a better school? Low-income mothers face different and often distressing "choices" as they work out what can be sacrificed to protect their children from the stigma of not having the things considered normal for their peer group. In other cases, women may struggle to be seen as "real," let alone "good" mothers, because their children are dead or biologically unrelated, for example (Taylor, Layne, and Wozniak 2004). A key theme emerging from many studies of mothers as consumers (regardless of their economic, social, or employment status) is the challenge of working out for themselves, and negotiating with others, what constitutes being a good enough mother in the context of their particular circumstances. Consumption choices and practices are often bound up with these negotiations.

The commercialization and commodification of motherhood has been challenged in many contexts, nowhere more so than where motherhood itself is seen to be bought and sold, through expensive infertility treatment or surrogacy arrangements, for example, or through fees paid to adoption agencies or expenses paid to birth mothers.

SEE ALSO: Consumer Culture Theory (CCT); Consumer Socialization; Consumers, Flawed; Consumption and Identity; Femininities; Gender and Consumer Culture

REFERENCES

Cook, Daniel Thomas, ed. 2013. "Producing Motherhoods in/through Consumption." *Journal of Consumer Culture* 13(2) (special issue).

Miller, Daniel. 2011. "Getting THINGS Right: Motherhood and Material Culture." *Studies in the Maternal* 3(2). Accessed July 2, 2014. www.mamsie.bbk.ac.uk.

O'Donohoe, Stephanie, Margaret Hogg, Pauline Maclaran, Lydia Martens, and Lorna Stevens, eds. 2014. *Motherhoods, Markets and Consumption: The Making of Mothers in Contemporary Western Cultures*. London: Routledge.

Taylor, Janelle S., Linda L. Layne, and Danielle F. Wozniak, eds. 2004. *Consuming Motherhood*. New Brunswick, NJ: Rutgers University Press.
Thomson, Rachel, Mary Jane Kehily, Lucy Hadfield, and Sue Sharpe. 2011. *Making Modern Mothers*. Bristol: Policy Press.

Music and Consumer Experience

JOHN T. LANG
Occidental College, USA

Consumers are besieged by music. Corporations use music to shape consumer experience and purchasing behaviors, to build emotional connections with consumers, and to enhance the corporate brand image.

Auditory cues can and do modulate many different aspects of consumer perception and behavior in retail environments. For example, people move more slowly in retail environments featuring slow tempo or quiet music. This means that retailers often use slower, softer music when they want customers to linger. However, in fast-paced restaurants or bars, where there is quick table turnover, increasing the loudness, or beats per minute, of background music can result in a significant increase in rate of consumption of food and drink as well as in the overall amount that people consume.

Moreover, ambient music and purposefully programmed sound is such a taken-for-granted element of a built space that consumers notice only when they enter a music-free environment. Although it is a typically overlooked aesthetic structure, sound is an important design element of a built space devoted to consumerism. Music directs consumers to places of consumption. It also keeps out the unwanted noises of the commercial infrastructure such as heating and cooling systems, hard vertical and horizontal surfaces that produce echoes, random utterances and conversations, as well as the general social scene and traffic noise outside of the commercial space. As such, companies use background music and prepared soundscapes to mask undesirable noise and sounds in their environment and to enhance the aesthetic appeal of their business.

Stores often use these preprogrammed playlists to be heard by consumers, not listened to. This means that many, if not most, consumers are not entirely aware of the programmed soundscape. Though background music may be music-like in its content, it is noise-like in its purpose in that it is creating an atmosphere. For example, playing the sounds of a babbling brook would promote a soothing atmosphere, just as uplifting popular music in the hallways of a shopping mall promotes a social atmosphere.

Founded in 1934, Muzak carved out a longstanding niche by providing and distributing background music to retail stores and other companies. The company was so successful that its name became synonymous with benign background music, a connotation that was not often flattering. Despite providing background music to about 300,000 US locations such as restaurants, malls, and hotels, with revenues of almost US$200 million, the company filed for bankruptcy in 2009. After emerging from bankruptcy in 2010 and restructuring their corporate offerings, Mood Media purchased Muzak in 2011. Though Mood Media officially retired the name "Muzak" in 2013, the company will be remembered as a pioneer in the commercial use of music to produce a certain mood or response from consumers.

Music that consumers experience is, today, likely the result of planning, organization, and monitoring by a multi-sensory branding company such as Mood Media or PlayNetwork who sell plentiful preprogrammed playlists to all manner of clients. Whether you are in a library, a café, a shopping mall, or a restaurant, the scene is likely (unobtrusively) filled with music or some aural backdrop.

Of course, multi-sensory branding firms have not cornered the market on music commoditization, and many companies have moved their background music business in-house. Starbucks, for example, treats music as an active commodity, incorporating music into its global corporate culture. Though their strategy regarding in-store music sales and promotion has changed several times in the last decade, an in-house team selects all of the music played in their stores, helping to maintain a consistent brand image.

Music is a significant part of popular culture and people's everyday lives. Advertisers and agencies have understood this for a long time, leading them to incorporate jingles and popular music into advertising. Jingles are short tunes that explicitly promote a product or a brand. For example, State Farm has used Barry Manilow's "Like a Good Neighbor" jingle for 40 years. In contrast, popular music originally intended for a general listening audience is increasingly being used for specific commercial interests. For example, in the last decade the Apple corporation has used a variety of pop music in its ads for the iPod, iPhone, and its laptop computers. Both of these forms of music, jingles and pop, can become uniquely attached to a brand.

As a characteristic aesthetic element, particular music in advertising can become a distinctive asset for a company and an extension of a brand for consumers. This form of sonic distinction can extend to sound logos and sound trademarks. A sound logo is a short distinctive melody or other sequence of sound, mostly positioned at the beginning or ending of a commercial. It can be seen as the acoustic equivalent of a visual logo. For example, Walter Werzowa composed the five musical tones heard in every commercial for Intel Corporation and for computers that use its chips. Those tones are intended to evoke innovation and trouble-shooting skills while also sounding corporate and inviting. The 1996 World Trade Organization Agreement on Trade-Related Aspects of Intellectual Property Rights expanded the legal definition of trademark to encompass sound. A sound trademark is when sound is used to perform the trademark function of uniquely identifying the commercial origin of products or services. The National Broadcasting Company (NBC) chimes were the first sound trademark to be officially accepted by the US Patent and Trademark Office.

In summary, music provides a set of aesthetic and commercial cues, beyond visual and other sensory practices, for consumers and corporations. In this manner, music is intricately intertwined with commercial symbols, practices, and environments.

SEE ALSO: Advertising; Brands and Branding; Marketing/Marketing Science; Shopping; Shopping Malls

FURTHER READING

Allan, David. 2006. "Effects of Popular Music in Advertising on Attention and Memory." *Journal of Advertising Research* 46(4): 434–444.

DeNora, Tia. 2000. *Music in Everyday Life*. Cambridge: Cambridge University Press.

DeNora, Tia, and Sophie Belcher. 2000. "'When You're Trying Something on You Picture Yourself in a Place Where They Are Playing This Kind of Music'– Musically Sponsored Agency in the British Clothing Retail Sector." *The Sociological Review* 48(1): 80–101. doi:10.1111/1467-954X.00204.

Garlin, Francine V., and Katherine Owen. 2006. "Setting the Tone with the Tune: A Meta-analytic Review of the Effects of Background Music in Retail Settings." *Journal of Business Research* 59(6): 755–764. doi:10.1016/j.jbusres.2006.01.013.

Klein, Bethany. 2010. *As Heard on TV: Popular Music in Advertising*. Farnham, UK: Ashgate.

Lanza, Joseph. 2004. *Elevator Music: A Surreal History of Muzak, Easy-Listening, and Other Moodsong*. Ann Arbor: University of Michigan Press.

Milliman, Ronald E. 1982. "Using Background Music to Affect the Behavior of Supermarket Shoppers." *Journal of Marketing* 46(3): 86–91.

Milliman, Ronald E. 1986. "The Influence of Background Music on the Behavior of Restaurant Patrons." *Journal of Consumer Research* 13(2): 286–289.

North, Adrian C., Amber Shilcock, and David J. Hargreaves. 2003. "The Effect of Musical Style on Restaurant Customers' Spending." *Environment and Behavior* 35(5): 712–718. doi:10.1177/0013916503254749.

Prichard, Craig, Marek Korczynski, and Michael Elmes. 2007. "Music at Work: An Introduction." *Group & Organization Management* 32(1): 4–21. doi:10.1177/1059601106294485.

Scott, Linda M. 1990. "Understanding Jingles and Needledrop: A Rhetorical Approach to Music in Advertising." *Journal of Consumer Research* 17(2): 223–236. doi:10.2307/2626814.

Sterne, Jonathan. 1997. "Sounds Like the Mall of America: Programmed Music and the Architectonics of Commercial Space." *Ethnomusicology* 41(1): 22–50. doi:10.2307/852577.

Zampini, Massimiliano, and Charles Spence. 2010. "Assessing the Role of Sound in the Perception of Food and Drink." *Chemosensory Perception* 3(1): 57–67. doi:10.1007/s12078-010-9064-2.

N

Narcissism

YOK-FONG PAAT
University of Texas at El Paso, USA

The concept of narcissism encompasses excessive self-love, self-aggrandizing, and self-serving. While it has been studied as a bidirectional model that calls for two continua, in which one characterizes the grandiose sense of self while the other features vulnerable self-confidence, it is regarded as a social maladjustment that can put a person at risk for relational strain and self-destructive lifestyle. The consumption behaviors of narcissistic consumers parallel their extravagant personality in other aspects of their lives. Overall, their overemphasis on self-importance and craving the spotlight are detrimental to their financial welfare and general well-being.

Narcissism, which is frequently characterized by a personality disorder that connotes self-absorbed behaviors such as an excessive and inflated sense of self-centeredness, egocentrism, and self-admiration, was first introduced in Greek mythology. In ancient Greek folklore, Narcissus was a young man who fell in love with his self-image but died from obsession with his own beauty. While pathological narcissism is diagnosed based on the distinguishing criteria outlined in the American Psychiatric Association's *Diagnostic and Statistical Manual of Mental Disorders* (i.e., DSM-IV-TR), the modern operationalization of the narcissistic personality disorder often falls on the spectrum between an overly confident, grandiose narcissist and an exploitative but vulnerable narcissist. Under the broad domain of this dysfunctional disorder, however, individuals exhibiting certain levels of narcissistic behaviors tend to hold a self-inflated perception about themselves, leading them to exaggerate their self-importance in relation to others. In his book *The Culture of Narcissism* (1978), historian Christopher Lasch argues that the contemporary generation has become increasingly enmeshed in the culture of self-absorption that propels them to seek constant gratification in many aspects of their lifestyle.

Due to a strong belief in their superiority, narcissists value themselves highly with respect to their intelligence, abilities, popularity, as well as appearance. Becoming arrogant about their own capacities is just one of the hallmarks of their socially impaired expression; many narcissists fantasize about future success, crave admiration, and seek social approval publicly and frequently at the expense of others in order to bolster

The Wiley Blackwell Encyclopedia of Consumption and Consumer Studies, First Edition.
Edited by Daniel Thomas Cook and J. Michael Ryan.

their self-worth and attain personal interests. Although projection of high confidence is part of their everyday defense mechanism, in reality, narcissists are extremely fragile emotionally and psychologically. Consequently, they can become jealous, hostile, dominant, and even competitive about getting ahead. It is therefore not surprising that many relationships that go well in the beginning often become sour due to narcissists' lack of empathy, egotistical tendency, high sensitivity to constructive criticism, and false sense of entitlement.

Just as their social maladjustment strains relationships with others, narcissists' motivational traits can impact their consumers' behaviors as well. In particular, empirical evidence, such as Lee and Seidle (2012) and Sedikides et al. (2007), suggests that narcissists exhibit consumer behaviors that are consistent with their narcissistic personality. Both theoretical and empirical work has postulated that individuals with a narcissistic predisposition show preference for the symbolic value rather than the utilitarian value of a consumer product. Stated simply, to maintain their grandiose sense of self-importance, narcissists are more inclined to purchase items that are deemed to enhance their social status even if purchasing such products serves no use for them. This supposition indicates that narcissists may opt for customized and scarce items since possession of these products uniquely distinguishes themselves from others. Further, to impress and compete with others, narcissistic consumers might engage in regular searches for fashion-sensitive products, especially those in great demand, thus making them more susceptible to attractive advertisement. At the other end of the continuum, some may join private clubs that offer exclusive membership or visit expensive restaurants frequented by certain privileged members. Thus, narcissism can propel a person to become fond of luxury and personalized products, often without careful thought and consideration, since acquiring these items fulfills their exhibitionistic tendency. The preoccupation with unrealistic expectations and craving that drives them to purchase expensive but unnecessary products has consequences for their general well-being since not all narcissists can, from a financial point of view, afford these luxuries. Consequently, those who are not able to sustain this lavish lifestyle often have to give up valuable necessities and endure excessive financial costs they can ill afford.

SEE ALSO: Conspicuous Consumption; Consumer Culture; Hyperconsumption

REFERENCES

American Psychiatric Association. 2000. *Diagnostic and Statistical Manual of Mental Disorders*, 4th ed., text rev. Washington, DC: American Psychiatric Association.

Lasch, Christopher. 1978. *The Culture of Narcissism: American Life in an Age of Diminishing Expectations*. New York: W. W. Norton.

Lee, Seung Y., and Russell Seidle. 2012. "Narcissists as Consumers: The Effects of Perceived Scarcity on Processing of Product Information." *Social Behavior and Personality* 40: 1485–1500. doi:10.2224/sbp.2012.40.9.1485.

Sedikides, Constantine, Aiden P. Gregg, Sylwia Cisek, and Claire M. Hart. 2007. "The I that Buys: Narcissists as Consumers." *Journal of Consumer Psychology* 17: 254–257.

Needs, True and False

GEORGIOS PATSIAOURAS
University of Leicester, UK

Human needs vary considerably across different historical periods, cultures, and economic contexts. Traditionally, the conception of fundamental and "economic" human needs has been approached, examined, and classified via hierarchical order

(Maslow 1943) and ontological taxonomy (Max-Neef 1989), among other perspectives. From the mid-twentieth century, several scholars associated with the Frankfurt School began to discuss an emerging distinction between "true" and "false" needs which could be found primarily in advanced capitalistic and industrial societies. With a focus on the US context, members of the Frankfurt School highlighted the gradual replacement of individuals' "true" needs by "false" ones through their observations of the rise of consumer culture, conspicuous consumption practices, mass production, marketing techniques, and advertising as means of creating new desires, consumption lifestyles, archetypes, and increased consumer demand.

The German philosopher and sociologist Herbert Marcuse elaborated on how one can identify the difference between true and false needs. Marcuse (1964) suggested that there are few essential human needs that should be satisfied in every society, arguing that "the only needs that have an unqualified claim for satisfaction are the vital ones – nourishment, clothing, lodging at the attainable level of culture" (p. 5). The satisfaction of these basic and universal human needs can alleviate injustice, oppression, and poverty. In the majority of contemporary societies the provision of shelter, medical care, food, and water can satisfy "true" human needs. On the other hand, "false" or unnecessary needs can be viewed as socially created (Galbraith 1987/1957) or other-directed (Veblen 1899), and Marcuse (1964) argued that there are needs "superimposed upon the individual by particular social interests in his repression: the needs which perpetuate toil, aggressiveness, misery, and injustice" (p. 5). In most developed and industrial countries, during the twentieth century, existing labor and technological expertise contributed to the satisfaction of basic human needs; therefore capitalistic production focused on the creation of a plethora of false needs. Industrial growth and manufacturing competition, mass media, advertising, and consumerism constitute some of the vehicles for generating and fostering more consumer demand for the satisfaction of false needs.

In contemporary contexts, individuals construct their identities, social relationships, and sense of self via commodities, luxury goods, services, affluence, and material prosperity to the extent that they "find their soul in their automobile, hi-fi set, split-level home, kitchen equipment" (Marcuse 1964, 9). The cultural, industrial, and ideological processes around the formation of emerging "false" needs increase individuals' aspirations for more spending, public display of wealth, indulgence, and social approval without necessarily leading to higher levels of happiness and well-being. On the contrary, the popularity and spread of false needs triggers a vicious cycle of novel desires and wants for insatiable, passive, status-driven, and compulsive consumers whose needs for emulative spending and positional goods can turn into powerful sources of frustration and dissatisfaction with their current social position. Apart from suppressing self-expression, creativity, and critical thinking, the satisfaction of false needs fosters and encourages consumerism and contributes to waste, obesity, environmental pollution, excessive materialism, and social inequality in the twenty-first century.

SEE ALSO: Conspicuous Consumption; Frankfurt School; Needs and Wants; Veblen, Thorstein

REFERENCES

Galbraith, J. Kenneth. 1987/1957. *The Affluent Society*, 4th ed. London: Pelican Books.

Marcuse, Herbert. 1964. *One-Dimensional Man*. Boston: Beacon Press.

Maslow, Abraham. 1943. "A Theory of Human Motivation." *Psychological Review* 50(4): 370–396.
Max-Neef, Manfred. 1989. *Human Scale Development: Conception Application and Further Reflections*. New York: Apex Press.
Veblen, Thorstein. 1899. *The Theory of the Leisure Class: An Economic Study of Institutions*. New York: Random House.

Needs and Wants

PIERGIORGIO DEGLI ESPOSTI
University of Bologna, Italy

The terms "needs" and "wants" are part of the vocabulary of sociology, especially of the sociological branch devoted to the study of consumption and the economy, often with reference to the analysis and transformation of the modern consumer. A need is essential for organisms to live a healthy life. Deficiency of a need would cause a clear negative outcome, such as dysfunction or death. It is in this way that needs are distinguished from wants. Needs can be categorized as objective and physical, such as food, or as subjective and psychological, such as the need for self-esteem. The need derived from the primordial instinct of survival (primary needs) is understood also as the achievement of psychophysical (secondary) needs.

Karl Marx coined the famous definition in which he describes humans as "creatures of need" or "needy creatures" (1959/1932) who are subject to a complex and painful journey to achieve their needs, regardless of whether they are physical or emotional needs. Marx affirmed that as an individual meets certain needs, he/she immediately creates new ones. The subject naturally and constantly follows this cyclical process of recreation.

The influence of the Marxian conceptualization remains relevant: the political economist Michael Lebowitz develops the Marxian theories in *Beyond Capital* (1992). György Márkus, beginning with Marx's reflections, develops a theory in which he compares the human being and the animal: the difference is linked to the human's ability to take advantage of nature and use it as a means to satisfy their needs through the development of his/her skills, becoming a historical-universal being. Another fundamental conception of the analysis of the nature of human needs is Abraham Maslow's hierarchy of needs. While Maslow's hierarchy is still very popular in both sociology and management theories, it has been used in recent times by marketers and advertisers who have relied heavily on Maslow's ideas to fuel the modern consumer society. From a psychological perspective, Maslow's theory has been overtaken by the so-called "attachment theory."

Needs, unlike wants, are born to be satisfied. Wants, however, are born to induce "man," understood as a consumer, to the next desire, creating a vicious cycle, where the market and the self-regulation of the latter play a crucial role (Fabris 2010). Thus was born a new modernity, and it coincides with the civilization of desire and the model of the hamster consumer, always seeking the satisfaction of a want that, once attained, creates a new want (Lipovetsky 2006).

A civilization characterized by consumption, where consumption is an end in itself, is self-sustaining and does not produce gratification (Bauman 2000) because it is precisely the lack of sense of accomplishment, of satiety, that kick-starts the market. Wants, as opposed to needs, seek an object, but cannot define it. This mechanism comes from the fact that the representation of desire remains symbolic in the sense of polysemic; this is because desire arises to a level not transcribed into words or representations (Fabris 2010, 27).

The concept of "want" is subject to different interpretations. In ancient societies it was linked with other similar concepts such as emotion and desire, topics that became focal points for psychological and sociological explorations and theories. This concept was also analyzed from an economic point of view inasmuch as it highlighted a leading role or point of origin in the evolutionary process of capitalism and in its later expressions in the consumerism movement. When examined through the lens of spirituality, such as Buddhism, where the concept of "want" is linked to "desire," an evaluation can be made of the impact it has on the individual's life.

According to Campbell (2004), "new age" and "postmodernism" are viewed as movements that share the same ontological idealism – or emanationism – in which the "external" or "material world" is generally considered to be directly subject to the power of human thoughts and desires. The consumer society is oriented toward the production of desires, which are "satisfied" by the market, creating a vortex of consumption. Needs remain silent and excluded from this vicious cycle.

SEE ALSO: Advertising; Authenticity; Marx, Karl; Needs, True and False

REFERENCES

Bauman, Zygmunt. 2000. *Liquid Modernity*. Cambridge: Polity.

Campbell, Colin. 2004. "I Shop therefore I Know that I Am: The Metaphysical Basis of Modern Consumerism." In *Elusive Consumption*, edited by Karin M. Ekström and Helene Brubeck, 27–43. 2004. New York: Berg.

Fabris, Gianpaolo. 2010. *La società post-crescita*. Milan: Egea.

Lebowitz, Michael. 1992. *Beyond Capital: Marx's Political Economy of the Working Class*. London: Macmillan.

Lipovetsky, Gilles. 2006. *Le bonheur paradoxal. Essai sur la société d'hyperconsommation*. Paris: Éditions Gallimard.

Márkus, György. 1978. *Marxism and Anthropology*. Assen: Van Gorcum.

Marx, Karl. 1959/1932. *Economic and Philosophic Manuscripts of 1844*. Moscow: Progress Publishers: Moscow.

FURTHER READING

Maslow, Abraham H. 1943. "A Theory of Human Motivation." *Psychological Review* 50(4): 370–396.

Maslow, Abraham H. 1987. *Motivation and Personality*. New York: Addison-Wesley.

Niche Marketing

SUNG-CHANG CHUN
Mercy College of Ohio, USA

Niche marketing is a popular concept among both academics and practitioners. Indeed, niche marketing has been applied to numerous industries, products, and services over the last few decades. However, at a fundamental level, it remains unclear whether niche marketing is a theory, a generic strategy, an applied marketing strategy or an extreme case of a marketing segmentation strategy. Further, no single conceptual definition of *niche marketing* is widely accepted. Most definitions are based on versions of Dalgic and Leeuw's (1994) definition: "positioning into small, profitable homogeneous market segments … ignored or neglected by others." Since the late twentieth century, researchers in the field of marketing management have made little progress in developing a more generally acceptable definition of this term. One reason for this might be that the concept is studied in other fields of general strategy and segmentation research. More recently, Toften and Hammervoll (2013) suggested a more comprehensive definition of niche marketing: "The process of carving out, protecting and offering a valued product to a narrow part of a market that displays differentiated needs."

Marketing strategy in general involves identifying the desired customers and deciding how to get these customers to purchase the firm's offerings. This view is supported by traditional textbooks (e.g., Kotler and Keller 2009). Within this marketing strategy, micromarketing has become more widely adopted, with more companies now practicing individual and mass customization. Niche markets consist of groups within the larger marketplace who have similar geographic, demographic, psychographic, and behavioral characteristics. Increasing diversity in consumer tastes and habits and the changing needs of business and organizational markets are likely to favor firms that can better tailor their offerings to this fragmented market. Niche marketing enables customer needs to be better matched and, as a result, the niche marketer can charge a premium because of the added value. Larger companies have lost pieces of their market to niche marketers in confrontations labeled "guerrillas against gorillas."

Niche marketing is reported to have been applied successfully throughout the world, with claimed benefits that include increased profits, prices, sales, growth, and market share. Less frequently reported benefits include value creation, increased competitiveness, and better protection from competition. Successful niche marketing generally evidences most of the following characteristics: a high quality, unique product or service that is perceived by customers to have value but that can quickly be altered to adapt to changing market conditions; buyers who feel a relationship with and commitment to the brand; and partial protection from competition.

It should be noted that globalization and the internet have made niche marketing more feasible to many firms. Many markets have historically been dominated by a small number of bestselling products. The Pareto principle, also known as the 80/20 rule, describes this common pattern of sales concentration. However, information technology, and internet markets in particular, have the potential to substantially increase the collective share of niche products, thereby creating a longer tail in the distribution of sales. In his 2006 book, *The Long Tail: Why the Future of Business Is Selling Less of More*, Chris Anderson argues that the sudden availability of niche offerings more closely tailored to their tastes will lure consumers away from homogenized hits. The "tail" of the sales distribution curve, he says, will become longer, fatter, and more profitable. Anderson argues that the internet has directly contributed to the shifting of demand "down the trail, from hits to niches" in a number of product categories, including music, books, clothing, and movies. This "long tail" thesis has been supported by researchers. One study found that consumers who used both online and catalog channels of a mid-sized retailer purchased a more even distribution of products than consumers who bought solely through the catalog. Many companies that compete in the business of creating hits are beginning to develop ways to evolve niche successes in the long tail. However, others have countered that blockbusters are capturing even more of the market than they used to, and consumers in the tail don't really like niche products. This observation challenges the premise that old business paradigms have changed as much as Anderson suggests.

Although there is an abundance of successful niche marketing examples in the literature, several researchers warn about possible problems associated with the strategy, such as product cannibalization, lack of market and customer knowledge, competitor attacks and aggressive responses from generalists, price pressure, and temptation to go public. Thus, there is still room for more applied examples of both success and failure stories in regard to niche marketing. More examples describing how firms have managed to carve out a narrow part of a market would be of particular interest.

SEE ALSO: Globalization and Consumption; Internet, The, and Consumption; Marketing/Marketing Science; Mass Marketing

REFERENCES

Anderson, Chris. 2006. *The Long Tail: Why the Future of Business Is Selling Less of More*. New York: Hyperion.

Dalgic, Tevfik, and Maarten Leeuw. 1994. "Niche Marketing Revisited: Concept, Applications and Some European Cases." *European Journal of Marketing* 28(4): 39–55.

Kotler, Philip, and Kevin Lane Keller. 2009. *Marketing Management*. Upper Saddle River, NJ: Pearson Education.

Toften, Kjell, and Trond Hammervoll. 2013. "Niche Marketing Research: Status and Challenges." *Marketing Intelligence & Planning* 31(3): 272–285.

FURTHER READING

Bell, David R., Jeonghye Choi, and Leonard Lodish. 2012. "What Matters Most in Internet Retailing." *MIT Sloan Management Review* 54(1): 27–33.

Brynjolfsson, Erik, Yu "Jeffrey" Hu, and Michael D. Smith. 2006. "From Niches to Riches: Anatomy of a Long Tail." *MIT Sloan Management Review* 47(4): 67–71.

Elberse, Anita. 2008. "Should You Invest in the Long Tail?" *Harvard Business Review* 86(7–8): 88–96.

Hsu, Greta, Oezgecan Kocak, and Michael T. Hannan. 2009. "Multiple Category Memberships in Markets: An Integrative Theory and Two Empirical Tests." *American Sociological Review* 74(1): 150–169.

Nike

VIVIANE RIEGEL
Goldsmiths, University of London, UK

The name Nike comes from the Greek goddess of victory. Nike's brand logo is the Swoosh, created by Carolyn Davidson, a graphic design student at Portland State University. In addition to the Nike and Jordan brands, wholly owned subsidiaries include Converse (athletic and lifestyle footwear, apparel, and accessories), Hurley (action sports and youth lifestyle footwear, apparel, and accessories), and Nike Golf (since 1996, when Tiger Woods became a Nike spokesperson). The company's mission statement is: To bring inspiration and innovation to every athlete in the world. Nike co-founder Bill Bowerman said, "If you have a body, you are an athlete."

According to the Forbes Global Leading Companies (2013), Nike (www.nikeinc.com) had worldwide annual revenue of US$25 billion in 2013 (the company sells its products in 170 countries), and its market value was US$49 billion, meaning it was ranked 160 in the US market (public since 1980 in the Dow Jones). The BrandZ Top 100 Report (2013) ranked Nike the 57th most valuable global brand, with a brand value of US$15,817 million.

It all started in 1964, when Bill Bowerman and Phil Knight met and began a partnership. Bill Bowerman was a track and field coach at the University of Oregon and Phil Knight was a middle-distance runner from Portland, who enrolled at Oregon in the fall of 1955 and competed for Bowerman's track program. They incorporated in 1967 as BRS Inc. (Blue Ribbon Sports) and the brand Nike was created four years later, along with its logo, the Swoosh. The company's drive for innovation became stronger with the concept of athletic shoes with rubber spikes (with the first prototype made in a waffle iron), lighter than traditional training shoes. By then, Nike had a new logo, a new name, and a new design innovation.

Nike brand became a global icon by attaching sports to popular culture, and by elevating the cult of the athlete to a point never before imagined. The culture of the Nike brand focuses on building heroes and telling their stories. The main idea is that through sports competition, common men become heroes. Nike has created superior value by utilizing celebrity endorsers, such as Michael Jordan, John McEnroe, and Tiger Woods, to represent their brand. The idea is that the celebrity image is embedded into the consumer's mind and will cause the consumer to associate the endorser with Nike's products, making the brand more desirable and valuable. The sports celebrity conveys the idea of athleticism and becomes a heroic, iconic symbol people strive to emulate.

McCracken (1989) noted that celebrities encapsulate the values of a culture. Celebrity athletes date at least to the Olympics, and continue to signify the spirit of the games, of competition, and of winning, as resonant with national, town, or school teams or players. Following its endorsement strategy to celebrities and games, Nike also started investing in international sports events, such as the World Cup and the Olympics. It is the official provider of uniform and products to the International Olympic Committee, and is currently the sponsor of the Brazil, Netherlands, France, and England soccer squads (2014).

Nike's brand logo, the Swoosh, is so recognizable it often appears instead of the name. Nike's Swoosh has become the symbol of athleticism, power, fitness, and all other aspects that Nike attempts to incorporate into its brand image. The shape evokes an image of speed and, paired with Nike's tagline "Just Do It," gives the message of serious athletic shoes that help you perform better.

Nike and its many categories of products and sports were summarized by the slogan "Just Do It," from an extensive marketing campaign in 1988. The original campaign was aimed at Nike's traditional target, 18–40-year-old males. The campaign reached consumers on a humorous level and tapped into the fitness craze happening at the time. Later, Nike started spreading this target by releasing a series of ads aimed at women athletes (with the website NikeWomen.com), and by creating the P.L.A.Y. (Participate in the Lives of America's Youth) Foundation, with projects involving games that support health and fitness for children.

In 1990, the company also started investing in a new strategy of retail, opening its first NikeTown store in Portland, Oregon. In these stores, consumers could outfit their sporting life, whether they were aspiring practitioners or committed athletes, with different product lines for different purposes. NikeTown is an important site of cultural construction, conveying cultural meanings throughout the store in its design and displays. The architectural space is ideological, in the sense that its design and displays place consumers in particular relations to meaningful symbols and artifacts. NikeTown is part of a larger trend of major consumer products companies, joining Coca-Cola, Sony, and others in developing multisensorial, experiential venues in major upscale locations (see Sherry 1998).

Naomi Klein notes three ways Nike has strived to become the very definition of sport itself: creating sports celebrities, destroying the competition, and selling pieces of the brand "as if it was the Berlin Wall" (Klein 2000). By selling the brand, more than just products, Nike, the world's largest sporting goods brand, pioneered the outsourcing movement of production, which eventually became a global standard. Nike does not manufacture any of the products it sells; what Nike means is a brand, a signature on the products. Therefore, the company concentrates its work on marketing intelligence, design, and innovation.

The outsourcing strategy developed by Nike was translated into the search for low-cost production in Third World countries. The company was shamed in public for its labor practices, and problems started in 1991, when activists published a report documenting low wages and poor working conditions in Indonesia. Among other actions, Nike created the Fair Labor Association, a non-profit group that combines companies and human rights and labor representatives to establish independent monitoring and a code of conduct. However, this issue of working conditions is still present, as a recent factory collapse in Bangladesh (in 2013) shows.

SEE ALSO: Body and Consumer Culture; Brands and Branding; Consumption and Sport; Leisure and Consumption; Outsourcing

REFERENCES

BrandZ 2013 Top 100 Report. 2014. Millward Brown. Accessed July 3, 2014. http://www.millwardbrown.com/brandz/Top_100_Global_Brands.aspx.

Forbes Global Leading Companies. 2013. "Nike." Accessed July 3, 2014. http://www.forbes.com/companies/nike/.

Klein, Naomi. 2000. *No Logo*. London: Flamingo.

McCracken, Grant. 1989. "Who is the Celebrity Endorser? Cultural Foundations of the Endorsement Process." *Journal of Consumer Research* 16(3): 310–321.

Sherry, John. 1998. "The Soul of the Company Store: Nike Town Chicago and the Emplaced Brandscape." In *Servicescapes*, edited by John Sherry, 109–146. Chicago: American Marketing Association.

No Logo: *SEE* CONSUMER RESISTANCE MOVEMENTS

Nostalgia

MINNA AUTIO
University of Helsinki, Finland

Nostalgia comes from the Greek words *nostos*, meaning to return home, and *algia*, a painful condition. Thus, it refers to a sentimental yearning for the "dear departed past," which causes longing for things missing from one's personal life (e.g., homesickness). In modern times, however, the meaning of nostalgia has evolved, and the concept has many connotations. In consumer research, nostalgia has mainly been interpreted as a positive feeling and experience – longing for a happy former time or place. These enjoyable feelings are conceptualized through goods and services when, for example, people sense nostalgia through sound, smell, and taste. These sensory experiences are distinctive in food culture, where former eating and cooking practices and dishes are emphasized.

Consumption of nostalgia has been particularly promoted through cultural products such as films, music, advertising, and clothes. Perception of time is an essential part of nostalgia. For example, during the Christmas period people become sentimental and they reminisce about traditions. It is partially a leap back to former times. Places also have an importance in the construction of nostalgia. Museums or the city center of a medieval town connect us to the past, our history. Following the collapse of communism, a new form of nostalgia has arisen in Europe in recent years. The phenomenon, called "Ostalgie," is based on former East Germans' glorification of their communist past and rediscovery of former consumer products, such as toys, cameras, films, and fairy-tale animation (*Sandmännchen*).

Davis (1979) has emphasized the meaning of nostalgia for identity work. When people relate their past to the present and future, they are able to sense who they are, what they are about, and where they are going. Thus, nostalgia serves the continuity of identity by cultivating a positive understanding of former selves and a screening out of unpleasant memories. For example, through photographs people can see how "funny" they looked 10 or 20 years ago, when fashions were different. At the same time, they realize how young they look in those pictures, and how their appearance has changed over time. Nostalgic feelings are constitutive elements of identity, and those experiences are reinforced through age.

Young people do not usually focus on nostalgia, because they have energy and romance in their lives and new things to discover in the world. However, the transition from adolescence to adulthood also entails anxieties, uncertainties, and a feeling of strangeness, which makes this stage of life memorable. It seems that the experiences of youth generate the ground for future nostalgia in the middle-aged, when people consume the music, styles, films, and fads of their late teens and early twenties. Nostalgia suggests that things were better in the past, and people attempt to return to the past through the cultural symbols of their youth.

Postmodern consumer culture has been seen as favorable for nostalgia. People have lost their connection to the "real," which then leads to a nostalgia for the real – a fascination and desperate search for real people and real values (Featherstone 1994). Thus, nostalgia connects with the desire for authenticity. By romanticizing the past, people are able to construct "authentic" consumer experiences, or at least recapture past feelings. In postmodern culture it is even possible to witness the nostalgic consumption of goods and services that the consumer has not previously experienced "first hand." Young people can enjoy the products of *Ostalgie* without being East German or even German. Nostalgia is part of a globalized and shared consumer culture that emphasizes collective emotion. Nostalgic authenticity can also create alternative consumer behavior. People favor old marketplaces (e.g., the market square, farm markets) by separating themselves from the mass market and industrial production. Consumers escape from the conventional marketplace to the niche market, which indicates their commitment to traditions and alternative consuming habits and nostalgia.

SEE ALSO: Authenticity; Emotions and Consumption; Farmers' Markets; Niche Marketing; Slow Food Movement

REFERENCES

Davis, Fred. 1979. *A Yearning For Yesterday: A Sociology of Nostalgia*. London: Collier Macmillan.

Featherstone, Mike. 1994. *Consumer Culture and Postmodernism*. London: Sage.

O

Obesity

CHENJERAI KUMANYIKA
Clemson University, USA

The Centers for Disease Control and Prevention (CDC) in the United States define obesity as "ranges of weight that are greater than what is generally considered healthy for a given height." The term also identifies ranges of weight that have been shown to increase the likelihood of certain diseases and other health problems. Common scientific criteria for obesity include a body mass index (BMI) (measurement of the relationship between weight and height) over 30 or a percentage of body fat over 24 percent for men and 31 percent for women. Other methods of estimating body fat and body fat distribution include measurements of skinfold thickness and waist circumference, calculation of waist-to-hip circumference ratios, and techniques such as ultrasound, computed tomography, and magnetic resonance imaging (MRI). According to the CDC, more than one-third (35.7 percent) of adults in the United States are obese. According to the World Health Organization, 11 percent of adults worldwide aged 20 and over were obese in 2008.

The first documented usages of the term "obesity" date back to the early seventeenth century; however, obesity scholars argue that the concept of obesity in some form existed even for prehistoric humans. The word derives from the Latin *obesus* (nominative), and *obesitas* meaning "having eaten to a state of corpulence."

In addition to the strict scientific definition denoting the condition as an important risk factor for other diseases, the term has come to be associated with a variety of other cultural meanings related to both moral character and consumption. Factors such as dramatic changes in food production and the marketing of food products, more sedentary modern lifestyles, the proliferation of public and private sector intervention strategies, cultural influences, and representations of obesity in the mass media have influenced societal understandings of the relationship between obesity and consumption.

FACTORS THAT CONTRIBUTE TO OBESITY

Increased energy intake and energy imbalance

The primary cause of obesity is the consumption of more calories than one's body is able to burn. Scholars who research energy intake find that various changes in the environment

The Wiley Blackwell Encyclopedia of Consumption and Consumer Studies, First Edition.
Edited by Daniel Thomas Cook and J. Michael Ryan.

have led to a general per capita increase in energy intake. For example, according to the US Department of Agriculture in the United States (Golan and Waquiu 2007), between 1970 and 2003 the daily per capita energy intake increased from 2234 kcal to 2757 kcal. Some of the factors that contribute to this increase include the increased production and availability of food with a higher calorific content, bigger portion sizes, an increase in eating out, increasing ease of food preparation, increases in the consumption of high calorie, sugary beverages, and other factors. When combined with more sedentary lifestyles, or lifestyles with fewer opportunities for calorie-burning physical activity, this increased energy intake creates obesity.

Genes

Genetic change in the overall human population is a slow process and is therefore not a likely cause of the widespread and rapid increase in obesity. However, there is some variation in how individuals respond to environments that promote sedentary lifestyles and increased consumption of high-calorie foods. Only some people in these environments will become obese, and the nature of obesity also differs. There are differences within ethnic and racial groups and in the same families. These factors point to the fact that genes might play some role in the development of obesity.

Changes in the food environment

An important perspective on obesity arises at the intersection of obesity scholarship and scholarship on the political economy of food production. Scholars working in these areas argue that the dramatic rise in obesity from 1980s onward can be seen as a result of developments in the strategies of the food industry. Among these strategies, scholars identify three as particularly important. First, since the 1980s there has been a dramatic increase in the production of food products. Second, advertising and packaging of these products make a variety of claims that conceal their relationship to health risks and promote alleged health benefits. Third, there has been an effort to intensify the chemically addictive properties of food products while also resisting attempts to regulate food production and policies that would force producers to be more transparent about their processes and products. These environmental factors combine with cultural differences to produce higher rates of obesity in some American minority populations. Recent studies have documented the fact that several large food companies target sugary beverages disproportionately at African American and Latino youth.

CONSEQUENCES OF OBESITY

Obese individuals have increased risk for health problems and reduced life expectancy due to a number of factors. These include cardiovascular disease, type 2 diabetes, cancer, osteoarthritis, asthma, elevated blood and triglyceride levels, high blood pressure, metabolic syndrome, and obstructive sleep apnea. There is also significant social stigma associated with being obese and this can lead to discrimination in employment and professional opportunities as well as depression and psychological problems.

OBESITY AND CONSUMER CULTURE

In addition to these scientific links with obesity, the condition is also linked to the idea that overconsumption in general represents character flaws such as gluttony. The use of the term in antiquity suggests early worries about the relationship between the overconsumption of food and obesity. However, both historically and in some current cultural contexts, obesity has also been understood as a symbol of wealth and access to food and other needs. Before the industrial revolution it was not possible for most individuals to accumulate the amounts of food required to become obese. Furthermore, lack of access to proper nutrition was associated with the lack of health. Thus, depictions of individuals as obese were used to represent states of both financial and physical health.

Obesity is also linked to consumption and consumer culture through the proliferation and widespread influence of various interventions, communities, products, and processes that claim to address or prevent the condition.

Obesity-related consumer products include remedies, diets, the rebranding of food products, weight loss and fitness services, medical procedures, devices, clothing, weight loss- and fitness-focused software applications, and social media.

In addition to a rise in exercise/fitness television shows, the past two decades have also seen a rise in weight-loss and fitness reality genre mass media products such as NBC's *The Biggest Loser*, Bravo's *Thintervention*, MTV's *I Used to Be Fat*, VH1's *Celebrity Fit Club*, A&E's *Heavy*, CW's *Shedding for the Wedding*, and several others.

The proliferation of these products has led to some concern about the rise of an obesity "industry" in which in which decreasing health creates opportunities for increased profits and widely varying information about health-promoting behaviors.

SEE ALSO: Body and Consumer Culture; Fast Food; Food; Food Deserts

REFERENCES

Centers for Disease Control and Prevention. 2012. "Defining Overweight and Obesity." Accessed July 3, 2014. http://www.cdc.gov/obesity/adult/defining.html.

Golan, Elise, and Helen Waquiu. 2007. *Economics of Food Choice: Income, Price, and Availability.* Economic Research Service, United States Department of Agriculture. Accessed July 3, 2014. http://www.nifa.usda.gov/nea/food/pdfs/roundtable_presentations_golan.pdf.

World Health Organization Fact Sheet. 2014. "Obesity and Overweight." Accessed July 3, 2014. http://www.who.int/mediacentre/factsheets/fs311/en/.

FURTHER READING

Kumanyika, Shiriki. 2004. "Cultural Differences as Influences on Approaches to Obesity Treatment." In *Handbook of Obesity: Clinical Applications*, 2nd ed., edited by George A. Bray and Claude Bouchard, 45–67. New York: Marcel Dekker.

Nestle, M. 2013. *Food Politics: How the Food Industry Influences Nutrition and Health.* Vol. 3. Berkeley: University of California Press.

Stern, Judith, and Alexandra Kazaks. 2009. *Obesity.* Santa Barbara, CA: ABC-CLIO.

Obsolescence: Planned, Progressive, Stylistic

GASPAR BRÄNDLE
Universidad de Murcia, Spain

The current production system has an almost unlimited capacity to produce. It is arguably necessary, therefore, that objects of consumption have a planned and progressive obsolescence, either by natural wear due to normal use (loss of functional value) or by an artificial wear due to a change in the aesthetic canons (loss of its symbolic value). The key is that, either way, there is a created capacity for the arrival of renewed commodities.

In developed societies people are surrounded by a myriad of objects. The impressive capacity of the production system allows this material abundance, which contrasts with the shortage that many argue existed only a few decades ago. At that time, objects were few and their fundamental value was measured by their durability. An object that served its function for a long period of time was considered to be a good investment. In contrast, now the number of goods available to consumers has increased exponentially but their life has shortened dramatically under a market logic characterized by innovation and accelerating production and sales cycles. This means that the consumer gets used to the constant presence of new products, properly disseminated by advertising, and subordinated to the dictates of fashion, but it also means that the consumer is ready to get rid of goods as soon as possible to make space for the new range of commodities. The route between the mall and the dump is getting shorter (Bauman 2007).

Generally, objects combine at least two attributes – one related to functional use value and the other to symbolic value linked with its social value as a sign of status. However, in most cases one function prevails over the other: consider, for example, the difference between a jewel and a washing machine. In the current consumption system symbolic value usually prevails over functional value. Consumers fully appropriate goods, not only in their materiality and functional use, but also in their symbolic and immaterial use. Objects are signs (Baudrillard 1996/1968) that allow us to communicate with others (Douglas and Isherwood 1996), which could help in understanding the process by which objects that still have a material utility become obsolete in their symbolic value, losing the meaning they had conveyed before. So, most of the objects remain unaltered for a limited period of time during which they retain all of their functional and symbolic attributes. When the time comes, however, they disappear, leaving space for new products even though they still remain fully functional. The need that was still being satisfied by an object's material usefulness gives way to the exacerbated and inexhaustible desire to be renewed by a higher symbolic status. Furthermore, although the symbolic aspect of the commodity remains unchanged over time, and even though there are regulations to ensure the functional durability of the goods, the facility to produce often makes it more profitable to replace the product than to repair it.

The stylistic obsolescence of consumer goods is part of a broader process of the stylization of everyday life, where the utilitarian function of things is receding into the background to become a basically aesthetic issue. Ours is a "society of the spectacle" (Debord 1994/1967) where the boundaries between public and private are blurred so that one's life becomes a performance. A prime example of this is the importance attached to the body as an element of this symbolic culture – it transcends the private sphere to be displayed in public spaces and has the same status as other obsolescent sign-objects.

If in production capitalism the consumer pace was fast (but always conditioned by the duration of the process of manufacture and sale), in consumer capitalism, the urgent need for commercial novelties, technical innovation, and so on, makes shortening time – being reduced to instantly, if possible – a desirable goal. In this society the consumption process acquires a vertiginous pace, an immediacy that predestines consumer goods to have a short lifespan that is shortened more and more. Social death (obsolescence), which occurs when the object has lost its symbolic function, comes long before functional death (wear), at which time its practical usefulness disappears. Thus, the product's lifespan due to its symbolic durability overshadows its technical durability.

We are witnessing what can be referred to as a "novelties inflation," the end result being the overabundance of products on the market, which in most cases are designed to reach premature obsolescence. In this context, competition between firms intensifies and eventually becomes a vital factor in the struggle to get ahead in the marketing of new products. One aspect that is taken to the limit in some commercial sectors occurs when new products are announced well in advance of their launch to retail. This strategy gives visibility to the product and the brand, while establishing and promoting a strong desire for its possession. Thus, the hyperconsumer not only consumes things and symbols, but also consumes what has not yet even reached a state of material concretion (Lipovetsky 2007).

This progressive and accelerated obsolescence is not just the heritage of consumer goods, but is also part of a set of shared values and a new way of understanding everyday life. People are also part of this cycle of throwaway and renew: temporary workers are replaced by others, relationships become fleeting and repeated throughout life, etc. This adaptation to constant change and renewal has arguably become one of the archetypes of contemporary societies.

SEE ALSO: Consumption and Identity; Fashion; Hyperconsumption; Symbolic Value; Waste

REFERENCES

Baudrillard, Jean. 1996/1968. *The System of Objects*. London: Verso.

Bauman, Zygmunt. 2007. *Consuming Life*. Cambridge, UK: Polity.

Debord, Guy. 1994/1967. *The Society of the Spectacle*. New York: Zone Books.

Douglas, Mary, and Baron Isherwood. 1996. *The World of Goods: Towards an Anthropology of Consumption*. London: Routledge.

Lipovetsky, Gilles. 2007. *La Felicidad Paradójica. Ensayos sobre la Sociedad de Hiperconsumo*. Barcelona: Anagrama.

Occupy Movement

JACQUELIEN VAN STEKELENBURG
VU University Amsterdam, Netherlands

In the fall of 2011, the occupy movement occupied the headlines for weeks. Photos showed activists, or Occupiers, and their tents on squares in major cities like New York, London, and Amsterdam. What makes this movement so newsworthy? This entry explains what the occupy movement stands for, who the Occupiers are, and what strategies and tactics they use.

WHAT IS THE OCCUPY MOVEMENT?

From September 17, 2011, activists occupied New York's Manhattan using the name "Occupy Wall Street." What began as a small group of protesters quickly spread; at first this was only in New York but soon occupy camps were established in other cities, in the United States and worldwide. The Occupiers protest against inequality, the power of the financial sector and large multinationals, and the failure of politics. Although their claims may be vague, many Occupiers seem to agree with the short but powerful message "We are the 99%," by which they mean that 1 percent of the population possesses 40 percent of the world's wealth, while the remaining 99 percent shares the remaining 60 percent.

WHAT INSPIRED THEM?

The protesters in New York say that they were inspired by the demonstrators on Tahrir Square in Egypt, and protests in Spain, where tens of thousands started to occupy public squares from May 2011 onwards (the M15 movement or the *Indignados*). Inspiration was also found in Israel, where in July 2011 the protest movement J14 occupied squares in Tel Aviv. Facilitated by a strong symbolic media-magnet message, the simply translated frame resonated worldwide with citizens frustrated about the global economic recession. The occupation of the worldwide financial center Wall Street, seen as the kernel of the financial crisis and financial evil, became another global symbol. Finally, footage of brutal policing of clearings of the explicitly nonviolent occupy sites snowballed from new media to classic media; consequently the already strong symbolic message made it to the news worldwide for months.

WHAT TACTICS DO THEY USE?

The urban tent camps are perhaps the most prominent tactic. Occupy confronts and builds a movement by occupying public space with urban tent camps which visualize who they are and what they stand for. Symbolism and rituals are important "weapons." The camps are little microsocieties, inclusive, equitable, and ruled by deliberative democracy, in contrast to the individualistic, privatized, nontransparent, top-down, multinationals-dominated society they are diametrically opposing. Locations are strategically chosen, symbolic places where the opponent is omnipresent. This war of positioning not only strengthens symbolism, but also provides a free haven. Indeed, urban occupations are not just an innovative transgressive form of collective action, but free spaces that allow activists to connect with one another and develop movement frames, ideologies, and a shared identity. They are interactive encounters in which activists meet, debate earnestly, engage in lively study groups and workshops, plan future activities, organize political action, but also inspire and mobilize the general public. The urban camps form a place to build a collective identity and the related rituals.

WHO ARE THEY?

Occupiers are said to be marginal types, peripheral isolated individuals, dismissed by many as hippies or lazy scum. However, the opposite appears to be true. Research on the Spanish *Indignados*, for example, shows that compared to other austerity demonstrations in Spain, the so-called Plaza Protests show some noteworthy characteristics. Mobilization through digital media and particularly through social media managed to channel collective outrage through many small organizations with little mobilization experience and brought an unusual crowd into the streets. Participants were significantly younger, better educated, more likely to be women and unemployed, and less likely to have been previously politically engaged (Anduiza, Cristancho, and Sabucedo 2013). Moreover, rather than being peripheral isolated individuals, the activists were firmly socially embedded (Tejerina et al. 2013).

WHY DO THEY PROTEST?

Amr Mchanna – a young entrepreneur at Tahrir Square in Egypt – had much to lose. He had a good job and had just become a proud father. He was neither an outsider, nor did he see himself as a victim of the system – contrary to that, the Mubarak regime offered him every opportunity. So why did he go to Tahrir Square? Amr told the Dutch newspaper *NRC*: "Perhaps the idea that I can do something against a hated dictator. If my daughter grows up, she does not want to hear that her father had stayed at home today." His moral obligation and shared feelings of efficacy conquered Amr's biographical barriers.

But another motive has also emerged: the criticism of modern democracy (Della Porta 2011), as so aptly framed in the slogan of the Spanish *Indignados* "*Democracia real ya!*" ("real democracy now!"). Almost without exception, Occupiers find the system of parliamentary democracy outdated. An increasing number of people seem to be converging on the belief that the way democracies function and the political outcomes they generate are often frustrating, disappointing, shortsighted, unfair, and thus seriously deficient.

WILL OCCUPY HAVE ANY EFFECT?

Gamson (2012) argues that whatever the institutional and political changes are in the long run, the occupy movement will already have been a great success in terms of raising awareness. Sobieraj (2011) and Gamson both write about the avalanche of media attention the occupy movement garnered. Sobieraj compared two months of media attention to the Seattle protests in 1999 to two months of coverage of the occupy protests to show that the Seattle protests received only 10 percent of the media attention the occupy protests received.

One may wonder how sustainable this cultural change will be and how the occupy movement will change the political and public discourse. The fact that the movement floats on a potpourri of grievances and is not able to forward a coherent political agenda is fodder for critics. How politicians and other opponents will react to this assortment of grievances is an interesting but open question. Part of the answer, suspects Gamson, is determined by the extent to which major institutional or policy changes are made to actually reduce the growing inequality and the influence of multinationals on national and international politics. Should this not occur, the occupy movement and its issues are likely to remain on the global sociopolitical radar for a longer period.

SEE ALSO: Capitalism; Consumer Movements, Contemporary; Culture Jamming; Glocalization/Grobalization; Mass Media

REFERENCES

Anduiza, Eva, Camilo Cristancho, and Jóse M. Sabucedo. 2013. "Mobilization Through Online Social Networks: The Political Protest of the Indignados in Spain." *Information, Communication & Society* 17(6): 750–764.

Della Porta, Donatella. 2011. "The Road to Europe: Movements and Democracy." Open Democracy, August 24. http://www.opendemocracy.net/donatella-della-porta/road-to-europe-movements-and-democracy.

Gamson, William. 2012. "Cultural Outcomes of the Occupy Movement." Mobilizing Ideas, January 2. http://mobilizingideas.wordpress.com/2012/01/02/cultural-outcomes-of-the-occupy-movement.

Sobieraj, Sarah. 2011. "A Sociologist's View of the 'Occupy' Camps: Movements in a Shifting Media Landscape." *Footnotes* 39(9): 9–10.

Tejerina, Benjamin, Ignacia Perugorria, Tova Benski, and Lauren Langman, L. 2013. "From Indignation to Occupation: A New Wave of Global Mobilization." *Current Sociology* 61(4): 377–392.

FURTHER READING

Van Stekelenburg, Jacquelien. 2012. "The Occupy Movement: Product of This Time." *Development* 55(2): 224–231.

Van Stekelenburg, Jacquelien, and Marije Boekkooi. 2013. "Mobilizing for Change in a Changing Society." In *The Future of Social Movement Research: Dynamics, Mechanisms, and Processes*, edited by Jacquelien van Stekelenburg, Conny M. Roggeband, and Bert Klandermans, 217–234. Minnesota: University of Minnesota Press.

Open Source and Consumption

YU-WEI LIN
University for the Creative Arts, UK

Open sourcing, aligned with "crowdsourcing," has emerged as a viable methodology for collaborative co-production in today's knowledge society. Largely inspired by the computer hacker culture and the Free/Libre Open Source Software (FLOSS) movement that originated in the late 1970s and early 1980s, open sourcing refers to the practice of releasing product source codes or recipes for the general public to scrutinize, study, change, share, distribute, and redistribute the original and/or the modified work. Normally, open source products (be it software or hardware) or services, identifiable by open source licenses, feature higher modularity, transparency, openness, compatibility, interoperability, and sustainability than proprietary ones.

Though it is often implicit or invisible, a considerable quantity of goods or services that modern societies consume every day are based on FLOSS, co-developed (largely voluntarily but sometimes paid) by people from diverse backgrounds in distributed environments. These goods and services include embedded digital infrastructures or technologies used in airplanes, transportation, or the banking system. In fact, it would be accurate to say that the Web 2.0 and social media boom is enabled by the availability of FLOSS. Contemporary society is also witnessing parallel movements such as open standards, open content, open access, and open data, which are closely associated with the open source software movement. Notable examples include Wikipedia and OpenStreetMap.

Scholarly research has found that people are motivated to contribute voluntarily to open source projects for different reasons: pragmatic, political, cultural, social, religious, for hacker ethics, or personal. For example, through open sourcing, users and consumers can be empowered to have more choice in products, to configure and reconfigure, distribute and redistribute, and share goods and ideas. The freedoms of doing so are important inasmuch as freedom of expression and freedom of information are essential human rights in modern societies. Novel business models have also been built around open source projects, mainly provision of customized bespoke software solutions, datasets, or items. It is therefore inaccurate to consider open sourcing a purely voluntary activity. Through sharing, reusing, and recycling source codes, recipes, and ideas, new values can be added to existing work without reinventing the wheel. To successfully realize an open source project, new roles in FLOSS development that require specialization in project facilitation, coordination, and management have emerged.

As Lin (2005) argues, the FLOSS social world allows diverse actors to engage in the innovation process and therefore it contains more innovation resources than other relatively conventional software models. The strategic collaboration between the public (i.e., the free software communities) and the private (i.e., information technologies corporations) sectors symbolizes a pattern of hybrid innovation that entails complex communications and networks. The development of FLOSS democratizes software innovation processes and allows lay people/amateurs to develop their understanding and knowledge of a shared problem/issue, especially through the web, to challenge established views on the issue.

This open source movement has also gained momentum in the area of culture, food, and beverage production and consumption. For example, the instructions for making home brew drinks such as OpenCola and LinuxCider are freely available, modifiable, and can be redistributed as long as the terms and conditions of the GNU General Public License (GPL) – the open source license under which the original recipes were released – are met. With the emergence of Web 2.0 and other social media technologies, users (or audience) are invited to (re-)mix, (re-)distribute, and (re-)generate new content. Recently, hack spaces around the world (creative, independent coworking laboratories in cities) observed an even broader trend of "making." These can be broadly linked with amateurism, do-it-yourself (DIY) culture, grassroots artisan activism, prosumption (Tapscott and Williams 2006), or produsage (Bruns 2008).

The trend of utilizing, customizing, localizing, situating, domesticating, reappropriating, repurposing, reusing, recycling, remixing the technologies in users' local contexts not only emphasizes diverse consumers' needs but also (implicitly) reflects a resistance to being controlled by big companies (stereotypical and presumed roles and activities envisioned, designed, and devised by developers). Consumption is no longer simply a passive activity; it can be creative and varied. It can be a form of performance to challenge the intentions of producers and express resistance to dominant structures and values. Participants in open source projects, too, demonstrate "a growing interest in novelty – a willingness to reject existing goods and practices in favor of new ones. In this regard, open source can be considered a lifestyle, elected and subscribed to by some.

As in other consumer goods, open source products are cultural and sociotechnically constructed, mediating relationships and embodying meaning (Lin 2005). FLOSS goods can be associated with a range of social activities, and symbolize the desire of modern consumers for greater independence and individual everyday practices. For example, the recent growth of hacking events or maker fairs that celebrate open source practices and DIY mindsets in the areas of arts, crafts, engineering, and (citizen) science fosters a culture in which building things and taking things apart – tinkering, experimenting, making, and hacking – are encouraged. These events are usually associated with ideologies of sustainable living and ethical consumption. An open source turn not only blurs the boundary between professional experts and amateurs/hobbyists; more importantly, it demonstrates a shift in consumer attitudes and behaviors which may result in institutional and societal changes.

SEE ALSO: Digital-Mobile Consumption and Marketing; Do-It-Yourself (DIY); Prosumption; Social Media

REFERENCES

Bruns, Axel. 2008. *Blogs, Wikipedia, Second Life, and Beyond: From Production to Produsage*. New York: Peter Lang.

Lin, Yu-Wei. 2005. "*Hacking Practices and Software Development: A Social Worlds Analysis of ICT Innovation and the Role of Open Source Software*." Unpublished PhD diss., University of York, UK.

Tapscott, Don, and Anthony D. Williams. 2006. *Wikinomics: How Mass Collaboration Changes Everything*. New York: Portfolio.

FURTHER READING

Coleman, E. Gabriella. 2013. *Coding Freedom: The Ethics and Aesthetics of Hacking*. Princeton, NJ: Princeton University Press.

DiBona, Chris, Sam Ockman, and Mark Stone, eds. 1999. *Open Sources: Voices from the Open Source Revolution*. Sebastopol, CA: O'Reilly.

Lin, Yu-Wei. 2011. "A Qualitative Enquiry Into OpenStreetMap Making." *New Review of Hypermedia and Multimedia* 17(1): 53–71.

Torvalds, Linus, and David Diamond. 2011. *Just for Fun: The Story of an Accidental Revolutionary*. New York: HarperCollins.

Outsourcing

CRAIG D. LAIR
Gettysburg College, USA

Outsourcing traditionally refers to a process whereby an entity lifts an activity out from its organizational confines and transfers it to a source that is located in the market (e.g., an automaker deciding to transfer the building of its engines to a supplier instead of building this part itself). Often this idea is expressed in terms of the "make" versus "buy" decision: does an entity make the goods and services it needs itself, or does it buy them from others? Thought of in these terms, there can be little doubt that outsourcing is becoming an increasingly popular practice as a variety of entities are buying much of what they used to make. In particular, outsourcing is becoming increasingly prevalent in the realms of business (e.g., companies outsourcing their call center activities), the government (e.g., the use of private prisons and military contractors), and even in individual and family life (e.g., eating out or the use of errand running services): in each of these spheres entities are buying much of what they used to make. In order to get a sense of this phenomenon it is important not only to place outsourcing within a historical context, but also to look at the causes and consequences of outsourcing.

In terms of historical context, outsourcing is not new. Indeed, businesses, governments, and individuals and families all have long histories of buying needed goods and services. For example, in its infancy the Ford Motor Company was labeled as being "a mere assemblage place" since it did not make many of its own parts (Klier and Rubenstein 2008, 38). Rather, it relied on parts built by others. Similarly, governments as far back as the Ancient Greeks have hired private entities to perform a variety of public functions (e.g., the use of private tax collectors and mercenaries). Even individuals and families have a long history of paying others to perform a variety of services for them (e.g., the use of wet nurses and laundresses). That being said, beginning in the early part of the twentieth century and lasting through roughly 1970, the general trend was for entities in all these spheres of life to insource more and more of their activities (i.e., to move activities that were being performed in the market back into their organizational confines). Thus, in the business realm Fordism, the dominant business model of the time, was centered on high levels of vertical integration. For example, this model's namesake, Ford, attempted to own and operate virtually every aspect of automobile production all the way from the extraction of raw materials to the final sale and distribution of its goods. During the same period the state took over functions that had traditionally been performed by a variety of private actors. This can be seen in the development of the public education and prison systems. At the same time many individual and family activities that were formerly outsourced (e.g., laundry) were moved in-house as a result of various developments (e.g., the development of domestic appliances such as dishwashers and washing machines).

Beginning around 1970 this trend of insourcing again reversed itself as outsourcing became increasingly popular. A number of factors have caused this development to occur and a number of significant consequences have resulted from it. In the business realm this trend was fueled, at least in part, by a radical change in terms of what companies actually make. As Naomi Klein documents in *No Logo* (2002), many businesses have come to realize that what sells products is less their physical qualities and more the meanings attached to them (e.g., Apple has tried to frame its computers as being hip and cool in contrast to the square and stodgy PC). Thus, many companies, such as Nike and Apple, have freed themselves of the task of actually making their goods by outsourcing this activity to others (both Apple and Nike are manufacturers without factories). This leaves these companies to concentrate their efforts on the high-value-adding activity of brand building.

Another factor fueling the rise of outsourcing has been the desire of companies to lower their production costs. This is done by outsourcing their activities to suppliers that are located in lower cost environments. While in theory companies could save a great deal of money by moving their activities to suppliers that, while paying well below Western standards, offered their workers a decent wage and working conditions, in practice this has not been the case, as Klein and many others have noted. In fact, often these activities are outsourced to environments where such things as labor and other social protections are low or altogether absent (e.g., the movement of activities to firms located inside export processing zones). As a result of this, many workers who are (indirectly) employed by some of the world's biggest and most powerful brand name companies face a variety of exploitative conditions such as long hours, low pay, abusive managers, and unsafe work environments.

In the realm of government perhaps the biggest factor promoting outsourcing has been the growing dominance of neoliberalism. Neoliberalism is a political philosophy which advocates that virtually all activities, including those of the state, are best produced through the market. As this philosophy has gained dominance not just in America but in many other parts of the world, many governmental activities that were once "made" have become things that governments "buy" from the private sector. This has been particularly true for the military: just as companies have used outsourcing to free themselves of certain activities (e.g., manufacturing) in order to concentrate on others (e.g., developing one's brand), so too has the military used outsourcing to concentrate on its war-fighting efforts by moving a number of activities that it used to perform itself, such as base construction, food services, and the distribution of supplies, into the private sector. A particular concern in the context of military outsourcing is that a lack of oversight of private contractors has led to significant amounts of waste, fraud, and abuse. For example, the US Commission on Wartime Contracting in Iraq and Afghanistan (2011, 1) estimated that between their inceptions and 2011 anywhere between US$31 billion and US$60 billion were lost to contractor waste and fraud in the war efforts in Iraq and Afghanistan. Another concern is that contractors' desire to maximize profit could undermine the quality of government services. For example, private prisons tend to use fewer and less experienced guards, presumably because this is more cost effective for their bottom line. The result of this appears to be that private prisons experience higher levels of violence than their public counterparts. For example, conditions at one private youth correctional facility were so bad that a federal judge characterized them as "a picture of such horror as should be unrealized anywhere in the civilized world" and chastised this facility for allowing "a cesspool of unconstitutional and inhuman acts and conditions to germinate, the sum of which places the offenders at substantial ongoing risk" (cited in Burnett 2012).

In terms of individual and family life, perhaps the biggest factor promoting outsourcing has been the increased labor force participation rate of women. Since women have historically performed the bulk of housework, the fact that more women are working means that much of the time that was previously devoted to domestic activities is now being taken up by paid work. And since men have not significantly altered their schedules in order to take on more domestic activities, this development has fueled the demand for this type of outsourcing. That being said, it is also the case that outsourcing can be used to free women to work. This is particularly true for mothers who use child care services in order to give them the time needed to work.

One particularly interesting development in this area has been the outsourcing of increasingly intimate and sentimental affairs. Arlie Hochschild has been at the forefront of exploring this issue and her work has focused on the emotional tolls associated with the outsourcing of our personal affairs, or what she calls "the human story behind a world of everything for sale" (Hochschild 2011, 22). Of particular concern to Hochschild is the fear that this type of outsourcing allows the market not only to penetrate our most intimate activities but also to commodify them. Along similar lines, in *What Money Can't Buy: The Moral Limits of Markets* (2013) Michael Sandel argues that the buying of certain activities that we once made can be corrupting of them. For example, outsourcing the writing of a toast for someone's wedding would seemingly undermine the personal and symbolic value of this activity.

Whether we view it as something that is good or bad, the fact remains that ours is increasingly an age of outsourcing.

SEE ALSO: Apple; Fordism/Post-Fordism; Global Markets; Nike; Sweatshops

REFERENCES

Burnett, John. 2012. "Miss. Prison Operator Out; Facility Called A 'Cesspool.'" *NPR*, April 24. Accessed July 4, 2014. http://www.npr.org/2012/04/24/151276620/firm-leaves-miss-after-its-prison-is-called-cesspool.

Commission on Wartime Contracting in Iraq and Afghanistan. 2011. "Transforming Wartime Contracting: Controlling Costs, Reducing Risks." Accessed July 4, 2014. http://www.whs.mil/library/Reports/CWC_FinalReport-lowres.pdf.

Hochschild, Arlie. 2011. "Emotional Life on the Market Frontier." *Annual Review of Sociology* 37(1): 21–33.

Klein, Naomi. 2002. *No Logo: No Space, No Choice, No Jobs*. New York: Picador.

Klier, Thomas H., and James M. Rubenstein. 2008. *Who Really Made Your Car?: Restructuring and Geographic Change in the Auto Industry*. Kalamazoo, MI: W. E. Upjohn Institute for Employment Research.

Sandel, Michael. 2013. *What Money Can't Buy: The Moral Limits of Markets*. London: Penguin.

P

Peer-to-Peer File Sharing

PIERGIORGIO DEGLI ESPOSTI
University of Bologna, Italy

Technically, the term "peer to peer" (P2P) refers to the architecture of a network in which each node is not hierarchically connoted as simply a client or a server, but categorized according to its capabilities of hosting or receiving data. The fact that any node can be a peer means that it is both a client and a server at the same time. The only distinction is in the terminal nodes defined as host, which is essentially an exception or a new paradigm in the logic architecture of a network. According to this structure each and every node can begin and carry out an entire communication process, even if each node is different from the others in terms of speed, size, and memory. The main advantages of such a structure are the cost effectiveness and the speed of the upload/download process.

These systems have become quite popular, beginning in 1999 with Napster, a software that allowed the exchange and downloading of music (especially of .mp3) without paying royalties. Napster struggled with music's major labels and copyright laws, which led to the evolution of a P2P-based system for illegally sharing and downloading digital content such as audio/video and software.

After the shutdown of Napster, the technological evolution of P2P downloading went through second-generation platforms such as Kazaa, Gnutella, and Bit Torrent, which skip the central vulnerability of the system by connecting users directly to each other (see Watson, "How Kazaa Works"). Since 2004, more than 70 million people have used P2P services for file sharing, and the vast majority of them consider this behavior ethically acceptable, especially the younger generations.

If P2P has been often labeled by the mainstream media industry as a system for aiding and abetting media piracy through file sharing, it is also important to note that this is based upon a political and ethical vision about how digital technologies may empower the consumer as a citizen. According to P2P Foundation (2013):

> the distributed network format, expressed in the specific manner of peer to peer relations, is a new form of organising and subjectivity, and an alternative for many systems within the current socio-economic and cultural-political order, which though it does not offer solutions per se, points the way to a variety of dialogical and self-organizing formats … it ushers in a era of "nonrepresentational democracy."

The Wiley Blackwell Encyclopedia of Consumption and Consumer Studies, First Edition.
Edited by Daniel Thomas Cook and J. Michael Ryan.

The American software freedom activist and computer programmer Richard Stallman (2009) argues that P2P and file sharing have to be recognized as a legal system of exchange if they do not have a commercial purpose, for education, encyclopedic, and research material.

According to Lawrence Lessig (2004), piracy is brutally copying and selling copyrighted material without the permission of an author, but file sharing is not synonymous with piracy. His analysis is grounded upon the will of the user and the type of content downloaded. Based on this hypothesis he identified four categories of file sharing users: those who download instead of purchasing content, those who download as a way of sampling content, those who download to get access to copyrighted material no longer sold, and those who download to get access to content that is not copyrighted. Each of these four categories has different ethical implications. The so-called "free culture" that arises from the P2P and file sharing movements, according to Lessig, may be considered as a process of empowerment of the user in the direction of what he defines as the "remix culture" (Lessig 2009), creating meaning through the remix of different kinds of digital content.

SEE ALSO: B2B Marketing; Consumer Resistance Movements; Counterfeiting/Piracy; Culture Jamming

REFERENCES

Lessig, Lawrence. 2004. *Free Culture: The Nature and Future of Creativity*. New York: Penguin.

Lessig, Lawrence. 2009. *Remix: Making Art and Commerce Thrive in the Hybrid Economy*. New York: Penguin.

P2P Foundation. http//p2pfoundation.net.

Stallman, Richard M. 2009. "Viewpoint: Why 'Open Source' Misses the Point of Free Software." *Communications of the ACM* 52(6): 31–33.

Watson, S. "How Kazaa Works." HowStuffWorks.com. Accessed July 4, 2014. http://computer.howstuffworks.com/kazaa.htm.

Pets

DAVID D. BLOUIN
Indiana University South Bend, USA

The term"pet" (also "companion animal") is used to distinguish between different categories of animals (e.g., livestock, wild animals) and different human–animal relations. Although dogs and cats are by far the most prevalent, many other types of animal are kept as pets, including reptiles, birds, and fish. Thomas (1983) claims there are three criteria that differentiate pets from other animals: pets are allowed in homes, they are given names, and they are never eaten. Franklin (1999) asserts that pets are animals that people treat the way they do infants and children. Indeed, many pet owners prefer to adopt baby animals and may be drawn to pets because they elicit parental tendencies (Franklin 1999). Additionally, Serpell and Paul (1994) argue that pets, unlike other domestic animals, are valued for the emotional support they provide, not for their economic utility.

Pet keeping likely began with the domestication of the wolf in the Near East about 12,000 years ago, followed by the domestication of cats 3000 to 4000 years ago in Egypt. Although there are competing explanations for how certain animals were domesticated, the primary account is that early hunter-gatherer societies introduced the infants of wild animals into their societies and selectively and accidentally bred those animals that were best suited for living with people. Over time the domesticated animals began to resemble the infants and adolescents of their original species. In contrast to their wild counterparts, domestic animals tend to be relatively docile, curious, nonterritorial, and less distrustful of other animal species.

Despite notable exceptions among some aristocratic and religious elites, throughout much of their history domestic animals were viewed negatively and as mere means to an end (Ritvo 1988). At the turn of the nineteenth century, attitudes began to change as pet keeping became increasingly widespread among the middle classes (Ritvo 1988). Evidence of the increased prevalence of pets, especially dogs, includes increased profits from the dog tax, the first formal dog show, held in Newcastle, England in 1859, and the founding of the Kennel Club in 1873. Ritvo (1988) argues that this major change was made possible by a shift in humans' relationships with, and attitudes toward, nature. Due to increasing urbanization and scientific and economic development, nature was less often perceived as threatening and beyond human control.

The prevalence and status of pets has been expanding even more in recent decades. Franklin (1999) cites increases in pet populations, expansion in pet services industries, increased media attention, and a rising awareness of the benefits of companion animals. In Britain, for example, the number of dogs increased from 4.4 million in 1963 to 7.3 million in 1991; cats increased from 4 million to 7 million. In the United States the percentage of households with dogs grew from 31.6 percent in 1996, to 36.5 percent in 2011; and from 27.3 percent to 30.4 percent for cats (AVMA 2012). Veterinary expenditures have increased even more. From 1996 to 2011 payments grew from US$7 billion to US$19.1 billion for dogs and from US$4 billion to US$7.4 billion for cats. Pets are now commonly regarded as part of the family in many households across the world.

SEE ALSO: Leisure and Consumption; Markets, Moral Aspects of; Symbolic Value

REFERENCES

AVMA (American Veterinary Medical Association). 2012. *U.S. Pet Ownership & Demographics Sourcebook*. Schaumburg, IL: American Veterinary Medical Association.

Franklin, Adrian. 1999. *Animals and Modern Cultures: A Sociology of Human–Animal Relations in Modernity*. London: Sage.

Ritvo, Harriet. 1988. "The Emergence of Modern Pet-Keeping." In *Animals and People Sharing the World*, edited by Andrew N. Rowan, 13–32. Hanover, NH: University Press of New England.

Serpell, James, and Elizabeth Paul. 1994. "Pets and the Development of Positive Attitudes to Animals." In *Animals and Human Society: Changing Perspectives*, edited by James Serpell and Audrey Manning, 127–144. New York: Routledge.

Thomas, Keith. 1983. *Man and the Natural World: Changing Attitudes in England 1500–1800*. London: Allen Lane.

Politics and Consumer Culture

FAYE LINDA WACHS
California State Polytechnic University, Pomona, USA

Theories focused on consumer culture are intimately related to politics. The development of consumer culture is necessarily tied to the expansions of industrial and postindustrial capitalism that have included both an expansion of democracy and inhibitions on democratic principles. Consumer culture results from the advent of mass production and global trade and the requisite systemic need for mass consumption (Lury 2011). This shift emerges with the transition, for some, from feudalism to capitalism, and for others, from colonialism to postcolonialism. For the colonizers, the advent of consumer culture coincided with the move to industrial production methods and then eventually postindustrial production. For those in core nations, this shift brought with it a rise in the credo of individualism and the rights of the individual. The movement away from feudal monarchical relations to democratic nation-states, codified in the Treaty of Westphalia in 1648, laid the groundwork for the development of the modern concept of sovereignty, nation-states, international relations, and multinational corporations. For those in the core, sovereignty, citizenship, and neoliberal business interests came to predominate as political ideals. For those in the periphery, the shift from colonial to postcolonial relationships saw a removal of direct intervention by foreign powers to indirect intervention. Many former colonies remain adjuncts to wealthy nations through foreign debt, subsidies, and outsourcing.

The mutually beneficial relationship between consumer culture and neoliberal market forces has resulted in a form of politics imbued with the ideologies of consumerism. Mike Featherstone (2007) highlights three approaches to understanding consumer culture. In the first view, the expansion and development of capitalism results in the increasing salience of consumption to every aspect of our lives. In the second case, the focus is more on the meaning with which goods are infused and how this relates to status, display, and social meaning. Finally, there is the experience of consumption and its effects on the self. Regardless of the approach, politics and consumerism are intimately intertwined.

The economics of capitalism and the politics of consumer culture are viewed as interrelated by theorists in the first camp. In this view, the expansion of industrial capitalism necessitated the growth of consumer wants and needs. An increasing array of needs is generated by the market and supported through political decisions commensurate with the needs of corporate interests. Classic critiques focus on exploitation, alienation, and corruption. Many of the problems of the industrial factory are viewed as being now the burdens of the periphery. Recent critiques focus on the relationship between the political system and the needs of the market system at the expense of consumers, the environment, and workers. Issues of global sustainability are central.

In an international context, inherently exploitative production and consumption patterns have emerged that lead many to critique relations between the First and Third Worlds as being a form of economic colonization. World systems and dependency theories developed in contrast to development theory perspectives which had tended to attribute failures to economic, social, and political flaws in culture, investiture, or worker ability. By contrast, world systems and dependency theories point to international politics and the fact that adjunct nations remain economically dependent and politically impotent precisely because of their relationship to First World nations. Today, globalization theories prevail and tend to problematize how postcolonial relations have come to dominate. Such views recognize imbalances in global market power that adversely impede development for some nations while enhancing the power and privilege of others. At the same time, the development of alternatives, challenges, and resistance are noted. It must be recognized, however, that there has been a tremendous expansion of corporate power, as the spending power of corporations comes to surpass that of many nations. In some views, this is presented as an unrelenting force from which there is little chance of escape.

In addition, the environmental costs and consequences of production are devastating for much of the world. In a national context, corporate interests are coming to predominate. For example, in the United States, the Citizen's United Supreme Court decision (2008) that allows corporations and labor unions unlimited spending in political campaigns has transferred a tremendous amount of political power to private corporations and effectively removed limits on corporate spending in American elections. Individual state efforts to prevent corporate spending in political campaigns have been largely unsuccessful (for example, Montana's attempt to limit corporate campaign spending was overturned by the US Supreme Court in 2012).

In the second view, consumerism becomes a way of demonstrating and validating status and position. Those in power are advantaged not only in acquiring these symbols, but also in promoting a culture of consumption. Understanding how politics invokes signs and symbols as part of political display while simultaneously undermining the meaning of these signs is central. Frequently influenced by Gramsci's views of hegemony – the idea that consent to the existing social order is achieved not through coercion but consensus – this view highlights the role of culture. The provision of distractions and comfort for the populace by the political establishment, or "bread and circus" politics, is noted by this view. Advertising's profound effect on political campaigns provides a potent example. In the United States, the use of Super-PACs (political action committees) allow for the subversion of campaign spending limits and restrictions on advertising. Hence, advertising spending in American campaigns has skyrocketed, making it nearly impossible for candidates who lack corporate backing to compete.

In addition, the use of imagery to replace substantive calls for political change is manifest in the co-option of symbols of rebellion. The concepts of commodity racism and commodity feminism highlight how consumers are marketed supposed solutions to social ills through the commodified display of the symbols of anti-racism or feminist campaigns. Scholars note how consumers are presented with the image of political activism or social equity as marketed through symbolic display. This promotes the belief that through consumption one can transcend the problems of racism and/or sexism. Hence, the symbols of social justice become marketing tools, rather than rallying points. Moreover, scholars note that the proliferation of space for public discourse, rather than leading to political dissent, has been co-opted into a space of "frenetic inactivity" (Wachs et al. 2012). In this view, the public engages in symbolic debate through social media, posting on blogs or other online content, but little meaningful change occurs. Hence, while racist comments or imagery results in a barrage of criticism, little is done to address structural constraints such as a continued wage gap, or the racial implications of the prison industrial complex. Indeed, increasingly, such events are manufactured attempts to demonstrate the "anti-racist" stances of candidates or corporations, rather than genuine calls for social equity.

The third camp focuses on the experience of political participation in the consumerist world and the impacts that has on identity. Scholars note the myriad of ways that political participation is undermined through its channeling into market-driven experiences (King 2008) or media/social media maelstroms (Wachs et al. 2012). While some highlight the potential for self-reflexive construction, others note that the seemingly endless array of options presented to consumers is usually a limiting of choices. For example, despite the impressive number of candidates that often run for office, the lack of variety of the political views covered by mainstream media is telling. Moreover, King (2008) highlights the commodification of experience in movements and events, as organizations compete to provide the most moving experience for fundraisers. For example, King (2008) points to the AVON pink ribbons campaign as generating a tremendous amount of positive media coverage without addressing the use of known carcinogens in such products. This highlights the ways that political and civic activism are undermined through individualistic market practices. By channeling activism into corporate sponsored events, the political will of the population is directed into largely innocuous forms. Some refer to this as the branding of politics. Scholars have also problematized how the market undercuts the potential for key figures in popular culture to take political stances. In the past, cultural icons frequently engaged in political debate, but now market forces have undermined this. Legal contracts with sponsors and media producers significantly limit the ability of celebrities to engage in any form of political debate.

The role of the mass media in politics is crucial. Two key theories have emerged that focus on the role mass media play in politics, agenda setting, and framing. Scholars note the role of media frames and agenda setting in inhibiting the functioning of democracy by limiting debates to best serve the interests of corporations (McChesney 2004; McCombs 2004). Agenda setting reveals the correspondence between media emphasis on specific issues and how much importance the public imbues these issues. To put it simply, the more attention the media give to an issue, the more importance that issue is thought to have. The failure of the media to cover issues leads one to believe they lack importance. Framing demonstrates how presentation shapes understandings. Information tends to be presented in schemas with which audiences are familiar. Media frames operate within and reinforce existing schemas or patterns and associations that the mind uses to understand the external world. According to media scholars, there is not a single overarching way in which an event is framed, but overlapping, sometimes contradictory and competing frames. However, the tendency is for these frames to create a climate favorable to business interests, and specifically neoliberal business agendas. It is not so much that this is promoted, but rather that it is simply presented as the way that things are. Climate change presents an example. It is commonly presented as something up for debate, despite overwhelming evidence in support of it. As such, the framing of politicians around this issue marks them as liberal or conservative, while little attention is paid to the actual facts.

Alternative political movements are emerging as a means to challenge neoliberalism and the influence of corporate money on politics. Emergent movements such as the voluntary simplicity movement resist the influence of consumer culture on politics through an ethics of moderate consumption. Promoting conservation and judicious manufacturing as an alternative is emerging in some communities.

SEE ALSO: Capitalism; Ethical Consumption; Globalization and Consumption; Occupy Movement

REFERENCES

Featherstone, Mike. 2007. *Consumer Culture and Postmodernism*. Thousand Oaks, CA: Sage.

King, Samantha. 2008. *Pink Ribbons Inc.: Breast Cancer and the Politics of Philanthropy*. Minneapolis: University of Minnesota Press.

Lury, Cecilia. 2011. *Consumer Culture*. London: Polity.

McChesney, Robert W. 2004. *The Problem of the Media: U.S. Communications Politics of the Twenty-First Century*. New York: Monthly Review Press.

McCombs, Maxwell E. 2004. *Setting the Agenda: The Mass Media and Public Opinion*. Malden, MA: Blackwell.

Wachs, Faye Linda, Cheryl Cooky, Mike Messner, and Shari L. Dworkin. 2012. "Media Frames and the Displacement of Blame in the Don Imus/Rutger's Women's Basketball Team Incident: Sincere Fictions as Frenetic Inactivity."

Critical Studies in Media Communication 29: 421–438. doi:10.1080/15295036.2011.646282.

Popular Culture

MARK RUBINFELD
Westminster College, Salt Lake City, USA

"Popular culture" is a generic term that defies precise definition. Like the broader culture that it emanates from and contributes to, any attempts to define popular culture typically invite controversy while requiring elaboration and qualification. Because popular culture covers such a wide array of forms and functions, products and productions, processes and practices, and symbolisms and significances, no single definition of popular culture can fully capture its essence since there is no single essence to capture. However, most definitions of popular culture tend to broadly characterize it in terms of contemporary cultural forms that are (1) widely liked by large segments of the general public, (2) mass produced and distributed by and for commercial interests, and (3) consumed by individuals and groups primarily for purposes of amusement, entertainment, escapism, and fantasy or, in the case of fashion, glamour, trend, and style. By adding to, subtracting from, or otherwise modifying this list of component characteristics, different critical approaches to understanding popular culture provide differing critical perspectives as to what popular culture is, includes, and involves. There are generally six major critical approaches to understanding popular culture, which can best be classified in terms of a cultural bifurcation approach, a production of culture approach, a mass culture approach, a textual/content analysis approach, an ethnographic/subculture analysis approach, and a postmodernist approach. Each of these approaches involves its own set of theoretical assumptions, methodological considerations, and practical applications, although, as with most classifications, there are overlaps and variations between and within a number of these approaches.

The first of the six critical approaches to understanding popular culture, the *cultural bifurcation approach*, entails splitting culture into two component parts: "high culture," consisting of all cultural forms that aesthetically, intellectually, or spiritually inspire, uplift, and enhance the individual and society; and "low culture," that is, all "leftover" cultural forms which, falling under the rubric of popular culture, serve to mindlessly engage the masses while appealing to society's lowest common denominator (Gans 1977). Differentiating popular culture from the more refined high culture of the aristocracy, wealthy, privileged, upper classes and/or more highly educated, the cultural bifurcation approach concedes popular culture's democratic appeal in terms of its affordability, accessibility, and apprehensibility while, at the same time, disparages popular culture as morally inferior to those forms of culture one finds in the arts, fine arts, and classics. This disparagement often extends to both the audiences that consume popular culture and the societies that sustain it, leading to calls for constraining, curtailing, or censoring those forms of popular culture – usually associated with sex or violence – that are viewed as most objectionable.

While accepting the general premise of the two distinct cultural types, some variations of the cultural bifurcation approach discount the approach's moral concerns and judgments to focus, instead, on how high culture can serve as cultural capital. That is, these approaches look at the ways in which familiarity and proficiency in various forms of high culture may provide economic advantages to individuals and groups from higher classes while, conversely, disadvantaging individuals and groups from lower classes that do not have equal access to that familiarity and proficiency. From this perspective, people with regular access to high culture activities and experiences tend to acquire higher cultural tastes and skills – distinct appreciations and mannerisms of dress, speech, presence, and comportment which, conveying good upbringing, tend to make them more professionally marketable. And since these appreciations and mannerisms get passed down from one generation to another, cultural bifurcation both reflects and reproduces society's social class divisions (Bourdieu 1984/1979). Other variations of the cultural bifurcation approach, however, tend to be more skeptical, questioning the very distinctions the approach is based on, due to, as they see it, a blurring of the lines between high culture and low culture over the past century that, increasingly, has all but rendered the two cultural types indistinguishable (Swirski 2005).

The second of the six critical approaches to understanding popular culture, the *production of culture approach*, sidesteps the moral and class dimensions of the cultural bifurcation approach to focus primarily on the economic processes that drive popular culture production. Viewing popular culture as a multibillion dollar industry with shareholders and stakeholders all over the world, the production of culture approach explores the commercial entities, interests, and relationships that largely determine what kinds of popular culture products get produced, for which markets, and for whose benefits (Peterson and Anand 2004). Here, the "creation" of popular culture is attributed to the advent of industrialization and urbanization and, subsequently, its ascendancy in the twentieth century to the rise in commercialism, consumerism, and mass communications. The production of culture approach thus is interested in how increasing hours of leisure time, greater amounts of discretionary spending power, technological innovations in mass communications, emerging new overseas markets, and the globalization of capitalism have significantly changed both the production and consumption dimensions of popular culture. From this perspective, all forms of popular culture are commercial products that are marketed and sold to the general public for purposes of big business and profits and, as such, any contemporary analysis of popular culture can only be understood in the context of consumer and corporate capitalism.

Applying this basic understanding, some variations of the production of culture approach examine how the rise in corporate acquisitions and mergers over the past several decades has created a worldwide popular culture industry in which the overwhelming majority of the world's popular culture is produced by an ever-shrinking handful of multinational corporations that control nearly all aspects of the popular culture production processes, and how this consolidation, in turn, may be contributing to an increasing homogenization of popular culture at the expense of authenticity, creativity, and originality (Koval 1988). Other variations of the production of culture approach focus on questions of diversity, analyzing how much – or how little – ethnic, racial, class, gender, and sexual diversity there is or isn't among the producers of popular culture and how underrepresentation at each and every level of the production processes may affect popular culture products and productions. And still other variations of the production of culture approach analyze the role of smaller, independent popular culture producers, looking into how much competition they truly offer and how much independence they truly have.

The third of the six critical approaches to understanding popular culture, the *mass culture approach*, adds an ideological dimension to the economic processes that drive popular culture production while incorporating many of the concerns of the production of culture approach. Building on Antonio Gramsci's theory of cultural hegemony (1971) and the critical theorists from the Frankfurt School who later applied Gramsci's theory to popular culture, the mass culture approach focuses on popular culture's role in sustaining the ideological underpinnings for advanced capitalism. From this perspective, popular culture is more than just big business and big profits; rather, it is one of advanced capitalism's most effective tools for deterring potential resistance by placating the public through an endless stream of consumer goods and promises (Adorno and Horkheimer 1979/1947). Furthermore, from this perspective, all the processes of popular culture production along with all the products these processes produce serve the same ideological purpose – to transform freethinking individuals into mindless masses of capitalistic consumption through endless modes of advertising, commercializing, marketing, merchandising, broadcasting, and programming (Marcuse 1964).

Expanding on the premise that popular culture serves as an extraordinarily efficient apparatus of ideological indoctrination and, from a cultural Marxist perspective, the belief that ideological systems sometimes can and do operate independent of economic systems, the mass culture approach leads to a number of avenues of critical inquiry. These include, among others, investigating the other apparatuses of ideological indoctrination that popular culture works in concert with and the relationships between these apparatuses; identifying the linkages between popular culture homogeny and cultural hegemony and the ramifications of these linkages; exploring the global dominance of American popular culture products and productions and how that global dominance adversely impacts local and national cultures in other parts of the world; and examining how, in addition to supporting capitalism and consumerism, popular culture can and has been used to bolster nationalism, militarism, and interventionism.

Shifting away from the processes and systems of cultural production, the fourth of the six critical approaches to understanding popular culture, the *textual/content analysis approach*, borrows from the fields of structural anthropology, linguistics, semiotics, literary analysis, and film studies to focus, instead, on popular culture texts. Defining a text, in simplest terms, as anything that can be "critically read" for its symbolic meanings, the textual/content analysis approach utilizes the tools of textual analysis and content analysis, together or separately, to critically deduce the symbolic meanings and social significances of popular culture texts (Barthes 1968). By identifying and interpreting the symbolic compositions (e.g., connotations, significations, representations, themes, iconographies) that are structurally embedded in popular culture texts, textual analysis seeks to uncover how these symbolic compositions reflect and reinforce dominant social arrangements, divisions, and hierarchies in the broader society. And by classifying and calculating the frequency distributions of these symbolic compositions, content analysis works to quantify as well as qualify these reflections and reinforcements.

In addition to decoding popular culture texts, some variations of the textual/content analysis approach expand their analyses to include popular culture genres, that is, collections of similarly structured popular culture texts (e.g., romance novels, action movies, country songs, women's magazines) that are easily identified by their distinct conventions. These analyses often add an historical context by tracking the continuities, trends, and shifts in the narrative structures and symbolic compositions of a particular popular culture genre over time and equating these continuities, trends, and shifts to what may be changing – or failing to change – in the structural and social orderings of the society that produced that particular genre (Rubinfeld 2001). Other variations of the textual/content analysis approach, however, are more dubious – rejecting the approach's underlying assumption that textual constructions are always predictable and decipherable. To the contrary, these variations incorporate poststructuralist theories to claim that textual constructions are never fully coherent – that there are always ideological ambiguities, contradictions, and gaps in the symbolic compositions of all popular culture texts.

From this perspective, rather than being linear and one-dimensional, popular culture texts are polysemic, that is, they contain multiple and often differing symbolic meanings and messages and, because they do, real popular culture readers, viewers, audiences, and consumers are able to choose which of these meanings and messages to accept, question, challenge, or reject. Any thorough textual analysis, therefore, has to look beyond the dominant symbolic orderings of popular culture texts to locate their disorderly compositions as well since it is precisely these compositions that shed the most light on the real-life social conflicts, struggles, and resistances in the broader society (Fiske 1989).

All of the approaches to understanding popular culture presented so far – with the one exception of the poststructuralist variation of the textual/content analysis approach – tend to view popular culture in mostly regressive or repressive terms. Picking up where the poststructuralist variation of the textual analysis approach leaves off, the fifth of the six critical approaches to understanding popular culture, the *ethnographic/subculture analysis approach*, is similarly interested in the subversive potential of popular culture with, however, two crucial distinctions. First, instead of focusing on popular culture texts, its unit of analysis is the actual readers, viewers, audiences, and consumers of popular culture texts. And second, instead of relying on textual analysis to uncover the symbolic meanings of these texts, it employs ethnography (interviews, observations, participant observations) to directly learn from these actual readers, viewers, audiences, and consumers what they get out of – and from – their popular culture experiences.

Delving into people's everyday interactions with popular culture, these ethnographic investigations reveal how people do more than just passively absorb and consume pre-existing popular culture forms; they also actively create their own unique, original forms of popular culture, challenging or circumventing dominant social norms and conventions, as well as modifying existing forms of popular culture to better fit their personal experiences, needs, and proclivities (Radway 1981). Adding subculture analysis to the ethnography provides further information, uncovering the ways in which people from marginalized groups, in particular, often construct their own subterranean forms and usages of popular culture – developing entire subcultures and, occasionally, countercultures around these constructions.

From this perspective, popular culture is more than just the sum total of its products, productions, and processes since it also includes practices. And from this perspective, these component parts do more than simply serve as instruments of repression since they also include expressions of resistance. Drawing on the tensions between repression and resistance, some variations of the ethnographic/subculture analysis approach go so far as to view popular culture as the central site in modern societies where dominant and subordinate groups, jousting for influence, play out their symbolic struggles for social power. Other variations of the ethnographic/subculture analysis approach tend to focus on more micro-level applications, picking out the different ways that people from different groups (racial, ethnic, gender, generational, sexual orientation, etc.) or different parts of the world (Africa, Asia, Europe, Middle East, Latin America, North America) interpret and employ popular culture. And still other variations of the ethnographic/subculture analysis approach are more process-oriented, exploring the cyclical patterns of popular culture creations, co-options, and regenerations – that is, how innovative, counter-conventional popular culture forms periodically spring from grassroots origins – getting quickly co-opted by commercial interests that sap them of their innovativeness and counter-conventionality only to be periodically regenerated, through appropriation, into new innovative, counter-conventional popular culture forms springing from "new" grassroots origins.

The last of the six critical approaches to understanding popular culture, the *postmodernist approach*, draws from postmodern theories to focus on the ways that new communications and computer-related technologies have irrevocably altered the speed, scope, substance, and significance of popular culture. According to this approach, these technological innovations, coupled with hyperconsumerism and celebrity obsession, have collapsed the boundaries between fact and fiction, information and entertainment, authenticity and artificiality, and reality and virtuality – contributing to a postmodern culture and mindset in which everything, including and especially meanings, are up for grabs (Lyotard 1984/1979). From McDonald's arches to Nike's Swoosh to Disney's ears, the signs are everywhere that popular culture's most iconic symbols no longer signify but have become significations in themselves – uniting people in their universal recognition of popular culture's global reach and influence (Baudrillard 1994/1981). At the same time, the increasing computerization and digitalization of popular culture has a "detaching effect" as the ways in which people convey information, tell stories, entertain themselves, and stay personally connected to one another keep getting more and more reduced to less and less meaningful forms of communications and interactions – from face-to-face conversations, for example, to voicemails to emails to text messages to posts to tweets to hashtags to smiley faces.

Applying postmodern theories to contemporary concerns, some variations of the postmodernist approach to critically understanding popular culture explore the ways in which culture is becoming increasingly defined by popular culture, popular culture is becoming increasingly defined by celebrity culture, and both popular culture and celebrity culture are becoming increasingly defined by American popular culture and American celebrity culture (Turner 2004). Other variations of the postmodernist approach focus on the psychosocial impact of these developments, examining whether there can be any genuine meanings or selves in a world that is becoming more and more defined by both popular culture and celebrity culture, particularly as more and more people spend more and more of their lives fictitiously watching other people live their lives on reality TV, Netflix, YouTube, Facebook, video games, and virtual worlds. Still other variations of the postmodernist approach worry about privacy concerns, probing the surveillance capacities of popular culture-related internet and social networking sites, while yet other variations are more optimistic, seeing subversive possibilities in the global reach and increasing availability of these sites for mass-communicating dissent and mass-organizing resistance. Finally, leaving technological considerations aside, still other variations of the postmodernist approach see similar subversive possibilities in the changing formulations and presentations of postmodern popular culture productions as irony, self-reference, parody, satire, narrative rupture, spatial discontinuity, and time distortion, among other disrupting devices, work to break down old structures and strictures.

As with any significant social phenomenon, no single approach to critically understanding popular culture can fully capture all that popular culture is, does, and means. All six of the presented approaches to critically understanding popular culture have their strengths and shortcomings. Some of these approaches lend themselves more easily to empirical investigation than others. Some can be integrated or synthesized with other approaches more easily than others. But only by taking all of these approaches and their variations into account can we have a full appreciation of the cultural, economic, political, social, and technological dimensions of popular culture. And only by taking all of these dimensions into consideration can we begin to fully appreciate why popular culture can't be defined by any one thing – artificial, authentic, commercial, organic, material, symbolic, repressive, transgressive, indoctrinating, liberating, cohesive, disruptive, static, dynamic, institutional, interactional, structural, poststructural, modern, postmodern – but by all of these things. While popular culture is neither determining nor omnipotent, it is pervasive, ubiquitous, and increasingly influential, which is why what we continue to make of popular culture will contribute to the future we make.

SEE ALSO: Adorno, Theodor; Barthes, Roland; Baudrillard, Jean; Capitalism; Celebrity; Consumer Culture; Consumer Society; Frankfurt School; Homogenization and Heterogenization; Mass Media; Semiotics

REFERENCES

Adorno, Theodor, and Max Horkheimer. 1979/1947. *Dialectics of Enlightenment*. London: Verso.

Barthes, Roland. 1968. *Elements of Semiology*. New York: Hill & Wang.

Baudrillard, Jean. 1994/1981. *Simulacra and Simulation*, translated by Sheila Faria Glaser. Ann Arbor: University of Michigan Press.

Bourdieu, Pierre. 1984/1979. *Distinction: A Social Critique of the Judgment of Taste*. Cambridge, MA: Harvard University Press.

Fiske, John. 1989. *Understanding Popular Culture*. Boston: Unwin Hyman.

Gans, Herbert J. 1977. *Popular Culture and High Culture: An Analysis and Evaluation of Taste*. New York: Basic Books.

Gramsci, Antonio. 1971. *Selections from Prison Notebooks, translated and edited by Quintin Hoare and Geoffrey Nowell Smith*. London: Lawrence & Wishart.

Koval, Howard. 1988. "Homogenization of Culture in Capitalist Society," *Popular Music and Society* 12: 1–16.

Lyotard, Jean-Francis. 1984/1979. *The Postmodern Condition: A Report on Knowledge*, translated by Geoffrey Bennington and Brian Massumi. Minneapolis: University of Minnesota Press.

Marcuse, Herbert. 1964. *One-Dimensional Man*. Boston: Beacon Press.

Peterson, Richard, and N. Anand. 2004. "The Production of Culture Perspective." *Annual Review of Sociology* 30: 311–334.

Radway, Janice. 1981. *Reading the Romance: Women, Patriarchy, and Popular Literature*. Chapel Hill: University of North Carolina Press.

Rubinfeld, Mark. 2001. *Bound to Bond: Gender, Genre, and the Hollywood Romantic Comedy*. Westport, CT: Praeger.

Swirski, Peter. 2005. *From Lowbrow to Nobrow*. Montreal: McGill-Queen's University Press.

Turner, Graeme. 2004. *Understanding Celebrity*. London: Sage.

Privacy

GARY T. MARX
Professor Emeritus, Massachusetts Institute of Technology, USA
STEPHEN T. MARGULIS
Grand Valley State University, USA

Privacy is a contentious, multidimensional concept. Its contours are fluid and often ill defined, contested, and negotiated, and these vary by the context and culture. There is little consensus on the framework within which to analyze it, on definitions within and across frameworks, on levels of analysis to which the concept is applicable (e.g., to transactions among individuals, the individual and the organization, or between organizations), and on how competing interests (e.g., transactional data involving buyers and sellers) and values in conflict (e.g., privacy versus freedom of expression) should be weighed or even measured.

An important approach to privacy (the limited access framework) emphasizes the individual's control over his or her information. In this framework, "privacy represents control over unwanted access or, alternatively, the regulation of, limitations on, or exemption from scrutiny, surveillance, or unwanted access" (Margulis 2009, 132). This approach is consistent with most everyday meanings of privacy, behavioral science definitions, and with most common-law concepts and the Fourth Amendment of the US Constitution. The major goals of privacy are minimizing vulnerability and/or enhancing autonomy (Margulis 2003).

Privacy refers to the rules regarding the protection of information and contrasts with rules regarding publicity. These, in turn, contrast with the actual state of information as being known or restricted, apart from what the rules require. Privacy can be linked to and differentiated from other terms such as anonymity, pseudo-anonymity, confidentiality, secrecy, and surveillance.

Some have argued (e.g., Margulis 2003) that the control that privacy as a normative phenomenon provides might include being unobserved and/or left alone, decisions about one's body, control over commercial uses or publication of one's appearance or of facts not generally known about a person, and protections against unwarranted discovery and use of one's "personal" information. Personal data may simply be that tied to an individual (much of it being "impersonal" in simply locating the person within a shared category such as car owner, while other information might be sensitive and/or intimate).

In an age of computerization with credit cards, the internet and email, embedded sensors and GPSs (global positioning systems), informational privacy has taken on increased significance. Technological advancements in softly (and sometimes covertly) collecting, storing, analyzing, mining, retaining, and distributing personal information has brought to the surface deep privacy concerns, particularly as this involves secondary uses of information for purposes other than those for which it was initially collected and for which varying degrees of informed consent (another difficult concept) may have been offered.

The breadth, depth, and amount of digital data collected are staggering. According to one estimate (Mearian 2012), the quantity of data collected between 2012 and 2020 (much produced by machines talking to each other) will exceed 5200 GB of data on everyone alive – that is equivalent to 57 times all the grains of sand on all the world's beaches. The amount of data collected doubles every year.

The speed with which data from different sources and in different formats can be merged, the analytical power unleashed, and claims about the data's predictive power are astounding. Two examples from the retail firm Target illustrate this. The firm offers customers individually created clothes based on its taking 500 distinct measures of the body. The same firm was criticized for sending expectant mothers solicitations for purchases about what they would soon need, as their bodies changed. In some cases the women did not even know they were pregnant. The store determined this by noting purchasing patterns associated with the early months of pregnancy (Duhigg 2012).

A considerable amount of this information involves online (or at least credit card) consumer transactions. Online commerce is big business and continues to grow rapidly. In the United States, in 2011, consumers spent about US$200 billion online. Online consumption behavior is characterized by the massive and systematic collection of data with varying degrees of "sensitiveness." The scale of the collection, retention, distribution, merging, sale, and use of personal information by online businesses and information brokers sets it apart from pre-computer consumption. Third party users (who the individual is usually unaware of and has not given consent to have his or her personal information sold by) play a prominent role here.

Those who collect and market data on individuals' consumption behavior claim that the information has been voluntarily and gladly provided by customers in return for quicker, better, and more convenient personalized service and products, not to mention discounts and rewards as a result of their cooperation. Their justifications for creating better data for their use are that it can enhance strategic planning, reduce their risks and liability, and enhance their efficiency and profitability by targeting those likely to be interested in their products, while also creating loyal customers (Culnan and Bies 2003).

But such practices also can lead consumers to feel they have lost control over the collection and use of their personal information; it might result in discriminatory social sorting based on unfair secret criteria and, when data security is weak, problems such as identity theft. A variety of kinds of privacy problems can be identified at various stages of the data and consumption cycle (Marx, forthcoming).

The major ways of responding to such problems are laws controlling the use of personal data; policies designed to anticipate and reduce problems and to certify that companies follow recommended privacy policies; and technical controls such as buffered (and often disposable) pseudo-anonymous forms of identification, enhanced security, and audit trails.

The United States tends to emphasize voluntary self-restraint by businesses coupled with consumer awareness as the way to respond. When there is legislation, Congress has resisted general consumer privacy legislation in favor of limited sectoral legislation (e.g., federal protection for children online and of video rental, medical, and financial records). This emphasis contrasts with stronger legislation and the use of consumer oversight committees in the European Union (Margulis and Marx 2013).

The US's Federal Trade Commission (FTC), the major government agency currently addressing consumer privacy questions, advocates five fair information practice principles (FIPPs) to address consumer privacy concerns. In brief, they are notice of information practices; consumer choice on how personal information is used beyond its intended use; reasonable access to one's personal information at a website and the ability to ensure its accuracy and completeness; the taking of reasonable steps to ensure the security of personal information at a website; and instituting an enforcement mechanism through self-regulation, enforceable regulations, or legislation. The FTC's new privacy framework, based on best practices, subsumes the five aforementioned principles and also addresses reasonable information collection limits, sound retention practices, and consumer education about commercial data privacy practices (Federal Trade Commission 2012). However, these policies are voluntary because the Congress has resisted supporting legislation for the five FIPPs and for the new best practices framework (Margulis and Marx 2013).

Another tool is an independent organization acting as a third party guarantor, such as TRUSTe, which offers a privacy seal of approval to companies. The TRUSTe seal provides consumers with two FIPPs: notice and choice. Privacy seals are associated with greater trust in a website and a more favorable attitude toward the company's privacy policies (e.g., Miyazaki and Krishnamurthy 2002). But a privacy seal does not necessarily mean better privacy practices or the collection of less personal information, nor is it a guarantee that a website is free of malware or spam (Margulis and Marx 2013). One study found a higher rate of malware and/or spam at websites with a TRUSTe privacy seal than those without it (Edelman 2009).

Another tool is privacy impact assessments (PIA) (Wright and de Hert 2012). This approach tries to anticipate problems, seeking to prevent, rather than to put out, fires. The PIA model is adopted *before* personal data practices are established. It involves a variety of stakeholders and tries to learn from the past and also imagine how new technologies and practices might bring new problems – including that intriguing class of the "unknown unknowns." PIA is very much a work in development, but offers a model for raising awareness and for trying to bring some balance to conflicting interests. On the other hand, the practice is voluntary with no necessary requirement of publicity or means of enforcement. In the final analysis, consistent with American political economy: *caveat emptor.*

SEE ALSO: Consumer Behavior; Consumer Protection Agency; Consumers, Flawed; Stealth Marketing

REFERENCES

Culnan, Mary J., and Robert J. Bies, R. J. 2003. "Consumer Privacy: Balancing Economic and Justice Considerations." *Journal of Social Issues* 59(2): 323–332.

Duhigg, Charles. 2012. "How Companies Learn Your Secrets." Accessed July 7, 2014. http://www.nytimes.com/2012/02/19/magazine/shopping-habits.html?pagewanted=all&_r=0.

Edelman, Benjamin. 2009. "*Adverse Selection in Online "Trust" Certifications.*" Paper presented at ICEC '09, August 12–15, 2009, Taipei, Taiwan.

Federal Trade Commission. 2012. *Protecting Consumer Privacy in an Era of Rapid Change: Recommendations to Businesses and Policymakers.* Washington, DC: Federal Trade Commission.

Margulis, Stephen T. 2003. "Privacy as a Social Issue and Behavioral Concept." *Journal of Social Issues* 59(2): 243–262.

Margulis, Stephen T. 2009. "Privacy and Psychology." In *Contours of Privacy*, edited by David Matheson, 131–152. Newcastle on Tyne: Cambridge Scholars Press.

Margulis, Stephen T., and Gary T. Marx. 2013. "Caveat Emptor: A Perspective on Consumer Privacy Online." *Surveillance and Society* 10(3/4): 351–355.

Marx, Gary T. Forthcoming. *Windows Into the Soul: Surveillance and Society in an Age of High Technology.* Chicago: University of Chicago Press.

Mearian, Lucas. 2012. "By 2020 There Will Be 5,200 GB of Data for Every Person on Earth." Accessed July 7, 2014. http://www.computerworld.com/s/article/9234563/By_2020_there_will_be_5_200_GB_of_data_for_every_person_on_Earth.

Miyazaki, Anthony D., and Sandeep Krishnamurthy. 2002. "Internet Seals of Approval: Effects on Online Privacy Policies and Consumer Perceptions." *Journal of Consumer Affairs* 36(1): 28–49.

Wright, David, and Paul de Hert. 2012. *Privacy Impact Assessment.* New York: Springer.

Prosumption

WHITNEY ERIN BOESEL
University of California, Santa Cruz, USA
NATHAN JURGENSON
University of Maryland, USA

Prosumption is characterized by the blurring of production and consumption. Prosumption analyses therefore focus on both production and consumption simultaneously, rather than on either independently (Ritzer and Jurgenson 2010). Prosumers consume what they produce and/or produce what they consume (Toffler 1980).

Alvin Toffler first discusses "the rise of the prosumer" in his book *The Third Wave* (1980, 265), yet the majority of interest in both "prosumption" and related concepts (e.g., co-creation, peer-production, wikinomics, or crowdsourcing) has been more recent. Prosumption is therefore a contemporary term, but the blurring of production and consumption is itself not a new phenomenon (Toffler 1980; Ritzer 2009). Peasants on pre-industrial farms, for instance, often produced what they consumed. Toffler and Ritzer both argue that the industrial revolution divided production and consumption into separate spheres.

Prosumptive practices are increasingly common. Toffler (1980) cites the do-it-yourself (DIY) movement, the rise of self-help as a phenomenon, and the shift toward self-service in electronic banking and grocery stores to argue that consumers are increasingly active producers; there has since been a proliferation of ATMs, self-checkout machines at pharmacies and grocery stores, and electronic kiosks in hotels, movie theaters, and airports, etc. Ritzer discusses how customers are put to work through "McDonaldization," and others have written about productive craft consumers (such as hobbyists who brew their own beer). Prosumers also prosume collectively: consumers produce products and brands through market research, and the popularity of mass media products such as reality TV (e.g., *American Idol*), amateur pornography (e.g., "Girls Gone Wild"), "citizen journalism" (e.g., CNN's "iReport"), and user-created television (e.g., "Current TV," community cable access channels) indicates that, increasingly, consumers are also producers of the content they consume. Others note visual art, theatre and performance art, music, fan fiction, and even the festival Burning Man as examples of present-day prosumption.

The prosumption concept is particularly relevant to the explosion of user-generated content online, as the user-generated web (or "Web 2.0") marks a massive proliferation of simultaneous production and consumption (Ritzer and Jurgenson 2010). Consumers (users) collaboratively produce open source software (e.g., the operating system Linux, the content management platform Drupal, or the web browser Firefox), product listings (e.g., on eBay or Etsy), product and business reviews (e.g., on Amazon or Yelp), mobile phone applications (such as are sold in Apple's App Store and Google Play), Wikipedia (the world's largest encyclopedia), maps (e.g., OpenStreetMap), and even scientific or genealogical research (such as through the Citizen Science movement and on 23andMe or Ancestry.com). The content of social networking sites (SNS) such as Facebook, Tumblr, and Pinterest is largely created or curated by users, as is the content of blogs (including the microblogging service, Twitter), media sites (e.g., YouTube or Flickr), the community bulletin board Craigslist, and online digital environments (such as Second Life or World of Warcraft). Axel Bruns (2008) identifies a concept similar to prosumption of online content as "produsage."

It is debatable whether the expansion of prosumption online signifies empowerment or exploitation for consumers. Prosumption marks what has been called unpaid labor, free labor, or immaterial labor 2.0; some have speculated that prosumption may represent a hegemonic institution of exploitation and alienation. Alternatively, users do receive nonmonetary gains from online prosumer activities, such as socializing, building networks, gaining professional exposure, or feeling that they are part of a larger project or community. Users also produce individual and collective identities, as well as entire subcultures, through prosuming online content. Some theorists have argued that prosumption of online content may democratize social criticism.

Ritzer argues that prosumption should be treated as a continuum, with pure prosumption as the mid-point between pure consumption and pure production; he also differentiates between producers as consumers and consumers as producers. Accordingly, the relevance and applicability of the prosumption concept are nearly infinite, as it can also be used when either production or consumption is a primary focus. Producers consume raw materials in the production process, for instance, and many workers consume their identities while working.

Finally, prosumption has been analyzed through the Marxist labor theory of value, through Foucauldian notions of government, and through Bourdieusian theories of cultural/social (re)production. Prosumption characterizes what has been called "creationist capitalism," and Ritzer and Jurgenson (2010) situate prosumption within the literature on consumer capitalism to postulate prosumer capitalism.

SEE ALSO: Burning Man; Do-It-Yourself (DIY); Internet, The, and Consumption; McDonaldization; Social Media

REFERENCES

Bruns, Axel. 2008. *Blogs, Wikipedia, Second Life, and Beyond: From Production to Produsage*. New York: Peter Lang.

Ritzer, George. 2009. "Focusing on the Prosumer: On Correcting an Error in the History of Social Theory." Paper presented at Prosumer Revisited Conference, Frankfurt, Germany, March.

Ritzer, George, and Nathan Jurgenson. 2010. "Production, Consumption, Prosumption: The Nature of Capitalism in the Age of the Digital 'Prosumer.'" *Journal of Consumer Culture* 10(1): 13–36.

Toffler, Alvin. 1980. *The Third Wave*. New York: William Morrow and Company.

Public Relations

MELIKE AKTAŞ YAMANOĞLU
Ankara University, Turkey

Public relations (PR) is one of the central activities of economic and cultural life in contemporary societies, along with other works in creative industries dealing with presentation and representation, and mediating between production and consumption. Public relations is practiced on behalf of individuals, formally or informally structured organizations, and groups by in-house practitioners or consultants in order to promote particular discourses and interests. Public relations also has an active role in structuring society and culture. It shapes values, attitudes, and dispositions of publics and disseminates new trends and lifestyles.

As public relations activities are employed in a vast range of commercial and noncommercial contexts – and in each context particular goals, intentions, and tasks are attached to the practice – it is rather difficult to reach a universally agreed upon definition of the concept. The notion of public relations is multifaceted and can be characterized according to its objectives, target audiences, and tools.

Public institutions, private sector corporations, as well as nongovernmental organizations engage with public relations to build, alter, and maintain relationships with key publics. The term "publics" here refers to active or potentially active groups within a society who have interest, stake, influence, and power in particular organizations and those who are potentially affected by the actions of those organizations. An organization's publics generally include its employees, trade unions, local communities, financial investors, customers, suppliers, distributors, media, governmental institutions, and civil society groups.

Public relations is a persistent communication process achieved through various communication channels and tools. It utilizes interpersonal skills and persuasive techniques. Public relations can be employed to develop and/or mobilize public opinion, to obtain public legitimacy, to produce consent, to manage reputation, to build a positive image, to promote goods and services, to disseminate information, to monitor public issues, and to facilitate changes. On the other hand, public relations may also contribute to the development of civil society and enhance the political participation potentials of social groups. It can trigger public awareness, increase public screen, and raise public concern.

According to one of the latest definitions presented by the Public Relations Society of America (PRSA 2012), "public relations is a strategic communication process that builds mutually beneficial relationships between organizations and their publics." Similar types of functional conceptualizations of the notion that conceive public relations purely in an organizational context are common in the literature. In this frame, public relations is broadly defined as "management of communication between an organization and its public" (Grunig and Hunt 1984, 6) or managing organizational–public relationships. Yet, the effectiveness of public relations in the organizations is contingent upon meeting organizational interests and is measured in terms of organizational priorities. Functional approaches offer prescriptions and assign strategic roles to public relations practitioners about facilitating an organization to adapt to any changes in its external environment, guarding against any problems, and also developing the communicative capacity of the organization with its key publics. Specialties that are commonly described as, or part of, public relations include issues management, crisis communication, risk communication, fundraising, campaigning, public affairs, internal communication, media relations, financial public relations, and marketing communications that reflect strategically oriented activities of practice.

The managerial and functional portrayal of public relations has begun (starting in the 1990s) to be challenged and re-examined by multiple perspectives through highlighting its distinctive features and impacts on the wider society. Alternative views cover divergent schools of thought and mainly criticize the instrumental and technical mindset of public relations as a strategic and effective communications tool. Instead, these views situate public relations in a political, economic, and social context and offer a broader understanding of the notion. Critical, feminist, rhetorical, and cultural approaches expand the role of public relations and draw attention to the processes and outcomes of the practice. The normative portrayal of tasks is balanced with how public relations is actually practiced in society. Subjects such as power issues in relationships, inequalities in the professions, ideological function of public relations, persuasive communication initiatives and ethics of practice, and last but not least, the contribution of PR practices to the development and dissemination of material discourses and values extended the agenda of public relations research.

Societally and culturally oriented conceptualizations evaluate the complex roles and implications of public relations work. In this perspective, public relations is regarded as a subtle mechanism that structures society and culture. Public relations practices are linked to the sense making and production of discourses to secure, modify, or transform social and cultural structures. Public relations work involves crafting and circulating symbolic meanings, acceptable or legitimate values, attitudes, and actions. It also contributes to constructing frames of reference and interpretation guidelines for publics so that it serves as a medium for shaping social reality and building common sense. Thereby, public relations practitioners act as "cultural intermediaries" who aid in formulating or inculcating particular tastes, dispositions, lifestyles, and consumption patterns. Public relations professionals are important market actors and have critical roles in connecting production and consumption. They stimulate interest, produce demand, and promote new styles of consumption. Public relations has a pivotal role in the development of consumer culture and should be regarded as one of the driving forces of capitalism.

SEE ALSO: Capitalism; Consumer Culture; Cultural Intermediaries; Marketing/Marketing Science

REFERENCES

Grunig, James E., and Todd Hunt. 1984. *Managing Public Relations.* New York: Holt, Rinehart, & Winston.

PRSA. 2012. "Public Relations Society of America." http://www.prsa.org/AboutPRSA/PublicRelationsDefined/#.U7p6_igbKCY.

FURTHER READING

Edwards, Lee. 2012. "Defining the 'Object' of Public Relations Research: A New Starting Point." *Public Relations Inquiry* 1: 7–30.

Ewen, Stuart. 1996. *PR! A Social History of Spin.* New York: Basic Books.

Heath, Robert L., ed. 2010. *The Sage Handbook of Public Relations*, 2nd ed. Thousand Oaks, CA: Sage.

L'Etang, Jacquie. 2008. *Public Relations: Concepts, Practice and Critique.* London: Sage.

Moloney, Kevin. 2006. *Rethinking Public Relations: PR Propaganda and Democracy*, 2nd ed. London: Routledge.

Q

Quality of Life, Measurements of

CLAIR BROWN
University of California, Berkeley, USA

Defining and measuring the standard of living has a long history in economics and sociology, and is essential for understanding the role that consumption plays in how people live and their quality of life. The most commonly used national measure to compare the quality of life across countries and across time is gross domestic product (GDP) per capita or the closely related national income per capita. This approach has several weaknesses, and researchers have devised alternative measurements of the standard of living that are more comprehensive at both the national level and the individual level. There is no consensus on the best measure to use, and below is an overview of three alternative models and measures of quality of life: neoclassical, institutional, and Buddhist.

GDP AND NATIONAL INCOME: WHAT THEY MEASURE

GDP measures the market value of all final goods and services produced in a country in a given period, and national income, which is approximately 80 percent of GDP in the United States, measures the income earned through work and ownership of factors of production. Approximately 70 percent of US GDP is personal consumption. GDP per capita is used to indicate how well countries are doing economically, which is assumed to indicate the standard of living of the population. The weaknesses of the GDP as a measure of economic output and quality of life are widely discussed. They include exclusion of nonmarket activities (including unpaid work such as housework, volunteer work, and crime), work paid off the books (including the underground economy, bartering, and gift exchange), externalities (both negative, such as pollution, and positive, such as use of free public goods), unsustainable use of resources, and the distribution of income. However, official GDP, which is measured consistently and frequently across countries, provides a comparison of countries over time.

THE NEOCLASSICAL MODEL

The traditional neoclassical model assumes that individuals maximize utility (or satisfaction), which is usually measured as a combination of the income provided by work (hours multiplied by wage) and leisure (nonwork hours). Aggregation of utility across the

The Wiley Blackwell Encyclopedia of Consumption and Consumer Studies, First Edition.
Edited by Daniel Thomas Cook and J. Michael Ryan.

population provides a measure of total wellbeing, and this model justifies the use of GDP or national income per capita to measure wellbeing. The distribution of income is not relevant, and interpersonal comparisons of utility cannot be made because all individuals are maximizing income given their personal preferences (Becker 1978).

INSTITUTIONAL MODELS

Institutional economists assume that economic forces play out over a structure of rules, regulations, and norms, and the distribution of income is critical in evaluating how people live. A family's consumption is guided by social norms, and their wellbeing reflects their relative income as well as their total expenditures. Because a family judges its standard of living by what the income groups above it, as well as its own income group, are consuming, an increase in income inequality results in people trying to increase their consumption in order to keep up with the higher income groups. With more inequality, a society becomes less satisfied with the same national income (Frank 2010).

Institutionalists have traditionally divided family consumption into three categories: basics or necessities, variety or comforts, and status or luxuries. Basics are the goods and services that most families consume, and include expenditures made to meet fundamental physical needs and minimum requirements for social integration. Expenditures above the basic requirement can be broken down into variety, which makes life more comfortable and interesting, and luxuries, which provide status markings of social position through showiness or exclusion. With economic development and technological change, the required basics expand and change; basics vary across countries because of culture and level of economic development. Although the ability to purchase basics may be viewed as critical in defining a family's wellbeing, the family may be observed purchasing variety or even luxuries in place of some basics because of social norms. As income grows, families are assumed to emulate those in a higher income class. Economic distance between families in two adjacent income classes compares their consumption of basics, variety, and status, which describes how inequality translates into lifestyles. The United States has historically collected data on family consumption (Consumer Expenditure Survey, http://www.bls.gov/cex/). Measurement of a given family's quality of life includes consumption of basics and variety; the contribution of luxuries to the quality of life is controversial, because luxuries only mark social position and do not add to overall social wellbeing, even though consuming luxuries may make individuals happier. In 1918 wage earner families were spending 93 percent of their budgets on basics and 2 percent on luxuries. In 1988, they were spending only 55 percent of their budgets on basics, 23 percent on variety, and 22 percent on luxuries (Brown 1994).

A model based upon the capabilities and functionings that individuals achieve provides the framework for measuring quality of life across countries in a holistic manner (Sen 1999). Individual capabilities reflect social institutions and public goods and services as well as income, which is implicitly included through the capabilities it enables. Several indices have been developed from the capabilities and functionings approach in order to compare quality of life across countries and across time. The United Nations Human Development Index (HDI), introduced in the UN's first Human Development Report (1990), is a single index number that combines three dimensions – health (life expectancy), education (mean and expected years of schooling), and living standards (income per capita) – with minimum and maximum goalposts for each dimension. In 2010, the Inequality-Adjusted HDI (IHDI) was created to adjust the HDI for inequality in a country's distribution of the three dimensions of the HDI. In 2010, the Gender Inequality Index (GII) was created, using three dimensions – reproductive health, empowerment, and labor market – to indicate discrimination against women and girls in each country.

The OECD created a Better Life Index (BLI; see http://www.oecdbetterlifeindex.org/) to compare wellbeing across OECD countries. BLI has 11 dimensions, and an interactive online tool allows users to rate the dimensions according to their own ratings of importance. One of the dimensions is a subjective quality of life measurement that asks users to rate their own life in terms of the best possible life (10) through to the worst possible life (0), and also asks if they have more positive or negative experiences and feelings during an average day.

Although environmental degradation and sustainability were not part of the capabilities approach initially, indices that include these elements have been developed for a large number of countries. Genuine Progress Indicator (GPI) and the more detailed Index of Sustainable Economic Welfare (ISEW) adjust GDP for beneficial nonmarket activities (housework and volunteer work) and negative activities (pollution and crime) (Lawn 2003). The Happy Planet Index (HPI; see http://www.happyplanetindex.org/) is an index that measures human wellbeing (life expectancy and life satisfaction) per ecological footprint (environmental impact).

BUDDHIST ECONOMICS FRAMEWORK

The institutional model, which incorporates capabilities, environmental protection, and global sustainability, still lacks a spiritual element. The primary additions for a Buddhist economic approach would be relieving suffering of all people, and causing no harm or violence to others (Thubten and Brown 2013). A Buddhist economic approach puts less emphasis on personal consumption, especially after a person has adequate consumption (basics). For the individual, the wellbeing of others, especially relieving suffering of others, becomes more important than "more is better" for oneself.

Bhutan, a Buddhist nation, undertook a major project to define the components of happiness and create a Gross National Happiness (GNH) index, which includes 124 variables that measure nine equal domains: psychological wellbeing, health, education, culture, time use, good governance, community vitality, ecological diversity and resilience, and living standards. Each variable has a sufficiency level. It was noted that the ecological domain needed to be strengthened in future versions (Ura et al. 2012).

In 2010 Bhutan surveyed the entire population to create each person's happiness score and thus measure Bhutan's GNH. An important part of this program is to identify how people with different levels of education or employment and in different regions vary by their happiness, and to improve the conditions of "not-yet-happy" people. This GNH index and its measurement have attracted global interest.

SEE ALSO: Class; Consumer Behavior; Consumption in the United States; Lifestyle

REFERENCES

Becker, Gary S. 1978. *The Economic Approach to Human Behavior*. Chicago: University of Chicago Press.

Brown, Clair. 1994. *American Standards of Living*. Cambridge, MA: Blackwell.

Frank, Robert H. 2010. *Luxury Fever*. Princeton, NJ: Princeton University Press.

Lawn, Philip A. 2003. "An Assessment of the Valuation Methods Used to Calculate the Index of

Sustainable Economic Welfare (ISEW), Genuine Progress Indicator (GPI), and Sustainable Net Benefit Index (SNBI)." *Ecological Economics* 44: 105–118.

Sen, Amartya. 1999. *Development as Freedom*. New York: Alfred A. Knopf.

Thubten, Anam, and Clair Brown. 2013. "What Does Buddhism Have to Add to Economics?" Working paper, Center for Work, Technology and Society, IRLE, University of California Berkeley.

United Nations Development Programme. 1990–2013. *Human Development Report*. http://hdr.undp.org/en/reports/about/.

Ura, Karma, Sabina Alkire, Tshoki Zangmo, and Karma Wangdi. 2012. *A Short Guide to Gross Happiness Index*. Centre for Bhutan Studies. www.grossnationalhappiness.com/.

R

Recycling

MARKUS HADLER
Macquarie University, Australia

Recycling can be characterized as an intended environmentally significant behavior (Stern 2000) – if done with the intention to influence the environment. But, even when conducted for other reasons, such as monetary reward, recycling is still environmentally significant because it influences the distribution and use of environmental goods. Recycling is carried out mostly in the private sphere, similar to behaviors such as buying and boycotting certain products or improving the energy efficiency of one's home. This private nature differentiates it from public environmental behaviors such as activism and protest, and less costly political behaviors such as signing a petition, contacting a politician, and donating money to environmental organizations.

THE IMPACT OF RECYCLING

The United Nations Environmental Program fact sheet on resource efficiency (UNEP 2010) calls for efficient production and consumption and considers recycling an important factor in this process. UNEP promotes recycling, particularly in developing countries, by discussing a basic reduce, reuse, and recycle approach with national and local governments.

The use and reuse of resources is usually considered an important measure for achieving sustainable consumption. Nonetheless, its usefulness in financial terms and environmental impact is sometimes questioned. Shaw (2008) summarizes these arguments and discusses the following example of a possible negative impact: If newspapers were made from recycled paper only, areas devoted to growing trees might be used for less environmentally friendly purposes such as industrial developments. Furthermore, dependent on the material price, it is sometimes less costly to use landfills than to recycle.

THE PREVALENCE OF RECYCLING IN DIFFERENT COUNTRIES

Recycling behavior has become common. Based on representative population surveys collected by the International Social Survey Programme (www.issp.org) in 2010, the following percentage of the population "always" recycles: Above 70 percent in Austria, Belgium (Flanders only), Germany, Switzerland, Canada, and New Zealand; 50–69 percent in Denmark, Norway, Sweden, Finland, Slovenia, Spain, Japan, and South Korea; 30–49

The Wiley Blackwell Encyclopedia of Consumption and Consumer Studies, First Edition.
Edited by Daniel Thomas Cook and J. Michael Ryan.

percent in the Czech Republic, the Slovak Republic, the United States, Taiwan, and the Philippines; 10–29 percent in Bulgaria, Croatia, Latvia, Israel, Argentina, Chile, and Mexico; below 10 percent in Russia, South Africa, and Turkey. These numbers are a significant increase from 1993 when this data was collected for the first time. Among the 15 countries that took part in all ISSP environment surveys, the overall percentage of respondents who report recycling "always" has increased from 25 percent in 1993, to 29 percent in 2000, to 46 percent in 2010.

DETERMINANTS OF RECYCLING

The country differences pointed out above correlate with several national characteristics (Hadler and Haller 2011). Private behavior is more common in affluent societies, countries where environmentalism has been institutionalized in the form of ministries and other measures, in open political regimes, and in societies without a socialist past. The prevalence of recycling, thus, can be influenced by governmental actions – for example, providing recycling opportunities is one important measure that has become widespread. According to the ISSP environment data, the percentage of respondents who do not have access to recycling opportunities has dropped from 19 percent in 1993 to 7 percent in 2010 among the countries that completed all three environment surveys. Providing means to recycle conveniently, in fact, increases recycling rates beyond the mere increase in availability and opportunity. A possible explanation is that individual attitudes and behaviors tend to become more similar between individuals in close proximity (Schwab, Harton, and Cullum 2012). Observing other people recycling, therefore, can motivate individuals to do the same and, therefore, boost recycling rates additionally.

Considering the influence of contextual and attitudinal factors on behavior, attitudes are of particular importance when the effects of the context are weak (Stern 2000). As for environmental attitudes, research has pointed to a wide array of different attitudes, views, and concerns (Dietz, Fitzgerald, and Shwom 2005). The general idea is that such attitudes and views are of immediate importance for environmental behavior. Furthermore, differences also exist between various sociodemographic groups. Analyzing the 2000–01 ISSP data, Hadler and Haller (2011) identified that female, older, and higher educated respondents are more engaged in private environmental behaviors. The same is true for individuals who assess environmental risks as vast, are willing to make sacrifices, and are convinced that their actions can make a difference.

SEE ALSO: Consumer Behavior; Consumer Resistance Movements; Ethical Consumption; Green Consumption; Waste

REFERENCES

Dietz, Thomas, Amy Fitzgerald, and Rachael Shwom. 2005. "Environmental Values." *Annual Review of Environmental Resources* (30): 335–372.

Hadler, Markus, and Max Haller. 2011. "Global Activism and Nationally Driven Recycling: The Influence of World Society and National Contexts on Public and Private Environmental Behavior." *International Sociology* 26(3): 315–345.

Schwab, Nicholas, Helen C. Harton, and Jerry G. Cullum. 2012. "The Effects of Emergent Norms and Attitudes on Recycling Behavior." *Environment and Behavior. Online*. doi:10.1177/0013916512466093.

Shaw, Jane S. 2008. "Recycling." In *The Concise Encyclopedia of Economics*, edited by David R. Henderson. Indianapolis: Liberty Fund, Inc. Accessed July 7, 2014. http://www.econlib.org/library/Enc/Recycling.html.

Stern, Paul C. 2000. "Toward a Coherent Theory of Environmentally Significant Behavior." *Journal of Social Issues* 56(3): 407–424.

UNEP (United Nations Environmental Program). 2010. Six Priority Areas Factsheets – Resource Efficiency. Accessed July 7, 2014. http://www.unep.org/publications/.

S

Scarcity and Artificial Scarcity

ADEL DAOUD
University of Gothenburg, Sweden

Scarcity is a relational concept with both quantitative and qualitative properties. In its simplest form, scarcity refers to the quantitative relationship between means (resources, satisfiers, goods) and ends (wants, needs, desires). When the means (M) available to satisfy some ends (E) are not sufficient ($M < E$), then a situation of scarcity arises. If the reverse is true ($M > E$), then a situation of abundance is present. Sufficiency arises when means and ends are just about equal ($M = E$). Of these three intimately related concepts, scarcity seems to have played the most central role in the social sciences.

Scarcity of resources is different from resources being limited. Limited resources refers to the fact that there is a given amount of a resource (e.g., apples, cars, or arable land), but this in itself does not say anything about scarcity, abundance, or sufficiency. A limited resource can become scarce only if it is related to some human ends (wants, needs, desires), and if the available resources are less than the requirements for it.

Accordingly, the term *means* (M), or a resource, simply refers to how much an individual requires in order to satisfy some *ends* (E) or needs. It is thus the quantitative relationship between these terms that defines scarcity (and abundance and sufficiency). In a more complex analysis of scarcity, the qualitative aspects of scarcity are defined, which will also introduce a variety of scarcity forms, among them artificial scarcity – a situation where individuals are hindered from accessing given sufficient resources or where the systems production potential is not fully used.

The qualitative aspects of scarcity are as important as the quantitative for social analysis. There are at least two central questions in this instance, namely: "what causes scarcity to arise in a given social context?" and "what are the effects of scarcity on social behavior?". These two questions are largely dependent on what kinds of ends and means the analysis is about. Scarcity of food or water will certainly affect social behavior differently than scarcity of computers or cars. The former will hinder individuals from participating in society and the economy, and in severe situations it might even lead to death. Scarcity of cars, on the other hand, might hinder certain individuals from using personal transportation for reasons that are functional (e.g., speed

The Wiley Blackwell Encyclopedia of Consumption and Consumer Studies, First Edition.
Edited by Daniel Thomas Cook and J. Michael Ryan.

of transportation), economic (e.g., trade), or social (e.g., conspicuous consumption of certain luxurious cars). If an individual does not have a want or a need for a certain kind of good, then it implies that the given person cannot experience scarcity of that resource. The abolishment of excessive material wants, and thus indirectly scarcity, is the aim of some anti-consumerist social movements, such as voluntary simplicity, in the context of consumer society (Daoud 2011). Accordingly, some of the qualitative properties of the concept of scarcity are linked to the widely debated concepts of human needs and wants.

Another qualitative dimension of the concept of scarcity refers to the level of analysis. For example, Robinson Crusoe, who lives alone on an island, needs merely to think about his own wants and what resources he can use to satisfy them, whereas an average household, say in South East Asia, has a different needs–wants structure than Crusoe has, and their resources are also very different. A country as a whole has yet another aggregated structure of ends and pool of resources. This fact has at least two implications: the first is simply that scarcity can exist on an individual level, a household level, a country level, or at any other level of analysis. Accordingly, scarcity of resources is always relative to this level and does not necessarily exist globally. For example, there might be the case, as Amartya Sen has shown (1981), that famines can arise without there being scarcity of food on an aggregate level – a situation of artificial scarcity. Who is affected by starvation depends on other socioeconomic factors such as social class, ethnicity, or gender. The same argument can be true for other kinds of perceived scarcities.

This fact leads us to another important implication. Different individuals occupy different social positions in a given system of social structures (e.g., in their jobs or in their households), and so their ability to access resources varies. Children are largely dependent on their parents to access the resources which that household commands; the same household's ability to access resources in society or the economy depends on its socioeconomic characteristics (ethnicity, social class, education, etc.). This highlights the importance of property and thus the concept of entitlements, defined in a broad sense. Entitlements define the ownership structures of any given society and thus under which conditions exchange of goods between individuals are seen as legitimate (excluding exchange under threat or violence). In a market economy, money is regarded as the primary system of exchange. This defines one kind of trade-based entitlement. But exchange or access to goods can be defined by other kinds of entitlements such as by judicial, friendship, or family structures (Polanyi 1977). For example, a child usually accesses resources (e.g., food) just by the fact of being in a given family structure; friends might mutually acquire access to each other's pool of resources by lending (e.g., food, yacht, or money); similarly, citizens are given access to some resource provided by their community (e.g., education) just by the fact that they are citizens. There is accordingly a wide variety of entailment which can affect the quantitative and qualitative character of scarcity, abundance, and sufficiency.

Hence a situation of artificial scarcity arises when individuals have a need or want for some goods, but they are socially excluded from accessing them, even if there might be an actual abundance or sufficiency of that good in the system. They are simply excluded because they lack valid entitlements.

The concept of artificial scarcity can be used in another way also. Some scholars, for example John Maynard Keynes, have argued that given the level of technological development and available stock of capital in the world today there is a great potential to create an abundance of many types of goods (Galbraith 1958; Keynes 1972/1930). Others concur with this statement but they add that the contemporary capitalist system forces the economy toward artificial scarcity because of the market mechanism or due to vested interest of capital owners, as Karl Marx would argue. The internet economy (peer-to-peer exchange) and the use of intellectual property rights is a common example of this phenomenon. This situation, of potential abundance, is also known by some as a postscarcity system (e.g., Giddens 1990).

In the social sciences, neoclassical economics is one of the few frameworks that explicitly bases its approach on the concept of scarcity. The economic problem is often stated in a general sense, which encompasses universal scarcity. It is postulated that there are virtually infinite wants and limited means. Neoclassical economics is then about how individuals make choices between their wants in order to maximize utility. There are thus trade-offs and opportunity costs to each choice. This kind of scarcity is termed *relative scarcity* since the problem is formulated in terms of competing ends (a hierarchical list of preferences) relative to a given set of resources (budget constraint). The focus is on alternative use of a resource. This formulation of the problem was originally articulated in the writing of the early pioneers of marginal utility theory, more precisely, Carl Menger, William Stanley Jevons, and Léon Walras. The approach was later popularized by Alfred Marshall and Lionel Robbins.

The concept of scarcity can also be seen in terms of *absolute scarcity*. In the ecological economic framework, originating largely from Thomas Malthus's thinking, resources have an ultimate and finite limitation. For example, given population increase, there is a finite limitation of arable land in any given country, and thus there is a limit to how much food requirements can be satisfied at any point in time; energy in general is a finite resource, and the earth can only support some given amount of that demand. Accordingly, there is ultimately an absolute limitation, and so absolute scarcity regardless of how optimally we allocate resources (i.e., relative scarcity). In brief, the problem of absolute scarcity is about actual use of some resource (which is not substitutable), whereas the problem of relative scarcity is about alternative use of some resource (which is substitutable). These two perspectives are not necessarily mutually exclusive. They are, however, two different conceptual ways of regarding the relationship between means and ends. Additionally, in both systems of thought, scarcity seems to be naturalized (Daoud 2010), that is, the social and cultural dimensions of how ends and means are produced are usually not the main focus.

SEE ALSO: Capitalism; Commodities; Conspicuous Consumption; Downshifting; Needs and Wants; Needs, True and False

REFERENCES

Daoud, Adel. 2010. "Robbins and Malthus on Scarcity, Abundance, and Sufficiency: The Missing Sociocultural Element." *American Journal of Economics and Sociology* 69: 1206–1229.

Daoud, Adel. 2011. "The Modus Vivendi of Material Simplicity: Counteracting Scarcity Via the Deflation of Wants." *Review of Social Economy* 69: 275–305.

Galbraith, John Kenneth. 1958. *The Affluent Society*. London: Hamish Hamilton.

Giddens, Anthony. 1990. *The Consequences of Modernity*. Cambridge, UK: Polity.

Keynes, John Maynard. 1972/1930. "Economic Possibilities for Our Grandchildren." In *Essays in Persuasion*, 321–332. London: Macmillan.

Polanyi, Karl. 1977. *The Livelihood of Man*. New York: Academic Press.

Sen, Amartya Kumar. 1981. *Poverty and Famines: An Essay on Entitlement and Deprivation*. Oxford: Clarendon.

Semiotics

SILVER RATTASEPP and KALEVI KULL
University of Tartu, Estonia

Contemporary usage of the term "semiotics" is derived from John Locke's *Essay Concerning Human Understanding* (1690), which presents the requirement for a science that would study the "*signs* the mind makes use of" in acquiring knowledge. However, the concept *semeiotics* also existed in Greek, to denote the study of medical symptoms and "natural signs." The key difference with latter development of semiotics is the absence, in Greek thought, of a notion of sign that would be applicable beyond the nature–culture binary. Such a general notion of signs was introduced by Augustine of Hippo (354–430). Nevertheless, it was not until the late nineteenth century that semiotics began to develop as a separate branch of the sciences. The two leading figures and founders of contemporary semiotics were Charles Sanders Peirce (1839–1914) and especially Ferdinand de Saussure (1857–1913); the posthumous publication in 1916 of the latter's *Cours de linguistique générale* (*Course in General Linguistics*) laid the groundwork for much of twentieth-century semiotics in the West.

De Saussure proposed a science of semiology to cover the study of all arbitrary sign relations, which would be patterned after linguistic signs. He posited a dyadic or binary model for semiological analysis, consisting of linguistic terms, called "signifiers," and their conventional relation to cognitive states, called "signifieds." Language conceived as the full set of such arbitrary and therefore conventional sign relations is thus a total system of distinctions, in which every sign acquires its meaning by way of its distinctiveness as related to other signs within the same system. As a consequence, de Saussure limits sign action within the realm of culture.

Earlier, however, Charles S. Peirce had proposed a more general definition of signs, founded on convention conceived as a formation of habit, and divided into numerous classifications, of which the distinction between icons, indexes, and symbols has become the most widespread. Referring to the modes or mechanisms by which habitual sign usages are acquired, *icons* refer to the relation of similarity or resemblance, *indexes* refer to the relation of correlation or causality, and *symbols* to relations based on conventions, that is, the dispositions or factitious habits of their users. The sign is, in this instance, not an object in itself, but a set of conditions that have to be met in order for processes of meaning to appear and which, furthermore, require processes of habit formation. Unlike de Saussure's model, which was patterned after language, Peirce took a pragmatic or phenomenological route, defining a sign as cognizable, as something that can be experienced. Also unlike de Saussure, who proposed a binary conception of signs, Peirce's was a threefold one, comprising of an object, an interpretant, and a representamen. A sign is determined by something other than itself, called its object, but which, on the other hand, determines some mind or knower, called the *interpretant*, so that the interpretation of the object is related by way of a mediator, called the *representamen*. A sign is thus something which stands for somebody or something in some respect or capacity. With these general conceptions of sign action, Peirce laid the foundation for an understanding of semiosis that would not be limited to human culture.

Picking up on this theme, in 1963 Thomas A. Sebeok, a linguist and a biologist, introduced zoösemiotics as the study of animal semiosis. In addition to Peirce, this development became heavily based on the

Umwelttheorie of the German-Estonian biologist Jakob von Uexküll (1864–1944) and the theory of semiosphere developed by Juri Lotman (1990; 2009/1992). An *Umwelt* (a concept usually retained in its original German form in English-language texts) refers to the experienced, meaningful world of an organism, based on that organism's species-specific capacities for perception and action. *Umwelt*, the lived, sensed, recognized world of an organism, comprises those aspects of the environment that the organism is capable of perceiving, which are then rendered into capacities of action or behavior toward those aspects. The environmental objects which the organism can perceive and thus relate to take on a certain tone, a meaning for that organism. Humans, too, have their particular *Umwelten*, and hence biosemiotics is a comparative study of meaning in human and nonhuman worlds. This fruitful fusion of Peircean semiotics and Uexküllian biosemiotics led Sebeok to propose the thesis that since all living entities incorporate a species-specific model of their environment by means of signification and communication by signs, semiosis is coextensive with life.

The academic institutionalization of semiotics started to become more widespread from the 1960s onward, with the first major centers established in Paris, Bologna, Bloomington, Moscow, and Tartu. The International Association for Semiotic Studies was established in 1969. The oldest journals in the field are *Sign Systems Studies* (initially *Trudy po znakovym sistemam*, established in 1964) and *Semiotica* (established in 1969).

By the early twenty-first century, semiotics had generally replaced semiology as the name for the discipline, and emphasis has slowly shifted from the static, binary, and linguistic model of de Saussure toward the more encompassing and dynamic, triadic model of Peirce. Another development is the understanding that the sciences as based on experimental control of its objects depend fundamentally on the prior critical or conceptual control of objectification that would provide the framework within which sciences proper operate. Semiotics, the study of the action of signs, is the science of the latter. In consequence semiotics is necessarily an interdisciplinary or transdisciplinary perspective that requires input from more specialized sciences, and studies the premises and assumptions, the habits and methods that establish the boundaries of these sciences but which often go unnoticed within those sciences themselves. In general, semiotics serves both as a theoretical and methodological tool for the scientific study of cultural and living (communicative) systems.

Semiotics of culture as a major branch in semiotics owes much to the Tartu–Moscow school of semiotics, which was initiated by Juri Lotman (1922–1993). The aim of semiotics of culture is to study the whole set of sign systems that organize culture, including arts, media, everyday behavior, and material culture. The entirety of the cultural field comprises a semiosphere, a relational field of interconnected semiotic phenomena, characterized by various dynamical processes, such as those between the center and the periphery of any given semiosphere, as well as cross-border communication and translation between different semiospheres.

Since sign relations are acquired or learnt relations, they are therefore also modeling relations. They serve as modeling relations because a learnt relation can work as a sign relation only if it is about some particular existing regularity or recognizable difference, that is, there cannot be learning without some regularity to be learned. Accordingly, cultural sign systems are modeling systems that carry within themselves an acquired system of distinctions and discriminations.

Analyses of consumer culture, such as those of brand communication, consumer behavior, marketing, identity formation, and visual language, are a staple of cultural and media semiotics. Necessarily, the world of consumption is a web spun of various meanings, codes, and symbols, all furthermore embedded in a particular historical and cultural context. The goal of the semiotic approach to consumption is to pick apart those elements of interpretation which, for everyday consumers, may seem obvious and immediate, but which in fact consist of layers of meaning making of a highly complex nature. Applied semiotic analysis reveals the (often hidden) codes by which the object of analysis is constructed: the relational structure of the object or phenomenon that is responsible for its role and dynamics in an organization, including, for instance, that of consumers' behavior and preferences or values. Since semiotics studies the underlying conditions and premises of meaning making, it also eschews entrenched dichotomies, such as those between fact and value, for example, perceiving both as premised upon a prior construction of meaning (of objectivation).

As a result, a key element of the semiotic approach to consumer culture is the shift of focus from individual decision making and individualized examples of consumer culture, toward an analysis of dynamical cultural interaction and communicative phenomena. An important corollary to this, however, is that a semiotic study of consumer culture must also analyze the first-person perspective of consumers and their subjective and intersubjective meaning making, rather than remaining in the position of a supposedly impartial observer.

An early and influential example of consumer studies from a semiotic perspective is Jean Baudrillard's now-classic early work, such as *The System of Objects* (1996/1968) and *The Consumer Society* (1997/1970), according to which any analysis of the objects of consumption needs to be a study of the discourse *about* objects. Needs and desires, and their means of gratification, are symbolically or discursively constructed, and consumption is used to place the consumer within the symbolic field of the society. The system of objects is a system of symbolic goods that consumers use to signify themselves for the society.

A thorough overview of further semiotic developments in consumption and consumer studies is provided by Mick et al. (2004). The most pertinent issue has been to develop explanatory frameworks for conceptualizing the types of sign relations that constitute a product's potential meanings. For example, the influence on consumers of various signs may be based on "recognition, comprehension, learning, memory, and appreciation (aesthetic reactions)" (Mick et al. 2004, 13). Such analysis extends to the level of products, brands, and marketing (see also Danesi 2008; Rossolatos 2014; Williamson 1998). As in many other branches of semiotics, the Peircean and Saussurean schools are relatively distinct in consumer semiotics. The Saussurean paradigm (as developed by Louis Hjelmslev and Algirdas Julius Greimas) has focused on structural interpretation of textual meanings, with the purpose of identifying potential meanings of objects of consumer culture. The Peircean paradigm has focused on providing conceptual analyses for the development of theoretical frameworks for studying consumer culture. The fruitful cooperation of these two major paradigms is a present goal of general semiotics.

Beginning from the 1990s, semiotic methods have been used in commercial semiotics by companies providing semiotic consultancy, one of the first among which was the UK-based company Semiotic Solutions.

SEE ALSO: Barthes, Roland; Cultural Studies; Emotions and Consumption; Methods of Consumer Research; Needs and Wants; Symbolic Value

REFERENCES

Baudrillard, Jean. 1996/1968. *The System of Objects*. London: Verso.

Baudrillard, Jean. 1997/1970. *The Consumer Society: Myths and Structures*. London: Sage.

Danesi, Marcel. 2008. *Why it Sells: Decoding the Meanings of Brand Names, Logos, Ads, and Other Marketing and Advertising Ploys*. Lanham, MD: Rowman & Littlefield.

Lotman, Juri. 1990. *Universe of the Mind: A Semiotic Theory of Culture*. London: I.B. Tauris.

Lotman, Juri. 2009/1992. *Culture and Explosion*. Berlin: De Gruyter Mouton.

Mick, David Glen, James E. Burroughs, Partick Hetzel, and Mary Yoko Brannen. 2004. "Pursuing the Meaning of Meaning in the Commercial World: An International Review of Marketing and Consumer Research Founded on Semiotics." *Semiotica* 152(1/4): 1–74.

Rossolatos, George. 2014. *Brand Equity Planning with Structuralist Rhetorical Semiotics*. Kassel, Germany: Kassel University Press.

Williamson, Judith. 1998. *Decoding Advertisements: Ideology and Meaning in Advertising*. London: Marion Boyars.

FURTHER READING

Berger, Arthur A. 2010. *The Objects of Affection: Semiotics and Consumer Culture*. New York: Palgrave Macmillan.

Cobley, Paul, ed. 2010. *The Routledge Companion to Semiotics*. London: Routledge.

Danesi, Marcel. 2002. *Understanding Media Semiotics*. London: Oxford University Press.

Holbrook, Morris B., and Elizabeth C. Hirschman. 1993. *The Semiotics of Consumption: Interpreting Symbolic Consumer Behavior in Popular Culture and Works of Art*. Berlin: Mouton de Gruyter.

Krampen, Martin, Klaus Oehler, Roland Posner, Thomas A. Sebeok, and Thure von Uexküll, eds. 1987. *Classics of Semiotics*. New York: Plenum Press.

Nöth, Winfried. 1998. "The Language of Commodities: Groundwork for a Semiotics of Consumer Goods." In *European Perspectives on Consumer Behaviour*, edited by M. Lambkin, G. Foxall, F. van Raaij, and B. Heilbrunn, 354–369. London: Prentice Hall.

Sebeok, Thomas A. 1994. *Signs: An Introduction to Semiotics*. Toronto: University of Toronto Press.

Service Economy

CHRIS WARHURST
University of Warwick, UK

In a service economy, jobs, trade, and GDP are dominated by services provided through the public, private, and voluntary sectors: for example, retail, hospitality, and tourism; and education, health, and financial services. Even products in manufacturing are now more "servitized," through marketing services, for example, and many manufacturing companies now seek to add value to their operations through additional financial services.

Certainly, there has been a numerical shift in job types in recent years. In the middle of the twentieth century, manufacturing mattered in what are now called the advanced economies. Almost half of all jobs were in manufacturing, with the rest of jobs shared between services and still very strong primary industries such as mining, agriculture, and fisheries. By the century's end those same economies were dominated by jobs in services. Although there are variations by country, around three-quarters of all jobs are now in services. In some cities, where shopping has replaced shipbuilding and malls have replaced mills, more than four-fifths of jobs are in the service sector. Indeed, many of these so-called "postindustrial" cities in North America and Western Europe have deliberately sought to reinvent themselves as regional service hubs by promoting financial services and tourism.

Some caution is needed about this numerical shift. Long before manufacturing mattered in these countries, many thousands of working-class men and women went "into service" as the domestic servants of middle- and upper-class families. In recent years in these same countries, there has been a return to paid, home-based personal services such as childcare, as affluent families hire poor female workers from developing countries. In more modest homes, with the collapse of the Fordist Pact, "reproductive labor," undertaken by "traditional" stay-at-home wives and mothers supported by their husbands and the male "breadwinner" model of employment, is now being pushed and pulled out of the home into the market. Consequently, it becomes a paid job and is recast as "productive labor" and counted as part of the service economy. However, many of the women undertaking these jobs are simply doing the same work in the public sphere that they did in the private sphere – preparing and serving food, for example. Other jobs are similarly being recast as service jobs as manufacturing companies "debundle" jobs in noncore activities such as cleaning and catering. Now outsourced to contract cleaning companies, these jobs are again reclassified as part of the service economy. It should also be remembered that manufacturing jobs have not died. Instead, they have been offshored and relocated from the advanced to the newly developing economies. Importantly, this residual manufacturing and the new services are not separate. Manufactured products remain integral to many services. Retail work, for example, involves the shelf-stacking and selling of material goods – from tins of baked beans to cashmere sweaters. Even internet sales providers such as Amazon need manufactured trains, planes, and automobiles to deliver their goods.

THE QUALITY OF JOBS IN THE SERVICE ECONOMY

The quality, not just the quantity, of these service jobs is another issue. There are currently two accounts of the service economy. The first articulates a "new economy" of high skill, high wage jobs. Initially championed by Robert Reich in *The Work of Nations* (1991) as the knowledge economy, it has recently morphed into the creative economy following Richard Florida's *The Rise of the Creative Class* (2002). In this account of the service economy, brains have replaced brawn, with competitive advantage gained though the exploitation of ideas – or what's often called "intellectual capital" – and the provision of intangible, weightless products. Key occupations are those of management consultants, computer programmers, and university professors – most of whom are male. The second emphasizes a service economy of low-skill, low-wage jobs, with the physical labor of burger-flippers and hotel room attendants being sweated under increasing work intensity. Key occupations are those in the "3Cs" – cleaning, catering, and caring, employing mainly women, and often migrants.

Labor market data in the United States and the United Kingdom, as well as many other European countries, suggests that both accounts have empirical purchase, with a polarized economy emerging with a growing number of both good and bad service jobs. Figuratively, these polarized good and bad jobs are sometimes articulated as iMacJobs and McJobs respectively. Again, many of these jobs exist symbiotically, with cash-rich, time-poor workers in good jobs being dependent on workers in bad jobs to provide reproductive services such as childcare.

ARE SERVICES DIFFERENT?

There is consensus in much of the literature that service work is different from manufacturing work for two reasons. First, because service is intangible, perishable, and spontaneous, consumed at the point of production. Second, because it involves direct interaction with customers. In response to this second shift, as the number of service jobs began to expand in the mid-twentieth century, C. W. Mills identified an emerging "personality market." In his classic book *White Collar* (1951), Mills noted that what was now required were "skills with persons," not "skills with things." Workers' personalities, comprising their attitude and appearance, thus become commodified: bought and sold on this market as employers attempted to provide a favorable service encounter between employee and customer.

For Daniel Bell, this change was part of a transformation of society. In *The Coming of Post-Industrial Society* (1976), he used the metaphor of a game to outline three phases of capitalism. Pre-industrial society involved a "game against nature" – for example, agriculture. The industrial era involved a "game against fabricated nature" – for example, manufacturing – but has been usurped in the postindustrial era by a "game between persons," involving highly skilled and specialized occupations whose work centers on "handling people."

Use of another metaphor, this time dramaturgical and drawing on Erving Goffman's *The Presentation of Self In Everyday Life* (1959), is often used to explain this work. As Mills suggested, what creates a good performance in the service encounter are workers' attitudes and appearance. Analytically, the first is articulated as emotional labor (see Hochschild 1983) in which the task of workers is to manage their own and customers' feelings on behalf of their employing organization. The latter is articulated as aesthetic labor (see Warhurst et al. 2000), in which the service encounter is effected by workers having to manage (and have managed) their physical appearance, most obviously their looks and speech. The two concepts are combined in Alan Bryman's *The Disneyization of Society* (2004), in which he argues that service work requires employees to simulate their performances as if they are on stage and customers are an audience. Even the hardware or "servicescape" of organizations can be managed (Booms and Bitner 1981). Pine and Gilmore (2011) even argue that we have shifted to an "experience economy," with retail services providing memorable events or spectacles to lever sales, a tactic particularly useful in the battle with internet sales organizations.

Interestingly, contrasting with mainstream claims of difference between services and manufacturing in the literature on services, both good and bad service jobs can be organized and controlled as tightly by management as factory jobs were in the past. While jobs in the nascent computer industry of the 1960s were of the type now described by Reich and Florida, Philip Kraft (1979) notes how, as the industry matured, these jobs fell under managerial control and became routinized. Writing about already routine call-center jobs, Taylor and Bain (1999) describe this work as an "assembly line in the head," and workers' experience of these jobs is not dissimilar to those of the bygone industrial era. In other words, services too can be industrialized. For this reason, it might be better to articulate the broader economic shift to services in the advanced economies as less postindustrial and more post-manufacturing, driven by the outsourcing and offshoring noted above.

CONSUMPTION NOT PRODUCTION AS THE DEFINING FEATURE OF THE SERVICE ECONOMY?

It might be that these debates about the quantity and quality of service jobs miss the point. According to Zygmunt Bauman (2004), what defines the new phase of capitalism is the shift in emphasis from the production of services to the consumption of services. We are now what we buy, he proclaims. Shopping, not working, provides identity and meaning. Work is decentered, if not dead, according to Bauman.

Unfortunately this argument – as well as Bauman's subsequent books on "liquid modernity" – tends to be evidence-free. What evidence does exist points to work retaining its importance as a source of identity and meaning, even in a service economy – as Rachel Sherman's *Class Acts* (2007) highlights for workers in luxury hotels. Work also provides social inclusion in the service economy. Government often uses routine services as entry-level jobs into employment for the unemployed and economically inactive. Indeed, Bradley et al. (2004) argue that there is a cult rather than a death of work as the long working hours culture and welfare-to-work programs illustrate.

Nevertheless, the distinction between consumption and production again can be overplayed. Research on aesthetic labor reveals how consumers of retail and hospitality services become producers of these services, as employers hire customers to work because of their familiarity with the product (Warhurst and Nickson 2007b; Williams and Connell 2010). More broadly, Tom Baum (1997) points out that services have become "democratized." As services have become cheaper and more available, those who sell services are now the same people as those who buy them. To return to the opening point about service and class, service work is no longer servile work undertaken by a servant class as it was at the turn of the twentieth century. Seller and buyer, producer and consumer can be the same people. Middle-class students work as burger-flippers to pay their way through college; working-class families fly off to foreign holidays using low-cost airlines and hotels. This conflation of consumer and producer suggest that the "service" is being reconfigured, so that there are now three possible encounters between employer and customer: one in which the employee is subordinate, one in which the employee and customer have equivalence, and one in which the employee is superordinate, offering an aspirational benchmark for the customer (Warhurst and Nickson 2007a). As a consequence, the service economy becomes a lot more empirically and conceptually interesting than simply one in which the bulk of a country's jobs, trade, and GDP is based on something nebulously termed "services."

SEE ALSO: Body and Consumer Culture; Capitalism; Class; Consumption, Spectacles of; Disneyization; Mothers/Motherhood; Outsourcing; Servicescapes; Shopping; Tourism

REFERENCES

Baum, Tom. 1997. "Making or Breaking the Tourist Experience." In *The Tourist Experience*, edited by Chris Ryan, 141–142. London: Cassell.

Bauman, Zygmunt. 2004. *Work, Consumerism and the New Poor*, 2nd ed. Maidenhead: Open University Press.

Bell, Daniel. 1976. *The Coming of Post-Industrial Society*. New York: Basic Books.

Booms, Bernard H., and Mary Jo Bitner. 1981. "Marketing Strategies and Organization Structures for Service Firms." In *Marketing of Services*, edited by James H. Donnelly and William R. George, 47–51. Chicago: American Marketing Association.

Bradley, Harriet, Mark Erickson, Carol Stephenson, and Steve Williams. 2004. *Myths at Work*. Cambridge: Polity.

Bryman, Alan. 2004. *The Disneyization of Society*. Thousand Oaks, CA: Sage.

Florida, Richard. 2002. *The Rise of the Creative Class*. New York: Basic Books.

Goffman, Erving. 1959. *The Presentation of Self In Everyday Life*. London: Penguin Books.

Hochschild, Arlie Russell. 1983. *The Managed Heart*. Berkeley: University of California Press.

Kraft, Philip. 1979. "The Routinizing of Computer Programming." *Work and Occupations* 6(2): 139–155.

Mills, C. Wright. 1951. *White Collar: The American Middle Classes*. Oxford: Oxford University Press.

Pine, B. Joseph, and James H. Gilmore. 2011. *The Experience Economy*. Boston, MA: Harvard Business Press.

Reich, Richard. 1991. *The Work of Nations*. New York: Knopf Doubleday.

Sherman, Rachel. 2007. *Class Acts: Service and Inequality in Luxury Hotels*. Oakland, CA: University of California Press.

Taylor, Phil, and Peter Bain. 1999. "'An Assembly Line in the Head': Work and Employee Relations in the Call Centre." *Industrial Relations Journal* 30(2): 101–117.

Warhurst, Chris, and Dennis Nickson. 2007a. "A New Labour Aristocracy? Aesthetic Labour and Routine Interactive Service." *Work, Employment and Society* 21(4): 785–798.

Warhurst, Chris, and Dennis Nickson. 2007b. "Employee Experience of Aesthetic Labour in Retail and Hospitality." *Work, Employment and Society* 21(1): 103–120.

Warhurst, Chris, Dennis Nickson, Anne Witz, and Anne-Marie Cullen. 2000. "Aesthetic Labour in Interactive Service Work: Some Case Study Evidence from the 'New' Glasgow." *Service Industries Journal* 20(3): 1–18.

Williams, Christine L., and Catherine Connell (2010) "'Looking Good and Sounding Right' Aesthetic Labor and Social Inequality in the Retail Industry." *Work and Occupations*, 37(3): 349–377.

Servicescapes

ANNAMMA JOY
University of British Columbia, Canada

The term "servicescapes" was developed by Bitner (1992, 57) to refer to the environmental contexts within which economic transactions occur. How a given environment is structured, its interior and exterior design, sound, lighting, temperature, ease of access, and other such physical elements, will significantly affect a customer's potential purchase decisions. The signifiers inherent in a servicescape differentiate a given store from its competitors, and can instantly convey what demographic the store wishes to attract (e.g., quiet classical music versus the latest hits at ear-splitting volume). Well-curated servicescapes prime consumers' anticipatory expectations before they even enter a store, indicating the likely levels of prices, product quality, and sales attentiveness.

Throughout recorded history, the concept of the market has always been associated with a specific place in which trade took place. In the bustling markets of precapitalist economies, social interaction was as important as the goods being exchanged. Under capitalism, physical spaces serving as marketplaces are often deemed of even greater importance than the social interactions that accompany transactions. The physical impact of the department store, for instance, both demanded and depended upon new forms of conduct while simultaneously facilitating altered perceptions of space and relationship. Retailers' lack of focus on social interactions, other than those between employees and customers, aligns with an ideology of maximizing profitability, and is pragmatic regarding what lies within the control of the retailer. That said, the impact a given servicescape has on consumer actions is undeniable. The same product, available in different servicescapes, will be more or less desirable depending on its environmental context. A customer who is calmed by pleasant lighting, for example, who is not experiencing frustration in navigating a store's layout or worrying about getting a parking ticket, will be more inclined to linger, which, in turn, will affect their likelihood of making a purchase. Thus much is at stake in the creation of a servicescape: a particularly effective retail environment can mean the difference between a retailer's success and failure.

Bitner's definition of servicescapes follows Mehrabian and Russell's (1974) application of approach–avoidance theory to shopping behavior. If ambient conditions are pleasurable, consumers will respond positively; a carefully calibrated servicescape will increase customers' satisfaction, leaving them with enjoyable memories that will predispose them to future visits. If conditions are unpleasant, they will leave and not return. Sherry (2000) investigates how consumers perceive a servicescape in ways that help them form a highly personal sense of place. One consumer's noisy retailer, to be avoided at all costs, is another's favored spot, featuring familiar songs over the loudspeakers.

A broader view of the social atmospherics inherent in servicescapes recognizes the distinctions between private and group consumption. Does a consumer browse in solitude, searching for something unique? Or is a customer in pursuit of a trendy item, desired by many, buoyed by the energy of crowds within the store? Servicescapes that overtly reflect fashion trends reassure a consumer that whatever is purchased within this particular environment will be reliably *au courant*. Far from being a detached spectator, a consumer involved with a communal experience will be open to greater communication, not only with sales representatives, but also with fellow shoppers.

Within themed servicescapes, whether the theme is hushed high-status luxury or brash athletic youthfulness, consumers essentially buy into an overall retail narrative even as they buy a retailer's products, thereby co-creating a brand mystique. Dressed in impeccably tailored Prada, an affluent individual reinforces the elegance of the brand; casually slouchy in jeans and a simple T-shirt from Gap, a young consumer is a poster girl for the brand.

Servicescapes can also convey an implicit ideology, which can be effectively woven throughout a retail experience, one rich in values (e.g., in stores selling handmade children's toys, or those selling sustainable products, such as organic clothing). Buy a doll whose story embodies can-do American spirit (from the American Girl line, for example), and offer your child a sense of history and morality. Eschew fast fashion in favor of fair trade clothing, and experience or recapture a sense of social activism. Consumption never occurs in a vacuum; each element of a servicescape sets off responses, like ripples in a pond, within a consumer's emotional state.

Luxury brands use museum principles to become hybrid environments, part museum and part store, eliding the worlds of art and commerce to create a new retail phenomenon (Joy et al. forthcoming). A servicescape incorporating elements of a museum, such as original art and highly theatrical lighting and design, may spur consumers to seek education about a brand's heritage. The more welcoming and impressive a servicescape, the more communication between clientele and clerk is encouraged.

Such mainstays of a servicescape as ease of purchase and aesthetic appeal are as important online as in brick and mortar stores, with equal power to strongly influence a customer's sense of satisfaction. The site's ease of navigation, its overall appeal, and the simplicity or complexity of design will all attract specific target markets. Consumer interpretations of online environments can contribute to trust, which in turn strongly influences purchase intentions. Through live chat assistance and customer evaluations, consumers can replicate the experience, once limited to physical stores, of communicating with sales representatives and other customers.

Servicescapes, in sum, pay a crucial role in building and sustaining consumer trust and receptivity, leading to the ultimate goal of any retailer: brand loyalty.

SEE ALSO: Consumer Behavior; Consumption, Spectacles of; Department Stores; Experiential Consumption; Theming; Visual Consumption

REFERENCES

Bitner, M. J. 1992. "Servicescapes: The Impact of Physical Surroundings on Customers and

Employees." *Journal of Marketing* 56 (April): 57–71.
Joy, Annamma, Jianfeng Wang, Tsang-Sing Chan, John F. Sherry, and Geng Cui. (2014) "M(Art)Worlds: Consumer Perceptions of How Luxury Brand Stores Become Art Institutions." *Journal of Retailing*, forthcoming. 10.1016/j.jretai.2014.01.002.
Mehrabian, Albert, and James A. Russell. 1974. *An Approach to Environmental Psychology*. Cambridge, MA: MIT Press.
Sherry, John F., Jr. 2000. "Place, Technology and Representation." *Journal of Consumer Research* 27 (September): 273–278.

Sexualities and Consumption

YVETTE TAYLOR
London South Bank University, UK

Sexuality and consumption are interlinked in powerful and significant ways, perhaps even more so in contemporary, even postmodern, times, shaping various material and subjective possibilities and impossibilities, as sexuality is displayed and regulated via consumption. Consumption refers to a wide variety of spending patterns and behaviors and is typically equated with choice: what we choose to buy, where and when, and how we choose to use purchasable commodities, ranging from mundane everyday goods and services to extravagant one-off specials, which seemingly reinforce the uniqueness of our own individual consumer choice. Crane (2000) explores fashion and its various and shifting meanings, symbolically, culturally, and economically, across time and place, drawing on data from England, France, and the United States. Crane claims that class has become a less salient aspect of identity, with less effect upon clothing practices, consumption, and signification, which she describes as a shift from classed practices to those based around lifestyles (Taylor 2007a). The concept of subcultural affiliation is invoked as a way of capturing the proliferation of clothing styles and choices, which, it is claimed, mark the changes from industrial class-based societies to postmodern, postindustrial societies. The manifestations of class and gender are seemingly replaced by an erasure of fixed hierarchies, a blurring of certainty which these categories once represented, and a diffusion of meaning across and between other axes of "difference," particularly that of sexuality.

Yet to consume also implies a potential restriction in terms of what is being offered and to whom. Other market activities, such as employment, leisure activities, and citizenship, are related to consumption insofar as these afford possibilities for participating in certain markets, and create and foreground certain choices, while restricting and regulating individuals within multiple social domains. Heterosexuality is privileged, even expected, within many consumer spheres, but lesbian, gay, and bisexual sexualities are also increasingly affecting, and indeed affected by, marketization.

Sexuality, as an innately private and individual concern, has been interrogated and problematized by many feminist researchers, who have revealed its profoundly social and public regulation. While there has been longstanding attention to compulsory heterosexuality, as socially structured and institutionalized, others point to the increasing complexity, even fluidity, of sexual practices, identities, and regimes. The dichotomy existing around materialist versus queer conceptualizations of sexuality is strongly expressed through polarized critiques of sexuality and consumption (Jackson 2001). Here sexualities become either cynically commodified and thus inseparable from interconnecting inequalities, such as gender and class, or exist as evidence of potentiality and (market) possibility, affording diverse sexualities much cultural visibility.

Whether thought of as a resource or as a constraint, an equalizing force or a divisive battleground, it is difficult to ignore the ever-increasing spaces of sexual consumption, as manifest in the media, in commercialized scene spaces, and even in the realm of citizenship. The interconnection between sexuality and consumption provides for a series of inclusions and exclusions, in the market and in the state itself, which has been a dominant theme in the literature on sexuality studies.

Chasin (2000) uncovers the linkage between the development of the lesbian and gay movement in the United States and the growth of lesbian and gay niche markets that promise inclusion into the marketplace and the nation itself – but at a price. Within her account, social recognition is dependent on ability to consume as identity becomes branded, commodified, and consumed. Lesbians and gays are integrated, even assimilated, as consumers rather than as citizens. Money then represents the prerequisite for participation as well as the boundary. Chasin's catchy (and cutting) title *Selling Out* conveys notions of failure and possible fraudulence, hinting at the ways in which sexual identities have been depoliticized, as they become only another consumer possibility. The skepticism aired resonates with many other critiques (Warner 1993; Hennessy 2000). Many theorists have examined consumption in relation to the construction and reconstruction of identity. Warner looks at the pivotal role of the market in the construction of queer sexualities and notes its exclusionary tendencies. Here the "institutions of culture building have been market-mediated" (Warner 1993, xvi–xvii) and include bars, discos, newspapers, magazines, phone lines, resorts, and urban commercial districts, which are only accessible to those with the requisite social, cultural, and economic capital.

While popular discourses on the "pink pound" signal a new, consumer-based potential inclusion, many researchers have highlighted entrenched and compounded inequalities within this. Seemingly celebratory discourses on lesbians' and gay men's spending power invoke what Binnie (2004) describes as the "myth of the pink economy," which compounds the idea of a special, even privileged, group who can more than afford their rights: here rights are equated entirely with spending power, which is a highly gendered phenomenon. Lesbians have rarely been addressed as consumers, which may be set to change as they are identified as potentially profitable, whether that is in terms of new leisure pursuits, fostered by improving incomes, or in the commercialization of, for example, civil partnerships. Nearly half of the countries in the European Union offer some legal recognition to same-sex couples, ranging from full civil marriage to domestic partnerships. An array of legal and commercial services has sprung up in response to this demand.

As sexuality becomes marketed and commodified as a "lifestyle option," many note that not all lifestyles are equally visible or validated. Similarly, the existence of commercialized scene spaces, thought of as refuges and safe spaces for sexual minorities, is not unproblematic, and various theorists have given attention to inequalities operating within such commercialized space. Skeggs (1999, 2001) has shown that inequalities operate within leisure space, controlling entitlements to that space and affecting the appropriate "performance" (Taylor 2007b). Appearance in particular becomes the mechanism for inclusion and exclusion, a resource through which claims for legitimacy and entitlement are made whereby sexuality, gender, and class affect embodied presentations and a sense of entitlement versus a sense of exclusion. Having the money can buy access – having the right clothes, right style, and taste can indicate that entitlement to be there – but displaying sexual identity, and receiving affirmation may require unaffordable presentations. Hennessy (2000) has critiqued discourses of consumer choice and the necessity to display a "designer identity," given that it may only be accessible to those materially poised to occupy the position, those with the ability and opportunities to engage in lesbian or gay male chic.

Scene spaces are increasingly becoming leisurely spaces of consumption, where the claiming of a lesbian or gay identity is no longer necessary to consume such leisure space, but where the intrusion of a heterosexual presence into scene space is still far from unproblematic. Such intrusion, like the commercial scene space itself, appears to be highly gendered. Drawing upon longitudinal ethnographic research (Skeggs 1997) and research on violence, sexuality, and space in the UK, Skeggs (1999; 2001) highlights the contrast and tensions existing in scene spaces between a group of white working-class heterosexual women, whose identity is based on "dis-identification" (from being working class), and a group of lesbians who form their identity through visibility, recognition, and territorialization. Skeggs suggests that heterosexual working-class women enter commercialized scene venues in order to be safe from the male gaze, while their straight presence, or "lesbian masquerades," have negative consequences for others, namely lesbians and gay men.

Queer theory has been associated with the pursuit of a queer lifestyle, an "aestheticization of daily life" constructed through a "postmodern consumer ethic" (Hennessy 2000). Fraser (1999) argues that queer theory's stance on visibility and recognition further marks a connection between identity and aesthetics, whereby queer becomes a brand name, an identity project assuming the form of aesthetic, consumer-based lifestyles. The queer body, in displaying and signifying, is, from a queer perspective, seen to bestow a political value. But within this are important ramifications for escalating class inequality, given that appearance can be another signifier upon which to denigrate working-class bodies and tastes, in which they (again) become "flawed consumers" who cannot pay and display in proper, tasteful ways. Aesthetics, and identity constructed via consumption of cultural goods, may mark the self as tasteful, authentic, and thus entitled (for example, to occupy queer space), or it may exclude and mark as wrong, unentitled, and inauthentic. When considering intersections between consumption and sexuality, materialist feminists would suggest that it has been difficult to fully utilize and appropriate the theoretical readings of queer. Although Judith Butler (1993) may usefully illuminate aspects of the operation of queer identity, this reading of performance and performativity may mean little to the everyday enactment of sexuality.

In contrast, Roseneil (2000) charts the cultural valorizing of the queer in popular culture, fashion, magazines, and television, which is taken as evidence of the "aspirational status of queer" rather than as the class-exclusive "aestheticization of everyday life," which materialist thought would name as a perpetuation and extension of current inequalities (Fraser 1999). Culturally, there is a proliferation of films and literature where femininity is fetishized and naturalized as objects of female desire, while women can now choose the commodities and costumes from which to perform femininity, as part of their repertoire of self-identification. The burden faced is one of "having it all" whereby having it all, good career and good sex, becomes an imperative rather than a choice. Pick 'n' mix relationships and "identity umbrellas" become necessities in building an experienced, endlessly adaptable, and refashioned self, and multisexualism another sought-after and purchasable commodity. *Metrosexual* is becoming a new buzzword, apparently describing urban, fashion-conscious men who are not afraid to express an interest in fashion or beauty, areas typically thought of as the preserve of women and gay men. Nonetheless, multiplicity or metrosexuality does not necessarily translate into equality, and again choices are not equally available or validated on the (sexual) market. As one form of (male) sexuality is celebrated, other forms of (female) sexuality are problematized as excessive and simply wrong.

Romanticized representations seeking to reaffirm traditional femininity exist alongside representations that problematize and pathologize women's sexual behavior, appearance in public, especially leisure, space, and their uptake of a "laddish" drinking culture as resolutely unfeminine (McRobbie 2000; Harris 2004). A classed polarization between new celebratory (white and middle-class) femininities and sorrowful, pitiful, and excessive working-class sexuality, embodied in the pathological representations of the teenage mother, is articulated in the literature. Celebrations and denigrations of new femininity are challenged and resisted by the realization that gender, class, and sexual inequalities remain embedded within economic and social structures, something which materialist feminist approaches have been adept at highlighting.

Many feminist writers have explored young women's consumption of lifestyle magazines. McRobbie (2000) argues that contemporary femininity and masculinity are being reappraised with representations of sexuality now breaching traditional gendered boundaries of acceptance, whereas Tyler (2004) claims such resources bring managerial imperatives, such as efficiency and effectiveness, which must be incorporated into self-management of sexuality. Sexual pleasure may well be subject to rationalization, through a process of sexual modernization, whereby issues of efficiency and outcome again come to the fore in the "sexual mode of production" (Hawkes 1996). Tyler (2004) maintains that the focus on and overinvestment in "good sex," weighted toward success, entitlement, and mobility, deflects attention away from gendered inequalities, such as women's continued familial dependence and exploitation in family and work realms, potentially separating out interconnections between sexuality, gender, and the household, emphasized in feminist research.

The restructuring of flexible global capitalism offers new research directions. Binnie (2004) unravels the links between sexuality, the nation-state, and globalization, critiquing previous studies for their heteronormative assumptions and attentions and instead choosing to "queer" globalization, providing a queer perspective on the subject. The prevalence of class inequalities contests the link between globalization and inevitable and progressive mobility, movement, and liberation. Not only are there enduring citizenship and immigration restrictions, perhaps felt less by the monogamous high-earning couple, but the process of transnational movement is itself a highly gendered phenomenon. Maybe, as Binnie (2004) claims, we are all "sex tourists," tourism being a sexualized process, but gay men's tourism is often particularly problematized and pathologized as overtly, and deviantly, sexual. Thus a crucial reminder against collapsing important material and subjective differences and inequalities is highlighted in theorizing sexualities and consumption.

SEE ALSO: Beauty Industry; Citizenship and Consumption; Consumption and Identity; Femininities; Gay and Lesbian/Queer Markets/Marketing; Gender and Consumer Culture; Masculinity

REFERENCES

Binnie, Jon. 2004. *The Globalization of Sexuality*. London: Sage.

Butler, Judith. 1993. *Bodies that Matter: On the Discursive Limits of "Sex."* New York: Routledge.

Chasin, Alexandra. 2000. *Selling Out: The Gay and Lesbian Movement Goes to Market*. Basingstoke, UK: Palgrave.

Crane, Diana. 2000. *Fashion and its Social Agendas: Class, Gender, and Identity in Clothing*. Chicago: University of Chicago Press.

Fraser, Mariam. 1999. "Classing Queer: Politics in Competition." *Theory, Culture, and Society* 16(2): 107–131.

Harris, Anita, ed. 2004. *All About the Girl: Culture, Power, and Identity*. New York: Routledge.

Hawkes, Gail. 1996. *A Sociology of Sex and Sexuality*. Maidenhead, UK: Open University Press.

Hennessy, Rosemary. 2000. *Profit and Pleasure: Sexual Identities in Late Capitalism*. London: Taylor & Francis.

Jackson, Stevi. 2001. "Why a Materialist Feminism is (Still) Possible – and Necessary." *Women's Studies International Forum* 24(3/4): 283–293.

McRobbie, Angela. 2000. *Feminisms and Youth Culture*. London: Macmillan.

Roseneil, Sasha. 2000. "Queer Frameworks and Queer Tendencies: Towards an Understanding of Postmodern Transformations of Sexuality." *Sociological Research Online* 5(3). www.socresonline.org.uk/5/3/roseneil.html.

Skeggs, Beverley. 1997. *Formations of Class and Gender*. London: Sage.

Skeggs, Beverley. 1999. "Matter Out of Place: Visibility and Sexualities in Leisure Spaces." *Leisure Studies* 18(3): 213–232.

Skeggs, Beverley. 2001. "The Toilet Paper: Femininity, Class and Mis-Recognition." *Women's Studies International Forum* 24(3/4): 295–307.

Taylor, Yvette. 2007a. *Classed Outsiders: Working-Class Lesbian Life Experiences*. Basingstoke, UK: Palgrave.

Taylor, Yvette. 2007b. "'If Your Face Doesn't Fit ...': The Misrecognition of Working-Class Lesbians in Scene Space." *Leisure Studies* 26(2): 161–178.

Tyler, Melissa. 2004. "Managing Between the Sheets: Lifestyle Magazines and the Management of Sexuality in Everyday Life." *Sexualities* 7(1): 81–106.

Warner, Michael, ed. 1993. *Fear of a Queer Planet: Queer Politics and Social Theory*. Minneapolis: University of Minnesota Press.

Shopping

SHARON ZUKIN
City University of New York, USA

In a simple, material sense, shopping occupies a "downstream" position in the commodity chain where products, after being grown or manufactured, are "distributed" to consumers. But nothing about distribution is simple. The scale of global sourcing and overseas production gives rise to a complex logistics of long-distance freight transportation that brings goods to distribution hubs, warehouses, and stores, and sometimes directly to homes. Moreover, the geographical dispersal of housing in suburbs, exurbs, and rural locales, has led to dependence on a huge infrastructure of goods and services centered on individual ownership of automobiles, so shoppers can transport themselves to brick-and-mortar stores to select and pick up their purchases. Internet shopping does not reduce dependence on energy-intensive means of distribution, for goods are still transported by airplanes and trucks, and the selection of goods – as well as the coordination of their manufacture – requires a vast electronic infrastructure of mobile devices, computers, and data centers.

At the same time, the middle stages of the commodity chain involve producers' efforts, usually through cultural intermediaries, to influence shoppers' choices. Shopping may begin with either a concrete need or a vague desire, but it passes through reading of advertisements, magazine articles, product reviews, consumers' guides, and retailers' websites, as well as conversations with family members, friends, and sales clerks or customer service representatives at the point of purchase. It may also include comparing manufacturers' labels on packages and unit price tags in stores. What appears at first to be a single act of shopping is a learning process that is continually influenced by multiple peers and authorities, who become more numerous when consumer goods industries expand and compete, and the choice of goods is overwhelming (Zukin 2004).

Shopping is also a sensory experience where shoppers come into direct contact with tangible commodities. Though men who accompany women to shop for clothes often complain that women touch every garment on the rack, all shoppers run a finger over the upholstery while shopping for cars, smell fresh bread in a bakery, and listen to sample tracks before downloading music. This stimulation may make the process of shopping pleasurable in itself. Moreover, sensory perception is useful because it enables shoppers to do "research" on the commodities that are available. Shoppers' desire to "try" things before purchase is built into the design and staffing of Apple computer stores, where different models are set up so shoppers can try them and ask questions of technicians.

NEEDS AND WANTS

Shopping also occupies a significant position in the discursive opposition of needs and wants. Just as rich societies produce an abundance of materials that are processed into goods in many different sizes, shapes, and colors, rich shoppers have the financial resources to satisfy all their needs and a wide variety of their desires. But finding a balance between needs and desires poses a problem for everyone. Affluent men and women may shop "too much" and buy many more products than they need, while poor shoppers' lack of money and credit may make it difficult for them to shop at all.

Moreover, low-income shoppers may be forced to make economically irrational decisions. If they have only a small amount of disposable income, they cannot lay out the money for a larger size package of laundry detergent that has a proportionally lower price. Neither can they afford to buy enough items to take full advantage of sales, nor travel far to find the cheapest prices. Shopping for cheap goods may also pose long-term risks. Organically grown foods are often more expensive than factory-processed and fast food. Shoddy sneakers are likely to wear out faster than more durable but also more expensive items. From this viewpoint, shopping appears to be an investment opportunity where affluent shoppers enjoy an advantage. But both affluent and low-income shoppers make irrational decisions when they buy goods they don't need.

For this reason, shopping is often accused of leading to deviant, "excessive" behavior, like "maxing out" on credit cards or accumulating more goods than can be used. Shoppers, then, are criticized for violating a traditional cultural norm of self-restraint, and also ridiculed (or envied) for refusing to restrain their spending. These criticisms tend to emerge in eras when shopping opportunities expand, especially for high-income groups, and businesses cater to conspicuous consumption. Beginning in the 1980s, for example, the growth of high incomes in rich, industrial societies and the expansion of consumer goods industries intensified both a proclivity to shop for pleasure and a competition between stores where shoppers could indulge this habit. The visibility of celebrities and their luxurious lifestyle in the media encouraged shopping as a form of aspiration and imitation, aided by banks' aggressive expansion of their credit card business. Branded stores, selling a wide array of products associated with only one brand name, were introduced by many different firms, from The Gap to the Disney Company.

In this context, popular culture targeted excessive shopping as both a disease and an object of scorn. According to the *Oxford English Dictionary*, the word "shopaholic" first appeared in print in 1984, in a journalist's denial that the celebrity Diana, Princess of Wales, was addicted to shopping. At the same time, shopping for emotional compensation – to satisfy a psychic need to feel good – was recognized as "retail therapy." "Shop 'til you drop" became an ambiguous mantra for self-conscious shoppers and an aggressive marketing slogan for all the stores that wanted to attract them. It inspired a television game show of the same name in the 1990s and is still used in everyday conversations. In 1987, the conceptual artist Barbara Kruger created a silkscreen photograph that adapted the seventeenth-century philosopher Descartes' famous saying "I think, therefore I am" to "I shop, therefore I am." This motto of excess, which ironically equates shopping with human consciousness, has been widely reproduced.

HIDDEN INJURIES OF GENDER

Because the gender division of labor in most societies casts women in the role of shoppers, they are often criticized for being shopaholics. First, shopping is trivialized because it is women's work, and then women shoppers are accused of being frivolous, hedonistic, excessive spenders. Here again, however, it is important to recall the social context of such criticism.

In the late 1800s and early 1900s, shopping provided a legitimate opportunity for middle- and upper-class women in the West to go out in public without an escort. Department stores were expanding and welcomed women customers, channeling their aspirations for a fuller public life into dreams of consumption (Williams 1982). Shut out of the labor market and legally unable to get financial credit on their own, women depended on their husbands or fathers to pay their bills. When they exceeded the spending limits their male relatives set, they were disciplined at home and ridiculed in the media. Women shoppers were also accused of starting a criminal epidemic of shoplifting (Abelson 1989).

Even now, in the media, women are disproportionately associated with shoplifting (Shteir 2011). Although men and women apparently shoplift in equal numbers, women's supposed inability to control their desire for fancy goods is said to lead them to take those goods surreptitiously. Teenage girls and female young adults are described as victims of "compulsive buying disorder," a psychological illness that reflects an excessive expenditure of time, if not always money, in shopping.

Whether these are tragic gender stereotypes or realistic responses to pressures and opportunities, women are assumed to have an intimate relation with shopping. Visual images of shopping predominantly feature women, usually carrying armfuls of shopping bags. A popular series of novels by a British writer features a female "shopaholic." And the television series and movies *Sex and the City* show the four main female characters shopping often for either pleasure or consolation.

Nevertheless, women do the major share of routine, practical provisioning. This involves shopping for food, children's clothes and supplies, and gifts for social occasions. But domestic provisioning, no matter how mundane, cannot be separated from emotion. A shopper shows love by buying her child's favorite breakfast cereal. Women shoppers buy themselves a treat in return for doing the work of shopping for the family (Miller 1998).

SHOPPING PLACES

Though their built forms and geographical locations change over time, shopping places retain the basic model of a marketplace where buyers and sellers meet over goods. The sum of individual interactions in this marketplace creates a theater for the presentation of public personas as well as an incubator for public myths of community (Agnew 1986; de la Pradelle 2006).

Shopping begins historically in towns. Farmers and artisans sell what they have grown or made in open-air markets alongside long-distance traders who carry more exotic goods. When towns develop, shopping moves indoors into small, individual stores and market halls. Artisans and merchants who sell the same products organize into guilds and cluster in the same street, gradually creating not only local shopping streets and corner groceries but also districts that specialize in specific trades. With industrial production, supplies of goods increase, and investors amass capital to build larger stores that bring goods to a larger market. Both big and specialized stores cluster in the urban center where shopping becomes a major economic force as well as a mass entertainment. Smaller shops for daily needs cluster on specific streets in residential districts, where they support social networks and cultural ecosystems (Zukin 2012; Zukin, Kasinitz, and Chen 2015).

Just as corporations develop functional divisions, stores are differentiated both externally, by specializing in specific products, and internally, by establishing departments that offer a specific kind of good or a specific brand. Department stores, which developed in the 1860s in the cities of Europe and North America, were major innovators of internal, organizational differentiation that used new technology – elevators, escalators, colored lights, plate glass windows – to attract and seduce shoppers (Leach 1993). Also in the late nineteenth century, "variety" and five-and-ten-cents stores offered a broad array of small products at very low prices, leading the way to today's discount and dollar (or euro) stores. Each form of store made it easier – and, in a way, more democratic – for shoppers to enter, browse, and buy.

Supermarkets developed in a similar process during the first half of the twentieth century. They appealed to shoppers with a wide variety of products at very low prices, which were made possible by a chain's economy of scale. Early supermarkets also introduced self-service and shopping carts, which transformed shopping into a mobile experience inside the store and reduced interactions between shoppers and store owners (who were increasingly corporations) and individual employees.

With increases in car ownership and suburban housing, shopping moved outside cities (Cohen 2003). Real estate developers hired architects to design shopping centers or "malls" that housed dozens of stores side by side, "anchored" by a large supermarket or a branch of a department store chain, and surrounded by parking lots. The daily round of provisioning on a local shopping street that had been typical in cities, especially for women, was transformed into a weekly excursion for the whole family. Gradually developers built larger shopping malls offering more leisure activities, from food courts to multiplex movie theaters, aquariums, and theme parks, both to attract shoppers and keep them shopping longer (Goss 1993). Shopping malls became tourist destinations and resources for cultural consumption when they were integrated with art museums, hotels, and gambling casinos.

During the late twentieth century, a shared concern for fresh foods and urban amenities encouraged the resurgence of an old form of marketplace – farmers' markets. In contrast to supermarkets, shopping in these markets offers an opportunity for buyers to meet sellers who grow or make their foods, which promotes a return to shopping as both a more socially engaged, and more emotionally engaging, social activity.

Though the development of online shopping in the twenty-first century has reduced social interaction between buyers and sellers, it has increased shopping opportunities. This fosters the illusion of saving time and energy, for although shoppers do not physically travel to many stores, retail websites are designed, like shopping malls, to keep users shopping longer. Moreover, electronic commerce has broadened the integration of shopping in otherwise private spaces, for online shoppers search for goods at home, at work, and in many other places. They also post and read online reviews of consumer goods and services, which adds another stage to the shopping process.

Because it is ubiquitous and inescapable, shopping has become a major institution of modernity, a trope that paradoxically suggests modern consumers' mobility as well as their limitations (Slater 1997).

SEE ALSO: Arcades; Big-Box Stores; Consumption Rituals; Department Stores; Emotions and Consumption; Farmers' Markets; Shopping Malls; Supermarket; Wal-Mart

REFERENCES

Abelson, Elaine S. 1989. *When Ladies Go A-Thieving: Middle-Class Shoplifters in the Victorian Department Store*. New York: Oxford University Press.

Agnew, Jean-Christophe. 1986. *Worlds Apart: The Market and the Theater in Anglo-American Thought, 1550–1750*. Cambridge, UK: Cambridge University Press.

Cohen, Lizabeth. 2003. *A Consumers' Republic: The Politics of Mass Consumption in Postwar America*. New York: Knopf.

de la Pradelle, Michèle. 2006. *Market Day in Provence*. Translated by Amy Jacobs. Chicago: University of Chicago Press.

Goss, Jon. 1993. "The 'Magic of the Mall': An Analysis of Form, Function, and Meaning in the Contemporary Retail Built Environment." *Annals of the Association of American Geographers* 83(1): 18–47.

Leach, William. 1993. *Land of Desire: Merchants, Power, and the Rise of a New American Culture*. New York: Pantheon.

Miller, Daniel. 1998. *A Theory of Shopping*. Cambridge, UK: Polity.

Shteir, Rachel. 2011. *The Steal: A Cultural History of Shoplifting*. New York: Penguin.

Slater, Don. 1997. *Consumer Culture and Modernity*. Cambridge, UK: Polity.

Williams, Rosalind. 1982. *Dream Worlds: Mass Consumption in Late 19th-Century France*. Berkeley: University of California Press.

Zukin, Sharon. 2004. *Point of Purchase: How Shopping Changed American Culture*. New York: Routledge.

Zukin, Sharon. 2012. "The Social Production of Urban Cultural Heritage: Identity and Ecosystem on an Amsterdam Shopping Street." *City, Culture and Society* 3: 281–91.

Zukin, Sharon, Philip Kasinitz, and Xiangming Chen. 2015. *Global Cities, Local Streets*. New York: Routledge.

Shopping Malls

LAUREN LANGMAN
Loyola University Chicago, USA

The shopping mall is one of the most important social locations and symbols of contemporary consumer society and its cornucopia of goods. It is typically a "self-contained" social environment containing an assembly of stores and shops, carts and kiosks, and usually various eateries located in food courts. Shopping malls are the points of intersection between a vast globalized system where the production of highly advertised goods is distributed to individual consumers. They are sites of practices that mediate between the globalized factories and stores that sell the merchandise and individual interactions and identities that are today ever more dependent on the consumption of "branded" goods (Klein 1999).

Insofar as mall shopping is more frequent than church attendance in the United States and consumerism has taken on a religious hue, malls have often been termed "temples of consumption" (Kowinski 1985). They are special places apart from the "ordinary world," where people celebrate the "superior power" of the globalized commodity system through rituals of consumption that affirm their identities and lifestyles as they pursue beliefs that the "goods life" offers access to the simulated heaven on earth.

THE RISE OF THE MALL

From the earliest prehistoric times, people have traded goods with each other. Ever since people lived in permanent settlements, and merchant and artisan classes emerged, social places, such as markets, fairs, and bazaars, were designated as sites to trade various foods, spices, adornments, and handicrafts from rugs to pottery. Village squares and marketplaces were places where people might not only trade goods, but also exchange socially relevant information (or gossip). Traditional markets were as much concerned with maintaining social ties and relationships as with commerce.

This pattern of trade began to change after the Crusades, when silks, spices, and porcelain from the East became more readily available to Europe. When Marco Polo returned with tales of the Middle Kingdom, and as trade with the Levant (Eastern Mediterranean) began to flourish, a series of events would lead to one of the most significant social transformations in history: the rise of a rational, industrial, market society that would culminate in a now globalized, capitalist modernity. As markets expanded, the rising merchant classes sold and consumed more and more of the newly available goods.

Consumption accelerated with the growth of capitalism, modernity, and industrialization, and by the twentieth century the mass production of consumer goods. One early moment of this transformation was seen in the arcades of Paris around 1822 when a more or less self-contained collage of shops and stores erected glass roofs over its passageways to protect affluent shoppers from inclement weather. These arcades provided "phantasmagorias" of commodities for the growing, affluent middle classes (Benjamin, 1999). These new "dream worlds of the city" became backgrounds for the flaneur, the "urban dandy" with the conspicuous leisure to stroll through the city and create new experiences of urban life. They would be the harbingers of mass consumerism, valorized and celebrated lifestyles, and identities based on purchasing ever greater and more sophisticated amounts of goods and services. Together with the new department stores, this would mark the rise of consumer society – where most people partake in mass consumption. By the end of the nineteenth century, throughout Europe, with a growing middle class working in urban centers and with mass transportation improvements, came the department store: vast collections of goods from fashions to household goods. The latest fashions were elegantly displayed on mannequins. Magnificent "rooms" of furniture were displayed, with careful attention to the new forms of electric lights, colors, and arrangements (Leach, 1989). In little more than a century, we began to see the legacies of the nineteenth-century arcades and department stores.

Although some malls had been built in the 1920s, with the federally financed expressway system, department stores moved to the suburbs, where the people had moved, and commerce moved from "downtown" areas to the more distant environs, as suburbs, with relatively spacious and inexpensive housing, rapidly grew. Shopping malls began to mushroom. Vast tracts of land were transformed into malls with their parking lots. Major department stores became "anchors" for the many smaller shops of the mall whose architecture ensured that people would have to pass by many stores as shopping changed from instrumental acquisition of necessities to social activities and/or identity construction. There were four central features of the new shopping malls: (1) they had huge parking lots; (2) established department stores became "anchors" for the mall; (3) many tried to develop a particular theme to make them "different" from other malls and make customers feel special shopping there; and (4) malls were private property that attempted to recreate nostalgic forms of the "main streets" of the past, replete with casual interactions.

In order to create symbolic differences between malls selling more or less the same kinds and brands of goods, they were often "themed," given an overall motif perhaps connoting luxury, nautical, small-town nostalgia, or high tech fantasy, to create seeming distinctions. Malls provided amenities and activities such as lavish food courts and restaurants and even amusement park rides (roller coasters, submarines) and leisure activities such as ice skating or skiing to differentiate them from one another so that customers felt special shopping and would soon return (Gottdiener 1997).

With globalization fostering the growth of certain kinds of urban-based jobs in finance, law, and so forth, came the gentrification of urban-based malls in many cities. In the late twentieth century, shopping/entertainment centers and high rise urban malls began to emerge, such as Water Tower Place in Chicago or Rodeo Drive in Los Angeles. Many of the newer malls became vast collections of shops and entertainment and themselves became tourist attractions where people could travel hundreds of miles to buy things that for the most part were available locally. The largest mall in North America, West Edmonton in Canada, is 3.7 million square feet, while the world's largest, the New South China Mall in Dongguan, China, is over 6.4 million square feet. Baudrillard (1975) claimed that as society moved from the production of goods made by machines to the production of signs and meanings, we entered a new, "postmodern" age. While the "postmodern" may be debatable, there is little doubt that the mall became the ur site and symbol of modern consumerism where the products of factories across the globe fill the cornucopias of goods in the plethora of shops, stores, and kiosks.

Malls are more than stacks, racks, and shelves of goods. They are fantasy lands of abundance, spaces where otherwise frustrated desires are gratified and where consumption promises inclusion into emotionally gratifying, identity-granting communities of shared meanings – much like religions. Indeed, many scholars have noted that consumerism has displaced religion and malls have become sacralized "temples of consumption" (Kowinski 1985). They are magical places where people can overcome the sterility of a "disenchanted world" (Ritzer 1999).

SHOPPING MALL SELFHOOD

Malls stand apart from the "ordinary world." Here people celebrate the "superior power" of the globalized commodity system through rituals of consumption, insinuated by advertising that colonizes the lifeworlds where the consumptions of meanings can create and affirm identities and lifestyles that promise the "goods life" in the utopias of simulated abundance. Malls are the places where now ubiquitous advertising meets the self and its imagined identities and desires are expressed, if not engendered. Here people experience the pleasures of consumption with dopamine highs, and/or anticipate gratification in creating identities, appearances, and modes of self-presentations that enliven self, and become markers of status and inclusion into particular consumption-based subcultures of style (Langman 1992; Hebdige 1977). Certain accoutrements of identity provide realms of otherwise denied agency where they can fashion a "fantastic" subjectivity that provides recognition and gratifying self-presentations, especially in a "branded" world where a label provides a distinct, albeit often imaginary, yet valorized identity, lifestyle, and group membership (Klein 1999).

In the past decade or so, malls have lost some of their allure and pizzazz. While the megamalls may yet attract people as tourist destinations or meeting places, with leisure activities and entertainment zones, many smaller malls are facing a great deal of competition from online shopping, that not only provides access to all the goods sold in the malls, but often at a far lower price and the greater convenience of a mouse click. Further, we have also seen a growing number of hypermarkets and "big-box stores" such as Costco and Wal-Mart, that carry a wide range of goods including groceries, appliances, cookware, and furniture. Finally, we might note that the lingering adverse economic conditions and uncertainties since 2008 have had some lasting impacts on consumer behavior, especially for younger people in more precarious situations, who are more cautious and frugal in their spending patterns. Still others have become more aware of the exploited workers in the sweatshops that produce their goods or are concerned with the environmental consequences of production. Many are attempting to transform their identities away from consumption to social concerns ranging from the environment to social justice. But at the same time, many producers and retailers, responding to such concerns, are making and selling more goods from "approved" factories, more fair traded products, and more environmentally friendly goods. Shopping malls may change in many ways, but will remain with us for a long time.

THE SOCIOLOGY OF THE MALL

It is surprising that there has been very little sociological research and theory about shopping malls and mall-specific behavior. One of the first sociologists to study malls was Mark Gottdiener, whose work influenced many other sociologists, such as Crawford (1992), Ritzer (1999), and Zukin (2004).

The functions of malls

Malls are primarily places where consumer goods made anywhere in the world can be distributed to people according to their social locations, real and imagined, and their membership in particular cultures of taste, fashion, and sophistication – aspects of what Bourdieu (1984) has called "distinction." Almost two-thirds of the goods sold in the United States were purchased at malls.

There are two faces of mall functions: social and design. Mall design functions to disguise the exchange relation of producer and consumer by stimulating consumer fantasies (Gottdiener 1997). Malls are designed to lead consumers to walk through sequences of small and anchor stores, arranged on the basis of consumer behavior studies. Halls and fancy atriums are meant to enhance the leisure experience of mall visits to support consumption maximization and, as mentioned above, they are often "themed," with an overall motif (Gottdiener 1997). With the added symbolism provided by themes, malls now are not only about production and distribution, but also other phenomena related to goods and services: advertising, marketing, sales, individual taste, style, and fashion (Ritzer 1999, 6). Despite their goal to be "different," the motifs that are considered "successful" in attracting customers to the malls are often repeated in other malls.

Malls as social locations

Perhaps Benjamin's classical Arcades Project (1999) remains the most comprehensive attempt to frame the roofed passages as a new site of consumption with new modes of experiencing oneself and others. To Kowinski (1984), malls were spiritual places. Gottdiener emphasized the extent to which malls were exemplars of produced spaces that became essential moments of consumer society, exemplars of "theming," the creation of a coherent ambience in which symbolic differences attempt to give place a special leitmotif, and in turn loyalty to a specific place of consumption and location for the realization of the consumer-based self. For Ritzer (1999), malls, as "cathedrals of consumption," were places where the rationality of modernity was masked by a "re-enchantment of the world" to encourage consumption.

Some malls attempt to simulate public spaces for community events. For example, Christmas celebrations in shopping malls are typical, and may also perhaps encourage some more shopping. Some malls encourage visits at Halloween by suggesting they are considered safer places for children's trick-or-treating rather than knocking at doors at strangers' houses (Chin 2001). Meanwhile, the parents may happen to buy things. People wandering about in malls are perceived more positively compared to those in outdoor public spaces, since the "controlled environment" of the mall is absent from the actual downtown urban space. This keeps out "unwanted people" and/or political ideas.

Theories of shopping mall selfhood

Malls can be seen as sites where consumerism colonizes the lifeworld of the self. One can buy the accoutrements of identity to fashion a "fantastic" subjectivity, including modes of gratifying self-presentations and appearances that awaken an often moribund self, and incorporation into consumption-based subcultures (Langman 1992), especially in a "branded" world when a "brand" is a synecdoche for a distinct identity and lifestyle (Klein 1999).

Chin's study (2001) found that the consumer sphere in shopping malls is an almost imaginary world for African American girls from poor families, distracting them from threat and victimization from men and their childhood vulnerability at home. Malls are the places for subjective doing, being, and becoming, serving functional, existential, and imaginary purposes for the realization of consumer-based selfhood, often satisfying "needs" that are fostered by media-based programming and advertisement. "Being-in-the-mall," a fundamental ontological moment, results in being seen as a consumer and confirmed as one who can and does shop. For some people, being recognized as one who can and does buy a RL or DKNY jacket or Rolex watch are often the best experiences they have. The amount of money spent in the mall is influenced by the degree of exposure to the consumer culture and limitations of buying power.

SOCIOLOGICAL RESEARCH OF MALLS

How do people experience malls? Although the research is often impressionistic rather than systematic, it has been suggested that malls provide an adventurous rush of new experiences; there is a feeling of leisurely "timelessness" where people seem not to be in a hurry. They give a cosmopolitan feeling of being somewhere "special" rather than in a kind of fortress. An important topic has been the extent to which malls are used as public places, alternatives to schools or city centers. Yet they are private properties, and security guards often exclude political actions, such as leafleting or petitioning and thus act to constrain "free speech."

A number of research agendas have, however, looked at specific features of malls such as the impact of total CCTV surveillance as a disciplinary practice. Similarly, a topic that has warranted much attention has been the patterns of inclusion and exclusion. Malls generally don't want certain kinds of people: the poor, the unemployed (not there to buy but assumed to be there to steal), or the political. Those who are just likely to congregate and not buy much – teenage mall rats seeking hangouts – are observed closely or directed to inferior merchandise. Yet at the same time, they are the primary consumers of certain kinds of fashions, music, videos, and so forth.

Most research on malls has been done by developers and marketers studying the demographics and psychographics of a potential consumer base. For example, Weiss (1988) has shown how American consumer patterns readily differ according to the zip codes where people live. There are some 40 or more clusters of shoppers; some, like "young suburbia," are more likely to shop in malls than the more affluent, more educated, more urban "money and brains" or "new bohemians." Similarly, a great deal of marketing research has attempted to look at sales in terms of store location within the mall, store design, product placement, and even such things as lighting, scent, and the fashions of the sales staff as they impact consumers.

Methodological problems of mall research

Malls present major challenges for social research, not the least of which results from the many ways they can be studied: their historical evolution, impact on land use, class reproduction, job creation or semiotic analyses of their design, décor, and ambience. Much less has been charted about malls as sites for social practices. Ethnographic studies typically require a stable population; mall shoppers typically come and go.

THE DIALECTIC OF MALLDOM

Some elites criticize the banality and commercialization of malls, yet consumption of various goods can and does provide some people with various pleasures such as incorporation into peer groups, especially for the many people who do work that is both necessary and undesirable – "shadow work." Malls provide realms where shopping is fun and buying or using goods provides valorized identities with agency and creativity.

THE FUTURE OF MALLS

In the past decade, the dominance of the mall as the primary site for the distribution of mass-produced goods faced at least two major challenges. Foregrounded by growing inequality and wage stagnation, the standalone "big-box" superstores like Wal-Mart, Costco, and Target have been rapidly growing. While such stores do not have as wide a range of goods and brands, they do offer savings on quantity purchases. The other threat to the mall has been the proliferation of "virtual malls" on the internet. Most of the products available at the mall can be purchased online, and often for less cost in time and money than going to the mall.

Indeed given the economic and technological changes of the last decade or so a large number of smaller malls have closed and many of the larger established malls, with their lavish themes, have seen traffic decline. In a recent story in the *Guardian,* David Uberti (2014) charted the decline of the mall. First, as mentioned above, the economic stagnation of the last few years, especially exacerbated by the meltdown of 2008, has limited the disposable income of many – especially the young, who are avid consumers. Moreover, one of the major allures of the mall was social interaction – people went to malls to hang out with their friends. But that was in the days before Facebook and Twitter, and now many young people prefer to interact in virtual space rather than the physical spaces provided by malls. Second, many of the middle-range department stores like Sears have lost large numbers of their customer base who are more likely to prefer dollar stores and thrift shops, while those who can afford the more upscale goods will head to stores like Macy's and Nordstrom. Thus for many malls, the major anchor stores are showing economic decline, and when fewer people go to these stores there will be fewer people going to the other stores in the malls. Finally, and most significantly, many people today do their shopping online and in many cases the prices at Amazon, eBay, or the myriad of other purveyors is not only considerably less but require very little time and do not entail driving many miles to a mall.

If malls are to continue to stay in business, they will need to offer activities that cannot be easily done at home or online, as when movie theaters came to malls to take advantage of the empty parking lots in the evenings. Malls will need to offer people a lot more than goods in order to be able to sell them goods. For example, West Edmonton Mall and the Mall of America include a number of amusements such as rides for children and sophisticated restaurants for parents. However, it is unlikely that malls will fully become community and activity centers considering their abilities to exclude people, activities, and ideas. In a globalized world, the mall serves a central role in mediating advertising, fostering consumerism, and socializing the "emotion rules" and modes of experiencing the consumer self and the world.

But we should also note that given the fluidity of contemporary society, what Bauman (2000) has called "liquid modernity," major "heavy" structures like shopping malls have been displaced by the more flexible, fluid forms of virtual shopping as well as more fluid identities. Indeed, under these conditions, for people that can afford it consumerism becomes even more important for fashioning the plurality of self-presentations that now constitute subjectivity. But at the same time we might also note that consumer-based subjectivity is no longer based as much on the shopping mall as on the internet. Much as the great churches of Europe have emptied of congregants to be filled by tourists, so too as many of the great temples of consumption become emptied, they stand as markers to a way of life that has now passed.

SEE ALSO: Consumption Rituals; *Flâneur/Flanerie*; Globalization and Consumption.

REFERENCES

Baudrillard, Jean. 1975. *The Mirror of Production*. St. Louis: Telos Press.

Bauman, Zygmunt. 2000. *Liquid Modernity*. Cambridge, UK: Polity.

Benjamin, Walter. 1999. *The Arcades Project*. Cambridge, MA: Belknap Press of Harvard University Press.

Bourdieu, Pierre. 1984. *Distinction: A Social Critique of the Judgement of Taste*. Cambridge, MA: Harvard University Press.

Chin, Elizabeth M. Liew Siew. 2001. *Purchasing Power: Black Kids and American Consumer*

Culture. Minneapolis: University of Minnesota Press.

Crawford, Margaret. 1992. "The World in a Shopping Mall." In *Variations on a Theme Park: The New American City and the End of Public Space*, edited by Michael Sorkin, 3–30. New York: Hill & Wang.

Gottdiener, Mark. 1997. *The Theming of America: Dreams, Visions, and Commercial Spaces*. Boulder, CO: Westview Press.

Hebdige, Dick. 1977. *Subculture: The Meaning of Style*. London: Methuen.

Klein, Naomi. 1999. *No Logo*. New York: Picador USA.

Kowinski, William Severini. 1985. *The Malling of America: An Inside Look at the Great Consumer Paradise*. New York: William Morrow.

Langman, Lauren. 1992. "Neon Cages: Shopping for Subjectivity." In *Lifestyle Shopping: The Subject of Consumption*, edited by Rob Shields, 40–82. London: Routledge.

Leach, William R. 1989. *Consuming Visions: Accumulation and Display of Goods in America 1880–1920*, ed. Simon J. Bronner. New York: Norton.

Ritzer, George. 1999. *Enchanting a Disenchanted World: Revolutionizing the Means of Consumption*. Thousand Oaks, CA: Pine Forge Press.

Uberti, David. 2014. "The Death of the American Mall." *Guardian*, June 19. http://www.theguardian.com/cities/2014/jun/19/-sp-death-of-the-american-shopping-mall.

Weiss, Michael J. 1988. *The Clustering of America*. New York: Harper & Row.

Zukin, Sharon. 2004. *Point of Purchase: How Shopping Changed American Culture*. New York: Routledge.

Simulations

LAUREN LANGMAN
Loyola University Chicago, USA

The primary theorist of simulation/simulacra was sociologist Jean Baudrillard, who suggested (Baudrillard 1994) that there has been a transition from a society mass-producing goods to a postmodern order of mass-produced images and meanings wherein a world dominated by simulation has emerged. In this new order of simulation, it becomes ever more difficult to find the original until eventually there is total simulation and differences between true and false have disappeared. The simulacra, representations of representations, cannot be distinguished from the real – indeed one is led to believe that reality no longer exists. In 1961, Daniel Boorstin wrote of "pseudo events" that exist only in images or representations.

The first order of simulation, found in premodern society, was the counterfeit, the illusion, the fraud substituted for the real. The sign becomes more important than the physical reality it purportedly represented. The meaning of the sign, the signifier, became detached from what it represented, the signified. With the mass production and repetitive displays of images as part of the process of the commodification of information, we have the second order of simulation: the differences between images and what is represented begins to collapse. The image misrepresents, yet hides an underlying reality that can be discerned. For Marx, ideology is a set of understandings produced by elites, cloaking and obscuring the actual realities of capitalism. For Baudrillard, in the contemporary postmodern age of ultimate simulation, the third order takes place when there is a "precession of simulacra" – the representation comes before and defines the real. The real and imaginary are no longer distinguished; there is an implosion, a complete collapse of the simulacrum and reality. The representations of representations are the world. The simulacra do not hide the truth – there is no truth.

For Baudrillard, the importance of simulation for consumerism is the extent to which the endless proliferation of advertisements, from billboards to commercials to the adverts of media and now even the spam and pop-ups of the internet, collude to create an alternative, imaginary reality where, as with wishing upon a star, all your dreams come true. If you consume the right signs of self-presentation via materialized representations of self through fashion, cars, interior décor, clothes, jewelry, and even certain cultural tastes, you are promised a simulated, yet valorized, self.

There have been a number of criticisms of postmodernism, especially the reality of its hyperreality of simulation. Most of postmodern scholarship consists of media critics and cultural studies scholars "reading the texts." Very little empirical research has asked actual people how they experienced the simulations. Surely most people know that the castles of Disneyland or the Paris of Las Vegas were copies quite unlike the "originals." Moreover, for many people, consuming these diversionary simulations nevertheless provides a gratifying respite from the alienating labor still dominant in actually existing capitalist societies.

Some scholars have suggested that the demise of postmodernism was based on the ever more visible consequences of globalization, greater and greater inequalities, environmental despoliation and global warming. Notwithstanding the debates of scholars, corporate media controls the codes, the simulations and simulacra that are the main ingredient of both consumerism and its political economic base, and the differences have imploded. These images promise "the goods life" through buying and having the consumption of signs of selfhood, even if the self so produced becomes little more than a free-floating signifier of subjectivity. At the same time, consuming politics in which images displace reality has given us good-looking, pleasant leaders, whose ineptitude threatens our very viability. But that said, the domination by simulations, by images and appearances, erasing history and memory, serves hegemonic functions maintaining the status quo (Cubitt 2001). But this has already been said by modernists like Karl Marx and Antonio Gramsci whose imaginary included liberation from deceptive imaginaries.

SEE ALSO: Baudrillard, Jean; Consumption, Spectacles of; Las Vegas; Marx, Karl

REFERENCES

Baudrillard, Jean. 1994. *Simulacra and Simulation*. Ann Arbor: University of Michigan Press.

Boorstin, Daniel. 1961. *The Image*. New York: Random House.

Cubitt, Sean. 2001. *Simulation and Social Theory*. London: Sage.

University of Chicago: Theories of Media. "Simulation, Simulacrum." http://csmt.uchicago.edu/glossary2004/simulationsimulacrum.htm.

FURTHER READING

Eco, Umberto. 1986 (1967). *Travels in Hyperreality*. New York: Harcourt Brace.

Hedges, Chris. 2009. *Empire of Illusion: The End of Literacy and the Triumph of Spectacle*. New York: Nation Books.

Langman, Lauren. 2007. "Simulacra and Simulation." In *Blackwell Encyclopedia of Sociology*, edited by Georg Ritzer. Malden, MA: Blackwell.

Slow Food Movement

KOEN VAN BOMMEL
Vrije Universiteit, Netherlands
ANDRE SPICER
City University London, UK

Legend has it that the Slow Food movement began in 1986 with a demonstration against the opening of a branch of McDonald's near the Spanish Steps in Rome, organized by Italian food journalist and political activist Carlo Petrini. Petrini formed the action group Arcigola, out of which Slow Food emerged in 1989. Slow Food's actual history may be slightly more complex (see e.g., Chrzan 2004). This not-for-profit, member-supported association has firmly taken root, with a strong local and decentralized presence. It is organized around 1,500 local chapters (known as *convivia*) and has over 100,000 members across more than 150 countries. These branch organizations organize events such as markets, discussions, tastings, and protests. In addition, as a formal movement with defined aims, Slow Food International coordinates a range of activities from its offices in Bra, Italy, including the Slow Food Foundation for Biodiversity, Salone del Gusto (food fair), Terra Madre (meeting of food producers), and the University of Gastronomic Sciences.

Slow Food is part of "a much broader backlash against the high-speed, high-turnover culture of the global food industry" (Honoré 2004, 57). It has managed to transform itself from a somewhat snobbish middle-class gastronomic movement into one that appeals to a broad constituency of environmentalists and people concerned with fair trade and social justice. Groups that were previously relatively separate were thus linked and the reach of the movement extended as they infused existing products with novel meaning (Van Bommel and Spicer 2011).

Until the turn of the century Slow Food positioned itself as a gastronomic movement defending delicious, traditional, and varied local cuisine. The movement relied primarily on informal local grassroots strategies, epitomized by activities such as farmers' markets, tastings, community gardens, and school education. Realizing the limited appeal of this "strategy of autonomy," Slow Food started to emphasize the labels of "good, clean, and fair" as the key requirements for food products, thereby tapping into broader discourses of environmentalism, social justice, and fair trade. Movement members started championing *ecogastronomy*, a concept both clear and ambiguous enough to provide meaning and to appease constituents with different interests, backgrounds, and identities. Through a "strategy of engagement," Slow Food started to accompany its initial grassroots activities with more global and centrally coordinated formal activities such as the University of Gastronomic Sciences, the Slow Food Foundation for Biodiversity, and several large-scale events. The internal structure of the headquarters grew more complex and Slow Food started political campaigns and collaborations with elites.

As Slow Food transformed from a gastronomic movement into an ecogastronomic one it thus pursued centralized and overarching strategies, yet maintained a sense of consistency and authenticity by solidifying its grassroots convivia activities. By these means, the Slow Food movement created a dynamic field that included a range of organizations including farmers, research institutions, policy makers, restaurants, activists, food producers, and consumers. Its strategic and discursive positioning enabled the mobilization of new enthusiasts and the establishment of a collective identity, thereby extending and elevating the Slow Food ideology in today's products and markets.

SEE ALSO: Fair Trade; Fast Food; Farmers' Markets; McDonaldization

REFERENCES

Chrzan, Janet. 2004. "Slow Food: What, Why, and to Where?" *Food, Culture and Society* 7: 117–132.

Honoré, Carl. 2004. *In Praise of Slow: How a Worldwide Movement is Challenging the Cult of Speed.* London: Orion.

Van Bommel, Koen, and André Spicer. 2011. "Hail the Snail: Hegemonic Struggles in the Slow Food Movement." *Organization Studies* 32: 1717–1744.

Social Media

ANDREAS M. KAPLAN
ESCP Europe, France

DEFINITIONS

Social media are "a group of Internet-based applications that build on the ideological and technological foundations of Web 2.0, and that allow the creation and exchange of user-generated content" (Kaplan and Haenlein 2010, 61). In simpler terms, social media are a group of mobile and web applications which enable the creation and exchange of user-generated content. The term *social media* is often used as a synonym for Web 2.0 and user-generated content. However, this definition shows that these are three different concepts. Additionally, social media are closely connected to two further concepts: viral marketing and ambient awareness.

Web 2.0 describes a new way to make use of the World Wide Web (WWW). Whereas during the era of Web 1.0, content was created and uploaded by individuals, Web 2.0 allows the continuous modification of the web by users using a participatory and collaborative approach. While Web 2.0 does not stand for any particular technical revision of the WWW, there are some tools such as Adobe Flash or AJAX which have made its collaborative use possible. Web 2.0 therefore is the platform acting as a host for social media.

User-generated content (UGC) describes any type of media content which is publicly available and created by end users. According to the Organisation for Economic Co-operation and Development (2007), UGC must adhere to three conditions: first, the media content must be publicly available or accessible to a selected group of people; second, it must display a certain extent of creativity; and third, it must have been created outside of professional practices. UGC can be considered as a generic term to describe how people utilize social media.

Viral marketing is defined as "an electronic word-of-mouth in which some forms of marketing messages related to a company, brand or product are transmitted in an exponentially growing way, often through the use of social media applications" (Kaplan and Haenlein 2011b, 255; 2012b). Since a strong community element is embedded in social media, simplifying the publication of a message to a large group of people is particularly suited for viral marketing activities. Some researchers even use both terms, viral marketing and social media marketing, interchangeably (Kozinets et al. 2010).

The concept of ambient awareness, that is, "awareness created through regular and constant reception, and/or exchange of information fragments through social media" (Kaplan 2012, 132), can best be explained through the Greek philosopher Aristotle, who stated that sometimes the whole is greater than the sum of its parts. While the messages "She is the best ever" or "Queuing up for several hours to get concert tickets" do not make a lot of sense on their own, they are clear and less ambiguous when preceded by "Britney Spears is my absolute favorite." This is exactly what happens with status updates on social media applications such as Twitter or Facebook. Ambient awareness allows for the creation of a strong feeling of closeness and intimacy through the combination of several messages (status updates, tweets, etc.) sent out by a user, and enables the reader to draw a very precise picture of the user's activities.

CLASSIFICATION OF SOCIAL MEDIA

Applying a set of media theories and concepts (social presence, media richness, self-disclosure, and self-presentation), social media can be classified into six different

Table 1 Classification of social media

		Social presence / media richness		
		Low	Medium	High
Self-presentation / self-disclosure	High	Blogs and microblogs (e.g., Twitter)	Social networking sites (e.g., Facebook)	Virtual social worlds (e.g., Second Life)
	Low	Collaborative projects (e.g., Wikipedia)	Content communities (e.g., YouTube)	Virtual game worlds (e.g., World of Warcraft)

Source: Kaplan and Haenlein 2010, 62

groups: collaborative projects, blogs and microblogs, content communities, social networking sites, virtual games (MMORPGs) and social worlds (see Table 1).

On the one hand, social media differs in the degree of "social presence," that is, acoustic, visual, and physical contact, that can be achieved (Short, Williams, and Christie 1976) and in the degree of "media richness" they possess, that is, the amount of information they allow to be transmitted in a given time interval (Daft and Lengel 1986). On the other hand, it differs in the level of "self-disclosure" it requires, that is, the conscious or unconscious revelation of personal information that is consistent with the image one would like to give (Schau and Gilly 2003), and in the type of self-presentation it allows, that is, the desire to control the impressions other people form of oneself (Goffman 1959).

In detail, collaborative projects such as Wikipedia (Kaplan and Haenlein forthcoming) enable the joint creation of media content by many users. Blogs and microblogs such as Twitter (Kaplan and Haenlein 2011a) exhibit date-stamped entries in reverse chronological order. Content communities such as YouTube enable the sharing of media content between multiple users. Social networking sites such as Facebook enable users to set up personal profiles and connect with friends and colleagues by allowing them access to your profile. Virtual gaming worlds, or so-called "massively multiplayer online role-playing games" (MMORPGs) such as *World of Warcraft*, are a subgroup of virtual worlds, that is, simulated web environments through which users can interact with one another, and oblige their players to act according to strict rules in the context of the game world. Virtual social worlds such as *Second Life*, on the other hand, allow their users, more appropriately called "residents," to act more freely and to essentially live their virtual life as an extension of their real life (Kaplan and Haenlein 2009; 2010).

HISTORY OF SOCIAL MEDIA

The historical evolution of social media can be considered as the internet "going back to its roots" (Kaplan and Haenlein 2012a). Social media reconverted the WWW to its initial intention: being a platform which allows for the exchange of information between its users.

The internet started out very similarly in spirit to today's social media. In fact, it consisted of a set of newsgroups such as Usenet founded in 1979; individual users were able to read and post forum-like messages in different categories which mainly focused around "high tech" and "science fiction." Rapidly, these newsgroups evolved into powerful platforms enabling individuals to exchange UGC with each other – very similar to today's discussion forums. Simultaneously in 1979, the first internet-based MMORPG was developed, named *Multi-User Dungeon*, which can be considered as a direct precursor of the above-mentioned virtual gaming worlds.

During the second era, characterized through the arrival of industry giants such as Amazon and eBay in 1995, the internet no longer was in the possession of individuals, but was taken over by big corporations and their home pages. Corporate websites and e-commerce applications pushed individual activities to the margin, with the latter still being in existence, but not no longer visible for the broader public. This takeover of the virtual sphere through companies however, rapidly came to an end with the event of the burst of the dot-com bubble in 2001.

The same year, in 2001, Wikipedia started on January 15 with the simple posting: "Hello world. Humor me. Go there and add a little article. It will take all of five or ten minutes." For many, this date marks the beginning of today's social media revolution. Today, Wikipedia has 26 million articles and approximately 365 million readers worldwide, which makes it, de facto, the key information provider on the internet, and the initiator of the third era. The arrival of Facebook in 2004, YouTube in 2005, and Twitter in 2006 marked the reclaiming of individuals' power over the virtual sphere.

Does this historical U-turn with the internet's return to its roots mean that social media are nothing more than old wine in new bottles? This is not particularly true since technical advances of the last three decades nowadays enable the sharing of virtual media content which is much more powerful and different in comparison to the possibilities offered by 1979's Usenet. Thus, instead of describing the rise of social media as going "back to the roots," one could also look at it as traveling "back to the future." One example of the new communication opportunities given by social media are applications such as Foursquare or Facebook Places, so-called mobile social media.

MOBILE SOCIAL MEDIA

Building on the definition of social media described above, mobile social media can be defined as "a group of mobile marketing applications which allow for the creation and exchange of user-generated content" (Kaplan 2012, 131). This genre of social media accessed via a mobile device makes "traditional" computer-based social media look particularly dated (like a record player compared to an MP3 player). Due to the fact that mobile social media run on mobile devices, it differentiates them from traditional ones as it incorporates new factors such as the current location of the user, and/or the time delay between sending and receiving messages.

In order to classify mobile social media, four different types of applications can be created, depending on whether the message considers the user's specific location (location-sensitivity) and whether it is received and processed by the user instantaneously or with a time delay (time-sensitivity) (see Table 2). Applications that are neither location- nor time-sensitive are slow-timers (e.g., mobile YouTube or Wikipedia). Applications which take account of time and place simultaneously are space-timers (e.g., Facebook Places or Foursquare). Applications which only reflect one of these two dimensions are referred to as either "space-locators" (location-sensitive but not time-sensitive;

Table 2 Classification of mobile social media

		Location-sensitivity	
		No	Yes
Time-sensitivity	Yes	Quick-timers (The transferring of traditional social media applications to mobile devices to increase immediacy, e.g., posting Twitter messages or Facebook status updates)	Space-timers (The exchange of messages with relevance for one specific location at one specific point in time, e.g., Facebook Places, Foursquare, Gowalla)
	No	Slow-timers (The transferring of traditional social media applications to mobile devices, e.g., watching a YouTube video or reading a Wikipedia entry)	Space-locators (The exchange of messages with relevance for one specific location which are tagged to a certain place and read later by other others, e.g., Yelp, Qype)

Source: Kaplan 2012, 132

e.g., Yelp or Qype) or "quick-timers" (time-sensitive but not location-sensitive; e.g., mobile Twitter or Facebook).

In comparison to computer-based social media, mobile ones are more closely linked to how people engage themselves within the real world. For example, while with traditional Facebook one only knows the "status" of friends and acquaintances, the mobile version additionally discloses their current location. This further enables the possibility to actually go and see these friends in real life (Kaplan 2012).

SEE ALSO: Facebook; YouTube

REFERENCES

Daft, Richard L., and Robert H. Lengel. 1986. "Organizational Information Requirements, Media Richness, and Structural Design." *Management Science* 32(5): 554–571.

Goffman, Erving. 1959. *The Presentation of Self in Everyday Life*. New York: Doubleday Anchor.

Kaplan, Andreas M. 2012. "If You Love Something, Let It Go Mobile: Mobile Marketing and Mobile Social Media 4x4." *Business Horizons* 55(2): 129–139.

Kaplan, Andreas M., and Michael Haenlein. 2009. "The Fairyland of Second Life: About Virtual Social Worlds and How to Use Them." *Business Horizons* 52(6): 563–572.

Kaplan Andreas M., and Michael Haenlein. 2010. "Users of the World, Unite! The Challenges and Opportunities of Social Media." *Business Horizons* 53(1): 59–68.

Kaplan Andreas M., and Michael Haenlein. 2011a. "The Early Bird Catches the News: Nine Things You Should Know About Micro-Blogging." *Business Horizons* 54(2): 105–113.

Kaplan Andreas M., and Michael Haenlein. 2011b. "Two Hearts in 3/4 Time: How to Waltz the Social Media – Viral Marketing Dance." *Business Horizons* 54(3): 253–263.

Kaplan Andreas M., and Michael Haenlein. 2012a. "Social Media: Back to the Roots and Back to the Future." *Journal of Systems and Information Technology* 14(2): 101–104.

Kaplan Andreas M., and Michael Haenlein. 2012b. "The Britney Spears Universe: Social Media and Viral Marketing at its Best." *Business Horizons* 55(1): 27–31.

Kaplan Andreas M., and Michael Haenlein. "Collaborative projects (social media application): About Wikipedia, the free encyclopedia." *Business Horizons*, forthcoming.

Kozinets, Robert V., Kristine de Valck, Andrea C. Wojnicki, and Sarah J. S. Wilner. 2010. "Networked Narratives: Understanding Word-of-Mouth Marketing in Online Communities." *Journal of Marketing* 74(2): 71–89.

Organisation for Economic Co-operation and Development. 2007. *Participative Web and*

User-Created Content: Web 2.0, Wikis, and Social Networking. Paris: OECD.
Schau, Hope J., and Mary C. Gilly. 2003. "We Are What We Post? Self-Presentation in Personal Web Space." *Journal of Consumer Research* 30(3): 385–404.
Short, John, Williams, and Bruce Christie. 1976. *The Social Psychology of Telecommunications*. Hoboken, NJ: John Wiley & Sons.

Socially Responsible Marketing (SRM)

ELLIS JONES
Holy Cross College, USA

Socially responsible marketing (SRM), sometimes referred to as ethical corporate marketing or green marketing, refers to the practices that some companies adopt to acknowledge the larger social and environmental impacts of their products and services. SRM signals to consumers that the company takes responsibility for and aims to reduce the negative consequences of its operation. These practices fall under the larger rubric of corporate social responsibility (CSR) but are easily conflated with opposing practices: socially irresponsible marketing (SIM), more commonly referred to as greenwashing, the practice of masking poor social/environmental records with deceptive campaigns that falsely tout responsible behaviors or commitments.

Early calls for SRM included restrictions in marketing aimed toward children, particularly vis-à-vis products like tobacco, alcohol, and gambling. Consumer advocates recently added "junk food" to this list of products, in part due to increasing rates of childhood obesity. More recently, some consumers have expressed a desire for SRM that conveys specific, transparent, accurate, and easily understandable information about corporations' social and environmental responsibility. In other words, some consumers view SRM as a venue for educating the public about the consequences of the consumptive practices.

Authentic SRM involves claims that are easily verified using publically available information. Such claims clearly demonstrate that particular corporate practices, products, or services are more socially or environmentally responsible than the market competition. The most trusted sources for verifying SRM claims tend to be labels or certifications created and verified by third-party organizations such as USDA Organic, Fair Trade Association, Green Seal, Green-e, Energy Star, Forest Stewardship Council, Marine Stewardship Council, B Corporation, or Green America. Unfortunately, as the number of third-party certifications has increased, SIM (or greenwashing) has begun to muddy data even from these previously reliable sources.

As with other aspects of CSR, companies that wish to legitimately engage in SRM simultaneously face two struggles: (1) how to convey their responsible practices to consumers in ways that distinguish them from irresponsible companies engaged in greenwashing; and (2) how to accurately gauge their own social and environmental responsibility so that they, themselves, don't inadvertently engage in greenwashing.

GREENWASHING (SOCIALLY IRRESPONSIBLE MARKETING)

Greenwashing occurs when companies assert, through advertising and/or public relations, that they are environmentally virtuous despite a clear record indicating the opposite. The term "greenwash" combines "whitewash" (to cover up crimes/scandals) with "green" (environmentally sustainable). Although some consumer advocates employ terms such as "bluewashing" (human rights, poverty, and labor issues) and "pinkwashing" (LGBT and/or breast cancer research issues), greenwashing is more common and has evolved to encompass a broad span of issues beyond environmental responsibility.

As greenwashing has become increasingly common, it has also become more sophisticated, consisting of a wide range of techniques that companies use to obscure problematic records and/or "oversell" ostensibly responsible practices. Companies engage in greenwashing in order to increase their market share of the lucrative ethical consumer sector. Some of the most common greenwashing techniques include:

- *misdirection* (e.g., highlighting philanthropic donations to popular social and/or environmental causes as a way to distract from a troubled environmental/social record);
- *self-aggrandizement* (e.g., implying that a particular practice makes them exceptionally responsible when that practice is, in fact, standard within an industry);
- *ambiguity* (e.g., using vague language to describe a long-term commitment to broad social and environmental values);
- *magnification* (e.g., focusing attention on a positive practice that is not, in fact, particularly significant in terms of making change);
- *proclamations* (e.g., making social/environmental claims that cannot be verified or corroborated without access to confidential data);
- *implied association* (e.g., using language that is deceptively similar to official third-party social/environmental certifications or images that mimic those used by socially responsible competitors).

SRM is an important component of the ethical marketplace as it allows for clear communication between producers and consumers. SIM hinders the ability of ethical consumers in particular to effectively influence companies through their purchasing behavior, often construed as casting "economic votes" for responsible companies.

SEE ALSO: Green Consumption; Ethical Consumption; Fair Trade; Marketing/Marketing Science

FURTHER READING

Ekstrand, Susie S., and Kristine L. Nilsson. 2011. "Greenwashing?" *European Food & Feed Law Review* 11: 167–173.

Holcomb, Jeanne. 2008. "Environmentalism and the Internet: Corporate Greenwashers and Environmental Groups." *Contemporary Justice Review* 11: 203–211. doi:10.1080/10282580802295328.

Powell, Shaun M. 2011. "The Nexus Between Ethical Corporate Marketing, Ethical Corporate Identity and Corporate Social Responsibility: An Internal Organizational Perspective." *European Journal of Marketing* 45: 1365–1379.

Sport and Consumption: *SEE* Consumption and Sport

Starbuckization

NEWMAN CHUN WAI WONG
Midwestern State University, US

The term "Starbuckization" refers to the homogenized cultural force and phenomenon of Starbucks dominating other aspects of society. Starbucks was first founded as a coffee bean roaster and retailer in Pike Place Market in Seattle, Washington, in 1971. Originally, the founders of Starbucks aimed to provide quality coffee to customers, and the first shop only sold high-quality, dark-roasted coffee beans and coffee merchandise. In 1987, the current CEO of Starbucks, Howard Schultz, became the sole owner and started to expand the coffee house chain aggressively through licensing across the United States. In 1996, the first shop outside the United States was opened in Japan, and as of 2013 Starbucks has over 19,000 stores in 62 countries.

Explaining the rapid expansion of Starbucks, sociologist George Ritzer (2013) suggests that Starbuckization shares the characteristics of McDonaldization, the rationalized management practices of McDonald's, which are efficiency, predictability, calculability, and control by nonhuman technology. To achieve efficiency, Starbucks uses different strategies to minimize the time for providing services. For example, customers are expected to queue up, order, pay, wait for their order, and then fix their coffee at the cream and sugar stand. Some Starbucks stores have drive-throughs, and sometimes there are multiple shops within an airport terminal or a building for customers' convenience. For predictability, the production process is uniform, baristas are trained to make coffee in the same manner, and their tasks are often specific and repetitive. Customers know to expect very similar products when they enter any one of the shops, recognizing the logo and green aprons. In terms of calculability, the production process at Starbucks is quantifiable, and customers know to order by Starbucks sizes – tall (small), grande (medium), and venti (large) – and number of espresso shots. Starbucks uses nonhuman technology to ensure efficiency and predictability. For instance, automatic espresso machines now replace skillful baristas, and technology helps workers take orders from drive-through customers.

Although sharing some standardized practices with McDonalds, Starbucks projects a quality brand image. When Starbucks was founded, the quality of American coffee had been sacrificed for low prices, and the coffee culture was insignificant. Initially, Starbucks hand-brewed dark-roasted Arabica beans one cup at a time and served the coffee in ceramic cups, giving customers the Italian espresso bar experience. Over the years, Starbucks' brewing has become less hand-crafted and other food and drink products have been introduced, such as tea, frappuccino, pastries, sandwiches, and salads, as well as various merchandise that bolsters the café culture, like brewing equipment, mugs, music, and books.

According to Howard Schultz (Schultz and Yang 1997) Starbucks also emphasizes a personal connection with customers, with a mission to inspire and nurture the human spirit. Starbucks strives to build a "third place" for customers to relax outside of home (first place) and work (second place). The third place allows customers to have a taste of romance and luxury at an affordable price, an oasis in which customers can escape from reality, and an atmosphere that encourages casual interactions. Many Starbucks stores provide wi-fi and become a part-time office for some customers. In addition, Starbucks portrays itself as a socially responsible corporation and calls its employees "partners," who are instrumental in giving the Starbucks experience to customers. The company offers health care and stock options to eligible full- and part-time employees, but has also been accused of retaliation against pro-union employees. To demonstrate its social conscience, Starbucks is committed to fair trade coffee and green practices; however, Starbucks was criticized for paying too little to coffee growers in Ethiopia and refusing to trademark their coffee.

Starbucks has been successful in countries without a strong coffee culture, while facing challenges in countries with rich coffee cultures, such as Italy, France, and Turkey. When Starbucks enters foreign countries, glocalization (adaptation to local markets) and cultural heterogenization occur. For instance,

Starbucks in Japan not only promotes appreciation for consuming high-quality coffee, but also serves coffee-themed mixed drinks to increase revenues. At times, Starbucks partners with local enterprises for joint ventures, in order to develop new markets. Starbuckization has made the high coffee culture a way of life globally, and a taste of the original Starbucks in Seattle could now be found at some US university libraries, in major cities around the world like London and Seoul, and at iconic locations like the Great Wall in China.

SEE ALSO: Brands and Branding; Globalization and Consumption; Glocalization/Grobalization; Lifestyle; McDonaldization

REFERENCES

Ritzer, George. 2013. *The McDonaldization of Society*, 7th ed. Thousand Oaks, CA: Sage.

Schultz, Howard, and Dori Jones Yang. 1997. *Pour Your Heart Into It: How Starbucks Built a Company One Cup at a Time*. New York: Hyperion.

FURTHER READING

Simon, Bryant. 2011. *Everything but the Coffee: Learning About America from Starbucks*. Berkeley: University of California Press.

Stealth Marketing

DAVID GRAZIAN
University of Pennsylvania, USA

Stealth marketing refers to the surreptitious promotion of consumer goods, services, and experiences to unwitting potential customers. Its antecedents date back to the 1920s, when public relations firms attempted to promote their clients through creative event planning and targeted editorial placement in the popular press. Today, stealth marketing refers to a number of clandestine promotional tactics, including product placement, viral or buzz marketing, and reality marketing.

Starting in the 1990s, firms began relying on stealth marketing in response to a number of emergent concerns about the efficacy of more traditional advertising strategies, particularly the 30-second television commercial designed for a mass audience. Toward the end of the twentieth century, audiences had grown ever more media-savvy and therefore cynical about the ubiquity and transparency of traditional mass marketing and promotional media, as well as the advertising industry more generally. At the same time, digital innovations in television viewing, including digital video recorders, on-demand and pay-per-view services, and commercial-free media subscriptions available online, had increased consumers' ability to evade the broadcasting of traditional ads. Moreover, the mass communications landscape itself was drastically changing, as younger audiences shifted their media consumption habits from television to video games and other forms of online entertainment, and the television audience that remained was highly fragmented due to an exponential rise of cable TV offerings. Meanwhile, the costs of producing top-quality television commercials and purchasing media buys from broadcast networks remained very high, and did not provide the interactivity required to reach media audiences in the digital age. Stealth marketing therefore proliferated as a response to the expense, rigidity, and nonreciprocal nature of traditional television advertising.

Stealth marketing may take a variety of forms. Firms may engage in product placement, in which corporations or their agents embed references to a branded product in films, television programs, video games, or online content. Variants of product placement include hiring celebrities to wear, carry, or use a specific product when they appear in public, or paying them to "casually" mention a particular brand during the course of an interview or appearance intended for broadcast or reporting by a mass media outlet. Sometimes a stealth-marketing firm will simply pay attractive, stylish, or high-status men and women to use their product in public, just as if they were celebrities.

Viral or buzz marketing relies on the power of word-of-mouth communication among consumers, especially since (unlike more traditional advertising) such interactions are assumed to be independent of any material interest in a particular product, brand, or lifestyle. A common buzz marketing strategy involves hiring actors to work as brand pushers who ask strangers in public to take photographs of them with a specific camera, share their pack of newly marketed cigarettes, or else order them a particular brand of vodka at a nightclub, all while posing as tourists or otherwise "ordinary" consumers. Brand pushers are also employed as fake shoppers paid to promote new products in stores by talking aloud in the presence of unsuspecting customers. A more recent variant of this type of marketing is virtual marketing, which relies on paid individuals posting positive recommendations, reviews, user comments, and other kinds of promotional product placement on internet forums, blogs, and other online social media platforms.

Buzz marketing may also take place at the organizational level, as when a brand-name firm quietly underwrites a social event or public arts or cultural performance, and subsequently maintains a low enough profile to generate word-of-mouth among attendees without seeming too aggressive in its approach. Another strategy entails recruiting groups such as churches or charitable organizations to promote a new product or media offering to its members, sometimes in exchange for a donation of either money or goods and services.

Finally, reality marketing involves the recruitment of agents to promote brands, products, or consumer experiences to trusted members of their peer networks on a daily basis. For example, a select group of popular college students might receive cash payments or complimentary services to entice their classmates to show up for a happy hour at a designated campus bar. In the urban nightlife industry, there are professional reality marketers who are paid to send text messages to their vast social networks about their nightly comings and goings to particular client establishments throughout the city. In some instances, reality marketers are willing to promote brands or products for a stealth marketing firm without receiving *any* compensation, only the satisfying pleasure of socially interacting with one's intimates and acquaintances, and feeling like a trendsetter, as an insider within the world of consumer culture. Ironically, in such cases many participants tend not to see themselves as marketers at all.

There are some inherent weaknesses in stealth marketing as a business practice. Since firms rely on third parties (celebrities, brand pushers) for their buzz and reality marketing campaigns, they lose a certain control over the specific messaging directed to consumers. In many cases, stealth-marketing campaigns can have an unpredictable audience reach, and may be difficult to evaluate in terms of their efficacy. They also may not be appropriate for some kinds of products or services. Perhaps most of all, stealth marketers run the risk of alienating targeted customers if discovered, which could lead to the possibility of consumer backlash. Finally, given its proliferation since the 1990s, there has been widespread debate about the ethics of stealth marketing, both within the advertising industry and among members of the general public.

SEE ALSO: Advertising; Brands and Branding; Marketing/Marketing Science; Public Relations.

FURTHER READING

Bernays, Edward L. 1923. *Crystallizing Public Opinion*. New York: Liveright.
Grazian, David. 2008. *On the Make: The Hustle of Urban Nightlife*. Chicago: University of Chicago Press.
Grazian, David. 2010. *Mix It Up: Popular Culture, Mass Media, and Society*. New York: W. W. Norton.
Kaikati, Andrew M., and Jack G. Kaikati. 2004. "Stealth Marketing: How to Reach Consumers Surreptitiously," *California Management Review* 46(4): 6–22.
Walker, Rob. 2009. *Buying In: What We Buy and Who We Are*. New York: Random House.

Supermarkets

RACHEL SCHWARTZ
St. Joseph's College, USA

The "supermarket revolution" began in the 1930s in the United States with the novel idea that sales volume and profits could be increased by lowering prices and building bigger stores (Mayo 1993). Initially shunned by grocery store chains, the supermarketing format became ubiquitous in the United States less than a decade later. Supermarkets now have become both globally ubiquitous and the gatekeepers of the food system, controlling the flow of resources between retail consumers and the majority of the production process.

Three phases, not mutually exclusive, mark the rise of these supermarket superpowers: the "boom" of origination and steady growth through the 1990s; the shift from quantity to quality during the late 1990s and early 2000s; and the still ongoing broadening of the retail sector in scope and scale.

The first phase is characterized by the introduction of self-service, high-volume, low-cost selling and the technological advances that enabled these changes. The supermarketing sales strategy is epitomized by the concept of "one-stop shopping": a large store that sells meats, produce, dairy, bakery, canned and packaged foods, as well as nonfood items with self-service aisles and a location just outside the city center. Technological innovations such as free-standing shelving revolutionized the shopping, and retailing, experiences. Delivering items directly to the store and storing them on the large shelving units alleviated the expense of storing surplus in a warehouse. Customers were attracted as much to the *culture* of shopping as to the low prices (Humphery 1998). In ensuing decades, the supermarket industry pursued a strategy of consolidation and exclusive partnerships with manufacturers. By the 1990s, a strategy of mergers and acquisitions quickly enlarged the market share held by the top five food retailers in the United States by over 50 percent (Wrigley 2001; Schwartz and Lyson 2007). The entrance of "big-box" stores Wal-Mart and Costco prompted the traditional food retailers to diversify their strategies and focus on quality of experience by offering a wider variety of types of foods and services, managing store image, and negotiating brand development.

The second phase, emerging in the late 1990s, is marked by this shift in emphasis from quantity to quality of both products and shopping experience. During this period, supermarkets reconstructed themselves as trustworthy "brands," identifying themselves as reliable authority figures perfectly suited to alleviate the confusion (mainly created by the corporate food industry itself) about appropriate food choices (Nestle 2002; Dixon 2003). By providing "appropriate" private-label food products, they have managed to foster a belief in the supermarket as the "gatekeeper of food, nutrition and quality" (Burch and Lawrence 2005, 9). Because contemporary private-label goods are marked with the retailer's brand, retailers are invested not only in the potential success of the particular item, but the overall success of their brand.

The private-label market in the United States has only recently begun to develop and be exploited as a source of competitive gain for the food retailers but private-label goods emerged in the United Kingdom during the 1970s and now often occupy more shelf space than comparable branded foods. No longer merely cheaper versions of brand-name foods, private-label goods have become innovative market segment leaders and everything from canned corn to watermelon salsa is produced under a supermarket's brand label.

The second phase melds into the third during the early 2000s with the broadening of the retail sector in both scope and scale. Retailers are entering new territory, both figuratively and literally, as they structure production, rather than distribution, of consumer items and the construction of new stores in former state-controlled economies (FSCEs). Many supermarkets began outsourcing the production of their private-label products because traditional manufacturers were not able to meet constantly changing consumer demands, taking up to two years to move a new product through development and onto the shelves (Harvey et al. 2001). The food retailers funded and fueled a new type of production – the new manufacturers produce few, if any, products under their own name, but are guaranteed retail shelf space because they are contracted directly by the supermarkets. This also shifts financial risk and responsibility from the retailer to the new manufacturing sector.

The third phase also is marked by a second supermarket "boom" as regional corporations become transnational. In order to increase the scale of operation, many leading global food retailers began investing heavily in markets in developing countries and FSCEs as their relative domestic markets became saturated (Reardon and Swinnen 2004). The most recent "supermarket revolutions" are foreign direct investments that are spreading an industrial culture of retailer–manufacturer relations with retailers at the helm. The privatization of the entire food system in these countries occurred swiftly and the impacts of these changes are only beginning to materialize (Reardon and Swinnen 2004).

This final phase, although nascent, has already seriously impacted the global food system and numerous local food systems. The focus on expansion, in the form of increased control over relationships with manufacturers and global development, marks a new era for the food retailing industry.

SEE ALSO: Big-Box Stores; Farmers' Markets; Food; Food Deserts; Global Markets; Whole Foods Market

REFERENCES

Burch, David, and Geoffrey Lawrence. 2005. "Supermarket Own Brands, Supply Chains and the Transformation of the Agri-Food System." *International Journal of Sociology of Agriculture and Food* 13(1): 1–18.

Dixon, Jane. 2003. "Authority, Power and Value in Contemporary Industrial Food Systems." *International Journal of Sociology of Agriculture and Food* 11(1): 31–40.

Harvey, Mark, Andrew McMeekin, Sally Randles, Dale Southerton, Bruce Tether, and Alan Warde. 2001. "Between Demand and Consumption: A Framework for Research." Discussion Paper No 40. Centre for Research on Innovation and Competition, University of Manchester, UK. http://www.me.mtu.edu/~jwsuther/colloquium/Between_Demand_and_Consumption.pdf.

Humphery, Kim. 1998. *Shelf Life: Supermarkets and the Changing Cultures of Consumption*. Melbourne: Cambridge University Press.

Mayo, James. 1993. *The American Grocery Store: The Business Evolution of an Architectural Space*. Westport, CT: Greenwood.

Nestle, M. 2002. *Food Politics*. Berkeley, CA: University of California Press.

Reardon, Thomas and Johan Swinnen. 2004. "Agrifood Sector Liberalization and the Rise of Supermarkets in Former State-Controlled Economies: A Comparative Approach." *Development Policy Review* 22: 515–523.

Schwartz, Rachel and Thomas Lyson. 2007. "Retail Relations: An Interlocking Directorate Analysis of Food Retailing Corporations in the United States." *Agriculture and Human Values* 24: 489–98.

Wrigley, Neil. 2001. "The Consolidation Wave in US Food Retailing: A European Perspective." *Agribusiness* 17: 489.

FURTHER READING

Kaufman, Phil. 2000. "Consolidation in Food Retailing: Prospects for Consumers and Grocery Suppliers." *Agricultural Outlook* 273: 18–22.

Sustainable Consumption

KIM HUMPHERY
RMIT University, Australia

The term "sustainable consumption" is subject to a range of definitions, though all of them identify a need for change in consumption practices, especially in affluent economies. This perspective is driven primarily by a concern for the environmental impact of the consumption of goods and services in terms of both the depletion of unrenewable natural resources and the production and disposal of consumer waste. Some definitions attend also to issues of global economic equity and social and psychological wellbeing in challenging the logic of high-consumption economies and lifestyles. Beyond such generality, there are widely varying conceptions of how consumption should be transformed. Dominant policy approaches to sustainable consumption tend to emphasize informed consumer choice and improved production processes as vehicles for altering consumption patterns. This does not seek to challenge a global consumer capitalism, but to incrementally manage its environmental and social consequences. Less circumscribed approaches seek to change not only the patterns but the levels of consumption characteristic of affluent economies, as well as the values or conventions that drive unsustainable consumption practices. These approaches variously emphasize individual lifestyle change, collective and local forms of market provision, and/or transformations in the sociotechnical infrastructures and everyday conventions underlying consumption routines.

The terminological, if not conceptual, emergence of sustainable consumption can be conveniently traced to a specific historical moment. Unlike the related notions of ethical and green consumption, which have an ostensibly less definitive history, it is broadly acknowledged that it was the Agenda 21 report arising from the 1992 United Nations (UN) Conference on Environment and Development – the so-called Rio Earth Summit – that popularized the term sustainable consumption and gave birth to an international policy discourse. This was not so much invention as development: the Agenda 21 report built significantly on earlier attempts in *The Limits to Growth* (Meadows et al. 1972) and particularly *Our Common Future* (World Commission on Environment and Development 1987) to identify consumption patterns as integral to addressing problems of global environmental sustainability. More broadly, a critique of affluence and overconsumption was hardly news by the 1990s but was a consolidated theme of public intellectual and environmentalist critique, especially through the writings of critics such as J. K. Galbraith, Fred Hirsch, E. F. Schumacher, Tibor Scitovsky, William Leiss, and André Gorz.

Nevertheless, many commentators have identified the Rio Summit as heralding a key shift. As Maurie J. Cohen has noted, until the early 1990s Western industrialized nations had, in international forums, delimited discussion of global environmental degradation and uneven economic development to a problem of population growth. The Rio Summit (through the agitation of developing nations and nongovernment organizations) explicitly challenged this by placing Western consumption practices center stage. The result was that "consumption gained new stature, especially in European nations, as an organizing theme with which to interpret the widening gap in global economic equality and the environmental impact of consumer lifestyles" (Cohen 2001, 22). Indeed, as a newly minted concept with a UN imprimatur the imperative to render consumption sustainable quickly began to shape mainstream environmental policy rhetoric in the West, and a number of commentators have usefully traced the rise and consolidation of this policy terrain, mostly concentrating on United Nations and European initiatives which have been at the forefront of change (see Cohen 2001, 2010; Jackson 2006; Seyfang 2009; Hinton and Goodman 2010).

Internationally, UN agencies have, over the past two decades, continued to drive the further mainstream formulation of the sustainable consumption agenda through the Rio+5 Conference in 1997, by way of the 1998 *Human Development Report* (United Nations Development Programme 1998) and through the World Summit on Sustainable Development in Johannesburg in 2002. The latter gathering gave rise to a 2003 "International Expert Meeting" in Marrakech which inaugurated a 10-year framework of interventionist programs for sustainable consumption and production – thus dubbed the Marrakech Process. The United Nations Development Programme has also maintained since 1998 the information sharing and policy-oriented Sustainable Consumption and Production Network.

Beyond the UN, the Organisation for Economic Cooperation and Development (OECD) was quick to set up a working group in the 1990s on sustainable consumption and production designed to foster environmental policy initiatives by member states (see OECD 1997). A number of OECD countries have worked in tandem with this process (see OECD 2008). In the UK, for example, the sustainable consumption policy agenda has been driven through a series of government reports and bodies, especially centered on the establishment in 2002 of the Sustainable Development Commission (SDC). A year later, the UK government adopted a sustainable consumption strategy articulated in the *Changing Patterns* report (Defra 2003) – though this essentially carried forward earlier UK approaches, particularly the notion that sustainable consumption could be achieved by "decoupling" economic growth from environmental damage (Jackson 2006; Hinton and Goodman 2010). A more innovative move was the establishment in 2004 of the UK Roundtable on Sustainable Consumption which, through the SDC, published a number of influential reports including what would become the 2009 "bestseller," *Prosperity Without Growth* by the British environmental economist Tim Jackson (Jackson 2009). Other key European players in the field include the Netherlands. Indeed, from as early the 1970s the Dutch government adopted the language of "critical consumption" and "responsible living" in relation to environmental concerns, while from the mid-1990s both Dutch government agencies and environmentalist organizations targeted the "citizen-consumer" as central to altering consumption patterns (see Martens and Spaargaren 2006).

Despite these initiatives – and many others not mentioned in this brief discussion – governmental interventionism and commitment in relation to sustainable consumption has been highly circumscribed. This was clearly evident at the most recent UN Earth Summit in 2012. While this Rio+20 gathering promoted "green economies" as an overriding issue, the final outcome document – "The Future We Want" (United Nations 2013) – simply reiterated the Agenda 21 commitment to sustainable consumption and production, while explicitly refusing to set goals and targets.

For many observers this was a major lost opportunity, though hardly surprising. It has been noted often that the cost of sustainable consumption entering the mainstream policy realm was, from the outset, the dilution of its core message. As many critics have insisted, almost all of the policy documents pouring forth on sustainable consumption have predicated change on consumer-driven reforms, not on significant state intervention or infrastructural shifts – and least of all on a challenge to increasing levels of global consumption. Thus consumer-focused "green" behavior change programs, ecolabeling, and household energy use measurement (coupled in the production realm with strategies for improving resource productivity and minimizing waste) have been the preferred governmental strategies. Indeed, sustainable consumption policy has largely been the story of appealing to "rational" and "ethical" consumers and of the "technological fix," not of the abandonment of conventional, consumption-based economic growth. The tensions in the institutionalized rhetoric of sustainable consumption thus remain glaring and, as Gill Seyfang (2009) has noted, were originally embodied in the Agenda 21 report which both advocated a conventional use of market mechanisms to shift consumption patterns, while more radically suggesting the abandonment of conventional market notions of prosperity.

This tension, as signaled in the opening paragraph, undergirds the division between an incrementalist and a more radical politics of sustainable consumption. As Cohen (2011, 176–7) has argued, a "weak" or mainstream approach to sustainable consumption "is founded on notions of atomized consumer behaviour," whereas a "strong" or more encompassing approach seeks "to foster transformational changes" and adopts "a broad conception of moral responsibility." In the latter case, addressing sustainability entails confronting the problem of aggregate *overconsumption*, particularly in the affluent world, and of consumer excess. Moreover, the impact of high and ever-increasing levels of consumption – and an attendant "consumer culture" – is understood by many critics as resulting not only in environmental damage, but in a loss of social cohesion, personal wellbeing, and ethical commitment to reducing global economic inequality. Thus, a more comprehensive sustainable consumption agenda, as Seyfang has argued, moves to challenge not only mainstream sustainability policy but the very notion of "individualistic green consumerism"; while counterposed to this is the need for "the radical realignment of social and economic institutions" (2009, 2). In Seyfang's words, "the policy agenda has narrowed from initial possibilities of redefining prosperity and wealth and radically transforming lifestyles, to a focus on improving resource productivity and marketing 'green' or 'ethical' products" (Seyfang 2009, 3). Similarly, Emma Hinton and Michael Goodman (2010, 247) have observed, following arguments in relation to "green governmentality," that sustainable consumption rests heavily on the "responsibilization" of the citizen and, like Seyfang and Cohen, they look beyond the mainstream to alternative understandings of consuming sustainably. These alternatives run from movements such as voluntary simplicity and slow food, to discourses of degrowth and new economics, to theoretical interventions relating to infrastructures of provision, alternative hedonism, and concepts of sufficiency.

All this is not to imply a unity to the field of a more radical politics of sustainable consumption. On the contrary, there are significant theoretical and political differences between social movements advocating alternative forms of consumption, and especially between intellectual approaches focused on individual lifestyle change and those focused on collective economic responses and/or infrastructural transformation. One can also seek to temper some of the claims made by various opponents of overconsumption. A politics of ethical and green consumption, for example, is not easily characterized as simply "mainstream." While it has been extensively co-opted by conventional sustainability policy, responsible consumer choice remains a field of political possibility. Similarly, a caution is needed in making assumptions about the social and personal meaning and impact of contemporary consumption practices and their supposed connection to a rampant consumer culture destructive of moral sensibility and social bonds. Nevertheless, drawing distinctions between the mainstream and the alternative is certainly useful as a way of identifying the political fault lines – and the trajectory of political debate – that has come to characterize the terrain of sustainable consumption as analysis, policy, advocacy, and activism. Indeed, arguments over the need for an increased role for the state in regulating and reframing the infrastructures of consumption and production in the interest of sustainability, for broader ways of conceptualizing political action beyond the individualized practices of consuming "better," and for the adoption of alternative economic models of prosperity, remain paramount. Given the increasingly evident failure of much sustainable consumption policy worldwide, it is difficult to escape the conclusion that a more encompassing approach is urgently needed.

SEE ALSO: Capitalism; Ethical Consumption; Green Consumption

REFERENCES

Cohen, Maurie, J. 2001. "The Emergent Environmental Policy Discourse on Sustainable Consumption." In *Exploring Sustainable Consumption: Environmental Policy and the Social Sciences,* edited by Maurie Cohen, 21–37. Oxford: Elsevier.

Cohen, Maurie J. 2010. "The International Political Economy of (Un)Sustainable Consumption and the Global Financial Collapse." *Environmental Politics* 19(1): 107–126.

Cohen, Maurie J. 2011. "(Un)Sustainable Consumption and the New Political Economy of Growth." In *Beyond The Consumption Bubble,* edited by Karin M. Ekström and Kay Glans, 174–190. London: Routledge.

Department for Environment, Food and Rural Affairs (DEFRA). 2003. *Changing Patterns – UK Government Framework for Sustainable Consumption and Production.* London: Defra Publications. http://collections.europarchive.org/tna/20060810193049/http:/www.defra.gov.uk/environment/business/scp/pdf/changing-patterns.pdf.

Hinton, Emma D., and Michael K. Goodman. 2010. "Sustainable Consumption: Developments, Considerations and New Directions." In *The International Handbook of Environmental Sociology,* 2nd ed., edited by Michael R. Redclift and Graham Woodgate, 245–261. Cheltenham, UK: Edward Elgar.

Jackson, Tim. 2006. "Readings in Sustainable Consumption." In *The Earthscan Reader in Sustainable Consumption,* edited by Tim Jackson, 1–23. London: Earthscan.

Jackson, Tim. 2009. *Prosperity Without Growth: Economics for a Finite Planet*. London: Earthscan.

Martens, Susan, and Gert Spaargaren. 2006. "The Politics of Sustainable Consumption: The Case of the Netherlands." In *The Earthscan Reader in Sustainable Consumption*, edited by Tim Jackson, 197–221. London: Earthscan.

Meadows, Donella H., Dennis L. Meadows, Jørgen Randers, and William H. Behrens. 1972. *The Limits to Growth: A Report for the Club of Rome's Project on the Predicament of Mankind*. New York: Universe Books.

Organisation for Economic Cooperation and Development. 1997. *Sustainable Consumption and Production*. Paris: OECD.

Organisation for Economic Cooperation and Development. 2008. *Promoting Sustainable Consumption: Good Practices in OECD Countries*. Paris: OECD.

Seyfang, Gill. 2009. *The New Economics of Sustainable Consumption: Seeds of Change*. Basingstoke, UK: Palgrave Macmillan.

United Nations. 2013. "The Future We Want: Outcome Document Adopted at Rio+20." www.un.org/en/sustainablefuture/

United Nations Development Programme. 1998. *Human Development Report 1998*. Oxford: Oxford University Press.

World Commission on Environment and Development. 1987. *Our Common Future*. Oxford: Oxford University Press.

FURTHER READING

Southerton, Dale, Heather Chappells, and Bas Van Vliet, eds. 2004. *Sustainable Consumption: The Implications of Changing Infrastructures of Provision*. Cheltenham, UK: Edward Elgar.

Sweatshops

DENIS G. ARNOLD
University of North Carolina, USA

Sweatshops have been defined as workplaces where workers are subjected to at least two of the following conditions: wages for 48 hours that are less than the overall poverty rate for the nation (this means the wages are insufficient to avoid ill health and malnutrition, to obtain decent housing, and to obtain other basic goods), forced overtime, systematic health and safety risks resulting from a disregard for employee welfare, deceptive employment practices that put workers at risk (e.g., failing to disclose known workplace hazards), or the underpayment of earnings (Arnold and Bowie 2003). In most industrialized nations sweatshops are illegal and are shut down by law enforcement authorities when they are discovered. In developing nations the legal status of such working conditions is more complex. Some of these practices may be lawful (e.g., if minimum wage regulations have not kept up with inflation or if there are few occupational safety rules in place). However, sweatshop conditions are often illegal in developing nations but tolerated because of the inability of authorities to enforce their own laws or the fear that enforcing labor laws may lead employers to move the jobs to other poor nations given the large, surplus global labor supply. The most egregious working conditions violate international labor and human rights standards and conventions.

Economists, especially those with libertarian sympathies, often accuse critics of sweatshops of being naive for failing to recognize that sweatshops benefit the global poor by providing much needed jobs and foreign direct investment to nations with large supplies of uneducated workers. They point out that workers freely accept these jobs because these factory jobs are better than the alternatives. However, this analysis fails to take into account many of the most important ethical issues that are relevant to the evaluation of sweatshops. First, background conditions of injustice contribute to the desperation and poverty of many workers in developing nations. Critics of sweatshops argue that companies take advantage of background injustice in order to extract exploitative employment terms. Additionally, critics of sweatshops point out that workers are treated like disposable tools rather than as persons entitled to a basic level of respect and consideration (Arnold and Bowie 2003; Snyder 2010).

Sweatshops exist because consumers permit their existence. Consumers typically prefer to pay the lowest possible price for consumer goods and don't typically factor working conditions into their consumption preferences. Some studies indicate a willingness on the part of consumers to pay modestly increased prices for products made in factories with decent working conditions if they can be guaranteed that the premium is being passed on to workers in the form of improved working conditions or wages (Pollin, Burns, and Heintz 2004). However, few mechanisms exist to provide consumers with reliable information regarding the working conditions in which consumer goods are made. No widespread "sweat-free" labeling mechanism exists. Consumers who are concerned about working conditions in global factories must rely on the statements of companies and third-party auditors for information regarding working conditions in the overseas factories of companies and their suppliers. The accuracy of this information varies significantly between different companies.

The international business literature makes plain that simply issuing stipulations and additional requirements via unfunded mandates to overseas factories will not result in improved working conditions. For smaller companies with little influence over suppliers, this is unlikely to result in any change in behavior. For larger companies that threaten to cancel contracts for noncompliance with new standards, an adversarial stance is likely to result in deceptive practices such as the falsification of records regarding wages, coaching employees to lie about working conditions to auditors, and other strategies intended to placate large consumer goods companies or retailers. A partnership approach where companies provide suppliers with expertise and training, cover the costs of some factory improvements or wage increases, and work to develop long-term relationship with the supplier, is more likely to result in improved working conditions (Locke, Amengual, and Mangla 2009).

In the 1990s investigative journalism and field research brought to light labor rights violations in global factories supplying major apparel and footwear brands. Nongovernmental organizations such as the National Labor Committee, Campaign for Labor Rights, and Global Exchange, targeted specific companies and challenged those companies to improve their labor practices. Nike initially denied responsibility for the labor practices of its suppliers and was specifically targeted by the anti-sweatshop movement. Negative publicity from this campaign led Nike to accept some responsibility for labor practices in its supply chain and to initiate a gradual process of improving working conditions. Largely in response to the anti-sweatshop movement, apparel manufacturers and other interested parties founded the Fair Labor Association (FLA) to facilitate the monitoring and improvement of working conditions in factories. University students, administrators, and labor rights experts founded the Worker Rights Consortium (WRC) as an alternative labor monitoring organization without significant participation from industry. Activists claimed that the WRC's independence from industry would result in greater objectivity in monitoring sweatshops compared to FLA. In recent years, Bangladesh has been at the forefront of the global debate over sweatshops due to a weak regulatory and governance environment that has resulted in the deaths of thousands of factory workers. Consumers interested in improving working conditions can pressure individual companies and trade groups to adapt a partnership approach with their suppliers with the joint goal of maintaining low skill factory jobs while simultaneously respecting the dignity of workers.

SEE ALSO: Consumer Resistance Movements; Free Trade Zones/Export Processing Zones; Globalization and Consumption

REFERENCES

Arnold, Denis G., and Norman E. Bowie. 2003. "Sweatshops and Respect for Persons." *Business Ethics Quarterly* 13(2): 221–242.

Locke, Richard, Matthew Amengual and Akshay Mangla. 2009. "Virtue out of Necessity? Compliance, Commitment, and the Improvement of Labor Conditions in Global Supply Chains." *Politics & Society* 37(3): 319–351.

Pollin, Robert, Justine Burns, and James Heintz. 2004. "Global Apparel Production and Sweatshop Labour: Can Raising Retail Prices Finance Living Wages?" *Cambridge Journal of Economics* 28(2): 153–71.

Snyder, Jeremy. 2010. "Exploitation and Sweatshop Labor." *Business Ethics Quarterly* 20(2): 187–213.

Symbolic Exchange

MICHAEL T. RYAN
Dodge City Community College, USA

Symbolic exchange is the organizing principle, the cellular structure, of the earliest forms of society, the forms that Anthony Giddens designates as "tribal cultures." The exchanges that take place within and between clans, within and between tribes, and between chiefs and other members of the tribe are more than economic exchanges as we know them in modern societies, and their circulation integrates the members of these societies. Marcel Mauss conceptualizes these exchanges as a form of gift giving, and the gift is a "total social phenomenon" (1967, 1). They are multidimensional: economic, moral, religious, mythological, juridical, political, aesthetic, and historical.

Mauss, Émile Durkheim's nephew, created his concept from the work of nineteenth- and early twentieth-century anthropologists in Melanesia, Polynesia, and Northwest America. Like Durkheim, he also wanted to demonstrate the social basis for exchanges as a refutation of the utilitarian notion that individual interests were the foundation for the creation of market relations. There was no "natural" economy that had preceded political economy.

Further, while the tribes of the Americas, Africa, and Asia seemed so different, so "other," to Europeans, Mauss wanted to demonstrate through comparative analysis the underlying similarities as well. The complex structure of the gift made it more difficult for Europeans to see these groups as inferior primitives whose annihilation or assimilation would be of no loss to humanity.

Gift giving was obviously an economic phenomenon, although it did not involve the exchange of equivalent values as it does in market economies. In the Native American Kwakiutl tribe the *potlatch* ritual exchanges were competitive and required a reciprocal exchange at a later moment that was of more value than the original gift. This was how the chief, the clan, or the tribe maintained prestige and power; the chief would distribute the gifts later received to the members of his clan or tribe. The chief was the member of the tribe who shared the most. The goods exchanged were often destroyed in festivals, which made the accumulation of wealth impossible although it did enhance the personal power of the chief.

Gift giving also involved a relation with nature and created a balanced reciprocal relation between society and nature. For example, since tribes deified natural forces in their animistic religions, a wood carver would make an offering to the spirits of the forest before cutting down the tree that he would use. The domination of nature is a modern phenomenon; these tribes lived in nature.

Gift giving also included an ethic of reciprocity. The members of tribes were obligated to give gifts as well as receive gifts. Failure to do either would mean a loss of status, perhaps enslavement or possibly war if it occurred between two tribes. The norm of reciprocity bound clan to clan, men to women, and tribe to tribe, and the chronic circulation of gifts reproduced these tribes as tribes.

Thorstein Veblen brought the analysis of symbolic exchange to the consumer practices of wealthy Americans in his *Theory of the Leisure Class* (1953). Veblen developed his concepts of vicarious consumption and conspicuous consumption from the same sources as Mauss, from tribal cultures and agrarian societies. The leisure class originally derived its prestige from avoiding ignoble work and devoting its time to pursuits that had little practical significance: sports, indolence, war, religious activities, and government. They also derived prestige through the idleness and vicarious consumption of their families and servants. Further, as the members of the middle class took up practical positions as professionals and managers, they derived their prestige from conspicuous consumption, "keeping ahead of the Joneses." Further, the competitive logic of the rat race filtered down throughout the class structure. Although Veblen also recognized that, once his theory had become understood by the leisure class, the members of this elite could reverse course and practice asceticism. Old money has often adopted low profiles in their lifestyles, and the arts and crafts movement, with its functional aesthetic, was very popular for members of the professional managerial class in the early twentieth century. Veblen also recognized that the pursuits of the leisure class often had functional qualities and were not always a pure waste of time and wealth.

Jean Baudrillard (1998) developed his analysis from a critical reading of Mauss, John K. Galbraith, and Thorstein Veblen. Symbolic exchange for Baudrillard was a way to escape the consumer society and the political economy of the sign. He demonstrated in his early writings how the code of consumption and the system of needs had completed the system of production. The use value of the commodity provided no way out of the capitalist mode of production as it had for traditional Marxists – "to each according to his needs"; it only provided an alibi to exchange value. Consumers were even more alienated in their private lives than they were at work, engaging in unequal exchanges with capital and producing surplus value. They were unconscious of the process of semiosis that led through their acts of consumption of commodities with their coded differences to the reproduction of the social relations of production as well as the capitalist mode of production. The only way out of this system was a return to symbolic exchange where the accumulation of wealth and power was impossible and where exchanges were reciprocal and reversible.

Ryan (1982) has given us an analysis of what this could mean. The ideology of "fair exchange" in a market economy masks the unequal exchanges taking place in the labor process. Unpaid labor is the source of surplus value and capital formation. A return to symbolic exchange would restore the "expenditure without reserve" (Ryan 1982, quoting Georges Bataille) of tribal cultures, and this could be accomplished through a process of global gift giving. This would eventually create a level playing field so that wealth in the centers would not be accumulated at the expense of poverty in the peripheries. It would address the problem of uneven development between and within nations. It would inaugurate an era of freely donated labor and distribution according to need. Symbolic exchange will also likely restore a balance between society and nature, whereas the logic of the consumer society, predicated on continuous economic growth and the ideology of economic growth, is likely to destroy the environment.

What are the analytical problems with Baudrillard's analysis of symbolic exchange? A number of critics point out that he does not clearly define the concept of code in his writings. But it seems that what he means is that every commodity has a hierarchal structure with the originals at the top that are appropriated by the elite and models of descending quality that are appropriated by the other strata. The consumption of the sign value of each commodity reproduces the code *and* the relations of domination between the programmers of consumption and the consumers. George Ritzer, in his introduction to Baudrillard (1998) finds "commotion" in Baudrillard's appropriation of concepts from diverse theorists: Marx, Durkheim, Mauss, structural linguistics, Lévi-Strauss, Henri Lefebvre. But this *is* the procedure for dialectical method.

The most serious problem is the criticism that Baudrillard has given us a romantic possibility without identifying any actual agents or movements of social change. However, the Occupy Wall Street movement has given us a glimpse of a possible agency for social change. This movement brought together a number of different groups from the urban peripheries to the decision-making centers of our bureaucratic society of controlled consumption: youth, women, the unemployed, the homeless, working-class groups, intellectuals, anarchists, and so forth. They assembled to contest the technocratic decision making of the urban centers with unfettered speech and direct democracy. They put in question the homogenization, fragmentation, and hierarchization of social space. This may be a critical turning point in the "production of space" which has transcended the production of value as the total social phenomenon of late capitalism, according to Henri Lefebvre. This movement has revealed the possibility for a transition to an urban society and should be considered a moment in what Lefebvre calls the urban revolution. This movement has its historical precedents in urban uprisings of the past: the Paris Commune of 1871, the direct democracy evident in Barcelona in the Spanish Civil War of the 1930s, and the May events in Paris in 1968.

SEE ALSO: Baudrillard, Jean; Commodification; Commodities; Commodity Fetishism; Conspicuous Consumption; Veblen, Thorstein

REFERENCES

Baudrillard, Jean. 1998. *The Consumer Society: Myths and Structures*. London: Sage.

Mauss, Marcel. 1967 (1925). *The Gift*. New York: W. W. Norton.

Ryan, Michael. 1982. *Marxism and Deconstruction*. Baltimore: *Johns Hopkins University Press.*

Veblen, Thorstein. 1953. *Theory of the Leisure Class*. New York: Mentor.

FURTHER READING

Kellner, Douglas. 1988. *Jean Baudrillard*. Stanford, CA: Stanford University Press.

Kellner, Douglas. 1994. *Baudrillard*. Oxford: Blackwell.

Symbolic Value

MICHELE BONAZZI
University of Bologna, Italy

The symbolic value of an object refers to the semantic and cultural universe linked to it, which allows consumers to express their identity and social membership. Goods are symbolic as opposed to their supposed functionality; they are symbolic because they represent embodied symbols. The value of a good, therefore, is not only connected to its tangible aspects, that is, its structural characteristics and usefulness, but it is dematerialized and becomes sign, symbol, and communication. A commodity tells a story and at the same time becomes a form of identity expression, with a code and a language that are reflected in the system of meanings attributed to it. This process of signification is developed through a subjective reworking that, however, can be extended to the collective level, through rituals of exchange and sharing. Cultural anthropology has undoubtedly been a particularly fertile field for the study of consumption as a practice of signification.

In *The Gift*, Mauss (1990/1922) explains how the ritual exchange of goods, based on the principle of reciprocity, represents one of the most common and universal ways to create human relations. According to Mauss the gift exchange becomes a "total social fact," that is, a specific aspect of a culture that is related to all the others, and therefore through its analysis it is possible to understand by extension the different components of society. McCracken (1990) underlines the importance of the "possession rituals" inasmuch as they represent an essential step to allow consumers to actually enter into possession of goods. However, McCracken's analysis shows the absolute mobility of the meanings and the temporary nature of their relationship with objects. To the contrary, Miller (1987) argues that the re-appropriation of goods is a process through which mass culture is reworked and it is possible to give again personal values to an object. Both authors share the common vision whereby consumption activity and its rituals allow consumers to find a possible way of escape from the alienating condition that has its roots in the industrial production system in order to embed objects in their own system of meanings.

From a sociological perspective, the symbolic value of objects was emphasized by Baudrillard: in *The System of Objects* (1996/1968) he conceives goods as representations of a form of language, a "grammar." He highlights how commodities are primarily signs capable of expressing a syntax, to interact with each other as having a life of their own, escaping the Marxist concept of "use-value," linked to the usefulness and technical specifications of an object. According to Baudrillard, the analysis of commodities production proposed by Marx is to be considered outdated precisely because today's capitalism is no longer involved in material goods but in signs and images. This point of view is shared by Douglas and Isherwood, who affirm that consumption is a "joint production, with fellow consumers, of a universe of values" (Douglas and Isherwood 1979, 45). This process leads to a communicative approach that considers goods as a "semantics" through which consumption as language is realized.

An object can be changed in what is its common use and the figure of the craft consumer (Campbell 2005) is a form of subjective and structural reworking. There are also collective forms of semantic re-elaborations. Examples are the "neo-tribes" (Maffesoli 1996) that arise from cult objects who can now be identified as tribes of consumers, who are linked together by a common bond that has the product, the brand, and its rituals at the core of the system. Examples of these tribes are the consumption communities of lovers of products such as Nutella or Harley Davidson bikes. In this case, as affirmed by Roberts (2004), it is better to talk not about brands, but about *lovemarks*, which can create a deep and emotional connection that can lead to an identification process with consumers.

SEE ALSO: Commodities; Consumption and Identity; Gifts; Symbolic Exchange

REFERENCES

Baudrillard, Jean. 1996/1968. *The System of Objects*. London: Verso.

Campbell, Colin. 2005. "The Craft Consumer: Culture, Craft and Consumption in a Postmodern Society." *Journal of Consumer Culture* 5: 23–42.

Douglas, Mary, and Baron Isherwood. 1979. *The World of Goods*. New York: Basic Books.

Maffesoli, Michel. 1996. *The Time of the Tribes: The Decline of Individualism in Mass Society*. London: Sage.

Mauss, Marcel. 1990/1922. *The Gift: Forms and Functions of Exchange in Archaic Societies*. London: Routledge.

McCracken, Grant. 1990. *Culture and Consumption: New Approaches to the Symbolic Character of Consumer Goods and Activities*. Bloomington: Indiana University Press.

Miller, Daniel. 1987. *Material Culture and Mass Consumption*. Oxford: Basil Blackwell.

Roberts, Kevin. 2004. *Lovemarks: The Future Beyond Brands*. New York: Powerhouse Books.

T

Taxes

CHRISTINE A. WERNET
University of South Carolina, USA

There are many different taxes that are levied on citizens of a country. The two main reasons for taxation are to redistribute income among the population and to generate government revenue (Davies 1986). Redistribution of income can generate more equality in a society, and government revenue is needed to fund various endeavors from national security to education, all of which are necessary to maintain peace and prosperity. There are three main types of taxation: proportional, progressive, and regressive taxes.

Proportional taxes refer to taxes that equally burden all income groups in a society. Proportional taxes are sometimes referred to as a flat tax. For example, if a society had a proportional income tax of 15 percent, a family with an annual income of US$100,000 would pay US$15,000 a year in income taxes, while a family with an annual income of US$10,000 would pay US$1,500 a year in income taxes.

Progressive taxes are taxes that require those who earn more money to pay higher taxes. Federal income taxes in the United States are progressive. The breakdown of federal income tax rates for 2013 is listed in Table 1. The Internal Revenue Service (IRS) in the United States has a bracketed income tax system with the goal of generating government revenue without overburdening those who are less able to pay. The share of taxes that each group pays is similar to its share of the nation's total income: basically, the more money a person makes the more they pay in federal income taxes.

There were several changes put in place by Congress in 2013 that impacted taxes. One important change is that those who make the most, over US$400,000 for individuals and over US$450,000 for couples, saw their taxes increase by 4.6 percent, from 35 to 39.6 percent. Another change in the tax code is that capital gains taxes increased from 15 to 20 percent for individuals making over US$400,000, and estates valued at more than US$5 million will be taxed at 40 percent (Klein 2013).

Proponents of progressive taxes argue that wealthy individuals have a moral obligation to society to pay higher taxes. Opponents argue that progressive income taxation has a negative effect on capital formation and economic growth.

In a nonpartisan government study Hungerford (2012) found that drastic decreases in the tax rate for the richest Americans over the last 65 years do not appear to be correlated with economic

The Wiley Blackwell Encyclopedia of Consumption and Consumer Studies, First Edition.
Edited by Daniel Thomas Cook and J. Michael Ryan.

Table 1 Federal income tax rates, 2013

Tax Rate (%)	*Singles*	*Couples*
10.0	$0+	$0+
15.0	$8,700+	$17,400+
25.0	$35,350+	$70,700+
28.0	$85,650+	$142,700+
33.0	$178,650+	$217,450+
35.0	$388,350+	$388,350+
39.6	$400,000+	$450,000 +

Source: Federal Income Tax Brackets 2013

growth, saving, investment, or productivity. However, these tax cuts are correlated with increasing income disparities in the United States and an increase in income for the very wealthy. The share of income held by the top 0.1 percent of families increased from 4.2 percent in 1945 to 9.2 percent in 2009. At the same time the average tax rate paid by this same group fell from over 50 percent in 1945 to about 25 percent in 2009. In short, this study, as well as others, shows that multiple factors have resulted in the rich getting richer and the poor getting poorer.

Regressive taxes burden lower-income groups more than higher-income groups. Less affluent individuals spend a higher proportion of their income on regressive taxes, such as sales taxes and excise taxes, than do more affluent individuals. *Sales tax* is tax that is placed on all items that are sold: food, clothing, furniture, and so forth. *Excise taxes* are additional taxes placed on certain items such as alcohol, tobacco, and gasoline. Excise taxes and sales taxes place a heavier burden on the poor than on the rich because these taxes account for a larger proportion of the total income of the poor (Wernet 2007). For example, if someone who makes US$100,000 buys an item for US$1000 and pays US$70 in sales tax, that US$70 is a small percentage of their total income. If someone who makes US$10,000 needs to make a US$1000 purchase and has to pay US$70 in sales tax, that US$70 is a much larger percentage of their total income, and it is more difficult for individuals in this income bracket to pay the sales tax.

Data from the Congressional Budget Office show that lower-income households pay a significantly larger share of their incomes in federal excise taxes than middle- and upper-income households do. This is especially problematic because an excise tax is placed on gasoline. Additionally, many state and local taxes are also regressive. These taxes overburden low-income families, who pay a larger share of their total income on state and local taxes than do wealthier families (Marr and Huang 2012).

One exception to this is a luxury tax, a specific type of sales tax, which is more likely to be imposed on the rich than the poor because luxury taxes are placed on nonessential goods, such as expensive cars or jewelry or yachts, which the rich are more likely to buy. Luxury taxes are unlikely to inhibit consumption because acquisition of these expensive goods is more about increasing one's status than it is about the value or the utility of the product. Therefore an increase in price due to a luxury tax may even make the goods more desirable to the rich as they engage in conspicuous consumption.

In conclusion, 2011 data from the Institute on Taxation and Economic Policy show that the bottom 20 percent of households received 3.4 percent of the total income earned in the United States and paid 2.1 percent of the total taxes. The middle fifth of households earned 11.4 percent of income and paid 10.3 percent of taxes. The top 1 percent of households received 21.0 percent of income and paid 21.6 percent of taxes. This data shows that the tax system as a whole in the United States is only slightly progressive, at best (Marr and Huang 2012).

When all forms of taxation are considered, some countries, such as the United States, actually have nearly as much income inequality after taxation as they do before. Therefore, while taxation does generate revenue for the government, it may do little to redistribute income.

SEE ALSO: Economy, Informal; Markets, Moral Aspects of

REFERENCES

Davies, David G. 1986. *United States Taxes and Tax Policy*. New York: Cambridge University Press.

Devine, Joel A. 1983. "Fiscal Policy and Class Income Inequality: The Distributional Consequences of Governmental Revenues and Expenditures in the United States, 1949–1976." *American Sociological Review* 48: 606–22.

Federal Income Tax Brackets. 2013. http://www.tax-brackets.org/federaltaxtable.

Hungerford, Thomas L. 2012. Taxes and the Economy: An Economic Analysis of the Top Tax Rates Since 1945. Congressional Research Service. http://www.fas.org/sgp/crs/misc/R42729.pdf.

Klein, Ezra. 2013. "The Washington Post's Wonkbook: Everything You Need to Know About the Fiscal Cliff Deal." January 1. http://www.washingtonpost.com/blogs/wonkblog/wp/2013/01/01/wonkbook-everything-you-need-to-know-about-the-fiscal-cliff-deal.

Marr, Chuck, and Chye-Ching Huang. 2012. "Misconceptions and Realities About Who Pays Taxes." Center on Budget and Policy Priorities. September 17. http://www.cbpp.org/cms/index.cfm?fa=view&id=3505.

Wernet, Christine A. 2007. "Taxes: Regressive, Proportional and Progressive." In *The Blackwell Encyclopedia of Sociology*, edited by George Ritzer, 4946–4947. Oxford: Blackwell.

FURTHER READING

Bagwell, Laurie Simon, and B. Douglas Bernheim. 1996. "Veblen Effects in a Theory of Conspicuous Consumption." *American Economic Review* 86(3): 349–73.

Chait, Jonathan. 2012. "A Peek Into the Fantasy World of the Persecuted Rich." *New York Magazine*, September 25. http://nymag.com/daily/intelligencer/2012/09/fantasy-world-of-the-persecuted-rich.html.

Kerbo, Harold R. 2011. *Social Stratification and Inequality: Class Conflict in Historical, Comparative, and Global Perspective*. New York: McGraw Hill.

Teens

NATALIE COULTER
York University, Canada

The term "teen" refers to a category of young people loosely aged 13 to around age 17 or 18, who are no longer children but have not fully taken on adult responsibilities. The reference to young people as teens is a product of a developing youth culture that largely came about in the mid-twentieth century in the United States. The teen market is a distinct youth market and culture with particular patterns of consumption and tastes made possible by the affluence of the post-World War II economy when middle-class families could defer having their adolescent children enter the labor market. The term teens, along with teenagers, or sometimes even teeners, was beginning to be used as early as the 1930s, but came to prominence in the 1940s and 1950s in the United States. Advertisers and manufacturers referenced the teen as the new target market of affluent young people. In doing so, these industries started to play an active role in shaping and disseminating the tastes, styles, and attitudes of teenagers in the United States.

Prior to the nineteenth century, the liminal space between childhood and adulthood was not fully recognized as a separate stage in the life course. As a life stage this period of liminality, known as adolescence, was described by G. Stanley Hall in the early 1900s. Hall understood adolescence as a physiological stage of transformation, or awakening. He saw adolescence as a period of "storm and stress" in which adolescents' biology formed alternating and opposing emotions that youth had to learn to deal with. Hall's definition of adolescence privileges the psychodevelopmental discourses over social and cultural definitions that are ascribed to the teen. The term teen is different from adolescence in that adolescence marks a stage of psychosocial development while teen references a stage in the life course of participating in a youth culture with particular patterns of consumption and tastes.

By the 1940s there was a serious interest in the possibilities of a teen market by manufacturers, advertisers, marketers, and the media. The hero of the story of marketing to teenagers is the unlikely character of Eugene Gilbert who, at the age of 19, surmised that teens were the key to market expansion. In the 1940s, he hired a group of teenage surveyors to interview fellow teens, looking for answers about their tastes and spending habits, and eventually established the Youth Marketing Company, a prosperous research organization. Gilbert became the unofficial guide for the newly discovered youth culture and his market research was instrumental in shaping and defining what was meant by teen. He was quoted in *Advertising Age* stating that the "salient discovery is that within the past decade teens have become a separate and distinct group in society." Few companies acted upon his insight, leading Gilbert to complain that everyone was talking about advertising to youth, but "only a few (did) anything about it."

It was during the 1950s that the teenage consumer was solidified in the imagination of the social psyche as a separate and discrete segment of the population, and many companies began to cater to them. By the late 1950s, with the advent of rock 'n' roll and the coming of age of the early baby boomers, the teen demographic became a large force in the marketplace. The popular press described teens as "fun worshippers" and the "coolest customers" and estimated that in the United States the teen had between US$10 billion and US$12 billion of disposable income. These flattering descriptions of the teen market in the popular press further legitimized the teen as a viable consumer market while also communicating what it meant to be a teen to a generation of young people. Teen tastes and styles began to drive trends in the marketplace. The iconography of the youth market sold the idioms of "youth as fun" and promoted a new consumer value system that prioritized commodity consumption and immediate gratification. Teens were given the responsibility of encouraging and celebrating the prosperity that was promised in the postwar era.

Since the 1950s the teen has become reified as a separate stage in the life course. While originating largely in American consumer culture, there has been the growth of an international audience for teen youth culture in recent decades. Today the teen and teen culture are a global phenomenon, a situation often critiqued as a form of cultural imperialism. In the contemporary globalized marketplace the term teen is more about consumerism than it is about the connectedness of a cohort of young people. Anthropologists have observed that in the Global South, for example, the term teenager is used to teach the elite the language of consumption as the teenager is no longer an age category but a Western commercial lifestyle driven by the marketplace.

The expansion of teen culture is not just across geographic boundaries but across age boundaries as well. The tastes, styles, and attitudes of the teen push beyond the age borders of adolescence and down-age onto the tween at the younger end and up-age into adulthood as teen culture has become a major driver of marketplace trends.

It is important to note that the framing of the teen in the 1950s as a separate and independent stage in the life course is part of a larger historical project of the twentieth century in which youth culture has become intricately entwined with consumer culture and the spectrum of childhood and youth has been segmented into smaller, tighter market niches that offer more intense marketing opportunities.

SEE ALSO: Children's Consumer Culture; Cool; Coolhunting; Tweens; Youth Culture(s)

FURTHER READING

Fass, Paula. 1978. *The Damned and the Beautiful: American Youth in the 1920s*. Oxford: Oxford University Press.

Nash, Ilana. 2006. *American Sweethearts: Teenage Girls in Twentieth Century Popular Culture*. Bloomington: Indiana University Press.

Palladino, Grace. 1996. *Teenagers: An American History*. New York: Basic Books.

Theming

PER STRÖMBERG
Telemark University College, Norway

"Theming" involves the use of an overarching theme as an added value, for example, "pirates," "Wild West," "Egypt," or a self-referential brand such as Nike, to create a holistic and cohesive spatial, cultural, and social organization of a consumer venue. Theming as a method is mostly defined in relation to themed environments such as restaurants, hotels, theme parks, shopping malls, or any other servicescape based on a thematic concept, which serves as a narrative stage for human interaction in a commercial context.

A theme – a result of theming – is an all-encompassing narrative unit which provides a veneer of symbolism and meaning to a service, good, or location whose thematic source is external to the object or institution to which it is applied. In semiotic terms, a theme is a sign, or a "super sign," composed of several signifying elements. A theme is, like linguistic signs, arbitrary and polysemic, meaning that its unifying meaning always depends on the cultural context in which the theme is interpreted. Consumers relate and respond to themes in different ways; in other words, it is not a one-way communication. Themed environments are organized and arranged by suppliers (entrepreneurs, urban planners, and architects) and actively sought after – or avoided – by consumers as places for leisure and pleasure.

Over the last several decades, a number of scholars have observed an increased use of overarching themes. Today, various forms of symbol-driven environments pervade everyday life. Themed spaces of consumption are an instrumental way of attracting customers. This tendency can be understood in the light of a capitalist dilemma which the social theorist Mark Gottdiener (1997) calls the "realization problem": unless goods can be sold, no profit will be realized. In the capitalist world of today, it is not a problem to produce goods and services in large amounts; the problem is rather to sell them (leaving aside the problems of the lack of ecological and social sustainability related to industrial production). The abundance of producer goods and services, whose use values are equal and whose appearances are similar, forces suppliers to emphasize and articulate the symbolic aspect of goods and services as well as the spaces in which consumption takes place. From the supplier point of view, the benefit of theming is that of differentiation. Due to the homogenization, surplus, and standardization of goods and services, theming has thus become a widespread tool for distinguishing one service, good, tourist destination, or context from another in order to stand out from the competition.

Another benefit of theming is applying a theme as a management tool for structuring the business concept (Strömberg 2007). The theme determines and brings the different parts of the business concept together while the themed environment itself functions as a stage for the consumer venue. Merchandising, acting personnel, and other forms of commercial activities that are possible to generate from a theme – hybrid consumption – such as themed accommodation related to theme parks, are frequently structured and associated by themes in contemporary consumer society.

However, for service providers, there is a range of problems related to theming. First of all, theming is expensive and there is no guarantee that the providers' investments will pay off, that is, that the investment of capital will be successful. Furthermore, the frequent use of theming as a commercial method undermines its impact; theming itself becomes a standard practice and its motifs standardized. Increasing consumer expectations demand ever more innovative themes and more costly performances. Finally, if the use value of a service product is threatened – when, for example, the themed environment of a hotel restaurant affects its logistics – then the theming might be deprioritized.

Frequent motifs of themed environments are related to geography, history, popular culture, and social organization. According to Alan Bryman's (2004) taxonomy, the most frequent motifs and sources of theming are: place, time, sport, music, cinema, fashion, commodities, architecture, the natural world, literature, morality and/or philosophy. However, a theme may overlap and contain more than one of these motifs. In addition, one can speak about reflexive theming, which basically means self-referential brand extensions through theming. Here, the theme is not based on external devices for its narrative, but rather internally generated from the brand itself, such as Nike Town in New York City.

Even though theming perhaps is most related to an American context, with a variety of forms, motifs, and methods of theming, this practice cannot be related to one cultural context alone. Theming has a long history and is nowadays generally applied worldwide. The taxonomic way of ordering and staging cultural motifs as themes is a well-established method in Western society, together with exoticism and historicism. Historically, theming has its recreational precursors, such as the Egyptian valley at Hadrian's Villa outside Rome. This type of cultural appropriation was later adopted by the designers of English gardens in the eighteenth century, who included Turkish tents, Chinese pavilions, idyllic farmsteads, and so forth, in the gardens they created.

Theming in its modern and commercial meaning derives from the themed environments of the world exhibitions of the nineteenth century and the Parisian department stores and arcades, previously described by Walter Benjamin. Furthermore, modern scenographic practices of the nineteenth century such as dioramas and ethnographic sceneries have also played a role in this process. Together with a general taste for cultural exoticism in interior design and architecture over the centuries, theming has been established as one of the major methods for framing the experiences of consumerism. While modernist architects did not practice theming in the first place, except for the use of self-referential elements of modernism as themes, themed environments have become a part of the postmodern aesthetics of consumption, a specific marketing aesthetics. Since its inception, theming has primarily been associated with recreation, commerce, and leisure. Today, theming has come to be applied in other areas, at the dentist or in TV commercials for example, thus pervading people's daily life and influencing the way entrepreneurs structure their businesses in terms of concepts.

Theming as a practice has moreover been applied to urban development, notably influenced by new urbanism, whose principles are based on urban building typologies. For example, the Walt Disney Company is well known for their ideal city of Celebration, Florida, which was developed in 1990s. Today, we can find themed towns in many places around the world; the basic theme for the development of the city of Luodian, Shanghai, was the medieval city of Sigtuna, Sweden. We can also find corporate-themed skiing resorts and even themed shopping centers – outlet villages – that look like towns. The latter are especially numerous in the United States, the United Kingdom, and Italy. The significance of corporate-themed towns is that they play two contradictory roles: they carry the look of public spaces while they are privately owned.

Theming is a fairly recent object of research. The issue of the themed environments of the Walt Disney Company has been addressed extensively over the years – notably criticized by European scholars such as Baudrillard (1983), Marin (1984), and Eco (1986), and by American scholars

Figure 1 Castel Romano – a temple of consumption. Castel Romano is a themed outlet village outside Rome, built by the real estate company McArthurGlen. Here the theme is the architecture of the Roman Empire. Photo: Per Strömberg, 2006.

Figure 2 Magic Kingdom at Walt Disney World in Florida – a part of a Landscape of Power? Today, the theming strategies of Disney Imagineering are a part of a well-established practice in the world. Photo: Per Strömberg, 2004.

such as Zukin (1991) and Sorkin (1992). Earlier studies on themed environments had more or less the character of civilization criticism in which theme parks, notably those of the Walt Disney Company, were the main objects. The discussion basically took two directions: first, that themed environments make cultural expressions of civilizations banal; and second, that themed environments are a part of a corporate landscape of power.

Gottdiener's (1997) work on theming was one of the first to put the issue of theming in the context of consumption theory, social science, and urban studies. In his book, *The Theming of America*, Gottdiener seeks to understand theming as an economic, cultural, and social phenomenon of consumerism. Another example of this approach is Bryman's (2004) book *The Disneyization of Society*. This work was in certain aspects a counterpart to Ritzer's (1993) thesis on McDonaldization. A more recent anthology, *The Themed Space*, edited by Lukas (2007), is yet another example.

However, there are few anthropological and ethnographical studies on theming and how consumers actually respond to theming – studies from the user's perspective. Another important issue for future research is the transformation, distribution, and adaptation of theming as a commercial strategy in other areas of everyday life. As Gottdiener stresses, together with Baudrillard, there is a need for a critical theory of consumerist sign value as the hegemon of culture, but one without Baudrillard's fatalism and surrender.

SEE ALSO: Baudrillard, Jean; Benjamin, Walter; Capitalism; Consumer Culture; Department Stores; Disneyization; McDonaldization; Servicescapes; Shopping Malls; Symbolic Value

REFERENCES

Baudrillard, Jean. 1983. *Simulations*. New York: Semiotext(e).

Bryman, Alan. 2004. *The Disneyization of Society*. London: Sage.

Eco, Umberto. 1986. *Travels in Hyperreality: Essays*. San Diego: Harcourt Brace Jovanovich.

Gottdiener, Mark. 1997. *The Theming of America: Dreams, Visions and Commercial Spaces*. Boulder, CO: Westview Press.

Lukas, Scott A., ed. 2007. *The Themed Space: Locating Culture, Nation, and Self*. Lanham, MD: Lexington Books.

Marin, Louis. 1984. *Utopics: Spatial Play*. Atlantic Highlands, NJ: Humanities.

Ritzer, George. 1993. *The McDonaldization of Society: An Investigation into the Changing Character of Contemporary Social Life*. Thousand Oaks, CA: Pine Forge.

Sorkin, Michael, ed. 1992. *Variations on a Theme Park: The New American City and the End of Public Space*. New York: Hill and Wang.

Strömberg, Per. 2007. "Upplevelsesindustrins turistmiljöer: visuella berättarstrategier i svenska turistanläggningar 1985–2005." (Tourist Environments in the Era of the Experience Economy). Diss., Uppsala University; Fronton förlag.

Zukin, Sharon. 1991. *Landscapes of Power: From Detroit to Disney World*. Berkeley: University of California Press.

FURTHER READING

Hjemdahl, Kirsti Mathiesen. 2003. "*Tur-retur temapark: oppdragelse, opplevelse, kommers." (Round-Trip Theme Park: Education, Experience, Commerce)*. Diss. Kristiansand: Høyskoleforlaget.

Marling, Karal Ann. 1997. *Designing Disney's Theme Parks: The Architecture of Reassurance*. New York: Flammarion.

Warren, Stacy. 1999. "Cultural Contestation at Disneyland Paris." In *Leisure/Tourism Geographies: Practices and Geographical Knowledge*, edited by David Crouch, 109–125. London: Routledge.

Tourism

KEVIN FOX GOTHAM
Tulane University, USA

Tourism is a unique commodity that is spatially fixed and consumed at the point of production. Unlike other commodities that people buy and sell in markets, tourism is immobile and nontransportable. To participate as a consumer in the consumption of tourism, one has to travel to the actual place. At the same time, tourism is not just a singular commodity that people buy and sell in markets. Rather, tourism refers to a variety of social practices and institutional forms that involve the production, representation, and consumption of culture, history, and environment. In conventional accounts, tourism is a set of discrete economic activities, a mode of consumption, or a spatially bounded locality or destination that is subject to external forces producing impacts. Other research, in contrast, conceptualizes tourism as a highly complex set of institutions and social relations that involve capitalist markets, state policy, and flows of commodities, technology, cultural forms, and people.

Scholars have developed typologies of tourism and theories of tourist experience, and have investigated the impact of tourism on local economies and modes of cultural creation, among other concerns. One can find conceptualizations of tourism as a search for authenticity, an expression of leisure and performative identity for the postmodern consumer, a malevolent form of colonialism, conquest, and imperialism, a form of pilgrimage to culturally significant places, a type of ethnic relation, a force for historical and cultural commodification, and a process of mobility and demographic migration. In John Urry's (1990) famous concept of the "tourist gaze," tourists view or gaze upon particular sites and sights because "there is an anticipation, especially through day-dreaming and fantasy, of intense pleasures, either on a different scale or involving different senses from those customarily encountered" (p. 132). Influenced by Michel Foucault, Urry argues that a variety of nontourist practices, such as film, newspapers, TV, magazines, records, and videos, construct tourist experiences and circulate the signs and symbols by which consumers are coached to view tourist attractions and understand their experiences as tourists. In *Tourism Mobilities: Places to Play, Places in Play* (2006), Mimi Sheller and John Urry show how places to play are also places in play: made and remade by the mobilities and performances of tourists and workers, images and heritage, the latest fashions, and the newest diseases.

One major debate in tourism studies concerns whether tourism is a global process of simulation that reflects and reinforces people's alienation from society and social relations. Early, Dean MacCannell (1973) developed the concept of "staged authenticity" to refer to the manufacturing of local culture to create an impression of authenticity for a tourist audience. MacCannell conceived of culture as primordial and viewed tourists as alienated consumers who strive to experience an authentic experience and encounter with authentic sites, objects, or events. In contrast, Ritzer and Liska (1997) maintain that rather than seeking authenticity as MacCannell suggests, people prefer inauthentic and simulated tourist attractions and experiences because these can be made to be highly predictable and efficient vehicles for delivering fun and entertainment. Thus, for Ritzer (2006), tourism is about the global production of "nothing," which refers to a social form that is generally "centrally conceived, controlled, and comparatively devoid of distinctive content" (p. 7). Other scholars have used the concept of Disneyization to examine the spread of Disney theme-park characteristics to cities and urban culture. This city-as-theme-park explanation suggests that urban cultural spaces are being refashioned to attract visitors and enhance entertainment experiences through the production of fake histories and phony cultures that masquerade as authentic.

In contrast, more recent research eschews a conception of tourism as eroding urban culture and examines the ways in which tourism practices invigorate local culture and relations. Gotham (2007a) has elaborated on the concept of touristic culture to examine the actions of local elites in using tourism practices, images, symbols, and other representations to build a New Orleans community identity during the first half of the twentieth century (Gotham 2007b). As he points out, powerful groups and organized interests often deploy symbols and imagery in an attempt to unite local citizens and build a supportive constituency for tourism development. Tourism practices can support and invigorate existing modes of authenticity, help reconstruct old forms of authenticity, and promote the creation of new meanings of authenticity and local culture. Rather than viewing authenticity as immutable and primordial, Gotham (2007a) examines the process of authentication, focusing on how and under what conditions people make claims for authenticity and the interests that such claims serve. Findings suggest that tourism discourses, practices, modes of staging, and visualization can shape and constrain the availability of symbols and themes people use to construct meanings and definitions of authenticity. The implication is that tourism discourses, practices, and framings can mobilize people to create new authenticities, reinvent culture, and foster new conceptions of place identity.

The interconnections among tourism and culture are complex and fraught with conflict and antagonism. Economic and cultural globalization fosters new mobilities, generates new forms of tourism development, and encourages the proliferation of new modes of consuming local culture via tourism. Diverse scholars have all drawn attention to the rise of urban entertainment and tourism in the transformation of urban economies in the past several decades (for an overview, see Lloyd and Clark 2001). Gotham's (2007a; 2007b) concept of "touristic culture" suggests that tourism modes of visualization, staging, and discourse are now a central part of understanding cities and cannot be bounded off as a discrete activity. On the one hand, touristic culture involves enhanced spatial flows of people, commodities, capital, and cultures. On the other hand, touristic culture is a set of codes or repertoires that structure people's ability to think of places as objects of tourism, and to see themselves as reflective and acting agents who use tourist practices to affirm identities and construct culture. Thus tourism is an amalgam of conflictual processes that can disempower some groups of people, empower other interests, transform meanings of local authenticity, and create new pressures for local autonomy.

SEE ALSO: Consumer Culture; Disneyization; Las Vegas; McDonaldization

REFERENCES

Gotham, Kevin Fox. 2007a. *Authentic New Orleans: Race, Culture, and Tourism in the Big Easy*. New York: New York University Press.

Gotham, Kevin Fox. 2007b. "Selling New Orleans To New Orleans: Tourism Authenticity and the Construction of Community Identity." *Tourist Studies* 7(3): 317–339.

Lloyd, Richard, and Terry Nichols Clark. 2001. "The City as an Entertainment Machine." In *Critical Perspectives on Urban Redevelopment*, edited by Kevin Fox Gotham, 357–378. New York: Elsevier.

MacCannell, Dean. 1973. "Staged Authenticity: Arrangements of Social Space in Tourist Settings." *American Journal of Sociology* 79(3): 589–603.

Ritzer, George. 2006. *The Globalization of Nothing*, 2nd ed. Thousand Oaks, CA: Pine Forge Press.

Ritzer, George and Allan Liska. 1997. "'McDisneyization' and 'Post-Tourism': Contemporary Perspectives on Contemporary Tourism," In *Touring Cultures: Transformations in Travel and Leisure*, edited by Chris Rojek and John Urry, 96–112. London: Routledge.

Sheller, Mimi and John Urry. 2006. *Tourism Mobilities: Places to Play, Places in Play*. London: Routledge.

Urry, John. 1990. *The Tourist Gaze*. Thousand Oaks, CA: Sage.

FURTHER READING

Clark, Terry N. ed. 2004. *The City as an Entertainment Machine*. Oxford: Elsevier.

MacCannell, Dean. 1976. *The Tourist: A New Theory of the Leisure Class*. New York: Schocken.

Urry, John. 1995. *Consuming Places*. London: Routledge.

Tweens

RANDI WÆRDAHL
Agder Research, Norway

The term "tween" is used to describe the age group 8–12, who are not young children any more, but neither can be described as teenagers. The term is used to describe the consumer-savvy, brand-conscious preadolescent who stays informed about trends and fashion and is an active consumer. Tweening refers to the age compression processes in which younger children are being targeted with teen products, entertainment, and brands, and marketers often operate with an extended tween period from age 6 to 14 (Schor 2004).

In the latter part of the twentieth century, the interest in tweens as a consumer group grew intensely. In recognition of their increasing shopping behavior, individual purchasing power, and strong influence on family consumption, companies developed special lines of products catering to the trend- and brand-conscious tween.

The emergence of the tween has partially been ascribed to new family demographics, where children of two-income families, single parents and divorced parents, and reduced family sizes has rendered the child with more responsibilities in the family, and with a greater influence on family purchase decisions. Psychologists have argued that the preteen period coincides with a period of left brain development which makes them disposed to easy attachment to role models (Acuff 1997). Increased exposure to "adult" media and new digital technologies has also been cited as a factor in children becoming more knowledgeable at earlier ages. High media exposure has opened up the commercial world for increasingly younger children, as well as making children more vulnerable to age compression and commercial targeting. Some argue that a critical sense of product quality and value for money develops alongside extended experience with media advertising (Buckingham, 2000). KGOY (Kids Getting Older Younger) is an acronym that encapsulates these social and psychological developments.

Children's access to information and the commercial targeting of this group as receptive and conscious consumers have mutually reinforced the perception and definition of who they are. They are seen as a group that it is easy to promote products to, as they have not yet developed the critical thinking that characterizes adolescents and young adults. Their age-related striving for conformity and acceptance by their peers makes this group vulnerable to peer pressure, yet also receptive to ready-made style packages, where clothing, music, and leisure products go together. In effect, the tweens are now targeted as a brand- and trend-conscious consumer group who know what they want, yet with the age-related inclination to want to be like everybody else. For the child, tween products represent an alienation from a social age identity of a child and as transitional objects in the social processes of becoming youth, a process also known as *anticipatory socialization* (Wærdahl 2005).

When demographics relating to children change, there will always be concerns about the effects these changes have on the individual. For tweens, these concerns have mainly been about tween girls, who have been described as "too sexy, too soon" or "too old for toys, but too young for boys," which expresses a fear that girls do not participate in play, which is so significant in childhood development, but are rather being introduced to adulthood prematurely (Cook and Kaiser 2004). In the literature, tween boys are almost invisible. Although too much screen time, exposure to violence through games and media, excessive intake of sugar and fast food is often expressed as a concern for boys in this age group, boys are usually not described as tweens before they come into prepuberty and become preoccupied with clothes, cleanliness, and the desire to "smell good for the girls." This does not mean that boys are less malleable or less consumer-savvy than girls at this age. However, the consumption of young boys is more often inspired by competitiveness, sports, or fantasy or fictional worlds that are less likely to blur age categories in society, in particular those categories that regulate sexuality and sexual behavior.

SEE ALSO: Brands and Branding; Children's Consumer Culture; Consumer Socialization; Disneyization; Edutainment; Teens

REFERENCES

Acuff, Dan S. 1997. *The Psychology of Marketing to Kids: What Kids Buy and Why*. New York: The Free Press.

Buckingham, David. 2000. *After the Death of Childhood. Growing Up in the Age of Electronic Media*. Cambridge, UK: Polity.

Cook, Daniel T., and Susan B. Kaiser. 2004. "Betwixt and Be Tween. Age Ambiguity and the Sexualization of the Female Consuming Object." *Journal of Consumer Culture* 4(2): 203–227.

Schor, Juliet B. 2004. *Born to Buy*. New York: Scribner.

Wærdahl, Randi. 2005. "'Maybe I Need a Pair of Levi's Before Junior High?' Child and Youth Trajectories and Anticipatory Socialization." *Childhood* 12(2): 201–219.

V

Veblen, Thorstein

JUSTIN L. SCHUPP
Kenyon College, USA

Thorstein Bunde Veblen (1857–1929) was a US economist and sociologist who is often credited for the introduction of the concept *conspicuous consumption* to the academic lexicon. Veblen was also a major contributor to the field of institutional economics and was noted as being a witty and eccentric critic of the dominant forms of economic systems during his lifetime. He was one of the leading voices of the Progressive Era (1890s–1920s) where he wrote extensively about what he viewed as a wasteful production system that was focused too much on personal consumption of goods.

Veblen was born on July 30, 1857 in Cato, Wisconsin to parents who had recently immigrated from Norway. He spent most of his youth on a farm in rural Minnesota where his family put an emphasis on hard work and education – themes that Veblen focused on throughout much of his work later in life. He was married twice, and had two stepdaughters. Veblen attended numerous institutions, including John Hopkins, Yale, and Cornell, where his academic interests extended to several different disciplines, including philosophy, history, sociology, and economics. The works of Charles Darwin and Herbert Spencer had a significant influence on him as he considered how evolutionary processes could be applied to human societies. He utilized evolutionary principles to theorize how economic systems developed over long periods of time.

Veblen is best known for his seminal book entitled *The Theory of the Leisure Class*, first published in 1899, in which he outlines several prominent features of social stratification that existed in society, with a particular focus on economic inequality. His approach focused on how the division of labor in a society contributed to significant differences in life experiences between classes through a historical analysis from the feudal period up to the time the book was written, which demonstrated how an unequal division of labor led to the emergence of a leisure class – a social class Veblen accused of wasteful and irrational consumption patterns. Although Veblen was considered an accomplished scholar at the time of the book's publication, the attention given to the book, both in the form of praise and criticism, surprised many.

The major thesis in the book was that many forms of economic life are not driven by social or economic utility to the individual

The Wiley Blackwell Encyclopedia of Consumption and Consumer Studies, First Edition.
Edited by Daniel Thomas Cook and J. Michael Ryan.

or to the group, but instead by the desire to position one apart from the rest of society. To show how this occurred, Veblen suggested that many economic behaviors emerged within hunting and gathering societies. He contended that these cultures focused on ideals such as conquest, domination, and exploitation, which carried over to future societies. This led to the initial creation of a leisure class where the victors of either formal or informal contention would assign the labor tasks across society. Veblen argued that that the defeated segments of society would be appointed to take on the labor-intensive and low status positions, whereas the victors would assume the less labor-intensive occupations that were considered to be of higher status. Thus the victors continued to perform labor, but much of it went toward symbolic gestures to communicate that they were separate from the laboring peoples and classes, in this way assisting in retaining their superior status through direct and indirect forms of coercion. It is out of these conjectures that key concepts like leisure, conspicuous waste, and conspicuous consumption arise, with much of the text focusing on the consumption of the rich and emerging nouveau riche classes of his time.

While much of Veblen's legacy is tied to *The Theory of the Leisure Class*, he was also a founding thinker in the theory of institutional economics. Though typically dismissed by modern economists, this form of theorizing gained traction in the early part of the twentieth century. Rather than focusing on rational individuals as the basis of economic life, institutional economics suggested that there was a need to also consider the institutions of a given society. Veblen contended that economic systems could not be considered a separate entity from the political, cultural, and other social institutions with which they interacted, meaning that the economic system was intricately connected to the institutions that existed around them. Thus economic behavior, such as habits, taste, and motivation, was not just a product of the individual, but significantly tied to the system in which an individual lived.

SEE ALSO: Conspicuous Consumption

REFERENCE

Veblen, Thorstein. 1934/1899. *The Theory of the Leisure Class*. New York: The Modern Library.

FURTHER READING

Campbell, Colin. 1995. "Conspicuous Confusion? A Critique of Veblen's Theory of Conspicuous Consumption." *Sociological Theory* 13: 37–47.

Visual Consumption

ANNA SPARRMAN
Linköping University, Sweden

In its broadest sense, visual consumption concerns visually oriented consumer gazes and behavior such as window-shopping in urban and internet-based settings, the tourist gaze, the development of visual technologies for seeing, visual branding, and advertising. Historically, the idea of visual consumption derives from Walter Benjamin's (1999) interpretation and development of Baudelaire's 1860s literary modern male Parisian, the *flâneur*. The *flâneur* walks slowly through the boulevards of Paris, visually browsing people and the urban space through his gaze and, in the process, becoming a part of the space and scene by being gazed upon. In his own writing, Benjamin positioned the *flâneur* under the glass-roofed shopping arcades of Paris. The *flâneur* walks leisurely, glancing at the shopping windows and at the arcade mirrors, which reflect images of himself and other consumers. The *flâneur* does not necessarily purchase anything, but he is significant for the idea of the viewer and the viewed. In particular, he makes clear how consumers expose themselves to one another.

The establishment of department stores dates from the 1840s. It paralleled the mass production of goods and commodities, the founding of the packaging industry, and the emergence of the marketing professions to meet the needs of new markets and new consumer patterns. Thereby, as argued by Ulrika Torell, Roger Qvarsell, and Jenny Lee (2009) in their comprehensive visual study of the cultural history of food packaging, at the end of the nineteenth century the collaboration between branding, packaging, and advertising resulted in the development of important visual promotional instruments in support of the rising culture of consumption. The department stores' large shopping windows visually changed the urban space, making consumption, in part, an aesthetic experience and endeavor. Because almost all products were mass produced and thus had the same appearance, the shopping windows became advertising sites. Professional marketers worked out strategies for exposing commodities in the best way using repetition, clean lines, mass presentations, or by creating so-called "idea windows." In food retailing, self-service became the norm and consumers now walked up and down shopping aisles browsing the shelves with their gaze while choosing between different visually branded packages. Nicely designed everyday food packages colorfully covered in images were increasingly placed on the kitchen table instead of in the cupboard. The symbolic visual value of the products became consumer objects in themselves.

As has been pointed out in the research, the same thing is happening today when the stock market is presented on internet screens as a colorful and aesthetic product, thereby essentially transforming it into a visual commodity, just as internet shopping sites and mail-order catalogues are essentially commodities that are visually browsed by consumers for potential consumption. Today, department store shopping windows compete with new technologies for display, and everyday retail and shopping involve extensive vicarious explorations on the part of consumers.

The visual technology at hand is important for understanding visual consumption. Sociologist of tourism and mobility, John Urry (1992) has pointed out how tourism and camera technology developed in parallel in the 1840s. With the help of the camera, a tourist gaze was created. Tourist photographs built, and still build on, the principle of "being seen and recorded, and seeing others and recording them" (Urry 1990, 138). Consequently, the tourist gaze shares certain commonalities with the gaze of the *flâneur*: the mobility, the browsing, and a leisurely approach to looking. Just as camera technology made it possible to preserve visual memories of places tourists traveled to, it also helped establish an *image economy* of tourism. Visual commodities such as photographic reproductions, postcards, guidebooks, and souvenirs were created, along with mental memories. Places and sites for sight-seeing were created through special forms of *visual resource management*. Particular strategies for covering up what tourists should not look at and highlighting what they should look at were developed. Places, landscapes, and people (e.g., indigenous peoples) were transformed into objects of visual consumption for tourism.

Visual consumption has more recently also become a theoretical and methodological concept within interpretive marketing research. In his book *Visual Consumption* (2002), marketing researcher Jonathan Schroeder establishes visual consumption as a multidisciplinary concept by theoretically combining art history, semiotics, photography, consumer behaviorism, visual studies, and marketing and management theory. This combined theoretical and methodological starting point establishes an interpretative and qualitative approach within the area of marketing research. Schroeder's aim is to show how visual representations work within a cultural system of meaning-making, how they influence and are influenced by marketing, the internet, mass media, and consumer behavior. Central to the theory is understanding how marketing strategies produce brand images, customer satisfaction, and product identity and the attendant economical, psychological, and political implications. More specifically, images are equated with visual advertising and advertising photography. Vision and gaze are also central concepts for Schroeder, not least, as he points out, in relation to new technologies and e-consumption. Other researchers have drawn on Schroeder's theories and methods to conduct research on wedding parlors and wedding photography as visual consumption, on consumers browsing in magazine stands, and on advertising and marketing.

Theoretically and methodologically, research in the area of visual consumption focuses on presumed observers derived through marketing strategies, but also includes ethnographic and anthropological studies of how actual consumers consume through their gaze. Research on visual consumption on the screen and the internet is a growing research field. Few studies, however, have explored policies and legislation regulating visual consumption. Research focusing on that topic points to an area characterized by contradictions and blurriness between markets' self-regulations and state and governmental policies. One challenge for the future is to develop a comprehensive approach to studying regulations on the local, national, and global levels.

SEE ALSO: Advertising; Benjamin, Walter; Cities, Visual Consumption of; Department Stores; Internet, The, and Consumption; Tourism

REFERENCES

Benjamin, Walter. 1999 (1982). *The Arcades Project*, translated by Howard Eiland and Kevin McLaughlin. Cambridge, MA: Harvard University Press.

Schroeder, Jonathan E. 2002. *Visual Consumption*. London: Routledge.

Torell, Ulrika, Roger Qvarsell, and Jenny Lee, eds. 2009. "Burkar, påsar och paket: Förpackningarnas historia I vardagens konsumtionskulturer" (Tins, Bags and Packages: The Cultural History of Packaging in Everyday Consumer Culture). Stockholm: Nordiska museet förlag.

Urry, John. 1992. "The Tourist Gaze and the 'Environment'." *Theory, Culture and Society* 9: 1–26.

Urry, John. 1990. *The Tourist Gaze*. London: Sage.

W

Wal-Mart

NEWMAN CHUN WAI WONG
Midwestern State University, USA

Wal-Mart Stores, Inc. is an international retail corporation headquartered in Bentonville, Arkansas. Wal-Mart was founded by Sam Walton, a businessman and former employee of J. C. Penny Department Store. Prior to opening the first Wal-Mart in 1962, Walton ran a nickel and dime discount store, and was keen on selling products at lower prices than his competitors and still making profits with high sales volumes. Walton opened the first Wal-Mart in Rogers, Arkansas, with the principle of "the lowest prices anytime, anywhere." By 1967, Wal-Mart had expanded to 24 stores with sales of US$12.7 million. Wal-Mart was incorporated in 1969, and became a publicly traded company in 1970, as Walton needed cash to pay off debts and open more stores. In 1971, it established its first distribution center and home office in Bentonville, and in 1972 Wal-Mart was listed on the New York Stock Exchange. By 1975, Wal-Mart had become a regional store in the Southern United States.

Wal-Mart continued to expand and implement new concepts in the 1980s. In 1980, Wal-Mart's annual sales reached to US$1 billion with 276 stores and 21,000 employees. The first Sam's Club, the company's membership-based discount warehouse club, was opened in Midwest City, Oklahoma, in 1983. By its 25th anniversary in 1987, Wal-Mart's sales were US$15.9 billion with 1,198 stores and 200,000 employees, and the company installed the largest private satellite network, linking all operating units with the Bentonville headquarters through voice, data, and video communication. In 1988, the first Wal-Mart Supercenter, a general merchandise and grocery hypermarket, was opened in Washington, Missouri. In the same year, Sam Walton stepped down as chief executive officer, but remained as chairman of the corporate board of directors.

From the 1990s, Wal-Mart has grown rapidly from a national retail chain to a multinational corporation. By 1990, Wal-Mart was America's largest retailer, and the spread of Wal-Mart Supercenters made one-stop shopping popular. The company opened its first Sam's Club overseas in Mexico City in 1991. In 1992, Wal-Mart's founder Sam Walton died of cancer at the age of 74, and S. Robson Walton, his eldest son, succeeded as chairman of the corporate board of directors. In 1997, Wal-Mart had its first US$100 billion sales year. In 1998, the Neighborhood Market concept – grocery stores with quick

The Wiley Blackwell Encyclopedia of Consumption and Consumer Studies, First Edition.
Edited by Daniel Thomas Cook and J. Michael Ryan.

checkout – was introduced at three stores in Arkansas. During the 1990s, Wal-Mart entered the markets of Mexico, Canada, China, and the United Kingdom.

In the twenty-first century, Wal-Mart started focusing on internet sales and established Walmart.com in 2000. In 2002, Wal-Mart was named for the first time as America's largest corporation on the Fortune 500 list. In 2007, Walmart.com launched its Site-to-Store service, allowing customers to pick up online purchases in stores, and Wal-Mart also changed its longstanding slogan, "Always Low Prices. Always" to "Save Money, Live Better." From 2000, Wal-Mart expanded to Japan, Chile, and South Africa. In 2014, the global retail chain has more than 11,000 stores and 2.2 million employees in 27 countries.

As a successful enterprise, Wal-Mart shares the characteristics of McDonaldization: the rationalized management strategies used by McDonald's including efficiency, predictability, calculability, and control by nonhuman technology (Ritzer 2013). Efficiency is the optimum method of delivering services, and Wal-Mart Supercenters provide convenience by allowing customers to shop for different types of merchandise, ranging from groceries to electronics, all in one stop. For predictability, consumers know to expect discounted pricing when they enter any one of the Wal-Mart stores, and they will find the layout of departments and products available very similar in most stores. Wal-Mart also uses consumers' data to predict their shopping habits, in order to optimize operations. Calculability is important for Wal-Mart, as the company aims to make profits by selling products at low prices in high volumes, and cutting costs of supplies and labor. To reduce overheads, Wal-Mart employs aggressive supply-chain management and provides low wages and few benefits to workers. Wal-Mart utilizes technology to have more control over efficiency, predictability, and calculability. Wal-Mart has a long history of using technology to keep track of their inventory, such as building its own satellite network in 1987, and recently more self-checkout machines are used in stores to replace human cashiers.

As a powerful economic institution, Wal-Mart has economic and social impacts on various parties involved in their business, including customers, employees, local communities, and suppliers in America and abroad. Wal-Mart has successfully fulfilled its founder's mission to save customers' money. In 2007, Wal-Mart commissioned consulting firm Global Insight to study how much the retailer saved its customers. The research found the reduction in prices by Wal-Mart translated to US$287 billion annual saving for customers, which was equal to US$957 per person or US$2,500 per household. Wal-Mart also categorized its 200 million customers into three groups, including "brand inspirationals" who have low incomes but are obsessed with brand names, "price-sensitive affluents" who are wealthier shoppers but love deals, and "value-price shoppers" who cannot afford much and like bargains. Some argue that Wal-Mart has conditioned customers to low prices, without recognizing the cost of their savings.

Wal-Mart refers to its employees as "associates" but has been criticized for its treatment of its workforce. The content of the criticism includes low wages, insufficient benefits, poor working conditions, and anti-union policies. Paying low wages, providing limited benefits, and hiring part-time employees are major ways for Wal-Mart to control costs. Some low-paid workers qualify for welfare programs. According to a report released by congressional Democrats in 2013, Wal-Mart employees receive various federally funded social services, such as healthcare, subsidized school lunches, and Section 8 housing, costing taxpayers between

US$900,000 and US$1.75 million per year. Wal-Mart has been involved in some class action lawsuits, accused of forcing employees to work off-the-clock, and also accused of gender discrimination both during the hiring process and in the workplace. In recent years, Wal-Mart has started its Black Friday sales as early as Thanksgiving evening, and some employees participated in strikes along with unions to protest against Wal-Mart's treatment of workers. In 2013, the National Labor Relations Board found that in 13 states, Wal-Mart pressured employees not to participate in strikes on Black Friday and unlawfully disciplined those who participated.

Many studies have found that new Wal-Mart stores have effects on local economies. When Wal-Mart enters new markets in smaller towns, it often drives down the local prices for daily necessities and saves consumers money; however, the low prices may undermine the sales of local retail stores, or even drive some mom-and-pop stores out of business. Therefore, sometimes when Wal-Mart plans new store locations, local activists may protest against the plans, citing concerns like predatory pricing, low wages and benefits, and environmental issues. As a big client to many suppliers, Wal-Mart has the power to negotiate lower prices with vendors. When a supplier cannot keep prices competitive, their products are likely to be removed from store shelves and replaced by its competitors. With the pressure to produce at a low cost, many suppliers move to China and other countries with cheap labor to manufacture their products. Wal-Mart has been criticized for having foreign vendors that use sweatshops and having limited supervision over working conditions. For instance, a commercial building housing different garment factories collapsed in Savar, Bangladesh in 2013, and it was discovered that Wal-Mart used some of the clothing factories involved in the accident. Wal-Mart later became a founding member of the Alliance of Bangladesh Worker Safety along with other international retailers.

The founding of Wal-Mart has changed how manufacturers and how consumers shop over the years. As Wal-Mart continues to expand globally, more nations are likely to be exposed to its culture and values, and experience economic and social changes.

SEE ALSO: Big-Box Stores; Department Stores; Globalization and Consumption; McDonaldization; Shopping; Supermarkets

REFERENCE

Ritzer, George. 2013. *The McDonaldization of Society*, 7th ed. Thousand Oaks, CA: Sage.

FURTHER READING

Copeland, Nicholas, and Christine Labuski. 2013. *The World of Wal-Mart: Discounting the American Dream*. New York: Routledge.

Fishman, Charles. 2006. *The Wal-Mart Effect: How the World's Most Powerful Company Really Works – and How It's Transforming the American Economy*. New York: Penguin Press.

Lichtenstein, Nelson. 2009. *The Retail Revolution: How Wal-Mart Created a Brave New World of Business*. New York: Picador.

Warhol, Andy

VINCE CARDUCCI
College for Creative Studies, USA

Andy Warhol (1928–87) was an American artist, filmmaker, and pop culture avatar who first gained renown in the early 1960s as one of the founders of the visual art movement known as pop art. He subsequently came to be recognized as one of the most influential artists of the latter twentieth century by supporters and detractors alike. Warhol is known for his iconic representations of consumer products, advertisements, and celebrities. Subjects include: rows of Campbell Soup cans and Coca-Cola bottles, stacks of Brillo boxes, portraits of Elvis Presley, Jackie Kennedy, and Marilyn Monroe, and images derived from the media and other aspects of everyday life. He created paintings, sculptures, drawings, prints, photographs, films, videos, and multimedia installations and performances, mixing mechanical processes with hand-rendered techniques. By the end of his life he was a celebrity in his own right, featured as an endorsement personality in advertisements, making guest appearances on television programs and in motion pictures, and living the life of an international society figure whose activities were chronicled in the media.

Before entering the art world, Warhol had a highly successful career as a commercial artist in New York City, starting in the late 1940s after graduating from art school in his hometown of Pittsburgh, Pennsylvania, and continuing throughout the following decade. During that time, he designed retail advertisements and promotional packages, illustrated books and magazine articles, and won several creative awards in the process (Bourdon 1989). He was known especially for his technique of using blotchy lines of India ink to create whimsical drawings of shoes and other fashion items. His facility with commercial idioms and comfort with the dictates of commercial enterprise influenced his work as an artist and continued to be felt in all of his activities over his lifetime. Even at the height of his fame as an avant-garde artist, he continued to engage in commercial projects, such as designing long-playing record jackets for rock groups like the Velvet Underground, whose first recordings he also produced, and the Rolling Stones, as well as a series of advertisements for Absolut Vodka. He also founded the celebrity tabloid *Interview*.

As an artist, he is considered one of the progenitors of postmodernist art, generally considered a seismic shift in Western aesthetics. The philosopher and art critic Arthur C. Danto identifies Warhol's 1964 work *Brillo Boxes* as the culmination of Modernist art's quest to reveal its self-reflexive conditions, writing: "He in effect brought Modernism to an end by showing how the philosophical question of What is art? is to be answered" (2009, 52). Specifically, what constitutes a work of art, in Danto's estimation of the *Brillo Boxes*, is not any quality inherent within the work itself but an effect of something called the art world, a social-historical field that comprises a body of knowledge and network of relationships within which the work circulates (Danto 1964).

Erasing the apparent barrier between art and what Danto terms "mere things" registers an important aspect of Warhol's legacy in relation to consumption and consumer studies. Warhol's breaking down of the ostensible distinctions between high and low culture is a harbinger of the cultural omnivore, which Richard Peterson and Roger Kern (1996) identify as having become sociologically observable by the early 1980s. The embrace of Warhol in all his iterations stands as a repudiation of the culture industry critique put forth in the mid-twentieth century by the Frankfurt School that sought to establish autonomous art as an authentic respite from the base manipulations of the commercial marketplace. Instead, "the Warhol Economy" (Currid 2008) merges what were once considered the separate spheres of art and commerce into a seamless whole.

SEE ALSO: Celebrity; Consumption, Postmodern; Cultural Omnivores; Culture Industries; Frankfurt School; Popular Culture

REFERENCES

Bourdon, David. 1989. *Warhol.* New York: Abrams.
Currid, Elizabeth. 2008. *The Warhol Economy: How Art, Fashion, and Music Drive New York City.* Princeton, NJ: Princeton University Press.

Danto, Arthur C. 1964. "The Art World." *Journal of Philosophy* 61(19): 571–584.
Danto, Arthur C. 2009. *Andy Warhol*. New Haven, CT: Yale University Press.
Peterson, Richard A. and Roger M. Kern. 1996. "Changing Highbrow Taste: From Snob to Omnivore." *American Sociological Review* 61(5): 900–907.

Waste

SARA DI CHIAZZA
Universidade Nova de Lisboa, Portugal
DENNIS ZUEV
CIES-ISCTE, Portugal

Waste is a fundamental concept in understanding the variety of patterns in person–thing relations and the transformation of an object's value. Waste is a ubiquitous product of major human activities and also a part of human moral economy (Scanlan 2005) that has tended to stigmatize people related to waste management (cleaning, scavenging, recycling, dumpster diving).

Until the 1970s, the general tendency in social sciences was to focus on the production and the circulation of objects inside the life of consumers, neglecting the potentiality that things have to reveal the social and cultural bases that are established and renewed through consumption practices. Parallel to this, the social life of things and their value has been considered more important than the social death of things (Reno 2009). This created a vacuum in knowledge of what happens with things after they are thrown away and become waste. Consumption studies and material culture studies have failed to investigate the end product of the process of consumption – waste, and despite following analytically the life and destination of objects, they did not offer insights into the final resting place of waste.

Anthropologists provided important foundations for the study of relationships between waste and culture. Mary Douglas (1981) explored the issues related to what is considered clean and unclean in her influential work *Purity and Danger* (first published in 1966) and traced the words and meaning associated with dirt in different cultural contexts. Douglas wrote about the two stages of identity of dirt. Objects that were recognized as out of place and threatening to good order had half identity and were considered dangerous; after the processes of rotting, dissolving, and pulverizing, objects enter the "mass of common rubbish" and lose their identity. Recovering anything in the refuse can be considered dangerous as it revives the previous identities of things.

The Garbology Project, which started in 1973 at the University of Arizona and was directed by William Rathje, focused on changing patterns of modern household refuse and trash. Rathje's research uncovered some popular misconceptions about landfill in different states. The project was based on the contents thrown away from 69 households. One of the findings concerned with higher food waste disposal in times of food shortage led to the hypothesis of crisis buying and eventual increased wasting (Rathje and Murphy 2001). "Garbology" as a school subject was introduced in some North American schools in order to teach students about reuse of things and to make them aware of the excesses of consumption, as well as to introduce sustainable methods to managing waste.

In 2005 sociologist John Scanlan focused on the analysis of garbage in Western societies from a wide range of perspectives, from lexical to philosophical and aesthetic. He revealed that the "useless," the "unwanted," or the "uncanny" frameworks that we normally attribute to the universe of wasted things are instead a treasure trove of material and cultural evidence which show how the notion of garbage has been a product of particular cultural patterns of Western civilization and different fields of knowledge (philosophy, technology, science).

Sociology also provided a study of waste in private and public spheres (Magali 2002). One of the important aspects in the conceptualization of waste concerns the passage from household or small-scale collective waste management to domestic waste disposal delegated to municipalities. This passage has alienated and marginalized waste, which initially was assessed from a strategic resource perspective. In the end, delegation of waste management to municipal services meant a physical separation of the waste producer from the waste produced, which over time has led to a "practical disempowerment" (Schott 2004, 525) or detachment of people from the techniques of the reuse of waste as a resource. That is to say, people have lost control over the amount of waste they produce and are comfortable not knowing about what happens to waste when it is far away from them.

The waste recycling business in the current economic crisis holds an evident economic meaning and value. The recent functionalization of refuse materials in different and stable categories, such as plastic, paper, and glass, helps to separate waste and to recycle its components, although the categorization of waste can be locally established (e.g., in Portugal plastic goes with metal, in Italy metal goes together with glass, and in Germany there are different kinds of glass (green, white, brown)). But even though the amount of recycled material is increasing it gives rise to little optimism from an ecological perspective, as material consumption in industrialized and developing countries grows and creates a problem of reutilization of waste, which is often solved by exporting waste to poorer countries.

Several studies have also related the meaning of waste and decaying objects to nature, places, and things (Edensor 2005). Walter Benjamin developed a "natural history" approach to study decaying and outmoded objects that could reveal concrete facts about past "cultural imaginings" to discern their former lives and larger contexts in which they circulated and forces that contributed to their decay. This natural history approach was later used by Jennifer Gabrys in the study of digital rubbish (2011). A classical study in environmental history is Martin Melosi's *Garbage in the Cities* (1981), dedicated to the study of the relationship between urbanization, infrastructure, and technologies of refuse, but mostly limited to the cases of waste management in American urban centers. The work of Zsuzsa Gille (2007) on the historical evolution of the "waste regimes" in Hungary under various political ideologies demonstrated in a different geographic setting how garbage has to be understood first of all as a cultural and political issue.

From 2000 on, waste, waste governance, and cleaning management have become a hot issue in social sciences as new complex relationships develop between urban management actors, environmental NGOs, recycling businesses, and waste trafficking by organized crime groups like Camorra in Italy. Some of the contemporary issues related to waste and consumption are focused on the management of waste, practices of recycling, and anti-consumption strategies (e.g., dumpster diving and "freeganism") with much geographic focus on waste management politics in rapidly urbanizing countries like China and Brazil.

Waste is closely connected to the concept of repetitive consumption and is often associated with the "disposable culture" and "throwaway ethic" (Slade 2006). Different types of waste and human waste (Bauman 2004) categories have emerged as the global consumption patterns changed. One of the new material waste types is *e-waste*, which includes consumer electronics. Rapid changes in technology and the switch to new media, falling prices, planned obsolescence, or fashion trends all contribute to the multiplication of e-waste. The idea of *planned obsolescence* was investigated by Giles Slade (2006), who showed that in North America alone out of 315m still working computers only 10 percent are reused or repaired, while the rest go to the waste heap. Slade defines "deliberate obsolescence" as an assortment of techniques and marketing strategies which limit the durability of a manufactured good in order to stimulate repetitive consumption. As Slade argues, the development of disposable personal products not only habituated people to increasing levels of repetitive consumption but broadened the cultural acceptance of the throwaway ethic, a necessary accompaniment to planned obsolescence (Slade 2006).

In line with other forms of waste management, e-waste recycling has become an arena for political activism and promotion of reusing old unused electronics, while some organizations collect and repair electronics for educational purposes. In other cases e-waste is routinely transported to developing countries such as China, Ghana, India, Mexico where electronics are manually disassembled for the purpose of recovering reusable elements and secondary scrap (copper, steel, plastic) which become commodities.

E-waste recycling has created new geographies and routes for digital postconsumption. Consumer goods which are assembled in countries like China are used in the wealthy countries of the West in order to later be transported to trash towns like Guiyu in China or Bangalore, India with cheap labor and lax environmental laws. The economy of the trash towns becomes reoriented from rural activities to servicing the growing rates of consumption in the West, unable to recycle its own rubbish but concerned with the environmental dilemma of e-waste exportation.

Despite the vitality of modern waste scholarship it still appears to be largely fragmented and in need of a fuller engagement with materiality and the social consequences of waste production on a global scale.

SEE ALSO: Benjamin, Walter; Conspicuous Consumption; Consumer Resistance Movements

REFERENCES

Bauman, Zygmunt. 2004. *Wasted Lives: Modernity and its Outcasts*. Cambridge, UK: Polity.

Douglas, Mary. 1981 (1966). *Purity and Danger. An Analysis of the Concepts of Pollution and Taboo*. London: Routledge.

Edensor, Tim. 2005. *Industrial Ruins: Spaces, Aesthetics and Materiality*. Oxford: Berg.

Gabrys, Jennifer. 2011. *Digital Rubbish: A Natural History of Electronics*. Ann Arbor: University of Michigan Press.

Gille, Zsuzsa. 2007. *From the Cult of Waste to the Trash Heap of History: The Politics of Waste in Socialist and Postsocialist Hungary*. Bloomington: Indiana University Press.

Magali, Pierre. ed. 2002. *Les déchets ménagers, entre privé et public. Approches sociologiques (Household Waste, Between Private and Public. Sociological Approaches)*. Paris: L'Harmattan.

Melosi, Martin V. 1981. *Garbage in the Cities: Refuse, Reform, and the Environment: 1880–1980*. College Station: Texas A&M University Press.

Rathje, William and Cullen Murphy. 2001. *Rubbish: The Archaeology of Garbage*. Tucson: University of Arizona Press.

Reno, Joshua. 2009. "Your Trash is Someone's Treasure." *Journal of Material Culture* 14(1): 29–46.

Scanlan, John. 2005. *On Garbage*. London: Reaktion Books.

Schott, Dieter. 2004. "Urban Environmental History: What Lessons Are There to be Learnt?" *Boreal Environment Research* 9: 519–528.

Slade, Giles. 2006. *Made to Break. Technology and Obsolescence in America*. Cambridge, MA: Harvard University Press.

Weddings

PATRICIA AREND
Fitchburg State University, USA

Weddings are cultural rituals that, until the twenty-first century, have symbolized the entry point for primarily heterosexual couples into the social, economic, legal, and/or religious relations of marriage. In many places around the world, weddings are also considered to be rites of passage to adulthood. This meaning is de-emphasized in modern and postmodern consumer societies where individuals frequently establish households separately from their parents, sometimes with their partners, for many years before getting married. Some experts argue that this is because the meaning of marriage is changing (Cherlin 2004). In the United States, for example, marriage is now something many couples do for individual fulfillment, after completing their education and becoming financially stable. Having children can be a catalyst. That middle- and upper-class individuals are much more likely than their lower-class and poor counterparts to marry supports this contention. In this historical context weddings become opportunities for displaying that success through conspicuous consumption and/or displays of cultural capital. Weddings also serve this purpose in places around the world where new consumer classes are emerging, such as India. The most important trend to watch for the future is the recent spread of the legalization of same-sex marriage and its impact on weddings.

White weddings are the dominant type of marriage ritual in the Global North today, especially in the United States, Northern and Western Europe, and other places where Judeo-Christian culture dominates. Aspects of the white wedding are also becoming popular in other parts of the world. While some couples use only some aspects of what a white wedding may entail, at its most complete the US white wedding involves the following stages, events, and/or rituals: a proposal with a diamond ring, an engagement party or parties, the selection of bridesmaids and groomsmen, bridal showers and bachelor/ette parties, event planning (including the procurement of a church, synagogue, or other ceremonial site, reception hall, caterer and music entertainment), religious preparation where appropriate, the formation of a gift registry, a rehearsal and rehearsal dinner, a ceremony with vows, a reception with food, music, and dancing, and a honeymoon. They entail highly symbolic, often sacred objects such as a cake, invitations, flowers, photographs, and a white bridal gown. White weddings are also identified by specific practices, including preventing a groom from seeing the bride's gown until the day of the wedding, a processional, the announcement and presentation of the couple by name at the reception site, the best man and maid of honor toasts, the cutting of the cake, and the couple's first dance and dances with their parents (if an evening reception). The widespread popularity of the white wedding has led some to point to it as evidence of the democratization of consumption. However, closer inspection reveals that class status is now displayed at weddings through distinctions of taste, such as style and brand of bridal gown as well as the type of fabric out of which it is made (Arend 2011).

The wedding industry in the United States is now estimated at more than 160 billion dollars. Retailers target brides and grooms, not only for the business involved with the actual wedding, but because of the brand loyalty that can develop through items acquired through the gift registry, such as china and other kitchenware.

Few social scientists studied weddings prior to the 1990s and the research literature was comparably sparse. Diana Leonard Barker (then as Diana Leonard) published work such as *Sex and Generation: A Study of Courtship and Weddings* (1980), the first full social scientific study of the practice, meaning, and significance of traditional white weddings. Research on weddings grew somewhat in the 1980s, following the wedding of British royalty Prince Charles and Princess Diana. But, as the cost of weddings in the United States escalated in the 1990s, so too did the number of publications. Initially, most of the research came from consumer behavior studies, such as those by marketing professor Cele Otnes and her coauthors (Otnes and Lowrey 1993; Otnes and Pleck 2003), until Chrys Ingraham (1999) published her influential and oft-cited text *White Weddings: Romancing Heterosexuality in Popular Culture*. The first decade of the twenty-first century saw a plethora of publications related to weddings. Mass media remains a central concern, given the oft-used image of the white wedding in advertising and the many films, television shows (especially reality television shows), magazines, and internet websites that feature wedding-related content. This content reveals a dominant theme in the gendering of consumer society that has persisted since the eighteenth century, that is, the tension in consumption as a feminine activity that has the potential to both positively transform and negatively devour (Kowaleski-Wallace 1997) – Cinderella and Bridezilla respectively. Gender is another prominent theme in the contemporary consumption-related studies of weddings, as white weddings produce and exaggerate differences between hegemonic masculinity and emphasized femininity (Connell 1987).

SEE ALSO: Beauty Industry; Consumption Rituals; Femininities

REFERENCES

Arend, Patricia. 2011. "*Dream Weddings: Fantasy, Femininity and Consumer Desire.*" PhD diss., Boston College.

Cherlin, Andrew J. 2004. "The Deinstitutionalization of American Marriage." *Journal of Marriage and Family* 66(4): 848–861.

Connell, R. W. 1987. *Gender and Power: Society, the Person and Sexual Politics.* Stanford, CA: Stanford University Press.

Ingraham, Chrys. 1999. *White Weddings: Romancing Heterosexuality in Popular Culture.* New York: Routledge.

Kowaleski-Wallace, Elizabeth. 1997. *Consuming Subjects: Women, Shopping, and Business in the Eighteenth Century.* New York: Columbia University Press.

Leonard, Diana. 1980. *Sex and Generation: A Study of Courtship and Weddings.* London: Tavistock Publications.

Otnes, Cele, and Tina M. Lowrey. 1993. "'Til Debt do Us Part: The Selection and Meaning of Artifacts in the American Wedding." *Advances in Consumer Research* 20(1): 325–329.

Otnes, Cele, and Elizabeth Pleck. 2003. *Cinderella Dreams: The Allure of the Lavish Wedding.* Berkeley: University of California Press.

Whole Foods Market

JOSÉE JOHNSTON
University of Toronto, Canada

Whole Foods Market (WFM) is a large, US-based corporate grocery store chain that specializes in natural and organic foods and personal care products. The grocery chain offers consumers a place to purchase delicious foods that make them feel good, both about their own health and their impact on the environment. WFM's considerable market success speaks to the rise of natural, quality foods as a high-status arena of consumption, as well as the prominent (but contested) linkage between progressive social change and commodity consumption.

WFM opened its first store in Austin, Texas in 1980. It has since expanded considerably to more than 310 locations. Most of its locations are in the United States, but the chain has also opened stores in Canada and the United Kingdom. Much of WFM's growth has occurred by absorbing its natural-food store competitors (e.g., Fresh & Wild, Wild Oats Market). While WFM specializes in organic foods and is a certified organic grocer, part of the chain's consumer appeal is that they also carry a range of noncertified organic products and consumer staples produced by corporate food giants like Kraft, General Mills, and ConAgra. WFM has created its own standards for what is considered "natural" enough to carry in its stores. It maintains a list of banned food products and food chemicals (e.g., aspartame, artificial flavors and colors, sucralose, foie gras, live lobsters), as well as a five-tiered code of animal husbandry practices certified by an independent third party (The Global Animal Partnership).

WFM describes itself as a "mission-driven" organization with a win–win–win vision of environmental stewardship, consumer interests, and shareholder value. The firm aggressively promotes itself as a progressive capitalist enterprise with innovative environmental policies (e.g., buying wind energy credits, not using plastic bags), community projects (e.g., microloans to local producers and rural communities in the Global South), progressive labor relations (e.g., executive salaries are capped at 19 times that of an average worker), and happy employees (e.g., "team members" are organized into teams that control some elements of store operations). CEO John Mackey is one of the original founders of WFM, and is a controversial figure who publicly promotes his vision of morally responsible capitalism (see Welch and Bragg 2012). His libertarian corporate vision has raised eyebrows because of its seeming incompatibility with union organizing and state-organized health-care programs like The Patient Protection and Affordable Care Act (aka Obamacare) (Mackey 2009). Mackey refused to sign a United Farm Workers union petition to guarantee the rights of strawberry pickers in 1998 (Lubove 1998), and all unionization attempts in WFM stores have been defeated to date.

Research on consumers' experiences at WFM suggests that several features are critical to the store's considerable commercial success. First, WFM creates a highly pleasurable, luxurious shopping environment that many shoppers enjoy greatly; it is a place to attain specific high-quality food items, but it is also a destination, an "outing," a mini-vacation for consumers to find new products or treat themselves to specialty foods (Johnston and Szabo 2011). Shopping at WFM is constructed to be a pleasurable and entertaining experience; there are literally thousands of goods to choose from, artfully presented in a well-lit, luxurious setting that *Forbes* magazine described as "food porn" (Lubove 2005). Second, WFM satisfies some consumers' interest in having an ethical, or virtuous, shopping environment; the slogan, "feel good about where you shop" is prominently featured throughout the store (Johnston 2008). However, consumers also feel that the store is not *so* virtuous that it denies them culinary pleasures, like eating nonseasonal fruits shipped long-distances (see Johnston and Szabo 2011).

WFM has won numerous accolades as a good corporate citizen, is a major purchaser of green power, and is a prominent actor in the popular discourse of ethical consumption. However, it also has its share of critics and contradictions. A common nickname for WFM in popular discourse is "whole paycheck." Indeed, WFM does appear to open stores in affluent locations that service the needs of upper-middle-class consumers. In 2006, a journalist compared a basket of monthly food goods (based on a minimal, USDA-recommended "low-cost food plan") and found that the basket would cost US$232 plus sales tax at Wal-Mart, and US$564 at Whole Foods Market (Cox 2006). WFM has also been criticized for contributing to the corporatization of the organic food movement, and for not doing enough to support local growers and small producers (see, e.g., Marati 2012; Pollan 2006; Paul Hawken in Grist Staff interview (2004). Most recently, WFM has been criticized for its sale of products containing genetically modified organisms (GMOs) as well as its lukewarm support of organized efforts in California to mandate labeling of GMO products (Cummings 2012).

SEE ALSO: Ethical Consumption; Food; Green Consumption; Supermarkets

REFERENCES

Cox, Stan. 2006, "Natural Food, Unnatural Prices." *Alternet*, January 30. http://www.alternet.org/story/31260/.

Cummings, Ronnie. 2012. "Is Whole Foods Sincere About its Support for Labeling Genetically Modified Foods?" Organic Consumer Association. http://www.organicconsumers.org/articles/article_26366.cfm.

Grist Staff. 2004. "A Wide-Ranging Interview with Environmental Visionary, Paul Hawken." *Grist*, February 18. http://www.grist.org/news/maindish/2004/02/18/pauling/.

Johnston, Josée. 2008. "The Citizen-Consumer Hybrid: Ideological Tensions and the Case of Whole Foods Market." *Theory and Society* 37: 229–270.

Johnston, Josée, and Michelle Szabo. 2011. "Reflexivity and the Whole Food Market Shopper: Shopping for Change, or Cruising for Pleasure?" *Agriculture and Human Values* 28: 303–319.

Lubove, Seth. 1998. "New Age capitalist." *Forbes*, June 4. http://www.forbes.com/forbes/1998/0406/6107042a.html.

Lubove, Seth. 2005. "Food Porn." *Forbes*, July 2. http://www.forbes.com/global/2005/0207/050.html.

Mackey, John. 2009. "The Whole Foods Alternative to Obamacare." *Wall Street Journal*, August 11. http://online.wsj.com/article/SB10001424052970204251404574342170072865070.html.

Marati, Jessica. 2012. "Behind the Label: WFM's Everyday 365 Value." *Ecosalon*, May 23. http://ecosalon.com/behind-the-label-whole-foods-365-everyday-value/.

Pollan, Michael. 2006. *The Omnivore's Dilemma: A Natural History of Four Meals*. New York: Penguin.

Welch, Matt, and Meredith Bragg. 2012. "Whole Foods CEO John Mackey on the Moral Case for Capitalism." *Reason.Com.*, August 10. http://reason.com/reasontv/2012/08/10/whole-foods-ceo-john-mackey-on.

Williams, Raymond

ANDREA DASSOPOULOS
University of Nevada–Las Vegas, USA

POPULAR CULTURE

Raymond Williams (1921–1988) was an influential British literary critic, novelist, and founder of cultural studies. His work was explicitly political, and he was personally active in the New Left. Though a devoted Marxist his whole life, he was sometimes highly critical of Marxist theories for what he thought were ambiguous ideas about culture. His experience growing up in a working-class family in Wales and as a young adult during World War II heavily influenced his perspectives on culture and politics. In the 1950s, along with Richard Hoggart, he formed a new perspective toward ordinary, or popular, culture, and developed the conceptual and methodological foundations of cultural studies. He also pioneered the use of textual analysis as a research method, by which he explored the evolution of cultural meanings through history. Anti-deterministic, his work emphasized human agency and the capacity for political activism to be part of a long revolutionary process toward a socialist future. The point of studying culture was to become more conscious about inequalities, injustice, and marginalization and to contribute to the public discourse. Williams's approach would later be labeled *culturalist* to distinguish his work from the overly deterministic approach of structuralists, such as Louis Althusser, whom he criticized. Toward the end of his career, Williams focused his literary criticism on issues of representation and positionality. For him, all works were ideological; therefore it was crucial to understand the author's relationship to the subject.

In his influential 1958 book, *Culture and Society*, Williams traces the changing meaning of the word *culture* through the spread of industrialism and democracy in the late eighteenth century. He continued to develop his method of tracing language, and in his 1976 book *Keywords: A Vocabulary of Culture and Society*, he showed important cultural transformations by mapping changes in key words, such as industry, democracy, and culture. Through understanding the specific history of these words, he concludes that culture must be understood as a process. This method of analyzing important historical texts and situating their meanings in social processes led to the development of his theory of cultural materialism. A Marxist-influenced theory, cultural materialism takes culture as a productive process through which meaning is manipulated to reinforce the social order. Williams saw culture as an evolving productive process that played an important role in political activism. Cultural materialism combines historical context, theory, textual analysis, and politics. Williams saw cultural materialism as a historical semiotics, essentially adding a social dimension to the study of sign systems.

Williams believed that culture was an elusive concept that had been misunderstood and inadequately defined by the existing distinctions of high and low culture. Whereas cultural critic F. R. Leavis defined culture by the sophisticated tastes of the elite, and orthodox Marxists viewed the masses as cultural dupes, Williams's significant contribution to the understanding of culture is the idea that culture is ordinary, a position that he first detailed in his 1958 essay "Culture is Ordinary" (Williams 2001/1958). Ordinary culture is the shared meanings and practices of people, actively and creatively constructed. Williams shared the anthropological view of culture as an entire way of life that exists in every human society and explored cultural meanings through tracing changes in lifestyles, thoughts, and material contexts over time.

One of the ways Williams sought to deconstruct the distinctions between high and low culture was to take seriously the role of popular cultural forms such as novels, films, television, advertising, and popular newspapers. He thought film, in particular, had the ability to capture the "structure of feeling" or the culture of a historical moment. Thus art has the ability to constitute and express the consensus and values of a society. Williams's view of culture as a constitutive force differs from the Marxist position that culture is part of a superstructure that reflects an economic base. Williams argued against mass culture critiques that are predicated on viewing the masses as dupes and cultural receptors to be manipulated through cheap emotional appeals. Popular culture is full of opportunities for representing groups in new ways, but those who have control of the medium continue to reproduce the same mediocrity.

SEE ALSO: Cultural Studies, Semiotics

REFERENCES

Williams, Raymond. 1985/1976. *Keywords: A Vocabulary of Culture and Society*. New York: Oxford University Press.

Williams, Raymond. 1983/1958. *Culture and Society: 1780–1950*. New York: Columbia University Press.
Williams, Raymond. 2001/1958. "Culture is Ordinary." In *The Raymond Williams Reader*, edited by John Higgins, 10–24. Malden, MA: Blackwell.

FURTHER READING

Eldridge, John and Lizzie Eldridge. 1994. *Raymond Williams: Making Connections*. New York: Routledge.
Walton, David. 2012. *Doing Cultural Theory*. Thousand Oaks, CA: Sage.

World's Fairs and International Expositions

ROBERT W. RYDELL
Montana State University, USA

The world's fairs that swept the planet between London's Crystal Palace Exhibition (1851) and Shanghai's World Expo (2010) attest to the globalization of consumerism. The hundreds of expositions presented on the global stage during this period can be seen as overstuffed theaters of agricultural and technological commodities intended to promote the definition of the good life as being synonymous with the accumulation of consumer materials. Through towering displays of surplus fruits and vegetables, fashion shows and "pest-free" gardens, television sets and dishwashers, automobiles and model homes, world expositions have served as key vehicles for the rapid modernization of the world from the Victorian era through the present.

In addition to the displays of "things" themselves that occupied enormous pavilions dedicated to machines, electricity, agriculture, household products, and the like, world's fairs have also played a pivotal role in the development of saturation media advertising and tourism – both central components of consumerism. The 1893 Chicago World's Columbian Exposition organized an enormous publicity department that generated newspaper copy and broadside advertising that made its way across the Atlantic Ocean to Russia and the Middle East. Subsequent expositions followed suit and, as a result, tens of millions of people made these fairs into tourist destinations. The Thomas Cook agency gained prominence through its tours to the 1851 Great Exhibition at Crystal Palace in London, and several California fairs featured exhibits, organized by railroad companies, of national parks with a view to promoting tourists to travel by railroad and stay in hotels in parks that the railroads owned.

Closely related to world's fair tourism was the development of picture postcards, sold as souvenirs to world's fair visitors. Among the souvenirs that fairs generated were trinkets as well as commodity advertisements, often in the form of trade cards for new products: alcoholic beverages (Pabst beer), new building materials (like Formica), and countless other products that would enter first the mainstream of American consumer culture and then the world economy. Some reflected and advanced the prevalence of commodity racism in circulation in the cultures of the world's imperial powers. Racialized images of African Americans and Native Americans and other indigenous peoples were embedded in advertisements, just as people of color were often featured as "ethnological types" who performed in world's fair exhibits.

World's fair promoters embraced motion pictures after Eadweard Muybridge exhibited his famous Zoopraxiscope at the 1893 Chicago fair. By 1915, Hollywood was using world's fair sites as the backgrounds for filming motion pictures. American corporations by the 1930s were producing films about their products. One such film, the Westinghouse Corporation's *The Middleton Family at the New York World's Fair*, featured a competition between a "Mrs. Drudge," doing dishes by hand, and a "Mrs. Modern," using a Westinghouse dishwasher. The film also featured Elektro, a chain-smoking robot.

World's fairs promoted new forms of consumer experiences tied to amusement. Beginning with the Midway Plaisance at the 1893 Chicago Exposition, world's fairs included entertainment strips, generally called "midways," that blended mechanical rides with ethnological villages. From midways came the inspiration for many attractions at amusement parks like Coney Island. More recently, the 1964/65 New York World's Fair inspired the creation of both Disney World and EPCOT. The distinctive architecture designs of many midway shows spawned a vernacular architecture craze that would characterize building designs of everything from fast-food franchises to cemetery designs to automobile tire dealerships.

Perhaps the best example of how fairs promoted dreams of consumer abundance comes from the Panama-California International Exposition, where the Federal Housing Administration organized Modeltown, complete with miniature sample homes designed by famous American architects like Richard Neutra, and abundant information about how FHA mortgage loans would expand opportunities for middle-class Americans to own their own homes where they could live out their own fantasies of the American Dream.

World's fairs have reflected and advanced consumerist values. Between 1851 and 1940, world expositions attracted around one billion visitors. Since World War II, hundreds of millions more visitors have made world expos, as they are now called, a part of their lives. Expositions continue to propagate consumerism, but now do so with greater attention to green technologies, recycling, and products made from renewable materials. Whether the medium of the world's fair can adjust longstanding consumerist habits to a planet confronting limits to industrial growth remains to be seen.

SEE ALSO: Tourism

FURTHER READING

Gilbert, James. 1991. *Perfect Cities.* Chicago: University of Chicago Press.

Rydell, Robert W. 1984. *All the World's a Fair: Visions of Empire at America's International Exhibitions, 1876–1916.* Chicago: University of Chicago Press.

Rydell, Robert W., and Laura B. Schiavo. 2010. *Designing Tomorrow: America's World's Fairs of the 1930s.* New Haven, CT: Yale University Press.

Y

Youth culture(s)

MURRAY MILNER JR.
University of Virginia, USA

Most civilizations have had awareness that individuals between puberty and marriage were distinct from those younger and older, and that they often formed a relatively distinctive subculture that was concerned about consumption and how it affected their status. Shakespeare's plays indicate this. *Romeo and Juliet* focuses on a group of young men – Romeo, Mercutio, Benvolio, and Tybalt – and their sense of honor, romantic concerns, and their conflicts. *As You Like It* opens with the young Orlando complaining about his allowance: "he keeps me rustically at home, or, to speak more properly, stays me here at home unkept; for call you that keeping for a gentleman of my birth, that differs not from the stalling of an ox?"

It is, however, in contemporary developed societies that notions of youth and youth cultures are now especially salient to consumption patterns. While notions of youth are clearly linked to the process of biological and psychological development, these factors explain only a modest amount of the variations in the way that young people act. While young people in the United States in the nineteenth and early twentieth century obviously went through puberty and psychological maturation, there were no "teenagers"; most people left school after the eighth grade, had jobs, and were often married within a few years.

In contrast, with more extended schooling people may spend more than a quarter of their life interacting primarily with school peers. This tends to contribute to distinctive youth cultures and the formation of peer groups that have a significant degree of autonomy and insulation from adult supervision. When compared with families, schools have few adults relative to the number of young people, and their authority is narrower. Changes in family structures have also contributed to autonomy. In single-parent families or families in which both parents work away from the home, there tends to be less time spent with adult family members. While youth have more autonomy, they have little economic or political power. They have to be in school; they have little control over where they go to school, who teaches them, or what they have to learn. Adults control most of the major decisions that shape their lives. They may have spending money, but parents usually determine how much they have.

The key kind of power that they have is status power: the ability to express approval and

The Wiley Blackwell Encyclopedia of Consumption and Consumer Studies, First Edition.
Edited by Daniel Thomas Cook and J. Michael Ryan.

disapproval of one another. Hence popularity with peers becomes a primary preoccupation. This typically leads to social categories called "crowds," who share roughly the same interests, lifestyles, and status. Such groups often adopt distinctive symbols of membership with respect to clothing, language, attitudes toward adults, and other peers. In many developed societies high schools include crowds of preps, brains, skaters, punks, nerds, and freaks, or rough equivalents. In larger schools crowds may be further subdivided into cliques who tend to hang out together during lunch and other periods of free time.

Status and popularity are primarily a relative ranking and hence inherently scarce. To have an above average status means others have less. Hence, the competition for status can be intense and often involves not only elevating a popular individual or crowd, but demeaning others. Associating with high-status peers improves your status; associating with low-status peers does the opposite – especially in expressive relationships. Who eats with whom at lunch and who "goes with" whom affects status more than who you work with on a class project. High-status individuals and groups protect their status by changing the norms about what is considered "in." This can involve noneconomic matters such as language, but it most obviously relates to consumer commodities: what is considered "cool" and what is "so yesterday." Because adolescents are in the process of forming a personal identity they are especially concerned with items that symbolize this identity and their status. Hence there is a generally high sensitivity to fashion. In affluent societies where aggregate economic demand is not usually due to actual physical needs, instilling in people a concern with fashion can also be a crucial feature of the economy.

In addition to socializing people so that they take fashion-based consumption for granted, youth culture identifies an attractive market. Marketing to teenagers takes a wide variety of forms. There are numerous movies and TV programs aimed to appeal to youth, especially teenagers (e.g., *Freaks and Geeks, Smallville, Beverly Hills, 90210*). Advertisers pay about the same rates for advertisements on successful teen-oriented TV programs as they do for prime-time shows. An obvious example of youth-oriented programming is MTV. It originally played primarily music videos, but now includes an array of programs targeted primarily at adolescents and young adults. It has inspired or spun off a number of similar channels around the world. Many radio stations specialize in popular music that appeals primarily to young people, and recruit advertisers accordingly. There are also approximately one hundred magazines that are intended to appeal primarily to young women (e.g., *Cosmo Girl, Teen Vogue, Seventeen, Teen People, Sassy, Vivi*, and *Muslim Girl*). A number of these are published outside of the United States or have multinational editions.

Some companies specialize in marketing to both youth and adults through schools. Typically this takes the form of a school activity group or club (e.g., the band, the choir, the senior class) selling the company's fruit, cookies, T-shirts, and so forth in order to raise money for a trip. In order to raise revenues school systems have sometimes contracted with soft drink and candy companies and allowed them to install dispensing machines in schools. Similarly, some school systems have sold advertising space in their buses, hallways, and lunchrooms, as well as stadiums and other athletic facilities. One of the most controversial examples of youth marketing is Channel One. The company provides schools with TVs and satellite connections. The schools must agree to require the students to watch 12 minutes of news aimed at teenagers including two minutes of advertising. Another technique that has been used is peer marketing. Some marketers use "stealth or buzz marketing" by identifying students who are popular trendsetters and offering them "prizes" for encouraging their friends to buy these products. Marketers also try to influence the purchases of adults by influencing their children, as indicated by advertising in youth-oriented media for expensive automobiles, hotels, airlines, vacation spots, credit cards, and insurance – items that youth seldom purchase by themselves. The most noted development is marketing via the internet. There are many sites aimed specifically at youth (e.g., Cyberteens and Teenstarsonline). Ads can be targeted based on the person's demographic characteristics, browsing history, and past purchases. This technique is not, of course, aimed only at youth but young people disproportionately use many websites and services.

Are these marketing efforts successful and are they economically significant? Much of the research on the effectiveness of sales directed at youth is proprietary and not available to the public, or it is conducted by marketing research companies that are trying to convince other companies to buy their services. Hence the data from these sources may exaggerate the scope of the market and the effectiveness of advertising. With this in mind, a 2012 research report estimates that the value of products bought by and for teens in the United States was US$208.7 billion (Marketingvox 2012). To put this in perspective, the value of all of the new cars sold in the United States in the same year was US$237 billion (US Bureau of Economic Analysis 2013). Obviously the car industry is a major part of the economy – and so are sales to youth. Another way in which youth culture shapes the economy is that both younger and older age groups are adopting modified versions of youth culture. Popularity, fashion, and sexuality are increasingly important in middle schools. As adults tend to get married later their lifestyles and consumption interests are often closer to that of teenagers than to married couples with children. As the satirical novelist Tom Wolfe has said, "The social ideal [is] to look twenty-three and dress thirteen" (Wolfe 2000, 9-10). So the indirect economic and social effect of youth culture on those normally considered adults and children may be of an even greater significance.

It seems clear that through movies, TV programs, and the internet, American youth culture has affected youth cultures and consumption patterns in a wide array of other societies. An obvious example is the adoptions of jeans as the popular form of dress for young people in most parts of the world. For example, in their *Indian Youth in a Transforming World*, DeSouza, Kumar, and Shastri (2009) note: "A strong candidate for visually representing the new world of youth in India was the idea of a pair of jeans ... They have become a ubiquitous symbol of youth in India, from the large village, to the small town, to the big city" (p. xix).

This is not to deny that there are significant differences between societies. For example, in much of Europe schools are less the source and center of youth cultures. This is in part because many expressive activities such as competitive sports and dances are often organized by private clubs rather than within the school per se. In many less economically developed countries most youth leave school at relatively early ages and hence youth cultures are not primarily school-centered. In poorer societies young people may be interested in the latest fashions and knowledgeable about international brands, but the actual consumption patterns of all but the wealthy are more limited by lower incomes. There are an increasing number of studies of youth in non-Western cultures. Some elite groups may simply copy patterns from more developed countries, but more commonly imported consumption patterns are modified to fit local conditions. Often the adoption of such patterns is contested by some groups within the society. Nonetheless it seems clear that the long-term pattern is likely to be that youth will lead the way toward higher levels and new forms of consumption, especially in less developed countries. The key point is that as incomes increase and as the current teenagers in India become the adult consumers, levels of consumption are likely to follow those of developed countries. There are approximately 1.2 billion people in the world between the ages of 10 and 19 (United Nations 2012). A billion of this total is in less developed countries. The impact of these young people on future levels of consumption is likely to have crucial repercussions on the future of both the environment and the world economy. This is the reason that it is important that future consumer research pays careful attention to youth and youth cultures in less developed countries.

SEE ALSO: Coolhunting; Culture-Ideology of Consumerism; Fashion; Glocalization/Grobalization; Stealth Marketing; Teens

REFERENCES

DeSouza, Peter R., Sanjay Kumar, and Sandeep Shastri. 2009. *Indian Youth in a Transforming World: Attitudes and Perceptions*. New Delhi: Sage.

Marketingvox. 2012. "Rand Youth Poll, Seventeen, Packaged Facts, Research date: 9-8-2012." http://www.statisticbrain.com/teenage-consumer-spending-statistics/.

United Nations. 2012. "World Population Prospects: The 2012 Revision, Population by Age Groups – Both Sexes," File POP 7/1. http://esa.un.org/unpd/wpp/Excel-Data/population.htm.

US Bureau of Economic Analysis. 2013. "Personal Consumption Expenditures by Type of Product," Table 2.4.5. http://www.bea.gov/iTable/iTable.cfm?reqid=9&step=1&acrdn=2#reqid=9&step=3&isuri=1&903=70.

Wolfe, Tom. 2000. *Hooking Up*. New York: Farrar, Strauss, and Giroux.

FURTHER READING

Fung, Anthony. 2009. "Fandom, Youth and Consumption in China." *European Journal of Cultural Studies* 12(3): 285–303.

Lukose, Ritty A. 2009. *Liberalization's Children: Gender, Youth, and Consumer Citizenship in Globalizing India*. Durham, NC: Duke University Press.

Milner, Murray Jr. 2013. *Freaks, Geeks, and Cool Kids*, revised ed. New York: Routledge.

Nilan, Pam. 1999. "Young People and Globalizing Trends in Vietnam." *Journal of Youth Studies* 2(3): 353–370.

Warikoo, Natasha K. 2011. *Balancing Acts: Youth Culture in the Global City*. Berkeley: University of California Press.

YouTube

AARON HESS
Arizona State University, USA

YouTube is a video-sharing social media website and digital application found on desktop computers, tablets, smartphones, and smart televisions. Founded in 2005 by Steve Chen and Chad Harley and purchased by Google in 2006, YouTube is considered to be a hallmark of Web 2.0 culture and user-generated content. The site serves as a database of video content, featuring videos coupled with the ability for users to rate the video, comment, or find related content. YouTube videos are shorter than traditional broadcast television, around four minutes, and can be edited with embedded annotations or links. Advertisements, either in the form of commercials before a video or as banners that appear during the video, are a key revenue source for individual users and by Google. Research into YouTube has focused on both the production and consumption of content by individual users, drawn from a variety of methodological and theoretical approaches.

Designed as a destination for individually produced videos, such as home videos, do-it-yourself videos, personal video blogs (vlogs), and independent short films, YouTube invites the sharing of content across users via horizontal distribution. This many-to-many distribution contrasts with major media conglomerates and the vertical one-to-many distribution of content. While this potential remains, the predominant use of YouTube falls into the vertical distribution of content, with the top videos of all time consistently being music videos from major artists and labels. The first video to gain over one billion views, "Gangnam Style," is from K-Pop star, PSY. However, theorizing regarding the production of content for YouTube marks a collapse of the traditional boundaries of consumption and production, toward produsers or produsage (Bruns 2008), parallel with participatory convergence culture. For example, Beyoncé's hit music video in 2009, "Single Ladies," has been viewed well over 200 million times, but has also been replicated by countless YouTube viewers, including a dancing baby who has drawn four million views. This participation in the dance of "Single Ladies" or other mainstream performances displays how consumers simultaneously produce and consume. Concerns have been expressed about such "volunteer" labor that contributes to Google's coffers (Dijck 2009).

The Web 2.0 YouTube aesthetic has generated new forms of content and media. The vlog became a mainstay of the YouTube form, through which a user speaks directly to the camera and edits with a jumpy frame-to-frame style. Notably, the failed fiction vlog of LonelyGirl15 was an early experiment in combining the confessional style with episodic fiction writing, leading to a large fan base for a character, Bree, who, unknown to many of her followers, was completely fictional. Other common elements of YouTube video style include embrace of playful parody (Hess 2009) and remix culture, whereby videos are "mashups" of a variety of other previously recorded videos. One popular example is from a news story in 2010 about a home intruder who was caught by Antoine Dodson during an attempted rape of his sister. Video of Dodson explaining the attack, and an autotuned musical version, went viral and both attracted well over 160 million views.

Research into the political and democratic function of YouTube has been mixed, with some finding that YouTube has replicated existing hierarchies in news production and consumption, but that distribution of news has been altered on the video website (Dylko et al. 2011). YouTube has been a prime venue for posting top-down campaign commercials and bottom-up videos of incorrigible voters, candidate slip-ups, and other election year politicking (Hess 2010). This use has been linked to broadcast news cycles and political spectacle, which points to the website following a broadcast consumption model and questions the utility of the website for deliberative democracy. However, this same spectacular logic has been successful in gaining awareness for international political issues, such as the Kony 2012 video about rebel Joseph Kony's atrocities in Central Africa.

SEE ALSO: Consumption, Spectacles of; Do-It-Yourself (DIY); Internet, The, and Consumption; Social Media; Visual Consumption

REFERENCES

Bruns, Axel. 2008. *Blogs, Wikipedia, Second Life, and Beyond: From Production to Produsage*. New York: Peter Lang.

Dijck, Jose van. 2009. "Users Like You? Theorizing Agency in User-Generated Content." *Media, Culture & Society* 31: 41 – 58.

Dylko, Ivan B., Michael A. Beam, Kristen D. Landreville, and Nicholas Geidner. 2012. "Filtering 2008 US Presidential Election News on YouTube by Elites and Nonelites: An Examination of the Democratizing Potential of the Internet." *New Media & Society* 14(5): 832–849.

Hess, Aaron. 2009. "Resistance Up In Smoke: Analyzing the Limitations of Deliberation on YouTube." *Critical Studies in Media Communication* 26: 411–434.

Hess, Aaron. 2010. "Democracy Through the Lens of the Camcorder: Argumentation and Vernacular Spectacle on YouTube in the 2008 Election." *Argumentation & Advocacy* 47: 106–122.

FURTHER READING

Burgess, Jean, and Joshua Green. 2009. *YouTube: Online Video and Participatory Culture*. Cambridge, UK: Polity Press.

Snickars, Pelle, and Patrick Vonderau. 2009. *The YouTube Reader*. Stockholm: National Library of Sweden.

Index

Entries in **bold** indicate subjects covered by a main article; page ranges in **bold** indicate main articles.

6S model, 422–423

A

A-B-C-D paradigm, 332
absolute scarcity, 491
accountability, 131, 137
achieved celebrity, 71
activism *see* consumer activism; resistance
actor–network theory (ANT), 415, 425
adaptation, 332–333
Adbusters
  anti-consumption tactics, 17
  boycotts, 56
  consumer movements, 133
  consumer resistance movements, 140
  culture jamming, 226–227, 228
Adler, Alfred, 383–385
adoptive parents, 100
Adorno, Theodor, 1–2
  Benjamin, Walter, 2
  consumer culture, 123
  critical theory, 1–2
  culture industries, 1–2, 44, 222–223, 354
  Debord, Guy, 2
  Horkheimer, Max, 1
advertising, 2–9
  African Americans, 11
  anti-consumption tactics, 15, 17
  beauty industry, 39
  brand mascots, 59
  branded self, 6–7
  character licensing, **74–75**
  children's consumer culture, 76
  commodity fetishism, 98–99
  concepts and definitions, 2–3
  consumer culture, 121–122, 123
  consumer movements, 134–135
  consumer society, 4–5
  cosmetic surgery, 202–203
  culture jamming, 226–227
  emotions, 6, 264, 265
  Facebook, 277
  femininities, 292
  Fordism/post-Fordism, 302
  gay and lesbian/queer markets, 313, 315
  green consumption, 350–351
  historical development, 3–4
  infomercial, **363–364**
  internet-mediated consumption, 369–370
  joys of shopping, 5–6
  leisure consumption, 382
  mass culture, 408–409
  mass media, 413–414
  music, 436
  political advertising, 8
  politics and consumer culture, 465
  shopping malls, 512–513
  simulations, 516–517
  social consequences, 7–9
  spectacles of consumption, 191
  teens, 543–544
  visual consumption, 79
  youth culture, 574–575
aestheticization, 185–186, 215, 340, 503
aesthetics, 53, 79–80, 114, 115
  see also arts; taste
Africa, 157–158
African Americans, 10–12
  beauty industry, 39
  citizen consumers, 10
  citizenship, 83
  commodity racism, 100
  conspicuous consumption, 11–12

The Wiley Blackwell Encyclopedia of Consumption and Consumer Studies, First Edition.
Edited by Daniel Thomas Cook and J. Michael Ryan.

African Americans (*Continued*)
political activism, 10
popular culture, 12
purchasing power and exploitation, 11
agency, 147, 166
Agenda 21 report, 530, 532
agricultural commodities, 281 - 282
agricultural cooperatives, 201
alienation
Adorno, Theodor, 1 - 2
advertising, 2, 8, 9
Baudrillard, Jean, 37
Benjamin, Walter, 43
Debord, Guy, 233
gay and lesbian/queer markets, 315
gender and consumer culture, 319
altruism, 348, 349
ambient awareness, 519
ambient music, 435
ambiguity, 524
Americanization, 12 - 15
citizen consumers, 14
concepts and definitions, 12 - 13
credit cards, 207
culture-ideology of consumerism, 221
globalization, 12, 13 - 14
historical development, 14 - 15
popular culture, 469
anarchism, 16, 17
Anderson, Chris, 444
ANT *see* actor - network theory
anticipatory socialization, 552
anti-consumption tactics, 15 - 19
activism, 15 - 16
anarchism, 16
boycotting, 18
citizenship, 83
coca-colonization, 90
collaborative consumption, 18
concepts and definitions, 15
consumer behavior, 108
culture jamming, 17 - 18
do-it-yourselfers, 16 - 17
dumpstering, 16
freegans, 16 - 17
Latinos/Latinas, 379 - 380
lifestyle tactics, 16 - 17
performance art, 17 - 18
scarcity, 490
sharing and gifting, 17
typology and motivations, 15 - 16
voluntary simplicity, 16
anti-globalization movement, 71, 123, 137, 328
Anti-Oedipus: Capitalism and Schizophrenia (Deleuze and Guattari), 63 - 64
anxiety, 30
Apple Inc., 19 - 21, 458
approach - avoidance theory, 499 - 500
Arab Spring, 330, 365
Arab World, 174 - 179
colonial consumption, 175 - 176
global and multilocal consumption, 178 - 179
postcolonial and nationalist consumption, 176 - 178
trade routes, 174 - 175
arcades, 21 - 23
architectural dimensions, 21 - 22
concepts and definitions, 21
consumer culture, 122
economic dimensions, 22
flâneur/flânerie, 22, 43 - 44
functional dimensions, 22
historical development, 21
modern arcades, 22 - 23
public and private spaces, 21
shopping malls, 510
theming, 546
visual consumption, 556 - 557
Arcades Project (Benjamin), 43
artificial needs, 308, 309
artificial scarcity, 490 - 491
arts
Benjamin, Walter, 44
Burning Man, 66
cultural bifurcation approach, 467 - 468
cultural capital, 210
cultural omnivores, 215
culture industries, 222 - 223, 224
dandyism, 229
education, 258 - 259
experiential consumption, 274
Warhol, Andy, 561 - 562
Williams, Raymond, 570
Arts and Crafts movement, 141
ascribed celebrity, 71
Asian Americans, 23 - 25
demographics, 23
diversity, 23
entrepreneurship, 23 - 24
identity, 24
marketing, 23 - 24
popular culture, 24
remittances, 24
attachment theory, 442
attitude - behavior gap, 271, 347
audio agit-prop, 226 - 227
Aunt Jemima, 100

authenticity, **25–26**
  Barbie, 32
  concepts and definitions, 25
  cool, 198
  do-it-yourself, 248
  emotions, 265
  farmers' markets, 285
  gentrification, 322
  Hollywood, 354
  hyperconsumption, 361
  market offerings, 25–26
  nostalgia, 448
  originality, 26
  perceptual connections, 26
  personality and behavior, 25–26
  physical connections, 25, 26
  Slow Food movement, 518
  tourism, 549–551
  Warhol, Andy, 562
authorship, 204
automobile industry, 197
autonomy, 54

B
B2B marketing, **27–28**
background music, 435
Bakhtin, Mikhail, 69–70, 90
bankruptcy, **28–30**
  concepts and definitions, 28
  historical development, 28
  mortgage loans and pensions, 30
  older debtors and retirees, 29
  socioeconomic status, 29
  stigma, 29
  stress and anxiety, 30
  upward social mobility, 29
  US law and policy, 28–29
Barbie, **30–32**, 100–101
Barthes, Roland, **32–33**
  Baudrillard, Jean, 33–34
  consumer culture, 122
  cultural theory, 32
  globalization, 33
  literary theory, 32
  metalanguage, 33
  myth, 32–33
  signification, 33
Baudelaire, Charles, 43–44
Baudrillard, Jean, **33–38**
  activism, 36–37
  alienation, 37
  commodification, 37
  consumer society, 33–35, 37–38, 147
  critique of everyday life, 34, 35–36
  Frankfurt School, 37
  French Situationists, 33–34
  globalization, 334
  governmentality, 340
  major works, 34–36, 38
  mass culture, 408–409
  reification, 37
  semiotics, 494
  simulation and simulacra, 38, 516–517
  symbolic exchange, 537–538
  symbolic value, 539
  system of objects, 34–35
Bauman, Zygmunt
  consumer society, 148
  failed consumers, 153–154
  flawed consumers, 148, **154–156**
  identity, 164
B corporations, 143
BE *see* behavioral economics
beauty industry, **38–40**
  advertising, 39
  African Americans, 39
  body and embodiment, 51
  branding, 40
  Chinese consumers, 160
  cosmetic surgery, **202–204**
  critiques of, 39–40
  feminist theory, 39–40
  gender, 40
  historical development, 38–39
  masculinity, 405–406
  morality, 39
  sexuality, 504
Beauvoir, Simone de, 291
behavioral economics (BE), **41–42**
  concepts and definitions, 41
  critiques of, 42
  historical development, 41–42
  human biases, 42
  nudging, 42
  prospect theory, 41
  rational choice theory, 41
  standard economic model of consumer behavior, 41
belonging, 24
Benjamin, Walter, **42–45**
  Adorno, Theodor, 2
  Baudelaire, Charles, 43–44
  consumer culture, 122
  consumption of art, 44
  flâneur/flânerie, 22, 43–44
  historical materialism, 44–45
  life and works, 42–43
  mass culture, 44

Benjamin, Walter (*Continued*)
philosophy of history, 44–45
Simmel, Georg, 43
theming, 546
theology, 44–45
visual consumption, 556–557
waste, 564
Better Life Index (BLI), 483
big-box stores, 45–46
benefits, 46
concepts and definitions, 45
critiques of, 46
environmental issues, 46
historical development, 45–46
postcommunist countries, 182
shopping malls, 512, 514
supermarkets, 528
Wal-Mart, **559–561**
big data, 413
billboard banditry, 226–227
billboards, 3, 17
biodiversity, 518
Birmingham School, 47–49
Birth of Biopolitics, The (Foucault), 340
Black Friday, 190, 561
black markets, 180, 335
blaxploitation, 11
BLI *see* Better Life Index
blockbusters, 444
blogging, 79, 520
bluewashing, 143, 523–524
body and embodiment, 49–51
Bourdieu, Pierre, 50, 52–53
capitalism, 68
Cartesian dualism, 49
concepts and definitions, 49
cosmetic surgery, **202–204**
dressed body, 50–51
Elias, Norbert, 262
emotions, 263
fashion, 288
femininities, 292–293
Foucault, Michel, 49
Frankfurt School, 308
gender and consumer culture, 319
Giddens, Anthony, 49
identity, 49, 50–51
Merleau-Ponty, Maurice, 50
Schilling, Chris, 49–50
sexuality, 502–503
symbolic consumption, 50–51
Bon Marché, 122, 241
bottom-of-pyramid (BoP) consumers, 151–152
Bourdieu, Pierre, 51–55
body and embodiment, 50, 52–53
class, 88
classifiable practices, 53
cultural capital, 54–55, 209–210, 211
cultural, economic and symbolic capital, 54–55
cultural intermediaries, 212–213
culture industries, 222
emotions, 263
habitus, 50, 52–53
identity, 165
life and works, 51–52
lifestyle, 53–54, 55, 386
major works, 52
material culture studies, 415
social stratification theory, 210
taste, 53–55
theory of practice, 52
boycotts, 55–56
anti-consumption tactics, 18
buycotting, 55
concepts and definitions, 55–56
consumer activism, 103–104
consumer movements, 128
consumer resistance movements, 141–142
ethical consumption, 270
historical development, 55–56
Latinos/Latinas, 379–380
Middle East/Arab World consumers, 178–179
political boycotts, 56
brand aid, 85
brandalism, 17, 233–234
branded self, 6–7
branding, 59–63
advertising, 3, 6–7
Apple Inc., 19–20
beauty industry, 40
brand communities, 61
brand equity, 57–58, 61
brand identity, 61
brand image, 61
brand relationships, 61
citizenship, 85–86
concepts and definitions, 59
conspicuous consumption, 62
consumer culture, 62–63, 116–117
consumer perspective, 61
consumer resistance movements, 142
corporate perspective, 60–61
critiques of, 62
cultural perspective, 61–62
culture industries, 225
culture jamming, 227, 228
emotions, 264, 265, 267

Generation Y, 321
global branding, 61, 62
landscapes of consumption, 173
music, 435–436
Nike, 445–447
postcommunist countries, 181
servicescapes, 500
shopping, 506–507
shopping malls, 512
strategy, 60–61
supermarkets, 528–529
symbolic value, 539–540
theoretical approaches, 59–60
Wal-Mart, 560
brand loyalty, 19–20, **57–58**
brand mascots, **58–59**, 62
brand value, 98
BRIC nations, 333–334
bricolage, **63–65**
concepts and definitions, 63
de Certeau, Michel, 230–231
do-it-yourself culture, 63
identity, 64
key thinkers, 63–64
subcultures, 64
bridging goods, 243
broadcast media
advertising, 4
consumer culture, 123
infomercial, **363–364**
spectacles of consumption, 190
Buddhist economics framework, 483
Bureaucratic Phenomenon, The (Crozier), 231
Burning Man, **65–66**
carnivals/carnivalesque, 71
commodification, 92
consumer behavior, 107
business format franchising, 304–305
business-to-business *see* B2B
Butler, Judith, 291
buycotts
boycotts, 55
consumer activism, 103–104
consumer movements, 128
consumer resistance movements, 142
ethical consumption, 269, 270
Buy Nothing Day, 56, 133, 140
buzz marketing *see* viral marketing

C
CAB *see* Consumer Advisory Board
capital accumulation, 302–303
capitalism, **67–69**
Adorno, Theodor, 1–2
advertising, 4–5, 8
African Americans, 10
American consumers, 196
Americanization, 14
Baudrillard, Jean, 34–36
commodification, 91
concepts and definitions, 67
consumer activism, 104
consumer culture, 115–116, 121, 123
consumer society, 146–148
culture-ideology of consumerism, **220–222**
culture industries, 224–225
Debord, Guy, 233–235
emotions, 266–268
finance and financial markets, 294
Fordism/post-Fordism, 302–304
Frankfurt School, 305–309
globalization, 337
green consumerism, 344
historical development, 67
leisure consumption, 381–382
lifestyle, 386
Marx, Karl, 67, 305–306, 399, 402–403
money, 431
obsolescence, 452
politics and consumer culture, 464
postmodernism, 184
power, control, and freedom, 68–69
prosumption, 477
scarcity, 491
service economy, 497
servicescapes, 499
sexuality, 504
sociology and, 69
spectacles of consumption, 189
sport, 191–192
symbolic exchange, 537
Weber's five criteria, 67–68
Capital (Marx), 399, 402
carnivals/carnivalesque, **69–71**
activism, 70–71
concepts and definitions, 69
cooptation by consumerism, 70, 71
eroticism, 70
flea markets, 297
historical development, 69–70
key thinkers, 69–70
postmodernism, 185
Cartesian dualism, 49
cause related marketing (CRM), 84–85
CCCS *see* Birmingham School
CDA *see* critical discourse analysis
celebrity, **71–74**
celetoids, 71–72

celebrity (*Continued*)
concepts and definitions, 71
consumer culture, 73
endorsement and celebrity vamping, 73, 446, 526–527
fashion, 288
Nike, 446
popular culture, 471
role models, 73–74
shopping, 506
stealth marketing, 526–527
supply- and demand-side accounts, 72–73
celebrity ware, 7
celebrity worship syndrome (CWS), 73
celetoids, 71–72
Centre for Contemporary Cultural Studies *see* Birmingham School
Certeau, Michel de, 230–231
certification revolution, 132
CFPB *see* Consumer Financial Protection Bureau
character licensing, 74–75
chartalism, 431–432
childhood obesity, 301
childity, 77
children's consumer culture, 75–77, 124
access to money, 76
Barbie, 31–32
childity and tweens, 77
edutainment, **260–261**
girl culture, **326–328**
meaning making, 77
moral panics, 75–76
negotiation strategies, 76
prosumption, 77
sociology of childhood, 75
tweens, **551–553**
China, 159–161
fast-growing middle class, 159–160
process of diversification, 160–161
purchasing power, 159–160
social inequalities and luxury goods, 160
choice
culture industries, 225
governmentality, 340
mothers/motherhood, 433–434
paradox of, 153
Christmas, 77–78
consumption rituals, 187
gifts, 325
shopping malls, 513
circuits of commerce, 432
circumvention tourism, 418, 419–420
cities
consumer culture, 121–122
consumer society, 148
Indian consumers, 168
Las Vegas, **377–379**
visual consumption, **79–80**
waste, 564
citizen consumers
African Americans, 10
Americanization, 14
citizenship, 81–84
Latinos/Latinas, 379
sustainable consumption, 532
citizenship
branding, 85–86
civil rights, 82–83
concepts and definitions, 81
consumption and, **81–86**
corporate social responsibility, 84–85
democratic citizenship, 81–82
gender, 82–83
historical development, 81–82
market liberalization, 83–84
political consumerism, 85
political and economic controls, 82–83
Civilizing Process, The (Elias), 261, 298
civil rights
African Americans, 10–11
boycotts, 56
citizenship, 82–83
identity, 165–166
Clarke, John, 64
class, 86–89
Bourdieu, Pierre, 53
capitalism, 68
carnivals/carnivalesque, 69–70
Chinese consumers, 159–160
citizenship, 83
concepts and definitions, 86–87
conspicuous consumption, 88, 102
consumer culture, 120–121
consumption and, 88
cultural capital, 210–211
cultural intermediaries, 212
cultural omnivores, 214–215
culture-ideology of consumerism, 221–222
dandyism, 229
education, 259
Elias, Norbert, 262
ethical consumption, 272
failed consumers, 153
farmers' markets, 285
fashion, 287
food consumption, 298–299
gender and consumer culture, 318–320
gentrification, 322–323

housing market, 358
identity, 164, 165
inequality and status, 88, 102
Marx, Karl, 402–403
pets, 463
popular culture, 467–468
postcommunist countries, 182
service economy, 498
sexuality, 503
theories of, 87–88
Class Acts (Sherman), 498
classifiable practices, 53
clicktivism, 86
coca-colonization, 89–90
coercion, 207–208, 254–255
coffee culture, 525–526
cognitive developmental theory, 145
Coleman, James, 210–211
collaborative consumption, 18, 371
collective action
African Americans, 10–11
Baudrillard, Jean, 36–37
boycotts, **55–56**
carnivals/carnivalesque, 70–71
citizenship, 81
ethical consumption, 272
colonialism
African consumers, 158
consumer culture, 120–121
Middle East/Arab World consumers, 175–176
politics and consumer culture, 463–464
Coming of Post-Industrial Society, The (Bell), 497
commercial debt, 235
commercialization
capitalism, 68
cultural omnivores, 215
culture, 191
mothers/motherhood, 434
sexuality, 502
commodification, 90–93
African Americans, 12
Baudrillard, Jean, 37
Burning Man, 92
Christmas, 78
citizenship, 86
commodity fetishism, 91, **97–99**
commodity racism, 100–101
compassionate consumerism, 92–93
concepts and definitions, 90–91
cool, 198, 199
coolhunting, 199
cultural studies, 219–220
culture industries, 223
culture jamming, 228
death, 232
Diderot effect, 243
ecotourism, 257
environmental issues, 92
exchange value, 91
fair trade, 284
femininities, 292
global justice movement, 328–329
hegemony and cooptation, 91–92
housing market, 359
internet-mediated consumption, 370
leisure consumption, 382–383
masculinity, 406
mass media, 92
mothers/motherhood, 434
otherness, 91–92
outsourcing, 460
politics and consumer culture, 465
postcommunist countries, 182
postmodernism, 186
sport, 192–193, 194
tourism, 549–550
weddings, 566–567
commodities, 93–95
concepts and definitions, 93
emotions, 264–268
Frankfurt School, 305–306
liberal economics and cognitive sciences, 93
Marx, Karl, 399
sociocultural and postcolonial studies, 94
substitutability, 93
symbolic value, 539
theoretical approaches, 93–94
commodity chains, 94, **95–97**
activism, 96–97
concepts and definitions, 95
globalization, 97
producer driven chains, 95–96
world system theory, 95
commodity-experience, 266–267
commodity fetishism, 97–99
advertising, 98–99
commodification, 91, 97–99
consumer society, 146–147
labor and exploitation, 99
Marx, Karl, 91, 97–98, 399–400
commodity form, 2
commodity racism, 99–101
adoptive parents, 100
commodification, 100–101
concepts and definitions, 99–100
gender, 100–101
slavery, 100

commons
  anti-consumption tactics, 18
  citizenship, 81
  creative commons, 367
  Debord, Guy, 234
communication studies, 1
communism, 179–180
Communist Manifesto (Marx and Engels), 400
communitas, 187–188
community, 69–70
community-supported agriculture (CSA), 388
commuting, 197
companion animals *see* pets
compassionate consumerism, 92–93, 118, 132–133, 140–141
competitive altruism, 349
conceptual consumption, 106
conformity, 308, 309
conspicuous consumption, 101–103
  African Americans, 11–12
  branding, 62
  Christmas, 78
  class, 88, 102
  concepts and definitions, 101–102
  consumer culture, 120
  ethical consumption, 272
  Frankfurt School, 308
  hyperconsumption, 360
  leisure consumption, 102, 382
  trickle-down economics, 88, 102
  Veblen, Thorstein, 88, 101–102, 120, 555–556
consumer activism, 103–105
  advertising, 9
  African Americans, 10–11
  anti-consumption tactics, 15–16
  Baudrillard, Jean, 36–37
  Birmingham School, 47
  boycotts, **55–56**, 103–104
  buycotts, 103–104
  carnivals/carnivalesque, 70–71
  citizenship, 86
  commodity chains, 96–97
  concepts and definitions, 103
  consumer activism, **103–105**
  consumer behavior, 108
  consumer culture, 123–124
  corporate resistance, 104
  culture jamming, **226–228**
  Debord, Guy, 234–235
  gay and lesbian/queer markets, 315–316
  historical development, 104
  Latinos/Latinas, 379–380
  Occupy movement, **453–455**
  philosophical premise, 103
  see also anti-consumption tactics
Consumer Advisory Board (CAB), 130
consumer behavior, 105–110
  concepts and definitions, 105
  consumer culture theory, 105, 106–108
  consumer identity projects, 107
  experiential consumption, **273–275**
  global markets, 332
  green consumption, 348
  lifestyle, 384–385
  marketplace cultures, 107
  mass-mediated marketplaces, 108
  obesity, 449–450
  psychology, 105–106
  recycling, 486
  social media, 109
  sociohistoric patterning, 107–108
  theoretical approaches, 108–109
consumer capital, 211
consumer cosmopolitanism, 110–112
consumer culture, 112–118
  activism, 123–124
  Americanization, 14–15
  anti-consumption tactics, 15–18
  arcades, 122
  beauty industry, 38
  body and embodiment, 51
  branding, 62–63, 116–117
  brand mascots, 59
  celebrity, 73
  cities, department stores, and advertising, 121–122, 123, 242
  citizenship, 81
  class, 120–121
  colonial commerce, social competition, and hedonism, 120–121
  commodification, 91
  commodities, 94
  commodity fetishism, 98
  concepts and definitions, 112–113, 118–119
  conspicuous consumption, 120
  consumer behavior, 108–109
  consumer society and the internet, 122–124
  consumption and consumerism, 112–113
  consumption rituals, 188
  critiques of, 114–116
  decluttering, 239
  downshifting, 249
  emotions, 263, 268
  environmental issues, 117–118
  features and characterization, 113–114
  flâneur/flânerie, 295–296
  flawed consumers, 155
  gender, **316–321**

globalization, 117
governmentality, **339–342**
historical development, **118–124**
Latinos/Latinas, 380
leisure consumption, 381–382
luxury goods, 120
as moral/political judgment, 114–116
mothers/motherhood, 434
nostalgia, 448
obesity, 450–451
politics and, **463–467**
postconsumer culture, 116–118
postmodernism, 185–186
prosumption, 113–114, 117
public relations, 479
Renaissance, royal courts and bourgeois classes, 119–120
semiotics, 493–494
sport, 191
sustainable consumption, 532–533
see also children's consumer culture
consumer culture theory (CCT), 124–128
axiology, 125
concepts and definitions, 124–125
consumer behavior, 105, 106–108
consumer identity projects, 107, 125
critiques of, 127–128
historical development, 125–126
marketplace cultures, 107, 125–126
mass-mediated marketplaces, 108, 127
research domains, 107–108, 126–127
sociohistoric patterning, 107–108, 127
consumer debt, 235–238
Consumer Financial Protection Bureau (CFPB), 138
consumer identity projects, 107, 125
consumerism
carnivals/carnivalesque, 70, 71
compassionate consumerism, 92–93, 118, 132–133, 140–141
consumer culture, 112–113
culture-ideology of consumerism, **220–222**, 337
green consumerism, **342–346**
political consumerism, 85, 131–133, 259
postmodernism, 184–185
consumer movements, 128–133
1890s–1910s, 133–134
1920s–1930s, 129–130, 134–136
1960s–1970s, 130–131, 136–137
1990s–today, 131–133
advertising, 134–135
boycotts and buycotts, 128
compassionate consumerism, 132–133
concepts and definitions, 128–129
consumer protection, 131, 135–136
corporate accountability, 131, 137
deregulation, 137
fair trade organizations, 132
historical development, 129–133, **133–137**
product testing, 130
social justice and environmental sustainability, 131–133, 137
consumer protection agency, 137–139
consumer psychology, 105–106
consumer research methods, 422–427
6S model, 422–423
critical discourse analysis, 424
domains of study, 424–425
future directions, 426–427
interdisciplinary methods, 425–426
network theories, 424–425
neuroscience, 426–427
observation methods, 425
professionals and specialists, 426
qualitative and quantitative approaches, 423–424
questionnaires, 425–426
consumer resistance movements, 139–144
B corporations, 143
boycotts and buycotts, 141–142
classical and neoclassical economics, 140
concepts and definitions, 139–140
corporate social responsibility, 142–143
culture jamming, 142
do-it-yourself and prosumption, 140–141, 143
exit and voice, 140
marginal utility, 140
Marxist theory, 141
producer perspective, 141
slavery, 141
voluntary simplicity, 140–141
consumer socialization, 144–145
consumer society, 145–150
advertising, 4–5
American consumers, 195
Baudrillard, Jean, 33–35, 37–38, 147
carnivals/carnivalesque, 70–71
cities, 148
commodity fetishism, 146–147
concepts and definitions, 145–146
consumer culture, 122–124
flawed consumer, 148
Frankfurt School, 146, 148–149, 308–309
freedom, 147, 148–149
globalization, 146, 334–336
hegemony, 146
inequality and social division, 147–148

consumer society (*Continued*)
  lifestyle, 386
  Marx, Karl, 146–147
  mass media, 148
  needs, 147
  scarcity, 490
  spectacles of consumption, 190
  structure and agency, 147
Consumer Society, The (Baudrillard), 34–36, 147, 494
Consumers' Research (CR), 129–130
Consumers Union (CU), 129–130, 136
consumption epistemics, 294
consumption rituals, 187–189
  death, 187, 232–233
  Elias, Norbert, 261–262
  weddings, 187–188, **566–567**
consumption spectacles, 189–191, 361
content analysis, 469–470
continuous production, 374
Cook, Daniel Thomas, 77
cool, 197–199
  authenticity, 198
  commodification, 198, 199
  concepts and definitions, 197–198
  coolhunting, **199–200**
  counterculture and rebellion, 197–198
  culture jamming, 226–227
coolhunting, 199–200
cooperatives, 200–202
cooptation
  carnivals/carnivalesque, 70, 71
  commodification, 91
  consumer culture, 115
  culture, 12
  fair trade, 282–283
  locavorism, 388
  politics and consumer culture, 465
  popular culture, 471
corporate accountability, 131, 137
corporate culture, 374
corporate social responsibility (CSR)
  citizenship, 84–85
  consumer research methods, 426
  consumer resistance movements, 142–143
  free trade zones, 310
  greenwashing, 143, 523–524
  marketing, 392
  socially responsible marketing, **523–524**
  Whole Foods Market, 567–569
corporate sponsorship, 65
cosmetic surgery, 202–204
costly signaling, 349
counterculture, 65–66, 91, 197–198
counterfeiting/piracy, 204–206
  challenges to control of, 206
  concepts and definitions, 204
  digital technologies, 205–206
  division of labor, 205
  intellectual property, 204–205
  peer-to-peer file sharing, 461
court model of conduct, 261–262
CR *see* Consumers' Research
creationist capitalism, 477
creative capital, 210–211
creative commons, 367
creative industries, 2, 225
creativity, 496
credit cards, 206–209
  Americanization, 207
  debt, 236
  finance and financial markets, 293
  globalization, 336–337
  historical development, 206–207
  information asymmetry, 208
  payday loans, 208–209
  postcommunist countries, 207–208
  two-sided markets, 207
  usage types, 208
credit unions, 201
cremation, 232
critical advertising theory, 98
critical discourse analysis (CDA), 424
critical mass, 18
Critical Mass (social movement), 234
critical reading, 469
critical theory *see* Frankfurt School
CRM *see* cause related marketing
cross-cultural analysis, 331–332
crowdsourcing, 455–456
CSA *see* community-supported agriculture
CU *see* Consumers Union
cultural appropriation, 158
cultural bifurcation approach, 467–468
cultural capital, 209–212
  Apple Inc., 20
  Bourdieu, Pierre, 54–55, 209–210, 211
  concepts and definitions, 209–210
  cultural intermediaries, 212
  cultural omnivores, 215
  fans and fandom, 211
  gender and consumer culture, 320
  gentrification, 322–323
  gifts, 325
  human and creative capital, 210–211
  social stratification theory, 210, 211
  subtypes of, 209–210
  weddings, 566

cultural elitism, 215, 223, 224, 258–259
cultural imperialism
  Americanization, 12–15
  coca-colonization, **89–90**
  culture-ideology of consumerism, 221
  globalization, 337
  modernization theory, 429
cultural intermediaries, 55, **212–214**, 240
cultural materialism, 570
cultural omnivores, 213, **214–216**
cultural sociology of money, 432
cultural studies, **216–220**
  academia and, 218–219
  Barthes, Roland, 32
  Birmingham School, 47–48
  commodification, 219–220
  concepts and definitions, 216
  continuities across disciplines, 217
  difference and binaries, 218
  etymology of culture, 216–217
  hegemony, 217
  historical development, 216–217
  spatial trajectory, 216
  subcultures, 218–219
  subjectivity and power, 217–218
culturalized economy, 191
culture
  Baudrillard, Jean, 36
  Bourdieu, Pierre, 52, 53
  branding, 61–62
  consumption rituals, 188
  dandyism, 229
  debt, 237–238
  education, 258–259
  global markets, 331–332
  Indian consumers, 169
  needs, 441
  semiotics, 493
  sexuality, 503–504
  Starbuckization, 525–526
  teens, 544–545
  tourism, 550–551
  waste, 563
  weddings, 566
  Williams, Raymond, 570
culture-ideology of consumerism, **220–222**, 337
culture industries, **222–226**
  Adorno, Theodor and Horkheimer, Max, 1–2, 44, 222–223, 354
  coca-colonization, 89
  concepts and definitions, 222
  contemporary debate, 225
  creative industries, 225
  cultural studies, 220
  Frankfurt School, 222–223, 307, 309
  high culture, popular culture, and mass culture, 222–223, 224
  historical development, 222–225
  Hollywood, 354
  infotainment, 365
  mass production of culture, 222
  policy adoption, 223–225
culture jamming, **226–228**
  anti-consumption tactics, 17–18
  coca-colonization, 90
  concepts and definitions, 226
  consumer resistance movements, 142
  critiques of, 228
  modes of, 226–227
  situationism, 227–228
Culture and Society (Williams), 222, 570
customer relationship management (CRM), 392
customerization, 245
CWS *see* celebrity worship syndrome

D
daily routine, 230–231, 319
dandyism, **229–230**, 428
data collection and storage, 473–474
data protection, 278
dating websites, 370
death
  commodification, 232
  concepts and definitions, 231–232
  consumption and, **231–233**
  cremation, 232
  embalming, 232
  emotions, 232–233
  funeral services, 187, 231–232
de Beauvoir, Simone, 291
Debord, Guy, **233–235**
  Adorno, Theodor, 2
  Baudrillard, Jean, 33–34
  détournement and *dérive*, 234–235
  life and works, 233–235
  spectacles of consumption, 189–191
  spectacular society, 233–234, 235
debt, **235–238**
  concepts and definitions, 235
  consumer legislation, 237
  credit cards, **206–209**
  culture, 237–238
  finance and financial markets, 294
  financial crises, 237–238
  freedom and control, 236–237
  globalization, 336–337
  historical development, 235–236
  housing market, 359

de Certeau, Michel, 230–231
decluttering, 238–240
Deleuze, Gilles, 63–64
deliberate obsolescence, 565
dematerialization, 371
democratic citizenship, 81–82
democratization, 429, 456
demodernization, 343, 344–345
demographic targeting, 196
department stores, 240–243
  concepts and definitions, 240
  consumer culture, 121–122, 242
  credit cards, 206
  cultural intermediaries, 240
  flâneur/flânerie, 241
  gender, 241–242
  gender and consumer culture, 318
  historical development, 240–241
  Middle East/Arab World consumers, 176
  servicescapes, 499
  shopping, 508
  shopping malls, 510–511
  visual consumption, 557
dependency theory, 429
deregulation, 137, 303–304, 328–329
dérive, 234–235
Derrida, Jacques, 63
Dery, Mark, 226–227
de Saussure, Ferdinand, 492, 494
détournement, 234–235
development
  African consumers, 157
  emerging economies, **150–153**
  modernization theory, **428–430**
  quality of life, 482–483
diabetes mellitus, 450
Diderot, Denis, 243
Diderot effect, 243–244
digital divide, 244
digital-mobile consumption
  customerization, 245
  marketing, **244–246**
  pricing, 245–246
  primary adoption, 244
  prosumption, 245
  social relationships, 245
  technological change, 244
  traditional business disruption, 246
discrimination
  African Americans, 10–11
  identity, 165–166
  politics and consumer culture, 465
  Wal-Mart, 561
disguised observation, 425
Disneyization, 246–247
  children's consumer culture, 76
  concepts and definitions, 246–247
  hybrid consumption, 247
  merchandising, 247
  performative labor, 247
  theming, 246–247, 547–548
Disneyization of Society, The (Bryman), 497, 548
displaced meaning, 243
displacement, 323–324, 335
distinction, 512
Distinction (Bourdieu), 52, 210, 212, 299, 386
diversification, 160–161
diversity, 214–215
division of labor, 205, 336
Diwali, 187
DIY *see* do-it-yourself
docile body, 49, 68
do-it-yourself (DIY), 247–248
  anti-consumption tactics, 16–17
  bricolage, 63
  carnivals/carnivalesque, 70
  concepts and definitions, 247
  consumer resistance movements, 140–141, 143
  festivals, 248
  girl culture, 327
  historical development, 247–248
  masculinity, 406
  open source, 457
  popular culture, 248
  prosumption, 476
  YouTube, 576–577
domestic animals *see* pets
domination relations, 230
Douglas, Mary, 163, 563
downshifting, 248–250
  concepts and definitions, 248–249
  consumer culture, 249
  consumer movements, 133
  historical development, 248–249
  obstacles to, 249–250
dressed body, 50–51
dumpstering/dumpster diving, 16–17
Durkheim, Émile, 69

E
eating disorders, 31
eBay, 251–252
eBayization, 418
ecogastronomy, 518
ecological citizenship, 345
ecological modernization theory, 343–344
economic capital, 54–55, 323
economic imperialism, 13

Economic and Philosophic Manuscripts of 1844, The (Marx and Engels), 398–399
ecotourism, 255–257
education
Chinese consumers, 161
concepts and definitions, 257–258
consumption and, **257–260**
culture and the arts, 258–259
ethical and political consumption, 259
food and healthy lifestyles, 258
edutainment, 260–261
Electronic Frontier Foundation, 235
Elias, Norbert, 261–262, 298
email, 8–9
embalming, 232
embodied cultural capital, 209–210
embodiment *see* body and embodiment
emerging economies, 150–153
emotional commodities, 267–268
emotions
advertising, 6, 264, 265
authenticity, 265
bankruptcy, 30
as commodities, 267–268
concepts and definitions, 263
consumption and, **263–268**
creation of consumer as emotional agent, 264–265
death, 232–233
Elias, Norbert, 262
as independent category of consumption, 263–264
performativity, 266
semiotics of consumption, 265–267
Empire of Scrounge (Ferrell), 234
emulation, 164, 211
endorsement, 73, 446, 526–527
Engels, Friedrich, 398–403
entitlements, 490
entrepreneurship, 23–24, 254, 318
environmental issues
advertising, 2, 8
American consumers, 196
big-box stores, 46
boycotts, 56
citizenship, 84
commodification, 92
consumer behavior, 109
consumer culture, 117–118
consumer movements, 131–133, 137
consumer resistance movements, 141, 143
culture-ideology of consumerism, 221–222
downshifting, 249
eBay, 251–252
ecotourism, **255–257**
ethical consumption, 269
fashion, 288
green consumerism, **342–346**
green consumption, **346–352**
locavorism, 387–388
modernization theory, 430
politics and consumer culture, 464–465
recycling, **485–487**
Slow Food movement, 518
sustainable consumption, 530–533
waste, **563–565**
Whole Foods Market, 568
EPZs *see* export processing zones
eroticism, 70
ethical consumption, 268–273
attitude-behavior gap, 271
boycotts and buycotts, 269, 270
concepts and definitions, 268–269
critiques of, 272–273
education, 259
food consumption, 299
historical development, 270
identity, 271–272
norm-activation model, 271
research approaches, 270–272
social movements, 272
space and place, 272
sustainability, 269–270
typology, 269–270
Whole Foods Market, 568–569
willingness to pay, 271
ethical simplifiers, 249
ethnographic/subculture analysis approach, 470–471
e-waste recycling, 565
excise taxes, 542
exit, 140
experiential consumption, 273–275
export processing zones (EPZs), 310–312
extended self, 107
externalities, 98

F
Facebook, 277–279, 519–521
facework, 162
failed consumers, 153–154
failing consumption, 279–280
fair exchange, 537–538
fair information practice principles (FIPPs), 474–475
Fair Labor Association (FLA), 535
fair trade, 280–284
agricultural commodities, 281–282

fair trade (*Continued*)
certification and standardization, 281–282
concepts and definitions, 280–281
consumer movements, 132
critiques of, 282–283
eBay, 252
handicrafts, 281, 283
historical development, 281
mainstreaming of, 282–283
market sector, 282
marketing, 283–284
social movements, 280–281
social premium cost, 281
false advertising, 8, 135
false consciousness, 146
false needs, **440–442**
family-friendly mega-franchises, 355
fans and fandom, 192–193, 194, 211, 327
farmers' markets, **284–286**, 508–509
fashion, **286–289**
body and embodiment, 288
Bourdieu, Pierre, 54
celebrity, 288
concepts and definitions, 286–287
cool, 198
coolhunting, 199
dandyism, 229
dress, 286–287
ethics and sustainability, 288
failed consumers, 153
feminist theory, 288
gender, 288
Indian consumers, 168–169
Middle East/Arab World consumers, 178
sweatshops, **534–536**
trickle-down economics, 287–288
fast food, **289–290**, 300
fast-moving consumer goods (FMCG), 410–411
FDA *see* Food and Drug Administration
FDI *see* foreign direct investment
Featherstone, Mike, 386, 464
federal cooperatives, 201
Federal National Mortgage Association, 302
Federal Trade Commission (FTC), 82, 131, 135–137, 233, 474–475
Feeding the Family (De Vault), 319
femininities, **290–293**
advertising and mass media, 292
biological traits, 291
body and embodiment, 292–293
commodification, 292
concepts and definitions, 290
feminist theory, 291–292
forms, 290–291
gender and consumer culture, 319
gender roles and stereotypes, 291, 292–293
metrosexual, 406, 427–428
postfeminism and girl power, 291–292
sexuality, 503–504
sociocultural theory, 292
feminist theory
beauty industry, 39–40
fashion, 288
femininities, 291–292
gender and consumer culture, 316–319
sexuality, 501–502, 504
Ferrell, Joe, 234
fertility tourism, 420
festivals
Burning Man, **65–66**, 71, 92, 107
carnivals/carnivalesque, **69–71**
commodification, 92
consumer behavior, 107
do-it-yourself, 248
Field of Cultural Production, In the (Bourdieu), 54
file sharing *see* peer-to-peer
film industry, 11, 72, **353–356**, 571–572
finance and financial markets, **293–295**
capitalist transformation, 294
concepts and definitions, 293
credit, 293
financial instruments, 293–294
Fordism/post-Fordism, 303–304
investment and speculation, 293–294
risk and debt, 294
financial crises
consumer protection agency, 138–139
debt, 237–238
Fordism/post-Fordism, 303–304
globalization, 337
housing market, 359
financialization, 431–432
FIPPs *see* fair information practice principles
FLA *see* Fair Labor Association
flâneur/flânerie, **295–296**
arcades, 22, 43–44
Benjamin, Walter, 22, 43–44
concepts and definitions, 295
consumer culture, 295–296
department stores, 241
sport, 193
tourism, 295–296
visual consumption, 556–557
flawed consumers, 148, **154–156**, 503
flea markets, **296–297**
Florida, Richard, 211, 225
FLOSS *see* Free/Libre Open Source Software
FMCG *see* fast-moving consumer goods

fMRI *see* functional magnetic resonance imaging
folk culture, 408
food consumption, 297–300
  American consumers, 195–196
  Chinese consumers, 160–161
  concepts and definitions, 297–298
  do-it-yourself, 248
  education, 258
  ethical consumption and alternative food movements, 299
  farmers' markets, **284–286**, 508–509
  fast food, **289–290**, 300
  franchising, 304–305
  identity, 298–299
  locavorism, **387–388**
  music, 435
  obesity, **449–451**
  rise of food studies, 299–300
  scarcity, 489
  Slow Food movement, **517–518**
  social appetite, 298–299
  Whole Foods Market, **567–569**
  see also McDonaldization
food deserts, 300–301
Food and Drug Administration (FDA), 135–136
food security, 299
For a Critique of the Political Economy of the Sign (Baudrillard), 38
Fordism/post-Fordism, 301–304
  capital accumulation, 302–303
  concepts and definitions, 301–302
  financial crises, 304
  historical development, 301–303
  homeownership and the American Dream, 303
  limitations of Fordism, 303
  mass culture, 407
  outsourcing, 458
  policy reforms, 302–303
foreign aid, 429
foreign direct investment (FDI), 310–311
former state-controlled economies (FSCEs), 529
Foucault, Michel
  body and embodiment, 49
  capitalism, 68
  cosmetic surgery, 203
  cultural intermediaries, 213
  governmentality, 339–340
  identity, 166
franchising, 304–305, 318
Frankfurt School, 305–310
  Adorno, Theodor, **1–2**, 44
  Baudrillard, Jean, 37
  Benjamin, Walter, 42–43, 44
  capitalism, 305–309
  conformity, 308, 309
  conspicuous consumption, 308
  consumer culture, 115
  consumer society, 146, 148–149, 308–309
  culture industries, 222–223, 307, 309
  lifestyle, 386
  Marxist theory, 306–307
  mass culture, 408
  mass media, 306, 307–308, 309, 412
  Nazism, 306
  popular culture, 469
  postmodernism, 184
  sexuality, 308–309
  Warhol, Andy, 562
fraud, 207, 459
free culture, 462
free trade zones, 310–312
freedom
  capitalism, 68
  consumer society, 147, 148–149
  cultural studies, 220
  Frankfurt School, 308
  open source, 456
freegans, 16–17
Free/Libre Open Source Software (FLOSS) movement, 456–457
French Situationists, 33–34
Friedberg, Anne, 266–267
Frieden, Betty, 317–318
fringe banking, 237
Fromm, Erich, 307
FSCEs *see* former state-controlled economies
FTC *see* Federal Trade Commission
functional magnetic resonance imaging (fMRI), 426–427
functional value, 452
functionalism, 163–164, 428
funerals, 187, 231–232
fun morality, 364
futures, 294

G
Galbraith, John Kenneth, 408
gambling, 370–371, **377–379**
gamification, 260
Gandhi, Mohandas Karamchand, 167
Garbology Project, 563
gay and lesbian marketing, 313–316
  advertising, 313, 315
  coded appeals, 315
  concepts and definitions, 313
  critiques of, 315–316
  historical development, 313–314
  identity, 315–316

gay and lesbian marketing (*Continued*)
moral panic, 315
print media, 313–315
purchasing power, 314–315
GCC *see* global commodity chain
GDP *see* gross domestic product
gender
beauty industry, 40
body and embodiment, 319
Burning Man, 65
citizenship, 82–83
class, 318–320
commodity racism, 100–101
concepts and definitions, 316–317
consumer culture, **316–321**
department stores, 241–242
entrepreneurialism, 318
fashion, 288
femininities, **290–293**
feminist theory, 316–319
flâneur/flânerie, 295
food consumption, 298
identity, 318
masculinity, 101, 291–293, 295, **403–407**
outsourcing, 459–460
purchasing power, 319–320
quality of life, 483
sexuality, 503–504
shopping, 507
tweens, 552
Wal-Mart, 561
weddings, 567
Gender Inequality Index (GII), 483
Gender Trouble (Butler), 291
Generation Y, 321
genetically modified organisms (GMOs), 569
genetics, 450
genre, 354–355
gentrification, 322–324, 358
Genuine Progress Indicator (GPI), 483
German Ideology, The (Marx and Engels), 87, 398
gestation, 188
Getting Loose (Binkley), 198
Giddens, Anthony, 49, 385
gifts, 324–326
Burning Man, 65
concepts and definitions, 324–325
consumption rituals, 188
culture, 17
cycles of exchange, 325
identity, 325
socialization, 325–326
symbolic exchange, 536–537
symbolic value, 539
Gift, The (Mauss), 539
GII *see* Gender Inequality Index
girl culture, 31–32, **326–328**
girl power, 291–292
GJM *see* global justice movement
Gladwell, Malcolm, 199
global commodity chain (GCC), 94, 95–97
global justice movement (GJM), 328–331
concepts and definitions, 328
core characteristics, 329–330
future directions, 330
historical development, 328–329
market liberalization, 328–329
global markets, 331–333
A-B-C-D paradigm, 332
concepts and definitions, 331
consumer behavior, 332
cross-cultural analysis, 331–332
historical development, 331
standardization and adaptation, 332–333
globalization
American consumers, 196
Americanization, 12, 13–14
Barthes, Roland, 33
black markets, 335
brand mascots, 59
branding, 61, 62
carnivals/carnivalesque, 71
coca-colonization, 89–90
commodity chains, 97
concepts and definitions, 333
consumer behavior, 108, 109
consumer cosmopolitanism, 111
consumer culture, 117
consumer society, 146, 334–336
consumption and, **333–338**
credit cards, 207
credit and debt, 336–337
culture-ideology of consumerism, **220–222**, 337
culture industries, 224
ethical consumption, 270
fashion, 288
financial crises, 337
Fordism/post-Fordism, 303
global justice movement, 328, 329–330
global markets, **331–333**
goods and services, 335
homogenization and heterogenization, 356–357
hyperconsumption, 337
Middle East/Arab World consumers, 178–179
modernization theory, 429–430
multinational corporations, 334–335
niche marketing, 444
nostalgia, 448

nothingness and somethingness, 336
politics and consumer culture, 464
positive and negative flows, 336
postcommunist countries, 181–183
productivist bias, 333–334
sexuality, 504
shopping malls, 335, 509–510, 511
sites of consumption, 335–336
supermarkets, 529
teens, 544
tourism, 551
glocalization, 338–339
Americanization, 13
concepts and definitions, 338
consumer behavior, 108
grobalization, 338–339
homogenization and heterogenization, 356–357
Starbuckization, 525
GMOs *see* genetically modified organisms
GNH *see* Gross National Happiness
Goffman, Erving, 162–163
Goodman, Douglas, 357
governmentality
concepts and definitions, 339–340
consumer culture, **339–342**
consumption as production, 340
consumption as responsibility, 341
consumption as security, 341
Foucault, Michel, 339–340
Homo œconomicus, 340
human capital, 340
GPI *see* Genuine Progress Indicator
graffiti, 235
Grammatology, Of (Derrida), 63
Gramsci, Antonio, 48
gratification
advertising, 5–8
cultural capital, 210
debt, 236
education, 258
Generation Y, 321
infotainment, 364–365
needs and wants, 442
shopping malls, 512
teens, 544
Great Exhibition, 571
green advertising, 351
green capitalism, 344
green consumerism, 342–346
concepts and definitions, 342
demodernization, 343, 344–345
ecological modernization, 343–344
efficiency versus sufficiency, 343
key debates, 342–343
middle position on consumption, 345–346
green consumption, 346–352
altruism, 348
attitude–behavior gap, 347
concepts and definitions, 346–347
demographic factors, 348
environmental knowledge, 348
ethics, 350
green marketing and advertising, 350–351
historical development, 347
internet-mediated consumption, 371
market research, 347–350
models of, 351
opinion leadership and market mavenism, 349–350
responsibility, 346, 348–349
social identity theory, 349
status and prestige, 349
green marketing, 350–351
greenwashing
citizenship, 84
consumer resistance movements, 143
ecotourism, 257
ethical consumption, 273
socially responsible marketing, 523–524
grobalization, 338–339
gross domestic product (GDP), 150–151, 481–482
Gross National Happiness (GNH) index, 483
Guattari, Félix, 63–64

H
habitus, 50, 52–53, 262, 263
haggling, 297
Hall, Stuart, 47–48
Halloween, 513
handicrafts, 281, 283
happiness, 7
hard news, 364
Hart, Keith, 253–254
HDI *see* Human Development Index
Hebdige, Dick, 64, 386
hedonism, 120–121
Hegel, Georg Wilhelm Friedrich, 397–398
hegemonic masculinity, 404
hegemony
Adorno, Theodor, 2
Birmingham School, 48
commodification, 91–92
consumer culture theory, 127
consumer society, 146
cultural studies, 217
ecotourism, 256–257
politics and consumer culture, 465
popular culture, 469

hegemony (*Continued*)
prosumption, 477
heijunka, 373
heterogenization, 356–357
high culture *see* arts
Hills, Matt, 211
hip hop, 12
hire purchase, 236
Hirschmann, Albert O., 140
Hirschmann, Elizabeth, 275
historical materialism, 44–45
historical sociology, 431–432
hoarding, 238–239
Hochschild, Arlie, 460
Hoggart, Richard, 47
Holbrook, Morris, 274–275
Hollywood, 353–356
celebrity, 72
culture industries, 354
family-friendly mega-franchises, 355
film theory, 353–354
genre, 354–355
historical development, 354
media cross-promotion, 355
merchandising, 355
world's fairs and international expositions, 571–572
homeownership
American consumers, 196–197, 209
credit cards, 208
cultural meanings, 357–358
flawed consumers, 156
Fordism/post-Fordism, 303
gender and consumer culture, 317–320
historical development, 358–359
Japanese consumers, 171
homo clausus condition, 262
Homo œconomicus, 340
homogenization, 356–357
Americanization, 13
beauty industry, 39
coca-colonization, 90
globalization, 336
heterogenization, 356–357
Starbuckization, 525
theming, 546
Hoover, Herbert, 384–385
Horkheimer, Max, 1, 123, 222–223, 354
household debt, 235
housing cooperatives, 201
housing market, 357–360
American consumers, 196–197
Chinese consumers, 160
class, 358
commodification, 359
concepts and definitions, 357–358
cultural meanings of homeownership, 357–358
financial crises, 359
flawed consumers, 156
Fordism/post-Fordism, 303–304
gentrification, **322–324**, 358
historical development, 358–359
Japanese consumers, 171
mortgage loans, 359
human capital, 210–211, 340
Human Development Index (HDI), 482–483
Human Development Report (UNDP), 531
hybrid consumption, 247, 546
hyperconsumption, 360–361
concepts and definitions, 360
globalization, 337
historical development, 360–361
homogenization and heterogenization, 361
obsolescence, 453
spectacularization of consumption, 361
hypermarkets, 512
hypermasculinity, 406

I
icons, 492
ICPEN *see* International Consumer Protection and Enforcement Network
identity
Asian Americans, 24
authenticity, 25–26
body and embodiment, 49, 50–51
branded self, 6–7
bricolage, 64
civil rights and identity politics, 165–166
concepts and definitions, 162
consumer culture, 113
consumer society, 147
consumption and, **162–167**
culture industries, 225
discrimination and social exclusion, 165–166
emotions, 264
emulation, 164
ethical consumption, 271–272
farmers' markets, 285
food consumption, 298–299
functionalism, 163–164
gay and lesbian/queer markets, 315–316
gender and consumer culture, 318
gifts, 325
grobalization, 339
historical and modern meanings, 162
homogenization and heterogenization, 356–357
key thinkers, 162–166

Latinos/Latinas, 379
lifestyle, 385
masculinity, 404, 406
merchandising, 421
mothers/motherhood, 433
motility and reflexivity, 163
nostalgia, 448
performativity, 162
production and, 163–164
sexuality, 503–504
shopping malls, 511–512, 513
sovereignty, 166
tourism, 550–551
identity projects, 107
ideology
advertising, 8
American consumers, 195
coca-colonization, 90
commodification, 92
commodities, 94
commodity racism, 101
consumer behavior, 108
consumer society, 148, 149
culture-ideology of consumerism, **220–222**, 337
ecotourism, 256–257
failed consumers, 153
fair trade, 283
Fordism/post-Fordism, 302
green consumerism, 342
housing market, 358–359
Indian consumers, 167
Marx, Karl, 400–401
material culture studies, 415
needs, 441
popular culture, 469
servicescapes, 499–500
simulations, 516
symbolic exchange, 537
idling capacity, 18
IHDI *see* Inequality-Adjusted HDI
IKEAization, 418
illicit informality, 252–253
ILO *see* International Labour Organization
image economy, 557
IMF *see* International Monetary Fund
Imperial Leather (McClintock), 99–100
imperialism
Americanization, 12–15
coca-colonization, **89–90**
culture-ideology of consumerism, 221
globalization, 337
grobalization, 338–339
modernization theory, 429
implied association, 524
imported goods, 158, 177
Incense Route, 174
Index of Sustainable Economic Welfare (ISEW), 483
indexes, 492
India, 167–170
economic reforms of 1990s, 167–168
emerging economies, 150–151
localization, 169
luxury goods and leisure consumption, 168–169
Indignados, 453–454
industrialization, 171, 429–430
Inequality-Adjusted HDI (IHDI), 483
infomercial, 363–364
informal economy, 252–255
concepts and definitions, 252
illicit and licit activities, 252–253
institutional and market informality, 253
as integral part of system, 254
mercantilism, 254–255
state coercion, 254–255
structural articulation, 254
trust, 252
urbanization and migration, 253
information asymmetry, 208
infotainment, 233, **364–366**
institutional informality, 253
institutionalized cultural capital, 210
intellectual capital, 496
intellectual property, 366–368
concepts and definitions, 366
consumer movements, 136
counterfeiting/piracy, 204–205
creative commons, 367
critiques of, 366–367
legal context, 366–367
music, 436
peer-to-peer file sharing, 462
reforms and remedies, 367
scarcity, 491
typology, 366
Internal Revenue Service (IRS), 541
International Consumer Protection and Enforcement Network (ICPEN), 139
international expositions, 571–572
International Labour Organization (ILO), 254, 310
International Monetary Fund (IMF), 329
internet advertising, 8–9
internet-mediated consumption, 368–372
advertising, 369–370
collaborative consumption, 371

internet-mediated consumption (*Continued*)
commodification, 370
concepts and definitions, 368
consumer-to-consumer sales, 368
dating websites, 370
dematerialization, 371
gambling, 370–371
online auctions, 369
online gaming, 370
pornography and virtual sex, 370
technological developments, 369–370
tourism and travel, 369
virtual communities, 368–369, 371
interpretant, 492
Invention of the Daily Routine, The (de Certeau, Michel), 230–231
investment capital, 293–294, 429
IRS *see* Internal Revenue Service
ISEW *see* Index of Sustainable Economic Welfare

J
Japan, 170–173
economic growth, 170
growth in demand for consumer goods, 170–171
interwar period, 171–172
luxury goods and leisure consumption, 170–172
population aging, 172
Tokugawa period, 170, 172
urbanization and industrialization, 171
jiba sangyo, 374
jingles, 436
Jungle, The (Sinclair), 134
just-in-time production (JITP), 373–375
concepts and definitions, 373–374
continuous production, 374
corporate culture, 374
heijunka, 373
historical development, 373
jiba sangyo, 374
kaizen, 374
kanban system, 373–374
keiretsu, 374

K
kaizen, 374
kanban system, 373–374
keiretsu, 374
Keynesian economics, 82, 83, 104, 116
Keywords: A Vocabulary of Culture and Society (Williams), 570
Klein, Naomi, 98–99, 446–447, 458–459

L
labor
capitalism, 68
citizenship, 85
commodity fetishism, 99
consumer activism, 104
consumer movements, 137
consumer resistance movements, 140, 142–143
counterfeiting/piracy, 205
Disneyization, 247
Fordism/post-Fordism, 301–302
Frankfurt School, 305–306
free trade zones, 310–311
gender and consumer culture, 319
globalization, 336
informal economy, **252–255**
leisure consumption, 382–383
Nike, 447
outsourcing, **457–460**
politics and consumer culture, 464
prosumption, 477
service economy, 495–498
sweatshops, **534–536**
symbolic exchange, 537–538
Wal-Mart, 560–561
Whole Foods Market, 568
landscapes of consumption, 173–174
language and linguistics, 32–33
see also semiotics
Las Vegas, 377–379
Lasalle, Ferdinand, 398
Latinos/Latinas, 379–381
concepts and definitions, 379
consumer activism, 379–380
consumer culture, 380
identity, 379
marketing, 379–380
leisure consumption, 381–383
commodification, 382–383
concepts and definitions, 381
conspicuous consumption, 102, 382
consumer culture, 381–382
Elias, Norbert, 262
emotions, 266–267
Indian consumers, 168
Japanese consumers, 171–172
Las Vegas, **377–379**
narcissism, 440
visual consumption of cities, 80
work and spend arguments, 382–383
Lessig, Lawrence, 462
Lévi-Strauss, Claude, 63–64
LGBT community, **313–316**, 323, 501–504

liberalization of markets, 83–84, 328–329, 429–430
licit informality, 252–253
lifestyle, **383–387**
Adler, Alfred, 383–385
anti-consumption tactics, 16–17
Bourdieu, Pierre, 53–54, 55, 386
concepts and definitions, 383–384
consumer movements, 133
education, 258
Frankfurt School, 386
identity, 166
Indian consumers, 168
infotainment, 364–365
negative individual types, 384–385
Nietzsche, Friedrich, 385
Plato, 385
sexuality, 502–503
Starbuckization, 525–526
teens, 544–545
visual consumption of cities, 79–80
liminal spaces, 297, 544
Limits to Growth, The (Meadows et al.), 530
liquid modernity, 515
literary theory, 32
localization, 169
locavorism, **387–388**
Long Tail, The (Anderson), 444
Looking Backward: 2000–1887 (Bellamy), 207
Lotman, Juri, 493
lovemarks, 539–540
low culture *see* popular culture
loyalty cards/programs, 57
Luxury and Capitalism (Sombart), 120
luxury goods
Chinese consumers, 160
consumer culture, 120
cultural capital, 210
Indian consumers, 168–169
Japanese consumers, 170
narcissism, 440
servicescapes, 500
luxury taxes, 542

M

magnification, 524
mail order brides, 100
Making Ends Meet (Edin and Lein), 155
male grooming, 405–406, **427–428**, 504
Marcuse, Herbert, 146, 307–308, 441
marginal utility, 140
market informality, 253
market liberalization, 83–84, 328–329, 429–430
market mavenism, 349–350
market research, 199, 347–350, 514
market segmentation, 196
marketing, **389–393**
American consumers, 196
Americanization, 13
Asian Americans, 23–24
B2B marketing, **27–28**
brand loyalty, 57
character licensing, **74–75**
citizenship, 83, 84–86
concepts and definitions, 389–390
consumer cosmopolitanism, 111
consumer culture, 113–114, 121
consumer research methods, 426
consumer resistance movements, 142
customer relationship management, 392
debt, 237
digital-mobile consumption, **244–246**
experiential consumption, 275
Facebook, 277
fair trade, 283–284
franchising, 304
gay and lesbian/queer markets, **313–316**
Generation Y, 321
green consumption, 350–351
historical development, 389–390, 391–392
Latinos/Latinas, 379–380
macromarketing school, 391
marketing management school, 390–391
mass culture, 408–409
mass marketing, **410–411**
mass media, 413–414
micromarketing, 444
morality, 396
niche marketing, **443–445**
Nike, 446
postmodernism, 186
privacy, 474
schools of thought, 389–390
social marketing, 391
social media, 519
socially responsible marketing, **523–524**
stages of evolution, 391–392
stealth marketing, **526–528**
strategies, 390, 444
tweens, 552
youth culture, 574–575
marketplace cultures, 107, 125–126
marketplace trust, **393–395**
concepts and definitions, 393
dimensions of, 394
exchange agreements and expectations, 393–395
fostering trust, 395

marketplace trust (*Continued*)
social context, 395
Marx, Karl, 397–403
capitalism, 67, 305–306, 399, 402–403
class, 87–88
class consciousness, 402–403
commodity fetishism, 91, 97–98, 399–400
consumer society, 146–147
globalization, 333
Hegel, Georg Wilhelm Friedrich, 397–398
ideology, 400–401
life and times, 397
Manifesto and modernity, 400
Marxism and Marxist theory, 400–403
MEGA texts, 401–402
needs and wants, 442
Marxist theory
advertising, 5–6
Baudrillard, Jean, 38
class, 87
commodification, 91, 97–98
consumer culture, 115
consumer resistance movements, 141
Frankfurt School, 306–307
gender and consumer culture, 318
leisure consumption, 381
Marx, Karl, 400–403
mass culture, 407–408
popular culture, 469
symbolic exchange, 537
Williams, Raymond, 570
masculinity, 403–407
commodity racism, 101
concepts and definitions, 403–404
as consumable product, 405–406
consumption and, 405
doing masculinity, 404–405
femininities, 291, 292–293, 406
flâneur/flânerie, 295
hegemonic masculinity, 404
hypermasculinity, 406
metrosexual, 406, **427–428**
popular culture, 406
sex as commodity, 406
sexuality, 504
mashups, 577
Maslow's hierarchy of needs, 164, 442
mass consumption, 114, 317–318, 510
mass culture, 407–409
Benjamin, Walter, 44
concepts and definitions, 407
critiques of, 406–408
culture industries, 222–223
emotions, 266–267
Fordism/post-Fordism, 407
historical development, 407–408
marketing and advertising, 408–409
Marxist theory, 407–408
mass marketing, 408
popular culture, 468–469
social movements, 409
mass marketing, 408, **410–411**
mass media, 411–414
Adorno, Theodor, 1–2
advertising, 3–4, 6
commodification, 92
concepts and definitions, 411–412
consumer society, 148
cosmetic surgery, 203
culture-ideology of consumerism, 221
Debord, Guy, 233
early research, 412
femininities, 292
Frankfurt School, 306, 307, 309, 412
future research directions, 413–414
globalization, 337
historical development, 412
Hollywood, 354
infotainment, **364–366**
politics and consumer culture, 466
research trends, 412–413
sport, 192
weddings, 567
mass-mediated marketplaces, 108, 127
massively multiplayer online role playing games (MMORPGs), 109, 520–521
material culture studies, 414–416
concepts and definitions, 414–415
contemporary studies, 415
future directions, 415–416
historical development, 414–415
semiotics, 416
Mauss, Marcel, 324–325, 536, 539
McClintock, Anne, 99–100
McCracken, Grant, 243, 539
McDonaldization, 416–418
alternative explanations and paradigms, 418
Americanization, 13–14
children's consumer culture, 76
concepts and definitions, 416
credit cards, 207
critiques of, 416–417
fast food, 289–290
homogenization and heterogenization, 356, 361
hyperconsumption, 361
principles, 416
resistance, 417–418
Ritzer, George, 416–417

Starbuckization, 525
Wal-Mart, 560
Mecca, 174–175
media cross-promotion, 355
media hoaxing, 226–227
media richness, 520
medical tourism, 418–421
circumvention tourism, 418, 419–420
concepts and definitions, 418–419
fertility tourism, 420
health care ramifications, 419
legal and ethical issues, 419–420
regulation, 419
transplant tourism, 420
MEGA texts, 401–402
mercantilism, 254–255
merchandising, 421–422
concepts and definitions, 421
Disneyization, 247
Hollywood, 355
identity, 421
tactics, 421
theming, 546
Merleau-Ponty, Maurice, 50
metafunctional objects, 34
metalanguage, 33
metrosexual, 406, **427–428**, 504
microblogging, 520
micromarketing, 444
Middle East, 174–179
colonial consumption, 175–176
global and multilocal consumption, 178–179
postcolonial and nationalist consumption, 176–178
trade routes, 174–175
migration, 253
Mirror of Production, The (Baudrillard), 38
misdirection, 524
MMORPGs *see* massively multiplayer online role playing games
mobile devices, **244–246**, 521–522
modernization theory, 428–430
characteristics of modernity, 429
concepts and definitions, 428–429
critiques of, 429–430
cultural imperialism, 429
democratization, 429
dependency theory, 429
environmental issues, 430
globalization, 429–430
investment capital and foreign aid, 429
transitions from traditional society, 429
money, 430–433
chartalism, 431–432
circuits of commerce, 432
concepts and definitions, 430
cultural sociology, 432
financialization, 431–432
future research directions, 432–433
historical sociology, 431–432
morality, 432
power elites, 431
sociological study of, 430–433
monthly per capita expenditure (MPCE), 167–168
Moral Economy of the Peasant, The (Scott), 395–396
moral panic, 75–76, 315
morality
beauty industry, 39
children's consumer culture, 75–76
concepts and definitions, 395–396
ethical consumption, 270–271
fairness and inequality, 396–397
infotainment, 364
markets, **395–397**
money, 432
organ donation, 396
mortgage loans, 30, 209, 359
mothers/motherhood, 433–435
choice, 433–434
concepts and definitions, 433
consumer culture, 434
responsibility, 433
as social construct, 433
Motion Picture Association of America (MPAA), 354
movie business, 11, 72, **353–356**, 571–572
MPAA *see* Motion Picture Association of America
MPCE *see* monthly per capita expenditure
multiculturalism, 111
multilocalism, 178–179
multinational corporations (MNCs), 303, 311, 329, 334–335
Münsterberg, Hugo, 353
Musak, 435
music
ambient and background music, 435
branding, 435–436
consumer experience, **435–437**
do-it-yourself, 248
food consumption, 435
intellectual property, 436
jingles, 436
Musak, 435
programmed soundscapes, 435
sound logos, 436
YouTube, 576–577

myth, 32–33
Mythologies (Barthes), 32

N
Nader, Ralph, 82, 131, 136–137, 270
Napster, 461
narcissism, 439–440
National Consumers' League (NCL), 130
National Emergency Council (NED), 130
national identity, 357
national income, 481
National Negro Business League, 10
National Negro Convention, 56
National Recovery Administration (NRA), 130
National Sample Survey Organization (NSSO), 167–168
National Security Agency (NSA), 235
nationalism, 175–176, 180–181
Nazism, 306
NCL *see* National Consumers' League
NED *see* National Emergency Council
needs
  artificial, 308, 309
  concepts and definitions, 440–441, 442
  consumer society, 147
  Maslow's hierarchy of needs, 164, 442
  shopping, 506–507
  true and false, **440–442**
  wants and, **442–443**
neighborhoods, **322–324**, 358
neoliberalism
  citizenship, 83–84
  commodification, 91
  consumer society, 149
  culture industries, 223
  Debord, Guy, 234
  globalization, 333
  global justice movement, 328–330
  governmentality, 340–341
  modernization theory, 429
  outsourcing, 459
network theories, 424–425
neuromarketing, 426
neuroscience, 426–427
new age, 443
New Deal, 82, 130, 236, 302–303
new ecological paradigm, 351
New Left, 47
New Year's Eve, 188
niche marketing, 443–445
  concepts and definitions, 443–444
  consumer culture, 113–114
  critiques of, 444–445
  gay and lesbian/queer markets, **313–316**
  globalization, 444
  marketing strategy, 444
  Pareto principle and the long tail, 444
  sales distribution curves, 444
  successful applications, 444
Nietzsche, Friedrich, 385
Nike, 445–447
  branding, 445–447
  celebrity endorsement, 446
  historical development, 446
  outsourcing, 446–447, 458
  social justice, 447, 535
  sweatshops, 535
No Logo (Klein), 98–99, 458–459
nondisguised observation, 425
non-functional objects, 34
norm-activation model, 271
nostalgia, 172, 180–181, **447–448**
novelties inflation, 453
NRA *see* National Recovery Administration
NSA *see* National Security Agency
NSSO *see* National Sample Survey Organization
nudging, 42

O
obesity, 449–451
  changes in food environment, 450
  concepts and definitions, 449
  consequences of, 450
  consumer culture, 450–451
  contributing factors, 449–450
  energy intake and imbalance, 449–450
  fast food, 289–290
  food deserts, 300–301
  genetic factors, 450
objectified cultural capital, 209–210
objective journalism, 227
observation methods, 425
obsolescence, 451–453
  concepts and definitions, 451–452
  coolhunting, 199
  failed consumers, 153
  functional and symbolic value, 452
  novelties inflation, 453
  planned obsolescence, 451
  progressive obsolescence, 451, 453
  stylistic obsolescence, 452
  waste, 565
Occupy movement, 453–455
  concepts and definitions, 453
  consumer movements, 133
  demographics, 454
  global justice movement, 330
  historical development, 453–454

impacts and future directions, 455
infotainment, 365
reasons for protest, 454–455
symbolic exchange, 538
tactics, 454
OECD *see* Organisation for Economic Cooperation and Development
oil wealth, 177
Olympic games, 190–191
Omnivore's Dilemma, The (Pollan), 387
One-Dimensional Man (Marcuse), 307–308
online auctions, **251–252**, 369
online gambling, 370–371
online gaming, 109, 370, 520–521
online marketplaces, 246, 509, 514–515
open source, 455–457
concepts and definitions, 455–456
crowdsourcing, 455–456
do-it-yourself, 457
Free/Libre Open Source Software movement, 456–457
social media, 456–457
opinion leaders, 349–350
oppression, 44
organ donation, 396
organic foods, 388, 567–569
Organisation for Economic Cooperation and Development (OECD), 531–532
originality, 26
otherness, 91–92
Ottoman Empire, 175
Our Common Future (WCED), 530
outsourcing, 457–460
commodification, 460
commodity chains, 97
concepts and definitions, 457–458
Fordism/post-Fordism, 458
gender roles, 459–460
historical development, 458
neoliberalism, 459
Nike, 446–447
production costs, 459
social justice, 459
wartime contracting and private prisons, 459

P
P2P *see* peer-to-peer
Packard, Vance, 408
paradox of choice, 153
Pareto principle, 444
Passeron, Jean-Claude, 209
payday loans, 208–209
pecuniary emulation, 211
peer-to-peer (P2P) file sharing, 461–462
anti-consumption tactics, 18
concepts and definitions, 461
historical development, 461
intellectual property, 462
piracy, 461
Peirce, Charles S., 492, 494
pensions, 30
performance art, 17–18, 227
performativity
consumer culture, 112
consumption rituals, **187–189**
Disneyization, 247
emotions, 266
identity, 162
masculinity, 404–405
money, 432
personal debt, 235–236
personal information, 277–278, 473–474
personality disorders, 439
Peterson, Richard, 214
pets, 462–463
pharmaceutical industry, 205
Phenomenology of Mind (Hegel), 398
philanthropy, 85, 222–223
philosophy of history, 44–45
Philosophy of Right (Hegel), 397–398
PIA *see* privacy impact assessments
Picture of Dorian Gray, The (Wilde), 229
pinkwashing, 524
piracy *see* counterfeiting/piracy
planned observation, 425
planned obsolescence, 451, 565
Plato, 385
playboy philosophy, 405
politicized goods, 196
politics
advertising, 8, 465
colonialism and postcolonialism, 463–464
commodification, 465
concepts and definitions, 463–464
consumer culture and, **463–467**
consumerism, 85, 131–133, 259
discrimination, 465
environmental issues, 464–465
globalization, 464
hegemony, 465
mass media, 466
participation, 465–466
social justice, 464
social movements, 465–466
pop art, 123, 561–562
popular culture, 467–472
African Americans, 12

popular culture (*Continued*)
Asian Americans, 24
Birmingham School, 47
commodification, 91
concepts and definitions, 467
consumer culture, 123
consumer culture theory, 127
critical approaches, 467–471
cultural bifurcation approach, 467–468
cultural capital, 210
cultural omnivores, 214
cultural studies, 217
culture industries, 222–223, 224
decluttering, 238–239
do-it-yourself, 248
ethnographic/subculture analysis approach, 470–471
experiential consumption, 274
fast food, 290
future research directions, 472
girl culture, 327
Hollywood, 353
locavorism, 387
masculinity, 406
mass culture approach, 468–469
postmodernist approach, 471–472
production of culture approach, 468
shopping, 507
textual/content analysis approach, 469–470
Warhol, Andy, 562
Williams, Raymond, 569–570
youth culture, 574–575
population aging, 172
population growth, 377–378
porn chic, 70
pornography, 70, 370, 406
postcolonialism, 176–178
postcommunist countries, 179–183
communist consumption, 179–180
credit cards, 207–208
diverging consumption after communism, 181
nostalgic and nationalist consumption, 180–181
shifts in global consumption, 181–183
postconsumer culture, 116–118
postfeminism, 291–292
post-Fordism *see* Fordism/post-Fordism
postmodernism, 183–187
aestheticization, 185–186
Baudrillard, Jean, 34, 38
carnivals/carnivalesque, 185
concepts and definitions, 183–184
consumer culture, 116
consumerism, 184–185
everyday life, 185–186
finance and financial markets, 295
historical development, 183
homogenization and heterogenization, 356–357
marketing, 186
needs and wants, 443
nostalgia, 448
popular culture, 471–472
shopping malls, 511
simulations, **516–517**
theming, 547
Warhol, Andy, 562
poststructuralism, 183, 469–470
poverty
gentrification, 324
globalization, 336
medical tourism, 419–420
sweatshops, 534–535
symbolic exchange, 538
power
capitalism, 68–69
cultural studies, 217–218
de Certeau, Michel, 230–231
digital-mobile consumption, 245–246
money, 431
youth culture, 573–574
PR *see* public relations
practical disempowerment, 564
Presentation of Self In Everyday Life, The (Goffman), 497
prestation, 188
print media, 3, 11, 246, 313–315
Prison Notebooks, The (Gramsci), 48
privacy, 473–475
concepts and definitions, 473
data collection and storage, 473–474
fair information practice principles, 474–475
legal and policy issues, 474–475
marketing, 474
online commerce, 474
personal information, 473–474
privacy impact assessments, 475
third party guarantors, 475
privacy impact assessments (PIA), 475
privacy seals, 475
private-label market, 528–529
private prisons, 459
private sphere, 21, 81
privatization, 181
proclamations, 524
producer driven chains, 95–96
product franchising, 304–305
product placement, 526–527
product testing, 130
production of culture approach, 468

productivist bias, 333 – 334
programmed soundscapes, 435
progressive obsolescence, 451, 453
progressive taxes, 541 – 542
proportional taxes, 541
prospect theory, 41
Prosperity Without Growth (Jackson), 531
prostitution, 406
prosumption, 476 – 477
  Burning Man, 65 – 66
  capitalism, 477
  children's consumer culture, 77
  concepts and definitions, 476
  consumer culture, 113 – 114, 117
  consumer resistance movements, 143
  digital-mobile consumption, 245
  emotions, 268
  hegemony, 477
  social justice, 477
  sport, 193 – 194
  user-generated content, 476
Protagoras (Plato), 385
psychology, 105 – 106, 263, 264 – 265
public debt, 235
public funding, 222 – 223
public relations (PR), 477 – 479
  concepts and definitions, 477
  critiques of, 478 – 479
  managerial and functional portrayals, 478
  public relations-media hub, 71 – 72
  sociocultural portrayals, 479
public sphere, 21, 81
punk, 70, 91, 218 – 219, 248
purchasing power
  African consumers, 157
  Chinese consumers, 159 – 160
  de Certeau, Michel, 231
  gay and lesbian/queer markets, 314 – 315
  gender and consumer culture, 319 – 320
  Indian consumers, 167 – 169
  sexuality, 502
  shopping, 506
Purchasing Power (Chin), 156
Purity and Danger (Douglas), 563

Q
QoL *see* quality of life
qualitative consumer research, 423 – 424
quality of life (QoL)
  Buddhist economics framework, 483
  concepts and definitions, 481
  gross domestic product and national income, 481 – 482
  institutional models, 482 – 483
  measures of, **481 – 484**
  neoclassical model, 481 – 482
quantitative consumer research, 423 – 424
queer markets *see* gay and lesbian marketing
queer theory, 503
Quest for Excitement (Elias), 261 – 262
questionnaires, 425 – 426
quick-timers, 522

R
racial segregation, 301
racism
  commodity racism, **99 – 101**
  movie business, 11
  politics and consumer culture, 465
  world's fairs and international expositions, 571 – 572
radio broadcasting, 4
Ram, Uri, 357
Rathje, William, 563
rational choice theory, 41
reality marketing, 527
realization problem, 545
reasonable person model, 351
rebellion, 198
reciprocity, 325, 537
Reclaim the Streets, 234
recycling, 485 – 487
  concepts and definitions, 485
  determinants of, 486
  impact of, 485
  prevalence in different countries, 485 – 486
  waste, 564 – 565
reformulation, 188
regressive taxes, 542
reification, 37
relative scarcity, 491
religious fundamentalism, 142
remittances, 24, 177 – 178
remix culture, 462
repetitive consumption, 564 – 565
representamen, 492
repressive desublimation, 70
Republic, The (Plato), 385
resistance
  anti-consumption tactics, 16
  Baudrillard, Jean, 37
  Birmingham School, 47
  commodities, 94
  consumer activism, 104
  consumer behavior, 108
  consumer resistance movements, **139 – 144**
  de Certeau, Michel, 230
  fast food, 289 – 290

resistance (*Continued*)
McDonaldization, 417–418
resocialization, 144
responsibility
governmentality, 341
green consumerism, 345
green consumption, 346, 348–349
mothers/motherhood, 433
socially responsible marketing, **523–524**
see also corporate social responsibility
retail therapy, 507
Rio Earth Summits, 530–532
Rise of the Creative Class, The (Florida), 496
rites of passage, 188, 327, 406
rituals of consumption, 187–189
death, 187, 232–233
Elias, Norbert, 261–262
weddings, 187–188, **566–567**
Ritzer, George
homogenization and heterogenization, 356, 361
hyperconsumption, 360–361
landscapes of consumption, 173
McDonaldization, 416–417
prosumption, 476–477
Robertson, Roland, 356–357
role models, 73–74
Rousseau, Jean-Jacques, 81
rugged individualism, 384–385

S
sales distribution curves, 444
sales taxes, 542
Sandel, Michael J., 396–397, 460
Sassatelli, Roberta, 211
Satz, Debra, 396
Saussure, Ferdinand de, 492, 494
Savage Mind, The (Lévi-Strauss), 63–64
Scanlan, John, 563–564
scarcity, 489–491
absolute, 491
artificial, 490–491
concepts and definitions, 489
entitlements, 490
level of analysis, 490
means and ends, 489
qualitative aspects, 489–490
relative scarcity, 491
social movements, 490
Schilling, Chris, 49–50
Schroeder, Jonathan, 557–558
Scott, James, 395–396
SDC *see* Sustainable Development Commission
Sebeok, Thomas A., 492–493
Second Sex, The (Beauvoir), 291
security, 341
Security, Territory, Population (Foucault), 339–340
self-actualization, 386
self-aestheticization, 40
self-aggrandizement, 524
self-image, 6–7
self-interest, 351
self-presentation/self-disclosure, 520
Selling Out (Chasin), 502
semiotics, 492–495
advertising, 5
Barthes, Roland, 33
Baudrillard, Jean, 33–34, 37
bricolage, 63–64
concepts and definitions, 492
consumer culture, 493–494
culture, 493
emotions, 265–267
historical development, 492–494
icons, indexes and symbols, 492
key thinkers, 492–494
material culture studies, 416
signifier/signified, 492
theming, 545
Williams, Raymond, 570
Sen, Amartya, 490
sensory experience, 506
service economy, 495–499
class, 498
concepts and definitions, 495–496
consumption as defining feature of, 497–498
differences from manufacturing work, 496–497
numerical shift in job types, 495–496
quality of jobs, 496
servicescapes, 499–501
approach–avoidance theory, 499–500
concepts and definitions, 499
ideology, 499–500
luxury goods, 500
SES *see* socioeconomic status
sex industry, 370, 406
sex tourism, 100, 406, 504
sexism, 465
sexuality
advertising, 7
body and embodiment, 502–503
concepts and definitions, 501
consumption and, **501–505**
culture, 503–504
feminist theory, 501–502, 504
Frankfurt School, 308–309
gender, 503–504
globalization, 504
identity, 503–504

LGBT community, 501–504
lifestyle, 502–503
masculinity, 405–406
metrosexual, 428, 504
purchasing power, 502
queer theory, 503
weddings, 567
see also LGBT community
Shakespeare, William, 573
share ownership, 68
sharing culture, 17
shopping, **505–509**
concepts and definitions, 505–506
hidden injuries of gender, 507
needs and wants, 506–507
places of, 508–509
popular culture, 507
sensory experience, 506
shopping malls, **509–516**
concepts and definitions, 508, 509–510
consumer culture, 123
department stores, 510–511
dialectic of malldom, 514
function of malls, 512–513
future directions, 514–515
globalization, 335, 509–510, 511
historical development, 510–511
identity/selfhood, 511–512, 513
landscapes of consumption, 173
methodological problems of mall research, 514
postcommunist countries, 182
social locations, 513
sociological research, 512–514
themed malls, 511
signifier/signified, 33, 492, 517
Simmel, Georg, 43, 298
simulations, 38, **516–517**
Sinclair, Upton, 134
situationism
culture jamming, 227–228
Debord, Guy, 189–190, **233–235**
spectacles of consumption, 189–190
slavery, 100, 141
Slow Food movement, **517–518**
concepts and definitions, 290, 299, 518
ecogastronomy, 518
historical development, 517–518
locavorism, 387
McDonaldization, 418
slow-timers, 521–522
smartphones, 244–245
social appetite, 298–299
social class *see* class
social competition, 120–121
social distinction, 272
social engineering, 302
social exclusion, 165–166
social identity theory, 349
social inequality, 147–148, 160, 182
social justice
consumer movements, 131–133, 137
consumer resistance movements, 140, 142–143
education, 259
fashion, 288
free trade zones, 311
global justice movement, **328–331**
Nike, 447
outsourcing, 459
politics and consumer culture, 464
prosumption, 477
sweatshops, **534–536**
Wal-Mart, 560–561
social learning theory, 145
social marketing, 391
social media, **519–523**
ambient awareness, 519
brand mascots, 59, 62
carnivals/carnivalesque, 70
classification of, 519–520, 521–522
commodification, 92
concepts and definitions, 519
consumer behavior, 109
Facebook, **277–279**
historical development, 520–521
infotainment, 365
mobile social media, 521–522
open source, 456–457
popular culture, 471–472
prosumption, 476
sport, 192, 193–194
user-generated content, 519, 521
viral marketing, 519
visual consumption, 79
YouTube, **576–578**
social mobility, 29, 87, 149, 164
social movements
African Americans, 10–11
Birmingham School, 47
carnivals/carnivalesque, 70–71
commodities, 94
consumer activism, 103
cooperatives, 201
cultural studies, 219
ethical consumption, 272
fair trade, 280–281
food consumption, 289–290, 299
mass culture, 409
politics and consumer culture, 465–466

social movements (*Continued*)
scarcity, 490
symbolic exchange, 538
social networking, 79
social premium cost, 281
social presence, 520
social preservationists, 324
social stratification theory, 210, 211, 244
socialization
consumer socialization, **144–145**
gifts, 325–326
tweens, 552
youth culture, 574
socially responsible marketing (SRM), 143, **523–524**
Society of the Spectacle, The (Debord), 189–190, 226, 233
socioeconomic status (SES)
African Americans, 11–12
bankruptcy, 29
digital-mobile consumption, 244
food deserts, 301
sociohistoric patterning, 107–108, 127
soft news, 365
solidarity economics, 141
sound logos, 436
sovereignty, 166, 167
space-locators, 521–522
space-timers, 521–522
spam, 8–9
spectacles of consumption, 189–191, 361
spectacular society, 233–234, 235
speculation, 293–294
Spongebob Squarepants, 74
sponsorship, 113–114, 121
sport, 191–195
accumulation and incorporation, 191–192
commodification, 192–193, 194
concepts and definitions, 191
consumer culture, 191
flâneur/flânerie, 193
involvement and spectatorship, 192–193, 194
mass media, 192
prosumption, 193–194
social media, 192, 193–194
spectacles of consumption, 189
SRM *see* socially responsible marketing
staged authenticity, 550
Stallman, Richard, 462
standardization
global markets, 332–333
hyperconsumption, 361
Starbuckization, 525
theming, 546
see also homogenization
Starbuckization, 418, **524–526**
Star Wars, 74
state power, 68–69
status power, 573–574
stealth marketing, 526–528
celebrity endorsement, 526–527
concepts and definitions, 526
critiques of, 527
forms of, 526–527
historical development, 526
product placement, 526–527
reality marketing, 527
viral marketing, 527
youth culture, 575
stereotypes
femininities, 291, 292
gay and lesbian/queer markets, 315–316
Latinos/Latinas, 380
stigmatization, 29, 235
storytelling, 424
Strawberry Cheesecake, 74
street performance, 17–18
stress, 30
strike action, 36
structural articulation, 254
stylistic obsolescence, 452
subcultural capital, 211
Subculture: The Meaning of Style (Hebdige), 64
subcultures
bricolage, 64
commodification, 91
cultural studies, 218–219
fashion, 287–288
girl culture, 326–327
lifestyle, 386
popular culture, 470–471
sexuality, 501
subliminal messaging, 6
substitutability, 93
suburbanization, 70
subvertisements, 17, 226–227
Super Bowl, 190–191
superbrands, 62
supermarketing, 335
supermarkets, 528–530
branding, 528–529
globalization, 529
historical development, 528–529
private-label market, 528–529
shopping malls, 508
surveillance, 514
survey research, 214–215

sustainability
American consumers, 196
anti-consumption tactics, 16, 18
Chinese consumers, 161
consumer culture, 114
consumer movements, 131–133
consumer resistance movements, 141, 143
culture-ideology of consumerism, 221–222
eBay, 251–252
education, 259
ethical consumption, 269–270
farmers' markets, 285–286
fashion, 288
food consumption, 299
green consumerism, 342, 344–345
green consumption, 346
Las Vegas, 377
locavorism, 387–388
recycling, **485–487**
theming, 545
sustainable consumption, 530–534
concepts and definitions, 530
consumer culture, 532–533
historical development, 530–531
international organizations, 530–532
policy agenda, 532–533
Sustainable Development Commission (SDC), 531–532
sweatshops, 534–536
citizenship, 85
concepts and definitions, 534
consumer activism, 104
consumer resistance movements, 140
critiques of, 534–535
fashion, 288
Nike, 447
Wal-Mart, 561
willingness to pay, 535
symbolic capital, 54–55
symbolic consumption, 50–51
symbolic exchange, 536–538
concepts and definitions, 536
critiques of, 538
fair exchange, 537–538
gift giving, 536–537
reciprocity, 537
social movements, 538
symbolic value, 538–540
branding, 539–540
concepts and definitions, 538–539
gift giving, 539
obsolescence, 452
outsourcing, 459
symbols, 492
System of Objects, The (Baudrillard), 34–35, 494, 539

T
taste
Bourdieu, Pierre, 53–55
class, 88
cultural capital, 210–211
cultural omnivores, 214–215
education, 258–259
food consumption, 299
Frankfurt School, 308
teens, 543
taxes, 541–543
Tearing Down the Streets (Ferrell), 234
teens, 543–545
advertising, 543–544
concepts and definitions, 543
globalization, 544
historical development, 544
lifestyle and teen culture, 544–545
teleshopping, 363–364
television broadcasting
advertising, 4
consumer culture, 123
infomercial, **363–364**
spectacles of consumption, 190
textual analysis, 469–470
Themed Space, The (Lukacs), 548
theming, 545–549
arcades, 546
architecture, 546–547
concepts and definitions, 545
Disneyization, 246–247, 547–548
historical development, 545
hybrid consumption, 546
motifs and environments, 545–546
realization problem, 545
research approaches, 547–548
Theming of America, The (Gottdeiner), 548
theology, 44–45
theory of planned behavior (TPB), 351
Theory of the Leisure Class, The (Veblen), 537, 555–556
theory of practice, 52
third party guarantors, 475
Third Wave, The (Toffler), 476
Thornton, Sarah, 211
Thus Spoke Zarathustra (Nietzsche), 385
TNC *see* transnational corporations
tobacco industry, 4, 5
Toffler, Alvin, 476

tourism, 549–551
authenticity, 549–551
concepts and definitions, 549
cosmetic surgery, 203
culture, 550–551
ecotourism, **255–257**
emotions, 266–267
flâneur/flânerie, 295–296
globalization, 336, 551
Indian consumers, 168
internet-mediated consumption, 369
Japanese consumers, 171
Las Vegas, 377–378
leisure consumption, 383
masculinity, 406
medical tourism, **418–421**
sex tourism, 100, 406, 504
typology, 549–550
visual consumption, 80, 557
world's fairs and international expositions, 571–572
TPB *see* theory of planned behavior
trade liberalization, 83–84, 328–329, 429–430
trade name franchising, 304–305
trade routes, 174–175
trade secrets, 136
tragedy of the commons, 18
transformation, 187, 234–235
transformative consumer research, 94, 95
transnational corporations (TNC), 96
transplant tourism, 420
trickle-down economics, 88, 102, 287–288, 360
true needs, **440–442**
trust, 18, 252, **393–395**
TRUSTe, 475
Tupperware parties, 318
tweens, 551–553
anticipatory socialization, 552
children's consumer culture, 77
concepts and definitions, 551
historical development, 551–552
marketing, 552
media exposure, 552
Twitter, 519–521
two-sided markets, 207

U
UGC *see* user-generated content
Umwelten, 493
UN *see* United Nations
uncooling, 226–227
underclass, 153–154
United Nations (UN)
consumer protection agency, 139
green consumerism, 342
quality of life, 482–483
sustainable consumption, 530–532
United Nations Educational, Scientific, and Cultural Organization (UNESCO), 223–224
United Nations Environmental Program (UNEP), 485
United States, consumption in the, 195–197
United Students Against Sweatshops (USAS), 140
Unsafe at Any Speed (Nader), 136
Unsettling of America, The (Berry), 387
urbanization
informal economy, 253
Japanese consumers, 171
modernization theory, 429
theming, 547
waste, 564
Urry, John, 549–550, 557
USAS *see* United Students Against Sweatshops
use value, 98, 114
user-generated content (UGC), 414, 476, 519, 521
usury laws, 235–236

V
value-belief-norm model, 351
value chains, 95
value-for-money movement, 270
vandalism, 233–234
Veblen, Thorstein
conspicuous consumption, 88, 101–102, 120, 555–556
cultural capital, 211
hyperconsumption, 360
life and works, **555–556**
symbolic exchange, 537
veganism, 16–17
venture capital, 378
viral marketing
Facebook, 277
social media, 519
stealth marketing, 527
youth culture, 575
virtual communities, 368–369, 371
virtual environmentalism, 345
virtual malls, 514–515
virtual sex, 370
visual consumption, 556–558
advertising, 79
arcades, 556–557

cities, **79–80**
concepts and definitions, 79, 556–557
department stores, 557
flâneur/flânerie, 556–557
leisure consumption, 80
research approaches, 557–558
social media, 79
tourism, 80, 557
Visual Consumption (Schroeder), 557–558
visual resource management, 557
vlogs, 577
voice, 140
voluntary simplicity, 16, 140–141, 466, 490
volunteering, 65
voyeurism, 383

W
Wal-Mart, 559–561
critiques of, 560–561
efficiency and calculability, 560
historical development, 559–560
McDonaldization, 560
social justice, 560–561
Walmartization, 335
wants, 442–443, 506–507
Warhol, Andy, 561–563
wartime contracting, 459
Washington, Booker T., 10
waste, 563–565
concepts and definitions, 563
culture, 563
Garbology Project, 563
recycling, 564–565
repetitive consumption, 564–565
sociological perspective, 563–564
urbanization, 564
Web 2.0, 519, 577
Weber, Max, 67–68, 87–88, 360–361
weddings, 566–567
commodification, 566–567
consumption rituals, 187–188
culture, 566
gender, 567
mass media, 567
research approaches, 567
visual consumption, 558
white weddings, 566–567
Wedgewood, Josiah, 121
welfare state, 208, 237
WFM *see* Whole Foods Market
What Money Can't Buy (Sandel), 396–397, 460
White Collar (Mills), 497
White Negro, The (Mailer), 197
white weddings, 566–567
Whole Foods Market (WFM), 567–569
ethical consumption, 568–569
genetically modified organisms, 569
historical development, 567–568
organic food movement, 567–569
wholesale societies, 201
Wikipedia, 520–521
Wilde, Oscar, 229
Williams, Raymond, 569–571
Birmingham School, 47
cultural materialism, 570
life and works, 569–570
popular culture, 569–570
willingness-to-pay (WTP), 271, 347, 535
Window Shopping: Cinema and the Postmodern (Friedberg), 266
word-of-mouth, 278, 519, 527
see also viral marketing
Work, Consumerism, and the New Poor (Bauman), 155
Work of Nations, The (Reich), 496
Workers' Rights Consortium (WRC), 535
world system theory, 95
World Trade Organization (WTO), 329
world's fairs, 571–572
WRC *see* Workers' Rights Consortium
WTP *see* willingness-to-pay

Y
Yes Men, 18, 227
youth culture, 573–576
advertising, 7
concepts and definitions, 573
coolhunting, 199
developing nations, 575–576
fast food, 289
Generation Y, 321
girl culture, **326–328**
historical development, 573
marketing, 574–575
nostalgia, 448
popular culture, 574–575
power, 573–574
shopping malls, 514
socialization, 574
teens, **543–545**
tweens, **551–553**
YouTube, 576–578
broadcast news cycles, 577
do-it-yourself, 576–577
historical development, 576
infotainment, 365
internet-mediated consumption, 369

YouTube (*Continued*)
mashups, 577
social media, 520–521
vlogs, 577
yummy mummy, 434

Z
Zapatistas, 234
Zelizer, Viviana, 395–396, 432
zoösemiotics, 492–493
Zukin, Sharon, 173

Printed and bound by CPI Group (UK) Ltd, Croydon, CR0 4YY

16/09/2026

14963392-0002